A bridge in Bruges, Belgium, spanning a canal that links the ancient manufacturing city with the North Sea. Centuries ago, the river that served that purpose became clogged with silt. Vance Henry–Taurus Photos

FUNK & WAGNALLS NEW ENCYCLOPEDIA

VOLUME 3

AUSTRALIAN BALLOT to BLIZZARD

LEON L. BRAM
Editorial Director

ROBERT S. PHILLIPS
Editor

NORMA H. DICKEY
Executive Editor

FUNK & WAGNALLS, INC., NEW YORK

FUNK & WAGNALLS NEW ENCYCLOPEDIA
IS REVISED AND UPDATED EVERY YEAR
FOLLOWING THE YEAR OF COPYRIGHT

ISBN 0-8343-0033-8
Library of Congress Catalog
Card Number 72-170933

MANUFACTURED IN THE UNITED STATES OF AMERICA
PRINTED AND BOUND BY RAND McNALLY & COMPANY

FUNK & WAGNALLS NEW ENCYCLOPEDIA

LIST OF ABBREVIATIONS USED IN THE TEXT*

abbr.	abbreviated
AC; a-c	alternating current
A.D.	*anno Domini* (Lat., in the year of the Lord)
alt.	altitude
A.M.	*ante meridiem* (Lat., before noon)
AM	amplitude modulation
amu *or* AMU	atomic mass unit
anc.	ancient
Ar.	Arabic
AS.	Anglo-Saxon
A.S.S.R.	Autonomous Soviet Socialist Republic
at.no.	atomic number
at.wt.	atomic weight
b.	born
bbl	barrel
B.C.	before Christ
bd.ft.	board feet
bev *or* BeV	billion electron volts
b.p.	boiling point
B.T.U.	British Thermal Unit
bu.	bushel
Bulg.	Bulgarian
C.	centigrade
cent.	century
Chin.	Chinese
cm	centimeter
Co.	County
colloq.	colloquial
cu.	cubic
Czech.	Czechoslovakian
d.	died
Dan.	Danish
DC; d-c	direct current
Du.	Dutch
E.	east; eastern
ed.	edition; editor
Egypt.	Egyptian
Eng.	English
est.	estimated
ev *or* EV	electron volt
F.	Fahrenheit
fl.	flourished
FM	frequency modulation
fr.	from
Fr.	French
ft.	foot
g	gram
Gael.	Gaelic
gal.	gallon
Ger.	German
Gr.	Greek
Heb.	Hebrew
Hind.	Hindustani
h.p.	horsepower
hr.	hour
Hung.	Hungarian
Hz	hertz or cycles per second
I.	Island
i.e.	*id est* (Lat., that is)
in.	inch
Ind.	Indian
Ir.	Irish
It.	Italian
K.	Kelvin
kg	kilogram
kHz	kilohertz
km	kilometer
kw	kilowatt
kw hour	kilowatt hour
lat.	latitude
Lat.	Latin
lb.	pound
long.	longitude
m	meter
M.	Middle
mev *or* MEV	million electron volts
mg	milligram
MHz	megahertz
mi.	mile
min.	minute
M.L.	Medieval Latin
mm	millimeter
mod.	modern
m.p.	melting point
m.p.h.	miles per hour
Mt(s).	Mount, Mountain
N.	north; northern
Norw.	Norwegian
N.T.	New Testament
OE.	Old English
OF.	Old French
OHG.	Old High German
ON.	Old Norse
ONF.	Old Norman French
O.T.	Old Testament
oz.	ounce
P.M.	*post meridiem* (Lat., after noon)
Pol.	Polish
pop.	population
Port.	Portuguese
prelim.	preliminary
pron.	pronounced
q.v.	*quod vide* (Lat., which see)**
r.	reigned
R.	River
rev.	revised; revision
R.R.	railroad
Rum.	Rumanian
Russ.	Russian
Ry.	railway
S.	south; southern
sec.	second
S.F.S.R.	Soviet Federated Socialist Republic
Skr.	Sanskrit
Sp.	Spanish
sp.gr.	specific gravity
sq.	square
sq.mi.	square mile
S.S.R.	Soviet Socialist Republic
St.; Ste.	Saint
Sum.	Sumerian
Sw.	Swedish
temp.	temperature
trans.	translation
Turk.	Turkish
U.K.	United Kingdom
U.N.	United Nations
U.S.	United States
U.S.A.	United States of America
U.S.S.R.	Union of Soviet Socialist Republics
var.	variant
vol.	volume
vs.	versus or against
W.	west; western
yd.	yard

*For a more extensive listing of abbreviations, widely used by authoritative sources in many fields, *see* ABBREVIATION. Charts of pertinent abbreviations also accompany the articles BIBLE, CANON OF THE; DEGREE, ACADEMIC; ELEMENTS, CHEMICAL; MATHEMATICAL SYMBOLS; and WEIGHTS AND MEASURES. Accent marks and special letters are explained in the article DIACRITIC MARK.

**The abbreviation (q.v.) stands for the Latin words "quod vide", meaning "which see". The placement of this abbreviation after a word—or a name or term—indicates that the word itself is the title of a separate article in the encyclopedia. By looking up the article on this word, or the entries on each word in a series that is followed by the plural form (qq.v.) of the abbreviation, the reader will find specific information about the words used as well as data about the main topic of the article he is reading.

FUNK & WAGNALLS NEW ENCYCLOPEDIA

AUSTRALIAN BALLOT. *See* BALLOT.

AUSTRALIAN CAPITAL TERRITORY, federal district of the Commonwealth of Australia, in the S.E. section of the State of New South Wales. The territory, including the site of Canberra (q. v.), the capital city of Australia, was formally acquired by the Australian government in 1911. Port Jervis Bay Territory, situated at Jervis Bay on the coast, is attached to the Capital Territory for administrative purposes. Sheep raising is important in rural areas of the Capital Territory. Area, 939 sq.mi.; pop. (1972 est.) 153,900.

AUSTRALIAN FEDERATION. *See* AUSTRALIA: *History.*

AUSTRALIAN LITERATURE, literature written by the English-speaking settlers of the continent of Australia and their descendants.

Poetry. The first Australian-published poetry, remembered now because of its primacy, was *First Fruits of Australian Poetry* (1819) by Barron Field (1786–1846), an Englishman serving in the Australian judiciary. Four years later the founder of Australian colonial self-government, William Charles Wentworth (q.v.), a native-born Australian, published a single poem, "Australasia, an Ode", which is invariably cited as the first poetic expression of anything resembling a national spirit. The first volume of poetry by a native-born Australian is *Wild Notes from the Lyre of a Native Minstrel* (1826) by Charles Tompson (1806–83), who spent the greater part of his life as a government official. Charles Harpur (1817–68), also a native-born government employee and a farmer as well, is the author of *Thoughts: a Series of Sonnets,* which appeared in 1845. He continued to publish occasionally during the rest of his life and was the earliest poet of any merit. It was not, however, until the time of Henry Clarence Kendall (1841–82), an Australian by birth, and Adam Lindsay Gordon (1833–70), an English immigrant, that Australian poetry really became significant. Gordon's sporting poems and narratives, which had great popularity, may be seen at their best in *Sea Spray and Smoke Drift* (1867) and *Ashtaroth* (1867). Kendall, often called the national poet, developed a personal idiom to deal with Australian subjects in *Leaves from an Australian Forest* (1869) and *Songs from the Mountains* (1880), and was especially successful in describing the scenery of the wooded valleys along the Pacific coast.

These pioneers prepared the ground for a number of poets whose work shows greater distinction and is more clearly expressive of the national character. Bernard (Patrick) O'Dowd (1866–1953), a lawyer by profession, was a didactic poet of wide learning who published verses in pamphlet form after 1903. There is little emotion in his work; he is rather a rhetorician of ideas, notably of the belief that Australia is a land in which there is an opportunity to build a cultured nation free from contamination by such evils of European culture as economic, political, and social inequalities. The classical scholar Christopher (John) Brennan (1870–1932) was the most learned poet Australia produced at this time. His work, largely in the symbolist tradition, is characterized by depth of feeling and force of imagery. Not popularly known, Brennan's poetry is esteemed by a small group of discriminating readers. (John) Shaw Neilson (1872–1942), who had little schooling, but is considered by some critics to be the best poet of his era, reflects the experience of ordinary people in the simple lyricism of his verse.

The journalist and lawyer Andrew Barton Paterson (1864–1941) gave the greatest literary development to the bush ballad, a kind of popular poem about life in the scrub country of the interior. His ballad "Waltzing Matilda" (1917), which was sung by Australian troops in both World Wars, gained great popularity among all English-speaking people. *The Man from Snowy*

Christopher Brennan Australian News & Information Bureau

River contains Paterson's best ballads. C. J. Dennis (1876–1938) was another popular versifier who expressed in dialect the feelings and experiences of the "dinkum Aussie bloke", or true Australian guy, notably in *The Songs of a Sentimental Bloke* (1915).

A number of contemporary Australian poets have written works of the highest distinction. Notable among them is Robert Fitzgerald (1902–), whose long, semiphilosophical discourses in verse blend themes of Australian experience with those of more universal interest. Kenneth Slessor (1901–71) is important for his collection of verse, *One Hundred Poems* (1944), all written between 1919 and 1939. His work ranges from examples of pallid aestheticism to amusing realistic sketches of historical characters done in a variety of forms. Among other distinguished modern poets are Judith Wright (1915–), adjudged by some critics to be the most considerable woman poet writing in English today; the verse-drama author Douglas Stewart (1913–); A. D. Hope (1907–), not only the exemplary poet of his time in Australia, but a poet of large and growing reputation overseas; and James McAuley (1917–). A useful sampling of Australian poetry, beginning with the work of Harpur, is *A Book of Australian Verse* (1956; 2nd ed. 1968), edited by Judith Wright.

Early Fiction. The earliest fictional work commonly cited is *Tales of the Colonies* (1843) by Charles Rowcroft (d. 1850), but the most frequently reprinted is *Geoffrey Hamlyn* (1859) by Henry Kingsley (1830–76), brother of the British novelist Charles Kingsley (q.v.). Kingsley originated the novel of Australian pastoral life. Kingsley's main characters are, however, Englishmen who come to Australia for colonial experience and then return to England, as he did. Two fairly prolific early novelists were Marcus Andrew Hislop Clarke (1846–81) and Thomas Alexander Browne (1826–1915), the latter of whom wrote under the name of Rolf Boldrewood. Clarke is most famous for his classic story of the convict era, *For the Term of His Natural Life* (1874), which exploits the horrors of convict life in the realistic manner of the British novelist Charles Dickens (q.v.). Browne's reputation rests on *Robbery Under Arms* (1888), a classic story of bushranging. It may be described as an Australian Western, a narrative about bush life full of vivid adventures.

In recent years two important works, both on the borderline between fiction and reportage, one published long ago and one belatedly discovered and printed, have come to notice. These are *Ralph Rashleigh* (1952), probably written in the early 1840's by James Tucker (1808–66?), and *Settlers and Convicts* (1852), written under the pen name "An Emigrant Mechanic" by Alexander Harris.

Among the 20th-century authors, Henry Hertzberg Lawson (1867–1922) is noteworthy as a writer of sketches. Poorly educated, he identified himself with the working people and wrote prolifically about them and their feelings toward Australia. His best work appeared during the 1880's in the weekly newspaper *The Bulletin,* which was devoted to expression of a char-

Kenneth Slessor Australian News & Information Bureau

acteristic Australian viewpoint. There is humor as well as bitterness in his sketches, which range from sentimental vignettes to strongly realistic studies. Perhaps the volume for which he is best known abroad is *While the Billy Boils,* published in *Travellers' Library* in 1927. The finest single work of fiction expressing basic Australian attitudes is *Such Is Life* (1903) by Joseph Furphy (1843–1912), who used the pen name Tom Collins. Furphy's life was spent in the pastoral hinterland as a farmer and driver of bullock teams before the days of the railroad. His book, written in diary form, is a compound of episodic adventures, philosophic, and literary opinions, and homely observations about men and conditions in Australia. Katharine Susannah Prichard (1884–1969), whose work began to appear before World War I, wrote in almost every form. She interprets Australian life in terms of class struggle and was for many years an important literary figure in the Australian Communist Party. Her best fiction is contained in *Working Bullocks* (1926), a story of lumbering in western Australia, and *Coonardoo* (1930), a study of miscegenation.

Later Fiction. One of the finest craftsmen of Australian fiction is Frank Dalby Davison (1893–1970), whose writings were first published when he was thirty-eight years of age. He is known primarily for his animal tales, the most distinctive of which is *Man-Shy,* published in the United States as *Red Heifer* (1934). It is a subtly conceived story of a maverick on a Queensland cattle station. In *Dusty* (1946), Davison describes the life of a dog with equal success. He is quite as discerning in his stories of human character, as, for example, in the collection *The Woman at the Mill* (1940), and his study of pre-World War II suburban life in Sydney, the novel *The White Thorn Tree* (1968). Eleanor Dark (1901–), another prose writer of literary skill, wrote excellent historical novels, especially *The Timeless Land* (1941), which is about the founding of Australia; she wrote also novels of contemporary life. Both types of her fiction are distinguished by psychological perceptiveness and brilliant descriptions of the Australian landscape.

The Australian writer of the middle generation who was best known in the U.S. is Henry Handel Richardson (1870–1946), whose real name was Henrietta Richardson. Her earliest novel of note is *Maurice Guest* (1908), but her trilogy *The Fortunes of Richard Mahoney* (1917, 1925, 1929) is by far her most widely appreciated work. The latter novel, based on the life of the author's father, begins with the gold rushes of the 1850's and then penetratingly describes various aspects of Australian life in later decades. The main character, after whom the trilogy is named, is an unstable Irish doctor who intensely dislikes Australian life; he is considered by Australian critics to be one of the major creations of the literature. With profound insight, Richardson develops Australian themes in the European tradition of psychological realism.

Patrick White Australian Information Service

Several other 20th-century Australian novelists enjoy reputations outside their own country. One of them is Mrs. Lewis Charles Rodd, better known as Kylie Tennant (1912–), whose first novel, *Tiburon* (1935), was a distinguished achievement. Among her major works are *The Joyful Condemned* (1953), a novel concerned with working girls in the Sydney slums, and *The Battlers* (1954), a regional novel of caravan life in southwestern Australia. These hardheaded studies in realism are characterized by a fine sense of comedy and are written in a racy Australian idiom. The major figure among contemporary Australian novelists is Patrick Victor Martindale White (q.v.), the first Australian to win a Nobel Prize in literature (1973). His *The Tree of Man* (1954), set in the Australian bush country, marks an ambitious attempt to describe the courage, dignity, and loneliness encountered among the people of the open farmlands. *Voss,* which White wrote in 1957, is a novel about a 19th-century German explorer who tries unsuccessfully to penetrate to the remote interior of the continent. It is written in an involuted style with great imaginative boldness. His novels *The Solid Mandala* (1966) and *The Vivisector* (1970) also attained favor outside Australia. Hal Porter (1917–), author of *The Tilted Cross* (1961), and Jon Cleary (1917–), author of *The Sundowners* (1952), scored notable popular success. John O'Grady (1907–), under the pen name Nino Culotta, wrote *They're a Weird Mob* (1957), a comic novel that became the best seller of all Australian novels. Worldwide fame was achieved by Christina Stead (1902–). Morris Langlo West (1916–) wrote several international best sellers, including *The Devil's Advocate* (1959), *The Shoes of the Fisherman* (1963), and *The Summer of Red Wolf* (1971). Thomas Michael Keneally (1935–) has received overseas acclaim for the novels *A Dutiful Daughter* (1971) and *The Chart of Jimmie Blacksmith* (1972). Other important novelists are Xavier Herbert (1901–) and the venerable Martin a Beckett Boyd (1893–). Dal Stivens (1911–) and Gavin Casey (1907–64) are writers of short stories of original quality.

Other Genres. Although the theater has flourished in Australia since the earliest days and Australian actors have made brilliant careers at home, in New York City, and in London, dramatists comparable in outlook and skill to the poets and fiction writers have been scarce. Louis Esson (1882–1943) is usually cited as the writer who most consistently devoted himself to Australian drama, but many others before and since have also helped to build a theatrical tradition. In 1954 there appeared on the stage *Summer of the Seventeenth Doll* by Ray Lawler (1921–). It scored a resounding success and was produced in New York City on Broadway (1956) and off-Broadway (1968), and as a film, *Season of Passion* (1961). Since World War II, perhaps a dozen important plays by native authors have been produced successfully on the Australian stage. A promising young playwright is Alexander Buzo (1944–); his play *Rooted* was performed by the Hartford (Conn.) Stage Company in 1972.

The writer A. G. Stephens (1865–1933) has a reputation as a literary critic, and penetrating critical articles by other writers may be found in literary journals. In general these articles are produced by poets, fiction writers, and academics as a by-product of other activities. The Scottish-born educator and anthologist Walter Murdoch (1874–1970) was a well-known essayist.

Contemporary literary opinion finds expression in the quarterlies *Meanjin* of Melbourne and *Southerly* of Sydney and in the weekly journal of opinion *The Bulletin*. The latter has been a force in Australian literature for at least seven decades. Australian literature is now a recognized academic subject in educational institutions. The academic journal *Australian Literary Studies* is an adjunct of these courses. In addition, many popular periodicals carry reviews and articles on contemporary publications and developments.

Australian literature has developed certain well-defined qualities: a love of the vast, empty land, with its unexampled flora and fauna, a compelling sense of the worth of the common man, and freedom from the bondage of European traditions. Although the English language has not been radically transformed in Australia, it has undergone distinctive changes of style with colorful additions to vocabulary, about which Australians were once apologetic but which are now regarded as a dynamic and valuable contribution to the language. Indeed, several studies of Australian transformations of the English language have appeared. Some of these are short vocabulary lists, with a history of the first appearance and subsequent usage of the word or phrase in question; others are studies of pronunciation or intonation that is peculiarly Australian. C.H.G.

AUSTRIA (Ger. *Österreich*), republic of central Europe, bounded on the N. and N.E. by Czechoslovakia, on the E. by Hungary, on the S. by Yugoslavia, Italy, and Switzerland, and on the W. by Liechtenstein, Switzerland, and West Germany. It lies between about lat. 46°25′ N. and lat. 49° N. and long. 9°30′ E. and long. 17° E. Somewhat larger than South Carolina, Austria is 360 mi. long and ranges in width from an average of 130 mi. in the E. to an average of 37 mi. in the W. The area of Austria is 32,369 sq.mi.

THE LAND

Austria is predominantly a mountainous country, with an average elevation of about 3000 ft. Most of the land falls within the E. division of the Alps. In general the major mountain ranges of Austria run in an east-to-west direction and are separated from one another by rather broad valleys. The northernmost line of ranges includes the North Tirol Alps and the Salzburg Alps. Among the central ranges is the Hohe Tauern, which culminates in the Grossglockner (12,457 ft.), the greatest elevation in the country. The southernmost ranges include the Ötztal Alps, the Zillertal Alps, the Noric Alps, and the Karawanken Mts. Besides these east-to-west ranges, there are also several series of mountain spurs which extend in a north-to-south direction. The mountain barriers of Austria are broken in many places by passes, including the Brenner Pass and the Semmering Pass.

Austria. Plate 1. *Saint Wolfgang (above, left), a market village near Salzburg in the Salzkammergut, a lake district in the eastern Alps. The charm of the setting makes the region a favorite summer resort. The Gloriette monument (above, right) in Schönbrunn Park, the summer residence of the former Austrian royal family, on the outskirts of Vienna. Situated on a hill at an elevation of about 800 ft., the colonnade affords a view of the park and the city below. Monument to Saint Anne (left) erected in 1706 in the middle of the picturesque Maria Theresien Strasse, the main thoroughfare of Innsbruck. Encircled by a series of jagged Alpine peaks, the city is one of the most scenic in Austria.*

Plates 1 through 4 in this series courtesy of the Austrian Information Service

Austria. Plate 2. *The village of Lech (above), near the Alberg peak, a famous Alpine ski resort. The Europa bridge (below) over the Sill R., is a link in the Brenner Autobahn between Austria and Italy.*

Austria. Plate 3. *Austrian traditions come to life (left) in the rifle contest held annually near Saint Jacob am Thurn in the Tirol. The mountain people, divided into many separated communities, express their individuality through costume, dialect, and customs. Girl in original Tirolean costume (below, left) playing the zither, probably the most popular musical instrument in Austria. Man in military garb (below, right) reflects the national pride of the people and is reminiscent of the spirit of the Austrian hero of the late 18th century Andreas Hofer, who resisted the separation of the Tirol from the mother country during the Napoleonic Wars.*

Austria. Plate 4. *Interior of the chapel of the Hofburg (left), the former imperial palace of the Hapsburg rulers at Innsbruck. The chapel houses twelve bronze statues of Austrian nobles called Schwarze Mander, or "black figures". Altar of Verdun (below) in the Augustine abbey at Klosterneuberg, near Vienna. The altar, completed in 1181 by the German goldsmith Nicholas of Verdun, depicts scenes from the Old and New Testaments in gilt and enamel.*

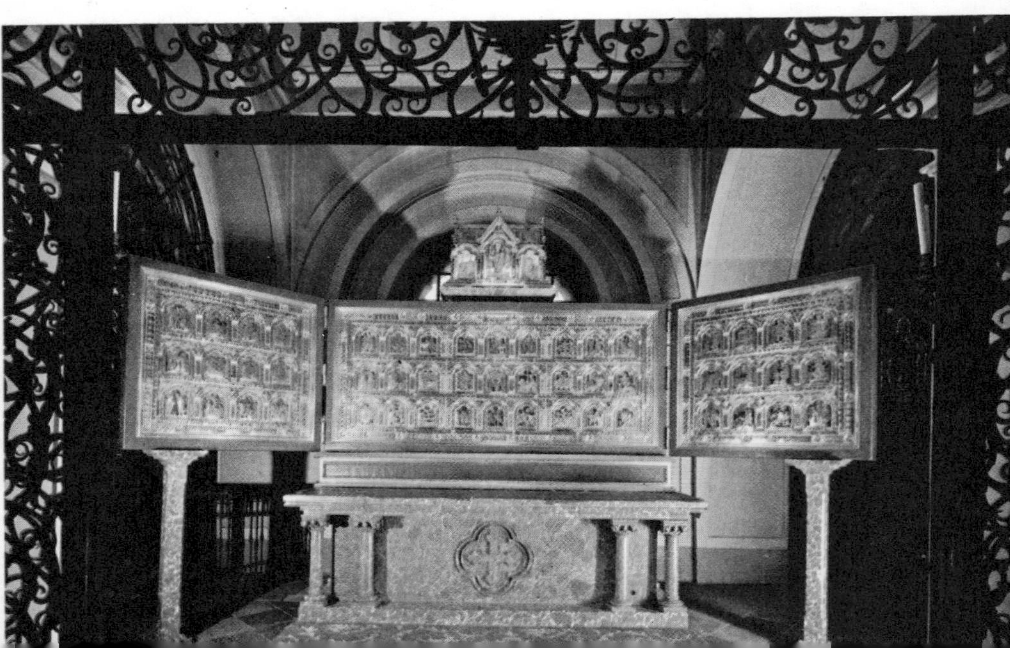

The Burgtheater in Vienna, reopened in 1955 after having been severely damaged in World War II, is the major theater of Austria. Across the roofs can be seen the baroque dome of Saint Peter's Church and the spire of Saint Stephen's Cathedral.

Fred Grunert–Bruce Coleman

The principal areas of Austria which are not within the Alps are the N. and E. border sections. The N. section consists of rolling upland ranging in elevation from 1300 to 2400 ft. The E. border section comprises part of the Danube basin. The Danube-basin region, including Vienna, leads the rest of the country in agricultural and industrial production.

The principal river is the Danube, which flows through the N. section of Austria from Passau at the German border, past Linz and Vienna, to Bratislava on the Czechoslovakian border. Austrian tributaries of the Danube include the Traun, Enns, and Ybbs rivers. In the S., important rivers are the Mur and the Mürz. The hydrographic system of the country includes numerous lakes, notably in the south-central and the N.W. areas.

CLIMATE. The Austrian climate varies with altitude; with location in relation to Atlantic, continental, and Mediterranean influences; and with certain local wind characteristics. Mountainous regions are partially subject to moderate Atlantic conditions and experience more precipitation than the E. lowlands, which are under continental influences. Spring and fall are usually mild throughout the country. Summers are short, with moderate temperatures. Cold and often severe winters last about three months in the valleys, where they are usually ended by the foehn, a warm, dry wind from the S. that is often accompanied by damp fog and sudden thaws that precipitate avalanches. Mean annual temperatures range between about 44° F. and 48° F. throughout the country. Average annual rainfall is between about 40 and 50 in. In the Vienna region, in the S.E., and in some interior valleys, the average annual rainfall reaches about 60 to 80 in.

Natural Resources. Austria has sizable deposits of iron ore, lignite, magnesite, oil, and natural gas, and is a prime world supplier of high-grade graphite. Some small deposits of bituminous coal have been mined, in addition to deposits of lead, zinc, copper, kaolin, gypsum, mica, quartz, salt, bauxite, antimony, and talc.

PLANTS AND ANIMALS. Deciduous trees, mainly beech, oak, and birch, are predominant in the lower altitudes; spruce, fir, larch, and stone pine extend to the timberline. The higher altitudes have a very brief season during which Alpine plants, including edelweiss, gentians, primroses, buttercups, and monkshoods come into brilliant flower.

Wildlife is generally scarce in Austria. Chamois, deer, and marmots are still represented; however, bear, which were once abundant, are almost completely absent. Hunting is strictly regulated to protect the remaining species.

SOILS AND WATERPOWER. Rich *terra rosa* (red) soils predominate in Austrian valleys. At slightly higher elevations, the soil is chiefly of a brown forest type. Alpine meadow soils are found in high-altitude regions. Austrian waterpower resources are among the largest in Europe. In 1970, Austrian electric power production averaged 30,000,000,000 kw hours annually, of which about 70 percent were generated by hydroelectric plants. About 3,500,000,000 of the total wattage was exported to the German Federal Republic, Italy, and Switzerland. Two thirds of the hydroelectric potential of Alpine streams remains untapped.

THE PEOPLE

Although the Austrian people are primarily Germanic, Austria has a varied ethnic mixture including significant minorities of Croat, Magyar, and Slovene stock, as well as smaller groups of Rumanians, Serbs, and Italians.

Population. The population of Austria (census 1971) was 7,443,809. Overall population density was estimated by the United Nations (1970) at about 229 per sq.mi. Almost one third of the people live in the five largest cities—Vienna, Graz, Linz, Salzburg, and Innsbruck.

Political Divisions. Austria is divided into nine provinces: Vienna, Lower Austria, Upper Austria, Salzburg, Styria, Carinthia, Tirol, Vorarlberg, and Burgenland.

PRINCIPAL CITIES. Vienna (q.v.), the capital and largest city, had a population (1971) of 1,614,841. Other important cities include Graz, a center for heavy industry, with a population of 249,211; Linz, the provincial capital of Upper Austria and a port on the Danube, with 204,627; Salzburg, a cultural and tourist center, with 127,455; and Innsbruck, the provincial capital of Tirol and a tourist attraction because of the beauty of the city and its situation, with 115,293.

Religion. Roman Catholicism is the religion of about 89 percent of the population of Austria. Various Protestant denominations account for about 6 percent, and a small minority of the population is Jewish.

Language. German is the official language of Austria. About 2 percent of the population speak languages other than German, chiefly Croatian, Slovene, and Czech.

Education. The basis of the Austrian educational system is the national law that requires school attendance for all youths between the ages of six and fifteen. Austria's long tradition of free education dates from the Educational Reform Act of 1774, instituted by Empress Maria Theresa (q.v.) and continued under her son, Emperor Joseph II (*see under* JOSEPH). This law was expanded in 1867 and again in 1962, and largely accounts for the fact that 99 percent of the population of the country is able to read and write.

Although the foundations of Austria's present educational system were laid in the 18th century, its roots can be traced to the monastic schools of the Middle Ages. One such school, the Schottengymnasium in Vienna, has been in continuous operation by the Benedictine order since 1155. Under German occupation (1938–45) the country's schools suffered severe restraints on their teaching programs, but the end of the war brought a restoration of freedom, as well as expanded educational programs and greater equality of educational opportunities.

Since World War II, various programs have been inaugurated to expand and strengthen the educational system. These include: (1) a one-year extension in required school attendance; (2) the addition of one year to the secondary-school program as further preparation for university training; (3) the training of primary-school teachers in universities and other institutions of higher education; (4) an increase in religious instruction and in the number of schools in which such instruction is compulsory; and (5) expanded opportunities in adult education, providing the equivalent of a secondary-school education in both general and technical studies.

During the 20th century, Austria has received international recognition for the high quality of its medical training. In the arts it has sought new approaches to the awakening of students' creative interests, especially in the field of art education under the leadership of Franz Čizek (1865–1947). In many respects, Austrian schools were among the first to be marked by a general trend toward progressive education.

ELEMENTARY AND SECONDARY SCHOOLS. All students attend elementary school (*Volksschule*) for four years. Thereafter, children who will end their schooling at fifteen either enter vocational school or continue at the *Volksschule*. Secondary-school education is limited to ages ten to eighteen; it is required for admission to a university. In the early 1970's some 960,000 students attended more than 5000 elementary schools, and more than 219,000 students were enrolled in some 480 secondary schools.

One of the elegant rococo rooms of the Schönbrunn Palace. Dating from 1750, the huge palace near Vienna was a summer residence of Austrian royalty, and Napoleon also lived there for a time.
J. Launois–Black Star

SPECIALIZED SCHOOLS. Austria has an extensive system of special schools and adult-education centers. In the early 1970's more than 10,000 students attended some 45 commercial academies and more than 21,000 were enrolled in about 85 schools for technical and industrial training. Other schools offered courses in trades, women's professions, and social work.

UNIVERSITIES AND COLLEGES. The largest of the four state-maintained universities, in Vienna, had an average annual enrollment of 19,000 in the early 1970's. Other universities are established in Graz, Innsbruck, and Salzburg. Austria also has two technical universities; colleges of mining, agriculture, veterinary medicine, and commerce; and five academies of fine arts and music, which also offer summer programs that attract many foreign students.

Culture. Throughout the 18th and 19th centuries, Vienna was a world center of culture, particularly in music and literature. Austrian fine art usually is considered with the art of S. Germany; *see* GERMAN ART AND ARCHITECTURE. A distinctive Austrian style, however, is manifested in the refined baroque architecture and sculpture of the 17th and 18th centuries, notably in Vienna and Salzburg.

LIBRARIES AND MUSEUMS. The largest of the nearly 3000 libraries in Austria is the National Library, founded in 1526, which contains more than 1,800,000 volumes. Important research collections are housed in the various universities, in several old monasteries, and in a number of scientific libraries. The collection of the former royal house contains state papers dating from 816; collections of the Holy Roman Empire date from 1555; and documents concerning the history of the Austrian Empire, the Austro-Hungarian monarchy, and the period since 1918.

The art and natural-science museums of Vienna are internationally known, as are many individual collections. The Kunsthistorisches Museum (Museum of Art History) is famous for its paintings by various members of the Brueghel family (*see under* BRUEGHEL) and for the works of Dutch, Italian, and German painters. The Albertina print collection, the collections of jewelry and relics of the Holy Roman Empire, the Austrian Gallery, the technical museum, and the museum for folklore and ethnography are all well known. Salzburg, the birthplace of the composer Wolfgang Amadeus Mozart (q.v.), has two museums housing collections of his manuscripts and other memorabilia.

ARCHEOLOGY. At Hallstatt, 30 miles S.E. of Salzburg, on the S.E. shore of Lake Hallstatt, archeol-

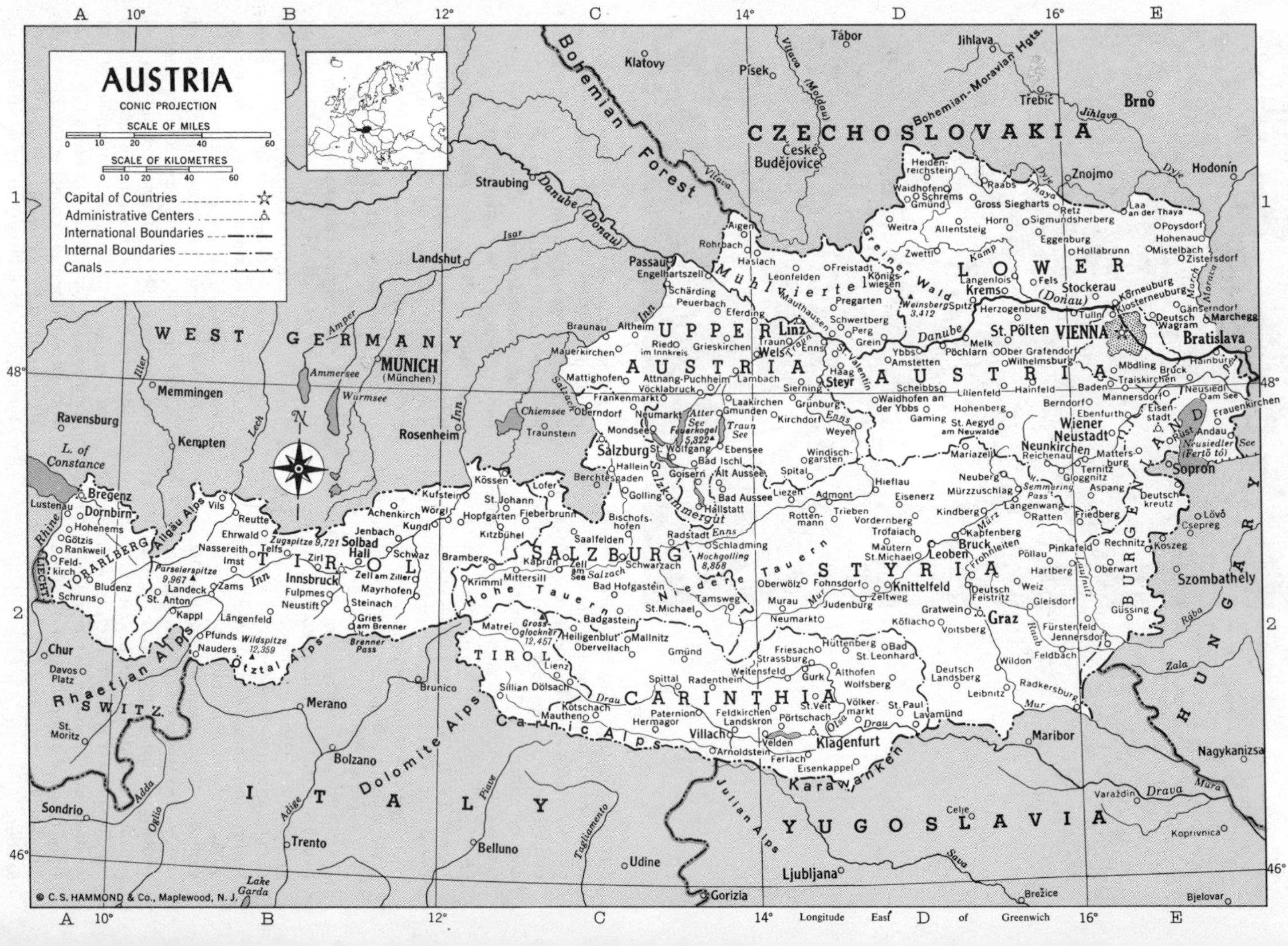
AUSTRIA
CONIC PROJECTION
SCALE OF MILES
0 10 20 40 60
SCALE OF KILOMETRES
0 10 20 40 60
Capital of Countries
Administrative Centers
International Boundaries
Internal Boundaries
Canals
WEST GERMANY
MUNICH (München)
CZECHOSLOVAKIA
LOWER AUSTRIA
UPPER AUSTRIA
VIENNA
STYRIA
CARINTHIA
SALZBURG
TIROL
VORARLBERG
BURGENLAND
YUGOSLAVIA
ITALY
SWITZ.
HUNGARY
LIECHT.
Bohemian Forest
Danube (Donau)
Hohe Tauern
Niedere Tauern
Carnic Alps
Karawanken
Dolomite Alps
Julian Alps
Rhaetian Alps
Ötztal Alps
Allgäu Alps
Zugspitze 9,721
Grossglockner 12,457
Wildspitze 12,359
Longitude East of Greenwich
© C. S. HAMMOND & Co., Maplewood, N. J.

INDEX TO MAP OF AUSTRIA

Haystacks in the sun at Dormitz, west of Innsbruck in the pasturelands of the Tirol. Cattle grazing and dairying are among the chief occupations of this peaceful area of western Austria. Keith Gunnar–Bruce Coleman, Inc.

ogists have uncovered relics of a stable society of herdsmen that flourished in the period of transition between the Bronze and Iron ages, about 700–400 B.C. Hallstatt was the center of a Celtic culture, the outgrowth of early warrior-nomad invasions from the E. Not far to the S. evidence of a Roman settlement of a later date has been found. Greek coins, and urns and pottery from N. Italy, found in this settlement, indicate that the residents of the region were active traders.

LITERATURE. *See* AUSTRIAN LITERATURE.

ART. Important art contributions include early wood carvings, Gobelin (q.v.) tapestries, hand-carved and hand-painted chests, intricately forged grates and other ironwork, stained-glass windows, porcelain made in Augarten (a suburb of Vienna), lace, and leatherwork. Wood carving and sculpturing have long been popular among the men of the Alpine valleys. Among the best-known modern painters of Austria are Egon Schiele (1890–1918) and Oskar Kokoschka (q.v.).

MUSIC. "The Land of Music" is a name often given to Austria. The symphonic and operatic music of Wolfgang Amadeus Mozart and Ludwig van Beethoven, the symphonies of Anton Bruckner and (Franz) Joseph Haydn, the songs and symphonies of Franz Peter Schubert (qq.v.), the waltzes of the two Johann Strausses (*see under* STRAUSS), and the operettas of Franz von Suppé and Franz Lehár (qq.v.) made Austrian music world-famous. Composers Gustav Mahler, Richard Strauss (qq.v.), Franz Schmidt (1847–1939), and Arnold Schönberg (q.v.), as well as conductors Felix Weingartner (1863–1942), Clemens Kraus (1893–1954), and Herbert von Karajan (q.v.), are just a few of those who have enriched Austrian cultural life. The Vienna Choir Boys and the Vienna Philharmonic Orchestra are celebrated organizations. Vienna has two famous opera houses, the *Volksoper* (People's Opera), opened in 1904, and the Vienna State Opera, completed in 1869 and known for its beautiful architecture and fine performances. In addition, every provincial capital has its own theater, and the summer festivals in Vienna, Salzburg, and Bregenz are outstanding musical events. *See also* MUSIC: *History of Music: Preclassic and Classic Periods.*

THE ECONOMY

The Austrian economy is based on a balance of private and public enterprise. All of the basic industries have been nationalized since 1946; these include all oil production and refining, the three largest commercial banks, and the principal companies in river and air transportation, railroad equipment, electrical machinery and appliances, mining, iron, steel, and chemical manufacturing, and natural-gas and electric-power production. In addition, the government, at all levels, has broad regulatory powers in regard to the economy. Self-administering public bodies, such as the chambers of agriculture, commerce, and labor (to which all farmers, businessmen, and employees, respectively, must belong), are required by law to participate in consulting bodies that influence economic legislation.

In a recent year the national budget showed revenues of more than $4,800,000,000 and expenditures of slightly more than $5,100,000,000.

Agriculture. Of the total land area, about 20 percent is considered suitable for cultivation. Meadows and pastures comprise about 28 percent of the total land area, and market gardens and vineyards account for slightly more than 1 percent. More than 60 percent of Austrian farms are under 25 acres in size.

Major products and yields in 1970 included potatoes, 2,704,000 metric tons; barley, 913,000 tons; wheat, 810,000 tons; corn, 612,000 tons; oats, 272,000 tons; and milk, 3,328,000 tons. Livestock included 3,200,000 pigs; 2,400,000 head of cattle (of which about one half were milch cows); 121,000 sheep; and 53,000 horses.

Forest and Fishing Industries. Approximately 40 percent of the total land area is forest or woodland, and about one quarter of the population derives its income directly or indirectly from forestry. A comprehensive reforestation and conservation program has been in progress since the early 1950's to compensate for damage inflicted during World War II and for postwar overcut of forest trees. More than 80 percent of the forests are conifers, mostly spruce, which are important in the paper and pulp industry as well as in building construction. Forest holdings, like agricultural holdings, are small, the average single holding amounting to about 17 acres. Cutting averaged about 13,000,000 cu.yd. per year in 1970.

Processing and consumption of fish are low, and most table fish is imported. Fishing for sport in the mountain streams is popular. The annual consumption of fish in Austria averages about 4 lb. per person.

Mining. The average annual production of principal minerals in 1970 included lignite, 3,670,000 metric tons; iron ore, 1,304,000 tons; crude oil, 2,798,000 tons; magnesite, 1,609,000 tons; salt, 564,000 tons; and zinc, 15,700 tons. Other minerals commercially mined included copper, lead, and bauxite.

Manufacturing. The Austrian manufacturing industry consists of a few large organizations, many of which operate under government auspices, and a great number of small- and medium-sized production units. Because of the traditional popularity of Austrian wood, glass, textile, and ceramic handicrafts, some 20 percent of the labor force is employed by more than 100,000 establishments producing such goods. The principal industrial products are pig iron, crude steel, rolled steel, motor vehicles, cement, fertilizers, rayon, cotton, and woolen yarns and fabrics, and paper. Production of crude steel totaled almost 4,000,000 metric tons in 1971 and of pig iron about 2,848,000 tons.

Because of its wealth of cultural and recreational facilities, Austria has a major tourist industry; in 1970 almost 9,000,000 foreigners visited the country.

Fine cut glass is an Austrian tradition. Here, an artisan in cut glass works at his trade in the Tirolean village of Rattenberg, near Innsbruck. Completed stemware is in the foreground. Ralph Boxter–Monkmeyer Press

Currency and Banking. The schilling, consisting of 100 groschen, is the official currency (17 schillings equal U.S.$1, in August, 1973). The Austrian National Bank has authority over the nation's currency and bank credit policies. Austria has more than forty commercial and savings banks.

Commerce and Trade. The value of imports in 1970 was about $3,500,000,000. Construction and industrial machinery, chemicals, electrical apparatus, coal, coke, petroleum, coffee, tea, corn, and foodstuffs were among the chief import commodities. Austrian exports totaled about $2,800,000,000 in that year. The principal products exported included iron and steel, wood and lumber, paper, paperboard, synthetic fibers and fabrics, electric power, and lace and embroidery. The Federal Republic of Germany was the largest market for and supplier to Austrian industry. Italy and the other nations of the European Economic Community (q.v.), or Common Market, and Switzerland are also major trade partners.

Transportation. Austria has a highly developed system of rail, air, water, and highway transportation. In the early 1970's the country had some 3700 mi. of railroads, all of which were owned by the state. As a landlocked and mountainous country, Austria depends on rail passage for more than two thirds of all imports and half of all exports. Improved highways and roads totaled about 20,000 mi. Water transportation is confined largely to the Danube R. The state-owned Danube Steamship Co., the largest shipping company in Austria, provides both freight and passenger service on the river. More than twenty international carriers serve Austrian airports, with most traffic to Schwechat, the airport serving Vienna. Austrian Airlines (A.U.A.), the national airline, serves many European and domestic routes.

Communications. Radio, television, telephone, and telegraph systems were all state monopolies, but the broadcasting system was converted into a joint-stock company in December, 1957. Three programs are broadcast throughout the day by Austrian Radio, Ltd. Licenses must be obtained, for a small fee, when radios are purchased. A television service was begun in 1955, and more than 1,400,000 receivers were in operation in 1970.

Telephone and telegraph communications are directed by the Austrian postal service. More than 1,300,000 telephones are in service, most of which operate on an automatic dialing system. Some 150 daily newspapers and periodicals are published. Daily newspaper circulation averages 2,300,000. The *Kurier, Express,* and *Illustrierte Kronen-Zeitung* have the largest circulation.

Labor. Nearly two thirds of the total Austrian labor force of 3,400,000 belong to the sixteen unions comprising the Austrian Trade Union Federation. Membership in unions is on a voluntary basis, but all wage earners are required by law to join their respective chambers of labor. Chambers are organized on a provincial basis, and represent workers on legislative matters. Women make up about 40 percent of the total work force.

GOVERNMENT

Austria is a democratic, federal republic governed according to the constitution of 1920, as amended in 1929 and subsequently modified. Like the constitutions of many other Western democracies, that of Austria provides for a distinct division of power among the executive, the legislative, and the judicial branches of government. Laws having their origin in 1862 and 1867 guarantee basic human rights and liberties; the rights of minorities also are guaranteed by the constitution. Executive power is exercised by the president of the republic, who is elected by popular vote every six years, and by the federal cabinet, which is headed by a chancellor, appointed by the president for a term not exceeding four years. Suffrage is universal, and minimum voting age requirements are set by the provincial legislatures.

HEALTH AND WELFARE. The Austrian system of social insurance is comprehensive, including sickness, disability, accident, old-age, and unemployment benefits, allowances for families with children, and rent aid. The program is financed by compulsory employer and employee contributions. Health insurance and some other benefits are voluntary for those who are self-employed.

Legislature. Federal legislative power is vested principally in the National Council (*Nationalrat*), or lower house, composed of 183 members elected by popular vote for four-year terms. The cabinet may remain in office only so long as it enjoys the confidence of the National Council. The Federal Council (*Bundesrat*), the upper house, consists of 54 members chosen by the provincial legislatures in proportion to population for terms ranging from four to six years. Although the powers of the Federal Council are principally advisory, the council can delay passage of bills.

Political Parties. Following parliamentary elections held in the fall of 1971, the National Council consisted of 93 members of the Socialist Party, 80 members of the People's Party, and 10

Salzburg, ancient and atmospheric, is a renowned cultural center permeated by the spirit of Mozart, a native son. This spire-skimming view is toward an 800-year-old fortress atop a hill of rock. H. Gritscher-Peter Arnold, Inc.

members of the Freedom Party. Other parties not included in the government were the Liberal, Communist, and Democratic Progressive parties.

Local Government. Each of the nine provinces has a unicameral legislature elected on the same basis as is the National Council. The legislature chooses a provincial governor. All legislation must be submitted by the governor to the competent federal ministry for approval. The provincial legislature, however, may override a ministry veto by majority vote. Cities and villages are administered by elected communal councils, which in turn elect mayors, or burgomasters.

Judiciary. Supreme judicial authority is exercised by the Supreme Court of Justice. The judicial system includes 4 high provincial courts and 18 lower provincial and district courts. There is also a Supreme Administrative Court, which deals with violations of administrative powers.

Defense. An Austrian army was authorized by the state treaty of May 15, 1955. There is no limitation on its size, but it may use only conventional weapons. Austria has compulsory military service; the period of service is two years in the army and three years in the navy and air force. In the early 1970's the army numbered about 47,000 (including 6000 volunteers), the navy about 3000, and the air force 6000.

HISTORY

At the beginning of the Christian era, Austria was sparsely inhabited by Illyrian and Celtic peoples who from time to time advanced into the northern plains of Italy.

Early Period. Much of the region south of the Danubius (Danube) R. was known as Noricum. The western uplands region between the upper Rhine R., the lower course of the Inn R., and the Bavarian and subalpine plateau was known as Rhaetia. The plains region in the east and southeast was known as Pannonia. The Romans invaded all three regions about 15 B.C. and made them provinces of the empire. Under Roman control, the provinces eventually became outposts for offensive and defensive action against various barbarian tribes. To a large extent Roman strategy was based on the fact that the region contains important passes through the eastern Alps and thus commands vital transportation arteries between northern, southern, western, and eastern Europe. One of the first Roman military posts in the region was Vindobona (now Vienna), which was located on the site of a Celtic settlement on the edge of the eastern Alps and on an arm of the Danube. Vindobona became an important strategic crossroad for two main trade routes and for numerous roads leading into the fertile basin of Lower Austria. Carnuntum (now Petronell), built in 73 A.D., was another important Roman center in the area.

As a result of periodic overpopulation and land hunger, combined with pressure from remote peoples and the attraction of the wealth of the peaceful Roman provinces, the Germanic tribes attacked the provincial frontiers at various times starting in 166 A.D. The frontiers completely broke down during the 4th century A.D. Goths, Rugians, Lombards, Vandals, Ostrogoths, and Huns at one time or another crossed the Vienna basin. The Alamanni advanced into Rhaetia, the Herulians captured Juvavum (now Salzburg), and the Goths advanced along the Drau R.

The Slavs and the Avars moved into Pannonia from the east and southeast at about the same time the Germans invaded the northwest. By the middle of the 6th century the Bavarians had occupied Tirol and the Alamanni had settled to the west. The Slavic people were split into northern and southern groups by Avars and Bavarians contending for control of the Danube R. valley. The Avars left only superficial traces in the country, but the Slovenes built settlements in the depopulated valleys of the eastern Alps. The Germans finally overwhelmed the Slovene settlements which could not depend upon a continuous stream of new settlers. In a few areas of what are now Carinthia and Styria the Slovenes managed to establish permanent settlements.

Medieval Era. During the 8th century, after fratricidal strife among the Germans, the Franks secured the throne of Bavaria. Fighting continued during that century between the Avars and the Bavarians in the Danube R. valley. At the end of the century the Frankish emperor Charlemagne (q.v.) devastated the territory of the Avars and established a series of outposts (military districts) of the empire in the country between the Enns and Raab rivers to serve as buffer territories against further encroachment from the east. One of these outposts was the Ostmark (Eastern March), which later became known as Ost Reich (Eastern Country) or Österreich (Austria). Other marches in the east and southeast were Carantania and Carniola, later Styria. However, these marches were too weak to hold back intrusions from the east.

The Magyars, a nomadic people migrating slowly from the east, advanced easily along the Danube R. valley until they were finally defeated by the German king Otto I (*see under* OTTO) at Augsburg in 955 in the Battle of the Lechfeld. Otto I revived the Eastern March and gave the more influential title of margrave to its administrator; these moves marked the emergence of Austria as a political entity. The boundary of the Eastern March was slowly extended eastward until in the early 11th century it reached what is now called Moravia. The margrave of Austria was subordinate to the duke of Bavaria, whose domain included this march. The main function of the margrave was the defense of the march and the outlying areas, and for that purpose the margraves enjoyed exceptional power. Between 976 and 1230 the Babenberg rulers of Austria contributed much to the growth of the march. They built cities and roads, encouraged trade, and enhanced their prestige by participation in the Crusades.

The death of the last Babenberg was followed by a period of trial and unrest. King Ottokar II (1230?–78) of Bohemia occupied Austria, Styria, and Carniola. His power was opposed by Rudolph von Hapsburg (*see* RUDOLF I), who was crowned Holy Roman Emperor in 1273. In 1278 Ottokar was defeated in battle by Rudolf's forces and slain. By 1283 most of the former domain of Ottokar had come under the rule of Rudolf's son Albert I (1250?–1308).

Austria under the Hapsburgs. The rise of the house of Hapsburg is closely linked to the rise of Austria. During the 14th and 15th centuries the Hapsburgs steadily increased their holdings in the eastern part of the Holy Roman Empire. With acquisition of the region surrounding the Brenner Pass, the Hapsburg holdings extended from the upper Danube to the upper Rhine and to the edge of the eastern Alps. Between 1438 and 1806 the rulers of Austria, with one exception, also held the title of Holy Roman Emperor.

The Austrian rulers enlarged their holdings by political agreements and by marriage. It was said that while other states made war, it was the good fortune of Austria to make marriages. Flanders, Burgundy, Spain, Trieste, Styria, southern Tirol, and all the present Austrian provinces (with the exception of Salzburg which was governed by an archbishop) became Hapsburg possessions through marriage. With the acquisition of the Netherlands through marriage in 1477, of the crown of Bohemia in 1526, and the crown of Hungary in 1527, the Hapsburgs made Austria the center of a vast empire. Again through marriage, Austria and Spain were united. Charles V (q.v.) of Hapsburg, son of Philip I (1478–1506) of the Netherlands and Juana of Spain (1479–1555), became heir to the united monarchies in 1516 and was elected Holy Roman Emperor in 1519. However, Charles V left (1556) all his German territories to his younger brother Ferdinand I (q.v.) who was the founder of the Austrian, as distinguished from the Spanish, branch of the Hapsburgs.

Under Ferdinand and his successors the power of Austria and the Holy Roman Empire greatly increased. During the 17th century, however, and, in particular, during the Thirty Years' War (q.v.), rebellion, religious disputes, and weak rulers threatened the disruption of the empire. At the Peace of Westphalia (1648) Austria had to cede Alsace to France.

Before the end of the century the empire was threatened by Turkish hordes. The climax came in 1683 when Vienna was besieged by the Turkish grand vizier Kara Mustafa (d. 1683), defended by the Austrian field marshal Count Ernst Rüdiger von Starhemberg (1635–1701), and rescued by an army of Poles and Germans under the Polish king John III Sobieski (q.v.). The imperial armies won important victories toward the end of the century under the command of Eugene, Prince of Savoy (q.v.). The death of Charles II (q.v.), the last of the Hapsburg sovereigns in Spain, led to the War of the Spanish Succession (*see* SPANISH SUCCESSION, WAR OF THE). Concluded in 1713 by the Peace of Utrecht, the war secured for Austria the Spanish Netherlands and Spanish possessions in northern Italy.

With continuous wars on Austrian borders, trade and agriculture declined and the state treasury was exhausted. Less and less attention was given to domestic affairs. Upon the death of Charles VI (q.v.) in 1740 the male line of the Hapsburgs became extinct. Charles' daughter Maria Theresa, who was married to Francis, Duke of Lorraine, assumed the government under a so-called Pragmatic Sanction (q.v.). Her succession led to the War of the Austrian Succession (*see* SUCCESSION WARS) and culminated in the Seven Years' War (q.v.), as a result of which Austria lost part of Silesia. Maria Theresa, a good ruler, gave much attention to economic, administrative, and cultural reforms.

During the following years Austria acquired part of Poland by participating, with Russia and Prussia, in the partition of that country. Later Austria was forced by Louis XV (q.v.), King of France, to exchange Lorraine for certain disputed French possessions in northern Italy. The execution of Louis XVI, King of France, and of his queen, Marie Antoinette (qq.v.), who was an Austrian princess, during the French Revolution brought (1793) Austria into a war with the French Republic. As a result, Austria lost the Netherlands and later came into conflict with Napoleon I (q.v.), Emperor of France. In 1804 Francis II (q.v.) declared himself hereditary emperor of Austria, resigning the empty honor of German and Holy Roman Emperor. His power and territory, which were greatly reduced by the Napoleonic victories, were for the most part restored by the Congress of Vienna in 1815. The diplomatic skill of the Austrian chancellor Prince Klemens von Metternich (q.v.) made the empire the center of the new European order that followed. Austria lost some territories in the Netherlands and in Baden, but added Lombardy, Venetia, Istria, and Dalmatia to its realm. Austrian influence, both in the Germanic Confederation and the Holy Alliance (q.v.), was at a peak.

From 1815 to 1848 the course of the Austrian Empire was essentially reactionary; the preservation of the status quo was the policy of the Hapsburg rulers after 1815. In 1848 the people of the Austrian Empire, including Germans, Slavs, Magyars, and Croats, revolted against the imperial regime. The revolution took place in an empire that was overwhelmingly rural in character. Peasant discontent, together with city revolutions led by unemployed, landless laborers, led to short-lived changes in the domestic structure of the empire. Metternich was forced to resign. Ferdinand I (*see under* FERDINAND) abdicated in favor of his nephew; *see* FRANCIS JOSEPH

REIGN OF FRANCIS JOSEPH. A favorable foreign political situation was helpful to the empire during those critical days: Prussia was not strong, the French revolution of 1848 did not show the strength of that of 1789, and Russia, itself conservative, was on the side of Austria. A rebellion in Hungary, led by Lajos Kossuth (q.v.), was suppressed with the help of Russia.

After the revolution of 1848 the empire had to deal with many internal problems, as well as with difficult situations in Italy and Germany. The Hapsburg position in Italy was secured by Austrian armies; in Germany, however, it deteriorated, making inevitable an ultimate Austro-Prussian conflict for leadership. On the domestic scene the new emperor dropped liberal pretenses, and a new form of absolutism, based on complete loyalty of all people of the empire, was again reinstated.

During the 1850's the empire tried to protect its territorial acquisitions against the pressures of nationalism and Russian advances into southern Europe. Austria was defeated by France and

Schloss Montfort, a medieval walled castle near Feldkirch, western Austria; in the background are the Alps. Toni Schneiders-Lindau-Bruce Coleman, Inc.

Italy in 1859 and deprived of Lombardy. The struggle for supremacy in Germany between the empire and Prussia reached its climax on the battlefield of Sadowa (1866). As a result of the Prussian victory the German Confederation was dissolved and then reorganized without Austria. Prussia assumed the leadership and control of the confederation and took the lead for unification.

The Austrian government introduced a new policy in the postwar period. Hungary won (1867) recognition and the restoration of its constitutional liberties; a compromise (*Ausgleich*) became the basis of the Dual Monarchy of Austria-Hungary (q.v.). The various peoples within the monarchy, including Czechs, Poles, Slovenians, Croatians, Slovaks, and Italians, demanded a greater role in government. Foreign policy had been reoriented toward the east. The failure of the Austrians and the Hungarians to agree on a satisfactory solution for the Slavic members of the monarchy and the disastrous policies of the joint foreign ministry, however, culminated in a declaration of war against Serbia in 1914, and, in turn, brought about World War I, which ended in the collapse of the monarchy.

THE LAST AUSTRIAN EMPEROR. Charles I (q.v.) was forced to abdicate and was exiled by the victorious Allies in 1919. The monarchy disintegrated completely and its various peoples formed independent states.

The First Austrian Republic. The Austrian republic, which came into being after World War I, entered the comity of nations as a disorganized and impoverished state. Austrian resources had been exhausted by the war. Furthermore, the dismemberment of the Austro-Hungarian Empire deprived Austria of the industrial areas of Bohemia and Moravia and ended the prewar balance between agriculture and industry. Immediate help was urgently needed. In 1919–20 an American Relief Administration provided food to relieve the desperate situation. An Austrian application for permission to borrow funds abroad was at first rejected by the League of Nations, but in 1922 Great Britain, France, Italy, and Czechoslovakia lent about $35,000,000, thus preventing the collapse of the Austrian economy. In December, 1923, a large international loan was made available, and Austria slowly returned to more normal conditions.

The internal political situation continued to be uneasy throughout the postwar years because of the antagonism between the Conservatives and the Social Democrats. There was much unrest caused by private left-wing and right-wing armies. On July 15, 1927, a riot broke out in Vienna over the acquittal of three members of the principal right-wing group, the *Heimwehr,* on trial for the death of two Socialists, and during a demonstration the Palace of Justice was burned. The police fired on the mob, killing seventy persons and wounding hundreds.

ANSCHLUSS. A succession of governments, mostly dominated by the Clerical Party, could overcome neither the continuously brewing unrest nor the financial misery. A movement for Anschluss (unification with Germany), though prohibited by the peace treaties, was revived, and the two countries proclaimed agreement in March, 1931, on plans for a customs union. Austria and Germany renounced this project on Sept. 3 after vigorous protests by various countries, including France and Italy.

With the rise of National Socialism (q.v.) in Germany, Austria was faced with new difficulties. Internal unrest increased and the Anschluss movement, promoted by the German dictator Adolf Hitler (q.v.), became stronger. In February, 1934, the *Heimwehr,* with the support of the government, crushed the Socialists. During a Nazi Putsch (July) Chancellor Engelbert Dollfuss (q.v.) was assassinated. The new chancellor, Kurt von Schuschnigg (1897–1977), formerly minister of culture and education, attempted to preserve Austrian independence by treaties with neighboring nations, especially Italy. The Italian dictator Benito Mussolini (q.v.) promised to preserve the status quo, but following the establishment (1936) of the Rome-Berlin Axis, he reversed his position and became an advocate of unification of Austria and Germany. In February, 1938, Schuschnigg, in an attempt to secure his country's independence, reached an agreement with the German Führer Adolf Hitler regarding Austro-German relations. Immediately thereafter the Austrian Nazi leader Artur von Seyss-Inquart (1892–1946) was made minister of the interior in charge of Austrian police. As a consequence the authority of the state was rapidly undermined, and the road was cleared for the Nazis to gain control of the country. On March 12, 1938, Hitler declared Austria to be part of Germany. German troops immediately occupied the country.

As a division of Germany, Austria lost not only its freedom, but also its name; called the *Ostmark,* it was divided into seven administrative districts under the central authority of the German Third Reich.

World War II. In October, 1943, during World War II, the chiefs of state of the United States, Great Britain, and the Soviet Union signed the so-called Moscow Declaration, which proclaimed the reestablishment of an independent Austria as a major Allied war aim. The resistance movement in Austria was weak, however, and could provide little assistance to the Allied troops, which liberated the country in April, 1945. Later that month, a provisional government was set up under the leadership of the Socialist statesman Karl Renner (1870–1950). This government was recognized by the occupation powers in October, 1945. In November, 1945, national parliamentary elections were held, with ten parties participating. The People's Party, a centrist grouping consisting mainly of Roman Catholics, won 85 of a total of 165 seats in the National Council, the Socialist Party won 76 seats, and the Communist Party won 4 seats. In December, 1945, the newly elected upper and lower houses of parliament elected Renner president of the republic. A coalition government, with the People's Party leader Leopold Figl (1902–65) as chancellor, was then formed.

In the meantime Austria had been divided into four zones of occupation controlled respectively by the U.S., Great Britain, France, and the Soviet Union. The city of Vienna was also divided into four zones.

By the terms of an agreement (June, 1946) with the occupation powers, the Austrian government received qualified authority over the entire country, including the right to legislate and to administer the national laws. The occupation powers retained authority on such matters as demilitarization, restitution of property belonging to Allied nationals, and the disposal of German-owned property. Austria was required to pay the costs of occupation. The Soviet government assumed control of the petroleum and other important industries in its zone and proceeded to divert their output to the Soviet Union. Various restrictions were imposed on the press, on travel, and on other activities of Austrian nationals in the Soviet zone.

The Austrian government was faced with immediate domestic problems that severely taxed its limited powers. The war had shattered much of Austrian industry and had disrupted its transportation and communication systems. There was much suffering, even starvation, among the Austrian people. The first task of the Figl government was to institute a relief program. The United Nations Relief and Rehabilitation Administration (UNRRA) contributed substantially to the program, and by the beginning of 1947 the danger of starvation had ended. Economic recovery was greatly facilitated by the European Recovery Program (q.v.), which Austria formally endorsed in July, 1947. Between 1947 and 1951, when the E.R.P. was officially terminated, it had contributed well over $1,000,000,000 to the Austrian economy. Partly as a result of this assistance, Austrian industrial production increased steadily. By 1951 it had exceeded prewar peaks, and it continued to rise in the succeeding years. Agriculture lagged somewhat behind industry, however.

The most significant event in the postwar era

was the restoration of Austrian sovereignty in July, 1955. Negotiations among the four occupying powers had begun in 1947, proceeding intermittently and with few results. The main points at issue between the Soviet Union, on the one side, and the U.S., Great Britain, and France, on the other, were Soviet claims to German-owned property in Austria and Soviet demands that Austria pay its occupation costs. In 1950 the Soviet Union made the implementation of the Allied agreement to establish a Free Territory of Trieste a condition for signing an Austrian peace treaty. Agreement on payment of occupation costs was reached in 1951, but other issues remained deadlocked. Early in 1952 the Soviet Union made demilitarization of the occupation zones of the Western powers prerequisite to a treaty; later that year it revived the Trieste issue. The death of the Soviet dictator Joseph Stalin (q.v.) in 1953 resulted in a softening of Soviet attitudes.

Restoration of Austrian Sovereignty. The deadlock was finally broken in April, 1955. In bilateral talks between Soviet and Austrian representatives, most of the issues were resolved. Austria, in exchange for Soviet concessions, promised ". . . not to join any military alliances or permit military bases on her territory. . .". On May 5, 1955, a peace treaty was signed which, among other things, pledged Austria to guarantee free elections and fundamental human rights and freedoms, denied Austria the right to own or manufacture nuclear weapons or guided missiles, and obligated Austria to give most of its oil output to the Soviet Union for ten years. The signatories ratified the treaty on July 27, restoring Austrian sovereignty.

In August, 1955, the Soviet Union relinquished control of the Austrian oil fields, 300 formerly German-owned industrial enterprises, and 240,000 acres of land, leaving Austria in full charge of its own economy. By October all occupation troops had been withdrawn. The first major action of Austria as a sovereign state was to authorize (Sept. 14) the creation of a national army. In October the legislature adopted a law pledging Austrian neutrality, and in December Austria was admitted to membership in the United Nations. Austria completed payment of reparations to the Soviet Union, totaling $150,000,000, in July, 1961.

The coalition of the Socialist and People's parties governed throughout the entire postwar era, despite occasional differences and the passing of prewar and wartime leaders from the scene. President Renner died in December, 1950. Theodor Koerner (1873–1957), the Socialist Party leader and mayor of Vienna, was elected to succeed him in May, 1951.

The coalition was split in October, 1952, over economic policies; elections held the following February gave 74 seats to the People's Party and 73 to the Socialists, thus necessitating another coalition, formed under Chancellor Julius Raab (1891–1964), the leader of the People's Party. In

Police clash with protesters in Vienna as U.S. Vice-President Walter Mondale and South African Prime Minister John Vorster held talks there in 1977. UPI

1956 the government was divided over the future of properties returned by the Soviet Union. The Socialists urged nationalization, whereas the People's Party sought to have private enterprise participate in their control. In the May elections, the two parties retained their dominant positions, and a new coalition was formed, again headed by Raab. The crisis that had caused this division was settled by compromise; the government created a holding company headed by two Socialist and two People's Party ministers to adminster the former German properties. In 1957 the government reached agreement with Germany regarding German assets in Austria. During the same year, however, Austria became embroiled in a dispute with Italy over the status of Austrians in the South Tirol, which had been under Italian rule since 1919. The dispute continued until 1970, when an agreement was reached.

In 1960 Austria became a signatory to the pact establishing the European Free Trade Association (q.v.). The government announced on July 31, 1961, that it would seek such association with the European Economic Community (E.E.C.) as was compatible with Austrian neutrality. The initial Socialist Party opposition to participation waned gradually, however, and in July, 1964, negotiations began with the E.E.C.

The coalition broke in October, 1965, because of a budget dispute that eventually forced the resignation of Chancellor Joseph Klaus (1910–), leader of the People's Party. His party gained a narrow majority in the National Council in the elections of March, 1966. A People's Party government under Klaus took office after the Socialists rejected an invitation to form a coalition. Four years later the Socialists won a narrow victory and formed a government under a former foreign minister, Dr. Bruno Kreisky (1911–). In the elections of 1971 the Socialists won 50.04 percent of the vote, the first time in Austrian history that one party had gained more than 50 percent. Kreisky returned as chancellor in a Socialist government. After this election, Foreign Minister Kurt Waldheim (q.v.) became secretary-general of the U.N.

In July, 1972, Austria signed a free industrial trade pact with the E.E.C. Later in the year, in answer to a warning memorandum from the Soviet Union, Austria asserted that its association with the E.E.C. would have no effect on Austria's "permanent neutrality". On Dec. 7, 1972, as a result of international accords, Austria recognized East Germany.

AUSTRIA-HUNGARY, officially the AUSTRO-HUNGARIAN MONARCHY, known also as the DUAL MONARCHY, former constitutional monarchy of Europe. It was a political union in which the Austrian Empire and the kingdom of Hungary were separate states, each with its own constitution, parliament, courts, and language. They were linked by a single flag and a single Hapsburg (q.v.) ruler, known as emperor in Austria and king in Hungary. Certain matters of state, notably war, finance, and foreign affairs, were controlled by joint ministries. The union lasted for about fifty years, from the formal enactment in 1867 until the dissolution at the end of World War I in 1918.

The Austrian part of the Dual Monarchy had an area of 115,823 sq.mi. and comprised provinces of Lower Austria, Upper Austria, Salzburg, Styria, Carinthia, Carniola, Trieste, Görz and Gradisca, Istria, Tirol, Vorarlberg, Bohemia, Moravia, Silesia, Galicia, Bukovina, and Dalmatia. Bosnia and Hercegovina, occupied in 1878 and annexed in 1908, had an area of 19,768 sq.mi.

The kingdom of Hungary had an area of 125,641 sq.mi., including Hungary itself and the provinces of Transylvania, Croatia, Slavonia, and the district of Fiume.

The Dual Monarchy was established by the Austrian Empire to bolster its waning international prestige and to reduce domestic tension caused by dissident minorities and conflicting nationalist movements.

Austrian preeminence in Europe had been considerably damaged by the rise of Italy and Prussia. Italy, aided by France, defeated Austria in the War of Italian Liberation (1859) and conquered the province of Lombardy, last Austrian possession in Italy. Moreover, the decisive Prussian victory over Austria in the Seven Weeks' War (q.v.) of 1866 led to the expulsion of Austria from the Germanic Confederation, which it had dominated since it was established in 1815 by the Congress of Vienna (*see* VIENNA, CONGRESS OF).

Domestically, more than a dozen national minorities, notably the Hungarians and the Czechs, clamored for autonomy, especially regarding their own languages and schools. Hungary, long under Hapsburg rule, had a particularly strong nationalist movement, with a Magyar population second only to the majority group of Austrian Germans. Hungary, however, had remained loyal to the empire during the Seven Weeks' War.

Hoping to ease the domestic situation and to regain Austrian international prestige, Emperor Francis Joseph I (q.v.) turned to Hungary. The Hungarian leaders Count Gyula Andrássy (q.v.) and Ferencz Deák (1803–76) and the Austrian foreign minister Friedrich Ferdinand von Beust (1809–86) worked out the compromise (*Ausgleich*) of 1867, giving Hungary a constitution and independence. This compromise was the basis of the Dual Monarchy.

The new monarchy did not fulfill all the emperor's ambitions. With the unification in 1871 of all the German states into an empire dominated by Prussia, Austria was forced to abandon hope for Hapsburg ascendancy in central Europe. Although the problem of Hungarian nationalism was settled, similar demands of other minorities continued. Hungary and Austria, with different cultures and languages, had only one bond, the hereditary Hapsburg ruler.

Aside from Austrian Germans and Hungarian Magyars (about 10,000,000 each), the Dual Monarchy controlled over 30,000,000 people of about a dozen national groups, with at least as many languages, including Czechs, Poles, Ruthenes, Slovenes, Slovaks, Serbs, Rumanians, and Italians. Of these groups, the Czechs, including almost 5,000,000 Bohemians, Moravians, and Silesians, were the largest and most vociferous minority. Czech leaders demanded autonomy equal to that granted Hungary, but Austria, backed by Hungary, rejected their demands. The Slavs in the Balkan provinces also demanded autonomy, to no avail; *see* BALKAN PENINSULA. Resenting political and cultural discrimination, the minorities became more and more nationalistic and openly rebellious.

As Hungarian influence in Austrian affairs increased, the Hungarian leader Andrássy replaced von Beust as foreign minister of Austria-Hungary. Satisfied with what Hungary had attained, Andrássy was determined to maintain the status quo. Adopting a policy of friendship with the new unified Germany he promised that Austria-Hungary would not interfere with German internal affairs in return for which Germany backed Austro-Hungarian policy in S.E. Europe. This policy, intended to prevent Russia (q.v.) from expanding to the Dardanelles, was aimed at preserving Turkey (q.v.) as a Balkan power.

The Austro-Hungarian government knew, however, that Russia could not be kept completely out of the Balkans. In 1876 and 1877, therefore, Russia and Austria-Hungary signed two secret treaties; Russia agreed to limit its ambitions to Bessarabia and to back the Dual Monarchy in Bosnia and Hercegovina. Accordingly, Austria stayed neutral during the Russo-Turkish War (*see* RUSSO-TURKISH WARS) of 1877–78, but was so completely defeated that Russia imposed complete submission, ignoring the secret treaties. Austrian protests, supported by Germany and Great Britain, led to the Congress of Berlin in 1878 (*see* BERLIN, CONGRESS OF). The treaty of Berlin restricted Russian expansion into S.E. Europe. It also permitted Austria-Hungary to occupy the Turkish provinces of Bosnia and Hercegovina and to station a military garrison in the Turkish district of Novi Pazar, an area between Serbia and Montenegro, thus preventing these two Balkan states from uniting. German support of Austria-Hungary cemented the friendly relations of the two powers, and in 1879 they signed a formal alliance which, with the addition of Italy in 1882, became known as the Triple Alliance (q.v.).

Austro-Hungarian occupation of Bosnia and Hercegovina contributed to World War I. The occupation lasted until 1908, when the Young Turk revolution forced parliamentary government on the Ottoman Empire and brought Turkish demands that the two provinces be represented in the new parliament at Constantinople (now İstanbul, Turkey). *See* TURKEY: *History*. The Dual Monarchy promptly annexed them, antagonizing Turkey and the neighboring Slav states, particularly Serbia.

Serbia, made independent of Turkey by the Congress of Berlin, had long hoped to bring the two provinces plus other Slav sections of the Hapsburg Empire into a Greater Serbia. Furthermore, the annexation blocked Serbian access to the Adriatic Sea. Serbia was backed by Russia, and only German intervention prevented war. Mounting Serbian resentment finally produced the spark that set off World War I.

In June, 1914, while on a visit to Sarajevo, capital of Bosnia and Hercegovina, Archduke Francis Ferdinand (q.v.), heir to the Austro-Hungarian thrones, was assassinated by a fanatic believed to be a Serbian nationalist. Despite diplomatic maneuvers and Serbian attempts at conciliation, Austria-Hungary declared war on Serbia on July 28.

Austro-Hungarian military activity during the first years of World War I was concentrated against Italy (which left the Triple Alliance and joined the Allies in 1915), Russia, and Serbia. The Dual Monarchy, weakened by decades of internal dissension, began to disintegrate after the death (1916) of Emperor Francis Joseph I, for sixty-eight years almost the only link between the far-flung parts of the Hapsburg possession. His grandnephew Charles I (q.v.) of Austria succeeded him as emperor.

The death of the old emperor weakened the bonds between Austria and Hungary, and a movement for a separate peace with the Allies

Austria-Hungary, known also as the Dual Monarchy, as it existed in 1914 before World War I. Shaded portion of the map represents the Austrian Empire.

Bettmann Archive

gained force among Hungarian leaders. At the same time representatives of the Czechs, the Poles, and the Slavs set up organizations in the Allied countries to gain sympathy and official recognition.

During the spring and summer of 1918 Austro-Hungarian forces were defeated on every military front. Recognizing that collapse of the Hapsburg Empire was inevitable, the nationalist groups within the borders took action. On Oct. 5, 1918, representatives of all Slav provinces met in Zagreb and elected a Yugoslav national council. Two days later, the 4,000,000 Poles under Austrian rule joined their Russian and German compatriots and declared Polish independence. A provisional Czechoslovak government was organized in Paris on Oct. 14, recognized by France the next day, and proclaimed in Prague on Oct. 28. On Nov. 3 the Hungarian government announced the end of dualism and complete separation from Austria.

Realizing that the Hapsburg Empire had disintegrated, Charles I officially renounced his rights to the thrones of Austria and Hungary on Nov. 11, the day the armistice was signed, and left the country. Within a week Austria and Hungary declared themselves republics, and the Dual Monarchy ceased to exist. *See also* AUSTRIA; HUNGARY; WORLD WAR I. G.W.H.

AUSTRIAN LITERATURE, literature written in the German language by people of Austrian nationality and distinguishable Austrian national consciousness. Although the unknown author of the medieval *Nibelungenlied* (q.v.) and the greatest German minnesinger, Walther von der Vogelweide (1170?–1230?), were both Austrian, a distinct Austrian literature did not exist in the Middle Ages. An Austrian culture distinct from that of Germany developed only after the Counter Reformation (*see* REFORMATION: *Results of the Reformation*), when in the 16th century Catholic Austria and Protestant Germany were separated. The Hapsburg (q.v.) and Hapsburg-Lorraine dynasty, rulers of Austria until 1918, fostered Spanish and Italian influences which still distinguish Austrian culture. Spanish drama and Italian opera both influenced Austrian literature.

The first uniquely Austrian literary genre was the magic play of the 18th century, depicting supernatural events in allegorical terms. A magic play that attained worldwide fame was *Die Zauberflöte* ("The Magic Flute", 1791), by Emanuel Schikaneder (1751–1812), set to music by the

Austrian composer Wolfgang Amadeus Mozart (q.v.). Ferdinand Raimund (1790–1836) elevated the magic play to tragicomedy. Johann Nepomuk Nestroy (1801–62) wrote plays of political satire and literary parody, but still within the magic-play tradition.

Franz Grillparzer (q.v.), on the other hand, fused the tradition of the German classics with the typically Austrian spirit that Catholicism and the Hapsburg empire had shaped. In the play *König Ottokars Glück und Ende* ("King Ottokar: His Rise and Fall", first performed in 1825) he contrasts the arrogance of the enemies of Austria with the Christian humility of Austrian heroes. His verse dramas treat national histories and legends, Oriental in *Der Traum, ein Leben* ("The Dream, a Life", first performed in 1834), Biblical in *Esther* (1868; Eng. trans., 1953), Spanish in *Die Judin von Toledo* (1872; Eng. trans., *The Jewess of Toledo*, 1953), and Czech in *Libussa* (1872; Eng. trans., 1941). Greek themes provide the material for *Sappho* (1819; Eng. trans., 1953), and *Das Goldene Vlies* ("The Golden Fleece", first performed in 1821). Like Grillparzer, his contemporary Adalbert Stifter (1805–68) demonstrated a concern for tradition, literary form, and morality. The well-ordered life is idealized in his novel *Der Nachsommer* ("Indian Summer", 1857). Stifter's prose is an expression of the quiet desperation underlying the era dominated by the Austrian statesman Prince Klemens von Metternich (q.v.). The poems and verse dramas of Nikolaus Lenau (q.v.) express the Romantic world-weariness of the same period. An important contribution to Austrian literature was made by the dramatist Ludwig Anzengruber (1839–89). His realistic presentation of dialect and social issues, as in *Der Pfarrer von Kirchfeld* ("The Village Priest of Kirchfeld", 1870) and *Das Vierte Gebot* ("The Fourth Commandment", 1877), mark him as a pioneer of naturalism (q.v.). He is a humorous and sentimental observer of peasant life in *Der G'wissenswurm* ("The Worm of Conscience", 1874), the forerunner of the regional *Heimatkunst* ("homely art"), popular tales of the late 19th century.

Franz Grillparzer — Austrian Information Service

The 20th Century. Modern Austrian literature, developing while the Austrian empire was disintegrating, began with Hermann Bahr (1863–1934). He was the author of the sophisticated comedy *Das Konzert* ("The Concert", 1909) and the essayist who promoted impressionism (q.v.) and other new movements. His contemporary Arthur Schnitzler (q.v.) bared the hypocrisies of men and women in such plays as *Anatol* (1893; Eng. Trans., *The Affairs of Anatol,* 1911) and *Der Reigen* (published 1903; first performed in 1921; Eng. trans., *Hands Around,* 1920). Influenced by impressionism, Schnitzler excelled in the short dramatic episode, such as *Der Grüne Kakadu* (1899; Eng. trans., *The Green Cockatoo,* 1913); and, anticipating the Irish novelist and poet James Joyce (q.v.), he used the stream-of-consciousness method in his stories *Leutnant Gustl* (1900; Eng. trans., *None But the Brave,* 1919) and *Fräulein Else* (1924; Eng. trans., 1925).

Hugo von Hofmannsthal (q.v.) at first turned to a new Romanticism. His early verse plays, such as *Der Tod des Tizian* (published 1892; first performed in 1902; Eng. trans., *The Death of Titian,* 1920) and *Der Tor und der Tod* (1894; Eng. trans., *Death and the Fool,* 1913), were stylized Renaissance legends or timeless fairy tales. He later sought to escape from his neo-Romanticism by drawing inspiration, as did Grillparzer, from a universal cultural heritage. He wrote in a variety of forms, including Greek drama in *Elektra* (1903; Eng. trans., 1908); miracle play in *Jedermann* (1911; Eng. trans., *Everyman,* 1917); drawing-room comedy in *Der Schwierige* ("The Difficult One", 1920); and opera libretto. In the last-named form he provided librettos for several operas by German composer Richard Strauss (q.v.), such as *Der Rosenkavalier* ("The Cavalier of the Rose", 1911), *Ariadne auf Naxos* ("Ariadne at Naxos", 1912), and *Die Frau ohne Schatten* ("The Woman Without a Shadow", 1919).

Like Hofmannsthal, the influential critic Karl Kraus (1874–1936) stressed the preservation of good language. For him the work of his contemporaries, castigated in his periodical *Die Fackel* ("The Torch", 1899–1936), was a symptom of moral degeneration. His play *Die Letzten Tage der Menschheit* ("The Last Days of Mankind", 1919–22), consisting partly of actual war communiques and street conversations, paints an apocalyptic picture of Vienna in World War I.

Universality and preoccupation with psychological analysis merge in the biographies written by Stefan Zweig (q.v.). These include *Triumph und Tragik des Erasmus von Rotterdam* (1934; Eng. trans., *Erasmus of Rotterdam,* 1934), *Maria Stuart* (1935; Eng. trans., *Mary, Queen of Scotland and the Isles,* 1935), and *Marie Antoinette* (1932). His fiction plumbs the depth of emotional aberration, as in *Amok* (1922; Eng. trans., 1931), *Verwirrung der Gefühle* (1925; Eng. trans., *Conflicts,* 1927), and *Ungeduld des Herzens* (1938; Eng. trans., *Beware of Pity,* 1939).

Anton Wildgans (1881–1932) heralded expressionism (q.v.) in the emotional intensity of his poetry. Expressionism also appears in the plays of Franz Theodor Csokor (1885–1968). The poetry of Georg Trakl (1887–1914) presents dreamlike patterns expressing a personal, terrifying universe. Josef Weinheber (1892–1945), however, returned to classical verse forms. He presented in *Adel und Untergang* ("Nobility and Decline", 1934) an aristocratic ideal opposed to the modern age.

Of 20th-century novelists, Hermann Broch (1886–1951) is closest to James Joyce. His *Der Tod des Vergil* (1945; Eng. trans., *The Death of Virgil,* 1946) uses an inner monologue to express the despair of the Roman poet Vergil (q.v.) over the discrepancy between art and truth. Robert Musil (1880–1942) wrote the monumental unfinished novel *Der Mann ohne Eigenschaften* (1931–43; Eng. trans., *The Man Without Qualities,* 1953–60), which probes the possibility of the freedom of men, emancipated from prejudices and habits. The novel also analyzes the process of disintegration beneath the complacency of Viennese life. Philosophically more modest than Musil, Heimito von Doderer (1896–1966) wrote the voluminous novels *Ein Mord den jeder begeht* (1938; Eng. trans., *Every Man a Murderer,* 1964); *Die Dämonen* (1956; Eng. trans., *The Demons,* 1964), and *Die Wasserfälle von Slunj* (1963; Eng. trans., *The Waterfalls of Slunj,* 1966). Doderer, influenced by Russian novelist Fëdor Mikhailovich Dostoevski and French novelist Marcel Proust (qq.v.), used a web of human relationships in a Viennese social circle to give substance and structure to his novels. The novels of Joseph Roth (1894–1939) are

Hugo von Hofmannsthal Granger Collection

less experimental in form and smaller in scope than those of Doderer. Roth depicted the modern world of a refined style, in such works as *Tarabas, ein Gast auf dieser Erde* (1934; Eng. trans., *Tarabas, a Guest on Earth,* 1934).

Apart from Doderer, probably the most outstanding force in post-World War II Austrian literature, other writers must be mentioned. Friedrich Kantor-Berg (1908–), writing under the pseudonym Friedrich Torberg, was the author of a strong novel of adolescence, *Der Schüler Gerber Hat Absolviert* ("Student Gerber Has Graduated", 1930). Fritz Hochwalder (1911–) achieved renown in Europe with neatly structured intellectual dramas. His play *Das Heilige Experiment* (1941) was produced in New York City as *The Strong Are Lonely* (1953). Ilse Aichinger (1921–), a writer of short stories, and Ingeborg Bachmann (1926–73), a poet, were widely read. Fritz Habeck (1916–), author of *Der Ritt auf dem Tiger* ("The Ride on the Tiger", 1958) and *Der Piber* (1965), and Johannes Mario Simmel (1924–), who wrote *Liebe Ist Nur ein Wort* ("Love Is Only a Word", 1963), produced realistic novels deeply concerned with life in postwar Vienna. They were also representative of the many Austrian authors who wrote extensively for German-speaking television. Two versatile younger authors wrote novels, plays, short stories, and verse. They are Wolfgang Bauer (1941–), whose *Magic Afternoon* (1969) is one of several plays in German with English titles, and Peter Handke (1942–), whose *Kaspar* (1969) was produced (1972) in New York City.

Austrian literature is essentially that of Vienna and the Alpine hinterland of the city. Certain writers, including Gustav Meyrink (1868–1932) and Paul Kornfeld (1889–1942), and Franz Kafka, Max Brod, and Franz Werfel (qq.v.), who lived in Prague and wrote in German, are sometimes improperly classified as Austrian. Although Bohemia was for centuries part of the Austrian empire, the Prague authors did not share the Austrian national consciousness; their affinity with German literature was greater. *See also* GERMAN LITERATURE. G.H.

AUSTRIAN SUCCESSION, WAR OF THE. *See* SUCCESSION WARS.

AUSTRONESIAN LANGUAGES, or MALAYO-POLYNESIAN LANGUAGES, family of languages spoken in Oceania (q.v.) and divided into three subfamilies: Indonesian, Polynesian, and Melanesian languages (qq.v.).

AUTISM, severe infant disorder of communication and behavior which develops before the age of three. The term has been used to describe many types of mental disorders, but as originally named in 1943 by the American child psychologist Leo Kanner (1894–   ), early infantile autism describes a rare cluster of symptoms. The incidence of the disorder is approximately 4 in 10,000, and autistic males outnumber females 4 to 1.

The autistic child is unable to use language meaningfully or to process information from the environment. About one half of all autistic children are mute, and those with speech often repeat only mechanically what they have heard. The term autism refers to their vacant, withdrawn appearance, but its connotation of voluntary detachment is inappropriate.

Other characteristics of autism include an attractive physical appearance, an uneven pattern of development, a fascination with mechanical objects, a ritualistic response to environmental stimuli, and a resistance to any change in the environment. Some autistic children have precocious ability, particularly in music or mathematics.

The cause, treatment, and prognosis of the disorder are still being researched, but many experts maintain that autism results from a biochemical imbalance. Preferred treatment for autism is special education, stressing learning in small increments, and strict behavioral control of the child. Some researchers claim success with large doses of certain vitamins, especially the B complex. The prognosis is poor for those autistic children who remain mute through their fifth year. Children with speech fare better, and some cases of recovery are known.

GAIL EVRA
NATIONAL SOCIETY FOR AUTISTIC CHILDREN

AUTO-DA-FE (Port., "act of faith"), public ceremony of execution of persons condemned to death by the Inquisition for heresy and other sins; *see* INQUISITION, THE. The auto-da-fé was observed in Spain, Portugal, and elsewhere. It was the most impressive of the judicial ceremonies of the Roman Catholic Church (q.v.) and was celebrated with great pomp and solemnity; it consisted of the procession of the condemned to a public place and the delivery of a sermon, followed by execution of the sentence, which was frequently burning at the stake. Most of these executions took place in Spain and Portugal and their colonies. The first one recorded was held by the Spanish inquisitor general Tomás de Torquemada (q.v.) in Seville in 1481; the last took place in the early part of the 19th century. Between 1481 and 1808 more than 340,000 persons suffered punishment preceded by the autos-da-fé. Of these, 32,000 were burned. The Americas also had autos-da-fé, Mexico celebrating one as late as 1815. Autos-da-fé were generally held on a Sunday between Whitsunday (*see* PENTECOST) and Advent, or on All-Saints' Day (qq.v.).

AUTOGIRO, trade name for a type of airplane invented in 1920 by the Spanish aeronautical engineer Juan de la Cierva (q.v.). The term is commonly applied to all planes that use the principle of autogyration to provide lift. The wings of an autogiro are rudimentary or nonexistent, the lift being supplied by a large, multibladed rotor mounted above the fuselage. The plane is equipped with a conventional engine and propeller that pull it forward through the air; the forward motion causes the rotor to gyrate automatically, like a windmill. The rotor of an autogiro, unlike that of a helicopter, is not connected with the engine during flight, except during takeoff in some models. If there is such a connection, the craft is sometimes called a gyrodyne.

As the rotor turns, each blade moves forward on one side of the aircraft and backward on the other, thus creating more lift on the forward-moving side. De la Cierva articulated each blade at the hub of the rotor so that an individual blade can rise automatically to avoid producing too much lift or fall to avoid producing too little.

Because of the large torque, or rotational inertia, produced by the rotor, an autogiro is difficult to maneuver. Because of gyroscopic effect, any attempt to turn the aircraft causes it to roll with possibly disastrous effect. To counteract the torque of the main rotor, de la Cierva mounted a small rotor at the tail. An aircraft so equipped is capable of direct control, and it requires no conventional rudders, elevators, or ailerons, control being effected by varying the pitch or speed of the rotor blades, or by tilting the rotors. More recent autogiros have used two main rotors turning in opposite directions, mounted either coaxially or at the tips of winglike struts projecting from the sides of the fuselage.

The autogiro can ascend or descend very steeply, and can therefore operate from extremely small airfields; it cannot, however, climb or descend vertically, or hover over one spot, like a helicopter. Autogiros were used during the 1930's for military liaison, for delivering mail, for exploration, and for agricultural purposes. They have now been generally replaced by helicopters. *See* AIRPLANE, HELICOPTER.
L.A.B.

AUTOMATIC SEQUENCER, in astronautics (q.v.), equipment that automatically triggers the mechanisms used in the reentry and splashdown of a manned spacecraft. The sequencer fires maneuvering rockets to keep the craft pointed properly toward the earth, fires retrorockets that control the speed and trajectory of the craft as it reenters the atmosphere (q.v.), and triggers parachutes that slow the craft and bring it safely to the surface of the earth. The sequencer is controlled by a computer on board the spacecraft, using data gathered by sensors (devices that respond to outside stimuli and transmit impulses for interpretation or for operating a control) in the craft, supplemented by information from ground tracking stations. If an astronaut doubts the functioning of the automatic sequencer, he can switch it off and operate manual controls on board the spacecraft, reading the sensed data for himself.

AUTOMATION, operation of manufacturing processes and business procedures by means of regulatory machines. A logical extension of the mechanization of labor that began with the Industrial Revolution (q.v.), automation utilizes machines that "tell" other machines what to do. In mechanization, a machine performs work formerly produced by human hands, but human judgment still directly guides the machine's program of operation. In automation, control mechanisms direct the entire operation, eliminating the need for continuous human guidance. Automation is a revolutionary development with profound economic and social implications. It has been hailed as initiating a second industrial revolution.

Feedback. All automatic-control mechanisms work on the feedback principle involving a capacity for self-correction. In such a system the output of a machine is linked to its input (*see* SERVOMECHANISM); information concerning actual performance (output) is fed back for comparison with intended performance (input). Departures from the desired condition automatically bring about the required adjustment.

There have been applications of the feedback principle for centuries. An outstanding early example is the flyball governor, invented in 1788 by the British engineer James Watt to control the speed of the steam engine. In this device a pair of weighted balls is suspended from arms attached to a spindle, which is connected by gears to the output shaft of the engine. At the top of the spindle, the arms are linked by a lever with a valve that regulates the steam input. As the engine speeds up beyond the desirable rate, causing the spindle to rotate faster, the flyballs are driven upward by centrifugal force. The action of the flyballs partly closes the input valve, reducing the amount of steam delivered to the engine. For a description of a more familiar feedback device, *see* THERMOSTAT.

Many other control mechanisms were devised long before the theoretical significance of the feedback principle was realized. Early in the 20th century the thermionic vacuum tube was developed and utilized to regulate the emission and flow of electrons in electrical circuits. Other electronic devices, such as the photoelectric cell (q.v.) and the piezoelectric crystal (*see* CRYSTAL), were adapted for control in communications systems and in industrial applications. The new science of cybernetics (q.v.), which provided the general theory of feedback control, arose after World War II.

Application. The automotive industry pioneered in the application of automation equipment to production lines. The basic unit of automated machining lines is the transfer machine, which moves parts from one operation to the next. Once an operator loads the rough part in the transfer machine, it is guided automatically through each successive operation until it is ready to be unloaded as a finished product. For complete automation such systems incorporate electronic feedback devices that supervise the work, checking each phase of the operation, correcting errors, and indicating by a signal on the control panel when a machine tool needs replacement. It was estimated that more than one fourth of all machines purchased by the automobile industry in 1956 was automation equipment; by 1957 the proportion had increased to one third.

The techniques of automation have been ap-

Consolidated Edison Co.

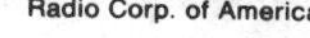

Radio Corp. of America

Cities Service Oil Co.

Applications of automation: At this modern accounting firm (opposite page, top) reference to bulky printed records is no longer necessary. Customer account records are available on microfilm, and supplementary data is retrieved from a random access computer memory and displayed on video screens. An optical scanning machine (opposite page, bottom) scans and sorts machine-printed ZIP-coded mail to 279 bins at a rate of 36,000 letters per hour. A control console (above) puts an instructor in touch with the electronic learning resources center at Oral Roberts University, Tulsa, Okla. The center provides playbacks of lesson material prerecorded on tape or in motion-picture or slide form. Computers (right) are used in petroleum refineries to direct the processing of vast quantities of crude oil into useful products.

plied successfully in the petroleum and chemical industries. In such industries, production may be accomplished by a type of operation known as continuous process, which is best suited to automation. For example, in an oil refinery there is a continuous flow of raw materials into pipes at one end of the plant and of finished products from the other end. Within the plant the entire operation is regulated by feedback control devices. Feedback control is essential in atomic-energy plants, in which human operators must be protected from exposure to radioactivity. Without automation it would be impossible to produce economically such products as nylon because of the high precision required in their manufacture.

Electronic Data-processing Equipment. Computer technology has broadened and accelerated the use of automation techniques since the early 1950's. Many areas of business and research, not previously amenable to automation, have been greatly influenced by this development. *See also* COMPUTERS.

Computers of many different sizes and capacities are now widely used to automate such tasks as general accounting procedures; the reporting and collection of business data; the compilation of statistics; and the auditing of business reports.

Additional applications include the storage and retrieval of large amounts of information; the calculation of complex mathematical equations, such as formulae in mass spectroscopy; and the step-by-step control of industrial processes and machine tools.

The use of computers has been significant in many areas of communication and transportation, such as the navigation and control of missiles and spacecraft; the control of air traffic moving into and out of large airports; the scheduling of ship movements; the design of bridges, tunnels, roads, and other civil-engineering projects; and the automatic routing of calls over telephone networks.

The information fed into a computer for processing, as well as the results of computer calculation, can be transmitted automatically over any distance in coded, high-speed bursts of information via ordinary telephone or cable circuits or via radio (including earth-satellite relays).

Computer installations are integral parts of industrial continuous-control systems in the petroleum and chemical industries. Computers regulate the output of electric generators and the distribution of the power according to changing consumer demand. Connected to automatic machine tools, computers perform the calculations that control the motions of the machines in performing such tasks as milling, boring, and shaping metal. At the same time, the computer can prepare a magnetic or punched-paper tape that enables the machine to perform the identical task at a later time.

Computers are the heart of comprehensive accounting and inventory-control systems used by large businesses, industries, and government. Airlines and hotel chains use computers to make reservations and to keep account of cancellations. Also, in the printing industry, computers automatically compute the spacing between words to justify, that is, properly to space the letters of each line and to hyphenate words broken at the end of a line. The computer then operates an automatic typesetting machine to set the type or it prepares a paper tape that is used later to operate the typesetting machine.

Agencies of the United States government are the largest users of computers, making intensive use of these machines to cope with the constantly increasing quantity of data required for efficient government operation. The examination of income-tax returns, compilations of census, labor, and economic statistics, and the preparation of payrolls and pension payments are some of the tasks performed by computers.

Automation is enabling industry to achieve unprecedented levels of productivity. It is an aid in relieving employees of monotonous, repetitive, and time-consuming jobs. The increasing use of automation, on the other hand, makes ever-increasing demands on individuals operating these systems, in terms of job skills and level of education. A continuously expanding economy and precautionary measures by government, labor, and industry have succeeded in avoiding serious job dislocations resulting from the constant elimination of routine jobs in the process of automation. N.W. & R.A.W-W.

AUTOMOBILE (Gr. *autos,* "self"; Lat. *mobilis,* "movable"), any self-powered vehicle capable of being steered by the operator and designed for use on a roadway or street. The term is used more specifically to denote any such vehicle designed to carry from two to seven people only; larger vehicles designed for more passengers are called omnibuses, or buses, and those designed to carry freight are called trucks. The term automotive vehicle includes all of the above, as well as certain specialized industrial and military vehicles.

HISTORY

After the invention of the steam engine in the early part of the 17th century, various attempts were made to apply this source of power to self-propelled road vehicles. Early attempts were unsuccessful, except for the production of interesting toys such as the machine developed about 1680 by the English scientist Sir Isaac Newton (q.v.), which was propelled by the back pressure of a jet of steam directed to the rear. The first successful self-propelled road vehicle was a steam automobile invented in 1770 by the Frenchman Nicolas Joseph Cugnot (1725–1804). It was designed for the transportation of artillery, and it ran on three wheels. In Great Britain the inventors William Murdock (1754–1839) and James Watt (q.v.) constructed another form of automobile in 1781, and in 1784 produced the model of a wagon, which used the power of a high-pressure, noncondensing steam engine. The British inventor William Symington (1763–1831) in 1786 built a working model of a so-called steam carriage.

The first automobile to carry passengers was built by the British inventor Richard Trevithick (q.v.) in 1801. In December of that year, Trevithick conducted a successful road test of his vehicle, which carried several passengers, on an open road near his native town. His success was due to the greater efficiency and smaller size of his power unit, which was the first to have the piston moved by steam at high pressure. Earlier power units had pistons which moved as a result of atmospheric pressure against the vacuum produced by the condensation of steam. The quantity of water required for this condensation necessarily precluded the use of these earlier engines for vehicles; their bulk and weight relative to the power developed, moreover, were such that they could not have moved themselves if mounted on a vehicle. Later, Trevithick successfully embodied his power plant in a locomotive for rails, so that he can be considered the founder of both automotive road and rail transportation.

In the United States, the inventor Oliver Evans (q.v.) obtained the first patent on a steam carriage in 1789. In 1803 he built a self-propelled steam dredge, which is regarded as the first self-propelled vehicle to operate over American

American inventor Henry Ford riding through the streets of Detroit in 1896 in the original model of his first car, called the quadricycle. UPI

roads. Improvement in the steam engine and in vehicles continued, in England especially, and by 1830 steam coaches were used in regular daily transportation of passengers over English roads. Starting in 1831, however, restrictive legislation in England forced the steam coaches off the highways, and by 1860 development of self-propelled vehicles virtually ceased. In France and Germany, meanwhile, attention turned to the development of the internal-combustion engine (q.v.).

The first internal-combustion engine was designed by the Dutch scientist Christian Huygens (q.v.) in 1678; it was to have been fueled with gunpowder, but was never built. About 1860 a French inventor, Étienne Lenoir (1822–1900), built the first practical internal-combustion engine, that burned illuminating gas. In 1866 two German engineers, Eugen Langen (1833–95) and Nikolaus August Otto (1832–91), developed a more efficient gas engine, and in 1876 Otto built a four-cycle engine, a prototype of the so-called the Otto-cycle engines used in most modern automobiles and airplanes. The high-speed internal-combustion motor of the German engineer Gottlieb Wilhelm Daimler (q.v.) revolutionized the automobile industry. His four-cycle, single-cylinder motor of 1885 achieved speeds many times those of any previous engine, thereby producing many times the power for the same weight. In 1889 he developed a V-type two-cylinder engine giving still greater power. This engine design was adopted by a French manufacturer Émile Levassor (1844–97), who launched experiments in 1891 that subsequently led his firm, Panhard et Levassor, into automobile manufacture, Levassor's first automobile, produced in 1894, not only incorporated the Daimler engine, but also was the first car in which the working parts were arranged in the operational sequence still used in present-day models; that is, with the engine in front, followed by the clutch, gear box, propeller shaft, and differential and driving axle. The superiority of the high-speed Daimler engine over the then highly developed steam engine was conclusively demonstrated at the famous Paris-Bordeaux Race of 1895; the first car, propelled by a Daimler engine, came in six hours achead of the second car, and the next three cars to finish were all propelled by Daimler engines.

Another pioneer with the gasoline engine was the German engineer Karl Friedrich Benz (q.v.), who in 1886, working independently of Daimler, produced a mechanically propelled tricycle.

In the U.S., pioneer automobile manufacturers were very active in the 1890's. Charles Edgar Duryea (q.v.) and his brother Frank Duryea brought out their horseless carriage in 1892–93; the design of 1894 had two cylinders. Elwood Haynes (q.v.) constructed his automobile at about the same time, and Alexander Winton (1860–1932) produced his in 1896. Henry Ford (q.v.) produced his first car, an experimental model, in 1896.

An important factor in the commercial and industrial history of the motor vehicle in the U.S. was the patent which was applied for in 1879 by George Baldwin Selden (1846–1922), a lawyer of Rochester, N.Y. By clever legal technicalities, the actual issuing of this patent was delayed until 1895, so that the original patent rights did not expire until 1912. This patent covered the idea of applying an internal-combustion engine to the propulsion of a vehicle. It included the combination of such a motor with a clutch, or similar engaging and disengaging device in the train of mechanism, by which the motor drove the propelling wheels; it also covered the use of reducing gear, by which the propelling wheels could be driven at speeds lower than that of the motor shaft. Several leading companies took licenses under the patent, while others, led by Ford, refused to do so, leading to litigation which continued from 1903 to 1911. This litigation terminated in a decision that Selden's patent was not infringed because it was valid only for an automobile driven by an engine of the specific type described in the patent, instead of the four-cycle engine then in universal use.

When the Selden patent suit ended, there were 600,000 automobiles in the U.S., some driven by steam, some by gasoline, and some by electricity. These cars were almost all open models of the roadster and phaeton, or touring-car, type. Before that time motoring had been regarded chiefly as a sport; from then on it was increasingly considered a means of transportation. To meet the increasing demand for automobiles of all types, Henry Ford greatly speeded up production by the introduction, in 1913, of the conveyor belt to carry automobile parts on assembly lines. Another important factor in the subsequent growth of the automobile industry was the formation at this time of the organization then known as the Automobile Board of Trade, and now named the Automobile Manufacturers Association. Members of the organization, which today embraces all of the automobile manufacturers in the U.S., made a cross-licensing agreement whereby any member company might use the patents controlled by any other member, without the payment of royalties. The virtue of the agreement was that it

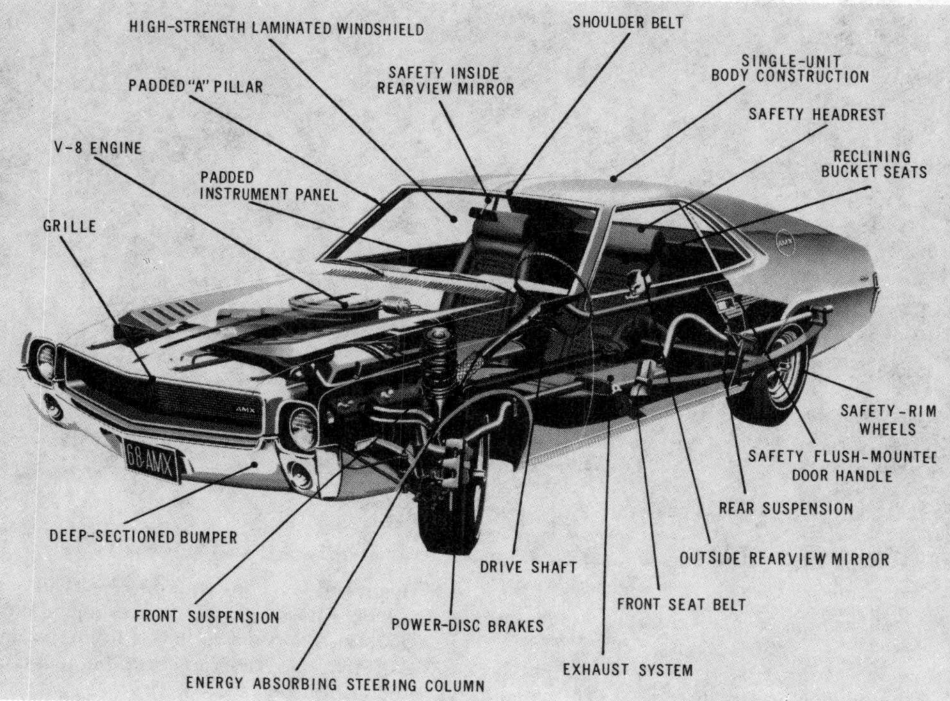

Cutaway drawing illustrating the major parts of an automobile. American Motors Corp.

established a custom of "patents for use", instead of patents as advantages to be monopolized and exploited. Under the agreement, patent rights were shared so that better automobiles might be made, no matter who might make them.

Many early U.S. manufacturers located their plants in and about Detroit, Mich., where the home establishments of the manufacturers of all the passenger-car and most of the motor-truck vehicles produced in the U.S. are now located. Since its inception, the automotive industry has shown a steady expansion, with the exception of the years during World War II when its plants were converted to the production of war materials. In 1973 motor-vehicle production reached an all-time high of 12,600,000 units, including about 9,700,000 cars. In the aftermath of the fuel shortages of 1973-74, U.S. motor-vehicle production was less than 9,000,000 units by 1975. In the late 1970's, however, production had recovered to about 11,200,000 units.

CONSTRUCTION

The chief component parts of an automobile are the power plant, the power transmission, the running gear, and the control system. These constitute the chassis, on which the body is mounted, and are discussed below.

Power Plant. The power plant includes the engine and its fuel, carburetion, ignition, lubrication, and cooling systems, and the starter or electric plant.

ENGINE. By far the greatest number of automobiles in the U.S. use piston engines but in the early 1970's, the rotary engine became popular. *Piston Engine.* The four-cycle engine requires four strokes of the piston per cycle: the first downstroke to draw in the gasoline mixture; the first upstroke to compress it; the second downstroke, the power stroke following the combustion of the fuel, to supply the actual power; and the second upstroke to evacuate the burned gases. Intake and exhaust valves in the cylinder control the intake of fuel and the release of burned gases. At the end of the power stroke the pressure of the burned gases in the cylinder is 40 to 50 lb. per sq.in. These gases escape with almost explosive violence with the sudden opening of the exhaust valve. They rush through an exhaust manifold to a muffler, an enlarged section of piping containing expanding ducts and perforated plates through which the gases expand and are released into the atmosphere.

Chassis buildup begins with the installation of the front suspension system and rear axle. The frame is inverted in the initial operations for ease and accuracy of assembly. Cadillac Motor Car Division

Continuous availability of power and smoothness of operation of the four-cycle engine was improved by the development of the four-cylinder engine, which supplies power from one or another of the cylinders on each stroke of the cycle. A further increase in power and smoothness is obtained in engines of six, eight, twelve, and sixteen cylinders, which are arranged either in a straight line or in two banks assembled in the form of a V.

Wankel Rotary Engine. In the early 1970's, as the auto industry came under intensified pressure to reduce air pollution, a dramatic breakthrough in the rotary-combustion or Wankel engine, invented by the German engineer Felix Wankel (1902–) in the early 1950's, offered prospects of major technical and ecological advances. The Japanese-built Maźda car, the only Wankel-engine vehicle on sale in the U.S., sold nearly 60,000 cars in 1972 and General Motors announced that it would consider making a rotary-engine economy car. The Wankel engine, in which the combustion movement employed rotors instead of vertical pistons, was up to one-third lighter than conventional vehicle engines because it needed fewer spark plugs, piston rings, and moving parts. Economy in engine weight, afforded through rotary combustion, therefore appeared to offset the penalties feared in the future in terms of overall car weight and fuel consumption. Use of additional or wider rotors with the Wankel engine process could raise horsepower levels to the maximum levels that have been found to be necessary in American-made cars.

CARBURETION. Air is mixed with the vapor of the gasoline in the carburetor. To prevent the air and the carburetor from becoming too cold for successful evaporation of the fuel, the air for the carburetor is usually taken from a point close to a heated part of the engine. Modern carburetors are fitted with a so-called float-feed chamber and a mixing or spraying chamber. The first is a receptacle in which a small supply of gasoline is maintained at a constant level. The gasoline in most makes of cars is pumped from the main tank to this chamber, the float rising as the gasoline flows in until the desired level is reached, when the inlet closes. The carburetor is equipped with such devices as accelerating pumps and economizer valves, which control automatically the mixture ratio for sufficient operation under varying conditions. Level-road driving at constant speed requires a lower mixture ratio of gasoline to air than that needed for climbing hills, for acceleration, or for starting the engine in cold weather. When an extremely rich mixture is necessary, a valve known as the choke cuts down the air intake drastically, permitting large quantities of unvaporized fuel to enter the cylinder.

IGNITION. The mixture of air and gasoline vapor delivered to the cylinder from the carburetor is compressed by the first upstroke of the piston.

This heats the gas, and both the higher temperature and the higher pressure favor ready ignition and quick combustion. The next operation is that of igniting the charge by causing a spark to jump the gap between the electrodes of a spark plug, which projects through the walls of the cylinder. One electrode is insulated by porcelain or mica; the other is grounded through the metal of the plug; and both form part of the secondary circuit of an induction system. The principal type of high-tension ignition now commonly used is the battery-and-coil system. The current from the battery flows through the low-tension coil and magnetizes the iron core. When this circuit is opened at the distributor points by the interrupter cam, a transient high-frequency current is produced in the primary coil with the assistance of the condenser. This induces a transient, high-frequency, high-voltage current in the secondary winding. This secondary high voltage is needed to cause the spark to jump the gap in the spark plug. The spark is directed to the proper cylinder to be fired by the distributor, which connects the secondary coil to the spark plugs in the several cylinders in their proper firing sequence. The interrupter cam and distributor are driven from the same shaft, the number of breaking points on the interrupter cam being the same as the number of cylinders.

The electric equipment controls the starting of the engine, its ignition system, and the lighting of the car. It consists of the storage battery, a generator for charging it when the engine is running, a motor for starting the engine, and the necessary wiring. In addition, electricity operates various automatic devices and accessories, including windshield wipers, directional signals, air conditioning, cigarette lighters, convertible tops, power windows, television sets, and radios.

LUBRICATION. In the force-feed system a pump forces the oil to the main crankshaft bearings, and thence through drilled holes in the crankpins. In the full-force system oil is also forced to the connecting rod and then out to the walls of the cylinder at the piston pin.

COOLING. At the moment of explosion, the temperature within the cylinder is much higher than the melting point of cast iron. Since the explosions take place as often as 2000 times per minute in each cylinder, the cylinder would soon get so hot that the piston, through expansion, would freeze, as it were, in the cylinder. The cylinders are therefore provided with jackets, through which water is rapidly circulated by a small pump driven by a gear on the crankshaft or camshaft. During cold weather, the water is generally mixed with a suitable antifreeze, such as alcohol, wood alcohol, or ethylene glycol.

In order to keep the water from boiling away, a radiator forms part of the engine-cooling system. Radiators vary in shape and style. They all have the same function, however, of allowing the water to pass through a large area of tubes, the outer surface of which can be cooled by the atmosphere. In air cooling of engine cylinders, various means are used to give the heat an outlet and carry it off by a forced draft of air.

STARTER. Unlike the steam engine, the gasoline engine must usually be put in operation before an explosion can take place, and before any

How the rotary engine works.

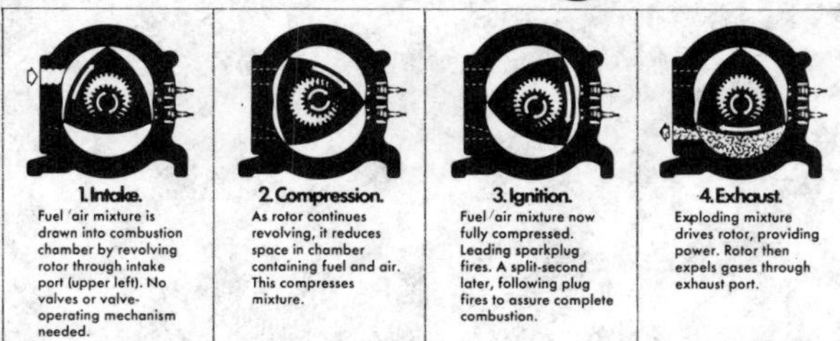

How your piston engine works.

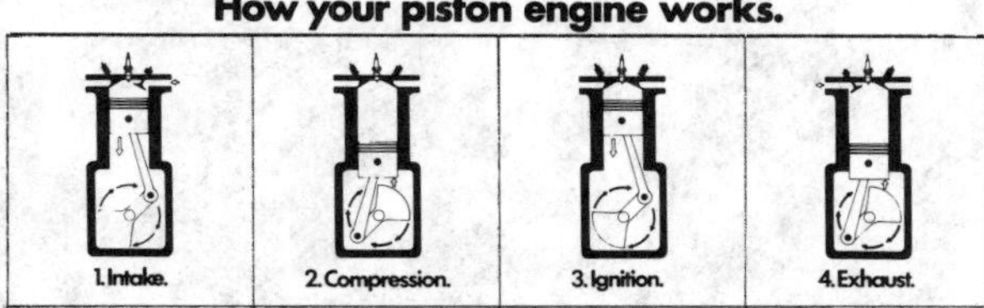

Mazda Corporation

power can be developed; moreover, it cannot develop much power at low speeds. These difficulties have been overcome by the use of gears and clutches, which permit the engine to travel at a speed higher than that of the wheels, or to work when the vehicle is at rest. Ease of starting and steadiness of operation are secured in the highest degree in a multicylinder engine. An electric starting motor, receiving its current from the storage battery, turns over the crankshaft, thus starting the gasoline engine. The starting motor is of a special type that operates under a heavy overload, producing high power for very short periods of time. In modern cars, the starting motor is automatically actuated when the ignition switch is closed.

Power Transmission. The engine power is delivered first to the flywheel and then to the clutch. From the clutch, which is the means of coupling the engine with the power-transmission units the power flows through the transmission in one of several speeds and is delivered into the rear-axle drive gears, or differential, by means of the drive shaft and universal joints. The differential delivers the power to each of the rear wheels through the rear-axle drive shafts.

Some type of clutch is to be found in every car. Formerly the clutch was operated almost exclusively by means of a foot pedal. In present-day cars it is generally automatic or semiautomatic. The friction clutch and fluid coupling are the two basic varieties. The friction clutch, which depends on solid contact between engine and transmission, consists of the rear face of the flywheel, the driving plate, mounted to rotate with the flywheel; and the driven plate, between the other two. When the clutch is engaged, the driving plate presses the driven plate against the rear face of the flywheel, and engine power is then delivered through the contacting surfaces to the transmission by means of a splined shaft.

Fluid coupling may be used either with or without the friction clutch. When it is the sole means of engaging the engine to the transmission, power is delivered exclusively through an oil medium without any contact of solid parts. In this type, known as fluid drive, an engine-driven, fan-bladed disk, known as the fluid fly-

The body of the automobile is lowered onto the chassis after subassembly and electrical wiring.

wheel, agitates the oil with sufficient force to rotate a second disk that is connected to the transmission. As the rotation of the second disk is directly dependent upon the amount of engine power delivered, the prime result of fluid coupling is an automatic clutch action, which greatly simplifies the requirements for gear shifting.

The transmission is a device that changes speed and power ratios between the engine and the driving wheels. Three general types of transmissions are in current use. The conventional, or sliding-gear, transmission, which requires manual operation for shifting gears, dominated the field for about thirty years. This type is now far outsold by Hydra-Matic and torque-converter type systems.

The conventional transmission provides for three or four forward speeds and one reverse speed. It consists of two shafts, each with gears of varying diameters. One shaft drives the other at a preselected speed by meshing the appropriate set of gears. For reverse speed, an extra gear, known as the idler gear, is required to turn the driven shaft in the oppposite direction from normal rotation. In high speed, the two shafts usually turn at the same speed. In low, second, and reverse speeds, the driven shaft turns more slowly than the driving shaft. When a pair of gears permits the driven shaft to turn more rapidly than the driving shaft, the transmission is said to have overdrive. Overdrive is designed to increase the speed of an automobile without taxing the engine beyond its normal operating limits.

The Hydra-Matic type of transmission combines the automatic clutch provided by fluid coupling with a semiautomatic transmission. A mechanical governor, controlled by the pressure exerted on the accelerator pedal, regulates gear selection through a system of hydraulically controlled shift valves. Hydra-Matic transmission provides for two or three forward speeds.

The torque-converter type of transmission provides an unlimited number of gear ratios with no actual shifting of gears. The torque converter is a hydraulic mechanism using engine power to drive a pump which impels streams of oil against the blades of a turbine (q.v.). The turbine is connected to the drive shaft and causes it to rotate.

Both Hydra-Matic and torque-converter systems are controlled by a selector lever on the steering column, which provides also for reverse and emergency-low speeds.

Running Gear. The running gear of the automobile includes the wheel-suspension system, the stabilizers, and the wheels and tires. The frame of the car may be considered the integrating member of the running gear. It is attached to the rear axle and to the front wheels by springs. These springs, along with the axles, control and support arms, and shock absorbers, constitute the wheel-suspension system. In modern cars the front wheels are independently suspended from the frame in a manner which permits either wheel to change its plane without appreciably affecting the other. This type of front-wheel suspension is known popularly as knee-action suspension. The stabilizers consist of spring steel bars, connected between the shock-absorber arms by levers, to decrease body roll and improve steerability.

Control System. Steering is controlled by a hand wheel, mounted on an inclined column and attached to a steering tube inside the column. The other end of the tube is connected to the steering gear, which is designed to provide maximum ease of operation. Power steering, adapted for passenger cars in 1951, is generally a hydraulic mechanism used as a booster to reduce the effort for steering; *see* HYDRAULICS.

An automobile has two sets of brakes, the hand or emergency brake, and the foot brake. The emergency brake generally operates on the rear wheels only, or it may operate on the drive shaft. The foot brake in modern cars is always of the four-wheel type, operating on all wheels. Hydraulic brakes on cars, and hydraulic vacuum, air, or power brakes on trucks, apply the braking force to the wheels with much less exertion of force by the operator on the brake pedal than is required with ordinary mechanical brakes. The wheel brakes are generally of the internally expanding type, in which a convex strip of asbestos or similar material is forced against a concave steel brake drum.

NEW DEVELOPMENTS

In 1966 Federal legislation was enacted, providing for government-mandated standards for passenger-car safety equipment. The newly organized National Highway Safety Bureau, which issues vehicle safety standards, required cars built after Jan. 1, 1968, to be equipped with so-called collapsible steering columns, that would absorb collision shock; seat belts for every occupant; front-seat shoulder harnesses; dual brake cylinders; reflective devices and side lights to make cars more visible at night; padded seat backs and instrument panels; breakaway switches, levers, and handles; better-locking door latches; gasoline tanks that are less likely to leak in the event of an accident; and, for 1969 models, front-seat head rests.

Finished automobiles pass through the paint oven to dry.

In addition, the National Traffic Safety Bureau issued seventeen highway safety standards for possible adoption by the States, in such areas as driver licensing and vehicle inspection.

Pollution and Oil Shortage. In 1966, separate legislation was enacted requiring exhaust-emission control devices on all cars built after Jan. 1, 1968. The Federal exhaust-emission control law followed the enactment of similar standards in California, where unburned hydrocarbons polluting the atmosphere over the city of Los Angeles had been a problem for many years.

The automotive industry introduced two exhaust-emission systems designed to control the emissions of the internal-combustion engines. One of the systems involves the injection of air into the exhaust gas as it flows from the cylinder to the exhaust manifold. The introduction of fresh air at combustion temperatures continues the oxidation process in the exhaust system, so that more of the hydrocarbons and the carbon monoxide are burned before being emitted into the atmosphere. The other system involves engine modifications to improve carburetion, distributor calibration, and combustion, measures that effectively control exhaust emissions.

The 1970 Clean Air Act required U.S. automobile manufacturers to design more efficient and "clean" engines in order to reduce harmful emissions by 90 percent before 1976. But the deadline for meeting these standards was postponed to the 1980 model year because of the fuel crisis of the mid-1970's and technological difficulties. It was also stipulated that the average mileage for all cars be 27.5 m.p.g. by 1985.

Rising gasoline prices led to an increased demand for small cars, and U.S. manufacturers turned out their own models to compete with foreign ones. But the future lay in "downsizing" even standard models to reduce weight and increase economy. High-strength plastics and aluminum replaced steel in many components, and smaller, more efficient engines were designed. Chief among these were dual displacement engines, stratified charge engines, and engines aided by turbochargers. Small computers began to be used to control carburetion. Plans for steam and electric cars were under study for the 1990's.

SPEED AND RACING RECORDS

Official speed records are usually calculated in terms of the average speed of two or more runs over a measured mile. Since 1935 these records have risen from about 300 to about 400 (m.p.h.). The world records listed below were set at Bonneville Salt Flats in Utah; *see* BONNEVILLE LAKE.

Automobile racing is popular throughout the world, in both cross-country and track events. Distances vary widely, and racing cars are classified according to weight and certain mechanical considerations, particularly piston displacement. The most important American event is the annual Indianapolis Speedway race, usually run over a distance of 500 mi. In 1967 a turbine-powered car finished second in the race. In recent years stock-car racing has become increasingly popular, and all U.S. producers, except General Motors, have sponsored entries at Daytona Speedway in Florida and at other tracks.

AUTOMOBILE MANUFACTURERS ASSOCIATION

OFFICIAL WORLD SPEED RECORDS

Date	Driver	Car	Speed (m.p.h.)
Sept. 3, 1935	Sir Malcolm Campbell	Bluebird Special	301.13
Nov. 19, 1937	Capt. G. E. T. Eyston	Thunderbolt #1	311.42
Aug. 27, 1938	Capt. G. E. T. Eyston	Thunderbolt #1	345.5
Sept. 15, 1938	John Cobb	Railton	350.2
Sept. 16, 1938	Capt. G. E. T. Eyston	Thunderbolt #1	357.5
Aug. 23, 1939	John Cobb	Railton Red Lion	368.9
Sept. 16, 1947	John Cobb	Railton Mobil Special	394.19
July 17, 1964	Donald Campbell	Bluebird	403.1
Oct. 2, 1964	Tom Green	Winged Foot Express	413.20
Oct. 5, 1964	Art Arfons	Green Monster	434.02
Oct. 13, 1964	Craig Breedlove	Spirit of America	468.72
Oct. 15, 1964	Craig Breedlove	Spirit of America	526.28
Oct. 27, 1964	Art Arfons	Green Monster	536.71
Nov. 2, 1965	Craig Breedlove	Spirit of America-Sonic One	555.13
Nov. 7, 1965	Art Arfons	Green Monster	576.55
Nov. 15, 1965	Craig Breedlove	Spirit of America-Sonic One	600.60
Oct. 23, 1970	Gary Gabelich	Blue Flame	622.407

INDIANAPOLIS SPEEDWAY WINNERS

Year	Driver	Average Speed (m.p.h.)
1911	Ray Harroun	74.59
1912	Joseph Dawson	78.70
1913	Jules Goux	76.92
1914	Rene Thomas	82.47
1915	Ralph de Palma	89.84
1916	Dario Resta	83.26
1917–18	No race	
1919	"Howdy" Wilcox	88.06
1920	Gaston Chevrolet	88.50
1921	Thomas Milton	89.62
1922	James Murphy	94.48
1923	Thomas Milton	90.95
1924	L. L. Corum and Joseph Boyer	98.23
1925	Peter de Paolo	101.13
1926	Frank Lockhart	95.88
1927	George Souders	97.54
1928	Louis Meyer	99.48
1929	Ray Keech	97.58
1930	William Arnold	100.488
1931	Louis Schneider	96.629
1932	Fred Frame	104.144
1933	Louis Meyer	104.089
1934	William Cummings	104.863
1935	Kelly Petillo	106.240
1936	Louis Meyer	109.069
1937	Wilbur Shaw	113.580
1938	Floyd Roberts	117.200
1939	Wilbur Shaw	115.035
1940	Wilbur Shaw	114.277
1941	Floyd Davis and Mauri Rose	115.117
1942–45	No race	
1946	George Robson	114.820
1947	Mauri Rose	116.338
1948	Mauri Rose	119.813
1949	William Holland	121.327
1950	John Parsons	124.002
1951	Lee Wallard	126.244
1952	Troy Ruttman	128.922
1953	Bill Vukovich	128.740
1954	Bill Vukovich	130.840
1955	Bob Sweikert	128.209
1956	Pat Flaherty	128.490
1957	Sam Hanks	135.601
1958	Jimmy Bryan	133.791
1959	Rodger Ward	135.857
1960	Jim Rathmann	138.757
1961	A. J. Foyt	139.131
1962	Rodger Ward	140.292
1963	Parnelli Jones	143.137
1964	A. J. Foyt	147.350
1965	Jim Clark	150.686
1966	Graham Hill	144.317
1967	A. J. Foyt	151.207
1968	Robert Unser	152.882
1969	Mario Andretti	156.867
1970	Al Unser	155.749
1971	Al Unser	157.735
1972	Mark Donahue	163.465
1973	Gordon Johncock	159.014
1974	Johnny Rutherford	158.589
1975	Robert Unser	149.213
1976	Johnny Rutherford	148.725
1977	A. J. Foyt	161.3
1978	Al Unser	161.363

AUTONOMIC NERVOUS SYSTEM, in vertebrate anatomy, one of the two great divisions of the nervous system (q.v.), comprising all the nerves not in the cerebrospinal system, which includes the brain and spinal cord (qq.v.) and their associated cranial and spinal nerves. The autonomic system controls the action of the glands, the functions of the respiratory, circulatory, digestive, and urogenital systems, and the involuntary muscles in these systems and in the skin. Controlled by nerve centers in the lower part of the brain, the system also has a reciprocal effect on the internal secretions, being controlled to some degree by the hormones (q.v.) and exercising some control, in turn, on the ductless glands.

Two antagonistic divisions comprise the autonomic nervous system: the sympathetic, or thoracicolumbar, division, which stimulates the heart, dilates the bronchi, contracts the arteries, and inhibits the digestive system, preparing the organism for physical action; and the parasympathetic, or craniosacral, division, which has the opposite effects, and prepares the organism for feeding, digestion, and rest. The sympathetic division consists of a chain of interconnected ganglia (groups of nerve cells) on each side of the vertebral column, which send nerve fibers to several large ganglia, such as the coeliac ganglion. They, in turn, give rise to nerves passing to the internal organs. The ganglia of the sympathetic chains are connected to the central nervous system by fine branches connecting each ganglion with the spinal cord. Fibers of the parasympathetic system arise in the brain and, with the cranial nerves, especially the vagus and accessory nerves, pass to ganglia and plexuses (networks of nerves) within the various organs. The lower part of the body is innervated by fibers arising from the lowest (sacral) segment of the spinal cord and passing to the pelvic ganglion, which gives rise to nerves for such organs as the rectum, the bladder, and the genital organs. See also separate articles on the various parts and functions of the body.

AUTOPSY *or* **NECROPSY** *or* **POSTMORTEM EXAMINATION,** medical examination of a dead human body, including the internal organs, to determine the cause of death or to study pathological changes. An autopsy is performed by a doctor trained in pathology (q.v.). After the exterior body is thoroughly examined, an incision is made to expose the internal organs. Their position is noted, and they are removed for examination by eye and further study under a microscope. Autopsies are commonly performed shortly after the death of a person; usually authorization by a surviving relative is required.

Most autopsies serve to advance medical knowledge, but autopsies also have legal uses. Deaths resulting from violence or poison, or occurring under suspicious circumstances, are investigated by a government officer, called either a coroner (q.v.) or a medical examiner; *see* INQUEST. In such instances, the autopsy is made to determine the time and circumstances of death, thereby providing evidence for legal action.

AUTUMN CROCUS, common name for a bulbous herb, *Colchicum autumnale,* of the Lily family (Liliaceae). Autumn crocus, native to Europe, is a garden plant that takes its name from its unusual pattern of flowering. In spring, several large, straplike leaves grow from the bulb, more or less erect, to a height of 2 ft. or more. Later in the summer, the leaves die and fall off. In the autumn, at the same location, a cluster of purple or white crocuslike flowers appears.

Autumn crocus contains poisonous alkaloids, the principal one being colchicine, which is extracted from the bulb and seed of the plant. Symptoms of colchicine poisoning are mainly those of severe digestive upset. Death may follow from the effects of the alkaloids on the nervous system. Colchicine is sometimes prescribed against acute gout. J.M.K.

AUX CAYES. *See* LES CAYES.

AVARS, Mongolian people who about 461 conquered the Uighurs (q.v.), a Turkic tribe sometimes called the pseudo-Avars, and with the Uigurs formed a confederation on the Volga steppes. In the middle of the 6th century the confederation was almost annihilated by the Turks. The survivors, mostly Uigurs led by Avar chiefs, took the name of Avar, by which they were thenceforth known, and split into two bodies. One part remained in eastern Europe; the other moved westward, eventually reaching the Danube R. The members of the second group settled in Dacia (q.v.) and inaugurated an era of conquest.

At the end of the 6th century the domain of the Dacian Avars extended from the Volga R. to the Baltic Sea, and they exacted enormous tribute from the Byzantine Empire (q.v.). During this period, under their khagan, or khan, Baian (d. 617), they were probably the greatest power in Europe, and they influenced tremendously the later development of a large part of Europe by driving most of the western Slavs to the areas that they have occupied ever since. After the death of Baian the power of the western Avars declined under blows struck by the Slavs (q.v.), Bulgars, and Croats. In 795–96 they were crushed by Charlemagne (q.v.), King of the Franks, and were later almost completely exterminated by the Moravians. The survivors were absorbed by the Slavs.

Of the Avars who remained in eastern Europe little is known; the available evidence indicates that they are the ancestors of the modern Avars of the Caucasus (q.v.), one of the twenty-seven Lezghian tribes of Dagestan. Estimated to number more than 150,000, the modern Avars profess Islam (q.v.) and possess a language with Arabic characters. The great Lezghian warrior and patriot Shamyl (1797–1871), who led the people of the Caucasus region in the 19th century in their struggle for freedom from Russia, was an Avar.

AVELLANEDA, formerly BARRACAS AL SUD, city and port of Argentina, in Buenos Aires Province, and capital of Avellaneda District, about 5 miles S.E. of Buenos Aires. Avellaneda is a suburb of the Buenos Aires Federal District and is connected to it by several bridges over the Riachuelo R. A major rail center, Avellaneda is also one of the foremost commercial and industrial centers of Argentina. The city contains textile mills, meat-packing and grain-processing plants, oil refineries, metallurgical works, extensive docking facilities, and markets for farm and ranch products. Pop. (1970) 337,538.

AVELLINO (anc. *Abellinum*), city in Italy, and capital of Avellino Province, in Campania Region, 25 miles E. of Naples. Modern Avellino is built on a site about 3 mi. from the ruins of Abellinum. The city is a center for marketing and processing the agricultural products of the region, including wine, grain, chestnuts, and hazelnuts. The marketplace at Àvellino contains beautiful obelisks, and the city has an academy and a theater. It is an episcopal see. Nearby on Monte Vergine is a famous monastery built in 1119 on the ruins of a temple of the goddess Cybele (q.v.). The abbey is visited every year by thousands of pilgrims, many of whom ascend the mountain barefoot and crawl on their hands and knees from the church door to the altar. Pop. (1971) 54,665.

AVE MARIA *or* **ANGELICAL SALUTATION,** name given by Roman Catholics to a form of address to the Virgin Mary (*see* MARY, SAINT), included in the divine office and in a few antiphons of the Mass. *Ave Maria* are the first two words of the prayer that is taken from the salutation (Luke 1:28) of the angel Gabriel (q.v.): "Hail, Mary, full of grace, the Lord is with thee; blessed art thou among women". Appearing in varying forms as early as the 6th century in the Liturgy of Saint James (*see* LITURGY) and others, the *Ave Maria* was finally adopted as a popular devotion in the 11th century. The present form was fixed by Pope Pius V (*see under* PIUS) in 1568 and has been used by the Roman Catholic laity as widely as the Pater Noster or Lord's Prayer.

AVENTINE HILL. *See* ROME.

AVENZOAR *or* **ABUMERON,** called also IBN-ZUHR or IBN-ZOHR (1091?–1162), Spanish-Arabian physician, born in Seville. A student of the works of the ancient Greek physicians, particularly of Galen (q.v.), he was one of the first to insist on the importance of the experimental method. Many of his experiments were performed on himself. In cases of obstruction of the alimentary tract, he prescribed introduction of food into the stomach through a silver tube and the use of nutrient enemas. He also described a method for setting fractures. He wrote several important medical treatises, one of which, *The Method of Preparing Medicines and Diet*, was translated into Hebrew (1280) and Latin (1490).

AVERAGE. *See* STATISTICS.

AVERNUS, LAKE (Gr. *aornos,* "without birds"), historic lake in Campania, Italy, about 8 miles W. of Naples; the modern name of the lake is Averno. It is about 2 mi. in circumference and occupies the crater of an extinct volcano. The sulfurous and mephitic vapors that rose from it in ancient times were believed to kill the birds that flew over it; hence the name. Because of the forbidding appearance of the lake, ancient Greek and Roman writers believed it to be the entrance to Hades (q.v.). It was the site, in mythology, of the grotto of the Cumaean sibyl, or prophetess, the most famous sibyl (q.v.), and of the grove in which the Greek goddess of the underworld, Hecate (q.v.), dwelt. The Roman general and statesman Marcus Vipsanius Agrippa (q.v.) transformed the lake into a naval base, called Portus Iulius, building a canal connecting it with Lake Lucrine and the sea. Changes in the surrounding terrain soon blocked the canal and restored the lake.

AVERROËS *or* **AVERRHOËS,** *or* (Ar.) ABU-AL-WALĪD MUHAMMAD IBN-AHMAD IBN-RUSHD (1126–98), Spanish-Arab Islamic philosopher, jurist, and physician, born in Córdoba, Spain. His father, a judge in Córdoba, instructed him in Muslim jurisprudence. In his native city he also studied theology, philosophy, and mathematics under the Arab philosopher ibn-Tufail (d. 1185), and medicine under the Arab physician Avenzoar (q.v.). Averroës was appointed judge in Seville in 1169 and in Córdoba in 1171; in 1182 he became chief physician to abu-

Yakub Yusuf, the Almohad caliph of Morocco and Muslim Spain (*see* ALMOHADES). During the reign (1184–99) of al-Mansur, Averroës was exiled because of his view that reason takes precedence over religion; he was restored to favor shortly before his death.

Averroës held that there are two ways to express metaphysical truths: through philosophy, as represented by the views of the Greek philosopher Aristotle (q.v.), and through religion, which is truth presented in a form that the ordinary man can understand. Although Averroës did not actually say that there are two kinds of truth, philosophical truth and religious truth, his views were interpreted in that way by Christian thinkers, who called it the theory of "double truth"; *see* SCHOLASTICISM: *Principal Characteristics.* He rejected the concept of a creation of the world in the history of time; the world, he maintained, has no beginning. God is the "prime mover", the self-moved force that stimulates all motion, who transforms the potential into the actual. The individual human soul emanates from the one universal soul. Averroës' extensive commentaries on the works of Aristotle were translated into Latin and Hebrew, and greatly influenced the Scholastic school of philosophy in medieval Europe and medieval Jewish philosophy. His main independent work was *Tahafut al-Tahafut* ("Incoherence of the Incoherence"), a rebuttal of the attack on Neoplatonic and Aristotelian philosophy by the Islamic theologian al-Ghazzali (q.v.). Averroës also wrote books about medicine, astronomy, law, and grammar.

N.N.G.

AVERY, Samuel Putnam (1822–1904), American connoisseur and dealer in art, born in New York City, where he studied engraving. In 1867 he was appointed commissioner in charge of the American art department of the Exposition Universelle de Paris. He was a founder, and for many years a trustee, of the Metropolitan Museum of Art (q.v.), New York City, and he founded the Avery Architectural Library at Columbia University, in memory of his son, Henry Ogden Avery, an architect, who died in 1890. In 1912 Avery Hall, in memory of father and son, was erected on the Columbia campus. The first floor of the building houses the Avery Library, one of the largest architectural libraries in the world. *See* COLUMBIA UNIVERSITY.

AVES. *See* BIRD.

AVESTA *or* **ZEND-AVESTA,** the prayer book of the Zoroastrian religion (*see* ZOROASTRIANISM). The Avesta forms the sacred books of the present-day Zoroastrians known as Parsis (q.v.), who live in small communities in India and Iran. The original home of these worshipers and of their holy scriptures was ancient Persia (Iran), and the faith they profess was that founded by the ancient Persian Zoroaster (q.v.), one of the great religious teachers of the East. The doctrines of this ancient belief and a record of the customs of the earliest period of Persian history are preserved in the Avesta.

Flourishing six centuries before the Christian era, the religion that the Avesta represents became the faith of the later Achaemenian kings (*see* PERSIA), if it was not already the creed of the Persian kings Cyrus the Great (q.v.), Darius I (*see under* DARIUS), and Xerxes I (q.v.). The religion lost adherents after the conquest of Persia by Alexander the Great (*see* ALEXANDER III), King of Macedonia, in the 4th century B.C., and many of the sacred books were lost. It revived again but was virtually destroyed in the 7th century A.D. by the Muslims in their victorious invasion. Most of the Zoroastrian worshipers were then compelled, through persecution, to accept the Koran (q.v.), the sacred scriptures of Islam (q.v.); many, however, fled to India for refuge and took with them what was left of their sacred writings. A few of the faithful remained behind in Persia and, though persecuted, they continued to practice their religion. These two groups, about 80,000 persons in India and 10,000 in Persia, were responsible for the preservation of the Avesta in its present form. The language of the Avesta is most closely allied to Sanskrit; *see* SANSKRIT LANGUAGE.

AVIATION, term applied to the science and practice of flight in heavier-than-air craft, including airplanes, gliders, helicopters, ornithopters, convertiplanes, V.T.O.L. (vertical takeoff and landing), and S.T.O.L. (short takeoff and landing) craft; *see* AIRPLANE; GLIDER; HELICOPTER. These are distinguished from lighter-than-air craft, which include balloons (free, usually spherical; and captive, usually elongated) and dirigible airships; *see* AIRSHIP; BALLOON.

Operational aviation is grouped broadly into three classes, military aviation, air-transport aviation, and general aviation. Military aviation includes all forms of flying by the armed forces, strategic, tactical, and logistical. Air-transport aviation embraces primarily the operation of scheduled and charter airlines. General aviation embraces all other forms of flying such as instructional flying, crop dusting by air, flying for sport, private flying, and transportation in business-owned airplanes, usually known as executive aircraft.

Early History. Centuries of dreaming, study, speculation, and experimentation preceded the first successful flight. The ancient legends contain numerous references to the possibility of movement through the air. Philosophers believed that it could be accomplished by imitating the wing motions of birds, and by using smoke or other lighter-than-air media. The first form of aircraft made was the kite (q.v.), about the 5th century B.C. In the 13th century, the English monk Roger Bacon (q.v.) conducted studies that led him to the conclusion that air could support a craft in the same manner that water supports boats. At the beginning of the 16th century, the Italian artist and inventor Leonardo da Vinci (q.v.) gathered data on the flight of birds, and anticipated developments that subsequently became practical. Among his important contributions to the development of aviation were his invention of the airscrew, or propeller (q.v.), and the parachute. He conceived three different types of heavier-than-air craft: an ornithopter, a machine with mechanical wings designed to flap like those of a bird; a helicopter, designed to rise by the revolving of a rotor on a vertical axis; and a glider, consisting of a wing fixed to a frame on which a man might coast on the air. Da Vinci's concepts involved the use of human muscular power, quite inadequate to produce flight with the craft that he pictured. Nevertheless, he was important because he was the first to make scientific proposals.

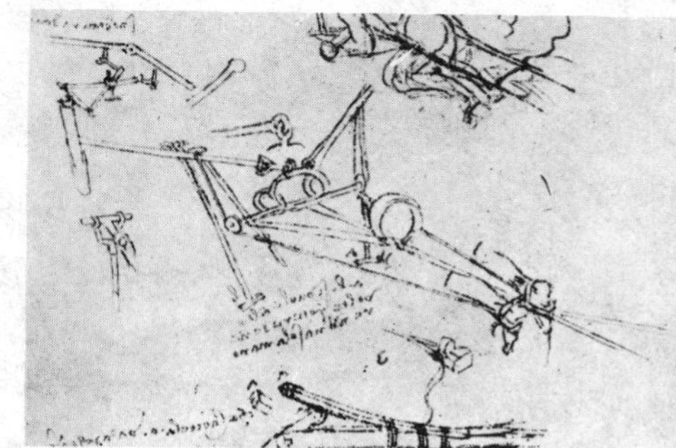

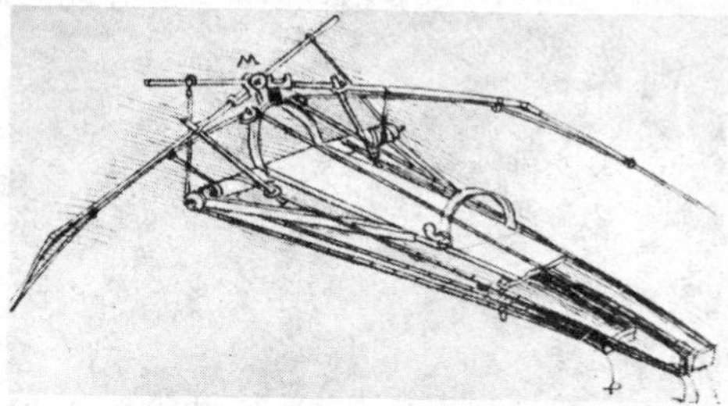

Sketches by the Renaissance genius Leonardo da Vinci for a birdlike ornithopter, designed to fly on flapping wings operated by a man working foot pedals.

IBM Corp.

The 19th Century. The practical development of aviation took various paths during the 19th century. The British aeronautical engineer and inventor Sir George Cayley (1773–1857) was a farsighted theorist who proved his ideas with experiments involving kites and controlled and man-carrying gliders. He designed a combined helicopter and horizontally propelled aircraft and deserves to be called "the father of aviation". The British scientist Francis Herbert Wenham (1824–1908) used a wind tunnel (q.v.) in his studies and foresaw the use of multiple wings placed one above the other. He was also a founder member of the Royal Aeronautical Society of Great Britain. Makers and fliers of models included the British inventors John Stringfellow (1799–1883) and William Samuel Henson (1805–1888) who collaborated in the early 1840's to produce the model of an airliner. Stringfellow's improved 1848 model, powered with a steam engine and launched from a wire, demonstrated lift but failed to climb. The French inventor Alphonse Penaud (1850–1880) produced a hand-launched model powered with rubber bands which flew about 115 ft. in 1871. Another French inventor, Victor Tatin (1843–1913), powered his model plane with compressed air. Tethered to a central pole, it was pulled by two traction propellers; rising with its four-wheeled chassis, it made short, low-altitude flights.

The British-born Australian inventor Lawrence Hargrave (1850–1915), produced a rigid-winged model, propelled by flapping blades that were operated by a compressed-air motor. It flew 312 ft. in 1891. The American astronomer Samuel Pierpont Langley (q.v.) produced steam-powered, large (15-ft. span) tandem-monoplane models in 1896. They repeatedly flew 3000 ft. to 4000 ft., for a period of about a minute and a half, climbing in large circles. Then with power exhausted they descended slowly to alight on the waters of the Potomac R.

Numerous efforts to imitate the flight of birds were also made with experiments involving muscle-powered paddles or flappers, but none proved successful. These included the early attempts of the Austrian Jacob Degen, who carried out various experiments from 1806 to 1813; the Belgian Vincent DeGroof, who crashed to his death in 1874, and the American R. J. Spaulding who actually received a patent for his idea of muscle-powered flight in 1889.

More successful were the attempts of aeronauts who advanced the art through their study of gliding and contributed extensively to the design of wings. They included the Frenchman Jean Marie Le Bris (1817–1872) who tested a gli-

Otto Lilienthal of Germany becomes airborne in 1894 in a batwing glider. Smithsonian Institution

der with moveable wings, the American John Joseph Montgomery (1858–1911), and the renowned Otto Lilienthal (q.v.), of Germany. Lilienthal's experiments with aircraft, including kites and ornithopters, attained greatest success with his glider flights in 1894–96. In 1896, however, he met his death when his glider went out of control and crashed. Percy S. Pilcher (1866–99), of Scotland, who had attained remarkable success with his gliders, had a fatal fall in 1899. The American engineer Octave Chanute (q.v.) had a limited success with multiplane gliders, in 1896–1902. Chanute's most notable contribution to flight was his compilation of developments, *Progress in Flying Machines,* published in 1894.

Additional information on aerodynamics (q.v.) and on flight stability was gained by a number of experiments with kites. The American inventor James Means (1853–1920) published his results in the *Aeronautical Annuals* of 1895, 1896 and 1897. Lawrence Hargrave invented the box kite in 1893 and Alexander Graham Bell (q.v.) developed huge man-carrying tetrahedral-celled kites between 1895 and 1910.

Powered experiments with full-scale models were conducted by various investigators between 1890 and 1901. Most important were the attempts of Langley who tested and flew an unmanned quarter-size model in 1901 and 1903 before testing his full-scale *aerodrome.* This model was the first gasoline-engine powered heavier-than-air craft to fly. His full-scale machine was completed in 1903 and tested twice, but each launching ended in a mishap. The German aviator Karl Jatho (1873–1933) also tested a full-scale powered craft in 1903 but without success.

Advances through the 19th century laid the foundation for the eventual successful flight by the Wright brothers (*see under* WRIGHT) in 1903, but the major developments were the result of the efforts of Chanute, Lilienthal and Langley subsequent to 1885. A sound basis in experimental aerodynamics had been established, though the stability and control required for sustained flight had not been acquired. More important, successful powered flight needed the light gasoline engine to replace the heavy steam engine.

Kitty Hawk and After. On Dec. 17, 1903, near Kitty Hawk, N.C., the brothers Wilbur and Orville Wright made the world's first successful flights in a heavier-than-air craft under power and control. The airplane had been designed, constructed, and flown by them, each brother making two flights that day. The longest, by Wilbur, extended to a distance of 852 ft. in 59 sec. The next year, continuing the development of their design and improving their skill as pilots, the brothers made 105 flights, the longest lasting for more than 5 min. The following year, their best flight was 24⅕ mi. in 38 min. 3 sec. All these flights were in open country, the longest involving numerous turns, usually returning to near the starting point.

Not until 1906 did anyone else fly in an airplane. In that year short hops were made by a Hungarian, Trajan Vuia (1872–1950), living in Paris, and by Jacob Christian Ellehammer (1871–1946) in Denmark. The first officially witnessed flight in Europe was made in France, by Alberto Santos-Dumont (q.v.), of Brazil. His longest flight, on Nov. 12, 1906, covered a distance of about 722 ft. in 22.5 sec. The airplane, the *14-bis,* was of his own design, made by the Voisin firm in Paris, and powered with a Levavasseur 40 h.p. Antoinette engine. The airplane resembled a large box kite, with a smaller box at the front end of a long, cloth-covered frame. The engine and propeller were at the rear, and the pilot stood in a basket just forward of the main rear wing. Not until near the end of 1907 did anyone in Europe fly for a minute; Henri Farman (q.v.) did so in an airplane built by Voisin.

In great contrast were the flights made by Wilbur Wright, when he went to France in August, 1908; he continued to fly until Dec. 31 of that year, when he was aloft in one flight of over 2⅓ hr. He demonstrated complete control of his *Flyer,* turning gracefully and climbing or descending at will. Meanwhile, arrangements were made by the U.S. Army for Orville to demonstrate another *Flyer* at Ft. Myer, Va., beginning Sept. 3, 1908. On Sept. 9 he made the world's first flight for more than an hour, and the same day he carried for the first time a military passenger, Lt. Frank P. Lahm, for a 6-min. 24-sec. flight. These progressive demonstrations were interrupted on Sept. 17, when the airplane crashed, injuring Orville and his passenger, Lt. Thomas O. Selfridge, who died about 2 hr. later from concussion. Selfridge was the first person to be fatally injured in a powered airplane. Orville recovered, and with Wilbur's assistance, he resumed the demonstrations in the following July. All U.S. Signal Corps requirements were met by the end of the month, and the airplane was purchased on Aug. 2, becoming the first successful military airplane. It remained in active service for about two years and was then retired to the Smithsonian Institution, Washington, D.C., at which it is displayed today.

Prominent among American designers, makers, and pilots of airplanes was Glenn Hammond Curtiss (q.v.), of Hammondsport, N.Y. He first made a solo flight on June 28, 1907, in a dirigible airship built by Thomas Baldwin (1854–1923). It was powered with a Curtiss engine, modified from those used on Curtiss motorcycles. In the following May, Curtiss flew alone in an airplane designed and built by a group known as the Aerial Experiment Association, organized by Alexander Graham Bell (q.v.). Curtiss was one of the five members. In their third airplane, the *June Bug,* Curtiss, on July 4, 1908, won the first American award given for an airplane flight, the Scientific American Trophy, covering a distance of 5090 ft. in 1 min. 42 ½ sec. At Reims, France, on Aug. 28, 1909, Curtiss won the first international speed event, at about 47 m.p.h. On May 29, 1910, he won the New York *World* prize of $10,000 for the first flight from Albany, N.Y., to New York City. In August he flew along the shore of Lake Erie, from Cleveland, Ohio, to Sandusky, Ohio, and back. In January, 1911, he became the first American to develop and fly a seaplane. The first successful seaplane had been made and flown by Henri Fabre (1882–   ), of France, on March 28, 1910.

The pioneer airplane flight across the English Channel, from Calais, France, to Dover, England, a distance of about 23 mi. in 35 ½ min., was

The biplane of the Wright brothers, in which they made four successful flights, under power and control, on Dec. 17, 1903. Civil Aeronautics Administration

made July 25, 1909, by the French engineer Louis Blériot (1872–1936), in a monoplane that he had designed and built.

During the period before World War I the design of both the airplane and the engine showed considerable improvement. Pusher biplanes, two-winged airplanes with the engine and propeller behind the wing, were succeeded by tractor biplanes, with the propeller in front of the wing. Only a few types of monoplanes were used. Huge biplane bombers with two, three, or four engines were introduced by both contending forces in World War I. In Europe, the rotary engine was favored at first, but was succeeded by radial-type engines. In Great Britain and the U.S., water-cooled engines of the V type predominated.

The first transportation of mail by airplane to be officially approved by the U.S. Post Office Department began on Sept. 23, 1911, at the Nassau Boulevard air meet, Long Island, N.Y. The pilot was Earle Ovington, who carried the mail bag on his knees, flying about 5 mi. to Mineola, L.I., where he tossed the bag overboard, to be picked up and carried to the post office. The service was continued for a week; *see* AIRMAIL.

In 1911 the first transcontinental flight across the U.S., from New York City to Long Beach, Calif., was completed by the American aviator Calbraith P. Rodgers. Rodgers left Sheepshead Bay, in Brooklyn, N.Y., on Sept. 17, 1911, using a Wright machine. He landed safely at his goal on Dec. 10, 1911, 84 days later. His actual flying time was 3 days, 10 hr., and 14 min.

World War I and After. During World War I both airplanes and lighter-than-air craft were used by the belligerents. The urgent necessities of war provided the impetus for designers to construct special planes for reconnnaissance, attack, pursuit, bombing, and other highly specialized military purposes.

Because of the pressure of war, more pilots were trained and more planes built during the four years of conflict than in the thirteen years since the first flight.

Many of the surplus military planes released after the war were acquired and operated by wartime-trained aviators, who "barnstormed" from place to place, using such fields as were available. Their operations included practically any flying activity that would provide an income, including carrying passengers, aerial photography, advertising (usually by writing names of products on their airplanes), flight instruction, air racing, and exhibitions of stunt flying.

Notable flights following World War I included a nonstop flight of 727 mi. from Chicago to New York City in 1919 by Captain E. F. White of the U.S. Army. In 1920 Major Quintin Brand and Captain Pierre Van Ryneveld, both of the British army, flew from Cairo, Egypt, to Cape Town, Union of South Africa. In the same year, five U.S. Army Air Service planes, each carrying a pilot and a copilot-mechanic, with Captain St. Clair Street in command, flew from New York to Nome, Alaska, and returned. In other army exploits, Lieutenant James Harold Doolittle (q.v.), in 1922, made a one-stop flight from Jacksonville, Fla., to San Diego, Calif.; Lieutenants Oakley Kelly and John A. Macready made the first nonstop transcontinental flight, May 2–3, 1923, from Roosevelt Field, Long Island, to Rockwell Field, San Diego, Calif., and the first flight completely around the world was made from April 6 to Sept. 28, 1924. Four Liberty-engined Douglas Cruisers, each with two men, left Seattle, Wash., and two returned. One plane had been lost in Alaska, the other in the North Sea, but there were no fatalities.

Transoceanic flying began with the flight of

The almost legendary "Spirit of St. Louis", the single-engine monoplane in which Charles A. Lindbergh made the first solo nonstop flight from New York to Paris in May, 1927. Smithsonian Institution

Commercial aviation between the World Wars. Flying boats like this four-engine Pan American craft carried passengers over international routes during the 1930's, encouraging the development of modern air travel.

Pan American World Airways

the NC-4, the initials denoting Navy-Curtiss. This huge flying boat flew from Rockaway Beach, L.I., to Plymouth, England, with intermediate stops including Newfoundland, the Azores, and Lisbon, Portugal; the elapsed time was from May 8 to May 31, 1919. The first nonstop transatlantic flight was made by the British aviators John William Alcock and Arthur Whitten Brown (qq.v.). They flew from St. John's, Newfoundland, to Clifden, Ireland, June 14–15, 1919, in a little over 16 hr. The flyers won the London *Daily Mail* prize of $50,000.

The first nonstop solo crossing of the Atlantic Ocean was the flight of the American aviator Charles A. Lindbergh (q.v.) from New York City to Paris, a distance of 3610 mi. covered in 33 ½ hr. on May 20–21, 1927. On June 28–29 of the same year Lieutenants Lester J. Maitland and Albert F. Hegenberger of the U.S. Army made a nonstop flight from California to Hawaii, a distance of 2400 mi. in 26 hr. Between Aug. 27 and Sept. 14 two other Americans, William S. Brock and Edward F. Schlee, flew from Newfoundland to Japan, covering 12,300 mi.

The first nonstop westward flight by an airplane over the Atlantic Ocean was made on April 12–13, 1928, by Captain Herman Köhl and Baron Guenther von Hünefeld, Germans, and Captain James Fitzmaurice, an Irishman. They flew from Dublin, Ireland, to Greenly Island, Labrador, a distance of 2215 mi. Between May 31 and June 9, 1928, Sir Charles Kingsford-Smith and Charles T. P. Ulm, Australian fliers, with Harry W. Lyon and James Warner, Americans, flew the *Southern Cross* across the Pacific Ocean from Oakland, Calif., to Sydney, Australia, 7400 mi., with stops at Hawaii, the Fiji Islands and Brisbane, Australia. The noted American woman flyer Amelia Earhart (q.v.), with pilots Wilmer Stultz and Louis Gordon, crossed the Atlantic Ocean from Trepassey Bay, Newfoundland, to Burry Port, Wales, on June 17–18; and from July 3 to 5 Captain Arturo Ferrarin and Major Carlo P. Del Prete, Italian army pilots, made a nonstop flight of 4466 mi. across the Atlantic Ocean from Rome, Italy, to Point Genipabu, Brazil.

In 1920 airlines were established for mail and passenger service between Key West, Fla., and Havana, Cuba, and between Seattle, Wash., and Vancouver, Canada. In 1924 scheduled transcontinental airmail service between New York City and San Francisco was inaugurated by the U.S. Post Office Department. Congress passed the Kelly Air Mail Act in 1925, authorizing the Post Office Department to contract with air-transport operators for the transportation of U.S. mail. Fourteen domestic airmail lines were established in 1926. Lines also were established and extended between the U.S. and Central and South America, and between the U.S. and Canada.

During the period from 1930 to 1940, commercial air transportation was greatly expanded, and frequent long-distance and transoceanic flights were undertaken. The transcontinental nonstop flight record was reduced by American aviators flying small planes and, subsequently, transport planes. In 1930 Roscoe Turner flew from New York City to Los Angeles in 18 hr. and 43 min.; Frank Hawks flew from Los Angeles to New York City in 12 hr. and 25 min. In 1937 Howard Hughes flew from Burbank, Calif., to Newark, N.J., in 7 hr. and 28 min. In 1939 Ben

Military aircraft. Two types of propeller-driven long-range heavy bombers, both produced by the Boeing Aircraft Company and both vital to the U.S. effort in World War II, fly in formation, a B-17 Flying Fortress leading a pair of B-29 Superfortresses.

N. W. Ayer & Son

Kelsey flew from Marsh Field, Calif., to Mitchell Field, N.Y., in 7 hr. and 45 min.

World War II. Most of the major countries of the world developed commercial air transportation in varying degrees, with the U.S. gradually gaining ascendancy. On the foundations of the U.S. air-transport industry were built the military-transport commands that played a decisive role in winning World War II.

Largest of all international airlines in operation when World War II began was Pan American Airways, which, with its subsidiaries and affiliated companies, served forty-seven countries and colonies on 82,000 route miles, linking all continents and spanning most oceans.

The demands of World War II greatly accelerated the further development of aircraft. Important advances were achieved in the development of planes for bombing and combat and for the transportation of parachute troops and of tanks and other heavy equipment. Aircraft became a decisive factor in warfare.

Small aircraft production expanded rapidly. Under the Civilian Pilot Training program of the Civil Aeronautics Administration, private operators expanded their facilities and gave training to thousands of students, who subsequently became the backbone of the army, navy, and marine-air arms. Types of aircraft designed for personal use found extensive military use throughout the world. Large contracts for light planes were awarded by the U.S. Army and Navy in 1941.

During 1941 American military aircraft were in action on all fronts. The number of persons employed in the aviation industry totaled 450,000 compared to about 193,000 employed before World War II. About 3,375,000 passengers, about 1,000,000 more than in 1940, were carried by 18 U.S. airlines. Mail and express loads increased by about 30 percent.

Toward the end of the war, airplane production attained an all-time high, air warfare increased in intensity and extent, and domestic airlines established new passenger- and cargo-carrying records. In the U.S., the number of planes produced in 1944 totaled 97,694, with an average weight of approximately 10,500 lb. An outstanding development in the same year was the appearance in air combat of German jet-engined and rocket-propelled fighter planes.

After World War II. In 1945 U.S. military-aircraft production was sharply curtailed, but civilian-aircraft orders increased considerably. By the end of the year, U.S. manufacturers held orders for 40,000 planes, in contrast to the former production record for civilian use of 6844 planes in 1941. Again the domestic and international airlines of the U.S. broke all records, with all categories of traffic showing substantial gains over 1944. Both passenger fares and basic freight rates were reduced. International commercial services were resumed in 1945.

The experience gained in the production of military aircraft during the war was utilized in civil-aircraft production following the close of hostilities, and larger, faster aircraft, with such improvements as pressurized cabins, were made available to the airlines. Improved airports, more efficient weather forecasting, additional aids to navigation, and public demand for air transportation all aided in the postwar boom in airline passenger travel and freight transportation.

The 345-passenger Lockheed-1011 TriStar, which went into service in 1972, has a cruising speed of about 620 m.p.h. Lockheed-California Co.

Experimentation with new aerodynamic designs, new metals, new power plants, and electronic inventions resulted in the development of high-speed turbojet planes, designed for transoceanic flights, and of turboprop aircraft; *see* AIRPLANE: *Commercial Airplanes;* JET PROPULSION. In the early 1970's more than 500,000 workers were engaged in the production of aircraft and parts in the U.S. The airframe industry is centered largely west of the Mississippi R.; the airplane-engine industry is situated mainly in the eastern section of the country.

Nine generally recognized classes operate in the air-transport industry in the U.S. The classifications are used by the Civil Aeronautics Board and the Federal Aviation Administration. Seven of the classes have certificates authorizing regularly scheduled services. They are the domestic trunk carriers (the airlines operating in the U.S.), the domestic local-service carriers (feeder lines), the intra-Hawaiian carriers, the intra-Alaskan carriers, the helicopter carriers, the international and territorial carriers (all U.S.-flag lines operating between the U.S. and foreign countries, except Canada, and flying over international waters), and the all-cargo carriers (operating within the U.S. and abroad; one line flies to the Caribbean area and another to Europe). The supplemental air carriers (nonscheduled) and intrastate air carriers are the two remaining classes. The scheduled airlines maintain a trade association known as the Air Transport Association of America. *See* AIR TRANSPORT.

After World War II a marked increase in the use of company-owned airplanes for the transportation of executives took place. More than 130,000 craft (planes and helicopters) were in general-aviation use in the early 1970's, comprising more than 96 percent of all aircraft active in the U.S. They flew more than 25,500,000 aircraft hours and 3,140,000 mi. within this period of time.

Conferences relative to the problems of international flight were held as early as 1889, but not until 1947 was an organization established to handle the problems of large-scale international air travel. This body is the International Civil Aviation Organization (q.v.), with head-

Poised for supersonic flight, the stubby-winged F-106 Delta Dart jet fighter plane is capable of carrying air-to-air missiles with nuclear warheads in operations of the North American air defense system. UPI

quarters in Montréal, Canada. Working in close cooperation with I.C.A.O. is the International Air Transport Association (I.A.T.A.), also with headquarters in Montréal, and comprising about a hundred airlines that seek jointly to solve mutual problems.

See also ASTRONAUTICS; AVIATION MEDICINE; FLIGHT, THEORY OF. L.A.B.

AVIATION INDUSTRY. *See* AIR TRANSPORT; AVIATION.

AVIATION MEDICINE, subspecialty of preventive medicine that treats the physiological and psychological reactions of man to the stresses of air travel. Medical specialists in both military and civil aviation are concerned with the proper screening of candidates for flight training, maintenance of maximum efficiency among flight personnel, and with clinically oriented research programs involving the physics, physiology, and psychology of flight. They are also concerned with the medical logistics of transporting the sick and wounded by aircraft; they cooperate actively with aeronautical engineers in the development of safe and efficient aircraft; and they seek to prevent the spread of disease by airborne carriers.

Lieutenant Colonel John F. Stapp awaits the beginning of a test run on the rocket-propelled decelerator sled in an experiment to determine how much impact a pilot wearing safety harness could survive in an airplane crash. Accelerometers are attached at his mouth, chest, and right knee to transmit signals during the test.
U.S. Air Force

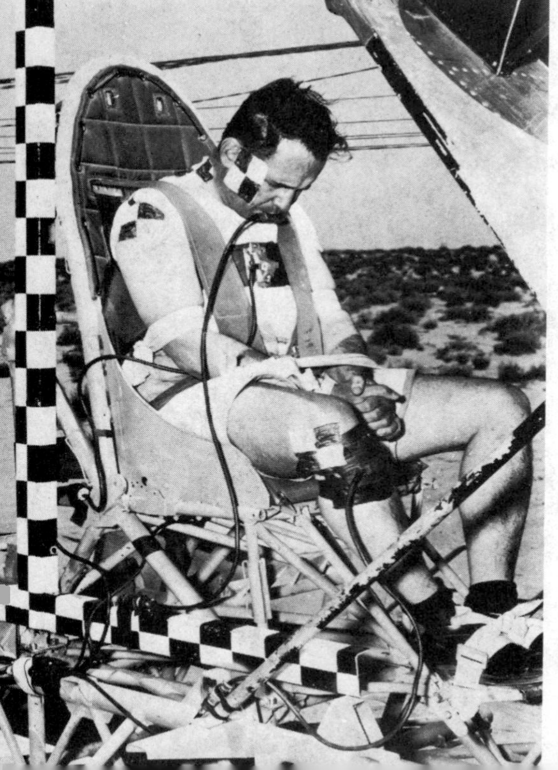

Air-Crew Selection Standards. Each of the military services, the army, navy, and air force, has issued regulations for its flying personnel. The Federal Aviation Administration (F.A.A.), now a part of the Department of Transportation, issues instructions concerning examinations for civil airmen. Physical standards in civil aviation are divided into three classes: Class I includes airline transport pilots, Class II covers the commercial pilot (for-hire class), and Class III covers the student and private pilot. Commercial airlines and other agencies may adhere to standards above those required by the F.A.A.

Certain basic requirements apply to all fliers, civilian and military. These include high standards for sight and hearing, normal color vision, and general physiological and psychological well-being. Among the common organic defects for which candidates may be disqualified are nasal obstructions, sinus abnormalities, hypertension, tuberculosis, severe allergies, and hernia. One important aspect of air safety is the assurance that the pilot-air controller team is medically fit, physically and emotionally, to cope with problems of guiding the takeoff, ascent, descent, and landing of aircraft. Because 50 percent of all accidents are attributed to error of the pilot or other members of the team, it is important to eliminate candidates who are poorly adjusted or emotionally immature.

PHYSIOLOGICAL CONSIDERATIONS IN FLIGHT

Aviation medicine is concerned primarily with the effects on the human mechanism of high speed and high altitude, involving such factors as acceleration and deceleration, atmospheric pressure, decompression, and the interrelationship of the atmospheric pressure and level of oxygen supply. In civil aviation, medicine is concerned with such discomforts of air travel as passenger airsickness.

High Speed. In itself, high speed does not produce harmful symptoms, provided the direction of flight and velocity remain constant. Acceleration or deceleration forces are expressed as multiples of the unit of force of 1 g (32.174 ft./sec.^{2} or 980.665 cm/sec.^{2}). The effects of one form of this force become apparent when a sharp change of direction occurs, as in pulling out of a dive. In such a maneuver the pilot may be subjected to an inertial force as high as 9 g. If a force of 4 to 6 g is sustained for more than a few seconds, the resulting symptoms range from visual impairment to total blackout. Protection is provided by a specially designed outfit, called

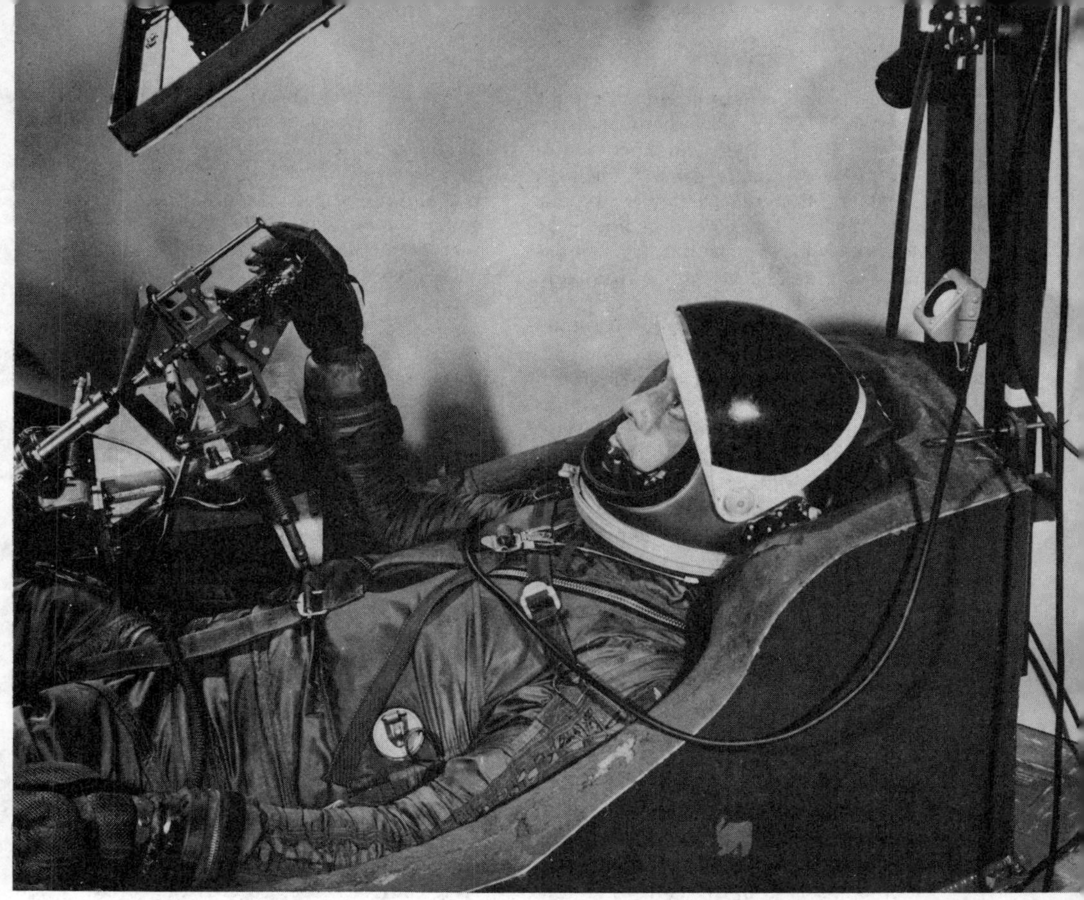

the "anti-g suit", which supplies pressure to the abdomen and legs, thus counteracting the tendency of the blood to accumulate in those areas. Proper support of the head is essential during extreme decelerations in order to avoid swelling of the sinuses and severe headaches. While facing backward in a seated position, human test subjects have been able to tolerate an impact of 50 g without severe damage.

High Altitude and Atmospheric Pressure. Because of the gravitational field of the earth, the atmosphere is compressed so that it is densest at the surface of the earth. As altitude increases, the atmospheric pressure falls rapidly at first and then more slowly as it becomes a vacuum at the outer limit of the atmosphere. At sea level, air mass and weight exert a pressure of more than 1 ton per sq.ft., 14.7 lb. per sq.in., or 760 mm of mercury under standard conditions. *See* BAROMETER.

A critical consideration in aircraft travel is the continuing physiological requirement for oxygen. The only oxygen stored by the body is that actually being transported by the bloodstream.

Astronaut Alan B. Shepard wears an MC-IV pressure suit as he undergoes test procedures in the Analog Flight Simulator at Langley Research Center, in preparation for a flight in the Mercury space flight series.
NASA

Although muscles can function temporarily without oxygen, the buildup of toxic fatigue products soon limits activity. The tissues most sensitive to oxygen deficiency are the central nervous system and the eyes.

The atmosphere, which contains 21 percent oxygen by volume, is capable of meeting the respiratory needs of man because the air he breathes is naturally under pressure. The barometric pressure existing at sea level and up to approximately 15,000 ft. is sufficient. However, above 15,000 ft., the air must be artificially put under pressure.

High-altitude military airplanes are provided with oxygen equipment, and military personnel are required to use oxygen at all times when participating in flight above 10,000 ft. Military aircraft that can fly above 35,000 ft. usually also have cockpits under pressure to altitude equivalents of 12,000 to 18,000 ft. Positive-pressure breathing equipment is used in aircraft capable of flight above 35,000 ft. Full or partial pressure suits with additional oxygen equipment are required in military aircraft capable of flight above 55,000 ft. Commercial carriers provide oxygen systems and pressurized cabins in accordance with civil air regulations. For example, an airliner flying at 22,000 ft. must maintain a "cabin altitude" of 6000 ft.

ALTITUDE SICKNESS. The physiological condition results from a state of acute oxygen deficiency, known medically as hypoxidosis, at high altitudes. Within the lower section of the atmosphere (called the troposphere), which extends upward to about 7 mi. from the surface of the earth, the atmosphere is sufficiently rarefied at 13,000 ft. to produce definite symptoms of hypoxia, also called oxygen hunger, the major limiting factor to life at high altitude. At the lower limit of the stratosphere, about 35,000 ft. above sea level, normal inhalation of pure oxygen no longer maintains an adequate blood-oxygen saturation; at 52,000 ft. unaided respiration is no longer possible, and oxygen must be introduced into the lungs under pressure, as in a pressurized cabin.

A high degree of variability exists in individual response to this effect of altitude, and a wide range of adaptability may be noted within a given individual. By a gradual process of acclimatization, mountaineers may sustain themselves at an upper limit of 25,000 ft. without requiring extra oxygen. On the other hand, the aviator in rapid ascent soon needs supplemental oxygen in ever-increasing concentration.

Hypoxia (reduced partial pressure of oxygen) produces a variety of reactions in the body. Mild intoxication and stimulation of the nervous system is followed by progressive loss of attention and judgment until unconsciousness supervenes. Respiration and pulse rate increase, the systemic oxygen content is lowered, large numbers of red cells are poured into the bloodstream from the spleen, the bone marrow is stimulated to increased activity, and urinary and intestinal functions are adversely affected. Prolonged lack of oxygen may cause brain damage.

AEROEMBOLISM. Because of the loss of barometric pressure at altitudes of about 30,000 ft., the body tissues can no longer retain atmospheric nitrogen in solution. As a result of the low atmospheric pressure, liberated gas bubbles and ruptured fat cells may enter the blood circulation, forming obstructions, or emboli, in the blood vessels. This condition, known medically as aeroembolism and popularly as the bends (q.v.), leads to confusion, paralysis, or neurocirculatory collapse, known as shock. Expanded intestinal gas produces abdominal distention and discomfort. The most characteristic symptom of bends is pain in the large joints resulting from pressure of the gas on tendons and nerves, together with spasm of the blood vessels. Unusually rapid ascents, severe physical exertion, and extreme cold aggravate the tendency to decompression illness. Preflight inhalation of pure oxygen to eliminate nitrogen from the system has proved valuable as a preventive measure. Rapid decompression, resulting from accidental failure at high altitudes of the pressure with the cabin, causes major damage to the heart and other organs by the "ram effect" of gross gases formed in the body cavities. Barometric pressure at 63,000 ft. is so low that fluids boil over explosively and evaporate.

AIRSICKNESS. This condition is produced by a disturbance of the labyrinthine mechanism of the inner ear, although psychogenic factors such as apprehension can also play a part. Only 8 percent of all airline passengers are affected; the incidence is highest among women and lowest among young adults. Medication such as some of the amphetamines is effective in preventing motion sickness. Since this type of drug produces drowsiness, it is of limited usefulness for personnel in actual control of aircraft.

See AEROSPACE MEDICINE; SPACE MEDICINE.

M.M.L.

AVICEBRÓN. *See* IBN-GABIROL, SOLOMON BEN JUDAH.

AVICENNA, *or* (Ar.) ABU-'ALI AL-HUSAYN IBN-SÎNA (980–1037), Persian Islamic philosopher and physician, born near Bukhara (now in the Uzbek S.S.R.). The son of a government official, Avicenna studied medicine and philosophy in Bukhara. At the age of seventeen he was rewarded for his medical discoveries with the post of court physician to the Samanid ruler of Bukhara. He remained in this position for about seven years, until the fall in 999, of the Samanid Empire, and then traveled extensively. He spent the last fourteen years of his life as scientific advisor and physician to the ruler of Isfahan.

Regarded by Muslims as one of the greatest Islamic philosophers, Avicenna is an important figure in the fields of both medicine and philosophy. His work *The Canon of Medicine,* largely based on Greek medical works, long was preeminent both in the Near East and in Europe as a textbook. It is significant as a systematic classification and summary of medical and pharmaceutical knowledge up to and including Avicenna's time. The first Latin translation of the work was made in the 12th century, the Hebrew version appeared in 1491, and the Arabic text in 1593, the second text ever printed in Arabic.

Avicenna's best-known philosophical work is *Kitab ash-Shifa* ("The Recovery [of the soul from error]"), a collection of treatises on Aristotelian logic, metaphysics, psychology, the natural sciences, and other subjects. Avicenna's own philosophy was based on a combination of Aristotelianism (*see* ARISTOTLE) and Neoplatonism (q.v.). Contrary to orthodox Islamic thought, Avicenna denied personal immortality, God's interest in individual men, and creation of the world in time. Because of his views, Avicenna became the main target of an attack on philosophy by the Islamic philospher al-Ghazzali (q.v.). Nevertheless, Avicenna's philosophy remained influential throughout the Middle Ages. *See* ISLAM: *Theology and Philosophy.* N.N.G.

AVIGNON, city in France, and capital of Vaucluse, Department, on the left bank of the Rhône R., about 55 miles N.W. of Marseille. The city is a commercial and transportation center with important trade in wines, fruits, and silk. Industries include flour mills, oil and leather works, and the manufacture of soap and chemicals.

Places of interest within the city include a huge 14th-century palace that once served as a residence and fortress of the popes. The beautiful Gothic Basilica of Saint Peter (14th century) is located nearby, and just north of the palace, on the rocky heights overlooking the Rhône R., are several public gardens. Only a fragment of the bridge of Saint Bénezét dating from the 12th century remains, but the city still retains its massive 14th-century ramparts, which were only slightly damaged during World War II. The modern districts of the city extend E. and S. of the old walled town.

From 1309 to 1377, the period often referred to as the "Babylonian captivity" of the popes, Avignon served as the seat of the papal court, and from 1378 to 1408 the city was the residence of several of the antipopes (*see* SCHISM, WESTERN). In 1475 the city was made an archiepiscopal see and became a flourishing commercial center. During this period, even though Avignon was part of the Papal States (q.v.) and was nominally ruled by legates, the citizens were actually free to govern themselves. The papacy lost the city during the French Revolution (q.v.) when Avignon was incorporated by plebiscite into France in 1791. Pop. (1971) 88,958.

ÁVILA, Pedro Arias de. *See* PEDRARIAS.

ÁVILA CAMACHO, Manuel (1897–1955), Mexican soldier and statesman, born in Teziutlán, State of Puebla, and self-educated. His mil-

The fortress-palace of the popes at Avignon, built in 14th-century Gothic style, dominates the city from a high hill. French Government Tourist Office

itary career began in 1941 with service in the revolutionary army of the Mexican soldier and political leader Victoriano Huerta (q.v.). Ávila Camacho was made general of a division in 1938 and in 1940 was elected president of Mexico as the candidate of the Mexican Revolutionary Army. As president he followed a more conservative economic and religious policy than did his predecessor, the Mexican soldier and statesman Lázaro Cárdenas (q.v.). During World War II, the Camacho government collaborated with the United States and the other Allied nations in the fight against the Axis powers (q.v.). In 1946 Ávila Camacho retired.

ÁVILA DE LOS CABALLEROS, *or* ÁVILA, city in Spain, and capital of Ávila Province, on the Adaja R., about 55 miles W. of Madrid. The city has little economic importance; the chief industry of the province is the raising of livestock. Many fine monuments of medieval architecture remain, however, including a Gothic cathedral dating from the 14th century, and the well-preserved dark granite walls of the ancient city, with imposing gates and surmounted by many turrets, dating from the 11th century. Pop. (1970) 30,983.

AVOCADO *or* **ALLIGATOR PEAR,** common name for a tree, *Persea americana,* of the Laurel family (Lauraceae), native to tropical America, and for the fruit of this tree. The fruit is a greenish, thick-skinned drupe (*see* FRUIT: *Types of Fruit*), the size and shape of a large pear. When ripe, the flesh has the consistency of firm butter and a faint nutlike flavor. It has a high fat content, containing 10 to 20 percent oil, and is rich in protein. In the United States avocado is popular as a salad vegetable, and in the tropics it is often used in soup to compensate for the scarcity of meat. The tree is extensively cultivated in the southern U.S.; *see also* LAUREL.

AVOCET *or* **AVOSET,** long-legged, web-footed shore bird of the genus *Recurvirostra* in the family Recurvirostridae, characterized by a long, slender, upcurved bill. Avocets frequent marshes and search shallow water with their sensitive beaks for crustaceans, snails, and similar prey. The several species are found in summer in the Northern Hemisphere; in winter they migrate to the tropics. They build simple nests upon the ground in marshy places and usually lay four olive or buff eggs, thickly spotted with dark brown. The principal American species, *R. americana,* has whitish plumage, with the wings black, and the head, neck, and breast a cinnamon color. It is common in the western States, where it is a popular game bird.

AVOGADRO, Count Amedeo (1776–1856), Italian physicist and chemist, born in Turin and educated as a lawyer. He became interested in mathematics and physics and, after several years of study, was appointed to a professorship at the Royal College of Vercelli. From 1820 until his death Avogadro was professor of physics at the University of Turin. Although he also carried on research on electricity and the physical properties of liquids, he is best known for his hypothesis, later known as Avogadro's Law (q.v.), first published in the scientific periodical *Journal de Physique* ("Journal of Physics") in 1811. Avogadro also made the important distinction between the atom and the molecule (qq.v.).

Avocet, Recurvirostra americana
Allan D. Cruickshank – National Audubon Society

AVOGADRO'S LAW, chemical law that states that under identical conditions of temperature and pressure, equal volumes of any two gases contain an equal number of molecules. The law was first proposed as a hypothesis by the Italian physicist Count Amedeo Avogadro (q.v.) in 1811. At that time this simple rule, providing an explanation for a wide number of apparently unconnected phenomena, was considered unacceptable by European scientists, principally because of exceptions in the case of ammonium chloride gas and nitrogen tetroxide gas. Some of the molecules of these gases decompose, however, at the temperatures at which the experiments were performed, thus yielding additional molecules and increasing the volume of the gas. Italian chemists and physicists continued to develop this hypothesis, and in the 1850's, largely through the efforts of the Italian chemist Stanislao Cannizzaro (q.v.), Avogadro's Law was universally accepted. It is now considered one of the fundamental laws of chemistry.

AVOGADRO'S NUMBER *or* **AVOGADRO'S CONSTANT,** the number of molecules in a gram molecule; that is, the number of molecules of any substance in that amount of grams of the substance which is numerically equal to the molecular weight. According to Avogadro's law (q.v.), this number must be the same for all substances; for example, the number of molecules in 32 grams of oxygen must be the same as the number of molecules in 2 grams of hydrogen. The exact value for Avogadro's number, 6.06×10^{23}, was initially determined by the American physicist Robert Andrews Millikan (q.v.). More recent experiments have assigned the values $6.0248 \pm 0.00016 \times 10^{23}$ (physical) and $6.0232 \pm 0.00016 \times 10^{23}$ (chemical).

AVOIRDUPOIS, system of weights applied in the English-speaking world to all goods except precious metals, precious stones, and medicines. *See* WEIGHTS AND MEASURES.

AVON (Celtic, "river" or "stream"), name of several rivers in England and Scotland. The most important, all of which are in England, include the Upper, or Warwickshire, Avon (93 mi. long), which rises in Northamptonshire and flows through Stratford, birthplace of William Shake-

Ambassador Saturo Kurusu reads the Japanese declaration following announcement on Sept. 27, 1940, of a military and economic pact between Germany, Italy, and Japan, in Berlin, Germany. Foreign Minister Count Galeazzo Ciano of Italy and Adolf Hitler, German dictator, are seated at his right. UPI

speare (q.v.), entering the Severn R. at the N. boundary of Gloucestershire; the East Avon, which rises in Wiltshire and flows S., entering the English Channel at Christchurch; and the Lower, or Bristol, Avon, which rises in Gloucestershire, flows through Wiltshire and Somersetshire, and enters the Bristol Channel 6 mi. below Bristol.

AWAJI, island in the Inland Sea of Japan, between the islands of Shikoku and Honshu, in Hyogo Prefecture. Farming, fishing, and pottery making are the chief occupations. Area, 228 sq. mi.

AWARD. *See* MEDAL; NATIONAL BOOK AWARDS; NOBEL PRIZES; PRESIDENTIAL MEDAL OF FREEDOM; PULITZER PRIZES; PURPLE HEART, ORDER OF THE.

AXEL. *See* ABSALON.

AXELROD, Julius (1912–), American biochemist, born in New York City, and educated at New York and George Washington universities. After working for nearly fifteen years as an industrial research chemist in New York City, he joined the National Heart Institute of the National Institutes of Health in 1949; in 1955 he was named chief of pharmacology of the laboratory of clinical science at the National Institute of Mental Health. For his investigation of the mechanisms that regulate the formation of the hormone noradrenaline, as an important nerve-impulse transmitter, Axelrod shared the 1970 Nobel Prize in medicine and physiology with the British biophysicist Sir Bernard Katz and the Swedish physiologist Ulf Svante von Euler (qq.v.). His research on the effects of drugs on the nervous system has included specific determination of the route taken by intravenously administered drugs.

AXIOM, general statement, the truth of which is self-evident and is accepted without proof. Among the ancient Greek philosophers, Plato (q.v.) probably limited the term to geometric propositions, but Aristotle (q.v.) applied it to statements of a more general nature. The Greek mathematician Euclid (q.v.) adopted Aristotle's use of the term, regarding axioms as common notions, not limited to geometry, such as, "If equals be added to equals, the sums are equal". He applied the term postulate to premises strictly geometric in character, such as, "Through a given point only one line can be drawn parallel to a given line". Mathematicians seek to limit the number of axioms and postulates to a minimum by furnishing rigorous proof of an assumption whenever possible, but an irreducible number remains; these axioms and postulates are not susceptible of proof and form the basic assumptions on which a science, such as geometry, is built. Different but self-consistent systems of geometry can be developed by altering one or more of the basic assumptions; *see* GEOMETRY: *Non-Euclidean Geometry.*

AXIS POWERS, coalition of powers that opposed the Allied powers in World War II (q.v.), comprising at the peak of German domination Germany, Italy, Japan, Bulgaria, Finland, Hungary, Rumania, Siam (now Thailand), the puppet states of Croatia, Manchukuo, and Slovakia, and the Nanking puppet regime in China. By the end of 1944 the Axis powers had been reduced to Germany and Japan (with puppet Japanese governments in Manchukuo and China) and four states in the process of being overrun by the Allies, that is, Hungary, Croatia, Slovakia, and Italy. The Axis came to a formal end with the ratification by the Allies of the unconditional surrender of Germany on May 8, 1945.

AXOLOTL, common name for the aquatic, larval form of the yellow-spotted, brown salamander (q.v.), *Ambystoma mexicanum,* which is found in Mexico and the western United States. Not all axolotls develop into salamanders. Those inhabiting lakes Chalco and Xochimilco near Mexico City do not metamorphose. They retain their gills, undeveloped legs, and finned tails, and merely increase in length to about 10 to 12 in. They attain sexual maturity in tadpole form. The phenomenon by which an animal becomes sexually mature in the larval stage is called neoteny. These Mexican axolotls do not become salamanders because the surrounding country is too dry and barren to sustain amphibious animals, whereas the lakes in which the axolotls are born provide plenty of cool, well-aerated water in which to swim and breathe, good shelter, and an abundance of insect and small animal life for food.

Until 1865 scientists considered the Mexican axolotl a distinct species, seeing no connection between it and the common salamander, *S. mexicanum,* but in that year a number of Mexican axolotls on exhibition in an aquarium in Paris, France, lost their gills and changed into salamanders. Later experiments proved that the addition of thyroid extracts to the tank will induce or hasten metamorphosis of tank-kept Mexican salamanders.

AYACUCHO, city in Peru, and capital of Ayacucho Department, 220 miles S.E. of Lima. The city was founded by the Spanish conquistador Francisco Pizarro (q.v.) in 1539. In Ayacucho on Dec. 9, 1824, the last Spanish army to set foot on the continent was defeated by the combined forces of Peru and Colombia. The city was formerly called Guamanga or Huamanga. Pop. (1972) 34,593.

AYE-AYE, common name for the rare lower primate *Daubentonia madagascariensis,* the sole species in the family Daubentoniidae, a division of the superfamily containing the lemurs. Found only in the dense bamboo forests of Madagascar, the aye-aye feeds at night on insects, fruit, bamboo, and the pulp of sugarcane. It is about the size of a large cat and has a long, bushy tail, a shaggy brown coat, and large ears. Aye-ayes sleep all day. The female rests with her single offspring in a ball-shaped nest of leaves and twigs about 2 ft. in diameter built high in a tree. The aye-aye prefers the traveler's tree, where it is thought to get some moisture from the watery sap in the leaves.

The aye-aye is a true lemur; the gnawing teeth were acquired through evolution. The fingers of the animal are unusually long. With the middle finger, the thinnest and longest of all, the aye-aye is said to pull insect larvae out of holes in the barks of trees. This finger is also used to comb the hair and clean the face and ears. In captivity the aye-aye has been seen using the middle finger to bring water to the mouth; it whips the finger through water and to the lips about forty times a minute. Like the lemurs, the aye-aye has an opposing thumb that meets the other fingers. *See* LEMUR.

AYESHA *or* **AYESHAH.** *See* AISHA.

AYMARA, name of an American Indian people centering in the high plateau about Lake Titicaca, in Peru and Bolivia. They are believed to have built the ancient city of Tiahuanacu (q.v.) in Bolivia. The Aymaras were conquered by the Incas in the 15th century and by the Spanish conquistadores in 1538. *See* AMERICAN INDIAN LANGUAGES; AMERICAN INDIANS: *Indians of South America: Andean Area.*

AYR, Great Britain, maritime county of Scotland, on the Firth of Clyde. The chief rivers are the Ayr and the Doon, both of which flow across the center of the county. Although principally agricultural, Ayrshire is rich in coal, ironstone, limestone, and freestone. The famous breed of Ayrshire cows come from this region, in which dairying is an important industry. Other industries are fishing, metal works, and the manufacture of woolens, carpet, tweeds, dynamite, and chemicals. The county town is Ayr (q.v.), which also has a coast fishery. The Scottish poet Robert Burns (q.v.), born in the parish of Alloway, celebrated many features and historical events of the county in his poetry. Important historical monuments include the ruins of the 13th-century abbey of Crossraguel; the battlefield of Largs, on which the Norwegians were defeated in the 13th century; and the castle of Turnberry, the family seat of the liberator of Scotland, Robert Bruce (q.v.). Area, 1132 sq.mi.; pop. (1971 est.) 361,785.

AYR, Great Britain, county town and seaport in Ayr Co., Scotland, at the mouth of the Ayr R., about 30 miles S.W. of Glasgow. Ayr exports coal and metals, and is also a resort area, with a beach, esplanade, and race course. Industries include metalworking and engineering, shipbuilding, fishing, and the manufacture of mining and agricultural machinery, switchgear, chemicals, textiles, and carpets. The town has a museum and statue of the Scottish poet Robert Burns (q.v.), who was born in Ayr in the parish of Alloway. The Scottish patriots Sir William

Wallace and Robert Bruce (qq.v.) are also commemorated at several memorial sites. Other historical sites include the 12th-century church of Saint John, and the remains of the fort castle, built in 1652 by the English soldier and statesman Oliver Cromwell (*see under* CROMWELL). Pop. (1971) 48,021.

AYRSHIRE, hardy breed of dairy cattle, named for Ayr, a county in southwestern Scotland, where the breed was developed in the late 18th century. The cows are medium sized, short legged, fine boned, and very active. The prevailing color is red and white, in spots variously proportioned, but not mixed. The cows are large and consistent milkers, but the fat globules are small, which causes the cream to rise slowly. A purebred herd will yield, on the average, 9500 lb. of milk and 340 lb. of butterfat per cow each year. The record production for an Ayrshire cow is over 31,000 lb. of milk and 1350 lb. of butterfat in a test year. The Ayrshire is raised in the northeastern United States, Canada, Australia, and Great Britain.

AYUB KHAN, Mohammad. *See* PAKISTAN: *History.*

AYUTTHAYA *or* **AYUTHIA,** city in Thailand, on the Chao Phraya R., about 40 miles N.W. of Bangkok. Ayutthaya is an important center of trade, and is in a rich rice-producing region. The city served as the capital of Siam (now Thailand) from about 1350 until 1767, when it was sacked by the Burmese and the capital was moved to Bangkok. Several magnificent Buddhist pagodas, built before the Burmese invasion, are still standing, as is a 16th-century palace, built on a nearby island as a summer residence for the king. Pop. (latest est.) 40,000.

AZALEA, group of plants in the Heath family (Ericaceae), considered by most botanists to be a subgenus of *Rhododendron,* but sometimes classified as a separate genus. The dividing line between the two groups is vague and indefinite, and the situation has been complicated by hybrids, some of which are called azaleodendrons. Azaleas are one of the most popular cultivated plants; the fragrant flowers of the plant bloom in a wide variety of colors.

Important species native to America include *R. nudiflorum,* pinxter flower, wild honeysuckle, or pink azalea, common in northeastern United States; *R. calendulaceum,* flame-colored azalea; *R. arborescens,* smooth azalea; and *R. viscosum,* clammy azalea or white swamp honeysuckle.

Significant among garden varieties are Indica azalea, *R. indicum,* a dwarf Japanese species with deep red flowers, found S. of Pennsylvania; Indian azalea, *R. simsii* and its hybrids, Asian species used principally as pot plants; Ghent azaleas, mostly hardy varieties, hybridized from the American species mentioned above and *R. luteum,* a yellow-flowered plant from the Black Sea region; Mollis azaleas, mostly hardy with large yellow or orange flowers, derived from *R. japonicum,* a native of Japan; and Kurume azaleas, mostly tender, dwarf varieties with white, pink, red, or purple flowers, derived from *R. obtusum,* another Japanese species; the popular hardy varieties Amoena and Hinodegiri are also derived from *R. obtusum.*

AZAÑA, Manuel (1880–1940), Spanish statesman, born near Madrid, and educated in law. After participating in the expulsion of Alfonso XIII (q.v.), King of Spain, in 1931, Azaña became minister of war in the provisional republican government. As such he reorganized the army. When Niceto Alcalá Zamora y Torres (1877–1949), the president, resigned in October, 1931, in protest against anticlerical legislation, Azaña became provisional president. In December, Zamora was elected as the first president under the new Spanish constitution and Azaña became premier. Azaña was premier from 1931 to 1933, and in that period the Jesuit Order was dissolved, church property nationalized, schools secularized, and a series of reform laws passed. Azaña's aim to form a socialist state was not fulfilled, however. The election in November, 1933, showed a conservative trend, and in protest against monarchist tendencies of the new government, the leftist parties called a general strike in October, 1934. In the ensuing confusion, bordering on civil war, Azaña was arrested and temporarily imprisoned. After his release from jail he became the leader of the left wing of the Republican Party and regained the post of premier in 1936. Elected president of the republic in May, 1936, he served in besieged Madrid during the Spanish Civil War (1936–39).

Pink azalea, Rhododendron nudiflorum

Shortly after the surrender of the city of Barcelona to the forces of General Francisco Franco (q.v.) in January, 1939, Azaña fled to the Spanish embassy in Paris, and one month later he resigned.

AZCAPOTZALCO, town of Mexico, in the Distrito Federal, just N. of Mexico City, of which it is a residential suburb. The town is an oil-refining center and produces metal and food products. It is believed to have been founded by the Tepaneca Indians in the 12th century; it was captured by the Aztec Indians in 1428 and became an important slave market. The name, meaning anthill, is illustrated by a figure on the side of a 17th-century church in the town. Pop. (1970) 8287.

AZEGLIO, Massimo Taparelli, Marchese d' (1798–1866), Italian writer and statesman, born in Turin, then a city in the Italian principality of Piedmont. He spent his youth in Rome, where he studied art and became known as a landscape painter. In 1830 he turned his attention to writing. His novels and pamphlets were commentaries on the state of Italian politics, and they served to stimulate Italian patriotism. He fought in the Italian war of independence and was severely wounded in the Battle of Vicenza; *see* ITALY: *History: Risorgimento.* In 1849 he was appointed prime minister of Sardinia, a position he held for three years. He became director of the art gallery at Turin in 1855, but four years later he reentered politics, completing successfully several diplomatic assignments before retiring in 1859.

Among his writings are *Ettore Fieramosca* (1833) and *Niccolò de' Lapi* (1841), historical novels; *Degli Ultimi Casi di Romagna* ("About the Last Cases in Romagna", 1846), a polemic against the papal government; and *I Miei Ricordi* ("My Remembrances", posthumously published, 1873), his memoirs.

AZERBAIDZHAN SOVIET SOCIALIST REPUBLIC, constituent republic of the U.S.S.R., bounded on the E. by the Caspian Sea, on the S. by Iran, on the W. by the Armenian S.S.R., and on the N. by the Georgian S.S.R. and the Dagestan A.S.S.R. The republic includes Nagorno-Karabakh Oblast and the Autonomous Republic of Nakhichevan', which is separated from the rest of Azerbaidzhan by a mountainous strip of the Armenian S.S.R. Two thirds of the population are Azerbaidzhan Turks; other nationalities are Russians, Armenians, and Georgians. The republic has twelve institutions of higher learning, including a state university in the capital city of Baku, which is also the site of the Azerbaidzhan S.S.R. Academy of Sciences.

INDEX TO MAP OF AZERBAIDZHAN S.S.R.

Cities and Towns	
Agdam	B 1
Alyaty-Pristan'	C 2
Astara	C 2
Baku (capital)	C 1
Barda	B 1
Dashkesan	B 1
Dzhul'fa	A 2
Geokchay	B 1
Karyagino	B 2
Kazi-Magomed	C 1
Khachmas	C 1
Kirovabad	B 1
Kuba	C 1
Kyurdamir	C 1
Lenkoran'	C 2
Mingechaur	B 1
Nakhichevan'	A 2
Neftechala	C 2
Neftyanye Kamni	D 1
Nukha	B 1
Sabirabad	C 1
Sal'yany	C 2
Shemakha	C 1
Stepanakert	B 2
Sumgait	C 1
Tauz	A 1
Yevlakh	B 1
Zakataly	B 1

Physical Features	
Alazan (river)	B 1
Apsheron (pen.)	D 1
Araks (Araxes) (river)	B 2
Bazar-Dyuzi (mt.)	C 1
Caspian (sea)	C 1
Caucasus (mts.)	B 1
Kura (river)	C 2
Mingechaur (reservoir)	B 1
Nagorno-Karabakh Autonomous Oblast	B 2
Nakhichevan' A.S.S.R.	A 2
Samur (river)	B 1
Terter (river)	B 1

Azerbaidzhan, located in E. Caucasia, is a mountainous area with ranges rising to 9000 ft. Except for the subtropical regions near the Caspian Sea, the climate is generally arid. Only one river, the Kura, is navigable, but the smaller streams are used for hydroelectric power and to irrigate about thirty-five percent of the arid land in the country. Cotton is the leading agricultural product; grains, tobacco, nuts, and grapes are also produced. In the mountains are large pastures used for the grazing of sheep and other livestock. In the lowlands, subtropical crops, including tea, citrus, almonds, pomegranates, pecans, and olives, are produced.

Industry is based largely on the great mineral resources of Azerbaidzhan and on the exploitation of the rich petroleum and natural-gas resources of the area adjoining the Caspian Sea N. and S. of Baku. Many large oil refineries are located in Baku, which is connected by a double pipeline with Batumi, Georgian S.S.R., on the Black Sea. Crude and refined petroleum products are also shipped from Baku by rail. Kirovabad and Sumgait are other important sites for the industries of the republic, which include steel, copper, cement and building materials, synthetic rubber, salt, timber, textiles, and fishing.

History. Known in ancient times as Albania, the area has been dominated by Arabs, Turks, Monguls, and finally by the Persians, who ceded part of the land to Russia in 1813 and the rest in 1828. In 1918, after the Russian Revolution (q.v.), Azerbaidzhan became an independent republic. On April 28, 1920, it was proclaimed a Soviet Socialist Republic and formed, with Georgia and Armenia, the Transcaucasian Federal Socialist Republic. Azerbaidzhan became a constituent republic of the U.S.S.R. in 1936. Area, 33,430 sq.mi.; pop. (1970) 5,117,081.

AZIMUTH. *See* MAP: *Map Projections: Plane Projections;* NAVIGATION: *Celestial Navigation.*

AZORES, group of nine islands in the mid-Atlantic Ocean belonging to Portugal, about 900 mi. to the W. of mainland Portugal. Extending over a distance of 400 mi., the islands form three distinct groups: São Miguel (largest in size and population) and Santa Maria in the S.E.; Terceira, Graciosa, São Jorge, Pico, and Faial in the center; and Flores and Corvo in the N.W. The islands are separated into three districts for political and administrative purposes. The district capitals, and also the chief seaports, are Ponta Delgada on São Miguel, Horta on Faial, and Angra do Heroísmo on Terceira.

The Azores are of volcanic origin and the highest mountain on the islands, Pico Alto (7611 ft.) is an active volcano. Textiles from Portugal and coal from Great Britain are the principal imports; exports include embroideries, pineapples, canned fish, and sperm-whale oil. Processing of agricultural products is the main industry, but dairying, fishing, and whaling are also important. Hot mineral springs, fine scenery, and a mild climate have made the Azores a popular winter resort area. Because they are distant from the mainland of Europe, the Azores are used to compile meteorological data essential to computing European weather forecasts.

Although the Azores were included on a map as early as 1351, Portuguese sailors are not

The great oil-producing seaport of Baku. Sovfoto

known to have reached them until 1427, and colonization did not begin until 1445. The islands were a place of rendezvous for fleets returning from the Indies, and they thus became a theater of sea warfare between the Spanish and the English when Portugal was under Spanish rule (1580–1640). The Portuguese later used the islands as a place of exile. The Azores became an Allied base in 1943, during World War II. The former United States base on Terceira is now a base of operations for the North Atlantic Treaty Organization (NATO). Area, 902 sq.mi.; pop. (1970) 291,028.

AZORÍN, real name JOSÉ MARTÍNEZ RUIZ (1873–1967), Spanish essayist, novelist, and critic, born in Monóvar, Alicante, and educated in law at the University of Valencia. He was active in politics during the early part of his career, and was elected twice to the Cortes (the Spanish parliament). The dominant theme of Azorín's writings is timelessness and continuity as symbolized by the changeless ways of the peasant. He won critical acclaim for his essays, collections of which include *El Alma Castellana* ("The Castilian Soul", 1900), *Los Pueblos* ("The Villages", 1904), and *Castilla* (1912). His most widely read novels are *La Voluntad* ("The Choice", 1902), *Antonio Azorín* (1903), and *Las Confesiones de un Pequeño Filósofo* ("Confessions of a Humble Philosopher", 1904), all of which are autobiographical with the same central character, Antonio Azorín.

Azorín also is noted for the perceptive literary criticism contained in such works as *Los Valores Literarios* ("Literary Values", 1913) and *Al Margen de los Clásicos* ("Marginal Notes to the Classics", 1915). In 1924 he was elected to the Spanish academy. Azorín, who is regarded as one of the most important contemporary Spanish writers, brought a new, invigorating style to Spanish prose.

AZOV, SEA OF, inland sea in the S. part of the European Soviet Union, connected with the Black Sea by the Strait of Kerch'. It is entirely shallow, from about 3 to 52 ft. in depth, and the water is almost fresh. Because it has an abundance of fish, the Turks call it *Baluk Deniz,* "Fish Sea". The smallest sea in the Soviet Union, it is roughly triangular in shape, narrowing at the N.E. extremity to form the Gulf of Taganrog. The three chief ports on the Azov are Taganrog, Zhdanov, and Berdyansk. Another large port, Rostov, is 28 mi. from the mouth of the Don R., the only important affluent of the Sea of Azov. The area of the sea is about 14,500 sq.mi.

AZRAEL, *or* RAPHAEL, in Islamic theology, one of the four highest angelic beings. The others are Gabriel, Michael (qq.v.), and Israfil (or Uriel). Azrael is called the "Angel of Death". According to the Koran (q.v.), it is Azrael who "separates men's souls and bodies" and either "tears them asunder with violence, or draws them apart with gentleness". He is sent by Allah (*see* ISLAM), having been promoted to his office for his faithfulness and fearlessness. Islam borrowed the concept of Azrael from Jewish theological literature, in which Azrael takes on the attributes of an evil genius and becomes the embodiment of evil. *See* ANGEL; ARCHANGEL.

AZRAQ, BAHR EL, Arab name for the Blue Nile. *See* NILE.

AZTEC, name popularly, although somewhat loosely, applied to all the tribes of Nahuatl (q.v.) stock in Mexico at the time of the Spanish conquest. More properly the name applies only to seven closely related Nahua tribes that inhabited the valley of Mexico. The name is restricted in its narrowest sense to one tribe, also known as the Mexica, that founded Tenochtitlán, or Mexico City, in 1325.

Aztlan, the Nahua word from which Aztec is derived, has been variously interpreted as "heron place", "place of the heron clan", "white place", and "seacoast"; in Aztec legend it signifies the original home of the Aztec, an unidentified place to the north from which they had migrated, finally reaching the valley of Mexico in the 12th century.

The Nahua builders of Tenochtitlán were numerically a small tribe among more powerful neighbors. During the 13th century they remained neutral, paying tribute to the tribes occupying territory around them. Growing in number, however, they gradually formed superior civil and military organizations. By the middle of the 15th century they had formed a military alliance, the Aztec Confederation, with several other Nahua tribes in the region, and by successive wars of conquest gradually acquired dominion over nearly all the tribes of southern Mexico. The confederation thus created the so-called Aztec Empire, which covered most of the area from Río del Fuerte on the Pacific coast to the borders of Guatemala. The empire was overthrown by the Spanish conqueror Hernando Cortes (q.v.) in 1521.

The dominant people of the Aztec Confederacy were the builders of Tenochtitlán; they were superior warriors, administrators, and builders. The empire, however, was not a unified political body, but rather a loosely knit aggregation of communities, some of which were allies of the Aztec, and others tributary to them. Moreover, within the Aztec domain itself were groups who resisted fiercely, notably the Tlascalan tribe, which voluntarily aided Cortes.

Although their culture was largely borrowed from their Toltec predecessors, the Aztec were a vigorous and highly developed people. They developed sculpture, metalwork, weaving, and picture writing. In common with certain other Mexican tribes, they possessed a calendar system based upon and essentially identical with the Mayan (*see* MAYA). The Aztec divided the solar year into 18 months of 20 days each, containing 5 intercalaries. Aztec society was divided into three distinct classes, the nobility, the priesthood, and the military. Education was widespread. Aztec religion, however, was distinguished by barbarism; it required a ceaseless stream of human sacrificial victims.

The descendants of the Aztec are especially numerous in the vicinity of Mexico City; they retain the Aztec-Nahua language.

See AMERICAN INDIAN LANGUAGES; AMERICAN INDIANS: *Northern and Central Mexico*; MEXICO; MONTEZUMA.

AZTEC RUINS NATIONAL MONUMENT, ruins of a great prehistoric Indian town near Aztec, northwestern N.Mex., in the valley of the Animas R. The main ruin, an E.-shaped pueblo (q.v.), built about 1100 around a plaza, has been largely excavated and stabilized. Constructed of masonry and timber, the pueblo was three stories high and contained 500 rooms and 36 kivas (ceremonial chambers), one of which, the Great Kiva, has been restored. Archeological studies have revealed that the community was agricultural, irrigating its land from the river. The prehistoric inhabitants wrought implements of stone, wood, and bone. The ruins, which cover 27.14 acres, were established as a national monument in 1923. The monument is administered by the National Park Service (q.v.).

A-Z TEST, abbreviation for Aschheim-Zondek test (q.v.).

AZURITE, blue mineral, also called blue malachite or chessylite. It is closely related to the green mineral malachite, although malachite is slightly more basic. Both are basic carbonates of copper, alteration products of other copper minerals, formed by the corrosive action of air and water. They are thus similar to the patina or verdigris that forms on ordinary copper. They are found together at Chessy, near Lyon in France, in the Ural Mts. of the U.S.S.R., in Australia, and in Arizona in the United States. Both are important copper ores. Their hardness is about 4, with sp.gr. 3.7. to 4.0.

Azurite and malachite have been used as pigments; when ground they yield blue verditer and green verditer, respectively. The minerals are translucent, with a fine vitreous luster, and when properly polished are highly ornamental. Although not hard enough for use as gems, they have been made into vases, and Siberian azurite has been used as a veneer for table tops.

The Aztecs represented their creator god, Quetzalcoatl, as a feathered or plumed serpent, as can be seen in this stylized figure. Mexican National Tourist Council

AZUSA, city of California, in Los Angeles Co., at the foot of the San Gabriel Mts., 15 miles E. of Los Angeles. Manufactures include jet engines, rocket motors and guided missiles, pipe, chemicals, fiber glass, construction equipment, and wire. Citrus fruits are packed and dairy products are processed in the city, and avocados and nuts are grown in the vicinity. Azusa College (1899) and Citrus Junior College (1915) are situated in Azusa. The city was founded in 1887 and incorporated in 1898. Azusa was originally the name of an Indian village on the site. Pop. (1960) 20,497; (1970) 25,217.

Bb

B, second letter in the English alphabet; a corresponding symbol has the same place in the Greek, Hebrew, Arabic, and other alphabets. In the runic alphabets (*see* RUNES) of Gothic and Anglian types, B is the eighteenth symbol, but in the Norse or Icelandic it is the thirteenth. Its position varies in different Eastern alphabets. The letter was derived by the Phoenicians from the Egyptian hieroglyph for "crane", but when taken over by them it was called *beth,* "the house".

The evolution of the symbol may be traced as follows:

B				
Roman	*Early Greek*	*Phoenician*	*Egyptian Hieratic*	*Egyptian Hieroglyphic Crane*

In Phoenician the derived letter, *beth,* meant "house"; in Anglo-Saxon it was called *beorc,* meaning "birch"; and in Russian it was called *buki,* which meant "beech". The simple phonetic naming began in the classic period of the Latin language (80 B.C.–180 A.D.), when *b* was pronounced in Latin as it is in English, French, Italian, Spanish, and other modern languages. In the 3rd century A.D. a colloquial pronunciation was introduced, which prevailed in the vernacular during the period of the later Roman emperors and ultimately degenerated into a carelessly pronounced *v.* The result, influenced by the fact that the Greeks pronounced *b* like *v,* as they do today, was that the letters b and v were often interchangeable.

Today the name of the Greek letter b (*beta,* like the Phoenician *beth*) is used in association with *alpha,* in the word "alphabet". See article on the letter A.

The sound of the letter b belongs to that class termed variously plosive, mute, or stop. It is defined by some writers as the voiced labial mute. Some languages do not make the sharp distinction that English makes between *b* and *p.* In southern Germany *b* is almost, if not altogether, voiceless, but is pronounced with a weaker expulsive effort than *p.* Thus *b* is merely a weak *p* and the sounds are indistinguishable to an unaccustomed ear. In Danish, *b* differs from *p* by being weaker.

An initial b in English is always pronounced when followed by a vowel. It is not pronounced when followed by d, as in "*bd*elloid" or "*bd*ellium". Final b, when preceded by m, as in "bo*mb*", "cru*mb*", or "to*mb*", is silent, except in "rho*mb*". B is silent before t when not in compounds, as in "de*bt*", "dou*bt*", or "su*bt*le", and in the word-final combination bs the s is pronounced as *z,* as in "cu*bs*".

In Roman notation the capital B stood for 300 or, in the form $\bar{B}$, for 3000. In Greek the value of B was 2000; the value of β was 2.

As an abbreviation, the capital letter B is used commonly for many words, such as bomber, Baumé, British, for bachelor in academic degrees, and for before, especially in the combination B.C. (before Christ). In chemistry, B stands for boron; in radio engineering it denotes a B battery; in spectroscopy it designates one of the Fraunhofer lines (q.v.) produced by oxygen; in music it is the seventh note of the diatonic scale (*see* SCALE). In bibliography B stands for Codex Vaticanus (*see* BIBLE: *Manuscripts, Versions, Editions, and Translations*), and in old books it denotes the reverse page of a leaf.

The lowercase b is used as an abbreviation commonly for book or born, in baseball for base, in cricket for bowled or by, in meteorological records for blue sky, and in nautical observations for broken sea.

Both the capital and lowercase b, Roman or italic, are used to denote a second division or subdivision, as of a classification, schedule, summary, or the like. On the stock exchange certain shares are designated Class B stock, and the letter has various commercial usages, as in indicating the grade of a lead pencil, 2B, 6B, or HB, or indicating the size of shot, B, BB, or BBB.

M.P.

BAADER, Franz Xaver von (1765–1841), German Roman Catholic theologian and philosopher, born in Munich, and educated in medicine at the universities of Ingolstadt and Vienna in Austria. In 1792 he went to England to study mining engineering. While there, he became familiar with the writings of the British philosophers David Hume and David Hartley and the German philosopher Immanuel Kant (qq.v.). Because of their insistence upon the supremacy of reason as a faculty distinct from faith, Baader regarded modern philosophy as misguided and atheistic. After returning to Germany in 1796, Baader discovered a method of making glass by using Glauber's salt (q.v.) instead of potash. He was superintendent of mines in Bavaria from 1817 to 1820.

In his major work, *Fermenta Cognitionis* ("Ferments of Understanding", 1822), he denounced modern philosophy because of its lack of understanding of spiritual truths and upheld the mysticism of the German philosopher Jakob Böhme (q.v.). On the basis of this book he became well known as a religious thinker and was appointed professor of philosophy and speculative theology at the newly established University of Munich in 1826. Because a state decree forbade laymen to teach theology, he was forced to resign in 1838.

Baader held that knowledge and faith are inseparable aspects of one phenomenon. Man's knowledge, he claimed, is largely derived from participation in God's knowledge. Faith, therefore, is a prerequisite of knowledge. Yet without the clarification effected by knowledge, or reason, it is imperfect. He drew from Böhme his belief in God as an all-embracing Being, a part of Whom resides in every man. All men are thus redeemable, and redemption is the result of man's endeavor to achieve harmony with the divine spark residing at the very core of his nature.

Baader's concept of the ideal society was strongly theocratic and essentially medieval. Because religion constitutes the very root of society, he maintained, the Church is entitled to wield direct authority in civil affairs. An advocate of inequality among social classes, the necessity of submission to a ruler by the people, and of the revival of medieval industrial associations, he opposed unrestricted industrial competition and free trade.

Baader's far-reaching influence as a Catholic thinker rests on his sociological, rather than his theological views. The former tended to affirm, in an age of drastic social change, the authority of the Church. The latter was, and is, at variance with Catholic theological tenets. Toward the end of his life Baader questioned the constitution of the Church and the Papacy. He also contrasted the Eastern and Roman churches to the disadvantage of the latter. He recanted these portions of his teachings, however, before his death.

BAAL (Heb. *ba'al* from the Phoenician *ba'al,* "owner", "lord"), among ancient Semitic peoples, name of innumerable local gods controlling fertility of the soil and of domestic animals. Because the various Baals were not everywhere conceived as identical, they may not be regarded as local variations of the same deity. In the plural, Baalim means idols or Baals collectively.

The name Baal formed a part of the names of various gods, as Baal-berith (the Lord of the covenant) of the Schechemites, and Baalzebub (the Lord of flies) of the Philistines. The Hebrews learned the worship of Baal from the agricultural Canaanites. Except for the offerings of fruits and the first-born of cattle, little is known of the rites employed. Their shrines were little more than altars with the symbol of the Canaanite and Hebrew female deity Ashtoreth (*see* ASTARTE) set beside them. Sacred pillars were often erected near the altars.

The name Baal was compounded with many Hebrew, Chaldean, Phoenician, and Carthaginian personal and place names, such as Baalbek, Ethbaal, Jezebel, Hasdrubal, and Hannibal.

BA'ALBEK, town of Lebanon, about 40 miles N.E. of Beirut and about 35 miles N.W. of Damascus, Syria. The name, which means City of Baal, is derived from the early association of the town with the worship of Baal (q.v.), a local sun deity whom the ancient Greeks identified with their sun-god, Helios; the Greeks and Romans called the town Heliopolis, "City of the Sun". It was once a splendid city, and is famous now for the imposing ruins of ancient temples.

The great Temple of the Sun was about 290 ft. by 160 ft. and contained fifty-eight Corinthian columns, each 75 ft. high and 7¼ ft. in diameter. Six of these columns are still standing. The entablature was 14 ft. in height. The temple appears to have been built on an artificial mound of earth, with great stones, or megaliths, employed to sustain this mass. Of these megaliths, three are in position at the west end, one of them measuring 64 ft. long by 14 ft. square. The

The six remaining columns of the Temple of the Sun, at Ba'albek. American Export Lines

Temple of Jupiter, also of the Corinthian order, measured 227 ft. by 117 ft. and was surrounded by a peristyle of forty-two plain columns, with ten fluted columns in the vestibule. The entablature was very profusely and richly ornamented. A smaller temple, known as the Temple of Venus, supported by six granite columns, adjoined the Temple of Jupiter. Clear traces also remain of a Christian basilica of later date.

Although the early history of Ba'albek is almost entirely unknown, abundant evidence indicates that the city is very ancient, portions of the masonry being attributed to Phoenician origin. The Roman emperor Augustus (q.v.) made the city a Roman colony; the Roman emperor Trajan (q.v.) consulted a celebrated oracle there. The city was sacked by the Arabs in 748 A.D., and pillaged by the Mongol chieftain Tamerlane (q.v.) in 1400. A severe earthquake in 1759 devastated what monuments still remained in the city. Present-day Ba'albek, connected by rail with Beirut and with Damascus and Aleppo in Syria, is the chief town in eastern Lebanon. Pop. (latest est.) 8000.

BAAL SHEM-TOB *or* **BAAL SHEM-TOV,** known also as BESHT, real name ISRAEL BEN ELIEZER (1700–60), Jewish religious leader, born in the region of Podolia (now in the Ukrainian S.S.R.). About 1740 he settled in Medzhibozh, Podolia. Rabbi Israel was called the Baal Shem, meaning "master of the Holy Name", because he professed to perform miracles by using the name of God. He was the founder of the 18th-century Eastern European sect called Hasidim or Chasidim. The Baal Shem stressed inner revival, personal piety, humility, charity, mystical and ecstatic experience of the divine presence, and a joyful attitude toward life, rather than traditional learning and fixed doctrine. The sayings and legends of the Baal Shem, preserved orally at first, were committed to writing as the Hasidic movement grew. *See* HASIDIM. N.N.G.

BABBAGE, Charles. *See* COMPUTER: *History.*

BABBITT, Irving (1865–1933), American critic and educator born in Dayton, Ohio, and educated at Harvard University and in Paris. After teaching for a year at Williams College, he entered the French Department of Harvard University, and became professor of French literature in 1912. Through his books and articles he became known as one of the leaders of the new humanistic movement in literature. He wrote *Literature and the American College* (1908), *The New Laokoön* (1910), *Masters of Modern French Criticism* (1912), *Rousseau and Romanticism* (1919), and *On Being Creative* (1932).

BABBITT METAL, any of several soft metal alloys used to line bearings and bushings in order to reduce friction. The metals usually contain large amounts of tin with smaller amounts of antimony, copper, and lead. The principal alloy consists of 89 percent tin, 7 percent antimony, and 4 percent copper. Babbitt metal is named after its inventor, the American Isaac Babbitt (1799–1862).

BABCOCK, Stephen Moulton (1843–1931), American chemist, born in Bridgewater, N.Y., and educated at Tufts and Cornell universities and the University of Göttingen in Germany. He taught agricultural chemistry at Cornell University and the University of Wisconsin and was a chemist at both the New York and Wisconsin State agricultural experiment stations. In 1890 he introduced the test, named for him, that is used to determine the richness of milk by measuring butterfat content. The Babcock test, which introduces concentrated sulfuric acid into a sample of milk, made possible fast and accurate milk grading. Babcock also conducted important research on the dietary needs of livestock.

BAB EL MANDEB (Ar. *Bab al-Mandab,* "gate of tears"), strait between Arabia and Africa, by which the Red Sea is connected with the Gulf of Aden. It is about 20 mi. wide; the strait is divided into two channels by Perim Island, near the Arabian mainland. The W. strait is 16 mi. wide and the E. one is 2 mi. wide. The hazards to navigation caused by the swift current in both channels have given the strait its name.

The Tower of Babel, as depicted in a 19th-century engraving, was to have "its top in heaven," according to Genesis. Granger Collection

BABEL, TOWER OF (Heb. *Bābhel,* fr. Assyr-Bab. *bāb-ili,* "gate of God"), according to the Old Testament (Gen. 11:1–9), tower erected on the plain of Shinar in Babylonia by descendants of Noah (q.v.). The builders intended the tower to reach to Heaven; their presumption, however, angered Jehovah (q.v.), who interrupted construction by causing a hitherto unknown language confusion among the builders. He then scattered these people, speaking different languages, over the face of the earth.

The story possibly was inspired by the fall of the famous temple-tower of Etemenanki, later restored by King Nabopolassar (r. 625–05 B.C.) and his son Nebuchadnezzar II (*see under* NEBUCHADNEZZAR) of Babylonia. The Genesis account appears to play on the Babylonian word *bāb-ili* ("gate of God") and on the Hebrew words *Bābhel* ("Babylon") and *bālāl* ("to confuse"). The English words "babel" and "babble" are derived from the story.

BABER *or* **BABUR** *or* **BABAR** (Mongol, "Tiger"), nickname for ZAHIR UD-DIN MUHAMMAD (1483–1530), first of the Great Moguls of India, who reigned from 1526 to 1530. He was a descendant of the Mongol conqueror Tamerlane (q.v.), succeeding his father in the sovereignty of the countries lying between Samarkand and the Indus R. By fast and daring movements he became master of the provinces of Kashgar, Kunduz, Kandahar, and Kabul. In 1526 he defeated at Panipat the army of 100,000 men and 100 elephants of Sultan Ibrahim Lodi (d. 1526), Emperor of Delhi. After this battle he made his entry into Delhi and a month later into Agra, the second city of the Empire of Delhi. The following year he secured his possession of his new realm by a victory over the Rajputs. In addition to being a capable soldier and statesman, Baber was an able writer and in the Tatar tongue wrote the history of his own life and conquests.

BABEUF, François Émile, pen name GRACCHUS BABEUF (1760–97), French revolutionist and the founder of revolutionary socialism, born in Saint-Quentin. His early years were spent in the service of the landed aristocracy. Babeuf, who hated inequality and injustice, enthusiastically supported the French Revolution (q.v.), but, at the end of the Reign of Terror, attacked the revolution because it had not developed along the lines of his own socialistic theories. He published a journal, *Tribun du peuple* ("Tribune of the People"), in which he bitterly condemned the enemies of the revolution. An advocate of common ownership of land and property and absolute economic and political equality of all citizens, he proposed doing away with all private ownership of property by confiscation and by the abolition of inheritance. These principles became known as Babouvism. Babeuf's participation in 1796 in a plot to overthrow the Directory, the executive branch of the government, and to establish a communistic state resulted in his execution.

BABINGTON, Anthony (1561–86), English conspirator, born in Dethick, Derbyshire. He served briefly as page to Mary, Queen of Scots (q.v.), during her imprisonment by the English in Sheffield. In 1586 Babington entered into a Catholic conspiracy to murder Elizabeth I (q.v.), Queen of England, and free Mary. He received letters from Mary approving the proposed assassination. The letters came into the hands of Sir Francis Walsingham (q.v.), Elizabeth's secretary, who had Babington and his accomplices arrested. They were executed in London.

BABIRUSSA *or* **BABIRUSA** *or* **BABIROUSSA** (Malay, *bābī,* "hog"; *rūsa,* "deer"), common name for a wild pig, *Babirussa babirussa,* of the family Suidae, which includes also the common domestic pig and the warthog. It is native to Celebes Island, Indonesia, and other islands east of Borneo. The babirussa has long upper tusks that pierce the skin of the snout and curve backward like horns. The tusks of the female are shorter than those of the boars, which grow upward and back to meet the skull between the eyes and therefore are almost useless as weapons. The babirussa is about 31 in. high at the shoulder. Wrinkled, thick-skinned, and hairless, its body may be as long as 3 ft. 6 in. and may weigh about 200 lb. The babirussa moves about mostly at night, either singly or in small herds, and has a keen sense of hearing, although the ears are relatively small. It is a good swimmer, and in the marshy forest where it feeds on fruits and grubs it is seldom far from water. The litter of the babirussa is one or two uniformly colored young. The babirussa is sometimes domesticated.

BABISM, religion that developed as an offshoot of the Shi'ite sect of Islam; *see* MUSLIM SECTS. Its principles were proclaimed at Shiraz, Persia (now Iran), on May 23, 1844, by Mirza Ali Mohammed of Shiraz (1821–50), who became known as the Bab (Persian, "the Gate") because he was considered the gate, or door, to spiritual truth.

In opposition to basic Islamic theology (*see* ISLAM), the Bab declared that the prophets were divine manifestations of God Himself and that he, Bab, was one of the prophets, equal to Muhammad (q.v.) in importance and the precursor of an even greater "Manifestation", which was to appear nineteen years after the founding of Babism. He also wrote a new holy book, the *Bayán* (or "Revelation") to supersede the Koran (q.v.). Babism forbade polygamy and concubinage and sought to alter many other Muslim customs. Babism also proclaimed the coming of an era in which all religions would be united under one spiritual head. The Bab soon founded a group of eighteen disciples, seventeen men and one woman, and the faith spread rapidly in Persia until the accession of Shah Nasr-ed-Din (1831-96) in 1848. Persuaded that the tenets of Babism were destructive of Islam and a danger to the state, the shah initiated violent persecutions of the Babists. The followers of the Bab revolted. After two years of civil war their rebellion was put down, and the Bab, although he had not taken part in the revolt, was imprisoned and executed at Tabriz on July 9, 1850.

After the death of the Bab, Babism continued to be preached throughout Persia and the Near East. In 1863 a follower of the Bab, Mirza Husayn Ali (1817-92), called Bahaullah ("the Splendor of God"), proclaimed himself the promised "Manifestation", and on the basis of Babism founded a new Bahai (q.v.) faith.

BABOON, common name applied most properly to African monkeys of the genus *Papio,* but designating also monkeys of the genera *Theropithecus, Mandrillus,* and *Comopithecus; see* MONKEY. The baboons belong to the family Cercopithecidae, which includes all Old World monkeys except the anthropoid apes; *see* APE. Some species are strong tree climbers, but baboons generally are adapted to life on the ground and most of them avoid the forests; they range in large troops over the rocky, barren areas of Africa and Arabia.

Powerful, ferocious animals about the size of a large dog, baboons have strong, elongated jaws, large cheek pouches in which they store food, and eyes placed close together. They have overhanging brows that are raised when the animal looks upward, and strong limbs. Unlike most other monkeys, baboons can distinguish colors and have a keen sense of smell. They have large, often brightly colored, hairless areas on their buttocks and thick, sturdy legs. The tail is generally short and is carried high in an arch.

Baboons eat various worms, eggs, insects, reptiles, fruits, and young shoots, as well as small animals. They live in herds, often composed of two or three hundred members. Baboons have several different calls, each of which appears to have a meaning. Herds of baboons often mix with herds of other wild animals.

The social life of the baboon is quite complex within the herd. A powerful male may have as many as seven females in his harem, jealously guarding them from other males. He often kills the female if she encourages another male. After a gestation period of about six months the female usually bears a single offspring, which clings to its mother's underside.

The chacma, *P. porcarius,* a native of South Africa, is one of the best-known species of baboon. The largest of the baboons, it is extremely strong and fierce; full grown, it weighs about 150 lb. The chacma, known also as the pig-tailed baboon, is grayish brown, tinted with green on the back. The face and long, blunt muzzle may be black or purplish. South African farmers fear it as a destroyer of crops. The chacma also kills lambs and kids and other domestic animals.

The olive baboon, *P. anubis,* found in western Africa as far north as the Congo R. and the borders of Sudan and Ethiopia, has a coat similar to that of the chacma, but it is a darker brown.

The yellow baboon, *P. cynocephalus,* is native to west and central Africa, south to Mashonaland in Rhodesia. The several subspecies of these baboons each have a light-yellow coat and a blackish face.

The mandrill, Mandrillus sphinx, *is a savage baboon of western Africa.* UPI

Another well-known species is the North African hamadryas baboon, *P. hamadryas,* known also as the sacred baboon because it was deified by the ancient Egyptians. The gelada, *Theropithecus gelada,* a baboon native to Ethiopia, has a long mane covering its neck and shoulders. It has a pink face and a long snout. The mandrill, *Mandrillus sphinx,* a large savage baboon of western Africa, has an enormous head, crested and bearded, and almost no forehead. Another western African species is the drill, *M. leucophaeus,* somewhat smaller than the mandrill, but similar in temperament.

BABSON, Roger Ward (1875–1967), American statistician, born in Gloucester, Mass., and educated at the Massachusetts Institute of Technology (q.v.). He pioneered in developing statistical information of special interest to businessmen, bankers, and investors, including forecasts of business conditions, and in presenting the data in unusual graphic form in *Babson's Reports,* which began publication in 1903. He founded two educational institutions; the first, Babson Institute (1919), located near Wellesley Hills, Mass., was designed to train men for business administration; the second, Webber College (1927), in Babson Park, Fla., was a special training school for women interested in business careers. In 1940, he was the candidate of the Prohibition Party for the Presidency of the

United States. Among the many books written by Babson on business, travel, and religion are the autobiography, *Actions and Reactions* (1935), and *Looking Ahead Fifty Years* (1942), a forecast of things to come.

BABUYAN, island group in Luzon Strait, belonging to the Republic of the Philippines, forming part of Cagayan Province, N. of Luzon Island, from which they are separated by Babuyan Channel. The principal islands of the group are Camiguin, Babuyan, Calayan, Fuga, and Dalupiri. Tobacco, grain, rice, and tropical products are grown. The chief occupation of the inhabitants is the raising of cattle, hogs, and horses, which, with lard, form the principal articles of export.

BABY BLUE–EYES, ornamental annual plant, Nemophila menziesi, in the family Hydrophyllaceae. Native to southern States of the United States, it blooms from April through May. It has alternate leaves and showy, white to deep blue, bell-shaped flowers from ½ to 1 in. wide. It is sometimes called California bluebell, a name more commonly applied to plants of the genus *Phacelia* in the same family.

BABYLON, village of New York State, in Suffolk Co., on Great South Bay, on S. Long Island, about 16 miles E. of Hempstead, and about 35 miles E. of Manhattan. The city manufactures candy, machinery, boats, and knit goods. Belmont Lake State Park is nearby. Pop. (1960) 11,062; (1970) 12,588.

BABYLON, ruined city in Iraq, and one of the oldest cities of antiquity and capital of Babylonia from the time of the ruler Hammurabi (q.v.), who ruled in the 18th century B.C., to the end of the Chaldean (Neo-Babylonian) Empire (539 B.C.). The ruins of Babylon are on the Euphrates R., about 55 miles S. of Baghdad. The Sumerian name of the city was Ka-dingir-ra, of which the Akkadian equivalent was Bābilu (*bāb-ili,* "gate of God"). The city existed in the time of the Babylonian ruler Sargon I (about 2637–2582 B.C.), who built a palace, introduced the worship of Anunitum, "she of the skirmish", a goddess of war, and seems to have given to the place its Akkadian name.

The city stood on both sides of the Euphrates R. and was built in the form of a square, the circumference of which was about 60 mi., according to the 5th-century Greek historian Herodotus (q.v.), whose eyewitness account is the earliest description of the city. It was surrounded by a wall that was said to be 200 cubits (about 300 ft.) high and 50 cubits (about 75 ft.) thick, having from 100 to 250 brazen gates. The city was built in an extremely regular pattern, with broad, straight streets crossing one another at right angles; the two parts of the city, on either side of the river, were connected by a roofed bridge built of hewn stones fastened together with iron clamps. Not a trace of this bridge has yet been discovered.

The western section of the city is undoubtedly the older, belonging to the early and properly Babylonian dynasty. In that section stood the famous sanctuary of Bel-Marduk which included the ziggurat (Etemenanki) that probably inspired the Biblical story of the Tower of Babel (*see* BABEL, TOWER OF). Also on the west side is the mass of ruins called Mujellibe, which was probably the royal citadel of the old Babylonian monarchy. On the east side of the river stood the buildings of the Neo-Babylonian period, among which were the "Hanging Gardens" of the legendary Assyrian queen Semiramis, one of the wonders of the ancient world; *see* SEVEN WONDERS OF THE WORLD: *Seven Wonders of the Ancient World.*

Their ruins may be recognized in the mound called El Kasr.

The city was captured by the Persian ruler Cyrus the Great (q.v.) in 539 B.C., and in the course of the fighting was badly damaged. One of its richest treasures, the sanctuary of Zeus Belos, was plundered in the next century by Xerxes I (q.v.) of Persia. Although the Persian kings made Babylon their residence, nothing was done to restore the city. The Macedonian king Alexander III (q.v.), known as Alexander the Great, on entering the city in 331 B.C., promised the inhabitants to rebuild the ruined temple, but he was unable even to clear away the rubbish, although he employed 10,000 workmen on the project for two months. Babylon rapidly declined after Alexander's death in 323 B.C., and after the city of Seleucia was founded on the Tigris R. by Seleucus I (*see under* SELEUCIDAE), the Macedonian general who founded the Seleucid Dynasty.

The remains of a Greek theater under the mound called Al Hamra show that the city continued to flourish in the Hellenistic period. The Sasanid kings are said to have resided there at times. Even after the founding of Baghdad (q.v.), Babylon remained the capital of a district, although later it became simply a village. The name remained attached to what at present is the northernmost mound, while the town of Hilla grew up farther south.

In 1616 the Italian traveler Pietro della Valle (1586–1652) recognized the ruins north of Hilla and near Jimjima as those of Babylon. They were visited by various archeologists between 1784 and 1818. The British archeologist Sir Austen Henry Layard (1817–94) began excavation in 1850, but he continued the work only a few weeks. Between 1851 and 1854 the French Orientalist Jules Oppert (1825–1905) conducted studies of the ruins. The most important work was done after 1899 by the Deutsche Orient Gesellschaft under the leadership of the German archeologist Robert Koldewey (1855–1925). He was able to trace the outermost wall, showing that the city extended over an area of about 12 sq.mi. Koldewey excavated the Processional Street and the Ishtar Gate, the foundations of two palaces of King Nebuchadnezzar II (*see under* NEBUCHADNEZZAR), the quays, the Marduk Canal, the great Marduk temple, Esagila, and the hole in the ground now called El Sahan, where stood the famous Tower of Babel. These excavations resulted in the discovery of numerous objects of art and a large number of inscriptions in cuneiform (q.v.) from different times.

BABYLONIA (Assyrian *Bābili,* "gate of God"; Old Persian *Babirush*), ancient country of Mesopotamia (q.v.), known originally as Sumer (q.v.) and later as Sumer and Akkad, lying between the Tigris and Euphrates rivers, and roughly coextensive with modern Baghdad Province in Iraq.

BABYLONIAN CIVILIZATION

The Babylonian civilization, which endured from the 18th until the 6th century B.C., was, like the Sumerian which preceded it, essentially urban in character, although it was based on agriculture rather than industry. The country consisted of a dozen or so cities, surrounded by villages and hamlets. At the head of the political structure was the king, a more or less absolute monarch who exercised legislative and judicial as well as executive powers. Directly under him was a group of appointed governors and administrators. Mayors and councils of city elders were in charge of local administration.

The Babylonians modified and transformed their Sumerian heritage in accordance with their own culture and ethos. The resulting way of life proved to be so effective that it underwent relatively little change for some 1200 years. It exerted influence on all the neighboring countries, especially the kingdom of Assyria (q.v.), which adopted the Babylonian social and economic system almost in its entirety. Fortunately, many written documents from this period have been excavated and made available to scholars. One of the most important of these documents is the remarkable collection of laws often designated as the Code of Hammurabi which, together with other documents and letters belonging to different periods, provides a comprehensive picture of Babylonian social structure and economic organization. *See* HAMMURABI, CODE OF.

Society. Babylonian society consisted of three classes represented by the *awelu,* a free man of the upper class; the *wardu,* or slave; and the *mushkenu,* a free man of low estate, who ranked legally between the *awelu* and the *wardu.* Most slaves were prisoners of war, but some were recruited from the Babylonian citizenry as well. For example, free men might be reduced to slavery as punishment for certain offenses; parents could sell their children as slaves in time of need; or a man might even turn over his entire family to creditors in payment of a debt, although for no longer than three years. The slave was the property of his master, like any other chattel. He could be branded and flogged, and he was severely punished if he attempted to escape. On the other hand, because it was to the advantage of the master that the slaves stay strong and healthy, they usually were well treated. Slaves even had certain legal rights and could engage in business, borrow money, and buy their freedom. If a slave, male or female, married a free person and had children, the latter were free. The sale price of a slave varied with the market, as well as with the attributes of the individual involved; the average price for a grown man was usually twenty shekels of silver, a sum which could buy some thirty-five bushels of barley.

The position of the *mushkenu* in Babylonian society can be surmised from a number of legal provisions in the Code of Hammurabi. To cite comparative examples, if a *mushkenu* was injured in eye or limb, he was indemnified by the payment of a mina (roughly 1 lb. of silver); in the case of an *awelu* similarly injured, the law of retaliation (*lex talionis*) was applied; whereas for an injured slave, the indemnity was to be simply half his market value. If his injury required surgical treatment, the *awelu* had to pay a fee of ten shekels, but the *mushkenu* paid five shekels; and, in the case of a slave, his master had to pay a fee of only two shekels.

The family was the basic unit of Babylonian society. Marriages were arranged by the parents, and the betrothal was recognized legally as soon as the groom had presented a bridal gift to the father of the bride; the ceremony often was concluded with a contract inscribed on a tablet. Although marriage was thus reduced to a practical arrangement, there is some evidence to show that surreptitious premarital lovemaking was not altogether unknown. The Babylonian woman had certain important legal rights. She could hold property, engage in business, and qualify as a witness. The husband, however, could divorce her on relatively light grounds, or, if she had borne him no children, he could marry a second wife. Children were under the absolute authority of their parents who could disinherit them or, as has already been mentioned, could even sell them into slavery. In the normal course of events, however, children were loved and at the death of the parents inherited all their property. Adopted children were not uncommon, and they too were treated with care and consideration.

The populations of the Babylonian cities cannot be estimated with any reasonable degree of exactness because the authorities, so far as extant documents reveal, took no census. The number of inhabitants of a city probably ranged from 10,000 to 50,000. The city streets were narrow, winding, and quite irregular, with high, windowless walls of houses on both sides. The streets were unpaved and undrained. The average house was a small, one-story, mud-brick structure, consisting of several rooms grouped around an open court. The house of a well-to-do Babylonian, on the other hand, was probably a two-story brick dwelling of about a dozen rooms, and was plastered and whitewashed both inside and out. The ground floor consisted of a reception room, kitchen, lavatory, servants' quarters, and, sometimes, even a private chapel. Furniture consisted of low tables, high-backed chairs, and beds with wooden frames. Household vessels were made of clay, stone, copper, and bronze, and baskets and chests were made of reed and wood. Floors and walls were adorned with reed mats, skin rugs, and woolen hangings.

Below the house was often located a mausoleum in which the family dead were buried. The Babylonians believed that the souls of the dead traveled to the nether world, and that, at least to some extent, life continued there as on earth. For this reason, pots, tools, weapons, and jewels were buried with the dead.

Technology. The Babylonians inherited the technical achievements of the Sumerians in irrigation and agriculture. Maintaining the system of canals, dikes, weirs, and reservoirs constructed by their predecessors demanded considerable engineering knowledge and skill. Preparation of maps, surveys, and plans involved the use of leveling instruments and measuring rods. For mathematical and arithmetical purposes they used the Sumerian sexagesimal system of numbers, which featured a most useful device of so-called place-value notation that resembles the present-day decimal system. Measures of length, area, capacity, and weight, standardized earlier by the Sumerians, remained in use. Farming was a complicated and methodical occupation requiring foresight, diligence, and skill. A recently translated document written in Sumerian but used as a textbook in the Babylonian schools is a veritable farmer's almanac; it records a series of instructions and directions to guide farm activities from the watering of the fields to the winnowing of the harvested crops.

Babylonian craftsmen were skilled in metallurgy, in the processes of fulling, bleaching, and dyeing, and in the preparation of paints, pigments, cosmetics, and perfumes. In the field of medicine, surgery was well known and often practiced, judging from the Hammurabi law code, which devotes several paragraphs to the surgeon. Pharmacology, too, doubtless had made considerable progress, although the only major direct evidence of this comes from a Sumerian tablet written several centuries before Hammurabi (q.v.).

Law and justice were key concepts in the Babylonian way of life. Justice was administered by the courts, each of which consisted of from one to four judges. Often the elders of a town constituted a tribunal. The judges could not reverse their decisions for any reason, but appeals from their verdicts could be made to the king. Evidence consisted either of statements from witnesses or of written documents. Oaths, which played a considerable role also in the administration of justice, could be either promissory, declaratory or exculpatory. The courts inflicted penalties ranging from capital punishment and mutilation to flogging, reduction to slavery, and banishment. Awards for damages were from three to thirty times the value of the object to be restored.

To ensure that their legal, administrative, and economic institutions functioned effectively, the Babylonians used the cuneiform (q.v.) system of writing developed by their Sumerian predecessors. To train their scribes, secretaries, archivists, and other administrative personnel, they adopted the Sumerian system of formal education, under which secular schools served as the cultural centers of the land. The curriculum consisted primarily of copying and memorizing textbooks and Sumero-Babylonian dictionaries containing long lists of words and phrases, including the names of trees, animals, birds, insects, countries, cities, villages, and minerals, as well as a large and diverse assortment of mathematical tables and problems. In the study of literature, the pupils copied and imitated various types of myths, epics, hymns, lamentations, proverbs, and essays in both the Sumerian and the Babylonian languages.

HISTORY

Long periods of the history of the Middle East in antiquity cannot be dated by an absolute chronology or according to our own system of reckoning. The *Sumerian King List* gives a succession of rulers to the end of the dynasty of Isin, about 1750 B.C., but it is quite unreliable for dates prior to the dynasty of Akkad, about 2270 B.C. A relative chronology is well established for the era from the beginning of the dynasty of Akkad to the end of the First Dynasty of Babylon, about 1530 B.C. This period, however, is followed by an obscure period of more than 700 years, during which dates are only approximate. Scholars follow at least three chronological systems for the ancient Near East: high, middle, or low, depending upon whether the date assigned to the first year of the reign of Hammurabi of Babylon is 1852, 1792, or 1728 B.C. The dates in this article, and in that on Sumer (q.v.), follow a system that is a compromise between the so-called middle and low chronologies, and date the first year of Hammurabi's reign to about 1750 B.C.

Toward the end of the 3rd millennium B.C., Sumer and Akkad was a kingdom of empire proportions ruled by a Sumerian dynasty known as the Third Dynasty of Ur (*see* UR). After a century or two, hordes of Semitic nomads, the Amurru, or Biblical Amorites (q.v.), who had migrated from the Arabian desert lands to the west, made themselves masters of some of the more important cities such as Isin, Larsa, Babylon, and Eshnunna (now Tell Asmar). About 1950 B.C. the last ruler of the Third Dynasty of Ur was carried off into captivity by the Elamites (*see* ELAM). The kingdom of Sumer and Akkad disintegrated, and civil strife became rampant. At first the city of Isin attempted to control Sumer and Akkad, but in the course of time its authority was challenged by Larsa, considerably to the south, and the two cities were constantly at war. About 1750 B.C. King Rim-Sin of Larsa conquered and occupied Isin, an event considered so important that it actually marked the beginning of a new, though limited, dating era in the scribal annals.

Rim-Sin was unable to exploit his victory, because at the same time in the previously unimportant city of Babylon to the north, the ruler Hammurabi came to the fore. As king, Hammurabi combined astute diplomacy and military leadership; he defeated Rim-Sin, as well as the kings of Elam, Mari, and Eshnunna, and about 1720 B.C. became the ruler of a united kingdom extending from the Persian Gulf to the Habur R. The history of Babylonia is considered to begin with Hammurabi.

An unusually active and capable administrator, Hammurabi gave his personal attention to such details as the cleaning of irrigation canals and the insertion of an extra month into the calendar. He was an outstanding lawgiver; the Code of Hammurabi is one of the most significant legal documents ever uncovered. He was also an inspiring religious leader; during his reign the Babylonian city-god Marduk became the recognized leader of the pantheon of deities.

During the reigns of Hammurabi and his son Samsu-iluna (r. about 1708–1671 B.C.) who succeeded him, Babylonian civilization reached the zenith of its cultural development and political power. Some of the more important cities of Babylonia began to seek independence, however, and, in the reign of Samsu-iluna the barbaric Kassites (q.v.) from the Zagros Mts. invaded the country. Although Samsu-iluna succeeded in beating them off, the Kassites continued to infiltrate Babylonia in the centuries that followed. Samsu-iluna suffered another serious setback when a rebel leader, Iluma-ilum, founded a dynasty in the southern Babylonian district, bordering on the Persian Gulf, commonly known as the Sea-land.

Under Samsu-iluna's successors Babylonia suffered a serious decline in power and territory. When, about 1530 B.C., a Hittite army penetrated as far south as Babylon and carried off Babylonian prisoners and wealth to far-off Anatolia, the kingdom became badly disorganized. Babylonia later fell under the rule of the Dynasty of the Sea-land, at least for a brief period. Finally, toward the end of the 16th century B.C., a Kassite ruler named Agum made himself master of Babylonia and extended its territory from the Euphrates R. to the Zagros Mts.

Under Kassite rule, Babylonia once again became a power of considerable importance. At the beginning of the 15th century B.C., for example, it was one of the four major powers of the Orient, the other three being the Egyptian, Mitanni, and Hittite empires (*see* HITTITES).

After Assyria (q.v.) made itself independent of Mitanni domination early in the 14th century B.C., its rulers began to interfere in the affairs of Babylonia and sought to control it politically. They were generally successful, and Babylonia became so weak that it fell prey to the Elamites who invaded it from the east, deposed its Kass-

The stele of Hammurabi shows Shamash, the sun god, presenting the Code of Laws to Hammurabi, King of Babylon. The stele dates from early in the second millennium B.C. Alinari

ite king, and practically reduced it to a state of vassalage. A revolt then broke out in southern and central Babylonia, and a new dynasty, known usually as the Second Dynasty of Isin, was founded. Toward the middle of the 12th century B.C., Nebuchadnezzar I (*see under* NEBUCHADNEZZAR), one of the kings of this dynasty, defeated the Elamites and even attacked Assyria with some success. Not long afterward Aramaean nomads began swarming into Babylonia. For about two centuries thereafter the country was in a state of political chaos and confusion.

Among the Aramaean tribes was one powerful group known as the Chaldeans. They settled in and dominated the district along the Persian Gulf which for centuries had been more or less an independent state. Beginning in the 9th century B.C., the Chaldeans were destined to play an important political role in the history of the Orient; their rulers helped destroy the Assyrian Empire and, at least for a brief period, made Babylonia, or, as it gradually came to be known, Chaldea, the dominant power of Mesopotamia.

One of the outstanding Chaldean kings was Merodach-baladan II (r. 721–710 B.C.), who fought bitterly and bravely, if unsuccessfully, against four mighty Assyrian monarchs: Tiglath-pileser III (r. 745–727 B.C.), Shalmaneser V (r. 727–722 B.C.), Sargon II (r. 722–705 B.C.), and Sennacherib (q.v.), the destroyer of Babylon. Sennacherib's successors, Esarhaddon (r. 681–669 B.C.) and Ashurbanipal (q.v.), retained political control of Babylonia in spite of numerous rebellions and defections. In 625, however, when Assyria was in turmoil and menaced by the Medes (*see* MEDIA), the Scythians, and the Cimmerians (qq.v.), a Chaldean named Nabopolassar (r. 625–605 B.C.) proclaimed himself king of Babylonia. Allying himself with the Medes, he helped them to destroy Assyrian might.

With Assyria no longer to be feared, Egypt began to menace Palestine and Syria. Nabopolassar's son Nebuchadnezzar II (*see under* NEBUCHADNEZZAR) marched against the Egyptians and defeated them at Carchemish. Nebuchadnezzar, who reigned for forty years, extended Babylonian political control over practically all of Mesopotamia. To students of the Bible he is known as the destroyer of Jerusalem and as the king who took the captive Jews to Babylonia; *see* BABYLONIAN CAPTIVITY. To archeologists and historians he is known as the great builder and restorer. He reconstructed Babylon, his capital, in elaborate style and completed the renovation of Marduk's temple (Esagila) and its ziggurat, or staged tower, called Etemenanki, which is probably the tower that inspired the Biblical story of the Tower of Babel (*see* BABEL, TOWER OF). He laid out a broad, processional avenue which passed through an imposing structure known as the Ishtar Gate, and he restored numerous temples throughout Babylonia. *See* BABYLONIAN ART.

The Babylonian revival did not long endure. After Nebuchadnezzar's death (562 B.C.), a struggle for power apparently went on among various parties and individuals for several years. In 556 B.C. Nabonidus, one of Nebuchadnezzar's governors, became king of Babylonia (r. 556–539 B.C.). A somewhat enigmatic figure, he in some way antagonized the influential priestly class of Babylon. Nabonidus left the city of Babylon under control of his son Belshazzar (q.v.) and lived for a while in the city of Harran and later in the oasis of Teima, in the Arabian Desert. In 539 B.C. the Babylonians were defeated by the Persian king Cyrus the Great (q.v.), who had defeated Media. Nabonidus was captured at Sippar (near modern Baghdad, Iraq), and the Persians entered Babylon itself without resistance. Babylonia was annexed to Persia (q.v.), and lost its independence for all time.

More than 1200 years had elapsed from the glorious reign of Hammurabi to the subjugation of Babylonia by the Persians. During this long span of time the Babylonian social structure, economic organization, arts and crafts, science and literature, judicial system, and religious beliefs underwent considerable modification, but

Three Lions, Inc.

Three Lions, Inc.

Babylonia. Plate 1. *Flood Tablet (above, left), one of twelve tablets comprising the Epic of Gilgamesh. Head of Hammurabi (above, right), the Babylonian lawgiver. Gold necklace (below) with pendants, an example of metalwork from the 16th century B.C.*

The Metropolitan Museum of Art – Fletcher Fund, 1947

Babylonia. Plate 2. *Colorful bulls and dragons still blaze forth on the lapis-lazuli blue walls of the Gate of Ishtar as they did when it was one of eight fortified entrances to the Babylon of Nebuchadnezzar II.* State Museum, Berlin

generally only in details, not in essence. Grounded almost wholly on the culture of Sumer, Babylonian cultural achievements left a deep impress on the entire ancient world, and particularly on the Hebrews and the Greeks. Even present-day civilization is indebted culturally to Babylonian civilization to some extent. For instance, Babylonian influence is pervasive throughout the Bible and in the works of such Greek poets as Homer and Hesiod (qq.v.), in the geometry of the Greek mathematician Euclid (q.v.), in astrology, and in heraldry. *See* BABYLONIAN LANGUAGE AND LITERATURE; BABYLONIAN RELIGION. S.N.K.

BABYLONIAN ART, architecture, painting, sculpture, and other art forms of ancient Babylonia (q.v.). This art generally continued a tradition in both style and subject inherited from the civilization of Sumer (q.v.).

The Babylonian temple, like its Sumerian precursors, consisted primarily of an elevated shrine approached through a court surrounded by subsidiary buildings. The main entrance consisted of a gateway between towers ornamented with stepped recesses, and the outside walls were decorated with flat buttresses. One or more courts were added to the larger temples. The stele of the god that is, the inscribed slab or pillar, occupied a special niche of the cella, the most sacred part of the shrine. The cella often was separated from the rest of the room or court by means of piers or a thin wall.

In the 15th century B.C., when Kassite kings (*see* KASSITES) ruled Babylonia, the architects introduced an impressive decorative scheme, essentially a novel application of a very ancient fertility motif. They placed male and female figures, each holding a water vase, in the stepped recesses of the towers. Symbolic life-bringing water flowing from the vases was represented by horizontal bands joining the buttresses between the figures, and by wavy double lines on the buttresses themselves. The figures were built up of molded bricks as structural components of the towers. This technique was applied very effectively much later, in days of Chaldean preeminence, to that remarkable structure known as the Ishtar Gate, part of which remains at the site of Babylon, near the modern city of Hilla; another part can be seen in the Museum of the Ancient Orient in Berlin, Germany. The walls of the Ishtar Gate were colorfully decorated with tier upon tier of brick panels showing mythological animal figures, some of which were enameled and in relief.

The Babylonians often built a staged tower, known in the Babylonian language as a ziggurat, in the vicinity of the temple. Also a Sumerian architectural development, the ziggurat continued to be an outstanding feature of Babylonian religious architecture throughout the centuries. For example, in the Sumerian city of Ur (q.v.), which passed into Babylonian hands, the famous ziggurat of the king Ur-Nammu (23rd or 22nd century B.C.) remained standing almost unaltered for some 1500 years. Babylon itself was the site of a celebrated ziggurat called Etemenanki, probably the structure known in the Bible as the Tower of Babel; *see* BABEL, TOWER OF. All that remains of the ziggurat are the ground plan and traces of three large stairways that led to its summit. According to a geometrical description found on a cuneiform (q.v.) tablet dated 229 B.C., the structure consisted apparently of two stories and a tower of five superimposed stages crowned by a sacred shrine at the summit. On the other hand, the Greek historian Herodotus (q.v.) described the ziggurat of Babylon as an eight-staged tower surrounded by a ramp and having a sanctuary on the topmost stage.

The palace of a king or governor was sometimes located next to the temple. Flanking the palace entrance were usually two guard rooms, and a brick-paved path led through the main court to the throne room. Beyond the latter lay the main administration hall, surrounded by government offices. Often the palace had its own chapel, constructed in a style similar to that of the adjoining temple. The palace might also contain the residential quarters of the king, or at least a suite of rooms from which he conducted the affairs of the state. The colonnade was sometimes a feature of the Babylonian palace.

Both the temples and the palaces of Babylon were often decorated with paintings. In the days of the dynasty of Hammurabi (q.v.), from the 18th to 16th centuries B.C., the painted themes were primarily mythological motifs, war scenes, and religious rites. The Kassites, on the other hand, had their palaces painted with geometrical and floral decorations and processions of human figures. Much later, in Chaldean times, a palace was decorated with a facade of glazed bricks showing a pattern of slender masts topped by volute and palmette capitals, and connected by graceful flower designs.

Babylonian sculpture-in-the-round is represented by cult statues of deities and rulers. Compared with their Sumerian forerunners, even the best pieces seem rather hard, insensitive, and not so finely modeled. The statues of the ruling princes are often inscribed. Some show broad but sensitive treatment of parts of

Babylonia drew upon the art traditions of ancient Sumer, represented by this lyre (about 2450 B.C.*) with a bearded bull's head. Gold, lapis lazuli, and mosaics decorate the lyre.* Scala New York/Florence

the body, particularly the muscles, combined with an extraordinary elaboration of ornamental details of dress and hair. One of the extant divine statues represents the goddess with the "flowing vase"; the statue has water pipes, and was thus once a true fountain.

Probably the most important surviving work of the Hammurabi dynasty is a head in black granite (now in the Louvre, Paris) which may well be that of King Hammurabi himself, the greatest figure in Babylonian history. The treatment, which is almost impressionistic, shows the finely modeled face of a rugged and powerful personality. Features similar to those of this head also characterize a remarkable Babylonian bronze statuette (also in the Louvre) of a man kneeling in adoration; the inscription states that it was dedicated to the Amorite god Martu. Hammurabi also appears in various relief sculptures, the most famous example of which is the relief stele, made of diorite (q.v.), inscribed with his code (*see* HAMMURABI, CODE OF). The king is shown confronting the sun-god Shamash, and the scene conveys a sense of earnest communication between the royal lawgiver and the divine lord of justice.

From the long period of Babylonian history following the Hammurabi dynasty, few important works of stone have survived. An exception is sculptured boundary stones, which usually were composed entirely of emblems representing the cult objects of different gods. Sometimes, however, these boundary stones show the image of a ruler in a style reminiscent of the reliefs of Hammurabi.

Babylonian seal engravings show relatively little vitality, variety, or unity. In the time of the Hammurabi dynasty the scenes depicted show a combination of unrelated motifs lacking harmony. In the Kassite period the inscription is made the most important feature of the seal engraving. Typical of the scenes in Chaldean times is a priest standing in prayer with hand upraised before an altar showing sacred emblems.

See SUMERIAN ART AND ARCHITECTURE. S.N.K.

BABYLONIAN CAPTIVITY *or* **BABYLONISH CAPTIVITY** *or* **BABYLONIAN EXILE,** term applied to the period between the deportation of the Jews from Palestine to Babylon by the Babylonian king Nebuchadnezzar and their release in 537 B.C. by the Persian king Cyrus. Two main deportations are recorded: one in 597 B.C., when Israelite nobles, warriors, and craftsmen were transported; and one in 586 B.C., when Nebuchadnezzar's army destroyed Jerusalem and the major part of the remaining Israelite community was taken to Babylon. At the time of the second deportation an important group of Israelites fled to Egypt; thereafter, only the poorest Israelite peasants were allowed to remain in Palestine, and the political dissolution of independent Israel was an accomplished fact. The majority of the Jews living in Babylon did not return to Palestine at the end of the exile period, but became a part of the Diaspora, or body of Jews dispersed among nations outside of Palestine. For an account of the historical background and consequences of the Babylonian captivity, *see* JEWS.

In the history of the Roman Catholic Church, the term "Babylonian Captivity" is frequently applied to the residence of the popes in Avignon, France, from 1309 to 1377. A.L.S.

BABYLONIAN LANGUAGE AND LITERATURE, the most important dialect of Akkadian, a language of ancient Akkad (*see* SUMER) and the literature written in that dialect. Akkadian belongs to the Semitic family of languages (*see* SEMITIC LANGUAGES) and is usually classified as East Semitic. From the very earliest times, the totally unrelated Sumerian language (*see* SUMERIAN LANGUAGE AND LITERATURE) strongly influenced Akkadian vocabulary and even grammar.

Sometime around 2400 B.C. Akkadian was first written down in the cuneiform (q.v.) script borrowed from the Sumerians. This script was not too well adapted to writing the Akkadian (Semitic) sounds, which were quite different from those of Sumerian. However, many of the difficulties were solved by a number of significant orthographic reforms, particularly in the time of the Babylonian king Hammurabi (q.v.), who reigned from about 1728 to 1688 B.C.

About 1950 B.C., when the breakup of the empire of Sumer and Akkad occurred at the end of the Third Dynasty of Ur (*see* UR), the Akkadian language was in general use throughout Mesopotamia (q.v.) and had already begun to replace Sumerian as the spoken language in Sumer itself. It appears also to have been adopted as a political and religious language by the Elamites (*see* ELAM) to the east, and by the Guti, Lullians, and Hurrians to the north and northeast.

After 1950 B.C. the Akkadian language itself broke up into two major dialects, Babylonian and Assyrian (*see* ASSYRIA), each of which gradually underwent a number of changes. Even in Assyria, however, the Babylonian dialect was used for literary purposes and, at least in certain periods, for historical and religious inscriptions; the Assyrian dialect was used primarily for economic and legal documents.

The history of the Babylonian dialect is usually divided into four periods: Old Babylonian (about 1950–1500 B.C.); Middle Babylonian (about 1500–1000 B.C.); Neo-Babylonian (about 1000–600 B.C.); and Late Babylonian (about 600 B.C.–75 A.D.).

During the Old Babylonian period the use of the Babylonian dialect spread over most of Syria as the diplomatic and commercial lingua franca. Later, after 1500 B.C., during the period of the bitter clashes between the rival empires of Babylonia and Mitanni to the north and northwest, the Hittites (q.v.) in Asia Minor, and Egypt, Middle Babylonian was the language of almost all diplomatic correspondence and of treaties between the great powers. In this period the chancelleries, even in Egypt and in the Hittite capital of Pteria (now Bogazköy, Turkey), not only employed scribes who wrote in the Babylonian language, but maintained schools in which Babylonian literature was read and studied. At this time too, within the Hurrian-speaking areas throughout the Mitanni empire, a form of Babylonian, considerably corrupted by the totally unrelated agglutinative Hurrian language, was used also as the language of commerce and of the law courts.

After 1200 B.C., when all of Syria and Anatolia (Asia Minor) were overrun by various waves of "Sea-Peoples" (maritime nations), Aramaeans, and others, the cultural and linguistic continuity in the western areas seems to have been radically disturbed, but within Mesopotamia itself it continued unbroken. Little by little, however, after 900 B.C., when the expanding Assyrian Empire came to include large numbers of Aramaeans, the Aramaic language began to supplant Assyrian as the spoken language, even in Assyria. Meanwhile Aramaic-speaking tribes, including the Chaldeans, had infiltrated Babylonia. Although these tribes soon assimilated Babylonian culture and religion, they gradually made Aramaic the speech of a large segment of the population. By the time of the Macedonian king Alexander III (q.v.), known as Alexander the Great, Babylonian had been replaced almost completely by Aramaic as the spoken language; nevertheless it was retained as the language of law, religion, literature, and science, and even for some historical writing, much as Latin was used in Europe after the breakup of the Roman Empire. This situation prevailed through the Hellenistic period (323–146 B.C.) into the period of Parthian rule (*see* PARTHIA), when, at least in the cities of Babylon and Erech, Babylonian was still used by the priesthood and by the Chaldean astronomers. The last known text in the Babylonian language is an astronomical tablet from Babylon datable to 75 A.D.

Babylonian Literature. Although nearly all of the literary compositions in the Akkadian language are in the Babylonian dialect, the largest extant body of this literature comes from the library of Ashurbanipal (q.v.), King of Assyria, in Nineveh, the ancient Assyrian capital. Most of the literature is written in the Neo-Assyrian script. Among the literary genres represented are epics and myths; historical chronicles and royal annals; historical romances in poetic form; hymns and prayers; incantations and rituals; collections of proverbs and precepts; disputations (fanciful literary debates between animals, trees, or the like); and poetic narratives dealing with the problem of human misery.

The longest Babylonian epic poems are the *Creation Epic,* known as *Enuma Elish* ("When Above", the first two words), and the *Epic of Gilgamesh.* The former, consisting of seven tablets, deals with the struggle between cosmic order and primeval chaos; the central figure is Marduk, the god of Babylon (in the Assyrian version, the national god Ashur was substituted). The secular *Epic of Gilgamesh,* consisting of twelve tablets, is concerned with the Deluge (q.v.), friendship, adventure, and the hero's fruitless search for immortality. Masterfully woven together from a series of separate Sumerian episodic tales, this epic poem had such popular appeal in antiquity that it was even translated into Hurrian and Hittite.

The *Epic of Zû* tells of the theft of the Tablets of Destiny from the gods by the evil bird Zû and of their recovery by the warrior-god Ninurta. The friendship of Etana, a shepherd who ultimately founded the first dynasty after the Deluge, with an eagle, who carried him to heaven in search of the "plant of birth" is related in the *Epic of Etana.* Other Babylonian epics and myths are *The Descent of Ishtar to the Nether World; Adapa and the South-wind; Atrahasis,* which deals with the sins of mankind and with its punishment through plagues and the Deluge; and *Nergal and Ereshkigal,* concerning the marriage of the divine couple who ruled the nether world.

The disputations include *The Tamarisk and the Date-palm; The Dog, the Wolf, the Lion, and the Fox;* and *The Ox and the Horse.* Other important Babylonian literary works include a long poem about a Joblike "righteous sufferer", *The Babylonian Theodicy,* a poetic dialogue on the subject of human misery; a satirical dialogue, *The Master and His Obliging Servant;* and a very recently discovered folk tale, *The Poor Man of Nippur,* which seems to be the ancestor of one of the stories in the *Thousand and One Nights* (*see* ARABIAN NIGHTS).

Among significant historical romances in poetic form are *The Cuthaean Legend,* concerning the defeat of King Naram-Sin (fl. about 2250 B.C.) of Akkad by the barbaric Guti and Lullians; *The King of Battle,* dealing with a military expedition led by Sargon I (r. about 2637–2582 B.C.) of Akkad far into Anatolia in support of Akkadian merchants; and *The Epic of Tukulti-Ninurta,* describing the overwhelming defeat of the Babylonians by the Assyrians under King Tukulti-Ninurta I (r. 1256–1233 B.C.) *See* BABYLONIA: *History.* E.I.G.

BABYLONIAN RELIGION, moral and supernatural beliefs and ritual practices of the ancient Babylonians; *see* BABYLONIA. The cosmogony and cosmology of Babylonian religion, that is, the gods and demons, cults and priests, and moral and ethical teachings, were taken almost entirely from the Sumerians; *see* SUMER. The Babylonians, however, whose dominant ethnic strain was Amorite (*see* AMORITES), undoubtedly modified many of the borrowed Sumerian religious beliefs and practices in accordance with their own cultural heritage and psychological disposition. To cite only two outstanding examples, it was the military success and political drive of the Semitic Amorites that made the city of Babylon (q.v.) the religious and cultural center of the land, and that gave the Amorite god Marduk preeminence in the Babylonian pantheon. Nevertheless, the Babylonian theologians found it necessary to justify Marduk's newly acquired exalted position by the legal fiction that his Sumerian predecessors, the gods An and Enlil, had themselves officially transferred their powers to him.

The Babylonians believed in a pantheon consisting of beings, manlike in form but superhuman and immortal, each of whom, though invisible to the human eye, ruled a particular component of the cosmos, however small, and controlled it in accordance with well-laid plans and duly prescribed laws. Each was in charge of one of the great realms of heaven, earth, sea, and air; or one of the major astral bodies, that is, the sun, moon, and planets; or, in the realm of the earth, of such natural entities as river, mountain, and plain, and of such social entities as city and state. Even tools and implements, such as the pickax, brick mold, and plow, were under the charge of specially appointed deities. Finally, each Babylonian had a personal god, a kind of good angel, to whom he prayed and through whom he found salvation.

At the head of this multitude of divine kings was Marduk, the Amorite tribal god, who had played only a minor and relatively unimportant role in the religious life of the land before the time of the ruler Hammurabi (q.v.) in the 18th and 17th centuries B.C. According to the Babylonian mythological poem known in world literature as *Enuma Elish* ("When Above", its initial two words), Marduk was granted the leadership of the pantheon as well as the "kingship over the universe entire" as a reward for avenging the gods by defeating Tiamat, the savage and defiant goddess of Chaos, and her monstrous host. Following his victory, Marduk fashioned heaven and earth, arranged and regulated the planets and stars, and created man.

Among the more important Babylonian deities, in addition to Marduk, were Ea, the god of wisdom, spells, and incantations; Sin, the moon-god who had his main temples at Ur (q.v.) and Harran, two cities associated in the Bible with the Hebrew patriarch Abraham; Shamash the sun-god and the god of justice, who is depicted on the stele, or tablet, inscribed with the code of Hammurabi (*see* HAMMURABI, CODE OF); Ishtar (q.v.), the ambitious, dynamic, and cruel goddess of love and war; Adad, the god of wind, storm, and flood; and Marduk's son Nabu, the scribe and herald of the gods, whose cult eventually rivaled that of his father in popularity. In addition to the sky-gods were the netherworld deities, as well as a large variety of demons, devils, and monsters, who were a constant threat to man and his well-being, and a few good, angelic spirits.

Each of the important deities had, in one or more of the Babylonian cities, a large temple in which he or she was worshiped as the divine civic ruler and protector. The larger cities also contained many temples and chapels dedicated to one deity or another; Babylon, for example, possessed more than fifty temples in Chaldean times (8th to 6th century B.C.).

Temple services were generally conducted in open courts containing fountains for ablution and altars for sacrifices. The cella, or inner part of the temple, in which the statue of the deity stood on a pedestal in a special niche, was the holy of holies, and only the high priest and other privileged members of the clergy and court were permitted to enter it. In the temple complexes of the larger cities a ziggurat, or staged tower, was often built, crowned by a small sanctuary, which probably was reserved for the all-important sacred-marriage ceremony celebrated in connection with the new-year festival.

The upkeep of the major Babylonian temples required large revenues, which were provided primarily by gifts and endowments from the court and the men of wealth. In the course of the centuries some of the major Babylonian temples accumulated immense wealth and came into possession of large estates and factories employing large numbers of serfs and slaves. Primarily, however, the temple was the house of the god, in which all the needs of the deity were provided for in accordance with ancient rites and impressive ceremonies carried out by a vast institutionalized clergy. The latter comprised high priests, sacrifice priests, musicians, singers, magicians, soothsayers, diviners, dream interpreters, astrologers, female devotees, and hierodules (temple slaves).

Sacrifices, which were offered daily, consisted of animal and vegetable foods, libations of water, wine, and beer, and the burning of incense. Numerous annual and monthly festivals were held, including a feast to celebrate the new moon. The most important festival of all was the celebration of the new year at the spring equinox; it was known as the Akitu festival because some of its more esoteric ritual was enacted in the Akitu, Marduk's shrine outside of Babylon. The festival lasted eleven days and included such rites as purification, sacrifice, propitiation, penance, and absolution, but it also involved colorful processions. The culmination was probably the sacred marriage ceremony previously mentioned, which took place in the sanctuary crowning the ziggurat.

Babylonian documents indicate that the ethical and moral beliefs of the people stressed goodness and truth, law and order, justice and freedom, wisdom and learning, and courage and loyalty. Mercy and compassion were espoused and special protection was accorded widows, orphans, refugees, the poor, and the oppressed. Immoral and unethical acts were considered transgressions against the gods and the divine order, and were believed to be punished by the gods accordingly. No man was considered to be without sin, and therefore all suffering was held to be deserved. The proper course for a Babylonian, unhappy with his condition in life, was not to argue and complain but to plead and wail, to lament and confess his inevitable sins and failings before his personal god, who acted as his mediator in the assembly of the great gods.

The religiosity of the Babylonians has come to be proverbial, and not unjustifiably so. Nevertheless, religious skepticism existed and may have been more prevalent than sources reveal.

One extant literary document known as the *Babylonian Theodicy,* for example, consists of a debate between a skeptic and a believer in which the latter finds it necessary to conclude with the patent and somewhat unsatisfying argument that the will of the gods is inscrutable. In another Babylonian essay, taking the form of a dialogue between a master and slave, the tone is similarly skeptical and the mood cynical; the relativist view is advanced that all human actions can be justified and are therefore fundamentally without meaning, particularly because death makes life itself insignificant.

For the Babylonians, death was indeed the consuming dread and a source of great despair. The Babylonian generally believed that at death the disembodied spirit descends to the dark nether world, and that man's existence beyond the grave is at best only a dismal, wretched reflection of life on earth. Any hope of an eternal reward for the righteous and deserving was absent; everyone was impartially consigned to the world below. It is not strange that the most popular, dramatic, and creative Babylonian literary work, the *Epic of Gilgamesh,* centers about a vain and pathetic quest for eternal life.

See also ASSYRIA; BABYLONIAN ART; BABYLONIAN LANGUAGE AND LITERATURE. S.N.K.

BABY'S BREATH, common name applied to several Old World plants with blossoms that are delicate in appearance and fragrance. They are often used in rock gardens and borders. The flowers of several of the plants are popular in mixed bouquets for their misty effect. **1.** Several species of the genus *Gypsophila* in the Pink family (*Caryophyllaceae*), particularly *G. paniculata,* an ornamental perennial with a slender, erect, forking stem about 2 to 3 ft. high, lanceolate leaves, and numerous small white or pink fragrant flowers in panicled cymes. **2.** Certain species of the genus *Galium* in the Madder family (Rubiaceae), also known as bedstraw (q.v.), including *G. sylvaticum,* known as baby's breath or Scotch mist, and *G. mollugo,* known as false baby's breath or wild madder. They have leaves without stalks and tiny yellow or white flowers grouped in clusters. **3.** Certain species of the genus *Muscari* in the Lily family (Liliaceae), also called grape hyacinth (q.v.). Their tiny flowers are usually blue but in some varieties are white; *M. botryoides* is the common garden species.

BACĂU, city of Rumania, capital of Bacău Region, on the Bistrita R., 150 miles N.E. of Bucharest. A Moldavian rail junction and industrial and trade center for petroleum products, fruits, and nuts, the city also mills flour, processes meat, and manufactures textiles, machinery, hardware, and leather and earthenware products. Major paper and pulp mills and several large hydroelectric plants are nearby. The city has two 15th-century churches and a cultural museum. During World War I, Bacău served as headquarters for the Rumanian army. Area of region, 5172 sq.mi.; pop. (1966) 1,110,000. Pop. of city (1971) 95,576.

BACCARAT, game of cards of French origin, dating from the end of the 15th century. The game is played in gambling; one or more decks of cards are used by two or more players, one of whom deals and acts as banker. The players may bet a total of any amount equal to or less than the amount of the bank. The cards count according to the number of marks, with tens and face cards counting zero; the object of the game is to form a combination of two or three cards totaling a count as close as possible to nine or nineteen. After the bets are made, the banker deals the cards, one at a time and face down, until each player has two. The player may ask for another card, which is dealt face up. After all have been supplied, the cards are faced and the bets are settled, the count nearer to nine or nineteen winning. In case of a tie, the bets are withdrawn. Two varieties of baccarat are played. In chemin de fer, the banker plays individually against each of the other players, or punters, betting on his hand against each of the hands held by the players. He retains the bank until he loses a bet, and the bank then falls to the winning player. In baccarat banque, the banker plays against only two hands, on which all the other players bet, holding the bank until he has lost his original stake or voluntarily resigns. Baccarat banque is played only in Europe.

BACCHANALIA. *See* BACCHUS.

BACCHANTES. *See* BACCHUS.

BACCHUS, in Greek and Roman mythology, the god of wine, identified with Dionysus (q.v.), the Greek god of wine, and Liber, the Roman god of wine. Bacchus is usually characterized in two ways. One is that of the god of vegetation, specifically of the fruit of the trees, who is often represented on Attic vases with a drinking horn and vine branches. As he came to be the popular national Greek god of wine and cheer, wine miracles were reputedly performed at certain of his festivals. The second concept of the god, that of a foreign deity whose mysteries inspired ecstatic, orgiastic worship, is exemplified by the Maenads, or Bacchantes, a group of women who were not permitted to worship him in the Olympian temples. They left their homes to roam the wilderness where the worship of Bacchus became centered.

Bacchus, god of wine, was also the protector of vines. He is often pictured crowned with grapes and vine leaves, as in this painting by Guido Reni in the Galleria Palatina, Florence, Italy. Scala

The name Bacchus came into use in ancient Greece during the 5th century B.C. It refers to the loud cries with which he was worshipped at the Bacchanalia, frenetic celebrations in his honor. These events, which supposedly originated in spring nature festivals, became occasions for licentiousness and intoxication, at which the celebrants danced, drank, and generally debauched themselves. The Bacchanalia became more and more extreme and were prohibited by the Roman senate in 186 B.C. In the first century A.D., however, the Dionysiac mysteries were still popular, as evidenced by representations of them found on Greek sarcophagi.

BACCHYLIDES (fl. 5th cent. B.C.), Greek poet, born in Iulis, on Ceos (now Kéa). According to tradition, he was a nephew and pupil of the poet Simonides of Ceos and the rival of the great Greek lyric poet Pindar (qq.v.). For a time he lived at the court of Hiero I (*see under* HIERO), tyrant of Syracuse, whom he celebrated in three of his poems. When exiled from his native town, Bacchylides resided in the Peloponnesus (now Pelopónnisos), and records of many of his victories in dithyrambic contests at Athens have been preserved. Though admired by the Roman lyric poet Horace (q.v.), and much read until 400 A.D., his works were later considered uninspired and ordinary. Until 1897 only 107 lines of Bacchylides' work were preserved in quotations, the longest one of only twelve verses. In 1896 the British Museum (q.v.), London, acquired two hundred fragments of a papyrus of Bacchylides. Pieced together, they came to 1070 lines. Fourteen are Odes of Victory. Six of them are the unique extant specimens of the dithyramb (q.v.), a type of Greek lyric poetry. Paeans (*see* PAEAN) and hymns also occur. In style Bacchylides is simple and clear, displaying a love of picturesque detail. He is a true and typical Greek poet in his smoothness, grace, and finish. As the youngest, he was placed last in the list of nine lyric poets deemed worthy of immortality by the canon of the Alexandrian critics (*see* ALEXANDRIAN AGE).

BACCIO DELLA PORTA. *See* BARTOLOMMEO.

BACH, name of a family of musicians originating in Wechmar near Gotha in Thuringia, Germany. Over a period of seven generations the family produced forty-nine musicians, twenty of whom, from Veit Bach (d. 1619) to Wilhelm Friedrich Ernst Bach (d. 1845) were prominent. The most famous members of the family were Johann Sebastian Bach and three of his sons, Johann Christian Bach, Karl Philipp Emanuel Bach, and Wilhelm Friedemann Bach.

Johann Sebastian Bach (1685–1750), organist and composer of the baroque era, born in Eisenach, Thuringia, Germany; *see* MUSIC: *History of Music: The Baroque Era.* He received his first musical instruction from his father, Johann Ambrosius (1645–95), a town musician. When his father died, he went to live and study with his elder brother, Johann Christoph (1671–1721), an organist in Ohrdruf. In 1700 Bach began to earn his own living. His first job was as a chorister at the Church of Saint Michael in Lüneburg.

In 1703 Bach became a violinist in the chamber orchestra of Prince Johann Ernst of Weimar, but later that year he moved to Arnstadt, where he became church organist. In October, 1705, he secured a one-month leave of absence in order to study with the renowned Swedish organist Dietrich Buxtehude (q.v.), who was then in Lübeck and whose organ music greatly influenced Bach's. The visit was so rewarding to Bach that he overstayed his leave by two months. He was criticized by the church authorities not only for this breach of contract, but also for the extravagant flourishes and strange harmonies in his organ accompaniments to congregational singing. He was already too highly respected, however, for either objection to result in his dismissal.

In 1707 he married a second cousin, Maria Barbara Bach, and went to Mülhausen as organist in the church of Saint Blasius. He went back to Weimar the next year as organist and violinist at the court of Duke Wilhelm Ernst, and remained there for the next nine years, becoming concertmaster of the court orchestra in 1714. In Weimar he composed about thirty cantatas including the well known funeral cantata *God's Time is the Best,* and also wrote organ and harpsichord works. He began to travel throughout Germany as an organ virtuoso and as a consultant to organ builders.

In 1717 Bach began a six-year employment as chapelmaster and director of chamber music at the court of Prince Leopold of Anhalt-Köthen. During this period he wrote primarily secular music for ensembles and solo instruments. He also prepared music books for his wife and children, that were designed to teach them keyboard technique and musicianship. These books included the *Well-Tempered Clavier,* the *Inventions,* and the *Little Organ Book.*

Bach's first wife died in 1720 and the next year he married Anna Magdalena Wilcken, a fine singer and the daughter of a court musician. She not only bore him thirteen children in addition to the seven he had had by his first wife, but helped him in his work by making copies of his music for performers.

In 1723 he moved to Leipzig, where he spent the rest of his life. His position there as musical director and choirmaster of St. Thomas' church and church school was unsatisfactory in many ways. He squabbled continually with the town council, and neither the council nor the populace appreciated his musical genius. They saw in him little more than a stuffy old man who clung stubbornly to obsolete forms of music. Nonetheless, the 202 cantatas surviving from the 295 which he wrote in Leipzig still endure, whereas much that was new and in vogue at the time has been forgotten. Most of the cantatas open with a section for chorus and orchestra, continue with alternating recitatives and arias for solo voices and accompaniment, and conclude with a chorale based on a simple Lutheran hymn. The music is at all times closely bound to the text, ennobling the latter immeasurably with its expressiveness and spiritual intensity. Among these works were the Ascension cantata and the *Christmas Oratorio,* the latter comprising of six cantatas. The *Passion of St. John* and the *Passion of St. Matthew* also were written in Leipzig, as well as the epic B minor Mass. Among the works written for the keyboard during this period are the famous *Goldberg Variations*; Part II of the *Well-Tempered Clavier;* and the *Art of the Fugue,* a magnificent demonstration of his contrapuntal skill in the form of sixteen fugues and four canons, all on a single theme. Bach's sight began to fail in the last year of his life, and he died shortly after undergoing an unsuccessful operation to restore his vision.

After Bach died he was remembered less as a composer than as an organist and harpsichord player. His frequent tours had insured his reputation as the greatest organist of the time, but his contrapuntal style of writing sounded old-fashioned to his contemporaries, most of whom preferred more homophonic music (*see* GERMAN MUSIC; MUSIC: *Pre-Classical and Classical Period*). Consequently, for the next eighty years his music was neglected by the public, although a few musicians admired it, among them the symphonists Wolfgang Amadeus Mozart and Ludwig van Beethoven (qq.v.). A revival of interest in Bach's music occurred in the mid-19th century. The German composer Felix Mendelssohn arranged a performance of the *Passion of St. Matthew* in 1829 which did much to awaken popular interest in Bach. The Bach Gesellschaft, formed in 1850, devoted itself assiduously to finding, editing, and publishing Bach's works.

Because the "Bach revival" coincided with the flowering of the romantic movement in music, performance styles were frequently gross distortions of Bach's intentions. Twentieth-century scholarship, inspired by the early enthusiasm of the French Protestant clergyman, medical missionary, organist, and musicologist Albert Schweitzer (q.v.), gradually has unearthed the correct principles of performance for Bach's music.

Bach was largely self-taught in musical composition. His principal study method, following the custom of his day, was to copy in his workbooks the music of French, German, and Italian composers of his own time and earlier. He did this throughout his life and often made arrangements of other composers' works.

The significance of Bach's music is due in large part to the scope of his intellect. He is perhaps best known as a supreme master of counterpoint (q.v.). He was able to understand and use every resource of musical language that was available in the baroque era. Thus, if he chose, he could combine the rhythmic patterns of French dances, the gracefulness of Italian melody, and the intricacy of German counterpoint all in one composition. At the same time he could write for voice and the various instruments so as to take advantage of the unique properties of construction and tone quality in each. In addition to these factors, when a text was associated with the music, Bach could write musical equivalents of verbal ideas, such as an undulating melody to represent the sea, or a canon (q.v.) to describe the Christians following the teaching of Jesus.

Johann Sebastian Bach

Bach's ability to assess and exploit the media, styles, and genre of his day enabled him to achieve many remarkable transfers of idiom. For instance, he could take an Italian ensemble composition, such as a violin concerto, and transform it into a convincing work for a single instrument, the harpsichord. By devising intricate melodic lines, he could convey the complex texture of a multi-voiced fugue on a single-melody instrument, such as the violin or cello. The conversational rhythms and sparse textures of operatic recitatives can be found in some of his works for solo keyboard. Technical facility alone, of course, is not the source of Bach's greatness. It is the expressiveness of his music, particularly as manifested in the vocal works, that conveys his humanity and that touches listeners everywhere.

Wilhelm Friedemann Bach (1710–84), German composer and organist, eldest son of Johann Sebastian Bach, born in Weimar and instructed in music by his father. From 1733 to 1746 he was organist in the Sophien Kirche in Dresden, after which and until 1764 he was organist at the Church of Our Lady in Halle. For the rest of his life he was a recitalist and private teacher in Brunswick and then Berlin. Much of his music contained sudden contrasts in mood that lent it an impulsiveness that was unusual for the time. This music is representative of the *empfindsamer Stil* (Ger., "expressive style"), one of the preclassic styles that flourished during the mid-18th century; *see* MUSIC: *Preclassic and Classic Periods.* Bach's output included 21 cantatas, 9 symphonies, several keyboard concertos, and many fantasies, fugues, preludes, and sonatas for keyboard instruments.

Karl Philipp Emanuel Bach (1714–88), German composer, third son of Johann Sebastian Bach, born in Weimar and trained under his father. He studied philosophy and law at the universities in Leipzig and Frankfurt-on-the-Oder before deciding on a musical career. From 1740 to 1768 he was a harpsichord player for Frederick II, King of Prussia (q.v.), after which he became music director of the five principal churches in Hamburg. K.P.E. Bach was one of the chief representatives of the *empfindsamer Stil* (German, expressive style), which emphasized frequent contrasts in emotion and contributed many technical features to the Classical style (*see* MUSIC: *Preclassic and Classic Periods*). His *Essay on the True Art of Playing Keyboard Instruments* is important for describing how music was performed during his lifetime (the printed notes themselves do not always indicate what composers intended). K.P.E. Bach wrote a large number of works, including 210 harpsichord pieces and 52 concertos. His church music includes oratorios, Passions, and cantatas.

Johann (John) Christian Bach (1735–82), German composer, youngest son of Johann Sebastian Bach, born in Leipzig and given his first musical training there under his father. In 1750, when his father died, he went to Berlin to study with his brother, Karl Philipp Emanuel Bach. He spent eight years in Italy, from 1754 to 1760 as music director for Count Antonio Litta in Milan, and then from 1760 to 1762 as organist at the Milan Cathedral. During this period he also studied in Bologna with the Italian composer Giovanni Battista Martini (1706–84). In 1762 Bach settled in London and soon became music master to the queen. Part of his success was due to the fact that he represented the pleasant, tuneful style of Italian opera, which was then fashionable in London. From 1764 until his death he and another German composer living in London, Karl Friedrich Abel (1725–87), produced a series of concerts that were famous because of the composers who wrote music for them. One such composer was the seven-year-old Austrian prodigy, Wolfgang Amadeus Mozart (q.v.). Bach himself wrote about a dozen operas and many symphonies, concertos, piano pieces, and chamber music. W.M.

BACHE, Alexander Dallas (1806–67), American physicist, great-grandson of the American statesman and scientist Benjamin Franklin (q.v.), born in Philadelphia, Pa., and educated at the United States Military Academy. He was professor of natural philosophy and chemistry at the University of Pennsylvania from 1828 to 1836 and first president of Girard College in Philadelphia from 1836 to 1842. He was appointed superintendent of the United States Coast and Geodetic Survey in 1843 and served until his death. At Girard College he established the first magnetic observatory in the United States, and his survey of Pennsylvania marks the beginning of the magnetic work carried on by the Coast and Geodetic Survey, now the Environmental Science Services Administration. His works include *Observations at the Magnetic and Meteorological Observatory at Girard College* (3 vol., 1840–47).

BACHELOR (fr. medieval Lat. *baccalaris,* "dependent or tenant farmer"; fr. Lat. *bacca,* "cow"), originally, in the early Middle Ages, a cowherd or farm servant. In the agricultural economy of this period, the term was applied to the tenant farmers or cultivators of certain portions of church lands, called *baccalaria.* At a somewhat later period the term was applied to novices in monasteries and to persons passing through the probationary stages of knighthood (*see* KNIGHT). When the earliest universities were established in Europe, in the 12th and 13th centuries, bachelors were those students who had just begun their academic careers. In the 13th century Pope Gregory IX (1147?–1241) bestowed the title upon those members of the University of Paris who had not yet reached the rank of master or doctor. From this usage, the term was finally standardized in educational practice as the title of the lowest academic degree (*see* DEGREE, ACADEMIC). In modern times the term is also used more generally to denote a man who has not married; this meaning rests upon a metaphoric view of such a person as a candidate or probationer for matrimony.

Regarded as a class in a community, bachelors, in the last meaning of the word, have been the subject of legislation from ancient times. Such legislation has imposed penalties upon unmarried males on the principle that a citizen is under an obligation to the state to rear legitimate children. This legal compulsion to marry has been especially severe in societies, such as those of ancient Sparta and Rome or of Fascist Italy and Germany, in which the interests of the state were regarded as superior to those of the individual.

BACHELOR, KNIGHT. *See* KNIGHT.

BACHELOR'S BUTTON, common name for any of several small, globular flowers which resemble cloth buttons worn by men in the 18th century. The cornflower, *Centaurea cyanus,* grows to a height of 3 ft. and has linear leaves. In bloom from June until the first frost, the flowers are mostly blue, but varieties of white, pink, and purple also exist. The bachelor's button, *Polygala lutea,* has densely clustered orange-yellow flowers, and grows wild in E. United States. Also known as bachelor's button are the field buttercup, *Ranunculus acris,* and the English daisy, *Bellis perennis.*

BACILLUS. *See* BACTERIA: *Scientific Classification.*

BACK, formerly GREAT FISH, river of Canada, in the Northwest Territories, rising in Aylme Lake and other lakes in Mackenzie District. It flows generally N.E. through Keewatin District and empties into Chantrey Inlet on the Arctic Ocean. The Back has a total length of 605 mi. and passes through several lakes, including Pelly, Garry, MacDougall, and Franklin. The river was named in honor of the British explorer Sir George Back (1796–1878), who explored the region between 1833 and 1835 and traced the river to its mouth.

BACK BAY, former inner harbor of Boston, Mass., drained and filled between 1856 and 1886. Straight, wide streets and squares were built on the reclaimed land, and the area is now one of the most exclusive residential districts of the city. Many of the finest streets, churches, and public buildings are in the Back Bay area, including the Public Garden and Copley Square.

BACKGAMMON, game played by two persons, each having fifteen counters on a special board with twenty-four points. Each player in turn rolls two dice and advances one or two of his counters the number of points indicated on the dice. If both dice show the same number, the player takes four moves of that number, rather than two. If a player has two or more counters on any point, that point is blocked, and his opponent may not move onto it. The object of the game is to move all fifteen counters around the twenty-four points and off the board. The first player to do so is the winner.

Games similar to backgammon were played in ancient Babylonia, Greece, and Rome. In North America, similar games were played by the Aztec (q.v.) Indians hundreds of years before the arrival of the Spanish conquistadores in the 16th century, and by the Iroquois (q.v.) Indians before the coming of European explorers and settlers. The modern form of the game was invented probably in the 10th century. Backgammon has been popular in the United States since about 1930.

Buttercup, Ranunculus acris — Museum of Natural History

BACKSWIMMER. *See* WATERBUG.

BACOLOD, city in the Republic of the Philippines, and capital of Negros Occidental Province, on the E. coast of Negros Island, about 300 miles S.E. of Manila. Sugar milling and fishing are the chief industries of the city, which is also a trade center. The surrounding area produces sugarcane and rice. Pop. (1970) 187,300.

BACON, Delia Salter (1811–59), American critic and writer, born in Tallmadge, Ohio. She wrote *Tales of the Puritans* (1837) and *Philosophy of the Plays of Shakespeare Unfolded* (1857), with a preface by the American writer Nathaniel Hawthorne (q.v.). In this book she advanced the theory that the plays of William Shakespeare (q.v.) were really written by the English writers Edmund Spenser, Sir Walter Raleigh, and Francis Bacon (qq.v.). Although she did not originate this theory, she gave it general currency. *See* BACON-SHAKESPEARE CONTROVERSY.

BACON, Francis, 1st Baron Verulam and Viscount Saint Albans (1561–1626), English philosopher and statesman, born at York House, in the Strand, London, and educated at Trinity

Sir Francis Bacon

College, University of Cambridge. Bacon was elected to the House of Commons in 1584, and served until 1614. He wrote letters of advice to Elizabeth I (q.v.), Queen of England, and, although the suggestions in the letters were sound, they were never implemented. He completely lost favor with the queen when, in 1593, he opposed a bill for a royal subsidy. He regained the respect of the court with the accession of James I (q.v.) to the English throne in 1603. Bacon proposed schemes both for the union of England and Scotland and for pacifying the Church of England (q.v.) on comprehensive lines. For these efforts he was knighted on July 23, 1603, was made a commissioner for the union of Scotland and England, and was given a pension in 1604. His *The Advancement of Learning* was published and presented to the king in 1605. Two years later he was appointed solicitor general.

In the last session of the first Parliament held (February, 1611), under James I, the differences between crown and Commons grew critical, and Bacon took the role of mediator, although he confessed his distrust of James' chief minister, Robert Cecil, 1st Earl of Salisbury (*see under* CECIL). On Salisbury's death in 1612, Bacon informed the king that he was willing to devote himself to the king's interests and undertook in Parliament to effect a reconciliation between crown and Commons. On Oct. 27, 1613, he was apointed attorney general.

In 1616 Bacon became a privy councilor, and in 1618 he was appointed lord chancellor and was raised to the peerage as Baron Verulam. In 1620 his *Novum Organum* was published; and on Jan. 26, 1621, he was created Viscount Saint Albans. In the same year he was charged by Parliament with accepting bribes. He confessed but said that he was "heartily and penitently sorry". He submitted himself to the will of his fellow peers, who ordered him fined, imprisoned during the king's pleasure, and banished from Parliament and the court. After his release from prison, he retired to his family residence at Gorhambury. In September the king pardoned him but prohibited his return to Parliament or the court. Bacon then resumed his writing, completing his *History of Henry VII* and his Latin translation of *The Advancement of Learning* (*De Augmentis*). In March, 1622, he offered to make a digest of the laws, but no further notice was taken of him in spite of the frequent petitions that he addressed to James I and James' successor, Charles I (q.v.).

Bacon's Works. His writings fall into three categories: philosophical, purely literary, and professional. The best of his philosophical works are *The Advancement of Learning* (1605), a review in English of the state of knowledge in his own time, and *Novum Organum,* or *Indications Respecting the Interpretations of Nature* (1620).

Bacon's philosophy emphasized the belief that man is the servant and interpreter of nature, that truth is not derived from authority, and that knowledge is the fruit of experience. Bacon is generally credited with having contributed to logic the method known as ampliative inference, a technique of inductive reasoning (*see* INDUCTION). Previous logicians had practiced induction by simple enumeration, that is, drawing general conclusions from particular data. Bacon's method was to infer by use of analogy, from the characteristics or properties of the larger group to which that datum belonged, leaving to later experience the correction of evident errors. Because it added significantly to the improvement of scientific hypotheses, this method was a fundamental advancement of the scientific method.

Bacon's *Novum Organum* was a contribution to science in that it successfully influenced the acceptance of accurate observation and experimentation in science. In it he maintained that all prejudices and preconceived attitudes, which he called idols, must be abandoned, whether they be the common property of the race due to common modes of thought ("idols of the tribe"), or the peculiar possession of the individual ("idols of the cave"); whether they arise from too great a dependence on language ("idols of the market place"), or from tradition ("idols of the theater").

Bacon's *Essays,* his chief contributions to literature, were published at various times between 1597 and 1625. His *History of Henry VII* (1622) shows his abilities in scholarly research. In his fanciful *New Atlantis* Bacon suggests the formation of scientific academies. Bacon's professional works include *Maxims of the Law* (1630), *Reading on the Statute of Uses* (1642), pleadings in law cases, and speeches in Parliament.

BACON, Henry (1866–1924), American architect, born in Watseka, Ill., and educated at the University of Illinois. He then joined the architectural firm of McKim, Mead & White in New York City. In 1897 he became one of the heads of the new firm of Brite & Bacon, and after 1903, when the partnership was dissolved, he maintained an individual practice. Among the best known of Bacon's works are the Lincoln Memorial (q.v.) in Washington, D.C., the Public Library of Paterson, N.J., the Court of the Four Seasons at the Panama-Pacific Exposition in San Francisco, Calif., and the World War Memorial at Yale University. Many of his historical and personal memorial structures were executed in collaboration with the American sculptor Daniel Chester French (q.v.).

BACON, Nathaniel (1647–76), English planter of colonial Virginia, born in Friston Hall, Suffolk, and educated at the University of Cambridge. His great-grandfather was a cousin of the English philosopher Francis Bacon (q.v.). Nathaniel Bacon settled in Virginia in 1673. Bacon, opposed to the Indian policies of William Berkeley (q.v.), governor of Virginia, led an expedition against the Indians in 1676. Although Berkeley denounced him as a rebel, Bacon was popular with the people. *See* BACON'S REBELLION.

BACON, Roger (1214?–94), English monk and philosopher, born in Ilchester, Somersetshire, and educated at the universities of Oxford and Paris. Bacon remained in Paris after completing his studies, and taught for a time at the University of Paris. Soon after his return to England in about 1251, he entered the religious order of the Franciscans (q.v.) and settled at Oxford. He carried on active studies and did experimental research, mainly in alchemy, optics, and astronomy.

Bacon was critical of the methods of learning of the times, and, at the request of Pope Clement IV (d. 1268), he wrote his *Opus Majus* ("Major Work"), in which he represented the necessity of a reformation in the sciences through different methods of studying the languages and nature. The *Opus Majus* was an encyclopedia of all science, embracing grammar and logic, mathematics, physics, experimental research, and moral philosophy. The response of the pope to Bacon's masterpiece is not known, but the work could not in any circumstances have had much effect in Bacon's time, because it reached Clement during the period of his fatal illness.

Because of his revolutionary ideas about the study of science, Bacon was condemned by the Franciscans for his heretical views. In 1278 the general of the Franciscan Order, Jerome of Ascoli, later Pope Nicholas III (*see under* NICHOLAS), forbade the reading of Bacon's books and had Bacon arrested. After ten years in prison, Bacon returned to Oxford. He wrote a *Compendium Studii Theologiae* ("A Compendium of the Study of Theology", 1292) shortly before his death.

Despite his advanced knowledge, Bacon accepted some of the scientifically inaccurate beliefs of his time, such as the existence of a philosopher's stone and the efficacy of astrology. Although many inventions have been credited to him, some of them undoubtedly were derived from the study of Arabian scientists. His writings brought new and ingenious views on optics, particularly on refraction, on the apparent magnitude of objects, and on the apparent increase in the size of the sun and moon at the

Roger Bacon

horizon. He found that with sulfur, saltpeter (qq.v.), and charcoal a substance (now known as gunpowder) could be produced that would imitate lightning and cause explosions. The previous use of gunpowder by the Arabs, however, has since been shown. He considered mathematics, applied to observation, to be the only means of arriving at a knowledge of nature. Bacon studied several languages and wrote Latin with great elegance and clarity. In 1263 he prepared a rectified calendar, of which a copy is preserved in the library of University College, Oxford. Because of his extensive knowledge he was known as "Doctor Admirabilis". Six of his works were printed between 1485 and 1614, and in 1733 the *Opus Majus* was edited and published.

BACON BEETLE. *See* DERMESTIDAE.

BACON-SHAKESPEARE CONTROVERSY, in English literary history, a question raised by proponents of the theory, often called the Baconian Theory, that the literary works attributed to William Shakespeare (q.v.) were actually written by the English philosopher and statesman Francis Bacon (q.v.). Adherents of this and related theories concede that William Shakespeare was an actor but deny that Shakespeare the actor became Shakespeare the playwright. The first statements of the theory appeared in fragmentary form as early as the middle of the 18th century. The complete theory was developed in *Philosophy of the Plays of Shakespeare Unfolded* (1857) by the American author Delia Salter Bacon (q.v.). Since the publication of this work a small number of students, often professionally engaged in fields other than literary history, have attempted to produce additional evidence in support of Delia Bacon's hypotheses. The vast majority of scholars trained in the literature and history of Elizabethan and Jacobean England have uncompromisingly rejected the Baconian Theory. The testimony of Shakespeare's friend the playwright Ben Jonson (q.v.) seems to be an absolutely conclusive argument for the identification.

The Baconian Theory displays both negative and positive aspects: on the one hand, it is an attempt to prove that Shakespeare could not have written the works attributed to him; on the other, it is an attempt to demonstrate Bacon's authorship. The first part of the argument rests upon the contentions that the historical Shakespeare, a moderately educated commoner raised in a provincial town, could not have acquired the wide learning and the close acquaintance with such fields as law and court life displayed in the plays; and that our knowledge of Shakespeare's life is insufficient to identify him with the author of the dramas. The claim that Bacon was the actual author rests mainly upon the existence of a few passages in Shakespeare's works which are similar to passages in Bacon's and the contention made by some adherents of the Baconian Theory, notably the American politician and writer Ignatius Donnelly (1831–1901) in *The Great Cryptogram* (1888), that a cipher or code containing cryptic disclosures of Bacon's authorship can be detected in the plays. The argument for Bacon's authorship is particularly weak; the parallel passages cited consist mainly of phrases in common use at the time, and the supposed ciphers are so tenuous and difficult to demonstrate that they have been rejected by many of the Baconians themselves. These crucial weaknesses in the second part of the Baconian Theory have led in recent times to fresh controversies in which one or another of several contemporaries of Shakespeare has been put forth as the true author of the plays. Of these theories the least weak is that supporting the English courtier and poet Edward de Vere (1550–1604), 17th Earl of Oxford. The explorer and author Sir Walter Raleigh (q.v.) has also been considered a possible author of the plays.

A new theory was added to the controversy by the American writer and dramatic critic Calvin Hoffman in his book *Murder of the Man Who Was Shakespeare* (1955). Hoffman maintained that the plays ascribed to Shakespeare were written by the Elizabethan dramatist Christopher Marlowe (q.v.). Hoffman claimed that Marlowe did not die in 1593, as is generally believed, but after that date lived in obscurity writing under Shakespeare's name. Hoffman's views have not gained the support of serious scholars.

The question of the supposed Shakespearean ciphers was reviewed in 1957 by the American cryptographer William Frederick Friedman (1891–), who had been largely responsible for breaking the Japanese diplomatic code during World War II, and his wife Elizabeth Smith Friedman (1893–), also a cryptographer. In their work *The Shakespearean Cipher Examined* (1957), the Friedmans considered the cryptographical evidence that someone other than Shakespeare wrote his plays and concluded that no ciphers are found in Shakespeare's writings that would tend to support rival claims to authorship. D.D.

BACON'S REBELLION, uprising in 1676 of Virginia farmers under the leadership of Nathaniel Bacon (q.v.) against the colonial authorities headed by William Berkeley (q.v.), governor of Virginia. Among the grievances of the colonists were the Navigation Acts of 1651 and 1660, which forced them to trade only with English firms and individuals at prices established in England, and the intolerably high export duties levied by colonial officials. With the restoration of Charles II (q.v.) to the throne of England, men who considered the colonies worthwhile only for the purpose of making money were brought to power in England. Governor Berkeley was suspected of sympathizing with them. The colonists were outraged by Governor Berkeley's monopoly of the fur trade with the Indians. To prevent effective protest by the colonists, Berkeley held the Virginia Assembly of 1662, which supported him strongly, in session from year to year, and he established a property qualification for the vote instead of granting universal suffrage.

Toward the end of 1675 the Indians began a series of attacks on the frontier plantations of Virginia, torturing and killing hundreds of colonists. Fearful of jeopardizing his trade with the Indians by too vigorous efforts against them, Berkeley made only a half-hearted attempt to fight them, and he refused to allow the colonists to march against them. The colonists formed an army of 300 and named as its leader Nathaniel Bacon, a plantation owner and member of the Governor's Council who had strong democratic leanings. Bacon marched his army against the Indians on his own authority. The Indians were defeated, and the entire colony was aroused. Berkeley was forced at last to dissolve his assembly and to order the election of a new one. He had Bacon arrested but released him on parole and promised him a commission. Berkeley kept his promise, however, only after Bacon and his army occupied Jamestown, the capital of the colony. As a major general, Bacon marched against the Indians once more and decisively defeated them at the Battle of Bloody Run. While Bacon was engaged in this effort, Berkeley began to raise a force to fight him. Marching against Jamestown a second time, Bacon captured the city and, on Sept. 19, burned it. The following month, while marching to meet a hostile force sent against him by the governor, Bacon died of malaria. His rebellion immediately collapsed. The governor took revenge upon Bacon's followers, executed some and confiscated the property of others. Some historians have interpreted Bacon's Rebellion as the forerunner of the American Revolution (q.v.).

BACTERIA (Gr. *bakterion,* "little staff"), large group of microscopic, unicellular organisms that lack a distinct nucleus. With blue-green algae (*see* ALGAE), they constitute the procaryotes ("before kernels"), one of the two great divisions of life. The eucaryotes ("true kernels"), which evolved later, may be single cells or multicellular, but all have cell nuclei enclosed in membranes as well as other structures.

Bacteria are among the smallest living cells, ranging from 1 to 10 microns (a micron equals 1/25,000 in.). They are an extremely variable group, with many specialized ways of obtaining energy and nourishment. Thus, species of bacteria occupy almost all the earth's environments: air, soil, water, ice, and hot springs. Certain types are found in nearly all food products and others in various forms of symbiosis (q.v.) with most plants and animals.

Classification. Bacteria make up the phylum Schizophyta in the kingdom Monera (q.v.). In the older two-kingdom system of plants and animals, they are considered plants of the class Schizomycetes; *see* CLASSIFICATION. About 1600 species are known, but identification can be difficult since outward forms may alter radically in different environments. (Some types are transformed into dormant spores under adverse conditions; *see* SPORE.) The main bacterial groups—which some consider separate phyla—are the Myxobacteria, Spirochetes, and Eubacteria; other significant groups are the sulfur bacteria and the photosynthetic green and purple bacteria. Myxobacteria are shaped in short rods and are similar to the slime molds (*see* MYXOMYCETES): they move by gliding and may form clumps with fruiting bodies. Spirochetes are long rods coiled around a single filament, which is thought to give the organism its motility (ability to move). Many are parasitic in humans. Eubacteria, the most diverse group, are distinguished by their relatively thick cell walls and are typed by their three characteristic shapes: bacilli (rods), cocci (spheres), and spirilla (spirals or commas). Many Eubacteria are not motile, but some are propelled by whiplike filaments called flagella, which may project from the entire cell or from one or both ends, singly or in tufts.

Reproduction. The genetic material of the bacterial cell is in the form of a roughly circular strand of DNA (*see* NUCLEIC ACIDS). Many have additional ringed strands, called plasmids, which are not essential for reproduction but may transfer genetic segments from one cell to another. Reproduction may be by conjugation, in which DNA is transferred from a donor to a host; by budding, as in yeasts; or by formation of spores. But most often, cells multiply by fission (q.v.). In this process, they elongate, constrict near the

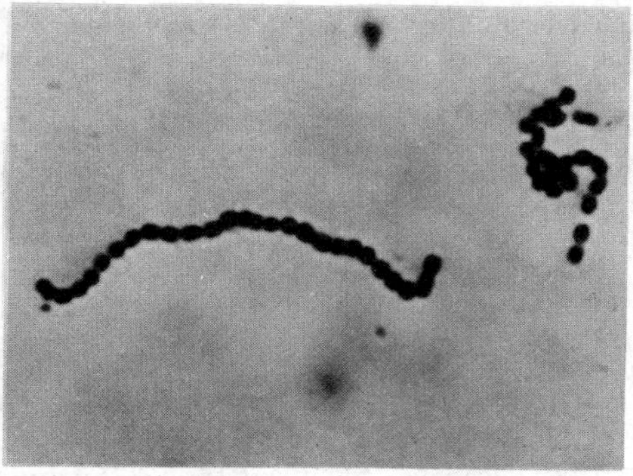

Photomicrograph of whiplike streptococci taken with an electron microscope. Chas. Pfizer & Co., Inc.

middle, and the organism then undergoes complete division, forming two daughter cells similar to the parent cell. The different species of bacteria preserve their identity as exactly as do the higher vegetable organisms, a given species of bacteria never producing any but the same species. The reproduction of bacteria by fission is, under favorable circumstances, exceedingly rapid, a bacterium reproducing itself in from 15 min. to 40 min. This rate of division would, in 24 hr., result in the production of many millions of bacteria from a single individual. Under favorable conditions, with one division every 30 min., a single cell at the end of 15 hr. will have produced roughly 1,000,000,000 progeny. Such a mass of bacteria is called a colony and may be seen without the aid of a magnifying lens.

Work of Bacteria. Two main groups of bacteria exist: the saprophytes, which live on dead animal or vegetable matter; and the parasites, which live on or in living animal or vegetable matter. This distinction is important because the bacteria that destroy dead matter are useful; they decompose dead animals and plants into their constituent elements, returning them to the mineral kingdom to furnish food for plants. Bacteria that live on animals or plants, however, can do harm by destroying life. Bacteria that require oxygen for growth are called aerobic; those that thrive without oxygen are anaerobic.

That bacteria are responsible for organic decomposition or putrefaction was long ago established. Further research has shown that they are the effective agents in various fermentative processes, for example, in tanning, tobacco curing, and ensilage. They have to do with various "diseases" of milk and wine, and their action on such foods as butter may render the foods unpalatable; on the other hand, bacteria are used deliberately to modify the flavor of milk and other dairy products. Some may produce poisonous ptomaines (q.v.) in the flesh of animals used for food, and some may increase the palatability of meat. Bacteria are usually absent from normal tissue, but they are usually present in the alimentary canal and are in many cases indispensable to normal physiological processes. They may produce light, such as the phosphorescence of dead fish; and they may produce enough heat to induce spontaneous combustion in hayricks or in hop granaries. By decomposing cellulose, certain anaerobic forms evolve marsh gas in stagnant pools; by oxidizing processes, other bacteria assist in forming deposits of bog iron ore, ocher, and manganese ore. *See* BIOLUMINESCENCE.

Bacteria have an immense influence on the nature and composition of the soil. One result of their important activities is the complete disintegration of organic remains of plants and animals and of inorganic rock particles. This action, carried on over the surface of the earth, produces in the aggregate vast quantities of plant food; in short, bacteria ensure the continued fertility of the soil. The family Leguminosae (including peas, beans, clover, and similar species), enriches the soil by increasing its nitrogen content; these plants draw nitrogen from the atmosphere with the help of *Rhizobium radicicola* and similar bacteria, which infect the roots of the plants and cause the growth of nitrogen-fixing nodules. Without the presence of bacteria the existence of human life on earth would be impossible.

Pathogenic Bacteria. Bacteria are called pathogenic if they produce disease, nonpathogenic if they do not. Among the various infectious diseases caused by known types of bacteria are cholera, lockjaw, gas gangrene, leprosy, plague, bacillary dysentery, tuberculosis, syphilis, typhoid fever, diphtheria, undulant fever, and several forms of pneumonia. Bacteria were considered the causative agents of all infectious diseases until the discovery of other disease-producing agents, such as the Rickettsiae and the viruses; *see* RICKETTSIA; VIRUS.

The pathogenic effects of bacteria upon body tissues may be grouped in three classes, as follows: (1) effects of the direct local action of the bacteria on the tissues, as the forming of lung cavities in tuberculosis; (2) mechanical effects, as when a clump of bacteria gets into a blood vessel and blocks it (infectious embolus); and (3) effects of the production in the body, under the influence of the bacteria, of certain chemical substances which act as poisons to the tissues. These poisons are in solution in the

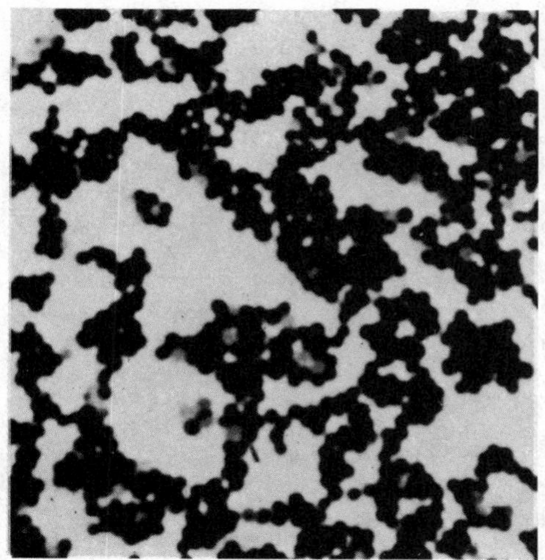

Grapelike clusters are characteristic of staphylococci, the bacteria responsible for wound infections, boils, and other diseases. Chas. Pfizer & Co., Inc.

body fluids, and each is peculiar to the species of bacteria which produces it; for example, the poison, or toxin, as it is called, of diphtheria is different from the toxin of typhoid fever.

Immunity. Since 1880, immunity against bacterial diseases has been systematically studied. The French chemist Louis Pasteur (q.v.) in that year discovered by accident that *Bacillus anthracis,* cultivated at a temperature of 42°–43° C. (108°–110° F.), lost its virulence after a few generations. Later it was found that animals inoculated with these enfeebled bacteria showed resistance to the virulent bacilli. From this beginning date the prevention, modification, and treatment of disease by serum inoculation, one of the most important medical advances in modern times. The present belief is that the body produces, as the result of the action of the bacteria, a chemical substance, or antibody, which is antagonistic to the proliferation of the bacteria. If the antibody persists in the tissues of an individual who has recovered from a disease such as measles, the individual may sustain an immunity to that particular disease. An antitoxin is an antibody that is produced when a toxin gains access to the body. Such antitoxins are produced even when the toxin is injected without the bacteria which formed it. This principle is the basis of the commercial preparation of antitoxins. For example, in the preparation of diphtheria antitoxin, a fresh culture of the diphtheria bacillus in a meat broth or extract is allowed to stand until toxins are formed in the broth. The broth is then strained through a fine filter, and a small amount is introduced into the body of a horse. Some days later a larger dose is given, and then constantly increasing quantities are injected for a period of several months. The animal is thus rendered immune to the action of the toxin, and the fluid part, or serum, of its blood contains the antitoxin successfully used in the treatment of diphtheria (q.v.) in humans. *See also* ANTITOXIN; IMMUNITY; TOXINS; VACCINATION.

Antibiotics. Various microorganisms, including certain bacteria, produce chemical substances which are toxic to specific bacteria belonging to other species. Such substances, which either kill the bacteria or prevent them from growing or reproducing, are known as antibiotics. In recent years antibiotics have played an increasingly important role in medicine in the control of bacterial diseases; *see* ANTIBIOTIC. For other types of chemotherapeutic agents, *see* CHEMOTHERAPY. *See also* ANTISEPTICS; BACTERIOLOGY; DISEASE; PROTOZOA. J.H.N.

BACTERIOLOGY, study of bacteria (q.v.), including their classification and the prevention of diseases that arise from bacterial infection. In practice, the subject matter of bacteriology is distributed not only among bacteriologists but also among chemists, biochemists, geneticists, pathologists, immunologists, and public-health physicians, as well as members of other scientific disciplines.

History. A bacterium was first observed by the Dutch naturalist Anton van Leeuwenhoek (q.v.), with the aid of a simple microscope of his own

Photomicrograph of pneumococci, one of the more common pneumonia-causing bacteria. Chas. Pfizer & Co., Inc.

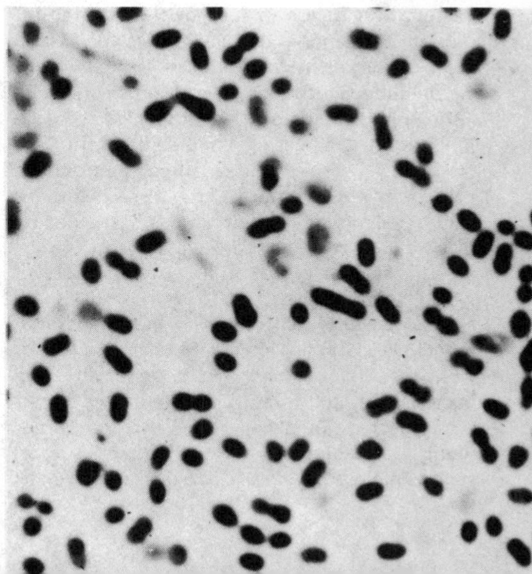

Louis Pasteur Chas. Pfizer & Co., Inc.

construction. He reported his discovery to the Royal Society of London in 1683, but the science of bacteriology was not firmly established until the middle of the 19th century. For nearly 200 years it was believed that bacteria are produced by spontaneous generation (q.v.). The efforts of several generations of chemists and biologists were required to prove that bacteria, like all living organisms, arise only from other similar organisms. This fundamental fact was finally established in 1860 by the French scientist Louis Pasteur (q.v.). Pasteur discovered that fermentation and many infectious diseases are caused by microorganisms. The systematic classification of bacteria was begun in 1872 by the German biologist Ferdinand J. Cohn (1828–98), who placed them in the plant kingdom. They are now usually included in the kingdom Monera (q.v.). In 1876 Robert Koch (q.v.), who had devised the method of inoculating bacteria into nutrient media as a means of studying them, found that a bacterium was the cause of the disease anthrax.

Other significant developments in the history of bacteriology were the discoveries of the organisms causing glanders (1862), relapsing fever (1868), typhoid fever (1880), tetanus (1885), tuberculosis (1890), plague (1894), bacillary dysentery (1898), syphilis (1905), and tularemia (1912).

Culture. A fundamental method of studying bacteria is by culturing them. The bacteriologist grows bacteria by placing them in a sterile medium and feeding them a nutritious substance, such as meat broth or blood. Agar-agar (a gelatinous substance derived from certain seaweeds) or gelatin is added to make a medium that is solid at some temperatures but may be liquefied by slight heating. After the bacteria have been added to the warm medium, the medium may be poured out in a thin layer onto a cold plate, on which it hardens, fixing the bacteria and preventing their moving. If the dilution has been sufficient to separate the growing bacteria, minute specks on the surface of the plate become visible to the naked eye. These specks are called colonies, and each such colony consists of a single species of bacteria. If a bit from one of these specks or colonies is transferred to another sterile medium, the resulting growth will be free of all organisms other than the single species of bacteria. This method produces what is known as a pure culture.

Many different species of bacteria so closely resemble one another in appearance that they cannot be differentiated under the microscope. Each species has, however, certain peculiarities of growth and development, making it possible to differentiate them by modifying the culture media. The medium is sometimes colored by litmus to show any acid or alkaline reaction the growth of the bacteria may produce. Sugar may be added to the medium, which is then placed in a V-shaped tube closed at one end, so that if the species causes fermentation, that fact may be noted by the collection of gas at the closed end of the tube.

Sterilization. The purpose of sterilization is to render an object free of all forms of bacteria potentially hazardous to life. Drying kills many species of bacteria and causes others to become inactive. Freezing destroys many bacteria and inhibits growth in others. The typhoid bacillus, however, can exist for many months frozen in a cake of ice, only to become active and dangerous again when the ice is melted. Heat or moist heat above a certain temperature kills all bacteria. Techniques for the sterilization of many different objects, such as spacecraft and surgical instruments, are important facets of bacteriological work. *See also* ANTISEPTICS.

Microscopic Examination. The microscope is one of the most important tools used in studying bacteria. Dyeing or staining bacterial specimens or cultures was introduced in 1871 by the German pathologist Karl Weigert (1843–1905) and has greatly helped the bacteriologist in identifying and observing bacteria under the microscope. A bacterial specimen is first placed on a glass slide. After the specimen has dried, it is stained to render the organism easier to observe. Stains also stimulate reactions in certain

Robert Koch Granger Collection

bacteria. For example, the tuberculosis (q.v.) bacillus can be recognized only on the basis of its reaction to certain stains; *see* GRAM'S METHOD. Bacteriologists were greatly aided in their work by the development of the electron microscope (*see* MICROSCOPE), which has far greater magnification powers than ordinary microscopes.

BACTERIOPHAGE *or* **PHAGE,** any of various viral parasites of bacteria, present in waste products of man and in soil and sewage, and possessing certain attributes of genes and living matter; *see* BACTERIA; BACTERIOLOGY; HEREDITY: *Gene Action.* Since the 1940's research with bacteriophages, or phages, has resulted in establishing nucleic acids (q.v.) as the genetic material of life, and has been central in the new field of molecular biology. In 1952 the American biologists Norton David Zinder (1928–) and Joshua Lederberg (q.v.) at the University of Wisconsin made the important discovery that genes of one bacterium can be transducted, or transplanted, to another bacterium by means of a phage. Other researchers discovered further that a phage could accommodate itself to its bacterial host and be transmitted from generation to generation. In the 1960's, pioneering research with so-called phage host-parasite systems was conducted by American physiologists Max Delbrück, Alfred Day Hershey, and Salvador Edward Luria (qq.v.), for which they became joint recipients in 1969 of the Nobel Prize in medicine and physiology (qq.v.). Although it is in its infancy, the study of phages has important implications in medicine and heredity (q.v.), specifically in the understanding of virus infection, genetic defects, human development and maldevelopment, the causes of cancer (q.v.), resistance of bacteria to antibiotics (*see* ANTIBIOTIC), and the unexplored field of viruses beneficial to man (*see* SYMBIOSIS). Research with phages is central to the plot of the novel *Arrowsmith* by the American novelist Sinclair Lewis (q.v.), a work published in 1924, when research with phages was rare. *See also* INFECTION; PARASITE; VIRUS.

BACTRIA, ancient Greek country of S.W. Asia, situated N. of the Paropamisus (now Hindu Kush) Mts. along the upper Oxus (now Amu Dar' ya) R. A branch of the same range separated it from the territories of the Sacae, a mixed Scythian, Tatar, and Chinese people, and it was bounded by Sogdiana on the N. and Ariana on the S. What was formerly Bactria is now included in Afghanistan and the Soviet Union. Its capital, Bactria (modern Balkh, Afghanistan), was the cradle of the Zoroastrian religion (*see* ZOROASTRIANISM). Subjugated in 545 B.C. by the Persian emperor Cyrus the Great (q.v.), Bactria became part of Persia and as such was conquered in 328 B.C. by the Macedonian ruler Alexander III (q.v.), known as the Great. At his death it formed a part of the kingdom of the Seleucidae (q.v.) until the foundation, about 250 B.C., by the Seleucid leader Diodotus I (d. 239? B.C.), of the Greek kingdom of Bactria, which extended to the Indus R. The kingdom was overrun during the 2d century B.C. by the Sacae. In early medieval times the Bactrian region became known as Balkh.

BADAJOZ, city in Spain, and capital of Badajoz province, on the Guadiana R., about 5 mi. from the border with Portugal, and 220 miles S.W. of Madrid. The see of a bishop, it has a 13th-century cathedral, in which are hung paintings by Luis de Morales (1510?–86), who was born there. Badajoz was an important Moorish town in the 11th century. After becoming a part of the kingdom of Castile in the 13th century, Badajoz withstood numerous attacks by the Portuguese. In 1811, during the Peninsular War, it was captured by the French, who held it until the following year, when it was taken by the British. In the Spanish Civil War, the Nationalists under General Francisco Franco

Sir Robert Stephenson Smyth Baden-Powell
Boy Scouts of America

(q.v.) captured Badajoz in 1936, and executed hundreds of the inhabitants. Trade is largely with Portugal. Foodstuffs, alcoholic beverages, and blankets are the chief products of Badajoz. Pop. (1970) 101,710.

BADALONA, city and seaport of Spain, in Barcelona Province, on the Mediterranean Sea, about 5 miles N.E. of the city of Barcelona. Industries include the manufacture of chemicals and glass, boatbuilding, wine making, and fishing. Pop. (1970) 162,888.

BAD EMS *or* **EMS,** town of West Germany, in Rhineland-Palatinate State, on the Lahn R., 11 mi. E. of Koblenz. The town is a resort noted for mineral waters, and has a casino and a large park. It has been the site of two important events. The Punctation of Ems, which protested the interference of the papacy in the affairs of the German Catholic Church, was formulated in Ems by an ecclesiastical delegation in 1786. The Ems Dispatch, or Ems Telegram, a communication artfully edited by Prince Otto Edward Leopold von Bismarck (q.v.) as head of the Prussian cabinet, precipitated the Franco-German War (q.v.). Pop. (1970 est.) 10,000.

BADEN-BADEN, city of West Germany, in Baden-Würrtemberg State, at the edge of the Black Forest, about 45 miles W. of Stuttgart. The city is noted chiefly for hot mineral springs that range in temperature from 115° to 153° F. The springs were known in the time of the Roman Empire, and remains of Roman baths have been discovered in the city. The city was ruled by the margraves of Baden-Baden from the 14th to the 18th century. Since the 19th century the city has been a popular health resort. Pop. (1970) 37,200.

BADEN-POWELL, Robert Stephenson Smyth, 1st Baron Baden-Powell of Gilwell (1857–1941), British soldier and founder of the Boy Scouts (q.v.), born in London, England, and educated at Charterhouse. He joined the 13th Hussars in India in 1876. From 1888 to 1895 he was stationed, successively, in India, Afghanistan, Zululand, and Ashanti. During the South African War (q.v.) he served as chief staff officer during the British campaign in Matabeleland (1896–97), colonel of Irregular Horse, South Africa, and lieutenant colonel of the 5th Dragoon Guards (1897–99). In recognition of his courageous defense (1899–1900) of Mafeking, he was promoted to the rank of major general. He organized the South African Constabulary toward the end of the war and became inspector general of cavalry in 1903. In 1908 he became a lieutenant general. Knighted in 1909, he retired from military service the following year. He founded the Boy Scouts in 1908, and two years later he helped to found the Girl Guides, a similar organization for girls. During World War I he served in the British Intelligence Department. He wrote many books on the Boy Scout movement, including *What Scouts Can Do* (1921), *Rovering to Success* (1922), *Pigsticking* (1924), and *Scouting and Youth Movement* (1929).

BADEN-WÜRTTEMBERG, State of West Germany bounded on the N. by the States of Hesse and Bavaria, on the E. by Bavaria, on the S. by Switzerland, and on the W. by the State of Rhineland-Palatinate and by France. Stuttgart (q.v.) is the capital and largest city. Other important cities are Mannheim, Karlsruhe, Freiburg, Heidelberg, and Ulm (qq.v.). Within Baden-Württemberg are several mountain regions, including the Black Forest (q.v.), the Swabian Forest, the Swabian Alb, and Odenwald. Cutting through these uplands are the Rhine, Neckar, and Danube rivers (qq.v.), and their tributaries. The Lake of Constance, the largest inland body of water in W. Europe, lies on the S. border of the State. Area, 13,804 sq.mi.; pop. (1971 est.) 9,055,100.

Baden-Württemberg is highly industrialized, producing textiles, automobiles, machinery, chemicals, leather goods, pottery, glass, furniture, clocks, and optical equipment. Crops, including wheat, barley, grapes, potatoes, and tobacco, are grown in the river valleys and foothill regions. Dairying and forestry are carried on in

The lovely houses of Tübingen, in the State of Baden-Württemberg, are reflected in the waters of the Neckar River.
German Information Center

the Black Forest and other highland regions. With its picturesque natural scenery, historic towns and castles, and famous health resorts, the State is second to Bavaria in tourism.

The State government, headed by a minister-president, is responsible to a popularly elected assembly. The State is divided into four administrative districts.

History. (For the early history of the Württemberg region of the State, *see* WÜRTTEMBERG.) The earliest known inhabitants of Baden were the Alamanni (q.v.), who fell under the dominion of the Frankish empire in the 5th century; *see* FRANKS. In the 11th century Berthold (d. 1078), a duke of the Austrian duchy of Carinthia, built the castle of Zahrringen in Breisgau, in Baden; a descendant of his second son took the title of margrave of Baden and founded a dynasty that ruled the region for more than eight centuries. One of the outstanding members of this dynasty was Charles Frederick (1728–1811), who became margrave in 1746. By favoring the French emperor Napoleon I (q.v.) and joining the Confederation of the Rhine (q.v.), Charles Frederick quadrupled his possessions in area and population and acquired in 1803 the dignity of elector and in 1806 the title of grand duke. In 1811 he was succeeded by his grandson Charles (1786–1818), who, after the battle of Leipzig, seceded from the Confederation of the Rhine and in 1815 joined the Germanic Confederation, a loose union of thirty-nine sovereign states, including Prussia, under Austrian presidency.

During the 1848–49 revolution in Germany, the reigning grand duke was deposed and then reinstated with the aid of Prussia. In 1867 Baden entered the North German Confedation (q.v.), and in 1871 it became a part of the German Empire. Under the empire, the grand dukes of Baden continued to reign with the help of an elected diet.

At the end of World War I the ruling dynasties of the German states were dethroned, and the grand duke Frederick II (1857–1928) abdicated on Nov. 22, 1918. On Jan. 15, 1919, a popularly elected national assembly met to draw up a new constitution. This constitution, issued the following May, abolished all privileges based on noble birth and religion; bestowed full legal rights on women; recognized the right of workers, including civil servants, to organize; and granted the vote to all men and women over twenty years of age. It vested executive power in a cabinet comprising the State president and his aides, all elected by the legislature. Legislative power was vested in a unicameral assembly. Baden became an administrative unit of the Third Reich in 1935. The area was invaded by the Allied forces in 1945, during the final stages of World War II.

Following the unconditional surrender of the Third Reich, about a third of the territory of Baden became part of the United States military occupation zone in Germany; the remainder became part of the French zone. The American-occupied sections of Baden and Württemberg, having been merged for administrative purposes, were organized as the autonomous State of Württemberg-Baden in 1946. French-occupied Baden became an autonomous State in the next year. In 1949 both States became components of the Federal Republic of Germany. In 1952 the States of Baden, Württemberg-Baden, and Württemberg-Hohenzollern merged to form the new State of Baden-Württemberg.

BADGER, common name for animals of the genera *Meles* and *Taxidea* in the family Mustelidae, the Weasel family of carnivorous mammals. The term is sometimes extended to related genera, thus including all animals of the subfamily Melinae, which is closely related to the Skunk subfamily. The group is characterized by short, strong legs, elongated and more or less plantigrade feet, and straight, strong, fossorial toes. All are heavily furred, distinctly marked, and possessed of strength, acuteness, and courage. They live in dens and are abroad mostly at night. They have perineal glands, which contain substances emitting a fetid odor. The pelts have

American badger, Taxidea taxus
North Dakota College of Agriculture

The Badlands of North Dakota U.S. Bureau of Reclamation

considerable value as furs, and the hairs are used in the manufacture of shaving and other types of brushes.

The American badger, *Taxidea taxus,* is native to the western regions of North America, as far east as Ohio, and north to southern Canada. About 2 ft. long, the animal has a squat, broad body and a short, thick tail. The powerful forelegs are armed with long claws, which serve as highly efficient digging tools. The shaggy fur is gray tipped with brown, and the head is white with characteristic dark-brown markings. The American badger is of great service to farmers because it feeds principally on gophers and other pests in agricultural areas. The badger lives in deep burrows that it digs in hillsides. Because pioneer Wisconsin lead miners burrowed into the hills for shelter during the winter months, Wisconsin is known popularly as the Badger State.

The European badger, *Meles meles,* is superficially similar to the American one in size and color, but different in dentition and other details. It lives in wooded places and digs a deep chamber, where it spends the winter and where in spring it bears four or five furless and blind young. It is omnivorous in a wild state as well as in confinement; fruits, roots, beechnuts, eggs, young birds, small quadrupeds, frogs, snails, worms, and insects constitute its natural food. It also feeds on honey and on the larvae of wasps and wild bees; the shaggy hair of the badger is protection against stings.

Other animals of the same subfamily include the teledu of Java, and the balisaur, or sand badger, of northeastern India. The so-called honey badger, or ratel (q.v.), of Africa belongs to another subfamily. In Australia, the wombat and the bandicoot (qq.v.) are sometimes called badgers.

The sport of badger baiting, once practiced in Great Britain, consisted of setting several dogs upon a badger trapped in an artificial hole, usually a barrel. After a long struggle, the badger was finally dragged out of the hole and was subjected to further baiting. The term "to badger", meaning in present-day usage to tease or worry persistently, arose from the practice of badger baiting.

BAD GODESBERG, southern suburb of Bonn, West Germany, in North Rhine–Westphalia State, on the Rhine R. Developed as a resort during the 19th century, Bad Godesberg has mineral baths, a casino established in a 12th-century castle, and ruins of a 13th-century bishop's castle. It is the site of many foreign embassies and has been host to several international conferences.

BADIA Y LEBLICH, Domingo (1766–1818), Spanish traveler, born in Barcelona. In 1803 he visited North Africa, disguised as a Muslim and calling himself Ali Bey. He traveled in Morocco, Egypt, and Arabia, and was the first European to visit the sacred city of Mecca after the establishment of the Islamic religion in the 7th century. He recorded his travels in a book, *Ali Bey en Asie et en Afrique* ("Ali Bey in Asia and in Africa", 1814).

BADLANDS, rugged, inhospitable regions of fantastically shaped rock masses and hills almost bare of vegetation, separated by labyrinthine valleys. Such formations are caused by erosion in regions of soft, unconsolidated rock where short periods of heavy rain alternate with long periods of drought. The little vegetation that grows during the dry period is insufficient to check erosion and is washed away with the soil by the rains. The principal Badlands in the United States are in the western parts of the Dakotas and in northwestern Nebraska.

BADLANDS NATIONAL MONUMENT, area of geologic interest in the Badlands (q.v.) of S.W. South Dakota, on the border of Pennington and Jackson counties, about 42 miles S.E. of Rapid City. It is in an arid region of layered sedimentary rock eroded into cliffs, ridges, hills, and canyons, containing numerous prehistoric animal fossils, some about 40,000,000 years old. The easily fragmented sedimentary rock formations are affected by the elements, and the appearance of the monument constantly changes. Less than half of the monument area can support vegetation. Trees and prairie grasses are found in the fertile pockets and passes. The monument, covering nearly 111,530 acres, was established in 1939, and is administered by the National Park Service.

BADMINTON, game that somewhat resembles tennis (q.v.). It is played by two or four players, either in or out of doors, on a marked-out space 44 ft. long by 20 ft. wide for the four-player and 17 ft. wide for the two-player game. Across the middle of the court a net is fixed, with the top edge 5 ft. from the ground at the center and 5½ ft. at the posts. Badminton is played with a shuttlecock, a cork ball fitted with stabilizing feathers. The players hit the shuttlecock back and forth over the net with lightweight rackets. When the receiving side fails to return it, the serving side scores a point. When the serving side fails to return the shuttlecock, it loses the service but no point is scored. Fifteen points win the game providing the score of the winner exceeds that of the loser by two points. The racket is strung with fine gut and weighs usually about 6 oz.

BADOGLIO, Pietro (1871–1956), Italian soldier, born in Grazzano Monferrato (now Grazzano Badoglio) and educated at the military academy in Turin. He participated in the Italian campaign in Tripoli during the Italo-Turkish War (1911–12) and served in World War I. He was commander in chief of the Italian army during the invasion of Ethiopia (1935–36), and during World War II was chief of the general staff of the Italian army during the disastrous campaign in Greece (1939–40). Following the resignation of the dictator Benito Mussolini (q.v.) as head of the Italian government, in July, 1943, Badoglio was appointed premier by Victor Emmanuel III (*see under* VICTOR EMMANUEL). In this capacity Badoglio signed the agreement, announced on Sept. 8, 1943, by which Italy surrendered unconditionally to the Allies. Subsequently his government declared war on Germany. He resigned the premiership in June, 1944.

BADRINATH, peak of the main Himalayan range, in Uttar Pradesh State (formerly United Provinces), Republic of India, about 23,190 ft. above sea level. On the slopes is a great temple containing a shrine dedicated to the Hindu deity Vishnu (q.v.).

BAEDA, Saint. *See* BEDE, SAINT.

BAEDEKER, Karl (1801–59), German book publisher, born in Essen and educated at the University of Heidelberg. In 1827 he established a printing business in Koblenz. Two years later he reprinted a guidebook to the Rhine R., and in 1839 he issued his own *Rhine Handbook,* inaugurating a series of travel handbooks that are still world-famous. Among the series, which was published in German, French, and English, were guidebooks to most of the countries of Europe, the United States, Egypt, and several European cities. The guidebooks, published in Leipzig, Germany, after 1872, were distinguished by excellent maps and accurate information. The Baedeker establishment in Leipzig was destroyed during World War II, but in 1949 the business was reestablished by the Baedeker family in West Germany.

BAEKELAND, Leo Hendrik (1863–1944), Belgian-American chemist, born in Ghent and educated at the University of Ghent. Baekeland emigrated in 1889 to the United States, where he spent the rest of his life. He became a manufacturer of photographic papers and developed a new type of paper called Velox that could be developed under artificial light. He is best known, however, for his invention, about 1906, of the synthetic resin Bakelite (q.v.). Baekeland received many honors, including the Nichols medal of the American Chemical Society in 1909 and the Franklin medal of the Franklin Institute in 1940.

BAER, Karl Ernst von (1792–1876), Russian naturalist and embryologist, born in the province of Estonia (now the Estonian Soviet Socialist Republic). From 1810 to 1814 he studied medicine at Tartu University; he subsequently studied comparative anatomy under the noted German physician Ignaz Döllinger (1770–1841) at the University of Würzburg (now in West Germany). In 1817 von Baer became prosector at the University of Königsberg (now Kaliningrad) in Russia. He was appointed professor of zoology there in 1819 and director of the Anatomical

Institute in 1826. In 1829 he became a member of the Academy of Sciences and professor of zoology at the University of Saint Petersburg (now Leningrad), but he returned the following year to Königsberg. After 1834 he was librarian of the Academy of St. Petersburg. He was one of the founders of the modern science of embryology and was among the most influential scientists of his day. Of his numerous works, the most important are *Epistola de Ovi Mammalium et Hominis Genesi* ("Papers on the Mammalian Egg and The Birth of Man", 1827), in which the mammalian egg is described for the first time; *Über Entwicklungsgeschichte der Thiere* ("On the Development of Animals", 1828-37); and *Untersuchungen über die Entwicklung der Fische* ("Research into the Development of Fishes", 1835).

BAEYER, (Johann Friedrich Wilhelm) Adolf von (1835-1917), German chemist, born in Berlin. He studied chemistry under the German chemists Robert Wilhelm Bunsen (q.v.) and Friedrich August Kekule von Stradonitz (*see* KEKULE VON STRADONITZ) and subsequently did graduate work at the University of Berlin. Von Baeyer was professor of chemistry at the University of Munich after 1875; and he is most renowned for the synthesis of indigo, about 1880, for which he received many honors, including the Davy medal of the Royal Society of London in 1881 and the Nobel Prize in chemistry in 1905. Among his other achievements was the synthesis of uric acid with the German chemist Emil Fischer (1852-1919). His theoretical research covered almost the entire field of organic chemistry.

BAFFIN, William (1584-1622), English navigator whose name was given to Baffin Island and Baffin Bay (qq.v.), born in London. In 1612 he served as chief pilot of the sailing ship *Patience* on a voyage to Greenland, seeking a northwestern passage to the Pacific Ocean. Three years later he was chief pilot of the *Discovery* on a similar expedition. He explored Hudson Strait during that voyage, making navigational observations that later proved to have been remarkably accurate. Piloting the *Discovery* on another expedition in 1616, he partially explored the bay subsequently named in his honor. He sailed as far north as lat. 77°45′ N. on that occasion, a record unsurpassed for 236 years. From 1617 to 1620 he was employed by the East India Company (q.v.), of England, for which he made surveys on the Persian Gulf and the Red Sea.

BAFFIN BAY, arm of the North Atlantic Ocean, between Greenland and several large islands of N.E. Canada. It is about 1130 km (702 mi.) long and up to about 650 km (404 mi.) wide. The bay is connected with the Atlantic Ocean by Davis Strait, to the S.E., and with the Arctic Ocean by several channels to the W. and N. Ice floes and icebergs prevent navigation on the bay for about nine months each year. Baffin Bay was visited by John Davis (q.v.), in 1585, and by William Baffin (q.v.), for whom it is named, in 1616.

BAFFIN ISLAND, island of Franklin District of the Northwest Territories, N.E. Canada. It is bordered by Baffin Bay and Davis Strait on the E., by Hudson Strait on the S., and by Foxe Basin and the Gulf of Boothia on the W. The largest island of Canada and the fifth largest in the world, Baffin Island is about 1600 km (994 mi.) long and has an area of 507,454 sq.km (195,928 sq.mi.). Geologically a continuation of Labrador, the island has an arctic climate and is treeless; there are many freshwater lakes. The E. coast is deeply indented, with many fjords. The central interior is dominated by ice-capped mountains rising to 2057.4 m (6750 ft.). The island is sparsely populated, mainly by Eskimo (Inuit). Baffin Island was visited by Sir Martin Frobisher (q.v.) during 1576-78 and by William Baffin (q.v.), for whom it is named, in 1616.

BAGATELLE, game, with many variations, somewhat similar to billiards. A bagatelle board is usually oblong and may be several feet in length. The game is played with small ivory balls and a cue or mace. The object of the game is to put the balls into holes or through wickets at one end of the board.

BAGDAD. *See* BAGHDAD.

BAGEHOT, Walter (1826-77), British economist and journalist, born in Langport, Somersetshire, England, and educated at the University of London. In 1858 he married a daughter of the British economist, the Right Honorable James Wilson (1805-60), founder of the *Economist,* and from 1860 till his death Bagehot was editor of that newspaper. Bagehot was active in high political and financial circles, and his writings, which deal with politics and business in a scientific manner, were based on his own observations. He wrote *The English Constitution* (1867), which was translated into several languages; *Physics and Politics* (1869); *Lombard Street* (1873), a study of the money market; and many essays on history, economics, and literature.

BAGGESEN, Jens Immanuel (1764-1826), Danish poet, born in Korsør, and educated at the University of Copenhagen. He won immediate recognition as a poet with the publication of *Komiske Fortællinger* ("Comic Tales", 1785), stories in verse form. A staunch classicist, he be-

View of Baghdad on the storied Tigris River. An Iraqi paddles his gufa, the round boat of wickerwork that has been used in Mesopotamia for countless centuries.
Ewing Galloway

came known as an uncompromising foe of the innovations of the Romantic writers (*see* ROMANTICISM). Baggesen left Denmark in 1789 and spent many years in Germany, France, and Switzerland. His most famous work, *The Labyrinth,* a long poem describing his travels, was published in 1791. In 1806 he returned to Denmark, where he later became involved in a prolonged literary feud with the Danish Romantic poet and dramatist Adam Gottlob Oehlenschläger (q.v.). Baggesen again became an expatriate in 1820.

Baggesen wrote many of his poems in German; of these, the most important is *Parthenaïs* (1804), a long epic. He also left a vast and entertaining correspondence. Baggesen introduced a high standard of elegance of form and diction in Danish literature, profoundly influencing subsequent literary development.

BAGHDAD *or* **BAGDAD,** capital of Iraq, situated on both E. and W. banks of the Tigris R., about 400 mi. upstream from the Persian Gulf. Baghdad is the center of air, road, and railroad transportation in Iraq. It is the leading manufacturing city of the country, with oil refineries, food processing plants, tanneries, and textile mills. Among the handcrafted wares produced in Baghdad are cloth, household utensils, jewelry, leather goods, felt, and rugs, which may be purchased in the bazaars, consisting of rows of small shops or stalls. These bazaars have long been a feature of the city. Among the noteworthy historical structures of Baghdad is the ruins of Bab al-Wastani, the last remaining of the famous gates of Baghdad; the gate has been converted into an arms museum. Other notable buildings are the ruins of Al-Mutansiriyah, a college founded in 1232, which has been restored as a museum; the Abbassid Palace, which probably dates back to 1179; and Marjan Mosque, completed in 1356. A few miles north of Baghdad is al Kadhimain, a city notable for its magnificent gold-domed mosque and the tombs of religious leaders venerated by the Shi'ite Muslims. (*see* SHI'ITES).

Baghdad was built by the Abbassid caliph al-Mansur (712?–75) in 762 on the W. bank of the Tigris R., opposite an old Iranian village also named Baghdad. The original city was round, with three concentric walls: the innermost wall enclosed the palace of the caliph; the second wall defined the army quarters; and the homes of the people occupied the outermost enclosure. The merchants' quarters, or bazaars, were located outside the city walls. Within the next half century the city reached a peak of prosperity and influence under the caliph Harun al-Rashid (q.v.), whose reign is celebrated in the famous tales, *Arabian Nights* (q.v.). During this period the city expanded to the E. bank of the Tigris, which later became the heart of Baghdad. Although past its zenith after Harun's time, Baghdad remained an important center of trade and culture for more than four centuries.

The decline of Baghdad began when Hulagu (1217–65), the grandson of the Mongol conqueror Genghis Khan (q.v.), sacked the city in 1258, putting an end to the Abbassid caliphate. Another Mongol, Tamerlane (q.v.), sacked the city in 1401. Baghdad was brought under Persian control in 1508. In 1534 it was captured by the Ottoman Turks. The Persians recaptured the city in 1623, holding it until 1638, when it was again annexed by Turkey. For almost three centuries thereafter Baghdad was ruled by Turkish governors. In 1917 it was captured from the Turks by British forces. In 1921 Baghdad was designated as the capital of the newly created kingdom of Iraq, which became a republic in 1958. Pop. (1970 est.) 1,028,083. *See also* CALIPH; IRAQ: *History;* MESOPOTAMIA.

BAGHDAD PACT. *See* CENTRAL TREATY ORGANIZATION.

BAGPIPE, musical instrument of wind family, with two or more reed pipes attached to and sounded by a wind chest or bag that is inflated, either by mouth or through a bellows, by the performer. Similar instruments seem to have been generally known, at least throughout Europe and Asia, from a very early period. In the 15th and 16th centuries bagpipes were common in Germany and England. The earliest Scottish bagpipe was probably made in 1409. Except that it lacked the large drone, introduced early in the 18th century, it was similar to the Highland bagpipe of the present day. The Scottish Highland bagpipe is the only form of the instrument still used in Britain. When it is played, the sound issues from three wooden pipes containing reeds of fixed tone, called drones, which furnish a continuous bass, and another reeded pipe of conical bore with holes in it, called the chanter, which produces the melody. The range is only nine notes, from G in the treble clef to A above the clef. In playing, the drones are thrown over the left shoulder, the bag tucked under the left arm, the blowpipe taken in the lips, and the chanter held with the fingers. The piper usually walks up and down while playing. The extensive musical literature written for the instrument includes reels, marches, the Scottish dance known as the strathspey, and the warlike music called pibroch. Each burgh in Scotland formerly had one or more pipers, and pipers formed a regular part of the retinue of Highland chieftains. The clan piper still plays an important part in Highland functions, and pipers are attached to all Highland regiments of the British army.

A Scottish piper of the Highlands strolls while playing.
Trans World Airlines

The chanter of the Irish bagpipe has a nearly full chromatic scale with a range from D below to D above the stave. The drones, which are all fixed on one stock, also possess keys, which are played with the wrist of the right hand. The Italian bagpipe is a crude instrument, a goatskin bag with a huge drone, on which the player performs by means of a mouth tube while another player carries the melody on a separate chanter. The Catalan bagpipe is similar to the Italian bagpipe.

BAGUIO, city of the Republic of the Philippines, in Benguet Province, on N. Luzon Island, 125 miles N.W. of Manila. The chief mountain resort and summer capital of the Philippines, with hot springs nearby, Baguio is called the "City of the Pines". It is the center of the chief gold-mining region of the country. Many handicrafts are produced in Baguio, and the City Hall Museum displays native products. The city is the site of the Philippine Military Academy. Baguio was designed in 1905 by the American architect Daniel Hudson Burnham (q.v.). Baguio was incorporated as a city in 1909. Pop. (1970) 84,538.

BAGWORM, *or* BASKET WORM, the caterpillar of any of several moths of the Psyche family (Psychidae), especially *Thyridopteryx ephemeraeformis,* common in the northern United States. The worm spins a protective silken bag into which it weaves pieces of leaves and twigs, and which it carries about attached to its abdomen. As the worm grows, it enlarges the bag and, when ready to pupate, fastens the bag to a tree branch and lives inside it. In about three weeks the adult male, with dark body and wings that are dark at first but later become transparent, emerges and sets out on the mating flight. The wingless female continues to live inside her bag, which later becomes a receptacle for her eggs. Another species of bagworm, *Oiketicus abboti,* is more frequently found in the southern U.S., where it is parasitic on orange trees.

BAHAI (Pers. *Bahā'ī,* "of glory"), religious faith founded late in the 19th century as the fulfillment of the prophecy of the Bab (*see* BABISM). The founder of Bahai was Mirza Husayn Ali (1817–92), born in Persia and later know as Bahaullah (Ar., "the Glory of God"). He became a follower of the Bab, and, in 1850 upon the martyrdom of the Bab, became the leader of one of the Babi factions. The Persian government, which had been persistently persecuting the Babis, in 1852 carried out a general massacre in which an estimated 20,000 died. Bahaullah, his family, and some of his followers were spared, but Bahaullah was first imprisoned and tortured and then exiled to Baghdad, then under Turkish control. A political prisoner for the rest of his life, Bahaullah was sent by the Turkish government, together with his family and followers, on successive rigorous marches from Baghdad to Constantinople (now İstanbul) to Adrianople (now Edirne) and finally to a penal colony in Acre, Palestine (now Israel), where he remained until his death.

Upon establishing the Babi faith in 1844, the Bab had foretold that in just nineteen years would appear a divine figure, "him whom God should manifest". In 1863, in Baghdad, Bahaullah proclaimed himself to be that divine manifestation. Bahaullah's followers, called Bahais, believe that he was the latest in a series of divine manifestations that includes Zoroaster, the Buddha, Jesus Christ, and Muhammad (qq.v.) and that he brought a new revelation to the world.

Bahaullah had sought above all to establish a universal religion; his teachings urging moral and social improvement were spread mainly by his eldest son Abbas (1844–1921), later called Abdul Baha (Ar., "the servant of the Glory"). Like his father, Abdul Baha was a political prisoner for years. But in 1908, when parts of the Ottoman empire were overthrown, he was freed, and he subsequently traveled to Europe and North America to introduce his father's teachings. Abdul Baha summarized the Bahai faith in a set of principles that included among its concrete social aims the abolition of racial and religious prejudice and the achievement of equality of the sexes, an international auxiliary language, universal education, a universal faith founded on the assumption of the essential identity of the great religions, and a universal representative government. The writings of the Bab and of Bahaullah and Abdul Baha constitute the sacred literature of Bahai, which has no other form of institutional authority; neither a priesthood nor a body of ritual is recognized. In his will, Abdul Baha named his eldest grandson, Shoghi Effendi (1896–1957), as guardian of the faith.

Although Bahai developed in Persia, by 1920 it had its greatest following in the United States. Under the direction (1921–57) of Shoghi Effendi, the U.S. Bahais developed an administrative system with headquarters in Wilmette, Ill.

Wherever nine or more Bahais reside, a "spiritual assembly" may be formed; more than 800 assemblies have been organized in the U.S. Delegates are sent from the local assemblies to an annual convention at the national headquarters, at which a National Spiritual Assembly is elected; by 1975, 114 national assemblies had been organized. Through their local and national assemblies the Bahais carry on extensive missionary, educational, and philanthropic work.

Bahai has adherents in more than 300 countries and dependencies, and Bahai literature has been translated into well over 350 languages. Bahai world headquarters is in Israel, on the slopes of Mt. Carmel overlooking Haifa and Acre; there, a shrine of the Bab, an archives building, and an administrative center have been constructed.

BAHAMA ISLANDS *or* **BAHAMAS,** officially COMMONWEALTH OF THE BAHAMAS, independent state in the West Indies, consisting of an archipelago of about 700 islands and islets and nearly 2400 cays and rocks, extending from a point about 70 miles S.E. of Palm Beach, Fla., to a point about 130 miles N.E. of Cap-Haïtien, Haiti. The Biminis, the westernmost of the group, are about 60 miles E. of Miami. Fewer than 30 of the islands are inhabited. New Providence (pop. 1970, 101,503), economically the most important of the group, lies about 190 miles S.E. of Miami. The other chief islands, often referred to as the out islands, include Acklins, Andros, Cat, Crooked, Eleuthera, Grand Bahama, Great Abaco, Great Inagua, Harbour, Long, Mayaguana, and San Salvador, or Watling. The capital of the islands is Nassau (q.v.), on New Providence.

Mild in climate, the Bahama Islands are one of the most popular year-round resorts in the

Nassau, capital of the Bahamas, is one of the most popular and beautiful resort areas of the islands. UPI

Western Hemisphere, visited annually by some 1,500,000 tourists. Besides tourism, which represents about 70 percent of the gross national product, other sources of income include salt production, farming, fishing, forestry, and livestock raising. The chief exports are cement, pulpwood, rum, salt, shellfish, and vegetables. Trade is primarily with Canada, Great Britain, and the United States.

Present-day San Salvador was the first part of the New World reached by the Genoese-born navigator Christopher Columbus (q.v.). The Spanish, however, did not colonize the islands. The first permanent European inhabitants were the British, who settled Eleuthera and New Providence about 1648. During its early years the settlement was repeatedly attacked by the Spanish. The islands were later the stronghold of various buccaneers, notably the Englishman Edward Teach (q.v.), or Thatch, popularly known as Blackbeard. The Bahamas were ruled by the proprietary governors of the British colony of Carolina from 1670 to 1717, when the British crown assumed direct control of civilian and military affairs. In 1776, during the American Revolution, Nassau was held for a short time by American naval forces. Spain held the islands in 1782–83. The Bahama Islands became a British colony in 1787. In 1964 Great Britain granted the Bahamas internal autonomy. Friction thereafter developed between the white-dominated United Bahamian Party (U.P.B.) and the black Progressive Liberal Party (P.L.P.). In an all-island election in 1967 the P.L.P. won control of the government, and Lynden O. Pindling became prime minister. On July 10, 1973, Great Britain formally withdrew and the Commonwealth of the Bahamas came into being. Area, 4404 sq.mi.; pop. (1970 census) 168,812.

BAHAULLAH. *See* BAHAI.

BAHAWALPUR, *or* BHAWALPUR, city of Pakistan, in the Punjab Province, near the Sutlej R., about 215 miles S.W. of Lahore. The city is located favorably for commerce, lying at the junction of trade routes from the E., S.E., and S. It is a center for trade in the wheat, cotton, millet, and rice grown in the surrounding region. Dates and mangoes are also grown there. A system of canals furnishes water for irrigation of the crops. The principal industries are cotton ginning, rice and flour milling, handweaving of textiles, and crafting of pottery. Pop. (1972 est.) 134,000.

BAHÍA BLANCA, city and seaport of Argentina, in Buenos Aires Province, at the head of the Bahía Blanca (White Bay), on the Atlantic Ocean, about 350 miles S.W. of the city of Buenos Aires. The leading city of S. Argentina, it is an important transshipping and commercial center, handling the large export trade in grain and wool from S. Buenos Aires Province, oil from Neuquén, and fruit from the Río Negro Valley. The National University of the South is in Bahía Blanca. The city was founded as a fort in 1828 and became commercially important after the construction of a railroad in 1885. Pop. (greater city, 1970) 175,000.

BAHRAIN *or* **BAHREIN,** independent sheikhdom, an archipelago in the Persian Gulf near the coasts of Saudi Arabia and Qatar. The 231-sq.mi. archipelago includes the main island of Bahrain, Muharraq, Umm An-Nasaan, Jidda, Sitra, the Hawar group just off the coast of Qatar, and several islets. For the location of Bahrain, see the map accompanying the article ARABIA.

The population of Bahrain (census 1971) was

216,078. The United Nations estimated the overall population density of Bahrain at about 936 persons per sq.mi. in 1970. Most of the people of Bahrain are Muslims. The principal cities are the capital, Manama (pop. 1971, 89,399), and Muharraq (pop. 49,450). A modern harbor, Mina Sulman, a free transit and industrial area, has supplemented the traditional position of Bahrain as the transshipment port of the southern part of the Gulf. The annual rainfall averages less than 4 in. Dates and vegetables are the most important crops.

The economy is based on the oil industry and transit trade. Oil, discovered in 1932, accounted for 63 percent of the 1967 revenue of $23,598,240. About one half of expenditures is devoted to development projects, with particular emphasis placed on improving the public water-supply system, roads, electric power, and airport and harbor facilities. According to the latest available statistics, annual production of oil in the early 1970's reached more than 3,840,000 tons.

Since 1783 Bahrain has been ruled by the Al Khalifa family. Under treaties signed in 1890 and 1892, the foreign affairs of the sheikhdom were entrusted to Great Britain. In 1968 the British government announced its intention of withdrawing all military forces from the Persian Gulf area by the end of 1971. Bahrain became an independent sovereign nation in August, 1971. Simultaneously, the island group stated that it would not seek membership in a proposed federation intended to unite nine states in the area. Bahrain is a member of the United Nations.

BAHR EL GHAZAL. *See* NILE.

BAIKAL. *See* BAYKAL.

BAIL. *See* CRIMINAL PROCEDURE.

BAILE ALTHA CLIATH. *See* DUBLIN, capital of the Republic of Ireland.

BAILEY, Liberty Hyde (1858–1954), American horticulturist and botanist, born in South Haven, Mich., and educated at Michigan State College. From 1882 to 1883 Bailey was assistant to the American botanist Asa Gray (q.v.) at Harvard University and from 1882 until 1888 was professor of horticulture and landscape gardening at Michigan State College. Bailey became professor of general and experimental horticulture at Cornell University in 1888 and from 1903 until his retirement in 1913 was dean of the College of Agriculture at that institution. A pioneer of scientific horticulture, Bailey is known for his horticultural research, his studies of rural economics and general rural problems, and his development of agricultural courses for farmers. An authority on North American flora and horticulture, he edited several standard horticultural reference works, including *Cyclopedia of American Horticulture* (4 vol., 1900–02), *Cyclopedia of American Agriculture* (4 vol., 1907–09), and *Standard Cyclopedia of Horticulture* (6 vol., 1914–17). His writings include *The Principles of Fruit-Growing* (1897), *Wind and Weather* (verse, 1916), *Manual of Cultivated Plants* (1924; rev. ed., 1949), *Hortus Second* (1941), and *Garden of Bellflowers in North America* (with G. H. M. Lawrence, 1954).

BAILEY, Solon Irving (1854–1931), American astronomer, born in Lisbon, N.H., and educated at Boston and Harvard universities. He was appointed assistant professor of astronomy at Harvard University in 1893, associate professor in 1898, professor in 1913, and acting director of the Harvard Observatory in 1919. In 1889 Bailey established in Arequipa, Peru, a southern station of the Harvard Observatory; in 1893 he set up another scientific station, at that time the highest in the world, on the summit of El Misti Mt. (19,199 ft.) in Peru. He spent 1908 and 1909 in southern Africa, making astronomical observations and investigating meteorological conditions at several possible observatory sites. His works include *The History and Work of Harvard Observatory, 1839 to 1927* (1931).

BAILLIE, Joanna (1762–1851), British dramatist and poet, born in Lanark, Scotland. Her finest works are generally considered to be the nine *Plays on the Passions* (1798–1836). The most popular of her works is *De Monfort,* a tragedy produced at the Drury Lane Theatre (q.v.) in London in 1800 with the British actors Charles Kemble (*see under* KEMBLE) and Sarah Kemble Siddons (q.v.) in the leading roles. Her *Family Legend,* produced in Edinburgh in 1810, was also very successful.

BAILY, Francis (1774–1844), British astronomer, born in Newbury, Berkshire, England and apprenticed to a merchant at fourteen. After a journey through the United States, Baily settled in London in 1797 and became a stockbroker. At the age of fifty-one, he retired from business to devote himself entirely to astronomy. Among his accomplishments were the founding of the Royal Astronomical Society, the improvement of the *Nautical Almanac,* the discovery of the solar phenomenon now known as Baily's Beads (q.v.), and the preparation of the catalog of stars of the Royal Astronomical Society, which included revising and codifying earlier star catalogs to create a usable body of information. In addition to contributions to the *Memoirs of the Royal Astronomical Society,* Baily wrote *The Doctrine* *of Interest and Annuities* (1808), *The Doctrine of Life Annuities and Assurances* (1810), and *An Account of the Rev. John Flamsteed, the First Astronomer Royal* (1835).

BAILY'S BEADS, phenomenon associated with total eclipses of the sun, first described in the 19th century by the English astronomer Francis Baily (q.v.). Just before the moon completely covers the sun, and again when the sun begins to re-emerge, the thin, crescent-shaped, unobscured portion of the sun suddenly appears discontinuous. It looks like a belt of bright points, varying in size and separated by dark spaces, an effect that looks like a string of beads. The phenomenon is caused by irregularities of the edge of the disk of the moon.

BAIN, Alexander (1818–1903), British psychologist and educator, born in Aberdeen, Scotland. He was educated at the University of Aberdeen, and taught philosophy there from 1841 to 1845 and logic and English literature from 1860 to 1880. In 1881 he became lord rector of the university. At various times from 1857 to 1863 he was an examiner for the University of London and for the India Civil Service. Bain was noted for his contributions to the improvement of Scottish education and to the study of psychology. Among his writings are *The Senses and the Intellect* (1855), *The Emotions and the Will* (1859), *Mental and Moral Science* (1868), and *Education as a Science* (1879).

BAINBRIDGE, city in Georgia, and county seat of Decatur Co., on the Flint R., about 53 miles S.W. of Albany. The city is situated in a timber and farm area, and is an industrial and trade center. Bainbridge manufactures paper, machinery, and clothing. Other industries include naval stores and peanut-shelling. The city was established in 1823 and incorporated in 1829. Pop. (1960) 12,714; (1970) 10,887.

BAINBRIDGE, William (1774–1833), American naval officer, born in Princeton, N.J. He joined the American merchant marine when he was fifteen years of age; at the age of nineteen he was in command of a merchant vessel. He was made a lieutenant when the United States Navy was organized in 1798, and was placed in command of the schooner *Retaliation*. Later that year he was captured by the French off the coast of Guadaloupe, but was released after several weeks. He was promoted to the rank of captain in 1800. In 1803, during the United States war with Tripoli that resulted from the molesting of U.S. shipping by Barbary pirates, he commanded the frigate *Philadelphia*. With this ship he captured the Moorish frigate *Meshboha*. Later he was himself captured and held in Tripoli until peace was declared in 1805. In the War of 1812, against Great Britain, in command of the famous *Constitution* ("Old Ironsides"), he defeated and captured the British frigate *Java* after a two-hour battle. In 1821 he became commander of the navy yards in Boston, Mass., and Philadelphia, Pa. Subsequently he was appointed president of the Board of Navy Commissioners.

BAIRAM (Persian and Turk., "festival"), either of the two principal festivals of Islam (q.v.). The Lesser Festival (or Sugar Festival, or Fast-Breaking Festival) begins the first day of the tenth Arabic month. Marking the end of Ramadan, the fasting month, its celebrations continue for three days. The Greater Festival (or Festival of Sacrifices) begins the tenth day of the twelfth Arabic month. To commemorate the saving from sacrifice of Ishmael son of Abraham and Hagar (qq.v.) through the sacrifice instead of a ram, every Muslim sacrifices an animal (usually a sheep), pilgrimages are made to Mecca, and festivities continue for three to four days. *See* MECCA.

BAIRD, Spencer Fullerton (1823–88), American zoologist, born in Reading, Pa., and educated at Dickinson College. He became professor of natural science at Dickinson in 1846. In 1850 he was elected assistant secretary of the Smithsonian Institution (q.v.), and in 1878, secretary. Baird became United States commissioner of fish and fisheries in 1871. His special work, while assistant secretary of the Smithsonian Institution, was the development of the National Museum, begun under his direction in 1850. With the American ornithologist John Cassin (1813–69), Baird wrote *The Mammals of North America* (1859) and *The Birds of North America* (2 vol., 1860), and with the American ornithologists Thomas Mayo Brewer (1814–80) and Robert Ridgway (1850–1929), Baird wrote *History of the Birds of North America* (5 vol., 1870–84).

BAIRNSFATHER, Bruce (1888–1959), British humorist, writer, and artist, born in Murree (now in Pakistan), and educated at the United Service College in Canada. He was an officer in the British army in World War I. His black-and-white sketches of life in the trenches, which appeared in the British periodical *Bystander,* won much acclaim. His successful play *The Better 'Ole* was based on the adventures of the "Old Bill" of those sketches. During World War II he was a war correspondent with the United States Army. His books about World War I include *Fragments from France* (6 vol., 1916) and *Bullets and Billets* (1917). Among his later works are

Wide Canvas (1939) and *Old Bill Does It Again* (1940).

BAJA CALIFORNIA *or* **LOWER CALIFORNIA,** peninsula of North America, lying between the Gulf of California and the Pacific Ocean, and forming two States of Mexico. The peninsula is about 760 mi. long and varies in width from 30 to 150 mi. It is mountainous, rising in the N. to more than 10,000 ft. above sea level.

Baja California Norte comprises the N. half of the peninsula; Mexicali is its capital. Baja California Sur occupies the rest of the peninsula; La Paz is its capital. Area of Baja California Norte, 27,653 sq.mi.; pop. (1974 est.) 1,102,250. Area of Baja California Sur, 27,976 sq.mi.; pop. (1974 est.) 157,390.

BAJAZET *or* **BAYAZID,** name of two Sultans of the Ottoman Empire (q.v.) in Turkey:

Bajazet I (1347–1403), called YILDERIM ("lightning"), Sultan (1389–1403). He succeeded his father Murad I (*see under* MURAD) and was the first of his dynasty to adopt the title Sultan. In three years Bajazet conquered Bulgaria, and parts of Serbia, Macedonia, and also subdued the greater part of Asia Minor. He blockaded Constantinople (now İstanbul, Turkey) for ten years, hoping to subdue it by famine. Bajazet might have destroyed the Byzantine Empire (q.v.), had not the Mongol conqueror Tamerlane (q.v.) attacked Ottoman possessions in Asia Minor and completely defeated the sultan in 1402 near Angora. Bajazet died a prisoner in the enemy camp and was succeeded as Sultan of Turkey by his son Suleiman I (q.v.).

Bajazet II (1447–1513), Sultan (1481–1512), succeeded his father Sultan Mohammed II (1430–81), the conqueror of Constantinople. His reign, an uninterrupted succession of wars against Hungary, Poland, Venice, Egypt, and Persia, strengthened the power of the Ottoman Turks in Europe. His submission to the Janizaries (q.v.) laid the foundation of their later importance. He was forced to abdicate in favor of his youngest son, Selim I (1467–1520). A patron of learning and lover of splendor, Bajazet built several magnificent mosques in Adrianople (now Edirne, Turkey) and Constantinople. The Mosque of Bajazet, built in 1505 in Constantinople, is considered one of the finest examples of Turkish architecture.

BAJER, Fredrik (1827–1922), Danish statesman and writer, born in Vester Egede. He was a member of the Folketing, the Danish legislature, from 1872 to 1895. Bajer participated in a number of peace conferences held in Europe in the 1880's. In 1882 he founded the Danish Peace Society. He established the International Peace Bureau in 1891 and was its president until 1907. He shared the 1908 Nobel Peace Prize with Klas Pontus Arnoldson (q.v.).

BAKELITE, trademark name for certain resinous products of the Union Carbide Corporation, applied particularly to the phenol-formaldehyde resins developed about 1906 by the Belgian-American chemist Leo Hendrik Baekeland (q.v.), for whom the material is named.

Although Bakelite is sometimes thought of as the first plastic material, it is not; natural plastics such as wax, amber, and rubber had been used for many years, and celluloid (q.v.) came into extensive use forty years before the development of Bakelite. Unlike earlier plastics, however, Bakelite was a wholly synthetic product. The phenol used for the synthesis is a constituent of coal tar (q.v.), and the formaldehyde is made by oxidation of methyl alcohol. Research into synthetic raw materials for plastics, stimulated by the development of Bakelite and of a number of similar plastics that appeared on the market about the same time, resulted in tremendous growth of the synthetic-plastics industry.

Bakelite is manufactured by heating phenol or a closely related compound with an aldehyde, usually formaldehyde, in the presence of a basic catalyst such as ammonia. The molecules of phenol condense with those of formaldehyde, forming giant molecules in the form of long and involved chains; the formula is $(C_6H_5OHCH_2)_n$, where *n* is a large number. When warm, this resin can be cast in any desired form; after it has cooled it becomes hard and inelastic and cannot be remelted. It is thus thermosetting, as opposed to thermoplastic resins, which can be warmed and remolded again and again.

Bakelite has a sp.gr. of 1.25. It may be molded into any desired shapes, or it may be cut, drilled, or ground after it has hardened. Dyes of various colors may be fused with the Bakelite during manufacture, so that the color cannot rub off, and the finished product may be given a high polish. It is an excellent insulator for heat and electricity, and has found extensive use in electrical appliances. It came into wide industrial and commercial use for electric insulators, fuse blocks, noiseless machine gears, fountain pens, pipe stems, display-counter tops, or wherever a hard, polished surface was desired; Bakelite serves as an adhesive and binder in the manufacture of grinding wheels, brake linings, plywood, and foundry molds.

BAKER, George Pierce (1866–1935), American educator, born in Providence, R.I., and educated at Harvard University. From 1905 to 1924 he was professor of English at Harvard University, at which he taught (1905–13) a course, "English 47: Techniques of Drama", that significantly influenced American theater. There he developed the experimental "47 Workshop" (after "English 47"), his now-famous "laboratory course" for drama students, which helped develop the American playwrights Eugene Gladstone O'Neill (q.v.) and Edward Brewster Sheldon (1886–1946), among others. In 1925 he became professor of the history and technique of the drama in the newly organized department of the drama at Yale University and director of the University Theater at that institution. Baker wrote *Dramatic Technique* (1919), and edited various Elizabethan plays.

BAKER, Newton Diehl (1871–1937), American lawyer and public official, born in Martinsburg, W.Va., and educated at Johns Hopkins and Washington and Lee universities. He practiced law in Martinsburg, 1896–97, then moved to Cleveland, Ohio, and from 1902 to 1912 was city solicitor. He was elected mayor in 1912 and was reelected in 1914. From 1916 to 1921 he served in the cabinet of President Woodrow Wilson (q.v.) as secretary of war. At the conclusion of his official service he resumed the practice of law in Cleveland. He was a zealous advocate of the League of Nations (q.v.), and at the Democratic National Convention in 1924 he made a strong but unsuccessful appeal for the inclusion in the platform of a plank favoring the League. In 1928 President Calvin Coolidge (q.v.) appointed Baker to the Permanent Court of International Justice at The Hague, Netherlands. *See* INTERNATIONAL COURT OF JUSTICE.

BAKER, Ray Stannard (1870–1946), American writer and publicist, born in Lansing, Mich., and educated at Michigan State University. Between 1892 and 1915 he was a member of the editorial staff of various publications, including *American Magazine.* After World War I he served as director of the press bureau of the American peace delegation in Paris. Under the pen name of David Grayson he wrote a series of idyllic sketches, including *Adventures in Contentment* (1907), *Adventures in Friendship* (1910), *The Friendly Road* (1913), *Great Possessions* (1917), and *Adventures in Understanding* (1925). In 1920 *The New Industrial Unrest* appeared under his own name. *What Wilson Did at Paris* (1919) and *Woodrow Wilson and World Settlement* (3 vol., 1922) were written in defense of the policies of President Woodrow Wilson (q.v.). Baker edited, with the American historian William Edward Dodd (q.v.), *The Public Papers of Woodrow Wilson* (6 vol., 1924–26). His eight-volume biography *Woodrow Wilson: Life and Letters* won the Pulitzer Prize for 1939. Two of his works, *Native America* (1941) and *American Chronicle* (1945), were autobiographical.

George Pierce Baker Harvard College Library

BAKER, Sir Samuel White (1821–93), British traveler and explorer, born in London, England, and educated in England and Germany. In 1859–60 he superintended the construction of a railway between the Danube R. and the Black Sea. In 1861 he set out from Cairo, Egypt, to search for the source of the Nile R. In 1862 he proceeded up the Nile to Gondokoro (in the Sudan), where he met the British explorers John Hanning Speke (q.v.) and James Augustus Grant (1827–92). Speke and Grant had left Bagamoyo (now in Tanzania) in 1860, and the former had discovered Lake Victoria to be the true source of the Nile. Informed by Speke of another lake, said to be crossed by the Nile on its course to Gondokoro, Baker continued his journey, despite hostile slave traders and a mutiny of his troops; on March 14, 1864, he discovered and named Lake Albert. From 1869 to 1873 he commanded an expedition to suppress slavery and open trade in the equatorial lake region. He explored and hunted in Cyprus, Syria, India, Japan, and the United States. He wrote *Eight Years Wandering in Ceylon* (1855), *The Albert Nyanza* (1866), *The Nile Tributaries of Abyssinia* (1867), and *Wild Beasts and Their Ways* (1890).

BAKERSFIELD, city in California, and county seat of Kern Co., on the Kern R., in the S. part of the San Joaquin Valley, about 85 miles N.W. of Los Angeles. Industries in Bakersfield include factories producing cement products, metal fabric, electronic products, carbon black, beauty aids, and plastics. Pop. (1960) 56,848; (1970) 69,515.

BAKING. *See* COOKERY: *Processes of Cooking.*

BAKING SODA. *See* SODA.

BAKST, Léon Nikolaevich, originally LEV SAMUILOVICH ROSENBERG (1866?–1924), Russian decorative designer, born in Saint Petersburg (now Leningrad), and trained there at the Academy of Arts and in Paris. Bakst worked as a painter at the Russian court until 1906, when he left Russia for political reasons. Soon after settling in Paris, he became known as a designer of stage settings. When the Russian ballet producer Sergei Pavlovich Diaghilev (q.v.) organized his famous ballet company, Ballets Russes, in Paris in 1909, Bakst became a stage designer. His designs for the early Ballets Russes productions quickly received international attention. They were followed by the remarkable designs for *Salome, Narcissus, Afternoon of a Faun,* and *The Butterflies.* He also designed stage settings for the operas *Boris Godunov* and *Secret of Suzanne.* In 1914 the ballet *Orientale* with Bakst's settings and the Russian ballet dancer Anna Pavlova (q.v.) in the leading role was performed in New York City. Bakst visited the United States for the first time in 1922. His designs are characterized by extraordinary richness and brilliance of color and by a fertile and exotic imagination. His influence on modern designing, both theatrical and costume, has been considerable.

BAKU, city and seaport in the Soviet Union, and capital of Azerbaidzhan S.S.R., on the Apsheron Peninsula along the W. coast of the Caspian Sea, about 200 miles E. of Kirovabad, and near the Soviet border with Iran. Situated within an extensive oil region, the chief industry of the city is oil refining. Pipelines carry kerosine and oil to Batumi, Georgian S.S.R., on the Black Sea. The city also has cable factories and shipyards, and is the chief port for Soviet-Iranian trade. Baku, fifth-largest city in the U.S.S.R., has an old quarter, dating from the 9th century, in which is located the fortress of Bad-Kube, with its medieval streets and mosques, and the khan's palace, dating from the 17th century. The newer and more modern sections of the city date from the 19th century. Baku is the site of Kirov State University founded in 1919.

Baku was a Persian town from 1509 until 1723 when it was taken by the Russians. In 1860 the city was incorporated into Russia, and for a brief period from 1918 to 1920 was the seat of an anti-Soviet regime. Pop. (greater city; 1972 est.) 1,314,000.

BAKUNIN, Mikhail Aleksandrovich (1814–76), Russian revolutionist and anarchist, born near Moscow, of an aristocratic family, and educated at a military school in Saint Petersburg (now Leningrad). He was an officer of the Imperial Guard but resigned and visited France, Switzerland, and Germany, and took part in the revolutionary movement of 1848–49 in Germany. He was arrested in Austria, condemned to death, then was surrendered to the Russians, who imprisoned him for several years. He was sent to Siberia in 1855, but he escaped in an American ship to Japan, and arrived in England in 1861. From that time until his death Bakunin was active in spreading his anarchistic views throughout Europe. In 1869 he founded the Alliance of the Social Democracy. As the leader of an anarchist group, he was the opponent of the German political philosopher and founder of Communism Karl Marx (q.v.) in the First International, from which he was expelled in 1872. Bakunin and his supporters, who called themselves autonomists, then founded a rival organization that was active in Spain and Italy for a short time. Bakunin wrote *Dieu et l'État* ("God and the State"), published in 1882.

BAL *or* **BRITISH ANTI-LEWISITE.** *See* LEAD: *Lead Poisoning.*

BALAAM, in the Old Testament, Gentile prophet from Pethor in the Euphrates Valley. According to Numbers 22–24 (*see* NUMBERS), Balak, King of the Moabites (q.v.), became alarmed at the entrance of the Israelites into his territories. He summoned Balaam to Moab and to pronounce a curse upon the Israelites, and thus drive them away. Balaam eventually consented to go, but on the way to Moab, the angel of the Lord met him in the famous incident of the talking ass, after which Balaam became a spokesman for the Lord (Num. 22:21–33). Balaam subsequently foretold happiness for Israel and foresaw the future ascendancy of the house of Jacob (q.v.), patriarch of Israel (Num. 24:17). Balaam, nevertheless, led the Israelites into sin by counseling them to consort with Moabite women and by causing them to eat food sacrificed to idols (Num. 25:1–3; 31:16). He is recalled for these deeds in the New Testament (Jude 11; Rev. 2:14). Balaam was killed in the fighting that subsequently took place between the Midianites and the Israelites (Num. 31:8). The story of Balaam expresses the idea that even foreigners testified to the greatness of Israel.

BALAKIREV, Mili Alekseevich (1837–1910), Russian composer, born in Nizhni Novgorod (now Gor'kiy), and trained in his native city and at the University of Kazan'. At the age of eighteen he went to Saint Petersburg (now Leningrad), where he became acquainted with the Russian composer Mikhail Ivanovich Glinka (q.v.). In 1861 Balakirev formed, with four other composers, a group known as the "Five"; under Balakirev's influence the "Five" broke away from classic musical forms, using Russian folk melodies in their compositions and Russian folktales as a basis for their operas. The four others were Modest Petrovich Musorgski, Nikolai Andreevich Rimski-Korsakov, Aleksandr Porfirevich Borodin (qq.v.), and César Antonovitch Cui (1835–1918). In 1862 Balakirev helped found the Free School of Music in St. Petersburg, and in 1869 he became director of the Imperial Chapel and Imperial Music Society. Important among his compositions are the symphonic poems *Tamara* and *Russia,* and the fantasia for orchestra and piano *Islamy.* He also wrote music for piano and for voice.

BALAKLAVA, village of the Soviet Union, in the Crimea, about 8 miles S.E. of Sevastopol', from which it is separated by a rocky peninsula. Fishing is the principal occupation of the inhabitants. The harbor, which affords secure anchorage for the largest ships, was a naval station till 1860. The harbor is well protected; in fact the harbor entrance is so narrow that it can barely admit more than one vessel at a time. From September, 1854, to June, 1856, it was the British headquarters during the Crimean War, the chief engagement occurring on Oct. 25, 1854. Balaklava was made famous by the British poet Alfred Tennyson, 1st Baron Tennyson (q.v.), in his poem "Charge of the Light Brigade", published late in 1854.

BALALAIKA. *See* MUSICAL INSTRUMENTS: *Stringed Instruments.*

BALANCE. *See* SCALE; WEIGHING.

BALANCE OF NATURE. *See* ECOLOGY.

BALANCE OF POWER, in international diplomacy, doctrine that approximate equality of military strength between individual states or groups of allied states is a fundamental prerequisite for the preservation of peace. The doctrine rests on the principle that states or groups of allied states with preponderant power constitute a menace to the independence of other states. Although nations of antiquity, especially the Greek city-states, often conducted their foreign affairs on the basis of this principle, the doctrine did not emerge as a distinctly formulated rule of international politics until relatively recent times. Specifically, the doctrine began to figure systematically in diplomacy after the development, during the 15th and 16th centuries, of various powerful European states, including England, France, and Spain.

Balance in the Old World. At the time of the great religious wars of the 16th century, the French, English, and Dutch individually resisted the aggressions of Hapsburg (q.v.) Spain, and later combined to subdue Spain. The close of these wars about 1600 saw the first formal proposal to preserve peace in Europe through maintenance of a balance of power. A plan called the Great Design, attributed to Henry IV (q.v.), King of France, or to his minister, Maximilien de Béthune, Duc de Sully (q.v.), proposed the establishment of a federation of states to create a balance between non-Hapsburg and Hapsburg Europe. The plan was considered fantastic at the time.

A similar combination of powers against Louis XIV (q.v.), King of France, when that monarch threatened the peace of Europe by seeking control of Spain, actually culminated in a Grand Alliance (q.v.), formed in 1689 and reconstituted in 1701. In the political maneuvers of the 18th century a new type of balance appeared; in place of all against one, Europe divided into rival camps of approximately equal power. England and France, competing for colonial advantages, remained hostile to each other; when France helped Prussia in a war against Austria in 1741, England sided with Austria; when the strength of Prussia grew and the balance of power appeared endangered, France changed sides, in 1756 deserting Prussia for Austria; whereupon England switched to aid Prussia.

The rise of Napoleon I (q.v.) in France early in the 19th century again resulted in a great alliance of powers against one nation, France, and the defeat of that nation in 1815. Members of the victorious coalition, Russia and Austria, along with France, under the restored Bourbon (q.v.) monarch, then formed the Holy Alliance (q.v.), with a program of preserving the status quo. The Holy Alliance considered the Latin American revolutions a challenge to its design and tried to suppress them; England supported the new American states.

The equilibrium of the Holy Alliance was finally upset by a series of revolutions and the rise of two new powers, Germany and Italy, in the last half of the 19th century. Again Europe split into two camps. Austria, Germany, and Italy formed the Triple Alliance (q.v.); England, France, and Russia formed the Triple Entente (q.v.). The balance was upset by relatively minor events in the Balkans in 1914, and the two camps battled each other in World War I (q.v.).

20th-Century Balance. After the end of the war, the powers tried to maintain peace through the League of Nations (q.v.); but not all the great nations were members of the league at any one time. The United States did not join. The U.S.S.R. was not admitted until 1934, by which time Japan and Germany had withdrawn. In World War II the major nations of the world divided into two camps, the so-called Axis Powers (q.v.), consisting of Germany, Italy, Japan, and various satellite states, and the Allies, which ultimately embraced most of the other nations of the world.

The victory of the Allies in 1945 left the problem of preserving peace, not merely in Europe, but on a worldwide scale, still to be solved. Five great powers emerged from World War II: the U.S., the U.S.S.R., and Great Britain in the first rank, followed by France and China (consisting of the Nationalist government now located on Taiwan). The organization, in October, 1945, of the United Nations (q.v.), to which these and most of the smaller countries belonged, provided a machinery to keep peace by avoiding conflicts arising through attempts to maintain a balance of power. Within the U.N. and in international politics generally, the nations of the world moved gradually during the postwar period into a new power alignment. The underlying cause of this new power struggle was the apparent impossibility of reconciling the economic and ideological systems of the U.S.S.R. and the Western democracies. The power struggle therefore was no longer based solely on relative military strength. In 1949 the North Atlantic Treaty Organization (q.v.), known as NATO, brought together many of the former Allies. When West Germany was admitted to NATO in 1955, the U.S.S.R. and other Communist nations, including East Germany, formed the Warsaw Treaty Organization (q.v.). Also in 1955, as Communist influence in the East spread outward from China, the Southeast Asia Treaty Organization (q.v.) was formed by a combination of the U.S., Great Britain, France, and five countries of Asia.

The Cold War and Détente. The state of military tension and political rivalry that existed between the Soviet and American blocs became known as the cold war (q.v.). It erupted into actual, although undeclared, warfare in the Korean War (q.v.) from 1950 to 1953. Other aspects of the period that affected the balance of power were the initiation of space exploration by both the U.S. and the U.S.S.R. and the testing of nuclear devices by the U.S., the U.S.S.R., Great Britain, France, the People's Republic of China, and India. Throughout the period further tensions were created by a series of what were known as wars of national liberation, as many smaller countries of the so-called Third World of Africa and Asia attempted to achieve their independence or struggled to maintain it successfully.

In the 1970's a more or less firm state of détente existed between the U.S. and both of the rival Communist powers, China and the U.S.S.R. But a new struggle for power began. Countries that produced raw materials, especially the members of the Organization of Petroleum Exporting Countries (q.v.), took political and economic advantage of the industrial nations that needed their products. A threat of open warfare existed, especially in the vulnerable area of the Middle East, where various oil-producing Arab countries and Israel, a U.S. ally, were engaged in what were almost constant hostilities.

BALANCE OF TRADE *or* **BALANCE OF PAYMENTS.** *See* DEVALUATION.

BALANCHINE, George (1904–), Russian-American choreographer, born in Saint Petersburg (now Leningrad), and graduated (1921) from the St. Petersburg branch of the School of the Imperial Ballet (now the Soviet State School). He left the U.S.S.R. for a European tour and in 1924 joined the Diaghilev Company as choreographer (*see* DIAGHILEV, SERGEI). At the request of Lincoln Kirstein (1907–), founder of the School of American Ballet (now the School

George Balanchine Fred Fehl

of American Ballet at the Juilliard School of Music), Balanchine came to the United States in 1933 to organize and direct the school and also the American Ballet Company. In 1947 he became artistic director of the newly reorganized performing company, the Ballet Society. The following year this company became the New York City Ballet, and under Balanchine's direction it has grown into one of the world's great performing companies, with a repertory consisting largely of Balanchine ballets.

Balanchine has choreographed over one hundred ballets, the best of which are noted for their musicality. Perhaps his masterwork in the romantic, lyric vein is *Liebeslieder Walzer* (1960). His balletic moods range from Americana (*Square Dance, Stars and Stripes*) to Russified dance (*Firebird*); from elaborate storytelling (*The Nutcracker*) to abstract dances without plots (*Agon, Jewels*). His close relationship with the Russian-American composer Igor Fëdorovich Stravinsky (q.v.) has produced a number of striking ballets, including the classic *Apollon Musagètes* (1928, revised as *Apollo* in 1957), *Orpheus* (1936, revised 1948), *Agon* (1957), *Monumentum Pro Gesualdo* (1960), *Movements for Piano and Orchestra* (1963), *Scherzo à la Russe* (1972), and *Violin Concerto* (1972).

See BALLET: *20th Century*.

BALANOGLOSSUS, genus of marine, wormlike animal of great zoological interest as a possible connecting link between invertebrates and vertebrates (q.v.). The genus is now usually considered to be chordate (*see* CHORDATA), part of the order Enteropneusta. The animals are found living in muddy sand in tropical and temperate climates all over the world. Like the common earthworm, the balanoglossus burrows through its surroundings, eating the muddy sand and digesting the organic content. Some species may attain a length of 8 in. or more. The body is divided into four distinct regions: a large proboscis in front of the mouth; a muscular collar of some length; a respiratory region, through slits in which water flows out from the gullet; and, lastly, a long gastric region that contains most of the body's digestive and reproductive systems.

BALATON, LAKE, largest lake in Hungary, about 55 miles S.W. of Budapest. It is about 426 ft. above sea level, 47 mi. long, and 7 to 9 mi. broad, with an area of about 260 sq.mi. and an approximate depth of from 15 to 40 ft. It is fed by more than thirty streams, the chief of which is the Zala.

BALBO, Italo (1896–1940), Italian statesman and aviator, born in Quartesana, and educated at the University of Florence and at the Institute of Social Science in Rome. He was an officer in the Italian army during World War I; later he became active in the Fascist movement in Italy. In 1922 he participated in the Fascist march on Rome, helping the Italian dictator Benito Mussolini (q.v.) to seize control of the government. Balbo held several important posts in the Fascist regime, notably in the Black Shirt Militia, in the Air Fleet, and in the Air Ministry, which he headed from 1929 to 1933. In 1933 he commanded a group of twenty-four airplanes on a flight from Italy to the United States. He was promoted to the rank of air marshal in that year, and appointed governor of Libya. He died in an airplane crash while serving as commander in chief of Italian armed forces in North Africa, a high-ranking post to which he had been appointed in 1937.

BALBOA, town in the Panama Canal Zone, at the Pacific terminus of the Panama Canal and adjoining the city of Panama. It is built on the site of a former tidal swamp that was filled with rock excavated in the construction of the Panama Canal (q.v.). The city has harbor installations, railway and ship-repair shops, oil-pumping plants, storage tanks for petroleum and diesel oil, and warehouses. The suburb of Balboa Heights, situated on a hill above the town of Balboa, is the United States administrative center of the Canal Zone. Pop. (1970 prelim.) 2568.

Vasco Núñez de Balboa

BALBOA, Vasco Núñez de (1475–1517), Spanish explorer, born in Jerez de los Caballeros. In 1500 he was a member of the trading expedition, organized by the Spanish explorer Rodrigo de Bastidas (b. 1460?), that visited the northern coast of South America. Later Balboa settled in what is now Santo Domingo, Dominican Republic, where he unsuccessfully engaged in farming. In order to escape from his creditors, he joined the expedition, commanded by Martín Fernández de Encisco (1470?–1528), that in 1510 established a settlement in Darien (now Panama). Balboa subsequently deposed Fernández de Encisco and, in 1513, led an exploratory party to the shores of the Pacific Ocean. Balboa thereupon claimed the ocean and all the lands in it as property of the Spanish monarchs. As a result of intrigues at the Spanish court, Balboa was replaced as governor of Darien by the Spanish soldier Pedrarias (q.v.). Balboa led several important expeditions thereafter, but he was accused by Pedrarias of treason and was beheaded.

BALCH, Emily Greene (1867–1961), American economist, educator, and writer born in Jamaica Plain (now part of Boston), Mass., and educated at Bryn Mawr College and at the universities of Paris, Chicago, and Berlin. In 1896 she joined the faculty of Wellesley College; her contract was not renewed in 1918 because of her activities as a pacifist.

She was international secretary of the Women's International League for Peace and Freedom, in Geneva, Switzerland, from 1919 to 1922; in 1936 she was elected honorary international president of the league. In 1946, when she shared the Nobel Peace Prize with the American evangelist John Raleigh Mott (q.v.), she donated her share of the prize to the league. Books by Emily Balch include *Public Assistance of the Poor in France* (1893); *Refugees as Assets* (1939); and *The Miracle of Living* (poems; 1941).

BALD CYPRESS. *See* CYPRESS.

BALD EAGLE. *See* EAGLE.

BALDER *or* **BALDUR,** in Norse mythology, the god of light and joy, son of Odin (q.v.) and Frigga, king and queen of the gods. Having dreamed evil dreams according to which Balder's life was threatened, Frigga exacted an oath from the forces and objects in nature, animate and inanimate, that they would not harm Balder. But she forgot the mistletoe. The gods, thinking Balder safe, cast darts and stones at him. The malicious giant Loki (q.v.), alone took no part in the play. Loki placed a bough of mistletoe in the hands of Balder's twin brother, the blind Hoder, god of war, and directed his aim against Balder, who fell pierced to the heart. After the death of Balder, Odin sent another son, the messenger Hermod, to the underworld to plead for Balder's return. The god would be released only if everything in the world would weep for him. Everything wept except one old woman in a cave, and Balder could not return to life.

BALDNESS. *See* HAIR.

BALDOVINETTI, Alessio, *or* BALDUINETTI, ALESSIO (1425?–99), Italian painter, probably born in Florence. He is believed to have studied with the Florentine painter Domenico Veneziano (active 1438–61). Besides painting on canvas and plaster, Baldovinetti was a master of painting on banners, shields, and chests; he was considered among the most capable mosaic workers of his time. His best-known surviving works are a series of frescoes in the Church of Santa Trinità, Florence.

BALDPATE, common name of the American freshwater duck, Mareca americana, belonging to the Waterfowl family (Anatidae) and known also as the American widgeon (q.v.). It is large (about 19 in. long), grayish brown above, and white below. The plumage of the adult male is characterized by a pure-white crown, which gives it the bald appearance on which the name is based. The wings have a large, white patch that is conspicuous in flight.

The baldpate breeds in the northwestern regions of North America, from Nevada to Canada and Alaska and winters as far south as Central America. It builds its nest on dry ground in a slight depression, lined with grass, weeds, and down, and lays from six to twelve white eggs. Baldpates feed mainly on seeds, grasses, and the stems of aquatic plants. Because of their habit of snatching food brought up to the surface of the water by diving ducks, baldpates often are called "poachers". Swift and erratic in flight, the baldpate is a challenge to the marksmanship of the sportsman. It is also a table delicacy.

BALDUR. *See* BALDER.

BALDWIN, borough of Pennsylvania, in Allegheny Co., immediately S.W. of Pittsburgh of which it is a residential suburb. Pop. (1960) 24, 489; (1970) 26,729.

BALDWIN, unincorporated village of New York State, in Nassau Co., in the town of Hempstead, on the S. shore of Long Island, 6 miles S. of Mineola. The chief manufactures are electrical and aircraft equipment, wood and food products, gas burners, clothing, and cement. Fishing is carried on in the Baldwin Harbor section, a summer resort on Middle Bay. The Hempstead area was settled in 1643. Pop. (1970) 34,525.

BALDWIN, name of two Latin emperors of Constantinople (now İstanbul, Turkey).

Baldwin I (1171–1205?), first Latin Emperor of Constantinople (1204–05?), born in Valenciennes. In 1200 he joined the Fourth Crusade (*see* CRUSADES: *Fourth Crusade*) and assisted in the recapture of Constantinople for the Byzantine emperor Isaac II Angelus (r. 1185–95; 1203–04). When Isaac failed to pay the Crusaders for their services, they turned against him and sacked the town. Both Isaac and his son were killed; Baldwin was chosen emperor, and was crowned in 1204. The Byzantines, invoking the aid of the Bulgarians, rebelled and seized Adrianople. Baldwin laid siege to the town, but he was defeated and taken prisoner. He died in captivity.

Baldwin II (1217–73), last Latin Emperor of Constantinople (1239–61), nephew of Baldwin I. At the age of eleven he inherited the throne but was not crowned until 1239, two years after the death of John of Brienne (1148–1237), former king of Jerusalem who had been chosen to rule as regent. At the time of John's death Baldwin was in western Europe, attempting to raise funds and an army to recover territories of his empire that had been conquered by the Greeks and Bulgarians. Unable to maintain his position after his return to Constantinople, he again, from 1245 to 1247, sought financial support in Italy and France. In 1261 his capital was taken by Michael VIII Palaeologus (1234–82), Emperor of the Eastern Roman Empire. Baldwin fled to Italy, ending the Latin empire in the East.

BALDWIN, name of five kings of Jerusalem who were descended from the Counts of Flanders (*see* FLANDERS).

Baldwin I (1058–1118), King (1100–18), brother of the French crusader Godfrey of Bouillon (q.v.). Following service in the First Crusade (*see* CRUSADES: *First Crusade*), Baldwin settled in Edessa (now Urfa, Turkey), a Christian stronghold that he helped to defend against Muslim attacks. He became ruler of Jerusalem upon Godfrey's death and assumed the title of king. Subsequently Baldwin extended Christian power in Palestine, defeated the Muslims at Acre and in Sidon, and invaded Egypt.

Baldwin II (d. 1131), King (1118–31), cousin and successor of Baldwin I. He also participated in the First Crusade. In 1104 he was captured by the Muslims, who detained him until 1108. After his election as king, on the death of Baldwin I, he campaigned against the Turks, winning control of Aleppo and Damascus. He was succeeded by his son-in-law Fulk V, the Young (1092–1143), Count of Anjou.

Baldwin III (1130?–62), King (1143–62), son and successor of Fulk V. His policies contributed to the loss of Edessa to the Muslims and to the collapse of the Second Crusade. He was succeeded on the throne by his brother Amalric I (1135–74).

Baldwin IV (1160–85), King (1174–83), son and successor of Amalric I. His reign was characterized by constant warfare with the Egyptians. Incapacitated in 1183 because of leprosy, he relinquished his crown to the child of his sister.

Baldwin V (d. 1186), King (1183–86), nephew of Baldwin IV. He died after a nominal reign of three years.

BALDWIN, James (1924–), American novelist and essayist, born and raised in the Harlem section of New York City. After high school, Baldwin supported his writing career by working at various jobs until he won a fellowship which enabled him to live in Paris. His first novel, written in Paris, *Go Tell It on the Mountain* (1953), established him as a leading Negro commentator on the condition of his race in America. *Notes of a Native Son* (1956) and *Nobody Knows My Name* (1961) are collections of essays and reminiscences based on his youth in Harlem. These and other works, such as *The Fire Next Time* (1963) and *No Name in the Street* (1972), reflect Baldwin's belief that the American Negro as an object of suffering and abuse represents a symbol of universal conflicts and problems. Baldwin states this position in a powerful and frank style. The novel *Tell Me How Long the Train's Been Gone* was published in 1968. His plays include *The Amen Corner* (1950) and *Blues for Mister Charlie* (1964). *One Day When I Was Lost* (1973) is a film script. *See also* AMERICAN LITERATURE: *20th Century*; NEGRO LITERATURE, AMERICAN: *1950 to the Present.*

BALDWIN, James Mark (1861–1934), American psychologist, born in Columbia, S.C., and educated at Princeton University. In 1900 he became the first recipient of an honorary D.Sc. degree from the University of Oxford, England. After teaching at other schools, he was appointed professor of psychology at Princeton (1893–1903) and at Johns Hopkins University (1903–09). His many books include *Mental Development in the Child and the Race* (1896), *Thoughts and Things, or Genetic Logic* (3 vol., 1906–11), *Darwin and the Humanities* (1909), and *Between Two Wars—Memories and Opinions* (2 vol., 1926).

BALDWIN, Stanley, 1st Earl Baldwin of Bewdley (1867–1947), British statesman, born in Bewdley, England, and educated at Harrow and at Trinity College, University of Cambridge. In

Stanley Baldwin UPI

1908 he was elected to Parliament from the Bewdley division of Worcestershire, representing the Conservative interests. He was financial secretary of the treasury (1917–21), president of the board of trade (1921–22), and chancellor of the exchequer (1922–23). In the latter position, he went to the United States in January, 1923, with the British Financial Mission, which funded the British war debt. When the British statesman Bonar Law (q.v.) resigned in May, 1923, Baldwin became prime minister. He believed in tariff protection, but he was bound by Bonar Law's pledge not to attempt to levy protective tariffs. After slightly more than six months in office, Baldwin appealed to the country on the protection issue. The subsequent election resulted in a Labour and Liberal majority; he resigned in January, 1924.

He was succeeded as prime minister by the British statesman James Ramsay MacDonald (q.v.), who formed a Labour government that remained in office only until November, 1924, when it was defeated by the Conservatives. Baldwin again became prime minister. In 1926, during the general strike that grew out of the coal strike of May 1, the country as a whole rallied to the support of the government, and the general strike was called off on May 12. Baldwin's support of the Trade Union Bill of 1927, which made another general strike virtually impossible, represented a return to the old Conservatism. In the same year he visited Canada, becoming the first incumbent premier to visit an overseas dominion. He resigned as prime minister in June, 1929, following a Labour victory in a general election. MacDonald again succeeded him. In September, 1931, Baldwin became lord privy seal and was again prime minister from 1935 to 1937. In 1936 his stand against the projected marriage of Edward VIII (q.v.), King of England, to a divorced American woman was instrumental in causing the abdication of the king that year. Baldwin retired in 1937 and was made 1st Earl Baldwin of Bewdley. He was one of the foremost British statesmen of his time, although he has been criticized for his failure to inform the British people of the preparations Germany was making for World War II. He wrote many books, including *Peace and Goodwill in Industry* (1925), *The Classics and the Plain Man* (1926), *This Torch of Freedom* (1935), *Service of Our Lives* (1937), and *An Interpreter of England* (1939).

BALDWIN PARK, city of California, in Los Angeles Co., in the E. part of the San Gabriel Valley, 16 miles E. of Los Angeles. Metal products and concrete are manufactured in the city, and the surrounding area is engaged in fruit growing and truck and poultry farming. Developed after the construction of an electric power station in 1912, Baldwin Park is on the site of the former Puente de San Gabriel ranch. The city was incorporated in 1956. Pop. (1970) 47,285.

BALE, John (1495–1563), English churchman, born in Suffolk. Educated as a Carmelite, he was converted to Protestantism. In 1540, persecuted by the Roman Catholics, he fled to Flanders. He was recalled to England in 1547 by Edward VI (q.v.), King of England, and in 1552 was appointed bishop of Ossory, in Ireland. By his Protestant zeal Bale so offended Roman Catholics, that on news of the death of Edward in 1553, the churchman's house was attacked and five of his servants killed. He escaped to Basel, Switzerland. On the accession of Elizabeth I (q.v.) as Queen of England in 1559 Bale returned to England and was made a prebendary in the cathedral of Canterbury. Bale's principal written work was a Latin history of English literature.

BALEARIC ISLANDS, *or* BALEARES, group of islands in the Mediterranean Sea, off the E. coast of Spain, forming the Spanish province of Baleares. Eleven islets and the four large islands of Majorca, Minorca, Ibiza, and Formentera constitute the group; the capital is the city of Palma on Majorca, the largest of the islands. Fishing and farming are the main occupations of the islands. Citrus fruit, grapes, olives, wheat, figs,

The Balearic Islands are dotted with many quiet coves such as this one, on the island of Minorca.

vegetables, and almonds are grown, and fruit, wine, olive oil, and hogs are exported. The chief industries are the manufacture of shoes and majolica pottery. The islands are especially well known as resort areas. First inhabited by the Iberians, the islands were later occupied successively by the Phoenicians, Greeks, Carthaginians, Romans, and Byzantines. In the 8th century the islands were conquered by the Moors, and became a base for pirates preying on the ships in the Mediterranean. James I, King of Aragon (*see under* JAMES) expelled the Moors in 1229. During the Spanish Civil War (1936–39), Majorca and Ibiza sided with the Nationalists, while Minorca sided with the Loyalists. Area, 1936 sq.mi.; pop. (1970) 558,287.

BALFOUR, Arthur James, 1st Earl of Balfour (1848–1930), British statesman, born in Scotland, and educated at Eton College and at Trinity College, University of Cambridge. He represented Hertford (1874–85) and Manchester (1886–1905) in the House of Commons. In 1891 he was made first lord of the treasury and government leader in the House of Commons. Upon the retirement of his uncle, Robert Arthur Talbot Gascoyne–Cecil, 3rd Marquis of Salisbury (*see under* CECIL), in July, 1902, he became prime minister. Dissensions within the Unionist Party finally led to Balfour's resignation in December, 1905. In the general election of January, 1906, the Unionists suffered a crushing defeat; Balfour himself was defeated in Manchester. He soon re-entered Parliament, however, as representative for the City of London.

With other Unionist leaders he discarded party differences at the outbreak of World War I and joined the first coalition cabinet of Prime Minister Herbert Henry Asquith (*see* ASQUITH, HERBERT HENRY, 1ST EARL OF OXFORD AND ASQUITH) in 1915 with the portfolio of first lord of the admiralty. When David Lloyd George (*see* LLOYD GEORGE, DAVID, 1ST EARL DWYFOR) became prime minister in December, 1916, Balfour was transferred to the Foreign Office; there he was employed in enlisting the support of the United States for the Allied powers; in 1917 he headed the British War Mission sent to the U.S. In the same year he made a statement to the effect that Great Britain would support the creation in Palestine of a homeland for the Jews; *see* BALFOUR DECLARATION. After World War I he attended the peace conference at Versailles (1919) as a British representative. Later in 1919 he resigned his foreign secretaryship, remaining in the cabinet as lord president of the council. In 1920 he represented his country at the first assembly of the League of Nations (q.v.) and in 1921 he represented England at the Washington Conference (q.v.). From 1925 until 1929 he was again lord president of the council.

In recognition of his services Balfour was awarded the Order of Merit in 1916, and in 1919 was appointed chancellor of the University of Cambridge. In 1922 he was created 1st Earl of Balfour and Viscount Traprain of Whittingehame. Balfour's writings display the questioning philosophical bent of his mind. Among his works are *Essays and Addresses* (1893), *The Foundations of Belief* (1895), *Theism and Humanism* (1915), and *Theism and Thought* (1923).

See GREAT BRITAIN: *History*.

BALFOUR DECLARATION, letter prepared in March, 1916, and issued in November, 1917, during World War I, by the British statesman Arthur James Balfour (q.v.), then foreign secretary in the cabinet of the British Prime Minister David Lloyd George (q.v.). Specifically, the letter expressed the "sympathy" of the British government with "Jewish Zionist aspirations", and a favorable attitude toward "the establishment in Palestine of a national home for the Jewish people" The letter committed the British government to making the "best endeavors to facilitate the achievement of this object, it being clearly understood that nothing shall be done which may prejudice the civil and religious rights of existing non-Jewish communities in Palestine, or the rights and political status enjoyed by Jews in any other country".

It has been commonly accepted that the Balfour Declaration was a unilateral undertaking by the British government. The immediate purpose was to win for the Allied cause in World War I the support of Jews and others in the belligerent nations and in neutral countries (such as the United States). In long-range terms, the motive behind British policy as set forth in the letter rested upon the importance of Palestine as a strategic point on the land and sea routes to India and, above all, as the terminus at the Mediterranean Sea of pipelines from the rich oil-bearing regions of the Middle East. The establishment of a Zionist state under British protection would give Great Britain possession of that coveted prize, while at the same time apparently implementing the Allied slogan of "self-determination of small nations". The long-range British plan met with success. In 1922 the Declaration was embodied in the League of Nations mandate for Palestine, which set forth terms under which Great Britain was entrusted with the temporary administration of the country in behalf of the Jewish people. For the subsequent history of the mandate, *see* ISRAEL: *History*.

BALI, island in the Republic of Indonesia, one of the Lesser Sunda Islands, in the Indian Ocean, situated between the island of Java to the W., from which it is separated by Bali Strait, and the island of Lombok to the E., from which it is separated by Lombok Strait. Bali is about 90 mi. long and about 50 mi. wide. The principal cities are the N. port and capital, Singaradja, and Denpasar near the S. coast. Mountain ranges cross the island from E. to W. The highest point on the island is Mt. Agung (10,308 ft.), a volcano that last erupted in March, 1963. In the S. the land descends to form an alluvial plain, watered by shallow rivers, dry in the dry season and overflowing during periods of heavy rains.

Economically and culturally, Bali is one of the most important islands of Indonesia. Rice is grown on irrigated, terraced hillsides. Other crops include sugarcane, coffee, copra, tobacco, fruits, and vegetables. Cattle and hogs are raised. The Balinese are skilled artisans, particularly in wood carving, and in fashioning objects of tortoiseshell, and of gold, silver, and other metals. The women of Bali are noted for their beauty, and for their skill in weaving cloth of gold and silver threads and in embroidering silk and cotton clothing. The principal religion on the island is a type of Hinduism that incorporates Polynesian religious rites.

Bali was first visited by the Dutch in 1597, but Dutch rule was not firmly established until 1908. In 1946, after the Japanese occupation of the island during World War II was ended, Bali was included in the newly formed State of East Indonesia, becoming part of the United States of Indonesia in 1948. In 1950 Bali became part of the unified Republic of Indonesia (*see* INDONESIA, REPUBLIC OF). Area, 2905 sq.mi.; pop. (1971) 2,120,000.

BALIKPAPAN, city and port of Indonesia, in East Kalimantan Province, on Makassar Strait, on the E. coast of Borneo, 210 miles N.E. of Bandjarmasin. An oil port, Balikpapan is the center of the major Indonesian petroleum region; oil refining and sawmilling are the chief industries. A battle between United States and Japanese naval forces was fought nearby in 1942. Pop. (1971) 137,340.

BALIOL, name of Anglo-Norman family prominent in Scottish history.

Guido de Baliol *or* **Guy de Baliol,** founder of the family, held Bailleul and other fiefs near Alençon in Normandy. He accompanied William I (q.v.), known as the Conquerer, to England in 1066. William II (q.v.), King of England, awarded extensive possessions in Durham and Northumberland to Guido.

Bernard de Baliol (d. about 1167), nephew and heir to Guido. He built the fortress of Barnard Castle in England, and was the first member of his family to hold land in Scotland.

John de Baliol (d. 1269), great-grandson of Bernard de Baliol. He was the founder of Balliol College, University of Oxford, donating lands for the endowment of the college about 1263 and awarding benefactions to a group of scholars. With the help of his wife Devorguila (d. 1290), a Scottish heiress wealthy in her own right, and monies left in his will, the endowment was greatly increased.

John de Baliol (1249–1315), King of Scotland (1292–96), son of John de Baliol (d. 1269). Upon the death of Princess Margaret in 1290, he became a competitor for the crown then claimed by Robert Bruce (q.v.), later King of Scotland as Robert I. Edward I (q.v.), King of England, was the arbiter in the dispute, and he chose in favor of Baliol, who in turn pledged his fealty to Edward. Feeling that his sovereignty was only nominal, and resenting various indignities to which he was subjected, Baliol concluded an alliance in 1295 with France, then at war with England. The English invaded Scotland, defeated the Scottish troops, took Baliol prisoner, and forced him to surrender his crown on July 10, 1296.

Edward de Baliol (d. 1363), King of Scotland (1329–56), son of John de Baliol, King of Scotland. He lived on the family estates in Normandy until 1324, when Edward II (q.v.), King of England, invited him to England in the hope of putting him on the Scottish throne. Baliol was not crowned king, however, until after the death of Robert I, King of Scotland, the accession of Edward III (q.v.) to the English throne, and a military victory against the Scottish nobles. In 1329 Baliol was crowned king of Scotland at Scone. His reign was marked by constant warfare with the Scottish nobility, and by frequent flights to England and the protection of Edward III. In 1356 Baliol surrendered the kingdom of Scotland to Edward III. The death of Edward de Baliol ended the house of Baliol.

Balinese women are considered among the most beautiful in the world.

BALKAN MOUNTAINS, mountain range of Europe, on the Balkan Peninsula, forming a continuation of the Carpathian system. They may be considered to begin at the W. extremity of the Transylvanian Alps, at the gorge known as the Iron Gate of the Danube, on the Yugoslav-Rumanian border. Bounded on the W. by the basin of the Morava R., the mountains form part of the border between Bulgaria and Yugoslavia, and turn E. across the center of Bulgaria, extending for about 350 mi. toward the Black Sea. The range varies in width from 12 to 20 mi.

The average height of the Balkans is about 3000 ft. above sea level; the highest point, Botev Peak, in central Bulgaria, rises to 7793 ft. Several other ranges including the Rhodope extend S. from the Balkans to the Aegean Sea. The princi-

INDEX TO MAP OF THE BALKAN PENINSULA

ALBANIA

Cities and Towns

Argyrokastron (Gjinokastër) B 3
Berat B 3
Durrës (Durazzo) B 3
Elbasan B 3
Gjinokastër (Argyrokastron) B 3
Korçë C 3
Scutari (Shkodër) B 3
Tiranë (Tirana) (capital) B 3
Vlonë (Valona) B 3

Physical Features

Adriatic (sea) A 3
Drin (river) C 3
Korab (mt.) C 3
Ohrid (lake) C 3
Otranto (strait) B 4
Prespa (lake) C 3
Scutari (lake) B 3

BULGARIA

Cities and Towns

Asenovgrad D 3
Blagoyevgrad C 3
Burgas D 3
Dimitrovgrad D 3
Dobrich (Tolbukhin) E 3
Gabrovo D 3
Gotse Delchev C 3
Kazanlŭk D 3
Khaskovo D 3
Kolarovgrad (Shumen) D 3
Kyustendil C 3
Lom C 3
Lovech D 3
Nova Zagora D 3
Pazardzhik C 3
Pernik C 3
Petrich C 3
Philippopolis (Plovdiv) D 3
Pleven D 3
Plovdiv D 3
Polyanovgrad D 3
Razgrad D 3
Ruse (Ruschuk) D 3
Shumen (Kolarovgrad) D 3
Silistra D 3
Sofia (Sofiya) (capital) C 3
Stanke Dimitrov C 3
Stara Zagora D 3
Svishtov D 3
Tolbukhin (Dobrich) E 3
Tŭrnovo D 3
Varna E 3
Vidin C 2
Vratsa C 3
Yambol D 3

Physical Features

Balkan (mts.) D 3
Iskŭr (river) D 3
Musala (mt.) C 3
Rhodope (mts.) D 3

GREECE

Cities and Towns

Agrínion C 4
Aíyion C 4
Alexandroúpolis D 3
Amaliás C 4
Árgos C 4
Árta C 4
Athens (capital) D 4
Candia (Iráklion) D 5
Canea (Khaniá) C 5
Corfu (Kérkira) B 4
Corinth C 4
Dráma C 3
Édhessa C 3
Ioánnina C 4
Iráklion D 5
Kalámai C 4
Kardhítsa C 4
Kateríni C 3
Kaválla D 3
Khalkís C 4
Khaniá C 5
Khíos D 4
Komotiní D 3
Kozáni C 3
Lamía C 4
Lárisa C 4
Levádhia C 4
Mytilíni D 4
Náousa C 3
Pátrai C 4
Piraiévs C 4
Pírgos C 4
Ródhos (Rhodes) E 4
Salonika (Thessaloníki) C 3
Sérrai C 3
Sparta C 4
Thívai C 4
Thessaloníki (Salonika) C 3
Tríkkala C 4
Tripolis C 4
Vérroia C 3
Vólos C 4
Xánthi D 3
Yiannitsá C 3
Zákinthos C 4

Physical Features

Aegean (sea) D 4
Ándros (isl.) D 4
Argolís (gulf) C 4
Áthos (mt.) D 3
Cephalonia (Kefallinía) (isl.) B 4
Corfu (Kérkira) (isl.) B 4
Corinth (gulf) C 4
Crete (isl.) D 5
Cyclades (isls.) D 4
Dodecanese (isls.) D 5
Euboea (isl.) C 4
Évros (river) D 3
Ionian (isls.) C 4
Ionian (sea) B 4
Itháki (Ithaca) (isl.) C 4
Kálimnos (isl.) D 4
Kefallinía (Cephalonia) (isl.) B 4
Kérkira (Corfu) (isl.) B 4
Khíos (isl.) D 4
Kíthira (isl.) C 4
Kíthnos (isl.) C 4
Kos (isl.) D 4
Lakonía (gulf) C 4
Lésvos (isl.) D 4
Matapan (Taínaron) (cape) C 4
Míkonos (isl.) D 4
Mirtóön (sea) C 4
Náxos (isl.) D 4
Northern Sporades (isls.) D 4
Olympus (mt.) C 3
Parnassus (mt.) C 4
Páros (isl.) D 4
Pindus (mts.) C 4
Rhodes (isl.) E 4
Sámos (isl.) D 4
Samothráki (isl.) D 3
Síderos (cape) D 5
Síros (isl.) D 4
Taínaron (Matapan) (cape) C 4
Thásos (isl.) D 3
Thermaic (Salonika) (gulf) C 4
Tínos (isl.) D 4
Toronaic (gulf) D 4
Zákinthos (Zante) (isl.) C 4

RUMANIA

Cities and Towns

Alexandria D 3
Arad C 2
Bacău D 2
Baia Mare C 2
Băileşti C 2
Bîrlad D 2
Bistriţa D 2
Botoşani D 2
Brăila D 2
Braşov D 2
Bucharest (Bucureşti) (capital) D 2
Buzău D 2
Călăraşi D 2
Caracal D 2
Caransebeş C 2
Carei C 2
Cîmpina D 2
Cîmpulung D 2
Cluj C 2
Constanţa E 2
Craiova C 2
Dej C 2
Deva C 2
Făgaraş D 2
Feteşti D 2
Focşani D 2
Galaţi D 2
Giurgiu D 2
Huşi D 2
Iaşi D 2
Lugoj C 2
Mediaş D 2
Oradea C 2
Paşcani D 2
Petroşeni C 2
Piatra Neamţ D 2
Piteşti D 2
Ploieşti D 2
Rădăuţi D 2
Reşiţa C 2
Rîmnicu Sărat D 2
Rîmnicu Vîlcea C 2
Roman D 2
Roşiori de Vede D 2
Salonta C 2
Satu Mare C 2
Sfîntu Gheorghe D 2
Sibiu C 2
Sighet C 2
Sighişoara D 2
Suceava D 2
Tecuci D 2
Timişoara C 2
Tîrgovişte D 2
Tîrgu Jiu C 2
Tîrgu Mureş D 2
Tulcea E 2
Turda C 2
Turnu Magŭrele D 3
Turnu Severin C 2

Physical Features

Argeş (river) D 2
Criş Alb (river) C 2
Criş Repede (river) C 2
Danube (river) C 3
Jiu (riv.) C 2
Mureş (river) C 2
Olt (river) D 2
Prut (river) E 2
Siret (river) D 2
Timiş (river) C 2
Transylvanian Alps (mts.) D 2

YUGOSLAVIA

Cities and Towns

Banja Luka B 2
Bečej B 2
Belgrade (Beograd) (capital) C 2
Bihač A 2
Bijeljina B 2
Bitola (Monastir) C 3
Bjelovar B 2
Brod B 2
Čačak C 3
Celje A 2
Cetinje B 3
Ćuprija C 2
Djakovica C 2
Dubrovnik (Ragusa) B 3
Fiume (Rijeka) A 2
Jesenice A 2
Karlovac A 2
Kikinda C 2
Koprivnica B 2
Kosovska Mitrovica B 3
Kragujevac C 2
Kruševac C 3
Kumanovo C 3
Leskovac C 3
Ljubljana A 2
Maribor A 2
Monastir (Bitola) C 3
Mostar B 2
Niš C 3
Novi Pazar C 3
Novi Sad B 2
Ohrid C 3
Osijek B 2
Pančevo C 2
Paraćin C 3
Peć C 2
Pirot C 3
Podgorica (Titograd) B 3
Pola (Pula) A 2
Požarevac C 2
Prilep C 3
Priština C 3
Prizren C 3
Pula (Pola) A 2
Ragusa (Dubrovnik) B 3
Rijeka (Fiume) A 2
Šabac B 2
Sarajevo B 3
Senta B 2
Sisak B 2
Skopje C 3
Smederevo C 2
Sombor B 2
Split B 3
Sremska Mitrovica B 2
Štip C 3
Strumica C 3
Subotica B 2
Tetovo C 3
Titograd (Podgorica) B 3
Titov Veles C 3
Titovo Užice B 3
Tuzla B 2
Valjevo C 2
Varaždin A 2
Vinkovci B 2
Virovitica B 2
Vranje C 3
Vršac C 2
Zadar (Zara) A 2
Zagreb A 2
Zaječar C 3
Zenica B 2
Zrenjanin C 2

Physical Features

Adriatic (sea) A 3
Brač (isl.) B 3
Cres (isl.) A 2
Dinaric Alps (mts.) B 3
Drava (river) B 2
Drina (river) B 2
Durmitor (mt.) B 3
Hvar (isl.) B 3
Korčula (isl.) B 3
Krk (isl.) A 2
Kvarner (gulf) A 2
Lošinj (isl.) A 2
Morava (river) C 2
Mura (river) C 2
Ohrid (lake) C 3
Pag (isl.) A 2
Rab (isl.) A 2
Sava (river) A 2
Scutari (lake) B 3
Vardar (river) C 3

BALKAN PENINSULA
CONIC PROJECTION
SCALE OF MILES
0 25 50 100 150 200 250
SCALE OF KILOMETRES
0 60 120 180 240 300
Capitals of Countries
Canals
International Boundaries
Copyright by C.S. HAMMOND & Co., N.Y.
A 16° B Longitude 20° East of C Greenwich 24° D 28°
A 16° B 20° C 24° D 28° E
1 48° 2 44° 3 40° 4 5 36°
CZECHOSLOVAKIA
POLAND
U. S. S. R.
AUSTRIA
HUNGARY
RUMANIA
YUGOSLAVIA
BULGARIA
ALBANIA
GREECE
TURKEY
ITALY
ADRIATIC SEA
IONIAN SEA
MEDITERRANEAN SEA
BLACK SEA
AEGEAN SEA
SEA OF MARMARA
SEA OF CRETE
TYRRHENIAN SEA
Prague
Vienna
Budapest
Belgrade (Beograd)
Bucharest (București)
Sofia (Sofiya)
Tiranë (Tirana)
Athens
Istanbul
Transylvanian Alps
Balkan Mts.
Dinaric Alps
Rhodope Mts.
Pindus Mts.
Danube
Delta of the Danube
Bosporus
Dardanelles
Crete
Dodecanese Is.
Cyclades
Northern Sporades
Ionian Is.

pal pass of the range is the Shipka, at an elevation of more than 4000 ft. The range is also crossed by about twenty highways, three railroads, and the Iskar R.

The Balkan range is composed largely of folded sedimentary strata of limestone and sandstone rock with crystalline schists. Resources include deposits of lignite and other coal, graphite, copper, lead, zinc, and iron; mineral springs with therapeutic properties; and coniferous and deciduous forests.

BALKAN PENINSULA, peninsula in S.E. Europe that is bounded on the E. by the Black and Aegean seas, on the S. by the Mediterranean Sea, and on the W. by the Adriatic and Ionian seas. It comprises the countries of Yugoslavia, Albania, Greece, Rumania, Bulgaria, and European Turkey.

The N. boundary is not easily defined. It may be geographically defined as the Sava R.; the lower Danube R. from the point, at Belgrade, Yugoslavia, where the Sava joins it; and a line drawn arbitrarily from the upper Sava to the Adriatic near Rijeka, Yugoslavia. This boundary is easily recognizable on a map and, with a few exceptions, encompasses the countries generally defined as Balkan states, but it has no physiographical justification. It is historically justifiable because the region so defined (together with Rumania, and excluding Montenegro, Dalmatia, and the Ionian Islands) constituted the European territory of Turkey from the late 15th to the 19th century.

Most of the Balkan Peninsula is mountainous, with streams flowing in every direction. The drainage area of the Danube is the most important hydrographic feature. From the S. slopes of the Rhodope Mts. the Vardar R. flows into the Aegean Sea and, at the most westerly point of the Balkan Mts., the Morava flows into the Danube. The Balkan Mts. form the largest continuous range; other mountainous sections are the so-called Dinaric Alps along the Adriatic coast of Yugoslavia, the Rhodope chain between Macedonia and the Maritsa valley, the Pindus range N. in Greece, and isolated summits of historical importance, including mounts Olympus, Pelion, and Óssa in Greece. Lakes Scutari and Ohrid, both on the Albanian-Yugoslav border, are the only lakes of importance in the peninsula. The S. part of the peninsula, which forms the mainland of Greece, has a mild climate, but the rest of the region is subject to the severe winters and hot summers of S. central Europe. The N.W. portion has few lowlands and is characterized by unbroken, jagged hills; the S. portion has much more level terrain.

The first peoples to migrate into the Balkans arrived from all directions: central Europe, S. Europe, Asia, Asia Minor. During the rule of the Roman and Eastern Roman (Byzantine) empires (1st cent. A.D. until the late Middle Ages) the region was periodically invaded by various ethnic groups. The Slavs appeared around the 3rd century A.D. and migrated to the peninsula in large numbers in the 6th century, and Bulgar tribes appeared in the 7th century; eventually the Bulgars were assimilated by the Slavs. The Slavonic and the various other ethnic groups who settled in the peninsula evolved in comparative isolation because of the natural barriers to communication, each group developing its own religion, language, and customs.

History. Balkan history is characterized by the emergence of political identity among the peoples of the area in the 19th century, and by military and political strife. Because the peninsula is politically and economically important as part of the land bridge between Europe and Asia and the overland route from the Mediterranean to the Black Sea, it was subjugated for centuries by a series of conquerors. Intra-Balkan conflict has been common, and the Balkans have played a key role in European power struggles. The Balkans once were Roman provinces and the peninsula remained part of the Byzantine Empire (q.v.) until the late Middle Ages, when the Ottoman Turks invaded and gradually took control of almost the entire peninsula.

In the 19th century, one Balkan nation after another won independence from the Turks. The various, small Balkan countries emerged from the revolt against Turkish rule as autonomous nations. Historically, the Balkan struggle for liberation was the first pan-Balkan phenomenon, uniting the history of the many Balkan states.

At the end of the 19th century the Balkan countries were Rumania, Walachia and Moldavia, Bulgaria, Greece, Albania, Serbia, Montenegro, and the Austrian provinces Bosnia and Hercegovina. The following years were marked by chronic friction and intrigue; in 1912 the Balkan Wars (q.v.) began and in 1914 World War I broke out.

After World War I the Austrian provinces Bosnia and Hercegovina; the provinces of Croatia, Slavonia, and Carniola; and the former countries of Serbia and Montenegro united into the Kingdom of the Serbs, Croats, and Slovenes, later named Yugoslavia. As a consequence of the Balkan Wars and World War I, European Turkey had virtually ceased to exist.

Between the two world wars statesmen tried to prevent the Balkan countries from becoming again the "powder keg of Europe". A Balkan Entente between Yugoslavia, Turkey, Greece, and Rumania was signed in 1934 but the international friction and open rifts that preceded World War II were not lessened. Turkey and Greece resisted the infiltration of the Axis Powers (q.v.), but the influence of Italy and Germany was strong in the other Balkan countries. In April, 1939, Italy seized Albania. After the outbreak of World War II Italy invaded Greece in October, 1940, but was thrown back into Albania, while the Germans swept through Rumania and Bulgaria. Yugoslavia and Greece fell to the Germans early in 1941 despite stubborn resistance, which continued throughout the war. Bulgaria and Rumania officially joined the Axis, but Yugoslavia and Greece established Allied governments-in-exile, which were replaced at the end of the war by provisional governments, and finally by the Kingdom of Greece and the Republic of Yugoslavia. Albanian resistance forces set up a provisional government that gained control after German withdrawal from the Balkans and proclaimed Albania the People's Republic of Albania. Upon the defeat of the Axis, a republic was also established in Bulgaria.

For recent history of the Balkan countries, see separate articles on each country.

BALKAN WARS, two consecutive wars among the various countries of the Balkan Peninsula (q.v.), fought during the interval between the gaining of their independence from the Ottoman Empire and World War I. At the close of the Russo-Turkish War of 1877–78, the Treaty of Berlin (July 13, 1878) provided for an autonomous principality of Bulgaria; the remaining Bulgarian province, called Eastern Rumelia, was placed under the control of the Ottoman Turks. In 1885 a revolution broke out in Eastern Rumelia and the province was joined to Bulgaria proper. That voluntary annexation led to trouble with Russia.

The czar withdrew all Russian officers then serving in the Bulgarian army, and Milan (1854–1901), King of Serbia thought it a propitious hour to realize the territorial aspirations of the Serbs. Serbia declared war on Bulgaria, Nov. 14, 1885, and, in a campaign that lasted less than five months, was defeated, but was saved from absolute destruction by the intervention of Austria. Then followed a series of conspiracies. The Bulgarian ruler, Prince Alexander I of Battenberg (1857–93), was abducted by Russian and Bulgarian conspirators but was recaptured in a few days. He was forced to abdicate, and left the country in September, 1886. Prince Ferdinand I (1861–1948) of the house of Saxe-Coburg-Gotha succeeded Alexander as ruler a year later.

Austria played a conspicuous role in Balkan disturbances and the chief policy of the Austrian foreign ministers seemed to be the establishment of internal discord between the Slav countries (Bulgaria and Serbia) and the non-Slav ones (Greece and Rumania). War almost broke

Terraced farmland like this is highly valued in Montenegro, Yugoslavia, where much of the land is mountainous. Tomas Friedmann–Photo Researchers

out again in 1908 when Austria annexed Bosnia-Hercegovina, a step bitterly resented by Serbia.

The Balkan states saw in the Turkish revolution of 1908–09 and the Turko-Italian War of 1911–12 an opportunity to even scores with an old enemy. In March, 1912, Serbia arranged a treaty of alliance with Bulgaria. Greece concluded a military convention with Bulgaria the following May. Tension increased steadily in the Balkan Peninsula during the summer of 1912, especially after Aug. 14, when Bulgaria dispatched a note to the Turks demanding that Macedonia, then a Turkish province, be granted autonomy. The Balkan states began to mobilize on Sept. 30, and eight days later Montenegro declared war on the Ottoman Empire. On Oct. 18 the Balkan allies entered the war on the side of Montenegro, precipitating what is commonly known as the First Balkan War. The Balkan Alliance won a series of decisive victories over the Turks during the next two months, forcing them to relinquish Albania, Macedonia, and practically all of their other holdings in southeast Europe. Late in November the Turks sued for an armistice. An armistice agreement was signed on Dec. 3 by all the Balkan allies except Greece, which continued military operations against the Turks. Later in the month, representatives of the belligerents and the major European powers met in London to decide the Balkan question. The Turks rejected the peace conditions demanded by the Balkan states, and the conference ended (Jan. 6, 1913) in failure. On Jan. 23, a successful coup d'etat brought an extreme nationalist grouping to power in the Ottoman Empire, and within a week hostilities were resumed.

In the subsequent fighting Greece captured Ioánnina, and Adrianople (now Edirne) fell to Bulgaria. The Turks obtained an armistice with Bulgaria, Greece, and Serbia on April 19, 1913. Montenegro accepted the armistice a few days later. Another peace conference, with the major European powers acting again as mediators, met at London on May 20. By the terms of the Treaty of London, concluded on May 30, the Turks ceded Crete to Greece and relinquished all territories in Europe west of a line between the Black Sea port of Midye and Enez, a town on the coast of the Aegean Sea. Boundary questions and the status of Albania and the Aegean Islands were referred to an international commission.

The Treaty of London created friction among the Balkan allies, especially between Serbia and Bulgaria. Among the causes of the friction was the Bulgarian refusal to recognize the Serbian claim to certain Bulgarian-held portions of Macedonia. In addition, Serbia was resentful because of its failure to obtain territory along the Adriatic Sea. On June 1, 1913, Greece and Serbia concluded an alliance obviously aimed at Bulgaria. The conflict known in history as the Second Balkan War began on June 29. On that date a Bulgarian general, acting without orders from his government, launched an attack on Serbian defensive positions. The Bulgarian government disavowed this attack, but on July 8 Serbia and Greece declared war. Within the next two weeks Montenegro, Rumania, and the Ottoman Empire entered the war against Bulgaria; on July 30 Bulgaria, totally unable to withstand this coalition, asked and received an armistice. As a result of the ensuing peace agreement, signed at Bucharest on Aug. 10, Bulgaria lost considerable territory, including nearly 3000 sq.mi. allotted to Rumania. The agreement, among other things, awarded most of Macedonia to Serbia and Greece. Through later agreements Bulgaria was also forced to yield a large amount of territory to the Turks.

The Balkan Wars profoundly influenced the subsequent course of European history. By creating a strong and ambitious Serbia, the peace settlements engendered fear and anti-Serbian sentiment in neighboring Austria-Hungary. The dismemberment of the Ottoman Empire and Bulgaria created equally dangerous tensions in southeastern Europe. Under these conditions the contemporary forces making for a general European conflict became irresistible. *See* EUROPE: *History;* WORLD WAR I.

BALKH, town of Afghanistan, in Balkh Province, on the Balkh R., about 14 miles W. of Mazar-i-Sharif. Although Balkh is now a town of merely a few hundred houses set in the midst of ruins and debris, in ancient times it rivaled such cities as Nineveh and Babylon in population and wealth. Zoroaster (q.v.), reputedly died within the city walls. Known as Bactra, it became the capital of Bactria (q.v.), a province of the Persian Empire, from the 6th to the 4th century B.C. Several important commercial routes passed through the city, extending as far E. as India and China. Bactra was conquered by the Macedonian king Alexander the Great (*see* ALEXANDER III) in 328 B.C. and became the capital of the Greek kingdom of Bactria about 256 B.C. It was sacked by the Mongol conquerors Genghis Khan in 1220 and Tamerlane (qq.v.) in the 14th century. After the 18th century it was held by various rulers before coming under the control of the Afghans in 1950. Impressive remains of past civilizations can be seen in and near the town. Pop. (1967 est.) 10,000.

BALKHASH, LAKE, inland lake of the Soviet Union, about 900 ft. above sea level, in the S.E. part of the Kazakh S.S.R. It has the shape of an irregular crescent, extending N.E. for about one third of the total length of about 375 mi. and then in a generally E. direction; the maximum width is about 51 mi. and the area is 6700 sq.mi. The Ili R., the principal affluent, enters Lake Balkhash near its S. extremity. Other affluents enter the lake from the S.E. and from the N.E. The S. shores of the lake, which has no outlet, are labyrinths of islands, peninsulas, and strips of shallow water. Extending southward from Lake Balkhash is the Semirech'ye Plain. The land W. of the lake consists of clay plains, barren except for patches of wormwood, but it has been made fertile by irrigation and produces cotton, grapes, and a variety of other fruits. Copper, mined at Kounradskiy, about 25 miles N. of the lake, is shipped by rail to Balkhash, on the shore of the lake, where it is smelted and refined.

BALL, John (d. 1381), English priest, known for his association with the peasant revolt of 1381 led by Wat Tyler (q.v.). Little is known of Ball's early life. He preached the doctrines of the English theologian and religious reformer John Wycliffe (q.v.) and advocated social equality. Ball was imprisoned by ecclesiastical authorities for his activities, and, upon his temporary release by the rebels, he preached from the famous text:

"When Adam dalf, and Eve span,
Who was thanne a gentilman?"

Ball was executed at Saint Albans in the presence of Richard II (q.v.), King of England.

BALLAD (OF. *balade,* Fr. *ballade,* "dancing song"), in literary usage, a short, narrative poem, adaptable for singing and sometimes as an accompaniment to a folk dance, and simple in plot and metrical structure. The narrator has no role in the story of the ballad, nor does he usually reflect or comment on it. The most common ballad stanza consists of four lines. The first and third lines, which sometimes rhyme, contain four iambic feet; the second and fourth, which always rhyme, contain three iambic feet. A characteristic of many ballads is the refrain.

The ballad was generally the earliest form of poetry developed by the various peoples of Europe. Primitive epics or heroic poems, such as the *Poema del Cid* (*see* CID, THE), the *Nibelungenlied,* and the *Iliad* and *Odyssey* (qq.v.), produced respectively in Spain, Germany, and Greece, are believed by many scholars to have originated in collections or cycles of ballads; *see* EPIC POETRY. Particularly rich collections have survived in the literature of Spain, Germany, and Denmark. Perhaps the most extensive and most intensively studied ballads are those of England and Scotland, which were transported to North America.

The English and Scottish popular ballads show characteristics common to the folk ballads of most nations. The earliest folk ballads are believed by some scholars to have been composed by a group or a community as a whole in the course of a dance or folk festival. Other scholars believe that they were the work of anonymous poets, who obtained material from other literary works, particularly, as in the English and Scottish ballads, from the metrical romances that flourished from about 1250 to about 1400. Regardless of origin, the ballads were at first oral, not written, literature; they were a cultural expression of a period when few people could write or read. Ballads were transmitted by word of mouth through generations until they were written down by some scholar, monk, or antiquarian. The long development makes assigning a date of composition or determining a single, authoritative version impossible.

The English popular ballads date from early antiquity. The Angles and Saxons (qq.v.) knew many ballads at the time they invaded Britain during the 5th and 6th centuries. According to medieval chroniclers, the singing of ballads was common among the English people of that period. Few of these early English ballads were written. Only one manuscript ballad of the 13th century, "Judas", is extant; a later extant manuscript ballad, "Saint Stephen and Herod", dates from about 1450. The 15th century was the period of the greatest production of ballads in the British Isles, and the border country of England and Scotland was the area where most of them originated. In the 17th century, printers sold ballads in the form of broadsides, single sheets that contained the words of a ballad and a notation of some well-known tune to which it could be sung. Many traditional ballads were issued in this form, but most of the broadside ballads were based on sensational contemporary events and have no literary value.

The popular ballads of the British Isles, as of other areas, were for generations the possession of the people alone, but in Elizabethan times they began to attract the attention of literary men. William Shakespeare (q.v.) worked snatches of English ballads into his plays. Ben Jonson (q.v.), the Elizabethan playwright and poet, said he would rather have been the author of the ballad "Song of Percy and Douglas" than of all his own works. It was not until the English antiquary and poet Thomas Percy (q.v.), however, edited *Reliques of Ancient English Poetry* in 1765, that Englishmen as a whole realized that their popular ballads had genuine poetic quality. In 1802–03 appeared the first two volumes of another important collection of ballads, *Minstrelsy of the Scottish Border,* edited by the Scottish novelist and poet Sir Walter Scott (q.v.). The influence of the popular ballad began to appear in the works of 18th- and 19th-century poets who created various forms of literary ballads. Notable examples of literary ballads by British poets are "The Rime of the Ancient Mariner" by Samuel Taylor Coleridge, "La Belle Dame sans Merci" by John Keats, and "The Lady of Shalott" by Alfred Tennyson, 1st Baron Tennyson (qq.v.).

The greatest American authority on ballads was the philologist Francis James Child (1825–96). He compiled a collection of more than 300 British ballads, *English and Scottish Popular Ballads* (5 vol., 1883–98). The work, part of which was published posthumously, also contains ballads from many other countries (including France, Germany, and Spain) that parallel closely the events and wording of the ballads of England and Scotland; the similarities indicate a common origin.

Among English and Scottish ballads published in the collections mentioned above are many that fall into the following classifications.

1. Ballads about the English outlaw Robin Hood (q.v.) and his companions, known as the Robin Hood cycle. Among these are "Robin Hood and the Monk", *A Lytell Geste of Robyn Hode* (eight ballads combined into a short epic), and "Robin Hood's Death".

2. Historical ballads, such as "The Battle of Otterburn" and "Hugh of Lincoln".

3. Ballads of tragic love, such as "Child Waters" and "Bonny Barbara Allan".

4. Humorous ballads, such as "The Gardener", "The Farmer's Curst Wife", and "Get Up and Bar the Door".

5. Ballads dealing with domestic tragedy, such as "The Cruel Brother" and "The Twa Sisters".

6. Ballads of the supernatural. Among these are "The Wife of Usher's Well", "Kemp Owynne", and "Sweet William's Ghost".

7. Border ballads, such as "Bonnie George Campbell".

Most folk ballads of the United States are of English or Scottish origin, in particular the ballads of the inhabitants of the southern Appalachian Mts. and the Kentucky highlands. American ballads may be classified according to subject, as follows.

1. Ballads dealing with occupations. Examples of this type are "Casey Jones" (railroad workers) and "Git Along, Little Dogies" (cowboys).

2. Ballads dealing with various regions of the country. An example is "The Roving Gambler" (Kentucky and Tennessee mountains).

3. War ballads, such as "Yankee Doodle" (American Revolution) and "The Battle of Shiloh Hill" (Civil War).

4. Ballads dealing with racial groups, for example, "John Henry" (Negroes).

5. Ballads dealing with outlaws and other unconventional characters, such as "Billy the Kid" and "Frankie and Johnny".

Notable among literary ballads by American poets are "The Skeleton in Armor" by Henry Wadsworth Longfellow, "Skipper Ireson's Ride" by John Greenleaf Whittier, "The Heathen Chinee" by Bret Harte, and "The Chinese Nightingale" by Vachel Lindsay (qq.v.).

See FOLKLORE; FOLK MUSIC.

BALLADE, in literature, form of verse found chiefly in French poetry of the 14th and 15th centuries. The ballade, which admits limited variations, consists of three stanzas and an *envoy,* or a final stanza of four lines in the form of a personal address to a patron or judge of poetry. The stanzas are each composed of eight lines rhyming *ababbcbc,* and the envoy has the rhyme scheme *bcbc.* The last line, or refrain, is repeated at the end of each division.

The origin of the ballade has been traced to medieval Italian and Provençal verse forms, and the French form was first elaborated by the poet and musician Guillaume de Machaut (1300?–77). Well-known examples of the form were composed by the French poets François Villon (q.v.) and Charles d'Orléans (*see under* ORLÉANS). The medieval English poet Geoffrey Chaucer (q.v.) wrote noted ballades, and in the 19th century the form was revived by several British poets, including Algernon Charles Swinburne (q.v.) and Dante Gabriel Rossetti (*see under* ROSSETTI). *See also* MUSIC: *History: Late Gothic Music.*

BALL BEARINGS. *See* BEARING.

BALLET, theatrical spectacle in which a dramatic, poetic, or allegorical theme, set to music and often lavishly staged and costumed, is interpreted in dance and pantomime by trained performers. Sometimes applied arbitrarily to any staged dance performance, the term refers strictly to a specific type of theatrical dancing in which a distinct technique is employed. The characteristic style and beauty of ballet derive from this technique. Ballet is, accordingly, a dance composition or performance based on a rigidly classical system of body mechanics and

The American Ballet Theatre performs Pëtr Tchaikovsky's ballet Swan Lake, *with Natalia Makarova (center, left) as the Swan Queen.* Kenn Duncan

techniques developed and perfected over more than three centuries.

As distinguished from other dance forms, classical ballet is founded on five fundamental positions of the feet. In these positions, which are determined functionally by the position of the pelvis, hips, and thighs, the feet are always turned outward. The basic positions are complemented by various positions of the head and arms and by a variety of definite steps, leaps, turns, and combined movements. This complex kinetic system is devised ideally to assure balance, ease, precision, and lightness of execution, as well as grace, harmony, fluency, and elegance of motion.

The performance of traditional ballet requires a complicated technical apparatus as well as a highly professional organization. Ballets are therefore usually produced only by a permanently established group or company. The company generally comprises leading dancers, or soloists, and a supporting group, called the corps de ballet. In theory, a dancer advances from the corps de ballet to increasingly responsible positions assigned according to merit and experience. In practice, however, exceptional talent frequently is apparent while the dancer is a student, early enough for him to be discovered, cultivated, and elevated to leading rank. The female dancer aspires to the rank of ballerina or prima (first) ballerina; the male dancer hopes to become premier danseur (first dancer). Training, practice, and maintenance of technical efficiency for the whole company are the responsibility of a *maître de ballet* (ballet master).

The creation and design of a ballet generally are called choreography; the artist who designs and plans the performance is known as a choreographer. Certain customs and practices, but no absolute rules, apply to the content, form, and scope of a ballet composition. Although the ballet is a composite work involving coordinated, collective efforts, the choreographer assumes artistic responsibility for the creation as a whole. Inasmuch as the ballet is performed with music, a carefully balanced, functional relationship exists between the musical score and the choreography. The character, style, mood, and structure of a ballet may be inspired and determined by an existing musical composition, or the music may be especially commissioned so that it suits the subject, plot, or outline of action.

Because ballet developed within the theatrical tradition of brilliant and elaborate spectacles, the stage settings and costumes are important ballet accessories that are organically integrated into the total production. Certain principles of design prevail for practical as well as esthetic reasons. Primarily, the setting must provide the largest possible floor area for free dance movement and at the same time create an illusionary stage effect. The costumes serve mainly to enhance the physical beauty and the beauty of movement of the dancers. With rare exceptions, both male and female dancers wear tights. The typical female costumes are variants of either the tutu, a short, many-layered skirt, or the Taglioni, a loose, calf-length, flowing tulle skirt named for the famous Italian ballerina Marie Taglioni (1804–84). These traditional costumes are always worn with "blocked" shoes, which permit the dancer to poise or pivot on the tips of the toes.

HISTORY

One of the most prominent, popular, and enduring dance forms in the Western cultural tradition, ballet originated in Italy during the Renaissance (q.v.). It was largely an incidental product of ambitious attempts by Italian scholars and artists to re-create the dramatic performances of antiquity; such efforts also led to the development of opera (q.v.). In its initial phase, ballet used, expanded, and adopted many existing traditions, such as the formal customs of social etiquette, the patterns of ballroom and folk dancing, and the intricate techniques and elaborate stagings of the festivals, pageants, and tournaments of the aristocracy. While still in its infancy, this aristocratic and spectacular entertainment was introduced into France as a novelty by the Florentine-born Catherine de Médicis (q.v.), Queen Consort of France. In 1581 she commissioned the *Ballet Comique de la Reine* ("The Queen's Comic Ballet"). An enormously ambitious production, it is usually thought of as the first genuine ballet because it presented a connected dramatic action combining poetry, music, dance, and pageantry. The success of this venture established the new art as a fashionable court entertainment; it grew increasingly popular because it was primarily a large-scale social event in which many courtiers actively participated.

France subsequently became the unchallenged ballet center of Europe, especially during the reign of King Louis XIV (q.v.). The pleasure-loving king, who was an enthusiastic dancer, patronized the ballet with unparalleled generosity. He officially recognized its importance and artistic autonomy in 1661 by chartering a royal academy of the dance. This organization was absorbed in 1672 by the *Académie Royale de Musique et de Danse* (Royal Academy of Music and Dance), a newly created institution for the performance of opera and ballet. This first professional dance organization occupied a central position in the subsequent development of the ballet. From its inception, the academy received support and guidance from a host of eminent individuals, among whom were the composer Jean Baptiste Lully (q.v.), who was in charge of the music department as well as of the opera, and Charles Louis Beauchamps (1636–1719), *maître de ballet* and first director of the academy. Many other distinguished artists, including dancers, choreographers, musicians, writers, and designers, contributed their talents to the institution. The close connection between music and dance drama, manifested in the performance of brilliantly staged *opéra ballets,* set a precedent that still prevails to some extent. The most significant consequence of these innovations, characterized essentially by the change in the status of ballet from amateur amusement to professional performance, was the standardization of all previously accumulated practices and techniques. Taught by experts, practiced by professionals, and performed by a permanent company in a public theater, the ballet became a formally systematized and accurately codified art form. From this period of consolidation also dates the comprehensive and exact French ballet nomenclature, which is still in universal use.

The *opéra ballets,* which were often as much opera as ballet, were distinguished by elegance and visual splendor; the form, however, became rigidly formalized, and remained more decorative than meaningful, being impeded by heavy costumes, masks, and wigs retained from the court ballets. Perpetuating many empty formulas and obsolete usages, these hybrid ballets had obvious limitations. Changes, moreover, occurred very slowly because of the conservatism of the royal patrons and the unwieldiness of the official apparatus. The pantomime ballet, known as the *ballet d'action,* or *choréodrame,* developed independently and broke with the operatic tradition altogether by introducing new principles of dramatic coherence and stylistic consistency. The trend toward reform was accelerated by the rival French ballerinas Marie Anne de Cupis de Camargo (1710–70) and Marie Sallé (1707–56), who scandalized conservative opinion by raising their long trailing skirts from the floor to a point well above the ankle. Subsequently masks were discarded, and the encumbrances of the standard costume were eliminated. These reforms facilitated greater freedom of movement and, more importantly, of expressiveness.

The most powerful and influential exponent of the new tendencies was Jean Georges Noverre (1727–1810), dancer, choreographer, and theorist. In a treatise of enduring significance, *Lettres sur la Danse et sur les Ballets* ("Letters on Dancing and the Ballet", 1760), he defined ballet as an autonomous art form. He advocated a relative realism with increasingly personal expression and characterization and pleaded for a reasonable dramatic structure of the plot as well as for many other reforms. Many of the reforms advocated by Noverre had been suggested earlier by the French ballet master Louis de Cahusac (1700–59) in *La Danse Ancienne et Moderne* ("The Ancient and Modern Dance", 1754). Neither Noverre nor his many disciples and successors, however, denied the validity of the classical doctrines and canons that distinguish ballet unmistakably from all related forms of theatrical dance, musical drama, or pantomime.

Scene from Ballet Comique de la Reine *by Balthasar de Beaujoyeux, the first dramatic ballet, performed in 1581 at the court of Henry II of France under the sponsorship of his queen, Catherine de Médicis. The illustration is the frontispiece of the book of the ballet, published in Paris in 1582.*

19th Century. Although the surface formalism of ballet was not disturbed, the sentimental spirit of the Romantic movement affected the substance of ballet. The Romantic revolution, so influential in other art forms (*see* ROMANTICISM), was reflected in ballet essentially by a change of tone and subject matter. The Romantic sentiment was merely superimposed upon the orthodox classic code, as exemplified in the ballet *Giselle* (1841), which has well-known music by the French composer Adolphe Charles Adam (q.v.). This ballet tells a highly romantic story of a young girl betrayed by her lover; its dance patterns, however, are elaborate and formal. Although sentimental and emotionally excessive, the Romantic ballet was sustained by a genuine and enduring impulse to achieve flawless technical virtuosity. The Romantic ballet is held in nostalgic affection, however, mainly because of the almost magical aura surrounding the names

A scene from an old ballet, Tobacco, *choreographed by Count Filippo Aglié San Martino (1604–67), and performed in 1650 at the court of Turin. Members of the court performed in the ballet during this age.*

of several unique ballerinas, notably Taglioni, the Austrian Fanny Elssler (1810–84), the Italians Carlotta Grisi (1819–99) and Fanny Cerrito (1817–1909), and the Dane Lucile Grahn (1819–1907). The spirit of the period is characterized by the idealization of evanescent beauty, symbolized in the ballerina through the ethereal, weightless grace of floating movement, the elevation on toe points (*sur les pointes*), effortlessly sustained balance, and slow, extended leaps supported by the partner.

The most important choreographer of this period was the Danish dancer and teacher August Bournonville (1805–79), who served as director of the Royal Danish Ballet from 1829 to 1877. This company still performs many of Bournonville's works, including *La Sylphide* (1836) and *Napoli* (1842). Among outstanding modern exponents of the so-called Bournonville style have been the Danish *danseur* Erik Bruhn (1928–), the Italian ballerina Carla Fracci (1936–), and the British Dame Alicia Markova (1910–).

In Italy, the Imperial Academy of Dancing and Pantomime, founded in 1812, became affiliated with La Scala (q.v.), the opera theater in Milan. The new academy gained international repute after the appointment in 1837 of Carlo Blasis (1795–1878) as director. Blasis became the most respected and admired ballet authority of the century in both choreographic practice and theory. His treatise on the dance code, which was published in 1830, provided the modern foundation of classic ballet technique, and his academy set the standard for the ballet schools of later generations. Thus, leadership in the ballet shifted gradually from France back to Italy; later it centered in Russia.

In Russia, Empress Anna Ivanovna (q.v.) had established an Imperial Academy in Saint Petersburg (now Leningrad) in the early 18th century. The academy supplied the dancers for the Imperial Russian Ballet. Another academy was founded in Moscow some years later. Both schools gave excellent training and performances, but instruction and direction were entrusted to foreign masters until late in the 19th century, and the leading dancers frequently were imported. By the end of the 19th century, when the other European ballet centers declined in importance, the Russian ballet, consistently patronized, supported, and directed, had developed the most exemplary training discipline, the best ensemble, and the most proficient virtuoso dancers in the world.

During this period in Russia many of the most famous works in the history of ballet were created. Largely the work of the great French choreographer Marius Petipa (1822–1910), these ballets include *The Nutcracker* (1892), *The Sleeping Beauty* (1890), and *Swan Lake* (1895), with music by the Russian composer Pëtr Ilich Tchaikovsky (q.v.); *Don Quixote* (1869) and *La Bayadere* (1877), scored by the French-Russian composer Ludwig Minkus (1827–90); *Le Corsaire* (1868), partly composed by the Italian Riccardo Drigo (1846–1930); and *Raymonda* (1898), with music by the Russian Aleksandr Glazunov (q.v.). Many of these works are still performed, especially by two notable companies in the Soviet Union: the Bolshoi Ballet (founded in 1776) of Moscow and the Leningrad Kirov Ballet. Famous Bolshoi ballerinas have included Galina Ulanova (1910–), Maya Plisetskaya (1925–), and Raissa Struchkova (1925–).

Numerous large-scale ballets were also produced in France, either by Petipa or under his influence. These productions include the popular *Coppélia* (1870) and *Sylvia* (1876), set to music by the French composer Léo Delibes (q.v.). At this time, ballets were included in almost all of the operas produced in Paris, although the German composer Richard Wagner (q.v.) refused to bow to this convention.

20th Century. Despite the great achievements of Petipa and Tchaikovsky, the Russian ballet at the beginning of the 20th century became artistically stale and lacking in creative vitality. At that crucial moment the young Russian dancer and choreographer Michel Fokine (q.v.) initiated reform that soon developed into a sweep-

A poster publicizing one of the great theatrical events of the Romantic age of ballet, the premiere of Pas de Quatre at Her Majesty's Theatre, London, on July 12, 1845. Featured were the four great ballerinas of the time —(left to right) Carlotta Grisi, Marie Taglioni, Lucile Grahn, and Fanny Cerrito. The ballet was choreographed by Jules Perrot, Grisi's husband, and the music composed by Cesare Pugni. Months of involved negotiation were required before the famous but temperamental ballerinas could be persuaded to take part. The production, which showed off the individual theatrical and technical skills of each of the dancers, was a phenomenal success. Theater Collection, Harvard University

Typical of the productions brought to the capitals of early 20th-century Europe by Sergei Diaghilev's Ballets Russes was Le Coq d'Or, *for which this set design was made.* Theater Collection, Harvard University

ing revolution. Without question the most illustrious single figure in the modern ballet, he rebelled against the lifeless mechanization and empty formalism prevailing in the Imperial Ballet. In many respects Fokine's reform was essentially a continuation and extension of Noverre's ideas. His central concept was that the ballet is a composite art in which dancing, music, setting, and costumes are of almost equal importance and must form a stylistically unified whole. This conception of the ballet implied, in practice, a break with almost all established conventions. The most famous Fokine ballets of this period are *Les Sylphides* (1903) and *Le Cygne* ("The Dying Swan", 1905).

The conservative Imperial Ballet offered Fokine little opportunity to put his theories into practice. Finally, in 1909, the astute ballet producer Sergei Diaghilev (q.v.) took Fokine and a group of talented young dancers to Paris, where they enjoyed considerable artistic freedom. Fokine's vision of ballet captivated the world, and Diaghilev provided the esthetic environment in which the vision could materialize. Among the dancers who appeared with the company was Anna Pavlova (q.v.), one of the great ballerinas of the world. Thus began a ballet era of unprecedented brilliance, originality, and excitement, lasting until Diaghilev's death in 1929.

The Diaghilev company, called the Ballets Russes, moved its headquarters in 1923 from Paris to Monte Carlo, where it became known as the Ballet Russe de Monte Carlo. During the years of its ascendancy, the roster of artists who worked occasionally or permanently in the company included almost every famous name in the worlds of ballet, music, and art. The only Russian ballet known to the Western world was the Ballets Russes.

After Diaghilev's death the original company broke up into a number of groups, each of which claimed legitimacy by adopting the name Ballets Russes, by hiring former Ballets Russes members, or by performing the original repertoire.

Among the remarkable personalities who

emerged from the original Diaghilev company were the Russian dancers and choreographers Waslaw Nijinsky, George Balanchine, and Leonide Massine (qq.v.), and the British dancer and choreographer Ninette de Valois (1898–).

Nijinsky was a legendary dancer and a choreographer of intuitive originality, but his works often aroused controversy. After the most auspicious beginnings, his career ended early because of mental illness.

Massine, for many years one of the most popular ballet dancers, was a versatile and inventive choreographer, noted especially for the production of intricate ballets set to great symphonies. Following Diaghilev's death, Massine became associated as director or choreographer with several ballet companies. The most influential of these during the 1930's and early 1940's was the Ballet Russe de Monte Carlo, which Massine left in 1943 in order to organize his own Ballet Russe Highlights.

George Balanchine, one of the foremost figures in contemporary ballet, was trained at the St. Petersburg Imperial School of Ballet. In 1933, when he was already a prominent choreographer with his own company in Paris, Balanchine was invited to organize an American ballet company. Although ballet was not alien to the United States, a continuous tradition had never existed there, and the outstanding ballet teachers, dancers, and companies had been imported. Supported by Lincoln Kirstein (1907–), one of the most important promoters of American ballet, Balanchine undertook the gigantic task of creating an indigenous American ballet company. Starting with a school, he slowly and methodically developed talented Americans into accomplished dancers. To this task Balan-

Waslaw Nijinsky and Tamara Karsavina (left), leading performers of Sergei Diaghilev's Ballets Russes, appear in the ballet duet Le Spectre de la Rose, *choreographed by Michel Fokine in 1911. Anna Pavlova (right) is shown on a poster in her most famous role, the solo dance* The Dying Swan, *created for her by Fokine in 1905.*

Theater Collection, Harvard University

MIRA-Hurok Concerts

Ballet. Plate 1. *Above: Antoinette Sibley and Derek Rencher in a Royal Ballet performance of* Romeo and Juliet, *choreographed by Kenneth MacMillan to music by Sergei Prokofiev. First presented in Leningrad by the Kirov Ballet in 1940, the work has become almost as much a part of the standard repertory as* Swan Lake *and* Giselle. *Below: Violette Verdy and Conrad Ludlow perform the first movement, "Emeralds", from the ballet* Jewels.

Martha Swope

Ballet. Plate 2. *John Prinz demonstrates the technical virtuosity and grace demanded of the male classical dancer in this leap, a grand jeté, during a male solo variation in Etudes, as produced by the American Ballet Theatre. The ballet was choreographed by Harald Lander to music by Knudaage Riisager, after piano pieces by Karl Czerny.*

Kenn Duncan

Poise, technical prowess, and theatricality characterize the art of Natalia Makarova, one of the outstanding ballerinas of today, shown here striking an "attitude" pose during the ballerina's solo in the Grand Pas de Deux from Don Quixote, produced by the American Ballet Theatre. Makarova, formerly a star of the Kirov Ballet of Leningrad, defected from the U.S.S.R. and now lives and dances principally in the United States.

Kenn Duncan

American ballet has produced outstanding works combining psychological motifs and expressive dancing, as in Fall River Legend, *in which this dramatic moment occurs. The work, choreographed by Agnes De Mille to music by Morton Gould, probes the causes of a Lizzie Borden-type murder. Shown here are (left to right) Gayle Young as the Father, Sallie Wilson as The Accused, and Lucia Chase as the Stepmother in the American Ballet Theatre production.* Kenn Duncan

Opposite page: Dances at a Gathering, *choreographed by Jerome Robbins to music by Frédéric Chopin, is a semiabstract ballet of poetic feeling and subtle relationships, in marked contrast to the choreographer's earlier works, in which he often adopted the idiom of jazz or Latin popular music and used contemporary themes as subjects. Shown here (left to right), are Patricia McBride, Kay Mazzo, and Sara Leland in the New York City Ballet production.*
Martha Swope

chine brought rare qualities of patience and faith, a mastery of choreography, unlimited imagination, and an extraordinary sense of classical style. The New York City Ballet, the result of Balanchine's efforts, is now one of the leading companies of the Western world.

Ninette de Valois, although not an original member of the Diaghilev group, nevertheless benefited considerably from her experience with the Ballets Russes. Capable and tenacious, she laid the foundations for a native British ballet academy and company. Both projects were very successful, and the ballet company gained a worldwide reputation as the Sadler's Wells Ballet. The company, renamed the Royal Ballet in 1956, has subsequently acquired even greater distinction, principally as a result of superb choreography by Sir Frederick Ashton (1906–), creator of such varied ballets as *Façade* (1931), *Symphonic Variations* (1946), and *Marguerite and Armand* (1963). The last work featured the combined artistry of guest artists: the British ballerina Dame Margot Fonteyn and the Soviet-born ballet dancer and choreographer Rudolf

Nureyev (qq.v.). These artists also appeared in the ballet *Romeo and Juliet* (1965), staged by the British choreographer Kenneth MacMillan (1930–) to music by the Russian composer Sergei Prokofiev (q.v.).

Another member of Diaghilev's Ballets Russes was the British ballet dancer and choreographer Anton Dolin (1904–), born Patrick Healy-Kay. Under the direction of Ninette de Valois, Dolin partnered Dame Alicia Markova from 1931 to 1935 in the Vic-Wells Ballet of London, predecessor of Sadler's Wells Ballet. The triumvirate helped establish national ballet in Great Britain. Dolin and Markova went on to dance in the Markova-Dolin Ballet Co. and in New York City with Ballet Theatre (now American Ballet Theatre). In 1950 they founded their own company in London, the Festival Ballet, for which Dolin, who was both premier danseur and artistic director from 1950 to 1961, choreographed various pieces. Featuring both new works and classical pieces including compositions by Fokine, Festival Ballet flourished initially under Dolin, and since 1968 under the guidance of the British prima ballerina Beryl Grey (1927–).

THE CONTEMPORARY SCENE

Current ballet activities are enlivened by a number of diversified companies, in addition to the established organizations mentioned previously. One of the oldest groups, the American Ballet Theatre, was launched in New York City as Ballet Theatre in 1939 and renamed in 1957; it has built up an impressive repertory that includes classical ballets as well as new and provocative creations. Among its outstanding contributions was the introduction to the U.S. of the psychological ballets of the British choreographer Antony Tudor (1909–). Tudor staged several productions of this type and created especially for Ballet Theatre what is usually considered to be his finest work, *Pillar of Fire* (1942).

Another member of Ballet Theatre, the American choreographer Jerome Robbins (q.v.), created the ballets *Fancy Free* (1944) and *Interplay* (1945), radically different works in which the traditional classical line was fused brilliantly with the modern jazz pattern. As associate artistic director (1949–63) of the New York City Ballet, Robbins contributed a number of highly

Dancers of the New York City Center Joffrey Ballet perform Trinity, *a ballet by choreographer Gerald Arpino that blends balletic and rock movement with music of great power and expressiveness written by Alan Raph and Lee Holdridge. Premiering in 1970, the work was acclaimed as an effective theatrical reflection of the youth culture of its day.*
Herb Migdoll

A ballet of the 1970's that recalls the commedia dell'arte, one of the theatrical forms of the Renaissance, is Theatre, *choreographed by Eliot Feld for the American Ballet Theatre. Shown here (left to right) are Terry Orr, Christine Sarry, and Eliot Feld in a lighthearted scene typical of the work. Its music was Richard Strauss' "Burlesque for Piano and Orchestra".*
Kenn Duncan

sensitive works to that company's repertory. *Dances at a Gathering* (1969), choreographed to piano pieces of Frédéric Chopin, marked his successful return to the company as choreographer and ballet master.

The City Center Joffrey Ballet, resident company of New York City Center since 1966, had its beginnings in the Robert Joffrey Ballet Concert of 1954, the first company formed by dancer, choreographer, and teacher Robert Joffrey (1930–). Joffrey's mixed-media ballet, *Astarte* (1967), a dazzling display of lights, film, dancers, and a rock band, soon became the greatest box-office success of the company. Exclusive to the company are the works of the principal choreographer and assistant director, Gerald Arpino (1929–), whose ballets range from the sheer exhibitionism of *Olympics* (1966), performed by the men of the company, to the elusive sensitivity of *Sea Shadow* (1962). The company's repertory is wide ranging and is particularly noted for its revival of works by Bournonville, Massine, and Kurt Joos (1906–).

The Nederlands Dans Theater, founded in 1959 by an American, Benjamin Harkarvy (1930–), with headquarters in The Hague, the Netherlands, has gained international recognition. Another notable company is the Stuttgart Ballet of Germany; since 1961, first under the direction of the British choreographer John Cranko (1927–73) and then under the American choreographer Glen Tetley (1926–), it has presented a wide variety of choreographic styles to international acclaim.

A striking feature of nearly all ballet companies today is their interest in both classical and contemporary works. Many of the latter reflect the influence of modern dance (*see* DANCE: *Modern Dance*), and some works represent combinations of new and old styles. Balanchine's *Jewels* (1967), for example, begins somewhat in the style of the Romantic Bournonville, then presents an athletic, jazzlike dance pattern, concluding with a grand Russian ballet in the style of Petipa. Like many contemporary choreographers, Balanchine utilizes the best elements of classical ballet, which include purity of line and form; but he also allows for the freedom of movement and emotional release that much modern dance provides. Modern ballets have also been freed from the conventional story patterns of the past, so that, on the one hand, choreographers may explore themes of psychological realism as in Tudor's ballets, and on the other, they can present ballets with no story at all, as in many of the works of Balanchine. Satire and parody, characteristic of many Ashton creations, have also enlivened contemporary dance. The continuing performances of classical ballet, moreover, assure that dancers will develop great physical mastery, allowing them to undertake new works of virtually unlimited diversity.

M.B.M.

BALL GAMES, games played, since ancient times, with balls of various materials, shapes, and sizes, which are thrown, kicked, struck with a hand or fist, or propelled by a racket, mallet, or other instrument. *See* BASEBALL; BASKETBALL; BILLIARDS; CRICKET; CROQUET; FOOTBALL; FOOTBALL, AMERICAN; GOLF; HANDBALL; LACROSSE; POLO; RACKETS; SOFTBALL; TABLE TENNIS; TENNIS; VOLLEYBALL.

BALLISTIC MISSILE EARLY WARNING SYSTEM. *See* COAST DEFENSE: *North American Air Defense Command.*

BALLISTICS, science dealing with the motion of bodies projected through space. Ordinarily, ballistics is concerned with projectiles fired from cannon or small arms, but it may be concerned also with the free flight of bombs and the powered flight of rockets.

The motion of a projectile, from the instant of firing until impact at the target, is divided into three distinct phases, namely, interior ballistics, which treats of the motion of a projectile while it is still in the gun; exterior ballistics, which considers the motion of the projectile from the time it emerges from the gun until it reaches the target; and terminal ballistics, which deals with the effect of the projectile upon the target.

Interior Ballistics. Interior ballistics deals with the temperature, volume, and pressure of the gases resulting from combustion of the propellant charge in the gun and also with the work performed by the expansion of these gases upon the gun, its carriage, and the projectile. Some of the critical factors determined by interior ballistics are the relationship of the weight of charge to the projectile, the length of bore, the optimum size, shape, and density of powder grains for different guns, and the related problems of maximum and muzzle pressures.

The British engineer Benjamin Robins (1707–51) conducted many experiments relating to interior ballistics. His findings justly entitle him to be called the "father of modern gunnery". Modern experiments verify most of Robins' conclusions, but disagree principally with respect to maximum temperature and pressure. Late in the 18th century the Anglo-American physicist Benjamin Thompson, Count Rumford (q.v.), made the first attempt to measure the pressure generated by gunpowder. The account of his experiments was the most important contribution to interior ballistics that had been made up to that time.

About 1760 French ballisticians determined the relationship of muzzle velocity to length of barrel by measuring the velocity of a musket ball and cutting off a portion of the barrel before taking the velocity of the next shot. From such experiments and the use of modern knowledge of chemistry and thermodynamics, ballisticians developed formulas showing the relationship between muzzle velocity and weight and shape of projectile; weight, type, and grain size of power charge; pressure and temperature in the barrel; and the size of the powder chamber and the length of the barrel.

Exterior Ballistics. In exterior ballistics, factors such as shape, caliber, weight, initial velocities, rotation, air resistance, and gravity help determine the path of a projectile from the time it leaves the gun until it reaches the target.

Until the middle of the 16th century it was

Terminal ballistics: The curving trails of the smoke rockets indicate the progress of the expanding spherical shock front upon the explosion of a hemispherically arranged 500-ton charge of TNT. U.S. Army

believed that bullets moved in straight lines from the gun to the target and that shells fired from mortars described a path made up of two straight lines joined by an arc of a circle. The Italian mathematician Niccolò Tartaglia (1500?–1557), in a published work on gunnery, claimed that no part of the path of a projectile could be a straight line, and that the greater the velocity of the projectile the flatter its path. Tartaglia invented the gunner's quadrant used to determine elevation of the muzzle of a gun. The Italian scientist Galileo Galilei (q.v.) proved that in a vacuum a projectile describes a parabolic arc. The discovery of the law of gravitation by the British scientist Sir Isaac Newton (q.v.) made plain the cause of the curvilinear motion of projectiles; *see* GRAVITATION. By the use of calculus he determined the momentum transferred from the projectile to the particles of air at rest; this method of calculating air drag has been superseded by the use of tables prepared from experimental firings.

Two methods are known for determining the velocity of a projectile after it leaves the gun. One is by measuring the momentum of the projectile and the other is by measuring the time required for the projectile to pass over a given space. The first method is the older, and many years ago, when guns and projectiles were small, velocities low, and ranges short, the results were sufficiently accurate for most practical purposes. Modern gunnery is indebted to the ballistic pendulum and gun pendulum, devices subsequently supplanted by cheaper and more accurate machines working on the principles of the second method.

The ballistic pendulum was developed about 1743 by Robins, who was the first to undertake a systematic series of experiments to determine the velocity of projectiles. The principle of the ballistic pendulum, as well as of the gun pendulum, which was developed by Count Rumford, is the transformation of the elements of the momentum of the projectile in a small mass with high velocity to a large mass with low velocity. At that time, the momentum of the large mass was more easily measured.

The ballistic pendulum consisted of a plate of iron to which was bolted a block of wood to receive the impact of the ball; the pendulum was suspended freely from a horizontal axis. The block, when struck by the ball, recoiled through a certain arc which was measured by the length of a tape pulled from a reel. The arc of oscillation having been determined, the velocity of the ball could be found by calculation. The ballistic pendulum was able to withstand the impact of musket balls only; however, by determining the relations which should exist between the caliber, length of barrel, and charge of powder, Robins substantially advanced the science of gunnery.

By the second method, the velocity of a projectile is determined by measuring the time required for it to travel a known length of its path. Numerous machines have been devised for this purpose; in 1840 the British physicist Sir Charles Wheatstone (q.v.) suggested the use of electricity for measuring small intervals of time. This suggestion led to the development of the chronograph, a device for recording, by electrical means, the time required for a projectile to pass between two screens of fine wire.

The formulas and tables of exterior ballistics, like those of interior ballistics, are more or less empirical and must be tested by actual experiment before being fully accepted.

Terminal Ballistics. The laws which govern the impact of the projectile upon the target are the special domain of the third branch of ballistics. Like interior and exterior ballistics, terminal ballistics involves many empirical formulas. Theoretical investigations and experiments, however, are carried on in penetration, fragmentation, detonation, shape of charge, and related blast phenomena, including combustion and incendiary effects. Ballisticians derive the principles governing such factors as number, size, velocity, and spatial distribution of fragments produced by detonations of cased high-explosive charges. Terminal ballistics includes study of the propagation and effect of shock waves in earth, rock, air, and water insofar as these factors are related to a target.

Ballistics Measurement. The development of high-speed photography and of the stroboscope (q.v.) by the American engineer Harold Eugene Edgerton (1903–) and others has led to greater understanding in all three branches of ballistics. By means of such devices any projectile can be "stopped" in flight, thus permitting accurate studies not only of its velocity, but of its position (to determine degree of wobble) and even of the air waves it produces.

The most important recent development in ballistics is the use of computers. The calculus of exterior ballistics generally involves sets of second-order partial differential equations. The mechanics of solving such a set of equations typically involves 100,000 multiplications and divisions and a larger number of additions and subtractions. To find the position of the projectile at various points along the trajectory, dozens of such solutions are required. For each of various elevations of the gun, the entire process must be repeated. Even with the aid of slide rules and ordinary calculating machines, such an operation would take a mathematician an inordinate amount of time. Electronic computers compile complete solutions within a few minutes. Computers are used also for digital simulation of missile flights.

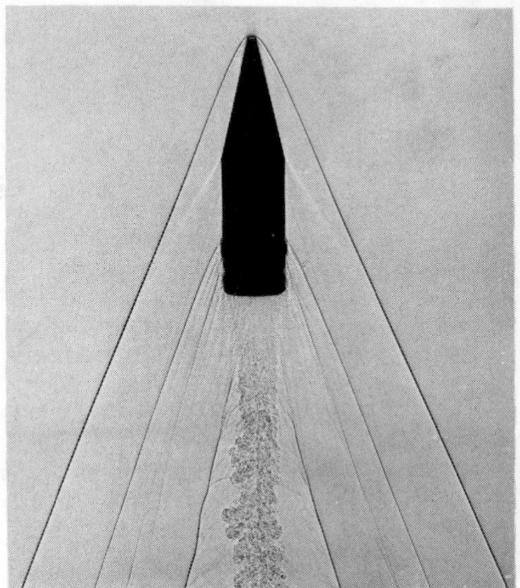

Exterior ballistics: Spark shadowgraph of the shock waves created by a 20-mm projectile at a 3600-ft.-per-sec. velocity. U.S. Army

The design, development, and calibration of a wide variety of highly specialized optical and electronic equipment in recent years have furthered considerably the advance of all ballistics research, particularly with respect to the performance of guided missiles. Examples of these instruments are long-focus tracking telescopes, photogrammetric cameras, and miniature radio transmitters and receivers installed in missiles. *See* GUIDED MISSILES. *See also* BOMBSIGHT; COMPUTER; ROCKET. U.S. DEPARTMENT OF THE ARMY

BALLOON, bag made of varnished silk, rubber, or other suitable material, and containing a gas that is lighter than air; it is usually approximately spherical in shape. The earliest balloons were filled with hot air and often carried a brazier to replenish the supply continuously. Modern balloons are filled with hydrogen or helium; helium has the great advantage of being noninflammable, but it is twice as heavy as hydrogen and has 7 percent less lifting power. Hydrogen weighs 0.071 lb. per cu.ft. less than air at standard atmospheric pressure and temperature, and

A contemporary sketch of the passenger balloon, built by the Montgolfier brothers, embarking on its maiden voyage in 1783. U.S. Air Force

a hydrogen balloon of 1000 cu.ft. is able to lift, therefore, about 70 lb. *See* ATMOSPHERE.

History. In 1783 Jacques Étienne Montgolfier (1745–99) and Joseph Michel Montgolfier (1740–1810), two wealthy papermakers of Annonay, France, sent up a balloon filled with hot air, and the French physicist, chemist, and areonaut Jacques Alexandre César Charles (q.v.) released one filled with hydrogen, which made a successful flight. The same year also marked the first actual balloon ascent by men, when the French physicist Jean François Pilâtre de Rozier (1756–85) made flights near Paris, first in a captive, and later in a free balloon. Two years later the French aeronaut Jean Pierre ("François") Blanchard (q.v.), accompanied by John Jeffries (1744–1819), an American, made the first balloon crossing of the English Channel. The first balloon ascent in America was made at Philadelphia, Pa. on Jan. 9, 1793. In 1836 *The Great Balloon of Nassau,* of 85,000 cu.ft. capacity, sailed 500 mi. from London, England, to Weilburg, Germany, in 18 hr. During the Franco-German War of 1870, balloons were used for military observation by the armies of both nations, and the French minister Léon Gambetta (q.v.) made a dramatic escape from the besieged city of Paris by balloon. The distance record for the flight of manned balloons was set during 1914, when the balloon *Berliner* traveled from Bitterfeld, Germany, to Perm', Russia, a distance of 1896.8 mi. The armies engaged in World War I made extensive use of balloons, especially for military observation. Interest in ballooning as a sport was stimulated by the Gordon Bennett Balloon Trophy Races, held annually, except during World War I, from 1906 when the American journalist James Gordon Bennett (q.v.) donated the trophy, to the start of World War II, when the races were discontinued.

Sport ballooning still enjoys limited popularity in Europe, where hydrogen-filled balloons are used almost exclusively. In the United States in recent years a resurgence in interest has taken place in sport ballooning, using hot-air balloons that are kept aloft with butane or propane burners.

High ascents in balloons have been made by a number of aeronauts. In 1931 the Swiss physicist Auguste Piccard (q.v.) ascended into the stratosphere in a spherical, airtight, metal cabin suspended from a specially-constructed, hydrogen-filled balloon of 494,400 cu.ft. capacity, reaching an altitude of 51,793 ft. The following year, in a second ascent, he reached 54,120 ft. In 1935, Capt. Orvil Anderson (1895–1965) and Capt. Albert William Stevens (1886–1949) of the U.S. Army ascended to a height of 72,394.795 ft.; their takeoff point was about 11 mi. from Rapid City, S.D., and they landed about 12 mi. from White Lake, S.D.

In August, 1957, Maj. David Simmons, a U.S. Air Force surgeon, ascended to about 102,000 ft., remained in the air 32 hr., and drifted 405 mi. from his takeoff point. The flight was designed to chart the reactions of man at high altitudes. On August 27, 1960, Capt. Joseph Kittinger of the U.S. Air Force bailed out of a polyethylene plastic balloon at 102,800 ft., setting a new altitude record for balloon flight and a new record for parachute descent. On May 4, 1961, the Americans Malcolm Ross and Victor Prather set a record of 113,700 ft. on a flight launched from a U.S. Navy aircraft carrier.

Modern Scientific Ballooning. Three types of balloons are in common use for scientific research or meteorological observations.

The rubber or neoprene balloon is used for vertical soundings, either as a pilot balloon or as a radiosonde-carrying balloon. The balloon, inflated with a lifting gas (hydrogen, helium, ammonia, or methane), stretches as it ascends into thin air. When the balloon has stretched from three to six times its unstressed length (that is, when its volume has increased 30 to 200 times its original amount), the skin ruptures.

The zero-pressure plastic (usually polyethylene) balloon is used to carry scientific instruments to a predetermined density level. The plastic balloon is filled only partially with gas while on the ground. As the balloon ascends, the expanding gas fills the envelope. This type of balloon has a valve that automatically discharges excess gas when the balloon reaches its constant-density altitude, so that the balloon can maintain this altitude. When the sun sets, the gas cools, the volume decreases, and the balloon descends to the ground, unless ballast is released.

The superpressure balloon is a nonextensible balloon that is sealed to prevent the release of gas. By the time the balloon reaches its constant-density level, the free-lift gas has become pressurized. Variations in the air pressure caused by the heat of the sun produce changes in the internal gas pressure but the volume of the balloon remains fixed. So long as the balloon remains under pressure, therefore, it continues to float at its predetermined constant-density level.

The highest balloon flight was made by an American-made balloon flown from West Germany on June 9, 1966, reaching an altitude of 168,000 ft. before bursting. This balloon was made of neoprene and carried a 5-lb. radiosonde instrument. The highest flight of a plastic balloon was made in September, 1959, when a balloon reached 150,000 ft. The heaviest payload carried by a plastic balloon was 10,620 lb. The largest balloon flown had a volume of 26,000,000 cu.ft. A number of flights were made with this balloon in 1967 to test instruments to be used for possible research on Mars.

Around the world each day radiosonde balloons make over 1000 soundings of the winds, temperature, pressure, and humidity in the upper atmosphere (*see* METEOROLOGY: *Upper-Air Observations*). These flights are made almost exclusively from land areas. As a result, adequate measurements of the atmosphere are made over less than 20 percent of the globe. To obtain coverage over ocean areas, Global Horizontal Sounding Technique (GHOST) balloons are being flown experimentally from the Southern Hemisphere. The longest flight so far made with this superpressure design was 313 days.

For information regarding lighter-than-air craft equipped with apparatus for power and steering, *see* AIRSHIP. V.E.L.

BALLOON VINE, common name for Cardiospermum halicacabum, a tropical, perennial vine of the Soapberry family (Sapindaceae). The balloon vine is characterized by alternate leaves, each having three groups of three leaflets, and by small, white flowers in axillary racemes. In the United States it is grown as an annual and reaches a height of 10 ft. The balloonlike capsules contain black seeds, each with a white, heart-shaped mark. Balloon vine is also known by several other names, as heartseed, heartpea, or Love-in-a-puff.

BALLOT (Fr. *balla,* It. *ballòtta,* "little ball"), in modern usage, a sheet of paper used in voting, usually in an electoral system that allows the voter to make his choices secretly. The term may also designate the method and act of voting secretly by means of a mechanical device. Used in elections in all democratic countries, the ballot method protects voters from coercion and reprisal in the exercise of their vote. Wherever the practice of deciding questions by free vote has prevailed, some form of secret voting has always been found necessary. In ancient Greece, the dicasts (members of high courts) voted secretly with balls, stones, or marked shells. Legislation was enacted in Rome in 139 B.C. establishing a system of secret voting. Long before the passage of this law, however, questions sometimes were decided in Rome in public meetings by means of the ballot. Colored balls were used as ballots during the Middle Ages (q.v.). This form has survived to modern times, particularly in clubs or associations in which voting decides the question of admitting or rejecting proposed new members. Each voter receives two balls, one white indicating acceptance and the other black indicating rejection; they are then deposited secretly in appropriate receptacles so as to indicate a favorable or unfavorable decision. According to the system in some organizations, candidates for admission are rejected if any black balls are found among the white balls.

In modern times, the most common form of ballot has been the written or printed ticket. Although the ballot had been used previously by the British Parliament for the purpose of concealing the voting record of its members, in 1710 the House of Lords rejected a proposal of the House of Commons providing for secret voting on matters before Parliament (q.v.). The French Chamber of Deputies voted by ballot from 1840 to 1845. With the development of democracy the practice of voting secretly in legislative assemblies responsible to the people was generally abandoned.

Toward the end of the 18th century, demands were made in Great Britain that elections to Par-

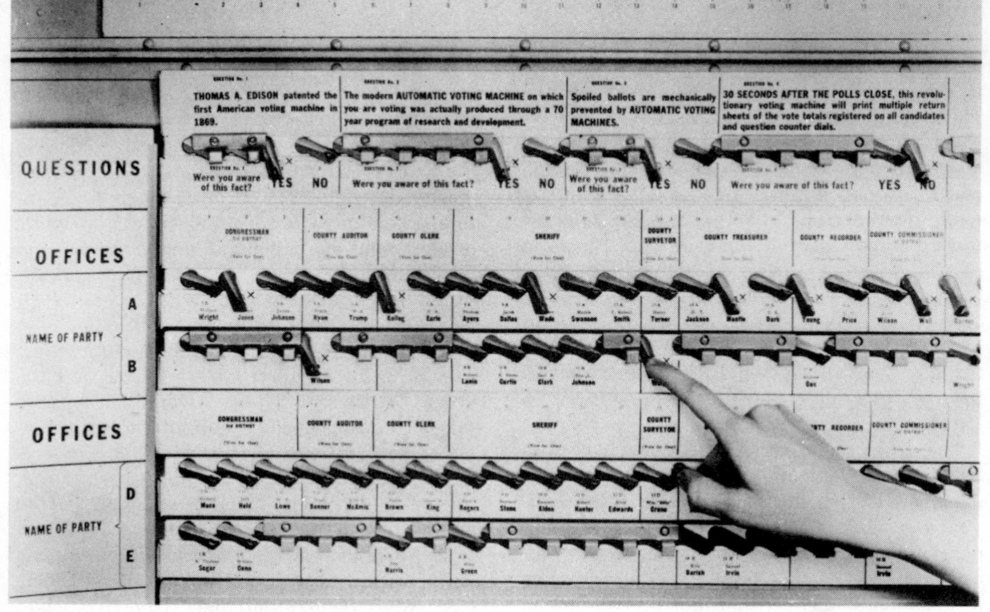

Simulated ballot being voted on an automatic voting machine. The voter indicates a choice by pressing the lever.

liament be conducted by secret ballot, but the first proposal of this kind was not introduced into Parliament until 1833. The proposal was rejected, but subsequently advocates of Chartism (q.v.) incorporated the demand in their petitions to Parliament. Despite repeated attempts by proponents of the legislation to secure its enactment, Parliament took no effective action until 1872. In that year the Ballot Act was approved, providing for secret voting at all parliamentary elections, except parliamentary elections held at universities, and at all municipal elections. Similar legislation had been previously adopted in France (1852) and Italy (1859).

BALLOTING IN THE UNITED STATES

Following the American Revolution (q.v.), the secret ballot, used universally during the period of British colonial rule, was adopted in most of the newly established States of the United States. Development of the political party system resulted in various abuses of the ballot system in many States during the first half of the 19th century, when the law permitted the printing and distribution of ballots to the voters both by candidates and by political organizations. This system, which led to confusion and fraud at the polls, produced widespread public sentiment for ballot reform. In 1888 the Massachusetts State legislature initiated remedial action, adopting legislation which provided for the so-called Australian ballot (q.v.) in State elections. The principal features of this method, first used in Australia in 1856 and subsequently adopted by every State in the Union, are: the preparation, printing, and distribution of the ballot by government agencies; the use of a blanket ballot listing the names and party designations of all candidates for all offices to be filled; and secret voting under government supervision.

Formerly, most States of the U.S. used the party-column type of blanket ballot, in which the names of candidates are arranged in columns allocated to their respective political parties. By 1967, however, most States had adopted the office-column type of listing, in which the names are arranged under the office sought, either alphabetically or by party, with the party label appearing after the name in either case. When the party-column ballot is used the party emblem is often added to the party column and the party circle. In some places a party emblem is used on the office-column ballot, as in New York State. The purpose of the emblem and the party circle is to make it easier for loyal but ill-informed party voters to vote a straight party ticket. In addition, some States, counties, and cities provide ballots with extra space for write-in votes for candidates not listed. The preferential ballot, now rarely used, allows voters to indicate with numerals the order of their preference among the candidates for the same office; *see* PROPORTIONAL REPRESENTATION. The so-called long ballot, on which candidates for administrative as well as for legislative office were listed, has gradually been replaced, through the efforts of such reformers as President (Thomas) Woodrow Wilson (q.v.), by the short ballot listing names of legislative candidates only, administrative offices often being filled largely by appointment.

Various methods have been devised for the nomination (q.v.) of candidates to assure that only the names of authorized office-seekers appear on the ballot. Many States and localities require a candidate to file a petition before his name can appear on the ballot. The petition must contain a certain minimum number of signatures of registered voters from a certain minimum number of counties in the State, or districts in the locality. The validity of the signatures may then be challenged by other candidates, with final adjudication of disputes to be made by the appropriate board of elections, or in some cases by the courts.

Voting Machines. To facilitate voting and to reduce the possibility of fraud, a mechanical device operated either manually or electrically began to be adopted in various parts of the U.S. after 1892, when New York State first authorized such use. The list of candidates is arranged on the face of a voting machine according to the office-column model, either horizontally or vertically. The voter indicates his preference by placing a pointer next to the name of the candidate of his choice. Space is also provided for write-in votes. Each voting machine is equipped with curtains, which the voter closes to form a complete, private polling booth. When the voter has completed his voting he pulls a special lever that opens the curtains, returns the pointers to their original positions, and starts the mechanical counting devices that record and add up the votes. The use of voting machines in U.S. elections depends on State legislation; in 1967, for example, 9 States required the use of voting machines in all localities, 12 States required it in the majority of areas, and 25 States required it only in certain specific areas; 4 States did not require the use of voting machines.

Despite the fact that the Australian ballot system, or a modification of it, is used in all of the States of the U.S., fraudulent voting, although greatly reduced, still occurs in some communities. This is accomplished chiefly by "repeating", an unlawful practice whereby citizens register and vote at more than one polling place, and by "stuffing", or putting fraudulent extra votes into the ballot box. All such frauds are generally accomplished with the connivance of dishonest election officials, but may be counteracted in some cases by calling for a recount after votes have been tallied. In some States, where voting machines are used exclusively, it is claimed that virtually no fraudulence occurs, although efforts are sometimes made to damage voting machines so as to reduce the number of votes given to a favored candidate. *See* ELECTORAL REFORM. C.A.B.

BALM, common name for a fragrant, perennial herb, *Melissa officinalis,* in the Mint family (Labiatae). It is a native to Europe and has been introduced into North America. It has long been cultivated in gardens. The stems and leaves, formerly widely used in medicine as a gentle stimulant and tonic, are still occasionally used as such. The taste is somewhat astringent, and the odor slightly aromatic. A variety of the common catnip, *Nepeta cataria,* with an odor like that of balm, is often mistaken for it. Balmlike properties are common among the Labiatae (*see* MINT). The name balm is applied also to several balsamic resins obtained from balsam fir trees; *see* CANADA BALSAM; FIR.

BALMACEDA, José Manuel (1842–91), Chilean statesman, born and educated in Santiago. He served as a member of the Chilean national assembly and as a diplomat from 1878 to 1886, when he became president of Chile. He was a liberal who sponsored many public construction projects and a reform of marriage laws. In 1891 he lost the confidence of the assembly and attempted by a coup d'etat to become dictator. Civil war broke out and, after severe fighting, his troops were defeated; Balmaceda committed suicide.

BALMONT, Konstantin Dmitrievich (1867–1943), Russian poet, born in the province of Vladimir, and educated at the University of Moscow. Balmont was one of the leading Symbolists (q.v.) of Russian literature. He also wrote many critical essays. Some of the best known of his volumes of poems are *Under the Northern Sky* (1894), *Silence* (1898), *The Bird of Flame* (1907), and *Mirage* (1922). He also wrote many short stories, translations, and a book of poems for children.

BALMORAL CASTLE, private residence of British royalty in Aberdeen County, Scotland, on the Dee R., 48 miles W. of Aberdeen. The castle, which replaced an older structure, was erected between 1853 and 1855 as an informal country residence by Victoria (q.v.), Queen of Great Britain. The estate now covers 40,000 acres.

BALSA, common name for a tropical American tree, *Ochroma lagopus,* of the Silk-cotton Tree family (Bombacaceae). The tree may grow to a height of 60 to 70 ft. Balsa wood, also called corkwood, weighs 6 to 8 lb. per cubic foot and is lighter and stronger than cork. In color it resembles white pine or basswood. Balsa has long been used, especially in South America, for raft and boat building, and the term "balsa" is applied to a type of raft made of two parallel cylindrical logs connected by a platform or grating. The wood is also used for life-preserver floats, surfboards, and model airplanes; it is used in the interiors of aircraft to reduce vibration and as a sound insulator. Its heat-insulating quality permits its use in lining refrigerators and ship holds.

BALSAM, *or* TOUCH-ME-NOT, common name for any of several succulent, herbaceous plants of the genus *Impatiens* of the Touch-me-not family (Balsaminaceae). A familiar example is the garden balsam, *I. balsamina.* More than one hundred species are known, natives chiefly of damp, bushy places in the East Indies; many are plants of great beauty. They are almost all annuals and generally have white, red, or yellow flowers. The genus is distinguished by extreme variation of the flowers and by the beakless fruit, which is a five-celled capsule, bursting when ripe if touched or disturbed.

BALSAM, *or* BALM, any of several resinous substances obtained from various trees. The word balsam is applied to oleoresins such as benzoin or Canada balsam (qq.v.), but is generally understood to mean balsam of Peru or Tolu. *Myroxylon balsamum,* the source of balsam of Tolu, is a tree indigenous to Ecuador, Venezuela, and Brazil; *M. pereirae,* common from Peru to Mexico, is the source of balsam of Peru. Both are dark, fragrant, viscid liquids, used in confectionery and perfumes; they serve as expectorants and tonics in medicine. Balm of Gilead, produced by *Commiphora meccanensis,* has long been used in the East for its fragrance and reputed medicinal properties. The finest variety of balm of Gilead, called opobalsam or Mecca balsam, has the color and consistency of honey. Tacamahac, a substance used for the same purposes, is produced by a species of poplar, *Populus balsamifera.*

BALSAM FIR. *See* FIR.

BALTIC PROVINCES, former Russian governments of Estonia, Livonia, and Kurland (Courland). The region occupied by those governments was divided in 1918 between the newly established independent republics of Latvia and Estonia (qq.v.). *See* BALTIC STATES.

BALTIC SEA, enclosed sea in N. Europe, bounded by East and West Germany, Denmark, Poland, Lithuania, Latvia, Estonia, Russia, Finland, and Sweden. It is connected with the North Sea by a series of winding channels known as Öresund, Store Baelt, Lille Baelt, Kattegat, and Skagerrak. From the peninsula of Denmark, which may be considered its W. limit, the Baltic Sea extends E. to long. 30° E., and N. to about lat. 66° N. The greatest length of the baltic, from Lübeck, West Germany, to Haparanda, Sweden, is about 930 mi.; the breadth varies from 425 mi. (Stockholm to Leningrad) to less than 50 mi. at the S. extremity. It covers an area of about 160,000 sq.mi.

The N. extension consists of two large bays or gulfs, the Gulf of Bothnia, between Finland and Sweden, and the Gulf of Finland, between Finland and Soviet Russia. The Gulf of Riga is a prominent feature of the Russian coast. On the coasts of Poland and Germany are smaller indentations, including the Polish Gulf of Danzig and the bay of Szczecin (Stettin) and the West German bays of Lübeck and Kiel. The principal islands are Rügen Island (East German), Bornholm and the Danish groups, Gotland and Öland islands (Swedish), Saaremaa (Ösel) and Hiiumaa (Dagö) islands (Estonian), and the Åland Islands (Finnish).

The Baltic receives the drainage of a large part of N. Europe, including W. Russia, N.E. Germany, and nearly the whole of Sweden. As a result of this drainage and the restricted channel to the North Sea, the surface water of the Baltic contains only a third as great a percentage of salt as the Atlantic Ocean, and the salinity shows a tendency to decrease toward the W. and N. Surface currents of a low degree of salinity flow constantly from the Baltic to the North Sea, while deeper currents, with a larger content of salt, flow in the opposite direction. Tidal action is apparent only in the S. part of the Baltic.

Storms are frequent and often cause severe damage to shipping. Easterly winds are particularly dangerous because they create huge tidal waves. Navigation in the N. part is suspended during the winter and early spring because of ice.

The Baltic is of great commercial importance to N. Europe. The most important ports are Copenhagen, Denmark; Kiel and Lübeck, West Germany; Szczecin, Gdańsk, and Gdynia, Poland; Kaliningrad, Leningrad, and Kronshtadt, Russian S.F.S.R.; Riga, Latvian S.S.R.; Tallinn, Estonian S.S.R.; Helsinki and Turku, Finland; and Stockholm, Karlskrona, and Malmö, Sweden. The Baltic is connected with the North Sea by an artificial waterway, the Nord-Ostsee Canal, about 60 mi. long.

BALTIC STATES, former republics of Estonia, Latvia, and Lithuania, on the E. coast of the Baltic Sea. The republics, established in 1918, comprised the territory formerly occupied by the

Baltic Provinces and parts of various other Russian governments, including Vilna and Kaunas. The Baltic States were incorporated into the Union of Soviet Socialist Republics in 1940, during World War II; the following year they were occupied by the Germans, who remained until the U.S.S.R. again took control in 1944.

BALTIMORE, largest city in Maryland, and one of the largest cities and principal seaports of the United States, at the head of navigation on the Patapsco R., about 12 mi. from Chesapeake Bay and about 170 mi. from the Atlantic Ocean. At the entrance to Baltimore harbor the Patapsco divides into three branches. The N.W. branch projects 2½ mi. into the heart of the business district of the city. The S.W. and middle branches envelop the S. and S.W. sections, providing a long expanse of waterfront close to the lines of the Baltimore and Ohio, the Western Maryland, and the Penn Central railroads. The main harbor, on the N.W. branch of the river, has a waterfront, measured on the pierhead line, of 6½ mi. and covers 630 acres. The harbor on the S.W. and middle branches has, within the city limits and measured on the pierhead line, a waterfront of 5½ mi., an area of 1300 acres, and channels that are 35 ft. deep at mean low water.

Baltimore is noted for its educational and cultural institutions. It is the site of Johns Hopkins University (q.v.), the University of Maryland, Goucher College, Saint Mary's Seminary and University, Loyola College, College of Notre Dame of Maryland, the Peabody Institute of the City of Baltimore, Maryland Institute College of Art, Coppin State College, Morgan State College, Mount Saint Agnes College, and the Baltimore College of Commerce. Cultural institutions include the Walters Art Gallery, the Baltimore Museum of Art, the Maryland Academy of Sciences, and the Maryland Historical Society. The city has a symphony orchestra and a civic opera company.

Baltimore has more than 600 churches of various denominations. It is the seat of the Roman Catholic archdiocese of Baltimore. Of particular architectural note is the Latin-cruciform Cathedral of the Assumption, the first cathedral in America. Dedicated in 1821, it contains paintings given by Louis XVIII and Charles X of France.

Among places of interest in Baltimore are Fort McHenry National Monument and Historic Shrine (q.v.); Westminster Churchyard, containing the grave of the American writer Edgar Allan Poe (q.v.); the home of Poe, typical of the straight-brick-front architecture of the period; and the Pimlico racetrack, in the northwest. In East Baltimore, the houses of the "Old Town" are characteristic of the 19th century, as are the row houses with white steps found throughout the city. The oldest house in Baltimore is Mount Clare, built about the middle of the 18th century. Numerous statues and monuments commemorate persons and events of historic interest. Among them are the Washington Monument (1815–29), on Mount Vernon Place; the first monument to Christopher Columbus in the Americas, dedicated in 1792; the Battle Monument; the World War I Memorial; and statues of Francis Scott Key, Edgar Allan Poe, and Martin Luther (q.v.).

Baltimore harbor, on the estuary of the Patapsco River, is one of the major ports and shipbuilding centers of the United States. Baltimore Chamber of Commerce

The park system of Baltimore comprises about 4000 acres and includes Druid Hill Park (674 acres), site of the city zoo and aquarium and of the museum of the Natural History Society of Baltimore. The city is the home of the Baltimore Colts professional football team and the Baltimore Orioles professional baseball team.

Baltimore is governed by a mayor and council. Although it lies within Baltimore County, the city is an independent political unit.

Baltimore is the third-largest foreign-tonnage port in the U.S. Leading exports include corn, iron and steel products and scrap, coal, tinplate, wheat, phosphates, soybeans, copper bars and slabs, and heavy machinery. Imports include iron, manganese, and chrome ores, crude oil, sugar, wood pulp, molasses, and bananas. The manufacturing enterprises of Baltimore are widely diversified. Situated in Baltimore or in the Baltimore Industrial Area (including Baltimore County) are a magnesium rolling mill, copper and petroleum refineries, and plants producing missiles and spacecraft, steel for

The Washington Monument in Baltimore, completed in 1829, houses a museum of history in its base.

Baltimore Chamber of Commerce

shipbuilding and repairs, radio and telephone equipment, automobiles and accessories, fertilizers, and chemicals. Other leading industries are shipbuilding, food processing, banking, insurance, and wholesale distributing.

History. Baltimore was founded in 1729 and named in honor of George Calvert, 1st Lord Baltimore (*see under* CALVERT), who was granted the territory comprising present-day Maryland by Charles I (q.v.), King of England in 1632. It received a city charter in 1797. Chiefly from Baltimore came the zeal and energy with which Maryland entered the American Revolution. The war interrupted foreign commerce and cut off all European supplies, but it stimulated local manufacturing. After the war Baltimore merchants engaged extensively in foreign trade, and the city became noted also as a shipbuilding center. During the French Revolution and, later, during the Napoleonic Wars, the city prospered as a large part of world trade fell temporarily into American hands. During the War of 1812 (as during the Revolutionary War), Baltimore was an active center of privateering. On Sept. 12, 1814, the British attempted to capture the city, but the attack was beaten off. During the bombardment of the city, the words of "The Star-Spangled Banner" were written by the American lawyer Francis Scott Key (q.v.), who, while imprisoned on a British man-of-war, saw the flag flying over Fort McHenry throughout the attack. The restoration of British ocean trade after the Napoleonic Wars ended in 1815 was a blow to Baltimore, as was the opening of the Erie Canal in 1825. Nevertheless, the city remained important both as a port and as a shipbuilding center; the Baltimore clipper, a type of ship used extensively in world trade, was one of the finest sailing vessels of the time.

On April 19, 1861, during the American Civil War, a mob attack upon a Massachusetts regiment passing through Baltimore led to the Federal occupation of the city. Martial law was maintained until the end of the war. Industry, trade, and commerce suffered during the war, but prosperity was merely interrupted.

On Feb. 7, 1904, a fire destroyed the business center of Baltimore, with a loss estimated at $125,000,000. Within three years, however, the area was completely rebuilt. Streets were widened, and a modern dock system and other improvements were installed, creating one of the most modern business districts in the U.S.

Population (1960) 939,024; (1970) 905,759.

BALTIMORE, David (1938–), American microbiologist and co-winner of the 1975 Nobel Prize for Physiology or Medicine.

Baltimore was born in New York City on March 7, 1938. He attended Swarthmore College, Massachusetts Institute of Technology (M.I.T.), and the Rockefeller Institute for Medical Research (later Rockefeller University), where he earned a PH.D. in 1964 for work with animal viruses. He then joined a virology research group at the Salk Institute for Biological Studies. Led by Renato Dulbecco (q.v.), the group made important contributions to an understanding of how viruses interact with the cells they invade. Baltimore returned to M.I.T. in 1968 and in 1970 reported the discovery of an enzyme called reverse transcriptase, which enables a virus containing only RNA to transform part of DNA in an animal cell and become part of the genetic material of the invaded cell. In 1973 Baltimore was awarded a lifetime research professorship by the American Cancer Society and in 1975 shared the Nobel Prize with Dulbecco and with Howard M. Temin (q.v.), who had independently found reverse transcriptase at the same time as Baltimore.

BALTIMORE, Lord. *See* CALVERT.

BALTIMORE CLIPPER, type of fast-sailing vessel built in the United States during the last half of the 18th century and the first half of the 19th. Though somewhat obscure in origin, it was probably a natural development of the known principles of fast-sailing-ship design popular in England in the 16th century. The basic hull form of the Baltimore clipper has a heart-shaped midsection, a short keel with very raking stern and stem outline, and a low-sided and sharp-ended hull. This hull form, in modified detail, is known to have been used in England in the 16th, 17th, and early 18th centuries and on the islands of Jamaica and Bermuda from late in the 17th century to well into the 19th. The Bermuda model was introduced into the American colonies, particularly in the Chesapeake Bay region, early in the 18th century. The first true Baltimore clipper appeared, presumably on the eastern shore of the bay, sometime before the American Revolution.

The Baltimore clipper was first referred to as Virginia Built during and soon after the revolution. Because the type was used as pilot boats in Norfolk, Va., and, later, in other ports, it also was referred to as pilot boat model or as of pilot boat construction. The name "Baltimore clipper" came into general usage in the U.S. shortly after the end of the War of 1812.

The type was usually schooner-, brigantine-, or brig-rigged, but some ship-rigged vessels of the model were built as early as the American Revolution. Baltimore clipper topsail schooners first attracted attention in Europe toward the end of the American Revolution because they had proved to be very fast privateers. By the early 19th century the Baltimore clipper had become known internationally as a fast-sailing, seagoing type suitable for naval service, for illegal trading, and for carrying light cargoes. The reputation of the ship was enhanced by its performance during the Napoleonic Wars and the War of 1812 (qq.v.); afterward most of the slavers and smugglers, as well as West Indian pirate craft, were Baltimore clippers.

The most common example of the type in the first quarter of the 19th century was a topsail schooner or brigantine, heavily sparred and canvased, with sharply raking masts, a low-sided and sharp-ended hull, and a rather deep draft greatest at the heel of the rudder. The draft forward was about half of that aft. The stem and stern had considerable rake, so that the keel was much shorter than the waterline length. The midsection had sharply rising, straight floors, a high, round bilge, and, usually, somewhat flaring topsides amidships. The entrance was moderately long and quite sharp, the run long and easy. Displacement was moderate for the hull dimensions, and the vessel was able to carry little cargo.

The early vessels of the type, at the time of the American Revolution, usually were built with high, short quarterdecks. By the end of the 18th century the deck was flush, without any break or rise. The largest two-masted vessels built in the last decade of the century were about 90 ft. long; in the next decade schooners and brigantines 100 ft. long appeared.

During the War of 1812 the vessels reached 120 ft. in length. This length was considered for years the maximum for two-masted vessels.

Vessels modeled after the Baltimore clipper were built all along the Atlantic coast after 1800 and were copied outside the U.S., notably in France and in the West Indies.

Because the Baltimore clipper was not especially suited for cargo carrying, it appears to have had very little influence on the later American clipper ships (*see* CLIPPER). The model had ceased to be used in legitimate trade by 1840 but remained, at least in North America, the basic form for small, fast-sailing craft, including fishing schooners, pilot boats, and yachts, until long after the American Civil War.

BALTIMORE ORIOLE *or* **BALTIMORE BIRD,** common name for a songbird, *Icterus galbula,* in the blackbird family, common throughout North America east of the Rocky Mts. during the summer and in Central or South America during the winter. The male is 7 to 8 in. long, with bright plumage, glossy black and brilliant orange. These colors are the same as those of the livery of George Calvert, 1st Lord Baltimore (*see* CALVERT), in whose honor the bird was named. The female is slightly smaller and much paler in color, having brown and greenish-yellow plumage. She constructs a nest in the form of a hanging pouch woven of grass, strings, hair, slender strips of bark, and other vegetable material. The top of the nest is woven around the tip of a branch, usually the drooping limb of an elm or willow. She lays four to six eggs, each nearly an inch long. The eggs are white and irregularly marked with black or brown. The young do not assume the full, bright plumage until the second year. The bird is known also as the hangnest.

BALUCHISTAN, region of Asia, in the S.W. part of Pakistan and in S.E. Iran. The greater part of Baluchistan, about 132,900 sq.mi., lies in Pakistan; there it forms the Quetta and Kalat divisions and part of the Karachi division of Pakistan. Iranian Baluchistan, comprising about 67,000 sq.mi., is incorporated in the Iranian administrative district of Seistan and Baluchistan.

The Baluchistan region is generally mountainous, cut through with deserts and barren plains. Rainfall is scant, and vegetation is stunted and sparse except in the upper highlands, the northeast highlands, and the date-palm groves of the coastal area. The inhabitants of Baluchistan belong mainly to three ethnic groups: the Pathan, the Baluch, and the Brahui. The Pathan, a tall, hardy people who are also a dominant group in Afghanistan, occupy the northeastern highlands. They speak a language related to Persian; *see* PERSIAN LANGUAGE AND LITERATURE: *New Persian*. The Baluch, from whom the name Baluchistan is derived, are spread throughout the region. They are of Iranian or Arabian origin. The Brahui, shorter and darker than the Pathan and Baluch, speak the Dravidian (q.v.) language of southern India. Most of the people are Muslims.

In the arid regions of Baluchistan, the camel and primitive plow are still used for subsistence farming.
United Nations

Baluchistan has traces of a civilization that is believed to date back about 5000 years. The first historic references to the region appeared in the *Avesta* (q.v.), the Zoroastrian sacred texts, and in the work of the Greek historian Herodotus (q.v.), who in the 5th century B.C. referred to the Mykian as inhabitants of a province of the Achaemenid Persian Empire. The Mykian are believed to have inhabited the Makran, the coastal area of Baluchistan that extends along the Gulf of Oman. In the 4th century B.C., Alexander III (q.v.), known as Alexander the Great, and his admiral Nearchus explored the coastal areas and waters of the region. In the centuries that followed, control of Baluchistan seems to have shifted among various dynasties ruling in Persia and the Indian subcontinent. The region was controlled by the Sassanian dynasty of Persia in the 7th century A.D. until Persia was annexed by the Arabs. In the 10th century the Persians again made Baluchistan part of their empire. Except for the four decades that the Mogul Empire (*see* INDIA: *History*) controlled it in the early part of the 17th century, Baluchistan remained Persian until 1747. At that time the beg (governor) of the region, Nasir Khan I (d. 1795), transferred his fealty from Persia to Ahmad Shah Durrani (q.v.), who had founded the kingdom of Afghanistan. In 1758, however, Nasir Khan rebelled against Ahmad and established in northeastern Baluchistan the khanate of Kalat, which was later designated as the capital of the province.

The British became involved with Baluchistan during the first Afghan War (1839–42). Marching toward Kandahar (q.v.) from India, the British army entered and attacked Kalat. After the war, in 1854 and 1876, the British negotiated treaties with the khan of Kalat under which the khan pledged to cooperate with the British who, in turn, recognized the independence of Kalat. In succeeding years the British established the province of British Baluchistan, which included not only Kalat but large tracts of land ceded by Afghanistan after the second Afghan War (1878–79). During their years under the British crown the Baluchistan states (Kalat, Las Bela, Kharan, and Makran) were governed by native rulers who were advised by British agents. When the British withdrew from India after World War II Baluchistan province voted to become part of Pakistan, which officially came into existence in 1947. In 1955 it became part of the province of West Pakistan; in 1970 it became a separate province.

Iran acquired its present holdings of Baluchistan territory piecemeal in the 19th century. The boundary which now divides Iranian Baluchistan from Pakistani Baluchistan, was established by an international commission in 1872. Iranian Baluchistan was part of the province of Kerman until 1959, when it was united with Seistan to form the present administrative district of Seistan and Baluchistan.

BALZAC, Honoré de (1799–1850), French novelist, born in Tours, and educated at a school of the Oratorian Order in Vendôme. At his father's insistence, he studied law in Paris from 1818 to 1821. After being licensed to practice law, however, he chose to embark on a literary career despite his father's objections. Between 1822 and 1829 he wrote bad plays and melodramatic novels that showed very little promise. In 1825 Balzac ventured into the publishing and printing business. When he finally withdrew in 1828, he had incurred debts that were to plague him for the rest of his life.

In 1829 he produced his first important novel, *Le Dernier Chouan,* later called *Les Chouans,* a story based on the conflict in Brittany between the Royalists and Republicans during the French Revolution (q.v.). Although the novel showed some of the weaknesses of his earlier works, it was far superior in quality and signaled Balzac's maturity as a writer. An indefatigable worker, he was to produce about ninety-five novels and many short stories, plays, and journalistic pieces within the next twenty years.

In 1834 he conceived the idea of collecting his novels, completed and projected, into one mammoth continuum entitled *La Comédie Humaine.* His objective was to create a panoramic view of French society in all its aspects from the Revolution to his own day. In an introduction written in 1842 he made explicit the underlying philosophy of the work, which reflected some of the views of the French naturalists Jean Baptiste de Lamarck (q.v.) and Geoffroy Saint-Hilaire (1772–1844). Balzac argued that just as differences of environment and heredity produce various species of animals, so do the varying pressures of society produce differentiations among human beings. The task he set for himself was that of depicting each of the so-called human "species". The work was to comprise 150 novels divided into three main groups, namely "Studies of Customs", "Philosophical Studies", and "Analytical Studies". The first group, that comprises most of the work actually completed, was subdivided into sections called "Scenes of Private Life", "Scenes of Provincial Life", "Scenes of Parisian Life", "Scenes of Military Life", "Scenes of Political Life", and "Scenes of Country Life". The novels were to involve about 2000 characters, the most important of whom would appear in several novels. Balzac ultimately accomplished about two thirds of this enormous project, writing about a hundred novels and stories. Among the best-known novels of the series are *Le Père Goriot* (1834), that deals with a father's sacrifices for his ungrateful daughters; *Eugénie Grandet* (1833), that concerns a miserly father who destroys his daughter's chance for happiness; *La Cousine Bette* (1846), about the machinations of a jealous old maid; and *La Recherche de l'Absolu* (1834), a compelling study of monomania.

Terra-cotta head, a study by Auguste Rodin (1891–92) for his monument to Balzac. Metropolitan Museum of Art

Meanwhile Balzac had begun in 1832 to correspond with a married Polish countess named Evelina Hanska (1801–82). The correspondence led to a prolonged and involved courtship and the countess promised to marry Balzac when her husband died. His death came in 1841, but although she and Balzac continued to meet, the marriage did not take place until March, 1850. Balzac died five months later.

Balzac is considered by most critics to be one

of the world's greatest novelists. His own avowed objective was to depict French society with the utmost realism (q.v.). Yet his greatness lies in his ability to transcend mere representation and to infuse his novels with a kind of "supra-realism". His description of background, for example, is almost as important as his development of characters in a story. Balzac once said that "the events of public and private life are intimately linked up with architecture", and consequently he portrays the houses and rooms through which his characters move in such a way as to reveal their passions and desires.

Although Balzac's characters are highly believable and real, they are nearly all possessed by their own particular type of monomania. Their very one-sidedness serves to expose under glaring light qualities which, in reality, would probably be obscured within the morass of a person's total personality. They seem all more active, more vivid, and more highly developed than their living models could be. What was mediocre in life Balzac made sublime in his writing by persistently deepening the shadows and heightening the luminosity. He gave to the usurer, the courtesan, and the dandy the grandeur of epic heroes.

Another aspect of Balzac's extreme realism lies in his attention to the prosaic exigencies of everyday life. Far from leading idealized or abstracted lives, Balzac's characters are obsessively embroiled in a materialistic world of business transactions and financial crises. More often than not such matters form the crux of their existence; avarice, in particular, is one of his most common themes. For dialogue, Balzac displays an extraordinary mastery in nearly all of his novels, adapting it with amazing skill to the portrayal of widely diversified characters. His general prose style, although on occasion pretentious, has a rich, dynamic quality that makes it compelling and absorbing.

Among his numerous important works, besides those already cited, are the novels *La Peau de Chagrin* (1831), *Le Colonel Chabert* (1832), *Le Lys dans la Vallée* (1835), *César Birotteau* (1837), *Le Curé de Village* (1839); the short stories *Contes Drolatiques* ("Droll Stories", 1832, 1833, 1837); the plays *Vautrin* (1840) and *Mercadet* (1840); and his correspondence with Evelina Hanska, *Lettres à l'Étrangère* (1906). W.F.

BAMAKO, city and capital of Mali, on the navigable headwaters of the Niger R., 425 miles S.W. of Timbuktu, and about 90 miles N.E. of the border with Guinea. A railroad connects Bamako with Dakar, Republic of Senegal. The city has several schools, including the Marchoux Institute and the School of Public Works. Meat processing is the chief industry, and the city has a large cattle market. In 1883 a fort was built by the French on the site of Bamako. The city that grew up around the fort was made capital of the French colony known as French Sudan in 1908. Bamako became the capital of the newly independent Mali in 1958. Pop. (1967 est.) 286,000.

BAMBERG, city of West Germany, in Bavaria State, on the Regnitz R., about 30 miles N. of Nuremberg. The principal industries of the city include brewing, and the manufacture of electrical equipment, textiles, and leather goods. The city is famous for its many fine examples of German architecture from the 15th through the 17th centuries. Bamberg is the site of an 11th-century cathedral and two episcopal palaces. A bishopric since 1007 and an archbishopric since 1802, Bamberg was ruled by bishop princes from the 13th century until 1801. It was annexed by Bavaria the following year. Pop. (1967 est.) 71,300.

BAMBOO, popular name for woody or arborescent plants in the tribe Bambuseae of the Grass family (Gramineae). It includes about 200 species of *Bambusa, Arundinaria, Phyllostachys,* and other genera of grasses (q.v.), many of which attain 70 to 100 ft. in height and have trunks a foot in diameter. The species are numerous and are found in tropical and subtropical regions of both the Eastern and Western hemispheres. The stems grow to nearly their full height unbranched, with straight, horizontal branches near the top. Bamboo forms dense thickets, and many species, being strongly armed with spines, are planted for fences and stockades. The stems, joined like those of other grasses, are very hard, although light and elastic. They are also hollow, containing only a light, spongy pith, except at the joints or nodes, where strong partitions divide the stem. They are therefore readily converted into pipes for conveying water. They are also widely used for the building of houses and bridges in tropical countries. Split bamboo is extensively used for weaving into nets, and for hats, umbrellas, and fishing rods. The smaller stems are converted into walking sticks and are used in light wickerwork and furniture. Some species of bamboo are well suited for the production of paper pulp.

The external covering of the stem is, in all the species, remarkably siliceous; the stem of *Bambusa tabacaria* is so hard that it produces sparks when struck with an ax. This species is a native of Amboina and Java; the slender stems are polished and used for the stems of tobacco pipes. The leaves of some kinds of bamboo are used for thatch. The young shoots of some species are eaten like asparagus or are pickled in vinegar. Certain bamboo seeds are used as rice and for making beer.

Bamboos generally grow rapidly and are often found in arid localities. The species common in the West Indies, *B. vulgaris,* is believed to have been introduced from the East Indies. Some species are hardy in parts of the United States, where they are used in landscape gardening. A number of species were introduced into the U.S. from Japan. *Arundinaria macrosperma* is native to the southern U.S., where it forms extensive canebrakes, or cane thickets.

BANANA, tropical, tree-like herb of the genus *Musa,* type genus of the banana family Musaceae, and also the fruit of the plant. Species of the genus are native to the Old World tropics, but are now grown extensively in all tropical countries for their fruit, fiber, or foliage. The banana is a large, herbaceous plant with a perennial root or rhizome, from which the plant is perpetuated by sprouts or suckers. In the tropics the stems are annual; that is, they die after perfecting the fruit, and fresh stems are developed from buds in the rootstock. These stems, or buds, are the common means of propagating and making fresh plantations, and the growth is so rapid that the fruit is usually ripe within ten months after the offsets are planted. When full grown, the stem attains a height of 10 to 40 ft. and is surmounted by a crown of large leaves, 6 to 10 ft. long by 2 to 3 ft. broad, with a strong fleshy footstalk and midrib. The flowers spring in great spikes from the center of the crown of leaves, and are arranged in whorllike clusters along the spike; the female flowers occupy the base of the spike, and the male the apex. The fruits vary in length from about 4 to 12 in., and in diameter from about 1 to 1½ in. The average weight of a bunch is about 25 lb., but individual bunches often exceed 40 lb. A stalk bears only once, dies down, and is replaced by sprouts, two or three of which are allowed to bear fruit.

The fruit of the plantain or cooking banana, *M. paradisiaca,* is larger, coarser, and less sweet than the kinds that are generally eaten raw. Of the latter kinds, the most common in cultivation is the Martinique, a variety of *M. sapientum* with large, yellow fruit growing in large dense clusters. The Cavendish banana, *M. cavendishi,* is a dwarf species grown commercially in Hawaii, and cultivated for fruit and for ornament in Florida and California.

The edible part of the banana contains, on the average, 75 percent water, 21 percent carbohydrate, and about 1 percent each of fat, protein, fiber, and ash. Other parts of the plant abound in fiber which is well adapted to the manufacture of paper and cordage. Another species, *M. textilis,* is the source of Manila hemp. The United States and its tropical possessions produce about 20,000,000 bunches of bananas and plantains a year.

Bamboo thicket in Ceylon. Ewing Galloway

BANAT, term formerly applied to any one of several districts in S.E. Europe under the jurisdiction of a provincial governor known as a ban. More recently, Banat was a large district of the former empire of Austria-Hungary, between the Mureş (Maros) R. on the N., the Transylvanian Alps on the E., the Danube (Duna) R. on the S. and S.W., and Tisza R. on the W., with an area of 11,013 sq.mi. After World War I, the eastern portion of this region, comprising about two thirds of the territory, became Rumanian; the western portion became part of Yugoslavia; and a tiny portion around Szeged (q.v.) in the N.W. remained Hungarian. The Yugoslavian portion is now approximately equivalent to the autonomous province of Voyvodina. The Rumanian portion of the historical region of Banat centers on the capital of Timiş District, the city of Timişoara (q.v.). The city was known as Temesvár, and the area was thus known as the Banat of Temesvár.

BANBURY, Great Britain, municipal borough of Oxfordshire, England, on the Cherwell R., about 23 miles N. of Oxford. The town has a large cattle market and plants manufacturing aluminum, electrical equipment, and agricultural machinery. Since the 17th century it has been noted for the Banbury cakes baked there. The Norman castle in Banbury, built in 1125, was subjected to several sieges during the civil wars (*see* GREAT REBELLION), and only ruins remain. During the 17th century the town was a stronghold of Puritanism, and the term Banbury man came to be applied, as a form of derision, to the typical Puritan. The old Banbury Cross, famous in the nursery rhyme, was destroyed by the Puritans; it was replaced in 1859. Banbury was incorporated in 1554. Pop. (1972 est.) 30,170.

BANCROFT, George (1800–91), American historian and statesman, born in Worcester, Mass. and educated at Harvard University and the University of Göttingen, at which he prepared for the ministry. From 1823 to 1831 he was a teacher at Round Hill School, a preparatory school that he helped to establish, in Northampton, Mass. He then moved to Springfield, Mass., where he began his career as a historian. In 1834 he completed the first volume of *History of the United States,* his most important work, nine additional volumes of which appeared during the next forty years. Bancroft had become prominent in Democratic Party circles in Massachusetts, meanwhile, and in 1838 President Martin Van Buren (q.v.) appointed him collector of the port of Boston, a position he held until 1841 In 1844 he was an unsuccessful candidate on the Democratic ticket for the governorship of Massachusetts. He was appointed secretary of the navy by President James Knox Polk (q.v.) in 1845. His most notable achievement in that office was the establishment of the United States Naval Academy (q.v.), at Annapolis, Md. He became U.S. minister to Great Britain in 1846, serving until 1849. During the American Civil War he broke with the Democratic Party and vigorously supported the policies of President Abraham Lincoln; *see* CIVIL WAR, THE AMERICAN. From 1867 to 1874 he was at Berlin, as minister to Prussia (1867–71) and to the German Empire (1871–74). In addition to *History of the United States,* his works include *The History of the Formation of the Constitution of the United States* (2 vol., 1882), and *Martin Van Buren to the End of His Public Career* (1889). Bancroft, often called the father of American history, wrote in the pretentious, dogmatic style popular in his time, but he did produce the first comprehensive, thoroughly researched U.S. history, however flavored by his personal partisan philosophy it might be.

BANCROFT, Hubert Howe (1832–1918), American historian, born in Granville, Ohio, and educated there in the public schools. In 1856 he settled in San Francisco, Calif., and in 1858 established a bookselling and publishing concern there. He gathered a large collection of historical material, which amounted to 60,000 volumes and many manuscripts when he presented it to the University of California in 1905. From this material, dealing mainly with the history and ethnography of western America, Bancroft directed the preparation of a pioneering *West American Historical Series* (39 vol., 1875–90). He employed a group of assistants and himself wrote less than a dozen volumes. The work includes *The Native Races of the Pacific States of North America* (5 vol., 1875–76) and six volumes of essays on California history.

BAND, in music, originally, any combination of instruments and executants employed in the performance of instrumental music. The term is still used in this sense in England, where even the full symphony orchestra is frequently called a band. In the United States, however, the term is now restricted in orchestral usage to any of the four groups of related instruments, such as the string or brass-wind bands, that make up the modern orchestra; and it is generally employed to denote a more or less complex combination of wind and percussion instruments, frequently devoted to music played on the march.

Until the 12th century, little or no attempt at musical organization had been made by instrumentalists. The prevailing musical medium had been provided by the unaccompanied vocal styles developed by the Church, and instrumental music had been played only by wandering musicians. By the 13th century, however, permanent bands of pipers and trumpeters were in existence. The original guild of musicians was probably that of the Brotherhood of Saint Nicholas, organized in Vienna in 1228. Later, town bands were formed in Germany and Austria, consisting of fifes, flutes, schalmeis, bombards, zinkers, or cornetti (six-holed horns, similar in shape to a cow's horn, and played with a special mouthpiece), bagpipes, viols, and drums. The development of the wind band (brass, woodwind, and reed instruments) was curiously influenced by the peculiar restrictions defining the social status of every calling during the Middle Ages. The trumpets and kettledrums, for example, were reserved exclusively for the nobility and were forbidden to ordinary minstrels. At the

Bandsmen of the Royal Fusiliers, titled the City of London Regiment since 1881, exercise for the last time the privilege of marching through London, England, with colors flying, drums beating, and bayonets fixed. The unit lost its unique title and privilege in 1967, when it was merged with other Fusilier regiments to form the Fusilier Brigade. UPI

end of the 16th century the band of Elizabeth I (q.v.), Queen of England, consisted of ten trumpets, six trombones, and a few other instruments.

TYPES OF BANDS

The specialized groups characteristic of modern musical performance originated at the beginning of the 18th century. The most elaborate of these groups, the full symphony orchestra, combines every type of instrumental medium; *see* ORCHESTRA. Certain highly specialized groups also survive, notably the brass or wind band, consisting solely of brass-wind instruments, and used in church and community music, especially for rendering chorales in the open air. Finally, two major types of modern band were developed: the military or marching band, used for playing music on the march and made up of brass-wind, woodwind, and percussion instruments; and the concert band, a more elaborate combination used for playing concert music especially written or arranged for band and containing large brass or percussion instruments (such as the kettledrum) that cannot be carried on the march, a group of solo instruments for virtuoso or display passages, and frequently a small number of stringed instruments such as violoncellos and harps. The brass or wind band has been closely connected with church services; in England it reached its highest development through the numerous workingmen's band organizations of Lancashire and Yorkshire. In England the progress of the military band was due largely to the efforts of Charles Godfrey (1790–1863), who joined the Coldstream Guards (q.v.) in 1813, became bandmaster in 1825, and held the office until his death.

Concert Bands. The concert band, which helped to develop band music, received its greatest impetus in the U.S. It may be said to have evolved from the Independence Day (q.v.) concerts given by the Boston city government toward the middle of the 19th century. These concerts brought the American bandmaster and composer Patrick Sarsfield Gilmore (q.v.) into prominence as a bandmaster. The leadership of the concerts was later assumed by the Irish-American composer and conductor Victor Herbert, who is said to have contributed as much as the American bandmaster John Philip Sousa (qq.v.) to the advancement of the concert band. The organization known as Sousa's Band was generally regarded as the best concert band of its time (1892–1932). A notable band of recent years is the Goldman Band, conducted by the American conductor and composer Edwin Franko Goldman (*see under* GOLDMAN), which presents open-air concerts in New York City.

In spite of the popularity of band music, there are few professional concert bands in the U.S.

today. The band in this country is primarily an amateur organization. During recent years the town and village concert band, prominent up to World War I, has been supplanted by high school and college marching bands. Thousands of such bands exist, organized mainly for educational purposes.

Military Bands. The military band is an organized body of musicians, under a bandmaster, generally assigned to each regiment of cavalry and infantry and to the headquarters of the branches of the service. In England, bandmasters are especially trained and the men are generally recruited as boys, from fourteen to sixteen years of age, usually from military institutions. The official establishment of British army bands is thirty-one men for infantry and twenty-three men for cavalry. This number may be increased at the expense of the officers.

In the U.S. Patrick Sarsfield Gilmore was the moving spirit in the development of bands in the military services. Although his first band, organized in Boston in 1859, was a private organization, he soon became a bandmaster in the Union Army. He served throughout the American Civil War and became world famous for the novel musical effects he produced. Bands in the United States Army now usually consist of twenty-eight players.

A notable development among service bands in the U.S. has been the organization of several elaborate and highly trained concert bands, such as the U.S. Marine Band, with members drawn exclusively from the armed forces. During World War II a particularly notable service band developed for concert work was the Army Air Force Band. This organization consisted of one hundred players, men from leading symphony orchestras, musicians from well-known dance orchestras, and musical educators. The Army Air Force Band, which gave weekly concerts at the Capitol in Washington, rivaled the best of the professional concert bands of the country.

BANDA ISLANDS, island group of the Republic of Indonesia, part of the Moluccas or Spice Islands, in the Banda Sea, about 60 miles S. of Ceram. The group consists of ten small islands, the most important being Bandalontar or Great Banda, Bandanaira, and Gunung Api. Great Banda, the largest of the group, is about 7½ mi. long and 2 mi. wide. All of the islands are volcanic in origin, and Gunung Api has an active volcano 2159 ft. high. Bandanaira, economically the most important of the group, Great Banda, and Gunung Api partly form the sides of an excellent harbor. The volcanic soil of the islands is extremely fertile and well suited for the cultivation of nutmeg, the principal crop. Mace, which is derived from the nutmeg tree, is the next-largest crop, and coconuts, cloves, tapioca, sago, fruit, and vegetables are grown.

The Banda Islands were discovered and occupied by the Portuguese in 1512 and remained under their control until the early part of the 17th century, when the Dutch expelled the Portuguese. Dutch rule of the group terminated in 1949 with the formation of the United States of Indonesia, later the Republic of Indonesia.

BANDELIER, Adolph Francis Alphonse (1840–1914), Swiss-American explorer, anthropologist, and archeologist, born in Bern, Switzerland. At the age of eight he was brought to the United States, but in 1855 he returned to Switzerland, where he studied geology at the University of Bern. In the late 1850's he returned to the U.S. and began to study Mexican archeology, on which he published several monographs. His later research among the Indians of the Southwest was published as *Final Report of Investigations Among the Indians of the Southwestern Portion of the United States* (2 parts, 1890, 1892). During an expedition (1892–1903) to Peru and Bolivia he unearthed valuable information about the pre-Columbian civilization of those areas. In 1903 he joined the staff of the American Museum of Natural History (q.v.), and he lectured on Spanish-American literature at Columbia University. In 1911 he went to Spain, where he worked until his death. The Bandelier National Monument, which includes the site of his investigations in north-central New Mexico, was named in his honor.

BANDELLO, Matteo (1480?–1562), Italian writer, born in Castelnuovo Scrivia, Piedmont, and educated in Milan and at the University of Pavia. In early life he became a Dominican monk. He is one of the best-known Italian writers of tales of his period. His stories are similar to those of the famous collection *The Decameron* (q.v.) and originate in the conversations of his social life. Bandello narrated, among others, the story of Romeo and Juliet, and it is thought that, through an intermediate source, a number of Elizabethan playwrights, including William Shakespeare, made use of Bandello's plots.

BANDICOOT, common name for any of seven genera of marsupials (q.v.) in the Bandicoot family (Peramelidae). About twenty species of bandicoot are found in Australia, New Guinea, Papua, and Tasmania.

The bandicoot is distinguished by two divergent characteristics: the presence of many incisor teeth, as in the flesh- and insect-eating marsupials, and a specialized foot structure in which the second and third toes are grown together, as in the herb-eating marsupial, the kangaroo (q.v.). The bandicoot ranges in length from about 10 to 20 in., depending on the species. The fur may be orange, grayish, or brown, and in some species is striped. The large hind legs, which are armed with claws, are longer than the forelegs, and are used for hopping.

The bandicoot is generally nocturnal and hides during the day in a nest, hollow log, or crevice. Most species are omnivorous, and will eat insects, small mammals, or plants, but some, including the pig-footed bandicoot, are mostly vegetarian; others, like the rabbit bandicoot, prefer a carnivorous diet, including small mammals and lizards. Although it digs holes in gardens while foraging, it is generally a useful animal, destroying mice and insect pests.

A peculiarity of the bandicoot is the way in which it fights, kicking furiously with its hind legs. It bites only as a last resort.

BANDICOOT RAT, *or* MALABAR RAT *or* PIG RAT, common name for a large, ratlike rodent, *Nesokia bandicota.* It is found in many parts of India and is plentiful in Ceylon. It attains a weight of about 2 to 3 lb. and is about 24 to 30 in. long, including the tail, which at the base is 2½ in. in circumference. The body is thick and arched upward; it is black above, grayish below. The animal feeds on grain and roots.

BANDJARMASIN, *or* BANDJERMASIN, city and port in the Republic of Indonesia, and capital of South Kalimantan Province, on the S.E. part of the island of Borneo, at the junction of the Barito and Martapura rivers, about 24 mi. from the Java Sea. The port, reached by ocean-going vessels, is a shipping point for the products of the surrounding region, including pepper, rubber, timber, rattan, coal, iron, and diamonds. Many of the structures in the city are built on piles over the river or on floating rafts. Pop. (1971) 281,673.

BANDUNG, *or* BANDOENG, city in the Republic of Indonesia, and capital of West Java Province, on the W. central part of the island of Java, about 75 miles S.E. of Djakarta. It is the third-largest city of Indonesia. Most important as an education and administrative center, Bandung is the site of the Pasteur Institute, the Bosscha Observatory, and several government departments. Manufactures include quinine, antibiotics, textiles, and rubber. It was the site of the Bandung Conference (April 18–24, 1955) of Asian and African nations; *see* AFRICA: *History.* Pop. (1971) 1,201,730.

BANEBERRY, common name for plants of the genus *Actaea* belonging to the Buttercup family (Ranunculaceae). Baneberries are deciduous plants of rich woods and are found in the northern United States and southern Canada, growing to about 2 ft. in height. They are sometimes cultivated in shady gardens as perennials. The small, feathery, white flowers bloom in the spring; the berries, which ripen in autumn, are white in *A. alba,* which is sometimes called "doll's-eyes", red in *A. rubra,* and black in *A. spicata,* a variety imported from Europe. The berries in all species are conspicuous, attractive to children, and poisonous. They contain an essential oil which produces severe gastroenteritis if eaten, but rarely with fatal results.

BANFF, town in Canada, in Alberta Province, on the Bow R., in the S. part of Banff National

Near Banff, Alberta. Canadian Pacific Railway

Park, Alberta Province. In Banff is located park headquarters. The park, oldest and best known of the Canadian national parks, was designated as a 10-acre preserve in 1885, but has since been enlarged to include 6640.76 sq.km (2564 sq.mi.) of scenic terrain. The town is noted for nearby Lake Louise and for its famous mineral hot springs. Banff is both a winter and summer resort; one of its most popular attractions is an annual winter sports carnival. The Banff School of Fine Arts, founded in 1933, is located in the town. Pop. (1976) 3849.

BANFF, Great Britain, county of N.E. Scotland, bordered on the N. by the North Sea, on the E. by Aberdeen, on the S. by Inverness, and on the W. by Moray. Most of the region is mountainous, interspersed with fertile valleys and pastures, but near the coast the terrain is comparatively level, though rocky. In the S. are the Cairngorm and Grampian mountains. The chief rivers are the Avon, Deveron, and Spey. The soil in many parts is very fertile and highly cultivated. Quarrying, fishing, cattle raising, and the manufacture of Scotch whisky are the most important industries. Banff has many remains of antiquity, including the churches of Gamrie and Mortlach, and the ruined castles of Auchindoun, Balvenie, Boharm, and Findlater. The county town is Banff. Area, 630 sq.mi.; pop. (1971) 43,503.

BANGALORE, city in the Republic of India, capital of Karnataka State, about 183 miles W. of Madras. The chief occupation in the region surrounding the city is farming. The city is an important rail center and has industries including textile mills, brickyards, and the manufacture of machine tools, telephones, and aircraft. Bangalore is the site of one of the two centers of the University of Mysore, the Indian Institute of Science, and the National Aeronautical Research Laboratory. Under British rule a large civil and military station was located in the city; thus much of the city is in European architectural style. Pop. (1971) 1,540,741.

BANGKA, *or* BANKA, island of the Malay Archipelago, in the Java Sea, belonging to the Republic of Indonesia, off the S.E. coast of Sumatra, from which it is separated by the narrow Bangka Strait. It is about 138 mi. long and about 62 mi. wide, and the terrain is generally hilly. The island is one of the leading tin-producing centers in the world. Both mining and production of tin are controlled by the Indonesian government. Pangkalpinang is the largest town of Bangka and the chief port is Muntok. Area, 4609 sq.mi.; pop. (latest census) 251,639.

BANGKOK, capital and principal city of Thailand, on the Chao Phraya R., about 20 miles N. of the Gulf of Siam. The site of the city, which is coextensive with the province of Phra Nakhon (area, 331 sq.mi.), lies in a generally low region. Numerous canals traverse the city, and as a precaution against floods many older structures are built on piles or rafts. The section of the city that adjoins the royal palace is of modern construction. One of the outstanding features of Bangkok is the large number of richly decorated temples. The most magnificent is Wat Phra Keo ("Chapel of the Emerald Buddha"), built in 1785 and located within the palace walls.

A high proportion of the export and import trade of Thailand is routed through Bangkok. Wharves, warehouses, and industrial establishments occupy both banks of the river for several miles below the modern section of the city. The chief exports are rice, tin, teak, rubber and hides. Rice milling is the principal industry of Bangkok. Other industries are sawmilling, petroleum refining, and the manufacture of aircraft. Bangkok has several universities.

History. Built on the site of a small fort, Bangkok became the capital of the Kingdom of Siam (now Thailand) in 1782. In December, 1941, during World War II, Japanese troops occupied Bangkok. The city was heavily bombed by Allied aircraft before it was liberated in 1945. The headquarters of SEATO (*see* SOUTHEAST ASIA TREATY ORGANIZATION) and of several other international organizations are in Bangkok. Pop. (greater city; 1970 prelim.) 2,132,000.

BANGLADESH, officially the PEOPLE'S REPUBLIC OF BANGLADESH, an independent country and a member of the Commonwealth of Nations (q.v.), located in the N.E. part of the Indian subcontinent. Bangladesh, formerly the province of East Pakistan, is bordered on the N. and W. by India, on the E. by Burma and India, and on the S. by the Bay of Bengal. It extends from lat. 21° N. to lat. 27° N. and from long. 88° E. to long. 92° 30′ E. The total area is 55,126 sq.mi. The capital is Dacca, located near the Bay of Bengal. The other leading cities are Chittagong, the principal port, Narayanganj, and Khulna.

THE LAND

A low-lying, water-logged area with a relatively narrow range of climatic variation, Bangladesh encompasses the lowlands of the Indo-Gangetic Plain which terminates in the alluvial plain of two great rivers, the Ganges and the Brahmaputra (qq.v.). The southern part of the delta is occupied by the Sundarbans, a region of marshes and swamps which extends W. into India. There are two hilly regions, varying in height from 200 to 1000 ft., including the Lashi Hills and the

Life in Bangladesh remains a struggle even after the historic achievement of independence from Pakistan. Using a team of emaciated buffalo, these farmers plow their fields in a continuing fight for survival against enormous hardships. UPI

Chittagong Hill Tracts (along the Burmese border).

The climate is normally hot and wet. Temperatures vary from 67° F. to 102° F.; rainfall varies from 70 to 170 in. and averages about 100 in. annually. Much of the rainfall takes place from April to October, during the S.W. monsoon (*see* MONSOONS).

Mainly because of the copious rainfall, plant life in Bangladesh is varied and abundant. Numerous species of tropical and subtropical plant life thrive at the base of the hills. The Ganges-Brahmaputra delta region contains banyan trees, coconut palms, mangroves, bamboo trees, a hardwood timber tree called the sal, and dipterocarps, a family of trees yielding timber, oils, and resins. The chief animals are elephants, tigers, and wild hogs, as well as poisonous and nonpoisonous snakes. Many varieties of fish abound in both the freshwater and saltwater areas.

THE PEOPLE

Because of heavy losses suffered during a cyclone in 1970 and the war of independence from Pakistan in 1971, exact population figures of Bangladesh are not available. At an estimated population (1974) of 75,000,000, it is the ninth most populous country in the world. In 1973, when the population was estimated by the United Nations at 71,614,000, the density was about 1260 people per sq.mi., with most of the people living in rural areas.

The ethnic composition of Bangladesh is predominantly Bengali or Bengalee, a people of mixed Aryan, Mongolian, and Dravidian extraction. Estimates for the non-Bengali or Bihari population vary from 500,000 to 2,000,000; most of these immigrants are Muslims from the Indian State of Bihar. Islam is the religion of 89 percent of the population; the rest comprises mostly Hindus, with a fraction of Buddhists, Parsee Sikhs, and Christians.

The official language is Bengali; *see* BENGALI LANGUAGE AND LITERATURE. English is spoken and written widely and is used in many schools and institutions of higher learning. The Biharis speak Hindi (q.v.) or Urdu. About 20 percent of the population is literate.

THE ECONOMY

Agriculture is the chief economic activity. The Gross National Product before attaining independence late in 1971 was $6,000,000,000. The principal products are jute and tea. According to Bangladesh government statistics, before independence, the area raised about 75 percent of the world's jute. Other exports include bamboo, pulp, hides, skins, forest products, natural gas, and fish. Fish and rice are staple items in the diet of the people. Rice is the most important crop; about 19,350,000 tons were produced in 1973. The annual per capita income is estimated at between $50 and $80.

The taka is the unit of currency (14 taka equal U.S.$1; 1975); it is divided into 100 piasas.

Manufacturing is sparse. It is comprised of about 1000 plants, including 22 textile mills, 18 match factories, 1 petroleum refinery, and 1 fertilizer factory. A few jute-processing and cement plants are in operation. A small scrap-melting industry is located in Chittagong.

The country has about 15,000 mi. of all-weather roads, 1750 mi. of railroads, and an airline. Communication facilities include about 48,000 telephones, government-run radio and television services, and several newspapers.

GOVERNMENT

Following a coup d'etat in August, 1975, Bangladesh was placed under martial law. Military officers took control of the government, although a civilian president was retained as head of state. Previously, under the 1972 constitution as amended in early 1975, the country had been a one-party parliamentary state headed by a president with extensive power.

HISTORY

For the history of the territory until 1947, *see* INDIA: *History;* for an account of the period from 1947 through the war for independence from Pakistan in 1971, *see* PAKISTAN: *History.*

The people of East Pakistan province declared their region independent as the nation of Bangladesh on March 26, 1971, amid fierce fighting with forces of the central government of Pakistan. The final separation from Pakistan took place, with extensive aid from India, on Dec. 16, 1971. Bangladesh soon was recognized by most other nations, but Pakistan withheld diplomatic recognition until 1974 and the People's Republic of China accorded recognition only in 1976. Bangladesh was admitted to the United Nations in 1974.

The country's initial government was formed in January, 1972, under the charismatic leadership of Sheikh Mujibur Rahman (1920–75), known as Mujib, who became prime minister.

Sheikh Mujibur Rahman (left) signs an official instrument making him prime minister on Jan. 12, 1972, not long after his return from imprisonment in Pakistan to independent Bangladesh. Then President Abu Sayeed Choudhury (right) swore in Rahman. UPI

His immediate tasks were to rebuild the war-ravaged nation, to reestablish law and order, and to reintegrate the numerous Bengalis returning from India, where they had fled during the independence struggle. A longer range problem was to foster economic growth in order to raise the very low living standards of the densely populated nation. In the first years of independence Bangladesh received massive amounts of aid from abroad, and Mujib nationalized various major industries as part of his program of developing the country along the lines of democratic socialism. Mujib had little success in improving the economy, however, and by late 1972 he was being criticized sharply at mass rallies.

In mid-1974 more than half of Bangladesh was inundated by devastating floods that destroyed much of the grain crop. At the same time, political disorder was increasing, and in late 1974 a national state of emergency was declared. In early 1975 Mujib became president of the nation under a remodeled constitution granting the president extensive power. But he was unable to stabilize the political situation, and, amid deteriorating economic conditions and allegations of official corruption, he was killed in a military coup d'etat on Aug. 15, 1975. Mujib was succeeded as president by Khandakar Mushtaque Ahmed, who placed the nation under martial law. In November military leaders ousted Khandakar and installed a leading jurist, Abusadat Mohammed Sayem (1916–), as president. By the end of 1975 Maj. Gen. Ziaur Rahmen had emerged as the most powerful person in the country. Economic conditions in Bangladesh improved somewhat in 1976, following excellent rice and wheat harvests.

BANGOR, city and port of entry in Maine, seat of Penobscot Co., at the confluence of the Penobscot and Kenduskeag rivers. Bangor is a commercial, industrial, and financial center. Its manufactures include forest products, textiles, and footwear. In the city are the Bangor Theological Seminary and the Northern Conservatory of Music. The site of Bangor may have been visited in 1604 by the French explorer Samuel de Champlain (q.v.), but it was not settled until 1769. Bangor was incorporated as a town in 1791, and chartered as a city in 1834. In the 19th century the city was an important lumber port. Pop. (1960) 38,912; (1970) 33,168.

BANGUI, city and capital of the Central African Empire, in the Ombella-M'Poko Prefecture, on the Ubangi R., which forms part of the border with the Republic of Zaire. The city is about 640 miles N.E. of Kinshasa. Bangui is the commercial, educational, and political center of the country, with an international airport and schools. A river-navigation and transshipment terminus for coffee plantations in the area, the city also handles products from Chad. Chief industries are palm-oil milling, food processing, and woodworking. Bangui was founded by the French in 1890. Pop. (1971 est.) 187,000.

BAN HAT YAI, city of Thailand, in Songkhla Province, and capital of Ban Hat Yai District, on the Malay Peninsula, about 475 miles S. of Bangkok. A major road and rail junction, the city is on the U Taphao R., in an area rich in tin. The name of the city is also spelled Hadyai, Haad Yai, and Hat Yai. Pop. (latest est.) 35,504.

BANIAN TREE. *See* BANYAN.

BANJA LUKA, city of Yugoslavia, in Bosnia and Hercegovina Republic, and capital of Banja Luka District, on the Vrbas R., 90 miles N.W. of Sarajevo. The city is a rail terminus and road center where textiles, tobacco, beer, and dairy products are produced. A hydroelectric plant and a coal mine are nearby. The city probably was the site of the Roman fort of Castra, and ruins of Roman baths are in the area. Banja Luka became important after the 15th century; it was the temporary capital of Bosnia from 1588 to 1638 and the scene of many Austro-Turkish battles. The name is spelled Banya Luka or Banialuka, and the city was also called Slatina Ilidže. Pop. (1971 prelim.) 89,866.

BANJUL. *See* BATHURST.

BANJO, musical instrument of the guitar type. It consists of a hoop or sound box of wood or metal over the top of which a parchment or vellum is stretched. The banjo has from four to nine strings, usually of metal or of catgut wound with metal. The strings are attached at the lower end of the hoop, pass over a low bridge set on the parchment or vellum, and then proceed up a long neck to a set of tuning pegs. The fingers of the player's left hand stop the strings, which are plucked with the fingers of the right hand or, more usually, a plectrum. The banjo reputedly originated in West Africa, where natives, who attempted to reproduce guitars obtained in trade with Arab merchants, developed in imitation a primitive banjo called *bania*. Brought to America by Negro slaves, the banjo became popular in the South and in minstrel shows (*see* MINSTREL SHOW) throughout the United States. The banjo today is used chiefly as a rhythm instrument in jazz bands, although it can be played as a solo instrument.

BANKHEAD, Tallulah (Brockman) (1903–68), American actress, born in Huntsville, Ala. She was the daughter of the American legislator William Brockman Bankhead (1874–1940), Democratic Party leader and Speaker of the United States House of Representatives (1936–40), and niece of the American legislator John Hollis Bankhead (1872–1946), United States Senator from Alabama (1931–46). Miss Bankhead left school at the age of fifteen. She made (1918) her theatrical debut in New York City, scored (1923–31) notable success on the stage in London, and returned to the United States to appear (1931–33) in several films. For her acting in *The Little Foxes* (1939) and *The Skin of Our Teeth* (1942) she was voted best actress of the theatrical season by the drama critics of New York City. Her films include *Lifeboat* (1944), *A Royal Scandal* (1945), and *Die! Die! My Darling!* (1965). She also performed extensively on radio and television and was the author of an autobiography, *Tallulah* (1952).

BANK NOTES. *See* CURRENCY; MONEY: *The Monetary System of the United States.*

BANK OF ENGLAND, central bank of Great Britain, a financial institution with special privileges and responsibilities. Located in London, it is often called the Old Lady of Threadneedle Street. It was projected by the English financier William Paterson (1658–1719) and was incorporated on July 27, 1694, as a private joint-stock association, with a capital of £1,200,000. In return for the loan of its entire capital to the government it received the right to issue notes and a monopoly on corporate banking in England.

From the outset the Bank of England was a servant of the government. In 1844 the bank was divided into two departments, the Issue Department and the Banking Department. The former, strictly regulated, was given the authority to issue notes covered by government securities in the amount of £11,015,100, representing the indebtedness of the government to the bank. Notes could be issued also on other securities, on gold coin and bullion, and on silver bullion. Gradually the right to issue notes, once a privilege of several British banks, was restricted to the Bank of England.

In the Banking Department, the Bank of England differs from other joint-stock banks because it is the banker for the government and the repository of the British monetary reserves.

On March 1, 1946, the bank, privately owned for 252 years, was placed under government ownership, the treasury holding the capital stock. The nationalized bank operating under the charters of 1694 and 1946, manages the British national debt, issues notes, and administers exchange control regulations. The bank is administered by a governor and a deputy governor serving five-year terms and by sixteen directors serving four-year terms; all are appointed by the crown. *See* BANKS AND BANKING.

BANK OF THE UNITED STATES. *See* BANKS AND BANKING: *United States Banking System;* JACKSON, ANDREW; UNITED STATES OF AMERICA: *History: Federalists vs. Democratic-Republicans.*

BANKRUPTCY, in legal terminology, the status of one who has been adjudged insolvent; in popular usage, the inability of a person to pay his debts, or the financial condition of one who has failed in business. The insolvent debtor was harshly treated under the legal systems of most countries until relatively recent times. During one period in ancient Rome, creditors were entitled literally to divide his body or to enslave him and his family. Under the laws of England in the reign (1603–25) of King James I (q.v.), a debtor who was unable satisfactorily to explain his insolvency was placed in the public pillory. The debtor might be put to death if his failure to pay his creditors was due to fraudulent practices. Savage reprisals of this kind were eventually halted, but for many years British courts ruled that a debtor who failed to pay a judgment against him was guilty of a breach of the peace and therefore subject to imprisonment. With the development of trade and commerce, steps were taken to ameliorate the condition of the debtor. Modern legislation dealing with bankruptcy generally contains the basic principle that a person who is unable to pay his debts in full may be discharged of them by giving up his entire property for ratable distribution among his creditors.

The Constitution of the United States (q.v.) empowers Congress "to establish . . . uniform laws on the subject of bankruptcies throughout the United States" (Art. 1, Sec. 8). This grant of power to Congress does not exclude the States from legislating on the subject, but a Federal bankruptcy statute suspends, while in force, operation of State statutes of a similar nature. The Congress adopted the first national bankruptcy law in 1800, modeling it on the British statute of that time. Because the provisions of the law applied only to tradesmen, public indignation resulted in its repeal in 1803. Two other, equally unpopular, national laws were in force from 1841 to 1843 and from 1867 to 1878. In 1898 Congress passed a fourth national bankruptcy law, which, as subsequently amended, remains in effect. By the terms of this amended legislation, a bankruptcy may be either involuntary or voluntary. In the latter case the insolvent person must declare in writing to the appropriate Federal court that he is insolvent and is willing to be adjudged bankrupt. The court then assumes control of his remaining property for the benefit of his creditors, and discharges the bankrupt from responsibility for all his debts, except those specifically exempted by law. The court is not obligated to discharge a bankrupt person until it is satisfied that his debts cannot be paid and that all assets have been assigned to creditors. Involuntary bankruptcies, which are initiated by the petition of creditors, may be adjudged against a debtor under the U.S. law on a number of grounds, notably if he has disposed of his property in order to defraud his creditors; if he has distributed his property among certain creditors in a fashion detrimental to the equity of other creditors; or if he has utilized a legal process, such as a lien, for the benefit of one or more preferred creditors. As amended in 1926 and 1938, the Federal law provides severe punishments, including prison sentences of from two to five years, for bankrupts found guilty of fraud. The statute of limitations of the amended law makes fraudulent bankrupts subject to prosecution for three years.

When a bankruptcy process begins, the United States District Court having jurisdiction assigns a referee to examine the various aspects of the petition. The referee, whose duties are essentially judicial, then submits to the court an opinion on whether or not the insolvent person should be discharged in bankruptcy. Subject to the approval of the court and after settlement of the bankrupt's debts has been arranged, he is discharged from debt.

BANKS, Sir Joseph (1743–1820), British naturalist, born in London, England, and educated at Christ Church College, University of Oxford. From 1768 to 1771 he collected biological specimens as a member of the expedition conducted by the British explorer James Cook (q.v.). In 1772 Banks visited the Hebrides and Iceland. He was elected President of the Royal Society in 1778, an office he held until his death, and a member of the Institute of France in 1802. Banks encouraged the development of the Kew Royal Botanic Gardens in London. He was created a baronet in 1781. His writings include *A Short Account of Blight, Mildew,* and *Rust* (1805).

BANKS AND BANKING. The term "bank" is applied to a variety of institutions established for one or more of the following purposes: to make loans and extend credit, to facilitate the transmission of funds by checks and by bills of exchange and other forms of commercial paper, to receive and hold money on deposit and to disburse it, to exchange the currency of one country for that of another, and to issue money.

Banks also act in fiduciary capacities, provide vaults for the safekeeping of valuables, buy and sell bonds and shares of stocks for their customers, and, in general, perform a variety of services not included in a strict definition of the term "banking". A number of banks in the United States sell life insurance.

Banks are generally classified according to their principal spheres of operations. Central banks of issue, such as the Bank of England (q. v.), issue paper currency, and act as government fiscal agents and as depositaries of the gold reserves of their countries. Commercial banks perform general banking services; the mutual banks of Europe provide credit facilities for farmers and small merchants. Investment and mortgage banks (*see* INVESTMENT BANKING) specialize in the financing of securities and mortgages. Savings institutions (q.v.) provide facilities for saving money, for which the banks pay interest to the depositors.

The principal sources of the income of banking institutions are the profitable investment (in industry, commerce, real estate, and government securities) of the funds entrusted to their care, interest on loans, and the discounting of commercial paper.

Trust companies (q.v.) and certain government agencies, herein discussed, also perform banking operations. Although the larger banks of various countries are engaged in international banking, in which their principal role is the transfer of capital from one country to another, recent international political and economic conditions have made it necessary to establish international banks, such as the Bank for International Settlements and the International Bank for Reconstruction and Development (q.v.).

History. Among the pastoral peoples of antiquity, banking comprised principally moneylending by individuals. As early as 2000 B.C. a banking system, comparable in many respects to modern banking systems, flourished in Babylon, where it was a monopoly of the temples. Later banking systems of antiquity in other countries were also religious monopolies. The first record of a privately owned banking business is that of the Igibi bank of Babylon, in the 6th century B.C. It made loans on objects deposited with it and on crops which it attached as security, received deposits of money on which it paid interest, and

Interior of an Italian banking house of the 15th century (from a Florentine woodcut). Bettmann Archive

acted as a buying agent for its customers. In Greece, two centuries later, banking operations were conducted by the governments of the city-states and by private bankers who specialized in moneylending, the assaying and changing of coins, the receipt of interest-paying deposits, and the issuance of letters of credit. In ancient Rome there were no state banks; banking was almost entirely a private enterprise carefully regulated by law. Beginning with the emperor Augustus (q.v.), however, the imperial government practically monopolized the banking business of the empire.

After the fall of the Roman Empire and the decentralization of temporal power in the major part of the civilized world, banking was confined to the illegal moneylending activities of private individuals who organized institutions known as poverty banks, which lasted until about the 8th century. For the most part they made small loans to relieve the distress of the needy. From about the 8th to the 13th century, banking services were performed by monasteries and churches.

With the growth of trade in the later Middle Ages and the breakup of feudal society, banking again became a large-scale private enterprise. The bank of San Giorgio was established in Genoa in 1148 and the Bank of Venice was established in 1157 to assist the government of Venice with loans. In the 14th century there were banks in Delft, Geneva, Florence, and other cities. The Bank of Barcelona in the Kingdom of Aragón, established in 1401, minted coins and handled the accounts of the ecclesiastical and military orders, including those of Saint James, Golden Fleece, and Saint George.

The era of discovery of the 15th and 16th centuries and the colonization of the New World led to an enormous expansion of world trade and resulted in the rise of great banking institutions that accepted money on deposit and made loans on commercial paper and bonds. Among the most prominent of these institutions were the enterprises of the Fuggers, the Bank of Amsterdam (founded in 1607), the Bank of Hamburg (1619), the Bank of Rotterdam (1635), the Riksbank of Sweden (1656), and the Bank of England (1694), which were among the first banks of issue. The industrial revolution (q.v.) of the 18th century in Great Britain and the subsequent industrialization of Europe and other countries created favorable conditions for the development of banks to their present position as essential and often dominant instruments in the circulation of currency, the operation of industry, and the movement of capital.

Most modern banking systems are privately or cooperatively owned enterprises, operating under government regulation, and consist of a small number of large banks, each with many branches. In the Soviet Union banking has been a state monopoly since December, 1917. After World War II the governments of Czechoslovakia and Finland, in 1945, nationalized the banking systems of their countries; and the governments of Great Britain and France, in 1945, and of Argentina, in 1946, nationalized their central banks.

The United States Banking System. Land banks, which issued notes secured by mortgages on land, but not redeemable in specie, were established in the 17th century in Massachusetts, Connecticut, New Hampshire, Rhode Island, and South Carolina. They were outlawed by the English Parliament in 1741. The colonial assembly of Pennsylvania in 1723 established a loan bank to make small loans, in the form of bills, secured by mortgages on the land of the borrowers. These bills were not redeemable in specie; by swelling the amount of paper money in circulation, they had an inflationary effect. In 1780, during the American Revolutionary War, on the initiative of the American political philosopher Thomas Paine (q.v.), a number of prominent men formed an association called the Pennsylvania Bank to raise money to underwrite the purchase of supplies for the Continental Army. The bank borrowed money and issued notes on which it paid 6 percent interest; it was liquidated in 1784. The Bank of North America was chartered by Congress in 1781 to supply a fund of sound currency and to act as fiscal agent for the government. It issued notes that were used in the payment of taxes and duties in the States. Other banks were established on private initiative in New York City and Boston in 1784. The notes issued by these banks were redeemable in specie and thus were instrumental in establishing a stable currency. The cause of a stable currency was still further advanced by the establishment in 1791, on the initiative of the American statesman Alexander Hamilton (q.v.), then secretary of the treasury, of the First Bank of the United States, the first nationwide banking institution in the country. It was chartered by Congress for a period of twenty years, had eight branches, furnished banking credit in the form of bank notes to the business community, and acted as a fiscal agent for the Federal government. Its capital was $10,000,000 and its notes were legal tender in the payment of debts to the U.S. government. This bank was successful, paying an average annual dividend of 8½ percent from 1791 to 1809. Congress, however, refused to renew the charter of the bank; it took this stand partly because of the opposition of the 88 State-chartered local banks, whose notes were not redeemable in specie and were not acceptable for deposit in the First Bank, and because of fear of the influence on the national economy of European interests, which held $7,000,000 of the capital of the bank.

Following the dissolution of the First Bank of the U.S., banking services were performed by the local banks which, largely because of the development of the western regions of the U.S., increased in number to 246 between 1811 and 1816. After the capture of Washington, D.C., by the British in the War of 1812, the banks of the country, with the exception of those in New England, refused to redeem their notes with specie. Since these banks continued to issue notes without restriction, the inevitable result was inflation of the currency.

In 1816 Congress chartered the Second Bank of the U.S. for twenty years with a capital of $35,000,000 to act as a fiscal agent for the Federal government and as a regulator of the national currency. In essential respects the Second Bank was like its predecessor, but mismanagement of the affairs of the bank during the first three years of its existence brought it to the verge of bankruptcy and contributed to the onset of the general economic crisis of 1819. Thereafter the bank prospered. Opposition by a variety of interests, chiefly agrarian, however, led by President Andrew Jackson (q.v.), who condemned it as a dangerous monopoly, resulted in the failure of Congress to pass a bill renewing the charter over the President's veto. Thus ended the effort to establish a central bank in the U.S.

A period of credit and monetary inflation followed the liquidation of the Second Bank, and, together with vast and frequently fraudulent speculations in land, led to the panic of 1837 and to the depression of 1837–43. In 1846 the Federal government, pursuant to an act of Congress, initiated the Independent Treasury System to act as custodian of public funds. Under this system all government moneys were held apart from the banks in subtreasuries in various cities, and all taxes and payments to the Federal government were made in specie; bank notes were not acceptable. In this way Congress hoped to avoid the establishment of a central bank and, at the same time, to restrain the local banks from inflating the currency by issuing excessive quantities of bank notes.

From 1847 to 1860 banks increased in number from 715 to 1562. Deposit banking and the use of checks developed in this period. The States enacted legislation regulating banking practices, but the absence of uniform legislation and the lack of a sound national monetary system led to confusion. Fraud was widespread; at one time more than 5000 kinds of counterfeit bank notes were in circulation.

The need to finance the Civil War and establish the credit of the U.S. and the later need to establish sound financial conditions for the development of industry led the Federal government to establish the National Banking System. A central bank was not established, but a number of strictly controlled, Federally chartered national banks were set up under legislation enacted by Congress, and severe restrictions were imposed on the practices of local banks. The national banks were formed by issuing Federal charters to existing banks, which, in order to realize the advantages offered them, agreed to observe the conditions regulating their operation. They issued notes that were secured by government bonds. Simultaneously, there was levied on State banks a tax in proportion to the bank notes they issued; this effectively eliminated an unstable and often counterfeit form of money. These actions were instrumental in establishing a uniform and sound currency within the control of the Federal authorities. From 1864 to 1866 the number of national banks rose from 139 to 1582, while the number of local banks decreased from 1089 to 297. Subsequent developments and revised legislation by the States, however, gave certain advantages to local banks, which increased in later years and outnumbered the national banks.

Thus developed the dual banking system of the U.S. that has no parallel in any other country. Experience revealed a number of defects in the operation of this system, and the economic crises of 1873–78, 1883–85, and 1893–95, and the panic of 1907 led to the movement that resulted, in 1914, in the establishment of the Federal Reserve System as a means of strengthening the banking system of the country. The Federal Reserve provided an elastic source of credit that had been lacking in previous crises; more importantly it gave a government agency continuous control over the required level and volume of legal bank reserves and ultimately over the loan and investment capacity of the banking system. For details of the structure, operation, and development of this system *see* FEDERAL RESERVE SYSTEM.

During World War I, in the development of the U.S. from a debtor nation to the leading creditor nation in the world, investment banks in Boston, Chicago, New York, Philadelphia, and other major cities played a leading role in the investment abroad, by American interests, of $10,000,000,000. Between 1927 and 1930 corporations known as investment affiliates, under the control of investment banks, sponsored more than 50 percent of the securities marketed in the U.S. in those years. Following the stock-market crash of 1929 and the onset of the general economic crisis, the Federal government in 1932 eliminated the issuance of bank notes by the national banks. Furthermore as a result of the failure of a large number of banks in 1932–33, all banks in the U.S. were temporarily closed on March 4, 1933, by a Presidential proclamation declaring a bank holiday. Laws intended to restore public confidence and improve the banking system were enacted by Congress in 1933 and 1935. Under the legislation, investment banks were prohibited from engaging in deposit banking, commercial banks were required to separate themselves from their investment affiliates, changes were made in the Federal Reserve System, and a Federal Deposit Insurance Corporation (F.D.I.C.) was created to insure all bank deposits. Initially, F.D.I.C. insurance covered deposits up to $5000 per account; later increases brought it to $100,000 in 1980. Federal legislation also established governmental agencies entrusted with outright banking functions or with functions directly related to the banking system of the country (*see* RECONSTRUCTION FINANCE CORPORATION).

A spacious, uncluttered banking office in New York City gives an impression of beauty as well as efficiency.
Chase Manhattan Bank

During the 1960's the proportion of liabilities on which banks pay explicit interest rose from ⅓ to ½ of all liabilities. This was the result of a broadening of the methods banks used to raise investable funds.

The most important new instrument was the negotiable certificate of deposit first issued in February, 1961, by the First National City Bank of New York. Prior to this, certificates of deposit were nonnegotiable. At the same time, several government-securities dealers announced that they would maintain trading markets; thus, banks encountered a major new competitive source of funds. In addition, many major banks became bank holding companies to allow themselves to be active in services that complemented their credit facilities, thus generating additional funds. The bank holding companies, in addition, provided investment, financial, and economic information services; the leasing of property and equipment; and the management of real property. Some banks also issued various types of ordinary commercial paper. As these services went beyond the provisions of the Bank Holding Company Act, the law was rewritten in 1971 to allow the Federal Reserve Board to exercise more control over banks and to prohibit banks furnishing services subject to tie-in arrangements requiring customers to accept credit services beyond the services they desired.

In March, 1980, Congress passed the Depository Institutions Deregulation and Monetary Control Act. The new law gradually eliminates many controls on banks and at the same time broadens the regulatory function of the Federal Reserve Board so as to standardize banking practices nationally.

With the growth in international banking in the 1960's, American national banks expanded abroad to borrow dollar claims (known in financial markets as Eurodollars) held by foreigners and by their own foreign branches. In the U.S., foreign-controlled banking offices totaled 175 in 1965 and 256 in 1977.

On June 30, 1974, 14,822 banks operated in the U.S. and U.S. possessions, including 4693 national commercial banks, 9644 State-chartered commercial banks, and 485 mutual savings banks. The combined assets of the commercial banks were $884,295,000,000. Their liabilities

Major banks frequently hold seminars on specialized aspects of banking for their executive trainees.
Chase Manhattan Bank

totaled $302,817,000,000 in demand deposits and $407,100,000,000 in time deposits. All but 229 of the commercial banks were insured with the F.D.I.C. Net income of the insured banks was $8,683,000,000 in 1973; of this total, $2,121,000,000 were paid in income taxes and $2,420,000,000 in dividends. J.M.L.

BANKS ISLAND, island of the Arctic Ocean, in Franklin District of the Northwest Territories, N.W. Canada. It is separated from the mainland by Amundsen Gulf and from Victoria Island by Prince of Wales Strait. The island is about 400 km (248 mi.) long and has an area of 70,028 sq.km (27,038 sq.mi.). The N. and S. portions are barren, rocky uplands; the W. section is a tundra-covered lowland. The island's small population is composed mostly of Eskimo (Inuit); the chief settlement is Sachs Harbour, in the S.W. The island, named for Sir Joseph Banks (q.v.), was discovered in 1820 by the British explorer Sir William Edward Parry (1790–1855).

BANKSTOWN, city of Australia, in New South Wales State, within the Sydney metropolitan area. An industrial center, it manufactures aluminumware, clothing and bricks and has a brass foundry. Pop. (1969 est.) 165,100.

BANNISTER, Roger (1929–), British physician and the first athlete in history to run a mile in less than four minutes, born in Harrow, England, and educated at the University of Oxford and at Saint Mary's Hospital Medical School. While in medical school he investigated the physiological factors that limit athletic performance and adopted special exercises that greatly increased his efficiency. At a meet in Oxford on May 6, 1954, Bannister ran the mile in 3 min. 59.4 sec., establishing a new world record. This remarkable feat was bettered less than two months later by the Australian athlete John Landy (1930–), who set a new record of 3 min. 58 sec. Bannister defeated Landy in a mile race held at Vancouver, Canada, in August, 1954. Although neither set a new record, both men again ran the mile in less than four minutes. Bannister retired from athletic competition in December, 1954, in order to devote himself to his medical duties. He wrote an autobiography, *Four Minute Mile,* published in 1955.

BANNOCKBURN, BATTLE OF, historic battle between Scottish and English armies, fought near Bannockburn, Scotland, on June 24, 1314, during the Scottish war of independence against England. The battle began when the Scottish forces, numbering about 40,000 troops under the command of Robert Bruce (q.v.), King of Scotland, intercepted an army of about 60,000 commanded by Edward II (q.v.), King of England, which was en route to the relief of a besieged English stronghold, Stirling Castle. After inconclusive skirmishing between patrols of the two armies, the English launched a mass attack, led by cavalry, on the Scottish positions. Bruce, however, had prepared the ground before his lines with a series of deep, camouflaged pits. The mounted English troops blundered into the pits and were slain by Scottish pikemen. In the fighting that followed, the demoralized English army was decisively defeated, losing an estimated 10,000 men. Bruce's victory, accomplished with about 4000 casualties, secured his throne and the independence of Scotland. *See* SCOTLAND: *History: The War for Independence.*

BANSHEE (Old Irish *ben sīde*; Scots Gaelic *bean-sīth,* "woman from the fairy abode"), in Celtic folklore, a female spirit said to announce an approaching death in the family she visits. The death was thought to be imminent when the spirit appeared to family members, or when the banshee was heard "keening" or wailing at night outside the family dwelling.

BANTENG *or* **BANTING,** common name for *Bos banteng,* the wild ox of Burma, Thailand, and the Malay Peninsula as far as Java. In color, shape, type of horns, and absence of dewlap, it resembles the gaur (q.v.) of India. It is black, with white legs; the hair is short and sleek, the limbs slender, and the muzzle sharp; the back rises into a high arch immediately behind the neck. The banteng is now extremely scarce, if not completely exterminated.

BANTING, Sir Frederick Grant (1891–1941), Canadian physician and physiologist, born in Alliston, Ontario, and educated at the University of Toronto. He entered the Army Medical Corps in 1915, becoming a captain. After World War I he practiced medicine in London, Ontario, until 1921. In 1922, working at the University of Toronto under the British physiologist John James Rickard Macleod and with the assistance of the Canadian physiologist Charles Herbert Best and the Canadian biochemist James Bertram Collip (qq.v.), Banting made the dramatic discovery of the hormone insulin (q.v.), used to alleviate diabetes. In 1923 Banting shared the Nobel Prize in medicine and physiology with Macleod. The following year he was made director of the Banting-Best Department of Medical Research at the University of Toronto. From 1930 until his death in an airplane crash, he was director of the Banting Institute for Medical Research at the university. In 1934 Banting was created Knight of the British Empire.

Female (left) and male banteng. The coloring of the male darkens with age. American Museum of Natural History

BANTU, name of a large group of Negroid tribes dwelling in equatorial and southern Africa and numbering about 60,000,000 people. The group includes more than 200 tribes, which vary in racial admixture and physical type. Among the most representative tribes are the Zulus (q.v.) of South Africa, the Congo of West Central Africa, the Swahili (q.v.) of Tanzania, and the Ganda of Uganda. The Bantu in general consist of tribes speaking the related Bantu languages, except that Pygmies (q.v.) are not generally called Bantu even though they speak Bantu languages. The term Bantu and similar words (*Abantu, Banto, Watu, Bar*) in various languages of the group mean "the people". *See* AFRICAN LANGUAGES: *The Niger-Kordofanian Family.*

The Bantu peoples migrated in all probability from the north, perhaps from the Cameroons (q.v.), and occupied all of the southern projection of Africa excluding a few areas where tribes unrelated to them remain. The Bushmen (q.v.) and Hottentots (*see* HOTTENTOT) of South Africa are the most important of these tribes.

The age and former accomplishments of Bantu culture are indicated by the great ruins of Zimbabwe (q.v.) in Rhodesia. Engineering and stone masonry were practiced there with high attainment at least 1300 years ago. These arts have not survived, but iron smelting, which was known to Bantu blacksmiths in early prehistoric times, is practiced in almost every tribe. Wood carving is an occupation of the forest tribes, and the masks and decorative carvings of the Congo basin represent a highly developed style which, with African Negro art in general, strongly influenced modern European artists after about 1906. *See* AFRICAN NEGRO ART. Contemporary Bantu artists show a remarkable aptitude for painting, and the styles which they are developing have been acclaimed by many critics. Above all, the Bantu tribesman is a master of rhythmic music. Intricate patterns of drum rhythms, accompanied by singing and dancing, are an important part of his work, play, and ritual.

Despite a general similarity in the artistic culture of the Bantu tribes, their material culture is characterized by striking differences, many of which are due to differing physical surroundings. Cattle raising predominates in the highlands of eastern Africa and the grasslands of southern Africa, and goats, sheep, and chickens are raised in small numbers everywhere. Wherever cattle have been domesticated, some milk but very little meat is consumed; however, livestock is actually prized more as a form of wealth than as a source of food. Because of cattle diseases, the tribes in some areas are forced to rely almost completely on crops for subsistence. White yams, cassava, plantains, and rice are the staple foods of most tribes in the heavy rainfall areas, such as the Congo rain forest. In drier regions, millet and corn are staple foods. Palm oil in forest lands and peanut oil elsewhere are also important items in the diet.

The Bantu women do most of the routine farm work and the men perform the heavier tasks, such as felling trees and building houses. Only men tend cattle. Axes, cutlasses, and spears have long been made locally, but imported tools from Europe and the United States have replaced local products to a large extent in recent years. Imported cloth also finds a ready market, although homespun cotton is not uncommon, and in some places bark cloth, skin, and simple leaves are used for clothing.

Social organization ranges from a relatively simple form in which tribes are divided into largely autonomous villages, each governed by a respected headman and a council of elders, to highly organized states with a hierarchy of hereditary chiefs, some of whom became powerful military leaders and conquerors. The Baganda and Watutsi states retained considerable power even under colonial rule. In the local community, individuals whose achievements are remarkable or whose personalities are outstanding are generally considered undesirable, possibly because they are potential competitors of the medicine man. The latter is often the most powerful person in the tribe, because he is believed to control evil spirits.

The basic social unit is usually the extended family, consisting of a patriarchal head and his sons with their wives and children. Sometimes the extended family is made up of a matriarchal head and her sons, including their wives and children. Many patriarchal tribes reflect matriarchal organization in prescribing the inheritance of goods from a maternal uncle rather than from the father. Sacrifices to ancestral spirits are characteristic of all Bantu tribes.

By about the 15th century, the southward movement of the Bantu peoples to the areas they now inhabit was completed. About that time the first Europeans, the Portuguese, arrived in Africa, and came into contact with them. During succeeding centuries the Bantu became known to the English, Dutch, Spaniards, and other European peoples whose soldiers, missionaries, and traders had penetrated Africa. Gradually trade agreements were concluded with local chiefs and the indigenous products of the Bantu came into commercial demand. Local products such as palm oil and copra were exported; coffee, cotton, and pyrethrum plantations were developed; rich diamond deposits were found in South Africa. By the 19th century the trade agreements had been transformed into treaties placing the Bantu tribes under foreign colonial administrations.

The contemporary Bantu tribes largely inhabit the area from Cameroon in the northwest to Kenya in the northeast, and all of Africa to the south except for a few islands of non-Bantu peoples. Along the northern fringe of this area, Bantu and non-Bantu tribes are interspersed. A few Bantu tribes are surrounded by non-Bantu peoples in northern Nigeria.

Many of the Bantu have been converted to Christianity through the efforts of missionaries. Within the last century, colonial governments and Christian missions have brought elementary education and modern medical facilities to many of the remotest villages. Although more than half of the Bantu are still illiterate and disease continues to be a major problem, the modern Bantu is rapidly becoming westernized. He may be found working as a uranium miner, a mechanic, a truck driver, or an office clerk, or attending institutions of higher education in Pietermaritzburg, Republic of South Africa; Nairobi, Kenya; and Kinshasa (formerly Léopoldville), Republic of Zaire.

W.E.W.

BANYAN, common name for a large Indian tree, *Ficus bengalensis* of the Mulberry family (Moraceae), remarkable for numerous aerial roots that, growing down from the branches,

The great banyan (Ficus benghalensis) *in the botanical garden of Calcutta, India, appears to be many trees intertwined, but is really a single tree with many aerial roots.* Ewing Galloway

take root in the soil and form prop roots or secondary trunks. In this manner the tree spreads over a large area. As the tree ages, the original trunk decays, and the tree breaks up into several sections, the props becoming separate trunks for the various sections. The banyan is a species of fig, with ovate, heart-shaped, entire leaves about 5 to 6 in. long. The fruit is scarlet, not larger than a cherry, and grows in pairs from the axils of the leaves. The seeds seldom germinate in the ground, but, deposited by birds in the crowns of palm trees, germinate there and send down roots that embrace and eventually kill the palms. A famous banyan in the Botanic Garden at Calcutta, India, is more than a century old. The main trunk is over 40 ft. in circumference; it has 230 prop roots 6 to 10 ft. around, and over 3000 smaller trunks. The banyan is called also Indian fig.

BAOBAB, common name for a tropical African tree, *Adansonia digitata,* of the silk-cotton tree family Bombacaceae. It grows to a height of only 70 ft., but extensive lateral growth makes it one of the largest trees. The trunk sometimes attains a diameter of 30 ft., and the branches, frequently as thick as the trunks of other large trees, form a hemispherical mass of foliage often 150 ft. in diameter. The fruit, called monkey bread, is about the size of a citron; the pulp, which has a pleasing acid taste, is used in the preparation of cooling drinks. The bark of the tree yields a strong cordage fiber. The baobab, native to Africa, is now cultivated in many tropical countries throughout the world.

BAPHOMET, idol said to have been worshiped by the Knights Templars (q.v.), a mediéval military and religious order. According to the oldest and most common interpretation, the word is a corruption of Mahomet (*see* MUHAMMAD), the name of the founder of Islam (q.v.). The image consisted of a small, human figure with two heads, male and female, and surrounded by serpents, the sun, and the moon.

BAPTISM (Gr. *baptein,* "to dip" or "to dip under"; *baptisma,* "the rite of baptism"), one of the sacraments of the Christian Church and the ceremony of admitting one to the Christian communion, performed by applying water in various ways to the person of the candidate, usually in the name of Christ or in the name of the Trinity (qq.v.). The ceremony is often called a christening, particularly when a baptismal name is given. The so-called Great Commission of Christ that enjoins baptism is found in the New Testament (Matt. 28:19).

Religious meanings were attached to rites of washing with water at an early date. Such rites were among the ordinances of the Jewish law, and it was the custom to baptize proselytes upon their admission into the Jewish faith. The Dead Sea Scrolls (q.v.) confirm that the Essenes (q.v.) practiced a ceremony of ritual purification similar to baptism. In Biblical references, however, the word "baptism" was not used until the time of John the Baptist (q.v.). John the Baptist baptized all who sought purification of the soul from sin. Jesus, and possibly His first disciples, were baptized by John, but in His teaching and practice Jesus did not make baptism a condition of discipleship. The Christian rite emerged after His death and was enjoined upon the Gentile converts.

One of the most important of the controversies that have agitated Christendom has been whether baptism should be administered to adults only, or to infants also. Some maintain that it was the practice from the time of the Apostles to baptize the infants of Christians. Others say that at first only adult converts who made a conscious decision to join the Church were baptized. They allege that infant baptism arose only when conscious choice ceased to be regarded as a necessary condition for sacramental efficacy.

Two modes of baptism are practiced, one by immersion and another by aspersion, or sprinkling. Infusion, or pouring, the common practice of the Roman Catholic Church, is regarded as essentially identical with sprinkling. The advocates of sprinkling universally admit the validity of baptism administered by immersion, but the advocates of immersion generally refuse to acknowledge that baptism by sprinkling is adequately grounded in Scripture. Some opponents of infant baptism generally insist upon immersion.

It is generally agreed, however, that at a very early period the ordinary mode of baptism was by immersion or partial immersion at some convenient place (such as the banks of a river) where water was abundantly available. Later baptisteries were erected. Males and females were usually baptized apart. Sprinkling became the common practice for both sick and well, partly because of convenience and partly because it was thought to be sufficient.

Baptism was accompanied, from an early period in the history of the Church, with various forms and ceremonies besides the simple rite of washing with water and the pronouncing of the formula. The traditional words of baptism contained the threefold phrase "Father (or God), Son, and Spirit" long before the ancient creeds (q.v.) were formulated. Later the renunciation of the world and the devil was included in the for-

"Baptism of Christ", left wing of the triptych "The Penitence of Saint Jerome", by the Flemish painter Joachim Patinir (1485?–1524). **Metropolitan Museum of Art – Fletcher Fund**

mulas of some churches. The giving of a name in baptism is not essential, but is a custom apparently derived from that of the Jews in circumcision. The Roman Catholic Church prefers the use of consecrated water (*see* HOLY WATER) in baptism, but regards any water as fit for the purpose in case of necessity. The administration of baptism in private houses was opposed by the Presbyterians in Scotland in the first half of the 17th century. Baptism in private houses is presently discouraged by many churches, but it has become common in England, Scotland, and the United States.

The Roman Catholic Church teaches that one of the effects of baptism is birth into the supernatural order. Some Protestant churches, particularly the Lutheran church, teach a similar doctrine of baptismal regeneration. But the Reformed Protestant churches in general hold that baptism is a sign and seal of regeneration by grace (q.v.) and of God's assurance that the sins of the penitent will be forgiven; an act of consecration and dedication upon the part of parents or sponsors in behalf of infants and children; and a profession of faith on the part of adults indicating their desire to be initiated into the community of Christ and His church. V.F.

BAPTIST, name of a Christian communion or denomination characterized historically by a belief in the spiritual regeneration of church members through baptism (q.v.), a congregational (*see* CONGREGATIONALISM) polity, and an insistence upon the complete separation of church and state. Baptist doctrine began with the conviction that the church is a fellowship of believers who, upon personal repentance and profession of faith, have been incorporated into the body of Christ through the activity of the Holy Ghost (q.v.). Local churches are held to be communities of believers voluntarily associated in Christian fellowship, witness, and service. Each local church is governed democratically by its own congregation. Forms of worship usually are simple, with special emphasis on preaching the Gospel.

Baptists observe two sacraments or ordinances, baptism of believers by immersion and the Lord's Supper (q.v.). Baptism by immersion was not the form originally emphasized by the Baptists. Immersion became the preferred practice in the middle of the 17th century, however, and is now virtually universal. Baptists also stress the inherent freedom of the individual in his relations with God, the priesthood of all believers, and the symbolic significance of the sacraments; *see* FREE WILL; SACRAMENT.

Membership in a Baptist church rests upon acceptance of a covenant that embraces the mutual obligations of the members, rather than upon compliance with a creed. Primary loyalty is to Jesus Christ, who is seen as the divine redeemer in whom man can receive forgiveness of sin and experience eternal life through faith. The New Testament is held as a divinely inspired, all-sufficient rule of faith and practice. Many Baptist groups have, nevertheless, formulated creeds (q.v.) or confessions as a means of expressing their faith. Such confessions of faith were published by the English Baptists in 1611, 1644, 1651, 1660, and 1679. In 1689 a general assembly of Baptists issued the Second London Confession, which had been written in 1677 in thirty-two articles together with a catechism. This became the most influential of all Baptist confessions. The best-known confessions of faith published in the United States are the Philadelphia and New Hampshire confessions.

The Baptists as a distinct denomination date from the time of the Reformation (q.v.), although the first known congregation of Baptists was organized among English refugees in Amsterdam, Holland, in 1609. The general, or Arminian (*see* ARMINIANISM), Baptists trace their history from this date. The particular, or Calvinistic (*see* CALVINISM), Baptists arose about 1638. The two groups were united in England in 1891.

Baptists who fled from England because of persecution (*see* DISSENTERS; NONCONFORMISTS) formed the nucleus of the Baptist movement in America. The first Baptist church in America was founded at Providence, R.I., in 1639 by Roger Williams (q.v.). A courageous advocate of religious freedom who defied the right of magistrates to interfere in matters of conscience and religion, Williams had been banished from the Massachusetts Bay Colony (*see* MASSACHUSETTS: *History*) in 1635 for advocating his views. Although he soon withdrew from the church he had established, Williams remained convinced that the Baptists were nearest the Apostolic Church in their understanding of the nature of the church and the meaning of baptism.

Despite the severe persecution they suffered in the early decades of their history, the Baptists experienced a steady growth. One hundred years after Roger Williams organized the Providence church, there were Baptist churches in all the colonies from Massachusetts to Georgia. During a long revivalist period beginning about 1740, the number of Baptist churches increased under the influence of Calvinistic evangelists, who gave momentum to the whole Baptist movement; *see* REVIVALS, RELIGIOUS. During the 19th century, the Baptists in the U.S. made rapid progress in spite of controversy and schisms. The most serious schism was that resulting in the establishment of the Disciples of Christ (*see* CHRISTIAN CHURCH [DISCIPLES OF

CHRIST]) as a separate body. Beginning about 1815, the Baptists had established churches in western Pennsylvania and Ohio, and eventually spread through the central west. By 1845 there were 686,870 Baptists in the U.S. Though the Baptists are currently divided into about twenty-five different groups, approximately 90 percent of all Baptists in the U.S. are included in the four largest conventions. In 1973 the Baptist World Alliance reported a world population of 32,804,398 Baptists, of which 28,764,903 were in the U.S. The 1971 census in Canada reported 667,245 persons who identified themselves as Baptists.

The following are the largest Baptist bodies in the U.S.

Southern Baptist Convention. A body organized in 1845 when Southern Baptists withdrew from the General Convention of the Baptist Denomination in the U.S. for Foreign Missions (commonly known as the Triennial Convention) because of tensions over slavery and denominational organization. It is the largest group of Baptists. The Southern Convention maintains a Foreign Mission Board with more than 1300 missionaries serving in 44 countries, a Home Mission Board with more than 1600 missionaries, and many educational institutions. The members of this body are Calvinistic in tradition and, for the most part, practice close communion. In 1971 the Southern Baptists reported 11,824,676 members in 34,420 churches.

American Baptist Churches in the U.S.A. Formerly the Northern Baptist Convention, then the American Baptist Convention (until 1973), a body organized in 1907 to coordinate and unify the work of the American Baptist Foreign Mission Society, the American Baptist Home Mission Society, the American Baptist Publication Society, and other missionary and educational agencies that had been organized many years earlier. It is continuous with the oldest of these groups, the General Convention of the Baptist Denomination in the U.S. for Foreign Missions, which was organized in 1814. The group maintains seminaries, training schools, junior colleges, colleges, and universities in the U.S., and churches, schools, and missions in foreign countries. It follows an ecumenical policy in its relations with other Christians, and almost all of its congregations practice open communion. In 1971 the American Baptist Convention reported 1,562,636 members in 6035 churches.

Negro Baptists. The largest groups of Negro Baptists include the National Baptist Convention, U.S.A., Inc., which in 1958 reported 5,500,000 members in 26,000 churches; the National Baptist Convention of America, which in 1956 reported 2,668,799 members in 11,398 churches; and The Progressive National Baptist Convention, Inc., which in 1967 reported 521,692 members in 655 churches. In common with most other Baptist groups, Negro Baptists adhere to a modified form of Calvinism. The three largest Negro conventions, the American Baptist Churches in the U.S.A., and the Seventh Day Baptist General Conference are members of the National Council of the Churches of Christ in the U.S.A. and the World Council of Churches.

Other Baptist bodies, in alphabetical order, include the following.

American Baptist Association. A group of Baptist churches that places extreme emphasis on the independence of the local congregation and that questions the validity of large organizational structures. Members of the association are widely known as "Landmark" Baptists. They organized the American Baptist Association in 1905, and they claim to belong to the historic succession of Baptist churches reaching back to the days of the Apostles (*see* APOSTLE). Their main area of concentration is in the Southwest. In 1972 the American Baptist Association reported 869,000 members in 3321 churches.

Baptist General Conference. Formerly the Swedish Baptist General Conference of America, organized as a conference in 1879. In 1971 it reported 108,474 members in 681 churches.

Baptist Missionary Association of America. A body organized in 1950 in Little Rock, Ark., by a secession from the American Baptist Association. Known as the North American Baptist Association until 1969, the group stresses Fundamentalism and premillennialism. In 1971 it reported 193,439 members in 1404 churches.

Bethel Ministerial Association, Inc. A body founded in Evanston, Ind., in 1934 as the Evangelistic Ministerial Alliance. In 1971 it reported 4000 members in 25 churches.

The Conservative Baptist Association of America. A body organized in 1947 at Atlantic City, N.J., as a Fundamentalist (*see* FUNDAMENTALISM) offshoot of the Northern Baptist Convention. It emphasizes the infallibility of the Bible and the independence of local congregations. In 1970 it reported 300,000 members in 1127 churches.

Duck River (and Kindred) Associations of Baptists. A body organized in Tennessee in 1807, which has associations in Alabama, Georgia, Kentucky, Mississippi, and Tennessee. It emphasizes Calvinistic doctrine, maintains close communion, and practices foot washing as a church ordinance. In 1968 it reported 8492 members in 81 churches.

Free Will Baptists (National Association of). A group organized by a Maryland-born Baptist minister, Paul Palmer, in North Carolina in 1727, later taking the name of Original Free Will Baptists. Another better-known group originated in New Hampshire in 1780 under the leadership of an evangelist, Benjamin Randall (1749–1808), and became known as the Free Baptists. In 1911 the Free Baptists united with the Northern Baptist Convention. The Free Will Baptists derive their name from the Arminian emphasis upon the freedom of man to determine his own response to God. They practice open communion, anointing, and foot washing. In 1972 they reported 210,000 members in 2250 churches.

General Baptists (General Association of). A group originating in Holland in 1609 among refugees whom John Smyth (d. 1612), an English Nonconformist clergyman, and Thomas Helwys (1550?–1616?), an English Brownist (*see* CONGREGATIONALISM), had led out of England in 1607 because of persecution. The association was transplanted to the American colonies in 1714, but later died out along the Atlantic coast. It was revived in the Midwest, however, in 1823 by a Baptist minister, Benoni Stinson (1798–1869). The association was organized in 1870. In 1971 it reported 65,000 members in 854 churches.

General Association of Regular Baptist Churches. A body organized in Chicago, Ill., in 1932 by a Fundamentalist secession from the Northern Baptist Convention. The association requires submission to the New Hampshire Confession of Faith and emphasizes premillennialism (*see* SECOND ADVENT OF CHRIST). In 1972 it reported 204,357 members in 1426 churches.

National Primitive Baptist Convention, Inc. Formerly known as Colored Primitive Baptists, a convention organized in 1907 and opposed to any centralized organization beyond that of the local church. In 1971 the group reported 1,645,000 members in 2198 churches.

North American Baptist Association. A body organized in 1960 in Little Rock, Ark., by a secession from the American Baptist Association. The group stresses Fundamentalism and premillennialism. In 1968 it reported 1650 churches with 275,000 members.

North American Baptist General Conference. A body organized among German Baptist immigrants who came to the U.S. and Canada in the early 19th century. The group manifests a strong spiritual unity and has a deep interest in mission work. In 1972 it reported 54,441 members in 341 churches.

Separate Baptists in Christ. A group of Baptists founded in Illinois, Indiana, Kentucky, Ohio, and Tennessee, which dates back to an association formed in 1758 in North Carolina. In 1962 the group reported 7496 members in 84 churches.

Seventh Day Baptist General Conference. A body of Baptists originating in England in 1617, and first established in America in Newport, R.I., in 1671. The group is distinguished from most Christian churches in that it observes Saturday as the Christian Sabbath (*see* SABBATH). In 1971 it reported 5376 members in 66 churches.

W.H.P.

In Canada, Baptist congregations were first formed about 1760, and the longest continuous history of a single Baptist church is claimed by a congregation in Horton, now Wolfville, Nova Scotia, organized in 1778. About 3 percent of all Canadians are Baptists, and the largest number of them live in New Brunswick and Nova Scotia. Baptists in Canada are likely to be rural, nonfarm residents.

Formal Canadian Baptist bodies include:

Baptist Federation of Canada. A coordinating body, with headquarters in Brantford, Ontario, for four federated member bodies—the United Baptist Convention of the Atlantic Provinces, the Baptist Convention of Ontario and Québec, the Baptist Union of Western Canada, and the French Baptist Union. In 1973 it reported 128,794 members in 1102 churches.

Baptist General Conference. A conservative, evangelical group, comprising three conferences in western Canada and the northwestern U.S. In 1971 it reported 12,432 members in 110 churches.

Canadian Baptist Conference. Affiliated with the Southern Baptist Convention of the U.S., with offices in British Columbia and Saskatchewan. In 1973 it reported 1746 members in 32 churches.

Primitive Baptist Conference of New Brunswick. A Fundamental, Arminian group. In 1971 it reported 5598 members in 18 churches.

BAPTISTERY, in Christian churches, name given sometimes to a separate building and sometimes to the portion of the church in which the ceremony of baptism (q.v.) is performed. Beginning during the reign of the Roman emperor Constantine I (q.v.) in the 4th century, many large baptisteries were erected. These baptisteries were usually circular or polygonal in plan and were commonly dedicated to John the Baptist (q.v.). The baptismal basin itself was surrounded by columns, between which hangings were drawn that concealed

The baptistery of Saint John at Siena, Italy, a landmark of Gothic architecture, was built in the early 14th century. The façade, completed in 1382, was probably designed by the Italian architect Giacomo di Mino del Pellicciaio. Alinari

from the public the actual scene of baptism. Above this central section usually rose a dome of masonry or wood, and around it was often an encircling aisle, or sometimes two aisles, to accommodate spectators. Early examples of such baptisteries are found in Italy and the Orient; one of the most notable is the 6th-century baptistery of Hagia Sophia (*see* SAINT SOPHIA) in İstanbul, Turkey.

In the 11th century the revival of architecture in Europe led to the building of superb baptisteries in Italy. An Italian city usually had, in addition to parish churches, a main group of three religious structures, consisting of cathedral, campanile, and baptistery. The most impressive of these groups are at Parma, Pisa, and Florence; others are at Pistoia, Novara, Cremona, Verona, Lucca, Volterra, and Siena. Of these baptisteries, that of Florence is the most famous; it is noted especially for internal mosaic decoration and for magnificent bronze doors by the Italian sculptors Andrea Pisano and Lorenzo Ghiberti (qq.v.). That of Pisa contains a famous pulpit by the Italian sculptor Nicola Pisano (*see under* PISANO). The Parma baptistery is filled with contemporary frescoes and sculptures.

BAR, in law, originally, the rail in the English Inns of Court that separated the court officials from the suitors, their advocates, and friends. When an action was brought to trial, the suitors presented themselves at the bar, accompanied by their advocates, who addressed the court from there. The term has been extended to apply to those whose profession it is to appear at the bar on behalf of suitors. The advocates or counsel attached to a certain judicial circuit or practicing their profession in a certain county (in Great Britain) or State (in the United States) are known collectively as the bar of such circuit, county, or State. The term is also used to designate all the lawyers of a country, as "the American bar" or "the English bar".

In common-law actions, a plea in bar is a plea or defense that, if supported by evidence, forms a conclusive answer to an action, such as a traverse, or denial, of all the allegations upon which a civil action or criminal prosecution is based.

BARABBAS, in the New Testament, name of a robber or, in some accounts, a rebel, who was condemned to death at about the same time as Jesus Christ. As was customary, the Roman governor of Judea, Pontius Pilate (*see* PILATE, PONTIUS), offered to pardon one prisoner at Passover (*see* PESACH). According to the accounts of the incident contained in the Gospels (*see* GOSPEL), the people of Jerusalem demanded that Barabbas, rather than Jesus, be released (Mark 15:6–15). In several versions of Matthew (*see* MATTHEW, GOSPEL ACCORDING TO SAINT), the name Barabbas appears as a surname preceded by the given name Jesus; this fact, which may be due to errors on the part of scribes, has been a source of confusion to readers of the Bible.

BARANOF ISLAND. *See* ALEXANDER ARCHIPELAGO.

BARANY, Robert (1876–1936), Austrian otologist, born in Vienna. As a student at the University of Vienna he began in 1902 a series of investigations on the internal ear. These studies culminated in his monograph *Physiologie und Pathologie des Bogengangapparates beim Menschen* (1912; Eng. trans., *Physiology and Pathology of Human Vestibular Apparatus*, 1912), for which he was awarded the 1914 Nobel Prize in medicine and physiology. From 1917 until his death he served as professor of otology at the University of Uppsala in Sweden.

BARBADOS, independent member of the Commonwealth of Nations (q.v.), easternmost island of the West Indies. The respective N. and S. limits are delineated approximately by lat. 13°2′ N. and 13°20′ N.; the respective E. and W. limits are delineated approximately by long. 59°25′ W. and 59°39′ W. The island is 21 mi. long, 14 mi. wide, and has an area of 166 sq.mi.

The Land. Barbados, which is surrounded by coral reefs, is generally flat along the coast and elevated in the interior. Mount Hillaby, the highest point, rises to 1104 ft. Barbados has a tropical climate tempered by sea breezes; the mean temperature is about 80° F. The rainy season lasts from June to December, with average

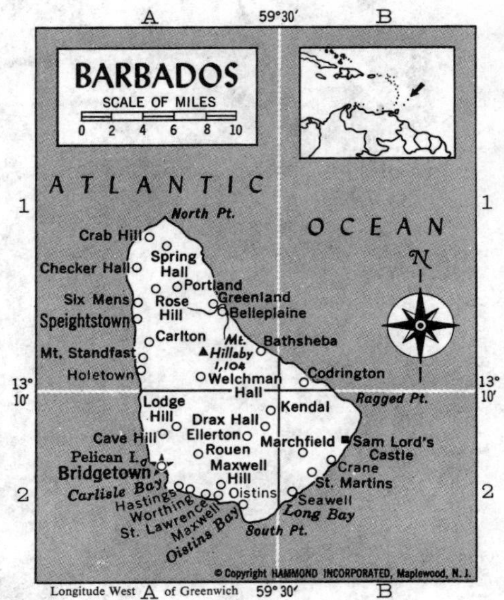

INDEX TO MAP OF BARBADOS

Cities and Towns	
Bathsheba	A 1
Belleplaine	A 1
Bridgetown (capital)	A 2
Carlton	A 1
Cave Hill	A 2
Checker Hall	A 1
Codrington	B 1
Crab Hill	A 1
Crane	B 2
Drax Hall	A 2
Ellerton	A 2
Greenland	A 1
Hastings	A 2
Holetown	A 1
Kendal	B 2
Lodge Hill	A 2
Marchfield	B 2
Maxwell	A 2
Maxwell Hill	A 2
Mount Standfast	A 1
Oistins	A 2
Portland	A 1
Rose Hill	A 1
Rouen	A 2
Saint Lawrence	A 2
Saint Martins	B 2
Sam Lord's Castle	B 2
Seawell	B 2
Six Mens	A 1
Speightstown	A 1
Spring Hall	A 1
Welchman Hall	A 1
Worthing	A 2

Physical Features	
Carlisle (bay)	A 2
Hillaby (mt.)	A 1
Long (bay)	B 2
North (point)	A 1
Oistins (bay)	A 2
Pelican (isl.)	A 2
Ragged (point)	B 2
South (point)	A 2

rainfall varying from 40 in. on the coast to 90 in. on the central ridge. Hurricanes occasionally cause severe damage.

The People. The population of Barbados (census 1970) was 238,141. The United Nations estimated the overall population density at 1420 persons per sq.mi. in 1973. Bridgetown, the capital and principal port, had a population (1970) of 8789.

About 88 percent of the total population are of black African and mixed descent; about 12 percent are of European descent; the remaining fraction of the population is of East Indian descent. English is the official language. The majority of the citizens are Anglicans. The culture combines English institutions, which were developed through centuries of English rule, with a folk culture of African origin. The music and dances are African.

Education is free but not compulsory for children between the ages of five and fourteen. A campus of the University of the West Indies was opened at Bridgetown in 1963.

The Economy. Barbados is dependent on the production and export of sugar, molasses, and rum. The government has been making an attempt to relieve the dependence on these products by establishing small manufacturing industries and by providing more facilities for tourists. Recent annual budget figures show revenues and expenditures nearly balanced at about $65,000,000. In 1972 a central bank was established and a new unit of currency adopted, the Barbados dollar, consisting of 100 cents (1 Barbados dollar equals U.S.$0.50; 1975).

Government. Under the constitution of 1966 legislative power is vested in a parliament consisting of a Senate of twenty-one members and a House of Assembly of twenty-four. A governor-general, who presides over a privy council, represents the queen as head of state; and a cabinet composed of a prime minister and other ministers responsible to the parliament directs and controls the government.

History. Barbados was probably discovered by Portuguese explorers in the 16th century. The first English ship probably arrived there between 1620 and 1624. Barbados was made a crown possession in 1663. The prosperity of the colony was gravely affected during the 18th century as a result of the warfare between the French and the British and the American Revolution. In 1834 the British government abolished slavery on Barbados. This move led to a substantial increase in agricultural production.

Severe riots, which resulted in bloodshed and loss of property, occurred in 1876 when the British government proposed the establishment of a confederation of Barbados and the Windward Islands, 78 mi. west of Barbados. Succeeding decades were marked by a slow rise to political power of the African and mixed majority, who eventually outnumbered the white landholders in the legislature.

In 1937 poor economic conditions caused serious unrest, and a British Royal Commission was sent to Barbados. The result of its report was the gradual introduction of social and political reforms, including, in 1950, universal adult suffrage. In 1958 Barbados joined the federation of the West Indies, but the federation was dissolved in 1962; *see* WEST INDIES.

In 1961 Barbados achieved full internal self-government, and it became independent on Nov. 30, 1966, under the leadership of Prime

View of the beach below Chalky Mountain at Saint Andrew, Barbados. British Information Services

Minister Errol Walton Barrow (1920–). Barbados is a member of the United Nations and of the Organization of American States (qq.v.). In 1973 Barbados helped form the Caribbean Community (CARICOM), an organization that promotes social and political cooperation and economic integration; in 1975 the group had twelve members. Barbados joined forty-five other developing nations in 1975 in signing a five-year trade and aid pact with the European Economic Community.

BARBADOS CHERRY, *or* ACEROLA, common name for the edible fruit of several plants of the genus *Malpighia* in the family Malpighiaceae. *Malpighia glabra* and *M. punicifolia* have shiny, oval leaves, red flowers, and tart, red fruit. *Malpighia urens* has pink flowers and oblong leaves, which are covered beneath with stinging hairs. The plants are found from Texas to tropical America and are an important crop in Puerto Rico. The fruit, which has a high vitamin-C content, is used in fruit-juice mixes and jellies.

BARBARA, Saint (fl. 3rd cent.), martyr and saint of the Roman Catholic Church. According to legend she lived and suffered martyrdom in the city of Nicomedia (now İzmit, Turkey). To protect her from the world, her father had a tower built, and there she spent her youth in solitude. While in this retirement she became converted to Christianity, against the will of her father, who then delivered her to the Roman governor. The governor failed to make her relinquish Christianity and at last the father offered to strike off his daughter's head. When he had beheaded St. Barbara, the father was struck by lightning and killed. Because of that event, St. Barbara has been associated with lightning and is prayed to in storms. For the same reason she is the patron saint of artillery, and her image was at one time frequently placed on arsenals and powder magazines; the powder storage room of a French warship is still called *Sainte-Barbe*. The feast day of St. Barbara is Dec. 4.

BARBARY APE, *or* MAGOT, common name for a tailless monkey, *Macaca sylvana,* of the family Cercopithecidae. The body is about 2 ft. long and covered with greenish-brown hair. It is the only monkey now found in Europe, where it is restricted, however, to Gibraltar (q.v.). It is abundant in some parts of North Africa.

BARBARY COAST, name applied to the coast of North Africa extending from the W. border of the Arab Republic of Egypt to the Atlantic Ocean, and bounded by the Sahara on the S. and the Mediterranean Sea on the N. The name is derived from the principal inhabitants of the region, the Berbers (*see* BERBER).

About the 12th century B.C., the Barbary Coast comprised principally the kingdom of Mauretania (now Morocco and part of Algeria) and, to the east of that kingdom, Numidia (most of modern Algeria). Phoenicians (*see* PHOENICIA) established colonies at Utica (q.v.) about 1100 B.C. and at Carthage (q.v.) about 800 B.C. Beginning with the 7th century B.C. the Greeks planted colonies W. of Egypt in the region now known as Cyrenaica (q.v.). The Romans conquered Carthage in 146 B.C. and, gradually extending their sovereignty over the entire Barbary Coast, by 114 A.D. had incorporated it entirely into the Roman Empire. In 429 the Vandals (q.v.), a Teutonic tribe that had settled in Spain about 400, crossed from Spain to the Barbary Coast and conquered the Romans. The Vandals held sway until 533, when they were in turn conquered by the Byzantine Empire. In the

The American fleet advancing on Tripoli in 1804 (lithograph by Nathaniel Currier, 1846). Granger Collection

7th and 8th centuries the Arabs conquered the Barbary Coast. From that time until the middle of the 19th century the Barbary Coast consisted of independent Muslim states and states under the sovereignty of the Ottoman Empire, which conquered various districts (middle of the 16th century). *See* ALGERIA; MOROCCO; TRIPOLI; TUNISIA. From the early 16th century the Barbary states were centers for Muslim pirates (*see* CORSAIR) who preyed upon the commerce of the Christian European nations in both Mediterranean and Atlantic waters. In 1785 the Barbary pirates began to molest the shipping of the United States. Following the example of European nations, the U.S. concluded treaties with the states of Morocco, Algiers, Tripoli, and Tunis, providing for immunity from attack by money payments. The breaking of these treaties by Tripoli and Algiers led to war. American naval action against Tripolitan ports (1801–05) and Algiers (1815), prosecuted by the American naval officer Stephen Decatur (q.v.), was instrumental in ending the piracy.

During the remainder of the 19th century and in the early part of the 20th century, European nations gradually established sovereignty over parts of the Barbary Coast. France established the colony of Algeria in 1847, the protectorate of Tunisia in 1881, and a protectorate over most of Morocco in 1911. After a war between the Turks and Italians fought on North African soil in 1912, Tripoli and Cyrenaica were consolidated into the Italian colony of Libya (*see* LIBYA, UNITED KINGDOM OF). During World War II the Barbary Coast was the scene of bitter fighting (1942–43) between the forces of the Axis Powers (q.v.) and British and American forces; *see* WORLD WAR II: *The War in Africa.*

BARBECUE. *See* COOKERY: *Recent Developments.*

BARBEL, common name for any fish of the genus *Barbus,* so called from the four fleshy feelers, or barbels, attached to the upper lip and used in the search for food. They are part of the Carp family (Cyprinidae). Found in fresh waters, chiefly in Europe, the fish feed on the leaves and roots of aquatic plants. In color they are greenish brown above, shading to white below. Fish of this genus attain a maximum weight of about 50 lb. The flesh is coarse and is seldom used for food.

BARBER (Lat. *barba,* "beard"), artisan who shaves, cuts, and dresses the hair of the head and face. The occupation of barber was practiced in Greece in the 5th century B.C. and in Rome in the 3rd century B.C. During the Middle Ages the occupations of barber and surgeon were combined, but in the Renaissance period the surgical practice of the barber was restricted to bloodletting and toothpulling. The functions of barber and surgeon had been entirely separated by law by the 17th century in France and the 18th century in Great Britain. The traditional sign of the barber was the spiral bandage used in bloodletting; it survives as the modern sign of a spiral red stripe on a white pole. *See also* HAIRDRESSING.

BARBER, Samuel (1910–81), American composer, born in West Chester, Pa., and trained at the Curtis Institute of Music, Philadelphia. One of the best-known American composers of the neo-Romantic school, he received a number of awards, notably the Prix de Rome (1935), Pulitzer Traveling Scholarships in Music (1935, 1936), a Guggenheim Fellowship (1945), and the Pulitzer Prize for Music (1958, 1963). Among his compositions for orchestra are *Overture to The School for Scandal* (1933), *Adagio for Strings* (1936), and two symphonies (1936 and 1944); concerti for violin (1940), cello (1945), and piano (1962); and the ballets *Medea* (1946), written for the American dancer Martha Graham (q.v.), and *Score For Poème* (1970). He also composed works for chorus, chamber ensemble, and piano, and many songs. His first opera, *Vanessa* (1958), has been recorded. His second opera, *Antony and Cleopatra* (1966), was commissioned for the opening performance at the new Metropolitan Opera House in New York City.

BARBERRY, common name for any plant of the genus *Berberis* of the Barberry family, Berberidaceae (q.v.). The species, which number about 175, are mainly natives of China, but are naturalized in temperate regions throughout most of the world. They are spiny shrubs, deciduous or evergreen, which in late spring or early summer put forth numerous small, yellow flowers. The stamens are sensitive, moving inward when irritated, so as to dust insects with pollen and so facilitate cross-fertilization. The fruit is a berry with two or three seeds; in some species it is rather acid in taste, but excellent for preserves and jelly. The berries of evergreen species are purplish black; those of deciduous species, red. *Berberis vulgaris,* a native of Europe, was introduced into the United States as an ornamental shrub. However, this species is an intermediate host in the life cycle of the stem rust, which is harmful to wheat, oats, rye, barley, and other small grains and grasses. Its cultivation in wheat-growing regions is prohibited by Federal plant-quarantine regulations. Two native American barberry species are also objectionable because of rust: the American barberry, *B. cana-*

American barberry, Berberis canadensis
American Museum of Natural History

densis, which is deciduous, and grows in the eastern Allegheny region; and the similar *B. fendleri,* called Colorado barberry, which is native to the Rocky Mountains. The Japanese barberry, *B. thunbergii,* also a deciduous species, is immune to the rust, and may safely be planted. A Chilean species, *B. buxifolia,* and a Chinese species, *B. julianae,* are commonly cultivated evergreen barberries. *Berberis vulgaris* and *B. buxifolia* grow to about 9 ft.; *B. canadensis, B. fendleri, B. thunbergii,* and *B. julianae* grow to about 6 ft.

BARBERTON, city of Ohio, in Summit Co., adjacent to the city of Akron, and about 35 miles S. of Cleveland. The city is an important industrial center. Among the manufactures are boilers, chemicals, matches, metal products, rubber products, and sporting goods. Barberton was named for the American match manufacturer Ohio Columbus Barber (1841–1920), who laid out the city in 1891. It was incorporated in 1892. Pop. (1960) 33,805; (1970) 33,052.

BARBET (Lat. *barbatus,* "bearded"), common name for any bird of the tropical family Capitonidae in the order Piciformes, so called in reference to the prominent bristles about the mouth. The family includes more than one hundred forms, distributed through the tropical forests of both the Old and New World and absent only from the West Indies and Australia. The birds are stockily built, usually less than 6 in. in length, and often richly colored. Barbets make their nests in holes in trees and feed mainly on insects and fruit.

BARBEY D'AUREVILLY, Jules Amédée (1808–89), French novelist and critic, born in Saint-Sauveur-le-Vicomte, Normandy, and educated at the Collège Stanislas, in Paris. He was of an aristocratic family and was a staunch Roman Catholic and a royalist. He studied law at Caen (1829–33) and later worked as a journalist. He became literary critic for *Le Pays* in 1851 and for *Le Constitutionnel* in 1868. His novels, which are tragic stories of violent emotions, deal with everyday character types on the Cotentin Peninsula in Normandy. In his critical work Barbey d'Aurevilly was noted for his acute literary evaluations. Among his fictional works are *Une Vieille Maîtresse* ("An Old Mistress", 1851), *L'Ensorcelée* (1854; Eng. trans., *Bewitched,* 1928), *Un Prêtre Marié* ("A Married Priest", 1865), *Les Diaboliques* (1874; Eng. trans., *The Diaboliques,* 1925), and *Ce Qui ne Meurt pas* (1884; Eng. trans., *What Never Dies,* 1909). Most of his critical work is included in *Les Oeuvres et les Hommes* ("The Works and the Men", 26 vol., 1860–1909).

BARBIROLLI, Sir John (1899–1970), British conductor, born in London, England, and educated at the Royal Academy of Music. He began his musical career as a cellist, making his first solo appearance in London in 1911. He played with the International String Quartet from 1920 to 1924. He was later conductor of the Scottish Orchestra and the Leeds Symphony Orchestra (1933–37), and conductor and music director of the New York Philharmonic Symphony Orchestra (1937–43). In 1943 he was appointed conductor and in 1959 conductor-in-chief of the Hallé Orchestra, Manchester, England. In 1961 he became conductor of the Houston Symphony Orchestra and remained in that post until he was made conductor emeritus in 1967. Barbirolli was knighted in 1949.

BARBITURATES, salt derivatives of barbituric acid. Barbituric acid is $C_4N_2O_3H_4$. The hydrogen atoms in barbituric acid may easily be replaced by alkyl or aryl radicals, resulting in barbiturates. Pentothal, Seconal, Luminal, Allonal, Amytal, Nembutal, phenobarbital, and amobarbital are barbiturates. Veronal, first synthesized in 1903, is derived from barbituric acid.

The duration of action of these drugs may be long, intermediate, short, and ultra short. One form may be prescribed in the prevention of medical management of convulsive disorders. Another is used in the induction of sleep prior to surgery. Others are temporarily useful in medicine as sedatives and hypnotics (sleep-inducing preparations).

Infectious disease or harmful effects (such as pneumonia, aspiration pneumonia, and gastric hemorrhage) may result from depression in activity of the central nervous system, and may require emergency hospital treatment. The habitual use of barbiturates, for example, may sometimes cause drug addiction. Other undesirable side effects, such as dizziness, headaches, nausea, and mental depression, sometimes occur. Frequent use of barbiturates increases the user's tolerance, thereby requiring ever-greater dosages to achieve the desired effect. Consequently, he may inadvertently take a dose that may result in death. Because of the misuse of barbiturates, Federal and State laws have been passed restricting their sale in the United States. *See* DRUGS, ADDICTION TO.

BARBIZON SCHOOL, name given to a group of French painters who from about 1830 to 1870 lived in or near the town of Barbizon, at the edge of the forest of Fontainebleau, France. There they painted the animals, landscapes, and people of the region. The group was distinguished for the fact that its members painted in the open air instead of in studios as had been the invariable practice before then. Their work had a wider scope of subject matter, greater reality, and fresher color than that of the French painters of the time who followed the traditions of the conservative French Academy. They were the precursors of impressionism (q.v.) in their informality and insistence on naturalness. Members of the Barbizon group included its nominal leader, Théodore Rousseau, Jean François Millet, Jules Dupré (qq.v.), and Charles François Daubigny; *see under* DAUBIGNY. Jean Baptiste Camille Corot (q.v.) occasionally joined the group and most dramatically represented the transition to impressionism with his silvery landscapes. Paintings by the members of this group are exhibited in nearly every museum in the world; the Metropolitan Museum of Art, New York City, and the Louvre, Paris, have especially large collections.

BARBOUR, John (1316?–95), Scottish poet, born probably in Aberdeen County, and educated at the University of Oxford and the University of Paris. He became archdeacon of Aberdeen possibly before 1357. He is known chiefly for his national epic poem *The Brus* (1375), which relates the history of Robert Bruce (q.v.), King of Scotland, during the Scottish war for independence from England in the early 14th century, and of the Battle of Bannockburn (q.v.), a major engagement in this struggle. The poem, in twenty books containing in all nearly 14,000 lines, was the first important poem in Scottish literature. Barbour is also the probable author of a long poem on the Trojan War (q.v.) entitled "Legend of Troy", and of a devotional poem, "Legends of the Saints".

BARBUSSE, Henri (1873–1935), French novelist, born in Asnières, and educated at the Collège Rollin. He worked as a dramatic critic on various Paris newspapers and acquired international fame with the publication of his war novel, *Le Feu* (1916; Eng. trans., *Under Fire,* 1917). The story of a squad of soldiers in the trenches during World War I, it is told in the language of infantrymen who philosophize on the future of humanity. Despite pacifist tendencies that stood in sharp contrast to the official policy of France, *Le Feu* was awarded the Prix Goncourt. *Le Feu* was followed by *Clarté* (1919; Eng. trans., *Light,* 1919), and after the publication of this political novel Barbusse organized the Clarté Movement, which sought to interest the writers of the world in the social and political progress of humanity. Among the other works of Barbusse are the novels *L'Enfer* (1908; Eng. trans., *The Inferno,* 1918), and *Les Enchaînements* (1925; Eng. trans., *Chains,* 1925), collections of essays, and a critical biography, *Zola* (1932).

BARCELONA, city and seaport of Spain, in the Catalonia Region, and capital of Barcelona Province, on the Mediterranean Sea between the Llobregat and Besos rivers, about 300 miles N.E. of Madrid. Barcelona is the second-largest Spanish city in population and the principal industrial and commercial center of the country. The chief manufactures are textiles, precision instruments, machinery, railroad equipment, paper, glass, and plastics. The city is one of the major Mediterranean ports and a financial and publishing center of Spain.

Barcelona Province, the most populous and industrialized of the Spanish provinces, is mountainous with fertile plains and a low sandy coast. Agricultural products include cork, olives, grains, vegetables, grapes, almonds, oranges, and peaches. Cement and textiles are the major manufactures and lignite and potash are mined.

The oldest section of the city of Barcelona, formerly enclosed by walls, was built on the harbor. The section is traversed by the Rambla, a paved thoroughfare extending from the harbor to the Plaza de Cataluña, the focal point of the city. The streets of the old section are narrow and crooked; in the newer sections they are wide and straight and the buildings are modern. Points of major interest include the Church of

The Plaza de Cataluña, in the center of Barcelona.
Spanish National Tourist Office

San Pablo del Campo (914), the Gothic Cathedral of Santa Eulalia, the Church of the Holy Family, a monument to the Genoese explorer Christopher Columbus (q.v.), and the nearby peak Tibidabo (1745 ft.). Among the many cultural institutions are the National University of Barcelona, the Royal Archives of Aragon, and the Archeological Museum. The city is surrounded by heavily populated suburbs.

According to legend, Barcelona was founded as Barcino about 230 B.C. by the Carthaginian general Hamilcar Barca (q.v.). The region became part of the Roman Empire in the 3rd century B.C.; it was ruled by the Visigoths (*see* GOTHS) in the 5th century A.D.; was conquered by the Moors (q.v.) in 713; and was captured by the King of the Franks Charlemagne (q.v.) in 801. Under Frankish rule the city and the supporting region became the self-governing County of Catalonia (q.v.), or Barcelona. The region was absorbed into the Kingdom of Aragon (q.v.) in 1137. Barcelona thereafter gained in commercial and political importance as a Mediterranean trading and shipping center. The prosperity of Barcelona diminished after the union, in 1479, of the kingdoms of Aragon and Castile (q.v.), and the subsequent imposition of restrictive trade policies on the city. In 1833 Barcelona Province was established, with Barcelona as the provincial capital. In the 19th and 20th centuries Barcelona was a center of Catalan regionalism, anarchy, and industrial unrest. During the Spanish Civil War the city was the seat of the autonomous Catalan government and was a Loyalist stronghold. It was heavily bombed in 1938 by the insurgents, or Nationalists, who finally captured the city on Jan. 26, 1939; *see* SPAIN: *History.*

The area of the province is about 3000 sq.mi.; pop. (1970 est.) 3,600,000. Pop. of city (1970 prelim.) 1,742,000.

BARCELONA, NATIONAL UNIVERSITY OF, coeducational public institution of higher learning, located in Barcelona, Spain, administered by the Roman Catholic Church, and regulated by the ministry of national education. The university developed from an academy formed by the merger in 1377 of two 12th-century schools, one in Barcelona and the other in Lérida. The city magistrates of Barcelona raised the academy to university status in 1430, and the authority of the institution to confer degrees was confirmed in 1450 by a papal bull. Philip V (*see under* PHILIP: *Spain*) suppressed the university in 1714 and three years later had it transferred to Cervera. The status of the institution was restored in 1841 and it reopened in Barcelona in 1842. Instruction is offered in the faculties of law; political science, economics, and commerce; medicine; pharmacy; philosophy and letters; and science. The *licenciado* is awarded in all faculties at the end of a five- to seven-year course of study. The doctorate is awarded on the basis of a thesis and additional study. The main library, famed for its collections of manuscripts and incunabula, contains about 590,000 volumes. In 1968–69 the student body numbered 13,270 and the faculty, approximately 1250.

BARCLAY, John (1582–1621), Scottish writer of satire and Latin verse, born in Pont-à-Mousson, France, where his father was professor of law. Because of persecution by the Jesuits, with whom he probably had studied, Barclay went with his father to England about 1603. There he wrote *Satyricon,* a politico-satirical romance directed chiefly against the Jesuits, and supplemented this work with a second part (1607), the *Apologia* (1611), and the *Icon Animorum* (1614). In 1616 he left England and went to Rome. In the same year *Argenis,* an allegory on political conspiracy and the work for which he is best known, appeared.

BARCLAY, Robert (1648–90), Scottish Quaker, born in Gordonstown, Moray County, and educated at the Scots College in Paris, France. Opposed to the doctrines of both Calvinism and Catholicism, he joined the Society of Friends (*see* FRIENDS, SOCIETY OF) in 1667. In 1672 he startled the city of Aberdeen by walking through its streets in sackcloth and ashes. He suffered much persecution and was frequently imprisoned. In later years he was in favor with the Duke of York, later James II (q.v.), King of England, Scotland, and Ireland. With other Quakers, including William Penn (q.v.), Barclay was granted a patent to East Jersey. Barclay was nominal governor of the province from 1883 to 1888 but never went to America. The best known of his works is *An Apology for the True Christian Divinity, as the Same is Held Forth and Preached by the People Called in Scorn Quakers* (1678). His *Treatise on Universal Love* (1677) dealt with the criminality of war. Barclay's collected works were published in a volume entitled *Truth Triumphant* (1692).

BARCLAY DE TOLLY, Prince Mikhail (1761–1818), Russian field marshal born in Livonia, and descended from an old Scottish family settled there. Having entered a Russian regiment, he fought in the Turkish War of 1788–89, in the campaign against Sweden in 1790, and in those against Poland in 1792 and 1794. Although disliked by the Russian National Party as a foreigner, he was appointed minister of war by Alexander I (q.v.), Emperor of Russia in 1810. In 1812, during the war against Napoleon I (q.v.) of France, Barclay was made commander in chief of the Army of the West. His tactics of continual retreat into the depths of Russia aroused the opposition of the Russian National Party to a greater extent than ever, and when the French captured Smolensk on Aug. 17 he was obliged to yield his command to Marshal Mikhail Kutuzov (1745–1813). Kutuzov, realizing the wisdom of Barclay's strategy, continued it with success, and after Kutuzov's death Barclay was again appointed commander in chief of the Russian army in the campaigns in Germany and France. His tactics finally brought about the defeat of Napoleon. Barclay took part in the invasion of France in 1814 and in that year was made a field marshal. At the end of the war he was created a prince.

BAR COCHEBA, Simon *or* **BAR KOKBA, Simon,** real name SIMEON BAR KOSBA (d. 135 A.D.), Jewish revolutionary leader. Nothing is known of his life before he emerged as the leader of the Jews in their insurrection against the Romans in 132–35 A.D. Stirred by the attempt of the Roman Emperor Hadrian (q.v.) to Romanize Judea (*see* JEWS: *Subject Judea*), the Jews rose in revolt in Cyrene, Eygpt, Cyprus, and Mesopotamia (qq.v.) in 118, and in Judea in 132. The revolt in Judea was the most violent. It was organized by Bar Cocheba with the support of Akiba ben Joseph (q.v.), one of the most influential rabbis of the period. Akiba proclaimed Bar Cocheba the Messiah, or leader believed by the Jews destined to be sent by God to put an end to their adversities under foreign rule. A large army of Jews of Judea and other parts of the Orient was formed under Bar Cocheba.

With this army Bar Cocheba defeated the Romans and captured Jerusalem and fifty towns and many villages. Hadrian sent against the Jews another army that was also defeated by Bar Cocheba. Finally Hadrian put in the field a force under his ablest general, C. Julius Severus. After a long campaign, the Romans crushed the Jewish army at Bethar near Jerusalem in August, 135. Bar Cocheba fell in this battle, though the exact circumstances of his death are obscured by legend. At Bethar and elsewhere in Judea half a million Jews were said to have been killed by the Romans and thousands of women and children sold into slavery. These and other reprisals taken by the Romans forced many Jews to leave Judea and settle elsewhere in Asia, and in Europe and Africa. This movement was the final exile or dispersal of Jews from their homeland, which was not again a state governed by Jews until the establishment of the republic of Israel in 1948. In 1960 fifteen messages by Bar Cocheba were found in one of the caves in the Dead Sea region. N.N.G.

BARD COLLEGE, coeducational privately controlled institution of higher learning, located in Annandale-on-Hudson, N.Y., and associated with the Protestant Episcopal Church. The college was established by the American philanthropist John Bard (1819–99) in 1860 as Saint Stephen's College, primarily a training school for candidates for the Episcopalian ministry. Affiliated with Columbia University in 1928, it was rechartered as Bard College in 1935. In 1944 the tie with Columbia was broken and coeducation was introduced. Bard provides four divisions of study leading to the B.A. degree: art, music, drama, and dance; languages and literature; natural sciences; and social studies. Instruction is mainly in tutorial conferences and seminars. In 1972 the college library housed 117,000 bound volumes; there were 759 students and 89 teachers. The endowment was about $267,000.

BARDEEN, John (1908–), American physicist, born in Madison, Wis., and educated at the University of Wisconsin and Princeton University. He taught (1938–41) at the University of Minnesota and was (1941–45) principal physicist at the United States Naval Ordnance Laboratories, Washington, D.C. As a research physicist (1945–51) at the Bell Telephone Laboratories in Murray Hill, N.J., he was a member of the team that developed the transistor (q.v.), a tiny electronic device capable of performing most of the functions of the vacuum tube (*see* VACUUM TUBES, THERMIONIC). For this work, he shared the 1956 Nobel Prize in physics with two colleagues, the American physicists William Shockley and Walter H. Brattain (qq.v.). Meanwhile he had joined (1951) the faculty of the University of Illinois. In 1972 he shared the Nobel Prize in physics with the American physicists Leon N. Cooper and John Robert Schieffer (qq.v.) for the development of a theory to explain superconductivity, the disappearance of electrical resistance in certain metals and alloys at temperatures near absolute zero; *see* CRYOGENICS. Bardeen thus became the first scientist to win two Nobel Prizes in the same category.

BARDS. *See* ENGLISH LITERATURE: *Poetry.*

BAREBONE'S PARLIAMENT, the Little Parliament summoned by the English soldier and statesman Oliver Cromwell (q.v.), which met July 4, 1653. It was derisively nicknamed for one of the members, Praisegod Barbon or Barebone (1596?–1679), a leather merchant. The assembly was made up of 140 members selected from lists of nominees submitted by Congregational churches in each county. Although the legislative measures enacted by this assembly were subjected to ridicule by contemporary jurists, their provisions were related to the contemporary laws of the New England colonies and anticipated some essential principles of the modern British legal system by nearly two hundred years. Included in the program, for example, was the abolition of ecclesiastical tithes, and among the ordinances was one providing for a civil-marriage celebration before justices of the peace and for civil-marriage registration by elected parish registrars. Cromwell dissolved the Parliament on Dec. 12, 1653; *see* PARLIAMENT.

BAREILLY *or* **BARELI,** city of the Republic of India, in Uttar Pradesh State, and capital of Rohilkhand Division, on the Ramganga R., about 130 miles E. of Delhi. It is a center for the manufacture of furniture and for trade in cotton, grain, and sugar. Pop. (1971) 296,248.

BARENTS, Willem (d. 1597), Dutch navigator. Barents made three voyages from the Netherlands in search of a Northeast Passage to Asia. The first vessel sailed June 5, 1594, reached the northeastern extremity of Novaya Zemlya, and returned. A second expedition of seven vessels was sent out the following year, too late in the season to be successful. On the third expedition, which started in May, 1596, Barents discovered and named Spitsbergen (now Svalbard). There his two vessels separated to conduct independent explorations. Barents and his crew spent a miserable winter frozen in north of Novaya Zemlya. On June 13, 1597, they left in two open boats; Barents died shortly afterward. The survivors reached the shores of Lapland and were rescued by the second ship of the expedition. The Barents Sea (q.v.), which he crossed in 1594, 1596, and 1597, and Barents Island in the Svalbard archipelago were named for him.

BARENTS SEA, part of the South Arctic Ocean, named for its discoverer the Dutch navigator Willem Barents (q.v.). Bounded on the W. by the Norwegian archipelago of Svalbard and on the E. by the two islands of Novaya Zemlya, which belong to the Soviet Union, the sea extends northward from Norway, Finland, and the Soviet Union for about 900 mi., where it is bounded by Franz Josef Land. The sea is shallow and the S. part is free of ice all year. Trawlers from N. European ports fish its waters for cod and haddock. During World War II the Barents Sea served as an important traffic route; it was the only direct approach to the Soviet Union other than by air. At present it forms the westernmost part of the 5000 mi. seaway established by the Soviet Union leading from Murmansk in Europe to Vladivostok on the Pacific Ocean.

BARETTI, Giuseppe Marc'Antonio (1719–89), Italian writer, born in Turin, and educated in Milan and Venice. In 1751 he became a teacher of Italian in London. He subsequently became the friend of such notable British personalities as the author Samuel Johnson and the actor David Garrick (qq.v.). In 1769 he stabbed a London hoodlum in self-defense, but was acquitted of a murder charge through the assistance of Johnson. His thirty-six works include a *Dissertation on Italian Poetry* (1753).

BARGHOORN, Elso S(ternenberg) (1915–), American paleobotanist, born in New York City, educated at Miami University in Ohio, and at Harvard University. He was an instructor (1941–43) and assistant professor (1944-46) in the department of biology at Amherst College. He was appointed assistant professor of botany at Harvard in 1946, associate professor in 1949, and full professor in 1955. Barghoorn is known for his discovery, in Precambrian rock from South Africa, of microorganic fossils of bacteria that lived over 3,000,000,000 years ago, thereby proving that life on earth began much earlier than had been thought.

BARHAM, Richard Harris, pen name THOMAS INGOLDSBY (1788–1845), British writer, born in Canterbury, England, and educated at Brasenose College, University of Oxford. He was ordained in 1813, received a minor canonry of Saint Paul's Cathedral in 1821, and became a priest of His Majesty's Chapel Royal in 1824. In the early numbers of the periodical *Bentley's Miscellany* in 1837 he began his series of burlesque metrical tales, *Ingoldsby Legends,* with which he gained immediate fame.

BAR HARBOR, town of Maine, in Hancock Co., on Mount Desert Island, on Frenchman Bay, about 40 miles S.E. of Bangor. Bar Harbor is at the gateway to Acadia National Park (q.v.). Since the middle of the 19th century Bar Harbor has been a popular summer resort. The town was settled in 1763 and incorporated in 1796. Pop. (1960) 3807; (1970) 3,716.

BAR-HEBRAEUS, Gregorius, *or* ABULFARAJ (1226–86), Jacobite Syrian scholar, born in Melitene (now Malatya), Turkey. He was the son of a Jewish physician who embraced Christianity. Bar-Hebraeus first studied medicine under his father and later turned to theology and philosophy. He became a monk about the age of seventeen and was later successively appointed bishop of Gubas, Lakabhin, and Aleppo. With his seat at Tikrit, on the Tigris R., he became *mafriana,* or primate, of the Eastern Jacobites in 1264, an office ranking next to that of patriarch. He compiled a Syriac grammar and wrote many works. Bar-Hebraeus is best known for his *Mákhtbhānúth Zábhnê* ("Chronicle"), a secular and ecclesiastical history, and *Auçár Râzê* ("Storehouse of Secrets"), a compendium of theology, philosophy, and metaphysics based on the text of the Scriptures.

BARI (anc. *Barium*), city and seaport in Italy, in the Apulia Region, and capital of Bari Province, on the Adriatic Sea, 135 miles N.E. of Naples. It is a major commercial center, having an especially extensive trade with E. Mediterranean ports, and is one of the principal cities of S. Italy.

Major industrial establishments include petroleum refineries, textile and flour mills, steelworks, food canneries, and plants producing machinery and tobacco products.

The old section of the city occupies a promontory separating the old and new harbors. It is the site of two notable Romanesque churches: the Basilica of San Nicola (11th–12th centuries), in which the relics of Saint Nicholas, patron of Bari, are preserved in a silver-covered altar, and the cathedral, built late in the 12th century. A castle begun in the mid-13th century by Holy Roman Emperor Frederick II (q.v.) overlooks the new harbor. The modern section of the city, which covers part of the adjacent plain, is regularly laid out, with broad avenues and streets. Points of interest include the buildings of the University of Bari, founded in 1924, and the fairgrounds of the Fiera del Levante, an important annual trade fair dedicated to stimulating commerce between Europe and the Near East. Bari was a major Italian naval base during World War II. The port area was heavily bombed by the Allies and, after 1943, by the Germans. Pop. (1967) 345,108.

BARILOCHE, city and resort center of Argentina, in Río Negro Province, on the S. shore of Lake Nahuel Huapi, about 600 miles S.W. of Buenos Aires. In full, the name is San Carlos de Bariloche. A resort of international renown since the early 1960's, it is connected with Buenos Aires by air, rail, and a paved road that was completed in 1969. The tourist and commercial center of Nahuel Huapi National Park, the city is at the S. edge of the extensive, forested Patagonian lake country, bounded on the W. by Andean peaks, some of which are snowcapped the year round. Skiing is the favorite sport in winter, and boating, fishing, and hiking are popular in summer. Settled primarily by Austrians and Germans about 1895, Bariloche has the appearance of an alpine town. Pop. (1969 est.) 15,022.

BARING, Evelyn, 1st Earl of Cromer, (1841–1917), British diplomat and administrator, born in Norfolk, England, and educated at Woolwich Academy. From 1872 to 1876 he was private secretary to the viceroy of India. In 1877 he was appointed British commissioner of the public debt office of Egypt, where he served until 1880, when he became finance minister of India. In 1883 he began a twenty-four-year stay in Egypt as British consul general and agent with plenipotentiary powers. Baring headed a staff of

British officials charged with the administration of Egypt then under the nominal authority of the khedive; *see* EGYPT: *Egypt under the Caliphate.* During his administration the financial system of Egypt was modernized, the army was reorganized, trade and communications were extended, and the interests of Great Britain were protected. In 1892 Baring was created Baron Cromer. When Mohammed Tewfik Pasha (1852–92), the khedive, died, Cromer secured the peaceful succession of Tewfik's son Abbas II (1874–1944). Cromer enforced the agreement by which Great Britain and Egypt exercised power over the Sudan (*see* SUDAN, REPUBLIC OF THE: *History: Mahdist Revolt; British-Egyptian Sovereignty*) after the former Egyptian province was regained by an Anglo-Egyptian army in 1898. Because of the efficiency of his administration, Cromer was called the Maker of Modern Egypt. He was created a viscount in 1897 and an earl in 1901. He returned to England in 1907, entered the House of Lords in 1908, and was active in Parliament until his death.

BARING-GOULD, Sabine (1834–1924), British clergyman and writer, born in Exeter, England, and educated at Clare College, University of Cambridge. In 1881 he was appointed rector of Lewtrenchard, Devonshire, his ancestral home. He edited *The Sacristy,* a quarterly ecclesiastical review, from 1871 to 1873. Although a prolific writer of fiction as well as of works on folklore, history, travel, and theology, Baring-Gould is remembered chiefly as the author of the words of the famous hymn "Onward, Christian Soldiers" (1865). His many other works include *The Book of Werewolves* (1865), *Curious Myths of the Middle Ages* (1866), and *Lives of the Saints* (15 vol., 1872–77). He wrote also an opera, *The Red Spider,* which was produced in 1898.

BARISAL, city of Bangladesh, capital of Barisal District, near the mouth of the Ganges R., about 70 miles S. of Dacca. The city is a center for trade in rice, betel nuts, jute, sugarcane, and fish. The chief industries are rice and flour milling, and the manufacture of soap and bricks. Three colleges, branches of Dacca University, are located in Barisal. In this region occurs the phenomenon known as Barisal guns (q.v.). Pop. (latest census) 69,936.

BARISAL GUNS, mysterious sounds, as of distant cannon, heard in many parts of the world, especially on or near the water; now generally believed to be caused by earth tremors that are too feeble to be felt. This phenomenon is known scientifically as brontides and commonly as barisal guns because it is particularly prevalent near the city of Barisal (q.v.) in Bangladesh. The sounds have various other names in different countries; in the Netherlands and Belgium they are known as *mistpoeffers,* in Italy as *baturlio marina,* or *brontidi,* and in Haiti as *gouffre.* In the United States, on Seneca Lake, N.Y., they are called *lake guns.*

BARITO, river of Indonesia, in the S.E. part of the island of Borneo. It rises in the Müller Mts. in the central part of the island, flows S. for about 550 mi., and below Bandjarmasin enters the Java Sea.

BARITONE (fr. Gr. *barytonos,* "deep sounding"), male singing voice intermediate in range between the bass and the tenor (qq.v.). Having both tenor and bass qualities (notably weightiness and brilliance in its upper register), it is much used in opera. The normal range of the baritone is two octaves, with its lowest note being A, a tenth below middle C.

BARIUM, element of the alkaline earth family with at.no. 56, at.wt. 137.35, b.p. over 1500° C. (2732° F.), m.p. 710° C. (1310° F.), sp.gr. $3.6^{20°}$, and symbol Ba. Although barium sulfate, or barite, had been known for some time, the pure element was first prepared in 1808 by the English scientist Sir Humphry Davy (q.v.). It is a soft, silvery metal that reacts vigorously with water and is rapidly corroded by moist air. Barium, the sixteenth most common element, makes up $\frac{1}{2000}$th of the crust of the earth. The pure metal does not occur in nature; the most important minerals are barite and witherite (barium carbonate). Barium metal has few practical applications, although it is sometimes used in coating electrical conductors in electronic apparatus and in automobile ignition systems. Barium sulfate is used as a filler for rubber products, in paint, and in linoleum. Barium nitrate is used in fireworks and barium carbonate in rat poisons. A form of barium sulfate is given to patients when X-ray photographs are to be taken of their stomachs.

BARK, hard covering or rind of the stem, branches, and roots of a tree or other plant, as distinguished from the wood. The bark consists of an inner and outer layer; *see* TREE. Principal commercial uses of bark are for the tanning of leather, for the building of boats, for basket-making, for shoes, for garments, for food flavoring, for medicine, and for cork (q.v.) and cork products.

For tanning, barks rich in tannin (*see* TANNINS) are usually used, although other properties also determine the value of a bark for preparing leather. Bark from several species of oak (*Quercus velutina, Q. prinus,* and *Q. falcata,* in the east; and *Q. densiflora,* west of the Rocky Mts.)

and the Eastern hemlock (*Tsuga canadensis*) supply much of the tannin in northern United States. In recent years the production of barks for tannin has been reduced by the increased use of the wood or fruit of many trees as a source of tannin, and by the development of synthetic tannins.

Bark has been used by primitive peoples for many purposes. The North American Indians used birchbark to cover canoes and tepees. Natives of Guyana make canoes of the bark of purple heart (*Copaifera pubiflora*) and of the locust (*Hymenaea courbaril*). In Lapland bark is used for baskets and shoes. Coats are made by the natives of British Columbia from pine bark, and garments of an elm bark are worn by the Ainu of Japan. Many peoples of Africa and Oceania make cloth from the bark of several trees.

The principal barks used for medicines and flavorings are discussed in separate articles; *see also* CASCARA SAGRADA; CINCHONA; CINNAMON; WITCH HAZEL.

BARK BEETLE, *or* ENGRAVER BEETLE, common name for any of the minute, cylindrical beetles of the family Scolytidae, found throughout the world. About 150 species of this family are recognized in the United States. Most of them burrow between the bark and the sapwood of trees, but a few forms tunnel through the wood. The female lays her eggs in pockets at intervals along the tunnel, and each larva forms its own tunnel, at an angle to the original burrow, and pupates there. When the adult is formed, it burrows directly to the surface; the young female migrates to a new place and starts another burrow. When numerous, the beetles kill trees by girdling with their burrows. Their burrowing forms characteristic patterns, giving rise to the name engraver beetle. They also carry plant diseases. *Scolytus multistriatus,* a small bark beetle with black thorax and red wing cases, is a principal carrier of the Dutch elm disease (q.v.). The Department of Agriculture estimates the damage to trees in the U.S. by Scolytidae to be many millions of dollars annually. *See* BEETLE.

BARKING DEER. *See* MUNTJAC.

BARKLA, Charles Glover (1877–1944), British physicist, born in Widnes, Lancashire, England, and educated at University College, Liverpool, and at the universities of Cambridge and Liverpool. He taught physics at the University of Liverpool from 1902 to 1907, was appointed professor of physics at the University of London in 1909, and was professor of natural philosophy at the University of Edinburgh from 1913 until his death. Barkla discovered the fluorescence polarization, and scattering of X rays, the characteristic X rays of elements and of X-ray spectra, the laws governing the transmission of X rays through matter, and the excitation of secondary rays. He was made a fellow of the Royal Society in 1912 and was awarded the Nobel Prize in physics in 1917.

BARKLEY, Alben William (1877–1956), American statesman and thirty-fifth Vice-President of the United States, born in Graves Co., Ky., and educated at Marvin College, Clinton, Ky., Emory College, Oxford, Ga., and the University of Virginia law school. In 1901 he was admitted to the Kentucky bar. After holding various county offices in Kentucky, he was elected as a Democrat to the House of Representatives in 1912 and served until 1927. He was elected U.S. Senator from Kentucky for four successive terms beginning in 1927. Barkley was majority leader of the Senate from 1937 to 1947, and minority leader from 1947 to 1948. In the latter year he was elected U.S. Vice-President on the Democratic ticket headed by Harry S. Truman (q.v.). He was again elected U.S. Senator from Kentucky in 1954.

BARK LOUSE. *See* SCALE INSECT.

BARLACH, Ernst Heinrich (1870–1938), German sculptor and playwright, born in Wedel. As a sculptor he worked in wood, terra-cotta, porcelain, and bronze, and was chiefly influenced by the French artists Honoré Daumier and Auguste Rodin (qq.v.), and by Russian wood carvings. Barlach produced monuments and memorials to the soldiers killed in World War I, for several German cities. His sculptures are shown in many European museums and in American collections. He made numerous portrait busts and illustrations (woodcuts and drawings) for books. After a career as a sculptor, he became a playwright. Among his best-known plays are *Der Arme Vetter* ("The Poor Cousin", 1918) and *Die Sündflut* ("The Deluge", 1924).

BARLETTA (anc. *Barduli*), city of Italy, in Bari Province, in the region of Apulia, on the Adriatic coast, 200 miles E. of Rome. The city, situated near the most important saltworks of Italy, is a seaport and an agricultural and industrial center. In Barletta are distilleries, tanneries, and plants manufacturing drugs, chemicals, and foodstuffs. Notable edifices include a cathedral built between the 12th and 15th centuries, the church of Santo Sepolcro containing 12th-century frescoes, and a medieval castle. Nine miles W. of the city is the site of ancient Cannae, where in 216 B.C. the Carthaginian general Hannibal (q.v.) defeated the Romans. Pop. (1971 prelim.) 76,405.

BARLEY, any cereal grass of genus *Hordeum* Native to Asia and Ethiopia, it is one of the most ancient of cultivated plants or grasses. Cultivation of barley is mentioned in the Bible, and it was grown by the ancient Egyptians, Greeks, Romans, and Chinese. In the United States and Canada, as well as in the greater portion of Europe, barley is sown in the spring. Along the Mediterranean Sea, and in parts of California and Arizona, it is sown in the fall. It is also grown as a winter annual in the southern U.S. Barley germinates at about the same temperature as wheat. The different cultivated varieties of barley belong to three distinct types: two-rowed barley, *H. distichum;* six-rowed barley, *H. vulgare;* and irregular barley, *H. irregulare.* The varieties grown in the U.S. are generally of the six-rowed type, in Europe the two-rowed type predominates, and the irregular type is found in Ethiopia. The finest malting varieties are the six-rowed and the two-rowed types.

Barley grain, hay, straw, and several by-products are used for feed. The grain is used for malt beverages (*see* BEER) and in cooking. Like other cereals, barley contains a large proportion of carbohydrate (67 percent) and of protein (12.8 percent). In the late 1960's annual production of barley in the U.S. totaled almost 8,000,000 tons; world production was about 115,000,000 tons.

BARLOW, Joel (1754–1812), American poet and diplomat, born in Redding, Conn., and educated at Dartmouth and Yale colleges. After serving in the American Revolution as chaplain, he was admitted to law practice in Hartford, Conn., in 1786. His epic poem *The Vision of Columbus* appeared in 1787 and *The Columbiad,* an enlarged version of the former, in 1807. He lived for a time in Paris and London, where he wrote various political works, the most noteworthy of which was *Advice to the Privileged Orders* in 1792. He was sent by President James Madison (q.v.) to negotiate a commercial treaty with the French emperor Napoleon I (q.v.) in 1811. On his way to meet Napoleon at Vilna, Russia, Barlow became involved in the disastrous retreat of the French army from Russia, during which he died of exposure.

BAR MITZVAH (Heb., "son of the commandment"), in Jewish religion, a boy entering his fourteenth year. At that age he assumes religious duties and responsibility. In the synagogue on the Sabbath, typically that nearest his birthday, it is customary for him to read sections of the Torah (q.v.) and to deliver an address. The religious ceremony usually is followed by a social function, and the boy receives gifts from his family and friends. *See* CONFIRMATION. S.L.

BARNABAS, surname given by the Apostles (*see* APOSTLE) to Joseph, one of the members of the early Christian Church in Jerusalem, and interpreted in the New Testament as "Son of Consolation" (Acts 4:36). A Levite and a native of Cyprus, Barnabas is credited with having founded the Cypriot Church. Barnabas introduced Saul of Tarsus, later the Apostle Paul (q.v.), to the other Apostles in Jerusalem following Paul's conversion (Acts 9:27); he later accompanied Paul on missionary journeys to Antioch, Cyprus, and Asia Minor. At the council held in Jerusalem (Acts 15), Barnabas was in harmony with Paul's views that the Church had a mission to the Gentiles. He and Paul later separated, however, when Barnabas insisted that his nephew Mark (q.v.), who had deserted them on a previous journey, should accompany them again (Acts 15:36–38). Barnabas and Mark together continued missionary work in Cyprus (Acts 15:39).

The writings ascribed to Barnabas have been the source of dispute among Biblical scholars. The early Christian writer Tertullian (q.v.) assigns to him the authorship of the New Testament Epistle to the Hebrews (*see* HEBREWS), in accordance with 2nd-century Church tradition. The apocryphal *Acts of Barnabas,* a work of late date, recounts his missionary tours and his death by martyrdom in Cyprus. The extant *Epistle of Barnabas,* found in a New Testament manuscript (part of the Codex Sinaiticus in a monastery at Mount Sinai (*see* SINAI), is a didactic work, full of allegorical interpretations of the Old Testament and attacks on Judaism. Although Barnabas was said to be its author by early Christian writers, the epistle itself makes no such claim and authorship by him is held to be improbable.

BARNACLE, popular name for the crustaceans of the subclass Cirripedia; *see* CRUSTACEA. The name was originally applied to the barnacle goose of northern Europe, and its transfer to these crustaceans was due to the fable formerly current that the bird develops from the stalked, or "goose", barnacle (*Lepas*).

Most barnacles are hermaphrodites; all species inhabit salt water. The larvae are free-swimming, but the adults always attach to foreign objects, such as ship bottoms, wharf piles, rocks, floating timbers, whales, large fish, and shellfish. The subclass is divided into five orders, four of which are minute parasitic forms on other shellfish. The other order includes the acorn barnacles common to temperate and cold waters, and the stalked barnacles, which are usually found in warm waters but, because they attach them-

Barnacle-covered rocks. UPI

selves to ships, are well distributed throughout the world. This habit is economically important because of the expense involved in the periodical removal of barnacles from the bottoms of ships.

A method of controlling barnacle infestation by means of ultrasonic vibrations was introduced in 1955; *see* ULTRASONICS. The hull of the ship is fitted with thin metal plates that are vibrated by a generator at 25,000 cycles per sec.; the vibrations repel the barnacles.

BARNARD, Christiaan Neethling (1922–), South African surgeon, born in Beaufort West. He received an M.D. degree from the University of Cape Town in 1953 and a Ph.D. degree from the University of Minnesota in 1958. He returned to the University of Cape Town in 1958 to teach surgery. Barnard specialized in open-heart surgery and in designing new artificial heart valves. On Dec. 3, 1967, he performed the first human heart-transplant operation, transferring the heart of a twenty-five-year-old woman into the body of Louis Washkansky, a fifty-five-year-old grocer; Washkansky died eighteen days later. The subject of Barnard's second transplant, performed Jan. 2, 1968, was a dentist, Dr. Philip Blaiberg (1909–69), who lived 563 days after the operation. Barnard's autobiography, *One Life*, was published in 1970. *See* HEART: *Heart Transplants*.

BARNARD, Edward Emerson (1857–1923), American astronomer, born in Nashville, Tenn., and educated at Vanderbilt University and the University of the Pacific. From 1887 to 1895 he was astronomer at Lick Observatory, Mt. Hamilton, Calif. Subsequently he became professor of astronomy at the University of Chicago and astronomer of the Yerkes Observatory, Williams Bay, Wis. In 1916 he discovered Barnard's Star, the star with the greatest motion. He also obtained excellent results in celestial photography and discovered sixteen comets and the fifth satellite of Jupiter.

BARNARD, Frederick Augustus Porter (1809–89), American mathematician and educator, born in Sheffield, Mass., and educated at Yale College (now Yale University). He was professor of natural philosophy, mathematics, and English literature at the University of Alabama from 1837 to 1848 and of chemistry and natural history until 1854. In 1855 he was professor of astronomy and mathematics at the University of Mississippi, and in 1856 became president of that institution, serving as its chancellor from 1858 to 1861. Barnard became one of the incorporators of the American Association for the Advancement of Science and also its president in 1860, and in 1863 was one of the incorporators of the National Academy of Sciences. He became president of Columbia College, now one of the schools of Columbia University, New York City, in 1864, and served in that office until 1889. Barnard was an advocate of higher education for women, and Barnard College (q.v.) was named in his honor.

BARNARD, George Grey (1863–1938), American sculptor, born in Bellefonte, Pa. He studied at the Art Institute of Chicago and at the École Nationale des Beaux-Arts, Paris. His early important works are "Two Natures", two figures in marble, in the Metropolitan Museum of Art, New York City; and the colossal bronze, "Great

God Pan", on the campus of Columbia University. His large statue "Abraham Lincoln" in Manchester, England, caused criticism because of its realism but is today generally acknowledged as a masterpiece. Among other of his works are "The Urn of Life" (Carnegie Museum) and "Adam and Eve" (Rockefeller estate, Pocantico Hills, N.Y.). Barnard's personal collection of Gothic art formed the nucleus of the collection housed at the Cloisters, a branch of the Metropolitan Museum of Art, New York City.

BARNARD, Henry (1811–1900), American educator, born in Hartford, Conn., and educated at Yale College (now Yale University). He was a lawyer and served in the Connecticut legislature, where he worked to effect educational reforms. He was president of Saint John's College, Annapolis, Md., in 1865–66. After becoming the first United States commissioner of education in 1867, Barnard organized the Bureau of Education, and many of his suggestions have been adopted in the educational system of the U.S. He is the author of several works on education, science, and art, and was the founder and editor of the periodical *American Journal of Education,* which was issued in thirty-two volumes between 1855 and 1882.

BARNARD COLLEGE, privately controlled nonsectarian school of liberal arts for men and women, in New York City, and affiliated with Columbia University (q.v.). Barnard was founded with the informal sanction of the trustees of Columbia and opened for instruction in 1889. The following year the college was officially incorporated in the university, but continued to be separately financed and administered. Barnard offers courses of instruction in the arts and sciences leading to the B.A. degree, which is conferred by Columbia. Seniors may elect first-year training in one of the professional schools of the university. Students have access to the 3,000,000-volume Columbia library, in addition to their own library which housed 119,000 bound volumes in 1973. Student enrollment in 1973 totaled about 1950, the faculty numbered almost 200, and the endowment of the college was approximately $19,-590,000.

BARNAUL, city of the Soviet Union, in the Russian S.F.S.R., and capital of Altai Territory, on the Ob' R. at the junction of the Turkestan-Siberian and South Siberian railroads, 110 miles S.E. of Novosibirsk. The city is one of the major industrial centers of Siberia, manufacturing cotton textiles, diesel motors, machine tools, and chemicals. Pop. (1970 est.) 439,000.

BARNBURNERS. *See* FREE SOIL PARTY.

BARNEGAT BAY, inlet of the Atlantic Ocean, in Ocean County, N.J. It is about 30 mi. long and is separated from the ocean by long, narrow islands called Island Beach and Long Beach. On the shouth shore of the bay is a lighthouse, 163 ft. high.

BARNES, Harry Elmer (1889–1968), American historian and sociologist, born in Auburn, N.Y., and educated at Syracuse, Columbia, and Harvard universities. He taught history, sociology, and economics at Syracuse, Columbia, Clark, Washington State, and other universities, at the New School for Social Research in New York City, and at Amherst and Smith colleges. He was a newspaper columnist and editorial writer from 1929 to 1940. His works include *Sociology and Political Theory* (1924), *The Genesis of the World War* (1926), *World Politics in Modern Civilization* (2 vol., 1935), *An Intellectual and Cultural History of the Western World* (1937), *Society in Transition* (1939), *New Horizons in Criminology* (1943), and *An Introduction to the History of Sociology* (1948). Barnes edited *Perpetual War for Perpetual Peace* (1953).

BARNES, Joshua (1654–1712), English classical scholar, born in London, and educated at Emmanuel College, University of Cambridge. He became regius professor of Greek at Cambridge in 1695. Among his best-known works are *Gerania: a New Discovery of a Little Sort of People Anciently Discoursed of, Called Pygmies* (1675), a sketch from which the British satirist Jonathan Swift (q.v.) may have derived the idea for *Voyage to Lilliput.* Barnes' other works include *History of That Most Victorious Monarch Edward III* (1688) and editions of Euripides and Homer (qq.v.).

BARNES, William (1801–86), British poet, philologist, and clergyman, born near Salisbury, England, and educated at Saint John's College, University of Cambridge. His first three volumes of poems were collected in 1879 and published as *Poems of Rural Life in the Dorset Dialect.* An attempt to teach the English language in exclusively Anglo-Saxon words is presented in his *Outline of English Speechcraft* (1878).

BARNEVELDT, Jan van Olden *or* **BARNEVELD, Jan van Olden** (1547–1619), Dutch statesman, born in Amersfoort, and educated as a lawyer. During the Dutch revolt (1568–1648) against Spanish rule he attained prominence as a militant fighter for independence. He became grand pensionary, or prime minister, of Rotterdam in 1576, and in 1579 he was instrumental in securing the election of William I (q.v.), known as William the Silent, as the first stadtholder, or chief executive, of the United Provinces of the Netherlands. After William's assassination in 1584 Barneveldt successfully supported William's son, Maurice of Nassau (1567–1625), for the stadtholderate. In 1586 Barneveldt became grand pensionary of the province of Holland, the most influential member of the Union. The chief accomplishment of his subsequent political career was the conclusion in 1609 of a twelve-year truce with Spain in which the independence of the Netherlands was recognized. In negotiating this pact, which was favored by the Dutch Republican Party and mercantile class, he incurred the enmity of a powerful anti-Spanish grouping, including Maurice and the Calvinist clergy, who felt that the Spanish would take advantage of the peace to strengthen their forces. The consequent controversy merged with the current religious conflict between Arminianism and Calvinism (qq.v.), with Barneveldt and the Republicans supporting the former. In August, 1617, during the height of the strife, the Holland provincial legislature voted, at his urging, to boycott a national synod which had been convoked by the States-General, the legislative body of the Netherlands. In retaliation against this move and other defiant gestures by the Holland legislature, the States-General ordered Maurice and a contingent of troops into the province. The Hollanders offered no resistance, and Barneveldt and his closest colleagues were arrested on Aug. 23. He was brought to trial before a commission especially appointed by the States-General in February, 1619, and was convicted of treason on May 12 after a trial in which he was denied a lawyer; he was beheaded the next day.

BARN OWL, common name for any bird of the family Tytonidae in the order Strigiformes. Barn owls differ from the typical owls (family Strigidae in the same order) in having a heart-shaped rather than circular face, and in not having ear tufts. Barn owls also have smaller eyes and longer legs. They are generally light in color, ranging from light brown to white flecked with black. Both male and female are colored alike. Like the true owls, they have nocturnal habits, and their food consists principally of harmful rodents; *see* OWL. Of the twenty-five species distributed throughout the temperate and tropical regions of the world, only one, the common barn owl, *Tyto alba,* is found in the United States. It is common in the southern States, ranging northward to Canada in the summer, and southward into Mexico in the winter. It nests in barns, abandoned buildings, belfries, or hollow trees. The eggs, usually five to seven in number, are chalky, unmarked white.

Young barn owls. UPI

BARNSLEY, Great Britain, county borough of West Riding, Yorkshire, England, on the Dearne R., 12 miles N. of Sheffield. The borough is an important industrial center, with plants manufacturing textiles and glass. In the vicinity are highly productive coal mines. Pop. (1967 est.) 75,910.

BARNSTABLE, town of Massachusetts, in Barnstable Co., on Cape Cod, about 70 miles S.E. of Boston. The county seat, also called Barnstable, a village of the town, lies on the N. shore of Cape Cod. Other villages of the town, which has an area of 64 sq.mi., are Cummaquid and West Barnstable, on the N. shore, and Hyannis, Hyannis Port, Centerville, Osterville, and Cotuit, on the S. shore. The town is a popular summer resort, catering to vacationists and tourists. Leading year-round industries are fishing and cranberry raising. First settled in 1637, Barnstable was incorporated as a town in 1639. It is the birthplace of the American revolutionary statesman James Otis (q.v.). Pop. (1960) 13,465; (1970) 19,842.

BARN SWALLOW, common name for a North American bird, *Hirundo rustica erythro gaster,* of the Swallow family. Found as far north as Alaska and Greenland in the summer, it migrates as far south as Brazil in the winter. The male is glossy blue above and pale reddish brown below. The forehead and throat are bright chestnut, bordered by a band of blue across the chest; the coloring of the female is similar, but slightly duller. In both sexes the tail is deeply forked, and each tail feather, except the central pair, has a white spot on its inner web. The barn swallow makes its nest inside barns and similar buildings. It should not be confused with the cliff swallow (q.v.), which has a square tail, and attaches its nest to the outside walls of buildings.

BARNUM, Phineas Taylor (1810–91), American showman, born in Bethel, Conn. His career in the amusement field began in 1835 in New York City, where he purchased Joyce Heth, a Negro slave, reputedly 161 years old, and alleged to have been the nurse of the American President George Washington (q.v.). Barnum exhibited her profitably throughout the country until her death in 1836. In 1841 he purchased Scudder's American Museum, in New York City, where in 1842 he placed on exhibition the American midget Charles Sherwood Stratton (q.v.), commonly known as General Tom Thumb. Also in his show were the original Siamese twins, Chang and Eng (1811–74). In 1850 he arranged an American concert tour for Jenny Lind (q.v.), the famous Swedish soprano. After several terms as a Connecticut State legislator, he launched, in Brooklyn, N.Y., in 1871, his greatest undertaking as a showman, a mobile circus. The circus included a menagerie and a museum containing many freaks; it was publicized as The Greatest Show on Earth. This organization merged in 1881 with the circus operated by another American showman, James Anthony Bailey (1847–1906), and as Barnum and Bailey's Circus it became internationally famous. Barnum wrote several books, notably his *Autobiography* (1854), *The Humbugs of the World* (1865), and *Moneygetting* (1883). *See* CIRCUS, MODERN.

Advertisement written by Phineas T. Barnum for his mobile circus "The Greatest Show on Earth".
Newark Public Library

BAROCCI, Federigo *or* **BAROCCIO, Federigo** (1528–1612), Italian painter, born in Urbino. He studied in Rome and was influenced chiefly by the works of the Italian painters Antonio Allegri da Correggio and Raphael (qq.v.). Upon his return to Urbino he executed many paintings that survive for the most part in the churches of that city, the most important being "Saint Sebastian", in the cathedral. On a later visit to Rome he was employed in painting frescoes in the Vatican. Among his most important paintings in Rome is the "Burning of Troy", in the Borghese Palace; others are in the Vatican collections and in the galleries of Florence. His finest work is considered to be "Christ Crucified", painted for the doge (chief magistrate) of Genoa and now in the Cathedral of Genoa.

BARODA, city in the Republic of India, in Gujarat State, on the Viswamitri R., about 230 miles N. of Bombay. The city has considerable trade in grain, flax, cotton, and tobacco. The chief manufactures are textiles, chemicals, and pottery. Located in the city are Baroda College, founded in 1885, and the Maharaja Sayajirao University of Baroda, founded in 1949. Baroda has several palaces, the largest of which is Lakshmi Vilas, and several temples, including the Kirti. The city was capital of the princely state of Baroda until 1949, when Baroda merged with Bombay State. Pop. (1971) 467,422.

BAROJA Y NESSI, Pío (1872–1956), Spanish novelist, born in San Sebastián, and educated in Madrid as a physician. He practiced his profession briefly, later managed a bakery, and before his thirtieth birthday began to write for a livelihood. Early in the 20th century he twice ran unsuccessfully as a Republican for a seat in the Cortes, or national parliament. His first novel was *La Casa de Aizgorri* (1900; Eng. trans., *The House of Aizgorri,* 1958). It forms part of the trilogy *La Tierra Vasca* ("The Basque Country", 1900–09), which also includes *El Mayorazgo de Labraz* (1903; Eng. trans., *The Lord of Labraz,* 1926), one of his most admired novels. The work for which he is best known outside Spain is the trilogy *La Lucha por la Vida* (1904; Eng. trans., *The Struggle for Life,* 1922–24), a moving description of life in the slums of Madrid. His *Memorias de un Hombre de Acción* ("Memories of a Man of Action"; 20 vol., 1913–31), consists of a series of loosely connected episodes revolving around one of his ancestors who lived in the Basque country at the time of the Carlist uprisings early in the 19th century; *see* CARLISTS. Baroja's published writings total more than one hundred volumes, including numerous volumes of essays and three of autobiography.

Working in the Spanish picaresque tradition (*see* PICARESQUE NOVEL), Baroja chose for his protagonists the misfits and outcasts of society, and his novels, though crammed with lively incident, usually lack plots. A master of the realistic portrayal of character and setting, especially when he draws on his knowledge of the Basque (*see* BASQUES) country and people, his style is abrupt, vivid, and impersonal and his philosophy is pessimistic. Many critics regard him as the leading Spanish novelist of the 20th century.

BAROMETER, instrument for measuring atmospheric pressure, that is, the force exerted on a surface of unit area by the weight of atmosphere. Since this force is transmitted equally in all directions through any fluid, it is most easily measured by observing the height of a column of liquid which, by its weight, exactly balances the weight of the atmosphere. A water barometer is far too large to be used conveniently, as normal atmospheric pressure will sustain a column of water 34 ft. high. Liquid mercury, however, is 13.6 times as heavy as water, and the column of mercury sustained by normal atmospheric pressure is only 30 in. high.

An ordinary mercurial barometer consists of a glass tube about 33 in. high, closed at the upper end and open at the lower. When the tube is filled with mercury and the open end placed in a cup full of the same liquid, the level in the tube falls to a height of about 30 in. above the level in the cup, leaving an almost perfect vacuum at the top of the tube. Variations in atmospheric pressure cause the liquid in the tube to rise or fall by small amounts, rarely below 29 in. or above 30.5 in. at sea level. When the mercury level is read with a form of gradated scale, known as a vernier attachment, and suitable corrections are made for altitude and latitude (because of the change of gravity), temperature (because of the expansion of the mercury), and the diameter of the tube (because of capillarity), the reading of a mercurial barometer can be relied on to within 0.1 mm. (0.004 in.).

A more convenient form of barometer, and one that is almost as accurate, is the aneroid, in which atmospheric pressure bends the elastic top of a partially evacuated drum, actuating a pointer.

Accurate prediction of weather is made possible only by delineation of the size, shape, and motions of continental air masses, and can be accomplished by simultaneous barometric observations at a number of separated observation points. The barometer is thus the basis for all meteorological prediction. Inasmuch as an approaching storm is generally heralded locally by falling atmospheric pressure, even a single barometer can be used with some accuracy for weather prediction. *See* METEOROLOGY.

A suitable aneroid barometer is often used as an altimeter, because pressure decreases rapidly with increasing altitude (about 1 in. of mercury per 1000 ft. at low altitudes).

Three types of aneroid barometer (left to right): pocket, engineering, surveying. The aneroid is light and sturdily constructed, making it more convenient for general use than the mercury barometer.

Taylor Instrument Co.

Normal atmospheric pressure is usually taken to be 760 mm (29.921 in.) of mercury, which is equal to 14.696 lb. per sq.in., or 1.0133 bars.

See also TORRICELLI, EVANGELISTA.

BARONIUS, Caesar (1538–1607), Italian prelate and ecclesiastical historian, born in Sora, Frosinone, and educated in Veroli and Naples. He joined the Fathers of the Oratory, the religious society founded in 1564 by the Italian priest Saint Philip Neri (1515–95). Baronius became superior of the society in 1593 and within the next five years was made successively confessor to Pope Clement VIII (*see under* CLEMENT), cardinal, and librarian of the Vatican. Baronius is best remembered for his compilation of the Roman Catholic *Annales Ecclesiastici a Christo Nato ad Annum 1198* ("Ecclesiastical Annals from the Nativity to 1198"; 12 vol., 1588–1607). Despite its polemical character and numerous minor errors of fact, which were corrected by later editors, the *Annales* proved to be a storehouse of learning of permanent value to scholars. Baronius also prepared a new edition of the *Martyrologium Romanum* ("Roman Martyrology", 1586).

BARONS' WAR, in English history, rebellion of the nobility against Henry III (q.v.), King of England, staged between 1263 and 1267. The rebellion, led by the English statesman Simon de Montfort (q.v.), Earl of Leicester, was precipitated by Henry's refusal, abetted by Pope Urban IV (*see under* URBAN), to effect the Provisions of Oxford, amendments to the Magna Charta (q.v.) that had been adopted by the nobility in 1258 in an effort to curb Henry's abuse of his powers. In 1263 the dispute between the barons and Henry was submitted for arbitration to Louis IX (q.v.), King of France, whose decision favored the English sovereign. Refusing to accept the decision, Montfort and his supporters, including sections of the middle class, resorted to arms, inflicting a severe defeat on Henry's forces at Lewes in 1264 and taking Henry prisoner. Montfort, who became virtual ruler of the kingdom, summoned a Parliament for 1265, establishing democratic principles of representation that figured significantly in the eventual development of the House of Commons; *see* PARLIAMENT. The war was renewed, however, and on Aug. 4, 1265, Henry's troops, led by Prince Edward, later King of England as Edward I (q.v.), won a decisive victory over the barons at Evesham, where Montfort was killed. The reforms for which Montfort fought were generally put into effect during the reign of Edward I.

BAROQUE (possibly from Port. *barroco,* "a rough, irregularly shaped pearl", It. *verucca,* "wart", or Gr. *baros,* "heavy"), term applied to the style prevalent in European art from the middle of the 16th century to the latter part of the 18th century. Baroque style developed in reaction to the austere and rigid formality of classical forms. It is characterized by freedom in the use of line and color, resulting in great vitality, fluidity, and complexity of detail. Baroque architecture features twisted columns, convoluted scrolls, and elaborate decorative figuration. Baroque painting utilizes romantic color, strong emotion, and heavy contrast in light and dark. In music, the term "baroque" is applied to the period during which many new forms, such as the opera, sonata, and concerto, were invented, and melody became freed from the strictures of classical rules.

The term "baroque" is sometimes wrongly used interchangeably with rococo (q.v.), a style in art of extravagant curvature and ornament, developed in France chiefly in the period of Louis XV (q.v.), King of France. *See* ART: *History: Baroque Art;* ARCHITECTURE: *The Renaissance;* MUSIC: *The Baroque Era.*

BARQUISIMETO, city in Venezuela, capital of Lara State, on the Barquisimeto R. and on both the Pan-American and Trans-Andean highways, in a fertile agricultural region about 100 miles S.W. of the Caribbean port of Tucacas. Fiber bags, sandals, hammocks, leather goods, and tobacco products are manufactured in the city, and it is a trading center for coffee, sugar, cacao, cereals, cattle, and hides. Founded in the 16th century, the city was destroyed by an earthquake in 1812 and has been completely rebuilt. The Spanish adventurer Lope de Aguirre (q.v.) was defeated and killed there in 1561. Pop. (1970 est.) 281,600.

BARRACUDA, *or* BECUNA, common names for fish of the genus *Sphyraena,* the only genus in the family Sphyraenidae, in the same suborder with the gray mullets and the sand smelts. They are pikelike, generally tropical fish, the largest attaining a length of about 8 ft. and a weight of about 40 lb. Voracious in habit, they have many sharp teeth. The picuda or great barracuda, *S. barracuda,* of the West Indies region, is often over 6 ft. long and is dangerous to swimmers. The European barracuda, *S. sphyraena,* also called spet or senet, is smaller. The California barracuda, *S. argentea,* the best food fish of this family, rarely exceeds 4 ft. in length.

BARRANQUILLA, city and seaport in Colombia, and capital of Atlántico Department, on the Magdalena R., a main traffic route between the Caribbean Sea and the interior, about 60 miles N.E. of Cartagena. The city is the leading interna-

Works of the baroque period: Church of Santa Maria della Salute (left) in Venice, Italy, designed by the Italian architect Baldassare Longhena (1598–1682), built in 1632. "The Meeting of Abraham and Melchizedek" (below) by the Flemish painter Peter Paul Rubens (1577–1640).

Alinari

National Gallery of Art

tional air center of Colombia. Cotton, sugar cane, and livestock are the principal products of the surrounding area. Industries in the city include sugar refineries and textile mills. Pop. (greater city; 1970 est.) 840,000.

BARRAS, Vicomte Paul François Jean Nicolas de (1755–1829), French revolutionist, born in Fox-Amphoux, of a noble family. In 1792 he was elected to the National Convention (q.v.), the revolutionary body which abolished the French monarchy and helped substantially to bring about the downfall of the radical French leader Maximilien de Robespierre (q.v.). Made commander in chief of the troops of the Convention in 1795, Barras called Napoleon Bonaparte (*see* NAPOLEON I) to keep order in Paris. Barras was made one of the five members of the Directory (q.v.) in the same year. Napoleon, suspecting him of monarchist intriguing, banished him to Rome in 1799. After the restoration of the monarchy Barras returned to Paris, where he died.

BARRAULT, Jean-Louis (1910–), French actor, director, and producer, born in Le Vésinet. He studied and taught art and attended the École du Louvre, Paris, until 1931, when he enrolled in the school of the Atelier Theatre, where he remained until 1935. Five years later he was sufficiently proficient to join the Comédie Française (q.v.). In 1946 he and his wife, the French actress Madeleine Renaud (1903–), resigned from the Comédie and formed the Renaud-Barrault Company at the Théâtre Marigny, Paris. In 1959 he was appointed director of the Théâtre de France and in 1965 of the Théâtre des Nations, both sponsored by the French government. Following a dispute over student riots in Paris in 1968, Barrault resigned, and he and his wife reformed the Renaud-Barrault Company. Although Barrault is internationally famous for his work in pantomime (q.v.), the range of productions which he has directed and acted in extends from Shakespeare and the French classics through contemporary comedy to experimental avant-garde works such as his own *Rabelais* (1968). Barrault directed productions for the Metropolitan Opera Company, New York City, and his companies toured the United States. He appeared in such motion-picture classics as *Les Enfants du Paradis* (1944; *Children of Paradise*, 1946). His books, expressing his dedication to theater as a total emotional and intellectual experience, include *Nouvelles Reflexions sur le Théâtre* (1959; Eng. trans., *The Theatre of Jean-Louis Barrault*, 1961).

BARRE, city of Vermont, in Washington Co., about 6 miles S.E. of Montpelier. Granite has been quarried in the surrounding area since the early 19th century. In addition to the local granite industry, Barre manufactures wood products, electronics, machinery, and tools. It is a winter sports area. Pop. (1960) 10,387; (1970) 10,209.

BARRÉ, Isaac (1726–1802), British soldier and political leader, born in Dublin, Ireland. He held the rank of lieutenant colonel in the expeditionary force, commanded by the British general James Wolfe (q.v.), which captured Québec in a battle of the French and Indian War (q.v.). Barré returned to England and was elected in 1761 to Parliament, where he became known for his opposition to the policies of the British statesman, the elder William Pitt (*see under* PITT). Subsequently, however, he supported Pitt's efforts to prevent the taxation of the American colonies. He fought against the Stamp Act (q.v.) of 1765, distinguishing himself then and later by his strenuous defense of the American cause. A laudatory reference to the Americans in one of his speeches on colonial taxation provided American patriots with the name of one of their most effective revolutionary organizations, the Sons of Liberty (q.v.). Several cities of the United States, notably Barre, Vt., and Wilkes-Barre, Pa., were named in his honor. He retired from Parliament in 1790.

BARREL, unit of capacity or volume in the United States, equivalent in liquid measure to 31 ½ gal., as compared to the British liquid barrel of 37 imperial gal.; but equivalent for petroleum and beer to 42 and 31 gal., respectively. The U.S. dry barrel equals 105 dry quarts or about 3.9 bushels. The term barrel also denotes any cylindrical or bulging, flat-bottomed container larger than a can. *See* WEIGHTS AND MEASURES.

BARREL ORGAN, musical instrument, usually portable, in which the music is produced by a revolving barrel or cylinder, set with pins and staples that open valves for admitting wind to pipes from a bellows worked by the same revolving cylinder. The pieces are usually arranged with a harmonic accompaniment.

The first barrel organs appeared in England in the early 18th century, and the instrument was adopted soon afterward on the Continent. At first, the instrument was adapted to religious uses; more or less primitive barrel organs, equipped with pipes for diatonic scales in the major keys, became popular in churches as accompanying instruments for hymn and psalm singing, particularly in evangelistic or revivalist services. Barrel organs have continued to be used in this capacity up to the present day. At the beginning of the 19th century two other types of organs appeared. One was the extremely light and portable barrel organ developed for the use of itinerant musicians; such hand organs, provided with limited repertoires of light secular music, are still to be heard on the streets of most modern cities. The other was the large and elaborate barrel organ called orchestrion, developed for use in restaurants, music and dancing halls, and carrousels. In the 20th century, recorded or live music replaced the orchestrion in all fields but that of the carrousel. During their vogue, however, the larger orchestrions were famous both for the richness of their repertoires and for the variety of sounds that they produced by ingenious mechanical arrangements of such additional instruments as drums, cymbals, triangles, and castanets. *See also* HURDY-GURDY.

BARRENNESS. *see* STERILITY.

BARRÈS, Maurice (1862–1923), French novelist and politician, born in Charmes, Lorraine, and educated at the Lycée of Nancy. In 1889 he was elected to the Chamber of Deputies from Nancy as a supporter of Boulangism (*see* BOULANGER, GEORGES). He served until 1893, and in 1906 he was again elected, this time as a Nationalist. His earlier works are highly introspective, but in his later writings he is concerned chiefly with expounding his views on making France a strong nation.

Barrès was a talented novelist whose life and work were an indissoluble fusion of literary and political endeavor. He profoundly influenced such French writers as André Gide and André Malraux. (qq.v.).

Among his numerous works are the trilogies *Le Culte du Moi* ("The Cult of the Self", 1888–91), consisting of the novels *Sous l'Oeil des Barbares* ("Under the Eye of the Barbarians", 1888), *Un Homme Libre* ("A Free Man", 1889), and *Le Jardin de Bérénice* ("The Garden of Berenice", 1891), and *Le Roman de l'Énergie Nationale* ("The Novel of National Vigor"), consisting of *Les Déracinés* ("The Uprooted", 1897), *L'Appel au Soldat* ("The Appeal to the Soldier", 1900), and *Leurs Figures* ("Their Faces", 1902); and the novel *La Colline Inspirée* (1913; Eng. trans., *The Sacred Hill,* 1929).

BARRETT, John (1866–1938), American writer and diplomat, born in Grafton, Vt., and educated at Dartmouth College. He served as United States minister to Siam (1894–98), Argentina (1903–04), Panama (1904–05), and Colombia (1905–06). He was presiding officer of the first and second Pan-American Commercial Conferences in 1911 and 1919, the director of the Pan-American Union (q.v.) from 1907 to 1920, when it was reorganized, and a member of the governing board of the General Committee on Limitation of Armaments (1921–22). He wrote extensively on Latin-American subjects. Among his works are *Pan American Union-Peace, Friendship, Commerce* (1911) and *The Call of South America* (1924).

BARRETT, Sir William Fletcher (1844–1925), British physicist, born in Jamaica, West Indies, and educated at the Royal Institution, London, under the Irish physicist John Tyndall (q.v.). From 1873 to 1910 he was professor of experimental physics at the Royal College of Science, Dublin, Ireland. A founder, in 1882, of the Society for Psychical Research, he established a branch of the society in the United States in 1885. He is known for original investigations in magnetism, radiant heat, sensitive flames, and the recalescence of iron. His writings include *A New Form of Polarimeter* (1909), *Creative Thought* (1911), *Swedenborg, the Savant and the Seer* (1913), and *On the Threshold of the Unseen* (1917).

BARRIE, Sir James Matthew (1860–1937), British dramatist and novelist, born in Kirriemuir, Forfar County (now Angus County), Scotland, and educated at the University of Edinburgh. He began writing (1883) for the *Nottingham Journal*; two years later he settled in London and wrote for the *St. James's Gazette* and many other periodicals. His first published volume was *Better Dead* (1887). *Auld Licht Idylls* (1888) and *A Window in Thrums* (1889) contained sketches of Scottish village life. *The Little Minister* (1891), a romantic novel of love and adventure, was followed by *Sentimental Tommy* (1895) and its sequel *Tommy and Grizel* (1900).

Barrie's play *Walker, London* (1893) was a success at its London premiere. His next dramatic work was the comedy *The Professor's Love Story* (1894). Productions of *Quality Street* (1902), *The Admirable Crichton* (1902), and *Little Mary* (1903) preceded the first performance of Barrie's now world-famous fairy tale play, *Peter Pan* (1904). In this fantasy, Barrie dealt with his two favorite themes, the retention of childish innocence and the feminine instinct for motherhood. Other plays by Barrie include *What Every Woman Knows* (1908), *A Kiss for Cinderella* (1916), *Dear Brutus* (1917), and *The Boy David* (1936). Throughout his works, both theatrical and nontheatrical, Barrie stressed his personal, ironic view of life as a romantic adventure. His whimsical and sentimental plays are occasionally revived; *What Every Woman Knows* and *Peter Pan* in particular have been popular vehicles for leading actresses, including for instance, the American actresses, Maude Adams and Mary Martin (qq.v.). Several musical versions of

Peter Pan, including two on the stage in New York City (1950; 1954) and an animated feature film (1953) by the American cartoonist Walt Disney (q.v.) have been produced.

Barrie was made a baronet in 1913 and received the order of Merit in 1922. He was named chancellor of the University of Edinburgh in 1930.

BARRIER REEF. *See* GREAT BARRIER REEF.

BARRIOS, Justo Rufino (1835?–85), Guatemalan politician and general, born in San Lorenzo. He studied law and became a revolutionist. In 1871, for his aid in a successful revolt against the government, he was made commander in chief of the army. He became president of the republic in 1873. His ambition was to consolidate the five independent states of Central America (q.v.) into one nation. Opposition to his plans on the part of El Salvador led in 1885 to war between El Salvador and Guatemala. Barrios was killed while leading his troops into the village of Chalchuapa, El Salvador.

BARRON, Clarence Walker (1855–1928), American financial editor and publisher, born in Boston, Mass., and educated in the public schools of that city. In 1887 he founded *The Boston News Bureau,* which supplied daily financial information. He established a similar organization, *The Philadelphia News Bureau,* in 1896. Barron purchased *The Wall Street Journal* in 1901. He founded *Barron's, the National Financial Weekly* in 1921. His writings include *The Federal Reserve Act* (1914), *The Audacious War* (1915), *The Mexican Problem* (1917), *War Finance* (1919), and *A World Remaking* (1920).

BARROW, name applied to two prominent localities of the Arctic regions, in honor of the British traveler and writer Sir John Barrow (1764–1848) for his interest in arctic exploration, and for his aid in obtaining British governmental sanction and help for a number of important arctic expeditions. **1. Point Barrow,** the northernmost extremity of Alaska, on the Arctic Ocean, the starting place for many arctic expeditions. **2. Barrow Strait,** a channel, about 40 mi. wide, N. of Prince of Wales and Somerset islands, and leading W. from Lancaster Sound to Viscount Melville Sound.

BARROW, Isaac (1630–77), English mathematician and theologian, born in London, and educated at Trinity College, University of Cambridge. After traveling abroad, he became a priest in the Church of England and in 1663 became Lucasian professor of mathematics at Cambridge, a post he resigned in favor of his pupil, the famous English scientist Sir Isaac Newton (q.v.). In 1672 Barrow became master of Trinity College. His principal mathematical works are *Lectiones Geometricæ* (1669) and *Lectiones Opticæ* (1674). One of his chief theological works is *Treatise on the Pope's Supremacy* (posthumously published, 1680).

BARROW-IN-FURNESS, Great Britain, county borough of Lancashire, England, on the S.W. coast of Furness Peninsula, opposite Walney Island, 36 miles N.W. of Lancaster. In the borough are shipyards, specializing in submarine construction, steelworks, paper mills, and armament factories. About 1840 the borough became an important steel center, but by the mid-20th century the rich deposits of hematite iron ore in the area had been exhausted, and shipbuilding became the leading local industry. Pop. (1971) 63,860.

BARRY, Sir Charles (1795–1860), British architect, born in London, England. He designed the Royal Institution of Fine Arts in Manchester (1824), Saint Peter's Church in Brighton (1826), and other buildings. Barry is best known as the codesigner, with the British architect Augustus Welby Northmore Pugin (q.v.), of the House of Parliament (1840–60). In 1852 he was knighted.

BARRY, Comtesse du. *See* DU BARRY.

BARRY, John (1745–1803), American naval officer, born in Ireland. He came to America about 1760 and, settling in Philadelphia, acquired wealth as master of a merchant vessel. During the American Revolution (q.v.) he was appointed to command the brig *Lexington* in 1776 and captured the British tender *Edward,* the first ship ever taken by a commissioned officer of the United States Navy. In 1778 he became commander of the *Raleigh,* which was soon afterward pursued and driven ashore by a British man-of-war. In 1781, while in command of another ship, the *Alliance,* he captured two vessels. He was first senior officer, with rank of commodore, after the reorganization of the U.S. Navy in 1794.

BARRY, Philip (1896–1949), American dramatist, born in Rochester, N.Y., and educated at Yale and Harvard universities. At Harvard he studied drama with the American writer and educator George Pierce Baker (q.v.). Barry wrote many plays, including *You and I* (1922), *In a Garden* (1925), *White Wings* (1926), *Paris Bound* (1927), *Holiday* (1929), *The Philadelphia Story* (1939), and *Without Love* (1942). A number of his plays were made into motion pictures.

BARRYMORE, name of a celebrated family of American actors, of whom the most distinguished were Maurice Barrymore and his three children, Lionel, Ethel, and John.

Maurice Barrymore, real name HERBERT

The Barrymores. Left to right: John, Ethel, and Lionel.

BLYTHE (1847–1905), British-American actor, born in India, and educated at the University of Cambridge. After appearing on the stage in England he came to the United States in 1875 to play in *Under the Gaslight* in New York City. In 1876 he married Georgiana Emma Drew (1856–93), an actress and a daughter of the American actor John Drew (*see under* DREW). Barrymore was the leading man for the Polish actress Helena Modjeska, the American actress Minnie Maddern Fiske, the British actress Lily Langtry (qq.v.), and many other stars. He wrote a play, *Nadjeska,* for Helena Modjeska, in which she appeared in 1884.

Lionel Barrymore (1878–1954), born in London, England, and privately educated. He made his debut in the theater in New York City in 1893, appearing with his grandmother, Louisa Lane Drew (*see under* DREW), in *The Road to Ruin.* Among the plays in which Barrymore had leading roles were *Peter Ibbetson* (1917), *The Jest* (with his brother John, 1919), *Macbeth* (1921), *Laugh, Clown, Laugh!* (1923), and *Man, A Devil* (1925). He began a career in motion pictures in 1907 and, after leaving the stage in 1925, appeared in numerous film and radio dramas and on television. In one of his best-known film roles he portrayed Dr. Gillespie in the *Doctor Kildare* series, which began with *Young Doctor Kildare* (1938) and included *Dark Delusion* (1947). He wrote *Mr. Cantonwine* (1953).

Ethel Barrymore (1879–1959), born in Philadelphia, Pa., and educated there at the Convent of Notre Dame. In 1894 she made her debut in New York City in *The Rivals* by the British dramatist Richard Brinsley Sheridan (q.v.). Ethel Barrymore played opposite the British actor Sir Henry Irving (q.v.) in England in 1898, appearing in the popular plays *The Bells* and *Peter the Great,* and was the star of *Captain Jinks of the Horse Marines* in the United States in 1900. A succession of later performances, including leading roles in *A Doll's House* by the Norwegian dramatist Henrik Ibsen (q.v.) in 1905, and

Alice-Sit-by-the-Fire by the British dramatist James Matthew Barrie (q.v.) in 1906, established Miss Barrymore as one of the foremost actresses in the American theater. She played Juliet in *Romeo and Juliet* in 1922, and Ophelia in *Hamlet* and Portia in *The Merchant of Venice* in 1925. In December, 1928, she opened the Ethel Barrymore Theater in New York City, appearing in *The Kingdom of God.* Other plays in which Ethel Barrymore was the star include *School for Scandal* (1931) by Sheridan, *The Twelve-Pound Look* (1934) by Barrie, and *The Corn Is Green* (1941–45) by the British playwright Emlyn Williams (1905–). Ethel Barrymore also played in motion pictures, with her brothers John and Lionel in *Rasputin and the Empress* in 1933, and as a star in a number of other films. Her autobiography, *Memories,* was published in 1955.

John Barrymore (1882–1942), born in Philadelphia, Pa., and privately educated. He made his stage debut in 1903 in Chicago in *Magda,* by the German playwright Hermann Sudermann (q.v.). In the same year Barrymore made his first appearance in New York City, and in 1905 he acted in London and also toured Australia with the company of the American comedian and playwright William Collier (1866–1944). Subsequent appearances in the United States and England made Barrymore one of the most famous actors of his day. Among his best-known performances were the leading roles in *Justice* (1910) by the British playwright John Galsworthy (q.v.), *The Jest* (1919) by the Italian playwright Sem Benelli (q.v.), and *Richard III* and *Hamlet* (1920 and 1924–25, respectively). In 1912 Barrymore began to appear in motion pictures, and after 1925 he confined himself almost exclusively to that medium. He made his last stage appearance in 1939–40 in *My Dear Children,* a topical comedy.

BARSTOW, city of California, in San Bernardino Co., in the Mojave Desert, about 56 miles N. of San Bernardino. The surrounding area is important for dairy and agricultural products and for silver, borax, and salt mines. The city is a railroad junction and an outfitting point for Death Valley expeditions. It is the site of Barstow College, established in 1960. Pop. (1960) 11,644; (1970) 17,442.

BARTER. *See* MONEY.

BARTH, Karl (1886–1968), Swiss Protestant Reformed theologian and educator, born in Basel and educated at the universities of Bern, Berlin, Tübingen, and Marburg. He held professorships successively at Göttingen and Münster universities from 1923 to 1930, when he was appointed professor of systematic theology at the University of Bonn. He opposed the Hitler regime in Germany and supported church-sponsored movements against National Socialism (q.v.). In 1934 he was expelled from Bonn. Barth's further defiance led, the following year, to deportation to his native Switzerland, where he accepted a professorship at the University of Basel. He remained in Basel until his death.

Karl Barth Wide World

The principal message of Barth's work, known as "neoorthodoxy" and "crisis theology", is the transcendence of God. He sought to turn theology (q.v.) away from its positive attitude toward the activity of man and its sympathy for mysticism (q.v.) and feeling and return it to the prophetic teaching of the Bible. He regarded the Bible, though, not as the revelation of God, but only as the record of that revelation; *see* BIBLE, INTERPRETATIONS OF THE. For Barth, God's sole revelation of Himself is in Jesus Christ. God is the "wholly other", totally unlike man, who is utterly dependent on that encounter for any understanding of ultimate reality. Barth saw the task of the Church as that of proclaiming the "good word" of God and as serving as the "place of encounter" between God and man. All human activity he regarded as being under the judgment of this encounter. *See* TRANSCENDENTALISM.

Barth is widely regarded as one of the most notable Christian theologians of the current century. His remarkably extensive work prepared the way for such writers as the German

Protestant cleric Dietrich Bonhoeffer (q.v.) and the radical theologians in America. Among Barth's writings are *Der Römerbrief* (1919; *The Epistle to the Romans,* (1933), *Das Wort Gottes und die Theologie* (1924; *The Word of God and the Word of Man,* 1928), *Kirchliche Dogmatik* (vol. I–IV, 1932–62; *Church Dogmatics,* 1936–62), and *Credo* (1935; Eng. trans., 1937). *Theologische Fragen und Antworten* ("Theological Questions and Answers") appeared in 1957, and *Einführung in die Evangelische Theologie* and its English-language version, *Evangelical Theology,* appeared in 1963.

BARTHOLDI, Frédéric Auguste (1834–1904), French sculptor, born in Colmar, Haut-Rhin, and trained in Paris. He is best known in the United States for his colossal statue "Liberty Enlightening the World" (now on Liberty Island, in the New York City harbor), which was presented by France to the U.S. in commemoration of the centenary of American independence. The sculptor was largely responsible for the success of the gift plan in France, personally supervising the collection, by voluntary donations, of the money needed by the French nation to make the gift. *See* LIBERTY, STATUE OF.

BARTHOLIN, family of Danish scholars, the most important of whom were the following.

Kaspar Bartholin (1585–1629), born in Malmö, Sweden. He was successively professor of rhetoric, medicine, and theology at the University of Copenhagen, and author of *Institutiones Anatomicæ* (1611), a textbook of anatomy used throughout Europe in the 17th century, in German, English, French, and other translations.

Thomas Bartholin (1616–80), born in Copenhagen, son of Kaspar Bartholin. Thomas was a physician, naturalist, and philologist. In 1641 he revised his father's work on anatomy and investigated the function of the lymphatic system.

Kaspar Bartholin (1655–1738), son of Thomas Bartholin, an anatomist. He discovered the duct of the submaxillary salivary gland and identified the female vulvovaginal glands or Bartholin glands.

BARTHOLOMEW, Saint, in the Christian Church, one of the twelve Apostles (*see* APOSTLE) of Christ (Mark 3:14–19). He is identified by many Biblical scholars with Nathanael, a native of Galilee described in John 1:45–51 (*see* JOHN, GOSPEL ACCORDING TO SAINT). Unsubstantiated tradition relates that he was a missionary in many countries and preached the Gospel (q.v.) in India (properly Arabia), where he left behind him a copy, in Hebrew, of the Gospel of Matthew (*see* MATTHEW, GOSPEL ACCORDING TO SAINT). Saint Bartholomew's feast day is Aug. 24 in the

"Saint Bartholomew", a 14th-century egg tempera on wood by Simone Martini. Metropolitan Museum of Art

Roman Catholic Church and the Church of England, and June 11 in the Orthodox Church.

BARTHOLOMEW'S DAY. *See* SAINT BARTHOLOMEW'S DAY, MASSACRE OF.

BARTLESVILLE city in Oklahoma, and county seat of Washington Co., about 45 miles N. of Tulsa. The city serves as a distribution center for the surrounding agricultural and oil-producing area. Located in Bartlesville are an oil refinery, a zinc-smelting plant, and a United States Bureau of Mines experimental station. Local manufactures include leather, metal products, ventilators, seismographs, and oil-producing equipment. Bartlesville was founded in 1877 and incorporated in 1897. Pop. (1960) 27,893; (1970) 29,683.

BARTLETT, John (1820–1905), American publisher and compiler, born in Plymouth, Mass. At sixteen he went to work for a bookstore in Cambridge, Mass., of which he became the owner in 1849. In his spare time he compiled *Familiar Quotations: Being an Attempt to Trace to Their Sources Passages and Phrases in Common Use* (1855). That work, which has been reissued in numerous editions, continues to be a standard reference book. Bartlett also compiled *The Shakespeare Phrase Book* (1882) and a *Complete Concordance to Shakespeare's Plays and Poems* (1894). In 1863 he joined the Boston publishing firm Little, Brown & Co., where he was a senior partner from 1878 until his retirement in 1889.

BARTLETT, John Russell (1805–86), American writer, born in Providence, R.I., and educated at Lowville Academy in New York and in Montréal, Canada. A founder of the American Ethnological Society, he also was secretary of the New York Historical Society. Bartlett first worked as a merchant and banker in Providence. In 1836 he moved to New York City, where he owned a bookstore. He was employed by the United States government from 1850 to 1853 as a commissioner for determining the Mexican boundary line and in 1854 wrote an account of his explorations. In 1855 he became secretary of state of Rhode Island, and in 1861–62 he was acting governor of the State. He wrote *The Progress of Ethnology* (1847), *A Dictionary of Americanisms* (1848), *Primeval Man* (1868), and *Bibliotheca Americana* (4 vol., 1865–82), a critical bibliography of early American books that is still valuable to scholars.

BARTLETT, Josiah (1729–95), American physician and statesman, born in Amesbury, Mass., and privately educated. He began medical practice in Kingston, N.H., in 1750 and in 1754 successfully introduced Peruvian bark in the treatment of a throat disease, angina maligna. From 1765 to 1775 he served in the New Hampshire legislature. A delegate in 1775 and 1776 to the Continental Congress, he was the first member to vote for the Declaration of Independence, and the first, after the American patriot John Hancock (q.v.), president of the Congress, to sign the document. Bartlett became chief justice of the New Hampshire Court of Common Pleas in 1779, a judge of the State Supreme Court in 1784, and chief justice in 1788. He was president of New Hampshire from 1790 to 1793, when, under the new constitution, he was elected governor. He retired in 1794. In 1791, he helped found the New Hampshire Medical Society.

BARTLETT, Paul Wayland (1865–1925), American sculptor, born in New Haven, Conn., and trained in Boston, Mass., and at the École des Beaux-Arts, Paris. At first interested in animal sculpture, he contributed animal figures to many groups by European sculptors. His early work includes the "Bear Tamer" in the Metropolitan Museum of Art, New York City, and "Ghost Dancer" in the Pennsylvania Academy of the Fine Arts, Philadelphia. Bartlett divided his career between the United States and France, maintaining a studio in Paris and another in Washington, D.C., or New York City. In 1908 he was awarded the French Legion of Honor, and in 1911 he became a member of the American Academy of Arts and Letters and a corresponding member of the Institute of France (qq.v.). In 1908–09 Bartlett collaborated with the American sculptor John Quincy Adams Ward (q.v.) on the "Genius of Integrity", a group for the pediment of the Stock Exchange in New York City. From 1909 to 1916, Bartlett sculpted the group "Democracy Protecting the Arts of Peace", on the pediment of the House wing of the Capitol Building in Washington, D.C. He is best known, however, for his historical portrait statues, including "Columbus" and "Michelangelo" in the Rotunda of the Library of Congress, Washington, D.C.; "Joseph Warren" in Boston, Mass.; "Lafayette", a monumental equestrian statue in the court of the Louvre Museum, Paris; "Benjamin Franklin" in Waterbury, Conn.; and "Robert Morris" in Philadelphia, Pa.

BARTLETT, Robert Abram (1875–1946), Canadian-American explorer, born in Brigus, Conception Bay, Newfoundland, and educated at the Methodist College at Saint John's and at the Halifax Nautical Academy. He accompanied the American explorer Robert Edwin Peary (q.v.) on an arctic expedition in 1897 and 1898, and from 1905 to 1909 commanded the *Roosevelt* on the voyages leading to Peary's discovery of the North Pole. On the final dash he accompanied Peary on land as far north as the 88th parallel. Bartlett became an American citizen in 1911. He was captain of the *Karluk* on the Canadian arctic expedition of 1913 and 1914. After his ship was crushed by ice near Wrangel Island, Bartlett crossed the ice to Siberia with one Eskimo and led back a party that rescued thirteen survivors. He headed other expeditions to the arctic in 1917 and each year from 1925 to 1935. He wrote *The Log of Bartlett* (1928) and *Sails over Ice* (1934).

BARTÓK, BÉLA (1881–1945), Hungarian composer, born in Nagyszentmiklós, Hungary (now Sînnicolau, Rumania), and trained in Pressburg (now Bratislava, Czechoslovakia) and Budapest. In 1907 he was appointed a piano teacher at the Hungarian Royal Academy of Music in Budapest, a post he retained until he emigrated as a refugee to the United States in 1940. Later he worked at Columbia University and taught music in New York City.

Late-19th-century romantic music and Hungarian folk music influenced his early compositions. About 1905 Bartók began to suspect that the compositions generally considered to be Hungarian folk music actually consisted of gypsy music arranged according to conventional central European standards. With the Hungarian composer Zoltán Kodály (1882–1967), Bartók systematically collected and analyzed the folk music of his own and other peoples. This

Béla Bartók with pianist György Sándor.

work resulted in the publication of twelve volumes comprising 2700 Magyar, 3500 Magyar-Rumanian, and several hundred Arabic folk songs.

Bartók's musical style, generally characterized by great emotional intensity and frequently by extreme dissonance, utilized both uncommon and conventional harmonies and every type of scale and rhythm. He is generally ranked among the most original and profound of modern composers. Among his compositions are *Kossuth* (1903), a symphonic poem; *For Children* (4 vol., 1908–09), piano pieces using Hungarian and Slovak themes; *Rhapsody* (1904), for piano and orchestra; six string quartets (1908–39); *Bluebeard's Castle* (1911), an opera; *The Miraculous Mandarin* (1921), a ballet; three piano concerti (1926, 1931, and 1945); *Music for Two Pianos and Percussion* (1937); a violin concerto (1938); and *Concerto for Orchestra* (1943).

BARTOLOMMEO, Fra, familiarly called BACCIO DELLA PORTA (1475–1517), Italian Renaissance painter, born in Florence and trained there under the Italian painter Cosimo Rosselli (1439–1507). In his youth he became a follower of the Italian reformer Girolamo Savonarola (q.v.), under whose influence he destroyed all his nonreligious works. In 1498 Bartolommeo contracted to paint the fresco "Last Judgment" (Museo di San Marco, Florence) but left it unfinished. After Savonarola's death in 1498 Bartolommeo renounced painting entirely, and in 1500 he joined the Dominican order at the Convent of San Marco in Florence. In 1504, however, the prior of his convent persuaded him to paint again. The first work of his second period was the "Apparition of the Virgin to St. Bernard" (Florentine Academy). Until 1508 Fra Bartolommeo worked under the influence of the Italian painters Leonardo da Vinci, Il Perugino (qq.v.), and Filippino Lippi (*see under* LIPPI). Then, at Venice, he encountered for the first time the work of such Venetian masters of color as Giovanni Bellini (*see under* BELLINI) and Il Giorgione (q.v.). From that time he figured as one of the chief colorists of the Florentine school.

From 1509 to 1512 he worked mainly in collaboration with his lifelong friend the Florentine painter Mariotto Albertinelli (1474–1515); among the works that they executed jointly is the "Madonna with Six Saints" (Museo di San Marco). The years following Bartolommeo's visit to Venice are generally considered his finest pe-

"Saints Mary Magdalen and Catherine" by Fra Bartolommeo. Alinari

riod. His independent works during that time include "Marriage of St. Catherine" (Louvre, Paris), and "Madonna with Saints John the Baptist and Stephen" and "God the Father with Saints Mary Magdalen and Catherine of Siena" (both in the Cathedral of Lucca). In 1514 he visited Rome for several months and there came under the last of the major influences upon his work, that of the Italian painters Raphael and Michelangelo (qq.v.). The pictures painted during the last years of Bartolommeo's life reflect Raphael's more monumental style and Michelangelo's more intensified sense of movement. His best-known works of this period include "Salvator Mundi" and "Pietà" (both in the Pitti Palace, Florence). R.S.M.

BARTOLOZZI, Francesco (1727–1815), Italian engraver, born in Florence, where he studied painting. Later he studied engraving in Venice and for a time he worked in Rome. In 1764 he settled in England, where he produced many line engravings of works by other artists, as well as original compositions. Bartolozzi was one of the original members of the Royal Academy, which was formed in 1768, and he executed the diploma of the Academy, which is still in use. In 1802 Bartolozzi went to Lisbon, Portugal, as director of the Royal Academy, a position he held until his death. His prints are among the most numerous ever executed by a single engraver.

BARTON, Clara, in full CLARISSA HARLOWE BARTON (1821–1912), American philanthropist, born in Oxford, Mass., and educated at home, chiefly by her two brothers and two sisters. She was a teacher in early life and the founder of various free schools in New Jersey. In 1854 she became a clerk in the Patent Office, Washington, D.C., but resigned at the beginning of the American Civil War to work at distributing supplies for wounded soldiers. She received no compensation for this work, and carried it on partially at her own expense. After the war she supervised a systematic search for missing soldiers. Between 1869 and 1873 she lived in Europe, where she assisted in establishing hospitals in the Franco-German War, followed the German army, and was honored with the Gold Cross of Baden and the Iron Cross of Germany. Through her efforts the American Red Cross Society was formed in 1881, and she served as the first president of the organization from 1881 until 1904. In 1884 she represented the United States at the Red Cross Conference and at the International Peace Convention in Geneva, Switzerland. She was responsible for the introduction at this convention of the "American amendment", which established that the Red Cross was to serve victims of peacetime disas-

Clara Barton American Red Cross

ters as well as victims of war. She superintended relief work in the yellow-fever pestilence in Florida (1887), in the Johnstown, Pa., flood (1889), in the Russian famine (1891), among the Armenians (1896), in the Spanish-American War (1898), and in the South African War (1899–1902). The last work which she personally directed was the relief of sufferers from the flood at Galveston, Texas, in 1900. She wrote *History of the Red Cross* (1882), *History of the Red Cross in Peace and War* (1898), *Story of the Red Cross* (1904), and *Story of My Childhood* (1907). *See* RED CROSS, THE AMERICAN NATIONAL.

BARTON, Derek Harold Richard (1918–), British chemist, born in Gravesend and educated at the Imperial College of Science and Technology of the University of London. He joined the faculty of the Imperial College in 1945. He also served as visiting professor at many institutions, including Massachusetts Institute of Technology, the University of Glasgow, the University of Western Ontario, and Harvard University. Barton shared the 1969 Nobel Prize in chemistry with the Norwegian chemist Odd Hassel (q.v.). They were cited for their independent work in the 1950's, which led to a new concept of conformation analysis in chemistry through study of the three-dimensional geometric configurations of molecules. *See* CHEMISTRY; CHEMISTRY, ORGANIC.

BARTOW, city in Florida, and county seat of Polk Co., on the Peace R., about 12 miles S.E. of Lakeland. The city is a processing and shipping center for the agricultural products and the phosphate of the surrounding region. The city produces fertilizer, cigars, and fishing tackle. It is the site of Polk Junior College, established in 1963. Pop. (1960) 12,849; (1970) 12,891.

BARTRAM, John (1699–1777), American botanist, born at Marple, near Darby, Pa. Orphaned at the age of thirteen, he taught himself botany, medicine, and surgery when he was not working as an agricultural laborer. The Swedish botanist Carolus Linnaeus (q.v.) called Bartram "the greatest botanist in the world", and Bartram is known as "the father of American botany". He corresponded with distinguished naturalists in Europe and in 1765 was appointed "Botanist to the King" by George III (q.v.), King of Great Britain. Bartram traveled extensively about the American colonies, observing wild life, writing, collecting plants, and making maps. The first botanical garden in America was founded by Bartram in 1728 at the town of Kingsessing, near Philadelphia, Pa.; the garden is still maintained by the city of Philadelphia as Bartram's Garden. Bartram was a charter member of the American Philosophical Society (q.v.). Bartram's best-known work is *Observations on the Inhabitants, Soil, Divers Productions, etc. Made by John Bartram in His Travels from Pennsylvania to Onondaga, Oswego, and the Lake Ontario* (1751).

BARUCH, book of the Old Testament Apocrypha (*see* BIBLE), in the King James Version, BARUCH. It is attributed to Baruch, who figures prominently in chapters 36 and 45 of the book of Jeremiah (*see* book of JEREMIAH) as Jeremiah's scribe and companion. The work, which is addressed to the Jews exiled in Babylon, and is partly in prose and partly in poetry, approximates the spirit and style of Old Testament prophecy more than any other Apocryphal book. The prose section (1–3:8) comprises an admission of sin, a promise of deliverance after repentance, and a prayer asking mercy and praising God. The poetry section (3:9–5:9) consists of verses in praise of wisdom and of God's commandments, and verses urging the exiles to be courageous and comforted. Baruch, which is preserved in Greek, may have been compiled as late as the 1st or 2nd century A.D. by an Alexandrian editor using original Hebrew manuscripts. Some versions of the Bible, including the King James Version, append as chapter 6 of Baruch, The Letter of Jeremiah (*see* JEREMIAH, THE LETTER OF).

BARUCH, Bernard Mannes (1870–1965), American financier, economist, and statesman, born in Camden, S.C., and educated at the College of the City of New York. In 1896 he became a member of the brokerage house of A. A. Housman & Co., in New York City. After an exceptionally successful business career he was appointed by the American President Woodrow Wilson (q.v.) in 1916 to serve on the advisory committee of the Council of National Defense. The Council was created to ascertain what critical materials the United States would lack in case of war with Germany. In 1917 Baruch served on the Allied Purchasing Commission, which had charge of all purchases made in the U.S. for the allied governments. During World War I he was chairman of the War Industries Board. While directing the work of the latter board, charged with converting industry from peacetime to wartime production, Baruch exerted great influence on the economic policies of the U.S. After the war, he was a member of the American delegation to the 1919 Paris peace conference.

Baruch was often consulted by Presidents Warren G. Harding, Calvin Coolidge, and Herbert Hoover (qq.v.) on economic matters. As a confidential advisor to President Franklin Del-

Bernard Baruch and friend in Central Park, New York City. UPI

ano Roosevelt (q.v.), Baruch played a considerable part in the drafting of the National Industrial Recovery Act (q.v.) of 1933. In 1943 he served as advisor to the American statesman James Byrnes (q.v.), war mobilization director. In 1946–47 Baruch held the post of U.S. representative on the United Nations Atomic Energy Commission.

Baruch wrote numerous pamphlets on economic subjects and the books *Taking the Profits out of War* (1935), *American Industry in the War* (1941), and, with the American banker John Milton Hancock (1883–1956), *Text of Official Reports and Related Documents: Post-War Adjustment Policies* (1946). Baruch was also the author of *A Philosophy for Our Time* (1954), and *Baruch: My Own Story* (2 vol., 1957–60).

BARYE, Antoine Louis (1795–1875), French sculptor, born in Paris. He began his career by working with an engraver and a goldsmith. He turned his attention to sculpture in 1818, when he studied modeling under the French sculptor François Joseph Bosio (1769?–1845) and drawing under the celebrated historical painter Baron Antoine Jean Gros (q.v.). In 1819 Barye took a second prize at the École des Beaux-Arts and a little later he began devoting himself to the study of animals, a branch of sculpture in which he achieved fame. In the Salon of 1831 Barye exhibited his famous "Tiger Tearing a Crocodile" (Louvre, Paris). He gained even greater success with his "Lion Battling with a Serpent" (1832), purchased by France for the Tuileries Gardens. Because he was not receiving the recognition that he believed his due, Barye ceased sending to the Salon and devoted his energies to the production of bronzes for commerce, and through those little masterpieces he is most widely known. His works are highly regarded for the accuracy of the anatomy, character, and movements of the various animals he represented. The architect of the Louvre employed him to sculpt four stone groups, "War", "Peace", "Order", and "Force" (1855) for the pavilions on the Place du Carrousel. In 1868 Barye was elected to the Académie des Beaux-Arts. Examples of his work are included in the collections of the Brooklyn Museum and the Metropolitan Museum of Art in New York City and the Walters Museum in Baltimore, Md.

BARZUN, Jacques Martin (1907–), American historian and educator, born near Paris, France. He received his early education at the Lycée Janson de Sailly, Paris. In 1920 he moved to the United States and began his long association with Columbia University, first as a student and later advancing in increasingly important and prestigious teaching and administrative positions. Barzun was naturalized a U.S. citizen in 1933. At Columbia he served as dean of the graduate faculties, 1955–58, and dean of faculties and provost, 1958–67. In 1967 he was appointed university professor and special adviser to the President on the arts; he retired in 1975. Among his many important and influential works are *Teacher in America* (1945), an analysis of the American educational system; *Berlioz and the Romantic Century* (1950); *The House of Intellect* (1959), an analysis of culture in a democracy; *Science: The Glorious Entertainment* (1964); and *The American University: How It Is Run, Where It Is Going* (1968).

BASAL METABOLISM. *See* METABOLISM.

BASALT, dark grayish, igneous rocks composed essentially of calcic feldspars (*see* FELDSPAR), with augite, olivine (q.v.), and, generally, magnetite (q.v.). They show all varieties of texture, from smooth compact to coarse crystalline, and vary in color from pale blue to dark grayish-blue, brownish, and black. When seen under the microscope, the compact and fine-grained basalt rocks often show glassy or vitrified matter lying between the various crystalline minerals of which the rock is chiefly composed. Basalt rocks often have a vesicular texture showing the bubbles produced by expanding steam as the rock solidified. Sometimes basalts occur as lava flows; at other times they appear as intrusive sheets, dikes, and masses. Two fine examples of columnar structure in basalt rocks are Fingal's Cave in West Scotland and the Giant's Causeway on the north coast of Ireland.

BASANITE. *See* TOUCHSTONE.

BASEBALL, competitive athletic game of skill played with a hard ball and a bat by two opposing nine-man teams, widely regarded as the American national sport. Although among the oldest, baseball goes unchallenged as the most popular professional game in the United States, daily attracting crowds of fans to parks and stadiums where it is played, followed by millions more over radio and television, and reported extensively in almost every newspaper in the country. By no means, however, is the game limited to a spectator-sport category. Baseball is played by amateurs of all ages, including numerous sandlot clubs and athletic associations, virtually every high school and college in the U.S., and scores of junior leagues. Games of baseball spontaneously organized by friends or neighbors on a summer afternoon have become part of the typical American scene. The game is now also played almost everywhere in the world and has gained popularity in Canada, Mexico, and other countries of the Western Hemisphere, and in Japan. The excitement of the sport, from both players' and fans' point of view, is vividly expressed in the poem "Casey at the Bat" (1888), written by American balladeer Ernest Lawrence Thayer (1863–1940), which recounts a tragic, game-losing strikeout by the hero of the Mudville Nine.

Origins and Early History. Although the modern game is indigenous to the U.S. and developed gradually, the actual origins of baseball are relatively obscure. The historical evidence indicates that in its earlier forms baseball represented a modified synthesis of cricket (q.v.) and rounders. Both games were imported from Great Britain to the American colonies and have features in common with baseball and all its early American variants. For example, both cricket and rounders, as well as baseball, involve contending teams equipped with a ball and a bat, in one form or another, with which to strike the ball. In addition, all three games require the use of a level playing field containing stations or bases to which the players advance in their attempts to score.

By the end of the 18th century several primitive varieties of baseball, each known by a different name, were being played in the U.S. One version popular in New York City was called one old cat, or one o' cat, and is still played by children in some sections of the U.S. By 1835 other varieties, such as town ball and New York ball, were played by established teams in the larger eastern cities. Most early variations of baseball were played on a square field, with stakes at the corners serving as stations and a striker's box situated about midway between the first and fourth stations. Shortly after 1840 the stakes, which frequently caused injuries to the players, were replaced by stones. Sand-filled sacks were subsequently substituted for the stones. These sacks soon became known as bases, and thereafter the players began calling the game baseball. The exact time and place of the origin of this term is, however, unknown.

The next important development in the history of the game occurred in 1845, when the Knickerbocker Baseball Club was organized in New York City. The team sponsored by this organization established the foundation of modern baseball, but the origin of the rules by which the team played has been the subject of considerable controversy. In 1907 an investigating commission headed by A. G. Mills (1844–1929), a former National League president, reported that certain basic rules of play as well as the design of the first diamond (the placement of the bases on the field formed a playing area in this shape) had been devised at Cooperstown, N.Y., in 1839. The American soldier Abner

BASEBALL WORLD'S CHAMPIONSHIPS

Year	Winner	Won	Lost
1912	Boston, A. L.	4	3
1913	Philadelphia, A. L.	4	1
1914	Boston, N. L.	4	0
1915	Boston, A. L.	4	1
1916	Boston, A. L.	4	1
1917	Chicago, A. L.	4	2
1918	Boston, A. L.	4	2
1919	Cincinnati, N. L.	5	3
1920	Cleveland, A. L.	5	2
1921	New York, N. L.	5	3
1922	New York, N. L.	4	0
1923	New York, A. L.	4	2
1924	Washington, A. L.	4	3
1925	Pittsburgh, N. L.	4	3
1926	St. Louis, N. L.	4	3
1927	New York, A. L.	4	0
1928	New York, A. L.	4	0
1929	Philadelphia, A. L.	4	1
1930	Philadelphia, A. L.	4	2
1931	St. Louis, N. L.	4	3
1932	New York, A. L.	4	0
1933	New York, N. L.	4	1
1934	St. Louis, N. L.	4	3
1935	Detroit, A. L.	4	2
1936	New York, A. L.	4	2
1937	New York, A. L.	4	1
1938	New York, A. L.	4	0
1939	New York, A. L.	4	0
1940	Cincinnati, N. L.	4	3
1941	New York, A. L.	4	1
1942	St. Louis, N. L.	4	1
1943	New York, A. L.	4	1
1944	St. Louis, N. L.	4	2
1945	Detroit, A. L.	4	3
1946	St. Louis, N. L.	4	3
1947	New York, A. L.	4	3
1948	Cleveland, A. L.	4	2
1949	New York, A. L.	4	1
1950	New York, A. L.	4	0
1951	New York, A. L.	4	2
1952	New York, A. L.	4	3
1953	New York, A. L.	4	2
1954	New York, N. L.	4	0
1955	Brooklyn, N. L.	4	3
1956	New York, A. L.	4	3
1957	Milwaukee, N. L.	4	3
1958	New York, A. L.	4	3
1959	Los Angeles, N. L.	4	2
1960	Pittsburgh, N. L.	4	3
1961	New York, A. L.	4	1
1962	New York, A. L.	4	3
1963	Los Angeles, N. L.	4	0
1964	St. Louis, N. L.	4	3
1965	Los Angeles, N. L.	4	3
1966	Baltimore, A. L.	4	0
1967	St. Louis, N. L.	4	3
1968	Detroit, A. L.	4	3
1969	New York, N. L.	4	1
1970	Baltimore, A. L.	4	1
1971	Pittsburgh, N. L.	4	3
1972	Oakland, A. L.	4	3
1973	Oakland, A. L.	4	3
1974	Oakland, A. L.	4	1
1975	Cincinnati, N. L.	4	3
1976	Cincinnati, N. L.	4	0
1977	New York, A. L.	4	2
1978	New York, A. L.	4	2
1979	Pittsburgh, N. L.	4	3
1980	Philadelphia, N. L.	4	2

Doubleday (q.v.), then a cadet at West Point, was credited with establishing the ground rules. Some authorities later contended that the findings of the commission were based on inconclusive evidence. At any rate, in recognition of Doubleday's purported contribution to the sport, Cooperstown was later selected as the site of the National Baseball Hall of Fame and Museum; *see* BASEBALL HALL OF FAME AND MUSEUM, NATIONAL. Subsequent investigators attributed the design of the field to Alexander Joy Cartwright (1820–92) of New York City, a member of the Knickerbocker Baseball Club, and the playing regulations to a committee of that club.

The Knickerbockers played their first game on June 19, 1846, at Hoboken, N.J., losing to the New York Nine, another New York City club. In all important respects the playing field, the position of the players, and a number of the rules closely resembled the corresponding features of modern baseball. About two years after their first game the Knickerbockers adopted a rule eliminating plugging, the practice of retiring a base runner from play by hitting him with a thrown ball. In 1849 the Knickerbocker team introduced the first baseball uniforms.

Baseball became increasingly popular in the U.S. between 1850 and 1860. The National Association of Baseball Players, representing various clubs, was organized in 1857 for the purpose of drafting a standard code of playing rules. A rule was adopted in 1859 prohibiting remuneration of players. In that year Amherst College defeated Williams College in the first intercollegiate baseball game. Admission fees to a baseball game were charged for the first time in 1858, when a New York team played a Brooklyn club at Fashion Race Course, West Flushing (now part of the New York City borough of Queens), Long Island.

Professional baseball was introduced in 1869 by the Cincinnati Red Stockings, a club that had been organized on an amateur basis three years earlier. During 1869 and 1870 this team won ninety-one of ninety-three games, playing before crowds that totaled more than 200,000. Other professional clubs were organized in various parts of the country, and in 1871 the National Association of Professional Baseball Players was organized, representing clubs in Boston, Mass.; Philadelphia, Pa.; Chicago, Ill.; Brooklyn, N.Y.; New York, N.Y.; Cleveland, Ohio; and four other cities. This event marked the end of amateurism as a significant factor in the development of the game. Professional baseball flourished until public support dropped off drastically during the 1875 season as the result of conflicting schedules, gambling on the outcome of games, and reports of corruption and dishonesty among players.

Development of Baseball Leagues. As in many other sports, a league in baseball signifies

BASEBALL PENNANT WINNERS—NATIONAL LEAGUE

Year	Winner	Won	Lost	Year	Winner	Won	Lost
1902	Pittsburgh	103	36	1942	St. Louis	106	48
1903	Pittsburgh	91	49	1943	St. Louis	105	49
1904	New York	106	47	1944	St. Louis	105	49
1905	New York	105	48	1945	Chicago	98	56
1906	Chicago	116	36	1946	St. Louis	98	58
1907	Chicago	107	45	1947	Brooklyn	94	59
1908	Chicago	95	55	1948	Boston	91	62
1909	Pittsburgh	110	42	1949	Brooklyn	97	57
1910	Chicago	104	50	1950	Philadelphia	91	63
1911	New York	99	54	1951	New York	98	59
1912	New York	103	48	1952	Brooklyn	96	57
1913	New York	101	51	1953	Brooklyn	105	49
1914	Boston	94	59	1954	New York	97	57
1915	Philadelphia	90	62	1955	Brooklyn	98	55
1916	Brooklyn	94	60	1956	Brooklyn	93	61
1917	New York	98	56	1957	Milwaukee	95	59
1918	Chicago	84	45	1958	Milwaukee	92	62
1919	Cincinnati	96	44	1959	Los Angeles	88	68
1920	Brooklyn	93	61	1960	Pittsburgh	95	59
1921	New York	94	56	1961	Cincinnati	93	61
1922	New York	93	61	1962	San Francisco	103	62
1923	New York	98	58	1963	Los Angeles	99	63
1924	New York	93	60	1964	St. Louis	93	69
1925	Pittsburgh	95	58	1965	Los Angeles	97	65
1926	St. Louis	85	65	1966	Los Angeles	95	67
1927	Pittsburgh	94	60	1967	St. Louis	101	60
1928	St. Louis	95	59	1968	St. Louis	97	65
1929	Chicago	98	54	1969	New York	100	62
1930	St. Louis	92	62	1970	Cincinnati	102	60
1931	St. Louis	101	53	1971	Pittsburgh	97	65
1932	Chicago	90	64	1972	Cincinnati	95	59
1933	New York	91	61	1973	New York	82	79
1934	St. Louis	95	59	1974	Los Angeles	102	60
1935	Chicago	100	54	1975	Cincinnati	108	54
1936	New York	91	62	1976	Cincinnati	102	60
1937	New York	95	57	1977	Los Angeles	98	64
1938	Chicago	89	63	1978	Los Angeles	95	67
1939	Cincinnati	97	57	1979	Pittsburgh	98	64
1940	Cincinnati	100	53	1980	Philadelphia	91	71
1941	Brooklyn	100	54				

BASEBALL PENNANT WINNERS—AMERICAN LEAGUE

Year	Winner	Won	Lost	Year	Winner	Won	Lost
1902	Philadelphia	83	53	1942	New York	103	51
1903	Boston	91	47	1943	New York	98	56
1904	Boston	95	59	1944	St. Louis	89	65
1905	Philadelphia	92	56	1945	Detroit	88	65
1906	Chicago	93	58	1946	Boston	104	50
1907	Detroit	92	58	1947	New York	96	57
1908	Detroit	90	63	1948	Cleveland	97	58
1909	Detroit	98	54	1949	New York	97	57
1910	Philadelphia	102	48	1950	New York	98	56
1911	Philadelphia	101	50	1951	New York	98	56
1912	Boston	105	47	1952	New York	95	59
1913	Philadelphia	96	57	1953	New York	99	52
1914	Philadelphia	99	53	1954	Cleveland	111	43
1915	Boston	101	50	1955	New York	96	58
1916	Boston	91	63	1956	New York	97	57
1917	Chicago	100	54	1957	New York	98	56
1918	Boston	75	51	1958	New York	92	62
1919	Chicago	88	52	1959	Chicago	94	60
1920	Cleveland	98	56	1960	New York	97	57
1921	New York	98	55	1961	New York	109	53
1922	New York	94	60	1962	New York	96	66
1923	New York	98	54	1963	New York	104	57
1924	Washington	92	62	1964	New York	99	63
1925	Washington	96	55	1965	Minnesota	102	60
1926	New York	91	63	1966	Baltimore	97	63
1927	New York	110	44	1967	Boston	92	70
1928	New York	101	53	1968	Detroit	103	59
1929	Philadelphia	104	46	1969	Baltimore	109	53
1930	Philadelphia	102	52	1970	Baltimore	108	54
1931	Philadelphia	107	45	1971	Baltimore	101	57
1932	New York	107	47	1972	Oakland	93	62
1933	Washington	99	53	1973	Oakland	94	68
1934	Detroit	101	53	1974	Oakland	90	72
1935	Detroit	93	58	1975	Boston	95	65
1936	New York	102	51	1976	New York	97	62
1937	New York	102	52	1977	New York	100	62
1938	New York	99	53	1978	New York	100	63
1939	New York	106	45	1979	Baltimore	102	57
1940	Detroit	90	64	1980	Kansas City	97	65
1941	New York	101	53				

CHAMPION BATTERS AND THEIR AVERAGES

NATIONAL LEAGUE

Year	Player	Club	Average
1917	Roush	Cincinnati	.341
1918	Wheat	Brooklyn	.335
1919	Cravath	Philadelphia	.321
1920	Hornsby	St. Louis	.370
1921	Hornsby	St. Louis	.397
1922	Hornsby	St. Louis	.401
1923	Hornsby	St. Louis	.384
1924	Hornsby	St. Louis	.424
1925	Hornsby	St. Louis	.403
1926	Hargrave	Cincinnati	.353
1927	P. Waner	Pittsburgh	.380
1928	Hornsby	Boston	.387
1929	O'Doul	Philadelphia	.398
1930	Terry	New York	.401
1931	Hafey	St. Louis	.349
1932	O'Doul	Brooklyn	.366
1933	Klein	Philadelphia	.368
1934	P. Waner	Pittsburgh	.362
1935	Vaughan	Pittsburgh	.385
1936	P. Waner	Pittsburgh	.373
1937	Medwick	St. Louis	.374
1938	Lombardi	Cincinnati	.342
1939	Mize	St. Louis	.349
1940	Garms	Pittsburgh	.355
1941	Reiser	Brooklyn	.343
1942	Lombardi	Boston	.330
1943	Musial	St. Louis	.357
1944	Walker	Brooklyn	.357
1945	Cavaretta	Chicago	.355
1946	Musial	St. Louis	.365
1947	Walker	Philadelphia	.363
1948	Musial	St. Louis	.376
1949	Robinson	Brooklyn	.342
1950	Musial	St. Louis	.346
1951	Musial	St. Louis	.355
1952	Musial	St. Louis	.336
1953	Furillo	Brooklyn	.344
1954	Mays	New York	.345
1955	Ashburn	Philadelphia	.338
1956	Aaron	Milwaukee	.328
1957	Musial	St. Louis	.351
1958	Ashburn	Philadelphia	.350
1959	Aaron	Milwaukee	.355
1960	Groat	Pittsburgh	.325
1961	Clemente	Pittsburgh	.351
1962	T. Davis	Los Angeles	.346
1963	T. Davis	Los Angeles	.326
1964	Clemente	Pittsburgh	.339
1965	Clemente	Pittsburgh	.329
1966	Alou	Pittsburgh	.342
1967	Clemente	Pittsburgh	.357
1968	Rose	Cincinnati	.335
1969	Rose	Cincinnati	.348
1970	Carty	Atlanta	.366
1971	Torre	St. Louis	.363
1972	B. Williams	Chicago	.333
1973	Rose	Cincinnati	.338
1974	Garr	Atlanta	.353
1975	Madlock	Chicago	.354
1976	Madlock	Chicago	.339
1977	Parker	Pittsburgh	.338
1978	Parker	Pittsburgh	.334
1979	Hernandez	St. Louis	.344
1980	Buckner	Chicago	.324

AMERICAN LEAGUE

Year	Player	Club	Average
1917	Cobb	Detroit	.383
1918	Cobb	Detroit	.382
1919	Cobb	Detroit	.384
1920	Sisler	St. Louis	.409
1921	Heilmann	Detroit	.394
1922	Sisler	St. Louis	.419
1923	Heilmann	Detroit	.403
1924	Ruth	New York	.378
1925	Heilmann	Detroit	.393
1926	Manush	Detroit	.377
1927	Heilmann	Detroit	.398
1928	Goslin	Washington	.379
1929	Fonseca	Cleveland	.369
1930	Simmons	Philadelphia	.382
1931	Simmons	Philadelphia	.390
1932	Alexander	Det. Bost.	.367
1933	Foxx	Philadelphia	.356
1934	Gehrig	New York	.363
1935	Myer	Washington	.350
1936	Appling	Chicago	.388
1937	Gehringer	Detroit	.369
1938	Foxx	Boston	.349
1939	Di Maggio	New York	.381
1940	Di Maggio	New York	.352
1941	T. Williams	Boston	.406
1942	T. Williams	Boston	.356
1943	Appling	Chicago	.328
1944	Boudreau	Cleveland	.327
1945	Stirnweiss	New York	.309
1946	Vernon	Washington	.353
1947	T. Williams	Boston	.343
1948	T. Williams	Boston	.369
1949	Kell	Detroit	.342
1950	Goodman	Boston	.354
1951	Fain	Philadelphia	.344
1952	Fain	Philadelphia	.327
1953	Vernon	Washington	.337
1954	Avila	Cleveland	.341
1955	Kaline	Detroit	.340
1956	Mantle	New York	.353
1957	T. Williams	Boston	.388
1958	T. Williams	Boston	.328
1959	Kuenn	Detroit	.353
1960	Runnels	Boston	.320
1961	Cash	Detroit	.361
1962	Runnels	Boston	.326
1963	Yastrzemski	Boston	.321
1964	Oliva	Minnesota	.323
1965	Oliva	Minnesota	.321
1966	F. Robinson	Baltimore	.316
1967	Yastrzemski	Boston	.326
1968	Yastrzemski	Boston	.301
1969	Carew	Minnesota	.332
1970	Johnson	California	.329
1971	Oliva	Minnesota	.337
1972	Carew	Minnesota	.318
1973	Carew	Minnesota	.350
1974	Carew	Minnesota	.364
1975	Carew	Minnesota	.359
1976	Brett	Kansas City	.333
1977	Carew	Minnesota	.388
1978	Carew	Minnesota	.333
1979	Lynn	Boston	.333
1980	Brett	Kansas City	.390

an association of teams that compete chiefly among themselves. Early in 1876 a group of influential club owners, headed by William A. Hulbert (1832–82) of Chicago, founded the National League of Professional Baseball Clubs, causing the collapse of the National Association. The National League, which is still in operation, then represented clubs in Boston, Mass.; Hartford, Conn.; Philadelphia, Pa.; New York, N.Y.; Saint Louis, Mo.; Chicago, Ill.; Cincinnati, Ohio; and Louisville, Ky. Chicago won the first league championship in 1876.

During the next quarter of a century numerous other leagues were organized throughout the U.S. Among the first of these were the International League and the Northwestern League, both composed of teams representing smaller cities than the clubs in the National League and known for that reason as minor leagues. In 1882 the American Association was established as a major league. Two years later, the champions of this league met the National League champions in the first series of postseason games. After the American Association disbanded in 1891, the National League clubs played each other at the end of the season.

The American League was founded in 1900 and the following year demanded that the National League recognize it as an equal. The original eight American League teams were Chicago, Ill.; Milwaukee, Wis.; Cleveland, Ohio; Detroit, Mich.; Washington, D.C.; Philadelphia, Pa.; Boston, Mass.; and Baltimore, Md. Recognition of the American League by the National League was gained finally in 1903, when the modern World Series, a postseason play-off between the two leagues, was inaugurated.

An attempt to maintain a third major league ended in failure in 1915 with the dissolution of the Federal League, organized two years previously.

Professional Baseball Government. In 1903, the same year as the first World Series competition, the major and minor leagues established a National Commission of three members and endowed it with supervisory control of professional baseball. During the World Series of 1919 between the Chicago club of the American League and the Cincinnati club of the National League, eight Chicago players conspired with gamblers to bring about the defeat of their own team. The subsequent scandal resulted in public demands for stricter control of professional baseball.

In 1921 the National Commission was replaced by the Advisory Council headed by a commissioner. The American jurist Kenesaw Mountain Landis (q.v.) became the first commissioner, holding the position until his death in 1944. He was succeeded in 1945 by Albert Benjamin ("Happy") Chandler (1898–), a prominent political leader of Kentucky. In 1951 Ford Christopher Frick (1894–), former president of the National League, was elected commissioner. In 1965 Frick was succeeded by William Doyle Eckert (1909–71), a retired United States Air Force general. The current commissioner of baseball is Bowie K. Kuhn (1926–), a lawyer who was named to the post in 1969.

The baseball commissioner is elected by the club owners for a seven-year term. He has the authority to investigate any action that he regards as harmful to the sport of baseball and may penalize, in the form of fines or suspensions, the personnel involved. He also rules on disputes between leagues, teams, and players.

Current Major and Minor Leagues. The two major leagues are the American League, with 14 teams, and the National League, with 12 teams. The teams in each league are grouped into two divisions, known as the eastern and western divisions.

The American League Eastern Division is composed of the New York (N.Y.) Yankees; Boston (Mass.) Red Sox; Baltimore (Md.) Orioles; Detroit (Mich.) Tigers; Milwaukee (Wis.) Brewers; Cleveland (Ohio) Indians; and the Toronto (Ontario) Blue Jays. The American League Western Division consists of the Chicago (Ill.) White Sox; Minnesota (Minneapolis, Minn.) Twins; Kansas City (Mo.) Royals; California Angels (based at Anaheim, Calif.); Texas (Arlington, Texas) Rangers; Oakland (Calif.) Athletics; and Seattle (Wash.) Mariners.

The National League Eastern Division is composed of the New York (N.Y.) Mets; Philadelphia (Pa.) Phillies; Pittsburgh (Pa.) Pirates; Montréal (Québec) Expos; Chicago (Ill.) Cubs; and Saint Louis (Mo.) Cardinals. The National League Western Division consists of the Atlanta (Ga.) Braves; Cincinnati (Ohio) Reds; Houston (Texas) Astros; Los Angeles (Calif.) Dodgers; San Diego (Calif.) Padres; and San Francisco (Calif.) Giants.

During the baseball season (April to September or early October), every team plays 162 games. A club plays 81 games at home and 81 games away against the teams in its own league. League championships are determined by a 3 out of 5 game play-off between the 2 division leaders; the victorious team takes the league pennant for that year. Pennant winners then meet at a final, 7-game play-off, called the World Series; the first team to win 4 of these games is the World Series Champion.

The minor leagues are governed by the National Association of Professional Baseball Leagues, organized in 1901. In 1970 the association numbered twenty-one leagues. Some teams in the minor leagues are referred to as the farm system and are used by the major league clubs as testing and training grounds for young talent. Most notable of the minor leagues are the Pacific Coast League, the International League, and the American Association.

The Playing Field. Baseball is played on a level field, usually about 2 acres in size. The field is divided into the infield and the outfield.

The infield consists largely of a square-shaped plot, called the diamond, measuring 90 ft. on each side. At each corner of the square, within the right angle formed, lies a white slab. One of the slabs is a five-sided piece of rubber called home plate. The others, moving counterclockwise, are called first base, second base, and third base. These are canvas bags, sized 15 in. square and filled with soft stuffing to a thickness of 3 to 5 in. Thick white lines, called the base lines, connect the home plate with first and third base. Flanking home plate are the two

Pitcher	1	Initiates central action of the game by throwing the ball to batters at the plate. Works closely with catcher, with whom he shares special pitching signals. Backs up defensive plays at home, third base, and first base and defends against bunts. Usually bats last in lineup. Manager can replace pitcher at any time.
Catcher	2	Generally considered "field commander" of the team while it is in the field. Calls for pitches thrown by the pitcher and helps keep the ball rubbed up. Watches and instructs shifts in field positions for particular batters or situations. Tries to throw out base runners attempting to steal, and like pitcher tries to pick off runners.
First Baseman	3	Defends base to which batters first run and short right field. Holds runners on. Plays in hole between first and second when no runner on first to cut off base hits. Backs up catcher on throws from outfield.
Second Baseman	4	Defends middle base and area behind and to right of it. With shortstop is involved in most double plays when there are baserunners and relays throws from outfield to home plate.
Third Baseman	5	Defends left-field line and, with shortstop, short left field. Guards against bunts. Initiates many double plays by throwing to second base. Backs up catcher on throws to home plate.
Shortstop	6	Defends between second and third base. With second baseman is crux of most double plays and relays to home, and like second baseman works with pitcher to catch runner off second base. Both shortstop and second baseman try to prevent grounders from going through the middle for base hits.
Left Fielder	7	Defends outfield area between left-field line and center field.
Center Fielder	8	Defends central outfield area, generally more territory than that of left fielder or right fielder.
Right Fielder	9	Defends outfield area between right-field line and center field. Like left fielder makes mostly direct, rather than relay throws to home plate to cut off runs.

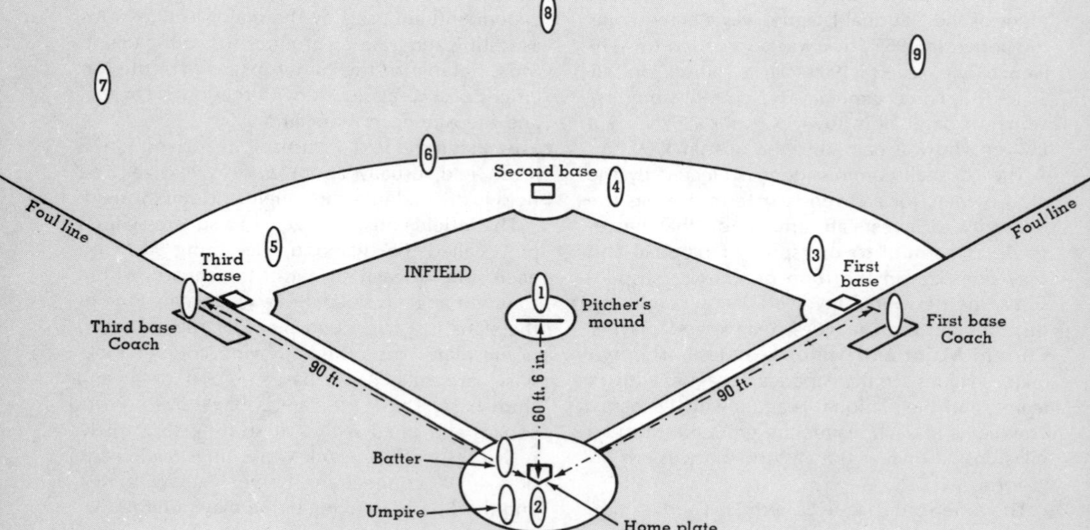

Dodger Stadium, home of the Los Angeles Dodgers, has a capacity of 56,000, sizable for a baseball arena. Football stadiums are usually larger, for the playing area in football is less concentrated. Los Angeles Dodgers

batter's boxes (batters may bat from either side of the plate), and behind the plate is the catcher's box. In the center of the diamond, 60½ ft. directly in front of home plate, is the pitcher's mound. The mound slopes gradually to its maximum height of 10 in. (lowered in 1968 from 15 in.), where the pitcher stands. Although most of the infield is made up of grass (either natural or artificial), the pitcher's circle is a sandy area. Set into the mound is the pitcher's rubber, an oblong strip upon which the pitcher must rest one foot while delivering the ball.

The outfield consists of the large grassy area that lies in back of the infield and is enclosed between extensions of the base lines that run from home plate to first and third bases. These lines are known as the foul lines. Any batted ball that strikes the ground outside the lines is said to fall into foul territory and is scored as a foul ball. Batted balls that stay between the lines are in fair territory, and play continues.

Other areas of the field, each outside the immediate playing area, include the two sunken shelters, called dugouts, located along the edges of the field and occupied by the players when they are not required to be on the field; two coaches' boxes, small rectangles located near first and third bases; and the bullpen, where relief, or substitute, pitchers practice prior to entering a game.

Equipment. The basic equipment for a baseball game includes a hard, horsehide-covered ball, which must measure between 9 and 9¼ in. in circumference and weigh between 5 and 5¼ oz.; a rounded wooden bat, not more than 42 in. long and 2¾ in. in diameter at its thickest section; and padded leather gloves, worn during the defensive phases of play. Players also wear spiked shoes for better traction on the field and, while at bat, don a protective plastic helmet to shield the skull. In addition the catcher wears a protective cagelike mask covering his face and chest and leg padding.

The Baseball Team. Each baseball team has nine players: the catcher, who occupies a position directly behind home plate; the pitcher, who, in delivering the ball to the catcher, attempts to prevent a batter from the opposing team, now standing beside home plate, from hitting the ball; three basemen who stand or crouch at or near the bases; a shortstop situated behind the line between second and third bases about midway between them; and three outfielders, who occupy positions in the left, center, and right of the outfield. While the players of one team are in these positions, the players of the other team take turns at bat according to the preestablished batting order. All the players wear identifying numbers on their uniforms.

The ultimate authority in matters concerning the team's training and performance rests with the team manager, who usually remains in the dugout while a game is in process. He is assisted

Kansas City Royals pitching ace Paul Splittorff faced the New York Yankees in the deciding game of the 1977 American League pennant playoff. The Yanks were victorious and went on to win the World Series.

Kansas City Royals

by several coaches, two of whom may occupy the coach's boxes when the team is at bat.

Basic Rules. The game is divided into nine periods of play, called innings. Each inning is further subdivided into halves, popularly called the top and the bottom of an inning, during which the two teams are alternately at bat and in the field. The team with the greatest number of runs at the end of nine innings wins the game. A run is scored when a batter completes a circuit of the bases and returns safely to home plate. In the event of a tie, the game continues until the tie is broken, in equal turns at bat unless weather or visibility conditions make this impossible. All decisions affecting the conduct of the game are made by the plate umpire, whose position is behind the catcher. Usually the plate umpire is assisted by base umpires, situated near the three bases. As a rule, the visiting team bats first; in organized baseball it always bats first. A team's half of an inning is completed when three of its batters have been put out. It then takes the field while the other team bats.

A batter is put out in a number of ways: (1) if the batted ball is caught by a defending player before it reaches the ground; (2) if a batted ball that is fair (within the foul lines) is retrieved by a defending player and delivered to a teammate in time for him to touch first base before the batter can reach it; (3) if three strikes are called, provided the catcher does not drop the ball on the third strike; (4) if the batter hits a fair ball and it touches him before he reaches first base. A strike is called (1) when the batter swings at a pitched ball and misses; (2) when the batter lets pass a ball pitched in the strike zone, that is, a ball that has been pitched so that it crosses over the plate between the batter's armpits and the top of his knees; and (3) when the batter hits a foul ball. A foul ball, however, is not counted as a third strike except on a bunt, which is a pushing stroke designed to move the ball only a few feet.

Players who have succeeded in reaching one of the bases may also be put out subsequently. Such players may be forced out, for example, when a runner on first is forced to run for second in order to make way for a batter who has hit the ball along the ground. He is out if the ball is retrieved and delivered to a defender at second before he arrives there. If the player at second then delivers the ball to a teammate at first before the batter arrives at that base, the batter is out also, in what is known as a double play. On the other hand, if the batter hits a ball to the outfield, the runner on first must stay there if he thinks the outfielder can make the catch on the fly, that is, before the ball touches the ground. After the catch the runner can tag up, or step on the base, and then try to advance to the next base at his own risk. If the outfielder fails to catch the ball, the runner must leave first base and attempt to reach second before the ball reaches that base from the outfield. These situations also occur when both first and second bases or all three bases are occupied. With two or more runners on the bases, the rare triple play may occur whereby three players are put out during one turn at bat. Any runner is out if he is hit by a batted ball and also if he leaves a base before a fly ball is caught and fails to return before the ball is delivered to that base.

The batter becomes a base runner (1) when he makes a safe hit, that is, bats a fair ball where it cannot be caught before it reaches the ground, or where it cannot be retrieved and delivered to first base (or any other base) before his arrival there; (2) after four balls have been called by the umpire, a ball being a pitch delivered outside the strike zone, which the batter deliberately allows to pass by (this is scored as a base on balls or, more popularly, a walk); (3) if the batter is hit by a pitched ball; (4) if the catcher interferes with the attempt of the batter to strike the ball; (5) if the catcher drops the ball on a third strike. In the last event, the batter must reach first base before the catcher delivers the ball to the first baseman or tags the batter with the ball; or (6) if an opposing player mishandles the batted ball, thereby allowing the batter to reach base safely. This is scored as an error.

Strong pitching is generally regarded as the key element in team success. Luis Tiant, shown here with the Boston Red Sox, turned in the best performance of any American League pitcher in 1968 and 1972.
Boston Red Sox

Through the slide into base, the runner achieves a low profile and may escape being tagged. Here, a base umpire signals the sliding runner is safe: the California Angel's tag was too slow. California Angels

George Herman ("Babe") Ruth, first a pitcher and later a power hitter, was officially recognized at a baseball centennial in 1969 as "The Greatest Player Ever". His record of 60 home runs was unbroken for 34 years. UPI

Baseball Strategy. The entire strategy and tactics of the game of baseball are built around scoring more runs than the opposing team. Of major importance is the batting order, the official schedule of a team's rotation at bat, usually determined by the manager prior to the start of a game. In setting up the batting order, the manager considers the important playing strengths of each player on his team (one player may be a particularly fast runner; another, a powerful hitter; a third, a dependable bunter) and arranges their sequence of batting to reflect the highest probability of players advancing each other to scoring position. Managers may make substitutions in the batting order at strategic points in the game. In addition, teams generally use a secret system of hand signals or body motions that allows strategy to be relayed among manager, coaches, and players without the opposing team's knowledge.

GETTING ON BASE. A batter tries to get on base by either a safe hit or a walk, also known as a free pass. Once he gets on base, his teammates attempt to advance him to home plate. If the next batter gets another safe hit, the first may advance more than one base at a time. A player may also hit a sacrifice bunt or a sacrifice fly, so called because the batter deliberately causes himself to be retired so that the runner may advance safely to the next base. A long sacrifice fly to the outfield will often enable a base runner to score from third base, perhaps with the deciding run of the game. A player may also advance a base by stealing it, that is, by dashing from one base to another before the ball can be brought into play against him.

PITCHING. For a pitcher the greatest achievement is a no-hit game, that is, a game in which he does not allow a single safe hit by any member of the opposing team. If he also prevents any player of the opposing team from reaching first base by a walk or by accidentally hitting a batter with the ball, and if none of his teammates commits an error (a fielding misplay) allowing an opponent to reach first base, it is possible for the pitcher to achieve a perfect game. Few perfect games have been played in baseball history.

In close-scoring games, managers frequently juggle, or change, their pitchers around as the situation of a game dictates. For example, it is commonly believed that left-handed pitchers are more effective against left-handed batters. One pitcher may be taken out of play at a critical moment to make way for another. Four, five, and even six pitchers may be used in a single game if the manager thinks it necessary.

Pitchers usually require at least two or three days of rest between each full game they pitch. Relief pitchers, brought into play for only a few innings, generally to rescue the previous pitcher from difficulties, are able to pitch more frequently.

HOME RUNS. Best of all, from the standpoint of the spectators as well as the players, is the home run, a long hit, usually out of the playing field, that enables all of the runners on the bases at the time to score ahead of the home-run hitter. One of the greatest home-run hitters was George Herman ("Babe") Ruth (q.v.) of the New York Yankees. His record of 60 home runs in 1927 stood for 34 years, until Roger Eugene Maris (q.v.) of the Yankees hit 61. Ruth held a record of 714 career home runs; but when Henry L. ("Hank") Aaron (q.v.) retired in 1976 he had hit 755. Ruth was at the peak of his fame during the era of the lively ball, when it is believed that baseball manufacturers were putting more rubber into the core of the ball. In the 1920's, 1930's, and 1940's, the batters were in the ascendancy, and many games had high scores. Leading batters in both major leagues usually averaged better than .350 and sometimes higher than .400 for the season; they hit safely at least once in every three turns at bat. (The batting average is determined by dividing a player's number of hits by the number of official times he batted, carrying the resulting figure to three decimal points.) In the late 1950's and the 1960's, the pitchers gained ascendancy, and low-scoring games were much more common than high-scoring games. Few batters hit above .300. In 1968 the leading batter of the American League, Carl Michael Yastrzemski (1939-) of the Boston Red Sox, posted an all-time low of .301 for a batting champion.

Player Records and Awards. Baseball enthusiasts follow and record individual as well as team performances with great enthusiasm. One of the most exciting contests of each season is the All-Star Game, first played in 1933. An All-Star Game pits the most outstanding players of the American League, regardless of their individual club affiliation, against the best players of the National League. The teams' members are selected on the basis of their distinguished playing, by their fellow players, managers, and coaches in the league.

Throughout the baseball season, records are tallied for nearly every facet of the sport, as most stolen bases, most three-base hits, fewest strikeouts, most consecutive games played, and even highest fan attendance. Records are usually determined in the single-game, the single-season, or a lifetime category.

At the close of each season, the Most Valuable Player Award is voted by the Baseball Writers Association of America and presented to one player in each major league. The Cy Young Award, also voted annually by the same organization, is given to the best pitcher of the season in each league. Perhaps the most coveted baseball honor, however, remains membership in baseball's Hall of Fame.

Boys Baseball. Throughout the world organized programs of baseball, similar in many ways to the professional leagues, have been developed for young boys. The largest such program is the Little League, first developed in the U.S. in 1939 and now being played in Canada, Latin Amer-

Batting is usually regarded as less important to team success than pitching, but nothing gets a crowd to its feet like a home run. Hank Aaron, shown here, took 755 round trips in his career, 41 more than Babe Ruth. UPI

NATIONAL BASEBALL HALL OF FAME

Alexander, Grover C.
Anson, Adrian C. (Cap)
Appling, Lucius Benjamin (Luke)
Averill, Earl
Baker, J. Frank (Home Run)
Bancroft, Dave J. (Beauty)
Banks, Ernie
Barrow, Edward G.
Beckley, Jake
Bell, James (Cool Papa)
Bender, Charles (Chief)
Berra, Lawrence P. (Yogi)
Bottomley, James (Sunny Jim)
Boudreau, Louis
Bresnahan, Roger (Duke)
Brouthers, Dan
Brown, Mordecai P. (Three Finger)
Bulkeley, Morgan C.
Burkett, Jesse C.
Campanella, Roy (Campy)
Carey, Max George
Cartwright, Alexander J., Jr.
Chadwick, Henry
Chance, Frank L. (Husk)
Charleston, Oscar
Chesbro, John D.
Clarke, Fred
Clarkson, John
*Clemente, Roberto
Cobb, Tyrus R.
Cochrane, Gordon S. (Mickey)
Collins, Edward T.
Collins, James
Combs, Earle
Comiskey, Charles A.
Conlan, John (Jocko)
Connolly, Thomas H.
Connor, Roger
Coveleski, Stanley A.
Crawford, Samuel E. (Candy)
Cronin, Joseph E.
Cummings, William A. (Candy)
Cuyler, Hazen S.
Dean, Jay Hanna (Dizzy)
Delehanty, Ed
Dickey, William M.
Dihigo, Martin
DiMaggio, Joseph P.
Duffy, Hugh
Evans, Billy
Evers, John J.
Ewing, William B. (Buck)
Faber, Urban Clarence (Red)
Feller, Robert W.
Flick, Elmer
Ford, Edward Charles (Whitey)
Foxx, James E.
Frick, Ford C.
Frisch, Frank
Galvin, James F.
*Gehrig, Henry Lewis (Lou)
Gehringer, Charles
Gibson, Joshua (Josh)
Gomez, Vernon L. (Lefty)
Goslin, Leon A. (Goose)
Greenberg, Henry B. (Hank)
Griffith, Clark C.
Grimes, Burleigh Arland
Grove, Robert M. (Lefty)
Hafey, Charles J. (Chick)
Haines, Jesse (Pop)
Hamilton, William R.
Harridge, William (Will)
Harris, Stanley (Bucky)
Hartnett, Charles L. (Gabby)
Heilmann, Harry E.
Herman, Billy
Hooper, Harry B.
Hornsby, Rogers
Hoyt, Waite C.
Hubbard, Cal
Hubbell, Carl
Huggins, James Miller (Miller)
Irvin, Monte
Jennings, Hugh
Johnson, Byron B.
Johnson, Walter P.
Johnson, William (Judy)
Joss, Addie
Kaline, Al
Keefe, Timothy J. (Smiling Tim)
Keeler, William (Willie)
Kelley, Joe
Kelly, George (Highpockets)
Kelly, Mike J. (King)
Kiner, Ralph
Klem, William J.
Koufax, Sanford (Sandy)
Lajoie, Napoleon
Landis, Kenesaw M.
Lemon, Bob
Leonard, Walter (Buck)
Lindstrom, Fred
Lloyd, John Henry (Pop)
Lopez, Al
Lyons, Theodore A.
Mack, Connie
MacPhail, Leland S. (Larry)
Mantle, Mickey
Manush, Henry Emmet (Heinie)
Maranville, Walter J. (Rabbit)
Marquard, Richard W. (Rube)
Mathews, Eddie
Mathewson, Christy
McCarthy, Joseph V.
McCarthy, Thomas F.
McGinnity, Joseph J.
McGraw, John J.
McKechnie, William B.
Medwick, Joseph M. (Ducky)
Musial, Stanley F. (Stan)
Nichols, Charles A. (Kid)
O'Rourke, James H.
Ott, Melvin T.
Paige, Leroy (Satchel)
Pennock, Herbert J.
Plank, Edward S.
Radbourne, Charlie (Old Hoss)
Rice, Sam
Rickey, Wesley Branch
Rixey, Eppa
Roberts, Robin
Robinson, Jack R. (Jackie)
Robinson, Wilbert
Roush, Edd J.
Ruffing, Charles H. (Red)
Rusie, Amos
Ruth, George H. (Babe)
Schalk, Raymond W.
Sewell, Joe
Simmons, Aloysius H. (Al)
Sisler, George H.
Snider, Edwin D. (Duke)
Spahn, Warren
Spalding, Albert G.
Speaker, Tristram E.
Stengel, Charles D. (Casey)
Terry, William H. (Bill)
Thompson, Sam
Tinker, Joseph B.
Traynor, Harold J. (Pie)
Vance, Arthur C. (Dazzy)
Waddell, George E. (Rube)
Wagner, Honus
Wallace, Roderick J.
Walsh, Edward A.
Waner, Lloyd J.
Waner, Paul G.
Ward, John Montgomery
Weiss, George
Welch, Mickey
Wheat, Zachariah D.
Williams, Theodore S. (Ted)
Wright, George
Wright, Harry
Wynn, Early
Young, Denton T. (Cy)
Youngs, Ross

* Required five-year waiting period was waived.

ica, Europe, North Africa, and the Near and Far East. Boys aged eight to twelve years are eligible to play on Little League teams. The league diamond is two thirds the size of that used in the major leagues, and games are limited to six innings. Local businessmen act as team sponsors, providing uniforms and equipment, and parents and other adults are the coaches. Girls were admitted to league play in 1974.

Other boys' baseball groups include the Junior League, for youths aged nine to twelve years; the Pony League, organized in 1951, for boys aged thirteen to fourteen years; the Babe Ruth League, organized in 1952, for boys thirteen to fifteen years; the American Legion League, founded as the American Legion Junior League in 1926, for players from sixteen through seventeen years of age; and the Connie Mack League.

See also SOFTBALL and separate biographies on outstanding baseball players. B.K.K.

BASEBALL HALL OF FAME AND MUSEUM, NATIONAL, memorial institution opened in 1939, in Cooperstown, N.Y. Displayed in the part of the building designated as a museum are uniforms, photographs, and trophies of famous players, paintings and lithographs of early games, photographs of the winning teams in the World Series, and many other baseball souvenirs and items of interest. The museum library is equipped to answer questions sent in by baseball enthusiasts of the United States and other parts of the world. In the part of the building designated the Hall of Fame are bronze plaques commemorating the "immortals" of baseball. Honor-roll members are mainly former players but include individuals who have contributed meritoriously to the advancement of the game.

The Hall of Fame Committee on Veterans selects the honor-roll members as well as players who have been retired from the major leagues for at least twenty years and who competed in at least ten championship seasons in the major leagues. Persons belonging to the Baseball Writers' Association of America for at least ten years elect the other Hall of Fame members; these must have retired as players five years prior to election, been active in the game during the preceding two decades, and competed in ten championship seasons in the major leagues. The Hall of Fame Committee on Negro Leagues elects members who were active at least ten years in the Negro baseball leagues prior to 1946 or whose service in them prior to 1946 and in the major leagues thereafter aggregates ten years or more.

BASEDOW, Johann Bernhard (1724?-90), German educational reformer, born in Hamburg. He was strongly influenced by the ideas of the English philosopher John Locke and the French philosopher Jean Jacques Rousseau (qq.v.) and in 1774 projected a reform of the primary educational system of Germany. Basedow's views were widely acclaimed, leading to the establishment in Dessau of a model educational institution called Philanthropinum, of which he was the director. Philanthropinum and similar institutions, which were subsequently established in other cities, strove to improve the quality of education by relating school work to the world outside the classroom. In 1778 Basedow resigned as director of Philanthropinum, which was closed fifteen years later. He wrote *Elementarwerk* (4 vol., 1774) and other works.

BASEL *or* **BASLE** (Fr. *Bâle*), city in Switzerland, and capital of the half-canton of Baselstadt, on the Rhine R. about 55 miles N.W. of Zurich. In 1833 the two independent half-cantons, Baselstadt and Baselland, were created from the former Basel Canton. Baselstadt, covering 14 sq.mi., is comprised of the city of Basel and two adjoining villages; Baselland, covering 165 sq.mi., has its capital at Liestal. The city of Basel is surrounded by a rich agricultural region where fruit trees and grapevines are cultivated and cattle are raised. The city is a major industrial center producing drugs, chemicals, machinery, and textiles. It is also the site of an annual Swiss Industries fair. Most of the inhabitants of the region speak German. In Basel are the Münster, consecrated as a cathedral in 1019 and as an abbey church in 1528, and the first Swiss university, founded in 1460 by Pope Pius II (*see under* PIUS). The Dutch scholar Desiderius Erasmus (q.v.) taught at the university and is buried in the Münster.

The city was founded in 374 A.D. as the Roman frontier post, Basilia. It was ruled by bishops of the Western Church after the 5th century, and in the 11th century it became an imperial city governed by bishop-princes. From 1431 to 1443,

A view of Basel showing the Rhine River and, in the left foreground, spires of the Münster, the venerable pre-Reformation cathedral that is now a Protestant church. Swiss National Tourist Office

the city was the site of a famous Roman Catholic council called to bring about reforms in the Church; *see* BASEL, COUNCIL OF. In 1501 Basel joined the Swiss Confederation and became a center of the Swiss Reformation movement; *see* REFORMATION: *Switzerland.* Pop. (1969 est.) 215,-600.

BASEL, CONFESSION OF, in ecclesiatical history, designation applied to two pronouncements of doctrinal belief in the Swiss Reformed Church.

First Confession of Basel, drafted in 1531 by the German theologian Johannes Oecolampadius (1482–1531), who presented it to the Synod of Basel, in 1534. It represented a compromise between the doctrines of the German religious reformer Martin Luther and those of the Swiss Huldreich Zwingli (qq.v.). The confession remained in effect until 1872.

Second Confession of Basel, known more correctly as the First Helvetic Confession, adopted in 1536. To a greater extent than the First Confession of Basel, it expressed the doctrines of Zwingli. It was modified by the Second Helvetic Confession (1566) and adopted as a declaration of doctrine by most Reformed churches throughout Europe. The Second did not replace the First Helvetic Confession in Basel itself.

BASEL, COUNCIL OF *or* **BASLE, COUNCIL OF** (1431–37), council of the Christian Church held in Basel, Switzerland, and the last of the three reforming Church councils held in the 15th century; *see* COUNCIL; ROMAN CATHOLIC CHURCH. The meeting at Basel had been decreed by the Council of Constance (*see* CONSTANCE, COUNCIL OF), second of the three ecclesiastical councils. The aim of the Council of Basel was to promote internal reforms in the Church. It was dissolved in 1437, when Pope Eugenius IV (*see under* EUGENIUS) transferred it to Ferrara, Italy. A rebellious group, however, remained at Basel; they voted the suspension of Eugenius IV in 1438, declared him a heretic in 1439, and elected an antipope, Felix V (*see under* FELIX). The pseudo-council at Basel lasted until 1449 when, with the resignation of Felix V, it ended the schism by accepting Nicholas V (*see under* NICHOLAS) as pope and decreeing its own dissolution. The Council of Basel, that is, the sessions that were held from 1431 to 1437, generally is considered one of the ecumenical, or world-wide, councils.

BASEL, UNIVERSITY OF, oldest university of Switzerland, located in the city of Basel. The university is under the jurisdiction of the department of education of the canton of Basel. The larger part of its expenses are met by the canton. Establishment of the university was authorized by a papal bull in 1459, and it opened the following year. During the Reformation (q.v.) it was reorganized and became the stronghold of Protestant scholarship throughout the world. Among its famous teachers were the Dutch scholar Desiderius Erasmus (q.v.), the German theological leader Johannes Oecolampadius (1482–1531), and the Swiss mathematicians Leonhard Euler (q.v.) and Jakob and Johann Bernoulli (*see under* BERNOULLI). Its major departments are those of philosophy and history, medicine, law, theology, and science. Depending on the field of study either a *Diplom,* the *Lizentiate* degree, or the degree of *Doktor* is awarded after a four year course of study, representing the equivalent of American master's-degree work. The university has a library of about 1,775,000 bound volumes and 3000 incunabula. In 1968–69 the student body numbered about 4600 and the faculty, about 360.

BASENJI, breed of the domestic dog belonging to the hound group. Long known, the breed is clearly shown in ancient Egyptian works of art. The animal is also called the African barkless dog; although it is barkless, it is not completely voiceless. Characteristics of the breed are upright ears, wrinkled forehead, moderately long legs, short, fine hair, a tightly curled tail, and small size. The basenji weighs about 22 lb. and is 16 in. high at the shoulder. The color varies from black to reddish and is often mixed with white. Because of its keen sense of smell and its quietness, the basenji is valuable as a hunting dog in the jungles of equatorial Africa.

BASES, in chemistry, opposites of acids. Originally the term referred to the oxides or hydroxides of metals, that is, to substances that react with acids, neutralizing them to form salts and water. When a base dissolves in water, it is transformed more or less completely into hydroxide ions (OH^-) and metallic ions. A strong base, or alkali (q.v.), such as sodium hydroxide ($NaOH$), is almost completely ionized in solution, but a weak base such as zinc hydroxide forms few ions (OH^- and Zn^{2+}). The solution is neutralized by the union of hydroxide ions from the base with hydrogen ions (H_3O^+) from the acid, forming water (H_2O).

The presence of hydroxide ions gives solutions of bases certain common properties in addition to their ability to neutralize acids. Solutions of bases are electrical conductors, are soapy to the touch, and have a soapy taste; they precipitate insoluble hydroxides and oxides when added to solutions containing ions of iron, nickel, mercury, and silver. Bases also cause litmus to turn blue, and affect the color of many dyes.

According to a wider concept proposed by the British chemist Thomas Martin Lowry (1874–1936), and the Danish physical chemist Johannes Nicolaus Brönsted (1879–1947), bases are those species, either neutral or ionic, that combine with protons (H^+). Water, ammonia (NH_3), carbonate ions (CO_3^{2-}), and hydroxide ions, therefore, are bases because each combines with protons. The products of these particular combinations have the formulas H_3O^+, NH_4^+, HCO_3^-, and H_2O respectively.

The most general idea of a base was suggested by the American chemist G. N. Lewis (q.v.), who considered a base to be any substance that can contribute a pair of electrons to be shared with another substance to form a chemical bond. According to this notion, substances classified by Lowry and Brönsted as bases continue to be regarded as bases because each of them can contribute a pair of electrons to share with a proton. The sharing, however, does not have to be with protons; a water molecule, for example, can supply a pair of electrons to be shared with a copper ion (Cu^{2+}). In contributing the pair of electrons, water functions as a base. Many Lewis bases give solutions that do not exhibit the properties of hydroxide ions. The Lewis point of view, therefore, represents a considerable extension of earlier ideas. T.W.D.

BASHKIR, Autonomous Soviet Socialist Republic of the Soviet Union, in the Russian S.F.S. R., in the s.w. Ural Mts., bordering on Asia. The republic, which was declared autonomous on May 23, 1919, is rich in copper, iron, manganese, and oil, and most industry is related to mining. The heavy forests of the mountains supply timber for paper and sawmilling, wood distilling, and veneering. Livestock raising and beekeeping are important occupations, and wheat, rye, oats, sugar beets, potatoes, and flax are grown on the rich farmland of Bashkir. The Bashkir A. S.S.R. has a larger population than any other autonomous republic. Many of the inhabitants of the republic are Bashkirs, a Turkic people of the Muslim religion, and the capital of the republic, Ufa, is the headquarters of Muslim life in Soviet Europe. Area of Bashkir, 54,233 sq.mi.; pop. (1967 est.) 3,757,000.

BASHKIRTSEV, Marie (1860–84), Russian painter and diarist, born near Poltava. She studied painting in Paris under the French painters Jules Bastien-Lepage (q.v.) and Tony Robert-Fleury (1837–1911). Everyday life and street scenes of the French capital were the chief subjects of her paintings, which achieved moderate success. Her fame, however, is based chiefly on her diary, written in French and published under the title *Journal de Marie Bashkirtseff* (1887). Because of its frankness in revealing the ambitions, the vanity, and the intimate experiences of a sensitive and talented person, many readers consider the *Journal* a classic of autobiographical literature comparable to the *Confessions* of the French philosopher Jean Jacques Rousseau (q.v.).

BASIC ENGLISH. *See* ENGLISH LANGUAGE.

BASIDIOMYCOTA, large phylum of fungi, comprising about 20,000 species, that includes rusts, smuts, puffballs, bracket fungi, and most mushrooms. Commonly called club fungi, the Basidiomycetes are characterized by the club-shaped reproductive structures known as basidia, with stalked spores at their tips. *See* FUNGI.

BASIE, William ("Count"). *See* JAZZ: *Early Jazz: Big-Band Jazz.*

BASIL, common name for any plant of the genus *Ocimum* of the Mint (q.v.) family (Labiatae). It is a sweet herb used for fragrance and as a seasoning for food. Sweet basil, *O. basilicum,* is an annual plant, a native of warm climates, about 1 ft. high, with ovate petioled leaves, and has long been cultivated in Europe. Bush basil, *O. minimum,* is a small cultivated form. Basil, or mountain mint, is a common name also for *Pyc-*

Basil, Ocimum campechianum

nanthemum, a North American genus of many species.

BASIL, Saint *or* **BASILIUS, Saint,** called also BASIL THE GREAT (330?–79? A.D.), doctor of the Church and patriarch of Eastern monks, born in Caesarea (now Kayşeri, Turkey) and educated in Constantinople (now İstanbul, Turkey) and Athens, Greece. He visited a number of noted hermits in Egypt and Syria, and subsequently founded the order of Basilian Monks (q.v.) about 360. After becoming bishop of Caesarea in 370, he defended the Nicene Creed (q.v.) against the followers of the heretical Alexandrian theologian Arius (q.v.). He was a brother of Saint Gregory of Nyssa (q.v.), and his feast day is June 14.

BASIL, name of two Byzantine emperors.

Basil I, called BASIL THE MACEDONIAN (812–86). He won the favor of Emperor Michael III (d. 867), who appointed Basil his chamberlain. In 866 Basil, with Michael's consent, murdered the latter's uncle, Caesar Bardas, regent during Michael's minority (842–856), and became co-ruler of the Byzantine Empire (q.v.) with Michael. In 867 Basil had Michael assassinated. As sole ruler of the empire, he reformed the legal code, introduced other administrative reforms, and tried unsuccessfully to terminate the schism between the Eastern and Western churches.

Basil II (958?–1025), great-great-grandson of Basil I. He was crowned emperor of Byzantium at the age of two, and from 976 ruled jointly with his brother Constantine VIII (960?–1028) who, however, took no part in the administration of the empire. Basil's reign was marked by continual warfare, in the course of which many revolts were suppressed and Armenia and Bulgaria were annexed. Basil is known as Bulgaroctonos, "slayer of Bulgarians", because of the cruelties he inflicted on the Bulgarians.

BASILAN, city and fishing port of the Republic of the Philippines, in Zamboanga del Sur Province, on the N.W. coast of Basilan Island, on Basilan Strait, 10 miles S. of Zamboanga. The metropolitan area includes all of Basilan Island and various smaller islands. Basilan produces rubber, coconuts, rice, and corn, and raises cattle. Formerly a part of Zamboanga municipality, the city was once called Isabela. Pop. of city (1970) 143,829; pop. of metropolitan area (1971 est.) 179,200.

BASILE, Giovanni Batista, Count of Torone (about 1575–1632), Italian writer, born in Naples. Written in his native Neapolitan dialect, his most important works include a well-known collection of fifty fairy tales and folk tales entitled *Lo Cunto de li Cunti* (1634; Eng. trans., *The Tale of Tales,* 1932). Among them are versions of the familiar stories "Cinderella", "Puss in Boots", "Snow White", and "Beauty and the Beast".

BASILIAN MONKS, *or* MONKS OF SAINT BASIL, order founded by St. Basil (q.v.), Bishop of Caesarea, about 360. Many monks of the Orthodox Church are of this order. In the Western Church Basilian monasteries existed after the Middle Ages, and the order became strong after the Reformation (q.v.) in Roman Catholic countries, especially Spain and Italy. A modern Basilian order, founded in France in 1822 and devoted to education, has colleges in Canada and the United States. The records of the order show that it furnished fourteen popes, many cardinals, and nearly 12,000 martyrs. There are also Basilian nuns, who call Saint Macrina the Younger (330?–79), sister of Basil, their founder.

BASILICA, in architecture, among the ancient Greeks and Romans, a public court or building, with a portico, nave, side aisles, a tribune, and an apse, in which justice was dispensed by archons or praetors and in which public business was transacted. The early Christian churches were built on a somewhat similar plan, and therefore the term basilica was applied to them as an architectural title; *see* CHURCH: *Architecture and Buildings.* Later the term was conferred as an honor or a dignity upon certain sacred edifices selected by the popes. As a technical architectural term, basilica describes a church built on a rectangular, as opposed to a cruciform, ground plan.

In classical architecture, many variations from the simplest form of basilica, a three-aisled type, were introduced. Some are halls with a single nave, having as many as five aisles, with four rows of columns, like the basilicas called Julia and Ulpia, in Rome. Two hemicycles, one at each end, characterize Basilica Ulpia, built for the Roman emperor Trajan (q.v.), while other basilicas are virtually square in form. The majority have no upper galleries. The Roman statesman and author Pliny the elder (*see under* PLINY) called the Aemelia and the Julia basilicas two of the most superb monuments of Rome. The Basilica Aemelia stood on the north side of the Forum (q.v.) near the Curia, or Senate House. After a fire it was restored in 14 B.C. at the expense of the Roman emperor Augustus (q.v.). The ruins now visible are those of a building on the site of an older structure, known as the Basilica Fulvia et Aemelia begun in 179 B.C. The Basilica Julia was located on the south side of the Forum, and was begun by the Roman statesman and soldier Gaius Julius Caesar (q.v.) and

The nave of St. Peter's Basilica, in Rome, looking toward the altar. Scala/EPA

opened in 46 B.C. Several times destroyed by fire and rebuilt, what remains at the present time represents chiefly modern restoration. The Basilica of Constantine, begun by the emperor Marcus Aurelius Valerius Maxentius (r. 306–312) and completed by the emperor Constantine I (q.v.), had a nave about 250 ft. long, with a vaulted roof over 100 ft. high and 80 ft. broad. Notable ancient basilicas, all in Rome, were Basilica Porcia, built in 184 B.C. and burned in 52 B.C.; the Fulvia (179 B.C.); the Sempronia (169 B.C.); and the Opimia (121 B.C.).

Examples of the early basilican type of church still standing are Saint Peter's (q.v.), Saint Mary Major, and Saint John Lateran in Rome. The plan of a Christian basilica consists of an oblong space, divided into a central nave and side aisles by two or four rows of columns, preceded at the entrance end by a porch or narthex (beyond which the neophytes and penitents were not admitted), and terminated at the opposite end with a wall. The wall is broken by an arch that leads into the sanctuary, out of which opens the apse, with the bishop's throne in the center, raised some steps above the floor, and the seats of the presbyters and deacons on each side. The altar stands between the bishop and the people. Attached to the narthex is the baptistery.

BASILICATA, formerly LUCANIA, region of Italy, in the S. part of the country, adjoining the Gulf of Taranto and the Tyrrhenian Sea, and comprising Potenza and Matera provinces, named for their capital cities. The regional capital is Potenza. The mountainous W. portion of Basilicata, with elevations of more than 6000 ft., is part of the Apennines. The hills slope S.E. to a low coastal plain on the Gulf of Taranto. The economy is primarily dependent on the cultivation of olives, oats, grapes and other fruits, and potatoes, and the raising of some sheep and goats. Traditional industries include the manufacture of ornaments, clothing, and furniture. In the mid-20th century discovery of methane gas in the Basento Valley of Matera spurred the building of factories for heavier industry. The sparse population of Basilicata lives mainly in hilltop villages. Basilicata was known as Lucania when it was under Roman rule in the 3rd century B.C. It later fell prey to the invasions of the Lombards and Byzantines, and in the 11th century it became part of the Norman duchy of Apulia. It was included in the kingdom of Naples in the 13th century and became part of the kingdom of Italy in 1861.

Area, 3856 sq.mi.; pop. (1971) 603,288.

BASILIDES (d. about 140 A.D.), teacher of Alexandria, Egypt, and founder of a heretical sect practicing Gnosticism (q.v.), born probably in

Syria. Known as Basilidians, his followers were numerous in Egypt, Syria, Italy, and France; the sect disappeared before the 4th century.

BASILISK, common name for lizards of the genus *Basiliscus* in the Iguana family, of which four species are found in tropical America from Mexico to Ecuador. The name is derived from a mythical monster, the basilisk, whose breath and glance were fatal. The basilisks are from about 2 to 3 ft. long when fully grown, most of the length being in the slender, whiplike tail. Their back legs are developed far out of proportion to the rest of their bodies, so that when at rest the basilisks squat like frogs. When moving, they either hop on the hind legs or run on all four. In appearance they are characterized chiefly by an erectile crest along the middle of the back and tail or on the head. This crest is rudimentary in the females. The banded basilisk, *B. vittatus,* is brown with a yellow band along each side of the body; the others are yellowish or greenish brown with red crests. They are lively animals, arboreal and omnivorous, and are harmless to humans.

BASIN. *See* GEOLOGY: *Geomorphology.*

BASKERVILLE, John. *See* TYPE.

BASKETBALL, athletic court game, usually played indoors, in which two competing teams attempt to throw an inflated ball so that it descends through one of two baskets suspended, at each end of the court, above their heads. The team scoring the most such throws, through field goals or foul shots, wins the game. Basketball is a popular spectator as well as a participants' sport in the United States and throughout the world.

Court and Teams. The basketball court is a rectangular area ranging in size from 94 ft. by 50 ft. to 74 ft. by 42 ft. At each end of the court is a vertical backboard, measuring usually 6 ft. by 4 ft. Each backboard is anchored to a wall, suspended from the ceiling, or otherwise mounted so that its lower edge is 9 ft. above the court. The baskets are attached firmly to the backboards 10 ft. above the playing surface. Each basket is 18 in. in diameter and consists of a horizontal metal ring from which a fringe of wide-meshed white netting is hung. The regulation basketball is an inflated, leather- or nylon-covered sphere that weighs from 20 to 22 oz. and has a diameter of about 9½ in.

A basketball team is made up of two forwards, two guards, and a center. At the beginning of play, called the opening jump or tap, the forwards of a given team are stationed in the forecourt, that half of the playing area containing the basket, or offensive backboard, at which their team is shooting. The two guards stand in the backcourt, near the basket their team is defending. The center, usually the tallest player on the team, stands inside a 2-ft. circle located mid-

Diagram of a regulation basketball court

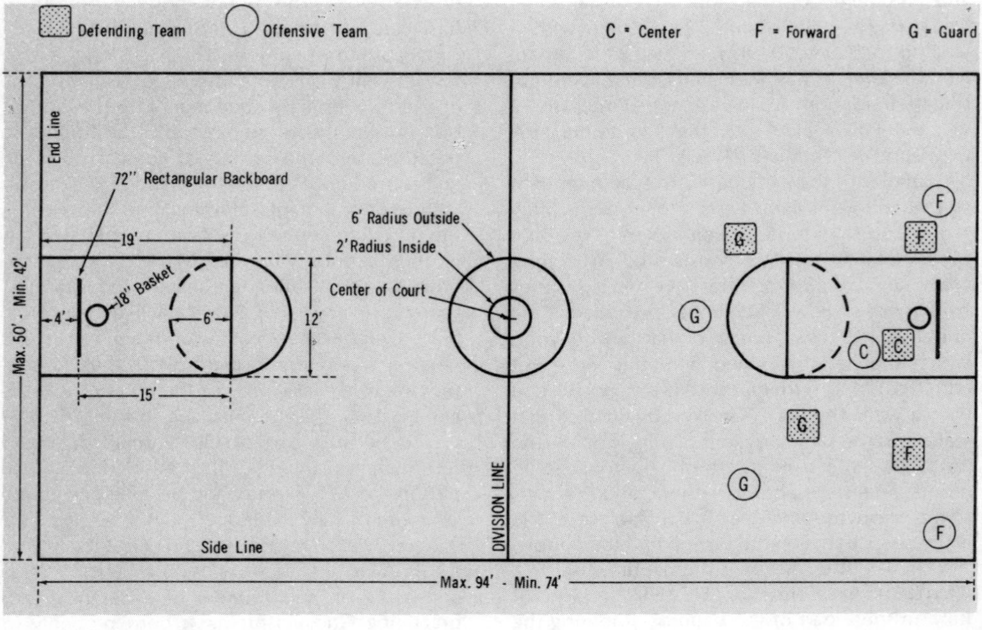

Dribbling, an art in itself, is the ground approach to advancing the ball. In this 1974 game, the New York Knickerbockers' Jerry Lucas dribbles into Atlanta Hawks territory and is double-teamed. UPI

way along a line painted across the center of the court.

Play. The game commences when the referee tosses the ball high into the air over the center circle, in which the opposing centers are standing face to face. The centers then leap into the air and attempt, with their hands, to tap the ball to teammates. The team that gets the ball attempts to advance it toward the basket defended by opposing side in order to try for a field goal, or two points. A player may advance the ball by passing it to a teammate or by bouncing it continually, or dribbling, along the floor while running toward the basket. If a player walks or runs with the ball without dribbling it, a violation called traveling, his team surrenders possession of the ball. When a player scores a basket from the floor during play, such a basket is known as a field goal and tallies two points for his team. The team scored on then puts the ball into play from behind its end line, and in turn tries to move the ball up-court to score.

Penalties and Free Throws. If a player is subjected to illegal body contact, termed a personal foul under the rules of the game, he receives one or two free throws, or uncontested shots, from a foul line 15 ft. from the basket. Each successful free throw counts for one point. Typical fouls include pushing, holding, charging, hacking, and tripping. When a player is fouled in the act of shooting, but scores the basket, he receives one free throw; this circumstance is called a three-point play. In professional basket-

That basketball is a tall player's game is never more evident than in the jump ball, where an agile big center outtaps an agile smaller center every time. Here, Denver plays Detroit; referee is at left. Denver Nuggets

ball, excessive fouls in a given quarter by a team are penalized by granting the opponents extra free-throw chances. A player who exceeds the maximum number of personal fouls allowed (in amateur play, five; in professional play, six) is eliminated from the game. Interference with certain shots that are near or about to drop through the basket is called goaltending, for which infraction the shot is ruled good.

Amateur games usually are divided into two halves, each containing 20 min. of actual play; professional games are divided into four quarters, each containing 12 min. of actual play. An added feature of professional games is the rule that a team must shoot at the basket within 24 sec. of putting the ball in play.

Offensive Skills. Many of the key skills and techniques of modern basketball are offensive.

Shooting and the prevention of shots—blocking—are what the game is all about. Here, a Denver Nuggets player tries to block a jump shot by a Philadelphia 76ers opponent. Denver Nuggets

Paul Westphal, a Phoenix Suns guard and field-goal virtuoso whom sportswriters voted one of the top professional players of 1977, goes for a two-handed lay-up in a game with the San Antonio Spurs. Phoenix Suns

The paramount offensive skills necessary to any player, besides adept dribbling or ball control, are passing and shooting. Passes to teammates, which may be thrown overhand, underhand, or laterally, include push passes, behind-the-back passes, jump passes, and bounce passes. A pass which leads directly to a basket being scored is called an assist.

The most important single basketball skill, however, is the ability to shoot accurately. Among the types of shots in the standard vocabulary of the basketball player are the one-handed or two-handed lay-up, made overhand or underhand and as close to the basket as possible; the one-handed jump shot, in which the shooter leaps into the air before releasing the ball; and the pivot or hook shot, an arched shot made over the head with one arm, going gener-

Fast scramble for a loose ball in a 1972 Los Angeles Lakers-Milwaukee Bucks game. Lakers and Bucks alternate from left to right: Wilt Chamberlain, Kareem Abdul Jabbar, Jerry West, Oscar Robertson. UPI

ally away from the basket. The one-handed or two-handed set or stationary shot, once popular when play was slower, is extremely rare in basketball today. Foul shots are usually made overhand from the foul line.

Rebounding is the art of out-positioning opponents and jumping high to gain possession of the ball off the backboard, as when a shot has been missed, or, where possible on offense, to tap the ball into the basket for a field goal. A high-speed offensive attack over the length of the whole court is called a fast-break, and is calculated to outrace or confuse the defending opponents for a quick score. Also essential in basketball is the screen, whereby a player or players interpose themselves so as to provide a temporarily unguarded teammate with a clear shot at the basket.

Generally speaking, team offensive strategy may involve deliberate weaves or patterns of attack or a looser, more improvisory style of play; but in each case the object is to evade the opposition and work for an unobstructed shot at the basket or to pass to the so-called open, or momentarily unguarded, man.

Defensive Skills. The main types of defensive strategy in basketball are the so-called zone and man-to-man defenses. In the zone defense, each player is responsible for defending a certain area of the court around the basket at which the opposing team is shooting. In a man-to-man or one-on-one defense, each player is assigned to closely guard a specific member of the opposing team. Zone defense is not permitted in the rules of professional basketball. Individual defensive skills include the ability to block shots without fouling, to break up passes, and to steal the ball. A change-of-hands of the ball in floor play, from one team to the other, is called a turnover. Intense or pressing defensive moves resorted to in many situations are double-teaming, whereby two players guard a particularly dangerous or vulnerable opponent; and the full-court press, in which the team with the ball is aggressively challenged the whole length of the court. Rebounding, to wrest possession of the ball under the opponent's basket, is just as vital to basketball defense as it is to basketball offense.

Competition. The amateur game in the U.S. is regulated by the Amateur Athletic Union (q.v.); the professional game is regulated principally by the National Basketball Association (N.B.A.) and the American Basketball Association (A.B.A.). Play-offs are held at the end of each basketball season among winning teams of the various intercollegiate conferences and among the leading teams of the N.B.A. and A.B.A. These play-offs determine the national intercollegiate champion and the champion in each professional league. In collegiate basketball, two important postseason tournaments also are held, namely the National Invitation Tournament (begun in 1938) and the National Collegiate Athletic Association (N.C.A.A.) elimination contests (begun in 1939), which determine the national N.C.A.A. champion. Since basketball was introduced in the Olympic Games (q.v.) in 1936, U.S. teams have won every gold medal except in the 1972 games when the Soviet Union won the gold medal.

History. Basketball was invented in December, 1891, by the Canadian clergyman and educator James Naismith (q.v.), then an instructor at the Young Men's Christian Association (q.v.), or Y.M.C.A., training school (now Springfield College) in Springfield, Mass. Naismith invented basketball to fill the need, voiced by Y.M.C.A. instructors, for a vigorous and entertaining form of indoor recreation. The first basketball was a soccer ball. The first teams comprised nine men each, and the original goals were wooden peach baskets affixed to the walls. In subsequent years the game spread to all parts of the country, and also became popular outdoors. Eventually it achieved popularity among both sexes in almost all parts of the world. A number of U.S. colleges adopted the game about 1895, and the first professional league was formed in 1898. The professional game was dominated during the 1920's by a team known as the Original Celtics, which played more than 150 games a season. Another notable professional team is the Harlem Globetrotters, a team specializing in amusing court antics and expert ball handling. Beginning in the mid-1930's, many college games and tournaments were held at Madison Square Garden in New York City. Famous players in the history of basketball include the U.S. stars Nat Holman; Joe Lapchick; Bob Kurland; George Mikan; and in more recent times Wilt Chamberlain; Bob Cousy; Oscar Robertson; Bill Russell; and Kareem Abdul Jabbar (qq.v.), formerly known as Lew Alcindor. A.J.A.

BASKET FISH, animal of the order Euryalida, of the same class (Ophiuroidea) of Echinoderms as the brittle star (q.v.), characterized by branched arms, in some species so numerously subdivided that when they are curled up the creature seems enclosed in a basket. The five-sided central body varies in size with age and species but may be 3 in. broad, is usually about 3 in. in diameter, while the arms may be 10 to 15 in. in length. On capture or disturbance the fish folds its arms closely about the body and assumes the basket shape. Basket fish are found in moderately deep water in all seas, but especially in the tropics. *See* ECHINODERMATA.

BASKING SHARK, common name for a shark, *Cetorhinus maximus,* of the North Atlantic Ocean. It attains a length of nearly 40 ft. The basking shark commonly lies near the surface, feeding on plankton; it is hunted for the oil of its liver, one shark sometimes yielding more than a ton of oil. *See* SHARK.

BASLE. *See* BASEL.

BASOV, Nicolai Gennadievich (1922–), Russian physicist, born in Leningrad and educated at the Moscow Engineering and Physics Institute. He became deputy director of the Lebedev Physics Institute in Moscow in 1958 and a member of the Academy of Sciences of the U.S.S.R. in 1968. In 1959 he shared the Lenin Prize in physics with the Russian physicist Alex-

Basking shark, Cetorhinus maximus

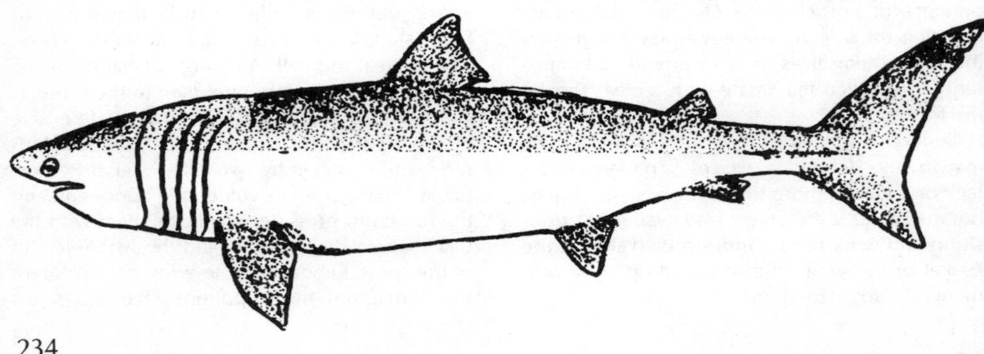

ander M. Prochorov (q.v.), and he and Prochorov shared the 1964 Nobel Prize in physics with the American physicist Charles H. Townes (q.v.). Basov, a specialist in quantum electronics, was cited for his work in development of the maser and the laser (q.v.). He has recently continued research in the field of gas-dynamic lasers and thermonuclear reactions produced by powerful lasers.

BASQUE LANGUAGE, language spoken by the Basques (q.v.), the people inhabiting north-central Spain and the department of Basses-Pyrénées in southwestern France. The Basque name for their language is Euskera. The language has a number of dialects, of which the chief are Guipúzcoan, Biscayan, and Navarrese in Spain and Labourdin and Navarrais in France. Basque is classified as an agglutinative language (*see* PHILOLOGY). The number of sounds varies according to the dialect; most dialects have five vowels. Basque words are accented as a rule on the last syllable; in most instances the latter ends with a vowel or s, r, l, n, or t. Although rules governing the use of nouns and pronouns are fairly simple, the conjugation of Basque verbs is extremely complicated. The transitive form of a verb may have as many as twenty-four variations. The Basque vocabulary contains no original words for abstract concepts and no words for tools or utensils brought into use in modern times. To designate such objects the Basques employ a Latin, French, or Spanish word with a Basque ending. For example, the word fork (Fr. *fourchette*) becomes "fourchetta" in Basque. The Roman alphabet is used in the written language, which is based on French or Spanish orthography and is phonetic.

Philologists have tried for a long time to trace the origin of the language, and attempts have been made to show an affinity between Basque and certain other languages such as Ligurian, an ancient language of northwestern Italy, or Japanese. Recent suggestions have linked Basque with Caucasian, a language of the Caucasus region of the U.S.S.R. All that can be safely maintained is that Basque was almost certainly spoken in ancient Aquitania, the region of Gascony (q.v.), France, although it probably was not related to the ancient Iberian language of the Spanish peninsula. Inscriptions in Iberian have been transliterated but not yet translated, in spite of the efforts of scholars.

Although the Basques speak one of the oldest languages, their literature is meager. The first Basque book on record was printed in 1545 and is a collection of religious and love poems called *Linguae Vasconum Primitivae.* The most important Basque work is the translation of the New Testament which appeared in 1571. Next in importance is a collection of religious and military chronicles published in the 17th century.

Following the Spanish Civil War (1936–39) the regime of Francisco Franco (q.v.) in Spain suppressed the use of the Basque language. Most present-day Basques speak their own tongue and that of their mother country. J.F.S.

BASQUES (Sp. *Vascongados;* in the Basque language, *Eskualdunak*), people living in the coastal region and western Pyrenees of Vizcaya, Guipúzcoa, and Álava provinces, Spain, and the department of Basses-Pyrénées, France. The origin of the Basques has long been a subject of scholarly research. Though possessing certain marked physical traits, such as a wedge-shaped face, the Basques are not considered a distinct race by most modern ethnologists. Their ancient language, customs, and traditions, however, distinguish them from all other peoples of Europe. Attempts have been made by various scholars to link the Basque language with a number of non-Indo-European languages (q.v.), but such connections are not accepted by the majority of linguists. *See* BASQUE LANGUAGE.

Among the outstanding characteristics of the Basques are their independent spirit, love of freedom, and respect for individual liberty; a favorite Basque motto is "Neither slave nor tyrant". These qualities are reflected in their ancient laws (called *fors* in France and *fueros* in Spain), which traditionally governed every area of their life and were strictly adhered to. These laws were maintained by democratically elected assemblies (juntas), and great care was taken to secure honesty at the polls. It was not uncommon for a fisherman to preside over meetings in which Spanish noblemen were seated.

The law of primogeniture (q.v.), of great importance in the life of the Basque people, gave the family structure great permanence. The importance of the family is reflected to some extent in the appearance of most Basque homesteads, which differ markedly from the one-story house of the average French or Spanish peasant. The typical Basque house has an air of dignity and stability; it is two stories high and has a wide doorway. The site includes a garden, vineyard, pasture, and woodland.

The Basques are devout Roman Catholics and have fought to prevent domination of their religious institutions by French and Spanish ecclesiastical authorities. Notable religious figures of Basque origin include Saint Ignatius of Loyola (q.v.), founder of the order of the Jesuits (q.v.), and the Jesuit missionary Saint Francis Xavier

Basque folk dancers wear the traditional boina (beret), which is part of their ancestral costume.
Spanish National Tourist Office

(q.v.). The Basques have retained many religious customs dating from medieval times. Among the most colorful are the Procession of the Crosses and the Corpus Christi processions. The latter are especially interesting because some of the national dances are introduced.

Dancing and games play an important part in the lives of the Basque people. One of the oldest and most picturesque Basque dances is the goblet dance, which has been performed for more than five centuries. The master dancer, called the Zamalzain, is dressed in elaborate costume, with a hobbyhorse around his waist. The climax of the dance occurs when he hops onto a glass of wine with his left foot, makes the sign of the cross with his right foot, then leaps up from the glass without spilling a drop of wine. The Basques are especially fond of a strenuous game known as jai alai (q.v.). They still preserve part of their ancient costume, notably the beret (boina), a blue or red cap like the Scottish broad bonnet.

Many Basques have emigrated to America. It is estimated that about 250,000 Basques live in South America and about 50,000 live in the United States. Most of those in the U.S. are employed as shepherds in California, Nevada, and Wyoming.

History. The Basques first appeared in written history late in the 1st century B.C., when they successfully withstood the Roman invaders of Spain; they maintained their independence throughout the period of Roman rule of the Iberian Peninsula. The Basques adopted Christianity between the 3rd and 5th centuries. In the 6th century they fought fiercely and successfully against the Visigoths. Late in the 6th century groups of Spanish Basques (Lat. *Vascones*) migrated northward across the Pyrenees to Aquitania (q.v.), which thereafter was known as Gascony (q.v.). Those who remained in Spain withstood the Moors, who dominated most of the peninsula from the 8th to the 11th century. The Spanish Basques preserved their tradition of autonomy throughout the Middle Ages. Biscay (Vizcaya), one of the provinces, was independent from 1093 until 1350; not until 1370 was it definitely part of the kingdom of Castile, to which Guipúzcoa had been united in 1200 and Álava in 1332. When a Spanish kingdom was established late in the 15th century, the Basque provinces still continued to preserve their own customs, laws, and diplomatic relations with foreign countries with slight variation until 1876, when the provinces were absorbed by Spain. During the Spanish Civil War (1936–39), an autonomous Basque state was established by the Republican government, with its capital at Guernica; but the victory of the Nationalists under General Francisco Franco (q.v.) ended this autonomous regime. Agitation for the reestablishment of Basque autonomy arose during the following three decades. In the 1970's the Basque separatist movement grew dramatically. After several violent incidents, the Spanish government in late 1977 provisionally granted limited autonomy to the Basque provinces, which were to be linked by a General Council. J.F.S.

BASRA, *or* BASRAH, city and principal port of Iraq, capital of Basra Province, on the Shatt-al-Arab R., 75 mi. from the Persian Gulf. The city has an international airport and is connected by rail with Baghdad, Iran, and with the sheikhdom of Kuwait. It is the terminal point for oil pipelines, and petroleum refining is a major industry. Ocean-going oil tankers reach Basra by means of the 30-ft.-deep Rooka Channel. Petroleum products, grains, and dates are the chief exports. Called Basorah in the collection of Oriental folk tales known as the *Arabian Nights* (q.v.), the city was founded by the caliph Omar I (q.v.) in 636. By the 8th century it had become an important trade and cultural center, but it declined with the fall of the Abbassid dynasty in 1258 (*see* CALIPH). Developed as a supply base by the British in World War I, Basra became a major port once more. Pop. (1970 est.) 370,875.

BAS-RELIEF. *See* RELIEF.

BASS, common name of many food fish, but not corresponding to any particular scientific classification. Most bass are included within three of the many families in the Perch suborder, but these families also include many fish not called bass. The common names black, white, or rock bass are applied to different fish in different localities.

In the United States the family Centrarchidae includes twelve genera and thirty species of fish, some of which are called bass and the others sunfish. *Pomoxis nigro-maculatus,* the calico bass, also called black crappie, is found from the Great Lakes and upper Mississippi valley to New Jersey, and southward to Florida, Louisiana, and Texas; it reaches a length of 12 to 14 in., but rarely weighs more than ½ lb. *Ambloplites rupestris,* the rock bass, rarely exceeds ½ lb. in weight, and is a poor food fish. It is abundant west of the Alleghenies, north into Manitoba, and south to Louisiana. *Paralabrax clathratus,* a saltwater rockfish of California in the same family, is also called kelp bass. The most important bass in this family are the black bass, of the genus *Micropterus.* The largemouthed black bass is *M. salmoides,* also called bayou, lake, or straw bass; the smallmouthed black bass is *M. dolomieu;* the Kentucky black bass, or spotted black bass, is *M. pseudoplites.* Largemouthed bass are found throughout central U.S. and may reach a weight of from 14 to 20 lb. Smallmouthed bass are found from Lake Champlain southwest on both sides of the Appalachians and reach a maximum weight of about 5 lb. *See also* CRAPPIE.

Although some are freshwater fish, the Serranidae are called sea bass (q.v.). *Centropristes striatus,* commonly called black sea bass or blackfish, is found on the Atlantic coast of the U.S. and is usually from 12 to 18 in. long. *Roccus saxatilis,* the striped bass, sometimes called rock bass, or rockfish, of the U.S. Atlantic coast, has been successfully introduced into the Pacific. It is an excellent food fish, and occasional speci-

A giant sea bass is fed by a diver at Marineland of the Pacific in Los Angeles, Calif. The 6 ft. 10 in., 500 lb. fish is believed to be the largest bass ever caught in American waters. UPI

mens reach a weight of 100 lb. *Lepibema chrysops,* the white bass of the Great Lakes and upper Mississippi valley, and *Morone interrupta,* the yellow bass of the lower Mississippi region, both reaching a maximum size of 18 in. and a maximum weight of 5 lb., are also in this family.

The family Sciaenidae, the croakers, includes the red drum (*see* DRUM), which is also called channel bass.

BASS (derived fr. Lat. *basis,* "base, foot, pedestal"; influenced by Fr. *basse* and It. *basso*), deepest or lowest male singing voice. The normal range of the bass voice is about two octaves, with its lowest note usually an octave and a sixth below middle C. Trained basses can reach notes considerably below and above the normal range, however; for example, the contrabass (the name given to an especially deep voice developed principally in Russia) can range nearly an octave below the normal lowest note.

Basses usually are classified as *basso profondo* (It., "deep bass"), a solemn, powerful, and low-ranging voice; *basso cantante* (It., "singing bass"), a voice with a well developed upper range, similar in quality to the lyric soprano (q.v.); and *basso buffo* (It., "comic bass"), an agile voice especially suited for comic operatic roles. A voice combining both *basso profondo* and *basso cantante* qualities, and with a slightly higher than normal range, is termed "bass-baritone"; *see* BARITONE.

The term "bass" also is used to denote the lowest member in range of a family of instruments, such as the bass-clarinet (*see* CLARINET); to denote the lower or grave part of the entire instrumental or vocal tonal range, as distinguished from the treble or higher part (*see* TONE); and to denote the lowest part in musical compositions, particularly in harmonic music (*see* HARMONY). *See also* MUSICAL NOTATION; OPERA; SINGING; VOICE AND SPEECH.

Basset hound

BASS, Sam (1851–78), American bandit leader, born near Mitchell, Ind. He moved to Texas about 1870 and was a millhand, cowboy, and deputy sheriff until 1875, when he began his career as an outlaw. In the Black Hills town of Deadwood, S.D., Bass formed a gang to rob stagecoaches, and in 1877 the gang held up a Union Pacific train at Big Springs, Nebr., stealing $65,000. Bass, pursued by lawmen, organized a new gang in Denton County, Texas, and robbed several trains in 1878. One of his followers became an informer for the Texas Rangers, and Bass was shot to death in an ambush during an attempted bank robbery.

BASSANO, Jacopo da, originally JACOPO DA PONTE (1510–92), a Venetian painter, born in Bassano del Grappa. He belonged to the school of genre painting (q.v.) and was also known for portraits and Biblical scenes. Only a few of his works are extant. Among them are "Christ Driving the Money Changers out of the Temple" (National Gallery, London), "Dives and Lazarus" (Cleveland Museum), and "Acteon and the Nymphs" (Art Institute, Chicago).

BASSEIN, city in the Union of Burma, capital of Irrawaddy Division and of the district of Bassein. The city is situated on the Bassein R., one of the mouths of the Irrawaddy R., 75 mi. from the sea, but it is accessible to the largest ocean-going ships. Inland water and rail connections enhance its importance as a commercial center. The principal trade is in rice. The town was captured by the British during the Second Burmese War in 1853, and by the Japanese during World War II. Pop. (latest est.) 175,000.

BASSE-TERRE. *See* GUADELOUPE.

BASSETERRE. *See* SAINT KITTS.

BASSET HORN (It. *corno di bassetto*), soft-toned musical instrument of the wind family, invented in Germany about 1770. It is similar to a tenor clarinet in tone and fingering, but is lower in pitch. The basset horn was part of the symphony orchestra until about the middle of the 19th century when it was replaced by the E-flat clarinet. *See* CLARINET.

BASSET HOUND, sporting dog originating in France from the French bloodhound and the Saint Hubert hound. The basset was popular in France, Belgium, and other parts of the European continent for hundreds of years before being exhibited for the first time at a British dog show in 1875. After 1880 it gained rapidly in popularity in Great Britain. Standing from 11 to 15 in. high at the shoulder, the basset has a long body and heavy bones and weighs from 25 to 40 lb. The English basset has deep-set eyes; long, soft, hanging ears; a long head; and a well-developed black nose. Smaller than the English type, the French basset is more agile. The type of basset common in America has crooked or half-crooked front legs, well-muscled hind legs, heavy shoulders, and a deep chest. Used for tracking and hunting small game and game birds, the basset has a keen sense of smell, second only to that of the bloodhound (q.v.).

BASSOON, double-reed musical instrument, the bass of the woodwind instruments. In 1539 a canon of Ferrara, Italy, reputedly conceived the idea of bending double the long *bombardon,* a heavy wind instrument with a deep tone, so as to make it easier for handling. The resulting instrument, resembling a bundle of wood, was called an Italian *fagotto,* "bundle". It is made of rosewood, maple, or plane-tree wood, with a long, S-shaped, metal mouthpiece, and generally has eight holes and ten keys. It has a very wide range of three chromatic octaves, from B flat below the bass clef to E flat above middle C in the treble. The notes for bassoon are written on the bass clef for the lower register and on the tenor clef for the higher. The double bassoon is an octave lower than the ordinary bassoon.

BASSORIN. *See* GUM.

BASS ROCK, THE, islet in the Firth of Forth, Scotland. It is composed of volcanic rock and is about 1 mi. in circumference and about 350 ft. high. Except on the S.W. side, precipitous cliffs make the rock inaccessible. A tunnel, usable at low tide, runs through the rock for some distance. Solan geese and other sea birds, which inhabit the rock in large numbers, give it a snowy appearance from a distance. In the 17th century a castle on the rock served as a prison for the militant Presbyterians known as Covenanters (q.v.).

BASS STRAIT, channel connecting the Tasman Sea on the E. with the Indian Ocean on the W., and separating Tasmania on the S. from Australia on the N. The strait is named for the British explorer George Bass (d. 1812?), who in 1798 sailed through the channel while proving that Tasmania was an island. The channel contains coral reefs and many islands, chiefly in its S. section. It runs almost due E. and W., is about 180 mi. long, and has an average breadth of about 140 mi.

BASSWOOD. *See* LINDEN.

BASTIA, city in France, capital of Haute-Corse department, on the N.E. coast of the island of Corsica. It is the chief city of the island. The principal industries are fishing and the manufacture of tobacco products, pâtés, and flour products. Bastia is an important trade center, exporting fruit, vegetables, wines, liqueurs, tannin, and fish. Settled in the 14th century by the Genoese, who built a fortress to protect it, Bastia was the capital of the island until 1791. The city was held by the British in 1745 during the War of the Austrian Succession (*see* SUCCESSION WARS), but was soon recaptured by the Genoese, who sold the entire island to France in 1768. It was occupied by the British again from 1794 to 1796 during the Napoleonic Wars (q.v.) and by the Germans in 1942–43 during a period of World War II. Pop. (1968) 48,858.

Young musicians playing the bassoon. UPI

BASTIAN, Adolf (1826–1905), German ethnologist, born in Bremen, and educated at the universities of Berlin, Heidelberg, and Prague. After completing his formal education in 1850, he traveled through Asia, Africa, Australia, and North and South America, and in 1860 published *Der Mensch in der Geschichte* ("Man in History"), an anthropological study. In 1866 he was appointed professor of ethnology at the University of Berlin and in 1886 was appointed director of the ethnological museum there. A prolific writer, he published nearly sixty anthropological works. He emphasized the importance of psychology in interpreting cultural history and contributed to the comparative study of different cultures.

BASTILLE, former prison fortress in Paris. It was built as part of the city fortifications about 1370 on the east wall of the city. During the 17th century the Bastille was used primarily for the housing of political prisoners, and from the time of the French statesman, Cardinal Armand du Plessis, Duc de Richelieu (q.v.), it was a symbol of terror throughout France. Citizens of every class and profession, if for any reason deemed obnoxious to the court, were arrested by secret warrants known as *lettres-de-cachet,* and imprisoned indefinitely in the Bastille without accusation or trial.

At the outbreak of the French Revolution (q.v.), the Bastille was attacked and captured by a mob assisted by royal troops. Two days later the destruction of the stronghold was begun amid great public rejoicings. The site is now an open square, called the *Place de la Bastille.* Bastille Day is celebrated annually in France on July 14.

BASTROP, city of Louisiana, parish seat of Morehouse Parish, about 23 miles N.E. of Monroe. The city manufactures chemicals, carbon black, glass, paper, lumber, and varnish. Bastrop is in an agricultural region which has peach orchards, truck-farming, and cotton. Pop. (1960) 15,193; (1970) 14,713.

BASUTOLAND. *See* LESOTHO.

BAT, the only mammal specialized for true flight, comprising the order Chiroptera (Gr. *cheiros,* "hand"; *pteron,* "wing"). About 850 species of bats are known, grouped in seventeen families, and undoubtedly many remain to be discovered. Bats are found throughout the world except for Antarctica, a limited area north of the Arctic Circle in Asia, the treeless areas of northern Canada and Greenland, and a few midoceanic islands.

Divisions. Bats are divided into two suborders, the Megachiroptera (greater bats) and Microchiroptera (lesser bats). The former inhabit the tropical regions of the Eastern Hemisphere, from the Red Sea to the Far East. They also range from the extreme south to New South Wales in Australia and to the Cape of Good Hope in Africa. Lesser bats, apart from the family Vespertilionidae, are not found north of 40° N. lat. or south of 30° S. lat., except in western Europe and eastern Asia.

The greater bats are predominantly fruit-eaters and include the largest of all forms, the great fruit bat or flying fox of Java, which has a body as big as that of a crow and a wing span of 5 ft. This group includes a species in w. Africa, however, having less than half the bulk of the largest Microchiroptera. Fruit bats gather by day in orchards and groves and their congregations sometimes extend for miles. Some fruit bats live in small groups under palm leaves; however, the hammerhead bat (*Hypsignathus*) of equatorial Africa, which takes its name from its long but blunt muzzle, lives alone or in small groups in caves of foliage. Most fruit bats fly to the feeding grounds shortly before sundown and return to their resting places about dawn.

Microchiroptera are varied in size, form, and habit. Unlike Megachiroptera, they have a more-or-less-fixed shoulder joint, rather than the ball-and-socket joint common to fruit bats, that permits greater arm movement and sustained power of flight. The largest of the Microchiroptera is the false-vampire of Australia (*Macroderma*) with a wing span of over 2 ft.; the smallest is a vespertilionid from central Africa with a body no larger than that of a bumblebee. There are sixteen families of lesser bats, the largest of which is the Vespertilionidae, the typical bat seen in the evening; the most anatomically primitive are the mouse-tailed bats of the Middle East.

Diets. Many of the American leaf-nosed lesser bats (Phyllostomatidae) of South and Central America eat fruit. The harelipped bats (Noctilionidae) are carnivorous, and catch insects, small birds, and other bats on the wing. They are known to take mice from the ground or to catch fish by dipping beneath the surfaces of lakes or the sea. Three forms, the true vampires (*Desmodus, Diaemus,* and *Diphylla*), have exceedingly short, almost straight intestines, and can lap and digest only fresh blood. They prey on all land animals, including man, and are carriers of several diseases, notably rabies (q.v.). An outbreak of this disease induced by rabid bats occurred in northern Argentina in 1925, and moved stead-

Vampire bat, Desmodus rotundus

ily northward thereafter. Herds of cattle have been decimated and human deaths reported from Trinidad to northern Mexico; bat-caused rabies on the United States border was confirmed in late 1955. Since then rabid bats have been found in various parts of the U.S.

Most lesser bats, however, feed on insects which they often catch on the wing, scooping them up in the membranes between the hind limbs and the tail. Some remarkable species of lesser bats in Madagascar and New Zealand have sucker cups under their "wrists" which enable them to adhere to glass-smooth surfaces.

Characteristics. Many bats hibernate, often huddling together in vast numbers; others migrate to warmer regions in the cold season. In some forms, one sex migrates while the other hibernates. There are bats in the far north that spend more than half of each year in total hibernation, during which time their metabolism is so reduced that hoarfrost may form on their pelts. The females of hibernating bat species retain viable male sperm all winter, the ova being fertilized the following spring after the hibernation period is ended. This is known as delayed implantation. While in flight many female bats carry their young clinging to their chests.

Perhaps the most remarkable characteristic of bats is their method of flight. In the lesser bats it is totally unlike the swimming or gliding motions peculiar to birds, but is rather a clawing of air by the elongated fingers and connecting membranes, which are extended in front of the head, curved outward, and pulled backward. The legs work in unison with the wings, causing a "swimming" action, which gives the bat extraordinary flight capability. Bats navigate by using principles akin to modern sonar and airborne location-finding devices: when in flight they emit extremely high-pitched sounds through their nostrils. The sound waves travel out in every direction and are reflected from objects in the vicinity, even from flying insects. These reflections are heard by the bats, enabling them to alter flight instantly to catch their prey or to avoid aerial snags. This phenomenon explains the unerring flight of bats, even in complete darkness.

The mastiff bats (Molossidae), found throughout the warmer regions of the world, have narrow, tapered wings, which make them the fastest of all, though lacking the maneuverability of the broader-winged forms. The mastiff bats, however, like the true vampires, can fold up their wings and run about on all fours like most other mammals.

Almost all bats sleep while suspended upside down, and they are very long-lived; fruit bats have lived for twenty years in captivity, and insectivorous forms, tagged with metal bands and released by naturalists, have been recovered after sixteen years.

BATAAN PENINSULA, mountainous area of Luzon Island, Republic of the Philippines, bounded by Manila Bay on the E., the South China Sea on the S., and Subic Bay on the W. During World War II it was the scene of heavy fighting between Allied and Japanese forces. Bataan fell to Japan on April 9, 1942, and was retaken by an American force on Feb. 17, 1945. *See* WORLD WAR II: *The War Becomes a Global Conflict: The Fall of the Philippines.*

BATAILLE, Félix Henri (1872–1922), French dramatist and poet, born in Nîmes and trained as a painter at the École des Beaux-Arts, Paris. He turned to writing in 1894 and from about 1900 to the outbreak of World War I was regarded as the foremost French dramatist. Among his plays, which are psychological studies of passion as a motivating force in human behavior, are *L'Enchantement* ("Enchantment", 1900), *Maman Colibri* ("Mother Colibri", 1904), and *La Femme Nue* ("The Naked Woman", 1908). His verse includes the book of war poems *La Divine Tragédie* ("The Divine Tragedy", 1917).

BATANGAS, city in the Republic of the Philippines, capital of Batangas Province, on Luzon Island, about 60 miles S. of Manila. It is an important seaport and trade center for the province, which is a sugar-growing region. Silk and cotton fabrics and coconut oil are manufactured in the city. Pop. (latest census) 14,182.

BATAVIA. *See* DJAKARTA.

BATCHELOR, Clarence Daniel (1880–), American cartoonist, born in Osage City, Kans. After attending the Art Institute of Chicago, he went in 1912 to New York City, where he studied at the Art Students' League. Batchelor was a cartoonist with a number of newspapers in New York before beginning, in 1932, his long association with the New York *Daily News,* for which he drew over 1000 cartoons concerned with the subjects of highway safety and politics. Batchelor's work won him a number of awards, including the Pulitzer Prize in 1937 for an antiwar cartoon.

BATES, Henry Walter (1825–92), British naturalist, born in Leicester, England, and largely self-educated. In 1848, with the British naturalist Alfred Russel Wallace (q.v.), he went to Brazil to study the native fauna, especially insects. Bates and Wallace separated after two years and Bates went to the upper Amazon region where he spent seven years. He returned to England in 1859, having found 8000 insect species new to science. After his return he published *The Naturalist on the Amazon* (1863), a work that has become a classic in the field.

In 1861 he read a paper before the Linnaean Society on the phenomenon of insects mimicry; *see* ADAPTATION: *Mimicry*. In 1864 he was made assistant secretary of the Royal Geographical Society and in 1881 he was elected a fellow of the Royal Society. A large part of his collections is in the British Museum (q.v.).

BATES, Katherine Lee (1859–1929), American educator and author, born in Falmouth, Mass. She was educated at Wellesley College and was professor of English at the college from 1891 to 1925. She wrote travel books, textbooks on literature and drama, books for children, short stories, and several volumes of poetry. Her most famous work is the patriotic poem "America the Beautiful", first written in 1893, rewritten in 1904, and cast in its final form in 1911. It has been set to music by many American composers, most familiarly by Samuel A. Ward (1848–1903).

BATES COLLEGE, nonsectarian coeducational institution of higher learning, located in Lewiston, Maine. The college was chartered in 1864, and was the first college in the eastern United States to grant a college degree to a woman, in 1869. The college is named after Benjamin Edward Bates (1862–1906), a prominent citizen of Lewiston, who gave the college considerable financial assistance. The college, which covers an area of 100 acres, has thirty buildings. It grants the B.A. and B.S. degrees. In 1968 the college library housed more than 150,000 bound volumes. In 1968 the enrollment at Bates College totaled 1001 students, and the faculty numbered 74. The endowment of the college in 1968 was about $7,867,000.

BATESON, William (1861–1926), British biologist and geneticist, born in Whitby, Yorkshire, England, and educated at Saint John's College, University of Cambridge. In 1894 he advanced the theory that the evolution of vertebrates proceeds in sudden, discontinuous steps, rather than by gradual progression. In support of his theory, he collected a mass of evidence that published in *Materials for the Study of Variation* (1894), led to the development of the theory of mutation (q.v.; *see also* HEREDITY: *Mutation*). He was among the earliest advocates of the principles of Mendel's Law (q.v.) and the leading British authority on the subject. In 1910 he became director of the John Innes Horticultural Institution, and in 1922 a trustee of the British Museum, holding both offices until his death.

BATFISH, common name for fish of the family Ogcocephalidae, related to the angler fish. The numerous species live on the bottom in relatively shallow marine waters. A few may be found at depths of several hundred fathoms, and some species are found in coastal rivers. In most species, the snout is pointed and the head and body flattened. The pectoral fins protrude laterally, giving the fish a superficial resemblance to a bat. The body, usually covered with hardened tubercles, may be black, brown, or red. Some species may exceed 1 ft. in length, but most are smaller. The batfish is not generally used for food.

BATH, usually, the washing or soaking of the body in water. The term is also applied to a building containing bathing facilities. The bath has been used as part of religious rituals and purification as in the *mikvah* of Judaism (q.v.); the immersion of Hinduism (q.v.); Christian Baptism (q.v.); and the ablutions required of the ancient Greeks and present-day Muslims.

ANCIENT AND MEDIEVAL BATHS

Bathing facilities have been found in the excavations of the royal palace of Knossos (q.v.) in Crete, built between 1700 B.C. and 1400 B.C., and in the ancient city of Tiryns (q.v.), in Greece. Paintings on ancient Greek urns show primitive shower arrangements and the Greek poet Homer (q.v.) mentions bathing in his *Iliad* (q.v.). The original Greek baths were adjuncts to the gymnasia, but by the 5th century B.C. baths in private homes and public baths with steam, hot, temperate, and cold rooms were common. Similar to later Roman baths, the Greek baths ended with the scraping of sweat from the skin of the bather and the anointing of his body with oil.

Rome. The earliest known Roman baths are the Stabian baths at Pompeii (q.v.), built in the 2nd century B.C. Their arrangement is similar to the public baths found in other parts of the Roman Empire. Around a central courtyard, used for exercise, were the *apodyterium,* or dressing room; the *calidarium,* or hot room, containing the *alveus,* or hot bath, and the *laconicum,* or steam bath; the *tepidarium,* or warm bath; and the *frigidarium,* or cold bath. These facilities were duplicated, on a smaller scale, for women. Floors were of mosaic tile. Between the 1st and 4th centuries A.D., five imperial *thermae* were built in Rome. Extensive ruins of three of these remain; the baths of Titus, Caracalla, and Diocletian (qq.v.). In addition to the facilities found in Pompeii, these had shops, lecture halls, elaborate gymnasia, gardens, and libraries. Floors and walls were heated by a hypocaust that circulated hot air through flues.

The public baths were the center of social life and a place for relaxation and recreation. Many works of art were discovered in the ruins. Separate times of the day or separate facilities existed for the use of women, but during the last years of the Roman Empire, mixed bathing was practiced, and the baths became the settings for debauchery.

The licentiousness of the Roman bathers incurred the censure of the Christian Church, and Christians were supposed to bathe only for cleanliness. Throughout the Middle Ages (q.v.), public baths existed in Western Europe but were little used by respectable people. During this period, however, the architecture of bathing places was progressing in the Islamic countries. In the Alhambra (q.v.) in Granada, Spain, are bathrooms in the style favored in Islamic art and architecture (q.v.); in İstanbul (q.v.) the baths, a series of square rooms, counterparts in function of those in the Roman baths, were in either the Islamic or the Byzantine style (*see* BYZANTINE ART: *Architecture*). Splendid baths were built by the rich in homes and gardens, and public baths were established in every town that had a mosque (q.v.). The Turkish bath involves the transition from one room to another, through constantly increasing temperatures, ending with a cold shower, a massage, and a cooling room. During the Renaissance (q.v.) in Europe, personal cleanliness was regarded as relatively unimportant, and bathing was considered unhealthy. This attitude persisted until the 19th century.

MODERN BATHS

With the onset of the Industrial Revolution (q.v.) sanitary reforms were initiated, and to compensate for the fact that only some of the wealthy had bathtubs, public bathhouses were built. In eastern Europe, the Russian baths were very like the Finnish saunas: small wooden rooms or huts with benches around the walls. Water was thrown on hot rocks or pebbles to create dense clouds of steam which brought the temperature to between 112° and 140° F. After a period of sweating, the bathers were soaped, rubbed, flogged with softened birch twigs, and washed with tepid water. Finally they had cold water dashed over them or they plunged into snow or an icy stream.

In Japan, almost every house has a bath, which may be either indoors or in a garden. One filling with very hot water provides baths for the entire family. Bathing is not a private function in Japan; there are many large public baths at mineral or hot springs and whole families bathe there in the company of others.

Ancient Roman white marble tub (about 4th to 1st century B.C.), the oldest known movable bathtub in existence.

French gilded "cradle" tub (about 1750). The cradle, with removable metal basin insert, is suspended between rococo columns set on an ornamental base.

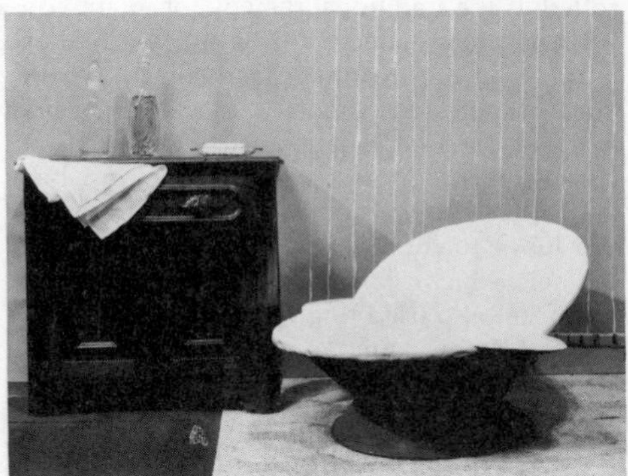

American sitz bath (about 1850). The bather sat in a basin, resting against the chairlike back, and allowed his arms and legs to protrude from the tub.

Cleanliness Bureau

Therapeutic Baths. As distinct from the medicated bath (see below), the therapeutic bath produces results through temperature of the water, aided in some instances by the stimulation produced by a jet such as a needle shower or a whirlpool. Baths at skin temperature (about 93° F.) are relaxing and sedative; those hotter or colder are stimulating. Baths may be given by submersion in water or, in the form of wet packs, by wrapping the body in wet sheets or towels. All of the body may be submerged, or only a particular part may be bathed as, for example, in the arm- or foot-bath, or the sitz-bath for the pelvic region. The hot bath stimulates, relieves pain, particularly of cramps, controls convulsions, and induces sleep. Quickening the pulse and respiration, it also increases perspiration, thereby relieving the kidneys of part of their work and temporarily decreasing weight. Hot packs are helpful in muscular disorders. The cold bath is helpful in reducing high fever and in limiting inflammation. Stimulating baths should be of short duration to avoid exhaustion; sedative warm baths may be continued for hours or, in the treatment of certain nervous diseases, for days. *Kinotherapeutic baths,* in which a routine of exercise is carried on while the member is submerged, have been very successful in restoring the use of muscles damaged by poliomyelitis (q.v.).

Medicated Baths. When any substance intended to effect, or assist in, the cure of disease is added to the bath medium, the bath is called medicated. Soap, bath salts, bath oil, and similar detergents are so common that they are not usually considered medicines. Alcohol sponge baths are cooling, and are useful in the prevention of bedsores. A hot bath, with mustard added, is the traditional remedy for infant convulsions, and alkaline baths have been used extensively in the treatment of rheumatic conditions. Medicated vapors, both natural and artificial, are used in steam baths. Often the vapors are allowed to fill a closed room in which the patient can walk about, exposing both skin and lungs to the effects of the vapors. Steam cabinets, which enclose the body from the neck down, are also used to give vapor baths.

Mineral Baths. Among the most popular medicinal baths are those in which the waters of natural warm mineral springs are used; *see* MINERAL WATERS. Many thousands of persons suffering from a wide variety of ailments frequent mineral baths in search of the cures attributed to local waters and muds. Resort communities, sometimes called spas, have grown up near springs to accommodate visitors. Perhaps the most famous European spa is the one at Karlovy-Vary (formerly Carlsbad), Czechoslovakia. Another famous spa is in the city of Bath, England. The Belgian city of Spa, and the cities of Wiesbaden, Bad Ems, and Baden-Baden, in West Germany, also are sites of popular mineral springs. The best-known American spas are the ones in Saratoga Springs, N.Y., Hot Springs, Ark., Warm Springs, Ga., and White Sulphur Springs, W. Va.

BATH, city and port of entry in Maine, and county seat of Sagadahoc Co., on the Kennebec R., 12 mi. from the Atlantic Ocean, and about 30 miles N.E. of Portland. The region surrounding the city is a popular summer-resort area. The chief industries in Bath include shipbuilding, sardine canning, and the manufacture of marine equipment and sportswear. The city has been a shipbuilding center since 1762. Bath was incorporated as a town in 1781 and as a city in 1847. Pop. (1960) 10,717; (1970) 9679.

BATH, Great Britain, county borough and city of Somersetshire, England, in the wooded valley of the Avon R., about 12 miles S.E. of Bristol. Bath has long been known as a health resort. The beneficial mineral springs were used by the Romans, who built baths there in the 1st century A.D. Extensive remains of the ancient baths were discovered in 1775 and in 1881. The temperature of the springs varies from 116° to 120° F. They rise near the riverbank, in the center of the city, and supply several health institutions, discharging over half a million gallons of water daily. Noteworthy edifices in Bath are the Abbey Church, dating from the 15th century, the Guildhall, the Pumproom, the Mineral Water Hospital, the City Markets, and the new baths. Pop. (1967 est.) 85,870.

BATH, ORDER OF THE, British order of merit, established in 1725 by George I (q.v.), King of Great Britain, with a membership consisting of the sovereign, a grand master, and thirty-six knights companions. Knights of the Bath were, originally, the men knighted ceremonially at coronations or other state occasions as opposed to those knighted on the field of battle. The title, which is derived from the practice of bathing, as a symbol of purity, by the men entering knighthood (q.v.), was used for the first time in 1399 at the coronation of Henry IV (q.v.), King of England. The last time it was used in that sense was in 1661 at the coronation of Charles II (q.v.).

In 1815 the order was separated into three classes: knight grand cross (G.C.B.), knight commander (K.C.B.), and knight companion (C.B.). Civil knights commanders and companions were admitted in 1847 and, apart from the sovereign, royal princes, and distinguished foreigners, the order is limited in membership to 55 military and 27 civil knights grand cross; 145 military and 108 civil knights commanders; and 705 military and 298 civil knights companions. The

Bath-Sheba and King David (engraving from a 15th-century Cologne Bible). Bettmann Archive

officers are the dean, who is also the dean of Westminster (q.v.), the Bath King of Arms, the registrar, and the usher of the Scarlet Rod. In Great Britain, the Order of the Bath is second in honor only to the Order of the Garter.

BATH-SHEBA, in the Old Testament, wife of Uriah, a Hittite soldier (*see* HITTITES). David (q.v.), King of Israel and Judah, wishing to marry Bath-Sheba, ordered Uriah to a dangerous battlefront, where he was killed (2 Sam. 11). As David's wife Bath-Sheba became the mother of his successor (2 Sam. 12:24), Solomon (q.v.).

BATHURST, former name of BANJUL, city and capital of Gambia, in Kombo Saint Mary's Division, on Saint Mary's Island, at the mouth of the Gambia R., 120 miles S.E. of Dakar, Senegal. Banjul is the chief port and trade center of Gambia, dealing in peanuts, palm products, fish, millet, rice, and corn. Products exported include peanuts, palm kernels, hides, skins, and beeswax. The city has fish- and vegetable-processing plants. Founded in 1816 as a British base of operations against the slave-trading centers of West Africa, the city was the capital of the British crown colony of Gambia from 1843 to 1866 and from 1888 to 1965. Pop. (1973 est.) 39,476.

BATHYSCAPHE, submarine vessel designed to operate at great depths. The first such vessel, invented in 1947 by the Swiss physicist Auguste Piccard (q.v.), could explore the ocean bottom at depths as great as 2 ½ mi. and operate under water pressure of 3 tons per square inch (sq.in.). The bathyscaphe *Trieste,* built in 1953, set a world record on Jan. 23, 1960, when it descended 35,800 ft. to the bottom of the Mariana Trench, deepest known point in the oceans, 250 mi. S.W. of Guam. It withstood pressure of 16,833 lb. per sq.in. at that depth. The craft, which carried gasoline for buoyancy and buckshot for ballast, sank when water was pumped into air tanks at either end and ascended when water was pumped out and buckshot released. The dive, manned by Jacques Ernest Jean Piccard, the son of Auguste Piccard, and U.S. Navy Lt. Donald Walsh, yielded important geophysical

The bathyscaphe Trieste *being lowered into the ocean to explore the bottom at a depth of 20,000 ft.* UPI

information. The *Trieste* was also used in the unsuccessful search for the hull of the nuclear submarine the U.S.S. *Thresher,* which plunged 8400 ft. to the ocean floor 220 mi. off the coast of New England in April, 1963. Although the hull of the *Thresher* was not found, some pieces of its equipment were recovered by the *Trieste.* *See* DEEP-SEA EXPLORATION; GEOPHYSICS: *International Geophysical Year.*

BATHYSPHERE, large, spherical, steel diving chamber designed for underwater exploration by American scientist William Beebe (q.v.). The bathysphere is suspended from a surface ship by a steel cable, and the observers manning it are connected to the mother-ship by telephone. In 1934, Beebe descended to a depth of 3028 ft. off one of the Bermuda Islands.

BATIK (Javanese, "wax painting"), process by which designs are printed on cloth by first painting them, on both sides of the fabric, in wax. When the wax hardens, the fabric is dipped into a dye bath; the parts covered in wax resist the dye while the remainder absorbs it. Batik, therefore, is known as resist-dyeing or reserve printing (*see* DYEING: *Dyeing Processes*). After the cloth has dried, the wax is removed and reapplied to the areas to be unaffected by the next dye-bath. This is done for each color to be applied, and the wax is removed by boiling the fabric or soaking it in gasoline. The process was first used by the Sumerians (*see* SUMER: *Sumerian Art and Architecture*) and was then introduced in the Orient. Java is the prime source of batik, which was first brought to Europe by Dutch traders in the 17th century. The term is applied to both fabric and design.

BATISTA Y ZALDÍVAR, Fulgencio (1901–73), Cuban political leader, born in Banes. He entered the army in 1921 and reached the grade of sergeant first class by 1928. As a member of a revolutionary organization known as A.B.C., he participated in the revolt against President Gerardo Machado y Morales (q.v.) and became a leader in the overthrow of Machado and of his successor, Carlos Manuel de Céspedes y Quesada (1871–1939), in 1933. Under the Provisional Government of 1933, Batista became chief of staff of the Cuban army, with the rank of colonel. During the following seven years he maintained total control of the Cuban government. As dictator he strengthened the Cuban army, combated illiteracy by establishing over 1000 schools, and initiated social services and reforms. He was elected president of Cuba for a four-year term in 1940. In 1948 he was elected to the senate. Backed by the Cuban army and police, he seized power on March 10, 1952, proclaimed himself chief of state, and suspended constitutional government. He was elected president of Cuba without opposition on Nov. 1, 1954. Two years of armed rebellion under the Cuban lawyer Fidel Castro (Ruz) (*see* CASTRO, FIDEL [Ruz]), who opposed the Batista regime, led to the overthrow of the dictator. On Jan. 1, 1959, he went into exile, first in the Dominican Republic, then in the Madeira Islands, and finally on the Portuguese mainland. *See* CUBA: *History: The Batista Regime.*

BATLLE Y ORDÓÑEZ, José. *See* URUGUAY: *History.*

BATON ROUGE, city and capital of Louisiana, and parish seat of East Baton Rouge Parish, on the E. bank of the Mississippi R., about 75 miles N.W. of New Orleans. Baton Rouge is the processing and distribution center for the surrounding agricultural and livestock-raising region. Industries within the city include oil refining and the manufacture of chemicals. Louisiana State University is situated approximately 3 miles S. of the city. Baton Rouge was one of the earliest French settlements in Louisiana. In 1779 the city came under Spanish rule, and in 1810 under American control as a part of the Louisiana Purchase (q.v.). Baton Rouge was incorporated as a city in 1817, and was the State capital from 1849 to 1862, when Shreveport became the capital. In 1882 Baton Rouge again became the seat of State government. Pop. (1970) 165,963.

BATSWANA, tribes of Bantu stock comprising a large majority of the population of Botswana (q.v.). The Batswana are divided into eight principle tribes, the most important and most numerous being the Bamangwato. Most of the Batswana speak Tswana, a Bantu language of the Sotho group. Considered the most peaceable of African tribes, the Batswana live primarily by subsistence farming and frequently tend herds of cattle. They are expert fishermen. Each year about 30,000 tribesmen spend nine months in the Republic of South Africa, working in the diamond mines.

BATTAMBANG, town in Cambodia, and capital of Battambang Province, 160 miles N.W. of Phnom Penh and 160 miles S.E. of Bangkok, Thailand. A junction for trains to Thailand, Battambang is divided by the seasonally navigable Battambang R., which flows through Tonle Sap Lake and into a major rice-growing area. Phosphate, cacao, betel nuts, cardamom, fruit, and fish are processed in the town. An ancient Khmer city with 10th-century ruins, Battambang was a part of Siam (now Thailand) from 1794 to 1907 and from 1941 to 1946. Pop. (1968 est.) 40,000.

BATTANI, Al-. *See* AL-BATTĀNI, ABU-'ABDULLĀH MUHAMMAD IBN-JĀBIR.

BATTERING RAM, engine of war used from ancient times until development of the cannon (q.v.). In earliest usage the ram was a wooden beam with a mass of metal on one end, carried on the shoulders of men; later the ram was mounted on a frame or rollers. The purpose was the breaching of fortifications, and some ancient writers have described rams weighing up to 150,000 lb. and requiring the energies of a thousand men for motive power.

BATTERY. *See* CELL, ELECTRIC.

BATTERY PARK, twenty-one acre park in New York City, at the extreme southern tip of Manhattan Island and locally known as The Battery. Because it commands the harbor approaches to the island, it was the site of early Dutch fortifications and, later, of Fort Clinton; *see* CASTLE CLINTON NATIONAL MONUMENT. Two bronze statues stand in the park: one of Florentine navigator Giovanni da Verrazano (q.v.) and one of Swedish-American engineer John Ericsson (1803–89), designer of the ironclad *Monitor* (q.v.).

BATTLE CREEK, city of Michigan, in Calhoun Co., on the Kalamazoo R., about 120 miles W. of Detroit. The city is a farm-trade center, and is noted for the manufacture of breakfast cereals. Other manufactures include machinery, and metal and paper products. The Battle Creek Sanitarium is within the city and a convalescent hospital for veterans is nearby. Battle Creek was settled in 1831 and was incorporated as a city in 1859. Pop. (1960) 44,169; (1970) 38,931.

BATTLE HYMN OF THE REPUBLIC. *See* HOWE, JULIA WARD.

BATTLESHIP. *See* SHIPS, NAVAL.

BATTLE, WAGER OF, *or* TRIAL BY COMBAT, method of adjudicating legal disputes by personal combat between the litigants or their appointed champions. The practice apparently originated among primitive German tribes about the 1st century A.D. and spread to many countries of Europe, notably to France where wager of battle was a recognized legal procedure after the 10th century. The last judicial duel in France was fought in 1547.

Wager of battle was one of the French customs imported to England in the 11th century by William I (q.v.), King of England. From 1133 to 1189, under Henry II (q.v.), King of England, no other legal means was recognized for the settlement of a suit involving recovery of land. By the end of the 16th century the custom was virtually obsolete. Judicial combat was, however, officially considered a principle of English law as late as 1817; in 1818 it was specifically outlawed.

BATU KHAN (d. 1255), Mongol ruler, grandson of Genghis Khan (q.v.). Batu's uncle, Ogadai (1185–1241), successor to Genghis Khan, sent him to invade eastern Europe, and his army conquered Russia, Poland, and Hungary (1237–41). In 1241, as Batu was preparing to invade Germany, he was recalled to Karakorum, Mongolia, on the death of Ogadai, whom he succeeded as khan. With his Golden Horde (q.v.) Batu lived in luxury at Sarai, on the Volga, until his death. His realm extended from Lake Balkhash in Russia to Hungary. *See* MONGOL DYNASTIES.

BATUMI, *or* BATUM, city of the Soviet Union, in the Georgian S.S.R., capital of the Adzhar A.S.S.R., on the E. coast of the Black Sea, about 150 miles W. of Tbilisi, near the border with Turkey. Batumi is a leading seaport and is the transport center for oil from Baku, with which it is connected by rail and pipelines. Other products that are exported include fruit, tea, manganese, raw silk, timber, wool, and cotton. The chief industries of Batumi are oil refining, shipbuilding and repair, food processing, and the manufacture of machinery, clothing, and furniture. The climate of the area is subtropical and health resorts are located nearby. Batumi was controlled by the Turks from the 16th century until after the Russo-Turkish War of 1877–78 when it was ceded to Russia (*see* RUSSO-TURKISH WARS). Pop. (1967 est.) 100,000.

BA U, Agga Maha Thiri Thudhamma (1887–1963), Burmese statesman, born in Burma, and educated in Burmese schools and at the University of Cambridge. Beginning in 1913 he served as a judge in various courts of Burma, including the supreme court. Ba U helped frame the Burmese constitution (adopted in 1947), and in 1948, when British supremacy in Burma ended, he was appointed the first chief justice of the Union of Burma. He served as president of Burma from 1952 until 1957.

BAUCIS. *See* PHILEMON AND BAUCIS.

BAUDELAIRE, (Pierre) Charles (1821-67), French poet and critic, born in Paris, and educated at the Collège Louis-le-Grand. His boyhood and adolescence were unhappy, for his father died when he was six, and shortly thereafter his mother married an army officer. Baudelaire disliked his stepfather and resented his mother for having married him. After completing his studies, Baudelaire announced his intention of pursuing a literary career. Opposed to his choice and hoping to distract him, his parents sent him on a sea voyage to India. He left the ship at the island of Réunion, however, and returned to Paris more determined than ever to devote himself to writing. At first his de-

Portrait of Charles Baudelaire by Émile Deroy.
French Embassy Press & Information Div.

cision was facilitated by a small inheritance from his father, but Baudelaire soon spent most of the money. In an effort to solve his financial problem he began to write critical journalism. His first important publications were two booklets of art criticism, *Les Salons* (1845–46), in which he discussed with acute insight the paintings and drawings of such contemporary French artists as Honoré Daumier, Édouard Manet, and Eugène Delacroix (qq.v.). He was first acclaimed as a skilled literary craftsman in 1848, when his translations, from English, of *Tales of Mystery and Imagination* (*Histoires Extraordinaires*) by the American writer Edgar Allan Poe (q.v.) began to appear. Encouraged by that success and inspired by his enthusiasm for Poe, with whom he felt a strong affinity both as a man and as an artist, Baudelaire continued to translate Poe's stories until 1857, when the entire five volumes were completed.

Baudelaire's major work, the volume of poetry *Fleurs du Mal* ("Flowers of Evil"), appeared in 1857. Immediately after its publication the French government prosecuted Baudelaire on a charge of offending public morals. Although the élite of French literature came to his support, he was fined, and six poems in the volume were suppressed in subsequent editions. His next work, *Les Paradis Artificiels* (1860), is a confessional, self-analytical book, based on his own experiences and inspired by *Confessions of an English Opium Eater* by the British author Thomas De Quincey (q.v.). From 1864 to 1866 Baudelaire lived in Belgium, where he had gone with the plan of lecturing and bringing out a complete edition of his work. Stricken by paralysis, however, he was brought back to Paris, where he died.

One of the great poets of French literature, Baudelaire possessed a classical sense of form, great skill at choosing the perfectly appropriate word, and a true gift for musical language; he produced some of the most mordant and lovely verse in the French language. His originality sets him apart from the dominant literary schools of his time. His poetry has been variously regarded as the last brilliant summation of Romanticism (q.v.), the precursor of symbolism (q.v.), and the first expression of modern techniques. Because he viewed man as a divided being, drawn equally toward God and Satan, he felt impelled to deal in his poems with all of man's experiences, from the most sublime to the most sordid. Yet despite his lurid subject matter, his obsession with death and decay, and his joyless carnality, Baudelaire is in essence a profoundly religious man grappling with the timeless conflict between the ideal and the sensual. He broke with an oratorical kind of poetry, initiating a new type of ruthless self-analysis that is not found in the typical Romantic poetry published in France between 1820 and 1840.

Among his other writings are *Petits Poèmes en Prose,* ("Little Poems in Prose"), a collection of prose poems; and his intimate journals *Fusées* ("Fireworks") and *Mon Coeur Mis à Nu* ("My Heart Laid Bare"). All were posthumously published in 1869. W.F.

BAUDOUIN, in full BAUDOUIN ALBERT CHARLES LEOPOLD AXEL MARIE GUSTAVE (1930–), King of Belgium, elder son of King Leopold III (*see under* LEOPOLD) and Queen Astrid (1905–35), born near Brussels, and educated privately and at a college in Geneva, Switzerland. He was in voluntary exile with his father in Switzerland from May, 1945, to July, 1950. Leopold's return to Belgium provoked much unrest, and in August, 1950, the king agreed to relinquish his royal prerogatives to Crown Prince Baudouin and to abdicate when Baudouin attained his majority. Leopold abdicated on July 16, 1951, two months before the twenty-first birthday of his son, and Baudouin took the oath of office the next day. He married Doña Fabiola de Mora y Aragon (1928–), of Spain, in 1960.

BAUER, Georg. *See* AGRICOLA, GEORGIUS.

BAUHAUS, famous art school founded in 1919 by the German architect Walter (Adolf) Gropius (q.v.) in Weimar, Germany. The curriculum at the Bauhaus was based on the principles that modern art and architecture must be responsive to the needs and influences of the modern industrial world, and that good designs must pass the test of both fine art and of sound engineering. The curriculum thus included classes in crafts, typography, and commercial and industrial design, as well as the traditional classes in sculpture, painting, and architecture. The Bauhaus style was marked by absence of ornament and ostentatious facades, and by harmony between function and the artistic and technical means employed. In 1925, the Bauhaus was moved into a group of buildings in Dessau especially designed for the school by Gropius. At Dessau the functional attitude became dominant. The newer style was marked by strong leanings in the direction of industrial realism, with an attempt to show the beauty and suitability of basic materials while maintaining the avoidance of ornamentation. In 1930 the Bauhaus came under the leadership of the German-American architect Ludwig Mies van der Rohe (q.v.), who moved the school to Berlin in 1932. By 1933, when the school was closed by the German National Socialist (Nazi) Party (*see* NATIONAL SOCIALISM), the principles and ideas of the Bauhaus were well known throughout the world and have since exerted an inestimable influence on architecture and on the industrial arts. In addition to the leaders of the school, other outstanding architects and artists on the staff of the Bauhaus included the Swiss painter Paul Klee, the Russian painter Vasily Kandinsky, the Hungarian painter and designer László Moholy-Nagy (qq.v.), who founded the Chicago Institute of Design on the principles of the Bauhaus, the American painter Lyonel Feininger (1871–1956), and the German painter Oskar Schlemmer (1888–1943).

BAUM, Lyman Frank (1856–1919), American writer, born in Chittenango, N.Y., and educated at Peekskill Military Academy. From 1880 to 1902 he was on the staff of newspapers in Aberdeen, S.Dak., and Chicago, Ill. In 1897 he wrote *Mother Goose in Prose* and in 1899, *Father Goose—His Book.* Following these two works he wrote a series of books in which he created an original fairyland, the land of Oz, a world of fantastic characters and gay adventures. The most famous of these books was *The Wonderful Wizard of Oz* (1900). In 1901 Baum adapted it as a musical extravaganza entitled *The Wizard of Oz*, and before his death Baum wrote fourteen books about Oz. After his death various writers continued the series, producing scores of volumes. A musical motion picture, *The Wizard of Oz* (1939), based on the original books by Baum, has become a classic.

BAUMGARTEN, Alexander Gottlieb (1714–62), German philosopher, born in Berlin. He studied with the German philosopher and mathematician Baron Christian von Wolff (q.v.) at the University of Halle and was influenced early by the work of another German philosopher, Baron Gottfried Wilhelm von Leibniz (q.v.). Baumgarten, the first modern philosopher to approach the question of beauty systematically, introduced the term aesthetics (q.v.), and defined the experience of beauty as the sensory recognition of perfection. In 1750–58 he issued two volumes of his *Esthetics.* He also wrote *Ethics* (1740), *Natural Law* (1765), and *General Philosophy* (1770). His brother, the theologian Siegmund Jacob Baumgarten (1707–57), was concerned with the Lutheran movement, Pietism (q.v.).

BAURU, city of Brazil, in São Paulo State, 175 miles N.W. of the city of São Paulo. The city is a rail junction and a trade center for a pioneer agricultural settlement area of the State. The industries of Bauru include food processing, tanning, woodworking, and textile manufacturing. Bauru ships coffee, cotton, fruit, and dairy products by rail to Atlantic ports. Pop. (1970 prelim.) 120,178.

BAUXITE, important ore of aluminum, consisting of aluminum oxide of various degrees of hydration, usually mixed with impurities, particularly iron. Among the specific aluminum-bearing minerals in bauxite are gibbsite, $Al(OH)_3$, and diaspore, $HAlO_2$. Bauxite is a soft mineral, the hardness varying from 1 to 3; sp.gr. 2 to 2.55. In color it may vary from white to brown, and it is dull in appearance. Bauxite usually occurs in aggregates in lumps about the size of a pea.

Although aluminum is the commonest of all metals on the surface of the earth, it most frequently occurs in the form of complex compounds such as those found in clay and granite, which cannot be used commercially as ores because of the difficulty of extracting the aluminum. Bauxite, on the other hand, can be easily purified and converted directly into either alum (q.v.) or metallic aluminum.

Bauxite is mined in large quantities in France, the name coming from the French town of Baux. It is also mined in the West Indies, Surinam,

Strip mining of bauxite in Arkansas.
Arkansas State Tourist office

Guyana, the U.S.S.R., Australia, and the United States. The major bauxite-producing States are Alabama, Arkansas, and Georgia. Total world production is about 40,000,000 tons a year.

BAVARIA (Ger. *Bayern*), State of West Germany, bounded on the N. by East Germany on the N.E. by Czechoslovakia, on the S.E. and S. by Austria, and on the W. by the States of Baden-Württemberg and Hesse. Munich (q.v.) is the capital and largest city. Other important cities are Nuremberg, Augsburg, and Regensburg (qq.v.). Bavaria is the largest State of West Germany. It is drained by the Main R. in the N.W., and by the Danube R. and two of its tributaries, the Inn River (qq.v.) and the Isar R. in the S. and central regions. North of the Danube the land is a rolling upland. Along the Czechoslovakian border is the Bavarian Forest, which reaches an elevation of 4780 ft. South of the Danube the land is a rising upland cut by numerous river valleys. In the extreme S. part of the State are the Bavarian Alps, the highest mountains in West Germany. Area, 27,239 sq.mi., pop. (1967 est.) 10,280,400.

The population, which is largely Roman Catholic, is engaged mainly in agriculture. The chief crops are grains (wheat in the S., rye in the N.), sugar beets, potatoes, hops, and grapes and other fruits. Cattle, hogs, and horses are raised, and dairying is carried on in the foothills of the Bavarian Alps. The forests yield a variety of wood products. Lignite, granite, iron ore, and salt are mined. Bavaria has extensive hydroelectric power, a key factor in its industrial growth. Industries center in Munich, one of the main transportation centers in West Germany, and in Nuremberg and Augsburg. In addition to the brewing of world-famous beer, industries include the production of glass and ceramics, machinery, textiles and paper, and optical and scientific equipment.

Bavaria is noted for many monasteries and baroque churches, picturesque castles, and universities.

Under the 1946 constitution, Bavaria has a cabinet government headed by a minister-president and responsible to a popularly elected diet. The State is divided into seven administrative districts.

History. Bavaria was conquered by the Romans in the 1st century B.C. and resettled by Germanic tribes in the 5th and 6th centuries. It became a possession of Charlemagne (q.v.), King of the Franks, in 787 and was ruled by the Carolingian dynasty (q.v.) until the 10th century. In 1180 it passed to the Bavarian family of Wittelsbach (q.v.). During the Reformation (q.v.) Bavaria remained staunchly Roman Catholic and was consequently ravaged by Protestant forces during the Thirty Years' War (q.v.). The fertile soil and strategic position of the region made it a highly prized possession, and it was frequently invaded by foreign armies in the 17th and 18th centuries.

During the Napoleonic Wars (q.v.) Bavaria was made a kingdom by Napoleon I (q.v.) of France. In the 19th century, Bavaria tended to support Austria against Prussia. After being defeated with Austria in the Seven Weeks' War (q.v.), however, Bavaria sided with Prussia and in 1871 joined the new German Empire. After World War I a Communist-led group belonging to the Independent Socialist Party seized power, but troops of the central government assisted by Bavarian volunteers crushed the rebellion. In the 1920's Bavaria was able to retain a large degree of autonomy, which it lost in the 1930's with the rise of the German dictator Adolf Hitler (q.v.). Munich became the headquarters of the National Socialist Party (*see* NATIONAL SOCIALISM) during the Hitler regime.

After World War II Bavaria was included in the Allied zone of occupation. A new constitution was drawn up in 1946, and in 1949 Bavaria became a constituent State of the Federal Republic of Germany. *See also* GERMANY: *History.*

BAVARIAN SUCCESSION, WAR OF THE. *See* SUCCESSION WARS: *War of the Bavarian Succession.*

BAX, Sir Arnold Edward Trevor (1883–1953), British composer, born in London, England, and trained at the Royal Academy of Music. Bax was noted for his symphonic works and songs based on the writings of modern Irish poets and dramatists. He was knighted in 1937. His compositions include three symphonic poems (written between 1916 and 1917), *The Garden of Fand, Tintagel,* and *November Woods;* a work for piano and orchestra, *Symphonic Varations* (1917); the score for the satiric ballet *The Truth About the Russian Dancers* (1920), based on a play by the British writer Sir James Matthew Barrie (q.v.); Sonata for Cello and Piano (1923); Quartet for Strings, No. 3, F major (1936); Symphony No. 7 in A-flat (1939); and Five Fantasies on Polish Christmas Carols (1945).

BAXTER, Richard (1615–91), English Puritan writer and scholar, born in Shropshire. He was ordained in 1638 and served as chaplain in the army of the Puritan general Oliver Cromwell (q.v.) in 1645. In his preaching, however, Baxter indicated opposition to the execution of Charles I (q.v.), King of England, and the usurpation of power by Cromwell. In 1660 after the Restoration (q.v.) of the monarchy, Baxter became court chaplain but was forced to leave the Church of England (q.v.) when the Act of Uniformity became law in 1662. He was tried for alleged sedition in his *Paraphrase of the New Testament* (1685) and was imprisoned for eighteen months. Chief among his works are *Saints' Everlasting Rest* (1650) and *Call to the Unconverted* (1657).

BAY, common name of various evergreen shrubs and trees of the Laurel family (Lauraceae) and to certain evergreen shrubs and also to trees resembling laurel, all of which are usually cultivated for their ornamental effect. The former group includes the red bay, *Persea borbonia,* which is native to the southern United States and belongs to the same genus as the avocado tree; and *Laurus nobilis,* commonly known as the bay tree, sweet bay, bayberry (q.v.), or Victor's laurel. Sprigs of *L. nobilis* were used to make garlands for winners in the Olympian games of ancient Greece. Associated since early times with superstitious ideas and practices, the wreath of bay leaves early became a symbol of rank and honor. Bay leaves are used often as an ornamental motif on monuments and statues; at Christmas time the long, oval, glossy green leaves are used to decorate doorways and altars of churches. The latter group includes two members of the Magnolia family (Magnoliaceae), *Magnolia grandiflora,* known as the bull bay, and *M. virginiana,* known as the white, sweet, or swamp bay, or laurel magnolia; the

Castle Neuschwanstein in Bavaria, built in the 19th century for King Louis II (Ludwig II in German), recalls castles of the Middle Ages. Pan American World Airways

cherry bay, English laurel, or cherry laurel, *Prunus laurocerasus,* belonging to the cherry group of the Rose family (Rosaceae) native to southern Europe; and the loblolly, or tan bay, *Gordonia lasianthus,* in the Tea family (Theaceae) a small tree or shrub native to the U.S.

The leaves of some kinds of bay tree are used in the seasoning of food. Oil of bay, made from the leaves of a tropical American bay tree commonly called the bayberry is used in the distilling of bay rum.

See LAUREL; MAGNOLIA; ROSE; TEA.

BAYARD, James Asheton (1767–1815), American lawyer and statesman, born in Philadelphia, Pa. He graduated from Princeton College in 1784, studied law, and settled permanently in Wilmington, Del. He became leader of the Federalist Party (q.v.), and served (1797–1803) in the United States House of Representatives. After the indecisive Presidential contest of 1800 between Thomas Jefferson and Aaron Burr (qq.v.), the House became responsible for the decision. Bayard was influential in securing the choice of Jefferson. From 1805 to 1813 Bayard was a United States Senator from Delaware. In 1814 he was a member of the commission that negotiated the Treaty of Ghent with Great Britain, thus ending the War of 1812.

BAYARD, Pierre Terrail, Seigneur de (1473?–1524), French knight, known in legend as *chevalier sans peur et sans reproche* ("fearless and blameless knight"), a model of chivalric virtue, born in the former province of Dauphiné, now the department of Isère. As a youth he won the favor of Charles VIII (1470–98), King of France. Bayard was knighted after the battle of Fornovo di Taro, Italy (1495). His reputation for valor was such that incredible stories were believed of him, such as that singlehanded he defended a bridge against 200 men. He was twice captured, but his gallantry and chivalrous qualities always secured his courteous release without ransom. During the war between Francis I (q.v.), King of France, and Charles V (q.v.), Holy Roman Emperor, Bayard with 1000 men held the fortress town of Mézières for six weeks against an army of 35,000. He was killed on the Sesia R. in Italy.

BAYAZID. *See* BAJAZET.

BAYBARS *or* **BAIBARS** *or* **BIBARS,** name of two sultans of Egypt, of a dynasty known as Bahri Mamelukes; *see* MAMELUKES.

Baybars I (1233–77), Sultan (1260–77), Turkish slave who rose to power through military skill. In 1260 he led the Mamelukes against the Mongols at the battle of Ayn Jalut, Palestine. In that same year he killed the sultan and was acclaimed chief by the military commanders. During his rule Egypt became the most powerful Muslim state in the Middle East. Baybars waged a successful war against the Crusaders (*see* CRUSADES) in Syria, and in 1268 put an end to the Norman principality of Antioch. His armies overran Armenia and penetrated deeply into Asia Minor, defeating the Seljuk Turks (*see* SELJUKS) and remnants of the Assassins (*see* ASSASSIN). His power toward the south extended over Nubia, and he controlled most of Arabia. His exploits gave rise to many legends, the most famous of which is the *Romance of Baybars.*

Baybars II (d. 1309), Sultan (1308–09), Circassian slave who became amir and prefect of the palace. He was proclaimed sultan in 1308 after he had usurped power and compelled the Sultan Malik al-Nāsir (1284–1340) to abdicate. Malik al-Nāsir, however, regained his authority as sovereign in 1309 and had Baybars executed.

BAYBERRY, common name for the wax myrtle, waxberry, or candelberry, *Myrica cerifera,* a small tree or shrub, 4 to 18 ft. high, found along the Great Lakes and the eastern coast of North America. It belongs to the Wax myrtle family (Myricaceae) and is characterized by naked flowers; small drupes or nuts (stone fruit), which are covered with a greenish-white wax; and evergreen, oblong, lanceolate leaves, which are sprinkled with resinous dots. Boiling the nuts, commonly called berries, yields the aromatic tallow used in making the bayberry candle, popular at Christmas time, and in making a soap with a balsamic odor. *Myrica gale* is the

Bayberry, Myrica cerifera

Detail of the Bayeux tapestry depicting the Norman fleet sailing to England in 1066.

sweet gale or bog myrtle of Scotland. Several species are also found in South Africa, one of which, *M. cordifolia,* bears the name of wax shrub. A Japanese species, *M. nagi,* is a tree from 40 to 50 ft. high that produces an edible fruit; *M. asplenifolia* is common in the United States, where it is known as sweet fern. Also known as bayberry are the laurel (q.v.) tree, *Laurus nobilis,* and its fruit; two tropical American trees, *Pimenta acris,* called also wild clove, the leaves of which are used in the preparation of bay rum; and a tree, *Aleurites moluccana,* of the Spurge (q.v.) family (Euphorbiaceae), which is native to South Pacific regions. *See* BAY.

BAY CITY, city in Michigan, and county seat of Bay Co., on Saginaw Bay, an arm of Lake Huron, about 100 miles N.W. of Detroit. Coal is mined in the vicinity of the city. Industries in Bay City include shipbuilding, woodworking, and the manufacture of magnesium products, cranes, power shovels, automobile parts, and welding machinery. Bay City was settled about 1831, and was incorporated as a city in 1865. Pop. (1960) 53,604; (1970) 49,449.

BAY CITY, city in Texas, and county seat of Matagorda Co., N. of Matagorda Bay, about 65 miles S.W. of Houston. Surrounded by a poultry- and livestock-raising, oil-producing, agricultural area, the city is a processing and shipping center. Bay City has flour and lumber mills, oil refineries, and cotton gins. Pop. (1960) 11,656; (1970) 11,733.

BAYEUX, city in France, in the department of Calvados, on the Aure R., about 5 mi. from the English Channel. The city is a market center for cattle and dairy products from the surrounding region. Lace making and the manufacture of pottery are the chief industries. Bayeux was called Augustodurum by the ancient Romans and later renamed Civitas Baiocassium, after a Gallic people of the region. The Gothic cathedral of Bayeux, reputedly the oldest in Normandy, has Romanesque sections dating from the 12th century. In the museum of the city is the famous Bayeux Tapestry (q.v.), which portrays the Norman Conquest of England. Pop. (1968 est.) 10,641.

BAYEUX TAPESTRY, needlework panorama, representing the invasion and conquest of England by William I (q.v.), called the Conqueror, preserved in the public library of Bayeux, France. It is made of woolen thread of various colors worked on a web of white canvas or linen cloth 231 ft. long by 20 in. wide. Traditionally considered the work of Mathilda (d. 1083), wife of William the Conqueror, it was actually made during the 11th century for Odo, bishop of Bayeux (1036?–97) and half-brother of William. It was used in the cathedral of Bayeux as a decorative hanging. The tapestry contains 1512 figures in 72 scenes, with Latin inscriptions giving the subjects and names. The heads and hands of the figures are crudely designed in embroidery work; the rest is formed of parallel woolen threads fastened down at intervals. A thread of a different shade gives the outlines. The border is of foliage, fantastic animals, and hunting scenes. The tapestry is most valuable for its representation of the costume, arms, and manners of the Normans before the Conquest; it gives more details of the events represented than does the contemporary literature (*see* ENGLAND: *History*).

BAYKAL, *or* BAIKAL, third-largest lake in Asia, and the largest freshwater lake of the Eurasian continent, in the Soviet Union, in S. Siberia. The area is about 12,150 sq.mi., and it has about 1220 mi. of shoreline. The crescent-shaped lake is about 386 mi. long and varies in width from about 9 mi. to about 50 mi. With a maximum depth of 5712 ft., the lake is the deepest freshwater lake in the world; the average depth is 820 ft. The lake is fed by the Selenga, Barguzin, and Verkhne Angara rivers and by more than 300 mountain streams. The only outlet is the lower Angara, which flows westward from the lake into the Yenisey R. The Baykal, Barguzin, and other mountain ranges surround the lake, rising on all shores except the S.E. Selenga delta. Baykal Lake has several islands, the largest of which is Olkhon. Nizhne-Angarsk and Listvyanka are ports on the lake. The sturgeon, salmon, and freshwater-seal fisheries of the lake are valuable, and large quantities of other fish are also caught. Petroleum wells, and mineral and hot springs are found in the vicinity. The S. shores of the lake are inhabited by tribes of the Buryats.

The discovery (1643) of Baykal Lake provided an important trade route between Russia and China, linking Listvyanka with points E. to the Mongolian frontier via the Selenga R. and tributaries.

In the 1950's and 1960's, much of the unique plant and animal life in Baykal was destroyed when refuse from a Soviet pulp- and papermaking complex on the S. shore was deposited in the lake. Because of the wide-spread pollution, efforts at purification have proved negligible.

BAYLE, Pierre (1647–1706), French philosopher and critic, born near Pamiers, in Ariège. Although born a Protestant, he was educated at the Jesuit College in Toulouse. He converted to Catholicism in 1669, but in 1670 he again adopted Protestantism. In 1675 he became professor of philosophy at the Protestant academy of Sedan; in 1681 he was appointed independent professor of philosophy and history at the Protestant academy of Rotterdam, receiving his salary from the city. His first well-known work was *Pensées Diverses sur la Comète de 1680* ("Diverse Thoughts on the Comet of 1680", 1682), a rationalistic discussion of the widespread fears aroused by the great comet of 1680. He was dismissed from his post at Rotterdam in 1693 because of the suspicion that he had written a tract expressing religious skepticism. He then compiled his *Dictionnaire Historique et Critique* ("Historical and Critical Dictionary", 1697). The skeptical tone of this work, which strongly advocated freedom of thought on all subjects, had great influence upon the French Encyclopedists and the rationalist philosophers of the 18th century. *See* ENCYCLOPEDISTS; RATIONALISM.

BAYLOR, Robert Emmet Bledsoe (1793?–1873), American jurist and clergyman, born in Lincoln County, Ky. He served in the United States Army during the War of 1812. After practicing law in Kentucky for some time, he moved to Alabama, where he engaged in politics and was elected to a term in the United States House of Representatives (1829–31). In 1839 he went to Texas, then an independent republic; was appointed a Texas supreme court justice in 1841; and, after the admission of Texas to the Union in 1845, became a Federal district judge (1845–61). His liberal donations of land and money were helpful in the founding, at Independence, Tex., of the first Baptist College in Texas in 1845. In 1886 the college was moved to Waco, where it merged with Waco University to constitute Baylor University (q.v.).

BAYLOR UNIVERSITY, private coeducational institution of higher education with its main campus in Waco, Texas, and owned by the Baptist General Convention of Texas (*see* BAPTIST). The university was founded in 1845, in Independence, Texas, as the Texas Baptist Educational Society; in 1886 it was moved to Waco, where it was consolidated with Waco University, and the present name was adopted. The divisions of the university include arts and sciences, business, education, law, and music, in Waco; a graduate division in the health sciences, in San Antonio; and nursing, dentistry, medical technology, and the Graduate Research Institute, in Dallas. The degrees conferred include B.A., B.S., B.F.A.; B.S. in home economics and physical education; B.MUS., B.B.A., M.A., M.S., master of education, music, and business administration; J.D., M.D., D.D.S., ED.D., and PH.D. In 1973 the university library housed more than 600,000 bound volumes. Armstrong Browning Library, on the Waco campus, contains a collection of art and materials related to the English literary figures Robert and Elizabeth Barrett Browning (*see under* BROWNING). Student enrollment in 1973 totaled 7500, the faculty numbered 413, and the endowment of the university was approximately $32,000,000.

BAYONET, weapon resembling a short sword or a dagger designed to be attached to the muzzle of a rifle or musket. The bayonet is believed to have been developed in Bayonne, France, about 1650. It consisted originally of a spike or dagger equipped with a handle that fitted into the muzzle of the musket. This first type, the plug bayonet, had several defects as a weapon. No shot could be fired until the bayonet was removed; if pushed in too tightly, it was difficult to remove; if not tight enough, it might fall out or remain in the body of an enemy. About 1700 the attachment was modified so that it fitted around the barrel of the musket and the gun could be fired with the bayonet in place. This type of attachment, the socket bayonet, is still in use, but the length and shape of the blade have been altered as required by changes in tactical use.

During World War I the American army used a bayonet resembling a short sword with a 16-in. blade. It was sharpened along the full length of one edge and on the back for about 5 in. from the point. The German army used a 15-in. sword; the French used a triangular blade about 22 in. long; the British used flat, triangular, and cruciform blades of various lengths. In World War II these armies reduced the length of their bayonets by 6 to 8 in., in order to decrease the load carried by the individual soldier and so increase his efficiency and mobility. Recent wars have demonstrated that the bayonet is not an obsolete weapon.

BAYONNE, city of New Jersey, in Hudson Co., on a peninsula at the S. end of the county, between Newark Bay on the W. and Upper New York Bay on the E. and S., immediately S. of Newark. The city has 9 mi. of water frontage on the bays, and is an important shipping center and oil terminal. Industries in the city include the manufacture of fabricated metals, foodstuffs, paper products, furniture, and wearing apparel. Bayonne was settled by Dutch traders about 1650, and was incorporated as a city in 1869. Pop. (1960) 74,215; (1970) 72,743.

BAY PSALM BOOK, first book published in the thirteen colonies in America and the first American psalmbook. It was prepared by several New England clergymen including Richard Mather and John Eliot (qq.v.), and was printed at Cambridge, Mass., Massachusetts Bay Colony, in 1640.

The book was the only work of its kind in New England churches for more than a century. In 1744 the 26th edition was printed in Boston. The early editions gave no music, but in 1690 an edition appeared containing twelve tunes. Among American book collectors the *Bay Psalm Book* is considered the most valuable of all American printed books because of its rarity and historical importance.

BAYREUTH, city of West Germany, in the State of Bavaria, on the Red Main R., 41 miles N.E. of Nuremberg. The principal industries of the city are brewing, the distillation of liquors, and the manufacture of machinery, textiles, chemicals, and pianos. From the 13th to the 18th century it was a possession of the Hohenzollern (q.v.) family. The principal buildings of the city are the Wagner Festspielhaus, the old palace, the new palace (containing a gallery of paintings), the opera house, and the town hall. Also in Bayreuth are the Villa Wahnfried, home of the German composer Richard Wagner (q.v.), who is buried here, and the home of the German writer Jean Paul (*see* RICHTER, JEAN PAUL FRIEDRICH). Both houses were badly damaged in World War II and have been rebuilt. Jean Paul and the Hungarian composer Franz Liszt (q.v.) are buried in the Central Cemetery. Bayreuth has numerous educational and charitable institutions.

From all over the world, people come to Bayreuth for the Wagner festivals, annual performances of Wagnerian operas. The performances are held in the Festspielhaus, a theater designed by Wagner and completed in 1876. Pop. (1970 est.) 64,200.

BAYTOWN, industrial city of Texas, in Harris Co., on the Houston Ship Channel and Galveston Bay, 20 miles E. of Houston. A port and pipeline terminus in an oil-producing area, Baytown has oil refineries and sawmills and produces synthetic rubber, chemicals, petroleum equipment, carbon black, paint, and cement. It is the site of Lee College (1934). The city was formed in 1947 by the consolidation of Baytown, Goose Creek, and Pelly. Pop. (1960) 28,159; (1970) 43,980.

BAY VILLAGE, city of Ohio, in Cuyahoga Co., on Lake Erie, about 11 miles W. of central Cleveland of which it is a residential suburb. Pop. (1960) 14,489; (1970) 18,163.

BAZAINE, Achille (1811–88), French military leader, born in Versailles. He joined the army in 1831 and, after serving in Algeria, Spain, the Crimea, and Italy, was appointed to the command of the French army in Mexico in 1863. He was accused of plotting to place himself at the head of a Mexican empire and, after quarreling with the emperor Maximilian (q.v.), returned with his army to France in 1867.

In the Franco-German War (q.v.) he commanded the Third Army Corps. He was defeated at Vionville, Mars-la-Tour, and Gravelotte. He was besieged in Metz from Aug. 18 to Oct. 27, 1870. While at Metz, Bazaine was not active in military service. He began negotiations with the Prussian statesman Prince Otto Eduard Leopold von Bismarck (q.v.). On October 27, however, Bazaine capitulated to the Germans and surrendered the city with 173,000 men, including 6000 officers. Because of his conduct of the campaign, Bazaine was found guilty of treason and received a death sentence; the sentence was commuted to imprisonment for twenty years. In 1874 he escaped from the fortress of Île-Sainte-Marguerite and found refuge in Madrid, Spain, where he later died. He wrote a defense of his leadership, *Episodes de la Guerre de 1870 et le Blocus de Metz* ("Episodes of the War of 1870 and the Siege of Metz", 1883).

BAZIN, René François Nicolas Marie (1853–1932), French writer, born in Angers, and educated at the Roman Catholic University of Angers. Bazin became professor of law at the university in 1878. In 1903 he was elected to the French Academy. He wrote novels about peasant life, including *Une Tache d'Encre* (1888; Eng. trans., *A Blot of Ink,* 1892) and *De Toute Son Âme,* 1897; Eng. trans., *Redemption,* 1908); and books of short stories, including *Récits de la Plaine et de la Montagne* ("Stories of the Plains and Mountains", 1904). Among his works, which are written in a patriotic and religious vein, are books on political subjects. He also wrote books on travel and an autobiography, *Étapes de Ma Vie* ("Stages of My Life"; posthumously published, 1936).

BAZOOKA, weapon consisting of a launching tube for military rockets, used by infantrymen against armored vehicles such as tanks. During 1941, American scientists developed an explosive projectile which, using the Munroe effect (*see* EXPLOSIVES), was able to penetrate armor without the high velocity that only a cannon could produce. The projectile was a 2.36-in., finned rocket that weighed 3.4 lb., and had a range of 700 yd. The launching tube, called the bazooka, was put into production in 1942 and was first used during the invasion of North Africa in World War II at the end of that year. Its introduction revolutionized antitank warfare. A 3.5-in. rocket launcher superseded the bazooka in the Korean War. The rocket launcher fired an 8.9-lb. rocket a distance of 800 yd.; the rocket could penetrate 11 in. of armor plate. The launcher was later replaced by a 66-mm. rocket preloaded in a disposable container.

BCG VACCINE. *See* CANCER: *Treatment: Chemotherapy; Environmental Causes of Cancer: Immunology*; TUBERCULOSIS: *Historical Background.*

BEACH, Chester (1881–1956), American sculptor, born in San Francisco, Calif. From 1904 to 1907 he studied sculpture in Paris. After winning recognition abroad, he returned to the United States in 1907 and settled in New York. He was a versatile artist and designed coins, medallions, and larger pieces of sculpture. Important among his larger works are "Twelve Signs of the Zodiac" and "Fountain of the Waters" in the Fine Arts Garden, Cleveland, Ohio; groups and figures for the Panama-Pacific Exposition (1915) and the New York World's Fair (1939–40); life-sized marble statues and groups in the Brooklyn Museum, Cleveland Museum, Newark Art Museum, Chicago Art Institute, and Barnard College; and portrait busts of notable Americans.

BEACH FLEA. *See* SAND FLEA.

BEACH PLANTS, *also called* STRAND PLANTS, SHORE PLANTS, *or* LITTORAL PLANTS, plants that grow along the shores of oceans or large lakes. They are specially adapted to their environment, being deeply rooted in the sandy or gravelly soil, capable of withstanding exposure to salt water, and resistant to drought. The last property is important because of the difficulty of drawing water from the saline solutions of the ocean and because of the porous nature of the sandy soil, which holds very little water.

Near the edge of the water, the most characteristic type of beach plant is the succulent annual, of which the sea rocket, *Cakile* of the Mustard family (Cruciferae) may be considered a good example, since it is a common beach plant along the ocean shores of America and Europe and along the shores of the Great Lakes. Biennials and perennials such as the beach pea, *Lathyrus maritimus* of the Pulse family (Legominosae), and the sand reed, *Ammophila* of the Grass family (Gramineae), are often found in higher places. Beach vegetation is usually sparse. *See* DUNE VEGETATION; GRASSES; MUSTARD.

BEACON, signal or system of signals, especially those designed to be observable from a great distance. In primitive civilizations, a beacon was any signal set upon a height used to spread word of fire, foreign invasion, or other events. Such signals are mentioned in the writings of ancient Persia, Palestine, and Greece. By obscuring the light or smoke, the signaler could indicate the nature of the news. Beacon fires were used by the North American Indians, who communicated in a smoke code by alternately smothering the fire with a blanket, and then allowing the fire to burn. In marine navigation, a beacon is a marker placed as a guide or warning to ships, generally erected on a high point near the shore or on dangerous rocks or shoals. Deep-water beacons generally are illuminated; shore beacons, occasionally. The lights are often arc lamps or neon lights, although some isolated beacons burn acetylene gas. *See* BUOY; LIGHTHOUSE. In aviation, beacons are of several types, one being a system of land markings used to indicate air stations or routes in the daytime when visibility is good and another being a system of arc lights to guide pilots flying at night. More recent is the radio beacon, which is now installed along all the principal air routes across the United States and many other countries. This beacon enables the pilot to navigate without difficulty in bad weather or at night. Radio beacons have been supplemented, but not displaced, by such modern electronic aids to navigation as radar, loran, shoran, and the omnidirectional radio range. *See* NAVIGATION; RADAR; RADIO AIDS TO NAVIGATION.

BEACON, city of New York State, in Dutchess Co., on the E. bank of the Hudson R., about 15 miles S. of Poughkeepsie. Beacon is in a summer resort area. It is a trade center, and manufactures furniture, chemicals, textiles, paper products, rubber goods, and bricks. Nearby Mt. Beacon, 1602 ft., is ascended by an incline railway. Pop. (1960) 13,922; (1970) 13,255.

BEACONSFIELD, Earl of. *See* DISRAELI, BENJAMIN, 1ST EARL OF BEACONSFIELD.

BEADED LIZARD, common name for a species of lizard, *Heloderma suspectum,* of the family Helodermatidae, so called because of the many beaded, brightly colored tubercles that cover its back. The beaded lizard and the closely related species, *H. horridum,* the American Gila monster, are the only two known venomous lizards in the world. The two animals are similar in habit and appearance, except for the entirely black head and longer tail of the beaded lizard. *See* GILA MONSTER.

BEADLE, George Wells (1903–), American biologist, born in Wahoo, Nebr., and educated at the University of Nebraska and Cornell University. He was assistant professor of genetics at Harvard University (1936–37), professor at Stanford University (1937–46), and chairman of the division of biology at California Institute of Technology (1946–61). He became president of the University of Chicago in 1961.

Beadle is noted for his pioneering research on the genetics of sac fungi, such as bread molds; *see* FUNGI; HEREDITY: *History.* For his achievements he shared the 1958 Nobel Prize in medicine and physiology with his associate Edward Lawrie Tatum and with another American geneticist, Joshua Lederberg (qq.v.). Beadle has also made studies of genes as biochemical regulators and their role in the synthesis of enzymes (q.v.); he also advanced the research of cancer. He wrote *Genetics and Modern Biology* (1963) and, with his wife Muriel (1915–), *The Language of Life* (1966).

UPI George W. Beadle

BEADS (M. Eng., *bede,* "prayer", "prayer bead"), small, perforated objects that may be strung to form necklaces or bracelets, or at-

Beaded necklace of the Zulu tribe, from Natal, South Africa. Brooklyn Museum

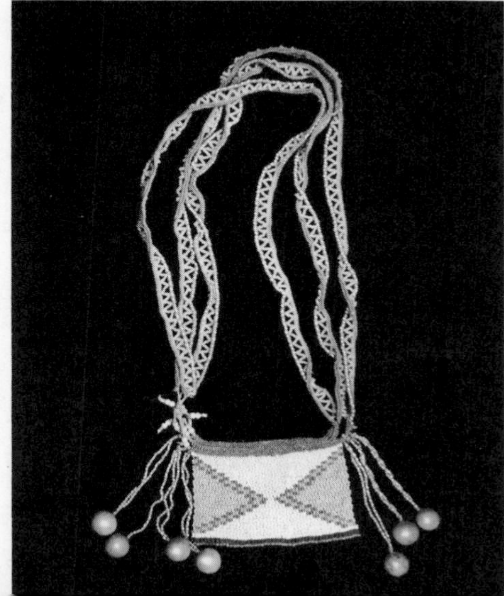

tached, for decorative effect, to articles of clothing. The word from which bead derives originally applied to the beads of a rosary (q.v.). Beads are made of a great variety of materials: glass, wood, ivory, bone, horn, shell, coral, pearl, jet, amber, minerals (including precious stones), metals, ceramics, and plastics. They are made in many different shapes and colors.

According to archaeologists, beads were used as early as the Stone Age for magical and decorative purposes. In ancient Mesopotamia and Egypt beads were worn as amulets, or charms, as they were centuries later in widely scattered parts of Europe; *see* AMULET. The manufacture of beads in Europe for commercial purposes dates from the Middle Ages. The American Indians (q.v.) and other primitive peoples used beads as ornaments and as money; hence beads served as a medium of exchange for explorers and colonizers dealing with native peoples.

BEAGLE, small hound of unknown origin that can be traced back to 16th-century England, where it is first known to have appeared as a distinct breed. Almost all modern English beagles are descended from a noted pack of beagles kept by a British clergyman in the middle of the 19th century. In the same century a type of beagle with some of the characteristics of the basset hound or the dachshund (qq.v.) was known in the southern United States. Since about 1870 beagle packs imported from Great Britain have greatly improved the American strain. The typical American beagle is short-legged, stands 12 to 16 in. high at the shoulder, and has a smooth coat that should be white with black and tan. It has a long, slightly domed head; brown or hazel eyes that have a gentle expression; pendulous ears; a straight and square-cut muzzle; sloping shoulders; muscular hips and thighs; and a short, slightly curved tail with a brush. In general, the beagle looks like a miniature foxhound (q.v.). The beagle, which hunts by scent, is used for tracking down small game such as rabbits, and is one of the most popular hunting dogs in the U.S.; *see* HOUND. The National Beagle Club of America sets the standard of points for show dogs.

Beagles running in characteristic hunting position.
Gaines Dog Research Center

BEAGLE EXPEDITION. *See* DARWIN, CHARLES ROBERT.

BEALE, Edward Fitzgerald (1822–93), American naval officer, courier, and pioneer, born in Washington, D.C., and educated at the United States Naval Academy. In 1846, shortly after the outbreak of the Mexican War (q.v.), Beale, was assigned to duty with the troops commanded by the American general Stephen Watts Kearny (q.v.). Kearny's troops were surrounded at San Pasquah, Calif., on Dec. 6, 1846, and Beale, accompanied by the American scout Kit Carson (*see* CARSON, CHRISTOPHER) and an Indian guide, succeeded in crossing the Mexican lines and obtaining help. Between 1847 and 1849 he made six crossings of the continent as a Federal courier. On his second crossing, made in 1848, Beale is said to have carried the first authentic report of the discovery of gold in California. He was appointed superintendent of Indian affairs for California and Nevada in 1852 and made several surveys of proposed railway and highway routes in the West.

BEAM TREE *or* **WHITEBEAM,** common name for a tree, *Sorbus* (or *Pyrus*) *aria,* growing in most parts of Europe. The red fruit is acid and astringent but becomes edible when fully ripe and is sometimes used as a constituent of beer. The tree, which has white foliage and flowers, is ornamental and is often cultivated in Europe. It reaches a height of about 20 to 40 ft. and the wood is valued for its hardness and fine grain.

BEAN, common name widely applied to many plants, most of which belong to several genera of the Pea family (Leguminosae). The seeds and pods of these plants are used for food and forage. The seeds themselves are also called beans, and are valuable as food because of their high protein content. The term bean is also applied to plants of other families, such as the Indian bean, which is a North American species of the *Catalpa* genus (*see* CATALPA) and the sacred bean, another name for both the plant and fruit of the Indian lotus (*see* LOTUS). The seeds or fruits of certain other plants, such as the coffee and the castor-bean plant (qq.v.), are also called beans.

The original bean, cultivated since prehistoric times and the one still most common in many parts of Europe, is the broad bean or horsebean, *Vicia faba,* also called the Windsor bean. Various species of the genus *Vicia* are cultivated in the United States under the name of vetch (q.v.). Most of the beans of the U.S. and the frijoles of Mexico belong in the genus *Phaseolus.* Species of the genera *Vigna* (cowpea and asparagus bean) and *Dolichos* (hyacinth bean) are also cultivated, particularly for forage. The soybean (q.v.), of the genus *Soja,* is the common bean of the Orient and has been more widely cultivated in the U.S. in recent years than native varieties of bean. Most soybeans are grown today for their oil, which is used in industrial manufacturing (*see* CHEMURGY).

The wild bean of the U.S., *Phaseolus polystachios,* is rarely cultivated. The common garden bean of the U.S. is *P. vulgaris.* Hundreds of varieties of this species are cultivated. The young pods are eaten as string, stringless, or snap beans if green, or wax or butter beans if yellowish. The seeds of the older pods are eaten as shell beans; the small variety is often called navy bean; the large and purplish variety, kidney bean.

The next most important species in the U.S. is *P. limensis,* the lima or sugar bean, regarded by some botanists as a variety of *P. lunatus,* the civet bean. Because it is drought-resistant, the tepary, *P. acutifolius,* is cultivated in Mexico and in the southwestern U.S. The scarlet runner, *P. multiflorus,* is often cultivated in Europe, as much for the attractive red flowers as for edible beans.

For cultivating, beans are divided into two groups: pole beans, vines requiring a pole for support; and bush beans, erect shrubs of low, spreading growth. Many of the species, notably *P. vulgaris,* have varieties in both groups, and the groups overlap one another. Although some of the bean plants are perennials, most of the important cultivated species are annuals, and should be sown in rich, loose, warm soil after all danger of frost is past.

The principal disease affecting beans is a form of anthracnose (q.v.), caused by a fungus, *Colletotrichum lindemuthianum.* The fungus attacks the stems, leaves, and pods of the bean. It is most visible on pods, in which it causes deep, dark pits. Infected seeds are wrinkled and discolored. The disease is more easily prevented than cured; seeds are carefully selected and care is taken not to spread the disease from one plant to another during wet weather. A rust, *Uromyces phaseoli,* is sometimes troublesome, defoliating the bean plants. It first appears as small, nearly circular, brown dots containing a

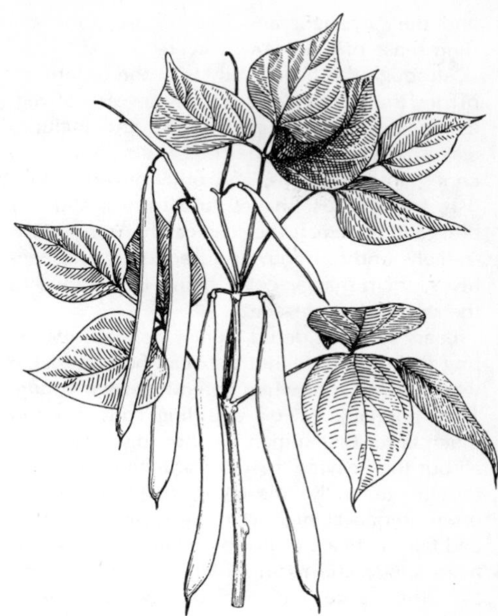

Garden bean, Phaseolus volgaris

brown powder, the spores of the fungus. Later the spots become larger and the spores black.

BEAN, Alan LaVern (1932–), American astronaut, born in Wheeler, Texas. He graduated from the University of Texas in 1955 with a B.S. degree and a commission in the United States Navy. After completing his flight training Bean was stationed at the Naval Air Station, Jacksonville, Fla., from 1956 to 1960 and at the Naval Air Test Center, Patuxent River, Md., from 1960 until 1963. He then joined the National Aeronautics and Space Administration (NASA) as an astronaut. As a member of the Apollo 12 mission in November, 1969, Commander Bean became the fourth man to set foot upon the moon, where he remained for 31½ hr. He was promoted to the rank of captain upon completion of the mission. Bean was the commander of the Skylab 2 space-station mission in 1973. *See also* ASTRONAUTICS.

BEAR, common name for carnivorous mammals comprising the family Ursidae. They are plantigrade; that is, they walk on the entire foot instead of only on the forefoot or toes as do most mammals. Bears are also characterized by the looseness of their skin, the length of the coarse fur of their coats, the short tail, and the comparative shortness of their legs. Most bears have broad, massive heads, and all have narrow jaws and long, sharp teeth. Their eyes are small and their eyesight and hearing are poor, but their sense of smell is very keen.

Although the bear family is in the order Carnivora, the diet of bears actually consists of vegetable as well as animal matter and includes leaves, roots, bulbs, berries, fruits, nuts, and cones; insects, snails, and other invertebrates; fish, frogs, toads, snakes, and turtles; and any birds and mammals they can catch. Bears are extremely fond of honey and frequently raid beehives, their shaggy coats being impervious to the stings of the insects.

Bears are considered clumsy animals, preferring flight to battle, but they can be formidable when cornered or when defending their young. They normally have a shuffling gait, can run much faster than a man for short distances, and all but the heaviest species can climb trees. Although generally diurnal in habit, bears are often abroad at night. During spring, summer, and fall the bears of northern latitudes have no fixed abode and roam widely. In winter, however, they retire into caves or holes and spend most of their time in deep sleep. Frequently they are partly enclosed by a wall of ice formed by the frozen moisture of their breath. This deep sleep is not considered hibernation because body temperature, pulse rate, and other physiological manifestations are not slowed down as much as in true hibernation.

Female bears usually give birth during the winter to a litter of one to four (usually two) extremely small cubs, weighing less than 1 lb. each.

Bears are not found in Africa, Australia, the Malagasy Republic, and the continent of Antarctica. The koala (q.v.), a marsupial indigenous to Australia, and resembling a toy teddy bear, is called a bear.

Bears resemble one another closely in their structure, appearance, and habits, and they were formerly all included in a single genus, *Ursus.* The scientific names of the various genera in present-day classification are derived from the Latin word *ursus* or the Greek word *arktos,* both meaning "bear".

Polar Bear. This species, *Ursus maritimus,* inhabits all of the arctic regions. Polar bears vary from almost pure white to yellow or dirty gray; the nose and claws are always black; they are slimmer than other bears, and have a long neck and pointed head. They eat mainly seals and, in the summer, fish, as well as large quantities of marine grasses and other plants. They are expert swimmers and have been seen more than 100 mi. from land. Polar bears are also at home on the ice, where the long hair on the soles of their feet enables them to obtain comparatively firm footing. These bears are up to 8 ft. long.

Brown Bear. The most widespread and varied group comprises the brown bears, all of which are classified as one species, *Ursus arctos,* and which once inhabited the whole of Eurasia north of the Himalaya, and the western third of North America from Alaska to Mexico. As their name suggests, most are brown, but grizzled forms are found in northeastern Asia and northwestern America. The famous "grizzlies", which once roamed the western prairies along with the bison, are brown bears. In addition, there are pale-cream and silvery-gray bears, such as the Isabelline bear of the Himalaya, and even a jet-black one, also classified as a brown bear. The American grizzly bear, one of the largest and most powerful of the brown bears, usually has a brownish-yellow coat. The largest terrestrial carnivorous mammal extant is a form of grizzly bear called the Kodiak bear, *U. middendorffi,* which may be 9 ft. long and stands 4 ft. high at the shoulder. These bears were discovered on the island of Kodiak, off the southern coast of Alaska, in 1895. Their principal food is salmon, and they sometimes weigh as much as 1600 lb. The Kodiak bear is golden brown. Large related bears inhabit other islands of this region, and the mainland of Alaska, in northeastern Siberia, and Kamchatka. The smallest brown bear probably is a subspecies native to Syria. The bears of Europe, found mainly in Scandinavia and in parts of the Alps, the Carpathians, and the Caucasus, are slightly larger. The common European bear, *U. arctos,* which was found in the British Isles until the 12th century, may weigh as much as 800 lb. Grizzly bears weighing over 1000 lb. are known, but despite their reputation for fierceness these animals do not appear to be any more aggressive than other bears. There are bears in many parts of the U.S.S.R.; a large bear, *U. pruinosus,* native to Tibet, probably represents a separate species. Brown-colored bears, belonging to the black group, are found in the Himalaya Mts. Like the Syrian bears, they may have a white mark on the chest.

Black Bear. This wholly North American species, *Euarctos americanus,* may be distinguished by the slight convexity of the muzzle when seen in profile. The black bears vary from jet black, with slight graying of the muzzle, to rich reddish brown and all intermediate shades of brown. A single litter may have different colors, however, with one of the twins in a litter being black and the other brown. A chestnut-colored variety of black bear is commonly called cinnamon bear. The latter was once scattered over al-

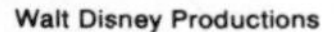

Walt Disney Productions

National Audubon Society

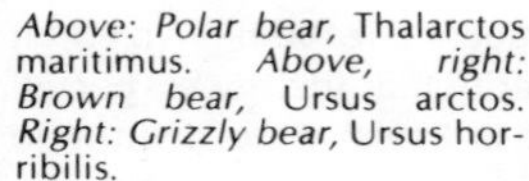

Above: Polar bear, Thalarctos maritimus. *Above, right: Brown bear,* Ursus arctos. *Right: Grizzly bear,* Ursus horribilis.

CBS

most all of North America, and its range even overlapped that of the brown or dish-faced bears in the far Northwest. After a drastic decrease in numbers following European settlement of the continent, the black bears recovered, and now live throughout a wide belt extending from Maine to Florida in well-wooded areas. Adults weigh from 400 to 800 lb. and are powerful creatures for their size. They consume almost everything edible in season, including skunk cabbage and pine cones, and they build up fat layers in the fall. Most black bears sleep during the winter.

Spectacled Bear. The spectacled bear, *Tremarctos,* is found in the Andes of Chile and Bolivia, as well as in Venezuela, Peru, and Ecuador. It is medium-sized and has a shaggy, black coat, yellow "spectacles" and usually a cream-colored muzzle, throat, and chest.

Sun Bear. This species, *Helarctos malayanus,* is found from Szechwan Province, China, south through Burma, Indochina, and Malaya to Borneo. The coat of the sun bear is sleek, short, and black, with an irregular white or yellow mark on the chest, and the muzzle is light. The sun bear is a tree climber. Because of its short, broad face and comic antics, strangers may believe that it has a gentle disposition but, on the contrary, it is dangerous.

Asiatic Black Bear. This species, *Selenarctos thibetanus,* known also as the moon bear, lives throughout the Himalaya and associated ranges from Iran to upper Assam, and in China, Japan, and the islands of Taiwan and Hainan. It is a large animal with a black, shaggy coat and a pronounced white V on its chest. The upper lip is usually white, as are the short claws, and the large ears are set low on the sides of the head. These bears grow to 5 ft. in length, are heavy-bodied, and carry much fat in winter. The Asiatic black bear is omnivorous. Apparently it is more indifferent to humans than are most other bears.

Sloth Bear. This species, *Melursus ursinus,* is found throughout the tropical forests of India and Ceylon. It has a very long, slender snout, and only four upper incisors instead of six. The fur is black, very long, and shaggy; the claws are long; and there is usually a white mark on the chest. The sloth bear spends much time in trees, but it is a poor climber, adapted mainly to hanging from limbs. It eats largely honey, fruit, and insects.

Extinct Bears. The fossilized remains of a considerable number of bears and bearlike animals dating back to the Miocene epoch (q.v.) have been found. Apparently the bears evolved from an extinct group of Carnivora known as the cynodonts. Fossilized bears occur in the Miocene strata of India, China, Italy, France, and Pennsylvania, and along with such remains are often found those of similar creatures, with very short muzzles, belonging to the group called Arctotherium. The best-known extinct bear is undoubtedly the cave bear, found in cave deposits throughout Eurasia and North America. This bear was larger than the greatest living brown bear, had a convex muzzle, and one less pair of upper teeth. The cave bear probably was not specifically a cave dweller; it doubtless retired to caves for occasional shelter, just as extant bears do.

BEARBAITING, former sport consisting of a contest between a bear chained to a stake and a pack of dogs. The bear was almost invariably torn to pieces by the dogs. In England the sport was known as early as the 12th century, and during the reign of Queen Elizabeth I (q.v.), it achieved such popularity that the queen herself attended bearbaitings. Bears were kept and publicly baited in public arenas called bear gardens. Bearbaiting and a similar sport, bullbaiting (q.v.), were both prohibited by Parliament in 1835.

BEARBERRY, common name for several unrelated plants with berries that are reputedly eaten by bears. The name most commonly refers to plants of the genus *Arctostaphylos* of the Heath family (Ericaceae), particularly the evergreen shrub *A. uva-ursi.* A native of northern Eurasia, introduced and now common in the northern United States and Canada, it is low and trailing and has leathery, green leaves, white to pink flowers, and red berries. It has been cultivated in northern gardens as a groundcover plant. *A. alpina,* the black or alpine bearberry, is a Canadian plant with deciduous, wrinkled leaves and black berries; it sometimes grows as far south as the northern U.S.

BEARD, heavy growth of hair on the chin, cheeks, and adjacent parts of the face of the adult male. The word may also refer to certain beardlike growths on birds and animals. Among human beings, usually only men have beards, although abnormal instances of bearded women occur. The beard generally begins to grow during puberty, when the texture is soft and downy. In maturity the beard, often the same color as the hair on top of the head, is, as a rule, more wiry. The amount of facial hair varies among the races of man. For example, the beard is especially luxuriant among Caucasian peoples, whereas among the North American Indians it is markedly thin. In ancient times among many peoples the beard was considered a sign of strength and manhood; it was highly prized and removal was regarded as a degrading punishment. The early Egyptians, however, usually shaved their beards, except in time of mourning. Among the Jews an unkempt, neglected beard was a sign of grief. In Greece all men wore beards until the 4th century B.C., when the Macedonian conqueror Alexander III (q.v.), known as the Great, ordered his soldiers to shave as a precaution against being seized by the beard in battle.

Shaving became popular among the Romans about the same time. The Roman general Scipio Africanus (*see under* SCIPIO), was the first Roman to shave every day, according to the Roman historian Pliny the Elder (*see under* PLINY). The beard was popular again among Romans during the 2d and 3rd centuries A.D. The ancient Germans considered a clean-shaven face evidence of servitude. In France, beards were fashionable until Louis XIII (q.v.) became King of France as a child in 1610; his beardlessness brought the clean-shaven face into vogue. About the beginning of the 18th century a similar attitude developed in Spain on the accession of Philip V (q.v.), who was unable to grow a beard. In 1705 a law was passed by the Russian emperor Peter the Great (*see* PETER I) making shaving compulsory. The law was not always observed, however, and those who persisted in wearing a beard were taxed in proportion to their rank.

A similar tax was imposed in England for a while during the reign of Henry VIII (q.v.), but about 1535 Henry restored the beard to fashion by wearing one himself. Beards were immensely popular during the reign (1558–1603) of Elizabeth I (q.v.), Queen of England, particularly among those who moved in court circles; the extreme styles in beard trims and the foppish behavior of the wearers frequently evoked criticism from the Puritans (q.v.). The fantastic fashions of the Elizabethan age were modified in time, and by the reign of Charles I (q.v.), in the second quarter of the 17th century, the Vandyke beard, a relatively conservative style of trim, was in favor. After the accession of Charles II (q.v.) to the English throne in 1660, beards became less fashionable in that country. During the 18th century few British wore beards, and even a moustache was regarded as the mark of a foreigner. Toward the close of the century, as wigs went out of fashion, beards again began to come into vogue. The dictates of fashion brought a large number of beard styles successively into favor. Most men wore at least a moustache, and a large minority wore beards of the widest possible range of styles and sizes. After World War I (q.v.) the custom of wearing beards largely disappeared in the Western world, except among certain Orthodox Jews who strictly observed the Biblical prohibition against cutting the hair, and among those who wore beards to proclaim their freedom from convention. In the 1960's beards again became popular, at first as a mark of unconventional taste and opinions.

Charles Austin Beard MacMillan Co.

BEARD, name of two American historians, husband and wife, who were also active in social causes.

Charles Austin Beard (1874–1948), educator and historian, born in Knightstown, Ind., and educated at DePauw and Columbia universities. He was a professor of political science at Columbia University from 1907 to 1917, when he resigned to protest the dismissal, during World War I, of a number of professors at Columbia who held pacifist views. In 1918 Beard helped found the New School for Social Research, an institution for adult education in New York City. In his teaching and writing he stressed the part played by economic forces in the development of American institutions. His many writings include *The Economic Interpretation of the Constitution* (1913), *The Economic Origins of Jeffersonian Democracy* (1915), *Public Policy and the General Welfare* (1941), and *American Foreign Policy in the Making, 1932–1940* (1946). He also collaborated on several books with his wife, Mary Ritter Beard.

Mary Ritter Beard (1876–1958), historian and feminist, born in Indianapolis, Ind., and educated at DePauw University. Until the ratification in 1920 of the Nineteenth Amendment to the Constitution of the United States (q.v.) she was prominent in the woman-suffrage movement; *see* WOMAN SUFFRAGE. She helped to organize women textile workers in New York City during part of this period, and after 1915 she traveled extensively in Europe and the Far East with her husband. The role of women in history and their rights are themes of a number of her works, which include *Woman's Work in Municipalities* (1915) and *Woman as a Force in History* (1946). Some of Mrs. Beard's most important writing was done in collaboration with her husband; among works in this category are *History of the United States* (1921) and *The American Spirit* (1942).

BEARD, Daniel Carter (1850–1941), American artist, author, and naturalist, born in Cincinnati, Ohio, and trained at the Art Students League in New York City. He contributed illustrations to leading magazines, and he also illustrated many books, the most notable of which is *A Connecticut Yankee at King Arthur's Court* (1889) by the American writer Mark Twain (*see* SAMUEL LANGHORNE CLEMENS). In 1905–06 Beard edited the periodical *Recreation.* Enthusiastic about outdoor life, he founded the first scouting society for boys in the United States. Known as the Sons of Daniel Boone, the organization became part of the Boy Scouts of America (q.v.) after the British Boy Scout movement reached the United States. Beard later became national commissioner of the Boy Scouts of America. Among his writings are *American Boys' Handy Book* (1882; 1903), *Boy Pioneers and Sons of Daniel Boone* (1909), and *Do It Yourself* (1925). He was also an associate editor of *Boys' Life* magazine.

BEARDSLEY, Aubrey Vincent (1872–98), English artist, whose sensitive, highly imaginative style and hedonistic, occasionally macabre subject matter were representative of the late 19th-century European artistic movement called decadent, or fin de siècle. In his short life (his productive career spanned only six years), Beardsley still managed to achieve a reputation as one of the most innovative illustrators in England.

Beardsley was born in Brighton on Aug. 24, 1872. In 1891 he attended evening classes at the Westminster School of Art in London for a few months. Essentially, however, he taught himself, learning to draw and paint by copying the work of the masters exhibited in the National Gallery. By the time he was twenty, he had developed his skill so far that he was already executing art commissions. His work is notable for its large areas of black and white, its hard, curving lines, rich ornamentation, and disregard of perspective, balance, and proportion. Recognizable influences include the great Japanese printmakers and the pre-Raphaelite painters. Because of the fantastic and occasionally erotic nature of his illustrations, they aroused great controversy.

Beardsley was successively art editor of the celebrated *Yellow Book* (1894–95) and *The Savoy* (1896), both of which featured his pictures. Among other works he illustrated were Sir Thomas Malory's *Morte d'Arthur* (1893–94), Oscar Wilde's *Salome* (1894), *The Works of Edgar Allan Poe* (1894–95), Aristophanes' *Lysistrata* (1896), and Ben Jonson's *Volpone* (1898). He also designed posters for the theater and book trade and wrote fiction, including *Under the Hill* (1904). By 1896 a recurrence of tuberculosis, which had afflicted him over the years, made him an invalid. He died on March 16, 1898, in Menton, France. Long after his death his

"Salome with the Head of John the Baptist", pen-and-ink drawing by Aubrey Beardsley for Salome *by Oscar Wilde.* Princeton University Library

distinctive style continued to influence book illustration and poster design in Europe and the U.S.

BEAR, GREAT and **BEAR, LITTLE.** *See* DIPPER, BIG; DIPPER, LITTLE.

BEARING, mechanical device for decreasing friction in a machine in which a moving part bears—that is, slides or rolls while exerting force—on another part. Usually in a bearing the support must allow the moving part one type of motion, for example, rotation, while preventing it from moving in any other way, for example, sidewise. The commonest bearings are found at the rigid supports of rotating shafts where friction is greatest.

Bearings were invented early in history; when the wheel was invented, it was mounted on an axle, and where wheel and axle touched was a bearing. Such early bearings had surfaces of wood or leather lubricated with animal fat. The bearing system used in modern railroad cars is essentially the same, though wheel and axle are made of steel. Two types of bearings are used in railroad cars. The modern antifriction roller bearing is presently used on all passenger cars and a large number of freight cars. The other type of bearing is lined with Babbitt metal and lubricated with a petroleum derivative.

Types. Modern bearings have arbitrarily been designated as friction bearings and antifriction bearings. The former comprises sleeve or journal bearings; the latter, ball and roller bearings. Friction and antifriction are misleading terms. Neither type of bearing is completely frictionless, and both are highly efficient in reducing friction. A large, modern aircraft engine, for example, has more than one hundred bearings, including both types; yet the total power consumed in overcoming bearing friction is less than 1 percent of the total power output of the engine.

Sleeve bearings, also called journal bearings, are simpler than antifriction bearings in construction but more complex in theory and operation. The shaft supported by the bearing is called the journal, and the outer portion, the sleeve. If journal and sleeve are both made of steel, the bearing surfaces, even if well lubricated, may grab or pick up, that is, rip, small pieces of metal from each other. The sleeves of

Cross section of a ball bearing.
Hyatt Co. (Div. of General Motors)

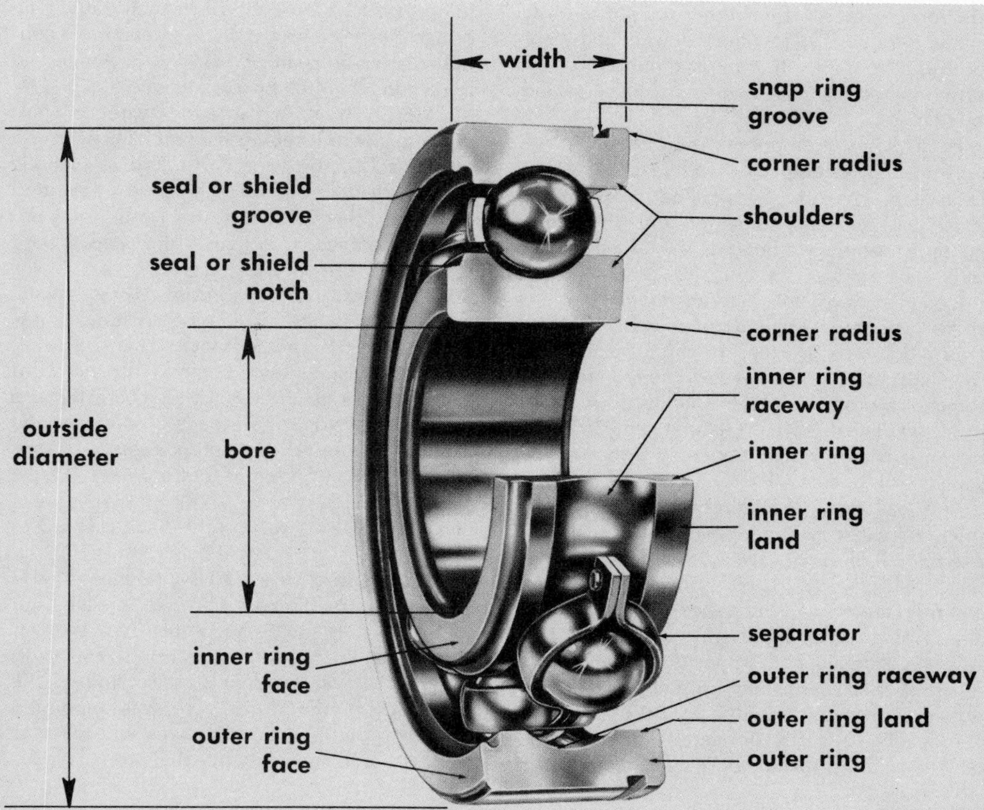

most bearings are therefore lined with brass, bronze, or Babbitt metal. Aluminum and certain other nonferrous metals and materials also provide suitable bearing surfaces against steel. Sleeve bearings are generally pressure-lubricated through a hole in the journal or from the housing that contains the bearing. The sleeve is often grooved to distribute the oil properly over the bearing surface.

Typical clearance (difference between the diameters of journal and sleeve) is nominally 0.001 in. for every 1 in. of journal diameter. When the journal is rotating, it may be about 0.0001 in. from the sleeve at the side with the greatest load. The journal is thus supported on an extremely thin film of oil, and the two parts have no actual contact. As the rotational speed increases, other variables remaining constant, the oil film becomes thicker, so that the friction increases in less than direct proportion to the speed. Conversely, at lower speeds the oil film is thinner if other factors are unchanged. At extremely low speeds, however, the film may rupture and the two pieces come into contact. Therefore, friction is high when the machine is started in motion, and the bearing may fail if high stresses are put on it during starting. Antifriction bearings, on the other hand, have low starting friction. A locomotive weighing hundreds of thousands of pounds, mounted on antifriction bearings, has been started and pulled by two men.

For all types of motion except rotation, a friction bearing is generally used. A poppet valve, for example, must be constrained to operate in a straight back-and-forth motion. The valve guide is essentially a bearing; it is usually made of bronze.

Jewel bearings are used to mount minute shafts such as those found in fine watches. They are friction-type bearings in which the ends of the shafts are mounted in extremely hard substances. Synthetic sapphires and rubies have now completely replaced natural gems in jewel bearings. The bearing is lubricated with a microscopic drop of fine oil.

In a ball bearing a number of balls rotate freely between an inner ring, which is rigidly fixed to a rotating shaft, and an outer ring, which is rigidly fixed to a support. Both balls and rings are made of hardened alloy steel, usually finished to extremely fine tolerances. The balls are generally held in position by a cage or separator that keeps them properly spaced and prevents them from rubbing against each other. The bearing is usually lubricated with grease or oil. The bearings that support a gyroscope (q.v.) in an instrument may be so tiny that the individual balls are barely visible. A bearing that supports the shaft of a large turbine may have balls about 6 in. in diameter.

A roller bearing is similar to a ball bearing, except that small steel cylinders, or rollers, are substituted for the balls. A needle bearing is a roller bearing in which the rollers are extremely long and thin. An ordinary roller bearing may have twenty rollers, each twice as long as it is wide, whereas a needle bearing may have one hundred needles, each ten times as long as it is wide. Needle bearings are particularly useful when space is limited.

BEAR MOUNTAIN, peak about 1314 ft. above sea level, on the W. bank of the Hudson R., in S. New York State, about 45 miles N. of New York City. The mountain is the center of a resort area with facilities for both winter and summer sports. From the tower at its summit the skyline of New York City is visible in clear weather. On the surrounding park grounds, which are crossed by the Appalachian Trail (q.v.), are a hotel, amusement areas, and a wharf for Hudson R. sightseeing boats. From the slope of Bear Mt. to Anthony's Nose, a hill across the river, runs the Bear Mountain Bridge, a 2257-ft.-long toll bridge for motor and pedestrian traffic. The bridge reaches a height of 155 ft. and has a central suspension span of 1632 ft., the longest in the world when the bridge was opened in 1924.

BEATIFICATION, an inferior degree of canonization introduced in the 12th century. It is a solemn act by the pope in the Roman Catholic Church, declaring a deceased person beatified (with the title "Blessed"), and worthy of a degree of homage. It is generally a step toward canonization (q.v.).

BEATITUDES (Lat. *beatitudo,* "blessedness"), in the New Testament, the nine opening clauses of the Sermon on the Mount (Matt. 5:3–11). Each of the statements begins with the word "Blessed". The Beatitudes list the characteristics that Jesus Christ (q.v.) expected of those who wished to follow Him. Another passage recording the Sermon on the Mount is found in Luke 6:20–49.

BEATLES, THE. *See* POPULAR MUSIC: *The 20th Century.*

BEATON, David *or* **BETHUNE, David** (1494–1546), Scottish Roman Catholic prelate and statesman, born in Fife, and educated at the universities of Saint Andrews, Glasgow, and Paris. In 1519 he was resident for Scotland at the French court and in 1528 he was appointed Keeper of the Privy Seal. He was sent twice as ambassador to France, to negotiate the two marriages of James V (q.v.), King of Scotland. In 1537 Beaton was appointed bishop of Mirepoix, in Foix, by Francis I (q.v.), King of France, and the following year the pope made him a cardinal. In 1539 Beaton succeeded his uncle as archbishop of St. Andrews and primate of Scotland and soon began a persecution of the Protestants. He induced the king to institute a Court of Inquisition (*see* INQUISITION, THE), to inquire after heretics in all parts of the kingdom.

When James died in 1542, Beaton produced a forged will of the late king appointing himself one of the regents of the kingdom during the minority of the infant Mary, Queen of Scots (q. v.), but the document was rejected by the nobility. Beaton was imprisoned in 1543 but was soon released. He then induced the regent, James Hamilton, 2nd Earl of Arran (d. 1575), to oppose the subjugation of Scotland by Henry VIII (q.v.), King of England, and to denounce the reformed religion. After the coronation of Mary in 1543, Beaton was again admitted to the council, and was appointed chancellor. He was assassinated in his castle by the followers of the Scottish reformer and martyr George Wishart (q.v.); Beaton had previously ordered the execution of Wishart.

BEATRICE, city in Nebraska, and county seat of Gage Co., on the Big Blue R., about 36 miles S. of Lincoln. Beatrice is a trade, industrial, and railroad center. Manufactures include hardware, wood products, and farm implements. Nearby, on the site of land first claimed under the Homestead Act of 1862, is the Homestead National Monument of America, which was established in 1937, and covers approximately 163 acres. Pop. (1960) 12,132; (1970) 12,389.

BEATRICE PORTINARI (1266–90), Italian noblewoman, born in Florence. According to most literary historians, she was the Beatrice whom the Italian poet Dante Alighieri (q.v.) loved and celebrated in his *La Vita Nuova* ("The New Life", about 1292) and *La Divina Commedia* ("The Divine Comedy", 1320). Dante first saw Beatrice when she was about eight years old and he was nine. He saw her only at rare intervals thereafter, and she ultimately married a Florentine nobleman, but from that first meeting until her death Beatrice was the object of his love. After her death Dante's feeling for her assumed a mystical form, and in his later work she is used as a symbol for theological concepts. *See* DIVINE COMEDY, THE.

BEATTIE, James (1735–1803), British poet and essayist, born in Laurencekirk, Scotland, and educated at Marischal College. In 1760 he became professor of moral philosophy at Marischal College. He had written several volumes of verse before his *Essay on Truth,* a critical attack on the rationalist theories of the British philosopher and historian David Hume (q.v.), appeared in 1770. Among other works by Beattie are *The Minstrel* (1771–74), a poem on the progress of genius; and *The Elements of Moral Science* (1790–93).

BEATTY, David, 1st Earl of the North Sea and of Brooksby (1871–1936), British admiral, born in County Wexford, Ireland. He entered the British navy in 1884, and served on a gunboat in the Nile R. from 1896 to 1898, and in Chinese waters in 1900, during the Boxer Rebellion (q.v.). In 1910 he became a rear admiral; from 1911 to 1913 he was naval secretary to the first lord of the admiralty, the British statesman Sir Winston Leonard Spencer Churchill (q.v.); and in 1913 he became the commander of the Battle Cruiser Squadron of the navy. In World War I, naval forces under his command fought at the battles of Helgoland Bight (*see* HELGOLAND BIGHT, BATTLE OF), Dogger Bank (q.v.), and Jutland (*see* JUTLAND, BATTLE OF). In 1916 he became commander in chief of the Grand Fleet; after the Treaty of Versailles (*see* VERSAILLES, TREATY OF) was signed in 1919 he received the surrender of the German navy. He became admiral of the fleet in 1919 and was first sea lord of the admiralty from 1919 to 1927. Beatty was knighted in 1914 and became an earl in 1919.

BEAU BRUMMELL. *See* BRUMMELL, GEORGE BRYAN.

BEAUFORT, Margaret, Countess of Richmond and Derby (1443–1509), prominent member of the English royal house of Lancaster (*see* LANCASTER, HOUSE OF) and patroness of learning. In 1455 she married Edmund Tudor, Earl of Richmond (*see under* TUDOR). Henry Tudor, the son of Margaret and Edmund, became Henry VII (q.v.), King of England, in 1485 at the end of the Wars of the Roses, the series of wars between the rival houses of Lancaster and York; *see* ROSES, WARS OF THE. In 1486 Margaret was instrumental in uniting the two houses by helping to arrange a marriage between Henry VII and Elizabeth of York (1465–1503), claimant to the throne as the eldest surviving daughter of Edward IV (q.v.), King of England. Margaret Beaufort was a patron of William Caxton (q.v.), the first English printer, and of Wynkyn de Worde (d. 1534?), Caxton's successor. She established divinity professorships at the universities of Oxford and Cambridge. The "Lady Margaret" professorship at Cambridge is the oldest in the university. In 1505 she founded Christ's College, and in 1508, Saint John's College, both at Cambridge.

BEAUFORT SEA, arm of the Arctic Ocean, bordered on the E. and S. by N.W. Canada and on the S.W. by N.E. Alaska. It is covered with ice floes for most of the year, but navigation is usually possible along the Alaska coast during the late summer. The sea receives the Mackenzie R. in the S. Extensive petroleum deposits are located below the S. and S.W. coasts and offshore. Named for the British naval officer Sir Francis Beaufort (1774–1857), the sea was explored by the Canadian-born American explorer Vilhjalmur Stefansson (q.v.) in 1914.

BEAUFORT WIND SCALE. *See* WIND.

BEAUHARNAIS, name of two members of a French family notable as the wife and adopted son of Napoléon Bonaparte, who subsequently proclaimed himself Napoleon I (q.v.), Emperor of the French; *see* FRANCE: *History*.

Joséphine de Beauharnais, (1763–1814), born Marie Joséphine Rose Tascher de la Pagerie in Martinique. In 1779 she married the French army officer Alexandre, Vicomte de Beauharnais (1760–94). Her husband was sympathetic to the republican cause in France, but in 1793 he was forced to resign as general of the army of the Rhine because he was a nobleman. During the Reign of Terror he was accused of counterrevolutionary activities, and in 1794 was guillotined (*see* FRENCH REVOLUTION). Two years later Joséphine became the first wife of the French soldier and statesman Napoléon Bonaparte, and in 1804, when he became Emperor as Napoleon I, she became Empress of France. Napoleon divorced her in 1809. By her marriage to Beauharnais Josephine was the mother of Eugène de Beauharnais and of Hortense de Beauharnais (1783–1837), later the wife of Louis Bonaparte (*see under* BONAPARTE) and the mother of Napoleon III (q.v.).

Eugène de Beauharnais (1781–1824), French army officer and nobleman, born in Paris, son of Alexandre, Vicomte de Beauharnais, and of Josephine de Beauharnais. After his mother married Napoleon Bonaparte, Beauharnais rose rapidly to the highest military rank, and in 1805, after the establishment of the empire under Napoleon I, he was made a prince of France and viceroy of Italy. In 1806, the same year Napoleon adopted him and made him heir to the kingdom of Italy, Beauharnais married Princess Amalie Auguste (1788–1851), of Bavaria. Shortly afterward, he was created prince of Venice. His military talents were displayed in the wars against Austria, and in the retreat from Moscow, where his judgment saved the French army from total destruction; *see* NAPOLEONIC WARS. Napoleon then sent him to command the French forces in Italy. Beauharnais took no part in the Treaty of Fontainebleau in 1814 but the Congress of Vienna (*see* VIENNA, CONGRESS OF) in 1815 granted him compensation for his Italian possessions and for the principality of Eichstatt, in Bavaria (now in West Germany). His eldest son, Auguste de Beauharnais, Duke of Leuchtenberg (1810–35), married Maria II (1819–53), Queen of Portugal. Another son, Maximilien de Beauharnais (1817–52), who succeeded his brother as duke of Leuchtenberg, married Maria Nikolaevna (1819–76) Grand Duchess of Russia.

BEAUMARCHAIS, Pierre Augustin Caron de (1732–99), French playwright, born in Paris. The son of a watchmaker he followed this trade himself and in 1754 became watchmaker to Louis XV (q.v.), King of France. Caron also taught the harp to the daughters of the king and became a court favorite. Young Caron married the widow of a court official in 1756 and took the name Beaumarchais. He bought the office of secretary to the king, which made him a nobleman. Subsequently he was employed in confidential missions by Louis XV and Louis XVI (q.v.). During the American Revolution (q.v.), Beaumarchais was instrumental in bringing about French secret aid to the American colonies before France openly declared war against Great Britain in 1777. He equipped a fleet of forty ships to trade with the American revolutionists, and influenced decisively the success of American arms.

Pierre de Beaumarchais

Beaumarchais first came to public attention as a writer through his *Mémoires* (1773–74), a series of witty attacks on judicial injustice. His literary fame, however, rests on his two comedies, *Le Barbier de Seville* ("The Barber of Seville", 1775) and *Le Mariage de Figaro* ("The Marriage of Figaro", 1784). In these plays Beaumarchais satirized the French ruling class, reflecting the growing dissatisfaction of the people with the nobility in the years preceding the French Revolution. The plays were later made into popular operas, *Le Nozze di Figaro* ("The Marriage of Figaro", 1786) by the Austrian composer Wolfgang Amadeus Mozart and the Italian poet Lorenzo DaPonte, and *Il Barbiere di Siviglia* ("The Barber of Seville", 1816) by the Italian composer Gioacchino Antonio Rossini (qq.v.) with libretto by the Italian Cesare Sterbini.

BEAUMONT, city in Texas, and county seat of Jefferson Co., on the W. bank of the Neches R., about 80 miles N.E. of Houston. Beaumont, connected to the Gulf of Mexico by a canal, is an important transportation, distribution, and industrial center for the surrounding region, which produces rice, oil, cattle, and lumber. Oil refining is the most important industry in the city. Other industries include the manufacture of chemicals, foodstuffs, machinery, transportation equipment, and paper. South of Beaumont is Spindletop oil field, discovered in 1901. Beaumont was settled before 1835, and was incorporated as a city in 1881. Pop. (1960) 119,175; (1970) 115,919.

BEAUMONT, Francis. *See* BEAUMONT AND FLETCHER.

BEAUMONT, William (1785–1853), American surgeon, born in Lebanon, Conn. He is noted for his discoveries about the physiology of digestion, made during his observations in the case of Alexis Saint-Martin. In 1822 St. Martin, a young Canadian trapper, received a gunshot wound through the stomach. Beaumont, then a United States Army surgeon stationed at Fort Mackinac, Mich., restored St. Martin to health, but part of his stomach protruded outside his body and healed there, covered only by a flap of skin that was easily lifted. By lifting the flap, Beaumont was able to observe the process of digestion and was the first to obtain samples of gastric contents at various stages of digestion. His observations and experiments, published in 1833, are regarded as the greatest single contribution to the knowledge of gastric digestion.

BEAUMONT AND FLETCHER, literary partnership of two English playwrights, **Francis Beaumont** (1584–1616) and **John Fletcher** (1579–1625). Beaumont was born in Leicestershire, and educated at the University of Oxford. Fletcher was born in Rye, Sussex, and educated at the University of Cambridge. From about 1606 to 1616, when Beaumont died, the two collaborated on many plays, the exact number of which is in dispute, on a masque, and on some poetry. Their plays are characterized by ingenious plots, diversified characters, and realistic dialogue. Their comedies, witty and sophisticated, foreshadow the licentious comedies of the Restoration (*see* DRAMA: *British Drama*).

Beaumont surpassed Fletcher in ability to write tragic scenes, construct plots, and express deep emotion. Fletcher was the better writer of comic scenes and of lyric blank verse. Notable among the plays they wrote together are *The Maid's Tragedy* (produced about 1611), *Philaster* (produced about 1608), and *A King and No King* (1611). Beaumont probably wrote one play alone, *The Knight of the Burning Pestle* (written about 1607), and was responsible for most of *The Woman Hater* (1607). Fletcher wrote several plays alone, including *The Faithful Shepherdess* (published about 1609), and several plays with collaborators other than Beaumont. Among these plays were, with the English playwright Philip Massinger (q.v.), *The Spanish Curate* (1622) and, probably, with William Shakespeare, *Henry VIII* (1613) and *The Two Noble Kinsmen* (1613). *See* ENGLISH LITERATURE: *Renaissance Drama and Prose.*

BEAUREGARD, Pierre Gustave Toutant de (1818–93), American soldier, born in New Orleans, La., and educated at the United States Military Academy. He entered the Engineer Corps as a second lieutenant in 1838. Between 1846 and 1848 he served with distinction in the Mexican War (q.v.) and afterward was superintendent of engineering works on the lower Mississippi R. and the Gulf of Mexico. After Louisiana seceded from the Union in February of 1861, Beauregard became a brigadier general, and later a full general, of the Confederate Army. On April 12, 1861, he directed the bombardment of Fort Sumter in Charleston, S.C., the first action of the Civil War (*see* CIVIL WAR, THE AMERICAN). He was second in command at the first Battle of Bull Run (*see* BULL RUN, BATTLE OF), in Virginia on July 21, 1861. In 1862, during the Battle of Shiloh (*see* SHILOH, BATTLE OF), in Tennessee, he was second in command to the Confederate general Albert Sidney Johnston (q.v.) and assumed full command when the latter was killed. He defended Charleston against the attacks of the Union naval officers Samuel Francis du Pont (*see under* DU PONT) and John Adolphus Dahlgren (1809–70) in 1863, and in 1864 he assumed command of the Department of North Carolina. On May 16, 1864, his troops defeated the Union forces led by General Benjamin Franklin Butler (q.v.) at Drury's Bluff (now Drewrys Bluff), Va.

Beauregard was president of the New Orleans, Jackson, and Mississippi Railroad from 1865 to 1870, became adjutant general of Louisiana in 1878, and for several years was manager of the Louisiana State lottery.

BEAUX, Cecilia (1863–1942), American painter, born in Philadelphia, Pa., and trained in that city and in Paris. She was especially well known for her portraits, particularly of women and children, and was the recipient of awards and medals from a number of societies and institutions. Her works include "Last Days of Infancy" and "A New England Woman" (both, Pennsylvania Academy of Fine Arts, Philadelphia), "Ernesta" (Metropolitan Museum of Art, New York), and "Portrait of Mrs. Dupont" (Boston Museum).

BEAUX-ARTS, ÉCOLE DES. *See* ÉCOLE DES BEAUX-ARTS.

BEAVER, common name for a mammal of the family Castoridae in the order of rodents. The family contains but a single genus, *Castor,* with but two species: *C. canadensis,* found in the New World, and *C. fiber,* found in the Old. The two species differ chiefly in the shape of the nasal bones, and are so much alike that some authorities consider them to be varieties of the same species. The average adult beaver weighs about 35 lbs., but specimens as heavy as 90 lbs. have been found.

American beaver, Castor canadensis

Ed Cesar – National Audubon Society

The beaver is usually about 2½ ft. in length. It stands under 1 ft. in height, and the broad, flat, scaly tail is about 10 in. long. The body is plump, the back arched, the neck thick, the hind feet webbed, and all the digits clawed. The fur is usually reddish-brown above, and lighter or grayish below. The eyes are small and the nostrils closable. The skull is massive, with marked ridges for fixing the muscles which work the jaws. The two front teeth on either jaw are like those of other rodents, wearing away more rapidly behind so as to leave a sharp, enameled chisel edge. With these the beaver can cut down large trees; it usually selects trees 2 to 8 in. in diameter, but can fell trees with diameters as large as 30 in. Beavers have a pair of anal scent glands called castors, that secrete a musklike substance called castoreum.

Characteristics. Beavers are social animals. In areas where food is abundant and the locality secluded, the number of families in a beaver community is rather large. The so-called beaver lodge is a unique structure. Three distinct kinds exist, their differences depending on whether they are built on islands, on the banks of ponds, or on the shores of lakes. The island lodge consists of a central chamber, with its floor a little above the level of the water, and with two entrances. One of these, the "wood entrance", is a straight incline rising from the water, opening into the floor of the hut. The other approach, the "beaver entrance", is more abrupt in its descent to the water. The lodge itself is an oven-shaped house of sticks, grass, and moss, woven together and plastered with mud, increasing gradually in size with year after year of repair and elaboration. The room inside may measure 8 ft. in diameter, and 2 to 3 ft. in height. The floor is carpeted with bark, grass, and wood chips, and there are sometimes special storerooms adjoining. The pond lodge is built either a short way back from the edge of the bank, or partly hanging over it, with the front wall built up from the bottom of the pond. The lake lodge is built on the shelving shores of lakes.

The dams used by beavers to widen the area and increase the depth of water around their homes are constructed either of sticks and poles, or more firmly and solidly of mud, brushwood, and stones. As time goes by the beaver repairs and adds to the dam; floating material lodges there; and vegetation grows on the top and its roots add to the strength of the dam. Frequently the beaver builds a smaller dam downstream in order to back up some water against

Baron Beaverbrook (right) with Earl of Halifax (far left), British ambassador to the United States, in Washington, D.C., in 1941. UPI

the original dam and thus decrease the pressure of water on it from the other side. The dams are about 5 ft. high, usually more than 10 ft. wide at the base and narrow at the top. A beaver dam more than 1000 ft. long was found in Rocky Mt. National Park, Colorado.

The building techniques employed by beavers provide some basis for belief that the animals possess a high degree of intelligence and the ability to reason. Much observation and some experimentation seem to disprove this belief but, nonetheless, the accomplishments of beavers are sometimes most extraordinary. For instance, although the beaver is a powerful swimmer, it has difficulty dragging over the ground the logs and branches it needs for building and to store as food. Colonies of beavers therefore often dig canals from the pond to a suitable grove of trees. Such canals are from 2 to 3 ft. wide and deep, and often hundreds of feet long. The timber is then readily floated down the canal toward the pond.

The favorite food of beavers is the bark and twigs of willow, poplar, and birch. Beavers also eat berries and roots, particularly waterlily roots. Sometimes beavers cut evergreen trees for building, but they do not eat any part of them. During the autumn beavers store enough food to last them the entire winter. Some of this is stored within the lodges, but most of it is in the form of branches stuck into the mud at the bottom of the ponds. A pond may freeze over during the winter, but it does not freeze all the way to the bottom. Whenever a beaver is hungry, it swims out through the underwater entrance to its home, and brings back as much food as it wishes from the storage pile.

Beavers have long been exploited for their fur. More than a hundred years before the discovery of America, the English poet Geoffrey Chaucer (q.v.) spoke of a "Flaundrish bever hat". For many years during the 18th and 19th centuries hundreds of thousands of beaver skins were exported to Europe from America annually. Ceaseless slaughter led to near extinction of beavers both in Europe and North America. The beaver is still almost extinct in Europe, but is becoming re-established in the forests of Canada and in protected areas of the United States. Beaver fur is highly valued and perennially popular for women's coats.

BEAVERBROOK, William Maxwell Aitken, Ist Baron (1879–1964), British politician and newspaper publisher, born in Maple, Ontario Province, Canada, and educated at the public school there. After amassing a fortune in the cement business, he emigrated to England in 1910; later that year he entered Parliament as Conservative member for Ashton-under-Lyne. He was knighted in the next year, and raised to the peerage in 1916. He became owner of the London *Daily Express* in 1916 and founded the London *Sunday Express* and *Evening Standard* in 1918 and 1923 respectively. Beaverbrook amassed a second fortune from his newspaper interests; he also attained an enormously influential position in political affairs. The Beaverbrook papers achieved unprecedented mass circulation, while emphasizing the strongly conservative philosophy of their publisher. In 1916 he represented the Canadian government as an observer with Canadian troops on the western front of World War I. In 1918 he joined the British cabinet as minister of information. During World War II he again joined the British cabinet, as minister of aircraft production in 1940 and minister of supply in 1941. In 1942 he was British Lend-Lease (q.v.) administrator in the United States, and he served from 1943 to

1945 as lord privy seal. Beaverbrook resigned from the Conservative Party in 1949; his newspapers thereafter were politically independent. From 1947 to 1953 he was chancellor of the University of New Brunswick. He wrote *Success* (1921), *Politicians and the Press* (1925), *Politicians and the War* (1928, 2nd ed. 1960), *Men and Power: 1917–18* (1956), *Friends* (1959), and *Decline and Fall of Lloyd George* (1963).

BEAVER DAM, city of Wisconsin, in Dodge Co., at the S.E. end of Beaver Lake, about 30 miles S.W. of Fond du Lac. Beaver Dam is a shipping center for the surrounding farm region. The city manufactures iron castings, stoves, electrical appliances, shoes, and dairy equipment, and produces beer, canned foods, and cheese. Pop. (1960) 13,118; (1970) 14,265.

BEAVER FALLS, city of Pennsylvania, in Beaver Co., on the Beaver R., about 27 miles N.W. of Pittsburgh. The city manufactures paints, cork and metal products, lumber, chinaware, and bricks. Bituminous coal is mined. It is the site of Geneva College, established in 1848. Pop. (1960) 16,240; (1970) 14,375.

BEAVER TREE *or* **BEAVERWOOD.** *See* MAGNOLIA.

BEBEL, August (1840–1913), German writer and political leader, born in Cologne. Bebel settled in Leipzig in 1860 as a journeyman lathe operator. Almost immediately he identified himself with the socialist movement among the working classes. In 1867 he was elected chairman of the permanent committee of the German workingmen's unions; later the same year he was sent to the North German Diet or legislature as a member of the Saxon People's Party. In 1869, in Eisenach, he joined in founding the Social Democratic Party, which was closely affiliated with the International Workingmen's Association (q.v.), the First International established in London by the German revolutionist and political philosopher Karl Marx (q.v.). In 1871 Bebel became a member of the newly formed German parliament, the Reichstag, in which he served almost continuously until his death. Bebel was imprisoned from 1872 until 1874, and again in 1886, convicted of treason against the German emperor. His forthright antimilitarism and devotion to progressive social measures earned him the enmity of the German chancellor, Prince Otto Eduard Leopold von Bismarck (q.v.). After 1890 Bebel lived in Berlin, known as an effective orator and the most influential member of his party, which he watched grow until in 1912 it represented a majority of the Reichstag. He was editor of the socialist periodical *Vorwärts* ("Forward"). His works include *Der Deutsche Bauernkrieg* ("The Peasants' War", 1876), *Die Frau und Socialismus* (1883; Eng. trans., *Women and Socialism,* 1910), *Charles Fourier* (1888), and *Aus meinem Leben* (1910; Eng. trans., *My Life,* 1912).

BECCAFUMI, Domenico, real name DOMENICO DI PACE, also called IL MECCHERINO (1486–1551), Italian painter and sculptor, born near Siena. He was the son of a peasant. He took the name Beccafumi from his patron, a wealthy citizen of Siena who fostered his natural taste for art by sending him to study in Siena and later in Rome. Beccafumi designed thirty-five mosaics for the pavement in the cathedral of Siena, each mosaic depicting a different Old Testament scene. He worked on these mosaics, considered his greatest achievement, from 1517 to 1525 and again in 1544 and 1546. His best-known paintings are the frescoes on the ceiling of the city hall in Siena and an altarpiece now in the museum of that city. His last years were devoted principally to sculpture, particularly to eighteen bronze figures of angels and twelve marble figures of the Apostles (*see* APOSTLE) for the cathedral of Siena. Beccafumi was also a talented engraver, and worked in both copper and wood.

BECCARIA, Cesare Bonesana, Marchese di (1738–94), Italian economist and jurist, born in Milan. His opinions were formed by study of the writers of the 18th-century French Enlightenment (*see* ENLIGHTENMENT, AGE OF), the Encyclopedists, especially Baron de Montesquieu (qq.v.). His chief work is *Trattato dei Delitti e delle Pene* (Eng. trans., "Crimes and Punishments", 1880), first published anonymously in Monaco in 1764, in which he argues against the severities and abuses of criminal law, especially capital punishment and torture. The work became extremely popular and was translated into all the European languages. The writings of Beccaria stimulated, and provided a guide for, reforms in the penal codes of Great Britain, Russia, and many European nations. He was among the first to advocate education as a means of lessening crime. From 1768 to 1771 Beccaria was professor of public law and economy at the Palatine College of Milan and held various public offices after 1771.

BECHER, Johann Joachim (1635–82), German chemist, physician, and economist, born in Speyer. He combined an extensive knowledge of the science and economics of his period with an adventurous spirit. In Munich he founded a chemical laboratory. He was interested also in German colonization, and urged the elector of Bavaria to establish colonies in South America.

In Vienna he proposed the building of a Rhine-Danube canal and attempted to change the sand of the Danube R. into gold. The phlogiston (q.v.) theory of combustion advanced by the German chemist and physician Georg Ernst Stahl (1660–1734) was based on Becher's views, as set forth in his *Physica Subterranea* ("Subterranean Physics", 1669), a study of the nature of minerals and other substances.

BECHUANALAND. *See* BOTSWANA.

BECHUANAS, former name of tribes of Bantu stock living in Botswana. *See* BATSWANA.

BECKET, Thomas à, *or* SAINT THOMAS BECKET (1118–70), English prelate, born in London, and educated in London and Paris. About 1142, Becket became a clerk in the household of Theobald (d. 1161), archbishop of Canterbury, who sent him to study canon law at the universities of Bologna (*see* BOLOGNA, UNIVERSITY OF) and Auxerre. While on the Continent, Becket obtained letters from the pope, Alexander III (*see under* ALEXANDER), forbidding the coronation of Eustace IV (d. 1153), son of King Stephen (q.v.) of England, as king. This action won him the favor of the king's cousin Henry, who succeeded Stephen, as Henry II (q.v.), in 1154. In 1155 Henry made Becket chancellor of England. He was elected archbishop of Canterbury in 1162 through the king's influence. Though he lived in splendor as archbishop, even maintaining 700 knights of his own, he was noted for his zeal, devotion, and piety. Soon, however, he came into conflict with the king. In 1163 he opposed Henry in a matter of taxation on behalf of the people. He also upheld the prerogatives of the Church despite the king's hostility, firmly resisting the royal authority. In 1164 he reluctantly assented to the laws, known as the Constitutions of Clarendon (*see* CLARENDON, CONSTITUTIONS OF), by which the king tried to subordinate the ecclesiastical to the secular courts, but soon repudiated them as contrary to canon law.

Under various pretexts the king mulcted Becket of large sums of money. Becket appealed to the pope in 1164, whereupon he was declared a traitor and compelled to flee to France. Henry confiscated Becket's property, but in 1170 the pope, by a threat of interdiction (*see* INTERDICT), forced Henry into a reconciliation with Becket and a promise to restore his property. Soon after returning (Dec. 1, 1170) to England, Becket resumed his quarrel with the king and influenced the pope to suspend certain bishops who remained in the king's party. On Dec. 29, 1170, four knights went to Canterbury Cathedral to demand in the king's name the restoration of the bishops to their office. Becket refused, and the knights withdrew, only to return with an armed band. Becket forbade his attendants to lock the doors, saying "God's house must be closed against no man". Then, by the altar, declaring that "for the name of Jesus and for the defense of the Church I am ready to embrace death", he was murdered. Henry was compelled to do public penance at Becket's tomb to avoid excommunication (q.v.).

"The Slaying of Thomas à Becket" (a miniature from a 13th-century Latin Psalter). Granger Collection

Becket was canonized by Pope Alexander in 1173, and the anniversary of his death was set apart as the day of his festival. In 1220 his bones were removed from the grave in the crypt where they had been hastily buried the day after his murder. By order of King Henry III (q.v.) they were deposited in a splendid shrine; for three centuries one of the great pilgrimages of Christendom was that to Becket's shrine. At the time of the Reformation (q.v.), Henry VIII (q.v.) despoiled the shrine and erased Becket's name from the calendar of the Anglican Church (*see* CHURCH OF ENGLAND). According to an account of dubious validity, Henry also ordered his bones to be burned and afterward scattered to the winds.

See also CANTERBURY. W.N.C.

BECKETT, Samuel (Barclay) (1906–), Irish-born poet, novelist, foremost dramatist in the theater of the absurd, and winner of the 1969 Nobel Prize in literature.

Beckett was born on April 13, 1906, in Foxrock, near Dublin. After attending Portola Royal Academy, a religion-steeped, middle-class Protestant school in the north of Ireland, he entered Trinity College, Dublin, where he earned an A.B. in Romance languages (1927) and later an M.A. (1931). In between the two degrees, he spent two years teaching in Paris. At the same time he continued his study of Descartes and wrote his critical essay *Proust* (1931)—work that laid the philosophical foundation for his life and literary production. Significantly, he also became acquainted with the Irish novelist and poet James Joyce (q.v.).

From 1932 to 1937 Beckett wrote, traveled restlessly, and held various jobs, his income supplemented by an annuity from his father, whose death in 1933 shocked him profoundly. In 1937 he settled permanently in Paris, except during World War II when, in 1942, he fled the Gestapo with his French wife Suzanne. He then worked as a farm laborer in unoccupied southern France, and there used his evenings to write the novel *Watt* (which was not published until 1953).

Back in Paris after the war, Beckett in three of his most productive years, 1947–1949, created four major works, all written in French: his trilogy *Malloy, Malone Dies,* and *The Unnamable,* novels that Beckett considered his greatest achievement; and the play, *Waiting for Godot* (first performed in Paris in 1953), which most critics, however, usually regard as his masterpiece.

Most of Beckett's works after 1945 were written in French and later translated. Other major works, with their English-language publication dates, include the plays *Endgame* (1958), *Krapp's Last Tape* (1959), *Happy Days* (1961), and *Play* (1964); the narrative prose works *Murphy* (1938) and *How It Is* (1964); and the verse collections *Whoroscope* (1930) and *Echo's Bones* (1935).

In his novels and plays alike Beckett focused on the wretchedness of living—not just to wallow in sordidness and misery, but to expose the bare-bones essence of the human condition, which he ultimately reduced to the solitary self, or to nothingness. Language, too, he pared down to its bare bones in a lean, disciplined prose verging on poetry but seasoned with sardonic wit and relieved by vaudevillian patter and clowning. His influence on subsequent dramatists, particularly those who followed him in the so-called absurdist tradition, was enormous, and the impact of his prose works, as well, was considerable.

BECKFORD, William (1759–1844), British writer and art collector, born at Fonthill Abbey, Wiltshire, England. In 1770 he inherited an enormous fortune. He traveled extensively in continental Europe, collecting books and objects of art. In 1782 he wrote his principal work, *Vathek: An Arabian Tale,* in French. It was published in English translation in London in 1786 and in the original French in Lausanne, Switzerland, and in Paris in 1787. The fantastic, grandiose, and exotic elements in this Oriental tale, as well as Beckford's extravagant homes in Fonthill and Bath and his aloofness from society, gave him the reputation of being a morose and eccentric genius. Beckford also wrote two burlesques of sentimental novels and sketches of his extensive travels.

BECKLEY, city in West Virginia, and county seat of Raleigh Co., about 45 miles S.E. of Charleston. The city is the center of an agricultural and coal-mining region. The most important industry in Beckley is the manufacture of electronic equipment. Pop. (1960) 18,642; (1970) 19,884.

BECKMANN, Max (1884–1950), German painter, born in Leipzig. He worked in Berlin and Frankfurt until 1937, when he moved to Amsterdam. Ten years later Beckmann moved to the United States, to teach first at Washington University, Saint Louis, Mo., and later at the Brooklyn Museum art school, New York City. His early work was in a monumental impressionistic style (*see* IMPRESSIONISM). Before World War I he joined the many German painters who turned to expressionism (q.v.). He produced works of considerable drama, energy, and symbolic power, characterized by heavy dark outlines and broadly contrasted areas of vivid color. Beckmann, whose later work dealt less abstractly and more realistically with problems facing mankind, painted nine triptychs, huge three-part allegorical works, after 1932. One of these, the celebrated "Departure", was painted in 1932–33, when the Nazis were coming to power in Germany. (They discharged Beckmann from his art professorship in Frankfurt, calling him a "degenerate" artist.) The picture is in the permanent collection of the Museum of Modern Art, New York City. He is also represented in the Boston Museum of Fine Arts, the Minneapolis Institute of Arts, and other museums.

BECQUE, Henry François (1837–99), French playwright, born in Paris, and educated at the Lycée Condorcet. After leaving school he became a clerk, working first for a railroad company and later for the French stock exchange. His first play, *L'Enfant prodigue* ("The Prodigal Son", 1867), a light comedy, was a well-received but insignificant work. His masterpieces are *Les Corbeaux* (1882; Eng. trans., *The Vultures,* 1913), and *La Parisienne* (1885; Eng. trans., *The Woman of Paris,* 1913), both naturalistic portrayals of French bourgeois life. *Les Corbeaux* depicts the plight of a widow and her family ruthlessly exploited by the business associates of her late husband, and *La Parisienne* sharply satirizes an unfaithful wife.

Becque was one of the first French playwrights to break with the formalism of classical drama and the pretentious emotionalism of romantic drama. He strove above all to depict Reality on the stage. His dialogue, with its revolutionary use of slang and colloquial expressions, contributed as much as the themes to the realistic effect of his plays. French drama has been influenced by the realism of Becque and, historically, by his rejection of neoclassicism.

BÉCQUER, Gustavo Adolfo (1836–70), Spanish poet, born in Seville. He spent most of his life in Madrid earning a meager living as a free-lance journalist and translator. The majority of his literary works were published posthumously in 1871. His best-known verse is in *Rimas* (1871; Eng. trans., *The Infinite Passion,* 1924), a collection of short, lyrical poems. Underscored by a deep, pantheistic faith, the poems deal chiefly with such themes as the struggle for perfection, despair, and the joys of love. His best-known prose works are the *Leyendas Españolas* (1871; Eng. trans., *Romantic Legends of Spain,* 1909), a collection of short stories. The stories are characterized by a quality of elusiveness and mystery and a remarkably delicate, musical prose. Bécquer is regarded as one of the most important lyric poets of 19th-century Spain and is widely read throughout the Spanish-speaking world.

BECQUEREL, name of a family of French physicists.

Antoine César Becquerel (1788–1878), born in Châtillon-Coligny. He studied electricity, including the electric conductivity of metals and atmospheric electricity, and was one of the founders of the science of electrochemistry. He also invented a thermoelectric needle that measured body temperatures. From 1837 until his death he was a professor of physics at the Museum of Natural History in Paris.

Alexandre Edmond Becquerel (1820–91), son of Antoine César Becquerel, born in Paris. He was professor of physics at the Conservatory of Arts and Science from 1853, and succeeded his father as professor of physics at the Museum of Natural History. He did important research on light and optics. He wrote *La Lumière, ses causes et ses effets* ("Light, Its Causes and Its Effects", 2 vol., 1867–68).

Antoine Henri Becquerel (1852–1908), son of Alexandre Edmond Becquerel, born in Paris. He became professor of physics at the Museum of Natural History in 1892 and at the Polytechnical School in 1895. In 1896 he discovered the phenomenon of radioactivity (q.v.), and he did important research on phosphorescence (*see* FLUORESCENCE AND PHOSPHORESCENCE), spectrum analysis (*see* SPECTRUM: *Spectrum Analysis*), and the absorption of light (q.v.). In 1903 he shared the Nobel Prize in physics with the French physicists Pierre Curie and Marie Sklodowska Curie (*see under* CURIE). His works include *Recherches sur la Phosphorescence* ("Research on Phosphorescence", 1882–97) and *Découverte des Radiations Invisibles Émises par l'Uranium* ("Discovery of the Invisible Radiation Emitted by Uranium", 1896–97).

BED, article of furniture designed for rest or sleep, comprising usually a bedstead, or supporting frame, a spring, and a mattress. In its broadest sense, the word refers to any sleeping place used by human beings or animals. The bed as an article of household furniture dates from remote antiquity. In ancient times only the wealthy and the powerful owned beds. These people used their beds both for sleeping and for eating meals in a reclining position everywhere except Egypt. An ancient sculpture in the collection of the British Museum, London, shows Ashurbanipal (q.v.), King of Assyria (r. 669–626 B.C.), reclining at dinner on a magnificent couch. Substantial evidence exists that beds were popular among leading Babylonians and Persians. The beds common in the homes of well-to-do Greeks, were, at first, somewhat less luxurious than those of the Persians. After the 7th century B.C., however, Greek bedsteads and couches were inlaid or veneered with ivory, tortoiseshell, and precious metals, and sometimes provided with feet of solid silver or gold; the cities of Miletus, Corinth, and Carthage (qq.v.), became famous centers for dyeing, weaving, and embroidering bedcovers.

Before the rise of Roman civilization, luxurious beds, similar to those in Greece, were manufactured in Etruria (q.v.). Two funeral bedsteads, veneered in ivory, were found by archaeologists in Etruscan tombs of the 4th and 3rd centuries B.C. The beds of the Romans were characterized by extreme simplicity until the dissolution of the Republic. Thereafter their beds surpassed in splendor those of the Persians, Greeks, and Etruscans.

Although a trend toward simplicity in bed design developed after the fall of Roman civilization, ostentatious beds reappeared during the Middle Ages. Beds of bronze tubing, similar to the brass beds of a later era, were made in the time of Charlemagne (q.v.), King of the Franks (r. 768–814). During the 12th and 13th centuries virtually all baronial mansions and castles were equipped with beds, which steadily increased in size and luxury. In the 14th century beds became smaller and such refinements as double mattresses wrapped in silk were introduced; by the 15th century, however, beds, notably those used by royalty, attained enormous proportions. Immense canopies, suspended over the beds from the ceilings or walls, became popular. Subsequently the canopies were attached to columns affixed to the corners of the bedsteads, a modification that led to the four-poster of later times. The bedsteads were heavily carved, with headboards extending to the top of the canopy. In the 17th and 18th centuries, during the reigns of the French kings Louis XIV, who owned 413 beds of all types, and Louis XV (qq.v.), the art of fine bed construction reached a peak, combining graceful design, fantastic ornamentation, and beautiful coloring. Kings, queens, noblemen, ministers, and fashionable ladies commonly held receptions in their bedrooms while they reclined in bed.

The extreme ostentation that characterized the beds of former times gradually disappeared as mass production made beds available to all classes, effectively ending their fashionableness. Although elaborate beds, such as four-posters, are still in use, the beds of modern times generally are constructed for comfort and simplicity of design. Emphasis is placed on well-designed, well-constructed mattresses and springs. Contemporary craftsmen achieve a certain beauty of line and grain, but the bed is no longer an *objet d'art.* Folding beds of various types, designed for saving space or for ease of storage or transportation, are widely used today; they range in complexity from the army cot, consisting of a canvas sheet attached to a collapsible frame, to the convertible couch or chair that opens out into a bed.

See also FURNITURE.

BEDA, Saint. See BEDE, SAINT.

BEDBUG, common name for a bloodsucking, wingless insect, *Cimex lectularius,* in the family *Cimicidae.* It is a small, flat, and oval bug (q.v.), reddish brown in color, with an unpleasant odor. The bedbug infests houses, particularly beds. It generally hides during the day and feeds at night. Sucking the blood of man and the higher animals, it is both a pest and a carrier of dangerous diseases. Two to four generations breed each year, depending on the temperature and the food supply. The larvae resemble the adult, and mature in about eleven weeks. Other bugs of the family Cimicidae and of the related family Reduviidae are also called bedbugs; *see* KISSING BUG.

BEDE, Saint *or* **BAEDA, Saint** *or* **BEDA, Saint,** often called THE VENERABLE BEDE (673–735), English historian and theologian, born in Durham, Kingdom of Northumbria (now in England), and educated at the monasteries of Monkwearmouth, in Sunderland, and Jarrow. He was ordained a priest in 703, and thereafter lived chiefly at Jarrow, devoting his life to teaching theology, Hebrew, Greek, and Latin, and to writing. He was probably the greatest Anglo-Saxon scholar of his time, and because of him, Northumbria was considered one of the leading centers of learning in Europe. Bede wrote about forty historical, scientific, and theological works, most of them in Latin. His writings, characterized by a vivid and concise style, reflect his piety and gentleness. The most important of them are *Historia Ecclesiastica Gentis Anglorum* ("Ecclesiastical History of the English Nation"), completed in 731, which earned him the appellation of father of English history; and *Historia Abbatum* ("History of the Abbots"), about the abbots of Wearmouth and Jarrow. He was canonized and created a doctor of the Church by Pope Leo XIII (*see under* LEO) in 1899. The feast day of St. Bede is May 25.

BEDFORD, city in Indiana, and county seat of Lawrence Co., about 22 miles S. of Bloomington. Bedford is in a high-quality limestone-quarrying region, and is a center for the quarrying industry. Manufactures include stoneworking machinery, work clothing, and tools. Pop. (1960) 13,024; (1970) 13,087.

BEDFORD, city of Ohio, in Cuyahoga Co., about 10 miles S.E. of central Cleveland. The city manufactures metal, rubber, and electrical products, and chinaware. Pop. (1960) 15,223; (1970) 17,552.

BEDFORD, Great Britain, municipal borough and county town of Bedfordshire, England, on the Ouse R., about 48 miles N.W. of London. The agricultural produce of the surrounding area is marketed in Bedford; agricultural implements, electrical equipment, boilers, and diesel engines are manufactured there. Located in the town are the well-known Bedford schools. The oldest,

Bedford School for boys, is one of the largest public schools in England. Maintained by the Newnham Priory since the 12th century, the school was in danger of closing when Sir William Harpur (about 1496–1573), a lord mayor of London, endowed it in 1556. Also administered from the Harpur Trust are the Bedford High School, a public school for girls, and two direct grant schools, Dame Alice Harpur Grammar School and Bedford Modern School. Direct grant schools are basically independent, but since they receive some money from the government, they must admit a certain number of students tuition free. Bedford was the scene of a battle between the Britons and Saxons in 571. It was a Danish borough until the 10th century, when the English captured it. The English preacher and writer John Bunyan (q.v.) was born in the neighboring village of Elstow and was a prisoner in the Bedford town jail from 1660 to 1672 and again in 1675 as a disturber of the peace. Pop. (1971) 73,229.

BEDFORD, Duke of. *See* JOHN OF LANCASTER.

BEDFORDSHIRE, Great Britain, county in central England. Because of a generally level surface and fertile soil the county is well suited to agriculture; stock raising, dairying, and truck farming are the leading occupations. Lace making and straw plaiting, formerly important industries, now survive on a limited scale. Located in the county is Woburn Abbey, the ancestral home of the dukes of Bedford. The principal towns are Bedford, the county town, Luton, Dunstable, Leighton, Buzzard, and Biggleswade. Area, 473 sq.mi.; pop. (1971) 464,277.

BÉDIER, Charles Marie Joseph (1864–1938), French scholar and writer, born in Paris, and educated at the École Normale Supérieure and the Collège de France. Between 1880 and 1903 he taught medieval French language and literature at the universities of Fribourg (Switzerland) and Caen (France), and in 1903 became a professor at the Collège de France. In 1920 he became a member of the French Academy. Bédier won international recognition in 1900 with his *Roman de Tristan et Yseult* ("Story of Tristram and Iseult"), an adaptation of the ancient legend, based on all the extant medieval versions; *see* TRISTRAM.

BEDIVERE, Sir, in Arthurian legend, a Knight of the Round Table. He threw King Arthur's sword Excalibur into the lake and carried the dying king to the boat that took him to the Vale of Avalon. *See* ARTHUR; ARTHURIAN CYCLE.

BEDLAM (corruption of "Bethlehem"), popular name for the first insane asylum in England. It was built in 1247 as a priory, became a hospital by 1330, and began to receive mental patients by 1403. In 1547 it was officially declared a hospital exclusively for the insane. As such, it became infamous for the brutality shown to patients. Formerly named the Hospital of Saint Mary of Bethlehem, and now called Bethlem Royal Hospital, it has been moved several times from the original site, Bishopsgate, London. The present location is Beckenham, Kent, just outside of London. The word bedlam has also come to signify any scene of uproar and confusion.

Bedlington terrier trimmed for showing.
Bedlington Terrier Club of America

BEDLINGTON TERRIER, fighting breed of terrier, used in hunting foxes, badgers, otters, and other small animals, and also much valued as a pet. The Bedlington terrier originated in 1825 in Bedlington, Northumberland County, England. The Bedlington stands 15 to 16 in. high at the shoulder and weighs from 22 to 24 lb. It has a lean, long head; a topknot lighter in color than the other hair on the body; long, pointed ears; and small, dark eyes. The thick, linty coat is usually blue or liver in color, although sometimes it is blue and tan or liver and tan. The body is muscular but flexible. An arched loin gives the impression that the hind legs are longer than the forelegs; the forelegs are straight and have hare feet. The tail of the Bedlington ranges from 9 to 11 in. long, tapering gracefully to a point. For the show ring the fur is clipped and trimmed so that the dog looks somewhat like a tiny lamb. *See also* TERRIER.

BEDLOE'S ISLAND. *See* LIBERTY ISLAND.

BED OF JUSTICE (Fr. *lit de justice*), the seat or platform occupied by the kings of France whenever they were present at sessions of the French royal court known as the *parlement*. In French judicial history, the term was also used to denote a session of the *parlement* held in the presence of the king and called specifically to overrule previous decisions of the *parlement* or to

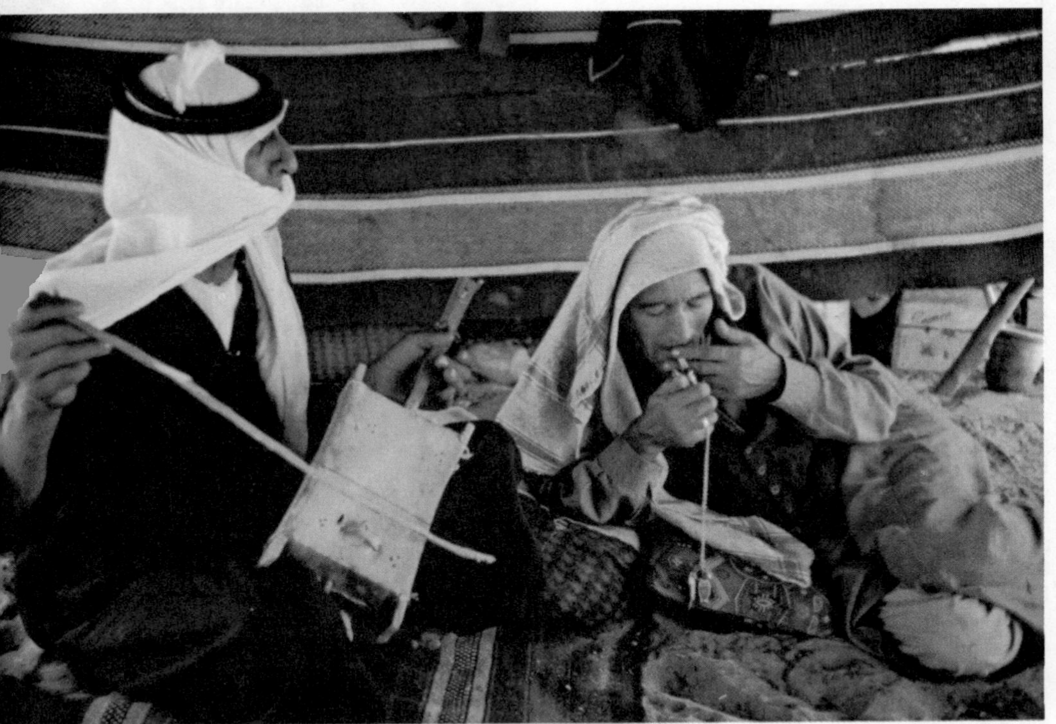

Bedouin nomads, members of a Jordanian tribe, relax in their tent. One (left) is playing a native musical instrument called a rababah. Mathias Oppersdorff

force the acceptance of royal edicts or ordinances that the *parlement* had rejected. This usage was based on the theory that the authority of the *parlement* was derived from the crown; and that in the presence of the king (the source of authority), this delegated authority ceased to exist. Under this legal fiction, the *parlement* was legally incapable of resisting any demand that the king might make from the bed of justice. French kings used the device frequently to control independent *parlements* from the earliest years of the nation until the end of the 18th century. The last bed of justice was held by King Louis XVI (q.v.) in 1787, during the period of unrest that immediately preceded the French Revolution (q.v.); as a result of this session the entire *parlement* was imprisoned.

BEDOUINS (Arab. *Badawi,* "dwellers in the desert"), nomadic Arabs inhabiting the deserts of Arabia, Syria, Saudi Arabia, the Arab Republic of Egypt, much of northern Africa, and parts of Israel. In ancient times their territory included only the deserts of Egypt and Syria. Later they entered Mesopotamia and Chaldea. The Muslim conquest of northern Africa in the 7th century opened vaster tracts to the Bedouins. At present they are to be found from the western boundary of Iran to the Atlantic Ocean, and from the mountains of Kurdistan to the Sudan. They form a small part of the population of these areas but utilize a great deal of territory. Bedouins are usually under medium height, with aquiline features and swarthy complexions. Virtually all Bedouins are Muslims. They manufacture their own woolen clothing. Members of many tribes shave their heads, but beards are worn by all.

Beginning about 1045 and continuing at a decreasing rate for several centuries, Bedouin nomads from central Arabia invaded northern Africa. These illiterate invaders took over all suitable grazing land and upset the balanced agricultural and urban civilization which the resident Berbers had achieved; *see* BERBER. The Bedouin flocks destroyed most of the natural ground cover; by overgrazing, the flocks turned pasture land into semidesert. A balanced civilization was restored, however, with the colonization of northern Africa by European powers, beginning in the 1830's.

The Bedouins have retained their nomadic and pastoral way of life. They subsist primarily on meat, milk, and dairy products provided by their herds. In general they leave crop agriculture and commerce to the native peoples of northern Africa and participate in such activities only when they have slaves available as a labor force. These slaves are captured members of other tribes, Arab or Negro. Exploitive and aggressive, Bedouins are disdainful of any kind of settled life.

The typical Bedouin tent is usually made from strips of cloth woven from goats' or camels' hair and vegetable fibers, sewn together and dyed black. In the rare instances in which they become sedentary and erect permanent dwellings, the Bedouins build rectangular houses several stories in height, with stone or adobe walls.

The political system of the Bedouins is based on an extended family unit with a patriarchal head. Each unit, from a minor family to an entire tribe, is led by a sheikh; the sheikhdom descends from father to eldest son. The actual political authority of each sheikh depends not upon the size of the unit he rules, but upon his wealth and the force of his personality.

The social system of the Bedouins is elaborately stratified into strongly differentiated, usually intra-marrying castes. Five castes can be distinguished: nobles, freemen, vassals or subservient landowners, slaves, and outcasts. Slavery remains a basic part of the Bedouin social system.

BEDSTRAW, common name for small herbs of the genus *Galium* in the Madder family (Rubiaceae), formerly used in the dried form for stuffing the mattresses of beds. The genus comprises about 300 varieties, including Our-Lady's-bedstraw, or yellow bedstraw, *G. verum;* rough bedstraw, *G. asprellum*; and wild madder, or white bedstraw, *G. mollugo.* The plant is a native of the northern parts of Europe, Asia, and America. Some of the species are called baby's breath (q.v.). Other plants that have been used for stuffing, particularly certain species of *Desmodium,* are sometimes called bedstraw. *See* MADDER.

BEE, common name for an extremely varied group of insects belonging to the superfamily Apoidea in the order Hymenoptera which are grouped conveniently as solitary bees and social bees. Together, the two divisions include some of the most highly evolved forms of insect life.

Solitary Bees. The majority of bees are solitary insects, that is, each female provides for her own offspring. Many solitary bees dig extensive tunnels while constructing their nests, boring into timber or banks of earth, for example. Some solitary bees utilize crevices in walls and rock ledges as nesting sites. Others, using highly specialized techniques, build their nests from various plant materials or from pebbles and bits of soil that they cement with saliva. A few solitary bees construct no nests of their own, but live as parasites in the nests of other bees. Of the solitary bees, four families are considered below.

Split-Tongued, or Wasplike Bees. These insects of the family Colletidae have short, notched, or deeply split, tongues and are extremely widespread and numerous. They fall naturally into two groups, one of which consists of small, black, almost hairless forms with yellow markings. The females lack pollen brushes on their hind legs. This group build their nests chiefly in the stems of plants or in ground cavities. They subsequently line the nests with a silky substance and stock them with a honey-and-pollen paste; the paste is stored in a series of sack-shaped compartments. The split-tongued bees of the other group have dense body hairs, and the females possess pollen brushes. Most bees included in this group have white bands upon the abdomen. They dig tunnels up to 2 ft. long in earthen banks and then dig lateral cells along the main tunnel. These cells are lined with a plastic material and are ultimately filled with liquid nectar. Eggs are laid in the central tunnel.

White bedstraw, Galium mollugo

American Museum of Natural History

Mining Bees. These bees, which belong to the family Andrenidae, are numerous and vary greatly in size and habit. They have pointed tongues, and the females bear pollen brushes on their hind legs. Most North American bees belong to this family. The mining bees dig tunnels in banks and clay walls and then line them with clay pellets obtained by puddling soil with water regurgitated from their stomachs. Small cells are dug along the sides of the tunnels and then filled with nectar on which a single egg is laid. The mining bees often are gregarious; sometimes they cooperate in digging clusters of nesting cells off a single tunnel. In such a community, a bee often stands guard just inside the narrow entrance and keeps out all but members of the community.

Leaf-Cutter Bees. The members of this family, known as the Megachilidae, are also numerous with widely varied habits. Most leaf-cutter bees nest in tunnels or natural cavities, frequently in wood. Some species dig in the ground, burrow under stones, or make plaster cells on rocks and walls. A few of the family are parasitic in the nests of allied species. Most of the leaf-cutters, as the name suggests, harvest sections of green leaves, especially of roses and related plants. They cut the leaves nearly symmetrically, chewing out two oblong sections and then a number of circular pieces. The oblongs are constructed into elongated thimbles for the burrows or tunnels and are then half filled with a mixture of pollen and honey. An egg is laid in this mixture, and then several circular pieces of leaf, cut somewhat larger than the diameter of the thimble, are forced down into the open end of the thimble, which is thus completely sealed. Other thimbles are added until the tunnel is filled. The larvae of several leaf-cutter species spin silken cocoons after hatching.

Social Bees. This division consists of bumblebees, stingless bees, and honeybees all placed together in the family Apidae, and all having certain distinguishing characteristics: they secrete wax as a nest-building material, produce many sexually imperfect females (workers), and practice progressive provisioning or feeding of larvae on hatching.

Bumblebees. The bumblebees, which constitute the tribe Bombini of the family Apidae, are large, hairy insects, usually black and gold and almost worldwide in distribution. Within the group are two varieties, one is parasitic in the nests of the other. Three castes are recognized: queens, workers, and drones. Both the queens and the workers, which are sterile females, bear pollen baskets on their hind legs. Young queens, the founders of new colonies, build nests of vegetable material in abandoned holes, such as mouse burrows. The nest consists of a spherical central chamber with a single exit, usually just large enough for passage. Next, a small dome of pollen paste is built in the middle of the nest, upon which a circular wax wall is erected. A batch of eggs is laid in this and sealed beneath a thin dome of wax. At the same time the queen constructs a hemispherical wax cup in the floor of the entranceway; this is filled with honey. The queen then sits upon the egg box continuously until the eggs hatch, feeding on the honey in the cup and maintaining an even temperature throughout the nest. The eggs hatch in a few days. The larvae partially consume the paste in their cell, but later are fed through a small opening by the queen. When the new brood is full-grown, the individual members spin cocoons which ultimately harden to parchmentlike rigidity. The queen then clears away the remains of the cell and broods her offspring like a bird. The first broods of a new nest are workers, who take over all nonreproductive duties. Eventually queens and males are produced, and these mate. The pregnant young queens then found new colonies.

The parasitic bumblebees lack pollen baskets. After invading the nests of allied species, they often kill the resident queen and force the workers to raise the young parasitic bees along with the rightful brood of the nest. Occasionally the invaders permit only their own young to be cared for, and the brood of the resident bees dies.

The carpenter bees drill geometrically exact holes, up to 12 in. deep, into soft-wood stems or sometimes into fence posts. Within these holes the insect constructs a series of platforms, either in sections or as a continuous spiral, of wood chips firmly cemented together. Nectar and an egg are deposited on each platform, and when the hole is nearly filled the nest-founding female occupies the exit to await hatching of her young. Hatching occurs from the bottom up: each young bee destroys the platform above it, until all are freed to follow the female on their first flights.

Stingless Bees. About 250 species divided between two genera (*Melipona* and *Trigona*) constitute this group, known as the Meliponidae. Although called stingless, these bees actually possess rudimentary stings and are well known for their darting mass attacks on molesters. Some species use caustic secretions when attacking. The greatest distribution of stingless bees is in Central and South America, but a few

Bee. Plate 1. *The bee develops from egg to pupa, larva, and adult. Above: A nest of bumblebee pupae and larvae. Inset: Alkali-bee larva, feeding on a mixture of pollen and nectar.*

Bee. Plate 2. *Above: An adult female sweat bee,* Halictus farinosus, *collecting pollen and nectar from an alfalfa flower. Below: The three castes—worker, queen, and drone—of the honeybee,* Apis mellifera.

All pictures in plates 1 and 2, U.S. Dept. of Agriculture – Entomology Research Division

forms are scattered throughout tropical Africa, Asia, and Australia. Organization of the stingless bees is in some respects as complex as that of the stinging honeybees. Most stingless bees encase their nests in clay masonry, leaving only one small entrance. This passage is constantly guarded by one, sometimes a few, or on occasion even a column of the insects. Many species store their honey in pots about the size of a pigeon egg at the bottom of the nest. The stingless bees gather nectar, pollen, and various resins, all of which they mix with wax in constructing their combs which sometimes resemble spiral staircases.

Stingless bees are small insects, the largest being a little more than ½ in. long; the smallest is less than 1/16 in. long. The latter are known as mosquito bees. Generally each colony has one queen, but a few species maintain several queens and produce very large numbers of males, or drones.

In Mexico and among many Amazonian tribesmen, stingless bees are kept in hollow logs, the ends of which are plugged with clay. When honey is desired, one of the clay plugs is removed and the whole nest is scooped out into a pot, mashed, and strained through a cloth.

Honeybees. Natives of the Old World, honeybees were introduced into North America about 300 years ago. The great Indian bees (*Apis dorsata*) and the lesser Indian bees (*A. florea*) are considered useless for apiculture. The third species (*A. mellifera*) is the common honeybee, widely cultivated for its honey. This species occurs in a dozen varieties, each with distinct characteristics. The most highly developed social bees, the honeybees have several specialized habits, including air-conditioning of hives by fanning air currents through them with their wings, communication with fellow bees through the medium of the so-called bee dance, and the specialization of workers, according to age, for care and feeding of the brood, cleaning and building in the hive, and foraging.

A subspecies *(Adansonii)* of the common honeybee, brought to an agricultural station in Brazil from South Africa for crossbreeding experiments, was accidentally freed in 1957. The bee is similar in appearance to the common honeybee but is a much more prolific honey producer and is much more aggressive when disturbed. Unlike the European variety, which gives up chase after about 100 yd., the African bee may continue for ½ mi.; massive stinging by large swarms caused at least eighteen human deaths over the years and led to highly publicized rumors of its spreading menace.

During the mid-1970's the African bee was reported to have moved northward to the coast of Guyana, and the United States Department of Agriculture sent several scientists to study its habits and migration patterns. They found that the African bee rapidly interbreeds with other honeybees and loses much of its aggressiveness while maintaining high honey output. At its current rate of advance there is the possibility that it could reach the U.S. in 1990 but probably could not survive cool winters. *See also* HONEYBEE.

BEEBE, (Charles) William (1877–1962), American explorer and naturalist, born in Brooklyn, N.Y., and educated at Columbia University. Appointed curator of ornithology of the New York Zoological Society in 1899, he originated the collection of living birds in the New York Zoological Park, the Bronx, New York City, making it one of the finest such collections in the world. In 1916 he became director of tropical research for the society. He headed scientific expeditions to Nova Scotia, Mexico, Venezuela, British Guiana (now Guyana), Borneo, China, Japan, the Himalaya Mts., and other regions. Particularly notable was his exploration in parts of Asia in search of data later published in his *Monograph of the Pheasants* (1918) and *Pheasants—Their Lives and Homes* (1926). In 1923 he headed an expedition to the Galápagos Islands in the ship *Noma* to study marine and land life, on the way making oceanographic studies in the Sargasso Sea. He made a record descent of 3028 ft. into the ocean off one of the Bermuda islands in 1934 by means of a spherical diving chamber, the bathysphere (q.v.). Beebe wrote about 300 articles and books. Among the books are titles such as *Jungle Days* (1925), *Beneath Tropic Seas* (1928), *Half Mile Down* (1943), *Book of Naturalists* (1944), and *Unseen Life in New York* (1953).

BEECH, common name for trees of the genus *Fagus* in the Beech family (Fagaceae), the same family to which the oak and chestnut (qq.v.) belong. The genus contains ten species; all of them are native to the temperate parts of the Northern Hemisphere. They are hardy, deciduous, ornamental trees growing, with spreading branches, to heights of about 80 ft. or more, sometimes reaching 100 to 120 ft. The hard, brittle wood is durable under water and therefore useful for the construction of weirs and sluiceways. It is also made into furniture, flooring, and novelties. The fruit is an edible, three-cornered nut (q.v.), widely used in Europe as feed for poultry and pigs. It yields a bland, fixed oil used as a substitute for butter.

American beech, Fagus grandifolia U.S. Forest Service

The European beech, *F. sylvatica,* forms pure forests in many parts of Europe. The thin, ovate, toothed leaves are dark, glossy green, and finely ciliated on the margins. The bark is smooth and gray, sometimes approaching white. The American beech, *F. grandifolia,* is smaller, with lighter leaves and usually lighter bark than that of *F. sylvatica.*

Evergreen or antarctic beeches, belonging to the closely related genus *Nothofagus,* differ chiefly in being evergreen and thriving in colder weather. About a dozen species are found in the mountainous, colder parts of South America, New Zealand, and Australia.

Blue beech and water beech are names for the American hornbeam, in the Hazelnut family (Betulaceae); *see* HORNBEAM.

BEECHAM, Sir Thomas (1879–1961), British conductor and opera impresario, born in Saint Helens, Lancashire, England, and educated at the University of Oxford, but in music largely self-taught. After touring in England with an opera company, he made his professional debut as a conductor with the Queen's Hall Orchestra in London in 1905. Between 1906 and 1909 he founded and conducted both the New Symphony Orchestra and the Beecham Symphony Orchestra. In 1910 he began the presentation of contemporary little-known operas and symphonic music. In 1911 he introduced the Russian ballet company, the Ballets Russes, to London, and two years later he conducted a series of Russian operas in which the Russian singer Feodor Ivanovitch Chaliapin (q.v.) made his first appearance in England.

Beecham was knighted in 1916 and when his father died later that year succeeded to his father's baronetcy. In 1928 he made the first of many appearances in the United States. In 1932 he founded the London Philharmonic Orchestra and in 1933 became artistic director of Covent Garden in London, at which he continued to present operatic productions. In 1940 he was conductor of the Seattle (Wash.) Symphony Orchestra; in 1941 a conductor at the Metropolitan Opera House in New York City; and in 1947 he formed the Royal Philharmonic Orchestra. Beecham wrote his autobiography, *A Mingled Chime* (1943), and *Frederick Delius* (1958), a biography of the British composer.

BEECHER, American family particularly noted as liberal clergymen and abolitionists. *See also* STOWE, HARRIET ELIZABETH BEECHER.

Lyman Beecher (1775–1863), American Presbyterian clergyman, born in New Haven, Conn., and educated at Yale College. He became pastor of the Presbyterian Church at East Hampton, Long Island, N.Y., in 1798. At this church, in 1804, he attained national prominence through his brilliant sermon on the death of the American statesman Alexander Hamilton, who had been killed in a duel with the American statesman Aaron Burr (qq.v.). Beecher held pastorates successively at Litchfield, Conn., and Boston, Mass., between 1810 and 1832, and during this period he became known as one of the most eloquent preachers of his time. He also was one of the leaders of a Presbyterian faction, called the New School, that opposed the strict doctrine and discipline of the conservative Presbyterians, called the Old School (*see* PRESBYTERIANISM: *Presbyterianism in America*). In 1832 he was appointed first president of Lane Theological Seminary, near Cincinnati, Ohio, and pastor of the Second Presbyterian Church of Cincinnati. His doctrinal liberalism soon brought him into conflict with his regional superiors. In 1835 he was tried by the presbytery on charges of heresy and hypocrisy, but was acquitted. The Presbyterian Synod, to which the verdict was appealed, sustained his acquittal in the same year. When the schism foreshadowed by the Old School–New School controversy finally developed in 1838, Beecher adhered to the New School. He continued to preach at his Cincinnati church until 1842 and retained the titular presidency of Lane Theological Seminary for the remainder of his life. He was the father of thirteen children. All seven of his sons became clergymen, and one of his daughters was the noted American writer Harriet Elizabeth Beecher Stowe. His writings include *Collected Works* (3 vol., 1852) and *Autobiography and Correspondence* (1863).

Henry Ward Beecher (1813–87), American clergyman, son of Lyman Beecher, born in Litchfield, Conn., and educated at Amherst College and at the Lane Theological Seminary. In 1847, after serving as pastor to Presbyterian congregations in Lawrenceburg, Ind., and Indianapolis, Ind., he became the pastor of the Plymouth Church of the Pilgrims in Brooklyn, N.Y. He held this post for the rest of his life and became one of the most famous pulpit orators and lecturers in American history. His theological views were fairly orthodox, but he attracted and held huge audiences in the United States and England with his brilliant speeches and leadership at services and revival meetings and his espousal of such controversial causes as the biological theory of evolution and scientific historical study of Biblical texts.

One of the earliest and best-known supporters of the abolitionists (q.v.), Beecher was also an effective proponent of women's rights, particularly woman suffrage (q.v.). From 1861 to 1863 he was editor in chief of the *Independent,* a religious and political periodical largely devoted to these causes, and from 1870 to 1881 he edited *The Christian Union* (later *The Outlook*), a similar publication. In 1874 Beecher's former friend and successor as editor of the *Independent,* the American journalist and writer Theodore Tilton (1835–1907), brought suit for damages against him, charging that Beecher had committed adultery with Tilton's wife. A trial held in that year ended in a disagreement by the jury, leaving Beecher's reputation uncleared, and though later investigations, including one by a council of Congregational churches, fully exonerated him, his later years remained clouded by the scandal.

Beecher's published works comprise mainly reprinted sermons, lectures, and magazine articles. His other writings include the novel *Norwood, or A Tale of Village Life in New England* (1867) and *The Life of Jesus the Christ* (4 vol., 1871–91).

Henry Ward Beecher

BEECHER, Harriet Elizabeth. *See* STOWE, HARRIET ELIZABETH BEECHER.

BEECHEY, Sir William (1753–1839), British painter, born in Burford, England, and trained in art at the newly founded Royal Academy. In 1793 he was made portrait painter to Charlotte Sophia (1744–1818), Queen Consort of Great Britain and in 1798 was knighted for his painting, now in the Hampton Court Picture Gallery at Hampton, England, of George III (q.v.), King of Great Britain, reviewing troops. Beechey was made a member of the Royal Academy, and in sixty-four years he exhibited 362 portraits at that institution. He painted portraits of such famous British people as the naval hero Horatio Nelson, the soldier Lord Charles Cornwallis, and the actress Sarah Kemble Siddons (qq.v.). Beechey is well represented in the National Gallery and the National Portrait Gallery, London, and in many American collections, including that of the Metropolitan Museum of Art in New York City.

BEECH GROVE, city of Indiana, in Marion Co., about 5 miles S.E. of central Indianapolis. Railroad shops are located in Beech Grove. Pop. (1960) 10,973; (1970) 13,468.

BEE EATER, common name for birds of the family Meropidae in the order Coraciiformes. The many known forms are widely distributed in the temperate and tropical parts of the Old World. Bee eaters receive the common name from their diet, which consists almost entirely of bees and wasps. Birds in the family have long, slender bills and swallowlike wings and are noted for their brilliant plumage.

The common bee eater, *Merops apiaster,* of Europe has a crown and mantle of chestnut, shading below into primrose; the head is black and white, the throat yellow, and the rest of the plumage greenish blue. It can be found as far north as Denmark, but its home extends from southern Spain and France through the Mediterranean area to Iran and beyond. It is migratory and winters in southern Africa.

Like the related family, the kingfisher (q.v.), the bee eaters nest in holes that they dig in earthen banks. When a colony is ready to nest, they select a bank and each pair digs a nesting burrow. A round chamber is formed, at the end of a passage about 6 to 8 ft. long, in which the white eggs are deposited on bare earth.

BEEF. *See* MEAT.

BEE FLY, common name for a fly of the family Bombyliidae, many species of which resemble bees in general appearance. Some bee flies resemble bumblebees while others are more slender. In general bee flies have large abdomens decorated with thickset hairs that may be yellow, orange, white, black, or any combination of these colors. The wings are transparent and have spots of black in patterns peculiar to each species. Bee flies tend to hover; their wings vibrate so rapidly they seem invisible, and the fly remains absolutely fixed over a spot. With wings still vibrating, a fly will dart off to hover over another spot a few feet away.

Adult bee flies live upon the nectar of flowers and are efficient agents in the cross fertilization of plants, the pollen adhering readily to the hairs on their abdomens. The larvae of bee flies are parasitic on other insects. Newly hatched maggots thrive on the egg mass of grasshoppers, caterpillars, beetle grubs, or the larvae of bees. *See* BEES; BUMBLEBEE.

BEELZEBUB *or* **BEELZEBUL** *or* **BAALZEBUB** (derived ultimately from the Heb. *ba'al zebub,* "Lord of flies"), in the Old Testament, god of the ancient Philistine city (*see* PHILISTINES) of Ekron, mentioned in 2 Kings 1:2. He was supposed to have the power of averting or controlling disease by dispersing the flies that infested the city. Beelzebub also is mentioned in the New Testament (Matt. 12:24) as the prince of demons; in Luke 11:15–20 Jesus denied that he cast out devils by the power of Beelzebub. In literature, notably in *Paradise Lost* by the English poet John Milton (q.v.), Beelzebub is described as a principal associate of Satan. *See* BAAL; DEVIL.

BEE MOTH *or* **WAX MOTH,** common name of a moth, *Galleria mellonella,* in the family Pyralididae. The bee moth has a slender, brownish or ashen-colored body and long legs. The larva of the bee moth feeds on the wax of the combs of the honeybee, often destroying the honey and injuring the bee brood. The larva of a smaller, but closely related, wax moth, *Achroia grisella,* also feeds on honeycombs.

BEER, term for fermented beverages made from cereal grains that have been converted to malt (q.v.). Beer may be brewed from any starchy grain, but in the United States it is generally made from malted barley, with corn, rice, or sugar as a malt adjunct, and is flavored with hops (*see* HOP). In the U.S., the word beer is usually understood to mean lager beer, which contains on the average 90 percent water, 3½ percent alcohol by weight, ½ percent carbon dioxide, and 6 percent extractives consisting of proteins, carbohydrates, minerals, and aromatic flavorings. It is a popular beverage because it does not deteriorate during long periods of storage and is adaptable to all climates. It is produced by bottom-fermenting yeasts; that is, yeasts that settle to the bottom, act slowly, and develop the brew at relatively low temperatures. Lager beer is stored for a time before being sold. Ale (q.v.) is usually produced by top-fermenting yeasts. These rise and act more violently. Ale has a higher alcoholic content and a more pronounced flavor and aroma of hops than beer. Porter is a type of ale that is sweeter and has less hop flavor. It is made with dark, or caramelized, malt which gives porter its rich dark color, heavy body, and creamy foam. Stout is similar to porter, but has a still heavier body, stronger hop flavor, and higher alcoholic content. Bock beer, high in flavor and alcoholic content, is brewed during the winter especially for use in the spring. In certain localities the composition of the water is especially favorable for production of a particular type of beer. Such beers are frequently named for the cities of their origin, as, for example, Munich, or Pilsener beer, and Burton ale. *See* BREWING.

History. Beer, by various names and in many forms, has been produced from the earliest times. It was made in ancient Mesopotamia and Egypt. Ale is believed to have originated among the early peoples of the British Isles. In Japan a kind of beer brewed from rice is called sake.

The Crimean Tatars prepare a beer from millet seed. Arabians, Ethiopians, and many African tribes make beer of grains native to the region, such as teff, millet, and grass seeds, in addition to the usual grains. The Russians use rye to prepare kvass. Weiss beer is made from malted wheat.

In the New World, the art of brewing was practiced by the Indians before the discoveries of Christopher Columbus. The first Europeans to brew beer in America were the Virginia colonists of 1587. Commercial breweries were set up as early as 1633 in New Amsterdam (later New York City), 1637 in Massachusetts Bay Colony, and 1638 by Roger Williams (q.v.) in Rhode Island. William Penn (q.v.) was among the pioneer brewers of Pennsylvania. His brewhouse, which stood for more than two hundred years, was erected in Pennsbury, Bucks County, Pennsylvania, in 1683. George Washington (q.v.) had his own brewhouse, and his recipe for beer, in his own handwriting, is in the archives of the New York Public Library. Samuel Adams (q.v.), the so-called Father of the Revolution, was briefly a brewer by profession.

Probably the most significant change from ancient to modern brewing occurred when the French biochemist Louis Pasteur (q.v.) proved that yeast is the cause of fermentation (q.v.). Scientists carried Pasteur's work further and differentiated many species of yeast, classifying them in several families and showing their different effects in the brewing process. As a result of these studies, brewers began to use pure cultures of yeast, and were soon able to maintain controls throughout the brewing process.

Manufacture of beer was encouraged in early colonial laws in America as a means of reducing the consumption of stronger alcoholic beverages. This traditional policy was followed generally in the laws of the various States and the Federal government until World War I. Under wartime restrictions the brewing of beer was first limited and then prohibited. Beer containing more than ½ percent of alcohol was included in the prohibition (q.v.) of intoxicating beverages by legislation under the Eighteenth Amendment to the Constitution. Congress legalized beer containing 3½ percent alcohol in March, 1933, and eight months later the prohibition amendment was repealed by the Twenty-first Amendment. The laws of the several States regulate the manufacture, distribution, and sale of beer within their jurisdictions, and provide for the licensing of brewers, distributors, and retailers. Direct taxes are laid on beer by all the States and by the Federal government. J.R.McB.

BEER, George Louis (1872–1920), American historian, born in New York City, and educated at Columbia University. A tobacco importer, he became an expert on British colonial history. In 1918–19, at the end of World War I, Beer was in Paris as chief of the Colonial Division of the American Commission to Negotiate Peace. In 1919 he was appointed director of the Mandatory Section of the League of Nations Secretariat (*see* LEAGUE OF NATIONS). The author of a number of historical volumes, his published works include *British Colonial Policy, 1754–1765* (1907); *The Origins of the British Colonial System, 1578–1660* (1908); and *The Old Colonial System, 1660–1754, Part I* (2 vol., 1912).

BEERBOHM, Sir Max (1872–1956), British essayist, critic, and caricaturist, half-brother of the actor Sir Herbert Beerbohm Tree (q.v.), born in London, England, and educated at Charterhouse and at Merton College, University of Oxford. He began his literary career with contributions to

Sir Max Beerbohm (self-portrait). Houghton Mifflin Co.

The Yellow Book, a quarterly illustrated by Aubrey Vincent Beardsley (q.v.). The British publisher Alfred Charles William Harmsworth, later Viscount Northcliffe (q.v.), recognized the talent of Beerbohm and employed him to work for his newspapers. Thus Beerbohm became a contributor to many London periodicals. He knew everybody and caricatured everybody, emphasizing the eccentricities and peculiarities of the leading figures of British social and political life in a long series of drawings which highly amused the London public. He became a favorite figure in London and was referred to as

"Max", the name with which he signed his caricatures. He was knighted in 1939 and thereafter was called "Sir Max".

Except for his one novel, *Zuleika Dobson* (1911), a satire on life at Oxford, his books are composed largely of material originally contributed to periodicals. Important among his works are the collections of essays, *The Happy Hypocrite* (1897), *More* (1889), *And Even Now* (1920), and *Variety of Things* (1928); his book of parodies of authors of his day, *A Christmas Garland* (1912); his volumes of pictorial caricatures, *Twenty-five Gentlemen* (1896), *The Poet's Corner* (1904), *Rosetti and His Circle* (1922), and *Observations* (1925); a volume of radio lectures delivered between 1935 and 1945, *Mainly on the Air* (1947); and a selected edition of articles on the London theater, *Around Theatres* (reissued in 1953).

BEERBOHM TREE. *See* TREE, SIR HERBERT BEERBOHM.

BEERNAERT, Auguste Marie François (1829–1912), Belgian statesman, born in Ostend. A lawyer by profession, he was elected to the Belgian Chamber of Deputies in 1873. In 1884 he received the portfolio of agriculture, industry, and art and soon afterward was appointed prime minister and minister of finance. In 1895 he was elected president of the Chamber of Deputies.

Beernaert was president of the International Law Association from 1903 to 1905. He was the first representative from Belgium at the Hague Conferences (q.v.) of 1899 and 1907. In 1909 he shared the Nobel Peace Prize with the French diplomat Baron d'Estournelles de Constant (q.v.).

BEERS, Clifford Whittingham (1876–1943), American humanitarian, born in New Haven, Conn., and educated at Yale University. As a result of a mental breakdown he was confined in an asylum from 1900 to 1903. After his recovery, he wrote a study of his experience, *A Mind That Found Itself* (1908), a book that was republished in successive editions for many years. Beers then devoted himself to the study and advancement of mental hygiene. He founded the Connecticut Society for Mental Hygiene in 1908 and similar organizations in later years, including, in 1931, the International Foundation for Mental Hygiene. In 1933 the National Institute of Social Sciences awarded him a gold medal for his "distinguished services for the benefit of mankind".

BEERSHEBA (Heb. *beer,* "well"; *sheba,* "oath, or seven"), in Biblical times, town in southern Judah in the territory of the tribe of Simeon. Its modern Arabic name is Bir es Saba. Several explanations are possible of the origin of the place and of the Hebrew name. According to a Biblical story (Gen. 21:22–31) involving Abraham and Abimelech, King of Gerar, the place received the name of either "well of oath", because the king exacted an oath of loyalty from Abraham, or of "well of seven", because, following a dispute over a well, Abraham gave Abimelech a gift of seven ewe lambs in witness of the fact that Abraham had dug the well. Abraham also planted a tamarisk at the place and invoked the name of God. Another account (Gen. 26:26–33) attributes the naming of the town to Isaac. Various other Biblical events are also set there (1. Sam. 8:2, 1 Kings 19:3, Amos 5:5, Neh. 11:27–30).

Beersheba was situated in the extreme southern part of Palestine, about 52 miles S.W. of Jerusalem. Its position led to use of the phrase "from Dan to Beersheba" to signify the extent of Hebrew territory from north to south (Judg. 20:1).

The new town of Bir es Saba has grown up in recent years S.W. of the old city and has a population of about 3000; the continuing excellence of the water supply in and about the town gives it importance as a source of irrigation for the surrounding area. By the terms of the United Nations decision (1947) to partition Palestine into independent Jewish and Arab states, the town was allocated to the proposed Arab state. Troops of the newly created state of Israel (q.v.), occupied the town, however, during the subsequent war (1948) between Israel and a coalition of Arab countries.

BEESWAX. *See* BEE.

BEET, common name for any plant of the genus *Beta* in the family Chenopodiaceae (*see* CHENOPODIUM). The genus contains few species, mostly biennials, that bear smooth, ovate, petioled root leaves, and, later, tall, leafy, flowering stems. Natives of the temperate parts of the Old World, they are now in general cultivation, chiefly for their large succulent roots, which are used as food for man and cattle and as a source of sugar. The most important species, *B. vulgaris,* has four recognized varieties. The var. *cicla,* called the leaf beet, has small roots and highly developed leaves. It is used mostly as an ornament in gardens. Others, such as chard (q.v.), called Swiss chard, have large leaves that are cooked for greens and thick leaf stalks that are also edible. Mangel-wurzel, var. *macrorhiza,* has large, coarse roots; it is also called the fodder beet, and is raised extensively as a field crop for cattle.

The var. *crassa,* called the garden beet or table

beet or red beet, has many subvarieties, distinguished by the depth of color and by the shape of the root, some being globular and others taprooted or carrot-shaped. The dark-red globular type, most esteemed as a table vegetable, is extensively grown as a truck-garden crop, and sometimes is cultivated under glass. Like all succulent roots, it has a high water content, 88 percent, and owes its food value chiefly to the 10 percent of carbohydrate it contains. Small percentages of protein, fat, fiber, and ash are also present, and the greens are rich in vitamins A and B. Most of the beet crop of the United States that is used as a table vegetable is frozen-packed or canned.

Another subvariety of *B. vulgaris crassa* is the sugar beet (q.v.), used as a source of sugar. It has large, white, conical roots containing a high percentage of sugar, which has been greatly increased by cultivation and selection; *see* SUGAR.

BEETHOVEN, Ludwig van (1770–1827), German composer, born in Bonn. His father, Johann van Beethoven (1739?–92), was a tenor in the choir of the elector's chapel at Bonn. When he began to teach his precocious five-year-old son the violin, he became the first of several incompetent teachers by whom the boy would be taught. Finally, when Ludwig was eleven, his musical education was taken over by the highly competent Christian Gottlob Neefe (1748–98), the organist of the elector's chapel. By 1784 Ludwig had been appointed assistant organist to Neefe, and in 1787 he was named violist in the court orchestra. Also in 1787 he made his first brief trip to Vienna, inspiring the well-known but apocryphal anecdote concerning his meeting and making a favorable impression upon the Austrian composer Wolfgang Amadeus Mozart (q.v.). During this trip Beethoven's mother, Maria Magdalena Keverich van Beethoven (1747–87), died. So he had to return to Bonn to support his family, his father having become a hopeless alcoholic. Soon he was hired as a music tutor for the wealthy von Breuning family, and Frau von Breuning, widow of the court counsellor Christoph von Breuning, became his devoted patron. Her son and daughter, Stephan and Eleanor von Breuning, became his lifelong friends.

Life in Vienna. His talent for playing the piano and his even more remarkable facility for improvisation gained him the patronage of several wealthy, titled Bonn music lovers. In 1792 Ludwig van Beethoven was sent to live and study in Vienna. When his father died later that year, he brought his two younger brothers, (Caspar Anton) Karl (1774–1815) and (Nikolaus) Johann (born 1776), to Vienna to live. During his first year in Vienna he studied music theory with the Austrian composer (Franz) Joseph Haydn (q.v.); after 1793 he studied with the Austrian teacher Johann Georg Albrechtsberger (1736–1809), the Austrian composer Johann Schenk (1753–1836), and the Italian composer Antonio Salieri (1750–1825), successively. At the same time he began a new career, becoming the first in the long line of struggling free-lance composers. Instead of holding a church or court appointment as other composers of his time did, Beethoven supported himself by selling his music. His compositions were priced according to their complexity; for example, a symphony cost more than a piano sonata. Some of these compositions were bought by music publishers; others were commissioned by his friends. He was also paid for playing the piano in the aristocratic salons of the city, and he had occasional piano pupils.

Ludwig van Beethoven (from a contemporary drawing).
Austrian Information Service

In 1798 he began to realize that he was growing deaf; in 1819 his deafness was total. By the beginning of the 19th century, when his deafness became noticeable to others, he had already achieved considerable fame, but more as a pianist and conductor than as a composer. Although he did write one letter in 1802 (later known as the "Heiligenstadt Testament") that expressed his agony over his approaching total deafness, he remained dedicated to his music.

He continued to conduct (until 1806), to play the piano (until 1814), and to compose (virtually until his death, although for many years he could only imagine the sound of his compositions).

Meanwhile, in 1815, his brother Karl had died and Beethoven's nine-year-old nephew, also named Karl, had become his ward. (Actually, the composer spent nearly five years contending with the boy's mother over the guardianship.) But the composer was not a wise choice to take charge of the boy, who soon grew into a frivolous, willful young man. There was enormous friction between the two, as Beethoven alternately spoiled and stormed at his nephew. These difficulties with his nephew epitomized Beethoven's stormy relationships with everyone with whom he came in contact.

The composer's personal characteristics have been vividly and extensively described by his contemporaries. His prime characteristic was his total, almost maniacal absorption with his work and its perfection. He was short and slender, with a heavily pocked-marked face and a mane of unkempt hair. He was unconcerned about his appearance, eccentric, irritable, frequently morose, and remarkably restless: during his years in Vienna he occupied nearly fifty different lodgings. Although he never married, he proposed to more than one woman and there has been a wealth of literary speculation as to the identity of the "Immortal Beloved" to whom he wrote one passionate undated letter. There has also been a wealth of literary speculation devoted to his death on March 26, 1827, accompanied, they say, by lightning and a violent thunderstorm.

Works. Beethoven composed 32 piano sonatas; 17 string quartets; 9 symphonies; 5 piano concertos; 1 violin concerto; 1 concerto for piano, violin, and cello; 5 sonatas for cello and piano; 10 sonatas for violin and piano; 1 opera; 1 ballet; 10 overtures; 2 masses; several cantatas; many songs; much chamber music for various instrumental combinations; and innumerable piano solos, including variations, bagatelles, and dances. His works have been grouped under a total of 259 opuses and added numbers.

When he arrived in Vienna, Beethoven already had a traveling case full of compositions. His musical life is usually divided by the critics into three periods. The Bonn compositions form part of the first period, which corresponds to the first 50 opus numbers he produced and includes more than 20 piano sonatas, the first 3 piano concertos, and his First and Second symphonies.

The second period begins in 1804. To this period belong the works often heard today in the concert halls of the world. The period begins with the composition of his Third Symphony, which Beethoven named the *Eroica*; it includes the Fifth (or *Fate*) Symphony; the Sixth (or *Pastoral*) Symphony; most of the familiar overtures; the Fourth and Fifth (*Emperor*) piano concertos; the opera *Fidelio*; the violin concerto; and several sonatas, including the *Kreutzer* for violin and piano and the *Appassionata* for solo piano.

In the third and final period, from 1816 until his death, Beethoven wrote the Ninth (or *Choral*) Symphony; the *Missa Solemnis*; the last five piano sonatas; and, during the last two years of his life, the string quartets opus 127 to opus 135. Throughout this third period, he composed exclusively for solo piano, for string quartet, or for symphony orchestra with solo voices.

Evaluation. It is virtually impossible to measure the impact of Ludwig van Beethoven on the history of music. Musicologists employ such phrases as the supreme genius or the titan and such adjectives as sublime, gigantic, and unique. They agree that after Beethoven music could not possibly be the same again. He had shaken up and recreated the old classical forms and brought to the composition of music a new element: the composer's personality. He was a Romantic (*see* ROMANTICISM), a part of, and a believer in, the movement that was reshaping artistic philosophies during his lifetime. He supported the Romantics' credo of freedom for the individual to express himself and the necessity for such expression to make some kind of personal statement. His own desire for perfection led him to rewrite, change, and develop his material incessantly.

Beethoven's early works were modeled on the sonatas, string quartets, and symphonies of Mozart and Haydn. But gradually he added his own touches. He employed sudden dramatic changes: in tempo, from loudness to softness, and from comic mood to tragic. His changes in chordal progression and from one key to another were previously undreamed of. He revolutionized accompaniment patterns, making the bass part more complicated by employing arpeggios (*see* ARPEGGIO) and heavy, repeated chords (*see* CHORD). He also included new instruments in his orchestrations, such as the piccolo, the trombone, and the contrabassoon. And he gave solo passages to the double bass, the cello, and the timpani for the first time. The major structural changes he introduced were in the formerly rigid sonata (q.v.) form, which he used in more than eighty of his compositions (one-third of the total). Beethoven was the first composer to link all four movements of the form thematically. He replaced the traditional minuet (q.v.) movement with the lighthearted scherzo (q.v.). But the more he experimented and changed, the less popular his works became. Early in his second period he began to be criticized for his lack of elegance and restraint. The monumental works of his last period were received with almost total rejection by contemporary critics. It was not until half a century later that they began to be regarded as masterpieces and that their profound influence on such later composers as the Germans Richard Wagner and Johannes Brahms (qq.v.) was acknowledged.

BEETLE, common name for insects of the order Coleoptera (Gr. *koleos,* "sheath"; *pteron,* "wing"), sometimes incorrectly applied to insects of other orders, such as roaches. The most prominent characteristic of the beetle is the *elytra,* the hardened, sheathlike front wings which in most beetles cover the entire abdomen when the insect is not in flight. In some beetles, such as the rove beetles, the elytra are short, covering only a portion of the abdomen; a few beetles are wingless. Although beetles vary greatly in size (from more than 6 in. to less than 1/50 in. when adult) and form, their anatomical structures are generally similar. Beetles undergo complete metamorphosis: the larvae are cylindrical grubs, with three pairs of legs on the thorax, and occasionally another pair on the last segment of the abdomen; the pupae are usually encased in a thin, light-colored skin with the legs free; the adults have biting mouth parts, in some cases enormously developed.

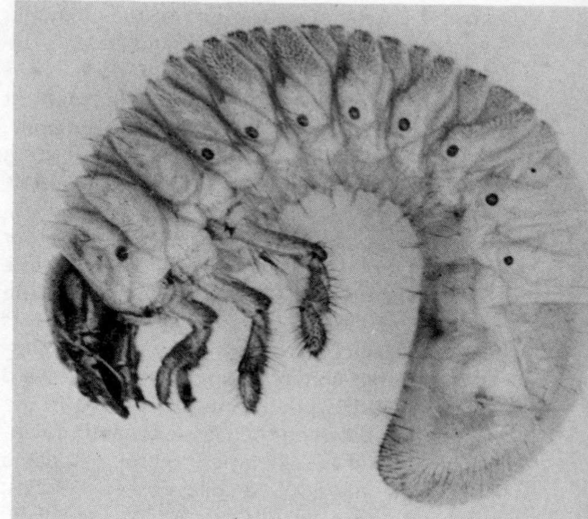

Beetle larva Cornell University

Striped cucumber beetle, Acalymma vittata

The order of beetles forms the largest major group in the animal kingdom. At least 200,000 kinds are known, of which more than 25,000 inhabit North America. Beetles constitute more than one quarter of all types of animals. Hundreds of families exist; some contain only one or two species, while others, such as the weevil (q.v.), contain 30,000 species, far more, for example, than the total number of different warm-blooded animals. The classification of this enormous number of forms is extremely difficult. The order is generally divided into several suborders, Adephaga, Clavicornia, Serricornia, Heteromera, Lamellicornia, Phytophaga, and Rhynchcophora; these are subdivided into series and superfamilies. The families are divided into subfamilies and subdivided into tribes and genera. Some coleopterists find still other groupings necessary to indicate the many relationships and differences among beetles.

Beetles vary widely in their habits and are found under the most diverse conditions. A few live in salt water, more in fresh water, and a small number breed in hot springs (*see* WATER BEETLE). Many beetles live under the bark of living and dead trees (*see* BARK BEETLE); numerous beetles feed on the roots, wood, leaves, flowers, and fruit of living plants, causing great economic damage; (*see* ENTOMOLOGY, ECONOMIC). Some beetles, such as the tiger beetle (q.v.), are carnivorous, hunting their prey in much the same way that a tiger does; others are scavengers, living on dung (*see* SCARAB) or dead animals. Some are parasites, or live in the nests of ants, bees, or termites, existing on food brought into the nest by the hosts or on the hosts themselves. Virtually every product of the animal or vegetable kingdom supplies some beetle, including the bookworm (q.v.), with food.

In addition to the articles noted above, most of which describe a single family or superfamily, *see also* BOMBARDIER BEETLE; DERMESTIDAE; FIREFLY; GROUND BEETLE; JAPANESE BEETLE; LADYBIRD BEETLE; LEAF BEETLE.

BEETS, Nikolaas (1814–1903), Dutch writer and pastor, born in Haarlem. As a student at the University of Leiden, he was influenced by the English poet George Gordon Byron (q.v.). Beets was one of the first to draw away from the classical school of Dutch writing and move toward romanticism. His poetry was an element in the controversy between the classicists and romantics. While still at Leiden he used the pen name Hildebrand, and wrote a collection of sketches, tales, and essays called *Camera Obscura* (1839). The collection continued the tradition of depicting domestic scenes in a realistic manner but combined it with a whimsical humor. *Camera Obscura* has been called the finest piece of prose in the Dutch literature of the 19th century.

Beets was ordained in 1839 and held pastorates between 1840 and 1874, when he became a professor at the State University of Utrecht. He left that position in 1884 and during his subsequent successful career in the church, he produced a great many works of prose and verse. His major works, however, were those written during his earlier years: *José* (1834), *Kuser* (1835), and the poetic tale *Guy de Vlaming* (1837). His later works include lyric songs and poetic tales. *See* DUTCH LITERATURE: *Romanticism.*

BEET SUGAR. *See* SUGAR; SUGAR BEET.

BEEVILLE, city in Texas, and county seat of Bee Co., about 49 miles N.W. of Corpus Christi. Located in an oil-producing, cattle-raising, agricultural region, the city is a processing, marketing, and trade center. Mattresses, saddles, boats, brooms, and oil-field equipment are manufactured. Pop. (1960) 13,811; (1970) 13,506.

BEGAS, family of German painters and sculptors.

Karl Begas (1794–1854), religious, historical, and portrait painter, born in Heinsberg, near Aachen. He studied painting in Paris from 1813 to 1822 with Baron Antoine Jean Gros (q.v.), and in Italy from 1822 to 1824 while he was court painter to Frederick William III (q.v.), King of Prussia. Begas successively adopted the viewpoints of the German Pre-Raphaelite, the Romantic, and the Realistic schools of painting. He is particularly noted for his historical and religious frescoes in Berlin churches, including "Baptism of Christ" and "Henry IV at Canossa"; and for his portraits of contemporary personages, including the German naturalist Baron Alexander von Humboldt, the German philologist and mythologist Jacob Ludwig Karl Grimm, and the German opera composer Giacomo Meyerbeer (qq.v.).

Oskar Begas (1828–83), painter, born in Berlin, son of Karl Begas. Oskar was a historical, genre, and portrait painter. Among his works are "Descent from the Cross" (Michaeliskirche, Berlin); portraits of William I, Emperor of Germany, and the German general Count Helmuth von Moltke (qq.v.); many landscapes; and mural decorations in Berlin Rathaus.

Reinhold Begas (1831–1911), sculptor, son of Karl Begas, born in Berlin. He was trained by the German sculptor Christian Daniel Rauch (q.v.) in Berlin. Begas' works are in the mode of the Romantic School. Among them are the group "Borussia" (surmounting the Berlin Bourse); the immense statue of William I, Emperor of Germany, in Berlin; and "Pan Consoling a Deserted Nymph".

Karl Begas (1845–1916), sculptor, son of Karl Begas, born in Berlin. He is most noted for his genre groups, portrait busts, and decorative monuments. Among his most famous works are "Boar Hunt" (Tiergarten, Berlin) and a monument commemorating the Franco-German War.

See GERMAN ART AND ARCHITECTURE.

BEGGAR'S-LICE, common name for certain sticky or prickly fruits that cling to the clothes of passers-by. The name is applied also to the plants that produce these adherent, burlike fruits. Plants given this name include the hound's-tongue and bed-straw (qq.v.).

BEGHARDS, semimonastic communities of laymen, the male counterparts of the Beguines (q.v.), originally composed of former artisans of the medieval craft guilds. Celibate and pious, the Beghards worked cooperatively, lived under a common roof, and shared their possessions. The oldest record of a Beghard community is that of the group in the city of Louvain (now in Belgium) in 1220. It is probable, however, that Beghard communities had been established earlier in a number of cities in the duchies of Brabant and Flanders. In the 13th century the Beghards spread throughout the Rhine valley and from there into Germany; a number of their communities were incorporated into the orders of the mendicant friars (q.v.).

As their communities became more numerous, the Beghards became involved in various social movements of the time, adopting some of the doctrines of the Apostolic Brethren, the Fraticelli (q.v.), and the Brethren of the Free Spirit, a sect of anarchistic freethinkers of southern Germany. In 1311 the Council of Vienne, under Pope Clement V (*see under* CLEMENT), denounced the Beghards as a heretical sect and decreed the suppression of their communities. Although Pope John XXII (*see under* JOHN) in 1321 allowed them to resume their original mode of life, they gradually disappeared.

BEGIN, Menachem *or* **BEIGIN, Menachem** (1913–), Israeli lawyer and political leader, born in Brest Litovsk, Russia (now Brest, U.S.S.R.), and educated in law at the University of Warsaw. He was head of Betar, a youth movement seeking the establishment of Palestine as an independent Jewish state, in Czechoslovakia (1936–38) and Poland (1939–40). In World War II he fought against Germany with the Polish army in exile. In 1943 he became commander in chief in Palestine of the Irgun Zvai Leumi (National Military Organization), the underground resistance force which fought to liberate Palestine from British rule. After the evacuation of the British forces in 1948 and the proclamation of the State of Israel, Begin and other members of the Irgun founded the Herut (Freedom Movement) Party. Begin was elected to the Knesset (parliament) in 1949. A conservative, he helped found the Gahal Party in 1965 and the Likud Party in 1973. After the Likud Party gained a plurality of parliamentary seats in the 1977 general election, Begin became premier.

BEGONIA, common and scientific name for a genus of tropical plants, the only important genus in the family Begoniaceae, which is related to the violet (q.v.) family (Violacea). Hundreds of species and varieties of begonias are cultivated, either for their flowers, some shade of red or pink, or for their large, showy leaves. The leaves, often colored or even variegated, usually have a curved axis, so that the leaves are longer on one side than on the other.

Begonias occur as either succulent herbs or low shrubs and are divided into three groups, according to the form of the roots, which are fibrous, tuberous, or rhizomatous. The groups hybridize freely. The genus *Begonia* was named in honor of the French colonial administrator Michel Begon (1638–1710), who was a patron of science.

BEGUINES, semimonastic communities of women, and the female counterparts of the Beghards (q.v.). The original members were widows of the Crusaders (*see* CRUSADES). Although the Beguines took no vows, they led pious lives and devoted themselves to the care of the infirm and the poor. Occasionally, they worked as teachers or performed manual labor. They retained what property they owned and were free to withdraw from their communities to marry.

The first Beguine community was established about 1180 in the city of Liège (now in Belgium). The movement has been associated with the name of Lambert le Bègue (d. 1177?), a priest of that city. Beguine communities, which included women of all classes, were established in several European countries. In the 13th century a number of Beguine communities were incorporated in the orders of the mendicant friars (q.v.); others remained independent, but became societies of religious beggars. Certain Beguine communities became involved in various social movements of the time.

In 1311 the Council of Vienne, under Pope Clement V (*see under* CLEMENT), denounced the Beguines as a heretical sect and ordered the suppression of their communities. Clement, however, had introduced a clause in which he exempted the orthodox communities of the West from suppression; and in 1319, his successor Pope John XXII (*see under* JOHN) took the Beguines of Brabant under his protection. Thus the sporadic persecution of the Beguines in the Rhineland during the 14th century was paralleled by their rehabilitation in Belgium. During the Reformation (q.v.) the Beguine communities were suppressed in the Protestant countries, and during the French Revolution, they were suppressed in France. A number of Beguine communities, organized according to the original rules of the order, still exist in the Netherlands, Belgium, and Germany; their members work among the poor.

BEHAIM, Martin *or* **BOHEIM, Martin** (1459?–1507), German geographer, born in Nuremberg. In 1484 he went to Portugal, where he acquired a reputation as a map maker. He claimed, probably falsely, to have accompanied the Portuguese navigator Diogo Cam (q.v.) in 1484 on a voyage along the western coast of Africa. In 1492 he fashioned a terrestrial globe, basing his work in part on the writings of the ancient Greek geographer and astronomer Ptolemy (q.v.) and in part on the discoveries of various medieval writers, notably the Italian traveler Marco Polo (q.v.). The globe, which is in Nuremberg, perpetuated many of the geographical misconceptions common among contemporary European cartographers.

BEHAN, Brendan (1923–64), Irish playwright and author, born in Dublin. Much of his life was spent in boisterous rebellion against authority in every form. He left school at the age of thirteen to join the outlawed Irish Republican Party (q.v.). Chiefly as a result of his subversive activities in England and Ireland, Behan spent much of the 1940's in reform school and prison. His observations of prison life were treated in a number of his works, perhaps the most noteworthy being *The Quare Fellow.* This play was produced in London in 1956, and in New York City in 1958, and was made into a motion picture in 1962. *The Hostage,* another of his highly successful plays, set in an Irish brothel, was staged in Dublin in 1958 and in New York in 1960. Behan's plays are marked by an abundant use of earthy dialogue and trenchant humor. His prose works include *Borstal Boy* (1958), an account of his first term in prison, *Brendan Behan's Island* (1962), a collection of Irish anecdotes, *Hold Your Hour and Have Another* (1964), and *The Scarperer* (1964).

BEHAR. *See* BIHAR.

BEHAVIORAL SCIENCES, those fields of study whose major concern is the understanding, prediction, or control of behavior, especially those types of human behavior that develop out of relations with other people. Although many fields of study contribute to behavioral science, a number of disciplines are so overwhelmingly concerned with past or present behavior that they can be classed together as the behavioral sciences. These disciplines include anthropology, economics, education, geography, history, linguistics, political science, psychiatry, psychology, and sociology. Investigators who work in these areas focus their attention on human behavior as it influences and is influenced by the behavior and needs of other people. Previously, these disciplines were referred to as the social sciences, a term that has increasingly become interchangeable with behavioral sciences.

The behavioral sciences may be approached in at least two different ways. One approach is professional, as when a university sets up a division of behavioral sciences. The other approach is functional, as when an investigator describes or explains the behavior of an organism. In this latter approach, a physiologist is not a behavioral scientist when he considers the influence of the pituitary upon the adrenal glands, but he is one when he considers the relation between the same glands and behavior.

A major application of behavioral science has been in the prediction of behavior. An example is the polling and testing movement, which includes political and marketing surveys, questionnaires, and attitudes tests, as well as psychological and industrial tests of aptitude, ability, achievement, and personality. Applied to the understanding of behavior, behavioral science has produced various theories of individual and social behavior and the disruption of such behavior, and these theories have had wide influence on social thought and practice. In the application of the behavioral sciences to the control of behavior, various procedures designed to influence behavior indirectly or to control it directly in a systematic manner are being developed, along with new procedures to facilitate training and instruction.

The behavioral sciences have not yet produced an organizing theory comparable with the periodic table of elements, possibly because their traditions, methods, and practices still display a bewildering variety. As relevant variables are slowly discovered, it becomes possible to predict and control behavior to an increasing extent. A technology of behavior is emerging that can be applied to education, correction, and psychotherapy, as well as to the problems of daily life. I.G.

BEHAVIORISM, name of an American school of psychology or, generally, the view that the subject matter of psychology is the behavior of animals, including man; or, more particularly, the responses of muscles and glands to variables in the physical environment.

History and Theory. The 20th-century American psychologist John B. Watson (q.v.), founder and leader of the behavioristic school, argued

John B. Watson

Ivan Pavlov National Library of Medicine

B. F. Skinner Boris and Milton, Boston

that neither the mind nor mental activity could provide measurable scientific data, and that previous methods of introspection were both unreliable and invalid. The task of psychology, he maintained, is to predict and control behavior by analyzing behavior into muscular and glandular elements, openly observable or detectable through the instruments of physical science, and by relating them to environmental events and internal physiological functions. Among the controversial aspects of his position were an emphasis on the influence of environment at the expense of instinct and hereditary traits, an extension of the conditioned-reflex principle of Ivan P. Pavlov (q.v.), to account for all learning, and the identification of covert speech or gesture as thought. Among philosophers, this position can be traced back to the Greek objectivists, the French materialists, and the positivist Auguste Comte (q.v.), among others. In natural science, its antecedents can be found in the study of reflex action, from the English physician and physiologist Marshall Hall (1790–1857) to Pavlov and the Russian neuropathologist Vladimir Mikhailovich Bekhterev (1857–1927); in the Darwinian belief in biological continuity; in the observations of trial-and-error learning by Conway Lloyd Morgan (1852–1936), English zoologist and psychologist, and Edward Lee Thorndike (q.v.); and in the investigations of animal tropisms by Jacques Loeb (q.v.) and others. In retrospect, Watsonian behaviorism seems often to have been an exercise in the translation of images, sensations, and feelings into the language of response. It did, however, induce an attitude of objectivity, and it had the salutary effect of encouraging a practical operationalism, well in advance of the work of the logical positivists.

Influence of Skinner, Hull, and Others. The diverse contributions of such men as the American psychologists Walter Samuel Hunter (1889–1954), Edwin Ray Guthrie (1886–1959), and Edward C. Tolman (1886–1959) set the stage for an account of animal and human behavior based on laboratory data instead of introspective observations. These contributions were made independent of physiology and were scientific in the spirit of both Pavlov and Thorndike. Such an account was provided in the 1930's by the American psychologist B. F. Skinner (q.v.) with the development of a new methodology, the completion of a brilliant series of animal experiments, and the formulation of a system of behavior. Skinner postulated a type of psychological conditioning known as reinforcement (q.v.). What Pavlov had done for reflex, or respondent,

Behaviorism. Plate 1. *Behavioral studies of primates took a major step forward in the 1970's as scientists at several U.S. laboratories attempted to learn if apes had the conceptual ability to understand a human-style language. At the Yerkes Regional Primate Research Center in Atlanta, Ga., researchers trained this female chimpanzee, Lana, to "communicate" by forming modified sentences in English using a computerized keyboard. In this sequence of four photographs, Lana presses the appropriate keys to form the sentence: "Please machine give piece of bread (period)" and in the last picture accepts her reward. Late in 1974 Lana stopped being a passive learner and began to "conceive" more sophisticated, abstract ideas, "asking" the names of unfamiliar objects, identifying six different colors, and requesting comforts such as the playing of music or movies.*

Yerkes Regional Primate Research Center

behavior, Skinner with his theory of reinforcement did for voluntary, or operant, behavior. Taking as his unifying concept this theory of reinforcement, Skinner gave Thorndike's "law of effect" a status comparable to Pavlov's conditioned reflex but rejecting physiological implication.

During the 1940's, another influential doctrine was developed at Yale University under the leadership of Clark Leonard Hull (1884–1952), an American professor of psychology. According to Hull, certain plausible assumptions are made about behavior and its causes; their consequences are deduced in detail and then put to empirical test in specially designed experiments. The outcome of these experiments is then used to verify, discard, or revise the assumptions. The initial postulates commonly came from conditioned-reflex generalizations; the type of experiment came primarily from Pavlov, Thorndike, and other students of animal maze-learning behavior, with latency, that is, the time between stimulus and response, as the most common measure. Reinforcement was equated with reduction of need, rather than with the mere operation of presenting or removing stimuli, as in the Skinner system; and organismic, or intervening, variables were inferred when their existence was deemed essential to the explanation of behavior.

Modern Experimental Research on Learning. The influence of Skinner and Hull dominates modern experimental research on learning, which increasingly approximates the field of psychology itself. Of the two positions, however, the one launched by Skinner is clearly in the ascendancy. This situation derives in part from the contributions of Skinner in the vital areas of textbook writing, analysis of language, and educational technique. The trend also results from the activities of a large and ever-increasing group of young psychologists in the United States and abroad. These men have notably advanced the experimental analysis of behavior within academic psychology or have applied it within such practical spheres as those of behavior therapy, psychopharmacology, rehabilitation, and programmed instruction (q.v.).

Very few present-day psychologists would readily accept the label "behaviorist". It could be argued, however, that most psychologists and certainly all experimentalists are at least methodological behaviorists who take behavior as their primary observable datum and deal with it in terms of objectively defined variables prior to any consideration of mental, physiological, or other inner states. F.S.K.

BEHEMOTH (Heb., plural of *b'hemah,* "beast", a word of Egyptian origin), in the Old Testament, the name of a large and strong four-footed beast (Job 40:15-24). Some scholars believe the term refers to a hippopotamus; others, to an elephant. *See also* LEVIATHAN.

BEHISTUN INSCRIPTION, cuneiform inscription in the relief panel carved in the precipitous limestone rock of a mountain, 500 ft. above the present village of Behistun, in western Iran, 22 mi. northeast of Kermanshah. The inscription was carved in parallel columns, repeating the same text in the Old Persian, Assyrian, and Elamite languages, by order of the Persian king Darius I (*see under* DARIUS), who reigned from 521 to 486 B.C.; it recounts his genealogy and conquests. In 1835 the British Assyriologist Sir Henry Creswicke Rawlinson (q.v.) began a study of the rock and by 1846 he had deciphered the Persian part of the inscription. As a result of this achievement, the parallel columns of the Behistun Inscription were deciphered and became the key to deciphering other ancient Elamite and Assyrian writings.

BEHN, Aphra *or* **BEHN, Afra** *or* **BEHN, Aphara** *or* **BEHN, Ayfara** (1640?–89), English novelist. As a child she was taken to live in Surinam, West Indies, an English possession, by a couple named Amis, who may have been her parents. In 1658, when Surinam was ceded to the Dutch and became part of Dutch Guiana, Aphra returned to England, where she married a merchant named Behn. Charles II (q.v.), King of England, employed Mrs. Behn as a spy in Antwerp during the war of 1665 to 1667 against the Dutch. She was not paid for her work and was jailed briefly for debt. Subsequently, she turned to writing for a living and became probably the first professional woman writer in England. Among her many works are poems and plays, the latter including *The Rover* (1677; second part 1681). Her novel *Oroonoko* (1688?), which influenced the development of the English novel, formed the basis of a tragedy of the same name written by the English dramatist Thomas Southerne (q.v.).

BEHRENS, Peter (1868–1940), German architect, painter, and designer, born in Hamburg, Germany. He received his early training as a painter, turning to architecture in 1900. Rejecting the florid art-nouveau style to which he had previously been attached, Behrens soon developed an austerely geometric style of architecture that, in time, became a standard in the design of highly functional modern industrial buildings. In 1909 he was appointed architect to an American electrical firm in Germany, and thereafter devoted himself largely to industrial architecture. Behrens-designed buildings were early examples of the use of modern techniques and materials. His buildings were constructed of poured concrete and typified by the lavish use of glass and exposed exterior steel supports. At the time he designed these structures, Behrens employed three architects who later became leading architects of the 20th century, Walter Gropius, Ludwig Mies van der Rohe, and Le Corbusier (qq.v.).

BEHRING, Emil Adolph von (1854–1917), German bacteriologist, born in Deutsch-Eylau, Prussia (now Iława, Poland), and educated at the University of Berlin. In 1880 he became an army surgeon. He was appointed professor at the University of Halle in 1894, and the following year became director of the Hygienic Institute at Marburg, a post he held until his death. In 1890, while working in the laboratory of the German bacteriologist Robert Koch (q.v.) in Berlin, Behring and the Japanese bacteriologist Shibasaburo Kitazato (1852–1931) discovered that injecting the blood serum of an animal that has tetanus into another animal will produce an immunity against the disease in the second animal. Serum from the immunized animal can then be injected into another individual in whom it will produce immunity to the same disease. This principle was applied the following year to fight diphtheria in children, with dramatically successful results. In 1901 Behring was awarded the first Nobel Prize in medicine and physiology. *See* VACCINATION.

BEHRMAN, Samuel Nathaniel (1893–1973), American playwright, born in Worcester, Mass., and educated at Clark College and Harvard and Columbia universities. At Harvard he was a member of the 47 Workshop, a playwriting class conducted by the American educator George Pierce Baker (q.v.).

S. N. Behrman, as he is usually known, wrote twenty-one plays for the Broadway stage. Almost all of them, from *The Second Man* (1927) through *But for Whom Charlie* (1964), are comedies of manners, noted for the sophistication and wit of their dialogue and the incisiveness of their characterizations. Among his most popular dramatic works are *Biography* (1933) and *No Time for Comedy* (1939). Behrman also wrote screenplays throughout his career.

He was also the author of *Duveen* (1952), a biography of the British art dealer Joseph Duveen (1869–1939). *The Worcester Account* (1954) and *People in a Diary* (1972) contain Behrman's memoirs, and *The Suspended Drawing Room* (1965) is a collection of his essays.

BEIDERBECKE, Leon Bismark, popularly BIX BEIDERBECKE (1903–31), American jazz cornet player, born in Davenport, Iowa, and educated at the Lake Forest (Ill.) Military Academy. Though he was one of the most original and accomplished of jazz musicians, he achieved popularity only after his death, through the wide circulation of his recordings. Beiderbecke first played professionally with a Chicago band called the "Wolverines". Upon his return to Chicago in 1925, he worked with the orchestra of Charlie Straight and occasionally with the bands of Louis Armstrong (q.v.), King Oliver (1889–1938), and others. The following year he played with the orchestra of Frank Trumbauer (1900–56) in Saint Louis and in 1926 played with the band of Jean Goldkette. From 1927 until just before he died of pneumonia, he was a featured player with the Paul Whiteman (q.v.) band.

BEIRA, city and seaport in Mozambique, capital of the province of Manica e Sofala, on Mozambique Channel, an inlet of the Indian Ocean, at the mouth of the navigable Pungwe R., about 450 miles N.E. of Maputo. It is connected by rail with Rhodesia, the Republic of Zambia, the Republic of South Africa, the Republic of Zaire, and Malawi, and it is the chief port for Malawi, Zambia, Rhodesia, and central Mozambique. The principal exports are sugar, tobacco, corn, cotton, sisal, chrome and copper ore, coal, and lead. The chief industries of Beira are cotton milling, food processing, and ship repair. Before 1942, when the province of Manica e Sofala was incorporated into Mozambique, Beira was the capital of the territory of the Portuguese-chartered Mozambique Company. Pop. (1970 prelim.) 113,770.

BEIRAM. *See* BAIRAM.

BEIRUT *or* **BEYROUTH** (anc. *Berytus*), capital, largest city, and chief seaport of Lebanon, on the Mediterranean Sea, at the foot of the Lebanon range of mountains, about 40 miles S.W. of Tarabulus. The city is linked by railroad and highway to Damascus, Syria, 50 mi. to the S.E., and to other major Middle East cities. It also has an international airport.

Silk and cotton fabrics and gold and silver articles are the chief manufactures of Beirut. The leading exports are silk, cotton textiles, fruits, hides, livestock, wool, and silk cocoons. Imports include building materials, clothing, and foods.

Beirut is an ancient town with modern suburbs. It has numerous mosques and Christian churches, several museums, and the American University of Beirut (q.v.), Saint Joseph's University, Lebanese University, and Beirut Arab University.

Beirut was mentioned in the Tell-el-Amarna (q.v.) tablets as early as the 15th century B.C. Under the Roman emperors it was the seat of a school of law. In 635 A.D. it was conquered by the Arabs and in 1110 was besieged and captured by Baldwin I (*see under* BALDWIN), King of Jerusalem. In 1187 it was taken by Saladin (q.v.), Sultan of Egypt and Syria, and in 1291 it fell to the Muslims. During the 16th century, the region became part of the Ottoman Empire, and control of the city was maintained by the Druzes (q.v.), a Syrian religious sect. On Oct. 8, 1918, during World War I, the city was captured by Allied forces under the command of the British general Edmund Henry Hynman Allenby, 1st Viscount Allenby (q.v.). Since Lebanese independence in 1941, Beirut has been the capital. Pop. (greater city; 1970 est.) 800,000.

BEISSEL, Johann Conrad (1690–1768), German-American clergyman, born in Eberbach. He was successively a baker, a violinist, and a theologian. Banished in 1720 for holding pietistic and inspirational views, he emigrated to America and settled in Germantown (now part of Philadelphia), Pa., where in 1725 he founded the sect of Dunkers. In 1732 he founded a monastic society for men and women and established a community at Ephrata (q.v.), Pa., where he became known to his followers as "Friedsam Gottrecht". He wrote and published both the words and music for over 400 hymns. Beissel's melodies influenced the contributions of later American hymn writers.

BEJA, city in Portugal, capital of Baixo Alentejo Province and of Beja District, about 85 miles S.E. of Lisbon. Pottery, olive oil, cheese, leather goods, and cloth are produced in the city. Beja is the seat of a bishopric and the site of a cathedral and a 14th-century citadel. An ancient Roman city, it was originally called Pax Julia. After the fall of the Roman Empire, the city became a Moorish stronghold. It was reconquered by Alfonso I (q.v.), King of Portugal, in 1162. Pop. (1970 prelim.) 37,205.

BÉJAÏA *or* **BOUGIE,** city and seaport of Algeria, in Constantine Department, on the Bay of Bougie, about 115 miles E. of Algiers. Wine, minerals, wool, hides, and oils are the chief articles of trade. Founded in ancient times by Carthaginians, the city became an important commercial and military center (called Saldoe) of the Roman Empire. In the 5th century it was seized and fortified by Genseric (q.v.), King of the Vandals. Occupied by Berbers in later times, the city in 1062 became the capital of a Berber dynasty; *see* BERBER. For a long period thereafter it was one of the chief ports of North Africa. After successive occupations of the region by Spain and Turkey, in the 16th century, the city declined in importance until, at the beginning of the 19th century, it contained little more than ruins. Following its capture by the French in 1833, however, Béjaïa regained a large part of its former importance. The harbor was enlarged and improved, and the town was connected by a spur line to the Tunis-Oran railroad. Pop. (latest census) 49,930.

BÉKÉSY, Georg von (1899–1972), Hungarian-American physicist, born in Budapest and educated at the University of Bern and the University of Budapest. He worked in the laboratories of the Hungarian telephone system from 1923 to 1946. In 1946 he went to Stockholm, where he did research in sound and hearing mechanisms. From 1949 until 1966 he taught at Harvard University. In 1966 he became professor of sensory science at the University of Hawaii. Békésy invented the audiometer, an instrument for measuring hearing ability, and was the first to demonstrate the functions of the cochlea within the inner ear. He was awarded the 1961 Nobel Prize in medicine and physiology.

BEL, supreme god, or one of the chief gods, of the Babylonians (Isa. 46). Bel is the Chaldaic form of Baal (q.v.), and is believed by some to be identical with that god. Like the equivalent Hebrew "Ba'al", the name "Bel" was used also in the sense of "lord" or "owner". Bel presided over the air. His consort was Belit. Bel was identified with the Greek god Zeus (q.v.) by the Greek historian Herodotus (q.v.) and was believed by the British Orientalist George Rawlinson (1812–1902) to have been different from the Syrian Baal. As Bel-Merodach the god was connected with the planet Jupiter, associated in astral mythology with the productive power of nature.

BEL AND THE DRAGON, book of the Old Testament Apocrypha (*see* BIBLE: *The Apocrypha*), in the King James Version, THE HISTORY OF THE DESTRUCTION OF BEL AND THE DRAGON. The book relates two legends about the prophet Daniel (q.v.). The first tells how Daniel proved the worthlessness of the Babylonian god Bel (q.v.) by revealing that food supposedly eaten by the god was actually eaten by the priests of Bel. The second tells of Daniel's miraculous delivery from a den of lions into which he had been thrown for killing a dragon revered by the Babylonians. In some versions of the Bible, Bel and the Dragon is attached to the canonical book of Daniel (*see* book of DANIEL), as are the two books Song of the Three Holy Children and Susanna (qq.v.).

BELASCO, David (1859–1931), American playwright, theatrical producer, and theater manager, born in San Francisco, Calif., and educated in local schools there and in Victoria, British Columbia, Canada, where his family lived for a time. He worked as an actor, writer, and stage manager in San Francisco from 1874 to 1882. His successful melodrama, *Hearts of Oak*, was produced in 1879. From 1882 to 1886 Belasco was manager of the Madison Square Theater and from 1887 until 1902, in association with the American theater manager Daniel Frohman (q.v.), he managed the Lyceum Theater (both in New York City). During this period Belasco established his reputation as one of the most popular of contemporary American playwrights, with such melodramas as *The Girl I Left Behind Me* (1893) and *Heart of Maryland* (1895).

Also famous as a producer, he staged plays as vehicles for many notable American actors. As owner and operator of the Belasco Theater in New York City from 1907 until his death, Belasco permanently influenced American production techniques through his insistence on natural styles of acting, elaborate theater facilities, and, above all, minutely realistic stage settings and properties.

Among Belasco's plays were *Madame Butterfly* (1900) and *The Girl of the Golden West* (1905), both later adapted by the Italian operatic composer Giacomo Puccini (q.v.). Belasco also wrote *The Return of Peter Grimm* (1911) and *Laugh, Clown, Laugh* (1923).

BELÉM, *or* PARÁ, city in Brazil, capital of Pará State and chief port of the lower Amazon R., near the equator, on the S. shore of the Pará R. estuary, about 90 mi. from the Atlantic Ocean, about 300 miles N.W. of São Luís. The port is accessible to oceangoing ships and includes a naval base. Founded in 1615 by the Portuguese, Belém owes its commercial importance to the opening of the Amazon to foreign trade in the late 19th century. The principal item of trade is rubber; other products include nuts, cacao, jute, and timber. In the city are sawmills, machine shops, shipyards, and brick, tile, and soap factories. One of the most attractive cities in South America, Belém has numerous public squares and well-paved streets, many of which extend to the edge of the jungle. The cultural center of N. Brazil, Belém is the site of the Teatro da Paz, the Goeldi Museum, and the Agricultural Institute of the North. Since 1723 Belém has been the see of a Roman Catholic bishopric. Pop. (1970 est.) 565,097.

BELFAST, city and port of entry in Maine, and county seat of Waldo Co., on the W. shore of Penobscot Bay, about 30 miles S.W. of Bangor. The city is a summer resort. Industries in Belfast include the manufacture of shoes, lumber and lumber products, and hardware. Settled around 1770, Belfast was incorporated in 1773 and chartered in 1853. Pop. (1960) 6140; (1970) 5957.

BELFAST, Great Britain, city and capital of Northern Ireland, county borough and administrative center of County Antrim, at the confluence of the Lagan R. and Belfast Lough, about 12 mi. from the North Channel of the Irish Sea and about 113 miles N. of Dublin, Ireland. Although the city forms a separate administrative district, it is partly in County Antrim and partly in County Down.

Belfast is a major commercial and industrial city. Long known as the center of the Irish linen industry, it also has a large shipyard and plants manufacturing aircraft, tobacco products, clothing, and canned goods. Ships, aircraft, dairy products, agricultural produce, livestock, and linen textiles are the chief exports. Located in the city are the Protestant cathedral of Saint Anne, Belfast Library and Society for Promoting Knowledge (1788), Queen's University of Belfast, and the College of Technology (1901).

History. Belfast was the site of a castle built about 1175 and destroyed by Edward Bruce (d. 1318) in 1315, the year he ascended the Irish throne. The English acquired control of the town in 1571. Belfast received a charter from James I (q.v.), King of England, in 1613, and widespread immigration, notably by Scottish Presbyterians, was encouraged by the government. Late in the 17th century large numbers of French Huguenot refugees settled in Belfast, bringing skilled manpower and valuable production techniques to the Irish linen industry. Cotton-textile manufacturing was introduced about 1770, and shipbuilding began on a large scale in 1796. Belfast was incorporated as a city in 1888, became a county borough in 1898, and in 1920 was made the capital of Northern Ireland. During World War II, Belfast was heavily damaged by German bombing raids. Beginning in 1969, the city was the site of civil-rights agitation, violent riots, and military skirmishes; *see* NORTHERN IRELAND: *History: Growing Violence*. Pop. (1971 prelim.) 360,150.

BELFAST, QUEEN'S UNIVERSITY OF, nonsectarian coeducational institution of higher learning, located in Belfast, Northern Ireland, and supported principally by government subsidies. The institution, founded in 1845, was incorporated in 1849 as Queen's College, a unit of Queen's University which also included colleges in Cork and Galway; *see* IRELAND, NATIONAL

UNIVERSITY OF. In 1908 Queen's College in Belfast was reconstituted a separate university. The university consists of faculties of agriculture, applied science and technology, the arts, theology, economics, education, law, medicine, and science. Courses in applied science are provided through the City of Belfast College of Technology. Theological studies for candidates for the Presbyterian ministry are available through the Presbyterian College, which is financially independent of the university. The university confers the degrees of bachelor, master, and doctor. The library contains more than 500,000 volumes. In 1970–71 enrollment totaled about 6390 students, and the faculty numbered about 565.

BELFORT, city in France, capital of Belfort Department, on the Savoureuse R., on the border with Switzerland, about 88 miles N.E. of Dijon. Textiles, engines, automobiles, and chemicals are manufactured in the city, and it is a center for trade in wines and grain. "The Lion of Belfort", a statue by Frédéric Auguste Bartholdi (q.v.), is located here. Belfort is strategically important because it lies in the Trouée de Belfort, a pass between the Vosges and Jura mountain ranges; this pass commands the roads between France, Switzerland, and Germany. Ceded to France by Austria in 1648, Belfort withstood many sieges, but was occupied by the Germans in World War II. The Allies recaptured it in November, 1944. Pop. (1970) 53,001.

BELFRY. *See* BELL TOWER.

BELGAE, Celtic-speaking people of antiquity, comprising one of the chief divisions of the Celtic linguistic stock found by invading Romans in Gaul (q.v.). According to the Roman general, statesman, and historian Gaius Julius Caesar (q.v.), who recorded the first written account of the Belgae, they inhabited mainly the region enclosed by what are now the Seine, Marne, Moselle, and Rhine rivers and the English Channel and the North Sea (now Belgium, part of northeastern France, and a portion of the Netherlands). Some of the Belgae had previously crossed the English Channel and settled in southern Britain, especially in what are now Sussex and Kent. Composed of numerous tribes, notably the Atrebates, Remi, Bellovaci, and Suessiones, the Belgae offered fierce resistance to Caesar's legions, which began the conquest of Gaul in 58 B.C., but were forced to lay down their arms in 57 B.C. Some authorities believe the modern Belgians are probably descendants of the Belgae.

BELGAUM, city of the Republic of India, in Karnataka State, capital of Belgaum District, 250 miles S.E. of Bombay. The chief industries are cotton, rice, and oilseed milling, tanning, and the manufacture of chemicals, textiles, cameras, truck bodies, and furniture. The district produces rice, timber, ghee (buffalo-milk butter), and jaggery (brown sugar made from palm sap). The city has colleges of arts and law. The records of the city date from the 6th century. Built on the site of ancient Venugrama, Belgaum was capital of the Ratta dynasty from 1210 to 1250. A fortress here dates from 1519. Pop. (1971) 192,427.

BEL GEDDES, Norman. *See* GEDDES, NORMAN BEL.

BELGIAN CONGO. *See* ZAIRE, REPUBLIC OF: *History.*

BELGIAN SHEEP DOG, breed of working dog existing in six varieties, the most important of which are the Groenendael and the Malinois. The Groenendael is named for the Belgian village where it was developed in the latter part of the 19th century and the Malinois for the town of Malines (Mechelen), Belgium. The two varieties have similar characteristics and differ greatly only in the nature and color of the coat. The Groenendael has a long-haired black coat, and the Malinois, a coat of short hair, fawn-colored with dark streaks. The male of both varieties is about 23½ in. high at the shoulder, and the female, about 22½ in.; the dog weighs about 50 lb. Both varieties have a flattened skull; brown eyes which have an alert, questioning, and intelligent expression; triangular ears held stiffly erect; a round neck; powerful back, loins, and hips; and a tail of medium length held low when the animal is at rest and raised and curled toward the body when the dog is in action. All varieties of the breed are used for guarding sheep, as watchdogs, and for police work.

Belgian sheep dog. Evelyn Shafer

BELGIUM (French, *Belgique*; Flemish, *Belgie*), kingdom of N.W. Europe, bounded on the N. by the Netherlands and the North Sea, on the E. by Germany and Luxembourg, and on the S. and S.W. by France. It lies between lat. 49°30′ N. and lat. 51°30′ N. and long. 2°35′ E. and long. 6°25′ E. The country is about 175 mi. long, measured in a southeast-to-northwest direction, and about 90 mi. wide, and is roughly triangular in shape. The area is 11,775 sq.mi.

THE LAND

Belgium has three main geographical sections: the coastal region, the central plain, and the Ardennes highlands.

The coastal region is a low-lying area consisting mainly of sand dunes and of polders. The polders, sections of land reclaimed from the sea and protected by dikes, were developed between the 13th and 15th centuries. The reclaimed land constitutes about 10 percent of the area of Belgium. The coastal district, extending about 10 to 30 mi. inland, is flat pastureland drained by canals. The altitude ranges from slightly below sea level to about 65 ft.

The central plain is a gently rolling, slightly elevated area irrigated by many waterways and containing a number of wide, fertile valleys with a rich, alluvial soil. Many caves, grottoes, and ravines are found in parts of this area.

The Ardennes highlands, a densely wooded plateau averaging 1500 ft. in elevation, extends into S.E. Belgium from N.E. France. The area is generally rocky and poorly suited to agriculture. The Ardennes region is one of the oldest inhabited parts of Europe, and many relics of prehistoric man have been found there.

The chief rivers are the Scheldt (Schelde) and the Meuse. Both rise in France and are for the most part navigable in Belgium. On the Scheldt, the principal waterway of Belgium, are the ports of Antwerp, Brussels, and Ghent. The chief tributaries of the Scheldt are the Lys, Dender, Senne, and Rupel rivers. The Sambre and Ourthe rivers are the main tributaries of the Meuse.

CLIMATE. The climate near the sea is humid and mild. Farther inland a marked increase in the range of temperature occurs. In the Ardennes section hot summers alternate with very cold winters. Heavy rains are confined almost exclusively to the highlands. Fog and drizzle are common, and April and November are particularly rainy months. The mean annual temperature in Brussels is 50° F. (36° F. in January, 65° F. in July). The average annual rainfall for the entire country is 27.5 in.; the average annual temperature is 47° F.

Natural Resources. The natural resources of Belgium are almost entirely mineral. Coal is mined in abundance. Deposits of zinc, lead, copper, and manganese are also exploited but are of little commercial significance.

PLANTS AND ANIMALS. Small animals, chiefly foxes, badgers, squirrels, weasels, martens, and hedgehogs, are found in Belgium. Abundant plants include the hyacinth, strawberry, goldenrod, periwinkle, foxglove, wild arum, and lily of the valley.

SOILS. Much of the region comprising Belgium is an extension of the geological formations characteristic of France and Germany. The Ardennes massif forms part of an ancient, worn-down mountain system. Outcroppings of Cambrian and Silurian rocks are found in the center of the massif along with slate, shale, and limestone of the Upper Devonian period. Extensive chalk downs extend in a northeast-to-southwest direction through the central plain. Most of the central plain consists of Tertiary deposits of clay and sand. Quaternary deposits of sands, peat, and alluvions occupy the coastal regions.

THE PEOPLE

The people of Belgium are chiefly of two ethnic stocks, the Fleming (Teutonic origin) and the Walloon (Celtic origin, probably with an admixture of Alpine elements). The Flemings, like the Dutch, are of fair complexion; southern Belgians resemble the dark-haired French. The predominantly Flemish provinces are in the N. half of the country and the predominantly Walloon provinces are in the S. half. The ratio of Flemings to Walloons is 5 to 3.

Population. The population of Belgium (census 1961) was 9,189,741; the United Nations estimated (1971) 9,726,000. The overall population density, one of the highest in Europe, is about 829 per sq.mi. (1971 est.). The largest concentrations are in the Brussels, Antwerp, Liège, and Ghent industrial areas, as well as in the narrow coal-mining region between Mons and Charleroi. In recent years the Limburg region increased in population owing to industrial expansion in that area. Over 10 percent of the inhabitants live in Brussels. Some 70 percent of the population lives in communities of less than 25,000 inhabitants.

Political Divisions and Principal Cities. Belgium is divided into the nine provinces of Antwerp, Brabant, East Flanders, Hainault, Liège, Limburg, Luxembourg, Namur, and West Flanders; and 2586 communes. The chief cities and their populations (1971 est., including suburbs) are Brussels, the capital (1,071,194), Antwerp (919,814), Ghent (473,597), and Liège (621,935).

Belgium. Plate 1. *The Belgian Ardennes (above), one of the oldest inhabited regions of Europe. The Brussels city hall (below, left), a 15th-century Gothic edifice. A churchyard (below, right) in Linkebeek, one of the many old villages near Brussels.*

All pictures in this series, courtesy Belgian Tourist Bureau

Belgium. Plate 2. *Three typical scenes. An open-air produce market (above), in Brussels, the capital. The officials of the famous pre-Lenten festival of Binche (right), in the province of Hainault. The curio section of the Brussels flea market (below), a popular Sunday-morning diversion.*

Religion. The majority of the population is Roman Catholic. Religious liberty is guaranteed, and part of the stipend of the ministers of all faiths is paid by the government. Other religions practiced within the country include various Protestant denominations and Judaism.

Language. On Sept. 1, 1963, a law was passed establishing three official languages within the country; Flemish was recognized as the official language in the N., French in the S., and German along the E. border. In the city and suburbs of Brussels, both French and Flemish are officially recognized. In 1971 legislation was enacted giving recognition to three language communities, providing cultural autonomy for them, and revising the bilingual and administrative status of Brussels, an enclave in the Flemish-speaking area. Local administrative bodies of the language communities were given specific powers in cultural matters, and fathers in Brussels were given the right to decide in which language their children should be educated.

Education. The modern school system of Belgium dates from 1830, when the nation declared its independence from the Netherlands. Although educational freedom was provided by the constitution of 1831, the first law for public elementary education was not passed until 1842. In that law religious instruction was made compulsory for all Roman Catholic children. It was not until 1959 that agreement occurred between Socialists and Catholics that acknowledges the right of each school-administering authority, whether government or church school, to devise its own curriculum as long as it meets the minimal requirements of the ministry of education.

Reforms continued into the 20th century, and in 1914 compulsory attendance was enacted for children between the ages of six and fourteen. Educational controversies involving language and religion that broke out in Belgium in the 19th century have continued to the present day. In an effort to resolve the language dispute, specific legislation was passed in 1963 and 1971; *see* LANGUAGE, *above*.

The oldest Belgian university dates from the Middle Ages. The University of Louvain, now a bilingual institution, was founded under religious auspices in 1425. The universities of Ghent and Liège were founded in 1817 during the period of Dutch rule, and the University of Brussels was opened in 1834 under an enactment by the newly formed Belgian government.

ELEMENTARY AND SECONDARY SCHOOLS. In the late 1960's, some 1,500,000 pupils were attending preprimary and primary schools, and about 850,000 students were enrolled in secondary schools, including general, vocational, and teacher-training institutions.

UNIVERSITIES AND COLLEGES. Annual attendance at the four universities numbered some 75,000 students in the early 1970's.

OTHER SCHOOLS. Royal academies of fine arts and royal conservatories of music are maintained in Antwerp, Brussels, Ghent, Liège, and Mons. State agricultural institutes are maintained in Ghent and Gembloux, and a state veterinary school is located in Cureghem. In the late 1960's the country had about 200 normal schools, with some 20,000 students.

Culture. Festivals play an important part in Belgian life. One of the most famous festivals is the three-day carnival at Binche, near Mons, held just before Lent. During the carnival, noisemaking and dancing are led by "Gilles", men dressed in high, plumed hats and bright costumes. Another famous pageant is the Procession of the Holy Blood, held in Bruges in May. December 6 commemorates Saint Nicholas' Day, an important children's holiday. Sports, too, are popular throughout the country. Archery, basketball, cycling, and soccer are among the favorite activities, as are boating, fishing, and swimming.

LIBRARIES AND MUSEUMS. General and specialized libraries are located in all of the principal cities. The main reference collection is the Bibliothèque Royale in Brussels, with some 2,250,000 volumes. Large libraries are maintained by the universities of Ghent, Liège, and Louvain.

The Royal Museum for Fine Art in Antwerp is noted for its collection of paintings by the Flemish painter Peter Paul Rubens (q.v.). The Royal Museum of Fine Arts of Belgium, located in Brussels, contains a collection of art works of many periods, as well as a concert hall and cinema.

LITERATURE. Belgium has contributed to both Flemish and French literature. Among the outstanding authors of the country are Philippe de Comines and Jean Froissart (qq.v.), who wrote in French during the Middle Ages. The works of Charles de Coster (1827–79) and Émile Verhaeren (1855–1916), both of whom wrote in French, and of Hendrik Conscience (1812–83), a Flemish author, were popular during the 19th century. Poet and playwright Maurice Maeterlinck (q.v.), who wrote in French, won the Nobel Prize in literature in 1911. *See* FLEMISH LANGUAGE AND LITERATURE.

ART. During the 15th and 16th centuries N. Europe was one of the centers of the Renaissance. Flemish painters Hubert and Jan van Eyck, Hier-

This small castle surrounded by fields is near Laarne, a small market town a few miles from Ghent.
Vance Henry–Taurus

onymus Bosch, and Pieter Brueghel the Elder (qq.v.) were among the outstanding artists of this period. The 17th century produced both Rubens and Sir Anthony Van Dyck (q.v.), who are regarded by many as two of the greatest Flemish painters. Among 20th-century painters of international fame are James Ensor (1860–1949), Paul Delvaux (1892–   ), and René Magritte (q.v.). Contemporary Belgian architecture is represented by the designs of Henry van de Velde (1863–1957). *See* FLEMISH ART AND ARCHITECTURE.

THE ECONOMY

Belgium is primarily an industrial nation. The country imports great quantities of raw materials that are processed mainly for export. The greater part of Belgian industry, including steel, coal, chemical, and petroleum firms, is controlled by six trusts. In 1975 installed electric-power capacity was about 11,100,000 kw; electric-power production was about 41.5 billion kw hours. Recent annual budget estimates set revenue at about $17.5 billion and expenditures at about 18.9 billion.

Agriculture. Farming engages 6 percent of the total labor force and supplies 80 percent of the food requirements of Belgium. About 65 percent of the farms are intensively cultivated units of less than twenty-five acres. About 60 percent of the land is used for field crops or stock raising, and nearly 3 percent for horticulture. In the mid-1970's the leading crops were sugar beets (4,900,000 metric tons), fodder beets (2,500,000 metric tons), potatoes (1,000,000 metric tons), wheat (677,000 metric tons), and barley (426,000 metric tons). Most fruits found in temperate climates are grown. Livestock and dairy farming are major agricultural industries; Belgium produces about 95 percent of the meat requirements of the country, and is totally self-sufficient in butter, eggs, and milk. In the mid-1970's the livestock population of Belgium numbered some 3,100,000 cattle, 4,800,000 pigs, 55,000 horses, and 84,000 sheep.

Forest and Fishing Industries. Forests cover about one fifth of the area of Belgium, and wooded areas are used chiefly for recreational purposes. Beech and oak are the most common trees, and in recent years stands of conifers have been planted.

The main fishing port of Belgium is Ostend. The fishing fleet exploits the North Atlantic Ocean fisheries from the North Sea to Iceland. The total annual catch in the mid-1970's amounted to about 38,000 tons valued at about $30,000,000. Most of the catch consists of herring, sole, shrimp, sprats, plaice, and ray.

Mining. Coal is the major mineral found within Belgium's borders. In the mid-1970's about 8,000,000 metric tons were mined annually. The coal-mining areas are centered around Mons, Charleroi, Liège, and Namur in the S., and in the Campine basin in the N. The rich Campine deposits are easily exploited and contain several good grades of bituminous coal. Belgium has begun to share in the exploitation of petroleum deposits under the North Sea.

Manufacturing. Belgium is one of the most highly industrialized countries of Europe, largely because of its geographical location and transport facilities. Industrial production increased steadily after World War II, but began to decrease in the 1950's. The establishment of the European Economic Community (q.v.) in 1957 (see *Commerce and Trade,* below) and the introduction by the government of an investment-incentive program, however, resulted in a new surge in Belgian industry. Belgium ranks high among world producers of iron and steel, and the greater part (about 65 percent) of the total output is exported.

The textile industry, dating from the Middle Ages, produces cottons, woolens, linens, and textiles of synthetic fibers. With the exception of flax, all raw materials are imported. Centers of the textile industry are Brugge (Bruges), Brussels, Limburg, Ghent, Liège, Courtrai, and Mechelen. In 1974 about 67,700 metric tons of cotton fabrics, 30,500 tons of wool fabrics, and 24,100 tons of rayon fibers were produced. Carpet making is an important industry in Saint-Nicolas, and Brussels and Bruges are noted for the manufacture of lace, fine lawn, and damask.

The Belgian chemical industry leads the world in the production of gelatin and radium salts and also ranks high in the production of coal tar, fertilizers, and plastics. Matches, pharmaceuticals, photographic supplies, paper and cartons, and cement are also important manufactures.

The nonferrous-metals industry, supplied by raw materials from the Republic of Zaire, furnishes the metallurgical, chemical, and other industries with a wide variety of metals, including copper, zinc, lead, platinum, germanium, and uranium.

The bulk of the metal-manufacturing industry is engaged in the production of heavy machinery, structural steelwork, and industrial equipment. Other important industries are shipbuilding, which is centered in Antwerp, and the manufacture of railroad equipment. The dia-

An Antwerp lacemaker at work. The city and Belgium itself have long been renowned for fine handmade lacework.
G. Sclarandis–Black Star

mond-cutting industry, also centered in Antwerp, supplies most of the demand of the United States for industrial diamonds.

Currency and Banking. The basic monetary unit is the Belgian franc (32 B.Fr. equal U.S.$1; 1978). At the head of the banking system is the National Bank of Belgium, established in 1850, which issues the bank notes of the country. Half the capital of the bank is owned by the government. In the early 1970's Belgium had about twenty banks and nearly 1300 branches and agencies. The National Society for Industrial Credit provides medium-term loans to exporters and business firms. The Postal Accounts Agency handles transactions involving payments by check and transfers of money.

Commerce and Trade. The foreign trade of Belgium and the Grand Duchy of Luxembourg is conducted jointly. The two countries formed a customs and currency union in 1922. On Jan. 1, 1948, the Netherlands entered a customs union, designated Benelux (q.v.), with Belgium and Luxembourg. In 1975 the chief Belgo-Luxembourg imports included ores and minerals, machinery and electrical equipment, motor vehicles, nonprecious metals, clothing accessories, and foodstuffs, valued at about $30.7 billion; exports, mainly iron and steel manufactures, textiles, chemicals, and cut diamonds, were valued at about $28.8 billion. In descending order West Germany, France, the Netherlands, the U.S., Great Britain, and Italy are the principal sources of Belgo-Luxembourg imports. The leading export markets are West Germany, France, the Netherlands, Great Britain, the U.S., and Italy. Belgium became a member of the European Coal and Steel Community (q.v.) on March 19, 1951. Six years later, on March 25, 1957, Belgium, France, West Germany, Italy, the Netherlands, and Luxembourg signed two treaties creating the European Economic Community (E.E.C.) and the European Atomic Energy Community (EURATOM).

Transportation. The chief access to the sea for Belgian shipping is via the Scheldt and Meuse estuaries, which lie within the territory of the Netherlands. Antwerp, on the Scheldt R., although some 52 mi. from the sea, is one of the busiest ports in the world. The rivers of Belgium are connected by an important system of canals. The aggregate length of rivers and canals totals about 1000 mi. Supplementing the waterways are about 7500 mi. of public roads and over 2700 mi. of railroads. No other country in the world has more railroad trackage per square mile. The railways are state-owned. Sabena, the Belgian national airline, operates routes to major cities throughout the world.

Communications. The Belgian National Radio, established by act of parliament in 1930, operates all radio- and television-broadcast sta-

Barges like these supply transportation in Ghent. A northern Venice, the city consists of numerous small islands separated by rivers and canals and joined by some 200 bridges. Herbert Lanks-Monkmeyer Press

tions. No commercial advertising is permitted. Broadcasting costs are defrayed through annual license fees on receiving sets. Separate services are broadcast in French and in Flemish. In the mid-1970's some 3,800,000 radio sets and 2,500,000 television sets were in operation. Belgium has about 600 telephone exchanges, with some 1,700,000 subscribers, and 1000 telegraph offices. About thirty daily newspapers with a circulation of 2,400,000 are published in the country.

Labor. The total labor force in the late 1970's numbered about 4,000,000 workers. About 72 percent is in manufacturing, services, and trade. More than 60 percent of the employees belongs to three trade-union groups: the General Federation of Labor, the Federation of Christian Trade Unions, and the General Federation of Liberal Trade Unions.

GOVERNMENT

Belgium is a constitutional, representative, and hereditary monarchy. Succession to the throne is determined by primogeniture. The present ruler is King Baudouin (q.v.).

In the late 1970's constitutional changes were under consideration to divide the country into three federal regions—Wallonia, Flanders, and Brussels.

Central Government. The Belgian constitution was promulgated in 1831 and revised in 1893 and 1920–21. Executive power is vested in the king, who appoints and removes cabinet ministers and judges. The king is commander in chief of the armed forces and, with the approval of parliament, has the power to declare war and conclude treaties. The rights of the king, according to the constitution, include convoking and dissolving parliament, conferring titles of nobility, and granting pardons. All royal acts, however, must be countersigned by a minister, who in turn assumes responsibility for those acts before parliament. Inasmuch as the ministers are responsible to parliament, the king must choose a cabinet that represents a majority in parliament. Cabinets are generally coalitions of two or more parties.

HEALTH AND WELFARE. Health and hospital services are the responsibility of public assistance committees located in each town. The committees pay for relief patients in private hospitals, administer public hospitals, and organize nursing services and clinics.

Social security, based on a law passed in December, 1944, applies to all workers subject to employment contracts. The Central National Office of Social Security collects from employers and employees all contributions for family allowances, health insurance, old-age insurance, holidays, and unemployment insurance, and distributes the funds to the respective administrative divisions.

Legislature. The Belgian parliament comprises the Senate and the Chamber of Representatives. The Senate consists of 178 members, elected directly and indirectly, for terms of four years. The number elected directly equals one half the number of representatives in the Chamber of Representatives; the rest are elected by the Senate and the provincial councils. The Chamber of Representatives, consisting of 212 members, is elected by direct suffrage. All persons over twenty-one years of age are required to vote in the parliamentary elections on pain of being fined.

Political Parties. The three major parties in Belgium are the Christian Social Party, the Belgian Socialist Party, and the Party for Liberty and Progress (formerly the Liberal Party). The Christian Social Party, founded in 1945, is the successor to the prewar Catholic Party; however, non-Catholics are now included among its adherents. The Belgian Socialist Party, founded in 1885, favors the development of trade unions and cooperatives. The Party for Liberty and Progress, founded in 1846, stands for free enterprise, moderate types of social reform, and reduced governmental expenditure.

Local Government. Each province has a council of fifty to ninety members who are chosen by direct vote. They are empowered to legislate in matters of local concern and to elect forty-eight members to the Senate. The councillors are elected for terms of four years by residents of the province who are over eighteen years of age. The council sessions are attended by a governor appointed by the king.

The provinces are subdivided into administrative districts, called communes. Each commune is administered by a burgomaster appointed by the king; and a town council, directly elected to six-year terms. The council elects an executive body called the board of aldermen. Local government on all levels possesses a large degree of autonomy, a tradition that originated in feudal times.

Judiciary. The Belgian constitution provides for an independent judiciary with powers equal to those of the executive and legislative departments. The highest tribunals are the courts of appeal, which sit at Brussels, Ghent, and Liège. Cases are referred to the courts of appeal by the courts of assize, which review both civil and criminal matters. In the assize courts twelve jurors decide all cases by majority vote.

Although capital punishment is still part of

the penal code, the death penalty is always commuted to life imprisonment by the king. There has been no execution since 1817.

Defense. The Belgian armed forces are recruited through voluntary enlistments and annual conscriptions. In 1959 the period of service was reduced from fifteen months to twelve months. Military training methods are coordinated with those of the Netherlands under the terms of a military and technical agreement signed between the two countries on May 10, 1948. The agreement provides also for staff contacts and standardization of equipment. The total strength of the Belgian armed forces, which include a navy, army, and air force, was some 100,000 in 1971.

HISTORY

Belgium takes its name from the ancient Celtic people called the Belgae (q.v.). The Roman province of Gallia Belgica embraced a much greater area than modern Belgium, extending from the mouth of the Scheldt R. almost to the Seine, and from the Strait of Dover to the range of the Vosges. After the disruption of the Frankish realm in the 9th century most of what is now Belgium was incorporated in the duchy of Lorraine (Lotharingia), which formed part of the realm of the eastern Franks (kingdom of Germany). In the extreme west arose the county of Flanders, a fief of the kings of France. In the 10th century the northern half of Lorraine became the duchy of Lower Lorraine, the name of which was supplanted by that of Brabant in the 13th century. In 1384 Flanders was united with Burgundy, the dukes of which had come into possession of the greater part of the Belgian and Dutch Netherlands by the middle of the 15th century. The rulers of Burgundy, though owing allegiance to the French crown, aimed at founding a powerful state between France and Germany. In furtherance of this objective they endeavored to repress the free republican spirit that manifested itself in the rapidly rising towns; but the work of establishing an absolute monarchy was interrupted by the death of the Burgundian duke Charles the Bold (1433–77).

King Leopold I of the Belgians. Belgian Information Service

By the marriage in 1477 of Mary of Burgundy (1457–82), daughter of Charles the Bold, to the German king Maximilian (*see* MAXIMILIAN I), all of the rich Burgundian realm except the duchy itself passed to the control of the Hapsburg (q.v.) family. Charles, the grandson of Maximilian, an heir apparent to the Spanish crown, inherited the Netherlands (consisting of what are now Belgium and the Dutch kingdom) in 1506. When, in 1516, Charles ascended the throne of Spain, the Netherlands became part of the Spanish dominions. In 1549 Charles, who had meanwhile been designated Holy Roman emperor as Charles V (q.v.), decreed the formal union of the Netherlands and Spain.

The despotic rule of the Spanish monarch Philip II (q.v.), the son and successor of Charles, provoked in the Netherlands a long and sanguinary struggle for political and religious freedom. Antagonisms arising out of the Protestant Reformation largely determined the nature and outcome of the revolt, which lasted from 1567 to 1579. The southern provinces (Belgium) remained loyal to the Roman Catholic Church and to the Spanish crown; the northern provinces, a stronghold of Protestantism, won their independence as the United Provinces of the Netherlands.

In 1598 King Philip II ceded the Spanish Netherlands to his son-in-law, Archduke Albert of Austria (1559–1621). The Spanish king, refusing to recognize Dutch independence, had meanwhile made several unsuccessful attempts to subdue the United Provinces. The struggle was resumed by Archduke Albert, but in 1609 he was compelled to conclude a twelve-year truce with his northern neighbors. During the ensuing period of peace the country, nominally an independent kingdom under the archduke, regained some of its former prosperity. After the death of Albert in 1621, his domain was returned to Spanish control; in the same year, the truce having expired, hostilities were renewed with the United Provinces.

The Spanish-Belgian forces suffered several severe defeats during the next decade, and in 1633 the Dutch arranged an alliance with France. A succession of Franco-Dutch victories finally forced the Spanish king Philip IV (q.v.) to accept in 1648 a separate peace with the Dutch. Considerable Belgian territory was ceded to the United Provinces by the terms of the settlement. In addition, the Dutch insisted on the perpetual closing of the Scheldt R., chief commercial artery of Belgium. The war between Spain and France continued until 1659, with disastrous results for the Spanish and their Belgian province. By the Treaty of the Pyrenees, several frontier points were given to France. Through subsequent conquests, France, at the Peace of Aix-la-Chapelle in 1668, won possession of more towns, three of which were restored in the Treaty of Nijmegen in 1678. As a compensation, however, Valenciennes, Cambrai, Saint-Omer, Maubeuge, Ypres, Poperinghe, Cassel, and Bailleul were given up. Some of these towns were regained at the Peace of Ryswick in 1697; *see* RYSWICK, PEACE OF.

The Spanish Netherlands became an important pawn in the next general European conflict, the War of the Spanish Succession (*see* SPANISH SUCCESSION, WAR OF THE). By the terms of the Peace of Utrecht, which concluded this conflict in 1713, Belgium was given to Austria. The Dutch received the right to garrison key Belgian fortresses along the French frontier. During the War of the Austrian Succession in 1744, the country was almost completely occupied by the French, but was restored to Austria by the Treaty of Aix-la-Chapelle (q.v.) in 1748.

Belgium remained undisturbed by the Seven Years' War, and during the long peace following the Treaty of Aix-la-Chapelle prosperity was restored. The ruling sovereign, Archduchess Maria Theresa (q.v.) of Austria, instituted a program of public works. Holy Roman Emperor Joseph II (*see under* JOSEPH: *Holy Roman Emperors*), son and successor of Maria Theresa, further improved conditions in the Austrian province, but some administrative reforms created widespread discontent. Popular opposition to Joseph's rule culminated in October, 1789, in a general uprising. Most of the Austrian garrisons in the province were forced to capitulate, and on Jan. 11, 1790, a Belgian republic was proclaimed. Factional strife soon developed among the rebels, insuring the speedy downfall of the republic. By the following December the troops of Leopold II (q.v.), who had meanwhile succeeded Joseph II, were in complete control of the country. Leopold revoked the objectionable reforms of his predecessor, but the new regime won little popular support.

Leopold II was succeeded by Francis II (q.v.) in 1792. In the same year Austria, one of the chief centers of opposition to the French Revolution, became embroiled in war with France, and Belgium was occupied by a French army. The Austrians regained control of the province in 1793, but were again expelled by the French in 1794. By the Treaty of Campoformio in 1797 Francis II formally ceded the province to France.

The revolutionary regime installed in Belgium by the French received little popular support, but lasted until 1814. In that year the country was occupied by the armies of the coalition of powers ranged against the French emperor Napoleon I (q.v.) in the Napoleonic Wars. By the terms of the peace settlement adopted in 1815 at the Congress of Vienna (*see* VIENNA, CONGRESS OF), Belgium was reunited with the Dutch Netherlands. The combined countries were officially designated the United Kingdom of the Netherlands.

Belgium Becomes an Independent Kingdom. This action of the Congress of Vienna was completely arbitrary, as the people of the northern and southern parts of the United Kingdom differed essentially in religion, language, interests, and traditions. Liberals and Catholics alike were ready to revolt against Dutch supremacy. The outbreak of a revolution in France in 1830 set the example, and on the birthday of the king on Aug. 24, 1830, several riots occurred in various towns of Belgium. Dutch occupation of Brussels by an army of 14,000 men brought the revolutionary ferment in the Belgian nation to a climax. In seven days the people deposed the royal authorities and appointed a provisional government. Prince Frederick, the son of the Dutch king, who commanded the troops, was compelled to retreat from Brussels to Antwerp. On Oct. 4, Belgium was declared independent by the provisional government. At a national congress on Nov. 10, only thirteen out of 200 votes were cast in favor of republican government. Meanwhile, representatives of Austria, Prussia, Russia, and Great Britain, the powers most concerned with the breach of the decisions reached at the Congress of Vienna, convened in London. On Dec. 20, 1830, the conferees recognized the

INDEX TO MAP OF BELGIUM

Provinces

Antwerp F 1
Brabant E 2
East Flanders D 2
Hainault D 2
Liège H 2
Limburg G 2
Luxembourg G 4
Namur F 3
West Flanders B 1

Cities and Towns

Aalst D 2
Aalter C 1
Aarlen (Arlon) H 4
Aarschot F 2
Aat (Ath) D 2
Alken G 2
Alost (Aalst) D 2
Amay G 2
Andenne G 3
Anderlecht B 4
Anderlues E 3
Antwerp (Antwerpen) E 1
Ardooie C 2
Arendonk G 1
Arlon H 4
Asse E 2
Assebroek C 1
Ath D 2
Athus H 4
Audenarde
(Oudenaarde) D 2
Auderghem C 4
Auvelais F 3
Baerle-Duc F 1
Balen G 1
Barvaux H 3
Bastogne (Bastenaken) H 4
Beaumont E 3
Berchem F 1
Berchem-Sainte-Agathe B 4
Bergen (Mons) D 3
Beveren E 1
Bilzen G 2
Binche E 3
Blankenberge C 1
Bocholt H 1
Boom E 1
Borgerhout E 1
Borgworm (Waremme) G 2
Bouillon G 4
Bourg-Léopold
(Leopoldsburg) G 1
Boussu D 3
Braine-l'Alleud E 2
Braine-le-Comte D 2
Bredene B 1
Bree H 1
Bruges (Brugge) C 1
Brussels (capital) C 4
Bruxelles (Brussels) C 4
Charleroi E 3
Châtelet F 3
Châtelineau F 3
Chimay E 3
Ciney G 3
Comblain-au-Pont G 3
Comines B 2
Couillet E 3
Courcelles E 3
Courtrai C 2
Couvin F 3
Deinze D 2
Denderleeuw E 2
Dendermonde E 1
De Panne B 1
Dessel G 1
Deurne F 1
Diegem C 4
Diest F 2
Diksmuide B 1
Dilbeek B 4
Dinant F 3
Dison H 2
Dixmude (Diksmuide) B 1
Doornik (Tournai) C 2
Dour D 3
Drogenbos B 5
Drongen D 1
Duffel F 1
Ecaussinnes d'Enghien E 3
Edingen (Enghien) D 2
Eeklo D 1
Eernegem B 1
Eigenbrakel
(Braine-l'Alleud) E 2
Ekeren E 1
Ellezelles D 2
Enghien D 2
Ensival H 2
Erquelinnes E 3
Esneux H 2
Essen E 1
Etterbeek C 4
Eupen J 2
Evere C 4
Evergem D 1
Flémalle-Haute G 2
Fleurus F 3
Florennes F 3
Forest B 4
Frameries D 3
Frasnes-lez-Buissenal D 2
Furnes (Veurne) B 1
Ganshoren B 4
Gaurain-Ramecroix D 2
Geel F 1
Geldenaken (Jodoigne) F 2
Gembloux F 3
Genk H 2
Gent (Ghent) D 1
Gentbrugge D 1
Geraardsbergen D 2
Ghent D 1
Gilly E 3
Gosselies E 3
Grammont
(Geraardsbergen) D 2
Haacht F 2
Hal (Halle) E 2
Halen G 2
Halle E 2
Hamme E 1
Hamont H 1
Hannut (Hannuit) G 2
Harelbeke C 2
Hasselt G 2
Heist C 1
Heist-op-den-Berg F 1
Herentals F 1
Herselt F 1
Herstal H 2
Herve H 2
Hoboken E 1
Hoei (Huy) G 3
Hoeselt H 2
Hoogstraten F 1
Hornu D 3
Huy G 3
Ieper B 2
Ingelmunster C 2
Ixelles C 4
Izegem C 2
Jambes F 3
Jemappes D 3
Jemeppe G 2
Jette B 4
Jodoigne F 2
Jumet E 3
Kalmthout F 1
Kapellen E 1
Kessel-Lo F 2
Knokke C 1
Koekelare B 1
Koekelberg B 4
Koersel G 1
Kontich E 1
Kortemark C 1
Kortrijk (Courtrai) C 2
Kraainem C 4
La Louvière E 3
Lanaken H 2
Landen G 2
Langemark B 2
La Roche-en-Ardenne G 3
Lede D 2
Ledeberg D 2
Leopoldsburg G 1
Lessines (Lessen) D 2
Leuven (Louvain) F 2
Leuze D 2
Lichtervelde C 1
Liedekerke D 2
Liège H 2
Lier F 1
Lierneux H 3
Lierre (Lier) F 1
Limbourg (Limburg) J 2
Linkebeek B 5
Lokeren D 1
Lommel G 1
Looz (Borgloon) G 2
Louvain F 2
Luik (Liège) H 2
Maaseik H 1
Machelen C 4
Maldegem C 1
Malines (Mechelen) F 1
Malmédy J 3
Marche-en-Famenne G 3
Marchin G 3
Marcinelle E 3
Mechelen F 1
Meerhout G 1
Menen (Menin) C 2
Merchtem E 2
Merelbeke D 2
Merksem E 1
Merksplas F 1
Mettet F 3
Meulebeke C 2
Moeskroen (Mouscron) C 2
Mol G 1
Molenbeek-Saint-Jean B 4
Mons D 3
Montegnée G 2
Montignies-sur-Sambre F 3
Mortsel E 1
Mouscron C 2
Namur (Namen) F 3
Neerlinter G 2
Neerpelt G 1
Neufchâteau G 4
Nieuwpoort
(Nieuport) B 1
Nijvel (Nivelles) E 2
Ninove D 2
Nivelles E 2
Oostende (Ostend) B 1
Oostkamp C 1
Opwijk E 2
Ostend B 1
Oudenaarde D 2
Oud-Turnhout F 1
Ougrée H 2
Overijse F 2
Overpelt G 1
Peer G 1
Péruwelz D 3
Perwez (Perwijs) F 2
Poperinge B 2
Putte F 1
Quaregnon D 3
Quiévrain D 3
Renaix (Ronse) D 2
Retie G 1
Rochefort G 3
Roeselare C 2
Ronse D 2
Roulers (Roeselare) C 2
Ruisbroek B 5
Saint-Georges G 2
Saint-Gilles B 4
Saint-Josse-ten-Noode C 4
Saint-Trond
(Sint-Truiden) G 2
Saint-Vith (Sankt-Vith) J 3
Schaerbeek C 4
Schoten F 1
Seraing G 2
's Gravenbrakel
(Braine-le-Comte) D 2
Sint-Amandsberg D 1
Sint-Andries C 1
Sint-Niklaas E 1
Sint-Pieters-Leeuw B 5
Sint-Truiden G 2
Soignies D 2
Spa H 3
Staden B 2
Steenokkerzeel C 4
Stene B 1
Strombeek-Bever C 4
Tamines F 3
Tamise (Temse) E 1
Temse E 1
Termonde
(Dendermonde) E 1
Tessenderlo G 1
Theux H 3
Thuin E 3
Tielt, Brabant F 2
Tielt, West Flanders C 2
Tienen (Tirlemont) F 2
Tongeren (Tongres) G 2
Torhout C 1
Tournai C 2
Tronchiennes (Drongen) D 1
Tubize (Tubeke) E 2
Turnhout F 1
Uccle (Ukkel) B 4
Verviers H 2
Veurne B 1
Vilvoorde (Vilvorde) F 2
Visé H 2
Vorst (Forest) B 4
Waarschoot D 1
Wandre H 2
Waregem C 2
Waremme G 2
Wasmes D 2
Waterloo E 2
Watermael-Boitsfort C 4
Wavre (Waver) F 2
Wemmel B 4
Wervik B 2
Westerlo F 1
Wetteren D 2
Wezembeek-Oppem D 4
Wezet (Visé) H 2
Willebroek E 1
Wilrijk E 1
Wingene C 1
Woluwe-Saint-Lambert C 4
Woluwe-Saint-Pierre C 4
Ypres (Ieper) B 2
Zaventem C 4
Zeebrugge C 1
Zele E 1
Zellik B 4
Zelzate D 1
Zinnik (Soignies) D 2
Zonhoven G 1
Zottegem D 2

Physical Features

Albert (canal) F 1
Ardennes (forest) F 4
Botrange (mt.) J 3
Dender (river) D 2
Deûle (river) B 2
Dommel (river) H 1
Dyle (river) F 2
Hohe Venn (plat.) H 3
Lesse (river) F 3
Lys (river) B 2
Mark (river) F 1
Meuse (river) F 3
Nethe (river) F 1
North (sea) B 1
Ourthe (river) H 3
Rupel (river) F 2
Sambre (river) D 3
Scheldt (river) C 2
Schnee Eifel (plat.) J 3
Semois (river) G 4
Senne (river) E 2
Vaalserberg (mt.) J 2
Vesdre (river) H 2
Yser (river) B 2
Zitterwald (plat.) J 3

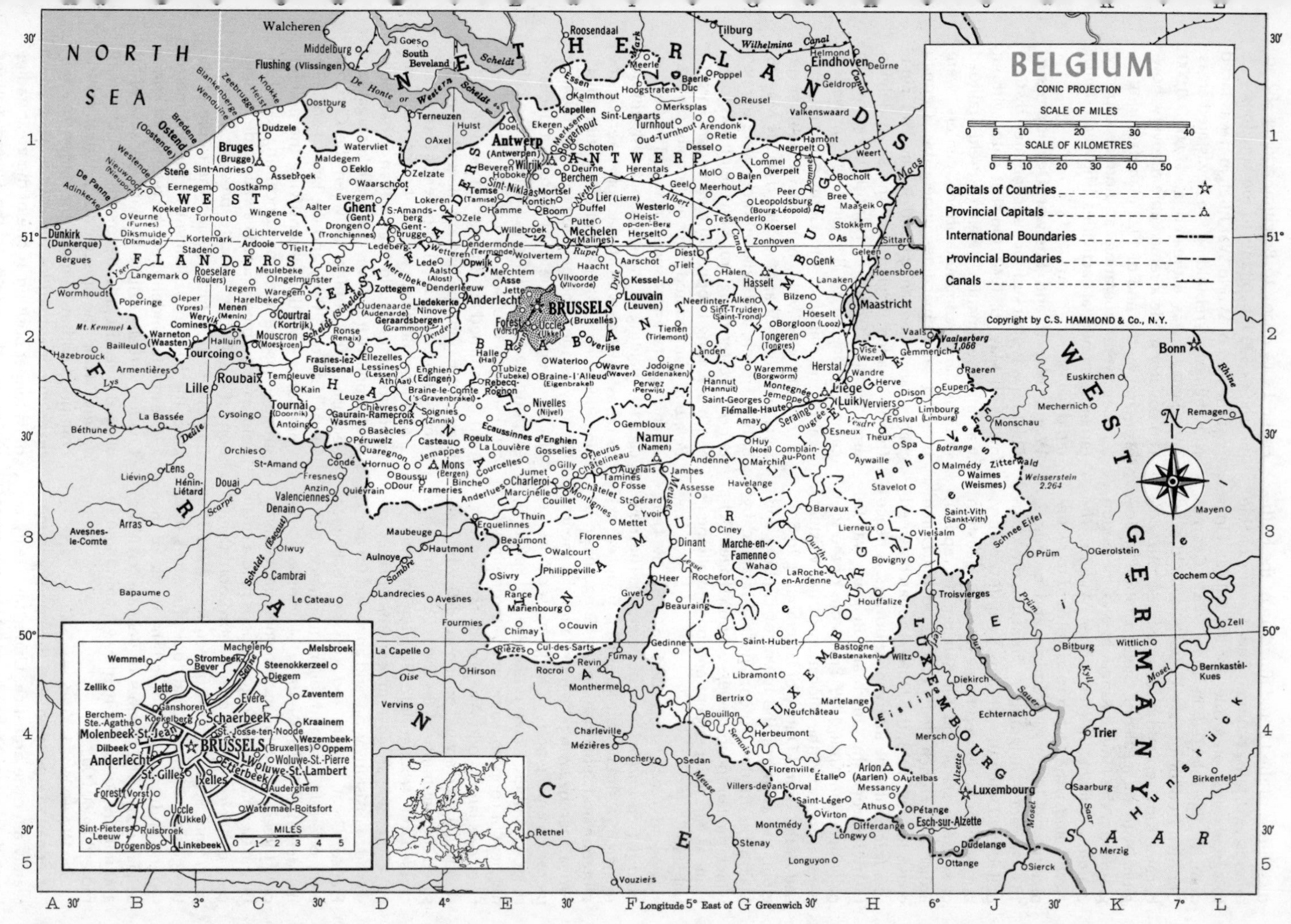
BELGIUM
CONIC PROJECTION
SCALE OF MILES
SCALE OF KILOMETRES
Capitals of Countries
Provincial Capitals
International Boundaries
Provincial Boundaries
Canals
Copyright by C.S. HAMMOND & Co., N.Y.
NORTH SEA
NETHERLANDS
WEST GERMANY
LUXEMBOURG
FRANCE
SAAR
WEST FLANDERS
EAST FLANDERS
ANTWERP
LIMBURG
BRABANT
HAINAUT
NAMUR
LIÈGE
LUXEMBOURG
BRUSSELS
Antwerp (Antwerpen)
Ghent (Gent)
Bruges (Brugge)
Ostend (Oostende)
Mechelen (Malines)
Louvain (Leuven)
Liège (Luik)
Namur (Namen)
Mons (Bergen)
Charleroi
Hasselt
Arlon (Aarlen)
Maastricht
Lille
Luxembourg
Bonn
MILES
Longitude 5° East of G Greenwich 30'

dissolution of the United Kingdom of the Netherlands as a fait accompli. The powers, unable to agree at first on a ruler for the Belgian kingdom, finally selected in June, 1831, Georges Chrétien Frédéric of Saxe-Coburg-Saalfield, who became King Leopold I; *see under* LEOPOLD: *Belgium.* A treaty legalizing the separation of Belgium from the United Kingdom was thereupon drafted. William III (*see under* WILLIAM: *the Netherlands*), the Dutch ruler, refused to recognize the validity of such a treaty and, on Aug. 2, 1831, invaded Belgium. A French army compelled the Dutch to withdraw from the country, but William III refused to yield on the question of separate statehood for Belgium. In reprisal, British and French fleets blockaded the Dutch coast. In May, 1833, the Dutch monarch agreed to a truce with the intervening powers. A peace treaty between the Dutch and Belgians was finally signed in April, 1839. Provisions of the settlement included the allocation of the western half of the Grand Duchy of Luxembourg to Belgium, the award of the towns of Limburg and Maastricht to the Dutch, and a guarantee by which the European powers acknowledged Belgium as "an independent and perpetually neutral State".

Leopold I was succeeded in 1865 by Leopold II (*see under* LEOPOLD: *Belgium*). The new monarch, a shrewd businessman, financed exploration and settlement in the Congo basin of Africa, thereby laying the foundations of the immense colonial empire of Belgium; *see* ZAIRE, REPUBLIC OF Albert I (*see under* ALBERT: *Belgium*), nephew of Leopold, came to the throne in 1909. Five years later World War I broke out. Notwithstanding the Treaty of London in 1870, which assured the neutrality of Belgium, German troops crossed the frontier into Belgium on Aug. 4, 1914; the Belgian government immediately resolved to resist invasion, and appealed for aid to France, Great Britain, and Russia. The Belgian army offered fierce and valiant resistance to the invaders, but by the end of November, 1914, only three Belgian towns remained unoccupied by the Germans. The Belgian troops held a small part of their country near Nieuwpoort (Nieuport) until Sept. 28, 1918, when they joined in the general offensive that took the Allies into Ostend and Bruges and freed the whole of the Belgian coast. The number of Belgians, civilians and military, killed during the war amounted to more than 80,000.

See WORLD WAR I; YPRES.

German troops evacuated the country immediately after the armistice. Under the Treaty of Versailles, Eupen, Malmédy, and Moresnet were ceded by Germany to Belgium, adding 382 sq. mi. and 64,520 inhabitants to the kingdom.

At the end of World War I Belgium was faced with the task of rebuilding the devastated areas. The damage was estimated at $7,600,000,000. The country made a remarkable recovery, however, and by the end of 1922 manufacturing industries were operating at normal capacity. Other commercial activities showed similar rapid gains.

World War II and Postwar Developments. Belgium was attacked for a second time by Germany on May 10, 1940. On that date, without warning or ultimatum, Belgian airfields, railroad stations, and communications centers were bombed and machine-gunned by German planes, and German ground forces and paratroops invaded Belgian soil. The small Belgian army and the French and British troops which came to the aid of Belgium were powerless against the might of the German forces. Antwerp fell on May 18, but Namur, with seven forts, held out for another five days. By May 26, British, French, and Belgian forces were trapped in northwestern Belgium, with their backs to the North Sea. King Leopold III (*see under* LEOPOLD: *Belgium*) surrendered unconditionally on May 28 and was taken prisoner of war. The Belgian cabinet, meeting in Paris, unanimously refused to be associated with the action taken by the king, declaring it "illegal and unconstitutional". On May 30, the cabinet voted to divest the king of all powers and the right to rule, a decision supported by the Belgian parliament. The cabinet established a seat in London on Oct. 22, 1940. It returned to Brussels on Sept. 8, 1944. Later that month, parliament elected as regent Prince Charles (1903–), brother of Leopold.

Although Belgium was in better economic condition after World War II than it had been after World War I, it was politically disorganized because of the conflict between the Christian Social (Catholic) Party and the Liberal-Socialist-Communist coalition. Intensifying the political struggle was the question concerning King Leopold, at that time in Austria awaiting determination of his future. Despite pressure from the Catholic Party, which favored the return of the king, the Belgian parliament in the summer of 1945 extended indefinitely the regency of Prince Charles, virtually exiling the king because of his alleged defeatist attitude toward the German invaders. While the struggle for political control continued within Belgium, the nation as a unit made important strides toward the assumption of its former position as one of the great trading nations of the world. In the United Nations, which Belgium joined as a charter member on June 26, 1945, the country gave consistent support to the other western democracies during the intense ideological and political struggle (the so-called cold war) with the Soviet Union and the states within the Soviet sphere of influence. Belgian diplomacy, in the realm of international politics generally, was marked by a similarly cooperative attitude toward the efforts of the democratic countries to accomplish economic recovery and to erect safeguards against possible Communist aggression. The country participated in the European Recovery Program, an American-sponsored plan (effectuated in April, 1948) designed to accelerate the rehabilitation of the war-torn economies of western Europe. Together with the other Benelux countries, France, and Great Britain, Belgium became, in 1948, a member of the Brussels Treaty Organization (*see* WESTERN EUROPEAN UNION). This step represented the final abandonment by Belgium of a traditional policy of neutrality. In April, 1949, Belgium joined the North Atlantic Treaty Organization (q.v.).

On March 12, 1950, after more than a year of successive governmental crises brought on by the controversy over the king, the Belgian electorate went to the polls in an advisory plebiscite on the question of Leopold's return. The return of the king from exile was favored by almost 57.7 percent of the voters. On July 20 the Belgian parliament voted (198 to 0) in favor of return. During the following week strikes, demonstrations, and riots occurred in many urban areas of the country, creating grave possibilities of a civil war. On Aug. 1, after consultations with government and political leaders, Leopold agreed to assign his royal prerogatives to his son, Crown Prince Baudouin. The king further agreed to abdicate in Baudouin's favor on the twenty-first birthday of the prince in the following year. Leopold III abdicated on July 16, 1951, and Baudouin was proclaimed king on July 17.

In May, 1952, Belgium became a signatory, along with France, West Germany, Italy, and the other Benelux countries, of the European Defense Community (E.D.C.) Treaty, a document providing for the creation of a supranational West European army.

In the spring of 1954, the Socialists and Liberals formed a coalition government. On Oct. 23 Belgium, along with the other members of the Brussels Treaty Organization and the North Atlantic Treaty Organization, signed agreements providing for the admission of West Germany into both organizations; the agreements were designed to replace the E.D.C. Treaty, which had been rejected by France in August. The Belgian parliament completed ratification of the agreements on April 6, 1955. Later that year, construction of an experimental nuclear reactor was begun in Mol-Donk, Antwerp Province.

Brussels was the site of a world's fair from April to October, 1958. Following elections in June, a Christian Social and Liberal government, under Gaston Eyskens (1905–), leader of the former party, took office.

Most of the Belgian coal miners were on strike from Feb. 13 to 24, 1959, in protest over Belgian compliance with a decision of the European Coal and Steel Community to shut uneconomic mines. The strike was ended after assurances were given that any miners made jobless by the shut-down would be resettled.

The 1960's and 70's. Major events in the early 1960's centered around the independence of the Belgian Congo, proclaimed by King Baudouin, June 30, 1960, and the adjustments in Belgian economic life necessitated by the loss of the former colony. In the general elections held in the spring of 1961 the Christian Socialists suffered a loss of 8 seats in the lower house and were left with a total of 96. The new premier, the Christian Socialist leader Theodore Lefèvre (1914–), formed a coalition cabinet with the Socialists.

The Belgian-administered United Nations trust territory of Ruanda-Urundi achieved independence on July 1, 1962, as two states, Rwanda and Burundi. A long-standing dispute between the Dutch-speaking Flemings and the French-speaking Walloons often erupted into street clashes in the early 1960's. A government settlement effected in September, 1963, changed the official language boundaries. The bitterness between the Belgian and Congolese governments which attended the granting of independence to the former Belgian colony was mitigated by a visit to the Congo in March, 1964, by Belgian Foreign Minister Paul-Henri Spaak (1899–1972). A crisis occurred on April 1, 1964, when Belgian doctors went on strike to protest a health-insurance law adopted in 1963. The government retaliated by mobilizing medical reserve officers and conscripting civilian physicians. On April 18 the strike was ended in the middle of the third week, and during subsequent negotiations the physicians were granted several concessions. In February, 1966, another strike by physicians was averted, but the government was forced to resign because of the dispute. In the general election in 1965 the coalition government suffered a setback. The Socialist Party won 64 seats, 20

In the Antwerp marketplace, automobiles are parked before guild houses dating from medieval times, when the city was already a flourishing northern European commercial center. Vance Henry–Taurus

seats fewer than they had won in the elections of 1961. The Christian Social Party lost 12 seats; the Party for Liberty and Progress gained 8, and joined the coalition on March 3, 1966.

In January, 1968, riots between the Walloons and Flemings led to the collapse of the government. The Christian Socialists, under Gaston Eyskens, formed a coalition with the Socialists in June. The coalition retained its majority in 1971 elections, but the cabinet resigned in November, 1972. In January, 1973, the Socialist leader Edmond Leburton (1915–) formed a cabinet including Liberal Party members as well as Christian Socialists and Socialists. Weakened by increasing linguistic-cultural tensions, the Leburton government fell in January, 1974. After elections were held in March, the Christian Socialist Léo Tindemans formed a coalition with the Liberals and the Rassemblement Wallon and held office, despite inflation, unemployment, and drought, until February, 1977, when the Walloon Federalists withdrew their support. Elections followed on April 17, but a new Tindemans government could not be formed until forty-six days later, when agreement was finally reached on a plan for greater regional autonomy, and the federalist Flemish People's Union and French Democratic Front joined the Christian Socialists and Socialists in the coalition.

BELGRADE (Serbian, *Beograd*), capital and largest city of the Socialist Federal Republic of Yugoslavia, and capital of the republic of Serbia, at the confluence of the Danube and Sava rivers, about 225 miles S.E. of Zagreb. Deposits of coal and lead are located nearby, and the city is an industrial center, manufacturing machinery, electrical equipment, pottery, and textiles. Belgrade is economically important also as a center, by rail and river, for the Yugoslavian export and import trade.

From the founding of the city, various peoples have fought for possession of it. From the 3rd century B.C. to the 7th century A.D., Belgrade, then a fortified town known as Singidunum, was held successively by the Celts, Romans, Huns, Sarmatians, and Goths; then it was taken by the Byzantines, the Franks, the Bulgars, and again by the Byzantines. Because of the strategic position on the route between Constantinople (now İstanbul) and Vienna, Austria, the city continued throughout the Middle Ages to be the prize of hard-fought contests; in addition Belgrade occupied a commanding post on the Danube R. The Byzantine Greeks, the Bulgars, the Serbians, and the Hungarians were masters of Belgrade at various times from the 12th century to the beginning of the 16th century. The Turks captured the city in 1521 and called it Darol-i-Jehad ("the home of the wars of the faith"). In 1866, some sixty years after the Serbian war for independence, which resulted in Serbian autonomy within the Ottoman Empire, Belgrade was finally freed of a Turkish garrison. After the withdrawal of the Turks, Belgrade gradually lost its Oriental atmosphere. During World War I the city was twice occupied by Austrian troops, and it was taken and held by German troops for the greater part of World War II. Pop. (1971) 741,618.

BELGRANO, Manuel (1770–1820), Argentine statesman and military leader, born in Buenos Aires and educated as a lawyer in Spain. Belgrano served as a government official until 1810, when he joined the revolt against Spanish rule in Argentina, and became a member of the revolutionary government. Subsequently he led Argentine troops against the Spaniards, winning major victories in northwestern Argentina, at Tucumán in 1812 and at Salta in 1813. Later that year Belgrano was defeated by Spaniards in what is now Bolivia, and in 1814 he yielded his command to the Argentine general José de San Martín (q.v.). Belgrano was later a diplomat in the Argentine government.

BELISARIUS (505?–65), Byzantine general, born in Germania, Illyria. He was given command of the army of the Byzantine Empire and was stationed on the frontier of Persia (now Iran), where in 530 he first gained eminence by a victory over a Persian army vastly outnumbering his own. In 532, when strife between political factions in Constantinople (now İstanbul) endangered the throne and the empire, and one group had proclaimed a new emperor to supersede the Byzantine emperor Justinian I (q.v.), Belisarius, at the head of the imperial lifeguards, quelled the insurrection by the slaughter of over 30,000 insurgents. In 533–34 he recovered Africa from the Vandals (q.v.) and brought their king, Gelimer (r. 530–34), a prisoner to Constantinople. In 535 Belisarius conquered Sicily and then recovered Italy from the Ostrogoths (*see* GOTHS: *Ostrogoths*) whose king, Vitiges (r. 536–40), was captured at Ravenna in 540. Belisarius was again engaged against the Persians in 541–42. In 544 he was back in Italy and recaptured Rome from the Ostrogoths. He was, however, left unsupported, and in 548 his command was transferred to his rival, the Byzantine general Narses (478–573?) who had rebelled against Belisarius' leadership in his earlier Italian campaigns. After a retirement of ten years Belisarius again came into prominence by defeating a Bulgarian invasion that threatened Constantinople. In 562 he was imprisoned for several months by Justinian on an accusation of conspiracy. The legend that Belisarius was later blinded and impoverished is unfounded.

BELITUNG, *or* BILLITON, island of the Republic of Indonesia, part of the Malay Archipelago (q.v.), in the Java Sea. About 55 mi. long and 43 mi. wide, it is generally rectangular in shape and has a diversified terrain, with hilly areas and extensive tracts of marshland. Climatic conditions are typically tropical. Belitung contains rich tin deposits, and tin mining is the chief industry. The principal town is Tandjungpandan, on the N.W. coast. Originally a part of the sultanate of Palembang, Belitung was ceded to the British in 1812. The British recognized Dutch claims to the island in 1824. Area, 1866 sq.mi.; pop. (latest census) 102,375.

BELIZE. *See* BRITISH HONDURAS.

BELIZE CITY, chief seaport and former capital of British Honduras, on the Caribbean Sea, at the mouth of the Belize R. It has been a trade center for the logwood and mahogany of the region for over three hundred years. Also produced in the district and exported are chicle, rice, fruit, and coconuts. Sawmilling and rice processing are the major industries. Belize was the site of an English settlement in the early 17th century, but British control of the city was not secured until the defeat of the Spanish in 1798. Pop. (1970) 39,257. *See also* BELMOPAN.

BELKIN, Ivan, pen name of the Russian poet Aleksander Sergeevich Pushkin (q.v.).

BELKNAP, Jeremy (1744–98), American historian, born in Boston, Mass., and educated at Harvard College. After teaching school for several years, he served as pastor of the Congregational Church, Dover, N.H., from 1767 to 1786, and of the Federal Street Church, Boston, from 1787 to 1798. During the American Revolution he supported independence from Great Britain, and after the war he advocated a strong union between the States and the abolition of slavery. He was a founder of the Massachusetts Historical Society in 1791. Among his works are *History of New Hampshire* (3 vol., 1784–92), and *American Biography* (2 vol., 1794–98).

BELL, cup-shaped, hollow, metallic instrument which produces a ringing sound when struck by clapper or hammer. The term is applied also to a modern electromechanical instrument in which hammers strike tiny rods of so-called bell metal; the resulting rod vibrations are amplified electronically. A true bell tone is not a simple tone but an intricate series of many partial tones, each produced by vibrations of different sec-

Bell in the tower of the Gothic cathedral at Bern, Switzerland. Swiss National Tourist Office

tions of the bell. Bells are rung singly or in concert. If tuning is not perfect, dissonance occurs.

Bells were in use in China before 2000 B.C. In the Bible (q.v.), the earliest reference to bells is in the Book of Exodus (28:33–34), which mentions the golden bells on the vestments of the Levitical high priests.

The introduction of bells in the services of the Christian church is ascribed usually to Paulinus (353–431 A.D.), Bishop of Nola, Campania, Italy. Church bells were introduced in France about the middle of the 6th century. The English historian and theologian known as the Venerable Bede (*see* BEDE, SAINT) mentions that Benedict, Abbot of Wearmouth, brought a bell from Italy for his church in England about 680. Bells were introduced in the Christian churches of the East in the 9th century, and to Switzerland and Germany in the 11th century.

Hand bells of the cowbell type came into use in Europe at an early date. Such bells were made of thin plates of metal bent into rectangles and fastened with rivets. One such bell, said to have belonged to Saint Patrick (q.v.) may still be seen in Belfast, Northern Ireland. This relic is called *Clog-an-eadhachta-Phatraic* (The Bell of St. Patrick's Will). The inscription indicates that the bell was made between 1091 and 1105.

Formerly, bells were a prize in warfare, because the metal of which they were made could be cast into cannon and other weapons. Many historic bells were destroyed in this fashion through the centuries, but the cycle often was completed in peacetime, when guns were melted and recast into bells.

Bells are suspended in towers of churches and public buildings or in separate bell towers or campaniles; *see* BELL TOWER. The largest bell in the world is the "Tsar Kolokol" of Moscow, cast in 1733, which is 19 feet high, more than 60 feet in circumference, and 2 feet thick, and weighs about 200 tons. Notable bells include a 53-ton bell in Peking, China; the 17-ton bell of the Cathedral of Notre Dame, in Paris; the 17-ton bell of Saint Paul's Cathedral, London; and the bell in Independence Hall, Philadelphia, Pa., known as the Liberty Bell (q.v.). The four bells of the Westminster Peal in the Metropolitan Life Insurance Building, New York City, weigh almost 7 tons and are the highest-hung in the world.

Fine cast bells are made of a bronze alloy called bell metal, which usually consists of four parts copper and one part tin. Other metals have been used, but the tones are usually inferior. The tone of a bell depends not only on the metal alloy, but on the proportions of height, width, thickness, and shape.

In founding (q.v.), or casting, a bell, a core is built up with clay, contoured to the exact size and shape of the interior of the proposed bell. A heavy outer shell, made of clay and other ingredients, is then built over the core; the inner surface of this heavy shell conforms to the exterior of the proposed bell. Molten bell metal then is poured into the space between the core and the outer shell. When the metal has cooled, the mold is opened and the exterior of the bell is smoothed and polished. The interior surface is machined with lathes to secure the wall thicknesses necessary for proper tune of the partials of the bell tone.

So-called tubular bells, consisting of tubes of metal suspended on hooks, were made in the early 1900's for use in musically-tuned sets. Most of these tubular bells have disappeared from bell towers and, like many of the traditional campaniform cast bells, have been superseded by the modern electromechanical bells; *see* CARILLON.

Of all musical instruments employed by man, perhaps none has had such wide acceptance as the bell. All metal-using societies use bells: church bells, school bells, clock bells, door bells, phone bells, dinner bells, train bells, ship's bells, and fire bells. *See also* SHIP'S CLOCK.

SCHULMERICH CARILLONS, INC.

BELL, city of California, in Los Angeles Co., about 10 miles S.E. of downtown Los Angeles. Bell has steel and iron-working plants. Pop. (1960) 19,450; (1970) 21,836.

BELL, Acton, pen name of the British writer Anne Brontë. *See* BRONTË.

BELL, Alexander Graham (1847–1922), American inventor, born in Edinburgh, Scotland, and educated at the universities of Edinburgh and London. He emigrated to Canada in 1870 and to the United States in 1871. In the U.S. he began teaching deaf-mutes (*see* DEAF), publicizing the system called visible speech. The system, which was developed by his father, the Scottish educator Alexander Melville Bell (1819–1905), shows how the lips, tongue, and throat, are used in the articulation of sound. In 1872 Bell founded a school for deaf-mutes in Boston. The school subsequently became part of Boston University, where Bell was appointed professor of vocal physiology. He became a naturalized U.S. citizen in 1882.

Since the age of eighteen, Bell had been working on the idea of transmitting speech by electric waves. In 1874, while working on a multiple telegraph (q.v.), he developed the basic ideas of the telephone (q.v.). His experiments finally proved successful on March 10, 1876, when the first complete sentence was transmitted, "Watson, come here; I want you". Subsequent demonstrations, notably at the 1876 Philadelphia Centennial Exposition, introduced the telephone to the world and led to the organization of the Bell Telephone Company in 1877.

In 1880 France bestowed on Bell the 50,000-franc Volta Prize for his invention. With this money he founded the Volta Laboratory in Washington, D.C., where, in that same year, he and his associates invented the photophone, that transmitted speech by light rays. Other inventions included the audiometer, used in measuring acuity in hearing; the induction balance, developed in 1881 and used to locate metal objects in human bodies; and the first wax recording cylinder, introduced in 1886. The cylinder, together with the flat wax disc, formed the basis of the modern phonograph (q.v.). Bell was also one of the cofounders of the National Geographic Society (q.v.) and served as its president from 1896 to 1904.

After 1895 Bell's interest turned mostly to aeronautics, and many of his inventions were first tested near his summer home at Baddeck on Cape Breton Island in Nova Scotia. His study of flight began with construction of large kites, leading to a man-carrying kite in 1907. With a group of associates, including the American inventor and aviator Glenn Hammond Curtiss (q.v.), he developed the aileron, a movable section of an airplane wing controlling roll, and the tricycle landing gear, which first permitted take-off from and landing on a flying field. Applying the principles of aeronautics to marine propulsion, his group started work on hydrofoil (q.v.) boats, which travel above the water at high speeds. His final full-sized "hydrodrome", developed in 1917, reached speeds in excess of 70 m.p.h. and for many years was the fastest boat in the world.

Alexander Graham Bell at the opening of the New York-Chicago long-distance telephone line, 1892.

Bell's continuing studies on the causes and heredity of deafness led to experiments in eugenics (q.v.), including sheep breeding, and to his book *Duration of Life and Conditions Associated with Longevity* (1918). He died at Baddeck, where a museum containing many of his original inventions is maintained by the Canadian government.

BELL, Andrew (1753–1832), British clergyman and educator, born in Saint Andrews, Scotland, and educated at the University of Saint Andrews. After several years as a tutor in Virginia and in Scotland, Bell was ordained a minister in the Church of England. In 1787 he went to India as an army chaplain, and two years later he was appointed superintendent of an orphan asylum in Madras, India. There he developed the monitorial system of teaching, under which older pupils learn by teaching younger pupils. Bell expounded his plan, known also as the Bell or Madras system, in the pamphlet *An Experiment in Education* (1797). He returned to Great Britain, and subsequently held clerical posts that permitted him to organize parish schools on the Bell system. He also became involved in a protracted controversy over the question of whether English grammar schools were to be controlled by the government or by the Church of England. The Bell system, widely adopted in British and European schools during Bell's lifetime, has been modified and is still used in many schools.

BELL, Sir Charles (1774–1842), British surgeon and anatomist, born in Edinburgh, Scotland, and educated at the University of Edinburgh. He studied with his brother John Bell (1763–1820), and assisted him in anatomical lectures and demonstrations. In 1799 Charles Bell became a member of the Edinburgh College of Surgeons and in 1812 of the Royal College of Surgeons in London. After serving at Middlesex Hospital in London from 1812 to 1836, he became professor of surgery at the University of Edinburgh.

Bell's contributions to anatomy made him one of the greatest scientists in medical history. He established the existence of motor and sensory nerves and showed the relationships of nerves to different parts of the brain and to different functions. His discoveries were described in several books, including *A New Idea of the Anatomy of the Brain* (1811) and *The Nervous System of the Human Body* (1830). For his discoveries he was awarded many honors, including the medal of the Royal Society (of which he was a member) in 1829. He was knighted in 1831.

BELL, Currer, pen name of the British writer Charlotte Brontë. *See* BRONTË.

BELL, Ellis, pen name of the British writer Emily Brontë. *See* BRONTË.

BELL, Gertrude Margaret Lowthian (1868–1926), British archeologist, writer and government official, born in Durham County, England, and educated at Lady Margaret Hall, University of Oxford. From 1899 to 1914 she made several archeological expeditions in Asia Minor and the Arabian peninsula. Her expert knowledge of those regions led her into service with British intelligence forces in the Middle East during World War I. In 1917 she went to Baghdad, Iraq, to serve in the British political office. She was influential in determining the British terms for Iraqi independence and in the election of Faisal I (*see under* FAISAL) as the first king of Iraq. Her works include *Poems from the Divan of Hafiz* (1897), *The Desert and the Sown* (1907), *Amurath to Amurath* (1911), *The Palace and the Mosque of Ukhaidir* (1914), and *Letters of Gertrude Bell* (2 vol., 1927).

BELL, John (1797–1869), American statesman, born near Nashville, Tenn., and educated at Cumberland College (now University of Nashville). He practiced law and served in the State senate before entering the United States House of Representatives in 1827 as a Democrat. In 1834 he joined the Whig Party (q.v.), and as a Whig he defeated James Knox Polk (q.v.), later President of the United States, as Speaker of the House. In 1841 Bell left the House to join the cabinet of President William Henry Harrison (q.v.). He resigned the following September, however, because of a split between the Whigs and President John Tyler (q.v.), who had succeeded Harrison. From 1847 to 1859 Bell served in the United States Senate as a Whig.

In 1860 he was the Presidential candidate of the Constitutional Union Party (q.v.). He won the electoral votes of Kentucky, Tennessee, and Virginia, but he lost the election to the Republican Abraham Lincoln (q.v.). Bell at first opposed the secession of the southern States, but he later endorsed the Confederate States of America (q.v.).

BELLADONNA, one of several common names for the Old World herb *Atropa belladonna* of the Nightshade (q.v.) family (Solanaceae) and for a crude drug obtained from the plant. Belladonna is a biennial or annual plant with large simple leaves and bell-shaped flowers. The flower tube is five-pointed, dull purple or red-purple, and surrounded by five green sepals. The fruit is a single green berry that becomes purple to black with maturity.

Belladonna is occasionally grown in gardens in North America but rarely becomes naturalized. It does not normally persist without cultivation. Through confusion of common names, other members of the Nightshade family are sometimes erroneously called belladonna. All parts of the true belladonna are poisonous and narcotic. The leaves and root contain tropane alkaloids that produce, among other effects, ex-

Belladonna, Atropa belladonna

treme dilation of the pupils of the eyes, and are used in medicine to facilitate eye examinations. In earlier times in Italy, extracts of belladonna were used by women for the cosmetic value of this dilating effect; such use explains the origin of the common name (It. "beautiful woman"). J.M.K.

BELLADONNA LILY, *or* CAPE BELLADONNA, common name for an African bulbous plant of the genus *Amaryllis* (q.v.), and the family Amaryllidaceae. This ornamental plant has fragrant red, white, purple, or white-striped flowers.

BELLAIRE, city of Ohio, in Belmont Co., on the Ohio R., about 85 miles S.E. of Akron, and about 4 miles S. of Wheeling, West Va. The city is in a coal-mining area, and manufactures stoves, glass and clay products, enamelware, and caskets. Pop. (1960) 11,502; (1970) 9655.

BELLAMY, Edward (1850–98), American essayist and journalist, born in Chicopee Falls, Mass., and educated at Union College. He worked briefly for the New York *Evening Post* and later joined the Springfield *Union* as editor and book reviewer. In 1880 he founded the Springfield *Daily News,* but he thereafter turned from journalism to literature. In 1888 Bellamy published his most important work, *Looking Backward,* a depiction of an ideal socialistic society in the year 2000. This best-selling novel inspired the formation of many socialistic clubs, and Bellamy, in 1891, founded the journal *New Nation* to expound his views. His other works include *Dr. Heidenhoff's Process* (1880), *Mrs. Ludington's Sister* (1884), *Equality* (1897), *The Blind Man's World and Other Stories* (1898), and *The Duke of Stockbridge* (1900).

BELL AND EVERETT PARTY. *See* CONSTITUTIONAL UNION PARTY.

BELLARMINE, Saint Robert, original name ROBERTO FRANCESCO ROMOLO BELLARMINO (1542–1621), Italian theologian and doctor of the Church, born in Montepulciano. He joined the Jesuits (q.v.) in 1560 and later studied and taught theology at Louvain. After 1576 he lectured in Rome on the conflicts arising from the Reformation (q.v.). He defended the Catholic position in his *Disputation on the Controversy of Christian Faith Confronting the Face of Heresy* (3 vol., 1581). He was elevated to cardinal in 1599. For the rest of his life Bellarmine was involved in the major Catholic controversies, including that with James I (q.v.), King of England. Bellarmine was canonized in 1930. His feast day is celebrated May 13.

BELLAY, Joachim du (about 1522–60), French poet, born near Liré. As a student in Paris he met the French poet Pierre de Ronsard (q.v.) who introduced him to the Pléiade (*see* PLEIAD), a Renaissance group restyling French literature on Greek and Roman models. In 1549 du Bellay wrote the Pléiade manifesto *La Défense* et Illustration de la Langue Française ("The Defense and Glorification of the French Language"). In the same year he issued *L'Olive,* 115 sonnets styled after the Italian poet Petrarch (q.v.). From 1553 to 1557 du Bellay was in Rome, where in 1558 he wrote two more sonnet collections, *Les Regrets* and *Les Antiquités* de Rome. The latter collection was translated in 1591 into *The Ruins of Rome* by the English poet Edmund Spenser (q.v.). Du Bellay returned to Paris, where he wrote and translated poetry until his death.

BELLBIRD, common name for several groups of songbirds of South America, Australia, and New Zealand, so named because their calls are similar to the sound of bells. The males of the South American genus, *Procnias,* are often white, or white with black or brown markings; the females are generally green with either brown or yellow markings. *Procnias* is classified in the family Cotingidae. The Australian and New Zealand bellbirds, *Manorina melanophrys* and *Anthornis melanura,* are honey eaters in the family Meliphagidae; *see* HONEY EATER.

BELL, BOOK, AND CANDLE, medieval form of excommunication administered by the Roman Catholic Church. The officiating ecclesiastic pronounced the formula of excommunication and closed the pronouncing of the sentence by shutting the book from which it was read, taking a lighted candle and casting it to the ground, and tolling the bell as for the dead. This appears to have been the mode of excommunication in the Western churches from the 7th to the 10th century. The Luxembourg State Museum has a painting by Jean Paul Laurens (1838–1921) on the Bell, Book, and Candle theme: "Excommunication of Robert the Pious".

BELLEAU WOOD, BATTLE OF, military engagement of World War I, fought between Germany and United States troops in Belleau Wood, a wooded tract of less than 1 sq.mi. in area, 5 mi. northwest of Chateau-Thierry, and about 40 mi. northeast of Paris, France. A German drive toward Paris had been halted and the Germans were entrenched in Belleau Wood when on June 6, 1918, a U.S. marine brigade, attached to the Second Division of the American Expeditionary Force (q.v.) and commanded by the American general James Guthrie Harbord (q.v.) attacked the Germans. The marines repeatedly attacked, fighting through matted underbrush and over rocky ground. On June 24 they launched a final successful drive to capture the wood. American casualties were more than 7800 officers and men killed, wounded, and missing. German losses were also severe. In 1923 the French government dedicated the battleground as a memorial to the Americans and renamed it *Bois de la Brigade de Marine* ("Wood of the Marine Brigade").

BELLEFONTAINE, city in Ohio, and county seat of Logan Co., about 30 miles N. of Springfield. The city is in an agricultural area, and is a railroad and trade center. Heating apparatus, furniture, and motor vehicles are manufactured, and food products and printed materials are produced. Pop. (1960) 11,424; (1970) 11,255.

BELLEFONTAINE NEIGHBORS, city of Missouri, in Saint Louis Co., near the W. bank of the Mississippi R., about 9 miles N. of central Saint Louis, of which it is a suburb. Pop. (1960) 13,650; (1970) 13,987.

BELLE GLADE, city of Florida, in Palm Beach Co., about 38 miles W. of West Palm Beach. Situated in a truck-farming area, Belle Glade is a canning and shipping center. Nearby is the Everglades Experiment Station. Pop. (1960) 11,273; (1970) 15,949.

BELLE ISLE, strait and granite island of the same name in the strait, between the coasts of S.E. Labrador and N. Newfoundland. The strait, which connects the Atlantic Ocean with the Gulf of Saint Lawrence, is 75 mi. long and between 10 and 15 mi. wide. Although much used by transatlantic vessels from June until the end of November, floating ice and fog make navigation difficult in all seasons. The island, at the Atlantic entrance to the strait, rises to about 700 ft. at its highest point. It is nearly 15 mi. from either coast, and has a lighthouse at its S. end. Area of the island, about 15 sq.mi.

BELLEROPHON, in Greek mythology, the son of Glaucus, King of Corinth (q.v.). Although a mortal, Bellerophon possessed so many godlike attributes that, in some legends, he was said to be the son of Poseidon (q.v.), god of the sea. Other legends attribute his divine characteristics to the fact that his mother Eurynome, a mortal, had been endowed with knowledge equal to the gods by her teacher Athena (q.v.), goddess of wisdom.

Bellerophon's greatest wish was to catch and tame the winged horse Pegasus (q.v.). With the aid of a bridle given him by Athena, he achieved this desire, and Pegasus became an invaluable help to him in the trials that lay ahead. Bellerophon aroused the jealousy of Proetus, king of Argos (q.v.), who sent him to his father-in-law Iobates, king of Lycia (q.v.), with a message requesting that the bearer be slain. The king, having entertained Bellerophon before he read the message, was afraid to anger the god Zeus (q.v.) by carrying out a request that would break the traditional bond between host and guest. Instead of killing Bellerophon, he asked him to kill the Chimera, a firebreathing monster, part goat, part serpent, part lion, which the hero did. Bellerophon also accepted the separate challenges of a warlike tribe called the Solymi (*see* LYCIA), a group of powerful female warriors known as the Amazons (q.v.), and several ambushers chosen by the king, emerging the victor each time. Iobates was impressed by his superhuman courage. He became Bellerophon's friend and married him to his daughter, by whom the young man had three children.

According to one legend, after a time of prosperity Bellerophon encountered misfortune and spent the rest of his life walking the earth. Another traditional story relates that Bellerophon defied the gods by trying to ride Pegasus up to Olympus (q.v.), but, thrown to the earth by the horse, he wandered in misery until he died.

BELLES-LETTRES, a body of writing comprising drama, poetry, fiction, criticism, and essays. In modern usage the term belles-lettres (Fr. "beautiful letters") denotes facile and sophisticated literature of an artistic, imaginative, or creative nature, as opposed to that which is utilitarian or scientific. Originally belles-lettres referred to the humanities in general. The English satirist Jonathan Swift (q.v.) was one of the first writers to employ the term, using it in the periodical *The Tatler*.

BELLEVILLE, city in Illinois, and county seat of Saint Clair Co., just S.E. of East Saint Louis. Situated in a rich coal-mining region, it is an industrial center, with a brewery and plants in which shoes, clothing, stoves and ranges, stencils and stencil machines, caskets, and corrugated boxes are manufactured. About 8 miles E. of the city is Scott Air Force Base, radio-training center of the United States Air Force. Belleville was incorporated as a city in 1819. Pop. (1960) 37,264; (1970) 41,699.

BELLEVILLE, town in New Jersey, in Essex Co., situated on the Passaic R., 3 miles N. of Newark, of which it is a suburb. Industries in Belleville include the manufacture of textiles, machinery, wire cloth, and cosmetics. Pop. (1970) 34,643.

BELLEVILLE, city of Canada, in Ontario Province, county seat of Hastings Co., at the mouth of the Moira R. on the Bay of Quinte, Lake Ontario, 45 miles W. of Kingston. A rail and road center and a port, Belleville has meat-packing and dairy industries and manufactures machinery, optical equipment, industrial alcohol, locks, cement, and radios. The city is the site of the Ontario School for the Deaf and of Albert College (1857), an affiliate of the University of Toronto. Pop. (1976) 35,311.

BELLEVUE, city of Washington, in King Co., near Lake Washington, about 8 miles W. of central Seattle. Bellevue is the site of Bellevue Community College, established in 1966. Pop. (1960) 12,809; (1970) 61,102.

BELLFLOWER. *See* CAMPANULA.

BELLFLOWER, city of California, in Los Angeles Co., 14 miles S.E. of downtown Los Angeles. Dairying, flower growing, and truck farming predominate; industrial products include lumber and metal products. Founded by Dutch settlers in 1906, Bellflower was called Somerset until 1909. The city was incorporated in 1957. Pop. (1960) 45,909; (1970) 51,454.

BELL GARDENS, city of California, in Los Angeles Co., 8 miles S.E. of downtown Los Angeles. Nursery products are grown here. An outgrowth of adjacent Bell, the city was incorporated in 1961. Pop. (1960) 26,467; (1970) 29,308.

BELLIGERENT, in international law, a state or organized community at war and subject to and protected by the laws of war. A state need not be politically independent to have the status of a belligerent. It must, however, be capable of maintaining itself by regular hostilities under a *de facto* government. A colony in revolt against the parent state, or a revolutionary section or party waging war against the general government, has no standing in international law. Without belligerent rights the insurgent is not entitled to have legal blockades, nor may rebel vessels be received in foreign ports. The insurgent acts of war are technically crimes, and certain maritime actions could be defined as piracy (q.v.). The recognition of an insurgent government as a belligerent by neutral powers (*see* NEUTRALITY) is often based on insurgent control over territory and the strength of the insurgent regime. Recognition of a belligerent status is often followed by recognition of the independence of the insurgent government.

The grant of belligerent rights carries with it certain benefits. The principal advantages are the powerful moral support gained from international recognition, respect of the flag, and the right to negotiate foreign loans. The status of belligerency also carries with it the obligation to observe the rules of civilized warfare set forth at the Geneva Convention (*see* RED CROSS, INTERNATIONAL), and it makes the belligerent liable for damage to neutral commerce and to citizens of neutral states. For example, during the American Civil War, Turkey did not recognize the belligerency of the Confederate States of America (q.v.) and was thus able to hold the United States government responsible for acts of the Confederacy. Conversely, Great Britain and France, having recognized the Confederacy, could not hold the U.S. government liable for damages inflicted by the Confederacy.

BELLINGHAM, city and port of entry in Washington, and county seat of Whatcom Co. on the E. shore of Padilla Bay, about 80 miles N. of Seattle. The surrounding region is noted for production of coal, timber, fruits, vegetables, and poultry, all of which are processed in, and shipped from, Bellingham. Other principal industries in the city are fishing, oil refining, shipbuilding, and the manufacture of lumber and wood products, paper and paper products, and aluminum products. The city is the site of Western Washington State College, and is the gateway to Mt. Baker National Forest. Pop. (1960) 34,688; (1970) 39,375.

BELLINGSHAUSEN, Fabian Gottlieb von (1778–1852), Russian explorer and naval officer, born on the Island of Ösel, Estonia (now Saaremaa, Estonian S.S.R.). He entered the imperial Russian navy in 1797, and received his training at the port of Kronshtadt. In 1809, as a commissioned officer, he participated in the Russian action against Sweden. Ten years later he was given command of two ships, *Vostok* and *Mirny,* and ordered to explore Antarctica. In 1819 he penetrated 70° S. lat. into the Antarctic sea bearing his name. In the sea he discovered and named Peter I and Alexander I islands. On his return trip to Russia in 1821, Bellingshausen explored the Society Islands (q.v.), one of which now bears his name. During the Russian war with Turkey (1828–29), he distinguished himself at Varna (now in Bulgaria), and was promoted to vice-admiral. He was later named admiral and was appointed governor of Kronshtadt.

BELLINI, name of a family of Italian painters who founded the so-called Venetian school of painting (q.v.).

Iacopo Bellini (1400–70?), born in Venice, a student of the Italian painter Gentile da Fabriano (q.v.). Iacopo's most important contribution was the education of his two sons and of his son-in-law, the Italian painter Andrea Mantegna (q.v.). Two sketchbooks (in the Louvre Museum, Paris, and the British Museum, London) provided the inspiration for the three younger men. Iacopo's extant works include "Christ Crucified" (Archbishop's Palace, Verona) and five Madonnas, the richest of which is in the Uffizi Gallery, Florence.

"Doge Loredano" (1501) by Giovanni Bellini.
National Gallery of Art, London

Gentile Bellini (1429?–1507), son of Iacopo Bellini, born in Venice. Gentile's fame rests with his portraits and his scenes of Venetian life. His most important works include several paintings of Muhammad II (1430–81), Sultan of Turkey, painted on the sultan's invitation in Constantinople (1479–80) and "Saint Mark Preaching at Alexandria" (1504, Brera Gallery, Milan).

Giovanni Bellini (1430?–1516), son of Iacopo Bellini, born in Venice. Giovanni, the most prolific of the Bellinis, was one of the greatest Venetian painters. He experimented with oil and was able to produce soft, glowing colors. Two of his students, the artists Il Giorgione and Titian (qq.v.), further developed his techniques. Giovanni's works include the San Zaccaria and Frari altarpieces, "Pietà" (about 1500, Galleria dell'Accademia, Venice), and "Allegory" (about 1490, Uffizi Gallery, Florence).

BELLINI, Vincenzo (1801–35), Italian composer, born in Catania, Sicily, and trained at the Conservatory of Music, Naples. The premiere of his first opera, *Adelson e Salvini* ("Adelson and Salvini"), in 1825 attracted Domenico Barbaja (1778–1841), the director of the San Carlo Opera, Naples and La Scala, Milan. Barbaja commissioned Bellini to compose *Bianca e Gernando* ("Bianca and Gernando") for San Carlo in 1826 and *Il Pirata* ("The Pirate") for La Scala in 1827. Both operas were very successful, as was *I Capuletti ed i Montecchi* ("The Capulets and the Montagues", 1830). In 1831 two of Bellini's most famous operas, *La Sonnambula* ("The Sleepwalker") and *Norma,* had their premieres. They were followed in 1833 by *Beatrice di Tenda* ("Beatrice of Tende") and in 1835 by his final work, *I Puritani* ("The Puritans"). Bellini was a master of *bel canto,* a singing style stressing vocal agility and precision, and *Il Pirata, La Sonnambula, Norma,* and *I Puritani* were noted for their charm and beauty.

BELLMANN, Karl Mikael (1740–95), Swedish poet, born in Stockholm, and educated at the University of Uppsala. He gained early fame with his religious songs and later became popular as a writer of pastorals, and of comic and drinking songs. Two of his collections are *Fredmans Epistlar* ("Fredman's Epistles", 1790) and *Fredmans Sanger* ("Fredman's Songs", 1791). Bellmann is ranked as the greatest Swedish lyric poet.

BELLO, Andrés (1781–1865), Latin-American poet, educator, and scholar, born in Caracas, Venezuela, and educated at the University of Caracas. In 1810 he went to London on behalf of the ruling Venezuelan junta, but after the overthrow of the junta he chose to remain in London. There he served as secretary to the legations of Colombia and Chile, and he wrote his famous epic *Silvas Americanas* ("American Woods", 1826–27). The epic, in a classical poetic style, celebrates the natural beauty and country life of South America. In 1829 Bello returned to South America to accept a post in the Chilean government, and in 1843 he became the first rector of the University of Chile in Santiago. Of his many works on law, philosophy, literary criticism, and philology, the most important are *Principios de Derecho Internacional* ("Principles of International Jurisprudence", 1832), a standard textbook on international law, and *Gramática de la Lengua Castellana* ("Grammar of the Castilian Language", 1847), the first scientific study of the Spanish language and the leading authority in the field. His complete works were published by the Chilean government in fifteen volumes (1881–93).

BELLOC, Hilaire, in full JOSEPH HILAIRE PIERRE BELLOC (1870–1953) writer, born in La Celle-Saint-Cloud, France, and educated at Balliol College, University of Oxford. He became a

British subject in 1902 and served (1906–10) in Parliament. His outspoken opposition to socialism attracted him to the British writer G. K. Chesterton (q.v.), and the two men founded (1911) a journal expounding their views. Belloc was a popular, versatile, and prolific writer. His first published works were *Verses and Sonnets* (1895), a delightful child's story, *The Bad Child's Book of Beasts* (1896), and two biographies, *Danton* (1899) and *Robespierre* (1901). In *The Path to Rome* (1902) he recounted a pilgrimage to Rome and showed his humor, love of travel, and piety. Belloc was a devout Roman Catholic and his religious and political convictions strongly colored his serious works. He offered an alternative to socialism in *The Servile State* (1912) and reinterpreted Anglican history in *History of England* (4 vol., 1925–31) and in the biographies *Charles I* (1933), *Cromwell* (1934), *Charles II* (1939), and *Elizabethan Commentary* (1942). His historical interpretation led to a public controversy with the British writer H. G. Wells (q.v.) over Wells' historical work *The Outline of History*.

BELLONA, in Roman mythology, the goddess of war. She is often identified with the Greek war goddess Enyo. In later mythology, Bellona was described as the sister, daughter, or wife of the Roman god of war Mars (q.v.), and sometimes as his charioteer or muse. Her temple, dedicated at Rome in 296 B.C., stood in the Campus Martius near the altar of Mars outside the gates of the city. Here the senate met to receive foreign ambassadors. At the *columna bellica* in front of Bellona's temple, the *fetialis* (Roman priestly officials) performed the declaration of war ceremony.

BELLOW, Saul (1915–), American novelist and Nobel laureate, born in Lachine, Québec, Canada. He graduated from Northwestern University in 1937 and subsequently taught at Pestalozzi-Froebel Teachers College in Chicago. For many years he was associated with the University of Chicago, after 1964 as a professor.

His first novel, *Dangling Man* (1944), deals with the anxiety and discomfort of a young man waiting to be drafted in wartime. It was followed by *The Victim* (1947). After winning a Guggenheim fellowship, Bellow lived for a time in Europe, where he wrote most of his best-known novel, *The Adventures of Augie March* (1953). A long, loosely structured narrative with a picaresque hero, the novel gives a vivid, often humorous picture of Jewish life in Chicago and of a young man's search for identity. These related themes of identity and Jewishness received further treatment in the novels *Seize the Day* (1956), *Henderson the Rain King* (1959), *Herzog* (1964), and *Mr. Sammler's Planet* (1970).

Bellow received the 1976 Pulitzer Prize in fiction for his novel *Humboldt's Gift* (1975). Three months later he was awarded the 1976 Nobel Prize in literature for "the human understanding and subtle analysis of contemporary culture that are combined in his work". His first book of nonfiction was *To Jerusalem and Back* (1976), a reflective study of his reactions to a visit to Israel.

BELLOWS, George Wesley (1882–1925), American artist, born in Columbus, Ohio, and educated at Ohio State University. He studied with the American painter Robert Henri (q.v.) and later taught in New York City and Chicago, Illinois. Bellows was strongly influenced by Henri, and both belonged to the American realistic art movement, the Ashcan school; *see* AMERICAN PAINTING: *20th Century*. Bellows received early recognition for his work, and in 1909 he became the youngest associate member of the National Academy of Design, an organization of artists. In the same year he completed his most famous painting, the realistic boxing scene "A Stag at Sharkey's" (Cleveland Museum of Art, Cleveland, Ohio).

He later concentrated on landscapes and por-

Hilaire Belloc Harper & Row

"Preliminaries to the Big Bout", crayon and wash drawing by George Wesley Bellows.
Boston Public Library — Wiggin Collection

traits. These included a family portrait "Emma and Her Children" (Museum of Fine Arts, Boston, Mass.), a portrait of his daughters, "Jean and Anna" (Buffalo Fine Arts Academy, Buffalo, N.Y.), a portrait of the British nurse, "Edith Cavell" (Museum of Fine Arts, Springfield, Mass.), the landscape "Up the Hudson" (Metropolitan Museum of Art, New York City), and a city scene, "Gramercy Park" (Whitney Museum of American Art, New York City). Bellows also produced lithographs of such fine quality that he inspired in those who followed him a renewed interest in the medium.

BELL ROCK, *or* INCHCAPE ROCK, a sandstone reef in the North Sea, about 12 mi. southeast of Arbroath, Scotland, and near the entrance to the Firth of Tay. The reef, about 2000 ft. long, is submerged at high tide, and is thus a navigational hazard. The British poet Robert Southey (q.v.) in *The Inchcape Rock* recounted the legendary placement of a warning bell on the reef and the subsequent theft of the bell. A lighthouse, about 100 ft. high, was built (1807–10) there.

BELL TOWER, *or* CAMPANILE (It. *campana,* "bell"), a tower standing free, attached to, or surmounting a religious or civic structure, and housing at least one bell. Originally the terms belfry and campanile were interchangeable, but now belfry refers to a structure atop a building in which the bell is placed and campanile to the entire bell tower.

Medieval bell towers were often tall and served also as watch towers and public monuments. Freestanding round campaniles date from about the 6th century in Italy. The campanile of Saint Apollinaire in Classe, Ravenna (534–38?) is representative of the early bell towers. It is round, brick, and multistoried, with arched windows, about 120 ft. high, and a slightly peaked roof. The tall, graceful, square-based campanile of Santa Maria in Cosmedin, Rome (772–95) is more representative of campanile style after the 8th century. A notable exception to the later square-based towers is the famous 12th-century Leaning Tower of the Cathedral of Pisa. This 180-ft.-high campanile is round and faced with columned arches that repeat the Gothic design of the cathedral.

In France during the 11th century bell towers were attached to the main building. The spired

Turreted bell tower (above), of the monastery of San Salvador, in northern Spain (from a 10th-century Spanish manuscript).
Metropolitan Museum of Art

Square bell tower of the Duomo of Florence, designed by the Florentine architect and artist Giotto (1276?–1337?).
Alinari

towers of Abbaye-aux-Hommes, Caen (1064–77) appear to sit atop the church; at Saint Pierre, Angoulême (1105–28), the towers were incorporated into the facade. The attached towers of the early-12th-century Sant' Ambrogio in Milan, Italy, are peaked, of unequal height, and flank the narthex.

Other important bell towers include the 320-ft. rectangular, freestanding campanile of Saint Mark's Cathedral, Venice, begun in the 9th century; the 275-ft. rectangular, freestanding campanile of Santa Maria of Florence, designed by the Florentine artist Giotto (q.v.) in red, white, and green marble; and the attached spired towers of Notre Dame of Chartres, France (12th to 13th century), which, although of unequal height and ornamentation, served as models for Notre Dame of Paris (1163–1235) and Notre Dame of Amiens (1220–88). In England the most notable bell towers are those designed by the English architect Sir Christopher Wren (q.v.) in the 17th century for Saint Mary-le-Bow, London, and Saint Paul's Cathedral, London.

More recent bell towers include the Victoria Tower of the Westminster Houses of Parliament, London; the Memorial Tower of Brown University, Providence, R.I.; and the campanile of the University of California, Berkeley, Calif.

BELLWOOD, village of Illinois, in Cook Co., on Addison Creek, 10 miles W. of Chicago. Situated in an area of dairying, livestock raising, and grain and truck farming, Bellwood manufactures metal and wood products, electrical appliances, radio and auto parts, and industrial machinery. The village was incorporated in 1900. Pop. (1960) 20,729; (1970) 22,096.

BELLWORT. *See* LILIACEAE.

BELMONT, city of California, in San Mateo Co., about 19 miles S.E. of central San Francisco. The city is a shipping center for flowers. It is the site of the College of Notre Dame, established in 1851. Pop. (1960) 15,996; (1970) 23,667.

BELMONT, town of Massachusetts, in Middlesex Co., 6 miles N.W. of Boston, of which it is a residential suburb. It was settled in 1636 as the Pequossette plantation and was later named for a local estate. Incorporated in 1859, Belmont is the site of an annual strawberry festival. Several sites in the town are referred to in the works of the American poet James Russell Lowell (*see under* LOWELL). Pop. (1960) 28,715; (1970) 28,285.

BELMOPAN, city, capital of Belize (British Honduras), near the Belize R. Situated in an interior area where the Maya (q.v.) once flourished, the city was founded in the 1960's to replace Belize City (q.v.), a seaport that had been badly damaged by several tropical storms. The construction of Belmopan began in 1967, and it became the capital in 1970. Pop. (1973 est.) 3500.

BELO HORIZONTE, city in Brazil, capital of Minas Gerais State, about 210 miles N. of Rio de Janeiro. The city is the center of a region containing rich gold, iron, and manganese mines. Cotton is the most important crop of the region. In the town diamonds are cut and cotton is milled. Other industries include metalworking and the manufacture of pottery, footwear, and furniture. The University of Minas Gerais is located in the city. Built in the late 19th century to become the capital of the State, replacing Ouro Preto, Belo Horizonte has rapidly increased in size and importance and is now the second-largest inland city in Brazil. Pop. (1970 prelim.) 1,106,722.

BELOIT, city of Wisconsin, in Rock County, on the Rock R., about 70 miles S.W. of Milwaukee. General farming, dairying, and stock raising are carried on in the surrounding region. Industries in the city include woodworking and the manufacture of papermaking and grinding machines, diesel engines, power pumps, machine tools, shoes, hosiery, and paper. Founded in 1836 by a group of New England immigrants, Beloit received a city charter in 1857. It is the site of Beloit College, a coeducational, liberal arts institution founded in 1846, and is notable as a winter sports center. Pop. (1970) 35,729.

BELOIT COLLEGE, coeducational privately controlled school of liberal arts, located in Beloit, Wis. It operates on a year-round trimester academic calendar. The college was chartered in 1846 and held its first classes in 1847. The degrees of B.A., B.S., and M.A.T. are conferred. The curriculum includes annual field trips in anthropology, archeology, biology, and geology, and an overseas study plan, as well as a term of off-campus work experience. The college offers qualified students a semester of study in Washington, D.C., in cooperation with The American University (q.v.). Selected science students are eligible for a semester of study at Argonne National Laboratory. By arrangement with several universities, Beloit students may elect a five-year course of study leading to both a degree of bachelor and a professional degree in engineering or forestry. In 1973 the college library housed more than 230,000 bound volumes. Student enrollment in 1973 totaled 1780, the faculty numbered 140, and the endowment was about $10,000,000.

BELORUSSIA. *See* WHITE RUSSIAN SOVIET SOCIALIST REPUBLIC.

BELSEN. *See* CONCENTRATION CAMP.

BELSHAZZAR, in the Old Testament, Babylonian prince mentioned in chapter 5 of the book of Daniel (q.v.) as the last Chaldean king of Babylon (q.v.). He was slain at the capture of Babylon by the Medes and the Persians (*see* MEDIA; PERSIA). Although no ancient historian mentions his name as one of the successors of the second Chaldean king, Nebuchadnezzar II (*see under* NEBUCHADNEZZAR), the Babylonian cuneiform inscriptions gave the name Belsaruzar as that of the son of Nabonidus (r. about 555–539 B.C.), the last king of Babylon. A later inscription suggested that Belshazzar was associated with his father on the throne. *See also* BABYLONIA: *History*.

BELTRAMI, Eugenio (1835–1900), Italian mathematician, born in Cremona. He taught mathematics at the universities of Rome, Pisa, and Pavia. He is best known for his research in non-Euclidian geometry (*see* GEOMETRY: *Non-Euclidian Geometry*), in which he proved the validity of hyperbolic geometry.

BELUGA, *or* WHITE WHALE, common name for *Delphinapterus leucas,* a marine mammal of the family Delphinidae, and closely related to the dolphin (q.v.). Belugas (Russ. *byelukha,* "white") are toothed whales with clearly defined heads and short flippers. They are born either black or dark brown, without dorsal fins, and turn milky white in about five years. Males can attain a length of 18 ft. and a weight of 1 ton; females are somewhat smaller. Belugas travel in schools of several hundred, feeding on fish and squid. Belugas are common to the Arctic Ocean and may be found as far south as the Saint Lawrence R. They are commercially important for their hides and oil. *See* WHALE.

BELVIDERE, city in Illinois, and county seat of Boone Co., on the Kishwaukee R., about 14 miles E. of Rockford. In a dairy, grain, and livestock region, the city serves as a processing and shipping center. Machine parts, hardware, and clothing are manufactured. Pop. (1960) 11,223; (1970) 14,061.

BELZONI, Giovanni Battista (1778–1823), Italian explorer and archeologist, born in Padua. He studied hydraulic engineering in Rome, and in 1803 he went to England. There he worked as a circus performer until 1815 when he went to Egypt. It is uncertain whether he ever attempted to use hydraulic machinery to raise the level of the Nile R., but he did meet the British consul in Cairo, who employed him to collect Egyptian antiquities for British museums. Within the next two years, he transferred from Thebes (q.v.) the colossal bust of the "Young Memnon" (now in the British Museum, London), explored the temple at Idfu, cleared the entrance to the huge temple at Abu Simbel (q.v.), and excavated at El Karnak (q.v.). In 1817 he traveled to the Valley of the Kings where he discovered the tomb of the Egyptian king Seti I (*see under* SETI) and Seti's sarcophagus (now in Sir John Soane's House and Museum, London). The following year Belzoni became the first modern man to enter the pyramid of Khufu at Giza (q.v.). He was one of the first Europeans to visit the oasis of Siwa, and he also identified the ruins of Berenice on the Red Sea. In 1819 he returned to England. The following year he published *Narrative of the Operations and Recent Discoveries Within the Pyramids, Temples, Tombs, and Excavations, in Egypt and Nubia.*

BEMBO, Pietro (1470–1547), Italian scholar, born in Venice and educated in Florence, Messina, and Padua. Following six years at the court of Urbino, in 1512 he went to Rome where he became secretary to Pope Leo X (*see under* LEO); in 1539 he was made a cardinal by Pope Paul III (q.v.). Bembo became historiographer of Venice and curator of Saint Mark's Library in 1529. He is credited with bringing about the 16th-century triumph of classic tradition in the Italian language and the creation of a style, written in imitation of the Italian poet Petrarch's poetry (*see* PETRARCH), known as bembism. His influence on Italian literature, art, and social life was felt for three centuries. His works include *Le Prose della Volgar Lingua* ("Prose in the Vernacular", 1525) and *Rerum Veneticarum Libri xii* ("A History of Venice", 1551).

BEMELMANS, Ludwig (1898–1962), American writer and artist, born in Meran, Austria (now Merano, Italy), and educated in Bavarian schools. He emigrated to the United States in 1914 and acquired citizenship four years later, while serving in the United States Army. For about a decade he worked as a busboy and then as assistant banquet manager in a New York City hotel; his books *Life Class* (1938) and *Hotel Splendide* (1939) are based on his experiences during this period. Among his other writings, for the most part satirical and humorous, are *My War with the United States* (1937), *Now I Lay Me Down to Sleep* (1943), and *On Board Noah's Ark* (1962). Bemelmans is also widely known for his books for children, notably *Madeline* (1939), a tale in verse about a little French girl, and its five sequels. He illustrated most of his own works in a distinctive style typically employing vivid watercolors and heavy black outlines. His more serious paintings are in the collections of several major museums, including the Metropolitan Museum of Art, New York City.

BEMIS HEIGHTS. *See* SARATOGA, BATTLES OF.

BENADRYL. *See* ALLERGY; HISTAMINE.

BENARES, former princely state of India, now forming part of Uttar Pradesh State (formerly United Provinces), Republic of India. The state, constituted in 1911, was in political association with Gwalior Residency, British India, until the termination of British paramountcy in India in 1947. Ramnagar, a town on the Ganges R. opposite the city of Varanasi (q.v.), formerly called Benares, is the former capital. Area of former state, 866 sq.mi.

BENARES *or* **BANARAS.** *See* VARANASI.

BENAVENTE Y MARTÍNEZ, Jacinto (1866–1954), Spanish playwright and critic, born in Madrid, and educated at the University of Madrid. After the publication of a book of his verse in 1886, he attracted public attention with a critical work, *Cartas de Mujeres* ("The Letters of Women", 1893), and a comedy, *El Nido Ajeno* ("Other Birds' Nests", 1894). Social climbers, the wealthy, and feudal institutions are among the subjects he attacks in a number of his plays. In 1922 he was awarded the Nobel Prize in literature; subsequently he toured Latin America and the United States with a company performing his works. In addition to plays for children, he wrote many comedies and tragedies. Many of his plays have been translated into French, Italian, and English; among them are *Noche del Sabado* (1903; Eng. trans., *Saturday Night,* 1923); *Los Intereses Creados* (1907; Eng. trans., *The Bonds of Interest,* 1917) and *La Malquerida* (1913; Eng. trans., *The Passion Flower,* 1917).

BEN BELLA, Ahmed. *See* ALGERIA: *History.*

BENCHLEY, Robert Charles (1889–1945), American humorist, editor, and actor, born in Worcester, Mass., and educated at Harvard University. From 1912 to 1940 he was a writer and editor, first with the Curtis Publishing Company; then with a newspaper, the New York *Tribune* (1916–19); and thereafter with the magazines *Vanity Fair* (1919–20), *Life* (1920–29), and *The New Yorker* (1929–40). Among his books are *Of All Things* (1921), *The Early Worm* (1927), *The Treasurer's Report* (1930), *From Bed to Worse* (1934), and *Benchley Beside Himself* (1943). In addition to writing many motion-picture scripts, he was a radio commentator, columnist, theater critic, and actor. *How To Sleep* (1935), which he wrote, directed, and acted in, won an award from the Academy of Motion Picture Arts and Sciences as the best short subject of the year. In all his work, Benchley showed an ability to find great humor in the pitfalls of everyday life.

One of his sons, Nathaniel Goddard Benchley (1915–), is a versatile writer of novels, books for children, a play, and *Robert Benchley: A Biography* (1955).

BEND, city in Oregon, and county seat of Deschutes Co., on the Deschutes R., about 86 miles E. of Eugene. Bend is in a timber and irrigated agricultural region and is a trade center for lumber and agricultural products. Bend is the site of Central Oregon Community College, established in 1949. Pop. (1960) 11,936; (1970) 13,710.

BENDS, in popular usage, name denoting the acute disease known medically as aeroembolism and caused by rapid decrease of the atmospheric pressure. Small bubbles or swellings under the skin characterize the disease, but its most striking symptom is excruciating pain, usually spread over many parts of the body. The victim is likely to double up in agony; this characteristic symptom gives the disease its name. Temporary paralysis of some part of the body may also occur, and sometimes permanent damage or even death may result. The disease is known also as caisson disease, decompression sickness, and diver's disease.

First observed in 1839, the disease soon became familiar to divers and caisson workers who had to work for long periods in compressed-air chambers. The symptoms appeared when those affected were brought back to ordinary atmospheric conditions. The only known cure was to put the victim immediately back into a pressure chamber and then to lower the pressure to normal very slowly. The cause of the symptoms was not known, although the liberation of air bubbles inside the blood stream and body tissues after a quick decompression was suspected.

During World War II airplanes were constructed that would climb within 6 min. to 30,000 ft., where the atmospheric pressure is less than one third the normal. Such rapid decompression could easily cause the aviator to be stricken with bends, and so an intensive study of the disease was undertaken. Bubbles of air liberated in the blood vessels were found to block some of the small terminal vessels, cutting off the blood supply of nerve endings and giving rise to the symptoms. Of the gases in the blood, oxygen and carbon dioxide are readily reabsorbed, so that nitrogen is the chief offender. The disease can therefore be prevented or made much less severe by having the aviator breathe pure oxygen not only during his flight, but for some time before it. In this way the nitrogen is eliminated from his system. This process is necessary only for interceptor pilots who fly rapidly to very high altitudes. In transport aircraft, equipped for long-range flight at high altitudes, the cabin is pressurized to control the drop in atmospheric pressure.

BENEDICITE, (Lat., "bless you"), canticle from The Song of the Three Children (q.v.), which is found in Daniel 3:57–87, 90, in Roman Catholic Bibles that are based on the Greek text. In the King James Version and other Protestant translations that adhere to Hebrew texts, it is placed in the Apocrypha (*see* BIBLE, CANON OF THE). The song stands as a prayer of Shadrach, Meshach, and Abednego in the fiery furnace. It was sung in the Christian Church as early as the 4th century and is still frequently used, especially during Advent, as a replacement for the *Te Deum.* In Anglican churches, the *Benedicite* can be substituted for the *Te Deum* in the morning prayer service.

BENEDICT, name of fifteen popes and several antipopes, among whom were the following.

Benedict VIII (d. 1024), born in Rome. He was the first of a line of Tusculan popes and the brother of his successor, Pope John XIX (*see under* JOHN). He was a layman before his election as pope. After his election, he was driven from Rome by an antipope, Gregory (r. 1012), who ruled for less than a year. Benedict was restored to the papal chair in 1014 with the aid of King Henry II (*see* HENRY II, called The Saint) of Saxony, whom he crowned Holy Roman Emperor in the same year. Benedict VIII distinguished himself as a reformer of the clergy, and prohibited, at the synod of Pavia in 1022, both clerical marriage and concubinage.

Benedict IX (about 1012–56), pope from 1032 to 1044, in 1045, and in 1047–48. He was a count of Tusculum and the nephew of his two immediate predecessors, Pope Benedict VIII and Pope John XIX. He bought the papal throne in 1032, at the age of twenty. His immoral character aroused much indignation, and in 1044 a Roman faction drove him from office as unfit to rule. He later reinstated himself, then resigned in favor of Gregory VI (d. 1048?), but regained the papal throne at the death of Clement II (d. 1047), who had succeeded the deposed Gregory VI. In 1048 Benedict was again driven from Rome.

Benedict XIII (1328–about 1423), original name PEDRO DE LUNA, antipope from 1394 to 1423, born in Illueca, Aragón (now in Spain). As a cardinal deacon he participated in the election of Pope Urban VI (*see under* URBAN) but later joined the French cardinals in the election of Robert of Geneva as Antipope Clement VII (*see under* CLEMENT). Benedict XIII was antipope of the Western Schism (*see* SCHISM, WESTERN OR GREAT) at Avignon from 1394 to 1423, having been chosen by the cardinals of Avignon after the death of Robert of Geneva. Although he was twice deposed, at the Council of Pisa in 1409 and the Council of Constance (*see* CONSTANCE, COUNCIL OF) in 1417, Benedict XIII still claimed to be the rightful pope until his death.

Benedict XIII (1649–1730), original name PIETRO FRANCESCO ORSINI, pope from 1724 to 1730. A member of a noble Italian family, he became a Dominican (*see* DOMINICANS) in 1667 and was created a cardinal in 1672. He was a pious, learned man, and as pope instituted various reforms that, however, were largely ineffective. In diplomatic affairs he yielded to unscrupulous advisers who took advantage of his trust.

Benedict XIV (1675–1758), original name PROSPERO LAMBERTINI, pope from 1740 to 1758, born in Bologna. He became a cardinal in 1728, and archbishop of Bologna in 1731. As pope, he encouraged commerce and agriculture, instituted various reforms, and, in his bulls and encyclicals, regulated mixed marriages, and settled controversies regarding Indian and Chinese rites. One of the most learned of the popes, Benedict greatly encouraged education and science, founding the chairs of physics, chemistry, and mathematics at the University of Rome, and reviving the academy of Bologna. In literature, he caused the best English and French books to be translated into Italian. His most important works are *On the Diocesan Synod, On the Sacrifice of the Mass,* and *On the Beatification and Canonization of Saints.*

Benedict XV (1854–1922), original name GIACOMO DELLA CHIESA, pope from 1914 to 1922, born in Pegli, Italy. After receiving a doctorate in jurisprudence from the University of Genoa at the age of twenty-one, he went to Rome to study theology and diplomacy. He was ordained as a priest in 1878, created archbishop of Bologna in 1907, and elevated to the cardinalate in 1914. Two months after the outbreak of World War I, he was elected pope. Benedict XV maintained a strict neutrality throughout the struggle, and made frequent efforts to bring about a peace settlement and to aid war victims. During his rule, official relations were restored between the Vatican and the French government, and a British representative was sent to the Vatican for the first time since the 17th century. His circulars were published in eight parts (1915–23), and in 1917 he promulgated the new *Codex Juris Canonici* ("Code of Canon Law").

BENEDICT, Ruth Fulton (1887–1948), American anthropologist, born in New York City, and educated at Vassar College and Columbia University. She joined the faculty of Columbia University in 1923 and served as a professor after 1930. Her most important field work, performed during periods of leave from Columbia, was done on trips that she made to the reservations of various American Indian tribes between 1922 and 1939. From 1943 to 1946 she was granted an extended leave in order to serve with the Bureau of Overseas Intelligence of the Office of War Information. A recognized authority on the ethnology of the American Indians, Ruth Benedict also earned a wide popular reputation through her work as a cultural anthropologist. Her works include *Patterns of Culture* (1934), *Zuñi Mythology* (2 vol., 1935), *Race: Science and Politics* (1940), and *The Chrysanthemum and the Sword: Patterns of Japanese Culture* (1946).

BENEDICTINES, monks and nuns following the rule of Saint Benedict of Nursia (q.v.). The first twelve Benedictine monasteries were founded early in the 6th century at Subiaco, near Rome, by Benedict, who later founded the famous abbey at Monte Cassino (q.v.) and there established the rule that organized and revitalized Western monasticism and gave it its particularly characteristics. Judged by the standards of the time, the Benedictine rule imposed no great amount of austerity or asceticism. It required the provision of adequate food, clothing, and shelter for the monks. Depending upon the season of the year and the festival celebrated, the monks each day devoted a period of four to eight hours to the celebration of the Divine Office (*see* BREVIARY) and one period of seven or eight hours to sleep; the remainder of the day was divided about equally between work (usually agricultural) and religious reading and study. The abbot (q.v.) was given full patriarchal authority over the community, but was himself subject to the rule and was required to consult the members of the community on important questions. During the lifetime of Benedict, his disciples spread the order through the countries of central and western Europe, and it soon became the only important order in those lands, remaining so until the founding of the Austin Friars (*see* AUGUSTINIANS) in the 11th century and of the mendicant orders (*see* MENDICANT FRIARS) in the 13th century.

Gregory the Great (*see under* GREGORY) was the first of fifty Benedictines who have occupied the papal throne; others were Leo IV (r. 847–55), Gregory VII (*see under* GREGORY), Pius VII (*see under* PIUS), and Gregory XVI (r. 1831–46). Saint Augustine (q.v.), the disciple of Gregory the Great who took the Benedictine rule to England late in the 6th century, became the first of a long list of Benedictine archbishops of Canterbury. As early as 1354 the order had provided 24 popes, 200 cardinals, 7000 archbishops, 15,000 bishops, 1560 canonized saints, and 5000 holy persons worthy of canonization (q.v.), a number since increased to 40,000, and it had included 20 emperors, 10 empresses, 47 kings, 50 queens, and many other royal and noble persons. The order had 37,000 monks in the 14th century; in the 15th century it had 15,107. The Reformation (q.v.) left not more than 5000, but this number has since increased to about 11,000 men and 25,000 women. During the 20th century the order has spread in the United States, and several large abbeys and a number of smaller monasteries, totaling about 30, are currently maintained there, most of which maintain schools or colleges attached to the monastery.

The Benedictine habit consists of a tunic and scapular, over which is worn a long full gown, or cowl, with a hood to cover the head. The color of the habit is not specified in the rule, and it is conjectured that the early Benedictines wore white, the natural color of undyed wool. For many centuries, however, black has been the prevailing color, and thus Benedictines have been called "black monks". *See also* MONASTICISM; NUN; ORDERS, RELIGIOUS. W.N.C.

BENEDICTION, formal invocation of the divine blessing upon men or things. Benedictions were specified (Num. 6:24–26) by the Hebrew lawgiver Moses (q.v.) and have been used by the Jews in public worship since Biblical times, especially on certain holy days; *see* PRAYER, JEWISH. Benedictions are also important parts of services in Christian churches. In the Roman Catholic Church (q.v.), the most solemn form of benediction is the Benediction of the Blessed Sacrament. This rite, during which a priest or bishop makes the sign of the cross over the congregation with a monstrance or ciborium containing the consecrated Host (q.v.), grew out of a popular 14th-century custom of exposing the Host for public adoration. Less solemn benedictions, usually called blessings, are given by making the sign of the cross with the right hand, while invoking the blessing of the Trinity (q.v.). The symbolism attached to the position of the fingers, the first three fingers extended symbolizing the Trinity, and the other two fingers flexed symbolizing the two natures in Christ, originated in the Orthodox Church (q.v.). The practice of benediction also is followed in the Church of England (q.v.). In most Protestant churches, however, the benediction is pronounced simply with the hands extended.

BENEDICT OF NURSIA, Saint (480?–543?), Italian prelate, born in Nursia (now Norcia), near Spoleto. At the age of fourteen he retired to an uninhabited area near Subiaco, where he lived in a cavern (later called the Holy Grotto) for three years. During this time his fame spread over the country and multitudes came to see him. Benedict established twelve monasteries near Subiaco and later founded the monastery of Monte Cassino and another monastery at Terracina. His rules of monastic discipline were adopted widely, and he became known as the founder of Western monasticism (q.v.). *See* BENEDICTINES.

BENEFIT OF CLERGY (*privilegium clericale*), in former British criminal law, a privilege accorded to the clergy and afterward extended to all who could read, by which one who had been convicted in a secular court of any lesser felony than treason could claim a hearing before the bishop's court, on his own declaration of innocence, in arrest of judgment. If the person who pleaded benefit of clergy was not actually in holy orders, the bishop's court would decide his case anyway but would have him branded on the fleshy part of the thumb so that he could not make the plea in other matters. Among the earliest enactments of the first Congress of the United States, held in 1790, was an act forbidding benefit of clergy, which had been recognized in the former British colonies of Carolina and Virginia. It was completely abolished in Great Britain in 1827.

BENELLI, Sem (1877–1949), Italian playwright and poet, born in Prato, Tuscany. He was one of the best-known Italian playwrights of his time, particularly for his historical plays in verse. Benelli's finest play is generally considered to be *La Cena delle Beffe* (1909; Eng. trans., *The Jester's Supper,* 1924–25), which was made into an opera by the Italian composer Umberto Giordano (1867–1948), and was produced in New York City after World War I both as an opera and as a play under the title *The Jest.* Benelli also wrote the libretto of the opera *L'Amore dei Tre Re* (1909; Eng. trans., *The Love of the Three Kings,* 1923), which was set to music by the Italian composer Italo Montemezzi (1857–1952). Although he wrote poetry and a prose work about World War I, Benelli wrote mostly for the stage. He is the author of thirty dramas and comedies.

BENELUX, collective designation for Belgium, the Netherlands, and Luxembourg, particularly in relation to their membership in the European Economic Community (q.v.). *See also* EUROPEAN COMMUNITIES.

Eduard Beneš

BENELUX ECONOMIC UNION, formerly BENELUX CUSTOMS UNION, trading agreement among Belgium, the Netherlands, and Luxembourg. The Benelux organization came into existence on Nov. 1, 1960, as a successor of the customs union formed on Jan. 1, 1948. The union levies uniform tariff rates on goods from nonmember countries and exempts duties on intra-Benelux trade. The fourth-largest trading bloc in the West, the union serves 20,000,000 people. *See also* EUROPEAN COAL AND STEEL COMMUNITY; EUROPEAN ECONOMIC COMMUNITY.

BENEŠ, Eduard (1884–1948), Czech statesman, born in Kožlany, and educated at the universities of Prague, and Paris. From 1909 to 1915 he was professor of economics at the Prague Academy of Commerce. During this period he met and became a disciple of the Czech statesman and nationalist leader Tomáš Garrigue Masaryk (q.v.), and from 1915 to 1918, as editor of the Paris newspaper *La Nation Tchêque* ("The Czech Nation"), Beneš was associated with Masaryk in the movement for an independent Czechoslovak state. In 1918, on the creation of the modern state of Czechoslovakia (*see* CZECHOSLOVAKIA: *History*), Beneš became foreign minister in the cabinet of Masaryk who was the first president of Czechoslovakia. In 1919–20, Beneš was chief of the Czech delegation to the Paris Peace Conference that followed World War I, and in 1920 was one of the founders of the political and economic alliance between

Czechoslovakia, Romania, and Yugoslavia known as the Little Entente (q.v.). Beneš held the post of prime minister as well as that of foreign minister from 1921 to 1922, and was a member of the Council of the League of Nations from 1923 to 1927; he also was professor of sociology at the University of Prague from 1922 to 1938.

Upon the retirement of Masaryk in 1935, Beneš was elected president of Czechoslovakia. Three years later, however, after the conclusion of the Munich Pact (q.v.), by which sections of Czechoslovakia were ceded to Germany, he resigned his office, and in October, 1938, he settled temporarily in Great Britain. He was appointed professor of sociology at the University of Chicago in the United States in 1939, but after the outbreak of World War II he returned to Great Britain, where he became president of the Czech government-in-exile. Beneš returned to Prague in May, 1945, after the liberation of Czechoslovakia. He was reelected president in 1946 for a seven-year term. A postwar period of increasing Communist control of the Czech government culminated in the spring of 1948 in a Communist seizure of complete power. In June, 1948, when a new Czech constitution legitimizing the Communist dictatorship was promulgated, Beneš resigned. He died about three months later. Beneš' writings include *The Spirit of the Czechoslovak Revolution* (1923), *My War Memoirs* (1928), and *Democracy—Today and Tomorrow* (1939).

BENÉT, name of two American men of letters who were brothers.

William Rose Benét (1886–1950), American poet, critic, and editor, born in Brooklyn, N.Y., and educated at Yale University. Benét was associate editor of the *Literary Review* of the New York *Evening Post* from 1920 until 1924. He was associated with the magazine *The Saturday Review of Literature* as a founder, editor, and columnist, from 1924 until his death. Benét's poetry, generally in extended narrative form, is romantic and spirited. It includes the volumes *Merchants from Cathay* (1913), *Moons of Grandeur* (1920), *With Wings as Eagles* (1940), and *The Dust Which Is God* (1941), an autobiographical poem for which he received the 1942 Pulitzer Prize for poetry. He also wrote a novel, *First Person Singular* (1922); a novel in verse, *Rip Tide* (1932); and a volume of essays, *Wild Goslings* (1927). He edited *The Reader's Encyclopedia* (1948), a reference work on world literature. His second wife was the American poet Elinor Wylie (q.v.).

Stephen Vincent Benét (1898–1943), American poet and novelist, born in Bethlehem, Pa., and educated at Yale University. As a student he published two highly creditable books of poetry, *Five Men and Pompey* (1915) and *Young Adventure* (1918). Among his later works are the volume of poetry *Heavens and Earth* (1920), the novels *Young People's Pride* (1922) and *Spanish Bayonet* (1926), and a popular narrative poem about the American Civil War, *John Brown's Body* (1928). For the latter work, Benét won his first Pulitzer Prize for poetry in 1929. *Thirteen O'Clock* (1937), a collection of short stories, includes "The Devil and Daniel Webster"; this story was adapted by Benét into the libretto for a folk opera (1939) with music by the American composer Douglas Moore (1893–1969) and was made into a motion picture, *All That Money Can Buy* (1941). For *Western Star* (1943), an unfinished narrative poem that was published posthumously, Benét won a second Pulitzer Prize in 1944. The works of Benét are remarkable in their imaginative evocation of the American scene.

BENEVENTO, city of Italy, in Campania Region, and capital of Benevento Province, on a hill between the Calore and Sabbato rivers, about 34 miles N.E. of Naples. The city is an archiepiscopal see. The city is a commercial and trade center of the surrounding agricultural region; manufactures include agricultural implements, foodstuffs, and distilled beverages. The original name, as chief town of the Samnites in the 4th century B.C., was *Maleventum* ("ill

William Rose Benét Mina Turner

Farmers selling produce in the marketplace in Bengal, India. United Nations

wind"). After the Roman victory of King Pyrrhus (q.v.) of Epirus at Maleventum, the name was changed to *Beneventum* ("fair wind"). In the 6th century A.D. the Lombards (q.v.) made it the capital of an independent duchy. From 1053 until the establishment of the modern Italian state in 1860, Benevento belonged to the Papal States, except during the years from 1806 to 1815, when it was the capital of a principality granted to the French statesman Charles Talleyrand-Périgord by Emperor Napoleon I (qq.v.). On the north side of Benevento is the famous memorial arch of the Roman emperor Trajan (q.v.), dedicated in 114 A.D. The reliefs show the emperor's life and his triumphs in the Dacian campaigns (101–06 A.D.). Pop. (1971) 60,025.

BENEVOLENT AND PROTECTIVE ORDER OF ELKS *or* **B.P.O.E.,** American fraternal, patriotic, and philanthropic society, founded in 1868 in New York City. A Grand Exalted Ruler, head of the organization, is elected at an annual convention of representatives from each of the subordinate lodges. Membership is limited to male citizens of the United States, twenty-one years of age or over, who believe in God and are of good character.

The Elks National Foundation Fund, maintained by the society, is devoted to various charitable projects, including scholarships for deserving students and aid to crippled children. The Elks National Veterans Service Commission, another agency of the B.P.O.E., aids hospitalized and disabled veterans. The order maintains a home for aged and indigent members in Bedford, Va. A memorial building in Chicago, Ill., is dedicated to members of the order who served in World Wars I and II; it also houses the organization's headquarters. The *Elks Magazine*, the official journal of the B.P.O.E., is published monthly. In the mid-1970's, membership exceeded 1,500,000.

BEN GABIROL, Solomon. *See* IBN-GABIROL, SOLOMON BEN JUDAH.

BENGAL, region of the subcontinent of India, bounded on the N. by Sikkim and Bhutan, on the E. by the Indian State of Assam and Burma, on the S. by the Bay of Bengal, and on the W. by the Indian State of Bihar. It has a total area of 82,812 sq.mi. The W. part of the region is occupied by West Bengal, a State of the Republic of India, and the larger E. section is occupied almost entirely by Bangladesh (formerly East Pakistan), with the Indian Territory of Tripura on the Assam border. Before 1947 the region of Bengal was almost entirely coextensive with the British Indian province of Bengal. The remainder was occupied by the princely states of Cooch Behar and Tripura, both on the Assam border.

Calcutta (q.v.), West Bengal, former capital of the British province, is the chief city; other important cities include Howrah and Dacca (qq.v.), in West Bengal and Bangladesh, respectively. The population of the region is predominantly rural. Muslims (a majority in Bangladesh), Hindus (a majority in West Bengal), native Christians, Buddhists, Sikhs, Jains, and Parsees are the chief religious groups. The principal language, Bengali, is spoken by more than 90 percent of the people; more than seventy-five other languages, however, are also spoken throughout the area.

Except for the mountainous N., which is part of the Himalaya, and the hill ranges along the E. and W., Bengal is a great alluvial plain, intersected by many rivers. In their course through Bengal the Ganges and Brahmaputra rivers bear the names Padma and Jamuna, respectively. These great rivers and their tributaries furnish easy and cheap transportation. More important, from their high Himalayan sources they bring down and distribute over the surface of their combined delta the rich silt that makes Bengal one of the most fertile regions of India.

The climate of Bengal is tropical and unhealthful, except during the cool season from November to February. Moist winds sweeping northward from the Bay of Bengal make the region very humid. The mean yearly temperature ranges from 80° F. to 75° F. Rainfall is heavy, averaging from 50 in. to 75 in. in the W., S.W., and central portions, and from 75 in. to 120 in. elsewhere, except in the mountainous N. region, where it is much heavier. During the rainy season from June to October, river floods and cyclones from the Bay of Bengal are common. In 1876 a cyclone accompanied by a tidal wave caused the death of 100,000 persons. The cyclone of 1937, accompanied by a huge tidal wave and the inundation of the Hooghly R., a channel of the Ganges, killed 300,000; a 1970 cyclone killed 500,000 and left millions homeless.

Most of the people of Bengal are engaged in agriculture. The chief crop is rice, the principal food of the people. Other important crops include jute, tea, the opium poppy, sugarcane, and cotton. Formerly large areas were devoted to the growing of indigo, but because of the cheapness of the synthetic dyes indigo cultivation is no longer important. Industrial establishments include jute mills and cotton mills, but there has been little industrial development. Many of the former craft industries of the region, such as the making of dyes, fine silks, and simple consumer goods, have almost disappeared. The decline of craft industries is due largely to modern rail transportation, bringing Western machine-made goods to compete with the more expensive local, handmade products.

Almost all of the Bengal region (except Cooch Behar and Tripura) became a presidency (division) of British India in 1699, sixty-six years after the arrival of the British. In 1937, after a series of changes in territorial and political structure, it became an autonomous province with a bicameral legislature. In 1945, however, administration was taken over by the British governor.

In 1947, with the achievement of Indian independence and the concurrent division of the country into Hindu India and Muslim Pakistan, the W. portion of former Bengal Province became part of India as West Bengal, and the E. portion became East Pakistan (now Bangladesh). Cooch Behar became part of West Bengal in 1947; Tripura is now a Territory of the Republic of India.

See BANGLADESH; INDIA, REPUBLIC OF.

BENGAL, BAY OF, arm of the Indian Ocean, between India on the W. and Burma and the Malay Peninsula on the E. Many large rivers flow into the bay: the Ganges and the Brahmaputra on the N.; the Irrawaddy on the E.; and the Mahanadi, the Godavari, the Kistna, and the Kaveri on the W. On the W. coast of the bay the harbors are poor, but on the E. coast are many good ports, such as Sittwe, Moulmein, and Tavoy, all in Burma. The islands in the bay, which is about 1300 mi. long and about 1000 mi. wide, include the Andaman and Nicobar groups.

BENGALI LANGUAGE AND LITERATURE, most important of the eastern group (including also Oriya, Assamese, and Bihari) of Indo-Aryan languages. A descendant of Old Indo-Aryan through Māgadhī Prakrit, the Bengali language is spoken by more than 70,000,000 people in West Bengal, in India, and in Bangladesh where it is the official language. Like other modern Indian languages, Bengali is an analytic language (possessed of a formal grammar, as are, for example, Latin and English) written in a form of the Devanagari alphabet (*see* ALPHABET). Literary Bengali differs from the colloquial dialect in its wide use of Sanskrit words; *see* SANSKRIT LANGUAGE.

Impetus was given to Bengali literature by the composition in the late 14th century of the *Mahabharata* or "Great Tale of the Descendants of the Prince Bharata" and the *Ramayana* (qq.v.) or "Life of Rama", epics inspired by their Sanskrit counterparts. Until the 19th century all Bengali literature was modeled after the Sanskrit classics; *see* SANSKRIT LITERATURE. In the 19th century, under European influence, Bengali writers began to use nonclassic and secular themes, in addition to the colloquial language, in literary works. As a result of this modernization Bengali has the most extensive literature of any modern Indian language (*see* INDIAN LANGUAGES), despite the fact that some writers still feel that Bengali literature should continue to follow the model of the Sanskrit classics. Western interest in Bengali literature was greatly stimulated in 1913 when the Indian writer and philosopher Sir Rabindranath Tagore (q.v.) was awarded the Nobel Prize for literature in 1913 for his volume of poetry *Gitanjali* (1912; Eng. trans., 1913).

BENGHAZI, *or* BENGASI *or* BENGAZI, second largest city of Libya, in the district of Benghazi, on the E. coast of the Gulf of Sidra, about 400 miles E. of Tripoli. It is located on a railroad and has a considerable caravan trade with the interior. Benghazi is the center for trade in the cereals, dates, olives, wool, and livestock produced in the surrounding area. In addition to farming, sponge and tuna fishing are important occupations. Sponges, hides, and wool are the chief exports. The National University of Libya, founded in 1955, is located in the city. Benghazi was the site of the ancient Greek colony, Hesperides. It was ruled by the Turks from the 16th century until 1911, when it was captured by the Italians during the Turko-Italian War; thereafter it was part of Italian Libya. During World War II, it was occupied by the British and served as the seat of British territorial administration until Libya gained independence in 1951. Pop. (1970 est.) 140,000.

BENGUELA, city and seaport in the Portuguese Overseas Territory of Angola, capital of Benguela District, on the Atlantic Ocean, about 250 miles S. of Luarda. Because Benguela lacks adequate port facilities, most export trade is handled at Lobito, 18 miles to the N. Refined sugar, dried fish, soap, tools, pottery, and lumber are the important products of the city. Benguela was founded by the Portuguese, who built a fort there in 1587. In the 19th century the city was a leading slave depot. Pop. (1970) 23,256.

BEN-GURION, David, original surname GRUEN (1886–1973), Israeli statesman and the first prime minister of Israel, who dedicated his life to the establishment of a Jewish homeland in Palestine (*see* ZIONISM) and who was regarded as the father of his country.

He was born in Płońsk, Russia (now part of Poland), on Oct. 16, 1886, the son of a lawyer who was an active Zionist. By the age of fourteen he had himself established a Zionist youth society. Gruen left Poland in 1906 to work on a farm in a Jewish settlement in Palestine, which was then under Turkish control. In 1910

David Ben-Gurion UPI

he gave up farming to edit the Zionist workers' Hebrew-language newspaper *Achdut* ("Unity"). By this time, he had adopted the surname Ben-Gurion, Hebrew for "son of the young lion". Expelled by the Turks early in World War I, he left Palestine; in 1915 he arrived in New York City.

In 1917 Great Britain issued the Balfour Declaration (q.v.), which revived Zionist hopes by its support of a "national home" for Jews in Palestine. Ben-Gurion helped to organize a Jewish Legion for the British forces, in which he himself enlisted in Canada in April, 1918. By the time he reached Palestine, however, the war was over and the British were in control. In 1922 the British mandate to govern Palestine became official. For nearly two decades the British generally supported the Jewish cause, in which Ben-Gurion remained active. In 1921 he became the general secretary of the Histadrut, a confederation of Jewish workers which was in effect a Jewish state within a state. In 1930 he formed the Mapai, the Zionist labor party, and by 1935 he was chairman of the executive committee of the Jewish Agency for Palestine, official overseer of the Jews in the Holy Land.

In 1939 Great Britain made a major change in policy; Jewish settlement was to be severely limited. A decade of Zionist warfare began. Throughout World War II Ben-Gurion continued his own battle. Finally, his dogged determination won out: The republic of Israel was proclaimed on May 14, 1948, with Ben-Gurion as prime minister. He welded the disparate underground forces into an army that defeated the invading Arabs, and for fifteen years (except for the period 1953–55) he continued to lead his country, promoting immigration, education, and the development of desert lands. In 1963 Ben-Gurion resigned, as he said, to study and write; he had also lost favor with his party. He did remain in the Knesset, the Israeli parliament, until his retirement from politics in 1970. For the last ten years of his life Ben-Gurion lived at Sede Boqer, a kibbutz in the Negev desert area; he died there on Dec. 1, 1973.

Ben-Gurion wrote extensively; among his works are *Israel: A Personal History* (1970) and *The Jews in Their Land* (1974).

BENI-ISRAEL, *or* BENE-ISRAEL, community of Jews living in India, principally in and near the city of Bombay. The Beni-Israel people claim to be descended from a group of Jews that was shipwrecked while trying to escape persecution more than 1600 years ago. In appearance the people differ little from the Hindus of the region, and some historians believe the Beni-Israel are more probably descendants of Indian converts to Judaism. When the community was discovered by Westerners, in the 18th century, the Beni-Israel observed only a few Jewish customs. Western Jews subsequently became much interested in them and built several synagogues in the Bombay area. As a result of the extensive educational work done among them, the Beni-Israel now adhere to most of the practices of Judaism. Many of them have emigrated to Israel since the republic was established in 1948.

BENIN CITY, city in the Federation of Nigeria, and capital of the Mid-Western State, on the Benin R., about 150 miles E. of Lagos. The city is connected by road to Lagos and Onitsha. Benin City has a rubber-processing plant and exports rubber and timber. Before the 15th century, when the Portuguese first penetrated the region, until the late 19th century, Benin was the center of a powerful kingdom with influence over the entire territory from the upper Niger R. to the Congo R. Benin craftsmen were noted for their skill in wood and ivory carving and bronze casting. The city was a center for trade in ivory and pepper. Pop. (1971 est.) 121,699.

BENIN, PEOPLE'S REPUBLIC OF. *See* DAHOMEY.

BENJAMIN, in the Old Testament (Gen. 42–45), youngest and most beloved son of the patriarch Jacob (q.v.), and eponym of the Israelite tribe of Benjamin. The warriors of the tribe were noted for their skill in archery and for their cleverness in using the left hand. The tribal territory lay on the west side of the Jordan R., between the regions inhabited by the tribes of Ephraim and Judah (qq.v.). Both Saul (q.v.), the first king of Israel (I Sam. 9:15–17), and Saint Paul (q.v.), the Apostle of Christ (Rom. 11:1), belonged to the tribe of Benjamin.

BENJAMIN, Judah Philip (1811–84), American lawyer and statesman, born in Christiansted, Saint Croix Island, brought to Charleston, S.C., as a child, and educated at Yale College (now Yale University). He practiced law in New Orleans, La., and early became prominent in politics, serving first with the Whigs (*see* WHIG PARTY), and afterward with the Democrats (*see* DEMOCRATIC PARTY). He was a United States Senator from Louisiana from 1852 until that State seceded from the Union in 1861. He then became attorney general in the cabinet of Confederate President Jefferson Davis (q.v.). During the American Civil War Benjamin also served as secretary of war for the Confederacy (*see* CONFEDERATE STATES OF AMERICA), and later was secretary of state. When Davis was captured in 1865, Benjamin escaped with some difficulty to Great Britain. There he began to practice law the following year, was appointed a queen's counsel in 1872, and until his retirement in 1881 was considered one of the most learned members of the British bar. His *Treatise on the Law of Sale of Personal Property* (1883) became a legal classic in Great Britain.

BENNETT, name of two distinguished American newspaper editors and publishers.

James Gordon Bennett (1795–1872), born in Keith, Scotland, and educated for the Roman Catholic priesthood. He emigrated to Halifax, Nova Scotia, Canada, in 1819. From there he moved to Boston, Mass., where he began his career in journalism. After 1822 Bennett worked on newspapers in Charleston, S.C., Washington, D.C., Philadelphia, Pa., and New York City. On May 6, 1835, from a cellar at 20 Wall Street and with a capital of $500, he published the first issue of the New York *Herald,* a four-page daily newspaper that was sold for one cent. His publishing venture was enormously successful and Bennett introduced many important journalistic innovations. The New York *Herald* was the first American newspaper to use telegraphy extensively in reporting, to use foreign correspondents, to illustrate news articles, to publish editorials critical of all political parties, and to print financial news from Wall Street. Bennett spent $525,000 to report the American Civil War, during which he employed 63 correspondents.

James Gordon Bennett (1841–1918), son of James Gordon Bennett, born in New York City, and educated chiefly in Europe. He became managing editor of the New York *Herald* in 1866 and chief executive officer of the newspaper upon the retirement of his father in 1867. In the same year Bennett founded another newspaper, the *Evening Journal,* which was oriented toward sensationalism (*see* NEWSPAPERS: *United States Newspapers*). In 1869 Bennett sent the American explorer Sir Henry Morton Stanley (q.v.) to Africa to search for the missing British missionary and explorer David Livingston (q.v.). To combat the existing Atlantic Ocean cable monopoly, he joined the American financier John D. Mackay (1831–1902) in founding the Commercial Cable Company in 1884. Bennett was a dedicated sportsman, who was particularly interested in yachting, and he donated money and trophies to various sporting organizations and events.

BENNETT, (Enoch) Arnold (1867–1931), British novelist, playwright, and essayist, born in Hanley (one of the "Five Towns" made famous by his writings), Staffordshire, England, and educated at the University of London. For a time he was editor of a magazine for women, but after 1900 he devoted himself entirely to writing. Bennett is best known for his novels. *Anna of the Five Towns* (1902), *The Old Wives' Tale* (1908), *Clayhanger* (1910), *Hilda Lessways* (1911), and *The Matador of the Five Towns* (1912) are psychological studies of commonplace people living in dingy manufacturing towns. Of his plays, two achieved considerable popularity: *Milestones,* written with the British dramatist Edward Knoblock (1874–1945) and produced in 1912, and *The Great Adventure,* a dramatization of his novel *Buried Alive* (1908), produced in 1913. Among his later works are the novels *Elsie and the Child* (1925) and *Lord Raingo* (1926). His autobiography is titled *The Truth about an Author* (1911).

BENNETT, Floyd (1890–1928), American aviator, born near Warrensburg, N.Y., educated in public schools and later trained as a garage mechanic. He enlisted in the aviation corps, United States Navy, in 1917, and became an instructor in aviation mechanics at the U.S. naval base at Hampton Roads, Va. In 1922 he was transferred to Norfolk, Va., where he met the American explorer Richard Evelyn Byrd (*see under* BYRD). Bennett piloted the plane in which Byrd flew across the North Pole in 1926. Byrd chose him as second in command of a projected flight to the South Pole, but Bennett did not live to take part in that expedition. Earlier while flying from Detroit, Mich., to Québec, to aid the crew of a transatlantic airplane stranded on Greenly Island, he contracted pneumonia and died soon after his return.

BENNETT, Richard Bedford, 1st Viscount Bennett (1870–1947), Canadian statesman, born in Hopewell Cape, New Brunswick, and educated at Dalhousie University. In 1911 he was elected to the Canadian House of Commons from Calgary. He later held a number of political offices, becoming leader of the Conservative Party in 1927 and prime minister in 1930; also in 1930 he became a member of the Imperial Privy Council of the British Commonwealth of Nations. When his party was defeated in the general election of 1935, Bennett resigned as prime minister, but he remained the leader of the Conservative Party until 1938. In 1939 he retired from politics. He later lived in Great Britain where he was created 1st Viscount Bennett of Calgary and of Hopewell in Canada, and of Mickleham in Great Britain.

BEN NEVIS, highest mountain peak in Great Britain, in Inverness County, Scotland, about 7 miles S.E. of Fort William. The peak lies in the Grampian Mts. Its height is 4406 ft., and it has a precipice of about 1500 ft. on the N.E. side.

BENNINGTON, BATTLE OF, battle of the American Revolution (q.v.), fought near the village of Bennington, Vt., on Aug. 16, 1777. The British general John Burgoyne (q.v.), on his march south from Canada to join the British forces in New York City, sent 800 Hessian dragoons and Indians, under the German colonel Friedrich Baum (d. Aug. 18, 1777), to capture the American supply base at Bennington. Detachments of the New Hampshire militia, led by the American Revolutionary general John Stark (1728–1822), decisively defeated the British forces, including reinforcements dispatched by General Burgoyne after the battle had begun. British casualties were 207 killed and wounded, and 600 men taken prisoner; American casualties were 14 killed and 12 wounded.

BENNINGTON COLLEGE, coeducational college, located in Bennington, Vt., founded as a college for women in 1932 by a group interested in progressive education. The college offers a four-year academic course leading to the bachelor of arts degree. Student programs are individually planned, no two following the same course. Fields of study are the natural sciences and mathematics; the social sciences; literature and languages; the performing arts of drama, music, and the dance; the visual arts of painting, sculpture, and architecture; and the graphic arts. The college year is divided into two fifteen-week terms at college and a nine-week winter term of nonresident work for various institutes and enterprises. Men were admitted in the fall of 1969. In 1972 enrollment at Bennington College totaled 595 students and the faculty numbered 65. In the same year the college library contained over 67,000 bound volumes, and the endowment of the college was about $2,500,000.

BENNY, Jack, original name BENJAMIN KUBELSKY (1894–1974), American comedian, born in Chicago, Ill. Benny began a successful career in vaudeville at the age of seventeen in Waukegan, Ill., where he grew up.

He began his career as a violinist, but he later became a monologuist, having discovered that he could convulse an audience with his deadpan stare and elegant style. His first motion picture was *Hollywood Review of 1929*; other films in which he appeared are *Love Thy Neighbor* (1940), *The Horn Blows at Midnight* (1945), and *A Guide for the Married Man* (1968). But it was as a radio performer that Benny achieved his greatest fame. His enormously popular program, "The Jack Benny Show", was introduced in 1932; it was heard every week for twenty-three years thereafter. He first successfully transferred his well-loved characterization of the acerbic penny pincher to television in 1950. For the next twenty-four years he appeared frequently as a guest star on various television programs, and his own "The Jack Benny Show" was seen biweekly from 1955 to 1960, weekly from 1960 to 1964, and on daytime reruns in 1964 and 1965. Benny also appeared in theaters and nightclubs in the late 1950's and 1960's, and after 1956 he appeared frequently, and with humorous effect, as a violin soloist with major American symphony orchestras in fund-raising concerts.

BENOÎT DE SAINTE-MAURE, *or* BENOÎT DE SAINTE-MORE (fl. 12th cent.), French trouvère or troubador (*see* TROUVÈRES), born in Sainte-Maure, Touraine (now in the department of Indre-et-Loire). Attached to the court of Henry II (q.v.), King of England, in 1150 he composed the *Roman de Troie* ("Story of Troy"), a poem of about 30,000 lines. The poem relates the story of the Trojan War (q.v.) as if it had occurred in the 12th century. The characters behave in conformity with contemporary feudal customs and standards. *Roman* tells for the first time in literature the story of Troilus (q.v.) and Briseida (Cressida) from which the Italian writer Giovanni Boccaccio and the English poet Geoffrey Chaucer drew material for poems and on which the English dramatist William Shakespeare (qq.v.) based his play *Troilus and Cressida.* Benoît is also the reputed author of *Chronique des Ducs de Normandie* ("Chronicle of the Dukes of Normandy"), a poem of 45,000 octosyllabic verses eulogizing the Plantagenet (q.v.) dynasty.

BENONI, city of the Republic of South Africa, in Transvaal Province, in the Witwatersrand gold-mining region, 16 miles E. of Johannesburg. In addition to the gold-processing industry, Benoni has brass and iron foundries and jute mills. It manufactures electrical equipment. The municipality was organized in 1907. Pop. (1971 est.) 149,563.

BENSON, name of two members of a British family who were father and son.

Edward White Benson (1829–96), British prelate, born near Birmingham, England, and educated at Trinity College, University of Cambridge. In 1875 he was named chaplain-in-ordinary to Victoria (q.v.), Queen of Great Britain, and in 1877 he was appointed bishop of Truro, where he began the building of the cathedral in 1880. In 1882 he became archbishop of Canterbury. Among his works are *Cyprian* (1897) and *The Apocalypse* (1900).

Arthur Christopher Benson (1862–1925), British writer and educator, educated at King's College, University of Cambridge. He became master of Magdalen College, University of Cambridge, in 1915. He was joint editor with Reginald Baliol Brett, 2nd Viscount of Esher (1852–1930) of the *Correspondence of Queen Victoria* (1907). Benson wrote many essays and biographies and the autobiography *Memories and Friends* (1924).

BENSON, Ezra Taft (1899–   ), American agricultural specialist and government official, born in Whitney, Idaho, and educated at Utah State Agricultural College, Brigham Young University, Iowa State College, and the University of California. He served as chairman of the department of agricultural economics and marketing for the University of Idaho extension service (1931–38). He was executive secretary of the National Council of Farmer Cooperatives (1939–44), was on the board of trustees of the American Institute of Cooperation (1942–52), and was United States secretary of agriculture (1953–61).

BENT GRASS, common name for grasses of the genus *Agrostis.* The genus is large and widely distributed. It includes species of valuable pasture grasses and of others excellent for lawns. White bent or red top, *A. alba,* is a good pasture grass, growing well in moist meadowlands; a variety, *vulgaris,* abounding on dry hills, is a pest in cultivated farmland. Brown or dog bent (*A. canina*), Rhode Island bent (*A. tenuis*), and creeping bent, (*A. palustris*), are extensively cultivated for lawns and golf greens because of their low, dense, spreading growth.

BENTHAM, Jeremy (1748–1832), British philosopher, born in London, England, and educated at Queen's College, University of Oxford. He was called to the bar in 1772. Bentham was always interested in reforming existing laws. His first book was *Fragment on Government* (1776), in which he criticized the *Commentaries* of the British jurist Sir William Blackstone (q.v.) for conservatism and dislike of reform. In his *Rationale of Punishment and Rewards* (1825) Bentham urged improvements in the then current methods of punishing criminals. His *Introduction to the Principles of Morals and Legislation* (1789) contained his fundamental ethical doctrine, called utilitarianism. This doctrine contends that an action is moral to the degree that it is useful, the usefulness of an action being its capacity to give pleasure or prevent pain. This principle leads to the idea that the purpose of all conduct and legislation should be "the greatest happiness of the greatest number". Bentham derived this phrase from a work by the British chemist Joseph Priestley and one by the British philosopher Francis Hutcheson (qq.v.); it became the basic tenet of his philosophy. In 1823 Bentham helped found the *Westminster Review* for the purpose of disseminating his philosophic views. At the time of his death he was working on a codification of laws, the first volume of which, *Constitutional Code,* had been published in 1827; other volumes appeared in 1841. Bentham's ideas had great influence on the reforms of the latter part of the 19th century in the administrative machinery of the British government, on criminal law, and on procedure in both criminal and civil law. The British philosopher and economist John Stuart Mill (q.v.) was a close friend of Bentham's, his disciple, and the editor of some of Bentham's works. *See* UTILITARIANISM; ETHICS.

BENTLEY, Richard (1662–1742), British classical scholar, born in Oulton, near Leeds, England, and educated at Saint John's College, University of Cambridge. In 1691 his *Letter to Mill,* a critical discussion of the ancient Greek dramatists, won him recognition as a scholar of profound learning. He is best known for his role in the so-called ancients and moderns controversy, in which many celebrated literary men of the time argued the relative merits of ancient and modern authors. In 1699 he exposed as spurious the *Epistles of Phalaris,* a work praised by the defenders of ancient literature. Although correct in his judgment, he was ridiculed by the British satirist Jonathan Swift (q.v.) in *The Battle of the Books* (1704). Bentley was master of Trinity College, University of Cambridge, from 1699 until his death. His critical editions of the works of classical writers, especially those of the Roman poet Horace and the Roman playwright Terence (qq.v.), established his reputation as one of the greatest British classical scholars.

BENTON, city in Arkansas, and county seat of Saline Co., about 21 miles S.W. of Little Rock. Benton is a railroad junction situated in a bauxite-mining area. The city manufactures furniture and wood products. Pop. (1970) 16,499.

BENTON, name of two prominent Americans.

Thomas Hart Benton (1782–1858), statesman, born in Hillsborough, N.C. He settled in Tennessee, where he studied law, and was elected to the legislature. In the War of 1812 (q.v.) he raised a regiment of volunteers and also served on the staff of the American general Andrew Jackson (q.v.), later President of the United States. Afterward Benton established a newspaper in Saint Louis, Mo. From 1820 to 1850 he was United States Senator from Missouri. In the Senate he was a determined opponent of nullification (q.v.). After Jackson became President, Benton supported his campaign against the United States Bank, and earned the nickname "Old Bullion" by his opposition to the issuing of paper currency. He wrote *A Thirty Years' View or a History of the Working of the American Government from 1820 to 1850* (2 vol., 1854–56) and *An Abridgment of the Debates of Congress from 1789 to 1856* (15 vol., 1857).

Thomas Hart Benton (1889–1975), grass-roots American painter known for his vigorous, color-splashed murals of the 1930's, mostly of rollicking scenes from the rural past of the American South and Midwest. President Harry Truman once called him "the best damned painter in America."

Benton was born in Neosho, Mo., April 15, 1889, and named after his granduncle, the famed pre-Civil War senator. He quit school at seventeen to work as a cartoonist on the nearby Joplin (Mo.) *American.* He left this job for a year of study at Chicago's Art Institute, and then spent three years in Paris. His enthusiasm for that city and its art world of cubism and impressionism having begun to pall, he returned to the United States in 1912.

Living in New York City, Benton continued to grope for artistic expression. By 1918 his search had ended. He abandoned symbolic art for a rugged naturalism that affirmed the old simple backwoods values, and by the 1930's he was riding a tide of popular acclaim along with his fellow Regionalists Grant Wood and John Steuart Curry. In 1931 Benton painted his masterpiece, "Modern America," at the New

"Cotton Pickers, Georgia" (1928–29) by Thomas Hart Benton. Metropolitan Museum of Art George A. Hearn Fund, 1933

School of Social Research, New York City. It breathed optimism with its sweeping panoramas of earthy, heroic figures and swirling color. Before he forsook New York City in 1935, he executed other major murals. Two were for museums of American art: in New Britain, Conn., and in New York City the Whitney (both in 1932).

Benton returned to Missouri, taught at the Kansas City Art Institute, and continued to paint—both smaller works and more murals. His mural in the State capitol in Jefferson City (1935) stirred protests because of its open portrayals of some of the seamier facets of Missouri's past. Benton insisted, however, that "warts" were history, too. Other, more recent, Missouri murals are in the Truman Memorial Library, Independence (1961), and in Joplin (1973). His last work, "The Origins of Country Music", was completed only three hours before his death on Jan. 19, 1975, in Kansas City, Mo.

BENTON HARBOR, city of Michigan, in Berrien Co., about 32 miles N.W. of South Bend, Ind. A resort city with mineral springs and beaches, Benton Harbor is surrounded by the leading fruit producing region of the State. The city manufactures hardware, machinery, furniture, and other products. It is the site of Lake Michigan College, founded in 1946. A religious colony, the House of David, is in the city and another religious colony, the Israelite City of David, is nearby. Pop. (1970) 16,481.

BENT'S OLD FORT NATIONAL HISTORIC SITE, remains of a famous trading post in southeastern Colorado on the Arkansas R. Built in 1833 by the American pioneer brothers Charles Bent (1799–1847) and William Bent (1809–69) in partnership with the American fur trader Ceran Saint Vrain (1802–70), it was for sixteen years the center of a trading empire that stretched from Texas and New Mexico to Wyoming, and from the Rockies to Kansas. With the influx of whites the friendly relations established by the Bents with neighboring Indian tribes deteriorated; in 1847 full-scale war between Indians and whites broke out, ending most of the profitable trade. In 1849, after a devastating cholera epidemic, William Bent, the sole remaining partner, set fire to the storerooms and powder magazine and abandoned the fort. The site, covering 178 acres, was established as a national historic site in 1963. It is administered by the National Park Service (q.v.).

BENUE *or* **BINUE,** river of W. central Africa and the largest tributary of the Niger. It rises in N. Cameroon, flows W. across E. central Nigeria, and joins the Niger 300 mi. from the coast. Its width varies from about 1600 to 3200 ft., and its navigable length is more than 600 mi. during the wet season. The river is about 850 mi. long.

BEN-YAHUDA, Elieser *or* **BEN-YEHUDA, Elieser** (1858–1922), Hebrew scholar, known as *Maskil* (Heb., "the enlightened one"), born Elieser Perlman in Lithuania. While studying medicine in Paris, France, in 1879, he became interested in Jewish problems. In 1881 he emigrated to Palestine, and four years later established a magazine dedicated to the revival of Hebrew as a living language. He also began to coin new Hebrew words needed in modern life, in most cases based on vernacular Arabic. Together with his son he founded the first Palestinian daily newspaper in 1912.

BENZ, Karl (1844–1929), German mechanical engineer, born in Karlsruhe. He was a pioneer in the automobile industry. In 1878 he developed a two-cycle internal-combustion engine, and later, a light four-cycle engine (*see* ENGINE). He invented the differential drive and other automotive accessories. In 1885 he built a three-wheeled vehicle with an internal-combustion engine. This vehicle was patented and driven through the streets of Munich in 1886. Benz shared with the German engineer Gottlieb Daimler (q.v.) the credit for building the first complete automobile. *See* AUTOMOBILE.

BENZEDRINE, trade name for the synthetic drug amphetamine (*a*lpha *m*ethyl *ph*en*et*hyl *amine*). In the common sulfate form, Benzedrine is a white, odorless powder, freely soluble in water, usually sold in tablet or capsule form, but also available as a liquid. Benzedrine is similar to adrenaline and ephedrine (qq.v.) in chemical structure and physiological action. Unlike adrenaline, which acts through the peripheral nervous system, Benzedrine acts primarily on the brain. Benzedrine Sulfate is administered internally as a stimulant in the treatment of mental depression and to induce wakefulness. Used as an inhalant, it gives symptomatic relief in head colds and allergic nasal congestion by shrinking the mucous membranes. In either form Benzedrine is habit forming but does not produce physical dependence. It is often used illegally for its euphoric effects. Overdoses are toxic, and the drug should be used only upon the advice of a physician. Benzedrine is not legally available without prescription. *See* DRUGS, ADDICTION TO.

BENZENE (less properly called BENZOL and often confused with benzine), colorless liquid, formula C_6H_6, of sp.gr. 0.88 at 20° C. (68° F.); m.p. 5.5° C. (42° F.); and b.p. 80° C. (176° F.). It is insoluble in water but miscible in all proportions with organic solvents. It also dissolves in mixtures of alcohol and water. Benzene itself is an excellent solvent for certain elements, such as sulfur, phosphorus, and iodine; for gums, fats, waxes, and resins; and for most simple organic chemicals. It is one of the most commonly used solvents in the organic chemical laboratory. It has a characteristic mild odor and burning taste. If inhaled in large quantities, benzene is poisonous. The vapors are explosive, and the liquid violently inflammable. Many compounds, such as nitrobenzene, are obtained from benzene. Benzene is also used in the manufacture of drugs and in the production of important derivatives, such as aniline and phenol (qq.v.).

Pure benzene burns with a smoky flame because of its high carbon content. When mixed with a large proportion of gasoline it makes a satisfactory fuel. Benzene also makes a valuable addition to fuels for internal-combustion engines because it is almost insusceptible to detonation (q.v.), its octane number being far above 100. In Europe, where gasoline is expensive, benzene mixed with some toluene and other re-

Three-wheeled automobile designed by Karl Benz in 1885. Bettmann Archive

lated compounds has long been added to motor fuels. In the United States this practice became common during the shortage of high-grade aviation fuels in World War II.

Benzene was first discovered in 1825 by the English scientist Michael Faraday (q.v.), and in 1842 it was made available in large quantities after it was found that coal tar contains benzene. A ton of coal, if coked in a by-product oven, yields about 2 gal. of benzene. Large quantities of impure benzene are now obtained from petroleum, either by direct extraction from certain types of crude oils or by chemical treatment of gasoline (hydroforming and cyclization). It can also be prepared synthetically, but this process is of no commercial importance. In 1978 the U.S. Department of Labor restricted worker exposure to benzene because of evidence that it could cause cancer.

The structure of the benzene molecule is of the utmost importance to the theory of organic chemistry. Benzene and its derivatives are included in the important chemical group known as aromatic compounds (q.v.). *See also* CHEMISTRY: *Major Divisions of Chemistry: Organic Chemistry.*

BENZINE. *See* LIGROIN.

BENZOATE OF SODA. *See* SODIUM BENZOATE.

BEN-ZVI, Izhak (1884–1963), Israeli statesman, born in Poltava, Ukraine (now in the Ukrainian S.S.R.), and educated at the University of Kiev and at Imperial Ottoman University, Constantinople (now İstanbul, Turkey). He became an active Zionist (*see* ZIONISM), in his youth. A founder of the Russian Zionist labor movement, he fled Russia in 1905 to escape arrest by the czarist police. He settled in Palestine in 1907, and the next year he helped to organize the first Jewish defense force in Palestine and the first Hebrew secondary school in Jerusalem. During World War I he was exiled by the Turks for pro-Allied and Zionist activities. He came to the United States in 1916 and helped organize the pioneer movement for the settlement of Palestine. Subsequently he helped recruit the American battalion of the Jewish Legion. He served with the legion in Palestine in 1918. Following the establishment of Palestine as a British mandate, Ben-Zvi became the official spokesman of the *Vaad Leumi,* the newly formed governing body of the Palestinian Jewish community. Meanwhile he was prominent in the Palestine labor movement and worked to further the cause of an independent Jewish state. In May, 1948, upon the termination of the British mandate, he became a member of the provisional government of the newly created State of Israel; later he was elected to the Knesset, or parliament. He succeeded the first president of Israel, Chaim Weizmann (q.v.), in December, 1952. Among Ben-Zvi's writings are *Arabs and Moslems* (1926), *Book of the Samaritans* (1935), and *Communities in Exile* (1953). *See* ISRAEL: *History.*

BEOGRAD. *See* BELGRADE.

BEOWULF, Old English epic poem. It is the most important work of Anglo-Saxon literature (*see* ENGLISH LITERATURE), and the oldest extant epic of the Teutonic peoples (*see* TEUTONS). The only surviving manuscript of the poem is now in the British Museum, London. It is written in the West-Saxon dialect and is believed to date from the late 10th century. The composition of the poem in its present form is placed as early as the 8th century. The poem consists of 3182 lines, which are alliterative and unrhymed (*see* RHYME). Each line has four accents and is divided by a caesura (*see* VERSIFICATION). The events described in *Beowulf,* in vigorous, rough, somber, and picturesque language, are as follows. The monster Grendel, a half man, half fiend, comes every night from the fens into the splendid hall of Hrothgar, King of the Danes, and carries off to his subterranean dwelling a number of the king's thanes, or feudal lords, and devours them. Beowulf, a prince among the Geats of south Sweden, hearing of this, crosses the sea with fourteen companions to rid Hrothgar of the sea fiend. In the hall at night, Beowulf engages in a mighty struggle with the monster. Grendel, after having an arm wrenched from its socket, flees to the fens to die. The next night Grendel's mother comes to the hall to avenge the death of her son and carries off one of Hrothgar's counselors. Beowulf, who had been absent, is sent for in the morning. He descends to the caves of the sea and slays the water demon with a sword wrought by the giants. Beowulf returns to his own country, where he becomes king and rules for fifty years. Then a dragon, robbed of a cup from an immense treasure hoard he had guarded for three hundred years, becomes enraged and devastates the land. Beowulf, although weakened by great age, kills the dragon with the aid of Wiglaf, a kinsman. Severely wounded during the encounter, however, Beowulf dies after viewing the treasures.

BÉRANGER, Pierre Jean de (1780–1857), French poet and writer of political songs, born in Paris. He lived in poverty until 1804, when one of his revolutionary songs brought him to the notice of Lucien Bonaparte, brother of the French emperor Napoleon I (qq.v.) and a strong republican sympathizer. Bonaparte supported the poet for several years, until Béranger obtained a clerkship in the office of the Imperial University. With the publication of the first collection of his songs in 1815, he was recognized as the poet of the republican faction in France. The chanson, in which the 18th-century writers had praised love and wine, became in his hands a powerful political weapon. He was imprisoned for the sentiments expressed in two of his works published in 1821, and again for a volume published in 1825. His works include *Chansons Nouvelles* (1830) and an autobiography (posthumously published 1858).

BERAR. *See* BRITISH INDIA.

BERBER, name given to the language and people of certain native, non-Arabic tribes inhabiting large sections of North Africa. Berbers are sparely built and range in skin color from white and near-white to dark brown. Through the centuries their blood has become mixed with that of so many other ethnic groups, notably the Arabs, that the people are identified usually on a linguistic rather than a racial basis. The Berber language is a branch of the Afro-Asiatic linguistic family (*see* AFRICAN LANGUAGES) and comprises about 300 closely related local dialects. It is primarily a spoken language; its written form is little known and rarely used. Berber-speaking peoples number between 8,000,000 and 10,000,000, more than 50 percent of the population of North Africa. Berbers constitute about 40 percent of the population of Morocco, about 30 percent of the population of Algeria, and about 1 percent of the population of Tunisia. The number of identifiable Berbers in North Africa is slowly declining as more and more tribesmen adopt the language and culture of the Arab majority. Like the Arabs, the Berbers are Muslims (*see* ISLAM); they are less orthodox, however, and their religious rituals include many elements, some animistic (*see* ANIMISM), which derive from ancient pre-Islamic and pagan religions. Most of the Berbers inhabit rural areas, where they dwell in tents and clay huts or, in the larger villages, in stone houses. The traditional Berber occupations are sheep and cattle raising, but increasing numbers of tribesmen raise crops. Other industries in which Berbers engage include flour milling, wood carving, the quarrying of millstones, and the production of domestic utensils, agricultural implements, pottery, jewelry, and leather goods.

The Berbers have lived in North Africa since the earliest recorded time. References to them date from about 3000 B.C. and occur frequently in ancient Egyptian, Greek, and Roman sources. For many centuries the Berbers inhabited the coast of North Africa from Egypt to the Atlantic Ocean. They continued to inhabit the region until the 7th century A.D., when the Arabs conquered North Africa and drove many Berber tribes inland to the Atlas Mts. and to areas in and near the Sahara. After the Arab conquest, the Berbers embraced the Muslim faith of their new rulers. Succeeding centuries were marked by almost continuous struggles for power in North Africa among the various Berber tribes, between the Berbers and the Arabs, and between both these peoples and Spanish, Portuguese, and Turkish invaders. During the same period the Barbary Coast (q.v.) of North Africa, the name of which derives from the word Berber, became famous as the principal base of Arab and Berber pirates, who preyed on Mediterranean shipping.

In the 19th and early 20th centuries France and Spain subjugated Morocco and Algeria. After World War I the Berber and Arab populations of North Africa began actively to seek independence. Beginning in 1926, Riff tribesmen, led by the Riff emir Abd-el-Krim (q.v.), repeatedly defeated Spanish troops occupying the Spanish zone of Morocco; Berbers advanced into French Morocco in 1926, but were repulsed the following year by combined French and Spanish troops. During the upsurge of native nationalism that swept French North Africa after World War II, the Berbers played a somewhat equivocal role. In French Morocco, Berber tribesmen, led by the pro-French Berber pasha Thami el-Mezouari el-Glaoui (1873–1956), constituted the chief bulwark of French control. In 1953 the French, aided by el-Glaoui, deposed and exiled the nationalist sultan of Morocco, Muhammed V ben Youssef (1913–61). Anti-French feeling grew steadily thereafter among the Berbers of Morocco, as well as among the Arabs. On Aug. 20, 1955, a force of Berbers from the Atlas Mts. region of Algeria raided two rural settlements in Morocco and killed seventy-seven French nationals. After a number of such anti-French outbreaks among the Berbers of Morocco, el-Glaoui, yielding to popular sentiment, adopted a nationalist position. The loss of Berber support helped to force the French to end the exile of Muhammed V in 1955, and to grant Morocco independence in 1956. In Algeria, violent resistance to French rule by segments of both the Berber and the Arab population continued until the country was granted independence in 1962.

BERBERIDACEAE, *or* BARBERRY FAMILY, family of plants belonging to the order Ranales. They are perennial herbs or shrubs, some evergreen and others carrying leaves into midwinter.

The fruit is a pod or berry. Some of the species have spiny stems and attractive berries of various colors, and are often used for hedges. The genera native to the United States are *Podophyllum,* may apple; *Jeffersonia,* twinleaf; *Diphylleia,* umbrella leaf; *Caulophyllum,* blue cohosh; and *Berberis,* barberry. *See* BARBERRY.

BERCEO, Gonzalo de. *See* SPANISH LITERATURE: *The Middle Ages.*

BERCHTESGADEN, town and year-round resort of West Germany, in Bavaria, in the Bavarian Alps, about 80 miles S.E. of Munich. The town is in a salt-mining region. The principal industry in the Berchtesgaden is wood carving. Near the town is Wachenfeld, or the Berghof, the palatial residence of the German dictator Adolf Hitler (q.v.). Berchtesgaden was captured by American forces in 1945 during World War II. Pop. (1970 est.) 39,100.

BERCHTOLD, Count Leopold von (1863–1942), Austro-Hungarian statesman, born in Vienna. Berchtold entered the diplomatic service at an early age. He was appointed ambassador to Russia in 1906, and foreign minister in 1912. In 1914, when Francis Ferdinand (q.v.), Archduke of Austria, was assassinated at Sarajevo, Serbia, Berchtold decided on an ultimatum that was calculated to ensure rejection by Serbia. He wanted war with Serbia, and his reckless policy resulted in the outbreak of World War I (q.v.). He resigned as foreign minister in 1915. After the collapse of the Austro-Hungarian monarchy in 1918, Berchtold retired from active political life.

BERDYAEV, Nikolai. *See* EXISTENTIALISM.

BEREA, city of Ohio, in Cuyahoga Co., about 11 miles S.W. of central Cleveland. The city quarries stone, and manufactures farm implements, bricks, and metal products. It is the site of Baldwin-Wallace College, established in 1845. Pop. (1960) 16,592; (1970) 22,396.

BERENGARIA (d. 1230?), Queen Consort of England (1191–99) as wife of King Richard I (q.v.), the daughter of Sancho VI, King of Navarre (d. 1194). She was betrothed to Richard shortly after his accession to the English throne in 1189 and joined him in Reggio, Italy, in 1191, while he was traveling to Palestine on the Third Crusade (*see* CRUSADES: *Third Crusade*); they were married later in the same year in Limassol, Cyprus. From 1191 to 1192, while Richard campaigned against the Saracens, she lived in Acre in Palestine, and from 1192 to 1194, while he was a prisoner in Germany, she lived in Poitou (now in France). After Richard's release from captivity the couple appear to have become estranged, and modern historians agree that they were probably never reunited. After Richard's death in 1199, Berengaria spent most of her last years in Le Mans, France, where she died.

BERENICE, name of two ancient towns of North Africa. **1.** Seaport in the Arab Republic of Egypt, on a bay on the W. coast of the Red Sea. It was founded about 275 B.C. by King Ptolemy II (*see under* PTOLEMY), who named it in honor of his mother. During the Macedonian dynasty and, later under Roman rule, Berenice was a flourishing commercial center. A caravan route that is still in use extended from the town N.W. across the desert to the Nile R. Various ruins, including remnants of a Roman temple, mark the ancient site. The harbor is navigable only by shallow-draft vessels. **2.** City of ancient Cyrenaica, the site of which is now occupied by Benghazi (q.v.), in Libya.

BERENICE *or* **BERNICE,** two princesses of the Herods (1st-century Jewish kings of Judea).

Berenice (fl. about 1 B.C.), niece of Herod the Great and mother of Herod Agrippa I (qq.v.), kings of Judea.

Berenice (fl. about 50 A.D.), daughter of Herod Agrippa I. She was successively the wife of Marcus, son of a magistrate in Alexandria; of her uncle Herod, ruler of Chalcis (d. 48 A.D.); and of Polemon II (d. 74 A.D.), King of Cilicia. Abandoning Polemon, she lived for a time with her brother Herod Agrippa II (q.v.), King of Judea, with whom she was accused of incest. During her residence at the court of her brother, Paul (q.v.), the Apostle, was placed on trial before a tribunal composed of Berenice, Herod Agrippa II, and Porcius Festus (d. about 62 A.D.), Roman procurator of Judea (Acts 25, 26); at the conclusion of the trial Paul was sent to Rome. In 75 A.D. she followed her brother to Rome, where she became the mistress of Titus (q.v.); when the latter became emperor of Rome (79 A.D.), he sent Berenice back to Judea.

BERENSON, Bernard (1865–1959), American art critic and writer, regarded during his lifetime as the world's foremost expert on Italian art. He was often employed by prominent art collectors, galleries, and museums to evaluate prospective acquisitions.

Born on June 26, 1865, in a Jewish village near Vilna, Lithuania, Berenson was taken by his parents to Boston, Mass., as a child. After attending Boston University and Harvard (B.A., 1887), he studied art history in Europe on a fellowship. In 1900 he married and settled at Settignano, near Florence, in a villa called I Tatti. His first book, *Venetian Painters of the Renaissance* (1894), was followed by others on the painters of Florence and central and northern

Bernard Berenson Wide World

Italy. In about 1906 he became consultant to the English art dealer Lord Joseph Duveen. This association and others, which utilized his skill in authenticating paintings, brought him substantial earnings. Although most famed for his expertise in Italian Renaissance art, he was one of the first to recognize the significance of such modern French artists as Pierre Auguste Renoir (*see under* RENOIR) and Paul Cézanne (q.v.). A prolific writer on art, he was also the author of *Sketch for a Self-Portrait* (1949), *Rumor and Reflection* (1952), and *Sunset and Twilight*, (1963). He died on Oct. 6, 1959, at Settignano.

BEREZINA, river of the Soviet Union, in the White Russian S.S.R., rising in the marshes near the town of Borisov. It flows S.E. for about 350 mi. to the Dnieper R., which carries its waters to the Black Sea. It is connected also with the Baltic Sea by a canal to the Dvina R. The Berezina is important commercially, especially for the transport of timber. From Nov. 26 to Nov. 29, 1812, during the retreat of the army of Napoleon I (q.v.) from Moscow, more than 10,000 French soldiers died under Russian artillery bombardment while crossing the Berezina near Borisov.

BEREZNIKI, city and port of the Soviet Union, in the Russian S.F.S.R., on the Kama R. about 90 miles N.E. of Perm'. The city is surrounded by an area rich in magnesium and potassium salts. It is an industrial center producing nitrate and phosphate fertilizers, aniline dyes, sulfuric acid, ammonia, and pharmaceuticals; it has one of the largest chemical plants in the U.S.S.R. Pop. (1970 est.) 145,000.

BERG, Alban (1885–1935), Austrian composer, whose music represents a flexible, emotionally intense use of the twelve-tone system (q.v.) of composition.

Berg was born in Vienna on Feb. 9, 1885, and trained under the Austrian composer Arnold Schönberg (q.v.), who was the originator of the twelve-tone system. Berg treated the twelve-tone method quite freely, integrating into it techniques and forms from 17th-, 18th-, and 19th-century music. His early works, such as the *Altenberg Lieder* ("Altenberg Songs", 1912) for voice and orchestra, show the influence of late-Romantic composers such as Richard Wagner and Gustav Mahler.

His opera *Wozzeck* (first performed in 1925) is considered an unmatched example of expressionist opera, and as such it is a document of post-World War I Europe. The music, based on earlier forms such as the symphony and invention, is highly structured, but the structure is not overtly apparent. The atonality characteristic of expressionistic music is abandoned when effect requires, as in the D-minor prelude to the last scene. Berg's second opera, *Lulu* (posthumously produced in 1937), is expressionistic, and it strictly uses the twelve-tone technique.

His final work, the Violin Concerto (posthumously premiered at Zürich, Switzerland, in 1937), was written in memory of Manon Gropius, daughter of the German architect Walter Gropius and his wife Alma, widow of Gustav Mahler. The twelve-tone sequence that underlies the work arouses listener associations with the sound of tonal music and includes the opening notes of a hymn melody used by Johann Sebastian Bach in his Cantata No. 60. After a determined struggle, against his failing health, to complete the opera *Lulu* (the third act of which remained unfinished), Berg died in Vienna on Dec. 24, 1935.

Berg, his colleague Anton Webern (q.v.), and their teacher, Schönberg, are often regarded as comprising the second Viennese school of music, so called after the 18th-century Viennese school of Franz Joseph Haydn, Wolfgang Mozart, and Ludwig van Beethoven. G.L.

BERGAMO, city of Italy, in Lombardy Province, and capital of Bergamo Province, 33 miles N.E. of Milan. It consists of a medieval upper city, built on a hill, and a modern, industrial lower city, built on the plain. Among the outstanding buildings of the upper city are the Romanesque Church of Santa Maria Maggiore, begun in 1137; the 12th-century Gothic Palazzo della Ragione, one of the oldest town halls in existence; and the 15th-century Colleoni Chapel, in early-Renaissance style. The Carrara Academy in the lower city is noted for its large picture gallery. Modern Bergamo is built on the site of ancient *Bergomum,* a Gallic settlement which received Roman municipal rights from the Roman general and statesman Gaius Julius Caesar and was destroyed in the 5th century by the Huns under King Attila (qq.v.). After it was rebuilt it became successively the capital of a Lombard duchy, a dependency of the city of Milan, and from 1428 to 1797 a part of the Venetian Republic. Later it became part of the Kingdom of Lombardy. It is now the principal industrial city of the province of Bergamo. Manufactures of the commune and the surrounding area include steel and steel products, silk, textiles, clothing, food products, aluminum, cement, machinery, and furniture. The operatic composer Gaetano Donizetti (q.v.) was born in Bergamo in 1797. Pop. (1971) 127,181.

BERGEN, Flemish name of the city of Mons (q.v.), in Belgium.

BERGEN, city and seaport, S.W. Norway, administrative center of Hordaland Co., located along inlets of the North Sea. The second largest city of Norway, it is a cultural, fishing, industrial, and shipping center. Its manufactures include steel, ships, fishing equipment, processed food, forest products, and electrical machinery.

Picturesquely situated near seven mountains, Bergen is a colorful city with numerous historic buildings. Among the notable structures are Saint Mary's Church (12th cent.), the city's oldest building; Bergenhus fortress, including Haakon's Hall (1261; rebuilt after World War II); and several steep-roofed, wooden quayside houses dating from the early 1700's. Educational institutions in the city include the University of Bergen (founded 1948), a school of economics and business administration (1936), and a music conservatory (1905). Also of note are a theater established (1850) by the violinist Ole Bornemann Bull (1810–80) and the Western Norway Museum of Applied Art (1887).

Originally named Björgvin, the city was founded about 1070 by King Olaf III and grew quickly as a commercial center. It was the capital of Norway during the 12th and 13th centuries. From the mid-1300's to 1560 the Hanseatic League (q.v.) held a monopoly over Bergen's trade, and Hanseatic merchants remained influential in the city until the late 1800's. Bergen suffered severe fires in 1702, 1855, and 1916, and the city was badly damaged during World War II, when it was occupied (1940–45) by the Germans. Pop. (1974 est.) 214,019.

BERGENFIELD, borough in New Jersey, in Bergen Co., 8 miles E. of Paterson. It is an industrial community, with plants engaged in the manufacture of clothing and machinery. Pop. (1960) 27,203; (1970) 33,131.

BERGER, Victor Louis (1860–1929), American Socalist leader, born in Austria, and educated at the universities of Budapest and Vienna. He emigrated to the United States in 1878 and later became a resident of Milwaukee, Wis. Elected to the United States House of Representatives in 1911, he was the first Socialist (*see* SOCIALIST PARTY) to serve in Congress. He opposed American participation in World War I even after the United States entered the war, and as a result, in 1918 he and four other Socialists were brought to trial, charged with violation of the Espionage Act of 1917 (q.v.). After a legal battle that attracted national attention, on Jan. 8, 1919, he was found guilty and sentenced to serve twenty years in a Federal prison. In November of the same year the House voted to exclude him from his seat. Berger's conviction was reversed by the Supreme Court of the United States in 1921, and in the following year the indictments against him were dismissed. He was again elected to Congress, was permitted to assume his seat, and served from 1923 to 1929 but he was defeated when he ran again in 1928. In 1924 he supported the candidacy of the American political leader Robert Marion La Follette (q.v.) for President. Berger was delegate of the American Socialist Party to the International Socialist Congress at Marseille, France, in 1925. After 1927 he was chairman of the National Executive Committee of the Socialist Party.

BERGERAC, Savinien de Cyrano de. *See* CYRANO DE BERGERAC, SAVINIEN DE.

BERGH, Henry. *See* ANIMALS, CRUELTY TO; CHILDREN, CRUELTY TO.

BERGIUS, Friedrich Karl Rudolph (1884–1949), German chemist, born near Breslau (now Wroctau, Poland), and educated at several German universities. He became interested in the synthesis of organic compounds under high pressure and wrote a book on this subject in 1913. After further research he produced synthetic gasoline by treating finely powdered coal with hydrogen gas at high temperature and pressure. Although only a small percentage of gasoline is produced by this process today, it is still a practical and important method.

Bergius made another outstanding chemical discovery, a method of manufacturing food from wood. Wood chips treated with cold, concentrated hydrochloric acid produce sugars that, after processing, may be used as food for cattle and, under certain conditions, for human beings. This process is in use in many parts of the world; the sugar thus produced is usually fermented to produce industrial alcohol. By-products include lignin, which may be converted into plastics, and other chemicals, such as acetic acid, usually produced by destructive distillation of wood. Bergius shared the 1931 Nobel Prize for chemistry with the German chemist Karl Bosch (q.v.).

BERGMAN, Ingmar (1918–), Swedish motion-picture director and producer, born in Uppsala, Sweden, and educated at Stockholm University. Possibly the most distinguished figure in Scandinavian cinema, Bergman has directed, produced, and written screenplays for films that range from light comedy to profound psychological and philosophical drama. His comedies, which include *Lesson in Love* (1953), *Smiles of a Summer Night* (1955), and *The Devil's Eye* (1962), are especially marked by their explicit sexual content. Among his serious films, *The Seventh Seal* (1956) is a somber allegory on the relationship of man to God and to death. His themes are frequently conveyed through the use of Christian symbols and are imbued with a dark sense of mystery. *Wild Strawberries* (1957) and *Persona* (1966), both profound studies of the human psyche, use the typical Bergman techniques of flashbacks, dream sequences, and visions. *Through a Glass Darkly* (1961) and *The Silence* (1964) contain such negative existential moods and themes as spiritual torpor and the inability to communicate or to feel or receive love. *Through a Glass Darkly* was named the best foreign film of 1961, by the Academy of Motion Picture Arts and Sciences. Bergman also wrote and directed *Hour of the Wolf* (1968), *Shame* (1968), and *Cries and Whispers* (1972).

BERGMAN, Ingrid (1915–), Swedish actress, born in Stockholm and educated (1933–34) at the school of the Royal Dramatic Theater, Stockholm. Within three years (1935–38) she became a star in Swedish motion pictures. Her performance in *Intermezzo* (1938) brought her to the attention of American motion-picture producers. Her first film in the United States was an English-language version of *Intermezzo* (1939). She appeared in more than a score of films in the next three decades, including *Casablanca* (1942), *For Whom the Bell Tolls* (1943), *Spellbound* (1945), *Notorious* (1946), *Stromboli* (1950), *The Yellow Rolls-Royce* (1965), and *Cactus Flower* (1969). For her performances in *Gaslight* (1944) and *Anastasia* (1956) she received awards as the best actress of the year from the Academy of Motion Picture Arts and Sciences. Miss Bergman acted on the stage in New York City in *Liliom* (1940), *Joan of Lorraine*

Contemplative Swedish film director Ingmar Bergman
Pictorial Parade/Camera Press

(1946), *More Stately Mansions* (1967), and *Captain Brassbound's Conversion* (1972), as well as in theatrical productions in Stockholm, Paris, and Guildford, England, and on British, French, and American television.

BERGSON, Henri Louis (1859–1941), French philosopher, born in Paris and educated at the École Normale Supérieure and the University of Paris. He taught in various secondary schools from 1881 until 1898, when he accepted a professorship at the École Normale Supérieure. Two years later he was appointed to the chair of philosophy at the Collège de France.

Meanwhile his doctoral dissertation, *Essai sur les donnés immédiates de la conscience* (1889; Eng. trans., *Time and Free Will*, 1910), was published and aroused great interest among philosophers. It presents Bergson's theories on the freedom of the mind and on duration, which he regarded as the succession of conscious states, intermingling and unmeasured. This work was followed by *Matière et mémoire* (1896; Eng. trans., *Matter and Memory*, 1911), emphasizing the selectivity of the human brain; *Le Rire* (1900; Eng. trans., *Laughter*, 1901), an essay on the mechanistic basis of comedy that is probably his most quoted work; and *L'Évolution créatrice* (1907; Eng. trans., *Creative Evolution*, 1911), probing the entire problem of human existence and defining the mind as pure energy, the élan vital, or vital force, responsible for all organic evolution. In 1914 Bergson was elected to the French Academy (*see* INSTITUTE OF FRANCE).

In 1921 he resigned from the Collège de France to devote his time to international affairs, politics, moral problems, and religion; he was converted to Roman Catholicism (his parents were Jewish). He published only one book during the last two decades of his life, *Les deux sources de la morale et de la religion* (1932; Eng. trans., *The Two Sources of Morality and Religion*, 1935), in which he aligns his own philosophy with Christianity. In 1927 he was awarded the Nobel Prize in literature. The influence of the earlier books cited above, as well as his many papers and lectures, on the philosophers, artists, and writers of the 20th century is virtually immeasurable. He was a master prose stylist and a brilliant lecturer, his mystical yet vital style contrasting with the formalistic materialism of his peers.

Although often associated with the intuitionalist school (*see* INTUITION) of philosophy (q.v.), Bergsonism is too original and eclectic a philosophy to be thus categorized. Bergson did, however, emphasize the importance of intuition over intellect, as he promoted the idea of two opposing currents, inert matter in conflict with organic life as the vital urge strives toward free creative action.

BERIA, Lavrenti Pavlovich. *See* BERYA, LAVRENTI PAVLOVICH.

BERIBERI, diet-deficiency disease caused by a lack of vitamin B_1. The disease is characterized by neuritis (q.v.), often with muscle atrophy, incoordination, and eventually paralysis. In advanced cases, progressive lassitude and edema (q.v.) appear. Death may follow from heart failure caused by edema and weakness of the heart muscle. The disease is prevalent in tropical and subtropical regions all over the world, but especially in those parts of the Orient where the diet consists mainly of polished rice. Recovery is prompt when adequate amounts of vitamin B_1 are restored to the diet. *See* VITAMIN: *Vitamin-B Complex.*

BERING, Vitus (1680–1741), Danish navigator, born in Horsens. He entered the newly formed navy of the Russian emperor Peter I (q.v.), called the Great, and, for the ability and daring he displayed in the wars with Sweden, Bering was appointed to conduct an expedition of discovery in what is now known as the Bering Sea. After some years spent in explorations on the coast of the Kamchatka Peninsula, the Sea of Okhotsk, and northern Siberia, he sailed in June, 1741, from Petropavlovsk toward the American continent. He sighted the continent north of what is now Cape Saint Elias, Alaska, on July 29, and shortly afterward landed on Kayak Island. During the return voyage his vessel, the Saint Peter, encountering storms and fog, was wrecked on an uninhabited island subsequently named Bering Island in his honor. Bering, who was ill at the time of the disaster, died there of exposure one month later. His companions built a vessel in which they returned to Kamchatka with more than $100,000 worth of furs they had trapped on the island.

BERING ISLAND, one of the largest of the Komandorskiye Islands (q.v.), E. of the Kamchatka Peninsula, in the S.W. portion of the Bering Sea, and forming part of Khabarovsk Territory, Russian S.F.S.R. Like the other islands of the Komandorskiye group, it is barren and treeless. Soviet naval and radio stations are located on the island, but it is otherwise uninhabited. The island was named in honor of the Danish navigator Vitus Bering (q.v.). Area, about 615 sq.mi.

BERING SEA, part of the North Pacific Ocean, between the Aleutian Islands on the S. and the Bering Strait, by which it is connected with the Arctic Ocean, on the N. On the W. are the Kamchatka and Chukotski peninsulas of N.E. Asia, and on the E. is Alaska. The sea is named in honor of the Danish explorer Vitus Bering (q.v.). The total area is about 873,000 sq.mi. The waters of the Anadyr' R. in Asia and of the Yukon R. in North America flow into the Bering Sea. Fog prevails and, in the winter, pack ice forms as far S. as Saint Matthew Island, and ice floes extend S. of the Pribilof Islands. Among other islands in the Bering Sea are Saint Lawrence Island, Nunivak Island, and the Komandorskiye Islands.

BERING SEA CONTROVERSY, international dispute arising in 1886 from attempts by the United States government to prohibit Canadian vessels from fishing for seals in the waters off the Pribilof Islands (q.v.), American-owned and protected fur-seal rookery. The United States Congress had adopted legislation forbidding pelagic (open sea) sealing in the waters adjacent to the rookery as early as 1868, one year after Alaska and the off-lying islands were acquired from Russia. The rookery itself had been leased to a commercial organization. Under the terms of the lease the slaughter was limited to 100,000 seals annually. In 1881, following protests from the American-licensed company against the indiscriminate slaughter of seals by foreign-flag vessels, the U.S. government ruled, in effect, that pelagic sealing was prohibited in the Bering Sea east of the line demarcating Russian and American territory; this ruling asserted American jurisdiction over part of the high seas. Implementation of the ruling was delayed until 1886, when three Canadian sealing vessels were seized by an American revenue cutter. After the seizure in 1887 of additional Canadian sealers, the British government protested to the U.S. Attempts by the two governments to arrange an international conference to deal with the points at issue ended in 1888 in failure. In 1889 the U.S. seized several Canadian sealers. Strong protests by Great Britain led to resumption of negotiations, and in February, 1892, the countries concluded an agreement providing for international arbitration of the dispute.

In August, 1893, the court of arbitration rejected American claims to territorial jurisdiction over the Bering Sea, but did adopt regulations restricting the operations of pelagic sealers. The regulations, however, proved to be completely ineffectual, and the herds were depleted by more than 66 percent during the next few years. Pelagic sealing was finally abolished under the provisions of a treaty concluded in 1911 by Japan, Russia, Great Britain, and the U.S.; since then the herd has gradually increased.

BERING STRAIT, body of water separating Asia from America and connecting the Bering Sea with the Arctic Ocean. It was first discovered and explored by the Russian navigator Simon Dezhnev (about 1605–73) in 1648. It was again explored by the Danish navigator Vitus Bering in 1728, and later by the British mariners James Cook (qq.v.) and Frederick William Beechey (1796–1856). The narrowest part of the strait is between Cape Dezhnev in Asia and Cape Prince of Wales in America. The distance between the two capes is approximately 40 mi. About midway are the Diomede Islands (q.v.).

BERKELEY, city in California, in Alameda Co., on the mainland shore of San Francisco Bay, 6 mi. across the bay from San Francisco. It is an educational and cultural center, and is the site of the University of California at Berkeley, Armstrong and Williams business colleges, several theological seminaries, and State schools for the deaf and blind. Berkeley is both a residential city and a commercial center. Industries in the city include the manufacturing of soups and other food products, chemicals, and machinery. Berkeley was incorporated as a town in 1878 and was chartered as a city in 1909. Pop. (1960) 111,268; (1970) 116,716.

BERKELEY, George (1685–1753), Irish philosopher and churchman, born in County Kilkenny, and educated at Trinity College. At Trinity he was deeply influenced by the views of the English philosopher John Locke (q.v.). In 1709 Berkeley completed his *Essay Towards a New Theory of Vision,* in which he extended Locke's ideas on the character of matter. This he followed with *Treatise Concerning the Principles of Human Knowledge* (1710) and *Three Dialogues Between Hylas and Philonous* (1713), works that further developed his philosophy of subjective idealism (q.v.). Meanwhile Berkeley had been ordained in the diaconate of the Church of England, and, after his *Discourse on Passive Obedience* (1711), an essay on theological utilitarianism, was published he became increasingly prominent as a churchman. In 1734 he was appointed bishop of Cloyne.

Generally regarded as the founder of the modern school of idealism, Berkeley developed his philosophy in an effort to discredit the materialism of his time. Locke already had reached the conclusion that some of the qualities of matter were subjective, but in his *Treatise Concerning the Principles of Human Knowledge,* Berkeley went even further. He maintained that matter cannot be conceived to exist independent of the mind. In other words, matter exists only to the extent that man perceives it. Since no external world exists, he argued, the phenomena of sense can be explained only by supposing a deity that continually and coherently evokes perception in the mind of man. Berkeley is regarded as one of the three or four most important English philosophers and among the most important of all modern philosophers.

BERKELEY, Sir William (1606–77), English colonial governor, born in Bruton, Somersetshire, and educated at the University of Oxford. He was appointed commissioner to Canada in 1632, and, in 1641, governor of the colony of Virginia. During the civil wars (*see* GREAT REBELLION) in England Berkeley kept Virginia loyal to the king until 1651, when the English lord protector Oliver Cromwell (q.v.) sent a fleet to depose him. Although Berkeley and his followers were forced to acknowledge Cromwell's rule, and Berkeley was removed as governor, he remained in the colony. At the Restoration in 1660, he was chosen governor by the general assembly, receiving his commission for the office from Charles II (q.v.), King of England. Berkeley soon lost favor with the people because of his arbitrary policy, his obstinacy, and his persistent refusal to furnish protection against the Indians. A rebellion against him led by the English colonial leader Nathaniel Bacon (q.v.) failed only because of Bacon's sudden death; *see* BACON'S REBELLION. A royal commission condemned Berkeley's policy, and he was forced to resign the governorship, returning to England in 1676. He wrote *A Discourse and View of Virginia* (1663) and a drama, *The Lost Lady* (1638).

BERKELIUM, transuranic radioactive element with at.no. 97, at.wt. 249, and symbol Bk. The first preparation of berkelium was announced in

January, 1950, by a group of American scientists working under the direction of Glenn Theodore Seaborg (q.v.) at the University of California laboratories in Berkeley, Calif. An isotope of mass number 243 with a half-life of 4.5 hours was produced by bombarding americium-241 with alpha particles (helium nuclei) accelerated in a cyclotron (q.v.). Subsequently another isotope, berkelium-249, with a half-life of 314 days, was synthesized. *See* TRANSURANIUM ELEMENTS.

BERKLEY, city in Michigan, in Oakland Co., about 12 miles N.W. of Detroit, of which it is a suburb. Berkley was incorporated as a village in 1923 and chartered as a city in 1932. Pop. (1960) 23,275; (1970) 22,618.

BERKSHIRE, Great Britain, county in S. England. The county is drained by the Kennet and Thames rivers. The administrative center of Berkshire is Reading (pop., 1971, 133,360). The principal occupations are dairying, and sheep and hog raising. The main industrial establishments are the aircraft plants in Newbury and Reading. Windsor Castle (q.v.), the royal residence, is in Windsor. In Abingdon and Reading are ruins of Benedictine abbeys (675 and 1121, respectively). Area, 725 sq.mi.; pop. (1971) 647,010.

BERKSHIRE FESTIVAL, annual music festival held in July and August at Tanglewood, a 210-acre estate in the towns of Lenox and Stockbridge, Mass., in the Berkshire Hills (q.v.). The festival was inaugurated in 1934 by the American composer and conductor Henry Kimball Hadley (q.v.) with three concerts by members of the New York Philharmonic-Symphony Orchestra in Stockbridge. Beginning in 1936 the orchestral concerts of the festival were given by the Boston Symphony Orchestra at Tanglewood under the direction of the Russian-American conductor Serge Koussevitzky (q.v.). In 1940 a music school, known as the Berkshire Music Center, was established at Tanglewood, also under Koussevitzky's direction. After Koussevitzky's retirement in 1951, the directorship of the concerts and the music school was held successively by the French conductor Charles Munch, the American conductor Erich Leinsdorf (qq.v.), and the German-American conductor William Steinberg (1889–1978). In 1973 the American conductor Gunther Schuller (1925–) was artistic director of the school, while the American composer and conductor Leonard Bernstein (q.v.) and the Manchukuo-born Japanese conductor Seiji Ozawa (1935–) were, respectively, adviser to and director of the concerts. The center offers an eight-week course of instruction and has departments of orchestral conducting, choral singing, orchestra and chamber music, ensemble playing, opera, and composition. The departments give public performances at the festival.

BERKSHIRE HILLS *or* **THE BERKSHIRES,** range of hills and mountains in Berkshire County, W. Massachusetts, noted for beautiful scenery and popular as a resort area. The Berkshires are an extension of the Green Mts. of Vermont. The highest peak of the Berkshires, Mt. Greylock (3491 ft.), is the highest point in Massachusetts.

BERLIN, city in New Hampshire, in Coos Co., at the junction of the Androscoggin and Dead rivers, about 90 miles N.E. of Concord. Factories in Berlin produce wood pulp, paper, chemicals, and textiles. Hydroelectric power is furnished by the Androscoggin R., which drops 200 ft. in a single mile near the city, forming Berlin Falls. Berlin, the site of one of the most famous ski jumps in the United States, was incorporated as a town in 1829 and as a city in 1897. Pop. (1970) 15,256.

BERLIN, partitioned city and former capital of Germany, within the German Democratic Republic (East Germany), approximately 163 miles S.E. of Hamburg, West Germany, and 300 miles W. of Warsaw, Poland. The city presently comprises East Berlin, considered by the East Germans to be the capital of the German Democratic Republic, and West Berlin, which has close ties with the Federal Republic of Germany (West Germany). At the end of World War II the entire city was placed under the joint control of the Big Four powers (the United States, Great Britain, France, and the Soviet Union), each of which occupied a sector. The Soviet Union withdrew from the Allied Control Council on July 1, 1948, and a few months later sanctioned the establishment within the Soviet sector of a separate municipal government known as East Berlin. After difficult negotiations among the World War II allies, an accord was ratified on June 3, 1972, which went far toward normalizing relations between West and East Berlin.

Berlin is divided from S.E. to N.W. into almost equal parts by the Spree R. The Havel R. traverses the W. section of the city. The site of Berlin is an irregular, sandy plain about 100 ft. above sea level. The three largest lakes within the city are the Tegelersee on the N.W., the Müggelsee on the S.E., and the Wannsee on the S.W.

The political dividing line between East Berlin and West Berlin extends N. and S. across Potsdamer Platz, the approximate center of the city. Berlin is the largest city in Germany and the third largest in western Europe. Before World

The Kurfürstendamm, the principal street of West Berlin.
German Information Center

War II, in which the city was virtually destroyed, Berlin was the transportation hub of northern Europe and one of the great financial, commercial, and industrial centers of the world.

The city is still the largest industrial center between Paris and Moscow. Several hundred thousand workers were employed in prewar Berlin in the production of electrical equipment and apparatus, machinery, steel and iron, locomotives, clothing, packaged foods, pharmaceuticals, precision instruments, musical instruments, printed matter, and textiles. Thousands of workers were engaged in banking, commerce, and insurance. The city was a leading inland port with extensive dock facilities and numerous canals connecting it with the Elbe R. and the North Sea, and with the Oder R. and the Baltic Sea. After the war many of the canals lost importance as inland waterways.

Before World War II the business and administrative districts occupied the center of the city, called the Mitte (now in East Berlin). Beyond the Mitte were the industrial sections and residential suburbs. Prewar Berlin had a metropolitan railway system, the Ringbahn, which encircled the heart of the city and joined eight large railway terminals. The present-day metropolitan railway system, the S-Bahn, runs in East and West Berlin but is boycotted by West Berliners because it is owned by East Berlin. A subway system, the U-Bahn, connects the sprawling city with its suburban surroundings, but West Berlin-based trains make no stops in the E. sector, nor do trains from East Berlin use stations in West Berlin. East and West Berlin have separate bus and tramway systems. Prewar Berlin was an outstanding center of air transportation. The chief airport was Tempelhof (rebuilt and enlarged in 1948–49), now in West Berlin. Other airports that have resumed operations are Tegel and Gatow airports in West Berlin and Schönefeld, adjacent to East Berlin.

Before World War II Berlin was the site of many architectural masterpieces, notably structures executed in the ornamental style prevalent in the 19th century and in the heavy Prussian style characteristic of the period after World War I. Most of the famous museums, churches, institutes, and theaters were destroyed or damaged in World War II. Berlin remained in ruins for more than six years, but by the early 1960's reconstruction had been virtually completed, including many new buildings.

Area of Berlin, 341 sq.mi.; pop. (1976 est.) 3,056,967.

WEST BERLIN

After 1949 the Allied nations retained only so-called reserved powers in West Berlin. The U.S. sector in the S.W. consisted of the districts of Tempelhof, Schöneberg, Neukölln, Kreuzberg, Steglitz, and Zehlendorf; the sector included the prewar municipal waterworks and residential quarters. The British sector in the W. consisted of Tiergarten, Charlottenburg, Wilmersdorf, and Spandau districts consisting principally of residential areas, parks, lakes, and forests. In the French sector to the N.W. were Wedding and Reinickendorf.

West Berlin has the nominal status of a *Land* ("State") of the Federal Republic of Germany and maintains twenty-two nonvoting observers in the *Bundestag* (lower house of the federal parliament). Legislative power of the municipal government is in a house of representatives; executive power, in a senate and burgomaster.

Very few industries were located in the W. part of prewar Berlin. However, after 1955, with American and West German aid, productive capacity rose sharply in West Berlin. Industrial establishments include electrotechnical works (notably in Siemensstadt), factories producing radios and electrical products, steelworks, automobile factories, and plants manufacturing garments, chemicals, precision machines, appliances, and food and tobacco products. West Berlin also possesses a thriving film industry and many publishing houses. Large numbers of the working population are engaged in construction, transportation, and commerce.

The heart of West Berlin is an area extending W. of the Lehrter railroad terminal to Stuttgarter Platz, and S. to Innsbrucker Platz. Many elegant retail stores and theaters have been constructed along the Kurfürstendamm and the Tauentzienstrasse, the principal streets. The State Opera, in Charlottenburg, has resumed its former importance. The Concert Hall (Philharmonic), opened in 1963, is located at the S. edge of the 630-acre Tiergarten park. It is the present home of the famed Berlin Philharmonic Orchestra. Tiergarten park and the Berlin zoo, both reduced to ruins during the war, have been restored.

The chief educational institution of West Berlin is the Free University (1948) in the suburb of Dahlem; it was built with American aid. The Technical University, located in Charlottenburg, is another important school of higher learning. Among other famous buildings and monuments in West Berlin are the American Memorial Library (opened in 1954), in Kreuzberg, containing approximately 405,000 volumes; the Dahlem museum (1914), containing the most comprehensive collection of painting and sculpture in all Berlin; and the Kaiser Wilhelm Memorial Church (1891–95), which was largely destroyed and has been left in its ruined state as a war memorial. Another famous ruin is that of the Reichstag, which was partly destroyed by fire in 1933 and virtually demolished during the war. The National Gallery, designed by the German-American architect Ludwig Mies van der Rohe (q.v.), was opened in 1968.

Area of West Berlin, 185 sq.mi.; pop. (1976 est.) 1,950,700.

EAST BERLIN

The Communist sector of the city is governed by a mayor and city council. East Berlin, which was proclaimed as the capital of the German Democratic Republic in 1953, comprises the central part of the city, N.E. of Potsdamer Platz, and the E. suburbs, including Lichtenberg, Pankow, Weissensee, Köpenick, Friedrichshain, Prenzlauer Berg, and Treptow. These suburbs formed the most highly populated and industrialized part of prewar Berlin and contained its administrative, financial, and business centers. Many of the industrial plants were removed as reparations by the Soviet Union early in the occupation period, but various new industries subsequently were established in East Berlin. The most important industry in East as in West Berlin is the manufacture of electrical equipment and machinery. Among other East Berlin industries are food processing and chemicals.

The best-known East Berlin street, and the most famous of all Berlin streets before the war, is Unter den Linden, a wide thoroughfare lined with linden trees. Unter den Linden extends from the Brandenburg Gate (1788–91), a neoclassical triumphal arch, in the W., to an island in the Spree R., in the E. Another principal street, called Frankfurter Allee at its east end and Karl-Marx Allee at its west end, extends E. from Alexanderplatz; it is lined with newly constructed government buildings and apartment houses. Unter den Linden remains a major center of interest because of the many historic structures ranged along it. At its east end is located the most distinguished educational institution of prewar Berlin, presently named Humboldt University, but better known under its old name of Friedrich Wilhelm University (1810). The Public Scientific Library, formerly the Prussian State Library (1661), and the State Opera House (built in 1741, destroyed by bombs in 1943, and reconstructed between 1952 and 1955), are also located on Unter den Linden. On Spree Island are the cathedral of Berlin, and the Dom (1894–1905), built in Italian Renaissance style, the upper half of which is damaged. The Imperial Palace, once a prominent landmark in this section, is no longer standing; it was razed in 1950 and the site is now a huge political rallying ground. The Leipzigerstrasse, the most exclusive shopping street before the war, runs parallel to Unter den Linden. Other well-known streets are the Friedrichstrasse, the main amusement district, and the Wilhelmstrasse, on which once stood the imperial government offices and the Reichschancery of the German dictator Adolf Hitler. A number of structures housing East German ministries presently are located on the Friedrichstrasse. The various theaters in East Berlin include the German State Opera, Comic Opera, German Theater, and Folk Theater. The Berliner Ensemble, the theatrical group founded by the poet and playwright Bertolt Brecht (q.v.), continues to perform.

Area of East Berlin, 156 sq.mi.; pop. (1976 est.) 1,106,267.

HISTORY

Berlin was originally a Wendish settlement (founded in 1244) on the S. bank of the Spree R. opposite the earlier Wendish settlement of Kölln (founded in 1237) on the N. bank. Both towns joined the Hanseatic League (q.v.) in the 14th century and prospered commercially. The towns lost their independence in the 15th century to Margrave Frederick II (1413–71), of Brandenburg, a member of the house of Hohenzollern. Subsequently Kölln was combined with Berlin, which became, toward the end of the 15th century, the residence of the Hohenzollern family and capital of Brandenburg. The commercial importance of Berlin declined during the Thirty Years' War (q.v.), but after the accession in 1640 of Elector Frederick William (q.v.), who encouraged the emigration of thrifty Protestant refugees from France and built a canal connecting the Oder and Spree rivers, the Berlin economy gradually recovered.

In 1709 King Frederick I (q.v.) of Prussia (the former Frederick III of Brandenburg) chose Berlin as his capital and merged various outlying sections with the city. Under King Frederick II (q.v.) the Tiergarten public park was laid out and the State Opera was built. The Austrians and later the Russians captured the city during the Seven Years' War (q.v.), but the occupations were too short-lived to hamper its expansion. Berlin suffered from the occupation by the French under Emperor Napoleon I (q.v.) in 1806 after the Prussian defeat at Jena during the Napoleonic Wars (q.v.). The populace agitated against the French, and Berlin became a focal point of German nationalism, especially after the overthrow of Napoleon in 1815. Subsequently Berlin began to rival Vienna as a center of culture. The founding of Friedrich Wilhelm University in 1810 was the beginning of a long period of cultural activity dominated by such figures as the philologist Wilhelm von Humboldt (*see under* HUMBOLDT), the philosopher

East German workers erect a second concrete wall behind the original Berlin Wall, a grim reminder of the division of the city. UPI

and mathematician Johann Gottlieb Fichte and the philosopher Georg Wilhelm Hegel (qq.v.).

In 1871 Berlin became the capital and parliamentary seat of the newly established German Empire. The city and some of the surrounding suburbs were organized as Greater Berlin in 1912, and in 1920, as a result of further extensions, the municipality became the largest city in continental Europe. Berlin was the center of great political and social unrest following World War I, but it also achieved renown in the fields of literature, art, and science. As the capital of the Third Reich from 1933 to 1945 the city was the target of frequent air raids during World War II. In the last two years of the war 75,000 tons of explosives were dropped on the city, and in the last ten days of April, 1945, Soviet artillery hurled 40,000 tons of shells into it. Property totally destroyed included 40 percent of the housing units in the city.

After the Germans surrender to Soviet forces, Berlin was partitioned into its present sectors. In 1948, after withdrawing from the united command, the Soviet occupation authorities blockaded all land traffic between West Berlin and West Germany. In order to supply West Berlin with food and provisions, the Allies organized an airlift on a huge scale. By May, 1949, when the blockade was lifted, more than 1,500,000 tons of supplies had been flown in by British and American aircraft.

In June, 1953, a demonstration for better living and working conditions in East Berlin, devel-

"The Congress of Berlin", painting by Anton von Werner (1843–1915). Bettmann Archive

oped into a general uprising. The rebellion quickly spread to other parts of East Germany, but it was soon suppressed by East German police and Soviet troops. In order to stem the tide of East Germans escaping through West Berlin, on Aug. 13, 1961, East German police constructed a barrier across the city, sealing off East Berlin. Despite military measures intended to make the so-called Berlin Wall impregnable, East Germans have found ways to escape. During the first six years of the wall, 26,383 fled to West Berlin and more than 70 others were killed in such attempts. Between 1963 and 1967 agreements signed by the East and West Berlin governments permitted limited visiting rights for West Berliners in East Berlin. Thereafter East Germany barred such visits. Under accords signed in 1972 West Berliners were granted freedom of access to East Berlin and East Germany.

BERLIN, Irving, original name ISRAEL BALINE (1888–), American composer of popular music, born in Russia, and educated in the public schools of New York City. He began his musical career in New York City as a singing waiter in restaurants and cafés. In 1911 the publication of "Alexander's Ragtime Band" established his reputation as a song writer. Among the numerous musical comedies and revues for which he wrote music and lyrics were *Watch Your Step* (1914), *The Century Girl* (1916 with Victor Herbert (q.v.), *Yip Yip Yaphank* (1918), the *Ziegfeld Follies* (1911, 1919, 1920, 1927), the *Music Box Revue* (1921–24), *As Thousands Cheer* (1933), *Annie Get Your Gun* (1946), *Miss Liberty* (1949), *Call Me Madam* (1950), and *Mr. President* (1962). In 1942 Berlin wrote and produced *This Is the Army,* using only military personnel. In 1955 President Dwight David Eisenhower (q.v.) presented Berlin with a special medal authorized by Congress for his composition of patriotic songs. Berlin wrote music for the motion pictures *Top Hat* (1935), *On the Avenue* (1937), *Second Fiddle* (1939), *Holiday Inn* (1942), *Blue Skies* (1946), *Easter Parade* (1948), and others. Among his many songs which achieved widespread popularity are "Everybody's Doin' It", "Oh, How I Hate to Get Up in the Morning", "Always", "Remember", "God Bless America", "White Christmas", and "Easter Parade".

BERLIN, CONGRESS OF, assembly of representatives of Germany, Russia, Austria-Hungary, Great Britain, France, Italy, and the Ottoman Empire that met in Berlin from June 13 to July 13, 1878, to revise the terms of the Treaty of San Stefano (*see* SAN STEFANO, TREATY OF), which had concluded the Russo-Turkish War in March, 1878. After winning the war, Russia by this treaty had imposed extremely severe terms on the Ottoman Turks. Other European powers, notably Austria-Hungary and Great Britain, alarmed at the growth of the power of Russia and of the independent states created in the Balkans by the treaty, and concerned for their own interests in the Middle East, insisted that the treaty be modified. Count Gyula Andrássy (*see under* ANDRÁSSY), foreign minister of Austria-Hungary, invited the European powers concerned to meet at Berlin. Prince Otto von Bismarck (q.v.) Chancellor of the German Empire, presided over the congress.

At the congress the Treaty of San Stefano was virtually abrogated, and the Treaty of Berlin was drawn up, with conditions much less favorable to Russia. The new treaty reaffirmed the principle that the status of the Ottoman Empire was to be decided by the powers jointly and not unilaterally by any one of them. It also reaffirmed the principle of nationalism for the Balkan peoples. Serbia and Montenegro (qq.v.) were made independent of the Turks, although the territory granted them by the Treaty of San Stefano was considerably reduced. Bulgaria was divided into three parts, and two of them were placed under Turkish control. Rumania gained its independence from the Turks, but Russia acquired the southern Bessarabian region of Rumania, for which Rumania was compensated by the Dobruja (now Dobrogea), a former Turkish region. Russia also received the territories of Batum (now Batumi), Kars, and Ardahan. The Turkish provinces of Bosnia and Hercegovina were mandated to Austria-Hungary; *see* BOSNIA AND HERCEGOVINA: *History.*

As a result of the Treaty of Berlin, the Turks lost most of their European territory, Russian influence was reduced in the Near East, and that of Austria-Hungary and Great Britain was increased. The Balkan countries and Russia were not satisfied with what they had obtained by the treaty; the tensions thus created in the Balkans and the Middle East were the cause of much future strife there, and eventually were one of the causes of World War I. *See* BALKAN WARS; TURKEY: *History.*

BERLIN, FREE UNIVERSITY OF, autonomous institution of higher learning, located in West Berlin, Federal Republic of Germany. The university is supported financially by the city of Berlin and the Federal government. The university was founded in 1948 by former students and faculty members of the University of Berlin (*see* BERLIN, UNIVERSITY OF). The university consists of the faculties of medicine, law, economic and social sciences, philosophy, mathmematical and natural sciences, and veterinary medicine. Several institutes are attached to the university, including the Osteuropa-Institut and the John F. Kennedy-Institut für Amerikastudien. The usual four- to six-year course of study leads to the *Diplom* or the degree of *Doktor* and represents about the equivalent of American master's-degree work. The main university library contains about 500,000 volumes and 220,000 theses. In 1971 the student body numbered about 15,060 and the faculty, about 940.

BERLIN, UNIVERSITY OF (officially HUMBOLDT-UNIVERSITÄT ZU BERLIN), before World War II one of the most important universities in the world. The university was established in Berlin as the Königliche (Royal) Friedrich-Wilhelms-Universität in 1810 by King Frederick William III (q.v.) of Prussia to take the place of the University of Halle, inasmuch as the French emperor, Napoleon I (q.v.), had incorporated the town of Halle into the newly formed kingdom of Westphalia. From the beginning the University of Berlin secured men of great ability to fill its professorial chairs; among the scholars connected with the university were the German philosophers Johann Gottlieb Fichte and Georg Wilhelm Hegel, the German classicist and historian Theodor Mommsen, and the American physicist Albert Einstein (qq.v.). The university comprised faculties of theology, jurisprudence, medicine, and philosophy (arts and science). The university was practically a self-governing body, with corporate freedom and responsibilities. It had police and judicial powers over its student body.

After World War II the university came under the control of the Soviet Union and its name was changed to Humboldt-Universität zu Berlin. It is currently under the jurisdiction of the minister for higher education of the German Democratic Republic and is supported by the government. The university consists of the faculties of philosophy, mathematics and natural sciences, law, economics, pedagogy, theology, medicine, veterinary medicine, and agriculture and horticulture. A *Diplom,* the approximate equivalent of an American baccalaureate degree, is awarded after a four- to five-year course of study. After an additional three years of study and the completion of a dissertation the doctorate is awarded. Further study and the completion of a second dissertation lead to a second doctorate (*Habilitation*), which qualifies the recipient to teach in a university. *Habilitation* represents the approximate equivalent of the American PH.D. The university library contains more than 1,910,000 bound volumes. In 1971 the student body numbered about 14,000 and the faculty, about 1900. *See* BERLIN, FREE UNIVERSITY OF.

BERLIOZ, Louis Hector (1803–69), French composer who was one of the principal forces in the development of 19th-century musical Romanticism.

Berlioz was born in La Côte-Saint-André on Dec. 11, 1803, and was originally educated in medicine in Paris. Abandoning medicine, he studied music from 1823 to 1825 at the Paris Conservatory under the French composer Jean François Le Sueur (1760–1837) and the Czech composer Anton Reicha (1770–1836). In 1830 he

Hector Berlioz

won the Prix de Rome. He became a librarian at the Paris Conservatory in 1838, toured the Continent and Great Britain several times as a conductor between 1842 and 1854, and from 1835 to 1863 wrote musical criticism for the periodical *Journal des Débats* ("Journal of Debates").

Berlioz's position in 19th-century music is that of a seminal figure, directly influencing symphonic form and the use of the orchestra as well as musical aesthetics; to many he exemplifies the Romantic image of the composer as artist. He labored ceaselessly to promote the new music of his time. Forced to train orchestras to meet the demands of this music, he educated a generation of musicians and became the first virtuoso conductor. His *Symphonie Fantastique* ("Fantastic Symphony", 1831) created an aesthetic revolution by its integral use of a literary program (inspired by his famous infatuation for the Irish actress Harriet Smithson) and established program music (q.v.) as a dominant Romantic orchestral genre. In this work and in his symphony with viola solo, *Harold en Italie* ("Harold in Italy", 1834), his use and transformation of a recurrent theme (the *idée fixe,* or fixed idea) foreshadowed the symphonic poem (q.v.) of the Hungarian composer Franz Liszt and the tone poem of the German composer Richard Strauss. The German composer Richard Wagner publicly acknowledged his debt to Berlioz. *See* ROMANTICISM.

Berlioz's profoundly influential *Traité d'instrumentation et d'orchestration modernes* ("Treatise on Modern Instrumentation and Orchestration", 1844), the first book on that subject, was an exposition of the aesthetics of musical expression as well as a handbook.

Berlioz's masterpiece is considered to be his monumental opera *Les Troyens* ("The Trojans", 1856–59), in which his Romanticism is infused with classical restraint. Other works include the symphony with chorus *Roméo et Juliette* ("Romeo and Juliet", 1836–38), the cantata *La Damnation de Faust* ("The Damnation of Faust", 1846), the requiem *Grande Messe des Morts* ("Requiem Mass", 1837), the oratorio *L'Enfance du Christ* ("The Childhood of Christ", 1850–54), and the overture *Le Carnaval romain* ("The Roman Carnival", 1844), an excerpt from his opera *Benvenuto Cellini* (1835–38). Important among his writings are his *Mémoires* (posthumously published in 1870) and *Soirées d'orchestre* ("Evenings with the Orchestra", 1853). Berlioz died in Paris on March 8, 1869. G.L.

BERMEJO, river of South America, rising in S.E. Bolivia and flowing through Argentina toward the Paraguay R., which it joins N. of Las Palmas, a short distance above the junction of the Paraguay and the Paraná rivers. The Bermejo is nearly 1300 mi. long, and it is navigable in its middle course, known as the Teuco, for more than half this distance for small steamers at all seasons, and for heavier craft during about six months of the year.

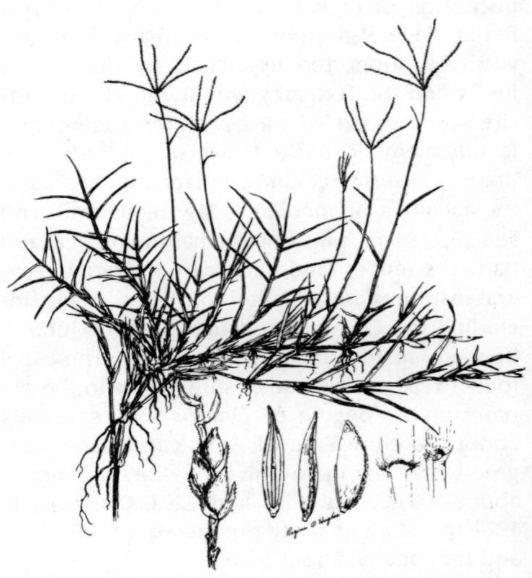

Bermuda grass, Cynodon dactylon

U.S. Dept. of Agriculture

An isolated beach on the southern shore of Great Bermuda Island. Picturesque scenery and a warm, sunny climate make the Bermudas a popular vacation resort.
UPI

BERMUDA GRASS common name for a perennial grass, *Cynodon dactylon,* in the Grass family (Gramineae), native to southern Europe and introduced throughout the warmer portions of the world. It is a low, creeping plant, rooting at the joints. In poor soils the leaves are short, and the plant sends up short flower stalks that divide into three to seven slender, divergent spikes. In good soil the grass is often 1 to 2 ft. high. The rootstocks grow rapidly, making a dense sod. Bermuda grass is resistant to heat and drought, and is valued in warm regions for grazing because it remains green after all other grasses are dry. It grows readily in sandy soil and is used in the southern United States as a lawn grass. Because it is hardy and grows readily in adverse conditions, it sometimes becomes a weed in fields of cultivated crops. *See* GRASSES.

BERMUDA ISLANDS *or* **BERMUDA** *or* **BERMUDAS,** island group in the North Atlantic Ocean, about 570 miles E. of Cape Hatteras, N.C., and 677 miles S.E. of New York City, constituting a dependency of Great Britain. The group consists of approximately 150 small islands, islets, and rocks, of which only 20 are inhabited and many are without names. Only six islands are of importance: Bermuda, called also Great Bermuda and Main Island, which is the largest (14 mi. in length), Somerset, Ireland, Saint George's, Saint Davids, and Boaz. The coral islands are enclosed on the N., W., and S. by reefs, which are mostly under water and which extend at some points 10 mi. from the islands, making navigation dangerous. The islands are separated from one another by narrow channels, but include several coral lagoons, or sounds, of which the most important are Harrington Sound and Castle Harbor. The highest point of land is 260 ft. above sea level. The total area of the islands is 20.59 sq.mi. Hamilton, on Bermuda Island, is the capital and chief town. Next in importance is Saint George, on Saint George's Island. The population of the islands in 1970 was about 52,700.

Lacking surface water and freshwater wells, the islands must depend on rainwater, which is collected from rooftops and stored in tanks, for water supply. The average rainfall is 58 in. per year. The climate is mild, the temperature averaging 63° F. in winter and 79° F. in summer. The ocean winds are tempered by the Gulf Stream, but when the south winds prevail there is much humidity and severe thunderstorms are frequent. Vegetation is luxuriant, and the small cultivated area of about 740 acres is very productive. Chief agricultural products are bananas, potatoes, onions, tomatoes, carrots, lily bulbs, and flowers (for the cut-flower market in the United States). The chief native growths are the

The "onion market", a Bernese tradition since the 15th century, is held yearly on the fourth Monday of November. Swiss National Tourist Office

Bermuda cedar, or juniper, bamboo, palm, and papaw. Hedges of oleander and thickets of mangrove are characteritistic features.

Economy. The picturesque scenery and the warm, sunny climate make the islands a popular resort for Americans. Tourism, ship repairing, and servicing the military bases on the islands are the major sources of employment. Pharmaceuticals, perfumes, flavoring extracts, mineral-water extracts, and essential oils are the most valuable exports. Food supplies form the major part of Bermudian imports. The United States, Great Britain, and Canada are the major trade partners. The islands are well equipped with telegraph, telephone, and postal facilities. Roads total 130 mi. Bermuda is serviced by several international airlines and shipping companies.

Government. Administration is based on a constitution adopted in 1968. The crown-appointed governor, responsible for external affairs, internal security, defense, and the police, is advised by an executive council on other matters. An appointed government leader heads the executive council. The legislature comprises an elected House of Assembly and an appointed legislative council. The currency is decimal and is based on the Bermuda dollar, at par with the U.S. dollar. Education is free and compulsory for children between the ages of five and sixteen.

History. The discovery of Bermuda is attributed to a Spanish navigator, Juan de Bermudez, who was shipwrecked there early in the 16th century. No settlement was established, however, until 1609, when a party of English colonists under the mariner Sir George Somers (1554–1610), sailing for Virginia, was also shipwrecked there. At first the islands were known as the Somers Islands, or Summer Islands. In 1612, Bermuda was included in the third charter of the Virginia Company, and a second group of English colonists arrived, but this charter was revoked in 1684 and Bermuda then became a crown colony. Shortly afterward the settlers imported Negro slaves and, later, Portuguese laborers from Madeira and the Azores. At the close of the American Civil War many colonists, particularly Virginians, immigrated from the U.S.; the islands also received Boer prisoners, sent by the British government during the South African War.

Because of the location the Bermuda Islands

are of considerable strategic importance. The group was formerly the winter naval station for both the British North Atlantic and West Indian squadrons; the West Indian squadron still maintains a station there. In 1941, during World War II, sites on the islands were leased to the U.S. for naval and air bases for ninety-nine years.

BERN *or* **BERNE,** city and capital of Switzerland, and capital of Bern Canton, about 59 miles S.W. of Zurich. It is situated on a lofty promontory surrounded on three sides by a bend of the Aare R. The old battlements of the city, converted into promenades, command a magnificent view of the surrounding Alpine scenery.

The bear is the heraldic emblem of Bern, and a bear pit, maintained since 1513, is one of the notable sights of the city. Principal public buildings are the houses of parliament; a Gothic cathedral, begun in 1421 and finished in 1611; and the town hall, dating from 1406. The University of Bern, founded in 1834, has departments of law, medicine, philosophy and science, and theology. Bern Library, which now includes the university library, contains many manuscripts and rare books. Bern has four museums, containing, respectively, collections of Swiss art and exhibitions dealing with history, natural history, and Alpine subjects.

The principal activities carried on in the city are governmental and administrative. Various international organizations, notably the International Postal Union, have headquarters there. Industrial activity is limited to the production of fine scientific instruments, textiles, machinery, and chocolates. Two great annual fairs are held at Bern, and it has a large horse and cattle market.

Bern was founded in 1191 and made a free imperial city in 1218. It joined the Swiss Confederation in 1353. The so-called Disputation of Bern between Catholics and Reformers in 1528 prepared the way for acceptance of the Reformed doctrine in Switzerland (*see* REFORMATION: *Switzerland*). The invasion of Switzerland in 1798 by the French revolutionary army overthrew the aristocratic regime, and during the 19th century the power of the church was limited, the constitution liberalized, and the principle of the referendum adopted. In 1885–86, Bern was the site of a conference held to formulate an international agreement on copyrights. The agreements, as well as the meeting itself, are known as the Bern Convention (*see* COPYRIGHT). Pop. (1970) 162,400.

BERN, Dietrich von. *See* THEODORIC.

BERNADETTE OF LOURDES, Saint, real name BERNADETTE SOUBIROUS (1844–79), French peasant girl, born in Lourdes. At the age of fourteen she claimed that she had experienced numerous visions of the Virgin Mary and that the Virgin had imparted miraculous powers of healing to the waters of a spring near a grotto in Lourdes (q.v.). The visions were declared authentic by the Roman Catholic Church, and the Lourdes grotto became a shrine for pilgrims. In 1866 Bernadette joined the Sisters of Charity, a group of women bound by annual vows to religious and charitable work. In 1877 she became a nun. She was beatified in 1925 and canonized in 1933. Her feast day is April 16.

BERNADOTTE, Folke, Count of Wisburg. *See* ISRAEL: *History;* UNITED NATIONS, THE: *The Role of the United Nations in Crisis Situations: Middle East.*

BERNADOTTE, Jean Baptiste Jules. *See* CHARLES XIV JOHN.

BERNARD, Claude (1813–78), French physiologist, born in Saint-Julien. He studied medicine at the Collège de France, and worked there under the French physiologist François Magendie (1783–1855), whom he succeeded as professor of experimental physiology in 1855. In 1854 he accepted the new chair of physiology at the Sorbonne, but relinquished the post in 1868 to accept a professorship at the Jardin des Plantes.

Bernard is regarded as the founder of experimental medicine. His specific discoveries in physiology include the function of the pancreas and its importance in the digestion of fats; the importance of the liver in the transformation, storage, and use of sugar in the body; and the existence of the vasomotor function and many other activities of the sympathetic nervous system. For these three discoveries he received the grand prize in physiology, in 1849, 1851, and 1853, from the French Academy of Sciences of which he became a member in 1854. Bernard was one of the great synthesizers and philosophers of science, making physiology a rational study. He wrote many books in his field.

BERNARDIN DE SAINT-PIERRE, Jacques Henri (1737–1814), French writer, born in Le Havre and educated by the Jesuits. After a period of travel followed by work as an engineer, he held a government post in Île de France (now Mauritius) from 1768 to 1771. On his return to France he became a friend and disciple of the French philosopher Jean Jacques Rousseau (q.v.); his writing was strongly influenced by Rousseau's concepts. Saint-Pierre's works reveal imagination, sentiment, and love of nature, as opposed to the emphasis on wit and external form that characterized most of the French literature of his time. His work foreshadowed the

Romantic movement in French literature (*see* ROMANTICISM). In 1795 Saint-Pierre was elected to the French Academy. He wrote *Voyage à l'Île de France* (1773; Eng. trans., *A Voyage to the Island of Mauritius,* 1775); *Paul et Virginie* (1788; Eng. trans., *Paul and Virginia,* 1789), part of the larger work, *Études de la Nature* ("Studies of Nature", 1784–88) and generally regarded as his masterpiece; and *Harmonies de la Nature* (1796; Eng. trans., *Harmonies of Nature,* 1815).

BERNARDINES. *See* CISTERCIANS.

BERNARDINO OF SIENA, Saint (1380–1444), Italian Franciscan monk, born in Massa Marittima. In 1402 he was made a member of the Franciscan Order and subsequently preached throughout Italy. He was the principal leader of the movement to restore the strict rule of Saint Francis of Assisi (q.v.) to the Franciscans (q.v.). Adherents to this rule, called Observants, greatly increased as a result of Bernardino's efforts. He was canonized in 1450, and his feast day is May 20.

BERNARD OF CLAIRVAUX, Saint (1090–1153), French ecclesiastic, born near Dijon. In 1113 he became a monk in the Cistercian (q.v.) monastery of Cîteaux, a small village south of Dijon, and in 1115 became abbot of a monastery at Clairvaux, north of Dijon. Under his rule the monastery at Clairvaux became the most prominent of the Cistercian order. Reputed miracles and the eloquent preaching of Bernard attracted numerous pilgrims. Between 1130 and 1145 more than ninety monasteries were founded under the auspices of the one at Clairvaux and Bernard's influence in the Catholic Church spread throughout the world. He is reputed to have established the rule of the order of Knights Templars (q.v.) and in 1128 obtained recognition of the order from the Church. In the contest between Pope Innocennt II (d. 1143) and Antipope Anacletus II (1130–38) for the papacy, Bernard was instrumental in the victory of Innocent. In 1146, at the command of the pope, Bernard began his preaching of the Second Crusade; *see* CRUSADES: *Second Crusade.* His sermon at Vézelay aroused enthusiasm throughout France; Louis VII (q.v.), King of France, was persuaded to join the crusade, and subsequently Bernard gained recruits from northern France, Flanders, and Germany. Its failure was a great blow to him. He was canonized in 1174 and named doctor of the Church in 1830. His feast day is Aug. 20.

Bernard was an uncompromising opponent of heresies and of rationalistic theology, such as that of the French philosopher and theologian Peter Abelard (q.v.). He wrote many sermons, letters, and hymns, some of the hymns are still sung in both Roman Catholic and Protestant churches. Important among his works are *De Diligendo Deo* ("The Love of God", about 1127) and *De Consideratione* ("Consideration to Eugene III", about 1148).

BERNARD OF MENTHON, Saint (923–1008), French priest, born in Menthon (now Menthon-Saint-Bernard) Savoie. He is also known as Bernard of Montjoux. As archdeacon of Aosta, in the Italian Alps, he spent most of his life spreading Christianity among the people of the Alpine regions. About 962 he founded hospices (rest houses for travelers) of the Augustinian Order (*see* AUGUSTINIANS) at the Great Saint Bernard Pass in the Alps between Switzerland and Italy, and at the Little Saint Bernard Pass between

Sarah Bernhardt in the role of Lady Macbeth in 1884.
Bettmann Archive

France and Italy (*see* SAINT BERNARD). He was canonized in 1681 and his feast day is May 28. He is the patron saint of mountaineers.

BERNE. *See* BERN.

BERNHARDI, Friedrich von (1849–1930), German military leader and writer, born in Saint Petersburg (now Leningrad, U.S.S.R.). He served in the Franco-German War, and from 1891 to 1894 was stationed in Bern, Switzerland, as military attaché; later he went to Berlin as head of the history department of the Grand General Staff. Bernhardi was general of cavalry and an army corps commander from 1907 to 1909, retiring then to write on military subjects. His *Deutschland und der Nächste Krieg* (1912; Eng. trans., *Germany and the Next War,* 1912) attracted international attention because in it he contended that his country could acquire its place in the sun by waging ruthless war. At the outbreak of World War I he was again given an army command and served with distinction. He also wrote *Deutschlands Heldenkampf 1914–1918* ("Germany's Heroic Struggle, 1914–1918", 1921).

BERNHARDT, Sarah, original name ROSINE BERNARD (1844–1923), French dramatic actress, born in Paris, and reared in a convent. She entered the dramatic school of the Paris Conservatory in 1858, and in 1862 made her debut as the Greek tragic heroine Iphigénie at the Comédie Française. She attracted so little notice that she soon left that company. She appeared for a short time in burlesque (q.v.), but she was also unsuccessful. In 1867 she played minor parts at the Théâtre de l' Odéon, Paris, gaining recognition by her portrayals of the queen of Spain in *Ruy Blas,* by the French writer Victor Marie Hugo (q.v.), and of Zanetto in *Le Passant,* by the French dramatist François Édouard Joachim Coppée (q.v.). She was recalled to the Comédie Française in 1872. After 1879 she appeared annually, with great success, in London, notably in *Adrienne Lecouvreur* and *Frou-Frou.* She made successful tours in North and South America, adding *La Dame aux Camélias* to her repertory, and in Italy, Russia, and other countries, becoming the best-known actress of her time.

With her appearance in *Fédora* by the French dramatist Victorien Sardou (q.v.), she began her long association with that author, who wrote for her *Théodora, La Tosca,* and, in collaboration with the French dramatist Émile Moreau (1852–1922), *Cléopâtre.* She visited the United States and Canada in 1886–87 and 1888–89, and toured the world between 1891 and 1893. On her return to Paris she became owner of the Théâtre de la Renaissance, and several years later leased the Théâtre des Nations (renamed Théâtre Sarah Bernhardt), appearing in leading roles in *L'Aiglon* by the French dramatist Edmond Rostand (q.v.) and a French version of *Hamlet* by William Shakespeare (q.v.).

Although she suffered the amputation of a leg at the age of seventy, she refused to abandon the stage. During World War I she played before audiences of soldiers close to the lines of battle and in the U.S. and Great Britain. She continued to produce plays and to act almost continuously until her death. In addition to her extraordinary dramatic gifts she showed talent in sculpture, painting, and writing and is the author of two plays and a volume of memoirs (1907). She was made a member of the Legion of Honor in 1914.

BERNICE. *See* BERENICE.

BERNINI, Giovanni Lorenzo (1598–1680), Italian sculptor, architect, and painter, born in Naples. He began sculpting at the age of eight and when he was eighteen finished his celebrated group, "Apollo and Daphne". Pope Urban VIII (*see under* URBAN) employed him to produce designs for the embellishment of Saint Peter's at Rome, and Bernini's greatest achievement in architecture is the colossal colonnade of the church. In 1663 he accepted an invitation from Louis XIV (q.v.), King of France, and traveled to

"The Ecstasy of Saint Teresa", a dramatically effective sculpture in which Bernini combined colored marble with bronze and stucco. Alinari

Paris, but his design for the Louvre was considered inferior to that of the French architect Claude Perrault (1613–88), and he confined himself thereafter entirely to sculpture. For fifty years Bernini dictated the artistic taste and achievements of the papacy, and his conceptions dominated the sculpture of Europe for a century.

BERNOULLI, name of a family, originally of Antwerp, Belgium, and later of Basel, Switzerland, distinguished in mathematics and physics.

Jakob Bernoulli *or* **Jacques Bernoulli** (1654–1705), mathematician, born in Basel, where he became professor at the university. He and his brother Johann were among the first to understand and use the new method of the German mathematician Baron Gottfried Wilhelm von Leibniz (q.v.). One of a famous group of problem solvers, he solved Leibniz' problem of the isochronous curve and discovered Bernoulli's numbers; *see* CALCULUS: *History of Calculus.*

Johann Bernoulli *or* **Jean Bernoulli** (1667–1748), born in Basel, brother of Jakob Bernoulli, whom he succeeded as professor of mathematics at the University of Basel. He was unrivaled in mathematics in Europe during his time. He proposed the problem of the minimum line between two points on a given surface, and was a pioneer in the work of constructing an exponential and an integral calculus (*see* CALCULUS).

Daniel Bernoulli (1700–82), son of Johann Bernoulli, born in Groningen, Holland. He became professor of mathematics at the Russian Academy in Saint Petersburg (now Leningrad) and later taught experimental philosophy and anatomy and botany at the universities of Groningen and Basel. He is credited with developing the first kinetic theory (q.v.) of gases, and formulating the basic energy relation for the flow of liquids (*see* BERNOULLI'S PRINCIPLE).

BERNOULLI'S PRINCIPLE, in physics, the interrelation between pressure, velocity, and gravitational effects in moving fluids. Originally formulated in 1738 by the Swiss mathematician and physicist Daniel Bernoulli (*see under* BERNOULLI), it states that for the steady flow of a frictionless and incompressible fluid, the total energy (consisting of the sum of the kinetic energy due to the velocity, the potential energy due to elevation in a gravitational field, and the pressure energy given by the pressure divided by the density) is a constant along the flow path. An increase in velocity at constant elevation must therefore be matched by a decrease in pressure. This concept is used in nozzles, where the flow is accelerated as the tube diameter is reduced and the pressure drops. It also applies to orifice or venturi flow meters, where measurements of the pressure difference between the low-speed fluid in the approach pipe and the high-speed fluid at the smaller orifice diameter are used to determine flow velocities and thus to meter the flow rate.

The principle also covers the flow over surfaces such as aircraft wings or ship's propellers. A wing is designed to permit air to flow more rapidly over its upper surface than its lower surface, with a consequently reduced pressure on the top surface as compared to the bottom surface. The resulting pressure difference provides the lift that sustains the plane in flight; *see* FLIGHT, THEORY OF. On a rotating propeller, which is also shaped like an airfoil, the corresponding pressure difference provides the thrust that propels the vessel. The curved motion of a spinning baseball or table-tennis ball can also be explained with the help of Bernoulli's principle. Because of the rotation, an additional velocity component is induced in the direction of rotation, which makes the total velocity around the ball higher on one side than on the other. This leads to a pressure difference causing the ball to drift in the direction of the lower pressure.

F.La.

BERNSTEIN, Eduard (1850–1932), German Social Democratic leader and writer, born in Berlin, and educated at Berlin University. In 1872 he joined the Social Democratic Party and from 1881 to 1890 he and the Social Democratic leader (Ferdinand) August Bebel (q.v.) jointly edited the newspaper *Sozialdemokrat* (*Social Democrat*). While living in voluntary exile in London from 1888 to 1901, Bernstein became acquainted with the German coauthor of the *Communist Manifesto,* Friedrich Engels, and studied the theories developed by Engels and the German revolutionist Karl Marx (qq.v.) dealing with the nature of capitalist society and the establishment of socialism; *see* COMMUNISM: *Modern Revolutionary Communism.* Bernstein rejected the arguments by Marx and Engels for the violent overthrow of capitalism; instead, he developed his own theory, known as revisionism, emphasizing evolutionary rather than revolutionary methods to bring about a socialist society; *see* SOCIALISM. In 1901, soon after his return to Germany, he was elected to the Reichstag, of which he was a member from 1902 to 1906, 1912 to 1918, and 1920 to 1928. His book, *Evolutionary Socialism* (1898; Eng. trans., 1909), presents his criticisms of the Marxist system.

BERNSTEIN, Leonard (1918–), American composer, conductor, and pianist, born in Lawrence, Mass., educated at Harvard University and Curtis Institute of Music, Philadelphia, Pa. He studied orchestral conducting under the Hungarian musician Fritz Reiner (1888–1963) and the Russian-American conductor Serge Koussevitzky (q.v.). In 1943 he made his debut, at the age of twenty-three, leading the New York Philharmonic Society Orchestra in place of the indisposed American conductor Bruno Walter (q.v.). Bernstein was, successively, music director of the New York City Symphony (1945–48), member of the faculty of the Berkshire Music Center (1948–55; *see* BERKSHIRE FESTIVAL), professor of music at Brandeis University (1951–56), and director of the New York Philharmonic Symphony orchestra (1957–69). He was also guest conductor for many other leading orchestras, and he made several European tours. Later he served as laureate conductor of the New York Philharmonic.

His eclectic and passionate compositions were created in an astonishing variety of forms; they range from three full-scale symphonies to the musicals *On the Town* (1944), *Wonderful Town* (1953), and *West Side Story* (1957). He also composed the operetta *Candide* (1956); the opera *Trouble in Tahiti* (1952); *Chichester Psalms* (1965) for chorus and orchestra; and the ballets *Fancy Free* (1944) and *The Dybbuk Variations* (1974). His *Mass* (1971), for singers, dancers, and players, was first performed at the opening of the John F. Kennedy Center for the Performing Arts, which is located in Washington, D.C.

Bernstein is the author of the books *The Joy of Music* (1959); *Young People's Concerts for Reading and Listening* (text and records, 1962), adapted from his television show of the same name; and *The Infinite Variety of Music* (1966).

BERNSTORFF, Johann-Heinrich, Count von (1862–1939), German diplomat, born in London, England, where his father was Prussian ambassador. Bernstorff entered the German diplomatic service in 1889, and in the same year was appointed attaché at the German embassy in Constantinople (now İstanbul), Turkey. From 1902 to 1906 he served as councilor to the German embassy in London, and from 1906 to 1907 was the German consul general at Cairo, Egypt (now United Arab Republic). In 1908 Bernstorff was appointed German ambassador to the United States; he held this post during World War I, attempting without success to strengthen German-American relations, until 1917, when relations were severed. He then served as ambassador to Turkey (1917–18) and as a member of the German Reichstag (1921–28). After the war Bernstorff became known as an advocate of world peace; he was a delegate to the League of Nations (q.v.), chairman of the educational organization called the German League of Nations Union, and a delegate to international disarmament conferences. In 1933, after the rise to power of the German dictator Adolf Hitler (q.v.), he went into exile in Switzerland. His writings include *My Three Years in America* (1920) and *Memoirs of Count Bernstorff* (1936).

BERRUGUETE, Alonso (1486?–1561), Spanish sculptor, painter, and architect, born in Paredes de Nava. He studied first under his father, the distinguished painter Pedro Berruguete (about 1483–about 1504) and after 1504 in Florence under the Italian artist Michelangelo (q.v.). After his return in 1520 to Spain, he established himself as the pioneer of the High Renaissance in his native country. In 1523 Charles V (q.v.), Holy Roman Emperor, bestowed upon him a judicial sinecure and named him court sculptor and painter, as well as court chamberlain.

Berruguete's most celebrated work is the thirty-five choir stalls (1539–1548) that he made for the Cathedral of Toledo. The backs of the stalls are adorned with wooden reliefs depicting events in the Old and New Testaments, and above the cornice are alabaster figures of the patriarchs, prophets, and saints. His other works include the retable (1529–31) of the Colegio Mayor de Santiago in Salamanca, with eight large pictures from the life of Christ, and the alabaster altar of the Holy Trinity (1538) in the Cathedral of Jaca. His final project, usually considered one of his best works, is the tomb of Cardinal Tavera in Toledo.

Berruguete was considered by his contemporaries to be the outstanding artist of Spain. Many important paintings, sculptures, and edifices have been ascribed incorrectly to him. His talents found their best expression in sculpture, and he was one of the foremost practitioners of that art in Renaissance Spain. The only authentic examples of his paintings are preserved in Salamanca and Valladolid. Berruguete's activity as an architect was confined to retables, portals, and similar decorative features.

BERRY. *See* FRUIT: *Types of Fruit.*

BERRY, Martha McChesney (1866–1942), American educator, born near Rome, Ga., and educated in private schools. In 1902 she opened a school in a log cabin, and began to teach children of the back-country regions of the Georgia mountains. As a result of her success, she established at Mount Berry, Ga., the Berry Schools for Mountain Children, which she maintained for the rest of her life.

Pierre Eugène Berthelot working in his laboratory.
Bettmann Archive

BERTHELOT, Pierre Eugène Marcelin (1827–1907), French chemist and public official, born in Paris, and educated at the Collège de France. He received his doctorate there in 1854, presenting a remarkable thesis that established the structure and synthesis of fats, the constitution of glycerin, and the nature of polyhydric alcohols. In 1856 he synthesized methane, the first of the hydrocarbons to be prepared in the laboratory from its elements. He contributed to the knowledge of almost every class of organic chemical compounds, and in particular did important work on explosives and dyes, and on the heat produced by chemical reactions. He became professor at the École Supérieure de Pharmacie in 1859 and at the Collège de France in 1865. He was elected a member of the French Academy of Sciences in 1873 and succeeded the French chemist Louis Pasteur (q.v.) as perpetual secretary in 1889. Berthelot was made inspector general of public education in 1876; was elected senator for life in 1881; was minister of public instruction in 1886–87; and was minister of foreign affairs in 1895–96). Among his works are *Les Origines de l'Alchemie* ("The Origins of Alchemy", 1885), *Traité Pratique de Calorimétrie Chimique* ("Practical Treatise on Chemical Calorimetry", 1893) and *Recherches Expérimentales* ("Experimental Inquiries", 1901).

BERTHIER, Louis Alexandre (1753–1815), French military leader, born in Versailles. He fought under the French military leader the Marquis de Lafayette (q.v.) in the American Revolution. At the outbreak of the French Revolution, Berthier was appointed major general of the National Guard of Versailles and rose to be a general of division and chief of staff in the French Army of Italy. He was chief of staff to the French soldier and statesman Napoleon Bonaparte (*see* NAPOLEON I) in the Egyptian campaign and was minister of war from 1799 to 1808. Berthier became marshal of France in 1804 and in 1809 was made prince of Wagram for his part in the battle of that name. Until 1814 he was constantly with Napoleon, superintending the movements of the French armies. When Napoleon began to suffer defeats, Berthier's loyalty wavered. After Napoleon's surrender at Neuchâtel Berthier made his peace with Louis XVIII (q.v.), King of France. On Napoleon's return from Elba, Berthier retired to Bavaria. According to one story, he committed suicide; according to another, he was murdered by members of a secret society.

BERTHOLLET, Comte Claude Louis (1748–1822), French chemist, born in Talloires, and educated at the University of Turin. In 1780 he became a member of the French Academy of Sciences, and in 1794 professor at the École Normale in Paris. In 1798 he was one of the scholars who accompanied the French soldier and statesman Napoleon Bonaparte (*see* NAPOLEON I) to Egypt and there formed an institute on the pattern of the Institut National in France. Napoleon made him a senator in 1804, later a grand officer of the Légion d'Honneur, and under the empire a count; nonetheless, he voted for Napoleon's deposition in 1814. Louis XVIII (q.v.), King of France, made Berthollet a peer.

In 1784 Berthollet became superintendent of dyeing processes for the French government and in 1785 proposed the use of chlorine as a bleaching agent. He was one of the original adherents of the antiphlogistic theory (*see* PHLOGISTON) of the French chemist Antoine Laurent Lavoisier (q.v.), although he opposed Lavoisier's erroneous theory that oxygen is the fundamental acidifying principle. In 1787, with Lavoisier and others, Berthollet devised a new system of chemical nomenclature that is the basis of the system currently used. He made important contributions to the knowledge of the chemistry of explosives (q.v.) and the metallurgy (q.v.) of iron. He also formulated important generalizations concerning chemical equilibrium, stressing the importance of the relative masses of the reactive substances; this concept was put forth in his most significant work, *Essai de Statique Chimique* ("Essay on the State of Chemistry", 2 vol., 1803).

BERTILLON, Alphonse (1853–1914), French anthropologist and criminologist, born in Paris, and privately educated. He became head of the identification department of the Prefecture of Police of the Seine, in Paris, and in 1879 he devised a system for identifying criminals (*see* BERTILLON SYSTEM). He was made a chevalier of the Legion of Honor. His writings include *Identification Anthropométrique* ("Anthropometric Identification", 1893) and *La Comparaison des Écritures et l'Identification Graphique* ("The Comparison of Handwriting and Graphic Identification", 1897).

BERTILLON SYSTEM, scientific method for identification of people, and especially identification of criminals, devised in 1879 by the French criminologist Alphonse Bertillon (q.v.). The system records anthropometric measurements and personal characteristcs, such as color of eyes, scars, and deformities. The following measurements are taken: (1) *body:* (*a*) height standing, (*b*) reach from finger tips to finger tips, (*c*) trunk and head or height sitting; (2) *head:* (*a*) length and width, (*b*) length and width of right ear; (3) *limbs:* (*a*) length of left foot, (*b*) left middle finger, (*c*) left little finger, (*d*) left forearm. These measurements are recorded on cards and classified according to the length of the head.

Bertillon measurements are difficult to take with uniform exactness, and physical dimensions are liable to change as a result of growth or surgery. For these reasons fingerprinting (q.v.) and other methods have for the most part superseded the Bertillon system as the principal means of identification in American and European police systems.

BERWICK, borough of Pennsylvania, in Columbia Co., on the Susquehanna R., about 15 miles N.E. of Hazelton. The city produces silk and manufactures railroad cars and clothing. Pop. (1960) 13,353; (1970) 12,274.

BERWICK, Great Britain, county in Scotland, bounded on the N. by East Lothian, on the E. by the North Sea, on the S. by Northumberland, in England, and Roxburgh, and on the W. by Midlothian. Physiographically the county may be divided into three districts: Lammermuir Hills, the highlands in the N.; Lauderdale, a hilly region in the W.; and the Merse valley in the S.E. The county is drained mainly by the Tweed R. The main occupations are agriculture and sheep raising. Duns, the county town, and Coldstream are the main agricultural markets. The chief industries are the woolen mills in Earlston and the paper mills in Ayton. Berwick was part of Northumbria (q.v.), the Anglo-Saxon kingdom. For several centuries the county was the site of border warfare between England and Scotland. Area, 457 sq.mi.; pop. (1971) 20,779.

BERWICK, Duke of, James Fitzjames (1670–1734), illegitimate son of the duke of York, who became James II (q.v.), King of England, born in Moulins, France, and educated in France. He received the title duke of Berwick in 1687. In 1689 he accompanied his father on the Irish expedition, undertaken to regain the English throne; *see* ENGLAND: *History: The Glorious Revolution.* Berwick also served in various campaigns on the Continent. In 1702 he became a French subject and in 1706 was made a marshal of France. He commanded a French army in Spain and there secured the throne for Philip V (q.v.), King of Spain, by the victory of Almansa in 1707; *see* SPANISH SUCCESSION, WAR OF THE. For this service Berwick was made a French peer by Louis XIV (q.v.), King of France, and duke of Liria and Xerica by King Philip V of Spain. In 1733 he commanded a French army intended to cross the Rhine R. during the War of the Polish Succession (*see* SUCCESSION WARS) and was killed at the siege of Phillippsburg, in Germany. Berwick is considered one of the greatest military strategists of his time.

BERWICK-UPON-TWEED, Great Britain, seaport and municipal borough of England, in Northumberland, at the mouth of the Tweed R., near the border with Scotland, about 380 miles N.W. of London. The principal occupations are coal mining, fishing, and shipbuilding. Among the notable structures are the town hall and church, which date from 1757, and the Royal Border Bridge, built in 1847. The town was involved in border disputes between England and Scotland from 1147 until 1482, at which time King Edward IV (q.v.) claimed Berwick-upon-Tweed for England. The town was incorporated into Northumberland in 1885. Area, 8 sq.mi. Pop. (1971 prelim.) 11,644.

BERWYN, city of Illinois, in Cook Co., on the outskirts of Chicago and about 9 mi. from Lake Michigan. It is a residential suburb of Chicago. Berwyn was founded in 1890 and was chartered as a city in 1908. Pop. (1960) 54,224; (1970) 52,502.

BERYA, Lavrenti Pavlovich *or* **BERIYA, Lavrenti Pavlovicki** *or* **BERIA, Lavrenti Pavlovich** (1899–1953), Soviet public official, born in Tbilisi (now Georgian S.S.R.). He joined the Bolshevik wing (*see* BOLSHEVISM) of the Social Democratic

Party in 1917 and participated in the Russian Revolution (q.v.), chiefly as an underground soldier in the Caucasus. Subsequently he served in the Cheka (q.v.) and became a high official of the Communist Party in the Caucasian region. Berya was called to Moscow in 1938 and appointed head of the Commissariat for Internal Affairs (N.K.V.D.), known after 1946 as the Ministry for Internal Affairs (M.V.D.); in this capacity he controlled the secret-police organization (*see* G.P.U.). He was a deputy premier after 1941, and in 1946 he became a member of the Politburo, the highest body of the Communist Party of the U.S.S.R. After changes in party organization in 1952 he was chosen a member of the newly created Presidium, which assumed the functions of the Politburo and other top party committees. Another reorganization of leading organs of the party and government occurred in March, 1953, following the death of Premier Joseph Stalin (q.v.). Berya emerged as second in command to Stalin's successor Georgi Maximilianovich Malenkov (q.v.), in the Soviet hierarchy. A power struggle ensued, and in July, 1953, Berya was arrested on charges of criminal and antistate activities. On Dec. 24 the Soviet government announced that he and six accomplices had been convicted of high treason and executed.

BERYL, common mineral and, in certain color modifications, a valuable gem material. It has hardness about 8 and sp.gr. about 2.8. Chemically it consists of aluminum beryllium silicate, and it is the chief commercial ore of beryllium (q.v.). Pure beryl is colorless and transparent. Emerald (q.v.), one of the most valuable of gems, is a variety that is colored green by minute amounts of chromium. Aquamarine (q.v.), also a gem stone, is a blue beryl, more common than emerald. Golden beryl and morganite or rose beryl are less valuable. Colorless beryl is occasionally used as a gem under the name goshenite. Beryl has a vitreous luster with little fire or brilliancy, and so its value depends principally on hardness, transparency, and color.

Beryl crystallizes in the hexgonal system, and crystals weighing over a ton are not uncommon. Crystals of that size, however, are invariably opaque and imperfect, and therefore valueless as gem material. Large, transparent crystals of the colored varieties are occasionally found.

BERYLLIUM, also called GLUCINIUM, element with at.no. 4, at.wt. 9.013, b.p. about 2500° C. (4532° F.) m.p. 1283° C. (2341.4° F.), sp.gr. $1.85^{20°}$, and symbol Be. Beryllium was named for its chief mineral, beryl (q.v.), an aluminum beryllium silicate.

Properties. Beryllium is a gray metal, more brittle than magnesium and aluminum which it resembles in appearance and chemical behavior. Beryllium is not as common as either aluminum or magnesium, but it is far more common than silver. The element has a high strength per unit weight. It was discovered as an oxide in 1798 by the French chemist Louis Nicolas Vauquelin (1763–1829), and the free element was first isolated in 1828 independently by Friedrich Wöhler (q.v.) and Antoine Alexandre Brutus Bussy (1794–1882). This important oxide is today known by the name beryllia.

Beryllium tarnishes only slightly in air, becoming covered with a thin layer of oxide. The ability of beryllium to scratch glass is usually ascribed to this oxide coating. Beryllium compounds are generally white (or colorless in solution) and show great similarity in chemical properties to the corresponding compounds of aluminum. This similarity makes it difficult to separate beryllium from the aluminum which is almost always present in beryllium ores.

Uses. The addition of beryllium to some alloys often results in products of high heat resistance, improved corrosion resistance, greater hardness, high insulating properties, and better casting qualities. Many parts of supersonic aircraft are made of beryllium alloys because of their lightness, stiffness, and dimensional stability. Other applications make use of the nonmagnetic and nonsparking qualities of beryllium or the ability of the metal to conduct electricity. Beryllium has important use in so-called multiplexing systems. In miniature, high-purity components made with beryllium, a single wire can carry hundreds of electronic signals. This advance has saved aircraft miles of cable.

Because its heat of oxidation is relatively high, 5.8 kilocalories per gram of oxide formed, beryllium is used in solid rocket propellants to increase total thrust of the rocket. Beryllium and its oxide, beryllia, are also used as a moderator, or so-called blanket, around the core of a nuclear reactor because of the tendency of the beryllium to capture neutrons. Beryllia is almost immune to nuclear radiation.

Although beryllium products are safe to use and handle, the fumes and dust released during fabrication are dangerous. Extreme care must be taken to avoid breathing or ingesting them. In working areas the total amount of beryllium dust should be kept below 1 gram per 1,000,000 cubic meters of air. Specially designed hoods are worn by personnel working with beryllium oxide.

Beryllium and its oxide are increasingly uti-

An emerald crystal, the green variety of beryl, surrounded by the matrix, or material in which it occurs in nature. Katherine H. Jensen

lized in industry. Besides its importance in aircraft and missiles, beryllium is used in computers, lasers, television, oceanographic instruments, and personal body armor.

BERZELIUS, Baron Jöns Jakob (1779–1848), Swedish chemist, born near Linköping. While studying medicine at the University of Uppsala, he became interested in chemistry. After practicing medicine and lecturing, he became a professor of botany and pharmacy at Stockholm in 1807. From 1815 to 1832 he was professor of chemistry at the Caroline Medico-Chirurgical Institute in Stockholm. He became a member of the Stockholm Academy of Sciences in 1808 and in 1818 became its permanent secretary. For his contributions to science, Berzelius was made a baron in 1835 by Charles XIV John (q.v.), King of Sweden and Norway.

Berzelius is considered the founder and organizer of modern chemistry. His research extended into every branch of chemistry and was extraordinary for its scope and accuracy. He discovered three chemical elements, cerium, selenium, and thorium (qq.v.), and was the first to prepare several others in pure form. He introduced the term catalyst into chemistry and was the first to elaborate upon the nature and importance of catalysis (q.v.). He introduced the present system of chemical formulation; this system uses one- or two-letter abbreviations for each element, yielding symbols such as the familiar H_2O for water. Berzelius was primarily responsible for the theory of radicals, which states that a group of atoms, such as the sulfate group, can act as an entity through a series of chemical reactions. He developed an elaborate electrochemical theory that, though greatly modified, was of fundamental importance in the development of concepts of chemical affinity. All of his theoretical work was supported by elaborate experimental measurement. His greatest achievement was the measurement of atomic weights.

BESANÇON, city in France, and capital of Doubs Department, on both sides of the Doubs R., about 50 miles E. of Dijon. The city is within a livestock-raising and agricultural region. Besançon is an industrial city noted especially for the production of clocks and watches. Other manufactures include foodstuffs, pottery, and textiles. Besançon is the seat of the University of Besançon, located in the city since 1691. In the area are ruins of a triumphal arch of the Roman emperor Marcus Aurelius (q.v.), an aqueduct, and an amphitheater. Later structures include a cathedral, parts of which date from the 12th century, and several buildings in the Spanish Renaissance style. The city is the birthplace of the French writer Victor Marie Hugo (q.v.). Besançon was a Roman military post. The city was incorporated into the historic French kingdom of Franche-Comté in the Middle Ages. Under Frederick I (q.v.), Holy Roman Emperor, Besançon was made a free city in 1184. In 1648 the city came under Spanish rule. Louis XIV (q.v.), King of France, incorporated Besançon into France in 1674. Pop. (1968) 119,471.

BESANT, Annie (1847–1933), British theosophist and nationalist leader in India, born in London, England, and privately educated. She early became interested in socialistic and freethought movements, and wrote pamphlets defending them. She became closely associated with the British social reformer Charles Bradlaugh (1833–91) and later with the Fabians (*see* FABIAN SOCIETY). She and Bradlaugh republished an old pamphlet, *The Fruits of Philosophy,* which advocated birth control, and for which they were brought to trial on a charge of obscenity. In 1889 she joined the Theosophical Society, serving as president from 1907 until her death. Shortly after joining the society she went to India, where she later became a leader of a Hindu nationalist movement. She founded Central Hindu College at Varanasi (1898) and organized the Indian Home Rule League, becoming president in 1916. She was elected president of the Indian National Congress in 1917, and general secretary of the National Convention of India in 1923. She lectured frequently on theosophy (q.v.) and in 1926 traveled widely with her Indian protégé Jiddu Krishnamurti (1897?–), whom she declared to be the new Messiah. Her works include *Reincarnation* (1892), *The Basis of Morality* (1915), *A World Religion* (1916), and *India, Bond or Free?* (1926).

BEŞIKTAŞ, city in Turkey, and residential section of İstanbul, N.E. of the city center, on the Bosporus. Once the Byzantine village of Diplokionion, it is now a cultural quarter of İstanbul. It is the site of the Dolmabahçe Palace and Museum (1854), the Yildiz Park and Palace (1844), the Çirağan Palace (1874), the Tanzimat and Naval museums, and Sinan Pasha Mosque, as well as a monument to Barbarossa (Khair ēd-Din, 1466?–1546, a Barbary pirate in the service of the sultan). A ferry crosses the Bosporus between Beşiktaş, in European Turkey, and Üsküdar, in Asian Turkey.

BESSARABIA, region of the Soviet Union, about 18,000 sq.mi. in area, between the Prut and Dniester rivers. It is roughly wedge shaped, with its base on the Black Sea, and extending in a N.W. direction about 300 mi. The land is flat and fertile, except for the N.W. corner, which is hilly and well forested, and the coastal strip, where sand and salt marshes predominate. The principal occupations are farming and the raising of horses, cattle, and other farm animals. Among agricultural products are grains, fruits, tobacco, and flax; leather goods and soap are manufactured.

History. Bessarabia has been fought over for many centuries. In ancient times it was occupied by many peoples, including the Romans, who made it part of the province of Dacia. From the 2nd century A.D.., it was invaded by Germanic and Asian tribes, including Goths, Bulgars, and finally, in the 13th century, Mongols. The territory was conquered and annexed by Moldavia in 1367. Throughout the 16th century, Bessarabia was ruled alternately by the Tatars and the Ottoman Turks and from 1700 to 1812 by the Russians and the Ottoman Turks. In 1812, by the terms of the Treaty of Bucharest, it became part of the Russian empire, in which it remained, with minor exchanges of territory, until it declared its independence during the Russian Revolution of 1917. In 1918 the ruling council approved union with Rumania, of which it became a province. The Soviet Union refused to recognize Rumanian control, and in June, 1940, forced Rumania to return the region. The S.E. part along the Black Sea coast and a small portion in the N.W. were then added to the Ukrainian S.S.R., and the remainder, together with a part of the Ukraine, was constituted as the Moldavian S.S.R. Rumanian and German troops occupied Bessarabia in June, 1941, when the Axis powers (q.v.) attacked the Soviet Union, and held the region for three years. When an armistice was signed between the U.S.S.R. and Rumania in 1944, the territory was returned to the Soviet Union.

BESSARION, Johannes, *or* BESSARION, BASILIUS (about 1395–1472), Greek scholar and Roman Catholic churchman, born in the Greek Empire of Trebizond (now Trabzon, Turkey) and educated in Constantinople (now İstanbul). He became archbishop of Nicaea (now İznik) in 1487 and went to Italy with the Byzantine emperor John VIII Palaeologus (*see under* JOHN: *Byzantine Empire*) in an unsuccessful effort to unite the Latin and Greek churches. Pope Eugenius IV (*see under* EUGENIUS) made him a cardinal in 1439; Bessarion remained in Italy, a patron of scholars and a collector of books. He was appointed Latin patriarch of Constantinople in 1463. Bessarion is the author of *In Calumniatorem Platonis* ("Upon the False Condemnation of Plato"), a work that attempted to reconcile the ideas of the ancient Greek philosophers Aristotle and Plato (qq.v.). His extensive collection of Greek manuscripts, which he gave to the senate of Venice, became the nucleus of the library of Saint Mark's Church, in Venice.

BESSEL, Friedrich Wilhelm (1784–1846), German astronomer, born in Minden. He supervised the construction of the Königsberg Observatory and served from 1813 until his death as director. He developed a theory of instrumental errors and applied it to the observations of 3222 stars made by the British astronomer James Bradley (q.v.). Bessel published his findings in his *Fundamenta Astronomiae* ("Fundamental Astronomy", 1818). He also established the uniform system of reduction (the computation of star positions) that is still in use. From 1821 to 1833 he accurately determined the positions of stars to the ninth magnitude (*see* MAGNITUDE), bringing the number of stars so catalogued to 50,000. His *Astronomische Untersuchungen* ("Astronomical Observations") was published in 1842. Bessel was the first to succeed in determining the parallax (q.v.) of a fixed star, 61 Cygni, thus giving final confirmation to the heliocentric theory that the sun, rather than the earth, is the center of the solar system (*see* GEOCENTRIC). He also determined the diameter, weight, and ellipticity, or deviation from the form of a true sphere, of the earth; *see* GEOPHYSICS: *Geodesy.* In the investigation of problems connected with planetary perturbation (q.v.), he introduced into mathematics the *Bessel functions* as the solutions of certain differential equations. The functions express the solution in the form of infinite series and are of great importance in determining the distribution and flow of heat or electricity through a circular cylinder, and in the solution of problems concerning wave theory, elasticity, and hydrodynamics.

BESSEMER, city of Alabama, in Jefferson Co., about 10 miles S.W. of Birmingham. Pig iron, steel, freight cars, cast-iron pipe, fertilizers, explosives, chemicals, brick, and cement are manufactured in Bessemer. The city was laid out in 1886 and incorporated in 1887. Pop. (1960) 33,054; (1970) 33,428.

BESSEMER, Sir Henry (1813–98), British inventor, born in Charlton, Hertfordshire, England, and largely self-educated. He was a prolific inventor, but is best known for his process for the manufacture of steel (*see* IRON AND STEEL MANUFACTURE). This method raised the annual production of steel in England enormously by making an excellent grade of steel available at a fraction of the former cost. Bessemer received many honors, including knighthood and a fellowship in the Royal Society, both awarded in 1879.

BEST, Charles Hebert (1899–1978), Canadian physiologist, born in West Pembroke, Maine, of Canadian parents, and educated at the University of Toronto. In 1921, while a medical student, he worked with the Canadian research physician Frederick Grant Banting (q.v.) in the extraction of insulin (q.v.) from pancreatic tissue. This work led in 1923 to the award of the Nobel Prize in medicine and physiology to Banting and to the Scottish physiologist John James Rickard Macleod (q.v.). Banting shared his part of the prize equally with Best. In 1923 the Banting-Best Department of Medical Research was established at the University of Toronto; Best became research associate of the department and director after Banting's death in 1941. From 1929 through 1965 he was full professor at the University of Toronto and director of the department of physiology. During World War II he was a member of several committees for military medical research, and was influential in organizing the Canadian program for procurement and use of dried human blood serum. In 1963 he was appointed advisor to the medical research committee of the World Health Organization.

BESTIARY, name given to medieval books by various authors describing all the animals of creation, real or fabled. Composed partly in prose and partly in verse, they generally were illustrated by drawings. They were highly popular in Europe during the Middle Ages, for both their moral allegories and their zoological information.

BETA CENTAUR. *See* STAR.

BETA RAYS. *See* RADIOACTIVITY.

BETATRON, apparatus designed to accelerate electrons (*see* ELECTRON) to high energies by means of magnetic induction. The machine was developed by the American physicist Donald William Kerst (1911–) in 1940. in the betatron an electron gun injects a stream of electrons into an evacuated, doughnut-shaped chamber located between the poles of an electromagnet. By applying an alternating current to the electromagnet, the electromotive force induced by the changing magnetic flux through the circular orbit accelerates the electrons to high energies. The particles are then directed at an internal metal target to produce X rays of equivalent energy (*see* X RAY), or are released from the betatron as a beam of high-speed projectiles for use in nuclear research.

Besides being valuable in the study of nuclear structure, the betatron has important applications in industrial and medical research. X rays produced by the betatron are very penetrating and hence are useful in the testing of metals. The X rays are also applied experimentally in medical therapy, notably for the treatment of

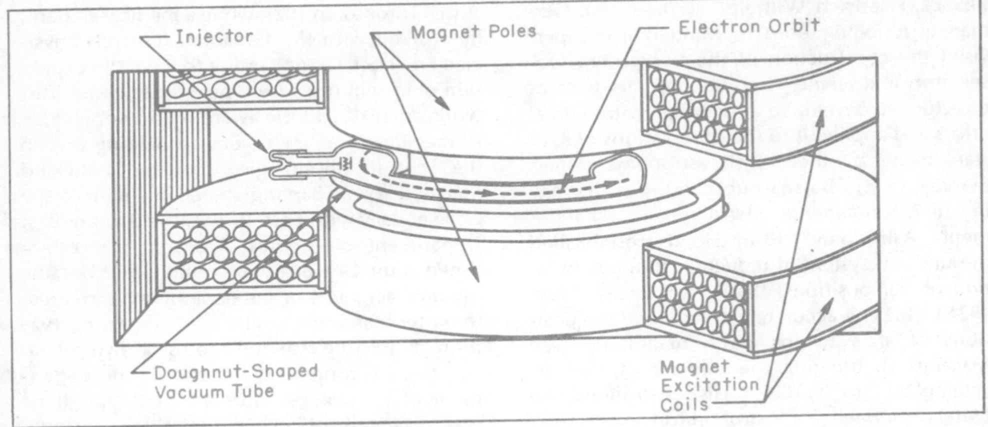

Operation of a betatron. The magnet poles are energized by alternating pulsed current passing through the primary coils. Electrons from a heated filament are injected into the vacuum tube and forced into a curved path by the magnetic field. When electrons reach the desired velocity, they are displaced onto a target for the production of X rays or for other purposes.
University of Illinois

cancer, and as a substitute for the surgeon's knife in several operative procedures, particularly those involving the brain. *See also* CYCLOTRON.

BETEL *or* **BETEL PEPPER,** common name for a vine, *Piper betle,* in the Pepper family (Piperaceae), and for its leaves. In India and the Malay Archipelago the leaves, together with a little quicklime, are used to wrap the areca (q.v.) nut (also called betel nut) for chewing. The chewing of this preparation (also called Betel) colors the saliva blood red and is reputed eventually to stain the teeth black; it is said to act as a stimulant and as a tonic. Approximately one third of the inhabitants of tropical Asia and the East Indies habitually chew the preparation.

BETELGEUSE, also known as ALPHA ORIONIS, reddish star that varies from magnitude 0.1 to 1.2, in the constellation Orion (q.v.), on the celestial equator. It is an irregularly variable star, with a diameter varying from 260,000,000 to 360,000,000 mi. The diameter was calculated at Mount Wilson Observatory, Calif., in 1920 by the American astronomer Francis Gladheim Pease (1881–1938), with the use of an interferometer (q.v.). Betelgeuse was the first star to be measured by this method.

BETHANY, city of Oklahoma, in Oklahoma Co., about 8 miles N.W. of Oklahoma City. The industries of the city include cotton-ginning and flour-milling. It is the site of Bethany Nazarene College, founded in 1909. Pop. (1960) 342; (1970) 21,785.

BETHANY (Ar. *el-Azariyeh,* "house of poverty"), small farming village of Jordan, on the southeastern slopes of the Mount of Olives (*see* OLIVES, MOUNT OF), 2 miles S.E. of Jerusalem (Mark 11:1). It is referred to in the Bible as the home of Lazarus (q.v.) and his sisters, Martha and Mary (John 11:1), and as a place frequently visited by Jesus Christ (Mark 14:3, Matt. 21:17).

BETHE, Hans Albrecht (1906–), American physicist, born in Strasbourg, Alsace-Lorraine (then a part of Germany). He was educated at the University of Frankfurt and the University of Munich, from which he received a Ph.D. degree in 1928. Bethe taught physics at various universities in Germany from 1928 to 1933 and in England from 1933 until 1935 when he began his long association with Cornell University, Ithaca, N.Y. His career at Cornell was interrupted in 1943 when he began work at Los Alamos, N. Mex., on the atomic-bomb project. After the explosion of the bomb in 1945 Bethe actively worked for international control of atomic energy, against atmospheric testing of atomic weapons, and against the development of the hydrogen bomb. He was a prime advocate of the partial test-ban agreement signed by the United States, the Soviet Union, and Great Britain in 1963. Bethe was awarded the 1967 Nobel Prize in physics for his studies of the production of energy by the sun and other stars, which he postulated occurs through a long series of nuclear reactions by which hydrogen is changed into helium. He was naturalized a U.S. citizen in 1941.

BETHEL (Heb., "the house of God"), ancient village of Jordan, 12 miles N. of Jerusalem. The village is called Beitīn by its Arab inhabitants, and it was sometimes referred to in the Bible as Luz (Gen. 28:19). Once the chief sanctuary of the Israelite tribes, Bethel is frequently mentioned in the Old Testament as a holy place. It was here that Abraham (q.v.) built an altar to God (Gen. 12:8), and Jacob (q.v.) had his vision of the ladder and angels (Gen. 28:12). Bethel later became a seat of idolatrous worship (1 Kings 12:26–33, 13:1–10). The village contains remains of churches dating from the 6th and 12th centuries, and is estimated to have been founded as early as the 21st century B.C.

BETHEL PARK, residential borough of Pennsylvania, in Allegheny Co., about 8 miles S. of central Pittsburgh. Industries include the manufacturing of steel and rubber products. In 1949 the borough was incorporated as Bethel and in 1960 it became known as Bethel Park. Pop. (1960) 23,650; (1970) 34,791.

BETHESDA *or* **BETHZATHA** (Heb., "the house of mercy"), pool or public bath in the city of Jerusalem (q.v.) at the time of Jesus Christ. Scholars now generally believe it to have been located between the Temple area (*see* TEMPLE: *Temple at Jerusalem*) and the Via Dolorosa. The pool is mentioned in the Bible as having had curative waters; it was also the scene of Christ's cure of an infirm man (John 5:2–9).

BETHESDA, unincorporated residential suburb of Maryland, in Montgomery Co., 6 miles N.W. of downtown Washington, D.C. Manufactures include electrical equipment, musical instruments, biological products, clothing, bricks, and building supplies. Bethesda is the site of the Naval Medical Center, the National Institutes of Health, the National Cancer Institute research center, the National Library of Medicine, and the Madonna of the Trail Monument, a tribute to pioneer women. Pop. (1970) 71,621.

BETHLEHEM, city of Pennsylvania, in Northampton and Lehigh counties, on the Lehigh R. about 50 miles N. of Philadelphia. One of the largest industrial centers in Pennsylvania, Bethlehem is the site of the main plant of the Bethlehem Steel Corporation, one of the largest steel producers in the world. Other products manufactured in the city include silk and other textiles, foundry and machine products, iron fences, electrical goods, and food products. The city is also an important railroad junction, and railroading is a major source of employment and income.

Bethlehem was founded on Christmas Eve, 1741, by a party of Moravians from the German States of Bohemia and Saxony. It is sometimes called the Christmas City because of special civic observances held annually at Christmas. A Bach Festival, developed from the rich musical tradition of the early Moravian Church, is given every year in May. In Bethlehem are Lehigh University, founded in 1865, and Moravian College, founded in 1807. Pop. (1960) 75,408; (1970) 72,686.

BETHLEHEM (Heb. and Aramaic, "house of bread"), town in Jordan, 5 miles S. of Jerusalem, specified in the Bible as the birthplace of both David, King of Judah and Israel, and Jesus Christ (qq.v.). Originally called Aphrath, the town also is referred to as Bethlehem-Judah to distinguish it from another Bethlehem (Josh. 19:15–16) in the territory of the tribe of Zebulon (q.v.).

Bethlehem first is mentioned in the Old Testament as the place where Rachel, the wife of the patriarch Jacob (qq.v.), was buried (Gen. 35:19). According to the book of Ruth (*see* book of RUTH), it later became the home of King David's ancestors and of David himself (1 Sam. 17: 12). In the book of Micah (*see* book of MICAH), Bethlehem is mentioned as the birthplace of the future Messiah (Mic. 5:2).

With the exception of Saint Mark (q.v.), the authors of the Gospels claim Bethlehem as the birthplace of Christ, and as such, it has been regarded by Christians as a holy place. Bethlehem contains one of the oldest churches in the world, the Church of the Holy Nativity, built by Constantine I (q.v.), Emperor of Rome, in 330 on the traditional site of the Nativity. Despite rebuilding by the Roman Emperor Justinian I (q.v.) in the 6th century, much of the original church

The bell tower of the Church of the Nativity in Bethlehem, one of the oldest extant examples of early Christian architecture. Israel Office of Information

still stands and the shrine is visited continuously by pilgrims from all branches of Christendom.

The modern Jordanian town is known as Beit Lahm. Pop. (1967) 23,240.

BETHLEHEMITES *or* **BETHLEHEMITE BROTHERS.** **1.** Order of monks mentioned by the English historian Mathew Paris (q.v.) as being at Cambridge, England, in 1257. On the front of their habits they wore a red star with five points and a blue disk, in allusion to the star of Bethlehem, but otherwise dressed as Dominicans (q.v.). **2.** Order founded in Guatemala by a Franciscan friar (*see* FRANCISCANS) named Pedro de Betancourt (1619–67). It developed from a congregation living under the rule of the Third Order of Saint Francis (*see* FRANCIS OF ASSISI, SAINT), and was devoted especially to the care of the sick and the education of children. A constitution was approved by Pope Clement X (1590–1676) in 1672, and the congregation was expanded into an order in 1687 and put under the rule of the Augustinians (q.v.). Members of the order dressed similarly to the Capuchins (q.v.) and carried on their right breasts a shield picturing the manger at Bethlehem and the figures of Mary (*see* MARY, SAINT) and Joseph (q.v.), her husband. The Bethlehemites especially were bound to exercise hospitality and to tend the sick. In 1668 a female order of the name was founded in Guatemala. The orders spread in South America, but they were secularized in 1820 and were extinct by 1845. **3.** Followers of the Bohemian religious reformer John Huss (q.v.), styled Bethlehemites from the Bethlehem Church in Prague, at which their leader preached.

BETHLEN, Gabriel *or* **BETHLEN VON IKTÁR, Gabriel** (1580–1629), Prince of Transylvania (1613–29) and King of Hungary (1620–21). A member of a prominent Protestant family of upper Hungary, he was noted for his military activities in behalf of the Protestant cause in the Thirty Years' War (q.v.). In 1619 he led a Protestant Hungarian army against the forces of the Roman Catholic Ferdinand II (q.v.), Holy Roman Emperor. Bethlen's success in penetrating to the gates of Vienna in the war led to his election as king of Hungary. As a result of his defeat at the Battle of the White Mountain, he was forced to relinquish the title in 1621. In 1623 and 1626 he again took up arms against Ferdinand. After 1626 Bethlen devoted himself exclusively to the internal affairs of Transylvania, which he made a center of Hungarian patriotism and culture.

BETHLEN, Count Stephen (1874–1950), Hungarian political leader, born in Transylvania, and educated at the University of Budapest. He entered the Hungarian parliament as a Liberal in 1901; in 1905, he transferred his allegiance to the Independent Party. In 1919 he led the counterrevolutionary movement against the communist regime set up by the Hungarian communist leader Béla Kun (q.v.). Bethlen became prime minister in 1921 at the request of Admiral Miklós von Nagybána Horthy (q.v.), and was able to obtain the aid of the League of Nations in the financial reconstruction of the country, which gradually emerged from chaos. Bethlen was prime minister until his resignation in 1931. During World War II, when German forces invaded Hungary, Bethlen went into hiding. In 1945 he was captured by Soviet troops and taken to the U.S.S.R. where he reportedly died.

BETHMANN-HOLLWEG, Theobald von (1856–1921), German statesman, born in Brandenburg, and educated at the universities of Strasbourg, Leipzig, and Berlin. In 1905 he became Prussian minister of the interior. In 1907 he was appointed imperial secretary of state for the interior; and in 1909 he succeeded Prince Bernhard von Bülow (q.v.) as chancellor of the German Empire. In 1914 Bethmann-Hollweg referred to the treaty of 1839 by which five great European powers had guaranteed the neutrality of Belgium as a "scrap of paper". Because he refused to accede to the policy of unlimited submarine warfare adopted by Germany in 1917, he was forced to resign the chancellorship. Bethmann-Hollweg wrote *Reflections on the World War* (1920).

BETHPAGE–OLD BETHPAGE, unincorporated residential area of New York State, in Nassau Co., on central Long Island, 3 miles S.E. of Hicksville and 27 miles E. of New York City. The area is governed as part of Oyster Bay town. Manufactures include aircraft, aircraft parts, and clothing. Bethpage has facilities for golf, polo, tennis, horseback riding, and winter sports. Bethpage State Park is nearby. Settled in 1697, Bethpage was called Central Park from 1841 to 1936. Pop. (1960) 20,515; (1970) 18,555.

BETHSAIDA OF GALILEE *or* **BETHSAIDA OF GAULONITIS,** ruined Biblical town in Syria, on the northeastern shore of the Sea of Galilee (now known as Lake Tiberias), near the influx of the Jordan R. To distinguish this town from a newer Greek town named Bethsaida, situated farther back from the shore, the Apostle John (*see* JOHN THE EVANGELIST, SAINT) refers to the former as Bethsaida of Galilee (John 12:21). Near Bethsaida of Galilee, the home of Philip, Peter, and Andrew (qq.v.), three of His disciples (John 1:44), Jesus Christ fed the multitude (Luke 9:10–17). Bethsaida was also the place that Jesus denounced for being unreceptive to His ministry (Matt. 11:21), and it was outside its walls that He healed the blind man described in Mark 8:22–26. After being rebuilt by Philip the Tetrarch (d. 34), the town was called Bethsaida Julias, in honor of the imperial house of Rome.

BETHUNE, David. *See* BEATON, DAVID.

BETHUNE, Mary (1875–1955), American educator, born Mary McLeod in Mayesville, S.C., and educated at Barber-Scotia College and the Moody Bible Institute. She taught school in Florida and Georgia from 1897 to 1903, and in 1904 she founded the Daytona Normal and Industrial Institute for Negro Girls (now Bethune-Cookman College). She remained president of the college until 1943. From 1936 until her death she held many other posts, including those of director of Negro affairs in the National Youth Administration (1936–42) and consultant to the United States secretary of war in the selection of the first female officer candidates for the armed services. She was appointed consultant on interracial affairs and understanding at the charter conference of the United Nations (q.v.). She was also the founder of the National Association of Colored Women and a vice-president of the National Association for the Advancement of Colored People (q.v.).

BETJEMAN, Sir John (1906–), poet laureate of England (1972–), often called the country's most popular contemporary poet.

Betjeman was born in Highgate, London, an only child and heir apparent to a four-generation family business. At the early age of seven he decided to become a poet and began his resistance to all efforts to groom him for his father's post. That long struggle and his memories of growing up to manhood are sensitively and humorously chronicled in Betjeman's autobiography in verse, *Summoned by Bells* (1960). From his *Mount Zion* (1931) to his *Collected Poems* (1971) his verse output was continuous and prodigious. In addition, starting with his *Ghastly Good Taste* in 1933, he wrote numerous scholarly works on English architecture, cities, and towns, as well as popular guides to old churches and other landmarks.

Betjeman was dubbed the "bard of nostalgia" for his lyrical skill in evoking the past, particularly the moods and images of actual places —gaslit depots, iron bridges, red-brick Victorian houses, and shadowy chancels. A militant preservationist, he aimed his wit and poetic shafts at planners, developers, and all others who, in the name of progress, threatened to destroy the past and despoil the English countryside that he loved so much.

BETTA. *See* FIGHTING FISH.

BETTENDORF, city of Iowa, in Scott Co., on the Mississippi R., about 4 miles E. of Davenport. Bettendorf is an industrial city that manufactures machinery, industrial gases, and foundry products. Dairy products are also produced. Pop. (1960) 11,534; (1970) 22,126.

BETTING. *See* GAMBLING.

BEUST, Count Friedrich Ferdinand von (1809–86), German statesman, born in Dresden. He entered the Saxon diplomatic service in 1830 and was minister to London in 1846 and ambassador to Berlin in 1848. In 1849 he became minister of foreign affairs of Saxony and in 1853 he was made premier of that State. An opponent of the Prussian statesman Otto von Bismarck (q.v.), Beust allied Saxony with Austria during the Seven Weeks' War (q.v.). In 1866 Beust entered the Austrian diplomatic service as minister of foreign affairs and in 1867 became chancellor of the Austrian Empire. During his term of office (1867–71) he reorganized the empire as the dual monarchy of Austria-Hungary (q.v.) and instituted liberal reforms. He served as the ambassador to Great Britain (1871–78) and to France (1878–82).

BEUTHEN. *See* BYTOM.

BEVAN, Aneurin (1897–1960), British political leader, born in Monmouthshire, Wales. After working in the coal mines, he attended the Central Labour College in London. He was elected to the House of Commons from Ebbw Vale, Monmouthshire, in 1929. In 1944 he was elected to the executive committee of the Labour Party (q.v.). As minister of health in the Labour government of British Prime Minister Clement Richard Attlee (q.v.) from 1945 to 1951, Bevan was instrumental in establishing the socialized National Health Service. In 1951 he became minister of labor and national service but resigned a few months after his appointment because of disagreement with government domestic policy. Bevan was best known as an outspoken leader of the left wing of the Labour Party. His writings include *In Place of Fear* (1952), which is an account of his political beliefs.

BEVATRON. *See* CYCLOTRON.

BEVELAND, NORTH *and* **SOUTH BEVELAND,** two former islands, Zeeland Province, S.W. Netherlands, strategically located in the Scheldt estuary. As part of the massive Delta Project begun in 1954 mainly to facilitate flood control in Zeeland, North Beveland (35 sq.mi.) was linked by a dike with Walcheren (q.v.), and South Beveland (135 sq.mi.) was attached to the mainland. Agriculture, especially livestock raising, is the chief occupation on both former islands, which were the scene of heavy fighting during World War II. Goes is the main town.

BEVERIDGE, Albert Jeremiah (1862–1927), American political leader and writer, born in Highland County, Ohio, and educated at Asbury University (now DePauw University). Admitted to the bar in 1887, he practiced law in Indianapolis, Ind. Having gained a reputation in Indiana as a political orator, he was elected as a Republican to the United States Senate in 1899 and served until he was defeated in 1911. In 1912 he joined the Progressive Party, but lost the election for governor of Indiana. He later returned to the Republican Party and in 1922 he again lost in a Senatorial election. He turned to the writing of history and won the Pulitzer Prize in 1920 for his *Life of John Marshall* (4 vol., 1916–1919). He also wrote *The State and the Nation* (1924) and other books.

BEVERIDGE, Sir William Henry, 1st Baron Beveridge of Tuggal (1879–1963), British economist, born in Rangpur (now in Pakistan), and educated at the University of Oxford. He was made director of labor exchanges for the city of London in 1908 and, as a member of the Food Ministry during World War I, he instituted a plan for wartime rationing. From 1919 to 1937 he was director of the London School of Economics and from 1937 to 1944 was master of University College, Oxford. Beveridge is particularly noted for the Beveridge Plan, a blueprint for social security and a welfare state. He was elected a Liberal member of the House of Commons in 1944 and in November of that year the House endorsed a government motion for an extensive social-insurance plan—the Beveridge Plan in a modified form. Other Beveridge proposals for medical insurance were adopted in subsequent legislation. Beveridge was knighted in 1919 and created baron in 1946. Among his published works are *Planning under Socialism* (1936), *Social Insurance and Allied Services* (1942), *Full Employment in a Free Society* (1944), *The Evidence for Voluntary Action* (1949), *Power and Influence* (autobiography, 1953), and *A Defence of Free Learning* (1959).

BEVERLY, city of Massachusetts, in Essex Co., on a narrow inlet of Massachusetts Bay, opposite Salem, and 18 miles N.E. of Boston. The city is a shoe-machinery manufacturing center. Other industries include the manufacture of shoes, grinding equipment, and electronic products. Important waterborne cargoes received at Beverly for transshipment are petroleum and coal. The city is also a popular summer resort. Points of historic interest are the site of what is believed to have been the first cotton mill in North America, established in 1788; Glover's Wharf, at which the first ship of the United States Navy was fitted out; and several 17th-century houses. Settled in 1626 by the British colonist Roger Conant (1592?–1679), Beverly formed part of Salem until 1668, when it was incorporated as a town under the present name. Beverly was chartered as a city in 1894. Pop. (1960) 36,108; (1970) 38,348.

BEVERLY HILLS, city of California, in Los Angeles Co., surrounded by the city of Los Angeles. A prosperous residential suburb, it is famous as the home of many celebrities of the motion-picture industry. Pop. (1960) 30,817; (1970) 33,416.

BEVIN, Ernest (1881–1951), British labor leader and statesman, born in Winsford, Somersetshire, England. About 1909, after working at a number of manual trades, he became a labor organizer. In 1920 he gained a nationwide reputation by making a speech before the Transport Workers' Court of Inquiry that resulted in a standard minimum wage for British dockworkers. In 1921 he organized the Transport and General Workers' Union, a national merger of thirty-two smaller unions; he served as general secretary of this group until 1940. He was a prominent member of the Labour Party (q.v.) and in 1940 joined the coalition cabinet of Prime Minister Sir Winston Leonard Spencer Churchill (q.v.) as minister of labor and national service, in charge of the mobilization of manpower and national resources throughout World War II.

In 1945 he became secretary of state for foreign affairs in the Labour cabinet of Prime Minister Clement Richard Attlee (q.v.) and participated in the formation of the North Atlantic Treaty Organization (q.v.). His foreign policy concerning the Middle East was controversial, however, and was opposed by proponents of Zionism (q.v.). At the time of his death he was Lord Privy Seal.

BEWICK, Thomas (1753–1828), British wood engraver, born near Newcastle upon Tyne, Northumberland, England. He became apprentice to and, in 1777, partner of an engraver in Newcastle. Bewick illustrated *A General History of Quadrupeds* (1790), which popularized natural history and led to the publication of a similar *History of British Birds* (1797 and 1804), which he also illustrated. Among his other works is an illustrated version of the *Fables of Æsop* (1818). His single best-known wood block is "The Chillingham Bull" (1789), from a painting by the British artist Sir Edwin Henry Landseer (q.v.).

BEXLEY, city of Ohio, in Franklin Co., about 4 miles E. of central Columbus. Bexley is a residential city. It is the site of Capital University, founded in 1850. Pop. (1960) 14,319; (1970) 14,888.

BEYLE, Marie Henri. *See* STENDHAL.

BEYOĞLU, residential section of Turkey, in the N. part of İstanbul, bordering the Golden Horn and the Bosporus. It is the site of European churches of many denominations and the largest hotels in the city. Beyoğlu includes historic Pera, the area reserved by the sultans for foreigners and noted for the 14th-century Genoese Galata Tower and an old mosque. In Beyoğlu are situated the Avenue of Independence, Taksim Square (site of the Monument of the War of Independence or Statue of the Republic), the Opera House, Tophane Fountain, the Technical University, Galatasaray College, and Kasimpaşa Naval College; nearby are the Caşino and Atatürk Museum. Two bridges, the Atatürk and the Galata, cross the Golden Horn on the south, linking residential Beyoğlu with the center of İstanbul.

BEYROUTH. *See* BEIRUT.

BÈZE, Théodore de, *or* THEODORUS BEZA (1519–1605), French theologian and Protestant reformer, born in Vézelay, Burgundy. In 1549 he began to teach Greek in Lausanne, Switzerland, and in 1559 he went to Geneva. There he became coadjutor to the French religious reformer John Calvin (q.v.) and was appointed professor of theology at Geneva Academy. After the death of Calvin he presided over the synods of French reformers held at La Rochelle in 1571 and at Nîmes in 1572. In 1581 he presented to the University of Cambridge the famous New Testament manuscript known as *codex D,* or *codex Bezae,* claiming to have obtained it from a monastery in Lyon. His works include a Latin translation of the New Testament and *Histoire Ecclésiastique des Églises Réformées de France, 1521–1563* ("Ecclesiastical History of the Reformed Churches of France, 1521–1563", 3 vol., 1580).

BÉZIERS (anc. *Baeterrae*), city of France, in Hérault Department, on the Orb R., about 40 miles S.W. of Montpellier. In the surrounding region are vineyards, coal mines, and factories. Béziers is a wine and alcohol-trade center, as well as an industrial city. In Béziers are distilleries and metalworking- and petroleum-refining plants. The chief products are candy, fertilizers, rubber, and wine-growing equipment. Points of interest in the city are a Gothic cathedral constructed in the 13th and 14th centuries, and the old city walls. In 1209 the inhabitants were massacred by troops under the Anglo-Norman soldier and crusader Simon IV de Montfort l'Amaury (1160?–1218) for protecting Albigensian fugitives (*see* ALBIGENSES). Béziers was an Episcopal see from the 4th to the 18th centuries. Pop. (1968) 80,382.

BEZWADA. *See* VIJAYAVADA.

BHAGALPUR, city of the Republic of India, in Bihar State, on the Ganges R., about 265 miles N.W. of Calcutta. It is an important railway and commercial center for the surrounding area, a fertile region that produces grain, especially rice, oilseeds, jute, and sugarcane. The chief industry of the city is the manufacture of coarse-silk goods. Pop. (1971) 172,202.

BHAGAVAD-GITA (Skr., "the Song of the Blessed One"), Sanskrit theosophical poem of about 700 verses, forming an episode in the religious epic *Mahabharata* (q.v.). It consists of a colloquy between Krishna, an incarnation of the god Vishnu, and Arjuna, the hero of the epic, and is a discourse on life, duty, and devotion to the Supreme Spirit. Long regarded by the Hindus as a sacred textbook, this passage has been translated into most modern Indian vernaculars and many other languages. *See* HINDUISM.

BHAKTAPUR, city of Nepal, about 7 miles E. of the capital, Katmandu, and about 75 mi. from the border with the Republic of India. Agriculture is the chief occupation of the surrounding area. Bhaktapur has several well-preserved buildings dating from the 17th and 18th centuries. Pop. (latest census) 33,075.

BHARAT, alternate name for India. *See* INDIA, REPUBLIC OF.

BHARATA NATYA. *See* DANCE: *Ethnic Dance: India.*

BHARATPUR, *or* BHURTPORE, city of the Republic of India, in Rajasthan State, about 100 miles N.E. of Jaipur. The city is a trade center, and is noted for such handicrafts as chowries, earthenware, and fans. Bharatpur was the capital of a princely State of the same name until 1949, when Bharatpur State merged with several neighboring princely States to form Rajasthan Union, now Rajasthan State. Pop. (1971) 69,442.

BHATPARA, city of the Republic of India, in West Bengal State, on the E. bank of the Hooghly R., 24 miles N. of Calcutta. The principal industries are cotton milling and paper production. Bhatpara is the ancient seat of Sanskrit learning. Pop. (1971) 204,750.

BHAVABHUTI (fl. 700 A.D.), Hindu dramatist, born in Berar, India. Little is known about his life, although it is judged from his writings that he was at the court of King Yasovarman (fl. 700 A.D.) of Kanauj. He is remembered as the author of three Sanskrit dramas. The first is a love story, the *Mālatī-Mādhava,* sometimes called the

Hindu "Romeo and Juliet"; the second, *Mahā-vīra-charita,* describes the fortunes of the great hero Rama (*see* RAMAYANA); and the third, *Uttara-rāma-charita,* relates the later adventures of Rama. Bhavabhuti is revered as one of the great dramatic poets of early Sanskrit Literature (q.v.).

BHAVNAGAR *or* **BHAUNAGAR,** city of the Republic of India, in Gujarat State, on the W. bank of the Gulf of Cambay, about 200 miles N.W. of Bombay. The city is a rail terminus and has an extensive trade in cloth and lumber. Leading industries include the manufacture or processing of bricks, candy, fertilizer, ice, plastics and rubber products, textiles, vegetable oil, and the making of handicraft objects. Bhavnagar was founded in 1723. The city was the capital of a princely State of Bhavnagar until 1948. Pop. (1969 est.) 217,533.

BHIL, *or* BHEEL, primitive tribal people of west-central India; found mostly in the hills of Rajasthan, Gujarat, and Maharashtra. They wear little clothing and subsist on wild grains, fruits, roots, and insects. When they engage in agriculture they use primitive instruments and methods. Their language is of Indo-European origin and is known as Bhili (*see* INDO-EUROPEAN LANGUAGES), but some Bhil use a dialect of Gujarati (*see* INDIAN LANGUAGES). Religious practices have been influenced by Hinduism (q.v.) in form but Bhil basically believe in witchcraft (q.v.). When the Rajput and Mogul were contending for power, the Bhil were pro-Mogul; under British rule, some moved from the hills to the plains and became farmers, while others became policemen and soldiers.

BHOPAL, former princely State of the Republic of India, absorbed in 1956 by Madhya Pradesh State. Traversed by the Vindhya Mts., it has large tracts of jungle. The chief occupation is farming and the chief crops are sugarcane, cereals, cotton, ginger, and tobacco. The principal city is Bhopal (q.v.). Established in 1723 by an Afghan chieftain, the State became a British protectorate in 1817. Female rulers, called begums, reigned from 1844 to 1926. Following the partition in 1947 of British India into India and Pakistan, the State joined India, which was predominately Hindu, although the population of Bhopal was mostly Muslim. From 1949 to 1956, Bhopal was a centrally administered area of the Federal government. Area of former State, 6921 sq.mi.

BHOPAL, city in the Republic of India, and capital of Madhya Pradesh State, about 180 miles N.W. of Nagpur. It is a railway junction and trade center. The main industries are the manufacture of cotton cloth and jewelry. Points of interest include two mosques. From 1723 until the end of British rule in India in 1947, Nagpur was the capital of the former princely State of Bhopal (q.v.). Pop. (1969 est.) 310,733.

BHUMIBOL ADULYADEJ. *See* RAMA IX.

BHUTAN, Monarchy in the eastern Himalaya mountains, bounded on the N., E., and N.W. by the Tibet Autonomous Region of China, and on the S. and S.W. by the Indian State of Assam and the protectorate of Sikkim. Sloping gradually from N. to S., the entire state is mountainous, with summits exceeding 24,000 ft. The area of Bhutan is about 18,000 sq.mi.; population (1970 est.) 1,000,000. Thimphu is the capital. The Bhutanese are of Mongolian stock; their language is Dzongkha, belonging to the Sino-Tibetan languages; and their religion is Buddhism of the Tibetan form.

Wild animals found in Bhutan include the elephant, leopard, deer, wild hog, bear, and rhinoceros.

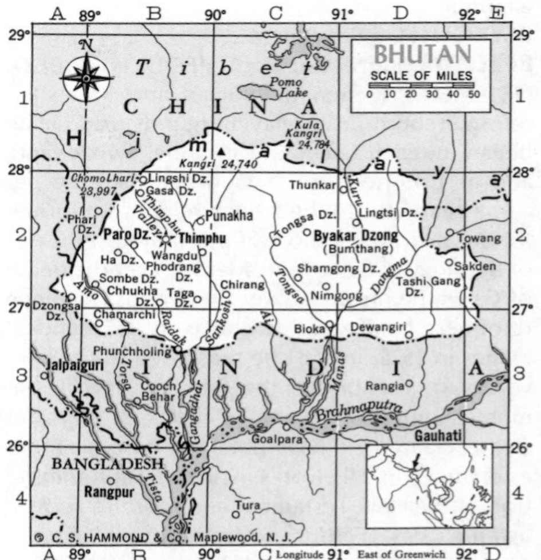

INDEX TO MAP OF BHUTAN

Cities and Towns

Bioka .... C 3
Bumthang (Byakar Dzong) .... C 2
Byakar Dzong (Bumthang) .... C 2
Chamarchi .... B 3
Chhukha Dzong ...... B 2
Chirang .... C 2
Dewangiri .... D 3
Dzongsa Dzong ...... A 2
Gasa Dzong .... B 2
Ha Dzong .... B 2
Lingshi Dzong .... B 2
Lingtsi Dzong .... D 2
Nimgong .... C 2
Paro Dzong .... B 2
Phunchholing .... B 3
Punakha .... C 2
Sakden .... E 2
Shamgong Dzong ..... C 2
Sombe Dzong .... B 2
Taga Dzong .... B 2
Tashi Gang Dzong .... D 2
Thimphu (capital) ..... B 2
Thunkar .... C 2
Tongsa Dzong .... C 2
Wangdu Phodrang Dzong .... B 2

Physical Features

Ai (river) .... C 3
Amo (river) .... A 2
Chomo Lhari (mt.) .... B 2
Dangma (river) .... D 2
Himalaya (mts.) .... B 1
Kangri (mt.) .... B 1
Kula Kangri (mt.) ..... C 1
Kuru (river) .... D 2
Raidak (river) .... B 3
Sankosh (river) .... C 2
Thimphu (valley) ...... B 2
Tongsa (river) .... C 2

History. Two centuries ago a band of colonists from Tibet subjugated the original inhabitants, the Tephus. From the mid-17th to the early 20th century, Bhutan was governed by both a spiritual ruler, the Dharma raja, and a temporal ruler, the Deb raja. By a treaty concluded in 1910, the Bhutanese government agreed to be guided by the advice of the British government on its external affairs, provided Great Britain did not interfere in internal administration. In 1971 Bhutan became a member of the United Nations.

Bhutan once included considerable tracts of territory that are now part of the region of Bengal and the State of Assam, both of which were annexed in 1841 by the British government. After this annexation, the Bhutanese were hostile to the British and frequently raided their frontier posts. When the British confronted the Bhutan government with a demand for reparations in 1863, the demands were rejected. In 1865, after the Bhutanese had rejected another ultimatum, the British sent a punitive expedition against them. A subsequent treaty concluded with the Bhutan government provided for payment by the Indian government of an annual subsidy in return for formal cession, by Bhutan, of the annexed territory in Assam and Bengal. This subsidy, which was payable on condition that Bhutan maintain peaceful relations with its neighbors, was increased from 50,000 rupees in 1865 to 100,000 in 1910 and 200,000 in 1942. In August, 1949, by the terms of a treaty concluded by Bhutan and the Republic of India, the subsidy was increased to 500,000 rupees (about U.S.$65,000). The treaty also provided for the return to Bhutan of about 32 sq.mi. of the territory ceded to the British in 1865.

The parts of Bhutan that are fertile produce corn, rice, wheat, buckwheat, mustard, and cardamoms. Cattle and considerable numbers of an unusual breed of ponies are raised. Manufactured products, which are intended for home consumption, include blankets and cotton cloth, swords and other weapons, and agricultural implements.

In 1907 Sir Ugyen Wangchuk was elected hereditary maharajah. Successors were (1952) Jigme Dorji Wangchuk (1927–72) and (1972) Jigme Singye Wangchuk (1956–).

BIAFRA. *See* NIGERIA: *History.*

BIAFRA, BIGHT OF. *See* BONNY, BIGHT OF.

BIALIK, Chaim Nachman (1873–1934), Hebrew poet, born in Zhitomir (now in the Ukrainian S.S.R.), and educated at a yeshiva in Volozhin. He published a book of poems, *Songs of Wrath* (1903), and one of the poems, "In the City of Slaughter", made him famous. It was inspired by his anger at the massacres in Kishinev, now in the Moldavian S.S.R. Bialik was influential in the revival of the Hebrew language (q.v.) and a strong supporter of Zionism (q.v.). He left the Soviet Union in 1921 to live in Germany but stayed there only until 1924, when he moved to Tel-Aviv, Palestine (now in Israel). In 1924 the first English translations of his work appeared; further English editions were published in 1926 and 1928. Bialik translated works from other languages into Hebrew and edited many books of ancient Hebrew legends and commentaries.

BIAŁYSTOK (Russ. *Belostok*), city in Poland, and capital of Białystok Province, about 110 miles N.E. of Warsaw. The province is a plain drained by the Bug, Niemen, and Narew rivers. Białystok Province is primarily agricultural, with a concentration of industries in the capital. The chief crops are flax, oats, potatoes, and rye. The city is a center of the Polish textile industry, and other manufactures include agricultural machinery, chemicals, cutlery, processed foods, tiles, and tools. The city was founded in 1310. In 1795 Białystok was annexed to Prussia, and in 1807 to Russia. In 1921 Białystok was returned to Poland. The city was captured by Germany during each of the world wars. The province was incorporated into the Soviet Union during World War II. In August, 1945, Białystok was ceded to Poland. Pop. (1973 est.) 182,300.

BIARRITZ, town and beach resort, Pyrénées-Atlantiques Department, S.W. France, on the Bay of Biscay, near Bayonne and the Spanish border. Once a small fishing and whaling port, the town became an elegant resort in the mid-19th century when it was patronized by Napoleon III, Empress Eugénie, and other members of European royalty. Today large numbers of visitors take advantage of its year-round mild climate, large white-sand beach, and mineral springs. Nearby is beautiful mountain scenery. Pop. (1968) 26,648.

BIBIENA, name adopted by a family of Italian architects, artists, and scene designers of the baroque (q.v.) period, descendants of the painter Giovanni Maria Galli (1620–65), who adopted the name of his birthplace as a surname. Three generations of Bibienas worked together and separately in the courts of Europe, patronized by many members of the Hapsburg (q.v.) family. Although much of their scenery for opera and for court functions was ephemeral, drawings have survived to indicate the brilliance and lavish imagination of their work. Noted members of the family were the following.

Ferdinando Galli Bibiena (1657–1743), the elder son of Giovanni Maria, born in Bologna.

He was an architect in the service of Francesco Maria, duke of Parma (1678–1727), and provided the decorations for the wedding and the coronation of Charles VI (q.v.), Holy Roman Emperor. He built a theater at Mantua and is the author of several important books about architecture and perspective.

Francesco Galli Bibiena (1659–1739), the younger son of Giovanni Maria, born in Bologna. He designed theaters in Vienna, Nancy, Verona, and Rome. He and his brother, Ferdinando, are credited with the typical baroque innovation of two-point perspective in theatrical scenery; *see* THEATER.

Alessandro Galli Bibiena (1687–1769), eldest son of Ferdinando, born in Parma. He was court architect to the elector of the Palatinate, Maximilian II Emanuel (1679–1726), and designed the opera house and a church at Mannheim.

Giuseppe Galli Bibiena (1696–1757), second son of Ferdinando, born in Parma. He is regarded as the most important member of the family. He designed scenery for plays, court functions, and for operas that were performed at the courts of Vienna, Austria, and Dresden, Saxony, and later published these designs in three sets of engravings. He was responsible (1748) for the interior of the extant court theater at Bayreuth, Bavaria. He is also credited with the first use of transparent scenery lighted from behind.

Antonio Galli Bibiena (1700–74), third son of Ferdinando, born in Parma. He was (1769) the architect of the extant theater of the Accademia Vergiliana, Mantua.

BIBLE, *called also* HOLY BIBLE, sacred Scriptures of Jews and Christians. The English term "Bible" is derived from the Greek plural *biblia* (from *biblos,* "papyrus" or "paper" that was exported from the ancient Phoenician city of Byblos), meaning "books". By the 8th century A.D., the various "books" of the Jewish and Christian sacred Scriptures came to be viewed as a united "book", especially after general acceptance of the "common version", the Latin Vulgate (q.v.). The term "Holy Bible" is derived from the Latin *biblia sacra* ("sacred books"). Because the term "Bible" has been applied almost exclusively to the Jewish and Christian sacred Scriptures, the sacred writings of other religions are only figuratively called "bibles"

Both Judaism and Christianity (qq.v.) are viewed as "historical religions", that is, historical events are regarded as the means by which God reveals his purposes to men. Thus, the Bible, viewed as a record of God's revelation in history, must necessarily be considered against the background of ancient Middle Eastern culture and history, wherein biblical literature developed. This literature—originating in the nomadic culture of the Fertile Crescent and continuously developing in the urban civilizations of Mesopotamia, Egypt, Greece, and Rome—includes law codes, poetry, history, philosophy, prophecy, and other genres written from the 2nd millennium B.C. to the 1st century A.D.

The Jewish Bible contains three sections—the Torah (q.v.), or "Law" (the first five books of the Bible), the *Nebiim*, or "Prophets" (historical and prophetic books), and the *Ketubim*, or "Writings" (psalms, proverbs, and other literary genres)—and is called by Christians the Old Testament. The Apocrypha are "hidden" or secret books written in the 1st and 2nd centuries B.C. by Jewish authors and regarded as canonical (scripturally acceptable) by Roman Catholic and Eastern Orthodox churches but not in Judaism or Protestantism; *see* DEUTEROCANONICAL BOOKS. The New Testament completes the Christian Bible and contains Gospels, letters, history, and apocalyptic writings (q.v.) that describe a sudden, dramatic intervention of God in history and the salvation of a faithful few, all written in the 1st century A.D.

Art, literature, music, everyday language, and basic underlying scientific views of modern civilization owe much to the Bible. Above all, however, the religious and ethical ideals of the Bible, inherited from Hebrew (*see* HEBREWS), Jewish (*see* JEWS), and Christian sources, have become generating forces within Western education and culture.

THE GROWTH OF THE BIBLE

The Old Testament and the Apocrypha are almost all the writings that remain from ancient Hebrew literature, although many other works are known to have existed. What distinguishes these surviving documents of Hebrew literature from other national literatures is an almost exclusively religious character. Other literatures contain numerous independent works of poetry, drama, satire, biography, history, or philosophy. In the Old Testament and Apocrypha, pure or mixed examples of some of these kinds of writing may be found (such as in the histories of 1 and 2 Kings, the poetry of the Psalms, or the dramatic dialogues of Job), but they are primarily characterized by the religious purpose that pervades the entire body of work. No real parallel to this situation can be found in any other literature. As one consequence, no other pre-Christian Western religion, except possibly that of ancient Greece, is so well documented as

The Bible. Plate 1. *The Old Testament. Above: A late-Byzantine mosaic depicting the prophet Jonah. Right: A 12th-century stained-glass portrait of the prophet Hosea. Below: A 14th-century illustration: "And the Lord appeared unto Abram . . ." (Gen. 12:7).*

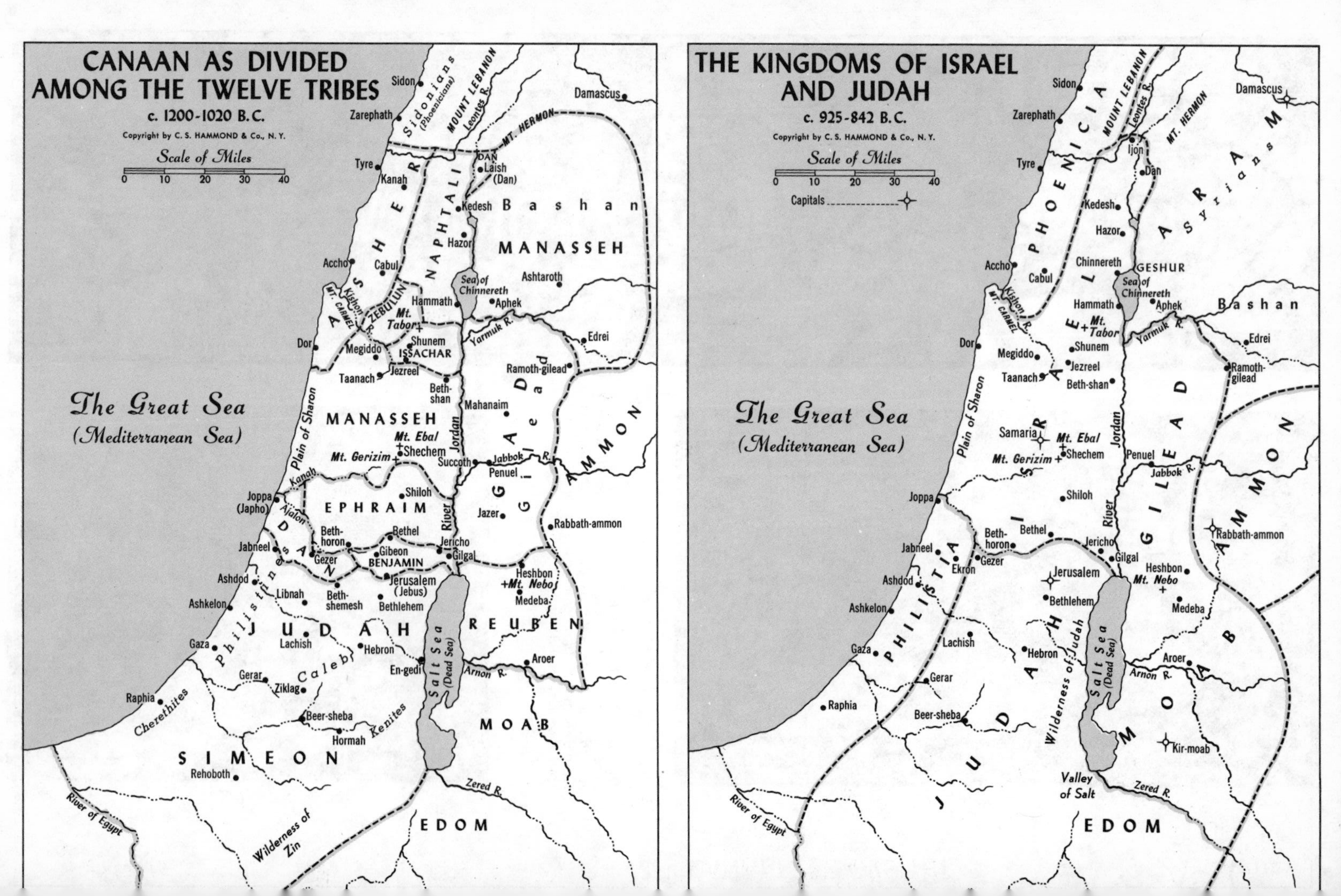
CANAAN AS DIVIDED AMONG THE TWELVE TRIBES
c. 1200-1020 B.C.
Copyright by C. S. HAMMOND & Co., N. Y.
Scale of Miles
0 10 20 30 40
The Great Sea
(Mediterranean Sea)
Sidon
Sidonians (Phoenicians)
Zarephath
MOUNT LEBANON
Leontes R.
MT. HERMON
Damascus
Tyre
Kanah
DAN
Laish (Dan)
ASHER
NAPHTALI
Kedesh
Bashan
Hazor
MANASSEH
Accho
Cabul
Ashtaroth
Sea of Chinnereth
ZEBULUN
Hammath
Aphek
Kishon R.
MT. CARMEL
Mt. Tabor
Yarmuk R.
Edrei
Dor
Megiddo
Shunem
ISSACHAR
Jezreel
Ramoth-gilead
Taanach
Beth-shan
Mahanaim
Plain of Sharon
MANASSEH
Gilead
GAD
AMMON
Mt. Ebal
Mt. Gerizim
Shechem
Jordan
Succoth
Jabbok R.
Penuel
Kanah
Joppa (Japho)
Shiloh
Ajalon
EPHRAIM
Jazer
Rabbath-ammon
Beth-horon
Bethel
River
Jabneel
DAN
Gezer
Gibeon
Jericho
Gilgal
BENJAMIN
Ashdod
Jerusalem (Jebus)
Heshbon
Mt. Nebo
Medeba
Ashkelon
Philistines
Libnah
Beth-shemesh
Bethlehem
JUDAH
REUBEN
Gaza
Lachish
Hebron
Salt Sea (Dead Sea)
Aroer
Gerar
Caleb
En-gedi
Arnon R.
Ziklag
Raphia
Cherethites
Beer-sheba
Kenites
MOAB
Hormah
SIMEON
Rehoboth
Zered R.
River of Egypt
Wilderness of Zin
EDOM
THE KINGDOMS OF ISRAEL AND JUDAH
c. 925-842 B.C.
Copyright by C. S. HAMMOND & Co., N. Y.
Scale of Miles
0 10 20 30 40
Capitals
The Great Sea
(Mediterranean Sea)
Sidon
Zarephath
PHOENICIA
MOUNT LEBANON
Leontes R.
MT. HERMON
Damascus
Ijon
Dan
Tyre
ARAM
Syrians
Kedesh
Hazor
Accho
Cabul
Chinnereth
GESHUR
Sea of Chinnereth
Hammath
Aphek
Bashan
Kishon R.
MT. CARMEL
Mt. Tabor
Yarmuk R.
Edrei
Dor
Megiddo
Shunem
Jezreel
Ramoth-gilead
Taanach
Beth-shan
ISRAEL
Plain of Sharon
Samaria
Mt. Ebal
Shechem
Mt. Gerizim
Jordan
Penuel
Jabbok R.
GILEAD
AMMON
Joppa
Shiloh
River
Rabbath-ammon
Beth-horon
Bethel
Jericho
Jabneel
Ekron
Gezer
Gilgal
Heshbon
Mt. Nebo
Ashdod
Jerusalem
Bethlehem
Medeba
Ashkelon
PHILISTIA
JUDAH
Lachish
Hebron
Wilderness of Judah
Salt Sea (Dead Sea)
Aroer
Gaza
Arnon R.
Gerar
MOAB
Raphia
Beer-sheba
Kir-moab
Valley of Salt
Zered R.
River of Egypt
EDOM

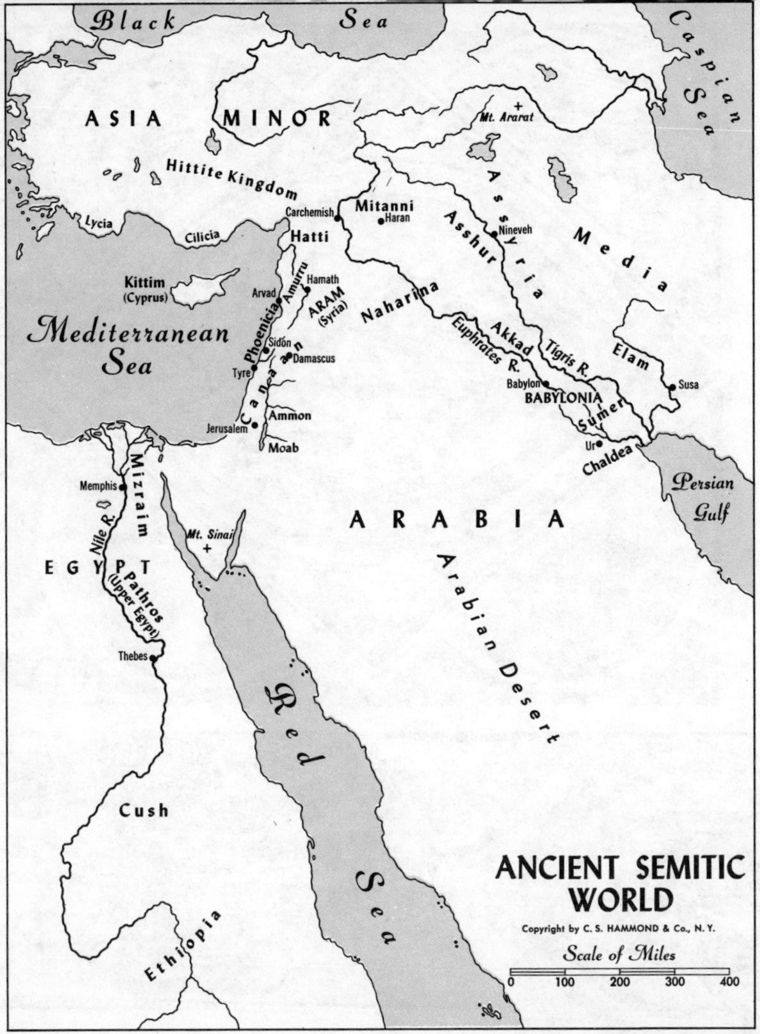
ANCIENT SEMITIC WORLD
Copyright by C. S. HAMMOND & Co., N. Y.
Scale of Miles
0
100
200
300
400
Black Sea
Caspian Sea
ASIA MINOR
Hittite Kingdom
Lycia
Cilicia
Carchemish
Hatti
Mitanni
Haran
Mt. Ararat
Assyria
Asshur
Nineveh
Media
Kittim (Cyprus)
Arvad
Amurru
Hamath
ARAM (Syria)
Naharina
Akkad
Tigris R.
Euphrates R.
Elam
Susa
Mediterranean Sea
Phoenicia
Sidon
Damascus
Tyre
Canaan
Ammon
Jerusalem
Moab
Babylon
BABYLONIA
Sumer
Ur
Chaldea
Persian Gulf
Memphis
Mizraim
Nile R.
Mt. Sinai
ARABIA
Arabian Desert
EGYPT
Pathros (Upper Egypt)
Thebes
Red Sea
Cush
Ethiopia

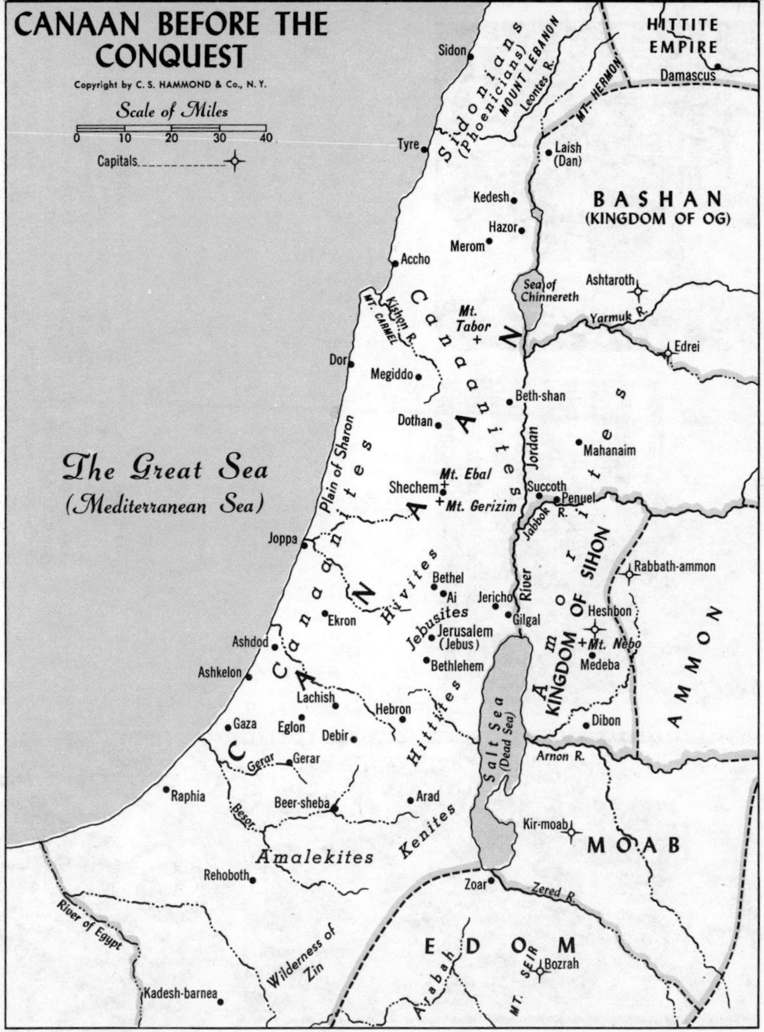
CANAAN BEFORE THE CONQUEST
Copyright by C. S. HAMMOND & Co., N. Y.
Scale of Miles
0
10
20
30
40
Capitals
HITTITE EMPIRE
Damascus
Sidon
Sidonians (Phoenicians)
MOUNT LEBANON
Leontes R.
MT. HERMON
Tyre
Laish (Dan)
BASHAN (KINGDOM OF OG)
Kedesh
Hazor
Merom
Accho
Sea of Chinnereth
Ashtaroth
Yarmuk R.
Edrei
Kishon R.
MT. CARMEL
Mt. Tabor
Canaanites
Dor
Megiddo
Beth-shan
Dothan
Mahanaim
The Great Sea (Mediterranean Sea)
Plain of Sharon
Mt. Ebal
Shechem
Mt. Gerizim
Jordan
Succoth
Penuel
Jabbok R.
Amorites
Joppa
CANAAN
Hivites
Bethel
Ai
Jericho
River
Rabbath-ammon
KINGDOM OF SIHON
Ekron
Jebusites
Jerusalem (Jebus)
Gilgal
Heshbon
Mt. Nebo
Ashdod
Bethlehem
Medeba
AMMON
Ashkelon
Lachish
Hebron
Hittites
Salt Sea (Dead Sea)
Gaza
Eglon
Debir
Dibon
Gerar
Arnon R.
Raphia
Arad
Beer-sheba
Besor
Kenites
Kir-moab
MOAB
Amalekites
Rehoboth
Zoar
Zered R.
River of Egypt
Wilderness of Zin
EDOM
Arabah
MT. SEIR
Bozrah
Kadesh-barnea

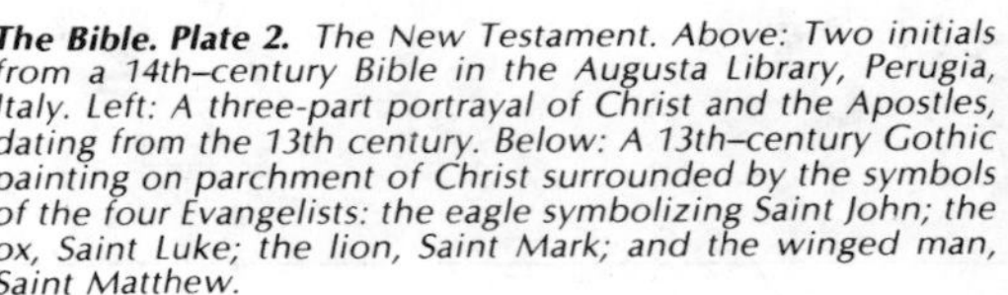

The Bible. Plate 2. *The New Testament. Above: Two initials from a 14th–century Bible in the Augusta Library, Perugia, Italy. Left: A three-part portrayal of Christ and the Apostles, dating from the 13th century. Below: A 13th–century Gothic painting on parchment of Christ surrounded by the symbols of the four Evangelists: the eagle symbolizing Saint John; the ox, Saint Luke; the lion, Saint Mark; and the winged man, Saint Matthew.*

"The Creation of Adam", a fresco by the 16th-century Italian artist Michelangelo on the ceiling of the Sistine Chapel, in the Vatican, Rome, Italy.

Brogi — Art Reference Library

that of ancient Israel. This circumstance is especially fortunate because the Old Testament enshrines many high and noble religious teachings and ideals.

The New Testament differs from the Old Testament in being not a national literature, or the literature of a national religion, but an international religious literature. It was basically Jewish in spirit, but was originally written in Greek, and arose in the Greek-speaking churches as the Christian supplement to the Greek translation, the Septuagint, of the Hebrew Bible, which included, as the Hebrew Bible did not, the writings known as the Apocrypha (see below). These early Christian writings, along with the Septuagint, were produced, preserved, copied, and made a part of Holy Scripture by the process of constant use in Christian worship, in the instruction of converts and youth, and in study, exposition, and preaching everywhere in the Christian Church. *See* BIBLE, VERSIONS OF THE.

Continuous research during the past four centuries (*see* BIBLE SCHOLARSHIP), and especially the combined scholarship of Jews, Roman Catholics, and Protestants since 1800, has made it possible to trace successive stages in the development of Biblical literature. Significant in this research has been the so-called documentary hypothesis, according to which various forms of linguistic usage found in the Biblical text presuppose the existence of certain original documents. Many scholars maintain that these documents were combined subsequently to form parts of the present text. Most agree, however, that the documents rest on earlier, oral traditions. The earliest of the presumed documents is called J because it uses a form of the Judean name for God, Jahweh or Yahweh; *see* JEHOVAH. A later document is called E because it uses a northern Israelite name for God, Elohim. Parts of J and E were combined in a single narrative, according to a modified chronology, and formed the JE source. Another document, the Deuteronomic, or D, source was another, later redaction of the earlier traditions. Another presumed document, the P (for Priestly) code was the latest to be compiled and is found in the priestly sections of the first five books of the Old Testament or the Pentateuch, plus Joshua (these six books are sometimes called the Hexateuch).

Viewed against their historical surroundings and in the light of such contextual clues as those already mentioned, the books of the Bible (*see* BIBLE, CANON OF THE) may be assigned in chronological order to eight categories, found in the three sections known as the Old Testament, the Apocrypha, and the New Testament.

The Old Testament. This is the oldest section of the modern Bible.

THE EARLY SOURCES. The earliest writings originated in folk traditions among the Semitic desert nomads who invaded Palestine in the 14th or 13th centuries B.C. These wandering tribes became known among nearby peoples as Hebrews. Later, some of them called themselves Israelites, after an eponymous ancestor. Many of the Hebrews' folk traditions concerned the patriarchs, Abraham, Isaac, and Jacob, and the Exodus, and were circulated orally for generations before being written down by the scribes as the national saga. Apart from such writings, two other distinct groups may be differentiated. One consists of certain ancient poems, such as the Song of Lamech (Gen. 4:23–24), the Song of the Well (Num. 21:17–18), and the Song of Miriam (Exod. 15:21). Another group consists of the primitive laws embedded in the Pentateuch, such as the Ten Commandments (Exod. 20:2–17, Deut. 5:6–21), and the Book of the Covenant

(Exod. 20:22–23:33 and elsewhere). The Book of the Covenant was, in part, a Canaanite (*see* CANAANITES) code that the Israelites adapted to their own use, along with some legal material that may go back to the time of Moses or even earlier.

FROM 1200 TO 922. Another group of writings originated in the period of the settlement in Palestine, of the early judges (12th and 11th centuries B.C.), and of the United Monarchy (11th and 10th centuries; that is, the reigns of Saul, David, and Solomon). After settling in Palestine, the Hebrew tribes adopted an agrarian way of life involving extensive domestic and international trade. The people were held together by "judges", or chief magistrates, principally Othniel, Ehud, Deborah, Gideon, Jephthah, and Samson, according to the book of Judges. A monarchy was begun under Saul (reigned about 1020–1000 B.C.), consolidated under David (reigned about 1000–961? B.C.), who established his capital at Jerusalem, and commercially expanded under Solomon (reigned about 961?–922 B.C.).

The fragments and traditions incorporated in later writings that originated in this period include a considerable number of traditional poems, such as the Blessing of Noah (Gen. 9: 25–27); the battle hymns (Josh. 10:12–13, Judg. 15:16, 1 Sam. 18:7); and the great heroic ballad known as the Song of Deborah (Judg. 5). To the same period belongs the vivid life of King David, a cycle of stories scattered through 1 and 2 Samuel and 1 Kings, and perhaps also the early narratives of the beginnings of human history found in the first part of Genesis (chapters 1–11). Psalm 24:7–10 may also come from this period; if so, it is the oldest of the Hebrew psalms. The Blessing of Jacob (Gen. 49:2–27) and the Oracle of Balaam (Num. 24:3–9, 15–24) probably belong to the period of Solomon.

THE LITERATURE OF ISRAEL, THE NORTHERN KINGDOM (about 922–722 B.C.). After the death of Solomon, the northern part of the kingdom revolted and established a separate dynasty and independent shrines, although it did not adopt substantially different religious practices. The name Israel henceforth refers to the northern kingdom as a political state, but also, and more enduringly, to the national entity of Jews, regardless of state. The height of power of the northern kingdom was attained under Jeroboam II (reigned about 786–746 B.C.). Israel continued as a separate state until Assyria, under Sargon II, finally conquered it and in 721 B.C. removed the inhabitants into captivity. Those who remained behind were largely Samaritans, who developed during the ensuing centuries a distinct type of worship within the Jewish religion.

The notable contributions of this period include the ancient poem called the Blessing of Moses (Deut. 33); the beautiful song for a royal marriage (Ps. 45); the two cycles of stories about Elijah and Elisha (1 and 2 Kings); the great E source or document underlying the Pentateuch; certain parts of the traditional Law; and the earliest prophetic writings, Amos and Hosea, which are among the most powerful and penetrating sermons ever delivered.

THE LITERATURE OF JUDAH, THE SOUTHERN KINGDOM (922–586 B.C.). Judah, which was smaller in size and population than Israel, became the most important state in Palestine under Uzziah (reigned about 783–750 B.C.). In 597 the Chaldean king Nebuchadnezzar overran the land and conquered the city of Jerusalem, capital of Judah. Most of the inhabitants were brought to Babylonia in captivity, like their northern brethren, although Judah was allowed to remain as a buffer state against Egypt until 586.

Many of the noblest writings of the Old Testament date from this period. First in importance was the source of document J, which traces the history of Israel from the call of Abraham to the conquest of Canaan; it was later supplemented by the book of Judges. The dominant prophetic figure in this period was the 8th-century prophet Isaiah of Jerusalem, whose prophecies are found in the first part of the present book of Isaiah (Isa. 1–39). Isaiah was a great patriot who rejected all political compromise with the competing nations of the south (Egypt) and east (Damascus, Syria, Babylon), and relied wholly upon divine intervention for the safety of Israel, soon to be limited to Judah. He also elaborated, in beautiful poetry, the hope of the coming Messianic king (Isa. 9:2–7), who would bring in a period of universal peace, safety, and welfare under the divine blessing. The Messiah was to be a descendant of King David. Other prophets were Micah, who lived in western Judah in the reign of King Hezekiah (715–687 B.C.), and proclaimed the impending doom of Samaria and Jerusalem because of their oppression of the poor (Mic. 1–3); and Nahum, who saw his prediction come true as to the fall of the Assyrian capital Nineveh, destroyed by the Babylonians in 612 B.C.

Jeremiah of Anathoth (a village north of Jerusalem), a prophet fully as great as Isaiah, was active until the fall of Jerusalem in 597 B.C. His "confessions" describe his call and the divine message with which he had been entrusted, and they set forth his hope for the future, as in the sublime prophecy of the "new" covenant. "Behold, the days come, saith the Lord, that I will make a new covenant with the house of Israel, and with the house of Judah. . . . I will put my law in their inward parts, and write it in their hearts; and will be their God, and they shall be my people. . . . for they shall all know me, from the least of them unto the greatest of them . . . I will forgive their iniquity, and I will remember their sin no more" (Jer. 31: 31–34). This passage marks one of the high points in religious history and looks forward to the goal of all spiritual individual religion.

Other products of the period are the legal code of Deuteronomy, supposedly the code found in the Temple in 621 B.C., although it probably is based in part upon older material; the single consecutive narrative formed by the combination of J and E; the prophecies of Zephaniah and Habakkuk; and parts of the book of Proverbs, most of Job, and many of the Psalms, such as Psalm 104.

THE LITERATURE OF THE PERIOD FROM THE BEGINNING OF THE EXILE TO THE COMING OF EZRA (597–438 or 397 B.C.). The Israelites remained in exile as deportees living in Egypt (as a result of capture in warfare) and in Babylonia until the Persian ruler Cyrus the Great added those kingdoms to his empire. In 538 B.C. they returned to Palestine with his permission, and were allowed to rebuild their Temple and to worship God without interference by their neighbors. They settled almost exclusively in the former kingdom of Judah; as residents of Judah or Judea they became known as Jews. The end of this period is traditionally marked by the priestly figure Ezra, who returned from Babylonia to establish certain religious standards of Judaism based upon ideas developed during the captivity. The widely diversified literature of this period begins with the Lamentations (over the fall of Jerusalem), attributed to Jeremiah, and various psalms and proverbs. The writings of the prophet Ezekiel come from early in the period (about 593–570 B.C.). About 550 B.C. the combined J and E narrative was supplemented by the books of Joshua, Judges, Samuel, and Kings, to provide a continuous account of Israelite history from the beginning of the world to the destruction (586 B.C.) of the First Temple (*see* TEMPLE: *Temple at Jerusalem*). The second part of the book of Isaiah (Isa. 40–55), which postdates the first part by about 200 years, belongs to the decades immediately preceding 538 B.C., when the rise of Cyrus the Great gave new hope to the exiled Jews. Haggai and Zechariah (Zech. 1–8) record the prophetic insistence, about 520 B.C., to have the people rebuild the Temple at Jerusalem. The Holiness Code (Lev. 17–26) also dates from about this time.

During the 5th century certain poems were added to the Pentateuch, namely, the Song of Moses (Deut. 32:1–43) and the Blessing of Moses (Deut. 33). The "memoirs" of Nehemiah were written some time after his visits to Jerusalem about 445 and 428 B.C. The beautiful idyll of Ruth, celebrating King David's Moabite ancestress, dates from this period; it constitutes a protest against a narrowly nationalistic view of Judaism. Many additions were made during the century to the earlier literature, among them the third part of Isaiah (Isa. 56–66). The most significant composition was, however, the P code, which provided a historical framework for the whole Pentateuch and Joshua. The P code was added to earlier historical narratives (J and E) and thus provided the setting for the great law codes, completing the Pentateuch in most essentials.

THE LITERATURE COMPLETING THE HEBREW OLD TESTAMENT (about 400–143 B.C.). For two centuries the Jews thrived under the rule of the Persian Empire. In 331 B.C. the King of Macedonia, Alexander III, known as Alexander the Great, defeated the Persian King Darius III (qq.v.) at the battle of Arbela (q.v.), in Assyria, and succeeded him as "Great King". Alexander introduced the age of Greek civilization, language, learning, and culture throughout the Near and Middle East; *see* HELLENIST. In 168 B.C. the Maccabees began their revolt against the Seleucid kingdom, a successor state of Alexander's empire. After a twenty-five-year struggle (recorded in the Apocryphal books of 1 and 2 Maccabees), the Jews won their independence in 143 B.C. The book of Joel and many additions to the poetic and historical books, such as the Song of Solomon, were written early in the period. The work of the chronicles (1–2 Chronicles, Ezra, Nehemiah) carries on the idealized historical narrative of the P code; the work finds the center of Jewish history in the Jerusalem temple and in the Jewish cult, and ignores the schismatic northern kingdom, whose Samaritan type of worship had developed independently, outside the Babylonian exile. The books of the Latter Prophets (*see* chart accompanying BIBLE, CANON OF THE), which consist of Isaiah, Jeremiah, Ezekiel, and the Book of the Twelve, the so-called Minor Prophets, come from this time and include such late additions as Zech. 9–14. The Psalter, or book of Psalms, was enriched by several additions during this period; the acrostic nature of some of the psalms, such as Ps. 110, in which the initial letters of the lines spell "Simon" (one of the Maccabees, son of Mattathias), shows that they belong to the Maccabean era. Quite clearly the book of Daniel refers to the crisis that led to the outbreak of the Maccabean War. It also predicts the victory of the Jews, as in chapter 7, in which "the saints of the Most High" are symbolically described as "one like the Son of man" (that is, a human figure, in contrast to the previous beast symbols) who is exalted to heaven and given world dominion. The later influence of this idea, especially after the figure had been literalized as "the" Son of Man, was enormous, particularly upon early Christianity. Some of the early books of the Apocrypha also date from this period.

Ecclesiastes, an essay in pious skepticism that seems to reflect Greek influence, also may belong to this period, although it is often dated earlier, as may Esther, the story read during the Jewish feast of Purim, which, curiously, fails to mention God. The attitude it reveals toward Gentiles apparently reflects the era of persecution that began in 168 B.C. *See* BIBLE, CANON OF THE: *The Old Testament.*

A 14th-century painting by the Sienese artist Bartolo di Fredi, depicting the adoration of the shepherds at the birth of Christ. Metropolitan Museum of Art

The Apocrypha (200 B.C.–100 A.D.). The period to which the Apocryphal books belong overlaps the periods that witnessed the completion of the Old Testament and the composition of the New Testament. The Jews enjoyed considerable freedom after regaining their independence as a result of the Maccabean wars, but were once again subjected to foreign rule in 63 B.C., when Pompey the Great, the Roman general in Syria, annexed Judea and Samaria. Successive revolts afterward were crushed by the Roman governors in Palestine, and the Jews as a nation did not again attain political independence until modern times.

The books known as the Apocrypha were composed chiefly during the last two centuries B.C., although 4 Ezra (known also as 2 Esdras) belongs to the end of the 1st century A.D. Several of the books were originally in Hebrew, and a few were in Aramaic, but the oldest surviving versions are in Greek (and, in the case of 4 Ezra, in Latin). Fragments of the Hebrew of Sirach have been discovered in modern times, in the Genizah or manuscript depository of the Synagogue of Fostat, near Cairo.

Contemporary with the Apocrypha is a still larger group of writings that was not included in any canonical, or authorized, collection, either Hebrew or Greek. These writings are known as the Pseudepigrapha, that is, writings of pseudonymous or fictitious authorship. Many are apocalyptic in style and subject, and purport to be revelations of events to come after the epoch of their composition. The most important are 1 Enoch, the Testaments of the Twelve Patriarchs, the Psalms of Solomon, the Book of Jubilees, the Assumption of Moses, the Apocalypse of Baruch, the Sibylline Oracles, and 3 and 4 Maccabees. Some of these works survive only in translation. Enoch, for example, was first found in an Ethiopic translation, although Latin and Aramaic fragments were found later. *See* BIBLE, CANON OF THE: *The Apocrypha.*

The New Testament (29–96 A.D.). Christianity began with the ministry of Jesus Christ (q.v.), usually dated about 29–30 or 28–30 A.D. The ministry is recounted in the Gospels (*see* GOSPEL), the first four books of the New Testament. The new religion expanded from Palestine to Syria, and then to Asia Minor, Macedonia, Greece, and Rome, as related in the Acts of the Apostles. The leading Apostle, or missionary of Christianity, was Saint Paul, whose letters form a large part of the New Testament, and who is believed to have died in Rome about 65 A.D. The remaining New Testament books reflect conditions and situations in the early Church, chiefly during the period about the end of the 1st century. The earliest books were not the Gospels but the letters of Paul. From, according to one scheme of chronology, the earliest (1 Thessalonians) of his many letters, written to the Christians in Thessalonica (now Salonika), to the last (Philippians), written from prison to the church at Philippi in Macedonia, Paul exercised his pastoral supervision and Apostolic ministry by means of his pen. He constantly communicated in this way with the churches he had founded, in order to deal with the serious problems that arose in the new communities, such as the threatened relapse into Judaic legalism in the Roman province of Galatia in Asia Minor (now part of Turkey), or the mixed marriages and the "speaking in tongues" (seizures of ecstatic utterance) common in Corinth.

The Gospels and the Acts of the Apostles, which is the continuation of the Gospel of Luke, were produced after Paul's death, during the second half of the 1st century, or perhaps a little later. These writings were intended to provide both encouragement and instruction to Christians, as well as a defense of the Christian cause against misrepresentation and persecution, and to explain the Christian faith to a new generation of believers in the somewhat philosophically minded Greco-Roman world. Thus the Gospel of Mark is addressed to the martyr church in Rome, under Nero; the Gospel of Luke and the Acts of the Apostles, to the Gentile Theophilus, perhaps a magistrate before whom Christians were being tried; the Gospel of Matthew, to a settled Christian community, possibly Antioch, where slow transition from the Law to the Gospel was in progress; and the Gospel of John, to a church or churches in which Gnosticism (q.v.) threatened to undermine faith in the reality of Jesus' human nature.

Other books, also written as letters, are intended to be homilies or sermons, such as the Epistle to the Hebrews and the Epistle of James, as well as 1 Peter, which some scholars now believe to incorporate a baptismal address. The last book of the New Testament, the Revelation, or Apocalypse, of Saint John (about 96 A.D.), is a work designed to encourage the Christians in the Province of Asia who were faced with persecution by the representatives of the Roman state cult in the time of the Emperor Domitian.

There is also a collection of New Testament Apocrypha, a significant number of which were composed in the 2nd century, but most were heretical or represented a fantastic growth of legend. Fragments of some early Apocryphal Gospels, such as "According to the Hebrews" or the "Ebionite Gospel", contain some interesting material, but most of it is simply borrowed from the four Gospels in the New Testament and then elaborated by writers with vivid imaginations. The discovery of the Gnostic library at Naj Hammadi, Egypt, in the 1950's, added several Apocryphal Gospels (Thomas, Philip, and the Gospel of Truth), acts (Thomas), letters, and apocalypses to the Apocryphal literature of the period succeeding that of the New Testament. *See* BIBLE, CANON OF THE: *The New Testament.*

BIBLE MANUSCRIPTS, VERSIONS, EDITIONS, AND TRANSLATIONS

The oldest surviving manuscript codexes of the Old Testament are the Leningrad Codex, containing the books of the Latter Prophets, dated 916 A.D.; another codex, the Cairo Codex, containing books of both Earlier or Former and Latter Prophets, dated 895 A.D.; a Hebrew manuscript, in Leningrad, of the whole Old Testament, dated 1008 A.D.; and the Aleppo Codex, now in Jerusalem, dated about 930 A.D. In addition to these oldest long manuscripts two copies survive of Isaiah, dating from the 2nd century B.C. or a little later. They were found in 1947 at Khirbet Qumran, Jordan, on the Dead Sea among the so-called Dead Sea Scrolls (q.v.). Surviving fragments of other Old Testament books include Habakkuk, and, in addition, an Egyptian papyrus of parts of Exodus and Deuteronomy, as well as many other fragments from the synagogue storeroom of Fostat.

The earliest printed editions of the Hebrew Old Testament were produced in Italy in the latter part of the 15th century. The modern editions by the British Biblical scholar Christian David Ginsburg (1831–1914) and the German Protestant theologian and Old Testament scholar Rudolf Kittel (1853–1929) rely largely upon those older publications that gave the exact text of the medieval manuscripts. In addition to the traditional Hebrew text, a Samaritan version, or recension, of the Pentateuch is also known. It contains about 6000 variations from the Hebrew text, which often agree with the Greek translation, but are sometimes clearly traceable to the peculiar views of the Samaritan sect.

The most important ancient version of the Old Testament is the Greek translation, usually called the Septuagint ("Seventy") because it is thought to have been translated by seventy Jewish scholars in Egypt in the 3rd century B.C. Several ancient editions of manuscripts survive, most of which were influenced by the Church Father Origen of Alexandria. A revised, enlarged edition of the Septuagint was published in

The crucifixion of Jesus, as depicted in a Latin missal and gradual made in Austria in the second half of the 13th century. Pierpont Morgan Library

English in 1954. In addition to the Greek translation, there are old Aramaic Targums ("Interpretations"), a Syriac translation, the Old Latin translation, the Vulgate Latin Version of Saint Jerome, and translations into Coptic, Ethiopic, Armenian, Gothic, Georgian, and Arabic.

The oldest complete New Testament collections include the extremely valuable Vatican manuscript, Codex Vaticanus (or B), and Codex Sinaiticus (S or the Hebrew letter *aleph*), which was discovered on Mt. Sinai in 1844, both from the 4th century; and Codex Alexandrinus (A) and Codex Ephraemi Syri (C), the latter a palimpsest or twice-written-upon manuscript, both from the 5th century. The bilingual Greek-

Latin manuscript Codex Bezae, containing the Gospels and Acts, is probably from the same century. A number of papyrus fragments of great value are extant, such as the Chester Beatty (bought in Egypt in the 1930's) and Michigan papyri (late 3rd century), the Papyrus Bodmer of John (about 200 A.D.), now at Geneva, and a tiny fragment of the Gospel of John, dating from 130–150 A.D., now in the Rylands Library in England. More than 150 New Testament manuscripts exist in codex form, written in uncial (that is, capital) letters. In addition, more than 3000 minuscule or cursive manuscripts (written in connected lower-case letters) are extant. The methods by which these manuscripts are studied are the same as those applied to ancient literature in general. *See* BIBLE SCHOLARSHIP: *Textual Criticism;* PALEOGRAPHY.

Valuable sources of information about the original text of the New Testament are found also in the ancient versions, especially the Old Latin and Old Syriac (both from about 150 A.D.). The quotations found in the writings of the Church fathers (*see* FATHERS OF THE CHURCH) are a valuable aid in recovering the text as it circulated in the early centuries. By the end of the 2nd century, three or four great "families" or "types" of text were distinguishable, including the Egyptian, or Neutral, the Western, and the Caesarean; each is identified in some measure with a particular locality or region. As a result of repeated revisions and the collation and copying of many manuscripts in the early Church, there arose the Byzantine or Ecclesiastical text, which prevailed in the East and was common in the West wherever Greek manuscripts were known. It became the basis of the Greek New Testament of the Dutch scholar and humanist Desiderius Erasmus, published in Basel in 1516, and of the Textus Receptus, published in Paris in 1550. Modern editors, such as the German classical philogist Karl Lachmann (1793–1851), the German Protestant theologian and Biblical scholar Konstantin von Tischendorf (1815–74), the British prelate and New Testament scholar Brooke Foss Westcott (1825–1901), and the British theologian and Biblical scholar Fenton John Anthony Hort (1828–92), always have taken account of the work of their predecessors; and each of their editions has been based upon an ever-increasing number of manuscripts. The widely used edition (1889 *et seq.*) of Eberhard Nestle (1851–1913), later edited by his son, combined the readings of Tischendorf, Westcott-Hort, and the German Protestant theologian Bernhard Weiss (1827–1918) and added a selection of important variant readings of manuscripts, versions, and Church Fathers. A complete Bible in modern Greek was published in Athens in 1954–55. A modern Greek paraphrase of the Textus Receptus was published in 1955.

From the time of the first translation, the Greek Septuagint, which was completed about the beginning of the Christian era, the Bible has been the most widely translated of all works. Among the most famous of the translations are Saint Jerome's Vulgate, regarded as the standard version by Roman Catholics, a translation into Latin made in the 4th century on the basis of Greek codices, some Hebrew texts, and earlier Latin versions; and the translation into German by the German religious reformer Martin Luther. In modern times the Bible, or parts of it, has been translated into more than 1100 distinct languages and dialects. *See* BIBLE, ENGLISH TRANSLATIONS OF THE; BIBLE, VERSIONS OF THE. See also individual entries under the names of persons, places, and portions of the Bible mentioned in this article.

BIBLE ARCHEOLOGY. *See* BIBLE SCHOLARSHIP.

BIBLE, CANON OF THE, the contents of the Bible (q.v.) accepted as standard or fixed by the Jews (q.v.) or by the Christian Church (*see* CHRISTIAN CHURCH, HISTORY OF THE) at various times. The canon (Gr., "measuring rod") was determined by the individual religious groups, according to criteria of inspiration, worth to the individual and to the group, and previous historical acceptance. The canonical list and arrangement differs for Jews and Catholics, and among the Protestant denominations; see accompanying chart. Thirty-nine (or twenty-four according to arrangement) books of the Old Testament are accepted as divinely inspired by both Jews and Christians. Twenty-seven books of the New Testament are accepted only by Christians. Fourteen books found in the Septuagint, or Greek version of the Old Testament, are known as the Apocrypha. The Apocryphal or deuterocanonical books (q.v.) are accepted, among Christians, only by the Roman Catholics, the Anglicans, and the Eastern Orthodox. The earliest standard list of Old Testament books was made by the Jews at a council in Jamnia in Judea (about 100 A.D.), but the term "canon" itself, borrowed from its Greek use in connection with literary works, was first applied to the Bible by Christians.

THE OLD TESTAMENT

No historical information exists concerning the stages in the development of the Old Testament canon among the Jews. It is generally supposed, however, that the present division of the Old Testament into three parts came about in three corresponding periods, ending about 187 B.C. in

THE BIBLICAL CANON

OLD TESTAMENT

Jewish (Hebrew)

The Law
Genesis
Exodus
Leviticus
Numbers
Deuteronomy

The Prophets
(Earlier Prophets)
Joshua
Judges
1 Samuel
2 Samuel
1 Kings
2 Kings
(Latter Prophets)
Isaiah
Jeremiah
Ezekiel
Hosea
Joel
Amos
Obadiah
Jonah
Micah
Nahum
Habakkuk
Zephaniah
Haggai
Zechariah
Malachi
(Hosea through Malachi: "Book of Twelve" or Minor Prophets)

The Writings
Psalms
Proverbs
Job
Song of Songs
Ruth
Lamentations
Ecclesiastes
Esther
Daniel
Ezra
Nehemiah
1 Chronicles
2 Chronicles

Roman Catholic (Douay)

The Pentateuch
Genesis
Exodus
Leviticus
Numbers
Deuteronomy

The Historical Books
Josue
Judges
Ruth
1 Kings
2 Kings
3 Kings
4 Kings
1 Paralipomenon
2 Paralipomenon
1 Esdras
2 Esdras, alias Nehemias
Tobias
Judith
Esther

The Didactic Books
Job
Psalms
Proverbs
Ecclesiastes
Canticle of Canticles
Wisdom
Ecclesiasticus

The Prophetical Books
Isaias
Jeremias
Lamentations
Baruch
Ezechiel
Daniel
Osee
Joel
Amos
Abdias
Jonas
Micheas
Nahum
Habacuc
Sophonias
Aggeus
Zacharias
Malachias

Historical Books
1 Machabees
2 Machabees

Roman Catholic (Jerusalem)

The Pentateuch
Genesis
Exodus
Leviticus
Numbers
Deuteronomy

The Historical Books
Joshua
Judges
Ruth
1 Samuel
2 Samuel
1 Kings
2 Kings
1 Chronicles
2 Chronicles
Ezra and Nehemiah
Tobit
Judith
Esther
1 Maccabees
2 Maccabees

The Wisdom Books
Job
Psalms
Proverbs
Ecclesiastes
The Song of Songs
Wisdom
Ecclesiasticus

The Prophets
Isaiah
Jeremiah
Lamentations
Baruch
Ezekiel
Daniel
Hosea
Joel
Amos
Obadiah
Jonah
Micah
Nahum
Habakkuk
Zephaniah
Haggai
Zechariah
Malachi

Protestant (King James)*

The Pentateuch
Genesis (Gen.)
Exodus (Exod.)
Leviticus (Lev.)
Numbers (Num.)
Deuteronomy (Deut.)

The Historical Books
Joshua (Josh.)
Judges (Judg.)
Ruth (Ruth)
1 Samuel (1 Sam.)
2 Samuel (2 Sam.)
1 Kings (1 Kings)
2 Kings (2 Kings)
1 Chronicles (1 Chron.)
2 Chronicles (2 Chron.)
Ezra (Ezra)
Nehemiah (Neh.)
Esther (Esther)

The Poetical Books
Job (Job)
Psalms (Ps.)
Proverbs (Prov.)
Ecclesiastes (Eccles.)
Song of Solomon (Song of Sol.)

The Prophetical Books
Isaiah (Isa.)
Jeremiah (Jer.)
Lamentations (Lam.)
Ezekiel (Ezek.)
Daniel (Dan.)
Hosea (Hos.)
Joel (Joel)
Amos (Amos)
Obadiah (Obad.)
Jonah (Jonah)
Micah (Mic.)
Nahum (Nah.)
Habakkuk (Hab.)
Zephaniah (Zeph.)
Haggai (Hag.)
Zechariah (Zech.)
Malachi (Mal.)

APOCRYPHA

Protestant
1 Esdras (1 Esd.)
2 Esdras (2 Esd.)
Tobit (Tob.)
Judith (Jth.)
Additions to Esther (Rest of Esther)
Wisdom of Solomon (Wisd. of Sol.)
Ecclesiasticus (Ecclus.)

Protestant (cont.)
Baruch, with the Epistle of Jeremiah (Bar.)
Song of the Three Children (Song of Three Children)
History of Susanna (Sus.)
Bel and the Dragon (Bel and Dragon)
Prayer of Manasses (Pr. of Man.)
1 Maccabees (1 Macc.)
2 Maccabees (2 Macc.)

Roman Catholic
Tobias
Judith
Wisdom
Ecclesiasticus
Baruch
1 Machabees
2 Machabees

NEW TESTAMENT

Matthew (Matt.)
Mark (Mark)
Luke (Luke)
John (John)
(Matthew through John: The Gospels)
Acts of the Apostles (Acts)
Romans (Rom.)
1 Corinthians (1 Cor.)
2 Corinthians (2 Cor.)
Galatians (Gal.)
Ephesians (Eph.)
Philippians (Phil.)
Colossians (Col.)
1 Thessalonians (1 Thess.)
2 Thessalonians (2 Thess.)
1 Timothy (1 Tim.)
2 Timothy (2 Tim.)
Titus (Titus)
Philemon (Philemon)
Hebrews (Heb.)
James (Jas.)
1 Peter (1 Pet.)
2 Peter (2 Pet.)
1 John (1 John)
2 John (2 John)
3 John (3 John)
Jude (Jude)
Revelation (Rev.) (Apocalypse)

* Standard abbreviations for this version, given in parentheses, are used in the text of this encyclopedia.

the days of the author of the book of Ecclesiasticus, that is, according to the King James Version of the text, of Jesus, son of Sirach of Jerusalem. The first stage is popularly thought to have been completed through the influence of Ezra, who in 438 or 397 B.C. returned to Judah from Babylonian exile, bringing with him either the first five books, or Law (*Torah,* Heb., "teaching"), or the core of that collection. Five books of the Law, known by Christians as the Pentateuch (Gr., "scroll of five"), or perhaps the first six books, or Hexateuch, constituted the earliest part of the Old Testament to be confirmed as authoritative. The second or later stage included the *Nebiim,* or Prophets, and the third or last stage included the *Ketubim,* or Writings, called by Christians the Hagiographa. The thirty-nine books of the Old Testament as customarily found in Christian usage correspond in contents with twenty-four books of the Hebrew Old Testament. The difference in number is accounted for by the subdivision of some of them (for example, Chronicles) into smaller units (that is, 1 and 2 Chronicles).

The main principle that determined the choice of all three collections of the Old Testament was that of providing a basis for the teaching and guidance of the new religious community that had been established since the exile. It was hoped that by obeying the will of God, as revealed in the sacred books, the type of destruction that had once overtaken the former northern and southern kingdoms thenceforth would be avoided; *see* ISRAEL, KINGDOM OF.

The Torah (q.v.), comprising the first group of Hebrew books to be singled out and set apart as inspired, is therefore absolutely authoritative. It consists of Genesis, Exodus, Leviticus, Numbers, and Deuteronomy, and embraces the earlier historical narratives and law codes of Israel and Judah.

During the second presumed stage of canonization, the historical and prophetic books, known as the Prophets, were added to the collection. These books apparently were used for reading and study in the synagogue, a custom that arose during the exile; *see* BABYLONIAN CAPTIVITY. The first six books of the Prophets (Joshua, Judges, 1 and 2 Samuel, 1 and 2 Kings) are often called the Earlier or Former Prophets; the remaining fifteen books, or Latter Prophets, are subdivided into Isaiah, Jeremiah, and Ezekiel, and into the "Twelve", sometimes called, because of their length rather than because of their importance, the books of the Minor Prophets.

The latter Prophets thus include the books of Isaiah, concerning the great 8th-century preacher in Jerusalem; Jeremiah, about the stern spiritual leader who lived just before and after the fall of the city in 597; and Ezekiel, about the prophet of the Babylonian exile who dreamed and planned a restored city, state, and Temple. These books are followed by the "Twelve", named for the prophets who figure in them. These "Twelve" prophetic books, listed below in approximate chronological order, were chiefly concerned with coming doom. Amos concerns the prophet who in the 8th century B.C. warned Israel of coming ruin; Hosea, the prophet who interpreted this disaster in terms of his own domestic tragedy; Micah, the prophet of Judea who lived through the final fall of the northern kingdom in 721 B.C. and foresaw a similar catastrophe for Jerusalem; Zephaniah concerns King Josiah's contemporary who, about 627 B.C., warned his people of the coming "Day of the Lord" when only a "remnant" of Judah would be saved; Nahum, the prophet who predicted the fall of the Assyrian capital city of Nineveh; Habakkuk, the prophet who dealt with the delay in God's judgment; Haggai and 1 Zechariah (Zech. 1–8), the prophets who preached during the rebuilding of the Temple in 520 B.C.; Obadiah, the prophet who composed a "song of hate" for Edom (q.v.), the old enemy of the Jews; Malachi (about 460 B.C.) and Joel (350 B.C.), the prophets who prophesied the coming Day of Judgment; Jonah, the disobedient prophet whose terrible adventure with a sea monster made him obedient to the word of Yahweh, and who eventually saw some hope for the conversion of the heathen, even the residents of barbarous Nineveh; and 2 Zechariah (Zech. 9–14), containing a glorious prophecy of the Reign of God. The books of the "Twelve" foresaw the approaching catastrophes of the nations, not only of Israel and Judah but of the others as well, in the light of divine judgment; but beyond the Day of Judgment, they saw hope for a better time to come. Out of this unconquerable hope grew the belief in the Messianic age, which characterized much of later Judaism and of early Christianity (q.v.). *See* MESSIAH.

The third collection of books, the Writings (or, Christian, Hagiographa), was added by the early scribes after the time of Ezra; the collection also came to be used as part of Temple worship and for study in the synagogues. It is primarily distinguished by the five books of poetry called the Psalms, comprising 150 Psalms in all. Many were old hymns sung in the Temple and some were more or less secular in origin, but all were pervaded by religious spirit. Other poetical works were Proverbs, brief wise sayings in verse form, and Job, a great poem dealing with the problem of human suffering and divine justice. The five "rolls" (Megilloth) also were added: Song of Songs (known to Roman Catholics as Canticles; to Protestants as the Song of Solomon), a collection of love and marriage poems; Ruth, the idyll of King David's Moabite ancestress; Lamentations, on the fall of Jerusalem; Ecclesiastes, a cynical tract on human vanity and futility; and Esther, the tale of the heroic Jewess who saved her people from massacre by the Persians. Finally, Daniel, written too late for inclusion with the "Twelve", was added. The work of the Chronicler, in the four books 1 and 2 Chronicles, Ezra, and Nehemiah, which contain the sacred annals of Jerusalem and the Temple, complete the collection.

THE APOCRYPHA

The Apocrypha may be viewed as a fourth collection, totaling fourteen books, that was accepted by the early Christians, and by Greek-speaking Jews outside Palestine, especially in Egypt. These books shed valuable light on the history and religious thought of the period between the two Testaments, called by some scholars the intertestamental period. In the Greek Bible and also in the Latin Vulgate, used by Roman Catholics, the books are dispersed through the Old Testament. In the Bibles used by most Protestant denominations, these books are either omitted or are made a separate section at the end of the Old Testament, in order to make clear their secondary value (see accompanying chart, *The Biblical Canon*). The books are not included in the Hebrew Bible.

The books called 1 and 2 Maccabees are two independent histories of the Maccabean War of the 2nd century B.C. The former is a more factual, the latter a more rhetorical and legendary, work. Tobit is a delightful short story that stresses the virtues of Pharisaism (*see* PHARISEES). Judith is the tale of a heroic Jewess who risked her life for her city, Bethulia. The Wisdom of Solomon is a treatise on wisdom and righteousness and an indictment of idolatry; it also teaches the immortality of the soul. Ecclesiasticus, or Sirach, is another wisdom book, the wise sayings of an aged teacher in Jerusalem early in the 2nd century B.C. Baruch, a book attributed to a fictitious author, warns the Jews to avoid idolatry while in exile in Babylon; chapter 6, known as the Letter of Jeremiah, reinforces this theme. Bel and the Dragon is a novelette that unmasks the trickery of the promotors of idolatry. The Additions to Esther, also made during this period, introduces the name of God and adds prayers and documents (it appears separately in some Protestant Bibles and as a part of Esther in Roman Catholic Bibles).

The Prayer of Manasses and the Song of the Three Children, further examples of pious fiction, emphasize prayer and devotion. Susanna is a short story designed to show that the two witnesses required at every trial should be examined separately to prevent collusion (Prayer, Song, and Susanna are included in the book of Daniel in Roman Catholic Bibles). The book numbered 1 Esdras (3, in the Vulgate), is a narrative of the fall of Jerusalem and the return of the Jews from exile under the leadership of Ezra (that is, of Esdras). Second, or 2, Esdras (4, in the Vulgate), is an apocalyptic work from the end of the 1st century A.D. existing only in Latin, Syriac, and other versions, but not in Greek; it deals with the religious problem created by the fall of Jerusalem and the further dispersion of the Jews, and contains Christian interpolations.

The view that the Pseudepigrapha was the result of a fifth wave of canonization succeeding the Apocrypha, but one that failed, is hardly supportable. Only a few copies of the Septuagint contain 3 Maccabees, the story of the attempted massacre of Jews in Alexandria in the reign of Ptolemy Philopator (222–205 B.C.); and 4 Maccabees, a discourse on "the triumph of mind over matter" using the story of the martyrdom of the seven brothers and other stories found in 2 Maccabees. In addition, only one or two of the pseudonymous writings, such as the Psalms of Solomon and the Testaments of the Twelve Patriarchs, ever were viewed as sacred Scripture in the early Christian Church or included in the great codices of the Greek Bible. Most of the others have never been regarded as divine in inspiration. *See* APOCALYPTIC WRITINGS.

THE NEW TESTAMENT

The full New Testament canon of twenty-seven books was not fixed until the 4th century A.D., although an almost complete collection was in use in Rome by about 180 A.D. These Christian additions to the Old Testament comprised the four Gospels; the Acts of the Apostles; the Letters, or Epistles, attributed to Paul, fourteen in all (although several are of doubtful authenticity); and the Revelation, or Apocalypse, considered to be by John. See accompanying chart, *The Biblical Canon*.

The stages by which the New Testament canon developed have not yet been established to the satisfaction of all Biblical scholars. Some of them maintain that the attempt of Marcion, a Gnostic heretic (*see* GNOSTICISM) who lived about 140 A.D., to provide a "Bible" that was to take the place of the Old Testament, was the starting point of the New Testament. His "Gospel" was supposedly an abridged copy of Luke and his "Apostle" a revision of ten Epistles of Paul. It is more probable, however, that the New Testament canon grew out of the use of the twenty-seven books in the preaching, teaching, and worship of the Christian Church through several generations. Gradually, these books stood out as the inspired writings that must be added to the Greek Old Testament, which had been the Bible of the Christian Church from the start.

Toward the end of the 1st century A.D. the Pauline letters were collected and others, including Hebrews, were added to them. The four Gospels were combined to form the "Four-fold Gospel" (that is, the four Gospels considered as a spiritual unity) about 140–150 A.D., with the Acts of the Apostles having been separated from Luke and located at the head of the "Catholic", or Apostolic, Epistles. Shortly afterward the Revelation (of John) was added, although the Eastern Church did not generally accept it until the first decade of the 5th century. It is certain, however, that during the theological crisis of the 2nd century all the books presently found in the New Testament proved invaluable as Apostolic witnesses to the historic Christian faith by refuting Gnostic speculations. The list of twenty-seven books finally agreed upon as canonical in the 4th century appears in the Festal Epistle (Ep. 39) of Saint Athanasius (q.v.) in 367 A.D.

The modern arrangement, intended to be more or less chronological, places the Gospels first, as records of the life of Christ. Matthew, supposedly written by the Apostle Matthew, therefore comes first; then comes Mark, which Saint Augustine and others described as an abridgment of Matthew, but which modern scholars view as the earliest of the Gospels; then Luke, originally the first part of a two-volume work, the other part being the Acts of the Apostles; and finally John, which was thought to supplement, complete, and even to correct the impression left by the first three Gospels. It is now, however, recognized as an attempt to restate Christian tradition in language that would be better understood among various groups in the Greco-Roman world, especially those influenced by Gnostic or theosophic speculation. The book of Acts, which came next, after being separated from Luke, tells the story of the spread of the Church from Jerusalem to Rome; it is the only early authoritative source for the history of the Jerusalem church in the 1st century and for the life and work of Paul. Without it, and with only the Gospels and Epistles, the interrelation of the latter would be almost wholly obscure. The letters of Paul came next. In order of inclusion, these are Romans, chronologically one of his last letters, dealing with the questions of justification by faith apart from obedience to the Law, and with the future of Israel, which had rejected the Gospel; 1 and 2 Corinthians, dealing with problems of the church in Corinth; Galatians, the great defense of the freedom of the Gospel from legalism; Ephesians, presently viewed by many scholars as a later selection from Paul's teachings made by one of his followers; Philippians, a letter from prison thanking the Christians at Philippi for a certain gift; Colossians, written to offset the Gnostic heresy that had sprung up at Colossae; 1 and 2 Thessalonians, probably the earliest of Paul's surviving letters, addressed to the Christians in Thessalonica and dealing with their problems; 1 and 2 Timothy and Titus, the so-called "Pastoral Epistles", dealing with Church problems about 100 A.D. from the point of view of Paul's teaching and activity; and Philemon, a brief, affectionate note urging the recipient to take back a runaway slave, Onesimus, who perhaps later became a Christian bishop. Hebrews is a homily designed to show that the exalted, heavenly Christ was superior to angels, to Moses, and to Aaron, and that His death was more efficacious for salvation than all the ancient sacrifices. James is a homily containing a variety of religious and moral exhortations. 1 Peter deals with problems faced by Christians in northwestern Asia Minor toward the end of the 1st century A.D., and 2 Peter is an apocalyptic tract and diatribe dating from about 150 A.D. The three Epistles of John belong with the Gospel of John; all four writings repudiate the Gnostic-Docetic misinterpretation of the life of Christ, which viewed Him as a phantom deity appearing only temporarily and intermittently in the likeness of a human body. Jude is another sharp rebuke to heretical teachers. The Revelation of John is an apocalypse that outlines the course of coming events, beginning with the persecution of Christians in western Asia Minor, up to the final consummation, the coming of the New Jerusalem from heaven to earth and the final reign of Christ in glory. *See* APOCALYPTIC WRITINGS; CHRISTOLOGY; SECOND ADVENT OF CHRIST.

For further information on the subjects within the scope of this article *see* BIBLE, ENGLISH TRANSLATIONS OF; BIBLE, INTERPRETATIONS OF THE; and articles on most of the various versions, editions, and books of the Bible mentioned. Individual entries should also be consulted on persons important in Biblical or church history.

Original woodcut illustration from a first edition of the 1522 Martin Luther translation of the New Testament.
New York Public Library

BIBLE, ENGLISH TRANSLATIONS OF THE, Holy Scriptures in English vernacular; *see* BIBLE. Prior to the 14th century, the only complete Bibles in England were in Latin, used by the clergy. Passages of the Bible were translated from Latin into Anglo-Saxon or Old English, however, as early as the 7th century, when some passages provided material for Caedmon (q.v.), the first English poet. In the 8th century the English scholar and theologian Bede (q.v.) translated parts of the Gospels. Other significant translations from the Scriptures into Old English were made by the scholar Alcuin, by Alfred, King of the West Saxons, and by the grammarian Aelfric (qq.v.). Virtually all the Scriptural manuscripts that circulated in England during the period of Norman dominance, following 1066, were in either French or Anglo-Norman, both unintelligible to the majority of the people; *see* ENGLAND: *History;* ENGLISH LANGUAGE: *History.* Although various books and parts of the Bible appeared in English during the first half of the 14th century, the first full translation was the *Wycliffe Bible,* sponsored by the English theologian John Wycliffe (q.v.) and completed about 1385; a second version appeared about 1395.

For nearly three quarters of a century after the printing of the first Bible in Germany in the middle of the 15th century, only manuscript copies of Wycliffe's Bible were available in England. The first printed Scriptural writing in English translation was a version of the New Testament completed in 1525 by William Tyndale (q.v.), an outspoken critic of the Roman Catholic Church. Based on the current Greek text, of which only two complete volumes and a few fragments are extant, 18,000 copies of this work were printed in Germany and many were smuggled into England. Tyndale subsequently translated the Pentateuch (1530) and other parts of the Old Testament, all of which were printed on the Continent. Tyndale's style, characterized by the use of popular idiom and a simple, rhythmic prose, became the model for English translations of the Bible for the next four centuries.

The first complete translation of the Scriptures to appear in English print was made by the clergyman Miles Coverdale (q.v.). This work, completed in 1535, was based chiefly on the Vulgate (q.v.) and the versions of other translators, including Tyndale and the German religious reformer Martin Luther (q.v.). In the next four years three additional versions of the Bible were issued in England: *Matthew's Bible* (1537), prepared by the English martyr John Rogers (1500?–55; also known as Thomas Matthew) mainly from Tyndale's and Coverdale's works; *Taverner's Bible* (1538), a revision, by the English religious reformer Richard Taverner (1505?–75), of *Matthew's Bible;* and the *Great Bible* (1539), edited by Coverdale and published in six editions. The second of these became known as *Cranmer's Bible,* in honor of Thomas Cranmer (q.v.), archbishop of Canterbury, who wrote a preface to it. The next important English version of the Bible was completed in 1560 in Geneva, Switzerland, by English Protestants in exile. The New Testament was translated by the English prelate William Whittingham (1524?–79), but revised by other scholars before inclusion in the completed Bible. Known officially as the *Geneva Bible,* it contained several innovations, including the division of chapters into numbered verses. This version became popular among the Puritans (q.v.). The Geneva Bible was followed, in 1568, by the *Bishops' Bible,* a revision of the Great Bible, by scholars and bishops of the Church of England (q.v.). In 1582 a commission of the Roman Catholic Church in England issued an official version of the New Testament. The entire Bible, completed in 1609–10, is known as the *Douai* (*Douay*) or *Douai-Rheims*

Bible, so named because of the work of Cardinal William Allen (1532–94) of Reims, France, and the scholar Gregory Martin (1540–82) of Douai, both English exiles in France. Based on the Vulgate, it was proclaimed the official Roman Catholic version in English. Since then it has undergone many revisions, the most recent being the Confraternity Version (1952–61), later issued in 1970 as *The New American Bible*. In the 20th century two other important translations to receive official Roman Catholic approval, both in modern idiom, are: a translation (New Testament 1945, Old Testament 1949), also based on the Vulgate, by Ronald A. Knox (1888–1957), and the *Jerusalem Bible* (complete Bible 1966), which was translated, with certain modifications, from the original French version.

The most notable translation of the Bible in English is the Authorized Version, completed in 1611. Sponsored by James I (q.v.), King of Great Britain, and thus also known as the *King James Version*, the Authorized Version is the work of fifty-four theologians and scholars, who completely revised the Bishops' Bible using Greek and Hebrew texts and earlier English translations. The style, closely modeled after that of Tyndale, and the spiritual content of the translation profoundly influenced the development of English literature during the next three centuries. A revision of the Authorized Version New Testament, containing an appendix of changes recommended by American scholars, was published in 1881. The Old Testament of this *English Revised Version* appeared in 1885, and the Apocrypha in 1895. In 1901 an *American Standard Version*, without the Apocrypha, was published, incorporating these changes and new readings by American scholars. A committee of the International Council of Religious Education (now the Division of Christian Education and Ministry of the National Council of the Churches of Christ in the United States of America, q.v.), representing forty leading Protestant denominations in the United States and Canada, undertook a comprehensive revision of the American Standard Version, with the object of utilizing data from newly discovered Bible manuscripts and ancient papyri and of eliminating archaic terminology. Known as the *Revised Standard Version*, it was completed in 1957 with the publication of the Apocrypha; the New Testament had appeared in 1946 and the Old Testament in 1952. The National Council of Churches published a complete Bible including the Apocrypha, known as the *Oxford Annotated Bible*, in 1965. In 1965 a Catholic-approved edition of the Revised Standard Version, sponsored by the National Council of Churches, was published. In 1961 the New Testament of an English project, rendered from original sources into more modern style, idiom, and vocabulary, was published; the complete translation appeared in 1970 as *The New English Bible*.

Jewish translations of the Hebrew Bible into English by individual scholars began appearing in the 18th century. The first volume of a new translation sponsored by the Jewish Publication Society of America, the Torah, appeared in 1962. The Scrolls (the Song of Songs, Ruth, Lamentations, Ecclesiastes, Esther, and Jonah), which are read on festival days, were published in 1969. Isaiah and Psalms were issued in 1973, and other books were scheduled for publication.

Since the beginning of the 16th century there have been many private translations, not under the sponsorship of any particular religious group. The most popular of recent versions is the *New Testament in Modern English* (1958) by J. B. Phillips (1906–). In 1964 *Genesis*, the first volume of the projected multivolume *Anchor Bible*, was published, and by 1975 more than thirty additional volumes had appeared. The publishers invited scholars of many nationali-

The first boke of Moses, called Genesis. Fo. i.

The first dayes worke. The seconde dayes worke. The thirde dayes worke.

The fourth dayes worke. The fifth dayes worke. The sixte dayes worke.

The first Chapter.

A

IN ẏ begynnynge God created heauen ⁊ earth: and ẏ earth was voyde and emptie, and darcknes was vpon the depe, ⁊ ẏ spirite of God moued vpõ the water.

And God sayde: let there be light, ⁊ there was light. And God sawe the light that it was good. Then God deuyded ẏ light from the darcknes, and called the light, Daye: and the darcknes, Night. Then of the euenynge and mornynge was made the first daye.

And God sayde: let there be a firmament betwene the waters, and let it deuyde ẏ waters a sunder. Then God made ẏ firmamẽt, and parted the waters vnder the firmamẽt, from the waters aboue the firmament: And so it came to passe. And God called ẏ firmament, Heauen. Then of the euenynge ⁊ mornynge was made the seconde daye.

And God sayde: let the waters vnder heauen gather thẽselues vnto one place, ẏ the drye londe maye appeare. And so it came to passe. And God called ẏ drye londe, Earth: and the gatheringe together of waters called he, ẏ See. And God sawe ẏ it was good. Iob 26. Pro. 8. c

And God sayde: let ẏ earth bringe forth grene grasse and herbe, that beareth sede: ⁊ frutefull trees, that maye beare frute, euery one after his kynde, hauynge their owne sede in them selues vpon the earth. And so it came to passe. And the earth brought forth grene grasse and herbe, ẏ beareth sede euery one after his kynde, ⁊ trees bearinge frute, ⁊ B

Page of a first edition of the 1535 Coverdale Bible, *the first complete Bible printed in English.*

New York Public Library

ties, without regard to religious background, to retranslate and annotate the Bible in the light of recent archeological and philological discoveries. The commentaries in many of the volumes are extensive.

BIBLE, INTERPRETATIONS OF THE, attempts to clarify the meaning of the sacred Scriptures of the Jews and Christians. All sacred books require interpretation because such books are assumed to contain the essential truths upon which theology (q.v.), ethics, and ritual are based. Careful interpretation presupposes accurate scholarship; all textual and linguistic obscurities must be removed before the significance of the religious message can be understood properly. Interpretation has taken the form of commentaries, expositions, and elaborations written by exegetes. The procedures for the purpose of interpretation have been applied to the Bible ever since it was compiled in the successive canons, or authorized collections. *See* BIBLE; BIBLE, CANON OF THE; BIBLE SCHOLARSHIP.

THE HISTORY OF JEWISH INTERPRETATION

The earliest interpreters of Old Testament manuscripts were the Jewish scribes (*see* SCRIBE) of the 5th century B.C. At first they were merely the copyists of the Bible manuscripts, but, because of their familiarity with the documents, their chief occupation soon became that of explaining the divine commandments contained in the Torah, or Pentateuch (qq.v.). The Ten Commandments (*see* DECALOGUE) required careful observance in Jewish religious life, and therefore had to be understood precisely. The scribes also extended their interpretation to the other two parts of the Old Testament, the Prophets and the Writings, because to some degree both were assumed to contain rules also requiring obedient observance.

Torah scroll inscribed on parchment with silver-mounted rollers, from 18th-century Germany.
Jewish Museum, N.Y.

Oral Law. Out of this intensive study grew the "tradition of the elders", that is, of scribal teaching, written down about 210 A.D. by the Jewish scholar Judah (135?–220?), called *ha-Nasi* ("the Prince"), in the work known as the Mishnah (q.v.). Beginning in the 3rd century, a body of interpretation began to be compiled, resulting in two collections, the Palestinian Talmud and the Babylonian Talmud; *see* TALMUD. These works drew principally upon the Mishnah and the teachings of the rabbis (*see* RABBI), the successors to the scribes, who, in their academies, studied and commented upon the Old Testament. The Tosefta (compiled 12th and 13th centuries) and the various Midrashim (earliest compilation about the middle of the 2nd century) also contain material from preceding periods (*see* MIDRASH). The Tosefta incorporates additions to the Mishnah; the writings in the Midrashim are mostly homiletical expositions of the various Old Testament books. Many of these homilies, or sermons, are popular in style, especially those gathered from the rabbis called the Tannaim (about 100 B.C.–200 A.D.) and their successors the Geonim (about 500–1000 A.D.). The purely fanciful and fictitious character of the many Midrashim stories used as illustrations and explanations of Scripture reflect their popular origin.

The primary purpose of this growing body of interpretive material, which came to be known as the Oral Law as distinguished from the Law itself, or Torah, was to elicit the literal meaning of the legal commandments and customary usages (*see* HALAKAH) and the ethical and religious principles upon which they were based (*see* HAGGADAH). During the course of the Middle Ages (q.v.), influential scholars and teachers, such as the French-Jewish commentator on the Bible and the Babylonian Talmud known as Rashi (Shelomoh ben Yishaq or Solomon Bar Isaac; 1040–1105) and the Jewish philosopher Maimonides (q.v.), similarly were concerned with the primary, literal, or historical meaning of the sacred text. They were also concerned, however, with its implication for the moral life in obedience to God's commandments and for the spiritual life in preparation for the world to come. Most Jewish scholars assumed that every situation in human life was covered by the sacred revelation in the Old Testament (Lev. 18:5) and that everything contained in the Scriptures had meaning, even the peculiarities in the spelling of words and the unusual shape of some of the letters in certain manuscripts. This view is made clear in Maimonides' two great works, the *Guide for the Perplexed* (about 1190) and the *Mishneh Torah* (known among scholars as "Strong Hand"), published in 1180. Certain other medieval works such as the *Zohar* (13th century) belong to the cabalistic system of esoteric speculation and are not part of the main Jewish interpretative tradition. *See* CABALA.

After the Middle Ages, Jewish exegesis of the Old Testament did not substantially change the insistence upon the primacy of the Law. However, the historical criticism of the 19th century, many aspects of which were anticipated by the Dutch philosopher Baruch Spinoza (q.v.) in his *Theological-Political Treatise* (1670), provided Jewish interpreters with new scholarly methods. Present-day Jewish scholars often interpret the New Testament as well as the Old. The work of the British-Jewish scholar Claude Joseph Goldsmid-Montefiore (1858–1938) has greatly enriched the study of the Gospels (*see* GOSPEL).

THE HISTORY OF CHRISTIAN INTERPRETATION

Christian exegesis began early in the history of Christianity.

Early Church Exegesis. The earliest Christians were Jews, but their interpretation of the Old Testament differed widely from the Jewish. Jesus Himself had rejected, on many points, the current "tradition of the elders" (Mark 7, Matt. 5–7, 23), and had approached the Scriptures with a direct, personal understanding and interpretation of Scriptural meaning. The Apostles, especially Saint Paul (q.v.), studied the Old Testament chiefly for evidence in support of the Christian gospel. In their view, the Gospel contains the true "meaning" of Scripture and reflects the divine plan from the creation of the world.

The Law, according to Paul, had been "holy, and just, and good" (Rom. 7:12). However, it also had been fulfilled in the coming of Christ, and was therefore no longer binding upon men, who now must live by "faith" or in "grace" and who were to be "justified", or acquitted, at the bar of divine justice by faith alone, apart from works of the Law (*see* ROMANS). Much of Paul's writing, and probably much of his preaching, centered on this theme, and became a legacy of interpretation for all later Christian theology, especially as expounded by the prelate and theologian Saint Augustine and the German religious reformer Martin Luther (qq.v.). For some thinkers, such as the heretic Marcion and the Gnostics (*see* GNOSTICISM), the consequence of this distinction between faith in Christ and obedience to the Law was the total repudiation of the Old Testament, and the rejection of the "God of the Jews", the Creator of the World, as an evil "demiurge" subordinate to the one supreme good God revealed by Jesus. This interpretation was a perversion of Paul's teaching; yet the strain of anti-Judaism and of antilegalism, and the tendency to depreciate the Old Testament, has survived to the present. Another result of the reevaluation of the Old Testament was that for many of the Christian Fathers (*see* FATHERS OF THE CHURCH), the Old Testament became a collection of proof texts for such Christian doctrines as the messiahship of Jesus, His resurrection, the final conquest of evil (especially of demons, as the pagan gods mentioned in the Old Testament were interpreted), and even the divine and human natures of Christ (q.v.) and the doctrine of the Trinity, *see* CHRISTOLOGY; TRINITY.

Allegory. To consider the Old Testament in this way, the early Church made use of allegorical interpretation, which Greek philosophers, especially the Stoics, had already applied to the Greek myths and to the works of the Greek poet Homer, and which the Jewish-Hellenistic philosopher Philo Judaeus had applied also to the Hebrew Bible; *see* ALLEGORY; HOMER; PHILO JUDAEUS; STOICISM. Consequently, many of the barbarous or indecent stories in the Old Testament, and those which lay on a lower level of religious meaning than the spiritual insights of the great prophets and psalmists, were interpreted allegorically. Such stories were considered veiled accounts of the conquest of vice by virtue or of human frailty and folly by divine goodness. Not all interpreters, however, regarded the allegorical meaning as the only possible one. For example, one of the most widely used methods applied to both Testaments was that of the Christian theologian Origen (q.v.) of Alexandria and of the Alexandrian school of thought during the 2nd and 3rd centuries. The theory behind this method assumed that Scripture contained a threefold meaning: literal, moral, and mystical, or allegorical. By this method even the earliest passages in the Old Testament were interpreted as foretelling (in cryptic terms) the Christian revelation; thereby one of the great arguments in favor of Christianity was supplied.

The greatest landmarks in the history of Christian exegesis all made use of allegory as part of a composite method of interpretation; two examples of this method were Origen's own work *On First Principles* (preserved in a Latin version of the 4th century), especially Book IV, and *Christian Teaching* (4 vol., written between 397 and 426) by Saint Augustine.

Despite the influence of the Church Fathers of the school of Antioch (4th and 5th centuries), who rejected all but the sober literal and historical type of interpretation, allegorism proved to have a lasting effect, especially in the medieval Western Church. In the classical education of the 4th and 5th centuries, flowery rhetoric and clever subtlety took the place of plain speaking and logical arguments, and partly gave rise to a widely popular system of Biblical interpretation. According to this system, there existed a fourfold type of Scriptural meaning; (1) the literal, which tells what happened; (2) the allegorical, which tells what to believe; (3) the moral, which tells what to do; and (4) the anagogical, which tells what to hope for, that is, "heaven". Thus, "Jerusalem", which is mentioned numberless times in Scripture, was accordingly taken to mean: (1) a city in Palestine; (2) the Church; (3) the orderly religious life; and (4) eternal life, as the heavenly "city of peace". Behind these connected meanings lay, however, a profound sense of the purely religious meaning which dominates the sacred writings. Nevertheless, the detailed interpretation was often trivial, especially when set forth by half-educated friars and monks.

Renaissance and Reformation. The Renaissance and Reformation (qq.v.) brought a new emphasis in the theory and practice of interpretation. It came to be accepted that a literal understanding of Scipture must precede any attempt to allegorize meanings of Scripture. Only then was it possible to allow other permissible senses that led toward spiritual, doctrinal, or practical understanding.

According to the Dutch scholar and humanist Desiderius Erasmus (q.v.) and the German humanists of the 15th and 16th centuries, the Church is not the sole interpreter entitled to determine and define the true significance of Scripture. On the contrary, Scripture determines what the Church must teach. The Bible is a revelation of God; He does not hide Himself in a mystery that only allegorical exposition can uncover. In this spirit, the English theologian John Colet (q.v.) began lecturing in 1494 on the Epistles of Paul, "explaining them as one would explain the letters of Cicero", that is, as one would study the works of the Roman orator and statesman Cicero (q.v.). In other words, as the ancient Jewish exegetes had maintained, Scripture is itself the best interpretation of Scripture. However, the Christian, as the French Protestant theologian and religious reformer John Calvin (q.v.) maintained, can rely also on the inner testimony of the Holy Spirit (*see* HOLY GHOST), which affirms and ratifies the true meaning of the Bible, as one reads it or hears it read. In the light of these assumptions, the Bible as a whole came to be interpreted as a divine message intended to be understood in human terms.

Modern Emphases. The greatest impetus to fresh interpretative studies has come from the scholarly analysis of the Bible and related documents on the basis of historical principles. These researches have reinforced the basic literal and historical approach toward the meaning of Biblical texts that is universally recognized in the exegetical studies of Jewish, Roman Catholic, and Protestant scholars. Differences among the scholars consist chiefly in their understanding of the purpose of Bible study.

MODERN JEWISH AND CHRISTIAN VIEWS

Jewish study of the Bible naturally centers on the Old Testament, which is the sacred literature and the classical documentation of Judaism. Judaism always has been the religion of the Torah, a divine revelation of God's will for man conveyed through the patriarchs and prophets, especially Moses. It is the "way" in which man must walk if he is to please God. Differences between Orthodox, Conservative, and Reform Jews consist largely in degrees of emphasis upon the literal force of these requirements.

For Protestants, the center of interest consists partly of the history of the divine revelation, viewed as reaching a climax and fulfillment in Jesus Christ, and partly of the doctrinal presuppositions or inferences to be drawn from Scripture. Protestantism has taken seriously the Reformation principle that even the Church itself is "under the divine judgment", and must conform to teaching what is revealed in Holy Scripture. Various Protestant churches have undertaken to conform not only their doctrinal teaching but also their patterns of organization and of worship to the models set forth in the New Testament, as these are understood in particular groups. Hence the variety in Protestant types of organization, ranging from pure congregationalism, or even Spirit-guided individualism with no formal organization or officers, to presbyterianism, episcopacy, and synodical authority. Similarly, Protestant forms of worship vary from free and unhindered spiritual utterance to the solemn observance of a prescribed ritual. In almost every case, a warrant for the particular preference of the church is sought and found in the Bible.

In the Roman Catholic Church, on the contrary, the interpretation of Scripture derives authority from the tradition of Church doctrine rather than from the Bible. As with the ancient Pharisees (q.v.), Catholics consider it inconceivable that there should be any disagreement between their church and the tradition that has been committed to it apart from the Bible as well as in and through the Bible. Consequently, although the Bible is regarded as a collection of inerrant documents, it does not establish the tradition of the church but supports it. The church therefore has the right, the authority, and the duty to define the true Christian teaching, without depending upon private study or interpretation of the Bible to arrive at the truth. This teaching office of the church cannot be abdicated or neglected in favor of even the most learned or pious private interpreter, who suffers from the disadvantage that the results of his studies may differ substantially from those of another individual.

Modern Roman Catholic exegesis is based upon the type of exegesis that came to prevail in the West after the 15th century, when the long reign of allegorism ended. Thus the important encyclical *Divino Afflante Spiritu* ("Under the Inspiration of the Holy Spirit", 1943) of Pope Pius XII (*see under* PIUS) asserts the right and the duty of the Catholic scholar to study not only the Latin Vulgate, which is the authorized version in the church, but also the original text, early manuscripts, and versions; *see* BIBLE, VERSIONS OF THE. The encyclical urges them also to devote themselves to textual criticism; to look for the "spiritual sense" of Scripture, that is, the genuinely religious meaning, not some allegorical interpretation read into it; to study the Church Fathers, who were the classical expositors, and many of whom spoke the language of the Scriptures from childhood; and to consider carefully the free use of figure, metaphor, and parable in much of ancient Near Eastern and Middle Eastern literature, to which the Bible, as a historical document, belongs. The Roman Catholic Church insists that its own scholars become proficient in Biblical studies and that the exegete has the right to pursue his researches in freedom.

ND I ſawe when the
Lambe opened one of the
ſeales, and I heard as it
were the noiſe of thunder,
one of the foure beaſtes,
ſaying, Come and ſee.
2 And I ſaw, and behold, a white
horſe, and hee that ſate on him had a
bowe, and a crowne was giuen vnto
him, and hee went foorth conquering,
and to conquere.
3 And when hee had opened the ſe-
cond ſeale, I heard the ſecond beaſt ſay,
Come and ſee.
4 And there went out another
horſe that was red: and power was
giuen to him that ſate thereon to take
peace from the earth, and that they
ſhould kill one another: and there was
giuen vnto him a great ſword.
5 And when hee had opened the
third ſeale, I heard the third beaſt ſay,
Come and ſee. And I beheld, and loe,
a blacke horſe: and hee that ſate on him
had a paire of balances in his hand.

Section of a page from the first edition (1611) of the King James Bible, or Authorized Version.

Bettmann Archive

In the Anglican Church and the Eastern Orthodox Church, the prevailing views share to some extent both the Protestant principle of intellectual freedom and the Roman emphasis upon the responsibility of the church as teacher of the divine truth. Both the Anglican and Eastern Orthodox churches rely upon traditional authority and view the patristic inheritance as invaluable and inalienable. Since the middle of the 19th century, Anglican scholars in particular have interpreted the Bible with great freedom in the light of historical methods of scholarship.

For further information within the scope of this subject, *see* BIBLE, ENGLISH TRANSLATIONS OF; BIBLE SCHOLARSHIP; and articles on the major religions and denominations, as well as on the books of the Bible mentioned in this article.

BIBLE SCHOLARSHIP, critical analysis of the texts and literary structure of the Bible (q.v.), and of the archeology and history of Biblical times. Scholarly study of the Bible was first undertaken by Jewish scribes in the 5th century B.C. and later by early Christians; it is historically continuous through the Middle Ages, the Renaissance, the Reformation (qq.v.), and modern times.

The most important methods of scholarship in both ancient and modern times have been textual criticism and literary criticism. In the 19th and 20th centuries, discoveries by archeologists of sites, buildings, artifacts, and manuscripts revealed much information about the history and culture of Biblical times. Biblical archeology may therefore be considered an additional method of Bible scholarship.

TEXTUAL CRITICISM

The science that undertakes to compare and classify the existing manuscripts of an ancient writing, arrange them in families or groups, and trace their interrelations is called textual criticism. This method of scholarship has been practiced from earliest times, that is, ever since copies were made of the oldest and most reliable manuscripts.

The Old Testament. The Old Testament was originally written in Hebrew, of which no autograph survives. The earliest manuscript fragment, a copy of Isaiah, which was among the so-called Dead Sea Scrolls (q.v.) found in 1947 at Wadi Qumran, Palestine, by Bedouin shepherds, dates only from the 1st and 2nd century B.C. The oldest complete manuscripts, all of which are in codex, or book form, date from the 9th and 10th centuries. Among the best of these complete manuscripts are the Cambridge Codex XIII (about 9th century); the Aleppo Sephardic Codex (early 10th century); and the Codex L (1008), presently in Leningrad, in the Soviet Union. All of these codices contain the standard text of the Old Testament as established by the Masoretic scholars (*see* MASORA) who flourished between the 6th and the 10th centuries. The first printed edition of the Hebrew Bible appeared in Soncino, Italy, in 1488. The authoritative critical text of the Hebrew Bible, based upon the Codex L at Leningrad, is the third edition of *Biblia Hebraica* (1937), originally (1905) the work of the German Protestant theologian and Old Testament scholar Rudolf Kittel (1857–1929).

The New Testament. The New Testament was originally written in Greek. Hundreds of surviving manuscripts have been traced to texts existing at the end of the 2nd century A.D. However, no manuscript even relatively complete in form comes from that period. The earliest complete manuscripts, two 4th-century codices, are the Codex Sinaiticus (known as "S" or by the Hebrew letter *aleph*), in the British Museum, which the German theologian and Biblical scholar Count Konstantin von Tischendorf (1815–74) discovered on Mt. Sinai in 1859; and the Codex Vaticanus (known as "B") in the Vatican Library, which contains also a complete Old Testament. The type of text represented by these codices generally conforms to that of certain early fragments of the New Testament, the so-called Chester Beatty papyri (about 250–300 A.D.), found in Egypt in 1931.

In Antioch and Byzantium, about 310 A.D., an eclectic type of text originated, based on earlier manuscripts. The copyists who transcribed this earlier material sometimes chose particular readings from certain of the manuscripts, but often they combined readings by blending textual differences. The text of the Septuagint, the earliest Greek Old Testament (known as the "Koine", or "common", text because it was written in a widely used type of everyday Greek), relied upon this earlier eclectic text. The Septuagint was accepted throughout the East during the Middle Ages and underlies many later editions and translations. This Greek text is referred to also as the *textus receptus,* or "received text", from the name the French printer Robert Estienne (1503–59) gave to his edition of it in 1550. The Dutch scholar and humanist Desiderius Erasmus (q.v.) published a text in 1516 that was practically identical with the medieval, or Byzantine, Koine; and the early English translations of the Bible, including the King James Version of 1611, also were based upon it. Only at the end of the 19th century, when the superior value of Codex Vaticanus was recognized, especially because it was supported by Codex Sinaiticus, was a better Greek text available to translators. Ever since the publication of the Revised English Version (1881–85), one of the earliest translations to adopt it, this better text has been in use.

Annotation. Many modern Bible editions contain footnotes giving the variant readings of the different manuscripts, as well as of the various ancient versions and of quotations by ancient authorities (for example, rabbinic for the Old Testament, patristic for the New Testament). A system of designating manuscripts was introduced by John Jacob Watstein, whose two-volume edition of the Greek New Testament was published in Amsterdam in 1751–52. Use of these designations makes possible a very compact statement of the facts about any given variant reading and saves the student the labor of consulting and collating the various manuscripts. As a rule, according to this system, capital letters are the symbols used for manuscripts written in uncial capitals. For example, "A" stands for Codex Alexandrinus, a 5th- or 6th-century manuscript in the British Museum; "C" for Codex Ephraemi Syri, a palimpsest dat-

The Isaiah Scroll, discovered in 1947 with the Dead Sea Scrolls at Khirbet Qumran, Jordan, dates from the 1st or 2nd century B.C.
Jewish Museum, N.Y.

ing from the 5th century and presently in the Bibliothèque Nationale in Paris; and "D" for Codex Bezae, a 5th- or 6th-century manuscript at Cambridge University. Small letters are used for manuscripts of the Old Latin Version, which was made perhaps about 150 A.D. but survives only in manuscripts dating from the 4th century through the 7th century. Italic numerals, *1, 2, 3,* etc., are used for minuscule, or cursive manuscripts, written in a connected, or "running", hand in lower case letters or script. These manuscripts are mostly later in date than the Old Latin manuscripts or those written in uncials. Tischendorf and later modern editors elaborated and improved upon this system of designating types of manuscript.

New discoveries of ancient manuscripts and fragments continue to increase the material available for textual criticism. In addition, the dating of newly found manuscripts by the use of various scientific devices and techniques has become extremely precise. At present, scholars can usually assign undated material to a span of approximately twenty-five years during which the writing must have taken place.

LITERARY CRITICISM

The literary study of the Bible is concerned with the analysis of language and style in Biblical manuscripts. One of the elementary devices used by the earliest Jewish scribes and Christian copyists in order to detect errors or omissions in transcription was the comparison of the number of lines or even of letters in the original and copy. Careful examination of the text of various manuscripts disclosed differences in spelling, grammar, and style, which were scrupulously noted. The historical background was investigated in order to date the author and his writing and to establish the course of events from various references in the text. Thus, the Psalms, assumed to be mainly by King David (q.v.), were referred by Jewish scholars to events in his life, as known from Samuel, Kings, and Chronicles. Parallel histories, as in the books of Kings and Chronicles, were compared, and differences were noted, especially in statements about the succession of events and about dates. Christians followed the same procedure in studying the Gospels, in attempting to "harmonize" them, and in correlating the letters of Saint Paul with the Acts of the Apostles. In general, these traditional methods of scholarship practiced in ancient times are still relied upon by modern researchers.

The solution of basic linguistic problems and the removal of obscurities and inconsistencies continually involved questions concerning the authenticity and meaning of Biblical writings. For example, in the Old Testament, Esther and Ecclesiastes were examined very carefully by Jewish scholars for their meaning and probable authorship and authority; and in the New Testament, the Epistle to the Hebrews and Revelation were similarly investigated by Christian scholars. The Christian writer and theologian Origen (q.v.) of Alexandria insisted that Hebrews could not have been written by Saint Paul. Saint Dionysus of Alexandria (fl. 3rd cent.) held that the style of Revelation was so different from that of the Gospel of John and the Epistles of John that if Saint John the Evangelist were presumed to be the author of the first work he could not have written the others. Aware of such divergencies, Origen noted carefully the variations between different manuscripts in his preparation of the Hexapla (written between 231 and 250), an edition of the Old Testament that contained parallel Hebrew and Greek versions. So, too, did Saint Jerome in the work he undertook for the Vulgate (4th cent.).

Eventually the books of the Bible were divided into chapters, each given a title indicating its contents. These chapters corresponded more or less to the "lessons" (that is, lections) read at public worship, and a list of them was placed, like a modern table of contents, at the beginning of the manuscripts. Tables of Gospel passages were drawn up, showing how they corresponded to or paralleled one another, and in how many of the Gospels these passages appeared.

Criticism. Modern literary criticism of the Bible rests upon a firm foundation of historical analysis involving internal literary evidence. This type of criticism, sometimes called "higher criticism", has been a continuous labor of scholarship since the middle of the 18th century. By 1753 the French physician Jean Astruct (1684–1766) had recognized the different strands of historical narrative in the Pentateuch, each characterized by a particular vocabulary and especially a particular form of the name for God. At the beginning of the 19th century the German Protestant theologian and Biblical scholar Wilhelm Martin Leberecht De Wette (1780–1849) had succeeded in tracing Deuteronomy to the 7th century B.C., largely on the grounds of internal historical and linguistic characteristics of the text. During the course of the 19th and 20th centuries, scholars also revealed that all of the various groups of Psalms, the later prophetic books, the Wisdom books, and the Apocrypha could be dated with some certainty by the distinctive vocabularies of each and that Isaiah was a composite work in which 2 and 3 Isaiah could be distinguished from 1 Isaiah by a comparison of vocabularies. Similarly, it has been shown that in the New Testament the language used by Saint Paul and Saint John the Evangelist, and by the writers of Hebrews and Revelation, is in each case characteristic of the respective authorship of the books and indicative of the dates of compositions. The Synoptic Gospels, those of Mark, Luke, Matthew, and the underlying sources of each have also been dated by scholars and clearly distinguished in style and language.

One of the great achievements of modern Biblical scholarship is the recognition of various types of Biblical literature. For example, with respect to the Psalms, which fall into various groups or classes, and the stories in Genesis, 1 and 2 Samuel, and 1 and 2 Kings, it is presently believed that each type of literature had its special place and use in the religious life of Israel and of the early Christian Church, and that much of the historical material, and of the Wisdom literature also, was based upon oral tradition. A special kind of research known as form criticism is devoted to studies of this nature with the aim of recovering the form in which the historical tradition circulated during the oral period.

Among the most important tools of literary criticism are reference works such as concordances, dictionaries, and grammars designed to facilitate the study of Biblical literature. The concordance, or alphabetical index of every term in the Bible (except such words as "a", "an", and "the") first came into use during the Middle Ages. The need for the concordance was based upon the assumption that the Bible is a unity, that every part of it sheds light upon every other, and that all words and phrases, especially divine titles and figures of speech, are significant parts of the whole work. By means of such an index, the references are arranged in the order of the books of the Bible for the purpose of trying to establish agreements among the books as integral parts of a system of revealed knowledge. Among the earliest of these works were the Latin Vulgate concordance compiled in 1230 by the French ecclesiastic Hugh of Saint Cher (1200–63?) and the Septuagint concordance, no copies of which survive, compiled about 1300. The leading present-day concordance of the Septuagint is the result of independent scholarly projects, notably an Old Testament concordance by Henry A. Redpath and the British theologian Edwin Hatch (1835–89), which appeared in 1897 and was supplemented by an additional volume issued in two parts in 1900 and 1906. The earliest Hebrew concordance of the Old Testament was compiled by the French philosopher Rabbi Nathan ben Kalonymus about 1438; the latest is the revised edition (1896; rev. ed., 1937) of the Russian poet and author Solomon Mandelkern (1846–1902). An early concordance of the English Bible was compiled by the theologian John Marbeck (d. 1585?) and published in 1550. The concordance (1737) of the King James Bible, compiled by the British bookseller Alexander Cruden (1701–70), has been the most widely used of any version published in English. Modern concordances include those of the Vulgate (1899), the American Revised Version (1922), the Douai Version (1942), and the Revised Standard Version (1957).

The many dictionaries and grammars of Hebrew and Greek, and especially of the Koine type of Greek in which much of the original New Testament is written, have been of inestimable value to Biblical scholars. Among such works are the Bible dictionary (5 vol., 1890–1904) of the Scottish clergyman and editor James Hastings (1852–1922); the *Encyclopedia Biblica* (4 vol., 1899–1903); the *Dictionnaire de la Bible* (1893–1912; Supplement 1912 et seq.) of the French Roman Catholic Biblical scholar Fulcran Grégoire Vigouroux (1837–1915); and in addition, many single-volume works, including grammars. A more popular work in English used by clergymen and educators is *The Interpreter's Dictionary of the Bible* (4 vol., 1962).

The more intensive type of literary criticism practiced since late in the 18th century and the availability of works of reference that incorporate the conclusions of various types of scholarship have brought the nature of Biblical literature into sharper focus. It is seen above all as a product of the life, thought, and aspirations of a living faith, that is, of the Hebrew-Jewish religion in the Old Testament and of the partly Jewish-Christian, partly Gentile-Christian religion in the New Testament. The word "literature" is not quite adequate therefore to describe the Bible, for most of its various books spring out of strong religious conviction and are in general, although not entirely, devoid of the conscious artistry that the word connotes.

Modern Trends. Current Biblical hermeneutics, or methods of interpretation (*see* BIBLE, INTERPRETATIONS OF THE), tend toward the application of general rules rather than of a particular principle of interpretation that is prejudiced or arbitrary in its origin. In the past, interpretation has been based on a variety of preconditioned assumptions, for example, that the Bible is to be understood only as the "Word of God", or as a definition of "justification by faith", or as a recounting of the *Heilsgeschichte* or "history of salvation". One more recent emphasis in hermeneutics has been concentration upon determining the *kerygma*, those Bible passages embodying the truth contained within the so-called Biblical myth, so as to redefine in more modern terms the original teachings of the early Christian Church. The Bible has also been studied as a source of historical and archeological information. To the present-day theologian, however, the essence of genuine Biblical hermeneutics is a constant interaction between the expositor and the texts.

BIBLICAL ARCHEOLOGY

The scientific study of historical remains and records related to the Jewish and Christian religions, and specifically to the Bible, lies within the province of Biblical archeology. The earliest information about Biblical sites came from Christian pilgrims who located holy places in Palestine (q.v.) and provided written descriptions of their travels. As early as the 4th century accounts of such journeys were in circulation; and during the period of the Crusades (11th through 13th centuries) and in the later Middle Ages (q.v.) the number of such accounts increased.

Work in Palestine. More scientific study and identification of Biblical sites was pioneered by the American scholar Edward Robinson (1795–1863). The publication of his book *Biblical Researches in Palestine* (1841) gained him title as the "father of Palestinian archeology". Further 19th-century efforts in this regard are well sum-

The Tomb of David, part of the Dormiton Church on Mt. Zion in Jerusalem, is the historic site of the Last Supper and of the death of the Virgin Mary. UPI

Looking down from the balustrade to the middle terrace of the fortress-retreat of Herod the Great at Masada. Eliot Elisofon – The Jewish Museum

marized in the *Historical Geography of the Holy Land* (1894) by the British clergyman Sir George Adam Smith (1856–1942). More recent treatments such as *The Westminster Historical Atlas to the Bible* (rev. ed., 1956) by George E. Wright and Floyd V. Filson (1896–), rest upon an additional half century of intensive exploration and excavation.

Archeological research in itself, involving deliberate excavation of specific Biblical sites, as distinguished from such general geographical study, belongs largely to the 20th century. In the 1890's the brilliant Englishman Sir Flinders Petrie (q.v.) introduced the principles of systematic excavation and recording into Palestinian work. Since his time technical archeology, employing the tools of refined ceramic typology, detailed stratigraphic observation, and newer methods of physical and chemical analysis, has made steady progress; *see also* ARCHEOLOGY. Under the auspices of such societies as the Palestine Exploration Fund (already founded by 1865) and the American Schools of Oriental Research (founded 1900) many ancient sites have been excavated. Early Palestinian work focused on such major Biblical sites as Jerusalem (1894–97), Gezer (1902–09), Megiddo (1902–05), Jericho (1907–09) and Samaria (1908–10).

The continued study and reinvestigation of these and other cities has revolutionized the understanding of the backgrounds of Biblical religion and history. For example, renewed excavations by British scientists at Jericho (1952–58) have revealed it to be one of the oldest cities in the world, with a history dating back to the 7th millennium B.C. This work also showed that the successive history of occupation of the city was abruptly terminated by the Egyptians in about 1600 B.C., leaving a sorely diminished target for the purported Israelite conquest several centuries later, as described in chapter 6 of Joshua. Important background and detail concerning the period of Kings David and Solomon (qq.v.) has also been provided by recent work. By identifying the earlier Jebusite walls well down on the eastern slopes, excavations in Jerusalem between 1962 and 1967 confirmed the details of the Biblical account of David's conquest of the city (2 Sam. 5:6). Continued investigations by Israeli scholars at Megiddo have shown that the now famous "Solomonic stables" must in fact be reassigned to the period of the prominent northern kings Omri and Ahab (see 2 Kings 16:23). Nonetheless, these efforts and new work undertaken between 1955 and 1958 at the huge site of Hazor in southern Galilee have served to reemphasize the extent of Solomon's provincial building enterprise. Characteristic of this work are the typical double "casemate" wall systems with four entryway gates that are found at both of these sites. In addition, the suggestion, offered by the Biblical account in 1 Kings 9:15, that a similar wall and gate plan might also exist at Gezer was recently proved by American excavations at that site. Doubtless the most dramatic recent work, however, was that undertaken between 1963 and 1965 at Masada along the western shore of the Dead Sea where the fortress-retreat of Herod the Great (q.v.) was located. The elaborate and well-preserved remains of a three-tiered palace built into the scarp at the northeast corner of the plateau well illustrates the scope of Roman culture at the turn of the Christian era.

Outside Palestine. Extensive excavations through the Middle East as well as in Greece and Italy have made the larger world of the Bible living and real. During a series of expeditions by the British in the mid-19th century, the great library of the 7th-century Assyrian king Ashurbanipal (q.v.) was uncovered at the site of ancient Nineveh (near modern Mosul in Iraq). In this library were found tablets with the Babylonian stories of creation and the flood (*see* CREATION EPIC, BABYLONIAN; DELUGE), a discovery that set the Biblical accounts in Genesis in a wholly new perspective. In the course of excavations at Dura-Europus (modern Qal'at es Salihiye in Syria) on the Euphrates R. (1928–37), a Yale University expedition found several Jewish synagogues containing lavish mural decorations depicting scenes from the Old Testament. A Christian church with similar New Testament scenes was found on the same site. Both of these discoveries indicate that, contrary to earlier conceptions, Judaism and early Christianity cultivated religious art and symbolism of a high order.

Literary Materials. Some of the most important archeological discoveries have been of literary materials. From 1929 to the present excavations by the French at Ras Shamra, site of ancient Ugarit along the northeastern Mediterranean coast, have produced thousands of tablets in a West Semitic language belonging to the period between 1400 and 1200 B.C. Many of these ritually describe the exploits of the gods of the Canaanite religion, including the storm deity Baal (q.v.) mentioned frequently in the Old Testament. Moreover, their poetry and language bear strong parallels with the Hebrew Psalms. In a similar way the discovery of the Qumran scrolls and other manuscript fragments along the western shores of the Dead Sea since 1947 has also revolutionized our understanding of later Jewish history and of New Testament backgrounds. These manuscript finds have also served to verify the antiquity and fidelity of Biblical Hebrew and Greek manuscript traditions. *See also* PALESTINIAN ARCHEOLOGY.

From the Masada excavations: leather sandals found near the skeleton of a woman, startlingly modern in design. Yigael Yadin – The Jewish Museum

For further information on the subjects within the scope of this article *see* BIBLE, CANON OF THE; BIBLE, ENGLISH TRANSLATIONS OF THE; and articles on many of the various versions, editions, and books of the Bible mentioned.

BIBLE SOCIETY, interdenominational association having as its object the diffusion of the Scriptures. The first such association is said to have been formed in 1710 at Halle, Saxony, Germany. The English society, founded in 1780, is now known as the Naval and Military Bible Society. In 1792 an association was formed in London under the name French Bible Society. The British and Foreign Bible Society, founded in 1804, has promoted the translation and distribution of the Bible in hundreds of languages and dialects. By 1969 some 1400 different languages and dialects had been used in translating the entire Bible or some portion of it. Well over 1,000,000,000 copies of the Scriptures have been distributed by the British and Foreign Bible Society and the American Bible Society (q.v.). The world fellowship of Bible societies, United Bible Societies, is located in London, England.

BIBLE SOCIETY, AMERICAN. *See* AMERICAN BIBLE SOCIETY.

BIBLE, VERSIONS OF THE, translations of the Bible (q.v.), or a part of it, for readers unfamiliar with the original languages in which it was written. The most important English versions of the Bible are described in the article BIBLE, ENGLISH TRANSLATIONS OF THE.

Among the ancient versions, the most important are the following. (1) Aramaic Targums (*see* TARGUM), translations or paraphrases of portions of the Hebrew Bible, produced by the Jews of western Asia in the last centuries B.C. (2) Greek versions, the most important of which is the Septuagint, a translation of the Hebrew Bible produced during the 3rd and 2nd centuries B.C. for the Greek-speaking Jews of Alexandria, Egypt. Other Greek versions include the so-called Hexapla edition of the Old Testament based on the Septuagint text, produced about the middle of the 3rd century A.D. by the Christian scholar Origen (q.v.). The Hexapla also included a translation of the Hebrew Bible produced by a Roman convert to Judaism, Aquila (q.v.), in the early 2nd century; a revision of the Septuagint based on the Hebrew text, produced by a Jewish writer of Ephesus, Theodotion, in the 2nd century; and a translation of the Hebrew Bible, produced by a Samaritan translator, Symmachus, in the late 2nd century. (3) Syriac versions, the most important of which is the Peshitta, a translation of the Hebrew Old Testament produced by either Jews or Christian Jews during the 2nd and 3rd centuries A.D. The Peshitta Version of the New Testament dates from the late 4th century and is based on the Greek text. (4) Latin versions, the most important of which is the Vulgate (q.v.), a late 4th-century translation of the Hebrew Bible and revisions of Old Latin versions of the New Testament produced by Saint Jerome (q.v.). (5) Armenian Version, a translation of both Testaments from either Greek or Syriac texts, produced about the 5th century. The translation into Armenian was at least begun by an Armenian bishop, Mesrob (350?–439), the inventor of the Armenian alphabet; *see* ARMENIAN LITERATURE. (6) Gothic Version, a translation of the whole Bible based on the Septuagint, by the 4th-century bishop Ulfilas (q.v.). (7) Egyptian Coptic versions, the most important of which were written in the Sahidic and Bohairic dialects. The Sahidic, or Thebaic, Version, used in upper Egypt, was translated during the 3rd and 4th centuries; the Bohairic, or Memphitic, Version, used in Lower Egypt, dates from between the 12th and 14th centuries. The Old Testament of both versions was based on the Septuagint. These translations are still in use among Egyptian Christians. (8) Ethiopic Version, a translation of the entire Bible, begun probably in the 5th century by a group of Syrian monks living in Ethiopia, who based their Old Testament on the Septuagint. This is the only authorized version among Abyssinian Christians.

Later versions of the Bible include the following. (9) An edition of the Greek text with a new Latin translation (1516), produced by the Dutch scholar Desiderius Erasmus (q.v.). (10) An influential translation into German by the German religious reformer Martin Luther (q.v.). Luther's translation of the New Testament, published in 1522, was based on Erasmus' earlier work; his translation of the entire Bible was published in 1534. This version was the first translation of the Bible from Greek or Hebrew into a modern European vernacular. (11) A translation from the Vulgate into French (New Testament, 1523; entire Bible, 1530), undertaken by a Roman Catholic scholar, Jacques Lefèvre d'Étaples (1450?–1537?).

BIBLIOGRAPHY (late Gr. *bibliographia*, "the writing of books"), originally, the writing or copying of books. In modern times the word is generally applied to a list or catalog of books, compiled for some specific purpose and including such information as authors, editions, dates and places of publication, styles of type, and other related details. The preparation of a bibliography is distinct from the collection and classification of books as practiced by librarians. The modern meaning of the word dates from about the middle of the 18th century. The word "bibliography" is applied to many types of listings of publications. Bibliographies may be general, including works on a wide variety of subjects, published in a number of countries and periods; or they may be selective. In the latter case they may be limited to works on a single subject, works published in a given place or time, or works by a single writer. Bibliographies or works published on a single subject are often appended to other works on that subject. Those dealing with the works of individual authors are often included either in biographies or in editions of the authors' collected works. Writers frequently append to their books bibliographies of the sources used in preparing their books. Bibliographies are used by collectors, librarians, booksellers, students, and specialists engaged in various commercial and cultural pursuits.

Universal Catalogs. Bibliographers have long wished to compile a work covering the whole realm of printed books. A notable attempt to achieve this aim was the *Bibliotheca Universalis* (4 vol., 1545–49), by the Swiss naturalist Konrad von Gesner (q.v.). Gesner recorded, under the names of their authors, all the books in Hebrew, Greek, and Latin about which he could obtain information. Since the 16th century many others have attempted to compile a universal catalog, among them the Scottish physician Robert Watt (1774–1819), who prepared the *Bibliotheca Britannica* (4 vol., 1824). But the latter's work, in respect to foreign books, is not universal; it is most useful in connection with works by British writers.

Also notable are *Manuel du Libraire et de l'Amateur des Livres* (1810) by the French bibliographer Jacques Charles Brunet (1823–94), and *Allgemeines Bibliographisches Lexikon* (2 vol., 1821–30) by the German bibliographer Friedrich Adolf Ebert (1791–1834). The library of the British Museum (q.v.) in London has so large a collection of books that its Catalogue of Printed Books (108 vol., 1881–1905) is one of the most important general bibliographies.

Selective Works. Important specialized bibliographies of British works, besides those already mentioned, include *The Bibliographer's Manual of English Literature* (4 vol., 1834) by the British bibliographer William Thomas Lowndes (1798–1843), the first systematic bibliographic compilation on this subject made in England; the *Reference Catalogue of Current Literature*, a quadrennial publication of publishers' lists; the trade publication *Book Prices Current*; and the annual *English Catalogue of Books.*

An important specialized bibliography of American publications is *American Bibliography, 1639–1820* (12 vol., 1903–34) by the American bibliographer Charles Evans (1850–1935). Current bibliographies of American publications include the trade publications *Publishers' Weekly,* which appeared for the first time in 1872; the monthly *United States Catalogue* (successor to the *American Catalogue*); the *Cumulative Book Index*; the *Standard Catalog for Public Libraries*; *The Publishers' Trade List Annual,* and two publications based on it, *Books in Print* and *Subject Guide to Books in Print*; and *American Book Prices Current.*

Lists of Bibliographies. Bibliographical literature has increased to such an extent that many bibliographies of bibliographies have been published. The best known of these is the *Bibliotheca Bibliographica* (1866) compiled by the German Julius Petzholdt (1812–1891), revised by the French editor Henri Stein (b. 1862) as *Manuel de Bibliographie Générale* (1897). Of great value to the general reader is the *List of Bibliographical Works in the Reading Room of the British Museum* (1889), and one of the most useful of all such lists is the *Register of National Bibliography* (1905–12) compiled by the British bibliographer William Courtney (1850–1928). In 1901 the Bibliographical Society of Chicago printed a *Bibliography of Bibliographies Chronologically Arranged*; a second edition was issued by the Bibliographical Society of America (1910–11).

See also Funk & Wagnalls New Encyclopedia Bibliography, in Vol. 27 of this set.

BIBLIOMANIA (Gr. *biblion,* "book"; *mania,* "madness"), term used to denote a compulsive preoccupation with books, especially with the acquisition and possession of rare or valuable books. The term, popular among book collectors, was first used in written English in 1750 by the British statesman Philip Dormer Stanhope, 4th Earl of Chesterfield (q.v.), who warned his son to "beware of the bibliomanie". *See also* BOOK COLLECTING.

BIBLIOTHÈQUE NATIONALE, French national library in Paris, the largest library in France. It contains more than 6,000,000 books, 155,000 manuscripts, and about 5,000,000 prints and engravings. The two chief sources of its origin were the Bibliothèque du Roi, which was founded in 1367 by King Charles V (q.v.) in the Louvre, Paris, and the library of the Orléans family at Blois. These libraries were united by King Francis I (q.v.). at Fontainebleau, and were later transferred to the Collège de Clermont in Paris by King Charles IX (q.v.). The library is now on the Rue de Richelieu. A decree of 1536 required that one copy of every work printed in France be filed in the national library. *See also* LIBRARY.

BICAMERAL SYSTEM, legislative system in which the power of making the law is vested in two chambers, or houses, both of which must approve a bill before it becomes law. In general the upper house is composed of members selected on a territorial basis, representing States or other political subdivisions rather than the people directly, and usually serving for longer terms than the members of the lower house. In principle the upper house provides the legislative experience necessary to control unwise legislation. The lower house is generally composed of members selected on the basis of population, each member representing an equal number of citizens. Because of more frequent election and closer identification with the districts they represent, members of the lower house reflect more strongly the contemporary mind of the electorate. Typical of the bicameral system is the United States Congress, which consists of a Senate, constituting an upper house, and a House of Representatives, constituting a lower. The bicameral system is in force in all of the States with the exception, since 1937, of Nebraska, which has a unicameral, or single-chamber, legislature. Throughout the world national parliaments are about equally divided between the bicameral and unicameral systems.

BICARBONATES. *See* CARBONATES.

BICEPS, muscle with two separate attachments at the origin. In the human body two pairs of muscles are called biceps: the biceps brachii and the biceps femoris. The biceps brachii, the bulging muscle of the upper arm, has two heads attached to the shoulder blade; the other end is connected to the bones of the forearm. Contraction of the muscle flexes the arm and turns the hand and wrist outward. The biceps femoris has two heads attached to the hip bone; the other end is connected to the bones of the lower leg. Contraction of the muscle flexes the leg and tends to turn the foot outward.

BICHAT, Marie François Xavier (1771–1802), French anatomist and physiologist, born in Thoirette, and educated in Lyon and Paris. In 1797 he lectured in Paris on anatomy and physiology. He was the first investigator to discern textural differences in the various parts of the body and to use the term tissue. Bichat isolated twenty-one kinds of tissue in the human body and his work became the basis of modern histology (q.v.) and pathological anatomy (*see* ANATOMY: *Microscopic Anatomy*). He wrote several books on membranes and tissues.

The Folklore Festival, held annually in Baden, Switzerland, attracts owners of unusual vehicles such as this high-wheeled bicycle, popular in the 19th century.
UPI

BICKERSTAFF, Isaac, pen name first used, in 1708, by British satirist Jonathan Swift (q.v.) in his parody of the astrological predictions made by the British cobbler and astrologist John Partridge (1644–1715). When the British writer Sir Richard Steele (q.v.) needed a pen name for use in the periodical *The Tatler* (1709–11) he also adopted the name. The American mathematician and almanac maker Benjamin West (1730–1813) published the first illustrated almanac in Massachusetts as *Bickerstaff's Boston Almanac for the Year of Our Lord, 1768.* He continued publication annually through 1779 and again from 1783 to 1793.

BICYCLE, vehicle consisting of two wheels fixed in tandem to a frame, steered by handlebars, and propelled by an arrangement of pedals and gears driven by the feet. The name of the modern vehicle dates from 1869. Various precursors of this machine were known as *vélocipèdes,* from a French name dating from the late 18th century.

Little is known about the earliest history of the bicycle, although crude two-wheeled vehicles propelled by the feet were popular as early as the second half of the 17th century. In 1690 a Frenchman invented the *célérifère,* consisting essentially of a wooden beam to which the wheels were affixed. The vehicle had no handlebar; the rider sat upon a cushion on the beam and propelled and steered the machine by pushing his feet against the ground. In 1816 a German nobleman designed the first two-wheeled vehicle with a steering device. This machine, named the draisine, had a handlebar that pivoted on the frame, enabling the front wheel to be turned. Various improvements were later developed by French, German, and British inventors. In England these early models were generally known as hobby horses; the name dandy horse was applied particularly to the expensive pedestrian curricle, invented in 1818. The curricle was lighter in weight than the *draisine* and had an adjustable saddle and elbow rest. It was patented in the United States in 1819 but aroused little interest. In 1839 driving levers and pedals were added to a machine of the *draisine* type. These innovations enabled the rider, for the first time, to propel the machine with his feet off the ground. The driving mechanism of this vehicle consisted of short cranks fixed to the rear wheel hub and connected by rods to

Professional European cyclists ride past the walled city of Ávila de los Caballeros during a strenuous race encompassing the whole of Spain. Embassy of Spain

long levers, which were hinged to the frame close to the head of the machine. The connecting rods were joined to the levers at about one third of their length from the pedals. The machine was propelled by a downward and forward thrust of the foot. In 1846 an improved model of this machine, designed by a Scotsman, acquired the name *dalzell* and was widely used in England.

The direct precursor of the modern bicycle was the French crank-driven, loose-pedaled velocipede, which became popular in France about 1855. The frame and wheels were made of wood. The tires were iron, and the pedals were attached to the hub of the front, or driver, wheel, which was slightly higher than the rear wheel. In England this machine was known as the boneshaker, because of its effect on a rider pedaling over a rough road or a cobblestoned street. In 1869 in England, solid rubber tires mounted on steel rims were introduced in a new machine, which was the first to be patented under the modern name bicycle. In 1873 James Starley (1830–81), an English inventor, produced the first machine incorporating most of the features of the so-called ordinary, or high-wheel bicycle. The front wheel of Starley's machine was as much as three times as large in diameter as the rear wheel.

The modifications and improvements of the next fifteen years included the ball bearing and the pneumatic tire. These inventions, along with the use of weldless steel tubing and spring seats, brought the ordinary bicycle to its highest point of development. The excessive vibration and instability of the high-wheel bicycle, however, caused inventors to turn their attention to reducing the height of the bicycle. About 1880 the so-called safety, or low, machine was developed. The wheels were of nearly equal size, and the pedals, attached to a sprocket through gears and a chain, drove the rear wheels.

The safety bicycle was universally adopted by manufacturers in the U.S. The improved safety machine had wheels of equal size, hollow steel tubing, coaster brake (a device incorporating both a braking mechanism and a free-wheeling arrangement for coasting), adjustable handlebars and other improvements. American cyclists increased greatly in numbers and became strong supporters of a nationwide movement for improved roads. In 1899 the American production of about 1,000,000 bicycles a year was valued at more than $31,000,000. By 1909, however, the bicycle industry in the U.S. was nearly nonexistent, the motorcycle and the automobile having largely displaced the bicycle. Bicycle riding was generally confined to children and to small groups of devotees, such as the members of the League of American Wheelmen, organized in 1880, and of the Century Road Club Association, organized in 1899. In European countries the bicycle remained an important means of transportation.

In the 1960's and 1970's, as air pollution (q.v.) from automobile exhaust aroused great concern and the energy crisis worsened, the popularity of the bicycle as a means of transportation and for recreational purposes increased tremendously. For several years before World War II, more than 1,000,000 bicycles were being produced annually in the U.S. for domestic use. During the mid-1970's about 80,000,000 bicycles were in use in the U.S. and some 10,200,000 were manufactured during 1974. Approximately 4,000,000 machines were imported annually. In Europe more bicycles than automobiles are in use but in the U.S., automobiles outnumber bicycles by about 10 percent.

Racing. Bicycle racing is popular as an amateur sport in Europe and to some extent in the U.S. Supervising the sport in the U.S. is the Amateur Bicycle League of America, an affiliate of the International Cyclist Union. Popular long-distance bicycle races include the 3000-mi. Tour of France, and the 2500-mi. Tour of Italy. In the U.S., professional six-day bicycle races, mostly held indoors, were popular during the late 19th and early 20th centuries. Interest declined after the 1930's but revived somewhat with outdoor races in the 1970's.

BIDAULT, Georges (1899–), French politician, born in Moulins and educated at the Sorbonne. Prior to World War II he was an editor of the Catholic newspaper *l'Aube*; head of the Popular Democratic Party, an organization of left-wing Catholics; and an outspoken opponent of the prewar appeasement of Germany which culminated in the Munich Pact (q.v.). Joining the French army at the outbreak of World War II in 1939, he was taken prisoner by the Germans. Released in 1941, Bidault was a leader of the underground resistance movement in France. In September, 1944, after the Allied invasion of France, Bidault became French minister of foreign affairs. He served as premier at the head of a coalition cabinet (1949–50), was vice-premier and minister of defense (1951–52), and foreign minister (1953–54). A member of the French National Assembly (1945–62), Bidault opposed the Algerian independence policy of President Charles de Gaulle (q.v.) and lived in exile in Brazil (1962–67) and Belgium (1967–68). He returned to France in June, 1968. Bidault is the author of *D'une Résistance à l'Autre* (1965; Eng. trans., *Resistance: The Political Autobiography of Georges Bidault,* 1967). *See also* FRANCE: *History: The Fourth Republic.*

BIDDEFORD, city of Maine, in York Co., on the Saco R., opposite the city of Saco and about 15 miles S.W. of Portland. In the surrounding region and nearby are several summer resorts, notably Old Orchard Beach and the coastal town of Biddeford Pool. An industrial center, the city has hydroelectric plants and diversified manufacturing industries, including plants producing automotive parts, boats, clothing, sheet-metal, shoes, and textiles. Biddeford was settled in 1630, and formed part of Saco until 1762, when it was incorporated separately as the town of Biddeford. It was chartered as a city in 1855. Pop. (1960) 19,255; (1970) 19,983.

BIDDLE, name of an American family, of whom the following are noteworthy.

Nicholas Biddle (1786–1844), financier, born in Philadelphia, Pa., and educated at the University of Pennsylvania and the College of New Jersey (now Princeton University). He was a member of the American legation in France that settled spoilation claims rising from the Napoleonic Wars (q.v.). He remained in Europe for three years to study and travel and returned home in 1807. He later became a contributor to *Port Folio,* a leading literary journal, which he edited after 1812. Biddle served one term in the Pennsylvania State House of Representatives. In 1819 he was appointed one of the directors of the Second Bank of the United States by President James Monroe (q.v.). Biddle became president of the bank in 1822 and embarked on a successful program to stabilize the currency; *see* BANKS AND BANKING: *United States Banking System.* He tried unsuccessfully to gain a new Federal charter for the bank, but in 1836 he secured a State charter and the bank was thereafter known as the Bank of the United States of Pennsylvania. Biddle resigned as president of the bank in 1839.

George Biddle (1885–1973), painter, born in Philadelphia, Pa., and educated at the Groton School and Harvard University. He was an administrator of the art projects of the Work Projects Administration (q.v.) during the 1930's and was appointed to the Commission of Fine Arts by President Harry S. Truman (q.v.) in 1950. Biddle is known both for his murals, which include five frescoes in the Department of Justice Building, Washington, D.C., and others in the National Library, Rio de Janeiro, Brazil, and the Supreme Court Building, Mexico City, Mexico; and for his easel paintings and lithographs which are part of the permanent collections of many museums. Biddle painted genre scenes and portraits in a monochromatic style that has been described as competent, linear, and precise.

Francis Biddle (1886–1968), jurist, brother of George Biddle, born in Paris, France, and educated at Harvard University. He served in 1911 and 1912 as private secretary to Justice Oliver Wendell Holmes (*see under* HOLMES) of the Supreme Court of the United States. Biddle served (1934–35) as the first chairman of the National Labor Relations Board (q.v.). In 1939 he became a judge of the United States Circuit Court of Ap-

peals, Third District; in 1940 he was named solicitor general of the U.S.; and from 1941 to 1945 he was attorney general in the Roosevelt cabinet. President Harry S. Truman appointed Biddle to serve as the American judge of the Tribunal in the war-crimes trials in Nuremberg, West Germany, in 1945 and 1946; *see* WAR-CRIMES TRIALS. Biddle was chairman of Americans for Democratic Action, an independent liberal political organization, from 1950 to 1953, and a member of the Permanent Court of Arbitration (q.v.) from 1951 to 1957. Biddle wrote *Mr. Justice Holmes* (1942), *The Fear of Freedom* (1951), and the autobiographical *A Casual Past* (1961) and *In Brief Authority* (1962).

BIDDLE, John (1615–62), English religious reformer, born in Wotton-under-Edge, Gloucestershire, and educated at Magdalen College, University of Oxford. Generally regarded as the founder of Unitarianism in England, Biddle was imprisoned for a short time in 1645 for having written a denial of the deity of the Holy Spirit (*see* HOLY GHOST). The published statement of this opinion was burned, in 1647, by order of Parliament. Later publications of his views, which denied the doctrine of the Trinity (q.v.), were also suppressed, and only by the intervention of Oliver Cromwell (q.v.), Lord Protector of England, did Biddle escape execution as a heretic. Thereafter he was imprisoned. He died in jail.

"The Headless Horseman of Sleepy Hollow" by George Biddle. George Biddle, with permission of the artist

BIDPAI *or* **PILPAY,** *or* PILPAI (fl. about 300 A.D.), reputed writer of Indian fables, written in Sanskrit (*see* SANSKRIT LITERATURE). Bidpai is not actually a name but a Sanskrit title meaning "master of knowledge" or "chief pundit". The original five fables, *Panchatantra,* are no longer extant in Sanskrit but have been translated into many languages; these fables are thought by scholars to be the basis of a number of European collections. Two English translations were published; one in 1924 and one in 1925.

BIEDERMEIER, style of furniture and decoration popular in Germany from 1815 to 1848. The name, derived from satiric poetry published toward the end of the era in the German periodical *Fliegende Blätter* ("Flying Papers"), is sometimes applied to the music, painting, sculpture, and literature of the same period and nationality. Characterized by a cheerful, homely massiveness, Biedermeier is an adaptation of the luxurious style known as empire (q.v.) that was popular in France from 1804 to 1830, but utilizes cheaper materials.

BIEL (Fr. *Bienne*), city of Switzerland, in Bern Canton, near Biel Lake, at the foot of the Jura mountain range, about 17 miles N.W. of the city of Bern. An important watch-making center, Biel also has plants engaged in the manufacture of automobiles, machinery, and pianos. Places of interest in the city include the Gothic town hall, a late-Gothic church, and the Schwab Museum, which houses a collection of relics from prehistoric settlements along the lake. The city was founded in the early 13th century. Pop. (1970) 64,333.

BIELA'S COMET, small periodic comet named for the Austrian soldier and astronomer Baron Wilhelm von Biela (1782–1856). He first observed the comet in 1826 and calculated the path of the elliptical orbit; he also confirmed that it appeared periodically at intervals of about six years. Before his observation, the comet had last been seen in 1772, but subsequently it appeared at the times forecast. In 1846 the comet was seen to break into two parts, each with a separate nucleus, and in 1852 the two parts were more than 1,000,000 mi. apart and very faint. In 1859, the location of the sun made observation impossible and the two parts were not found again. Showers of meteors, named Bielids, were seen in the path of the orbit until, at the stated intervals, 1899. *See* COMET; METEOR.

BIELEFELD, city of West Germany, in North Rhine-Westphalia State, at the foot of the Teutoburger Wald (a forested mountain range), about 110 miles N.E. of Düsseldorf. An industrial center, Bielefeld has plants producing bicycles, cars, machinery, sewing machines, and silks and linens. The city was chartered in the 13th century and became a part of the Hanseatic League (q.v.). From 1815 until the end of World War II Bielefeld was part of the Prussian province of Westphalia (q.v.). Pop. (1970 est.) 168,609.

BIEL, LAKE (Fr. *Bienne*), lake in N.W. Switzerland, located in Bern Canton, in the Jura Mts., at an elevation of about 1400 ft. It is about 10 mi. long and from 1 to 3 mi. wide and covers an area of about 16 sq.mi. The maximum depth is about 250 ft. The waters of Lake Neuchâtel, 3 mi. to the S.W., reach Lake Biel through the Schüss R. and Thièle Canal. *See* BIEL.

BIELSKO-BIAŁA (Ger. *Bielitz*), city of Poland, capital of Bielsko Province, on the Biała R., 40 miles S.W. of Cracow. Bielsko-Biała, a rail junction, has been a textile center since the Middle Ages; it also produces machinery and electrical equipment. Several health resorts are nearby. Bielsko was founded in the 13th century and fortified in the 15th century. It was a lordship in the Middle Ages and was made a duchy in 1752. From 1772 to 1919 it was in Austria-Hungary, and since the end of World War I it has belonged to Poland. In 1950 Bielsko was combined with adjoining Biała Krakowska; it was briefly called Biała Malopolska. Pop. (1973 est.) 114,200.

BIEN HOA, town in S. Vietnam, capital of Bien Hoa Province, on the Dong Nai R., 20 miles N.E. of Ho Chi Minh City. The town is on a main railroad; its manufactures include rubber and timber products, tiles, and pottery. In Bien Hoa Province are granite quarries, fruit orchards, and oil-palm plantations. The military airfield at Bien Hoa was the site of the initial buildup of United States air power following the Tonkin Gulf incident of 1964. During the Vietnam War Bien Hoa was headquarters for the surrounding military region. Pop. (1971) 177,513.

BIENNE, LAKE OF. *See* BIEL, LAKE.

BIENNIALS, *or* BIENNIAL PLANTS, plants that normally require two years for their life cycle. They store food in the first season of their growth, flower and bear fruit in the second season, and then die. Familiar examples of biennial flowers are foxglove, hollyhock, and pansy. Many cultivated vegetables are biennials, such as carrots, turnips, parsnips, parsley, and celery. Biennials often become annuals when early sowing, warm weather, or other factors cause the earlier development of a flowering stem. Less hardy varieties are often routinely treated as annuals.

See also GARDENING.

BIENVILLE, Jean Baptiste Lemoyne, Sieur de (1680–1768), French explorer and colonial administrator, born in Longueuil, Canada, a member of a notable family of French explorers. In 1699, with his brothers Pierre Lemoyne, Sieur d'Iberville (q.v.) and François Lemoyne, Sieur de Sauvole (1670–1700), he founded a settlement called Biloxi in the French province of Louisiana, across the bay from the present-day city of Biloxi, Miss. Upon the death of Sauvole, Bienville assumed the duties of governor of Louisiana, although he was not officially appointed to the post, and in 1710 founded the present-day city of Mobile, Ala. In 1712 the French soldier Sieur Antoine de la Mothe Cadillac (q.v.) was appointed governor of Louisiana and Bienville served as his second in command until 1717 when Cadillac returned to France and Bienville replaced him officially. In 1718, realizing its strategic importance, he laid out the city of New Orleans, which became his capital in 1722. His enemies accused him of incompetence, however, and in 1726 he was recalled to France and deprived of his office. Reinstated in 1732, he again served as governor of Louisiana from 1733 to 1743, when he retired and returned to France.

BIER, August (1861–1949), German surgeon and professor, born in Helsen. He taught at the universities in Kiel, Greifswald, Bonn, and Berlin, and introduced the use of spinal anesthesia in 1899 (*see* ANESTHESIA). Bier developed a new method for the treatment of amputees and developed an innovative method of treating chronic infections. This method, called Bier's passive hyperemia, involves the creation of an oversupply of blood in a vein by preventing outflow from that vein. His treatise on the subject was published in 1903.

BIERCE, Ambrose Gwinett (1842–1914?), American satirist, short-story writer, and journalist, born in Meigs Co., Ohio. He served in the Union army during the American Civil War and as a result of distinguished service went west with a military expedition. He settled in San Francisco and wrote political squibs and a column for the *News-Letter*; by 1868 he had become editor of the paper. He moved to London in 1872 and the caustic sketches and stories he wrote for the magazines *Fun* and *Figaro*, under the pen name of Dod Grile, were published as *Cobwebs from an Empty Skull* (1874). Bierce returned to San Francisco in 1877, writing for the *Argonaut*, editing the *Wasp*, and writing a column for the *Sunday Examiner*, owned by William Randolph Hearst (q.v.). Bierce's wit and fascination with death and horror earned him the nickname "Bitter Bierce"; his mastery of the short story earned him comparison with the American writers Edgar Allan Poe (q.v.) and Bret Harte (*see* HARTE, FRANCIS BRETT). From 1899 until 1913 he worked for the Hearst interests in Washington, D.C., and revised his own works. In 1913 he went to Mexico and disappeared; he is presumed to have died there. His *Collected Works* were published in twelve volumes (1909–12) and include the *Devil's Dictionary*, first entitled the *Cynic's Wordbook* (1906).

BIERSTADT, Albert (1830–1902), American painter, born in Solingen, Germany. After spending his childhood in New Bedford, Mass., he returned to Europe to study painting from 1853 to 1857. Bierstadt was a member of the Hudson River school of painting (q.v.). Among his works are "Rocky Mountains" (1871, Metropolitan Museum of Art, New York City), and two historical paintings, "The Discovery of the Hudson River" and "The Settlement of California" (both in the Capitol, Washington, D.C.).

BIFROST, in Scandinavian mythology (q.v.), the rainbow bridge connecting Asgard (q.v.), or heaven, and Midgard, or earth.

BIGAMY, in law, the criminal offense of contracting or purporting to contract another marriage by one who is at the time still married to his or her lawful spouse. In the United States a person can be tried for bigamy only by the courts of the State in which the second marriage occurs. The present statute in England continues this rule so far as aliens are concerned, but makes punishable in England the bigamous marriage of a British subject, wherever it may have been contracted. In some States of the U.S., a person who knowingly enters into a marriage with a bigamist is declared to be guilty of the same offense. It is a defense, however, that the person acted under a reasonable belief that he and the other party to the marriage were unmarried.

BIG BEN, great bell installed in the Clock Tower of the Parliament buildings in London, England; *see* PARLIAMENT, HOUSES OF. The bell weighs 13½ tons, is 7½ ft. high, and is 9 ft. in diameter at the mouth. It was first cast in 1852 but cracked on testing; the replacement, cast in 1858, also cracked but was filed to give a pure tone. The four-faced clock, illuminated at night except during World War II, is also called Big Ben. The great bell, which strikes the hours, is named for the commissioner of works, Sir Benjamin Hall (1802–67), who was in charge of the original installation.

BIG BEND NATIONAL PARK, American part of a planned international park to be shared with Mexico, in Brewster County, S.W. Texas, in the big bend of the Rio Grande (q.v.). Scenic features include the rugged Chisos Mts. and three deep canyons: the Boquillas, the Mariscal, and the Santa Elena. Remnants of prehistoric cultures, petrified trees, fossils, and rare forms of indigenous plant and animal life are found in the park. The park, covering 708,221.20 acres, was authorized in 1935 and established in 1944. It is administered by the National Park Service (q.v.).

BIG BLACK, river, 330 mi. long, flowing S.W. from Webster County, Miss., into the Mississippi R. about 20 mi. below Vicksburg.

BIG BROTHERS OF AMERICA, organization of men from all walks of life who volunteer to help fatherless, emotionally troubled and delinquent boys with guidance and companionship. Trained social workers employed by the organization investigate the cases of boys who have been referred by schools or social agencies or have appeared before juvenile courts. The boy is then introduced to a Big Brother, who takes a continuing personal interest in his welfare. All Big Brothers are screened before being accepted into the program and assigned to a boy. The social worker continues to work with the family of the boy.

The pioneer group of this type, Big Brothers, Inc., of New York, was founded in 1904; in 1968 the membership of this group was more than 500. Many others have since been formed in cities throughout the world. In 1946 the Big Brothers of America was founded in Philadelphia, Pa., to coordinate the activities of the various Big Brother agencies. The group are basically nonsectarian; however, in areas large enough to be served by several organizations, the major religious denominations are associated with separate organizations, such as the (Roman) Catholic Big Brothers and the Jewish Big Brothers. The organization also provides summer camps, neighborhood clubs, group activities, vocational guidance, employment service, and medical care. In the late 1960's the organization included some 120 Big Brother groups in the United States and Canada.

BIG DIPPER. *See* DIPPER, BIG.

BIGGERS, Earl Derr (1884–1933), American novelist, born in Warren, Ohio, and educated at Harvard University. After graduating in 1907, he wrote for the Boston *Traveler,* but left newspaper work in 1913, when his novel *Seven Keys to Baldpate* became successful, largely because of the dramatization by actor-playwright George Michael Cohan (q.v.). In 1925 Biggers' most famous character, the Chinese-American detective Charlie Chan, was introduced in *The House Without a Key.* Chan figured in five more novels, all of which were made into motion pictures. The last of these books was *Keeper of the Keys* (1932). Charlie Chan became the subject of many radio and television scripts.

Rocky Mountain sheep, Ovis canadensis
American Museum of Natural History

BIGGS, E(dward George) Power (1906–77), British-American organist, born in Westcliff, England, and trained at the Royal Academy of Music, London. He emigrated (1930) to the United States and became a citizen (1938). Emphasizing baroque (*see* MUSIC: *History of Music: The Baroque Era*) and 20th-century music, Biggs popularized classic organ literature through his concerts, recordings, and radio broadcasts.

BIG HOLE NATIONAL BATTLEFIELD, site of historic interest, in S.W. Montana, about 60 miles S.W. of Butte. It is administered by the National Park Service (q.v.).

BIGHORN *or* **ROCKY MOUNTAIN BIGHORN SHEEP,** *Ovis canadensis,* largest and best-known wild sheep of the North American continent, found from southern British Columbia to northwestern Mexico. A full-grown bighorn may average 40 in. at the shoulder and range in weight from 175 to 350 lb. The great curved horns, which may take more than one turn, attain a length of up to 50 in. The ewes have smaller horns, seldom exceeding 15 in. The coat is not woolly but long, full, and coarse, like that of a goat. The animals have a short mating season, during which the rams clash head-on in a battle for the ewes; for the rest of the year the sheep usually divide into separate male and female herds. The bighorns leap from ledge to ledge at great speed, appearing to be sailing through space, and grip slippery surfaces with the shock-absorbing elastic pads of the feet. The animals have exceptionally acute sight, smell, and hearing, and hunters must use high-powered rifles with telescopic sights to bring them down.

Two other varieties found in N.W. North America are the white sheep or Dall sheep, *O. montana dalli,* or *O. dalli,* and the deep gray or grayish brown Stone's sheep, *O. canadensis stonei.* The bighorn is related to the Asian argali (q.v.).

BIGHORN, river, 336 mi. long, formed in W. Wyoming by the Popo Agie and Wind rivers rising in the Absaroka Range. It is one of the main tributaries of the Yellowstone R., which it joins in Montana after flowing through Bighorn Basin, where it is joined by other rivers. The Bighorn provides water and hydroelectric power for a large area and is the site of several reservoirs.

BIGHORN CANYON NATIONAL RECREATION AREA. *See* NATIONAL PARK SERVICE.

BIGHORN MOUNTAINS, isolated range of the Rocky Mts., lying E. of the Bighorn R. and extending generally northward from Natrona County, Wyo., into S. Montana. The range averages over 7000 ft. in elevation; the highest summit is Cloud Peak (13,165 ft.). Along the upper levels are large coniferous forests, which are included in Bighorn National Forest.

BIG JAW. *See* ACTINOMYCOSIS.

BIGNONIACEAE *or* **BIGNONIA,** family of trees, shrubs, and woody vines in the order Polemoniales. The plants are found in tropical and temperate climates in Asia and the Americas and bear showy irregular flowers with two or four stamens. The catalpa, the calabash tree (qq.v.), and the jacaranda (*see* JACARANDA WOOD) are the best known of the ornamental trees of the family.

BIG SIOUX, river of South Dakota and Iowa, rising in Grant County, S. Dak. Flowing generally southward for about 400 mi., it empties into the Missouri R. at Sioux City, Iowa. From Lincoln County, S. Dak., to Sioux City, the river forms the boundary between South Dakota and Iowa.

BIG SPRING, city in Texas, and county seat of Howard Co., about 250 miles W. of Fort Worth. The city is in an agricultural and petroleum-producing region. A center of oil-related industries, Big Spring is also a trade center, and railroad center. In the city are gas-processing plants, oil refineries, railway shops, and plants manufacturing school supplies. Near the city is Webb Air Force Base. The city was founded in 1821 and incorporated in 1907. Pop. (1960) 31,230; (1970) 28,735.

BIG TREE, in the United States, synonym for sequoia (q.v.).

BIHAR *or* **BEHAR,** State of the Republic of India and the name of a city in the State. The State is bordered by Nepal on the N., Pakistan on the N.E., West Bengal State on the S.E., Orissa and Andhra Pradesh states on the S. and S.W., and Uttar Pradesh State on the W. The N. section of Bihar, which is crossed by the Ganges R., is primarily agricultural. The chief crops are barley, maize, rice, sugarcane, and wheat. Southeast Bihar is rich in coal, copper, and iron ore, and yields 60 percent of the supply of mica in the world. The State capital is Patna (q.v.), a market center for the surrounding agricultural area.

Most of the region comprising the State was occupied by the ancient kingdom of Magadha, which dates back to 600 B.C. The region subsequently formed part of the Maurya Empire and of the Gupta Empire (*see* INDIA: *History*). Seized

The Mahabodhi Temple, in the village of Buddh Gaya, Bihar, is one of the holiest places in the Buddhist world. Dating originally from the 2nd century A.D., the temple was extensively restored in the 19th century.

Government of India Tourist Office

by the Muslims in the 12th century A.D., it was held by them until 1497, after which it was annexed by the kings of Delhi. The British acquired Bihar in 1765 and merged it with Bengal. From 1912 to 1936 when it became a separate province of British India, Bihar formed part of the province of Bihar and Orissa. Bihar is considered the cradle of Buddhism (q.v.). About 528 B.C. Buddha (q.v.) is said to have experienced his "Great Enlightenment" in the town of Buddh Gaya, in the present-day State, and also to have begun his preaching there.

The city of Bihar is about 40 miles S.E. of Patna. Points of interest in the city include ruins of a Buddhist monastery built between the 8th and 9th centuries A.D.

Area of State, 67,113 sq.mi.; pop. (1971) 56,332,246. Pop. of city (1971) 100,052.

BIHARI, northeastern Indic language of the Indo-European family, spoken in Bihar State, India, and neighboring regions, including southern Nepal. Bihari has three main dialects: Maithili, or Tirhutia, and Magahi in the east; and Bhojpuri in the west. In conjugation and declension the language is more similar to Bengali (*see* BENGALI LANGUAGE AND LITERATURE) than Eastern Hindi (*see* HINDI). Spelling is not fixed, and the vocabulary has few borrowings from Arabic or Persian.

Only the Maithili dialect of Bihari has any real literature, the earliest writer being the court poet Vidyāpati Thakkura (fl. 15th century), who wrote of the loves of Rādhā and Krishna. The language is spoken today by about 40,000,000 people. *See* INDIAN LANGUAGES.

BIHZAD. *See* PERSIAN ART AND ARCHITECTURE: *Painting.*

BIISK. *See* BIYSK.

BIJAPUR, city of the Republic of India, in Karnataka State, about 240 miles S.E. of Bombay. Textile manufacturing is the principal industry. Formerly one of the most magnificent cities of southern India, present-day Bijapur consists of an inner section, surrounded by a massive wall with a circumference of 6 mi., and an outer section containing extensive ruins. The wall ranges from about 30 to 50 ft. in height and is of hewn-stone construction. Within the outer section are several splendid edifices in the Islamic architectural style, notably the restored mausoleum Gol Gunbaz, built between 1626 and 1656, and surmounted by a dome nearly 200 ft. high. Among other features of the outer city are remnants of a palace and numerous ruined mosques. The dominant feature of the inner city is a citadel measuring a mile in circumference. One of the outstanding historical treasures of Bijapur is "Malik-i-Maidan", a piece of bronze ordnance cast in 1549. Reputedly the largest bronze gun in existence, it was captured from the armed forces of Ahmadnagar in the 17th century. The importance of Bijapur dates from 1489, when it became the capital of an Islamic kingdom of the same name. Both the town and kingdom flourished for considerably more than a century thereafter. According to some accounts the town contained 100,000 dwellings and 1600 mosques at the height of its prosperity. The kingdom was conquered by the Mogul emperor Aurangzeb (q.v.) in 1686. During the ensuing period of decline the city was ceded in 1760 to the Maratha kingdom and annexed in 1818 by the British. Bijapur was attached to Bombay in 1848. Pop. (1971) 103,931.

BIKANER, city of the Republic of India, in Rajasthan State, about 247 miles W. of Delhi. Most of the city lies within a massive, battlemented wall, over 3 mi. in circumference and from about 15 to 30 ft. high. Noteworthy edifices include a number of Jain monasteries (*see* JAINISM) and a strongly fortified citadel. Bikaner is a famous carpet-weaving and blanket-making center, known also for pottery making and the manufacture of sugar candy. Founded in 1485, the city was formerly capital of the princely State of Bikaner. Pop. (1971) 188,518.

BIKINI, atoll in the Pacific Ocean, one of the Marshall Islands, in the Ralik Chain. The thirty-six islets of the atoll cover an area of about 2 sq.mi. and surround a lagoon 21½ mi. long by 11 mi. wide with an entrance through Enyu Channel. The native population was resettled on Rongerik, a nearby atoll, before the United States began tests of atomic weapons on Bikini in July, 1946. In 1949 the population was moved again, to the island of Kili, also in the Marshall Islands. Further nuclear weapons testing was carried out in 1954. In August, 1968, President Lyndon Baines Johnson (q.v.) announced plans for the resettlement of Bikini after experts concluded that a radiation hazard no longer existed. *See* MARSHALL ISLANDS.

BILBAO, city and seaport in Spain, and capital of Vizcaya Province, on both sides of the Nervion R., about 7 mi. inland from the Bay of Biscay, and some 200 miles E. of Madrid. The city consists of an old section lying on the right bank of the Nervión, and on the left bank a modern section dating from the late 19th century. Several bridges connect the old and new sections. Bilbao is served by several railroads, highways, and an international airport, which is just outside the city. One of the major industrial centers of Spain, the city is within a large iron-ore-mining region. The chief industries are shipbuilding and the manufacture of cement, chemicals, foodstuffs, iron, machinery, paper, steel, and textiles. An important seaport, iron ore, grain cereals, and wine comprise the bulk of exports. The chief imports are coal and timber.

Founded in 1300, Bilbao, by virtue of various privileges granted it, swiftly became one of the leading seaports of Spain. The fortunes of the city declined during the 17th and 18th centuries. In the 19th century the demand for iron ore and steel throughout Europe led to renewed industrial growth in Bilbao. The city withstood two great sieges by the Carlists (q.v.) in 1835–36 and 1874. During the Spanish Civil War from 1936 to 1939 Bilbao was the capital of an autonomous Basque state that was under Loyalist control. Pop. (1970) 410,490.

BILE, bitter, neutral, or slightly alkaline fluid secreted by the liver (q.v.), passed through a duct into the gallbladder (q.v.), where it is stored, and, as necessary, released into the duodenum (*see* INTESTINE). As formed in the liver, bile is a thin watery fluid to which the gallbladder adds a mucous secretion, forming a complex thickened and stringy substance consisting of salts and bile salts, proteins, cholesterol (q.v.), hormones, and enzymes. The gallbladder returns water containing salts and other materials to the circulation and concentrates the complex further by a tenfold reduction of the bile salts, which the liver synthesizes from cholesterol. Such foods as fats, egg yolk, and foods rich in cholesterol cause concentrated bile, together with secretions from the pancreas (q.v.), to be discharged into the duodenum to promote digestion (q.v.), to stimulate peristalsis and absorption, and to carry off excess cholesterol and the disintegration products of overage red blood cells. The hemoglobin (q.v.) of such disintegrating cells degrades rapidly into reddish-yellow bilirubin, predominant in the bile of carnivorous and omnivorous animals, and biliverdin, a green pigment that appears in the bile of herbivora. Under normal conditions, the liver efficiently clears these pigments.

Certain conditions create an inability to excrete bile that may create serious disabilities, such as jaundice (q.v.). In obese and immobilized persons, in pregnant women, and in cases of obstruction of flow of bile, gallstones may be formed by precipitation of bilirubin in combination with calcium and cholesterol. Stasis frequently coexists with inflammation and infection of the gallbladder; this may alter the concentration of bile constituents and create debris around which bile and its components may precipitate to form gallstones, which may then block the common bile duct to reduce or stop the flow of bile. Inflammation and infection, together with the consequent regurgitation of bile into the liver, may damage that organ, sometimes causing cirrhosis. *See also* DIGESTION.

BILHARZIA DISEASE. *See* SCHISTOSOMIASIS.

BILLAUD-VARENNE, Jean Nicolas (1756–1819), French revolutionist, born in La Rochelle, and educated in law at Paris and Poitiers. He became a member of the extreme revolutionary group, the Jacobins (q.v.). Elected a member of the National Convention of France in 1792, he advocated the establishment of a federal republic and the execution of King Louis XVI (q.v.), and in 1793 led the attack on the moderate Girondists (q.v.). He became a member of the Committee of Public Safety, the center of governmental power; and attacked the French revolutionary Maximilian de Robespierre (q.v.), whom he had previously supported. Following the overthrow of Robespierre's government in 1794, Billaud-Varenne was arrested and prosecuted as a terrorist, and, in 1795, was deported to Cayenne in French Guiana. In 1816 he went to Port-au-Prince, Haiti, where he died. *See* FRENCH REVOLUTION.

BILLFISH, common name applied collectively to marlin, sailfish, spearfish, and swordfish (qq.v.), large and popular sport fish of the families Istiophoridae and Xiphiidae. The fish are so named because of a common characteristic, an upper jaw that is prolonged beyond the lower jaw to form a bill or spear.

BILLIARDS, game played on a rectangular table with balls and tapering rods called cues. The three general types of billiards are carom billiards; pocket billiards, known as pool; and snooker. Challenging variations have been devised further in each of these categories. Basically, the game involves the propelling of one ball against another, by means of the cue, for the purpose either of simply striking another ball or of forcing balls off the tabletop. The sport requires both power and control, an unerring eye, and shrewd judgment and strategy. The ruling body of billiards in the United States is the Billiard Congress of America, with headquarters and a hall of fame in Chicago, Ill.

Equipment. Billiards is played on an oblong table half as wide as it is long. In the U.S. the regulation carom-billiards table and the snooker table may be 5 ft. by 10 ft., with a playing area of 56 in. by 112 in.; or 4½ ft. by 9 ft., with a playing area of 50 in. by 100 in. The regulation pocket-billiards table may be either of these sizes, or 4 ft. by 8 ft., with a playing area of 46 in. by 92 in. The billiards table is bordered on all sides by a narrow, slightly raised edge, or rail. Table height, from base to rail top, is 31–32 in. Both the playing surface of the table, which is made out of slate, and the rubber-padded inner part of the rail, called the cushion, are covered by felt. In pocket billiards and snooker, the table surface has six small openings, or pockets, one in each corner and one at the center of each long side; the carom-billiards table is pocketless. The side of the billiards table where play begins is called the head; the opposite side is the foot; and the two connecting borders are the side rails.

Billiards games are played with a differing number of small hard balls, about 5½ oz. to 6 oz. in weight. The white ball used for shooting is known as the cue ball, and the remaining colored balls are called object balls. In pocket billiards and snooker, a wooden triangle, called a rack, is used to arrange the object balls in pyramid formation, all balls touching, at the start of the game.

The billiard balls are propelled against one another by a tapering, leather-tipped wooden rod called a cue stick, or a cue. Cue sticks may be of variable lengths and widths, usually about 53 in. to 57 in. and from 12 oz. to 22 oz.; the diameter of the standard tip ranges from 11 to 15 mm. As a shooting aid, players often use a piece of chalk to roughen the leather tip of the cue.

General Rules. Opponents decide who will shoot first or the rotation of play in a game by a procedure called lagging. From a fixed position the players shoot against the foot cushion. The player whose ball returns nearest to the head rail wins the lag and may elect to begin play. The player's turn at the table is called an inning. The inning begins with the player's first shot and continues until that player either misses, fouls, or scores the maximum number of balls allowed. A foul is any infraction of the rules that govern the game in play and is usually also penalized by a loss of points.

Billiards players draw upon a wide variety of techniques in shooting, or stroking, the cue ball. Most billiardists hold one end of the cue alongside and behind the body with the right hand. The left hand, resting on the table, is used as a bridge across which the cue is guided toward its target. Expert players shoot so as to control the cue ball both before and after it strikes the object ball. Players usually bend low toward or over the tabletop and are required to execute shots with at least one foot touching the floor.

CAROM BILLIARDS

The surface of the carom-billiards table is marked by a head, center, and foot spot, and by imaginary head, center, and foot strings, or lines, which cross straight through the spots from diamonds, or markings, on the side rails. Three balls, two white and a red, each 2⅜ in. in diameter, are used. The object of the game is to make caroms, that is, to propel the cue ball by striking it with the tip of the cue so that the cue ball will hit both of the other balls in turn. The game is scored by points, with each carom counting for a single point. The contestants take alternate turns, and each contestant retires when he fails to make a carom. In tournament play the winning score is generally 100 points; in nontournament play, however, other winning scores, such as 25 or 33 points, are often agreed upon by the players.

To make the game more difficult and consequently of more interest to the expert player, various hazards have been introduced. In the balkline game, rectangular areas are marked off on the table by lines chalked either 14 in. or 18 in. from each cushion; a player may not score more than two successive caroms in the same area unless he drives a ball out of that particular rectangle. In the three-cushion game the cue ball must strike at least three cushions before completing a carom.

The professional carom-billiards championship tournaments in the U.S. were dominated for almost fifty years by the American billiardists William F. "Willie" Hoppe (q.v.), Jacob "Jake" Schaefer, Jr., and Welker Cochran (d. 1960). The national championship in 18.2 (18 in.–2 caroms) balkline billiards was held by one or another of these players from 1911 to 1935, except for the years 1926 and 1928. About 1933 the three-cushion game became the more popular version of the sport, and Hoppe and Cochran entered this field. Except in 1939 Hoppe or Cochran held the three-cushion championship every year from 1935 to 1952.

POCKET BILLIARDS

Pocket billiards, or pool, is played with one white cue ball and fifteen object balls, all 2¼ in. in diameter; the object balls are numbered 1 through 15 and are variously colored. The head and foot spot locations on the table are fixed by drawing a string line between the center of the side pocket diagonally to the center of the opposite corner pockets; where these lines intersect determines the spot locations.

Of the many varieties of pocket billiards the most popular is called straight pool. The purpose of the game is to drive the object balls into the pockets, utilizing the cue stick to propel the cue ball into contact with the object ball or balls; the player must call his shot, that is, announce the particular ball and the particular pocket into which he intends to drive each ball. The usual number of players is two, and the scoring consists of 1 point per object ball pocketed up to a prefixed number, usually 50. The first player to score 50 points is the winner.

At the beginning of this game the object balls are racked so that the first ball in the apex of the rack is placed on the foot spot, with the base of the rack below the spot and parallel with the short sides of the table. The cue ball is placed anywhere behind an imaginary line that passes through the head spot, parallel to the head rail.

The game begins with the break, which is the disruption of the triangular arrangement of object balls by propelling the cue ball toward the pack. The player must either call his shot on the break, or play safe, that is, send two object balls from the pack to the cushion that borders the table. If his cue ball misses the pack, or fails to send two balls to the cushion, or if the cue ball drops into a pocket whether he has called his shot or has played safe, he has committed a scratch and is penalized 1 point. Any object ball pocketed on a scratch does not count as a point and is spotted, that is, restored to the table on the foot spot, or if other balls are in the way, as

Irving Crane, three-time world champion in pocket billiards, lines up a shot. Billiard Room Proprietors' Assn.

close to the foot spot as possible and directly behind it. A scratch can also be committed during the course of the game, if the cue ball shot by a player fails to touch any other ball, if the cue ball is dropped into any pocket, or if no ball touches a cushion after a contact between the cue ball and any other ball. After the break, the players shoot in turn and keep shooting, until they fail to pocket a ball, or scratch. When all balls but one have been pocketed, the remaining fourteen balls are racked in the same position as at the start of the game, except that the apex position is left vacant. The player who pocketed the fourteenth ball then shoots at the fifteenth ball or at the pack. If the cue ball lies in the portion of the table that must be covered by the rack, it is moved back to the head of the table as in the beginning of the game; if the fifteenth object ball is in that area, all fifteen balls are racked and the player must break again. In a break other than the opening break, the player need not drive two object balls to the cushion.

In the course of the game, a player, confronted by a difficult arrangement of balls, may decide to play safe, causing also a difficult shot for his opponent. This play is done by calling "safe", and then sending the cue ball glancingly off one or more object balls so that the arrangement of balls is little changed, or even made more difficult for a successful shot. A player, in the course of the game, may call one ball in a particular pocket, and sink that ball and one or more others. He is credited with a point for each extra ball pocketed if he makes his original call good. If he sinks one or more balls not called, without making his original call good, or sinks a called ball into the wrong pocket, the ball or balls are spotted and do not count as points.

Popular variations of pocket billiards include Chicago or rotation pool (sometimes called 61), in which the object balls are played in numerical order; Kelly pool; bottle or pill pool; and eight ball. Among the world pocket-billiards champions since 1914 have been Frank Taberski (d. 1941), Ralph Greenleaf (d. 1950), Erwin Rudolph (d. 1957), Andrew Ponzi (d. 1950), and Willie Mosconi.

SNOOKER

American snooker is played with a white cue ball and twenty-one object balls, all 2⅛ in. in diameter. Fifteen of the object balls are colored red, and each of these has a scoring value of 1 point. The color and scoring value of the remaining six object balls are: yellow, 2 points; green, 3 points; brown, 4 points; blue, 5 points;

pink, 6 points; and black, 7 points. At the start of the game, the fifteen red balls are racked at the foot spot and the pink ball is placed so that it is touching the apex ball on the center line of the table. The black ball rests also on the center line but between the base of the rack and the foot of the table. The blue ball is placed on the center spot, and the green, brown, and yellow balls are placed on the balkline fixed near the head of the table. A semicircular area known as the D is formed by a line curving in the direction of the head of the table from the green to the yellow ball.

On the break or opening shot, the cue ball is put into play within the D. It must first contact a red ball, and if a red ball is pocketed on the break shot, the player scores 1 point. The next object is a numbered ball, which the player must call, or name, and which he is then said to be on. If the called object ball is pocketed, the player scores according to its value. Play continues to alternate between a red ball and a numbered ball. Numbered balls are spotted while there are red balls remaining on the table. When all the red balls are off the table, the remaining object balls are pocketed according to their numerical value. A player is "snookered" when he is blocked from shooting in a straight line directly at the ball he is on because of the placement of other balls on the table.

The first national snooker tournament, held in Chicago in 1950, was won by Benny Allen, a former world champion at pocket billiards.

History. The origin of the game of billiards is obscure. It is thought that the earliest versions were played outdoors on the ground, first with stones and later with balls. Subsequently the game was played indoors on a table in a form similar to croquet (q.v.), with two balls being struck by mallets or sticks through an iron arch. In France during the reign of King Charles IX (q.v.) in the 16th century, the design of the table was standardized and uniform rules were introduced. In the 18th century French players eliminated the arch and added a third ball, introducing the modern carom game.

The game became popular in the U.S. after the introduction of such technical improvements as leather cue tips and marble or slate tabletops or beds; these features enabled the player to give the ball a fast straight roll. In 1835 rubber cushions along the sides of the table were introduced, permitting a strong, accurately controlled rebound. From that time billiards rapidly developed into a game of scientific precision.

BILLINGS, city in Montana, and county seat of Yellowstone Co., on the Yellowstone R., about 180 miles S.E. of Helena. The city is served by several railroads, highways, and a municipal airport. Billings is the shipping and trade center for the surrounding region in which natural gas and oil are produced and alfalfa, livestock, and wheat are grown. Important industries in the city include construction, mining, oil refining, and the manufacture of farm machinery and foodstuffs. Billings is the seat of Eastern Montana College and Rocky Mountain College. The city was founded in 1882 by the Northern Pacific Railroad and was incorporated as a city in 1885. Pop. (1960) 52,851; (1970) 61,581.

BILLINGS, John Shaw (1838–1913), American physician and librarian, born in Switzerland County, Ind., and educated at Miami University of Ohio and the Medical College of Ohio. During the American Civil War he served in the field and in the office of the surgeon general. In his thirty years as director of the surgeon general's library, he made it into one of the largest and most comprehensive medical libraries in the world. With the American surgeon and bibliographer Robert Fletcher (1823–1912), he compiled and published two guides to medical literature: the *Index-Catalog of the Library of the Surgeon General's Office* (16 vol., 1880–95) and *Index Medicus,* a monthly guide to current publications. Upon his retirement from the army in 1895, Billings assumed the task of combining three separate collections into what is now the New York Public Library (q.v.). He cataloged the books in the new library and set up the present system of branches and free circulation. He retained his position as director of the library until his death.

BILLINGS, Josh, pen name of HENRY WHEELER SHAW (1818–85), American humorist, born in Lanesboro, Mass., and educated briefly at Hamilton College. After roaming about the country for more than twenty years, he settled in Poughkeepsie, N.Y., as an auctioneer and realtor. He began, at the age of forty-five, to write sketches in a rural dialect using intentional misspellings and the literary device of anticlimax. His writings attracted the American humorist Charles Farrar Browne (q.v.) who arranged the publication of the sketches as *Josh Billings, His Sayings* (1865). From 1870 to 1880 Billings published a popular annual called *Josh Billings' Farmer's Allminax.* His other works include *Everybody's Friend, or Josh Billings' Encyclopedia and Proverbial Philosophy of Wit and Humor* (1876).

BILLINGS, William (1746–1800), American composer of choral music, the foremost representative of early American music.

Born in Boston, Mass., on Oct. 7, 1746, and largely self-trained, he was a tanner by trade and a friend of such figures of the American Revolution as Samuel Adams and Paul Revere.

Billings' *New England Psalm-Singer* (1700), engraved by Revere, was the first collection of music entirely by an American. He was the first American to compose fuging tunes (a provincial English choral genre, in which an initial chordal section is followed by lively melodic imitation). He introduced pitch pipes into church choirs, and as an itinerant singing master for local singing schools was part of an American folk tradition. Many of his hymns, anthems, psalm settings, and fuging tunes remain in print in southern U.S. shape-note hymnals (folk hymnals in which pitch is shown by the note shape). Especially known among his compositions are his canon (round) "When Jesus Wept", the anthem "David's Lamentation", and the hymn "Chester", written to his own patriotic text and unofficially the national hymn of the American Revolution. Billings died in Boston, Sept. 26, 1800. G.L.

BILLINGSGATE. *See* LONDON: *Facilities.*

BILLITON. *See* BELITUNG.

BILL OF ATTAINDER. *See* ATTAINDER.

BILL OF EXCHANGE, unconditional order in writing, signed and addressed by one person (the drawer) to another (the drawee), requiring the drawee to pay on demand, or at a determinable or fixed future date, a specified sum of money to a third person (the payee). The payee is frequently the bearer of the bill. On accepting a bill of exchange, the drawee becomes the party primarily responsible for paying it. Bills of exchange are negotiable (*see* NEGOTIABLE INSTRUMENTS), and constitute one of the principal forms of commercial documents in most countries. The most common bill of exchange is the check.

The use and legal status of bills of exchange vary from country to country. In the United States their use is governed by the Uniform Negotiable Instruments Law, prepared in 1897 and, by 1927, adopted with little change by all the States.

BILL OF HEALTH, certificate to the master of a ship by the authorities of a port from which it sails, setting forth the condition of the port and vessel with respect to infectious diseases. A clean bill of health certifies the absence of diseases; a foul bill states that the ship has been exposed to contagion; and a touched or suspected bill indicates that infectious disease is suspected or feared. A ship entering a port must show a clean bill of health to avoid quarantine.

BILL OF RIGHTS, first ten Amendments to the Constitution of the United States, safeguarding fundamental individual rights against usurpation by the Federal government and prohibiting interference with existing rights. The precedents for these stipulations came from three separate English documents: the Magna Charta, the Petition of Right (qq.v.), and the Declaration of Rights (*see* WILLIAM III, King of England). Virginia, in 1776, and Massachusetts, in 1780, had incorporated bills of rights into their original constitutions (*see* MASSACHUSETTS: *Government;* VIRGINIA: *History*) and these two States, with New York and Pennsylvania, refused to ratify the new Federal Constitution unless it was amended to protect the individual. In 1790, Congress submitted twelve Amendments, ten of which were adopted in 1791 as Articles I through X. *See* CONSTITUTION OF THE UNITED STATES.

BILLY THE KID (1859?–81), famous desperado and outlaw of the American Southwest, probably born in New York City. He used many names, including William H. Bonney, Henry McCarthy, and Kid Antrim. He claimed to have shot and killed twenty-one men. Billy the Kid's first victim was killed in a barroom fight and the last two in his successful effort to escape from the guards taking him to jail. Shortly after his escape, he was trapped and shot by a sheriff. Legends have grown up around his name and his exploits have been romanticized in the stories based on his life and times.

BILOXI, city of Mississippi, in Harrison Co., on a peninsula formed by Biloxi Bay and the Mississippi Sound, about 13 miles E. of Gulfport. The city, a year-round resort, is a boatbuilding and fishing center, with extensive seafood-packing plants. Other industries include construction, shipping, and tourism. Biloxi is the site of Keesler Air Force Base, and of a veterans administration center. Historical points of interest include Beauvoir, the last home of the Confederate president Jefferson Davis (q.v.) and Fort Massachusetts, a Union fort used during the Civil War, on nearby Ship Island. Founded by the French in 1699, Biloxi was the capital of the vast French province of Louisiana until 1722. On Aug. 17, 1969, 190-m.p.h. winds of hurricane Camille devastated the gulf area causing severe damage in the area. Biloxi was incorporated as a town in 1838 and as a city in 1896. Pop. (1960); 44,053; (1970) 48,486.

BIMETALLISM, monetary policy based on the use of two metals, usually gold and silver, as legal tender (qq.v.), coined without limit (free coinage), and equalized by law in a fixed ratio. The ratio is expressed in terms of weight, usually with a fixed number of ounces of silver being made equal to one ounce of gold. Determined by law, this ratio does not necessarily reflect the relative abundance of the metals, and therefore may be changed by law, as it was in the United States in 1834, when the former ratio of 15 to 1 was changed to 15.988 to 1, or, as commonly expressed, 16 to 1. This weight ratio has no relation to the commercial ratio (value) of the metals, which may fluctuate. Adherents of bimetallism maintain that the fixed legal ratio prevents nearly all fluctuations in the commercial values of the two metals, and hence tends to stabilize the prices of commodities and to simplify foreign exchange. Most economists, however, are opposed to bimetallism on the grounds that the cheaper metal, which is valued commercially at less than its face value, drives the more precious metal from circulation; *see* GRESHAM'S LAW.

Practical difficulties, in the maintenance of concurrent circulation of the two metals, have led one nation after another to adopt a system of monometallism, with gold as its basis. In England the single gold standard, actually in operation since 1699, was finally legalized by successive steps, in 1717, 1774, 1778, and 1816. The U.S. adopted the double standard, as urged by Secretary of the Treasury Alexander Hamilton (q.v.) in 1792. France, in 1801, instituted a plan to make a five-franc silver piece standard money, but after the discovery of gold in Australia and California and the fall in the price of gold relative to silver, the French law favored the coinage of gold. In 1871 Germany, formerly operating on a silver basis, adopted the gold standard as one element in the unification of coinage following establishment of the German Empire. Thereafter the most important European nations abandoned the double standard for the single gold standard.

Bimetallism was abandoned in the U.S. in 1873. The Bland-Allison Act of 1878, however, allowed a limited number of silver dollars to be coined, thus creating the system termed limping bimetallism, a monetary system partially dependent on the use of silver, but primarily dependent on gold. Bimetallism was a major political issue in France and other European nations. It became a crucial issue in the U.S. during the last quarter of the 19th century, a period characterized by steadily falling prices and a commercial depression. The policy of limping bimetallism was ended by the Gold Standard Act of 1900, and with the gradual improvement in economic conditions, the issue was forgotten. It was revived, however, in the 1930's, following the depression of 1929, and although true bimetallism was not established, silver was added to gold as the U.S. monetary base; the amount of silver for which a silver certificate could be redeemed, however, had a lower commercial value than the monetary value of the certificate.

In 1967 the U.S. removed all connections to bimetallism; the 25 percent gold backing for the currency was eliminated as balance-of-payments difficulties reduced U.S. gold stock. Rising silver prices led to the virtual elimination of silver contents in coins, and to a discontinuation of redemption of any silver certificates presented after 1968; in 1970 the Federal government sold the rest of its silver supply.

See also GREENBACK-LABOR PARTY; MONEY; PEOPLE'S PARTY. J.M.L.

BINARY STARS. *See* DOUBLE STARS.

BINARY SYSTEM. *See* NOTATION.

BINDWEED. *See* CONVOLVULUS.

BINET, Alfred (1857–1911), French psychologist, born in Nice, and educated at the Sorbonne. At the Sorbonne he founded the first psychological research laboratory in France. In collaboration with psychologist Théodore Simon (1873–1961) he devised a test to measure the mental ability of children. *See* PSYCHOLOGICAL TESTING: *Intelligence Testing.* He was a founder and editor of the journal, *L'Année Psychologique* ("The Psychological Year"), from 1895 until his death.

BING, Sir Rudolf (1902–), opera manager, born in Vienna. He began his career as a singer and concert manager in Germany. In 1934 he emigrated to England and became a British subject in 1946. Bing was (1935–39, 1946–49) manager of the summer opera festivals of the Glyndebourne Opera Company, near Lewes, England. In 1950 he became general manager of the Metropolitan Opera Company, New York City. Among his contributions to American music (q.v.) are his expanding use of American singers and of opera sung in English. He also brought to the Metropolitan Opera many important designers and directors with previous experience in the dramatic theater rather than in opera. Bing retired in June, 1972, and joined the faculty of Brooklyn College. He is the author of *5,000 Nights at the Opera* (1972).

BINGEN, town of West Germany, in Rhineland-Palatinate State, on the Rhine R., about 85 miles S.E. of Cologne. The town is a busy port and railroad junction, with plants engaged in wine production and the manufacture of tobacco products. In the vicinity are the *Bingerloch,* a famous whirlpool in the Rhine R.; and the *Mäuseturm* (Mouse Tower), in which, according to legend, the German prelate Hatto II (d. about 970 A.D.) was devoured by mice. Prior to the arrival of the Romans Bingen was a town of the Belgae (q.v.), a Celtic-speaking people. The Romans fortified the town, and there, in 70 A.D. they inflicted a severe defeat on the Gauls. In 1254 it became a member of the Hanseatic League (q.v.). In 1689 Bingen was burned by the French, and from 1797 to 1814 the French ruled the town. In 1815 Bingen was included in the grand duchy of Hesse-Darmstadt (*see* HESSE). Pop. (1967 est.) 20,700.

BINGHAM, name of three members of an American family all of whom had the same given name; they were prominent in missionary work, translating, exploring, and public affairs.

Hiram Bingham (1789–1869), missionary born in Bennington, Vt., and educated at Middlebury College and Andover Theological Seminary (now Andover Newton Theological School). Ordained a Congregationalist minister in 1819, he was a member of the first group of Protestant missionaries sent to the Hawaiian Islands. Bingham served in Honolulu from 1820 to 1840. He was the first to adapt the Hawaiian language to writing, and with his fellow missionaries produced a grammar and a Bible translation in Hawaiian.

Hiram Bingham (1831–1908), missionary, son of Hiram (1789–1869), born in Honolulu and educated at Yale University and Andover Theological Seminary. Ordained a Congregationalist minister in 1857, he was missionary in the Gilbert Islands from 1857 to 1863 and from 1873 to 1875. Bingham was first to adapt Gilbertese, the language of the islands, to writing. He produced a translation of the Bible, a Bible dictionary, a hymnal, and a commentary on the Gospels, all in Gilbertese.

Hiram Bingham (1875–1956), educator, explorer, and legislator, son of Hiram (1831–1908), born in Honolulu and educated at Yale and Harvard universities and the University of California. He taught history at Harvard, Princeton, and Yale universities. As director of the Yale Peruvian Expedition (1911–12), he discovered the ruins of the ancient Inca city of Machupicchu; *see* PERUVIAN ARCHEOLOGY. He further explored (1912–15) the Inca lands for Yale and the National Geographic Society (q.v.). During World War I he was commander of the Aviation Instruction Center at Issoudun, France. A member of the Republican Party, Bingham served as lieutenant governor (1923–24) and governor (1925) of Connecticut and as United States Senator (1925–33). Of his many books the most important is *Lost City of the Incas* (1948).

BINGHAM, George Caleb (1811–79), American painter, born in Augusta County, Va. He spent a few months at the Pennsylvania Academy of the Fine Arts in 1837, but was otherwise self-taught. His most important works were naturalistic and vigorous paintings of Missouri frontier life. Apart from "Fur Traders Descending the Missouri" (1845?; Metropolitan Museum of Art) and "Result of the Election" (1854; National Gallery of Art), most of his paintings remain in Missouri in public collections. Bingham, also a political leader, served (1848) in the Missouri legislature and as State treasurer (1826–65) and State adjutant-general (1875–77).

BINGHAMTON, city in New York, and county seat of Broome Co., at the confluence of the Susquehanna and Chenango rivers, about 120 miles S.W. of Albany. It is served by several railroads, highways, and a nearby airport. Binghamton, Endicott, and Johnson City (qq.v.) comprise the so-called Triple Cities, famous for the manufacture of shoes. Industries in Binghamton include construction, metals and machinery production, and wholesale and retail trades. The city is the site of the State University at Binghamton, a liberal-arts college. Settled about 1787 as Chenango Point, Binghamton was renamed about 1820. In 1834 Binghamton was incorporated as a village, and in 1867 as a city. Pop. (1960) 75,941; (1970) 64,123.

BINGO, game of chance, widely popular in the United States, played with numbered cards and counters by any number of people. The object of the game is to cover a row of numbers with counters before any other players are able to do so; it is derived from lotto which in turn is based on lottery (*see* GAMBLING). In the U.S., bingo has become one of the favored means of raising funds for religious and charitable organizations, the sponsoring group taking a percentage of the moneys wagered. The proponents of bingo defend it as a harmless pastime providing participants with entertainment at small cost, while its opponents consider it nothing more than public gambling. The legality of bingo as a commercial game has been put to a vote in some States. In a New York State referendum, held in November, 1957, a majority of voters approved an amendment to the State constitution giving communities the right to legalize bingo.

Although there are many variations of bingo, in the basic game each player receives a card containing five horizontal rows of numbers ranging from one to ninety and a set of counters. The various cards have different arrangements of numbers and contain a center square, usually marked "Free", on which a player may immediately place a counter. Each player pays for his card and in some games he is free to buy more than one card.

One player, known as the banker, has in his charge a collection of tokens numbered from one to ninety which he draws from a box or other receptacle one by one. As he does so, he calls out the number of each token. Players with a corresponding number on their cards cover it with a token. The banker keeps track of the called numbers on a master chart visible to the players. As soon as any player covers a vertical or horizontal row of numbers with counters he cries "bingo". In some games diagonal rows may be played too. His covered numbers are then checked against the master chart to insure the correctness of his call. Winners receive either the sum total of all wagers or, if the game is commercially run, the total less a percentage for the "house". If two or more players go bingo at the same time, prizes are shared equally.

See also KENO.

BINOMIAL, algebraic expression that consists of exactly two terms separated by + or −, such as $x + y$ or $ab - cd$. The binomial theorem asserts that the general expansion of a binomial, such as $(x + y)$, raised to the nth power (*see* MATHEMATICS, TERMS IN) is given by

$$(x+y)^n = x^n + nx^{n-1}y + \frac{n(n-1)}{2}x^{n-2}y^2 + \frac{n(n-1)(n-2)}{2\cdot 3}x^{n-3}y^3 + \ldots + y^n$$

The general coefficient of the kth term in the above expression is

$$\frac{n(n-1)(n-2)(n-3)\ldots(n-k+1)}{2\cdot 3\cdot 4\cdot 5\cdot 6\ldots(k-1)k}$$

and is usually denoted by the symbol $\binom{n}{k}$. The expansion of $(x + y)^N$ contains $n + 1$ terms. Discovered by the English scientist Sir Isaac Newton (q.v.) about 1666, the binomial theorem is useful in many branches of mathematics, particularly in the theory of probability (q.v.). J.Si.

BINUE. *See* BENUE.

BIOASTRONAUTICS. *See* SPACE MEDICINE: *The Space Environment.*

BIOCHEMISTRY, science that studies the substances composing living organisms, and the details of the chemical changes, reactions, and products occurring in the life processes of plants and animals; *see* CHEMISTRY: *Major Divisions of Chemistry: Biochemistry.*

BIOENGINEERING *or* **BIOMEDICAL ENGINEERING,** application of engineering principles and design procedures to medical problems. The principal subdisciplines are biomechanical, biochemical, and bioelectrical engineering.

Biomechanical Engineering. The subdivision views the musculoskeletal system of the human body as a mechanical structure which can undergo certain motions and stresses. Thus it includes the analysis of human gait and the investigation of stresses on flesh and bone during accidents. Biomechanical engineering is also concerned with the flow of blood, the mechanics of respiration (q.v.) and energy exchange in the living human body.

Applications range from the development of protective automotive safety belts to the design and operation of heart-lung machines. An important early development was the iron lung (q.v.) which permitted victims of poliomyelitis (q.v.) to survive. Biomechanical engineering also forms the basis of reconstructive developments such as artificial implants and artificial limbs (q.v.). For instance, special artificial arms, driven by small electric motors and operated by bioelectrical signals from muscles, have given children born without limbs a nearly normal appearance and enough mobility to permit them to function socially and vocationally.

Biochemical Engineering. The field deals with the chemical interactions between the human body and artificial materials that, implanted into live tissue, may provoke adverse reaction or rejection; *see* IMMUNITY. For example, it took the development of woven acrylic artificial arteries to prevent the rapid clotting of blood in artificial blood vessels. Capsules of silicone (*see* SILICON) were developed to protect implanted electrical equipment, such as cardiac pacemakers, and to permit their integration into live tissues. Perhaps the most dramatic biochemical engineering development, however, has been the design and construction of the artificial kidney which serves to eliminate the toxic waste products of patients afflicted with incurable kidney diseases; *see* KIDNEY.

Bioelectrical Engineering. This area of biomedical engineering concerns itself with bioelectric activity, that includes the nervous system (q.v.), and regulates most life processes. The role of the bioelectrical engineer is to assist this regulation and to use bioelectric signals for diagnostic purposes. Developments in such engineering led to the invention of the pacemaker, the defibrillator, and the electrocardiograph. The pacemaker is a medical device that senses and restores the normal contraction rhythm of the heart muscle, by electrostimulation, in heart disease victims. The defibrillator sends a powerful but controlled electric current through the body of a patient whose heart has stopped, and restores normal heart action. An electrocardiograph records, through electrodes placed on the skin, the wave form and the frequency of the heart action; *see* HEART: *Heart Diseases.* Techniques for transmitting electrocardiograms via telephone to central computers and diagnostic centers have been developed, thus moving American physicians toward a nationwide diagnostic network. The monitoring of many other bioelectric functions by means of electrodes plays an important part in surgical recovery room and intensive-care units.

See also BIOPHYSICS; MEDICINE; THERAPEUTICS; TRANSPLANT, MEDICAL. E.R.T.

BIOGENESIS, theory in biology that life develops from preexisting life, specifically, that all living matter originated from similar organisms or parents. The hypothesis is opposed to the concept of spontaneous generation (q.v.), known as abiogenesis. Although biogenesis has been accepted by scientists for almost a century, recent scientific developments indicate that the theory may have to be modified to include such ultramicroscopic phenomena as the virus (q.v.).

BIOGENETIC LAW *or* **RECAPITULATION THEORY,** principle in biology that the embryological development of the individual organism recapitulates the evolution of the race or group. The German biologist Ernst Heinrich Haeckel (q.v.) formulated the law in 1867. It was originally interpreted to mean that in its development the embryo passes through exactly the same stages as did the race in its evolution. In modern biology the principle is no longer considered to apply strictly; the development of the embryo is now regarded as a condensed or superficial recapitulation of the development of the race.

BIOGEOGRAPHY. *See* GEOGRAPHY: *Physical Geography.*

BIOGRAPHY, the written account of an individual life. (An autobiography is an account of his life written by the subject himself.) The term biography now connotes an artful, conscious literary genre which employs a wide range of sources, strategies, and insights; which deals with the intimate, inconsistent textures of personality and experience; and which attempts to render through action and narrative the whole sense of its subject, not the life only but what it was like to have lived it at its several stages. Ideally, the writer molds complex biographical givens—birth and death, education, ambition, conflict, milieu, work, relationship, accident—into a book which has the independent vitality of any creative work but is, at the same time, "true to life".

Biography is as old as recorded history. Rulers and magnates of ancient Egypt, Assyria, and Babylonia had their deeds incised in stone and clay. The Old Testament contains many brief lives of patriarchs and prophets, while the four Gospels of the New Testament can be described as parallel lives of Jesus. Three notable examples of biographical writing in classical times are Xenophon's *Memorabilia,* his recollections and defense of Socrates; Plutarch's *Lives,* a source book for Shakespeare; and Suetonius' gossipy and anecdotal *Lives of the Caesars.* The practice of commemorating the illustrious dead continues, in a more objective manner, in multivolume modern compilations such as the *Dictionary of American Biography* and the British *Dictionary of National Biography.*

In Western culture until about the middle of the 17th century biography was generally commemorative, edifying, and inspirational, dealing didactically with the cautionary lives of malefactors and tyrants as well as the exemplary lives of heroes and heroines. Its chief subjects, once Christianity had triumphed, were saints, martyrs, and church fathers, who were depicted less as individuals than as actors in a stylized drama of salvation; the "saint's life" became one of the conventions of medieval literature. A late work in this hagiographic tradition was *Acts and Monuments* (popularly known as *The Book of Martyrs*), originally written in Latin by the English martyrologist John Foxe and published in 1559. In the same decade appeared the original Italian version of Giorgio Vasari's *Lives of the Painters,* a work that reflected a new, opposed spirit of Renaissance humanism in the fine arts and in the interpretation of lives.

An important transitional work is Izaak Walton's *Life of John Donne,* first published in 1640 and, in three successive editions over the next twenty-five years, revised and developed by its author in the direction of modern biography. Appropriately, the year of Walton's death, 1683, saw the first recorded use in English—by John Dryden, writing about Plutarch—of the word "biography".

The publication in 1791 of James Boswell's *Life of Samuel Johnson* is generally thought to have established Boswell as the first great modern biographer and to have inaugurated a "golden age of biography" that has extended to the present day. Yet somewhat the same claim of precedence could be made for Johnson himself—"The biographical part of literature", he said, "is what I love most"—and his remarkably candid, immediate, and existential life (1744) of his friend the English poet Richard Savage (1697?-1743).

During the 19th century, with the publication of such significant works as *Life of Sir Walter Scott* (7 vol., 1837-38) by John Gibson Lockhart (1794-1854) and two biographies of Thomas Carlyle (1882, 1884) by James Anthony Froude, the biographical impetus that sprang from Romantic celebrations of the individual (*see* ROMANTICISM) contended with and eventually survived social pressures toward reticence and propriety. At the same time, favored by conditions that later vanished with the advent of the telephone, rapid travel, and electronics, invaluable source materials for biography—personal letters, journals, diaries, and the like—proliferated and were frequently preserved.

In the 20th century Sigmund Freud and other scientific observers of self and society provided a further impetus for the exploration of personality through narrative. Meanwhile, literary standards for the writing of biography continued to rise along with a general level of sophistication. "A well-written life is almost as rare as a well-spent one", Carlyle said in 1827; the precise sentiment was echoed nearly a century later by Lytton Strachey, author of the popular and influential *Eminent Victorians* (1918) and *Queen Victoria* (1921). Strachey described biography as "the most delicate and humane of all the branches of the art of writing". Biography retained its broad appeal to different sorts of readers as various 20th-century literary fashions came and went. Among recent achievements by American biographers were Leon Edel's multivolume *Henry James* (5 vol., 1953-72), Richard Ellmann's several works on the Irish author James Joyce, and Erik Erikson's psychobiographical study, *Young Man Luther* (1958).

See biographies of most of the persons mentioned in this article whose life dates are not given. *See also* the various articles on national literatures, such as AMERICAN LITERATURE.

J.K.

BIOLOGICAL CHEMISTRY. *See* BIOCHEMISTRY.

BIOLOGICAL WARFARE, also called GERM WARFARE, use in war of living organisms, especially disease-producing agents, against the enemy, his animals, and his crops. Modern biological agents fall into several categories. The first group comprises pathogenic microorganisms, which include the protozoa (q.v.) that cause malaria and amoebic dysentery; the fungi (q.v.) that cause histoplasmosis and blastomycosis; the bacteria (q.v.) that cause anthrax, brucellosis, cholera, diphtheria, plague, tularemia, and typhoid fever; the rickettsia bodies (*see* RICKETTSIA) that cause typhus and Rocky Mountain spotted fever; and the viruses (*see* VIRUS) that cause encephalitis, hepatitis, influenza, smallpox, and yellow fever. The second group is the microbial toxins (q.v.) produced by bacteria, such as botulin and staphylococcal toxins. The third group consists of disease-carrying insects, birds, and animals. The use of plant and animal pests, such as locusts and grasshoppers, is sometimes considered a means of biological warfare. Chemical compounds such as plant-growth inhibitors and defoliants are usually included in chemical warfare (q.v.).

Essential characteristics for a military disease-producing agent are that it remain infectious and virulent long enough to be effective, yet stable during storage and transit; it should be economical to produce on a large scale, and be easily and efficiently disseminated, yet difficult to detect and immunize against. The agent should be capable of being introduced into the air or water supply as a concentrated liquid suspension or a dry powder. Research is being conducted in many countries to develop efficient biological weapons. Use of such agents, however, is banned by a 1925 international protocol signed by most nations. *See* DISARMAMENT: *Bans on Chemical and Biological Warfare.*

Defense against biological warfare consists of detecting the agent; immunizing the population beforehand; and establishing and maintaining effective procedures for quarantine and inspection to halt the spread of the disease, for protection during an attack, and for decontamination following an attack.

See also DISEASE; DISEASES OF ANIMALS; DISEASES OF PLANTS.

M.B.

BIOLOGY, the science of life. The term was introduced in Germany in 1800 and popularized by the French naturalist Jean Baptiste de Lamarck (q.v.) as a means of encompassing the growing number of disciplines involved with the study of living forms. The unifying concept of biology received its greatest stimulus from the English zoologist Thomas Henry Huxley (*see under* HUXLEY), also an important educator. Huxley insisted that the conventional segregation of zoology and botany was intellectually meaningless and that all living things should be studied in an integrated way. Huxley's approach to the study of biology is even more cogent today, for scientists now realize that many lower organisms are neither plants nor animals (*see* MONERA; PROTISTA). The limits of the science, however, have always been difficult to determine, and as the scope of biology has shifted over the years, its subject areas have been changed and reorganized.

Today, biology is subdivided into hierarchical levels based on the molecule, the cell, the organism, and the population.

Molecular biology, which spans biophysics (q.v.) and biochemistry (*see* CHEMISTRY), has made the most fundamental contributions to modern biology. Much is now known about the structure and action of nucleic acids and protein (qq.v.), the key molecules of all living matter. The discovery of the mechanism of heredity—the ability of the nucleic acids to control the synthesis of specific proteins—was a major breakthrough in modern science. Another important advance was in understanding the way in which molecules conduct metabolism, that is, how they process the energy needed to sustain life.

Cellular biology is closely linked with molecular biology. To understand the functions of the cell—the basic structural unit of living matter—cell biologists study its components on the molecular level. Organismal biology, in turn, is related to cellular biology, because the life functions of multicellular organisms are governed by the activities and interactions of their cellular components. The study of organisms includes their growth and development (developmental biology) and how they function (physiology). Particularly important today are investigations of the brain and nervous system (neurophysiology) and animal behavior (ethology).

Population biology became firmly established as a major subdivision of biological studies in the 1970's. Central to this field is evolutionary biology, in which the contributions of Charles Darwin (*see under* DARWIN) have been fully appreciated after a long period of neglect. Population genetics, the study of gene changes in populations, and ecology, the study of populations in their natural habitat, have been established subject areas since the 1930's. These two fields were combined in the 1960's to form a rapidly developing new discipline often called, simply, population biology. Closely associated is a new development in animal-behavior studies called sociobiology, which focuses on the genetic contribution to social interactions among animal populations.

Biology also includes the study of humans at the molecular, cellular, and organismal levels. If the focus of investigation is the application of biological knowledge to human health, the study is often termed biomedicine. Human populations are by convention not considered within the province of biology; instead, they are the subject of anthropology (q.v.) and the various social sciences. But the boundaries and subdivisions of biology are as fluid today as they have always been, and further shifts may be expected.

See BOTANY; CELL; CLASSIFICATION; ECOLOGY; EMBRYOLOGY; ETHOLOGY; EVOLUTION; HEREDITY; LIFE; MEDICINE; METABOLISM; REPRODUCTION; ZOOLOGY. J.T.B.

BIOLUMINESCENCE, emission of light from living organisms, without appreciable heat. The light results from a chemical reaction of enzymes (q.v.) and certain other substances in the organisms. Bacteria, algae, and fungi have bioluminescent species. Some deep-sea fish are equipped with organs that produce luminescence to which prey is attracted. The glow emitted by the female firefly (q.v.) attracts the male for mating. *See* FLUORESCENCE AND PHOSPHORESCENCE; LUMINESCENCE.

BIOMATHEMATICS, science of applying mathematics to biology (qq.v.). In a broader sense it includes mathematical biology as well as biostatistics. In mathematical biology, mathematics is applied to biology with the aim of explaining biological phenomena and understanding of the nature of life on the basis of developing mathematical theories and comparing their conclusions with observation and experiment. When organic life is explained in terms of physics, the term mathematical biophysics is preferred. In biostatistics (the statistical study of biological phenomena), mathematics is employed in evaluating the reliability of data and of establishing empirical relations which hold statistically between different characteristics of organisms. *See* BIOPHYSICS. N.R.

BIOMEDICAL ENGINEERING. *See* BIOENGINEERING.

BION (fl. 3rd or 2nd cent. B.C.), Greek poet born near Smyrna (present-day İzmir, Turkey). He was a younger contemporary and imitator of the Greek poet Theocritus (q.v.). His extant works consist of seventeen short poems and the longer "Lament for Adonis", which was the model for "Adonais", an elegy by the British poet Percy Bysshe Shelley (q.v.).

BIONICS, term used to describe the scientific study of living things as functional models for technical devices useful to man, especially when applied to cybernetics (q.v.) or systems engineering; *see* ENGINEERING: *Modern Engineering Trends*. The body of the porpoise (q.v.), to take an example of applied bionics, has helped shipbuilders to design better hulls. Biosonics, a field of bionics, attempts to adapt the ultrasonic sound waves observed in the acoustical patterns of animals, such as in the communication system used among whales and the sonar system of bats and moths, to man's benefit. Bionics is also closely related to bioengineering and biophysics (qq.v.).

BIOPHYSICS, interdisciplinary study of biological phenomena and problems using the principles and techniques of physics. The science of biophysics developed after World War II, stimulated in part by the application of nuclear physics (*see* NUCLEAR ENERGY) to biological systems, including the investigation of ionizing radiation effects on living matter; *see* ION; IONIZATION; RADIATION. In the course of these studies, physicists were introduced to biologists and biological problems, and biophysics evolved as a new scientific field. *See* BIOLOGY; PHYSICS.

Today biophysics is closely related to a number of areas in addition to radiation biology, including biochemistry, genetics, molecular biology, microbiology, physiology, neurobiology, histology, and virology. Being an extension of physics and physical chemistry, biophysics relies upon techniques derived from the physical sciences but focuses on biological problems.

An important field of biophysical study is the detailed analysis of macromolecular structure, the best known achievement in that respect being the model of deoxyribonucleic acid (DNA), built by the American molecular biologist James Dewey Watson and the British biologist Francis Harry Compton Crick (qq.v.). This model forms the basis of the greatest accomplishments of molecular biology and genetics in recent years, and was formulated from the X-ray crystallographic data of the New Zealand-born biophysicist Maurice Hugh Frederick Wilkins (q.v.). Similar crystallographic techniques have proven invaluable in determining the structures of myoglobin and hemoglobin (q.v.), which are oxygen-binding pigments of muscle and red blood cells, respectively; and of such enzymes (q.v.) as lysozyme and ribonuclease. *See* CRYSTAL: *Crystallography;* NUCLEIC ACIDS; X RAY.

Another important area of biophysics has been the study of information transmittal, in the form of impulses, in the nerve cells of organisms. Such information is transmitted as discrete events called action potentials, and is specified by the frequency at which these are transmitted and by the connections each nerve cell makes with its neighbors. For example, the British biophysicist Alan Lloyd Hodgkin (q.v.) and physicist Andrew Fielding Huxley (*see under* HUXLEY) studied nerve cells of the squid, whose large size permitted the insertion of several electrodes directly into the cell interior. With a judicious combination of electrochemistry, modern electronics, and mathematical modelling, they were able to formulate, test, and prove the theory that the action potential is caused by selective changes in the permeability of the cell membrane (q.v.) to sodium and potassium. The model of Hodgkin and Huxley has since been applied with minor modifications to other excitable tissues, and has come to form the basis for all modern attempts to understand the function of the central nervous system. *See* CELL; NERVOUS SYSTEM.

The domain of biophysics today can encompass biological subsystems which are so small that they are best studied with the techniques of quantum mechanics (q.v.). It can also be applied to larger biological systems and their interaction, such as several organs of the body, which can be analyzed by control theory.

BIOPSY, removal and miscroscopic examination of tissue from a living person for diagnosis of disease. The greatest use of biopsy is in early detection of cancer. In advanced cases biopsy is also used to determine the nature of the malignancy and to reveal the effects of treatment; *see* CANCER. It is used also in diagnosing other diseases and in determining the cause of chronic infections.

BIOSONICS. *See* BIONICS.

BIOSTATISTICS. *See* BIOMATHEMATICS.

BIOT, Jean Baptiste (1774–1862), French mathematician, physicist, and astronomer, born in Paris. He became professor of physics at the Collège de France in 1800 and was elected to membership in the French Institute at the age of twenty-nine. In 1804, with the French scientist Joseph Louis Gay-Lussac (q.v.), Biot made the first balloon ascent for the purpose of scientific observations. In 1806 he was sent to Spain to supervise the measuring of an arc of meridian, preparatory to the introduction of the metric system (q.v.) of weights and measures. Biot is best known for his optical law on polarized light, and was the first to use the polarimeter in determining the nature and amount of sugars in solution; *see* OPTICS: *Physical Optics: Polarization of Light.* He also formulated, with the French physicist Félix Savart (1791–1841), the Biot-Savart Law dealing with the effect of an electric current on a magnetic field; *see* MAGNETISM: *Magnetism and Electric Currents.*

BIOTITE. *See* MICA.

BIRCH, common name for deciduous, hardy trees of the genus *Betula* in the family Betulaceae, native to the temperate regions of the Northern Hemisphere. Most of the thirty-five species grow wild in cool woods and mountains and many are cultivated as ornamental trees.

The bark is dark in young saplings and varies from white to shades of orange and black in older trees, depending on the species. Foliage is usually light and thin and the leaves triangular. Blossoms are borne in separate male and female catkins on the same tree, and the seeds are contained in small cones. Most species of birch yield a hard, tough, close-grained wood, and the bark separates readily into thin, papery layers.

The black, sweet, or cherry birch, *B. lenta,* is a forest tree with dark bark that yields a volatile oil similar to oil of wintergreen. The yellow birch, *B. lutea,* grows in damp woods; its constantly peeling bark gives it a shaggy, silvery appearance. The white birch, *B. alba,* has many varieties. The bark of *papyrifera,* the paper or canoe birch, has been used as paper and for making canoes. It may be easily peeled from the tree, but it never regenerates; in its place a black scar is formed. Distillation of this bark yields birch oil or sweet-birch oil, used in treating certain skin diseases and in perfumes.

BIRCH SOCIETY. *See* JOHN BIRCH SOCIETY.

BIRD, warm-blooded vertebrate animal, usually completely covered with feathers and having forelimbs modified into wings for flight. Birds are found throughout the world, at almost all altitudes and in nearly every climate. Perhaps their most startling feature is their ability to soar through the sky, a power that has fascinated man through history. The popularity of birds is attested to by their universal adoption as household or backyard pets, by the great upsurge in the ranks of bird-watching hobbyists, and by the unusually high attendance figures recorded at the aviaries of major zoos.

Economic Importance of Birds. One of the earth's smallest animals, the bird, serves mankind in an amazingly large number of ways. Of primary importance is its role in pollination (q.v.), which enables man's vegetative food supply to flourish. Also significant is the bird's ability to devour insects, such as the locust, which are harmful to plants and animals. Certain birds also eat seeds poisonous to plants; and others eat rodents that destroy grains and materials.

Domestic birds, such as chickens and waterfowl, serve man directly as food. Bird meat and eggs are high in nutritional value and are part of the diet of many nations. In some parts of the world these foods are vital for human survival; in Greenland, for example, Eskimos store large quantities of eider ducks and dove-kies for their winter meals.

Bird products, too, are important. Guano (q.v.), the dried excrement of seabirds, is used as a fertilizer. Bird feathers, or plumage, are used in costume ornamentation, in upholstery for the stuffing of pillows and cushions, and in sports, as a part of the shuttlecock in badminton and as fishing flies. At one time, feathers were widely used as writing instruments; *see* PEN.

Birds can also do great harm to man. Some, in their search for seed and grain, may completely destroy a valuable crop. Birds of prey, such as the hawk, are killers of domesticated animals. Birds also transmit certain serious diseases, as psittacosis (q.v.), to man, and are suspected to be carriers of viral agents from one region to another.

Bird Study. The branch of zoology that deals specifically with the study of birds is called ornithology. Ornithologists examine both wild and domestic birds, investigating such factors as anatomy and behavior, historical development, ecology or the interrelation of plants and animals, classification, and species distribution.

Much of today's knowledge of birds comes also from a popular pastime known as bird watching. Bird watchers attempt to observe and identify birds in their natural environments. In part because of the refinement of optical aids, which permit clearer and more precise watching, the number of nonprofessional bird watchers has increased tremendously through the 20th century. Aside from its simple function as a hobby that gives one enjoyment, bird watching has contributed valuable data on the behavior and migration of birds.

As a result of the concern of bird watchers toward birds, many organizations have been established to educate the public in the protection and consideration of bird life. Two of these societies are the Royal Society for the Protection of Birds in Great Britain and the Audubon Society (q.v.) in the United States. Bird watching is extremely popular in North America, Australia, and England, where there are forty-seven natural history societies devoted to this study. On the international level, the International Ornithological Congresses, which originated in Vienna in 1884, are held every four years for amateur bird watchers and professionals alike. Two of the more popular journals among bird lovers are *Ibis,* which was started in 1959 by the British Ornithologists' Union, and *Auk,* begun in 1883 by the American Ornithologists' Union.

STRUCTURE

Birds exhibit certain singular structural features that mark them for their life in the air. The forelimbs, corresponding to the arms of man, are modified into a pair of relatively flat extremities called wings. As flight begins, powerful muscles

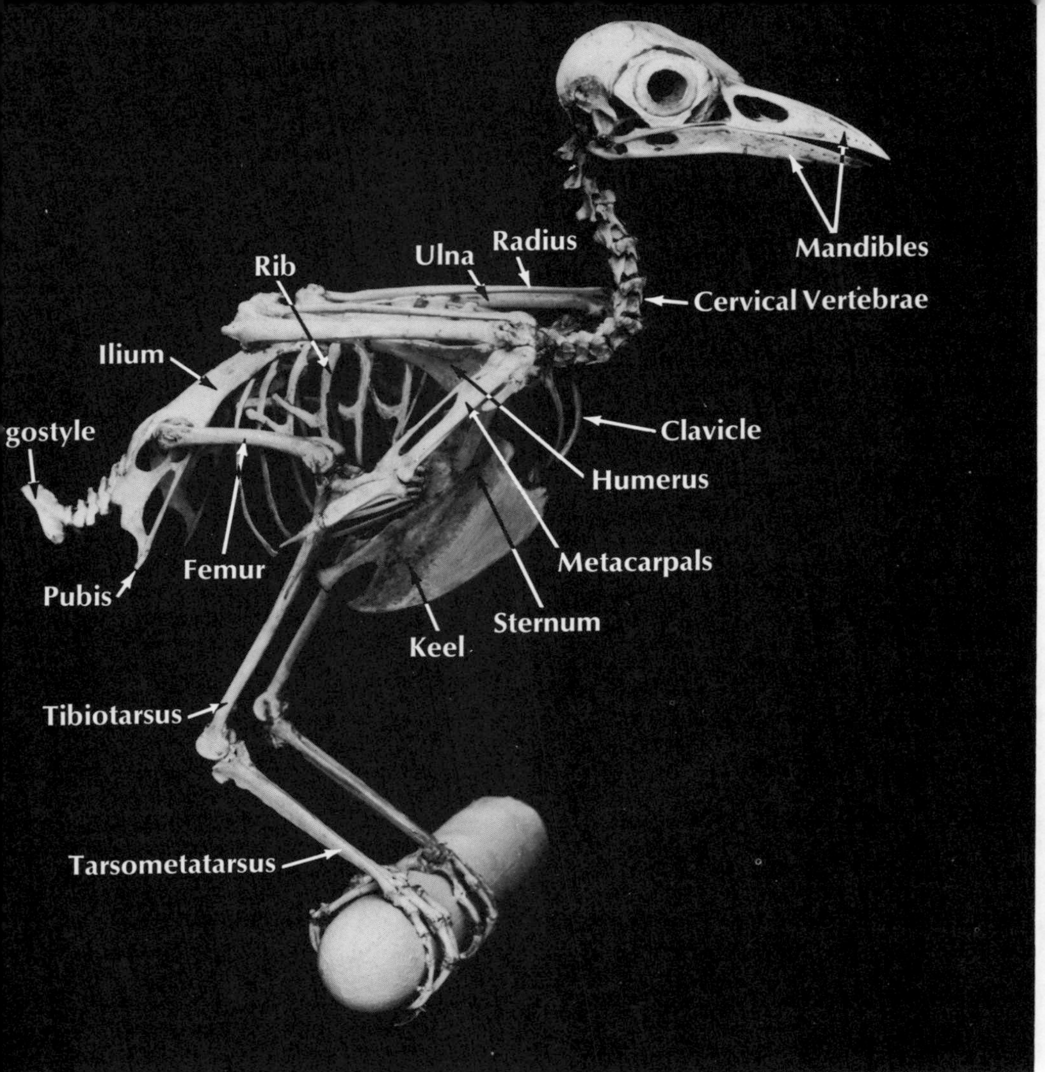

Bird skeleton Chicago Natural History Museum

in the breastbone extend and move, or flap, the wings. The flight is partially controlled by the wing feathers, which are manipulated so that air always exerts a greater pressure against the lower surfaces of the wings. By changing the position of the wing feathers, the bird can also change both its altitude and speed; for balance and steerage, it may also move the feathers in its tail. Other factors conducive to flight are the bird's largely hollow bones, which lessen weight in the air, and its rigid streamlined trunk, which offers little surface resistance to flight. Finally, as a result of the fusion of the ankle and foot into one long bone, the bird is able to use its legs to thrust itself up in takeoff and to absorb shock in landing.

Skeleton. The two main parts of the skeleton (q.v.) of a bird are the axial skeleton, made up of the skull, spinal column (qq.v.), and ribs, and the appendicular skeleton, composed of the pectoral, or breast, and pelvic girdles and the appendages. The bones, rather than being solid in structure, contain numerous air cavities, which make them lightweight and spongy.

The skull of a bird corresponds in general structure to that of other vertebrates (q.v.). Its distinguishing features include an early fusion and marked lightness of the component bones; the prolongation of the front bones to bear the bill, or beak; the absence of teeth; and large sockets for the eyes, separated from each other only by a thin partition. Much of the modern anatomical classification of birds has been based upon the nature of certain skull bones.

Courtship display in the peacock. Males of many bird species are larger and more colorful than females because the latter usually select mates that are impressive in appearance.
R. Austing–Bruce Coleman, Inc.

The backbone of the bird is different from that of other animals. The necks of most mammals consist of seven small connecting bones called vertebrae. In birds the neck is composed of a larger, variable number of vertebrae, from eleven in the parakeet to twenty-five in the swan. The vertebrae move easily, enabling the bird to turn its head quickly in all directions. They also allow the bird to use its bill in tasks such as feeding and nest building. Unlike the very movable neck, however, the dorsal region of the backbone tends to become rigid, especially the lower back where a large number of vertebrae enter into immovable connection with the pelvic girdle. The most anterior ribs are fused to the vertebrae, followed by a few that are free, but do not reach the breastbone. The next set meet at an angle, and the last ribs are again free.

The pectoral girdle consists of a pair of long bones called scapulae, or shoulder blades, which lie above the ribs in the thorax and run backward; a shorter bone, called the coracoid, connecting from the shoulder blades to the breastbone; and a right and left collarbone, or clavicle, which forms a broad uniting plate commonly known as the wishbone. In flightless birds the scapulae and coracoid may be greatly reduced, or, as in the ostrich, entirely absent.

The breastbone, or sternum, forms the base of attachment for the great muscles that work the wings. The breastbone is internally concave and in most birds bears a prominent ridge, or keel, on the midline in front. The wings consist of a strong upper bone, the humerus, that works in the socket formed by the scapula and coracoid. Also present are two bones, the radius and the stronger ulna, that form the forearm; two wrist bones; the three metacarpals fused together; and three fingers. The feathers attached to the hand are usually called primaries, and those borne on the radius and ulna, secondaries.

The most important part of the long pelvic girdle consists of two dorsal bones, called the ilia, which are fused to a large number of posterior vertebral bodies. A second portion, the ischium, extends backward on either side, nearly parallel to the hind part of the ilium, with which it is firmly fused. The third part, the pubis, also runs backward from the socket of the thigh and is a slender bone.

Connecting the hip with the knee is a short stout thigh bone called the femur. The knee usually includes a kneecap, or patella. In the lower leg, or crus, there are two bones, one of which is a long thin bone. The other, called the tibiotartus or drumstick, is actually a collection of fused bones. The legs of many birds are covered with scales instead of feathers. In most species the foot is made up of four toes, one of which usually points backward.

Muscular System. The most important muscles of the bird, those working the wings, are supported by the breastbone. One of these muscles is the great pectoral muscle, which forms the greater part of the breast and depresses the wing. A second smaller and deeper muscle, covered by the former, extends into a long tendon that passes through a hole at the shoulder joint, is attached to the back of the upper arm, and raises the wing. A third and much smaller breast muscle also assists in elevating the wing.

Nervous System. Although the brain (q.v.) of a bird is more complex than that of a reptile, it is not as highly developed as that of a mammal. Birds have a relatively small cerebrum; a large

A Western grebe sits on its nest of reeds, near the edge of a pond. Nest building is instinctive in birds, and the nests themselves vary enormously in shape, composition, and site. Joy Spurr–Bruce Coleman, Inc.

midbrain, which controls vision through the optic lobe; and a large cerebellum. In the hindbrain, and continuous with the spinal cord, is the medulla oblongata, from which eight of the twelve pairs of cranial nerves arise. *See* NERVOUS SYSTEM.

Sense Organs. The eyes of a bird are powerful and can be rapidly accommodated to different distances. A membrane, similar to a transparent eyelid, is conspicuously developed and can be drawn protectively across the eye. The ear differs from that of mammals by the absence of any external portion; a circle of fine hairlike feathers usually surrounds the external opening. Only one ear bone, the columella, is present, and in this particular, also, the bird ear differs from that of mammals. Taste and smell are less developed than sight and hearing.

Alimentary System. The character of the food canal varies according to the bird. The bill may be helped by the tongue in taking up food, but inasmuch as there are no teeth, chewing does not occur. Salivary glands open into the mouth cavity. In many birds the gullet dilates into a spacious thin-walled sack known as the crop, where large quantities of food can be retained. The succeeding portion of the canal is divided into two distinct parts. Soft glandular walls form the first part; the second part, or gizzard, is characterized by thick muscular walls and usually contains a number of small stones that were swallowed to assist in the grinding of food. The gizzard opens into the intestines, and these end in a common chamber, called the cloaca. The cloaca also receives urinary and genital products and discharges to the exterior.

Vascular System. The heart of a bird is more complex than that of a reptile in the separation of arterial and venous blood. Like that of mammals, the heart of the bird has four chambers. The blood-vessel arrangements also resemble those of mammals, having a single main branch, the aortic arch, which conveys blood from the heart to the body. The transfer system, however, runs to the right instead of to the left; *see* AORTA.

Respiratory System. The two lungs of the bird do not lie freely in a closed space, as in mammals, but are fixed to the back of the body cavity. A number of thin-walled air sacs surround the lungs and are connected to the bronchi and to the air spaces in the bones; they serve as auxiliary organs of respiration. The windpipe trachea is often long and coiled, strengthened by cartilaginous, or bony, rings. At its upper end the trachea opens into the pharynx through the larynx, and at its lower end it opens into the two bronchi through the syrinx which is the bird's vocal organ. Expiration, or the expulsion of air, is accomplished by the contraction of breast and abdominal muscles, which compress the enclosed cavities, forcing air from the sacs and lungs. The cavities expand and fresh air is drawn in when these muscles relax.

Excretory System. Two three-lobed kidneys lying one on each side of the backbone in the pelvic region are the principal organs of excretion. They are connected by a pair of ducts, called ureters, with the cloaca. The bird has no urinary bladder. The urinary secretion is semisolid and high in uric acid.

Reproductive System. The testes, which are the male reproductive organs, are paired in front of the kidneys. They are connected to the cloaca by the deferent ducts, which are comparable to the vas deferens, a spermatic duct in man. The sperm are brought to the cloaca by these ducts and can then be passed on to the female cloaca by touch.

Although two ovaries are present in the female embryo, the right ovary wholly degenerates. The end of the left oviduct is expanded to receive the ova as they burst from the ovary. The duct is glandular. The upper part secretes albumen to cover the yolk, and the lower secretes the limy shell. The end opens into the cloaca.

Feathers. The integument, or covering layer, of a bird differs markedly from that of other animals by being comprised of feathers (q.v.). These generally grow in uniform tracts, or paths, and vary in different species. The tracts are composed of contour, or outside, feathers; semiplumes, which resemble contour feathers but lack their interlocking construction; hairlike filoplumes at the base of the contour feathers; down feathers, which cover the young; and, in a few species, powder-down feathers, which serve as a means of cleaning the rest of the plumage. The typical contour feather consists of a midrib, called the shaft, and a web, or vane. The vane is composed of tiny branches, called barbs, barbules, and barbicels in descending order of size; all are interlocked to form a remarkable airtight structure.

The coloring of bird feathers varies markedly from species to species, with some birds, as the blue jay and the robin redbreast, taking their actual or popular name from their distinctive shading. Almost all species exhibit complex plumage patterns, and many, particularly in tropical areas, are brilliantly colored. Commonly, the male bird of a species is more strikingly patterned than the female. Many birds also exhibit unique feather groupings, called crests, about the facial area.

Bird feathers do far more than merely cover the bird, protecting it from injury and helping to conserve its body heat. It has already been shown that the feathers are of primary importance in initiating, controlling, and terminating flight. The feathers of some species also serve as a means of protective camouflage; the soft coloring pattern of the plumage enables the bird to blend into its background and thus remain hidden from its enemies. Birds also use their feathers to attract mates and to warn one another of nearby danger.

Structural Variations. Each type of bird has adapted the species' overall structural features for its own specific needs. The bill, or beak, of a bird frequently indicates its eating habits. Birds of prey, such as the hawk, have strong, hooked, sharp-edged beaks designed for tearing apart their victims. Fish-eating birds, such as the pelican, have broad lower beaks used to scoop prey from the water. Long pointed bills are typical of birds that peck for insects, and wide, sharp, rounded beaks are necessary for seed eaters.

Herring-gull chick hatching. First the chick cracks shell (top) by tapping with its temporary eggtooth and pressing with wings and feet. When hole is large enough (bottom), the chick struggles out. The process takes three days. David Overcash-Bruce Coleman, Inc.

Toes and claws indicate how a bird lives. Swimming birds have webbed feet, with one back toe free. Birds of prey have strong toes with sharp curved claws, or talons, which the bird uses to grab its victims. Birds that live primarily in trees have toes that curl and tighten automatically as the leg bends, permitting them to fasten onto a perch or branch. Birds remaining primarily on the ground usually have strong broad toes, all in a forward direction.

Birds that fly vary structurally from flightless birds by having air pockets, or sacs, in their bones; these reduce the bird's weight and help

A pair of black-throated blue warblers share the duties of caring for their large brood. The gaping mouths and begging calls of the nestlings automatically stimulate the parents to feed them. R. Austing–Bruce Coleman, Inc.

cool the body in flight. Flying birds also differ structurally from each other, as in wing length, width, and curvature, all of which are related to the type and pattern of flight required by a species. Tails, too, have been adapted for special uses. The woodpecker has developed a particularly stiff tail, which it uses as a support while working along a tree trunk.

HABITS

In addition to the anatomy and physiology of birds, ornithologists also study their unique patterns of behavior. Following are the most important or interesting of bird habits.

Nutrition. The food of birds varies greatly, depending upon the season as well as the bird type. Some birds are herbivorous, that is, feeding upon plants; some confine themselves to a diet of grain; and still others eat insects or small animals. Birds feeding primarily on grain have large crops and gizzards, and the glandular part of the stomach is small. In carnivorous or flesh-eating birds, the glandular portion predominates over the muscular portion of the stomach.

Locomotion. Most birds fly by raising and depressing their wings rapidly. This is controlled by means of the breast muscles. Strong birds, such as the albatross and birds of prey, can fly very rapidly for long periods. Many others, however, rarely take prolonged flights except during migration.

Birds also vary greatly in rate and manner of progression when on the ground. The swift strides of the ostrich, the rapid run of the partridge, and the hopping of the sparrow are examples of different gaits. The penguins walk with an awkward, waddling movement, but are fast, graceful swimmers, using their wings as flippers.

Song. With few exceptions birds have vocal organs and are able to produce sounds. Running birds, however, such as the ostrich and the American vulture, lack vocal organs. The song is most highly developed among the so-called perchers (order Passeriformes), and particularly among the songsters (suborder Passeres).

The purpose of song is to attract the other sex, to mark out nesting territories, to warn others of danger, or to intimidate or repel intruders. Although most marked during the breeding season, and among males, females of a few species also sing. The song of a bird may vary to some extent with its age, the time of day, and the season of the year.

Molting. After the reproductive period or sometimes at midwinter, birds undergo a molting process, whereby the entire coat of old feathers is shed. Many birds molt twice, and some three times a year, in addition to the normal annual molt.

Reproduction. Birds usually mate in the spring. Fertilization is internal, and all birds are oviparous, that is, they produce eggs that finish their development outside the body. The size of a bird's egg depends upon the number of eggs laid in the breeding season and the degree of maturity of the young when hatched.

A bird egg consists of a large yolk, formed in the ovary, upon which floats a small germinal disk, or blastoderm, from which the embryo develops. As the yolk descends from the upper portion of the oviduct, it becomes coated with white egg fluid or albumen, which is separated from the yolk by a membrane enclosing the latter. The yolk and the white nourish the developing embryo. In the lower portion of the oviduct the yolk and white are enclosed, first in a tough double membrane and then in a three-layered shell composed principally of calcium carbonate. The layers of the enclosing membrane separate at the broad end of the egg, leaving an air space that increases with the age of the egg. As the embryo grows, this space serves as an air reservoir from which the chick can breathe. The shape of the egg varies and may be an almost perfect circle, as in the case of owls' eggs, or an almost symmetrical oval, as the eggs of the redwing blackbird. The color of the shell also differs, in some instances serving as camouflage to conceal the eggs in the nest; hole-nesting species usually lay white eggs.

Fertilization of the egg occurs in the upper portion of the oviduct before the yolk is covered with albumen. Shortly before the shell has begun to form, the usual cell division begins in

Young red-bellied woodpecker searching for food. Driving its strong bill deeply into the bark of trees, the woodpecker probes for its insect prey with a long, sharp-tipped tongue. Stephen J. Kraseman–Peter Arnold, Inc.

Ground-nesting elegant terns squabble over living space on an island off the coast of Mexico. Ritualized threats establish a minimum distance between nest sites even in gregarious species.
Jen & Des Bartlett–Bruce Coleman, Inc.

the lower part of the oviduct; see EMBRYOLOGY. Owing to the vast amount of nutritive, as opposed to formative, material, the whole ovum does not divide, but only a portion of it, known as the germinal disk.

The number of eggs laid at one time, called the clutch, varies from one to twenty-one and is in inverse ratio to the likelihood of the embryo's reaching maturity; see EGG. Following the laying of the eggs is the incubation, or brooding, period. In order to provide the warmth that will ensure development of the embryo, one of the parents sits on the eggs throughout this phase. In most species of birds the requisite heat (about 40° C. or 104° F.) is supplied by the female parent; in some species, however, notably many of the order Passeriformes, the male parent is responsible for part or all of the incubation. Some birds, including the ostrich, allow their eggs to be incubated by the heat of the sun. Mound birds of the South Pacific build nests of decaying vegetable matter that generates heat in the process of decay, thus incubating the eggs. The incubation period of birds may vary from about twelve days, in the hummingbird, to eighty-one days, in the royal albatross.

Nest Building. The nest-building instinct is not limited to birds, but occurs also among insects, fishes, some reptiles, and mammals. Prolonged brooding, or hatching, periods; the frequent helplessness of the young; trees, or arboreal, living; and numerous enemies have necessitated many nest-building contrivances among birds. The nest is built before the eggs are ready to be laid. Each species has its own style and material of construction, though these may be adapted to prevailing conditions. The nests are usually solitary, rarely grouped, and only occasionally, as among cassowaries and ostriches, common property. Birds that do not build nests, but instead lay their eggs in the nests of other species, include the European cuckoo and many New World cowbirds.

Migration. Migration is the periodic passing from one climate or region to another, usually for specific purposes. Comparatively few birds remain in the same locality for the entire year. Some of the factors determining migratory behavior are length of day, changes in the temperature, and availability of food. These external conditions, however, act only upon those birds whose internal conditions have predisposed them to migrate. Such conditions are believed to be cyclic and closely tied to reproduction. The arctic tern migrates 22,000 mi. a year from the Arctic to the Antarctic regions. The Pacific golden plover flies from Alaska to Hawaii. Many shore birds migrate from the Arctic Regions to Patagonia in Argentina and back. In the tropics, migration is altitudinal or local.

Birds often gather in flocks before migrating. The return to the breeding grounds, which is generally the colder part of their range, is more rapid than the flight toward the winter area. By means of bird banding, that is, the attaching of an identifying strip, usually to the leg of the bird, ornithologists are able to trace the path, speed, and extent of migration. Sanctuaries, or protected

Bald eagle with deer carcass. Though strong and predatory, the eagle has not caused the death of the deer, but only profits from it. Its normal diet is fish, often stolen from other birds. G. Martin-Bruce Coleman, Inc.

Snow geese, in V-formation, in migratory flight. Migrations, thousands of miles long for some species, result partly from physiological changes induced by seasonal variation in day length. Joe Van Wormer-Bruce Coleman, Inc.

areas, have been established along popular migration routes so that flocks may stop and rest without danger. Various theories on the origin of migration have been propounded, but none is entirely satisfactory. *See* ANIMALS, MIGRATION OF; CONSERVATION: *Wildlife Conservation.*

Longevity. Few reliable statistics exist on the maximum life span of birds in the wild state. In general, longevity varies with the size of the bird; small field birds live for 2 to 6 years, and domestic fowl, for about 16 years. An eagle owl attained, in captivity, an age of 68 years, the all-time record for any species.

Preening and Bathing. The species' heavy reliance on its feathers requires that they be always in the proper condition. By means of a process called preening, or grooming, birds use their bill to comb through the feathers, keeping them smooth and straight. Many birds also have preen glands, located on the back in front of the tail; these secrete an oil, which the bird, rubbing its head against the gland, is able to spread over its body.

Bathing is commonly done by ducking the body in water and then flapping the water through the plumage. Birds also bathe in the rain and in sprays of any kind, such as the spray created from wet leaves. Some species prefer to bathe in dry soil, which the bird stirs up with its feathers. Sunbaths, whereby a bird lies stretched out on its back, with open feathers and beak, for several minutes, are also common.

Anting and Flocking. Anting is the name given to birds' baffling practice of putting ants on their bodies and moving them through the plumage or allowing them to run freely. The purpose or benefits of anting are unknown.

Similarly, the flocking phenomenon is not completely understood. The term indicates the tendency of birds to gather and remain in large groups. Flocking has been observed for such activities as feeding, migrating, and roosting.

Self-Protection. In addition to using their feathers to signal the presence of an enemy, birds employ several techniques to distract intruders from the nest. For example, the bird may run ahead of the intruder, enticing him to follow by limping or dragging a wing. The bird will always stay just out of range of its enemy, and when he has lured the intruder a safe distance from the nest, will take to the air and fly safely away. Another ruse used by birds is to scurry along the ground like a mouse or a chipmunk, distracting the attention of the outsider.

DEVELOPMENT AND DISTRIBUTION

Information obtained from the study of birds discloses that they evolved from the reptile (q.v.) during the Mesozoic Era (q.v.), some 200,000,000 years ago. Certain dinosaurs, who existed during the Permian Period (q.v.) about 40,000,000 years earlier, also developed from the reptile and are thought to have been warm-blooded ancestors of the bird. These creatures were egg laying, walked on hind legs, had thin ankle bones, and three toes on the front foot.

Evolution. The oldest known bird is the archaeopteryx, discovered in fossil (q.v.) form in 1861 in the Upper Jurassic slate of Solenhofen in Bavaria, Germany. The archaeopteryx appears to have been about the size of a crow. The bird's skeleton resembles that of a reptile with a vertebral column that extended into a long tail. The bird had wings and teeth, and its entire body was covered with feathers.

From then until about 45,000,000 years later, little is known about the bird. From the subsequent Cretaceous Period (q.v.), the remains of two birds are extant. The hesperornis, a toothed water bird, about 5 ft. long and resembling a loon, was found in marine deposits in Kansas;

Adélie penguins of the Hope Bay colony in Antarctica depart for the sea, where they may feed for 20 days. Penguins find their way back by using the sun as a directional aid. C. Haagner–Bruce Coleman, Inc.

the bird had bony, probably inactive wings. The skeleton of the Ichthyornis, a flying creature similar to the gull, was found in the same deposits.

In the Tertiary Period birds became more numerous and similar to those existing today. From the Oligocene Epoch (q.v.) onward, representatives of modern genera are found, many in regions far from their present habitats.

Extinct and Vanishing Birds. Birds that once flew in large numbers but today are known only by their fossils or by mention in literary or scientific chronicles are said to be extinct. Some of these were killed by animals in search of food; others died as their vegetation was destroyed. During World War II, rodents, inadvertently brought to Norway on ships, preyed upon and destroyed the entire population of the flightless rail in the country within two years. On Laysan Island in the North Pacific Ocean, rabbits, by destroying vegetation, caused the death of three fifths of all the birds on the island in only a 25-year period. Man, too, figures largely in the killing of birds as he hunts them either for food or for pleasure. The passenger pigeon, which numbered in the hundreds of millions in the 1800's, was slaughtered en masse and sold for pennies as food; it was extinct by 1914. The Carolina parakeet, hunted as a garden pest and also for its brightly colored feathers, was last seen in 1920. The moa, an ostrichlike bird that inhabited New Zealand; the Aepyornis of Madagascar; the Australian Dromornis, an ancestor of the emu; and others have also disappeared comparatively recently. The dodo of Mauritius, an island in the Indian Ocean, was last observed in 1681; the solitaire, a flightless bird of the island of Rodrigues, also in the Indian Ocean, was last seen in the late 18th century; and a sighting of the great auk of the North Atlantic Ocean was last recorded in 1852.

As human populations increase and industrialization accelerates, some modern species of birds are endangered. Current factors responsible for bird extinction include land clearage, swamp drainage, war, and disease. Birds that are threatened with annihilation are classified as endangered species, and special conservation measures are usually established for their protection. Still among the endangered species are the whooping crane, the ivory-billed woodpecker, the trumpeter swan, and the California condor.

Distribution. Some genera of birds are widely distributed and are represented in almost every land. Others, such as the bird of paradise and hummingbirds, are restricted in their habitat. Although birds have unusually great facility of dispersion, more species are found in the warmer countries.

CLASSIFICATION

In the 4th century B.C. the Greek philosopher Aristotle (q.v.) defined birds as feathered flying bipeds that lay eggs and catalogued them into three great orders, with the ostrich and a few others in separate subdivisions. The present system for classification (q.v.) of the animal kingdom was inaugurated in the 17th century by the English naturalist John Ray and perfected in the next century by the Swedish botanist Carolus Linnaeus (qq.v.). Naturalists toward the end of the 18th century attempted to apply and extend the system; much of our present knowledge of bird anatomy is due to the research of the French naturalist Georges Cuvier (q.v.) and his disciples. The present system of bird classification was developed near the end of the 19th century.

Divisions of Classification. The class Aves, or birds, comprises one of the major groups in the phylum Chordata. It is divided into twenty-seven orders, each further subdivided into families. The family is broken into genera, and the genus into species. About 8600 species of living birds exist. The number of different forms, including subspecies, totals approximately 30,000, of which nearly 1700 are indigenous to North America. In the Old and New Worlds several hundred fossil species are also known; *see* ZOOLOGY.

The following list includes all orders that contain living birds. One or more groups, each typical of a family, have been listed for each order. The list is not intended to be complete but rather an indication of the types of birds so classified. Where more than one family is noted, they are arranged in phylogenetic sequence, that is, in the presumed order of evolutionary development.

Sphenisciformes: penguins.
Struthioniformes: ostriches.
Rheiformes: rheas.
Casuariiformes: cassowaries, emus.
Apterygiformes: kiwis.
Tinamiformes: tinamous.
Gaviiformes: loons.
Podieipediformes: grebes.
Procellariiformes: albatrosses, shearwaters, petrels.
Pelecaniformes: pelicans, boobies, cormorants, gannets, darters.
Ciconiiformes: herons, storks, ibises, spoonbills, flamingos, bitterns.
Anseriformes: waterfowl (duck, geese, swans).
Falconiformes: vultures, hawks.
Galliformes: grouse, pheasants, turkeys, quail.
Gruiformes: cranes, rails, bustards, limpkins, coots, gallinules.
Charadriiformes: shorebirds, gulls, alcids, jacanas, skuas, terns, skimmers.
Psittaciformes: parrots.
Cuculiformes: cuckoos, anis, roadrunners.
Strigiformes: owls.
Caprimulgiformes: goatsuckers.
Apodiformes: swifts, hummingbirds.
Coliiformes: colies.
Trogoniformes: trogons.
Coraciiformes: kingfishers, bee eaters, rollers, hoopoes, hornbills.
Piciformes: woodpeckers, honey guides.
Passeriformes: perching birds (seventy families), including crows, thrushes, sparrows, swallows, wrens, warblers, flycatchers, larks, nuthatches, vireos, shrikes, blackbirds.

See also separate articles about most of the birds mentioned. H.H.C.

BIRD, Robert Montgomery (1806–54), American playwright and novelist, born in New Castle, Del., and educated in medicine at the University of Pennsylvania. He practiced as a physician only briefly. He wrote several successful tragedies for the American actor and producer Edwin Forrest (q.v.). The first, *The Gladiator* (1831), based on the life of the Roman slave Spartacus (q.v.), provided Forrest with one of his favorite roles. The other plays include *Oralloosa* (1832), based on the assassination of the Spanish conquistador Francisco Pizarro (q.v.), and his acknowledged masterpiece, *The Broker of Bogota* (1834), a domestic tragedy.

Bird began his career as a novelist after a disagreement with Forrest. In his most popular novel, *Nick of the Woods; or, The Jibbenainsay* (1837), he portrays the American Indian as a savage, in sharp contrast to the idealized aborigine made popular by the American novelist James Fenimore Cooper (q.v.). Bird's other novels include *Calavar; or The Knight of the Conquest* (1834), a tale of the conquest of Mexico; and *The Hawks of Hawk-Hollow* (1835), a romance of the American Revolution. Because his plays were not published until 1917, Bird's reputation as a playwright was long obscured.

BIRD, William. *See under* BYRD.

BIRD CHERRY, common name for either of two trees of the Rose family (Rosaceae), and for their fruit, which is often eaten by birds. **1.** The European bird cherry, *Prunus padus*. The tree is small, growing to a height of about 30 ft., and bears racemes of small, white flowers and black, bitter fruit, which is used for coloring wines and brandies. **2.** The North American wild cherry, *P.*

pennsylvanica, also called pin cherry. It grows to a height of about 30 ft., has reddish bark, and bears white blossoms and pea-sized, reddish fruit within an astringent taste. The tree is used as a grafting stock for orchard cherries and occasionally as an ornamental plant. Cough remedies are made from the bark.

See CHERRY.

BIRD OF PARADISE, common name for birds of the family Paradisaeidae, noted for the magnificent plumage of the adult male. They are native to New Guinea and the neighboring islands, and about forty species are known. Protected from their natural enemies by their dull color, the females and young gather in small flocks; the more conspicuous males are often solitary, but some indulge in elaborate social display. They have the omnivorous appetites characteristic of crows and jays, and their food consists largely of fruit, insects, and snails. Demand for bird-of-paradise plumage has resulted in a great decrease in some species.

The great emerald bird of paradise *Paradisaea apoda,* the largest species, is 1½ ft. in length, including the tail. It has a dense, erectile tuft of golden-orange plumes, about 2 ft. tall, arising under each wing, and its central tail feathers form into a bunch of long, wirelike bristles. The feet were removed from the first skins of this species sent, in the 15th century, to Europe, thereby giving rise to the name apoda, "without feet", and to the erroneous belief that the birds spent their entire lives on the wing.

Most of the paradise plumes once used for ornament were obtained from the lesser emerald bird of paradise. *P. minor,* which is smaller in size. Other species include the king bird of paradise, *Cincinnurus regius,* with two tail feathers modified into 6-in. spiral shafts bearing an emerald disk at the end, and the "twelve-wired" bird of paradise *Seleucidis melanoleuca,* which has twelve lateral plumes ending in 10-in. black, recurving filaments.

BIRDSEYE, Clarence (1886–1956), American food expert, industrialist, and inventor, born in Brooklyn, N.Y., and educated at Amherst College. He is best known as a pioneer in the preservation and marketing of quick-frozen and dehydrated foods; *see* FOOD PRESERVATION. He was also a technologist in incandescent lighting, wood pulping, and infrared heating.

BIRD'S-FOOT TREFOIL. *See* LOTUS.

BIRDS OF PREY, common name for the group of birds formerly comprising the order Raptores, and now classified in the orders Falconiformes (vultures, falcons, eagles, and hawks) and Strigiformes (owls and barn owls). For the most part, birds of prey feed on warm-blooded animals that they catch alive and tear apart with their hooked bills and strong talons. In general, birds classified within this group have acute sight and hearing and are above average in size and strength.

See separate articles under their present classifications.

BIR ES SABA. *See* BEERSHEBA.

BIRKENHEAD, Great Britain, county borough and seaport of Cheshire, England, on the Mersey R. estuary opposite Liverpool. The cities are linked by an electric railway tunnel, and a vehicular tunnel. Birkenhead is one of the chief shipbuilding and shipping centers of England, with extensive port facilities. Other major industries are flour milling, steel milling, and the manufacture of iron and steel products. The chief exports are coal, flour, and manufactured items. Cattle and grain are imported. The completion of new docks in 1847 led to the commercial development of the city. Pop. (1971) 138,090.

BIRLING. *See* LOGROLLING.

BIRMINGHAM, largest city in Alabama, and county seat of Jefferson Co., about 95 miles N.N.W. of Montgomery. It is served by railroad; Birmingham Airport, which ranks fourth in the Southeast in total activity and operations, is in the process of an extensive expansion program scheduled for completion in 1985. The region surrounding Birmingham has rich deposits of iron ore, coal, limestone, clay marble, graphite, bauxite, silica, and quartz, which have been important in the industrial growth of the city. The principal manufactures of the city are iron, steel, and iron and steel products, heavy machinery, electronics equipment, chemicals, textiles, clothing, coke, cement, lumber, and foodstuffs. Birmingham is the site of Samford University, Birmingham-Southern College, Miles College, and the schools of medicine and dentistry of the University of Alabama. The city is governed under the mayoral system.

Intensive exploitation of the mineral deposits in Jefferson County began in the 1860's. In 1871 the Elyton Land Company founded Birmingham and named it for the manufacturing center in England. The city was incorporated later in the same year, and in 1873 it became the county seat.

Between 1910 and 1950 the population of Birmingham increased from 132,685 to 326,037. In 1960 it was 340,887, but in 1970 it declined to 300,910.

BIRMINGHAM, city of Michigan, in Oakland Co., on the Rouge R., 8 miles N.W. of Detroit.

Manufactures include electrical equipment, steel and plastic products, bricks, and tile. Birmingham was settled in 1819, incorporated as a village in 1864, and as a city in 1933. Pop. (1960) 25,525; (1970) 26,170.

BIRMINGHAM, Great Britain, city in England, and county borough of Warwickshire, 110 miles N.W. of London, 102 miles S.E. of Liverpool, and 86 miles N. of Bristol. Served by a network of railways and roads and a municipal airport, the city is the center of the British metal-goods industry. Among the principal metal products manufactured are automobiles, machine tools, motorcycles, brassware, household utensils, sporting guns, jewelry, and electrical equipment. Other important manufactures include glass, rubber products, chemicals, plastic goods, paints and enamels, and candy.

Buildings and Institutions. Ecclesiastical edifices in Birmingham include the Cathedral Church of Saint Philip, consecrated in 1715; Saint Martin's Parish Church in the Bull Ring, dating from the 13th century; the Roman Catholic Cathedral of Saint Chad, recently renovated; and the Oratory of Saint Philip Neri, a memorial to Cardinal John Henry Newman (q.v.). Other important buildings include the Town Hall, opened in 1834 and modeled on the Temple of Castor and Pollux in Rome, the Victoria Law Courts, and the Bull Ring Shopping Center. The city has two universities, one of which is the University of Birmingham (q.v.). Other educational institutions include the College of Food and Domestic Arts, School of Music, and College of Art and Design. Cultural facilities include the Birmingham Art Gallery, the Museum of Science and Industry, and the City of Birmingham Symphony Orchestra, one of the few permanent orchestras to be maintained in English cities.

History. The *Domesday Book* (q.v.) recorded the worth of Birmingham as twenty shillings. In 1166 Birmingham was granted a market charter, and by the 16th century it had become established as a thriving manufacturing center, specializing in metal goods. At the time of the Great Rebellion (q.v.), one sword mill alone produced 15,000 sword blades for the Parliamentary forces opposing the Royalists, as a result of which the town was besieged. Birmingham became a Parliamentary borough in 1832, elected its first town council in 1838, and was raised to the rank of city in 1889. It is now the second city of Great Britain, famed for its great variety of industry and municipal enterprise and having the only municipal bank in Great Britain. Pop. (1971 prelim.) 1,013,366.

BIRMINGHAM, UNIVERSITY OF, coeducational institution of higher learning, located in Birmingham, England, and supported in part by government funds. The institution was founded as the Mason Science College in 1875 and opened for instruction in 1880. The name was changed to Mason College in 1892 and to Mason University College in 1897. In 1900 the institution obtained a royal charter as a university and adopted its present name. The university consists of faculties of arts, commerce and social science, medicine and dentistry, law, science and engineering, and a school of education. In the 1950's the university became a leading British center for research in nuclear physics and electronics. In addition, twenty-one institutes, centers, and nonfaculty departments are associated with the university. Among these are the Centre for Russian and East European Studies, the Centre of West African Studies, and a Shakespeare institute. The degrees of bachelor, master, and doctor are awarded. The university library contains more than 800,000 bound volumes. In 1972–73 student enrollment was about 7400; the faculty numbered about 1100.

BIRNEY, James Gillespie (1792–1857), American antislavery leader, born in Danville, Ky., and educated at the College of New Jersey (now Princeton University). In 1832 he gave up a prosperous law practice in Alabama to work for the American Colonization Society, which was dedicated to resettling Negroes in Africa. He freed his inherited slaves in 1834 and in 1835 moved to Cincinnati, Ohio, where he began publication of an antislavery newspaper, *The Philanthropist,* in January, 1836. The following year he became executive secretary of the American Antislavery Society (q.v.) and was vice-president of the World Antislavery Convention at London in 1840. In 1840 and again in 1844 Birney was the Presidential candidate of the Liberty Party (q.v.), which advocated the abolition of slavery by moral persuasion and political action. Among his writings are *A Letter on the Political Obligations of Abolitionists* (1839), and *The American Churches, the Bulwarks of American Slavery* (1840).

BIROBIDZHAN, oblast of the Russian S.F.S.R.; *see* JEWISH AUTONOMOUS OBLAST.

BIROBIDZHAN *or* **BIRO-BIDJAN,** city of the Soviet Union, in the Russian S.F.S.R., capital of the Jewish Autonomous Oblast (q.v.) on the Trans-Siberian Railroad, 100 miles W. of Khabarovsk. It is the industrial and cultural center of the oblast. Industrial establishments include railway-repair shops, shoe factories, clothing plants, lumber mills, brick works, and power plants. An agricultural college, several libraries, and a Jewish Art Theater are in the city. Pop. (1971 est.) 59,000.

BIRON, title of a French noble family, the most prominent members of which were the following.

Armand de Gontaut, Baron de Biron (1524?–92). During the religious wars (1562–98) in France between the Catholics and the Huguenots (q.v.), he supported the Catholics. In 1577 he was made marshal of France by Henry III (q.v.), King of France. In the wars for control of France that followed the accession to the French throne of Henry of Navarre (*see* HENRY IV), Biron supported the king and fought in the battles of Arques (1589) and Ivry (1590). He was killed during the siege of Épernay.

Charles de Gontaut, Duc de Biron (1562–1602), son of Armand de Gontaut. He served Henry IV, who made him admiral in 1592, marshal in 1594, and duke in 1598. In 1602, however, Biron conspired to overthrow the king and to seize the throne of the province of Burgundy, of which he was then governor. He was arrested and beheaded in the Bastille.

Armand Louis de Gontaut, Duc de Biron (1747–93), great-grandnephew of Charles de Gontaut. Under the name of the Duc de Lauzun, he fought for the Americans in the American Revolution. In 1789, during the French Revolution (q.v.), he was elected to the States-General, the French legislature, by the nobility, but he sympathized with the Revolutionary cause. He became a general in the Revolutionary army and in 1793 commanded the forces fighting counterrevolutionary insurgents in the La Vendée region. Accused of being too lenient toward the counterrevolutionists, Biron was removed from his command and guillotined.

BIRON, Ernst Johann, Duke of Kurland (1690–1772), Russian statesman, born in Kurland (now in the Latvian S.S.R.). He was in great favor with the duchess Anna Ivanovna (q.v.), and when she ascended the throne of Russia in 1730, he became chamberlain and virtual ruler of Russia. In 1737 he was made duke of Kurland. Biron ordered the execution or banishment of many of his enemies and rivals, and his entire career was characterized by cruelty. Upon the death of the empress in 1740, he assumed the regency for her adopted son Ivan VI (1740–64), Emperor of Russia (1740–41). Biron, however, was imprisoned by the nobles of Russia three weeks after the death of Anna Ivanovna and in 1741 was sent to Siberia. He was permitted to return the following year but never regained his influence.

BIRRELL, Augustine (1850–1933), British writer, lawyer, and statesman, born near Liverpool, England, and educated at Trinity Hall, University of Cambridge. From 1889 to 1900 he was a Liberal member of Parliament for West Fife, and from 1896 to 1899 he was professor of law at the University of London. He was chief secretary for Ireland in the British cabinet from 1907 to 1916, and during his administration the Irish Universities Act, the Irish Land Act, and the Home Rule Act were passed by Parliament. He resigned as a result of the Easter Rebellion (q.v.) in Ireland.

BIRTH, in mammals, beginning of independent life; expulsion of the young from the body of the mother. In humans, normal birth occurs after a period of gestation (q.v.) of 270 to 280 days and is accomplished by the physiological process called labor. Contractions of the uterus force the fetus through the birth canal, dilating the tissues of the cervix and vagina. The infant is completely separated from the mother when the umbilical cord is cut. Shortly after expulsion of the fetus, the uterus again contracts, expelling the placenta or afterbirth; *see* EMBRYOLOGY: *Nutrition and Respiration.* The duration of labor varies greatly, and the process may be complicated by various conditions, such as breech presentation, in which the lower extremities pass through the birth canal first. Although in underdeveloped countries the rate of infant mortality in childbirth is still high, in countries with more advanced medical knowledge infant deaths during childbirth have decreased greatly. *See* MULTIPLE BIRTH; OBSTETRICS.

BIRTH CONTROL. *See* PLANNED PARENTHOOD.

BIRTH DEFECTS, anatomical malformations or errors of metabolism (q.v.) present in an infant at birth and caused by faulty development of the embryo; *see* EMBRYOLOGY: *Normal Development.*

At conception (*see* FERTILIZATION), the fertilized egg receives from each parent a set of genes, which constitute instructions for the development of the organism. Genes control the structure of the polypeptide chains, the subunits of which proteins are composed. One pair of genes exist for each polypeptide; *see* PROTEIN. Proteins are of two classes: enzymes (q.v.), the biochemical catalysts that regulate the metabolism of the cell; and structural proteins, the main fabric of body tissues. Errors in development may be classified under four causes.

Mutant Genes. A change in the structure of a gene will result in a change in the structure of the corresponding polypeptide, sometimes modifying the function of the related protein. Errors in development attributable to an altered protein are of two kinds: (1) structural anomalies, such as polydactyly—the development of extra digits—or achondroplastic dwarfism; and (2) functional anomalies, such as hemophilia (q.v.), or phenylketonuria, faulty metabolism of phenylalanine that often leads to mental defects. These structural and functional birth defects, of which several hundred have been described, are hereditary and segregate in families according to Mendel's law (q.v.). The responsible altered protein has been identified for a number of functional, but few of the structural, anomalies. Perhaps 10 percent of birth defects fall in this category.

Chromosomal Aberrations. The genes are located on the chromosomes (q.v.); the human ovum has a set of 23 maternal chromosomes and receives a set of 23 paternal chromosomes from the sperm for a normal total of 46. If the egg or sperm carries an extra chromosome or lacks one, the organism will have either an excess or a deficiency of genes, leading to widespread developmental abnormalities, the nature of which depends on which chromosome is present in excess or is lacking. The most common birth defect resulting from a supernumerary chromosome is mongolism (q.v.). Abnormalities that are the result of errors in pairing or separation of chromosomes during formation of sperm or egg or division of a body cell do not tend to recur in a family; those that follow chromosomal rearrangement may be familial. Chromosomal aberrations account for perhaps 20 percent of birth defects; *see* CELL; HEREDITY.

Environmental Factors. Abnormal development may follow lack of a specific required factor; iodine deficiency may cause cretinism (q.v.; *see* MYXEDEMA; THYROID GLAND); brain damage may follow prenatal oxygen deficiency. Injury of developing tissues may follow maternal infection with German measles (q.v.). Relatively few such environmental factors are recognized.

Many Interacting Factors. Most common malformations, harelip, cleft palate, clubfoot (qq.v.), and other defects, seem to result from the interaction of numerous genetic and environmental factors, each with a small effect; they are familial, but do not follow the Mendelian principles.

Although the incidence of babies born with a defect sufficiently severe to require treatment remains at about 4 percent, progress is being made in developing methods for detection of inborn errors of metabolism. A technique called amniocentesis, for obtaining and culturing embryonic cells from the amniotic fluid surrounding the fetus (q.v.), has been used successfully for the detection of birth defects, including chromosomal aberrations, galactosemia (a congenital disability of the infant to convert galactose in the blood into glucose), and Tay-Sachs disease (a hereditary mental-deficiency disease with a high incidence among Jews).

Hemolytic disease of the newborn can be prevented by treating eligible cases with Rh antibody; *see* RH FACTOR. New approaches promise to protect the infant from the harmful effects of the gene by environmental control; dietary management of phenylketonuria and the development of a vaccine for German measles promise to prevent the damaging effects of these diseases. Finally, surgical management of congenital malformations is constantly improving. F.C.F.

BIRTHMARK *or* **NEVUS,** congenital mark on the skin of human beings that appears at birth or in later life and occasionally disappears spontaneously. The term nevus when unqualified refers to a benign cutaneous tumor consisting of blood capillaries. Such tumors, which rarely spread from their original site and which consequently are not dangerous to life, vary in color according to whether the capillaries composing them carry arterial or venous blood. The popularly termed cherry marks and port-wine stains or claret stains are nevi on a level with the surface of the skin. Certain other vascular nevi, commonly known as strawberry marks or raspberry marks, are slightly elevated above the surface. Vascular nevi comprise most birthmarks; two thirds are found on the face and head region. The term nevus is also applied with qualifying adjectives to superficial tumors derived from epithelium, nervous tissue, connective tissue, or fat. Among such tumors are pigmented spots and hairy moles. Although sometimes best left untreated, disfiguring nevi may sometimes be camouflaged by tattooing. Specific treatment, dictated by the type of blemish, is by electrocautery, small doses of radium, freezing with carbon dioxide, or removal by surgery. Nevi very seldom progress to malignancy. *See* SKIN: *Skin Diseases.*

Birthmarks have been mentioned in the literature of civilized countries for centuries. At first, because these marks sometimes resembled in outline animals or familiar objects, they were believed to be visitations of divine anger; later, this superstition was replaced by the belief that the marks are expressions of wishes or emotions of the mother during her pregnancy.

BIRTH RATE. See POPULATION STUDY.

BIRTHSTONE, any of various precious and semiprecious gems (*see* GEM) associated with the particular calendar months of the year, and considered lucky to those born in those months. The tradition of birthstones goes far back in history. Some attribute their origin to the twelve-jeweled breastplate worn by Aaron (q.v.), the brother of Moses, which is mentioned in the Bible (Exod. 39). Myths and superstitions gradually grew up regarding the stones, and symbolic meanings or virtues were ascribed to them. About half of the months of the year have alternate birthstones.

The various birthstones and the qualities they symbolize, as specified by the Jewelry Industry Council in New York City, are given in the accompanying table. See also separate articles on the gems listed in the table.

BIRTHSTONES

Month	Birthstone	Symbolizing
January	garnet	constancy
February	amethyst	sincerity
March	aquamarine, bloodstone	courage
April	diamond	innocence
May	emerald	love, success
June	pearl, alexandrite, moonstone	health, longevity
July	ruby	contentment
August	peridot, sardonyx	married happiness
September	sapphire	clear thinking
October	opal, tourmaline	hope
November	topaz	fidelity
December	turquoise, zircon	prosperity

BIRTHWORT. See ARISTOLOCHIA.

BISCAY, BAY OF, vast inlet of the Atlantic Ocean, bounded on the N. and E. by France and on the S. by Spain. The maximum width and length are about 400 mi. The depth of water ranges from about 120 ft. to about 1200 ft., with extreme depths along the Spanish coast. The S. coast is precipitious and rocky, in some places rising to a height of several hundred feet. In the S.E., between the mouths of the Adour R. and Gironde estuary, the coast is low and sandy, with many lagoons. Low marshland prevails for a distance of about 200 miles N. of the Gironde, but beyond the Quiberon Peninsula the coast is moderately elevated and rocky. Numerous streams run into the bay from the mountains of Spain and through the rivers Loire, Charente, Gironde, and Adour. The chief ports are Gijón, Santander, Bilbao, and San Sebastián in Spain; and Bayonne, Bordeaux, Rochefort, La Rochelle, Nantes, and Lorient in France. Among the principal islands in the bay are Belle-Île, Noirmoutier, Ré, and Oléron. Navigation is difficult and dangerous, because of the prevailing N.W. winds and a strong current.

BISCAYNE BAY, inlet of the Atlantic Ocean, on the S.E. coast of Florida. The bay is about 40 mi. long and between 2 and 10 mi. wide, and to the E. is a series of islands known as keys. The resort city of Miami Beach (q.v.) is built on several of these keys. To the S. of the city is Key Biscayne, the site of a home of the thirty-seventh President of the United States, Richard Milhous Nixon (q.v.).

BISCAYNE NATIONAL MONUMENT, area in Dade County, Fla., 25 miles S. of Miami. Only 4000 acres of the monument are on land. The remaining 101,000 acres comprise water areas in the southern parts of Biscayne Bay, constituting a part of the Intracoastal Waterway, and the coral-reef area of the Atlantic Ocean adjoining the northernmost of the Florida Keys (q.v.). Between the bay and the ocean are Sands Key, Elliott Key, Old Rhodes Key, and several smaller islets. The national monument was authorized in 1969 and is administered by the National Park Service.

BISHOP (Gr. *episkopos,* "overseer"), in the Christian churches from earliest times, the chief priest, ruler, and teacher of one or a number of churches, usually in a specific geographic area. In the Roman Catholic and Eastern Orthodox churches and in most of the Anglican churches a bishop is an ecclesiastic who, through sacramental consecration, holds special powers of the ministry as well as special administrative prerogatives; *see* ORDERS, HOLY. Few Protestant churches, other than the Anglican churches, recognize the office of bishop; in the churches that do, the bishop is not considered to have extraordinary priestly powers. He is simply a minister charged by the members of his church with superintendence of church affairs.

In the earliest days of Christianity the terms bishop and presbyter were often used interchangeably. Only gradually did the words acquire a distinction in meaning, with the title of bishop used to designate an overseer of pastors as well as laity. According to the theory of Apostolic succession held by the Roman, Orthodox, and Anglican churches, the order of bishop was instituted by Jesus Christ; the first bishops were the twelve Apostles, who ordained delegates and successors and transmitted to them the Apostolic authority and priority of rank. These churches claim an unbroken succession of bishops from Apostolic times. They consider Holy Orders a sacrament through which the bishop is endowed with certain sacred powers beyond those enjoyed by the priest (q.v.).

Consecration to the order of bishop is usually performed by three bishops (one of them a metropolitan), this number having been customary from post-Apostolic times. The bishop is the supreme ecclesiastical ruler of the diocese over which he presides. He is responsible for the spiritual welfare of all the faithful, both clergy and laymen, and for the government of all ecclesiastical institutions within his diocese. He has the power to ordain bishops, priests, and deacons, and in the Western rite of the Roman Church and in the Anglican Church, he is the ordinary minister of the sacrament of Confirmation (q.v.).

A certain jurisdictional hierarchy exists within the order of bishop. An archbishop (q.v.), or metropolitan, is a prelate in charge of several dioceses that have been grouped into a unit called an archdiocese. A residential bishop is in charge of a diocese. If that diocese falls within an archdiocese, he is also referred to as a suffragan bishop. The suffragan has full ecclesiastical authority within his diocese, but is subject to the archbishop in interdiocesan matters. Titular bishops, such as coadjutor and auxiliary bishops, are sometimes appointed to assist the resident bishop. Coadjutor bishops often succeed to the see in which they have assisted; they always succeed when appointed with right of succession. Certain superior bishops are known as exarchs or patriarchs; *see* ORTHODOX CHURCH.

In both the Western and Eastern rites of the Roman Catholic Church, a bishop is appointed by the pope; in the Eastern Orthodox churches the governing body of each rite or Holy Synod elects the bishop. Anglican bishops are, in theory, elected by the chapter of each cathedral church by virtue of a license from the crown; in actuality, however, the bishops of the Church of England are appointed by the crown on the advice of the prime minister, because no chapter ventures to disregard the nomination accompanying the license. In the Protestant Episcopal Church of the United States, which is a self-governing member of the Anglican Communion (q.v.), the bishop of a diocese is chosen by a convention of clerical and lay deputies from the diocese, subject to the consent of other diocesan bishops. This procedure is followed in various parts of the world by most independent branches of the Anglican Communion.

For the special vestments worn by bishops, *see* VESTMENTS, ECCLESIASTICAL.

BISHOP, Sir Henry Rowley (1786–1855), British composer and conductor, born in London, England. From 1810 to 1840 he was composer and musical director for various London theaters. He helped found the London Philharmonic Society in 1813 and served as one of its first conductors. In 1842 he was knighted by Victoria (q.v.), Queen of Great Britain, becoming the first musician ever to receive the honor. Bishop was professor of music at the University of Oxford from 1848 until his death. His compositions include numerous operas, glees, cantatas, and incidental music, but he is best remembered for his songs, notably "Home, Sweet Home", set to lyrics by the American playwright John Howard Payne (q.v.) and music for Shakespeare's poem "Lo! Hear the Gentle Lark".

BISHOP, William Avery (1894–1956), Canadian military aviator, born in Owen Sound, Ontario, and educated at the Royal Military College. After the outbreak of World War I in 1914, he was assigned to duty with the Canadian expeditionary force in France. He transferred to the Royal Flying Corps in 1915. Bishop was officially credited with having shot down seventy-two enemy aircraft, the third-highest record achieved by an aviator of the Allies. In 1938 Bishop became air marshal of Canada and in 1940, during World War II, was appointed director of air-force recruiting.

BISHOPS' BIBLE. *See* BIBLE, ENGLISH TRANSLATIONS OF THE.

BISHOPS' WARS. *See* COVENANTERS.

BISKRA, town of Algeria, in Constantine Department, about 175 miles S.E. of Algiers. The town lies in a fertile oasis of the Sahara desert and is a trading center for nomads. Fruit growing is a major enterprise; dates, olives, apricots, and pomegranates are the principal crops. Because of the equable climate the town is a popular winter resort. Fort Saint Germain, which was an important French military post during the French occupation of Algeria, is situated there. In antiquity a Roman military station stood on the site of Biskra. The Arab conqueror of North Africa, Okba (d. 683), was killed near the town; his tomb bears the oldest known Arabic inscription in North Africa. In 1844, after centuries of Moorish rule, Biskra was seized by the French. Pop. (latest census) 53,177.

BISMARCK, capital of North Dakota, and county seat of Burleigh Co., on the E. bank of the Missouri R., about 190 miles W. of Fargo. It is a trading and distributing center for the W. part of the State and for E. Montana, and is served by several railroads and airlines. In the surrounding region coal, natural gas, and oil are produced, and alfalfa, dairy cattle, grain, and poultry are raised. Industries in Bismarck include brewing, printing, trucking, woodworking, and the manufacture of brick and tile, and farm machinery. A junior college is located in the city, as is the capitol, which was completed in the early 1930's. On the grounds of the capitol are a State library and a historical museum.

Edwinton, the site of present-day Bismarck, was laid out in 1873 following the completion of

Prince Otto von Bismarck UPI

the Northern Pacific Railroad through the area. The name of the city was changed later that year. Bismarck became the capital of Dakota Territory in 1883. Upon the division of the Territory and the admission of North Dakota to the Union in 1889 Bismarck became the capital of the State. Pop. (1960) 27,670; (1970) 34,703.

BISMARCK, Prince Otto Eduard Leopold von *or* **BISMARCK-SCHÖNHAUSEN, Prince Otto Eduard Leopold von** (1815–98), Prussian statesman and first chancellor (1871–90) of the German Empire, born in Schönhausen, and educated at the universities of Göttingen and Berlin. He was a member of the United Prussian Diet in 1847 and 1849, and from 1851 to 1858 represented Prussia at the Germanic Confederation in Frankfurt am Main. In 1859 he became Prussian ambassador to Russia and in 1862 to France. In September, 1862, William I (q.v.), King of Prussia, made Bismarck prime minister and minister of foreign affairs. Bismarck then undertook his major lifework, the unification of Germany under Prussian leadership and the establishment of a unified Germany as the most powerful European nation.

To achieve his aim Bismarck provoked a series of wars. First he maneuvered Austria, the chief rival of Prussia in the Germanic Confederation, into alliance with Prussia in a war against Denmark for the control of Schleswig-Holstein (q.v.). When Denmark was defeated, Prussia and Austria disagreed on the disposition of the duchy of Holstein, and Prussia defeated Austria in the ensuing Seven Weeks' War (q.v.). After the war Bismarck transformed the Germanic Confederation into the North German Confederation (q.v.) and excluded Austria from membership. In 1870 Bismarck provoked the Franco-German War (q.v.), in which, under Prussian leadership, a coalition of German states defeated France. At the end of the war in 1871, all Germany was unified as the German Empire. William I of Prussia became emperor and Bismarck his chancellor.

As chancellor, Bismarck engaged in an unsuccessful struggle with the Roman Catholic Church (*see* KULTURKAMPF). He suppressed Socialist political activity (*see* SOCIALISM), but instituted a number of social reforms, including government ownership of some industries, and compulsory accident, sickness, and old-age insurance for workingmen. He arranged the Berlin Conference of 1884–85, which developed the conditions upon which Africa was subsequently partitioned (*see* AFRICA: *History*), and in 1878 presided over the Congress of Berlin (*see* BERLIN, CONGRESS OF), which dealt with the political status of the Balkans and the Middle East after the Russo-Turkish War. In 1882 Bismarck was instrumental in forming the military and political coalition known as the Triple Alliance (q.v.), consisting of Germany, Austria-Hungary, and Italy. William II (q.v.) became emperor in 1888, and Bismarck frequently disagreed with him over German foreign policy. In 1890 the emperor dismissed Bismarck from office, but granted him the title of Duke of Lauenberg.

Bismarck, known as the Iron Chancellor, is widely regarded as the greatest European diplomat of the 19th century. He transformed Germany from a group of conflicting kingdoms and principalities into a united nation and one of the great powers of the world. *See* GERMANY: *History*.

BISMARCK ARCHIPELAGO, group of more than 200 islands in the Pacific Ocean, once part of the Australian-administered Territory of New Guinea (q.v.) but now part of Papua New Guinea. The archipelago is N.E. of New Guinea and S. of the equator. The principal islands are New Britain (area, 14,150 sq.mi.), New Ireland (about 3340 sq.mi.), New Hanover (about 460 sq.mi.), Duke of York Islands (22 sq.mi.), and the Admiralty Islands (about 800 sq.mi.). Other groups in the archipelago are the Saint Matthias Group, the Vitu Islands, and the Umboi Islands. The archipelago is semicircular in shape and partly encloses Bismarck Sea. A majority of the population is Melanesian. Cacao, copra, and shellfish are the leading products. Known originally as New Britain Archipelago, the island group was proclaimed a German protectorate in 1884 and given its present name in 1885. Australian forces occupied the islands in 1914, after the outbreak of World War I. Australia obtained control of the archipelago under the terms of the League of Nations mandate (1920) establishing the Territory of New Guinea. The islands were invaded by Japanese forces in 1942, and were retaken by Allied troops in 1944. Area, about 20,000 sq.mi.

BISMUTH, metallic element with at.no. 83, at.wt. 208.99, b.p. estimated 1500° C. (2732° F.), m.p. 271.3° C. (519.8° F.), sp.gr. $9.8^{20°}$, and symbol Bi. It was known to the ancients but until the middle of the 18th century was confused with lead, tin, and zinc. In the crust of the earth bismuth is about as common as silver; most industrial bismuth is obtained as a by-product in the process of the refining of lead, copper, silver, and gold.

Bismuth is chemically a typical metal, although it sometimes shows nonmetallic properties (*see* ARSENIC). In compounds it has valences of 3 to 5, the compounds with trivalent bismuth being more stable. Even the latter compounds are generally unstable in the presence of water. There are several nitrates, notably bismuth nitrate $Bi(NO_3)_3$ or bismuth trinitrate; and bismuth nitrate pentahydrate, $Bi(NO_3)_3{\cdot}5H_2O$. The latter form decomposes into basic bismuth nitrate. The last-named is also known as bismuth oxynitrate or bismuthyl nitrate and may be used in medicine and cosmetics. Other common names for basic bismuth nitrate are pearl white and Spanish white.

Bismuth has a distinct pink tinge; it is the only metal other than copper and gold that is not silver-white in color. It shrinks on melting and expands on solidifying. Some of its alloys have unusually low melting points. Wood's alloy (4Bi, 2Pb, 1Sn, 1Cd), for example, melts at 65° C. (149°F.). One of the most strongly diamagnetic of all substances, bismuth is repelled by a magnet, and a bar of the metal tends to turn at right angles to a magnetic field. It is a poor conductor of heat and electricity, and its electrical resistance is further increased in a magnetic field; this property is utilized in instruments for measuring the strength of such fields. Among the stable elements bismuth has the highest atomic weight and atomic number; as it is opaque to X rays, it is sometimes used in fluoroscopy.

BISON, either of the two living species of the genus *Bison* in the family Bovidae. Although similar to the domestic ox (*see* CATTLE), it has a hump just behind the neck, a broader convex forehead, a larger head, and longer limbs. It has fourteen pairs of ribs; all other oxen (except the yak) have thirteen. The heavy, curved horns grow throughout life and are black in young bison, becoming grayish with advancing age. The American bison, *B. bison,* commonly called buffalo (q.v.), has shorter and thicker horns than the European bison, *B. bonasus,* called wisent, and its coat is thicker; both have very shaggy hair, much of which is shed each spring. A large bull of either species measures about 10 ft. in length and 6 ft. in height at the shoulder and weighs almost a ton.

A bull of the American bison, Bison bison*—the buffalo of the Wild West.* Leonard Lee Rue III-Bruce Coleman, Inc.

The European bison is now extinct, except for one or two small, protected herds. Until recent times the bison was abundant in North America, especially on the prairies beyond the Mississippi R., between Canada and New Mexico. Now it is nearly extinct, a result of hard winters, cattle ranching, railroads, and immigration. A few hundred are preserved in the Yellowstone National Park and in various zoological parks.

BISSAU *or* **BISSÃO,** city and capital of Guinea-Bissau, near the mouth of the Geba R., 250 miles S.E. of Dakar, Senegal. The main ethnic groups of the city are the Fulani (q.v.), Mandingo, and Balante tribes, and a large portion of them are Muslims. The principal products of the country, including nuts, hides, rice, and wax, are exported from Bissau, the chief port. Bissau was established as a slavetrading center for the Portuguese and became a free port in 1869. African guerrilla activities against the Portuguese originated in the city in 1962. Pop. (1970 prelim.) 8219.

BISTRIŢA, river of Rumania, rising in the Carpathian Mts. It flows S.E. through the regions of Bukovina and Moldavia, and joins the Siret R. just below Bacău, after a course of about 185 mi.

BITHYNIA, ancient country in N.W. Asia Minor, on the S. shores of the Pontus Euxinus (now the Black Sea), the Propontis (Sea of Marmara), and the Bosporus Thracius (Strait of Bosporus). A mountainous region, with heavy forests and fertile valleys, Bithynia acquired its name from the Bithyni, a tribe that had emigrated from Thrace. The country was conquered by Croesus (q.v.), King of Lydia, in 560 B.C. and after the subjugation of Lydia by the Persians four years later, it became a dominion of Persia. In 334 B.C. the Macedonian ruler Alexander III (q.v.), known as the Great, occupied Bithynia. After his death in 323 B.C., the country was ruled for a period by Antigonus I (*see under* ANTIGONUS), one of the Macedonian generals who partitioned Alexander's empire. About 316 B.C. Antigonus founded Nicaea (now İznik), later one of the chief cities of Bithynia. Led by a native prince, Ziboetes (about 327–about 279 B.C.), the Bithynians won independence from Macedonian rule early in the 3rd century B.C. The first dynasty of Bithynian kings was established by Ziboetes' son Nicomedes I (r. 278–250 B.C.), who founded Nicomedia (now İzmit) in 264 B.C. and made it his capital. Bithynia flourished under the succeeding kings of the dynasty, notably Prusias I (r. 237–192 B.C.), Prusias II (r. 192–148 B.C.), who founded Prusa (now Bursa), Nicomedes II (r. 142–91 B.C.) and Nicomedes III, (r. 91–74 B.C.). In 74 B.C. Nicomedes III, a close ally of the Romans, bequeathed the kingdom to Rome. It was then united with the Roman province of Pontus for administrative purposes. Later, under Byzantine rule, the territory of Bithynia was restricted to an area W. of the Sangarius R. (now Sakarya R.) It formed a province in the Diocese of Pontus. In 1298 A.D. Bithynia was overrun by the Seljuk Turks under Othman (q.v.), and thereafter the region formed an integral part of the Ottoman Empire. Bithynia is now part of Turkey.

BITOLA, city of Yugoslavia, in the Republic of Macedonia, capital of Bitola District, on the Dragor R., 65 miles S. of Skopje. The city, trade center of the Bitola Plain and the fertile Pelagonija Valley, produces hides, skins, leather, rugs, reed and rush matting, cordage, and grain. It is the site of a teachers' college. Nearby are the ruins of the Roman colony of Heraclea Lyncestis. Bitola became a bishopric in the 11th century and from 1382 to 1913 was ruled by the Ottoman Turks, under whom it was called Monastir. As a Yugoslav city it was formerly called Bitolj, sometimes spelled Bitolia or Bitol. Pop. (1971 prelim.) 65,851.

BITTER, Karl Theodore Francis (1867–1915), Austrian-American sculptor, born in Vienna, and trained at the Vienna Academy of Fine Arts. He came to the United States in 1888 and became a naturalized citizen. Among the works for which he won world renown are the Astor Memorial bronze doors of Trinity Church; sculptures for the Chamber of Commerce building and the Metropolitan Museum of Art; and the memorial to the German-American legislator and publicist Carl Schurz (q.v.), all in New York City.

BITTERN, common name for birds of the subfamily Botaurinae in the Heron family (Ardeidae). Although similar to other herons in habits and habitat, in general they have shorter necks and legs. The plumage is brown, yellow, and black, variously striped and speckled. Bitterns are solitary birds, inhabiting reedy and marshy places. At the approach of a human being, they stand motionless with head up and neck vertical, so that their brown-streaked plumage makes them almost indistinguishable from the surrounding reeds. The bird is sluggish, and its flight is slow and of short duration. When attacked, it fights desperately with bill and claws. The bittern makes a rude nest of sticks or reeds in its marshy haunts and lays four or five greenish-brown eggs each breeding season. *Botaurus stellaris,* the bog jumper, is the common bittern of Europe and is widely distributed over the Old World; *B. australis* is native to Australia; and *B. lentiginosus* can be found in all parts of the United States and most of Canada. The least bittern or little bittern (*Ixobrychus exilis*), found only in the U.S., attains a length of about 13 in. Species of *Botaurus* average 28 in. in length. In both genera the feathers can be erected so as greatly to increase the apparent size of the bird.

BITTERROOT. See PURSLANE.

BITTERROOT RANGE, chain of the Rocky Mts., extending for about 400 mi. on the border between Idaho and Montana. The name is derived from the bitterroot, a flowering plant that grows in the region.

BITTERS, any of various, usually alcoholic, flavoring agents distilled or infused from bitter herbs or roots. Extracts of quinine, orange, and angostura are among the most popular bitters on the market, and are used, sparingly, chiefly in mixed drinks and sauces. In addition to adding a bitter savor to food, bitters are valued for their tonic and digestive properties. In Great Britain a dry ale sold on draft is also known as bitter.

BITTERSWEET, *or* CLIMBING BITTERSWEET, common name for the plant *Celastrus scandens,* known also as false bittersweet and waxwork. This twining vine is native to eastern North America. It bears long-lasting, brightly colored, orange-yellow berries which are often used in ornamental arrangements of dried plants.

European or woody bittersweet, also called climbing nightshade, is an unrelated plant (*Solanum dulcamara*) of the Nightshade (q.v.) family (Solanaceae). This plant, native to Great Britain, has become naturalized throughout North America and is the commonest of the dangerous nightshades in many places, especially in the northern United States and southern Canada. It is a woody, bushy, or twining weed growing in woods, hedgerows, and thickets. Purple or blue flowers in drooping clusters are followed by ovate, red berries. The leaves are variable in outline, some without lobes and others with two basal lobes, similar to tomato leaves. All parts of this plant contain a complex poisonous principle, probably least in the berries. If eaten in any great amount, it produces severe gastroenteritis and is considered potentially fatal. J.M.K.

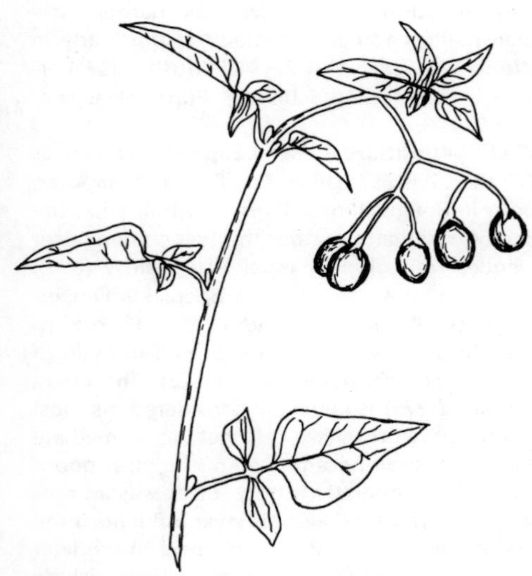

European bittersweet, Solanum dulcamara

BITUMEN, any of various, naturally occurring mineral substances, essentially mixtures of hydrocarbons (q.v.) with their nonmetallic derivatives. Crude petroleum, asphalt, and tar (qq.v.) are bitumens, which are characteristically dark brown or black in color and which contain little nitrogen, oxygen, or sulfur. Commercially the term bitumen refers chiefly to hydrocarbons in a solid or semisolid state, but in a wider sense it refers to all natural hydrocarbons, which may also occur in a liquid or gaseous state. Bitumen, distributed throughout the world, is found in all geological strata from the Precambrian Era to the Quaternary. In ancient times bitumen was the Roman name for an asphalt used as a cement and mortar.

BITUMINOUS COAL, *or* SOFT COAL, variety of coal intermediate in constitution and properties between anthracite (q.v.), or hard coal, and lignite (q.v.), or brown coal. See COAL.

BIVALVE, animal with a body covered by a shell consisting of two sides or "valves" joined on one side. The term specifically refers to a class of mollusks, such as the clam, scallop, or oyster (qq.v.), which have calcareous shells consisting of right and left valves joined dorsally by an elastic ligament. These mollusks are known also as Pelecypoda (Gr. *pelekys,* "hatchet"; *podon,* "foot") or Lamellibranchia (Lat. *lamella,* "little plate"; Gr. *branchia,* "gills").

As a rule the shell, when closed, covers the entire, highly compressed body of the bivalve and protects it against adverse conditions, such as exposure at low tide, brackish water, pollution, and predatory attack. In some burrowing species, notably the shipworm (q.v.), the shell covers only a small part of the body.

After the animal dies the ligament pulls the valves apart, but during life the opening and closing of the valves is regulated by the contractions of one or two abductor muscles. The mantle, a soft membrane, underlies both valves and secretes the shell. The mantle's edge usually bears a row of hightly sensitive tentacles.

Bivalves are filter-feeders in that they obtain their food by filtering large quantities of water through their gills and retaining plankton (q.v.) and organic debris. The current of water is maintained by the beating of millions of tiny, hairlike structures called cilia, which cover the gills; see GILL. Certain rows of cilia push the food toward the mouth. In clams and some other species the edges of the mantle are fused into two long tubes known as the siphons. Water is sucked in through one siphon and discharged through the other.

Some bivalves, such as oysters, are sedentary and never move after they have cemented themselves to rocks, whereas others such as scallops swim, and still others such as clams and fresh-water mussels (*see* MUSSEL) crawl or burrow by means of a strong muscular foot. Liquid waste products are excreted by the kidney. Blood is moved through blood vessels and irregular open spaces in the tissues by a heart which consists of one ventricle and two auricles. The head and the brain are absent. The nervous system consists of a number of ganglia joined by bands of nerve fibers (connectives). Typical sense organs are the otocysts, or statocysts, which are the organs of orientation; and the osphradia, or water-testing organs. Some bivalves, such as scallops, have a row of complex eyes along the edge of the mantle. Reproduction occurs when eggs are discharged into the water, or retained in the gills and developed inside the body. Fertility is high; for example, in oysters the female produces many millions of eggs each season. Larvae usually pass through two free-swimming stages, the trochophore and the veliger; however, these larval stages are absent in some fresh-water forms. The adult form is often developed from the egg within one year; some species have a life span of thirty years. In size the adults range from minute forms measuring 0.04 in. to the giant clam of the East Indies which becomes 3 ft. long.

About 14,000 species of bivalves are known; more than half of these are fossils. Classification is difficult, as it depends both on the anatomy of the body and the shell characteristics. Living pelecy-pods are found in both fresh and salt water in all parts of the world. Bivalves are an important food for many food fishes and birds and of mammals such as the walrus. Many are also eaten by man. The shells of many species contain the nacre, or mother-of-pearl, of commerce, and some of them produce pearls (*see* PEARL). *See* MOLLUSCA. P.S.G.

BIWA, largest lake of Japan, in the W. central part of Honshu Island, about 10 miles N.E. of Kyoto, and having an area of 268 sq.mi. A canal connects it with the Kamogawa Canal and supplies waterpower to Kyoto. Biwa Lake figures prominently in Japanese history and legends, and because of its beauty has frequently been the theme of Japanese poetry.

BIYSK *or* **BIISK,** city of the Soviet Union, in the Russian S.F.S.R., at the headwaters of the Ob' R., about 80 miles S.E. of Barnaul. The surrounding region has extensive agricultural enterprises, notably dairy and poultry farms. Wheat and flax are leading crops. Biysk is an important river port and headquarters for trade by caravan with Outer Mongolia. Among the chief articles of trade are furs, wool, lump silver, tea, and dairy products. Industries include food processing and textile manufacturing. Pop. (1970 est.) 186,000.

BIZERTE *or* **BIZERTA** (anc. *Hippo Zarytus*), city and fortified seaport of Tunisia, on the Mediterranean Sea, about 80 miles N.W. of Tunis. The outer harbor of the city is connected by canal with two inner harbors, the Bay of Sebra and the Lake of Bizerte. On the shores of the lake are important French naval installations, including Ferryville, a military post. Olives are grown in the surrounding region, and the lake contains valuable fisheries. Fish products, flour, and olive oil are among the chief manufactures.

Bizerte was occupied originally by colonists from the Phoenician capital Tyre. The town later became a Roman colony, and after the 7th century A.D. it was held by the Arabs. Following 1881 when France seized Tunisia and made it a protectorate the French dredged channels and canals and further modernized the harbor. German military forces occupied the port early in World War II. On May 7, 1943, British and American troops captured Bizerte. Pop. (latest census) 51,708.

BIZET, Alexandre César Léopold, known as GEORGES BIZET (1838–75), French composer, born in Bougival, near Paris, and trained at the Paris Conservatory under the French composer Jacques François Fromental Elias Halévy (q.v.). Bizet is best known for his operas, which include *Les Pêcheurs de Perles* ("The Pearl Fishers", 1863), *La Jolie Fille de Perth* ("Fair Maid of Perth", 1867), and *Djamileh* (1872). The opera *Carmen* (1875) is generally considered his most important work. Although not an immediate success, it soon became one of the most popular works in operatic history. Bizet was an outstanding dramatist, and his style influenced the realistic or *verismo* school of opera in the later 19th century. His other compositions include Symphony in C (1855), the symphonic suite

Roma ("Rome", 1866–68), incidental music (1872) to the play *L'Arlésienne* ("The Woman from Arles") by the French writer Alphonse Daudet (*see under* DAUDET), the dramatic overture *Patrie* ("Native Land", 1873), and works for piano and voice.

BJÖRNEBORG. *See* PORI.

BJÖRNSON, Björnstjerne (1832–1910), Norwegian writer, theater director, and political leader, born in Kvikne, and educated at Frederick University. He left the university before graduating to pursue a literary and journalistic career, during the course of which he wrote voluminously on the social, political, moral, and aesthetic questions of the time. He was influential in the creation of an indigenous Norwegian literature and a typically Norwegian school of writers of fiction, with roots in the early culture of Norway. His plays rank among the earliest and most important examples of native Norwegian dramatic literature. Between 1857 and 1872, he was at various times director of theaters in Bergen and Christiania (now Oslo). In 1903 he was awarded the Nobel Prize for literature.

Björnson was also regarded as the greatest contemporary orator of the Scandinavian countries. He was a leader in the political struggle that led to the dissolution, in 1905, of the union of Norway and Sweden and to the establishment of Norway as an independent country. His numerous works include the dramatic trilogy *Sigurd Slembe* (1862) and the plays *Mary Stuart in Scotland* (1864), *The Bankrupt* (1875), and *Beyond Human Power* (1883); the novel *The Fisher Maiden* (1868); and the cycle of epic poems *Arnljot Gelline* (1870).

BJÖRNSSON, Sveinn (1881–1952), Icelandic statesman, born in Copenhagen, Denmark, and educated in Reykjavík, Iceland, and at the University of Copenhagen. Björnsson began to practice law in Iceland in 1907. He was a member of the Althing, the Icelandic parliament, from 1914 to 1920 and served as special envoy to the United States and England in 1914 and 1915, respectively. From 1920 to 1924 and again from 1926 to 1941 he was Icelandic minister to Denmark. Björnsson became regent of Iceland in 1941, and three years later, when the country was proclaimed a constitutional republic, he was elected its first president. He served in that post until his death. *See* ICELAND: *History*.

BLACK, name of a number of rivers of the United States. **1.** A river, known also as the BIG BLACK RIVER, rising in S.E. Missouri and flowing in a southeasterly direction to a point near the State border. From there it flows S.W. through Arkansas, joining the White R. above Newport,

Georges Bizet French Embassy Press & Information Div.

Jackson Co. It is the largest affluent of the White R., with a total length of about 400 mi. The river is navigable for about 100 mi. from its mouth, except during the dry season. A Black R. flood-control project, including Clearwater Dam (4425 ft. long and 143 ft. high) was completed in 1948; it is situated about 6 mi. S.W. of Piedmont, Mo. **2.** A river, about 125 mi. long, rising in the S.W. Adirondack Mts., in New York State. It flows in a general northerly direction for the greater part of its length, and then turns W. and empties into Black River Bay, the extreme eastern end of Lake Ontario. Its numerous falls and rapids furnish abundant water power to Watertown, N.Y., and other localities. From Lyons Falls to the mouth of the river, about 72 mi., the fall is about 500 ft. **3.** A river, about 200 mi. long, rising in Taylor County, Wis., and flowing in a general southwesterly direction. It joins the Mississippi R. at La Crosse, Wis. **4.** A river of Windsor County, Vt., about 40 mi. long, flowing into the Connecticut R. It furnishes abundant water power to the towns along its banks. **5.** A river of eastern South Carolina, about 150 mi. long. It rises in Lee County and flows in a general southeasterly direction, entering the Waccamaw R. near Georgetown.

BLACK, Hugo La Fayette (1886–1971), American jurist, born in Harlan, Clay Co., Ala., and educated at the University of Alabama. He practiced law in Birmingham and was the prosecuting attorney of Jefferson County, Ala., from 1915 to 1917, when he entered the army. After World War I he resumed his law practice. As United States Senator (Democratic) from Alabama, 1927–37, he sponsored a number of New Deal (q.v.) legislative measures, including the Fair Labor Standards Act (q.v.). In 1937 President Franklin Delano Roosevelt (q.v.) appointed him associate justice of the Supreme Court of the U.S. During most of his long tenure Black supported the members of the court who viewed that body as an instrument of social reform. He wrote *One Man's Stand for Freedom* (1963).

BLACK, Joseph (1728–99), British chemist born in Bordeaux, France, and educated at Glasgow and Edinburgh universities. He was professor of chemistry, medicine, and anatomy at Glasgow University from 1756 to 1766; thereafter he was professor of chemistry at Edinburgh University. In about 1761 Black discovered the phenomenon of latent heat, and three years later he measured the latent heat of steam. His pupil and assistant James Watt (q.v.) later put these discoveries to practical use. About 1754 Black discovered the gas carbon dioxide (q.v.), which he called fixed air, and showed its function in the causticization of lime, thus helping to disprove the phlogiston theory of combustion; *see* CHEMISTRY: *History of Chemistry: Rise of Modern Chemistry;* PHLOGISTON. He also discovered that different substances have different specific heats.

BLACK AFRICA, general term used to identify African nations situated to the south of the Sahara Desert, the populations of which consist mainly of the people of the Negroid race; *see* AFRICA; NEGRO; RACES OF MANKIND: *Negroid Race;* SAHARA. See also separate articles on many of the peoples and place-names mentioned in this article.

Early History. Important evidence uncovered by the British anthropologist Louis S. B. Leakey (q.v.) in the 1950's and 1960's indicates that some 2,000,000 years ago, hominid ancestors of man lived in what is now northwestern Tanzania. Together with other tool-makers, the relics of whom were discovered in South Africa, these manlike creatures developed and spread through most of sub-Saharan Africa, and to this date are the earliest-known ancestors of man; *see* ARCHEOLOGY: *Early Man.*

By about 10,000 B.C., Bushmen lived in southern Africa, and other Negroid peoples were found elsewhere throughout the continent.

The Sahara, separating northern Africa from black Africa, nevertheless provided a passage for peoples and ideas passing north and south. Stock-raising cultures evolved on the Ethiopian plateau and elsewhere in East Africa, and new crops were widely introduced. Nomadic hunting and gathering peoples were gradually replaced by people following agricultural and industrial pursuits. By about 300 B.C. iron mining and forging was carried on in the Nok culture, probably the oldest culture in present-day Nigeria. Whether through diffusion from the ancient Egyptian city of Meroë or from other parts of North Africa, or by local invention, metal working had spread through sub-Saharan Africa by about 300 A.D. This phenomenon was associated with the migration of Bantu-speaking peoples from western Africa and the introduction of the Asian banana, a vital foodstuff brought to East Africa by trading caravans from Indonesia. The combination of iron tools and weapons and new foodstuffs helped to promote a sharp increase in population and the creation of new social and political organizations. More than 1000 distinct African languages (q.v.) emerged. Migrating groups often divided into small units, which in turn claimed new territories, but the basic unit was the extended family.

Growth of Political Units. Large-scale states began to emerge in northeastern Africa before the first millennium A.D., in the western Sudan region by about 400 A.D., and in the rest of sub-Saharan Africa between 1000 and 1600. Along the East-African coast, city-states were flourishing by the 13th century. These states were centered on a spiritually sanctioned king, were administered by nobles or headsmen, and peopled mainly by village-based farmers. The states that increased in power or wealth tended to do so because of control over trade routes or commodities. Gold, ivory, and salt were crucial, for example, to the growth of the medieval empires of Ghana, Mali, and Songhai in the western Sudan, and gold was crucial to the historic West African kingdom of Ashanti. As trade expanded, special groups such as the Mandingo, Ovimbundu, and Swahili developed as long-distance traders, and Muslim traders penetrated from North Africa. Islam (q.v.) introduced to many of the black-African states a unifying religion, and also the art of writing, and new consumer goods. Islam tended to dominate the courts and urban centers but made little headway in the countryside until the mid-18th century, when Muslim religious wars, spreading eastward from the Guinea highlands, extended and deepened its impact. In areas that were inaccessible, or lacked valuable minerals, or were inhabited by tribes that had little influence, large states usually did not emerge, and tribes such as the Masai and the Shilluk, both in East Africa, continued to practice their traditional ways of life.

European Impact. The initial European impact, which had started perhaps as early as 100 B.C., tended to be negative. When Europeans began to appear along the African coasts in the late 15th century, they brought Christianity, destroyed or helped alter trade patterns, and introduced new trade goods. Christianity also made inroads but failed in the Nubian states and had barely survived in Ethiopia. Reintroduced in the 15th century by the Europeans, it had its greatest effect in the short-lived Kongo kingdom. It was otherwise limited mainly to the coasts until the 19th century. By this time slave trading surpassed in importance and influence everything else, including Christianity. The slave trade generated violent warfare, made inroads on the population of western Africa, led to depopulation, and to increasingly arbitrary government; *see* SLAVERY. At the same time the import of consumer goods caused the decline of local industries.

Among the definite results of European colonization were the introduction of foodstuffs which probably supplied a more nutritious diet, from the New World, and the introduction of firearms, which permitted coastal and forest states to challenge the older inland states. Finally, the introduction of Western education helped prepare the indigenous Africans to deal with Europeans on their own terms, and to accommodate them to the concept of slavery in the New World; *see* NEGROES IN THE UNITED STATES.

By the late 19th century, European intervention to secure strategic areas and sources of raw materials and potential markets, to stop the slave trade, and to Christianize and Westernize the African, had led to the arbitrary division of black Africa into many European colonies. The initial African reaction to the European claims to political control was resistance, the most notable incidents being the Ndebele-Shona revolts in 1893 and 1896 in Rhodesia, which were the result of forcible seizure of land and cattle by white settlers, the Hut-Tax revolt (1898) in Sierra Leone against a new tax, and the Maji Maji rebellion (1905–07) in Tanganyika against the German disregard for local traditions, and forced labor. Inevitably, however, the resistance collapsed before the superior arms and organization of the Europeans.

As the Europeans conquered and consolidated control over African peoples, social change increased. With the introduction of a money economy, health services, Western education, and new religious beliefs, the old religious and social relationships were challenged and the old political leaders were isolated or adapted to the new systems.

Rise of Nationalism. With the increasing intrusion of European customs, values, and power during the early 20th century, the black Africans began to create new organizations, and to think in terms of loyalties beyond the family, lineage, or tribe. Political interest groups, which had begun to emerge as early as the 19th century in places such as the Gold Coast and Sierra Leone, were initially middle-class, civil-servant organizations. After World War II, however, they began to develop mass followings. Returning war veterans and Western-educated students aroused farmers, civil servants, clerks, and black youth generally to demand increased social and economic opportunities, an end to racial discrimination, and a voice in the government. In areas, such as most of western Africa, where there was little white settlement, the demands tended to be met after some initial resistance. In regions marked by extensive white settlement, as in Kenya and the Belgian Congo (now the Republic of Zaire), the change to black majority rule was less peaceful, or, as in the cases of South Africa and Rhodesia, has been prevented altogether by the superior power of the white minorities.

In the areas where black governments developed, the nationalist parties were gradually given increased power until independence was granted, first to Ghana in 1957 and by 1970 to some thirty-two new nations. After independence, the problems of government increased when experienced colonial administrators were replaced by poorly-trained politicians and party figures. Nevertheless, social and educational services increased slowly, as did economic and industrial development because industry, investment, and markets continued to be controlled from outside the continent by the developed countries. In several of the newly independent African countries, low wages, scarce goods and services on the one hand, and government extravagance, corruption, or favoritism on the other, set off military coups that toppled the new governments, for instance, in Nigeria and Ghana. In some states, such as Chad and Nigeria, tribes that felt discriminated against revolted and were suppressed. In a number of states, such as Tanzania and Zambia, however, dynamic leadership, lack of strong tribalism, an ideology of unity and development, and a shrewd use of natural and social resources is leading to the development of strong national states, each unified by language and loyalty to a common ideological identity. *See also* AFRICA: *History*. S.R.

BLACK AND TANS, members of an auxiliary force of constabulary serving in Ireland during the disturbances of 1920–21, so called from the colors of their uniform. They were recruited in England from unemployed veterans of World War I to carry on a ruthless campaign of counterterrorism against the Irish revolutionaries. Inadvertently, however, the Black and Tans actually aided the cause of Irish independence by uniting the general population of southern Ireland against British rule. Their tactics also aroused public opinion throughout England, thus influencing the British government to grant dominion status to the Irish Free State in 1921. *See* IRELAND, REPUBLIC OF: *History: The Irish Revolution.*

BLACK AND TAN TERRIER. *See* MANCHESTER TERRIER.

BLACKBEARD. *See* TEACH, EDWARD.

BLACK BELT, term for the low, prairie region of the southern United States, chiefly in Alabama, noted for its rich black soil and cotton production. The crescent-shaped belt extends along the Alabama R. in Alabama and into northeastern Mississippi, about three-fourths of its 5000-sq.mi. area being in Alabama. The region was settled in the 1830's after pioneers learned of the highly fertile black soil; the fertility is brought about by an underlayer of decayed soft limestone rock. The Black Belt soon became the most prosperous cotton-producing region of the South, although during the Civil War foodstuffs were grown there in order to supply the Confederate army with food. In recent times, livestock and diversified farming have been introduced, but the Black Belt remains the chief cotton-producing region east of the Mississippi. *See* COTTON; SOILS AND SOIL MANAGEMENT.

BLACKBERRY, common name for the fruit of plants of the genus *Rubus,* subgenus *Eubatus,* in the rose family (Rosaceae). The ripe fruit is an aggregate of small, purplish-black drupes attached to a cone-shaped receptacle, which readily separates from the plant when the berries are picked. In other subgenera of *Rubus,* the receptacle separates from the drupes and remains on the plant; *see* RASPBERRY. More than twenty-four species of blackberry are known, including several called dewberry (q.v.) and albino varieties called white blackberry. The most common species are the English *R. fruticosus* and the American *R. allegheniensis; see* BRAMBLE. Although it was highly developed as a wild fruit, the blackberry was rarely grown as a garden fruit until about 1850. Since then it has been widely cultivated, and has become an important commercial crop. Approximately 35,000,000 lb. of blackberries were produced in the United States in the late 1960's for marketing and canning.

BLACKBIRD, common name for several species of bird with black plumage of the family Icteridae in the order Passeriformes, all of which are native to the Americas. The family Icteridae, often called the Blackbird family, has about 240 species, and also includes the oriole, bobolink, cowbird, grackle, and meadowlark (qq.v.). All members of this family are heavy-billed birds with iridescent black plumage or black with yellow or orange markings. They have sharp, stout,

Cut-leaved bramble (blackberry), Rubus laciniatus

Black buck, Antilope cervicapra
American Museum of Natural History

cone-shaped bills with cutting edges. The two most familiar species of blackbird are the yellow-headed blackbird (*Xanthocephalus xanthocephalus*) and the redwing blackbird (*Agelaius phoeniceus*).

The common European blackbird (*Turdus merula*) is the blackbird of nursery-rhyme fame. Unlike the American blackbird, however, it is a species of thrush classified in the Thrush (q.v.) family (Turdidae).

BLACKBODY. *See* QUANTUM THEORY.

BLACK BUCK, common name for an antelope, *Antilope cervicapra,* of India. Adult males are about 32 in. high at the shoulder and weigh about 85 lb. Their ringed horns have a spiral twist of three to four turns and range from 16 to 28 in. in length. The upper parts of young males are dark brown and become black as the buck grows older; the under parts and a ring about the eyes are white. Does are usually hornless and are yellowish brown in color. Black bucks frequent open plains and travel in large herds. They are the fastest of the Indian antelopes and hunting them with greyhounds or cheetahs was once a popular sport in many parts of India. In danger of becoming extinct, the black buck is now protected by law.

The name black buck has also been applied to an African antelope, the sable antelope, which is related to the African antelopes known as oryxes. *See* ANTELOPE.

BLACKBURN, Great Britain, county borough of Lancashire, England, about 20 miles N.W. of Manchester. It has been an important textile-producing center since the late 18th century and also manufactures textile machinery, television equipment, chemicals, paint, and leather goods. The surrounding region contains coal mines, which have been worked out, and limestone quarries. In Elizabethan times Blackburn was already a center of handicraft clothmaking, and was known especially for a blue and white linen fabric called "Blackburn checks". Later it also became identified with a linen and cotton textile called "Blackburn greys". The British mechanic James Hargreaves (q.v.), who is generally credited with inventing the spinning jenny, was born near Blackburn. Pop. (1967 est.) 101,910.

BLACK CANYON OF THE GUNNISON NATIONAL MONUMENT, national monument of the United States, situated in Montrose County, Colo. Established by the Federal government in 1933 and occupying about 21 sq.mi., it contains the most picturesque section of Black Canyon, the gorge of the Gunnison R. This section of the gorge is 10 mi. long and 1730 to 2425 ft. deep in the deepest part. The shortest distance between its rims is 1300 ft., and along the bottom only 40 ft. Strata of the Archean era, the oldest in geological time, and of various other eras are exposed along the walls of the canyon, and the monument is consequently of great geological interest.

BLACKCOCK, male of a species of grouse known as black grouse, *Lyrurus textrix,* common in moorlands throughout Europe. It has dark plumage and laterally curved tail feathers. In Great Britain it is known as black game, or heath cock; the female, with lighter plumage, is called gray, or brown, hen. *See* GROUSE.

BLACK CODES. *See* NEGROES IN THE UNITED STATES.

BLACK DEATH. *See* PLAGUE.

BLACK DOUGLAS. *See under* DOUGLAS: *Sir James Douglas, Lord of Douglas.*

BLACK DRAFT. *See* SENNA.

BLACKETT, Patrick Maynard Stuart, Baron Blackett (1897–1974), British physicist, born in London, England, and educated at the Royal Naval College and the University of Cambridge. After teaching at various other institutions, he served (1953–65) as professor of physics at the Imperial College of Science and Technology of the University of London. During World War II he was chief adviser on operational research to the British navy. For his discoveries in the fields of nuclear physics and cosmic rays and his work with the cloud chamber (q.v.), he was awarded the 1948 Nobel Prize in physics. In 1969 he was created a life peer. He is the author of *Atomic Weapons and East-West Relations* (1956) and *Studies of War* (1962).

BLACK-EYED PEA. *See* COWPEA.

BLACK-EYED SUSAN. *See* RUDBECKIA.

BLACKFISH, common name for any of several fishes of dark color. In the United States the name is generally used to refer to the tautog, *Tautoga onitis.* Other blackfish are a bass (q.v.), *Centropristes striatus,* of the Atlantic coast, and a minnow, *Orthodon microlepidotus,* of the Pacific coast. In England the blackfish or black ruff is a food fish, *Centrolophus niger,* common in deep waters off southern Europe. Whales of the genus *Globicephala* are called blackfish; *see* CAAING WHALE.

BLACK FLY, any of the small insects of the family Simuliidae in the order Diptera (q.v.). The adult is about ¼ in. in length, with a black body and transparent wings. Black flies are diurnal in habit and live on blood sucked from men and animals. The eggs are deposited on rocks in swift streams, and the larvae develop in running water. Adult flies first emerge in spring, and several generations are born each summer. The northern, or Adirondack, black fly is a common pest in some woods and mountains of northeastern United States. A related species of the Mississippi Valley, known as the buffalo gnat, is sometimes a serious pest to cattle. Another species, the turkey gnat of southern U.S. is injurious to poultry. *See* FLY.

BLACKFOOT, a closely related confederacy of North American Indian tribes of Algonquian (q.v.) stock, formerly roaming the northern plains region between the upper Missouri and Saskatchewan rivers. The Blackfoot consists of the Siksika or Blackfoot proper, the Kainah or Bloods, and the Piegan. The entire group is known among its members as the Bloods. The Blackfoot were noted buffalo hunters and warriors; except for growing tobacco, they did no farming; their culture and economy were thus essentially typical of those of the Plains Indians (q.v.). In modern times the Blackfoot were settled on Indian reservations in the United States and Canada and are primarily farmers and ranchers. In 1962, 5804 members of the confederacy lived on the largest of these reservations, called the Blackfoot Reservation, situated in Montana.

BLACK FOREST (Ger. *Schwarzwald*), wooded mountain region in the S.W. part of Germany, in the West German State of Baden-Württemberg. The region is about 100 mi. long, varies in width from about 14 mi. in the N. to 38 mi. in the S., and occupies an area of about 2000 sq.mi. Its name refers to the heavy stands of fir on the upper slopes, especially above the 2000-ft. level. Below this level are extensive forests of oak and beech. Maximum elevations, situated mainly in the S. portion of the region, include the Feldberg (4898 ft.) and the Herzogenhorn (4642 ft.). The highest peak of the N. part is the Hornisgrinde (3819 ft.). Near Breisach, in the district of Freiburg, is situated the isolated volcanic mass of the Kaiserstuhl. A number of rivers, including the Danube and the Neckar, rise in the Black Forest, and on its E. slope are many lakes. Mineral springs are abundant; in the region are such well-known health resorts as Baden-Baden and Wildbad. The upland plains are suitable for farming and cattle raising.

BLACK FRIARS. *See* DOMINICANS.

BLACK FRIDAY, name applied to a short-lived financial crisis in the United States that occurred on Friday, Sept. 24, 1869. The panic (*see* PANIC, FINANCIAL) was precipitated when two financial speculators, James Fisk and Jay Gould (qq.v.), attempted to corner the U.S. gold market (*see* MONOPOLY AND COMPETITION: *History*). On Sept. 20 they began purchasing gold in New York City; by Sept. 24 they controlled enough of the available supply in the city to bid up the price from about 140 to 163½. This rapid increase in the price of gold threw the stock exchange (q.v.) into confusion, and the prices of commodities fluctuated wildly. The inflationary run on gold was halted toward the close of the business day when U.S. Secretary of the Treasury George Sewall Boutwell (q.v.) announced that the Federal government had made $4,000,000 of its gold reserves available for trad-

The dense masses of fir trees of the Black Forest surround and frame a scene in Baden-Württemberg, West Germany. German Information Center

ing. According to historians, Fisk and Gould made a profit of about $11,000,000 by their manipulations, but many other businessmen claimed to have been ruined by the panic.

The name Black Friday has occasionally been applied also to the Friday of Sept. 19, 1873, when the New York Stock Exchange suffered a major financial crash which ushered in the panic of 1873.

BLACK GUM. *See* TUPELO.

BLACK HAND, name and symbol of a secret Sicilian terroristic organization active in the United States in the early 20th century. Associated with the Mafia and the Camorra (qq.v.), the cabal was particularly powerful in New York

Chief Black Hawk

City. The Black Hand symbol appeared on blackmail letters to the Italian population and became synonymous with criminal threat.

BLACK HAWK (1767–1838), English name of MA-KA-TAE-MISH-KIA-KIAK, celebrated chief of the Sauk Indians. In 1804 the Sauk and Fox Indians (*see* FOX) agreed, for an annuity of $1000, to cede to the United States their lands east of the Mississippi R. Black Hawk promptly repudiated this agreement, and during the War of 1812 (q.v.) he fought against the U.S. The cession of the disputed territory was again arranged by treaties signed in 1815 and 1816, and in 1823 the majority of the Sauk and Fox settled west of the Mississippi. When white settlers began to occupy the vacated lands, however, Black Hawk once more refused to recognize the agreement. The Indians were, moreover, suffering from hunger in their new, less fertile lands, and so, in April, 1832, they returned to the disputed territory to plant crops. The white settlers shot a peaceful emissary sent out by Black Hawk and thus began the so-called Black Hawk War; *see* INDIAN WARS. The Indians were defeated near the Wisconsin R. on July 21, 1832, and again at the Bad Axe R. on Aug. 1–2; Black Hawk surrendered on Aug. 27. The Sauk and Fox were settled soon afterward on a reservation near Fort Des Moines, Iowa, where Black Hawk died. He wrote *The Autobiography of Black Hawk* (1833).

BLACKHEAD, scaup duck; *see* BLUEBILL.

BLACK HILLS, mountainous region of the United States, in N.E. Wyoming and W. South Dakota. The average elevation of the region, which occupies an area of about 6000 sq.mi., is about 4000 ft. Harney Peak (7242 ft.) in South Dakota is the highest point. To the N.E. of Harney Peak is Mount Rushmore (6040 ft.), also in South Dakota, site of Mount Rushmore National Memorial (q.v.). The region is drained by the Belle Fourche R. and by the South Fork of the Cheyenne R. On the slopes of the Black Hills are heavy stands of timber, mainly conifers. Nearly 1900 sq.mi. of the forested areas are preserved as a national forest. The region is one of the richest gold-mining districts in the U.S. and contains a wide variety of other mineral resources, including silver, lead, copper, tin, iron, coal, petroleum, salt, mica, and gypsum.

BLACK HOLE, in astronomy and astrophysics, term applied to the shrunken remnants of a high-mass star that has collapsed under the pull of its own gravitational force; *see* ASTRONOMY; GRAVITATION; STARS. The stellar matter constituting the contracting body becomes so dense that no light or any other signal can escape and the remnants of the star exist as a "black hole" in space. A low-mass star that is dying and losing its thermal pressure contracts and becomes a white dwarf star, or undergoes a violent explosion, called supernova, scattering debris far into space. It leaves behind a dense core, composed mainly of neutrons, and is known as a neutron star; *see* NEUTRON.

BLACK HOLE, term applied during the 18th century to a small chamber in the Calcutta fort of the British East India Company. The stronghold, known as Fort William, was captured by Bengalese insurrectionists under the leadership of Siraj-ud-daula, Nawab of Bengal (1728?–1757), on June 20, 1756. According to an account of the incident written in 1758 by a leading official of the East India Company, the British garrison of 146 men was confined in a cell measuring about 18 ft. by 14 ft., with only two small windows. After a night of agony from pressure, heat, and thirst, only twenty-three prisoners survived. In February, 1757, British forces under Robert Clive (q.v.) recaptured Calcutta.

BLACKJACK, *or* TWENTY-ONE, *or* VINGT-ET-UN, *or* PONTOON, wagering card game rivaling poker (q.v.) in popularity and derived possibly from the gambling casino game of baccarat (q.v.), which was known as early as the reign of the 19th-century French king Louis Philippe (q.v.). It is played with a fifty-two-card deck by two or more persons. The object of blackjack is

The Cathedral Spires of Custer State Park, in the Black Hills of South Dakota. South Dakota State Highway Commission

to draw cards totaling exactly 21, or to come as close to this count as possible without exceeding it. Cards have point values as follows: an ace counts as either 11 or 1 at the option of the player; any picture card counts as 10; other cards count at their face value. Two forms of the game are played, one with a permanent bank, the other with a changing bank; the latter form, which is more popular for home play, is described here.

First the banker is determined by shuffling a deck and dealing out cards face up to all participants until a black jack is turned. The recipient becomes the banker. He takes the deck, shuffles it, has it cut, and shows the top card to everyone. He then places it face up at the bottom of the deck, a process known as "burning" a card. When the "burnt" card is reached in dealing, the cards must be shuffled again.

The banker deals one card face down to each player in rotation, including himself. The players look at the card dealt them and, with the exception of the banker, each places a wager from the established minimum to the maximum. The banker then may require that all bets be doubled. Any player in turn may then redouble his own bet. The wagering completed, the banker gives one more card, face up, to each player, including himself. If his own two cards are a so-called natural, that is, an ace and a picture or ten, each player pays him double the amount he wagered, except that the holder of another natural pays only his original bet. Should some other player draw a natural when the banker does not, the latter pays him double, and when the current deal ends the bank passes to the holder of the natural. The latter player may sell the bank to anyone else.

If no natural shows up after two cards have been dealt, the banker works to each player, one at a time in rotation, dealing the cards singly until the player calls a halt. Should his total count exceed 21 he immediately loses. If he stops at or under 21, the banker turns to the next player and serves him as described. When all the players have been dealt to, the banker turns up his face-down card and draws until he goes over 21 or decides to stand. If he makes 21, he collects from all players. If he goes over, he must pay all those who stood. If he stands with less, he collects from those with lower counts and pays those still in the game with higher counts. Cards used in one deal are placed on the bottom of the deck.

The banker's opponents may play "splits" at their option; that is, if their first two cards are a pair they may request that each be dealt to as a separate hand and wagered on as such. Bonuses may be played, with the dealer's opponents receiving double their bets for hitting or staying under 21 on five cards, four times their bets for doing so on six cards, and double again for each additional card. Making 21 with three sevens may also collect double.

BLACK LEAD. *See* GRAPHITE.

BLACKLEG, *or* BLACK QUARTER, *or* SYMPTOMATIC ANTHRAX, infectious disease of farm animals characterized by subcutaneous swellings, especially in the legs, and caused by a bacterium, *Clostridium chauvoei.* It is confined almost entirely to cattle, but has occurred in sheep, goats, camels, pigs, and horses. Blackleg was, until recent years, generally confused with anthrax (q.v.) and malignant edema. The disease runs its course very rapidly and is fatal in nearly all cases. Cattle between the ages of six months and four years are most susceptible. In many cases infection takes place through wounds, but more frequently results from the consumption of infected feed or drinking water. Blackleg is found in nearly all countries of the world.

BLACK LUNG DISEASE. *See* COAL: *Mine Labor and Safety*; MINING: *Mine Safety*, OCCUPATIONAL DISEASES; SILICOSIS.

BLACKMAIL, in law, criminal offense of attempting to extort money or property by threats of exposure of crime or of disreputable conduct. It is distinguished from extortion (q.v.) in its widest sense, which is the use of any means of illegal compulsion or oppressive exaction. As a rule, defense to the charge of blackmailing does not include the claim that the person threatened with exposure of criminal or shameful conduct is guilty of the offenses imputed to him or that the attempt at extortion was not successful.

BLACK MARKET, term designating the illicit sale of commodities in violation of government rationing and price fixing. The term originated in Europe during World War I, when the introduction of rationing in belligerent countries tempted some persons with access to supplies to enrich themselves by selling unrestricted quantities of rationed items at inflated prices.

Black markets are phenomena of times of crisis. They flourish only when an abnormal scarcity of essential goods may cause a government to impose rationing and price controls as a means of assuring a more equitable distribution of supplies. At such times certain consumers will pay abnormally high prices to obtain the scarce items, and some profiteers are prepared to take legal and other risks to obtain and sell these items at high prices. Black markets flourished throughout World War II but disappeared after the war as soon as the production of civilian goods returned to normal and government controls were lifted.

Illicit currency exchanges are also sometimes defined as black market operations. These black markets develop when the official exchange value of a currency is fixed at a rate that does not reflect its real exchange value; *see* FOREIGN EXCHANGE. Such a situation is an incentive for holders of foreign currencies to engage in extralegal currency exchanges rather than to use the less profitable exchanges at official rates.

BLACKMORE, Richard Doddridge (1825–1900), British novelist, born in Longworth, Berkshire, England, and educated at the University of Oxford. He wrote several volumes of poetry before the publication of his first novel, *Clara Vaughn* (1864). His reputation was established by *Lorna Doone* (1869), a historical novel with a 17th-century setting that remains his best-known work. Among Blackmore's other writings are the novels *Cradock Nowell* (1866), *Alice Lorraine* (1875), *Springhaven* (1887), and *Dariel* (1897).

BLACK MOUNTAINS, range of the Allegheny Mts., forming the highest mountain group of the Appalachian system. The Black Mts. lie mainly in Yancey and Buncombe counties, w. North Carolina, and are so called because of the dark growth of evergreens covering their summits. The highest peak, Mt. Mitchell (6684 ft.), in Yancey County, is the highest point in the State. Several other peaks in the group are more than 6500 ft. high.

BLACKMUN, Harry Andrew (1908–), American jurist, born in Nashville, Ind., and educated at Harvard University. He was admitted to the Minnesota bar in 1932, served as a law clerk in Minneapolis for one year, and practiced law there from 1934 to 1950. During that time Blackmun also taught law at various institutions in Saint Paul and Minneapolis. From 1950 to 1959 he was resident counsel at the Mayo Clinic, a private medical facility in Rochester, Minn. In 1959 he was appointed to the United States Court of Appeals for the Eighth Circuit by President Dwight D. Eisenhower. He served on the circuit court until 1970, when President Richard M. Nixon appointed him an associate justice of the Supreme Court of the United States (q.v.).

BLACK MUSLIMS, popular name for the WORLD COMMUNITY OF AL-ISLAM IN THE WEST, a predominantly black religious group in the United States. It was formerly called the Nation of Islam and was committed to black nationalism. Black Muslims await what they believe is the inevitable establishment by Allah (God) of an "Afro-American homeland" in the U.S. Meanwhile, their leaders advocate black economic cooperation leading to self-sufficiency and enjoin a strict code of behavior governing such matters as diet, dress, and interpersonal relations. Members follow some Muslim religious ritual, but they are not part of the ancient Eastern Muslim community.

History. The group's origins are found in two black self-improvement movements that began shortly before World War I: the Moorish Science Temple of America, founded (1913) by Noble Drew Ali (d. 1929); and the Universal Negro Improvement Association, founded (1914) by Marcus Garvey (q.v.). When Ali died, leadership of his movement passed to Wallace D. Fard. In 1930 Fard founded a temple (later known as a mosque) in Detroit, Mich.; that was the actual beginning of the Nation of Islam. Fard, who used a variety of names (including Walli Farad and Master Farad Muhammad), is called "God", "Allah", and "the Great Mahdi" by Black Muslims.

The branch of the Nation of Islam in Chicago, Ill., was founded in 1933. In 1934, after the mysterious disappearance of Fard, the leader of the Chicago mosque became the Nation's leader. He was Elijah Muhammad, known as the "Last Messenger of Allah", who had been born Elijah Poole in Sandersville, Ga., on Oct. 7, 1897. Until his death in Chicago on Feb. 25, 1975, Muhammad was the supreme leader of the Nation of Islam. In the 1960's his supremacy was challenged by Malcolm X (q.v.), head of the New York City mosque. But Malcolm X was shot to death in 1965 by men said to be Black Muslims.

Formerly, Black Muslims held that the white man is "the Devil", who enslaves all nonwhites. Wallace D. Muhammad (1934-), who succeeded his father Elijah Muhammad in 1975, downplayed black nationalism, admitted nonblack members, and adopted the present name. But in the late 1970's, a purist faction wanted to return to original principles.

Importance. The Black Muslims established accredited schools in forty-six cities. They sent the produce of their 15,000 acres of farmland by their own trucks and airplanes throughout the U.S. Their weekly, *Muhammad Speaks* (after 1975 *Bilalian News*), was the most widely circulated black newspaper. They rehabilitated convicts, drug addicts, and alcoholics through their "doing-for-self" philosophy. Membership in 1978 was about 200,000.

BLACK PANTHER PARTY, political organization formed in Oakland, Calif., in 1966 by cofounders Bobby George Seale (1936-), later party chairman, and Huey P. Newton (1943-), later party defense minister. The party, named for a similar group in Lowndes County, Ala., first attracted national attention in May, 1967, when a group of armed party members invaded the California State legislature to protest gun-control legislation. Originally a kind of community-action club, the party subscribed to the political theories of Chinese Communist leader Mao Tse-tung (q.v.), holding that power is obtained through violence and that the U.S. must abandon racist tendencies and capitalism, through armed rebellion if necessary. Eventually the party considered itself to be an international movement for the liberation of the oppressed peoples of the world. Reports in early 1973 estimated U.S. membership at between 500 and 700, compared to 5000 in 1967; the decline was ascribed, in part, to disagreement within the leadership. The American author (Leroy) Eldridge Cleaver (1935-), who went into political exile in 1968, headed a Black Panther Party unit in Algiers, Algeria, until January, 1972, although he was expelled by the U.S. party in 1971. The Algiers office was closed early in 1973. Also in 1973 Seale, abandoning revolutionary rhetoric for progressive programs, ran for mayor in Oakland, Calif., but lost in a runoff election.

BLACKPOOL, Great Britain, county borough of Lancashire, England, on the Irish Sea, about 30 miles N. of Liverpool. A vacation resort, its recreational facilities include an excellent bathing beach, a 7-mi. promenade, and several piers. The city is visited by several million vacationists annually. Blackpool was known as Pool Houses during the 16th century. It became a popular vacation spot in the 1780's. Pop. (1971) 151,311.

BLACK PRINCE. *See* EDWARD, known as the Black Prince.

BLACK QUARTER. *See* BLACKLEG.

BLACK RACER. *See* BLACK SNAKE.

BLACK ROT. *See* DISEASES OF PLANTS.

BLACK SEA, *or* EUXINE SEA (anc. *Pontus Euxinus*), inland sea lying between E. Europe and Asia Minor, and connected with the Aegean Sea by the Bosporus, the Sea of Marmara, and the Dardanelles. Turkey in Europe, Bulgaria, and Rumania bound it on the W. The N. and E. shores are Soviet territory and the entire S. shore is Turkish territory.

The Black Sea has a length of about 750 mi. from E. to W., a maximum width of 380 mi., and an area (excluding its N. arm, the Sea of Azov) of about 168,500 sq.mi. The Crimean Peninsula projects into the Black Sea from the N., forming the shallow Sea of Azov and the Karkinitskiy Gulf. The former is almost entirely cut off from the Black Sea, which receives the drainage of a large part of central Europe through the Dnieper, Dniester, Bug, and Danube rivers. The sea also receives waters from a considerable section of E. Russia, through the Don R. (which flows into the Sea of Azov) and from the W. Caucasus region through the Kuban and a number of smaller rivers; and it drains N. Asia Minor through the Çoruh, Yeşilirmak, Kizilirmak, and Sakarya rivers. The floor of its single central basin lies 6000 ft. below the surface and the greatest depth exceeds 7000 ft. Severe storms occur frequently on the sea, particularly during the winter season. The prevailing winter winds are N.

The Black Sea is abundantly stocked with valuable sturgeon and other fish. As an outlet for the products of the Ukrainian S.S.R. and adjoining regions, it is of special importance in Soviet commerce. The principal ports on the Black Sea are Odessa, Poti, Batumi, Kherson, Sevastopol', and Novorossiysk in the Soviet Union, Constanta in Rumania, Burgas and Varna in Bulgaria, and Ereğli, Samsun, Sinop, and Trabzon in Turkey.

The Black Sea was navigated from a very early period. Many of the colonial and commercial activities of ancient Greece and Rome, and in later times of the Byzantine Empire, centered around it. For almost three centuries after 1453, when the Ottoman Turks occupied Constantinople (now İstanbul), modern capital and last stronghold of the Byzantine Empire, the sea was virtually closed to foreign commerce. The Russian Empire began to challenge Turkish supremacy in the Black Sea early in the 18th century. By the terms of the Treaty of Paris of 1856, which ended the Crimean War (q.v.), the sea was opened to the commerce of all nations and was neutralized. In 1870 Alexander II (q.v.), Emperor of Russia, repudiated the neutralization section of the Treaty of Paris and placed a naval force in the Black Sea. A conference of European powers, held in 1871, sanctioned this action, but reaffirmed the right of the Turkish sultan to close the Dardanelles and the Bosporus to war vessels. Following the defeat of Turkey in the Russo-Turkish War of 1877–78 (*see* RUSSO-TURKISH WARS), the Russians gained important rights for their Black Sea commerce. During World War I the Russian fleet in the Black Sea was active against Turkey.

With regard to traditional Russian ambitions for control of the outlet from the Black Sea to the Mediterranean Sea, *see* DARDANELLES AND BOSPORUS STRAITS QUESTION.

BLACK SHIRTS, name applied to members of the Fascist Party (*see* FASCISM) in Italy, which, under the Italian dictator Benito Mussolini (q.v.), ruled that country from 1922 to 1943. They were so called because they wore black uniforms.

BLACK SNAKE, common name for any snake predominantly black in color, particularly two nonpoisonous snakes of the United States. **1.** *Coluber constrictor,* the common black snake or black racer, is common throughout the eastern U.S. The adult is about 6 ft. long and is uniformly black, with smooth scales of satiny luster. It preys on small warm- and cold-blooded animals and swallows them alive. The blue racer, a variety of this species common west of the Mississippi R., is bluish green above and yellow beneath. **2.** *Elaphe obsoleta,* the pilot black snake, mountain black snake, or black chicken snake, is found in the eastern U.S. Growing to about 8 ft. or more in length, it is black above and white or gray beneath, with glossy, keeled scales. Small, warm-blooded animals are its only food, and it kills them by constriction. In some localities this snake is incorrectly regarded as a chicken killer, because it is often found near chicken coops. More probably, such snakes are interested in the rats that may be in the area.

BLACKSTONE, Sir William (1723–80), British jurist and legal scholar, born in London, and educated at the University of Oxford. A pioneer in instituting courses in English law at the universities, he became the first professor of English law at Oxford in 1758. In 1770 he was appointed a justice of the Court of King's Bench and shortly thereafter a justice of the Court of Common Pleas. He spent the remainder of his life in the discharge of his judicial duties and in activity for the reform of the inhuman prison system of his day. Blackstone's most important work, the *Commentaries on the Laws of England* (4 vol., 1765–69), was used for more than a century as the foundation of all legal education in Great Britain and the United States. Today, however, the *Commentaries* are significant chiefly as a comprehensive history of English law.

BLACK STUDIES, academic curricula designed to teach the history of the American Negro, including his African origins and his contribution to and place in American life.

Interest in such curricula began early in the 20th century with the work of the historian Carter G. Woodson (q.v.). He was the founder of the Association for the Study of Negro Life and History (1915) and of the quarterly *Journal of Negro History* (1916). He was the first to offer, as early as 1915, constructive criticism of the often distorted view of Negro life presented in textbooks on American history; he was the first to suggest that unbiased courses on Negro history should be offered in all schools, segregated and mixed, throughout the United States.

During the fifty years following Woodson's pioneer efforts, some progress was made toward presenting a more realistic image of the Negro in the classroom and awakening serious interest in his art, music, and literature. Some of this was a result of the work of the emerging Negro scholars of the U.S. Prominent among these was the bibliophile Arthur Schomburg (1874–1938), whose vast collection of books, papers, works of art, and microfilms related to the American Negro was purchased by the public library of New York City in 1926 and installed as the Schomburg Collection in the Harlem branch of the library. The literary critic Alain LeRoy Locke (1886–1954) edited an early anthology of Negro writing, *The New Negro* (1925); he also wrote histories of Negro art and music. Comprehensive sociological studies of Negro life in America were the work of the educator Charles Spurgeon Johnson (1893–1956); among his books are *The Negro in American Civilization* (1930) and *Growing Up in the Black Belt* (1941). The poet and critic Sterlin Brown (1901–) wrote *Negro Poetry and Drama* and *The Negro in American Fiction* (both 1928) and was Negro affairs editor for the Federal Writers Project of the U.S. government during the 1930's. Scholarly works on the American Civil War and the ensuing period of Reconstruction were produced by the historian John Hope Franklin (1915–); these include *From Slavery to Freedom* (1947) and *Reconstruction after the Civil War* (1961). Many educators, such as Mordecai Johnson (1890–), president of Howard University for thirty years, and Benjamin E. Mays (1895–), president emeritus of Morehouse University, played leading roles in the half-century during which interest in black studies gradually increased. Organizations, including the National Association for the Advancement of Colored People (q.v.) were also active.

At San Francisco State College late in 1968, Negro student activists agitated for a black-student program, to include not only black studies but also hiring authority, whereby the black-student union would hire teachers for the black-studies department, and give a full professorship to the black professor selected to direct the department. Thenceforth such a request was usually included when black students petitioned the administration of predominantly white institutions of higher learning throughout the U.S. The demand of some student activists for complete separatism, with black-studies programs unavailable to white students, was considered by some legal experts as conflicting with existing civil-rights laws.

By 1970, some 350 American colleges and universities had instituted black-studies curricula. The programs vary in scope from single courses to the Yale University plan, announced in December, 1968, to offer an undergraduate major in Afro-American studies, leading to a B.A. degree. Courses of study offered by these institutions include black history from its American origin to the Civil War; the Negro renaissance; black culture in the U.S.; the black experience in literature before World War I; and imperialism and race; as well as courses investigating the religion, art, music, and dance of the Afro-American.

See also NEGROES IN THE UNITED STATES; NEGRO LITERATURE, AMERICAN; NEGRO ORGANIZATIONS.

BLACK-TAILED DEER, common name for a species of deer, formerly *Odocoileus columbianus,* found in the Pacific coast region between Alaska and southern California. It is called the Columbia blacktail to distinguish it from the mule deer (q.v.), although it is now considered to be of the same species (*O. hemionus*). In appearance it is similar to the mule deer, but is considerably smaller; the tail is longer, and is dark above and white beneath. The Crook blacktailed deer, *O. crooki,* is a similar species found in Arizona and New Mexico.

BLACKTHORN. *See* SLOE.

BLACK WARRIOR, river of west-central Alabama formed by the junction of the Mulberry and Locust forks, and flowing in a S.W. direction. It empties into the Tombigbee R. after a course of about 180 mi. and is navigable S. of the city of Tuscaloosa.

BLACK WATCH *or,* officially, ROYAL HIGHLAND REGIMENT, famous Scottish infantry regiment. Raised by the British army in 1725, the first companies had the duty of controlling lawlessness on the Scottish highlands. In 1739 a regiment was formed. Unlike British regulars, with their uniforms of scarlet breeches and coats, the Scots wore dark-colored tartan kilts, and so were called the Black Watch. When absorbed by the regular army the Black Watch

The female black widow spider UPI

troops were allowed to retain their traditional name and dress. The regiment was designated the 42nd or Highland Regiment in 1749; in 1758 it was renamed Royal Highland Regiment, and use of the original title, Black Watch, was also authorized. The regiment distinguished itself in many wars, notably the French and Indian War, the Napoleonic Wars (qq.v.), and both World Wars.

BLACKWELL, name of American family of woman physicians and of woman-suffrage advocates.

Elizabeth Blackwell (1821–1910), physician, born in Bristol, England, and educated at the Geneva Medical School of Geneva College (now Hobart and William Smith Colleges). She and her sister Emily (see below) were pioneers in the practice of medicine by women, and Elizabeth in 1849 became the first woman in the United States to receive the degree of Doctor of Medicine.

Elizabeth and Emily founded the New York Infirmary for Indigent Women and Children (now New York Infirmary) in New York City in 1853. This institution has always had an entirely female medical staff, and was the first such institution ever founded. A medical college for women, added in 1868, was affiliated with the Cornell University Medical College when the latter was established in New York City in 1898. Elizabeth lived in London after 1869. She was one of the founders of the National Health Society (*see* NATIONAL HEALTH INSURANCE) of London and of the London School of Medicine for Women, where she was professor of gynecology from 1875 to 1907. Among her writings are *The Physical Education of Girls* (1852) and *Pioneer Work in Opening the Medical Profession to Women* (1895).

Henry Brown Blackwell (1825–1909), editor, brother of Elizabeth Blackwell, born in Bristol, England. He was one of the first men to advocate suffrage for women. In 1855 he married the American suffragette Lucy Stone (q.v.), and together they edited the Boston *Woman's Journal* from about 1870 to 1909. Their daughter Alice Stone Blackwell (1857–1950) also worked for woman's suffrage and assisted in editing *Woman's Journal.*

Emily Blackwell (1826–1910), physician, sister of Elizabeth Blackwell, born in Bristol, England, and educated at the medical school of Western Reserve University (now Case Western Reserve University), and in Edinburgh, Paris, and London. After completing her medical studies in Europe, she returned to the United States, where she practiced medicine and cofounded the New York Infirmary for Indigent Women and Children.

BLACKWELLS ISLAND. *See* WELFARE ISLAND.

BLACK WIDOW, common name for a spider, *Latrodectus mactans,* in the family Theridiidae. Found chiefly in the tropics, it is also common in the southern States of the United States and is occasionally found as far north as New England. The body of the female black widow is about ½ in. in length and jet black in color, with a red mark, shaped like an hourglass, on the underside of the abdomen. Males of the species are smaller, about ¼ in. in length; they are rarely seen and are harmless. The female, which is poisonous to man, usually devours the male immediately after mating, thus giving rise to its common name. Its bite is followed by local pain and swelling, nausea, and difficulty in breathing, and is sometimes fatal.

Two other species of *Latrodectus* found in the U.S. are also poisonous to man. The brown or gray widow, *L. geometricus,* occurring in southern Florida and southern California, and *L. bishopi,* found in southern Florida, are both venemous. In addition the brown recluse spider, (*Loxosceles reclusus*), inhabiting Missouri, Arkansas, and Texas, is dangerous to man and is probably second to the black widow in this respect. K.A.C.

BLADDER, in anatomy, organ that stores urine after its formation by the kidneys (*see* KIDNEY). In a man it is a membranous sac that is located behind the pubic bones. It consists of three layers: a lining of mucous membrane (*see* EPITHELIUM); an intermediate layer of involuntary muscle, with fibers arranged in three layers, each running in a different direction; and an outer layer of connective tissue, covered by the peritoneum above and to the back and blending with the connective tissues of the body wall in front and below. Urine enters the bladder from the kidneys through two ureters and is discharged through the urethra. The openings of the ureters lie in the basal part of the bladder, each about 1½ in. from the opening of the urethra, which is located in the midline of the bladder at its lowest point. Average normal capacity of the adult bladder is about one pint. *See also* URINE AND THE URINARY SYSTEM.

BLADDERWORT, common name for plants comprising the family Lentibulariaceae. The most widespread genus is *Utricularia,* containing about 275 species found in temperate and tropical regions throughout the world. Species of this genus grow in a wide variety of habitats; some are aquatic and others terrestrial. A number of tropical species are air plants, resembling orchids, and are sometimes cultivated in greenhouses. Among the aquatics, some root in the mud, and others, such as *U. vulgaris,* the common bladderwort, are rootless, floating freely in ponds. The common and scientific names of the genus refer to the numerous utricles, or bladders, borne on the leaves of *U. vulgaris.*

The bladders of the common bladderwort range from 1/25 to 1/5 in. in diameter, and each has an orifice guarded by bristles. When tiny aquatic insects or other animals, including minute fish, touch these bristles, the bladder suddenly dilates, sucking in and trapping the animal. By digesting its prey, the bladderwort obtains the food that is normally obtained by plants through a root system.

Among other plants in the family are *Vesiculina purpurea,* the purple bladderwort, common in ponds in eastern United States, and various species of *Stomosia* and *Pinguicula,* none of which is aquatic.

BLAGOVESHCHENSK, city of the Soviet Union, in the Russian S.F.S.R., administrative center of Amur Oblast, on the E. bank of the Amur R., at its junction with the Zeya R., on the border with China, about 500 miles W. of Khabarovsk. The Chinese Eastern Railway of Manchuria crosses into the Soviet Union at Blagoveshchensk, connecting 70 mi. to the N.E. with the Trans-Siberian Railway. The city is an important river port and commercial center, with an extensive trade in tea, grain, and cattle. Pop. (1970 est.) 128,000.

BLAINE, James Gillespie (1830–93), American statesman, born in West Brownsville, Pa., and educated at Washington College (now Washington and Jefferson College). From 1848 to 1854 he taught mathematics, first at a military school in Kentucky and then at a school for the blind in Philadelphia, Pa. In 1854 he moved to Augusta, Maine, to become editor and part owner of the newspaper *The Kennebec Journal.* He became prominent in Maine politics and in 1859 was elected to the State legislature as a Republican, serving until 1862. From 1862 to 1876 he was a member of the United States House of Representatives, serving as Speaker from 1869 to 1875. In the postwar years Blaine favored a strict policy of Reconstruction (q.v.) but opposed some of the most radical measures proposed by Congressman Thaddeus Stevens (q.v.) and his followers, who were especially vindictive toward the South. Economically, Blaine advocated railroad subsidies, high protective tariffs, and a hard-money policy.

Blaine sought the Republican Presidential nomination in 1876. Prior to the Republican National Convention, however, he was summoned before a House investigating committee to explain a series of letters, the so-called Mulligan Letters, which allegedly proved that Blaine had used his congressional influence to promote

Bladderwort, Utricularia vulgaris — Hugh Spencer – National Audubon Society

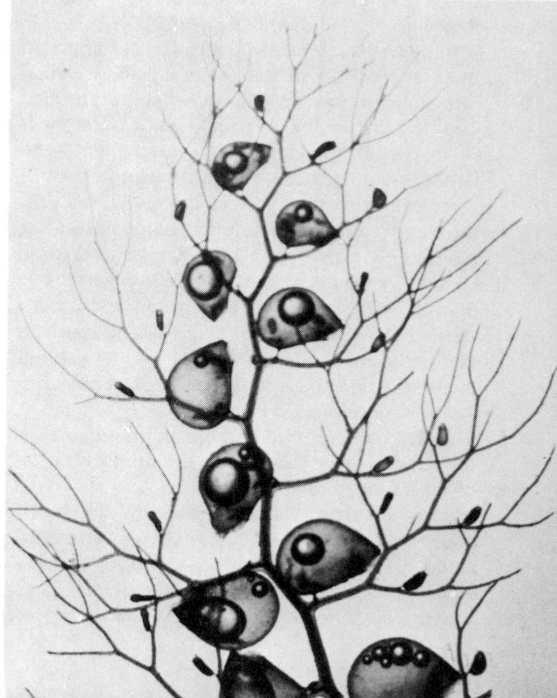

certain railroad interests for his personal gain. In spite of his efforts to vindicate himself he lost the nomination.

After the 1876 election, Blaine was appointed to fill a vacancy in the United States Senate and was subsequently elected to the seat. In 1880 he was again defeated for the Republican Presidential nomination by James Abram Garfield (q.v.), who won the election and appointed Blaine secretary of state. Several months later Garfield was killed by an assassin, and the Presidency passed to Chester Alan Arthur (q.v.). Arthur, who owed his position to Roscoe Conkling (q.v.), a political enemy of Blaine, induced Blaine to resign from the cabinet in December, 1881.

At the Republican convention of 1884 Blaine finally won the Presidential nomination and ran against Democrat Stephen Grover Cleveland (q.v.). After one of the fiercest campaigns in U.S. history, Blaine lost the election. Some historians have attributed his defeat to his tainted public image, which seems to have cost him the support of the independent Republicans, called Mugwumps (q.v.), and to a speech made on Blaine's behalf by the American Protestant clergyman Samuel Dickinson Burchard (1812–91). Burchard offended Irish Catholic voters in New York by characterizing the Democrats as "the party whose antecedents are rum, Romanism, and rebellion". Other historians, however, maintain that the Democratic Party would have had a resurgence in 1884 regardless of who the Republican candidate had been.

In 1889 Blaine received his second appointment as secretary of state from President Benjamin Harrison (q.v.). While in office he presided over the first of the Pan-American Conferences (q.v.). He also concluded an agreement with Great Britain to submit to arbitration a controversy over the right of Canada to catch seals off the American-owned Pribilof Islands (*see* BERING SEA CONTROVERSY). In 1892 Blaine was favored by some Republicans for the Republican Presidential nomination; this circumstance caused a strain on his relations with President Harrison and led to Blaine's resignation from the cabinet in June. A few days later the Republican convention renominated Harrison.

BLAIR, name of three American politicians, father and sons, active during the administration of President Abraham Lincoln (q.v.).

Francis Preston Blair (1791–1876), journalist and politician, born in Abingdon, Va., and educated at Transylvania University (now Transylvania College). A leader of the Democratic Party (q.v.), Blair was (1828–37) one of the group of advisers to President Andrew Jackson (q.v.) who were known as the kitchen cabinet. He founded and edited (1830–49) the newspaper the *Washington Globe* and cofounded (1834) the *Congressional Globe,* now known as the *Congressional Record* (q.v.). Active in the antislavery movement, Blair was a founder of the Republican Party (q.v.) and presided (1856) over its first convention. In 1864 Blair, with the consent of President Abraham Lincoln, conducted inconclusive private negotiations with Jefferson Davis (q.v.), president of the Confederate States of America (q.v.) in an attempt to end the Civil War (*see* CIVIL WAR, THE AMERICAN). During the administration of President Andrew Johnson (q.v.), Blair opposed the policies of Reconstruction (q.v.) and later rejoined the Democratic Party (q.v.).

Montgomery Blair (1813–83), lawyer and public official, son of Francis Preston (1791–1876), born in Franklin County, Ky. He was educated at the United States Military Academy and Transylvania University (now Transylvania College). While engaged in the practice of law in Missouri, Blair argued several cases before the Supreme Court of the United States; most notably he served as chief defense counsel in the Dred Scott case (q.v.). He became postmaster general in the cabinet of President Abraham Lincoln in 1861, and was responsible for such innovations as money orders, prepayment of postage by the sender, free rural delivery, and the sorting of mail on railway cars. Blair was forced to resign from the cabinet in 1864 because of his opposition to the radical leaders of the Republican Party. He later supported the Democratic Party.

Francis Preston Blair (1821–75), political and military leader, brother of Montgomery Blair, born in Lexington, Ky., and educated at Princeton University and Transylvania University (now Transylvania College). Active in the antislavery movement, Blair left the Democratic Party to help found (1848) the Free-Soil Party (q.v.). He served in the Missouri State legislature (1852–56) and in the United States House of Representatives (1857–59; June, 1860; 1861–62; January to June, 1864). He later returned to the Democratic Party, serving as Vice-Presidential candidate (1868), as Missouri State legislator (1870), and United States Senator (1871–73). Meanwhile, Blair had raised seven regiments of troops from Missouri for the Union army in the Civil War. Commissioned a major general he served with distinction in the Vicksburg, Chattanooga, and Atlanta (qq.v.) campaigns; *see* CIVIL WAR, THE AMERICAN.

BLAISE. *See* BLASIUS.

BLAKE, Edward (1833–1912), Canadian statesman, born in Middlesex Co., Ont., and educated at Upper Canada College and the University of Toronto. As a member of the Liberal Party he served from 1867 to 1872 in both the Ontario legislature and the Canadian House of Commons. He was premier of Ontario from 1871 to 1872; in the latter year a new law made it mandatory that he give up either his provincial offices or his seat in the House of Commons. Blake retained his House membership for the next two decades and was a minister in the government of Alexander Mackenzie (q.v.), whom he succeeded as leader of the Liberal Party of Canada in 1880. In 1891 he went to Ireland where, in 1892, he was elected to the British House of Commons as Nationalist member for South Longford. He served until 1907, when he retired to Canada.

BLAKE, Eugene Carson (1906–), American Protestant leader, born in Saint Louis, Mo., and educated at Princeton University, at New College of the University of Edinburgh, Scotland, and at Princeton Theological Seminary. In 1928–29 he taught at Forman Christian College, Lahore (then in India, now in Pakistan). He was minister of Presbyterian churches in Albany, N.Y., from 1935 to 1940, and Pasadena, Calif., from 1940 to 1951. He served as stated clerk of the General Assembly of the Presbyterian Church in the United States of America from 1951 to 1958 and of the United Presbyterian Church, a successor body, from 1958 to 1966. Dr. Blake was president of the National Council of the Churches of Christ in the United States of America (q.v.) from 1954 to 1957. He was a delegate to the assemblies of the World Council of Churches (q.v.) in Evanston, Ill., in 1954 and in New Delhi, India, in 1961, and was secretary-general of the council from 1966 until his retirement in 1972.

BLAKE, Robert (1599–1657), English admiral, born in Bridgwater, and educated at the University of Oxford. In the Civil War between Parliamentarians and Royalists (*see* GREAT REBELLION), he commanded the Parliamentary fleet of the English soldier and statesman Oliver Cromwell (q.v.), which defeated and sank, in 1650, most of the Royalist fleet in the Mediterranean Sea. In 1652 and 1653, during the naval war brought on by English economic restrictions aimed at Dutch trade, Blake commanded the English forces that won a series of notable victories over the Dutch navy, including a fleet commanded by the famous Dutch admiral Maarten Harpertszoon Tromp (q.v.). These victories led to the breaking of Dutch naval supremacy. In 1657, during a war with Spain over English seizure of Jamaica in the West Indies, Blake won a notable victory over the Spanish West Indian fleet. He was a member of both the Short Parliament and the Barebone's Parliament (q.v.).

William Blake (self-portrait) Bettmann Archive

BLAKE, William (1757–1827), British poet and artist, born in London, England, and largely self-trained. He began writing poetry at the age of twelve, and at fourteen was apprenticed to a London engraver by his father. Blake began to earn his living as an engraver at the age of twenty-one, and for the remainder of his life, he supported himself mainly by illustrating books. His first literary work, *Poetical Sketches* (1783), is a collection of verse written before he reached the age of twenty-one. In his mature literary and artistic work he is concerned principally with describing and interpreting visions that he claimed to have experienced of God, Jesus Christ, angels, and the spirits of great men of earlier times. Thus, his engravings, book illustrations, and paintings are characterized by a lack of realistic detail and an infusion of supernatural subject matter with intense, mystical emotion. His early poetry is notable for great purity and simplicity of diction, and for naïve, almost childlike eloquence; in his mature work, these lyrical qualities give way to power and grandeur, designed to express his complex personal theology.

Among Blake's poetic works are *Songs of Innocence* (1789), *Songs of Experience* (1794), and the *Prophetic Books,* a series of volumes published between 1793 and 1804, in which he described a new system of Christianity revealed to him in his visions. A prose work, *The Marriage of Heaven and Hell,* also belongs to the last-named group. Among Blake's notable color prints and watercolors are "The Day of Judgment", "Nebuchadnezzar", etchings for his symbolic poem *Jerusalem,* and watercolors to illustrate the Old Testament Book of Job. Blake died in obscurity and poverty, but time has brought a heightened appreciation of both his poetry and his graphic art.

BLAKELOCK, Ralph Albert (1847–1919), American painter, born in New York City, and largely self-trained as an artist. Blakelock is best known for his paintings of forest scenes and primitive American Indian life, and during the latter part of his life was considered one of the foremost American landscape painters. His work was not appreciated during his early career, however, and it brought meager financial returns. From 1901 to 1916 he was confined for mental illness. During this period, however, his reputation steadily increased. Among his paintings are "Sunset" (National Gallery of Art, Washington, D.C.), "Colorado Plains" (Corcoran Gallery, Washington, D.C.), "Brook by Moonlight" (Toledo Art Museum), and "Pipe Dance" (Metropolitan Museum of Art, New York City).

BLALOCK, Alfred (1899–1964), American surgeon, born in Culloden, Ga. He received an M.D. degree (1922) from Johns Hopkins University. From 1925 to 1941 he was resident surgeon at Vanderbilt University Hospital and held professorships at the university medical school. While at Vanderbilt, his discovery that surgical shock often resulted from the loss of blood led to the general use of transfusions and plasma infusions. In 1941, Blalock returned to Johns Hopkins as surgeon in chief at the university hospital, where he and Helen Brooke Taussig (q.v.) developed an operation for the relief of the so-called blue-baby condition caused by a malformation of the heart. The operation, first performed in 1944, has saved thousands of "blue babies" from invalidism or death.

BLAMEY, Sir Thomas Albert (1884–1951), Australian soldier, born in Wagga Wagga, New South Wales. In 1914 he became a member of the general staff of the Australian Imperial Forces (A.I.F.). During World War I he served on the Turkish front and in 1918 became brigadier general and chief of staff of the Australian Corps. He was made chief of staff of the A.I.F. in 1919 and in 1926 attained the rank of major general. As lieutenant general, Blamey commanded the A.I.F. in the Middle East from 1940 to 1942, during World War II, and for part of this period was deputy commander in chief of all British forces in the Middle Eastern area. From 1942 to 1945 he served as commander in chief of the Allied ground forces in the southwest Pacific. In 1950 Blamey became the first Australian to attain the rank of field marshal.

BLANC, Louis, in full JEAN JOSEPH CHARLES LOUIS BLANC (1813–82), French socialist leader and historian, born in Madrid, Spain, and educated in Paris. He contributed to various political periodicals and in 1839 he established the magazine *Revue du Progrès* as an organ for his socialist doctrines. In general Blanc's concept of the social order anticipated later theorists in declaring that the workers could solve their problems only by revolutionary action and in formulating the social principle, later adopted by the German revolutionist Karl Marx (q.v.), "to each according to his needs, from each according to his abilities". Blanc believed that this principle could be realized through the creation of "social workshops", associations of workers financed by the state and controlled by the workers.

In the revolution of 1848 Blanc became a leader of the provisional republican government which came to power following the abdication of King Louis Philippe (q.v.). After the bloody suppression of the uprising of workers of Paris, in June, 1848, however, he was forced to flee for his life, and lived for twenty-two years in exile in England. During his exile he wrote a 12-volume *Historie de la Révolution Française* ("History of the French Revolution", 1847–62). Following the fall of the Second Empire in 1870 Blanc returned to France and was elected a member of the National Assembly in February, 1871, but opposed the more extreme measures adopted by the Paris Commune; *see* COMMUNE OF 1871. He was a member of the Chamber of Deputies under the constitution of 1875 from 1876 until his death. Blanc is the author of *De l'Organisation du Travail* (1840; Eng. trans., *Organization of Work,* 1911) and *Histoire de Dix Ans, 1830–1840* (5 vol., 1841–44; Eng. trans., *The History of Ten Years, 1830–1840,* 1844–45). *See* FRANCE: *History: Reign of Louis Philippe.*

BLANCA PEAK, mountain of south-central Colorado, in the Sangre de Cristo range of the

Rocky Mts., about 8 miles S.E. of Great Sand Dunes National Monument (q.v.). It is 14,317 ft. high and is one of the highest mountains in the State.

BLANCHARD, Jean Pierre, known also as FRANÇOIS BLANCHARD (1753–1809), French aeronaut, born in Les Andelys. In 1784, a few months after the first manned balloon ascent by the French physicist Jean Pilâtre de Rozier (1756–85), Blanchard made a successful ascent in his own balloon. In 1785 he and John Jeffries (1744–1819), an American physician, made the first aerial crossing of the English Channel from Dover to Calais by balloon. In the same year Blanchard gave the first successful demonstration of the use of a parachute (q.v.); a basket containing a dog (or cat) was dropped from a balloon and parachuted to earth. In 1793 on a visit to the United States Blanchard made the first American balloon ascent in Philadelphia. *See* BALLOON: *History*.

BLANCHE OF CASTILE. *See* LOUIS IX, King of France.

BLANC, MONT (It. Monte Bianco), mountain mass in the W. Alps, on the French-Italian border. The highest peak of the Alps, also called Mont Blanc, is part of this mountainous area, which in geology is known as a massif. The peak is situated in the Haute-Savoie Department of France and is one of the highest points (15,771 ft.) in Europe. The entire massif forms part of the Savoy range. From the summit down to about the 8000-ft. level its slopes are covered by an icecap that is more than 75 ft. thick. On the lower slopes are a number of glaciers, notably Mer de Glace on the Northern slope. The first ascent of Mont Blanc was accomplished in 1786.

BLANCO, Antonio Guzmán. *See* VENEZUELA: *History*.

BLAND, James A. (1854–1911), American Negro minstrel and songwriter, born in Flushing, N.Y., and educated at Howard University. He gained considerable fame as a minstrel, especially in Great Britain, where he performed from 1882 to 1901. Bland composed several hundred songs, primarily for the minstrel shows in which he appeared. Some of his most famous songs are "Oh, Dem Golden Slippers", "In the Evening by the Moonlight", and "Carry Me Back to Old Virginny", which was adopted as the State song of Virginia.

BLAND, Richard Parks (1835–99), American legislator, born near Hartford, Ky., and educated in law. He began to practice law in Utah in 1860, and after 1873 served as a Democratic member of the United States House of Representatives from Missouri; he held this office continuously, with the exception of two years, until his death. An ardent advocate of free silver coinage, he introduced in 1878 a bill to restore silver as legal tender and require the U.S. Treasury to purchase and coin a certain amount monthly. This bill, which became known as the Bland-Allison Act, marks an important phase in American monetary policy (*see* BIMETALLISM). It remained in force until 1890, when the enactment of the Sherman Silver Law ended this policy of limited coinage.

BLANKETFLOWER. *See* GAILLARDIA.

BLANK VERSE, in versification, unrhymed lines, typically containing five feet (or measures), each foot having two syllables, with the accent usually on the second. Such lines, known technically as unrhymed iambic pentameter, are one of the most widely used forms in English poetry. Blank verse is especially effective in narrative poems and verse plays. The earliest appearance in English literature dates from the early 16th century, when the poet Henry Howard, Earl of Surrey, used it in his translation of the Latin epic the *Aeneid* (q.v.) by the Roman poet Vergil. It is used in the plays of the English dramatist Christopher Marlowe, and was perfected by William Shakespeare, principally in his tragedies. Among the greatest blank-verse poems in English literature is *Paradise Lost* by John Milton. Outstanding American poets who wrote in blank verse include Edwin Arlington Robinson and Robert Lee Frost. *See* VERSIFICATION; *see also* the articles on the individual authors mentioned.

BLANQUI, Louis Auguste (1805–81), French revolutionist, brother of the French economist Jérôme Adolphe Blanqui (1798–1854), born in Puget-Théniers. After studying law and medicine he joined the revolutionary movement in Paris and during his life participated in every revolutionary movement in France, becoming one of the first so-called professional revolutionaries. He took an active part in the overthrow in 1830 of King Charles X (*see* CHARLES: *France*). Blanqui subsequently agitated against the reactionary policies of Charles' successor Louis Philippe (q.v.). In May, 1839, after helping to organize an unsuccessful insurrection against the government, Banqui was arrested and condemned to life imprisonment. Pardoned early in 1848, he participated in the February Revolution, which was one of the immediate causes of Louis Philippe's abdication, and in the left-wing attempt (May, 1848) to overthrow the newly elected Constituent Assembly. He received a ten-year prison sentence for his part in the May, 1848, uprising. During his confinement in prison he studied socialist political philosophy and developed the theory of the dictatorship of the proletariat, a concept of revolutionary strategy that later strongly influenced the Russian communist leader Vladimir Ilich Lenin (q.v.).

Blanqui continued his revolutionary activities after his release (1859) from prison, and in 1861 was sentenced to jail for four years on charges of instigating a riot. In 1870 an armed force of revolutionary workers under his command figured decisively in the uprising that led to the establishment of the Third Republic. He and his followers opposed the conservatism of the government of the Third Republic and took part in the insurrection of March, 1871, which resulted in the formation of the Paris Commune (*see* COMMUNE OF PARIS, 1871). After the defeat of the Commune he was again sentenced to imprisonment for life, but was released in 1879. His most important work is *Critique Sociale* ("Social Criticism", posthumously published, 1885), a collection of writings on politics and economics.

BLANTYRE, city in Malawi, and administrative center of both the Southern Region and Blantyre District, on the Mudi R., 37 miles S.W. of Zomba. It is the largest city of Malawi and the transportation and trade center of the Shiré Highlands. Blantyre has government offices and several technical schools. The district produces tobacco, corn, coffee, tung oil, and wheat. The city, founded in 1876 by Scottish missionaries, was named for the birthplace of the explorer David Livingstone (q.v.). One of the oldest European settlements in the British dependencies of central Africa, Blantyre became a township in 1895, was combined as the municipality of Blantyre-Limbe in 1959, and became a city in 1966 when Limbe was incorporated into Blantyre. Pop. (1966) 109,795.

BLARNEY, village of the Republic of Ireland, in County Cork, about 5 miles N.W. of the city of Cork. Textile manufacturing is the chief industry. The town is the site of Blarney Castle, constructed about the middle of the 15th century and containing the so-called Blarney Stone, an inscribed slab near the top of one of the walls. According to legend, one who kisses the stone is thereupon endowed with the gift of eloquence and persuasive flattery. Large numbers of tourists visit Blarney Castle to see and kiss the stone. Pop. (1972 est.) 3586.

BLASCO IBÁÑEZ, Vicente. *See* IBÁÑEZ, VICENTE BLASCO.

BLASHFIELD, Edwin Howland (1848–1936), American painter, born in New York City, and trained under the French painter Léon Joseph Florentin Bonnat (q.v.). He is known especially for his genre paintings and his murals. Among his works are murals in the Library of Congress, Washington, D.C., and in the capitols of several States, including Wisconsin and Iowa. In collaboration with his wife he wrote *Italian Cities* (1900–13); his other writings include *Mural Painting in America* (1913).

BLASIUS, Saint *or* **BLAISE, Saint** (d. 316), early Christian martyr. He was bishop of Sebaste (now Sivas, Turkey). When the Roman emperor Licinius (270?–325) began to persecute the Christians, Blasius fled, but was captured. For refusing to deny his faith in Jesus Christ, he was flayed with wool-combing hooks, and finally beheaded. During ancient and medieval times Blasius was widely venerated, and his cultus is still popular. Because he saved the life of a child who was choking on a fishbone, he is invoked against diseases of the throat. He is regarded as the patron saint of wool combers because of the method of his martyrdom. In the Roman Catholic Church his feast day is Feb. 3; in the Orthodox churches it is Feb. 11.

BLASPHEMY, in common law, crime of speaking or publishing words that vilify or ridicule God, the Bible, or religious beliefs. It is a misdemeanor (q.v.) and two reasons formerly underlay its being a crime: (1) it tended to cause a breach of the peace between the blasphemer and those outraged by his words, and (2) because Christianity was a part of common law, blasphemy tended to undermine the law. Today only the first remains, for Christianity is no longer a part of the law. The manner rather than the content of the utterance or publication renders it blasphemous; a serious statement of opinion, however heretical (*see* HERESY) to a religion, is not punishable as blasphemy. Thus, scurrility and a resultant tendency to provoke a public disturbance are the criteria of blasphemy, and statutes condemning it are generally held to be in consonance with the laws that protect freedom of speech and religion (*see* RELIGIOUS LIBERTY; SPEECH, FREEDOM OF). Although blasphemy is still a crime in Great Britain and in a number of the States of the United States, prosecutions for the offense are now rare. *See* COMMON LAW; *see also* CRIME.

BLAST FURNACE, ore-refining furnace operating on the principle that a blast of air forced through a molten ore burns away unwanted impurities or converts them to insoluble slag, which can then be skimmed off. The name is usually restricted to metallurgical furnaces for the reduction of ores, and in particular to the furnace used for the manufacture of pig iron from iron ore. *See* ELECTROTHERMIC FURNACE; IRON AND STEEL MANUFACTURE; METALLURGY.

View of blast furnace, Pueblo, Colo. C F & I Steel Corp.

BLASTING, the use of explosives for the breaking, splitting, or loosening of massive bodies, such as rock, ore, tree stumps, and subsurface clay layers, or for the displacement of dirt or rock in such construction excavations as canals, channels, and foundations. The operation consists of (1) boring or excavating a hole to contain the explosive; (2) charging, or loading the explosive into the blast hole; (3) tamping, or filling the blast hole so as to confine and direct the force of the explosion; and (4) exploding the charge.

The first recorded use of blasting in mining operations dates from 1613, when German miners were reported as using both drilling and blasting. In 1670 blasting was introduced into England, and in 1724 into Sweden. The introduction in 1831 of the uniformly slow-burning "safety fuse" contributed greatly to the safety of blasting operations, and in the same year an American inventor was granted a patent on a method of exploding several blasting charges simultaneously by means of electrically fired blasting caps. In modern blasting practice, multiple charges are initiated by a safety fuse (burning at a rate of about 1 foot per minute) and connected by a detonating fuse (120 feet per second), or by an interconnected set of electric blasting caps fired by a single magneto or blasting machine.

The Atomic Energy Commission, under its "Plowshare" program established in 1958, is studying the use of nuclear explosions for blasting. There has been some speculation on the feasibility of using nuclear explosives to aid in the digging of a proposed sea-level canal across Central America. In May, 1973, the A.E.C. exploded three atomic bombs about 6000 ft. beneath the Western Slope in Colorado, creating a cavity of about 850 ft. by 140 ft. into which natural gas trapped in the surrounding sandstone was expected to seep over the next few decades. *See* GAS: *Natural Gas.*

BLATTARIAE, BLATTELA, *and* **BLATTIDAE.** *See* COCKROACH.

BLAVATSKY, Elena Petrovna (1831–91), Russian founder of theosophy (q.v.) born in Ekaterinoslav (now Dnepropetrovsk). After 1848 she traveled extensively. She became interested in spiritism and the occult during visits to India and Tibet. With the American theosophist Henry Steel Olcott (1832–1907) she founded the Theosophical Society in New York City in 1875, and established a branch of the organization in Bombay, India, in 1879. Through her demonstrations of psychic phenomena she won many followers in all parts of the world. In 1884 investigators of the Society for Psychical Research, a British organization, exposed many of her demonstrations as fraudulent. She wrote books on the esoteric doctrines of India, including *Isis Unveiled* (1877), *Key to Theosophy* (1889), and *Voice of Silence* (1889).

BLEACHING, process of whitening or removing the natural color of textile fibers and fabrics by treatment with chemicals or by exposure to the sun and weather. Chemically, the process of bleaching involves the change of a colored compound to a substance of little or no color. Many pigments and dyes are affected in this way by oxidizing agents (*see* OXIDATION); hence substances such as chlorine, hydrogen peroxide, and ozone (qq.v.) are most commonly used as bleaches. Heat, ultraviolet light, alkali, or any other agent producing chemical change may also act as a bleach. Many pigments and colored substances can also be decolorized by means of a reducing agent. This is the mode of action of sulfur dioxide when used as a bleaching agent.

The method of bleaching by exposure to the rays of the sun was practiced during ancient and medieval times in Egypt, China, and the countries of Asia Minor and Europe. In the 18th century bleaching solutions of potash and lye and of dilute sulfuric acid (q.v.) were used in Holland and France, and in 1785 the powerful bleaching properties of chlorine were discovered by the French chemist Comte Claude Louis Berthollet (q.v.). Bleaching powder, a solid chemical with the same action as the gas chlorine, came into use in 1799, and continued to be used as the standard bleaching agent until about 1920. Since that time the use of liquefied chlorine has increased, and new bleaching agents have been introduced, such as high-test hypochlorite (HTH), which has two to three times the effectiveness of bleaching powder.

Liquid bleach is a solution of sodium hypochlorite. The liquid bleach commonly sold in supermarkets for household use usually contains 5.25 g of available chlorine, that is, of effective oxidizing power, per 100 mm of solution. Solid bleach, or bleaching powder, contains 35 to 37 percent available chlorine, 10 to 15 percent water, and several percent of free calcium hydroxide. Bleaching powder was the most widely used bleach in the textile industry between 1800 and 1925. Most mills then changed over to the use of sodium hypochlorite, or liquid bleach, until about 1947 when they changed to hydrogen peroxide. The latter is presently the most widely used bleach for cotton cloth.

Chlorine dioxide is the bleaching agent most widely used in the pulp and paper industry, and is also the main bleach used for polyesters and acrylic fibers, as well as for blends of synthetics and cotton. Sodium hydrosulfite (sodium dithionate) is a reducing agent widely used for bleaching wool. So-called optical bleaches, now in widespread use, are not bleaching agents at all. They are substances which are deposited on textile fibers and serve to fluoresce, that is, to change ultraviolet light into blue or blue-green light, thus making the textile appear brighter to the eye.

BLEAK, common name for a European freshwater fish of the genus *Alburnus,* in the Carp family (Ciprinidae). Slim and minnowlike, it is usually about 6 in. long, with dark back and silvery side scales. It is popular with anglers as bait, and its scales are used in the manufacture of artificial pearls.

BLEEDING, *or* HEMORRHAGE, discharge of blood from blood vessels due to pathological conditions of the vessels, or traumatic rupture of one or more vessels. Toxic damage of bacterial or chemical origin may lead to the escape of blood into the skin, mucous membranes, or body cavities.

Hemorrhage is a frequent complication of many diseases. Peptic ulcer (*see* ULCER: *Peptic Ulcer*), for example, may cause gastric hemorrhage by eroding a blood vessel. Tuberculosis (q.v.) often leads to pulmonary hemorrhage. Apoplectic stroke (*see* STROKE) is usually due to hemorrhage in the brain, generally as a result of high blood pressure (q.v.). Hemorrhage is often the immediate cause of death in many forms of cancer. Hemorrhage is also the most frequent fatal complication of childbirth. Hemophilia (q.v.), a hereditary blood disease usually confined to males, is characterized by abnormal, uncontrollable bleeding, because of the failure of the blood to coagulate. Loss of one to three quarts of blood may lead to shock (q.v.), and unless the blood is replaced by transfusion, shock is often fatal; *see* BLOOD: *Blood Transfusion.*

Bleeding normally stops through the process of clotting of the blood, and methods used to stop hemorrhage depend on stanching the flow of blood sufficiently for a clot to form. In arterial bleeding (characterized by a pulsating stream of bright-red blood) it may be necessary to apply a ligature or tourniquet, which is seldom required in venous bleeding (a steady stream of dark, bluish-red blood). In either case the most direct method of stopping the hemorrhage is the application of pressure directly over the wound, preferably by means of a sterile dressing. Bleeding is also controlled through reducing the blood pressure by placing the patient in a recumbent position or by the use of drugs. Modern methods of controlling bleeding depend largely on increased understanding of the clotting mechanism. Thus, vitamin K is often administered to a patient, particularly before an operation, to minimize the danger of hemorrhage; *see* VITAMIN: *Vitamin K.* Fibrin film and fibrin foam, plastics made from the blood protein fibrinogen, are extensively used in surgery. Fibrin foam is used in the form of a surgical sponge that rapidly stops bleeding by forming clots. Fibrin film is used to wrap nerves or tendons or as a membrane to cover the brain or other organs. Either fibrin foam or fibrin film may be left, without harm, in the body, where it slowly dissolves.

BLEEDING HEART. See DICENTRA.

BLENDE. See SPHALERITE.

BLENHEIM, BATTLE OF, battle of the War of the Spanish Succession (*see* SPANISH SUCCESSION, WAR OF THE), fought on Aug. 13, 1704, near the village of Blenheim, Bavaria (now Blindheim, West Germany), 23 miles N.W. of Augsburg. Anglo-Austrian forces, led by the British military leader John Churchill, 1st Duke of Marlborough, and the Austrian general Eugene, Prince of Savoy (qq.v.), defeated the French and Bavarians under the French marshal Camille de Tallard (1652–1728) and Maximilian II Emanuel, Elector of Bavaria (1662–1726). The British and Austrian casualties were 4500 killed and 7500 wounded. The French and Bavarians lost a large but undetermined number; 11,000 were taken prisoner. After this defeat French military domination of Europe began to decline.

BLENNY, common name for small, spiny-rayed fishes of the family Blenniidae and related families, found in the seas of all parts of the world. Some blennies are able to use their ventral fins to aid them in moving about, out of water, among rocks and seaweeds. Many blennies of the family retain their eggs within the oviduct until they are hatched, so that the young are produced alive and capable of seeking their own food, which consists mainly of small crustaceans. Blennies are of little value as food.

BLÉRIOT, Louis (1872–1936), French engineer and pioneer aviator, born in Cambrai and educated at the École Centrale des Arts et Métiers. After designing and building various types of experimental aircraft, he concentrated on developing the monoplane, which has a single set of wings, as opposed to the biplane, which has two sets of wings. Most modern airplanes are monoplanes. *See* AIRPLANE: *Airplane Structure: Wings.* On July 25, 1909, he flew from Calais, France, to Dover, England, in one of his monoplanes, becoming the first aviator to cross the English Channel in a heavier-than-air machine. During World War I Blériot's factory produced about 10,000 airplanes for the armed forces of France and the other Allied powers.

BLESBOK, common name for a South African antelope, *Damaliscus albifrons,* closely related to the bontebok (*D. pygargus*). Both species are marked by a large, white spot on the forehead that in the blesbok is divided by a dark bar between the eyes. The blesbok is slightly smaller than the bontebok and has greenish, rather than black, horns. The coats of both species have a shining, purplish luster. Both the blesbok and the bontebok formerly roamed South Africa in enormous herds, the bontebok being restricted to the southern tip of the continent. They are now almost extinct; a few small herds raised on farms are the sole survivors.

See also ANTELOPE.

BLESSING. *See* BENEDICTION.

BLEULER, Eugen (1857–1939), Swiss psychiatrist, born near Zürich, and educated at the University of Bern. He was one of the first to accept psychoanalysis (q.v.), originated by the Austrian psychiatrist Sigmund Freud (q.v.). In the field of psychiatry he was noted for his conception of schizophrenia (*see* MENTAL DISORDERS: *Psychoses*), which he considered to be a split between the emotional life of the patient and his faculty of reasoning. Bleuler's writings include *Dementia Praecox, or the Group of Schizophrenias* (1911; Eng. trans., 1950) and *Textbook of Psychiatry* (1920).

BLICHER, Steen Steensen (1782–1848), Danish lyric poet and novelist, born in Vium, near Viborg, Jutland, and educated in theology at the University of Copenhagen. Blicher's earliest work was a translation into Danish (1807–09) of the Ossian poems of the British poet James Macpherson (q.v.). Blicher's own poems and novels at first attracted little attention, but his later work, particularly that written after 1826, won him a nation-wide reputation. He is best known for his sympathetic and humorous telling of the folk tales, legends, and simple peasant chronicles of his native province, notably in the poems and stories written in the Jutland dialect and collectively entitled *The Knitting Room* (1842). His collected tales and sketches were published in thirty-three volumes (1920–34).

BLIDA, town in Algeria, on a tributary of the Chéliff R., at the base of the Atlas Mts., about 25 miles S. of Algiers. Blida is the trading center for the surrounding region in which oranges and wheat are grown. Industries in the city include the manufacture of building materials, flour products, and olive oil. The city was founded in the 16th century, and was occupied by the French in 1839. In 1942 during World War II United States forces captured the nearby airfield. Pop. (1967 est.) 87,000.

BLIGH, William (1754–1817), British naval officer, born in Plymouth, England. He sailed under the British explorer and navigator James Cook (q.v.) on Cook's second voyage around the world (1772–75). In 1787 Bligh was sent by the British government to Tahiti as commander of the *Bounty* (q.v.). His crew mutinied, and on April 28, 1789, set him adrift in an open boat with eighteen loyal men. After tremendous hardship, Bligh arrived at the island of Timor, near Java, on June 14, having sailed 3618 mi. In 1805 he was appointed governor of New South Wales, Australia, but the colonists were dissatisfied with his harsh rule, and in 1808 the civil and military officers of the colony rebelled and arrested him. Bligh was imprisoned for two years and was sent back to England under arrest. He was, however, exonerated, and the mutineers found guilty at the subsequent inquiry. After Bligh's return to England he was raised to the rank of rear admiral (1811) and then to that of vice admiral (1814).

BLIGHT. *See* DISEASES OF PLANTS.

BLIMP. *See* AIRSHIP.

BLIND. *See* BLINDNESS.

BLIND, AIDS FOR THE. The earliest recorded instance of organized aid for the blind was the foundation of a hospice for the blind by Saint Basil in Cappadocia in the 4th century A.D. Since that time many hospitals and asylums for the blind have been established; not until the close of the 18th century, however, was any organized effort made to provide the blind with education, books, rehabilitation, or training in an appropriate occupational field.

Education. The first school for the blind was founded by the French educator Valentin Haüy (1745–1822) in Paris in 1785; known as the Institution Nationale, it is still in existence. During the 1790's, schools for the indigent blind were opened in several cities in England and Scotland. Their original purpose was the instruction of the blind in manual labor, but within a few years a system of general education was adopted. In 1806 Haüy established a school for the blind in Russia and aided in the establishment of a similar school in Berlin. These schools proved so successful that by 1811 similar institutions were established throughout Europe.

In the United States, the first institution for the blind was founded in Boston, Mass., by the American physician John Dix Fisher (1797–1850). This institution was incorporated in 1829, and is now known as the Perkins School for the Blind; since 1913 it has been located in Watertown, Mass. The New York Institute for the Education of the Blind (1831), the Pennsylvania Institution (1833), the Ohio School for the Blind (1837), the Virginia School (1838), and the Kentucky School (1842) are among the earlier private institutions established in the U.S. These schools are under private management, but have received State aid almost from their founding. About sixty other boarding schools for the blind have been established since the middle of the 19th century.

In 1900 the city of Chicago organized classes for blind children in the public day schools. The city thereby initiated the policy, which has since become a feature of American education of the blind, under which the blind attend regular classes with unhandicapped children and are segregated only for special classes required by their blindness. Nearly all of the larger cities in the U.S. have adopted this policy, and all of the States have established schools, or made arrangements with schools of other States, for free education of the blind from kindergarten through college.

Books and Writing. The first printing in raised letters on paper was introduced by Valen-

Trained fingertips serve as eyes for a blind person reading a book printed in Braille.
American Foundation for the Blind

tin Haüy in 1784. He used the italic style of type, embossing paper with large and small letters set in movable type by his pupils. Other styles of type were tried later, notably by the Scottish printer James Gall in 1827 and the American philanthropist Samuel Gridley Howe (1801–76) in 1833. Because of the large size of type required, however, the books produced were bulky and expensive. The only system of line type (type characters consisting of embossed lines) in current use is that invented by the Englishman William Moon (1818–94) in 1847. Based on outlines of the roman letters, the Moon type may be easily learned by persons who have become blind late in life, and whose hands, hardened by work, are not sufficiently sensitive to distinguish point type.

In 1821, a French army captain, Charles Barbier, invented the system of point type, a code based on groups of dots. Louis Braille (q.v.) adapted his system for the blind, using groups of from one to six dots. Many modifications of the Braille alphabet were devised in attempts to simplify or improve it. Such confusion resulted from the variety of systems, however, that a conference of workers for the blind was held in London in 1932 to standardize point systems. The conference adopted an alphabet known as Standard English Braille, which is the original Braille alphabet with a few modifications. This system is now in use throughout the English-speaking world and has been adapted to most other languages, including Chinese. Louis Braille also devised a system of point characters for musical notation.

The principal printing establishment in the U.S. for the production of books for the blind is the American Printing House for the Blind in Louisville, Ky. In 1879 Congress appropriated $10,000 a year to support this enterprise, and increased annual appropriations were made in later years. Other printing establishments have been founded and supported by private contributions; the best known is the Howe Memorial Press of the Perkins School for the Blind. The Perkins School also started the first circulating library for the blind in 1882. The Library of Congress, many State and municipal libraries, and private associations in most large cities provide circulating-library service for the blind. A more recent service of most of these libraries is the circulation of so-called talking books, phonograph records of readings from classical and popular literature. The magazine *Reader's Digest,* which in 1929 began publishing its complete edition in Braille for free distribution to the blind, added a further free service to the blind in 1939 by making its issues available in talking-book form as well.

In recent years a number of commercial publishers have produced books and periodicals in large print, using 18-point type for the benefit of two groups of people. One group, although classified as legally blind, has sufficient residual vision to permit the comprehension of large print. The other group includes those who are considered functionally blind because they are

Seeing-Eye dogs are most dependable in guiding their blind masters through the activities of everyday life.
UPI

unable to read ordinary print. Among the periodicals published in large print are *Reader's Digest* and a weekly edition of *The New York Times.* Among the commercial publishers that produce large-print books are Keith Jennison Books and Harper and Row.

Among the early appliances to aid the blind in writing was the grooved tablet, a sheet of metal or board grooved in small squares. The paper was placed on the tablet, and the pencil, guided by the grooves, indented the paper, forming a large, square handwriting that could be distinguished by both sight and touch. Modern methods employed in American institutions include the use of the typewriter for correspondence with persons who can see, and the use of tablets for guiding the writer in the formation of Braille characters for writing to the blind. The Braille tablet may in time be replaced by the Hall Braille writer, a modification of the typewriter, which embosses Braille characters on the paper instead of printing standard visible letters.

Rehabilitation. Pensions or similar forms of financial relief for the needy blind were first provided by New York City in 1866; the State of Illinois enacted relief measures in 1903; and by 1947 all of the States had made similar provisions. With the passage of the Social Security Act in 1935, the Federal government undertook to supplement State aid through the various branches of the Federal Security Agency. These branches include the Social Security Administration, which provides monetary benefits to blind persons; the Office of Vocational Rehabilitation, which cooperates with State, municipal, and private agencies in formulating plans for treatment and reeducation of persons disabled by blindness; and Services for the Blind, a division of the Office of Education which conducts surveys of industry and trains personnel executives to help the blind secure employment in suitable positions. All such Federal aid is distributed through State and municipal agencies and through local organizations supported by voluntary contributions.

The deaf blind, with or without speech, constitute a much more difficult problem than that presented by persons who lack only sight. These people must be dealt with individually; their rehabilitation usually requires special home teachers and always calls for infinite understanding and patience.

Specially trained guide dogs have proved successful in aiding some of the blind. At Morristown, N.J., The Seeing Eye, a nonprofit organization, began in 1929 to supply at least one hundred such dogs a year at a nominal charge. Inasmuch as only about 5 percent of blind people can use dog guides successfully, recipients are selected with great care, and are required to complte a rigorous training period with the dog selected.

During World War II, the United States Army Signal Corps developed an electronic eye that enables a blind person to perceive obstacles in his path. The apparatus is assembled in a small case and carried in the hand. It projects a beam of light that is reflected by any obstacle in its path within 20 ft. into a photoelectric cell (*see* CELL, ELECTRIC) inside the case. The cell operates an ear phone or buzzer; the intensity of the sound indicates the distance of the object, and the position of the case reveals its direction. as a result of subsequent research sponsored by the United States Veterans Administration an improved obstacle detector, more economical to operate and lighter in weight, was developed. The improvements were accomplished largely by the substitution of transistors (q.v.) for vacuum tubes. Another electronic device, known as the Step-down detector, warns its user when he is approaching a curb or a flight of stairs. The goal of current research is the combination of the two instruments into a single practical unit.

In practice, the majority of blind people today achieve relative mobility and independence without using either guide dogs or electronic detection devices. Because of recent refinements of techniques in the utilization of the

A long cane enables this blind girl to travel alone in the subway. American Foundation for the Blind

long cane, most blind people are able to guide themselves through the streets, at the office or factory, and about the home.

Persons who are blind because of a cornea rendered opaque by accident or disease can often have their sight restored by the transplant of a normal cornea to replace their own. To aid in this work, an eye bank (q.v.) was established in New York City in 1945, to collect and preserve corneal tissue. Within a year, the eye bank had a branch in Chicago, Ill., and had almost a hundred cooperating hospitals in many sections of the U.S. By the 1960's every major center of the country had an eye bank. In a number of the centers research is in progress to develop new techniques for prolonging the preservation period of corneal tissue. With present-day procedures, an eye must be used within two or three days in order to obtain satisfactory, clear transplants.

Occupations and Opportunities. Opportunities for the blind are limited more by the lack of self-confidence in individuals than by the actual defect of vision. Many blind persons successfully conduct their own business establishments or professions; many compete successfully in shops and factories with persons who can see. In most large cities, public and private agencies provide special workshops for those needing favorable conditions of employment, and home work for the blind who cannot reach the workshops because of disability or distance. Workshops for the blind are assured of a market for certain goods, such as brooms, mops, mattresses, and bed linen, because Federal and State laws require governmental departments to purchase goods made in such shops.

BLINDNESS, complete or almost complete absence of the sense of sight. Blindness may be caused by any obstacle to the rays of light on their way to the optic nerve, or by disease of the optic nerve or tract, or of that part of the brain connected with it. It may exist either under conditions of bright light or in situations of comparative darkness and may be permanent or transient, complete or partial. Few persons are born blind, although many lose their sight in infancy from preventable causes. Medical research has established the fact that considerable blindness is caused by the neglect or unsuitable treatment of inflammation of the eyes of newborn babies. Consequently legislation has been adopted in many countries specifying the treatment of all new-born infants to prevent this condition. Many persons become blind through accidents

A blind man learns to operate a broom-making machine. American Foundation for the Blind

or from complications arising from various diseases.

In the United States, Federal Social Security regulations define as blind any person whose corrected vision is less than one tenth of normal, or whose visual field is narrower than 20°. The number of such blind persons is estimated at 1.5 per 1000 of the population. Ten percent of the blind are under twenty years of age; fifty percent are over sixty-five years of age. *See* EYE: *Eye Diseases;* VISION. *See also* BLIND, AIDS FOR THE.

BLIND SPOT. *See* EYE: *The Human Eye.*

BLINDWORM, *or* SLOWWORM, common name for a small, limbless, snakelike lizard, *Anguis fragilis,* of the family Anguidae. The eyes are small but quite serviceable. The eyelids are scaly and movable. The blindworm rarely exceeds a foot in length. It has a feeble bite and is harmless and so timid that when frightened, it becomes momentarily rigid; at this time the tail becomes so brittle that when seized it snaps off, enabling the blindworm to escape. Blindworms bear between about eight and twenty-five living young in midsummer. They are found throughout most of Europe and are also known in North Africa and western Asia. The name blindworm is applied also to various other limbless lizards, to certain snakes of the family Typhlopidae with small or hidden eyes, and to certain reptilelike amphibians of the order Gymnophiona.

BLISS, Sir Arthur (1891–1975), British composer, born in London, England, and educated at the University of Cambridge. He studied at the Royal College of Music in London with the British composers Sir Charles Villiers Stanford (1852–1924), Ralph Vaughan Williams, and Gustav Holst (qq.v.). He experimented with unusual combinations of instruments and voices in such pieces as *Rout* (1920), scored for soprano and chamber orchestra, and *Rhapsody* (1919), for soprano and tenor with flute, English horn, string quartet, and double bass. His first major work was *Colour Symphony* (1922). Other works include *Pastoral* (1929), a musical setting for an anthology of pastoral verse; *Morning Heroes* (1930), a choral symphony based on an anthology of war verse; the scores for the ballets *Checkmate* (1937), *Miracle in the Gorbals* (1944), and *Adam Zero* (1946); the television opera *Tobias and the Angel* (1958); and the cantatas *The Beatitudes* (1961), *Mary of Magdala* (1963), and *The Golden Cantata* (1964). Bliss also wrote chamber music, film scores, songs, and piano pieces. He was knighted in 1950 and appointed Master of the Queen's Music in 1953.

BLISS, Tasker Howard (1853–1930), American army officer, born in Lewisburg, Pa., and educated at the United States Military Academy at West Point. During the Spanish-American War (q.v.) he participated in the Puerto Rican campaign (1898). He was made brigadier general in 1902 and commandant of the Army War College in 1903. From 1905 to 1909 he held commands in the Philippine Islands. Bliss was chief of staff with the rank of general during World War I and a member of the U.S. delegation to the Paris Peace Conference of 1918–19.

BLISTER BEETLES, common name for beetles of the family Meloidae, so called from the blister-raising properties of the dried bodies of certain of its species. The insects of this family pass through a complex metamorphosis, some having as many as nine distinct stages from egg to adult. The larvae are parasitic on other insects, some living in nests of wild bees, others on locust or grasshopper eggs. The adults are mostly black, gray, or striped with yellow and are pests in flower and vegetable gardens. The chief genera of the family are *Meloe,* the oil beetles; *Lytta,* the Spanish flies; and *Epicauta,* which includes potato and tomato beetles.

BLITZKRIEG. *See* WARFARE: *Total War.*

BLITZSTEIN, Marc (1905–64), American pianist and composer, born in Philadelphia, Pa. He gave his first concert at the age of five, composed his first work at seven, and made his debut as solo pianist with the Philadelphia Orchestra at fifteen. He later studied composition with the French composer Nadia Boulanger and the Austrian-American composer Arnold Schönberg (qq.v.) and eventually devoted his entire time to composing. Most of Blitzstein's works express his concern over the social injustices of his time. Among his works are the operas *The Harpies* (1931), *The Cradle Will Rock* (1937), and *No for an Answer* (1941); chamber and piano music; the symphonic poem *Freedom Morning* (1944); the symphony *The Airborne* (1946); the ballet *The Guests* (1948); and an English adaptation of the book and lyrics of *The Threepenny Opera* (1954).

BLIXEN-FINECKE, Baroness Karen Dinesen. *See* DINESEN, ISAK.

BLIZZARD, severe storm characterized by extreme cold, strong winds, and a heavy fall of fine, blinding snow. These storms are most common to the western United States, but sometimes occur in other parts of the country. The great blizzard of March 11–14, 1888, which covered the eastern U.S., was perhaps the most paralyzing of any storm on record. The blizzard of Dec. 26, 1947, covered New York City with 25.8 in. of snow and crippled the city temporarily. *See also* METEOROLOGY.